Have in
e

Have in
e

LATINO
AND
LATINA
WRITERS

LATINO
AND
LATINA
WRITERS

ALAN WEST-DURÁN, *Editor*

MARÍA HERRERA-SOBEK, *Associate Editor*
CÉSAR A. SALGADO, *Associate Editor*

VOLUME

I

Introductory Essays
Chicano and Chicana Authors

Latino and Latina Writers, Vol. 1

Alan West-Durán, Editor in Chief

Permissions Department
The Gale Group, Inc.
27500 Drake Rd.
Farmington Hills, MI 48331-3535
Permissions Hotline:
248 699-8006 or 800 877-4253, ext. 8006
Fax: 248 699-8074 or 800 762-4058

Since this page cannot legibly accommodate
all copyright notices, the acknowledgments
constitute an extension of the copyright
notice.

LIBRARY OF CONGRESS CATALOGING-IN-PUBLICATION DATA

Latino and Latina writers / Alan West-Durán, editor.
   p. cm. -- (Scribner writers series)
   Includes bibliographical references and index.
   ISBN 0-684-31293-X (set : alk. paper) -- ISBN 0-684-31294-8 (v. 1:
alk. paper) -- ISBN 0-684-31295-6 (v. 2 : alk. paper)
   1. American literature–Hispanic American authors--History and
criticism. 2. Hispanic Americans--Intellectual life. 3. Hispanic
Americans in literature. I. West, Alan, 1953- II. Series.
 PS153.H56 L39 2004
 810.9'868–dc22
                                          2003015728

Printed in the United States of America
10 9 8 7 6 5 4 3 2

Editorial and Production Staff

Contents

VOLUME 2

CUBAN AND CUBAN AMERICAN AUTHORS

DOMINICAN AND OTHER AUTHORS

PUERTO RICAN AUTHORS

CONTENTS

Introduction

Latino and Latina writing is a growing and diversifying field that is reshaping U.S. literature and culture. Although its indigenous, European, and African roots are irrefutable, it is a relatively new voice, since much of it has been created and published after 1960. Latino and Latina authors such as Sandra Cisneros, Oscar Hijuelos, and Julia Alvarez were unheard of fifteen years ago, as their works were published by small or academic presses. Now their works, and that of others, are widely read, reviewed by major media, and optioned for films, such as *Zoot Suit* (1981), *Mambo Kings* (1992), *Luminarias* (2000), *In the Time of the Butterflies* (2001), and *Real Women Have Curves* (2002). This is due, in part, to the growing population of Latinos and Latinas in the United States, which now constitutes the largest minority in the country.

Much of the research and scholarship published on Latino and Latina literature has focused on a specific group, be it Nuyorican poetry, Chicana feminism, or Cuban American fiction on exile. *Latino and Latina Writers* is more comprehensive because it brings together, for the first time, well crafted, in-depth studies of the works of some fifty-five authors representing different ethnicities and nationalities, in addition to five thematic essays treating autobiography and memoir, theater and performance, Chicana feminist criticism, Latino and Latina identity, and the historical antecedents of Latino literature.

The newness of Latino and Latina literature means it is under constant definition and redefinition. Does a Latino or Latina writer craft his or her work only in English, Spanish, Spanglish, or all three? Do they have to be born in the United States? How do these writers identify themselves racially, socially, culturally, and sexually? Have they experienced racism in the United States? Did they come to the United States as a small child, an adolescent, or as an adult? Did the family come for better economic opportunities, to flee a repressive regime or a civil war, or to study and then stay? If raised here, did they grow up in a large city like Los Angeles, Chicago, or New York, or in smaller, rural communities in Texas, Colorado, or Florida? The answers to these questions are neither simple nor straightforward, since many Latinos and Latinas are of mixed heritage, write in English, Spanish (and sometimes Spanglish), and consider themselves bi- or tri-cultural, pluri-racial, and multilingual.

As authors they might identify themselves as writers who happen to be Latinos rather than as Latino writers. The major—but not exclusive—focus of *Latino and Latina Writers* is on authors who write in English and whose characters, locations, and themes show some distinct commonalities. Their works stand as a testimonial commitment to create a literature that is ethically grounded and aesthetically innovative. For Latino and Latina writers, although expressed in individually unique voices, ethical concerns are embedded within a more collective consciousness—be it family, community, or nation—and directly or indirectly express the utopian yearnings of hope and transformation—a metamorphosis fashioned by recovering or affirming an identity, irreverently probing memory and history, and grappling with the intricate workings of power, injustice, resistance, and autonomy. This transformation generated by the creative tension between individual and collective concerns is perhaps best exemplified by the African proverb: "A person becomes human because of others."

What makes a literary work Latino or Latina? Are certain themes addressed, like personal or cultural identity, immigration to the United States, coming-of-age stories in an Anglo culture, an examination of the roots and problems of a community, either in the barrio or back in the home country? Is it the use of English and Spanish, the names and surnames of the characters, the settings and locations, or the cultural background in which a narrative, poem, or play takes place? What about the enormous weight and persistence of memoir, personal narrative, and autobiography within Latino and Latina letters? Many works might seem to fit these models, such as Ernesto Galarza's *Barrio Boy* (1971), Cristina García's *Dreaming in Cuban* (1992), or Piri Thomas's *Down These Mean Streets* (1967), novels like Ana Castillo's *Sapogonia: An Anti-Romance in 3/8 Meter* (1990), a book of poems like Juan Felipe Herrera's *Love After the Riots* (1996), or Guillermo Gómez-Peña's *The New World Border: Prophecies, Poems, & Loqueras for the End of the Century* (1996), with its mixture of poems, prophecies, performance pieces, essays, and a glossary of "borderismos," as prototypical coming-of-age works that reflect their respective milieu: the Mexican American barrio of Sacramento, the bleak neighborhoods of New York, and the Cuban exile experience. These works, however, elude easy classification by inhabiting hybrid and cross-genre spaces.

Criticism and theory about Latino and Latina literature and culture has emphasized its hybridity and multicultural dimensions, often drawing on such subjects as *mestizaje, rascuachismo,* and transculturation. Latino and Latina theorists have eloquently written on border theory or what has come to be known as "life on the hyphen." Chicana border theorists, as women of color, have made a significant contribution to social and aesthetic thought in the United States with their feminist-borderist work. To contextualize the significance of this thought, the origins of Latino and Latina culture must be examined.

SOURCES OF LATINO AND LATINA LITERATURE: INDIGENOUS, IBERIAN, AFRICAN

Latino and Latina literature was born out of conquest, colonialism, slavery, empire, and civil strife. Spain's influence in the southern parts of North America, Central America, the Caribbean, and Latin America was vast from 1492 to 1898. In Mexico and what is today the U.S. Southwest, the Spanish established the Viceroyalty of New Spain, which included Mexico, Central America, Cuba, Hispaniola (the Dominican Republic and Haiti), Puerto Rico, Venezuela, and Florida. Whether they were exploiting silver mines through coerced Indian labor or producing sugar through the importation of African slaves, the Spanish presence was ubiquitous. Its Counter-Reformation Catholicism and baroque aesthetics—which were simultaneously otherworldly and sensuous, mystical, and picaresque—and the Spanish language—enriched by contact with Arabic, indigenous, and African languages—became deeply rooted in the New World. Spain's legal system and thought, specifically its notions of *hidalguía* (whereby someone of noble character is granted land rented and worked by others) and honor, steeped in Stoic philosophy, were key elements that, within the limitations of a colonial society, supported individual autonomy, stimulation of conscience, and critical thinking. According to some scholars, these factors laid the groundwork for Father Bartolomé de Las Casas's work to protect the indigenous populations, thereby sparking the first transcontinental debate on human rights.

This Spanish legacy continues to be important artistically and culturally. Whether it be the extraordinary baroque churches (or the less ornate missions in the American Southwest), the power of its religious faith, the *romancero* (ballad) and flamenco traditions in music, its enormously rich and imaginative literature—particularly that of the Golden Age—and the vitality of its visual arts, Latino and Latina artists continue to draw on these Iberian cultural roots. These Iberian roots include Roman, Greek, Phoenician, and Gothic influences, and in the centuries preceding the Conquest, that of Arabs and Jews as well.

Spain's legacy was also one of political centralization and social conservatism, hierarchy, religious intolerance and persecution, obsession with blood purity and racial classification, hostility to scientific innovation, and eventually economic stagnation. Now less intrusive, Spain's influence is still pervasive, albeit in a very different manner than under colonial rule.

Spain's empire brought it into contact or collision with two other great ethno-cultural groups: the indigenous inhabitants of the Americas and Africans. From groups that lived in small chiefdoms like the Arawaks in the Caribbean to vast empires like that of the Aztecs in Mexico or the Incas in Peru, the Spanish empire interacted with and ultimately controlled tens of millions of people with different linguistic, cultural, and religious traits under vastly different forms of social organization. Despite the fact that in many areas—especially the Caribbean—the indigenous population was wiped out from overwork, mistreatment, war, but mostly disease, indigenous traditions survived and subtly influenced the new societies being built in the Americas.

The Spanish language now has hundreds of expressions that derive from Nahuátl, Quecha, Arawak, Guaraní, and Mayan languages, to name only the most widely spoken. Latin American culinary practices, religious beliefs, church buildings, popular festivals, music, poetry, textiles, pottery, stonemasonry and other crafts, healing methods, magic, and storytelling traditions all have origins in the indigenous traditions of the Americas.

Some writers have drawn on the rich mythological lore of the pre-Columbian period, invoking figures such as Quetzalcóatl (the "plumed serpent" associated with knowledge, the arts, and writing) or Coatlicue ("snake skirt," an aspect of the Earth Mother). Others follow the "flor y canto" (flower and song) tradition of Aztec poetry, which combines striking imagery with a powerful philosophical message. Many Chicana writers draw on Native American religions as well, developing a conceptual view of writing that incorporates healing methods and is linked to a deep attachment to the earth and an eco-feminist perspective. For example, *curanderas* and *curanderos* (female and male folk healers) have appeared as characters in novels. Native American oral and storytelling traditions are integral to the poetry, short fiction, and novels of many Latinos. Sometimes, stories like that of La Llorona (the Wailing Woman) or Cihuacoatl (an Aztec goddess who steals babies) are employed, while in other instances they are changed or given a different interpretation for more contemporary purposes, proving that tradition is not unchanging, that it becomes transformed as part of historical conditions.

Unlike their indigenous counterparts, Africans were forcefully brought to the Americas. The term African embraces a variety of cultures, languages, and religions, among them the Yoruba-Edo-Igbo, the Kongo-Angola-Western Bantu, the Akan-Ewe-Ga, the Jolof, the Fula, the Mandinga, and the Mina. Despite the brutality of slavery in the Caribbean and attempts to eradicate their native culture, wipe out ancestral memory, and violently force their assimilation into colonial regimes dominated by coerced labor, the vibrant cultures of Africa survived and even thrived. The African presence is indelible.

The Afrodiasporic presence has touched every aspect of Caribbean life, including music, religion, language, cuisine, sports, popular sayings, folk medicine, literature, ways of socializing, and personal hygiene. Latino and Latina writers of Caribbean descent have drawn on the *bomba* and salsa music of Puerto Rico, the mambo, *son, danzón,* rumba, and bolero traditions of Cuba, and the merengue and *bachata* genres of the Dominican Republic by imitating, re-creating their rhythms, or by using them as organizing metaphors for a narrative. The cosmology and *orishas* (deities) of the Yoruba pantheon have influenced authors who have included references to Regla de Ocha (also known as Santeria) or scenes of ritual ceremonies in their fiction. For Latina writers, *orishas* like Yemeyá, Ochún, and Oyá have provided inspiring female archetypes that are contextualized as symbols of creativity and agency for women. Moreover, the trickster figure common in traditional African storytelling traditions has been transformed by Latino and Latina authors into a modern or postmodern *pícaro* (rogue) who gets by through "shit, grit, and mother wit" (Ralph Ellison).

Along with the indigenous and African traditions, Latino and Latina writers have found inspiration in the Jewish, Arabic, and Asian elements of their heritage. Writers such as Tato Laviera, Ana Castillo, Marjorie Agosín, Ilan Stavans, Oscar Hijuelos, and Rudolfo Anaya have made all of these distinct cultural influences central to their creative work. Latino and Latina writers, whether they embody these influences literally or culturally, are, by adopting or reclaiming these heritages, reexamining the *mestizaje* myths of their cultures that under the banner of racial and cultural mixing often displace these indigenous, African, Jewish, Arabic, and Asian influences. In addition to developing a cultural and literary identity that is decidedly not Eurocentric—at least in outlook—these writers seem to be recovering lost memories or stolen documents of the past, which provide clues to their personal and cultural mosaic.

A myriad of cultural sources, such as the polyrhythmic voicings of *bomba* music from Puerto Rico, the multidimensional cosmology of Regla de Ocha, the pre-Columbian mythologies of Mesoamerica, the vivid teachings of the Maya, Zuni, or Pueblo folktales, the intimate and social rituals of Judaism or the Talmudic traditions of commentary and passionate textual scrutiny, are of paramount importance in understanding the textured legacies of Latino literature. This cultural density makes Latino and Latina writing notoriously difficult to neatly categorize, and Frantz Fanon's words in *The Wretched of the Earth* (1963) are still pertinent: "Culture has never the translucidity of custom; it abhors all simplification" (p. 224). While Fanon's opposition between custom and culture might obscure the continuities between the two, his definition emphasizes the dynamic, protean, historical, and performative nature of culture.

U.S. IMPACT ON LATIN AMERICA: FROM IMMIGRANT TO LATINO

The United States has also played a major role in the countries that account for three-quarters of the Latino and Latina population in the United States: Mexico, Puerto Rico, Cuba, the Dominican Republic, and El Salvador. In 1848, after a war with Mexico and through the Gadsden Purchase (1853), the United States annexed huge swathes of territory from its southern neighbor, creating what today are the states of Texas, New Mexico, California, Arizona, and parts of Colorado, Oklahoma, Nevada, Utah, and Kansas. Subsequent to this, Mexican-U.S. history, which includes the Mexican Revolution and its aftermath (1910–1929, 1934–1940), the Immigration and Naturalization Act (1924), the *bracero* program (1942–1964), and NAFTA (1994–), greatly affected immigration patterns and relationships between the two countries. In the ill-named Spanish–American War (1895–1898)—begun by Cubans in 1895 and fought on Cuban soil with many Cuban casualties—the United States acquired Cuba and Puerto Rico from Spain. While Cuba was a U.S. protectorate from 1898 until the communist revolution in 1959, Puerto Rico is still a U.S. possession. Occupation of the Dominican Republic by U.S. Marines (1916–1924) paved the way for the Trujillo dictatorship (1930–1961) and the subsequent invasion of the island in 1965. El Salvador witnessed bloody civil strife and war (1979–1992) that killed over 75,000 people, a conflict in which the United States, through billions of dollars in military and economic aid, backed several governments fighting a guerrilla insurgency. These events led to a massive exodus of Salvadorans from their country, and about a fifth of the nation lives abroad, mostly in the United States.

This brief historical overview is intended to signal two points. First, Hispanic culture has influenced the United States for centuries, and the Spanish language precedes the use of English within its borders by at least a century. Second, there is a long relationship between the peoples of Latin America, the Caribbean, and the United States, and these relationships have hardly been innocent. Latino and Latina literature continues to reflect the legacy of these antecedents as well as new circumstances. Witness, for example, the ever-growing influx of Colombians in the last decade. These factors point to a recognition that U.S. history, society, and its literature are deeply marked by a Latin American presence, and that the nation has been and is increasingly becoming more *mestizo*, or Latinized.

Many of the writers discussed in this volume deal with social and political themes, as well as issues of race, gender, sexuality, and identity. This should not be surprising: authors such as Luis J. Rodriguez, Ana Castillo, Demetria Martínez, Martín Espada, Cherríe Moraga, and Lorna Dee Cervantes have been or are still activists in their respective communities, working on education (bilingual or not), immigration policy, domestic violence, housing, U.S. foreign policy toward Latin America and human rights, the death penalty, AIDS among Latin Americans, and gang violence.

None of this should imply that their work is simply documentary or denunciatory. Indeed, its literary quality is first-rate, perhaps drawing on long-standing Latin American traditions, where the political and literary imaginations are deeply intertwined and not seen as antithetical. The antipathy toward social themes in U.S. literary circles is curious when one examines some of the most outstanding voices of that literature such as Walt Whitman, Ezra Pound, John Steinbeck, William Faulkner, Allen Ginsberg, Norman Mailer, Gore Vidal, E. L. Doctorow, and Kurt Vonnegut, in addition to Zora Neale Hurston, Richard Wright, James Baldwin, Alice Walker, and Toni Morrison. The poet Martín Espada admirably captured the dilemma in his foreword to *Poetry Like Bread: Poets of the Political Imagination from Curbstone Press* (1994):

> Political imagination goes beyond protest to articulate an artistry of dissent. The question is not whether poetry and politics can mix. That question is a luxury for those who can afford it. The question is how *best* to combine poetry and politics, craft and commitment, how to find the artistic imagination equal to the intensity of the experience and the quality of the ideas.
>
> (p. 17)

The writers discussed in these two volumes abundantly exhibit craft, imagination, and "intensity of the experience and the quality of the ideas." Even a playwright like María Irene Fornés, whose experimental work *The Successful Life of 3* (1965) focuses on personal relationships, invites the reader to make connections between power in an intimate setting and how it is wielded in a social context. Juan Felipe Herrera's *Love After the Riots* (1996), a hard-edged "love epic," is an erotic fantasy or recollection set in a post-apocalyptic Los Angeles (as well as in Rome) that discretely evokes the forces that have brought about urban desolation in the barrio.

Not all Latino and Latina writers' works are overt examples of the political imagination: some focus on family sagas and histories (Victor Villaseñor), myth (Rudolfo Anaya and Luis Valdez), music (Oscar Hijuelos), movies (Denise Chávez), language (Victor Hernández Cruz, Alurista, and Roberto Fernandez), historical themes (Martín Espada and Virgil Suárez), or the suffering of terminally ill patients and AIDS (Rafael Campo). Many have written exquisite if sometimes non-lyrical love poetry (Marjorie Agosín, Ana Castillo, Rafael Campo, and Demetria Martínez).

CRITERIA AND SCOPE OF *LATINO AND LATINA WRITERS*

Latino and Latina Writers is a comprehensive introduction to a core grouping of authors and themes of Latino and Latina literature. The essays will interest a wide audience of students, teachers, academics, researchers, editors, critics, and readers of literature. They give an overview of each author's work within a historical and biographical context, along with a thorough bibliography of the author's works and criticism of it. Because each pairing of author with essayist is unique, the essays vary in their outlook, creativity, and style. Some are intensely poetic, while others are more philosophical, and still others are polemical, engaging issues of politics, race, class, and sexual oppression.

Latino and Latina Writers is neither an encyclopedia nor a literary dictionary and does not seek to include every major Latino and Latina writer. The emphasis is on writers who have published after 1960, although some of the thematic essays address earlier periods. Only after 1960 does a group of writers arise who have sufficiently developed bodies of work to allow substantive criticism. Because *Latino and Latina Writers* is not a literary history, we have included thematic essays to offer broad overviews of issues and themes that are central to Latino and Latina literature. While in "Historical Origins of U.S. Latino Literature" by Harold Augenbraum, the approach is historical, in others it is concerned with genres (see Alicia Arrizón on "Performance Art and Theater" and Silvio Torres-Saillant on "The Latino Autobiography"). Another is on critical ideas and movements ("Chicana Feminist Criticism" by Debra Castillo) and still another discusses identity, language, history, and transculturation ("Crossing Borders, Creative Disorders" by Alan West-Durán). These essays were developed to offer historical, critical, and conceptual tools to aid the reader in better understanding the vast, varied, and constantly changing field of Latino and Latina literature, particularly since this field challenges more traditional notions of what constitutes ethnic literature.

Latino and Latina Writers is a member of the Scribner and Gale Group family, and the scope and style of the work is similar to the four-volume *Latin American Writers* edited by Carlos Solé (Vol. I–III, 1989; Supplement I, 2002) and Valerie Smith's two-volume *African American Writers,* 2nd edition (2001). With the former it shares a Latin American tradition that has informed or influenced U.S. Latino and Latina writers. With the latter it shares the experience of being a literature written by an ethnic minority. African American literature has inspired many Latino and Latina authors who write English in an ethnically specific register, and the important insights of black writers on the nature of American society, especially the twisted history of its race relations, has been invaluable to Latinos and Latinas. Directly or indirectly, Latino and Latina writers owe a debt to the likes of W. E. B. Du Bois, Langston Hughes, Audre Lorde, James Baldwin, Richard Wright, Zora Neale Hurston, Alice Walker, and Toni Morrison.

The rarity of published criticism demonstrates the newness of Latino and Latina literature as a field of study. Even more slippery is the constantly changing nature of this literature, the shifting demands of market forces, and the fact that several Latin American authors who are published and who receive critical attention are often controversial, sometimes for several decades. This is inevitable given that many of the writers in this volume are under the age of fifty-five and only two are deceased (Miguel Piñero and Tomás Rivera). This means that many of these authors have a productive future ahead of them, and their most important work might not have been written yet. Regardless of that risk, the authors included in this volume have already written works that merit dissemination and discussion, and any shortcomings from taking such a risk are far outweighed by the merits of this project.

LATINO AND LATINA LITERATURE: BEYOND THE "STAR" WRITERS

The future of the United States will be shaped by a Latino and Latina presence and enhanced by literature written by Latinos and Latinas. Already a significant body of literature has come to the attention of wider audiences. Latino and Latina authors have won several prestigious awards, such as the Pulitzer Prize, MacArthur Foundation grants, and Guggenheim Fellowhips. The bulk of Latino and Latina literature, however, resides in greater obscurity, in the absence of awards or prestigious grants, and is published by either university or small presses. Among the most supportive university presses are the University of Arizona and the University of New Mexico. Curbstone Press publishes both Latin American and Latino and Latina non-commercial authors. Arte Público Press (Houston), Tonatiuh Quinto Sol (formerly Quinto Sol), Tía Chucha Press, Chusma Press, and Red Salmon Press were founded by Latinos, the latter three by the writers Luis J. Rodriguez, Charley Trujillo, and Raúl Salinas, respectively. A central aim of *Latino and Latina Writers* is to ensure that important writers like Jack Agüeros, Graciela Limón, Juan Felipe Herrera, Lucha Corpi, and Dionisio Martínez are also discussed and valued as important contributors to U.S. and Latino literature.

Latino and Latina Writers seeks to expose and critically examine one of the most dynamic areas of U.S. culture. The themes written about are wide-ranging, complex, inspiring, and wrenching. They range from border crossing adventures to coming-of-age stories, from historical novels of epic sweep to intimate chronicles of the heart. The writing is realistic and poetic, fantastic and psychological, engaged, enraged, and experimental. The border crossings are not just geographical, but historical, linguistic, cultural, philosophical, and spiritual. In 1993 that tireless *borderólogo,* Guillermo Gómez-Peña, published a performance piece titled "1992: The Re-Discovery of America" in his collection *The Warrior for Gringostroika.* It is a hilarious, poignant, and deadly serious romp through the identity-soaked minefields that obsess U.S. culture, a work that questions and dismantles how U.S. culture constructs a notion of otherness that often leads to misunderstanding and violence. Here is a telling segment:

> I remember my first appointments
> with the guardians of cultural
> misunderstanding:
> I remember being thrown out of a deli
> 'cause I said I wanted a kidnap instead of a napkin
> . . . .
> I remember each of the 7 times
> the California police busted me for "looking suspicious"
> for "looking Iranian"
> . . . .
> for walking at night in a country
> that has forbidden darkness
> I'm glad I'm able to remember these moments
> & share them with you as art
> with all my love & all my anger.

(p. 114)

In this short segment of a much longer performance piece, Gómez-Peña captures all the delicacy, dispossession, and danger of the immigrant experience, never forgetting what it means to be Latino: to be misunderstood, to look "suspicious," to be known for doing things that seem to fall outside of the parameters of so-called acceptable behavior. Yet as he remembers, he shares these memories "as art, with all my love & all my anger." All of the writers in these volumes, consciously or not—some would even deny it—outspokenly or quietly, are warriors for *gringostroika,* changing U.S. culture and literature, defiantly, joyously, and with an integrity and passion that embraces their buoyant, baffling, and bracing histories and selves.

——ALAN WEST-DURÁN

List of Contributors

Paul Allatson is senior lecturer in Spanish studies and coordinator of the Spain and Latino U.S.A. study programs at the Institute for International Studies, the University of Technology, Sydney, Australia. He is the author of *Latino Dreams: Transcultural Traffic and the U.S. National Imaginary* (2002), and has published widely on Latino and Latina, hispanophone and postcolonial literary and cultural studies. ABRAHAM RODRIGUEZ JR.

Isabel Alvarez Borland is the author of the books *Cuban American Literature of Exile: From Person to Persona* and *Discontinuidad y ruptura en Guillermo Cabrera Infante*. Her articles on Cuban and Latin American authors have appeared in journals such as *Hispanic Review, Hispania, Symposium* and *World Literature Today*. She lives in Massachusetts, where she teaches Latin American and Latino literatures at the College of the Holy Cross. GUSTAVO PERÉZ FIRMAT.

Alicia Arrizon is an associate professor of women's studies and ethnic studies at the University of California, Riverside. She is the author of *Latina Performance* (1999) and coauthor of *Latinas on Stage* (2000). Her writings on theater and performance have been published in *TDR: The Journal of Performance Studies, Ollantay: Theatre Magazine, Theatre Journal,* and *Theatre Research International*. PERFORMANCE ART AND THEATER.

Harold Augenbraum is director of the Mercantile Library of New York and its Center for World Literature. His publications include *Growing Up Latino: Reflections on Life in the United States* (coedited with Ilan Stavans), *The Latino Reader: An American Literary Tradition*

from 1542 to the Present and *U.S. Latino Literature: A Critical Guide for Students and Teachers* (both coedited with Margarite Fernández Olmos), and Alvar Nuñez Cabeza de Vaca's *Chronicle of the Narváez Expedition*. HISTORICAL ORIGINS OF U.S. LATINO.

Debra J. Blake is an assistant professor of English at the University of Minnesota, Morris, specializing in Chicana and Chicano literary and cultural studies. She has published articles on Cherríe Moraga's writings and is completing a book manuscript comparing the feminist writings of Chicana authors with the oral narratives of working-class Mexican American women. CHERRÍE MORAGA.

Francisco Cabanillas is an associate professor at Bowling Green State University, Department of Romance Languages, Spanish Section. He has published articles on Puerto Rican, Dominican, and U.S. Latino literature and culture. TATO LAVIERA.

Roberto Cantú is a professor of Chicano studies and English at California State University, Los Angeles. Born in Guadalajara, Jalisco (Mexico), he has taught at Cal State L.A. since 1974. He has authored articles on Latin American, Spanish, and Chicano literatures, and translated José Antonio Villarreal's novel, *Pocho* (1994). ALFREDO VÉA JR.

Debra A. Castillo is Stephen H. Weiss Presidential Fellow and professor of romance studies and comparative literature at Cornell University. She is the author of several books, including *The Translated World: A Postmodern Tour of Libraries in Literature* (1984), *Talking Back: Strategies for a Latin American Feminist*

Literary Criticism (1992), and *Easy Women: Sex and Gender in Modern Mexican Fiction* (1998). Her most recent book (cowritten with María Socorro Tabuenca Córdoba) is *Border Women: Writing from La Frontera* (2002). ANA CASTILLO, CHICANA FEMINIST CRITICISM, HELENA MARÍA VIRAMONTES.

David de Posada is an assistant professor of French and Spanish at Macon State College and earned his Ph.D. from Florida State University. His areas of scholarly interest are sixteenth-century French poetry, U.S. Latino writers of Caribbean descent, and Diaspora studies. EDGARDO VEGA YUNQUÉ.

William O. Deaver holds a B.A. in English and an M.A. in Spanish from the University of Virginia. His Ph.D. is in Spanish from Florida State University. He is an associate professor of Spanish at Armstrong Atlantic State University in Savannah, Georgia. He has published numerous articles on writers from Spain and Spanish America as well as on Latino authors of the United States. MIGUEL PIÑERO.

María del Carmen Martínez teaches Latina and Latino literature at the University of Wisconsin and participates in various bridge-building projects between Cubans on both sides of the Florida Straits, including the St. Augustine-Baracoa Friendship Group. She has also taught creative writing, reproductive health care, and women's history at various women's detention centers. MARGARITA ENGLE.

Luis Duno Gottberg received his Ph.D from the University of Pittsburgh, and is an assistant professor at Florida Atlantic University. Recent works include *Solventar las diferencias: La ideología del mestizaje en Cuba, Iberoamericana* (2003) and the coordination of the special volume titled *Raza y Cultura en América Latina. Revista Estudios* (2002). He is also preparing a dossier about Colombian filmmaker Víctor Gaviria for the journal of Cinemateca Nacional de Venezuela, *Objeto Visual*. PIRI THOMAS.

Javier Durán is an associate professor of Spanish and border studies at the University of Arizona, where he received his doctorate in Hispanic literature. He is the author of *José Revueltas, una poética de la disidencia,* has written several articles, coedited five books on cultural studies, and has been an editorial collaborator for *Centennial Review.* Durán is working on a manuscript about border literature and culture titled *Crossing Lines, Crossing Lives: Memory and Self-Representation in Border Writing.* ALEJANDRO MORALES.

Martín Espada's seventh poetry collection is called *Alabanza: New and Selected Poems, 1982–2002* (2003). Another collection, *Imagine the Angels of Bread* (1996), won an American Book Award. Espada teaches at the University of Massachusetts-Amherst. JACK AGÜEROS

Adriana Estill received her Ph.D. from Cornell University in 1997 and is an assistant professor of English and American studies at Carleton College. Her articles on Latino literature and Mexican literature and culture have appeared in journals such as *Chasqui, Rocky Mountain Review, Confluencia,* and *Hispanofila.* She was recently awarded a Woodrow Wilson Postdoctoral Grant (2001–2002) to begin work on a monograph about the perceptions and constructions of Latina beauty in contemporary Latino literature and culture. GIANNINA BRASCHI, SANDRA MARÍA ESTEVEZ.

Roberto G. Fernández, a Cuban American writer, is the author of *Raining Backwards, Holy Radishes,* and *En la ocho y la doce.* He teaches Caribbean and Latino literature at Florida State University. VIRGILIO SUÁREZ.

Margarite Fernández Olmos is a professor of Spanish at Brooklyn College of the City University of New York. She wrote and coedited *Sacred Possessions: Vodou, Santería, Obeah and the Caribbean* (1997), *Healing Cultures: Art and Religion as Curative Practices in the Caribbean and its Diaspora* (2001), and *Creole*

Religions of the Caribbean: An Introduction from Vodou and Santería to Obeah and Espiritismo (2003) with Lizabeth Paravisini-Gebert, as well as *The Latino Reader: An American Literary Tradition from 1542 to the Present* (1997) with Harold Augenbraum. RUDOLFO A. ANAYA.

Licia Fiol-Matta is an associate professor of Latin American and Puerto Rican studies at Lehman College, City University of New York. She wrote *A Queer Mother for the Nation: The State and Gabriela Mistral* (2002), and articles on gender, race, and sexuality studies. She serves on the board of directors for the Center for Lesbian and Gay Studies, City University of New York, and is a member of the Editorial Collective of the journal *Social Text*. She is also the coeditor of the series *New Directions in Latino American Cultures*. ACHY OBEJAS.

Víctor Fowler Calzada. Born in Havana, Fowler has published five books of poetry, the most recent being *Malecón Tao* (2001) and several books of essays and criticism. *Rupturas y homenajes* (1998) won the 1997 UNEAC literary essay prize and his *La maldición: una historia del placer* (1998), is a collection of essays on eroticism in Cuban literature. He has also published thematico-critical editions on José Lezama Lima and Alejo Carpentier. RAFAEL CAMPO.

Flora M. Gonzalez has a Ph.D. in Hispanic studies from Yale University and has written essays on the Latin American novel, including her book *Jose Donoso's House of Fiction* (1995). She translated and edited a bilingual anthology of the Cuban poet Excilia Saldaña titled *In the Vortex of the Cyclone* (2002) with Rosamond Rosenmeier. She has also written articles on Afro-Cuban culture produced by women in the second half of the twentieth century and is working on a book-length study on the subject. GRACIELA LIMÓN.

Elisabeth Guerrero of Bucknell University has published articles on U.S. Latino and Latina

literature, Spanish American literature, and intellectual history in *Revista Monográfica, Chasqui, Hispanófila*, the *Arizona Journal of Hispanic Cultural Studies*, and the *Rocky Mountain Review of Language and Literature*. She is coediting the forthcoming *Steel and Glass: Women Write the City in Latin America*. VICTOR VILLASEÑOR.

Laura G. Gutiérrez received her Ph.D. from the University of Wisconsin-Madison in 2000. She is an assistant professor in the Department of Spanish and Portuguese at the University of Iowa. She has published essays in *Feminist Media Studies, Latin American Literary Review*, and *Velvet Barrios: Popular Culture and Chicana/o Sexualities* (edited by Alicia Gaspar de Alba), and is completing a manuscript titled *Unsettling Comforts: Sexualities in Mexicana and Chicana Performance*. MIGUEL ALGARÍN, MARÍA IRENE FORNÉS.

Amanda Nolacea Harris-Fonseca is a Ph.D. candidate in U.S. Latina and Latino literature in the Department of Spanish, Italian & Portuguese at the University of Illinois. As a Chicana Studies Dissertation Fellow at the University of California, Santa Barbara, she researches Chicana Feminist Theory. Additionally Harris-Fonseca coordinated research and translation for Dan Banda's *Indigenous Always: The Legend of La Malinche and the Conquest of Mexico*, which received five Emmy nominations and aired internationally. LORNA DEE CERVANTES..

Carmen Haydée Rivera, Ph.D, is an assistant professor of English at the University of Puerto Rico. Her areas of specialization include multiethnic literatures of the U.S. and contemporary U.S. Latino and Latina literature. She is coediting a collection of critical essays titled *Writing Of(f) the Hyphen: Critical Perspectives on the Literature of the Puerto Rican Diaspora*. JUDITH ORTIZ COFER.

María Herrera-Sobek received her Ph.D. from UCLA in Hispanic languages and literatures.

She is acting associate vice chancellor for academic policy and a professor of Chicano studies at the University of California, Santa Barbara. Herrera-Sobek holds the Luis Leal Endowed Chair in Chicano Studies and has written and edited more than fifteen books and has authored numerous articles and poems. PAT MORA.

Guillermo B. Irizarry teaches Caribbean and U.S. Latino and Latina literature at Yale University. He is affiliated with the Department of Spanish and Portuguese, the Department of American Studies, the Ethnicity, Race, and Migration Program, and the Council for Latin American and Iberian Studies. He has published articles on Caribbean and Mexican authors, and on studies dealing with the construction of identities based on race and ethnicity. His book, *José Luis González: el intelectual nómada,* was published in 2003. ROBERTO G. FERNÁNDEZ.

Amanda L. Irwin is an associate professor of modern languages at Rhodes College. Her areas of specialization are Paraguayan literature and U.S. Hispanic literature. Her publications include "René Ferrer" and "Sara Karlik" in the *Encyclopedia of Latin American Women Writers* (2002), "La escritura del 'monoteísmo del poder' y la experiencia del desarraigo en *El Fiscal,* de Augusto Roa Bastos" in *Hispania* (2003), and *El poeta de la revolución nacional: La vida y obra de Don Javier del Granado y Granado* (1991). DIONISIO MARTÍNEZ.

Héctor Jaimes holds a master's degree from New York University and a Ph.D. from the University of Pennsylvania in Latin American Literature. He teaches Latin American literature and culture at North Carolina State University. Jaimes is the author of *La reescritura de la historia en el ensayo hispanoamericano* (2001, literary criticism), *Salvoconducto* (1996, poetry) and *Abril* (1991, poetry). His forthcoming edition *Octavio Paz: La dimensión estética del ensayo* will be the first piece of literary criticism compiled on essays written by Paz. OSCAR HIJUELOS.

Francisco A. Lomelí is a professor in Chicano studies and Spanish and Portuguese at the University of California, Santa Barbara. He coedited *Chicano Literature: A Reference Book* (1985), *Dictionary of Literary Biography: Chicano Writers,* first series (1989), second series (1993), third series (1999), and *Handbook of Hispanic Cultures in the United States: Literature and Art* (1993). In addition, he has translated Latin American and Chicano literature including Alejandro Morales's novel *Barrio On The Edge* (1998) and has helped to organize a number of international conferences on Chicano literature and culture. ALURISTA.

Jacqueline Loss is an assistant professor of Spanish and Latin American literary and cultural studies at the University of Connecticut. She is finishing a manuscript on critical cosmopolitanisms called *Against the Destiny of Place: Cosmopolitas in a Globalizing World.* Her coedited *Cubanacán: New Short Fiction from Cuba* is forthcoming from Northwestern University Press. JUNOT DÍAZ.

Juan D. Mah y Busch received his Ph.D. from Cornell University in 2003. He recently completed a President's Postdoctoral Fellowship at the University of California, Santa Barbara, and begins his position as an assistant professor at Loyola Marymount University in the Department of English and as an affiliate of Chicana and Chicano studies. He lives in Los Angeles with his partner Irene and their daughter Izabel. GLORIA EVANGELINA ANZALDÚA.

Ellen McCracken is a professor in the Department of Spanish and Portuguese and the program in comparative literature at the University of California, Santa Barbara, where she teaches courses in Latin American and U.S. Latino literature. Her publications include *Decoding Women's Magazines: From* Mademoiselle *to* Ms. (1993); *New Latina Narrative: The Feminine Space of Postmodern Ethnicity* (1999); and the edited volume *Fray Angélico Chávez: Poet, Priest, and Artist* (2000). SANDRA CISNEROS.

Kirsten F. Nigro is a professor of Spanish at the University of Cincinnati where she teaches courses on Latin American and U.S. Latino literature and cultures. She has published on Latin American and Mexican theater as well as on women's writing and feminist theory. DO-LORES PRIDA, LUIS VALDEZ.

Patrick O'Connor is an assistant professor of Hispanic studies at Oberlin College and has taught English, comparative literature, and Spanish at Saint Ann's School, Deep Springs College, and the University of Chicago. He is completing a book titled *Paper Dolls and Spider Women: Latin American Fiction and the Narratives of Perverse.* JOHN RECHY.

B. V. Olguín is an assistant professor in the Department of English, Philosophy and Classics at the University of Texas at San Antonio. He has published poetry and scholarly essays in journals such as *American Literary History, Cultural Critique, Frontiers,* and *Nepantla* as well as in several anthologies. He is completing a manuscript titled "La Pinta: History, Culture, and Ideology in Chicana/o Prisoner Discourse," which is forthcoming from the University of Texas Press. JIMMY SANTIAGO BACA, LUIS J. ROD-RIGUEZ.

Karina Oliva will receive her Ph.D. in comparative ethnic studies from the University of California, Berkeley in 2007. In 2000 she worked for Jimmy Santiago Baca assisting the compilation of a poetry manuscript that became *Healing Earthquakes* (2001). She has published four books of poems, *Of Memory and Offering* (2001), *(Color) Rupture* (2002), *Atl Makuilli: Water from the Hand* (2002), and *Speaking Echoes from Within and Outside the Lost* (2003). ELÍAS MIGUEL MUÑOZ.

Alberto Julián Pérez received a Ph.D. in 1986 from New York University and is an associate professor of Spanish and director of Latin American and Iberian studies at Texas Tech University. He has published articles on con-temporary Hispanic American poetry and has written four books—*Poética de la prosa de J. L. Borges, Gredos* (1986), *La poética de Rubén Darío, Orígenes* (1992), *Modernismo, Vanguardias, Postmodernidad, Corregidor* (1995), and *Los dilemas políticos de la cultura letrada, Corregidor* (2002). TINO VILLANUEVA.

Tey Diana Rebolledo, Ph.D, is Regents' Professor and Chair of the Department of Spanish and Portuguese at the University of New Mexico. She is the author of *Women Singing in the Snow: A Cultural Analysis of Chicana Literature* (1995) and editor of *Infinite Divisions: An Anthology of Chicano Literature* (1993) with Eliana Rivero. A new book of essays, *The Chronicles of Panchita Villa,* will be published by the University of Texas Press in 2004. DENISE CHÁVEZ, LUCHA CORPI.

Eliana Rivero is a professor in the Department of Spanish and Portuguese at the University of Arizona in Tucson. Rivero has authored and coedited five scholarly books, has published over seventy articles, chapters in books, review essays, notes, bibliographies, and reference works. She is coeditor of the bestseller *Infinite Divisions: An Anthology of Chicana Literature* (1993) with Tey Diana Rebolledo and also coedited *Telling To Live: Latina Feminist Testimonios* (2001). CRISTINA GARCÍA.

Edna Rodríguez-Mangual is an assistant professor of Spanish and Latin American studies at Texas Christian University where she teaches courses on contemporary Hispanic literature and film. She is completing a book on the Cuban author Lydia Cabrera for the University of North Carolina Press, forthcoming in 2004. Her research has taken her to Cuba a number of times and she has had the opportunity to interview many of the leading writers and film directors working in Cuba today. ESMERALDA SANTIAGO.

Rolando J. Romero is an associate professor of Latina and Latino studies at the University of

Illinois, Urbana-Champaign in the Department of Spanish, Italian, and Portuguese. He is the general editor of *Discourse: Journal in Theoretical Studies in Media and Culture*, coeditor of the forthcoming *Malinche: Perspectives on the Mexican National Archetype*, and served as chief academic consultant for Dan Banda's *Indigenous Always: The Legend of La Malinche and the Conquest of Mexico*, a PBS documentary that explores the life of La Malinche. RICHARD RODRIGUEZ.

César A. Salgado is associate professor and has worked as academic adviser in the Spanish and Comparative Literature graduate programs at the University of Texas at Austin. Besides many critical articles, he has published two books: *From Modernism to Neobaroque: Joyce and Lezama Lima* (2001) and *Zona templada* (1993), a collection of poems that won the Puerto Rican Fifth Centennial Poetry Prize. MARTÍN ESPADA, VICTOR HERNÁNDEZ CRUZ.

Rosaura Sánchez received her Ph.D from the University of Texas at Austin and is a professor in the Department of Literature at the University of California, San Diego. She is the author of books and articles on Chicano sociolinguistics, Chicano and Chicana literature, and nineteenth-century Californio testimonios. ROLANDO HINOJOSA.

Lisa Sánchez González is the author of *Boricua Literature: A Literary History of the Puerto Rican Diaspora* (2001) and various other essays on Latino literary history and culture. Her forthcoming works are *Pura Belpré: Her Life and Writings* (2004) and a textbook, *Modern U.S. Latino Literature* (2004), selected and edited with John Christie. She teaches American studies at the University of Connecticut, Storrs. NICHOLASA MOHR.

Doris Sommer is a professor of Latin American literature at Harvard University. She is the author of *Foundational Fictions: The National Romances of Latin America* (1991), *Proceed*

With Caution When Engaged by Minority Writing in the Americas (1999), and the forthcoming *Bilingual Aesthetics: A New Sentimental Education*, among other works. VICTOR HERNÁNDEZ CRUZ.

Silvia Spitta teaches Latino and Latina American and comparative literature at Dartmouth College. She is the author of *Between Two Waters: Narratives of Transculturation in Latin America* (1995), and an edition on spaces and cities (with Boris Muñoz) titled *Más allá de la ciudad letrada: crónicas y espacios urbanos* (2003). She is working on a book tentatively titled *Misplaced Objects, Enacted Spaces*. ALICIA GASPAR DE ALBA.

Charles Tatum, Ph.D. Raised in Mexico—his mother is Mexican—is a professor of Spanish and Dean of the College of Humanities at the University of Arizona. He is the author of *Chicano Literature* (1982), coauthor of *Not Just for Children: The Mexican Comic Book in the Late 1960s and 1970s* (1992), and editor of *New Chicana/Chicano Writing* (1991–1993). He is also cofounder and coeditor of the journal *Studies in Latin American Popular Culture*. His book, *Chicano Popular Culture*, was selected as a Best of the Best of the University Presses book by the American Association of American Presses. GARY SOTO.

Silvio Torres-Saillant is an associate professor of English and director of the Latino-Latin American Studies Program at Syracuse University. He serves as associate editor of *Latino Studies* and as a senior editor for the *Encyclopedia of Latinos and Latinas in the United States*. He sits on the boards of directors for the New York Council for the Humanities and the University of Houston's Recovering the U.S. Hispanic Literary Heritage Project, and cochairs the MLA Committee on the Literatures of People of Color in the United States and Canada. THE LATINO AUTOBIOGRAPHY.

Fernando Valerio-Holguín obtained his Ph.D. from Tulane University and teaches Contemporary Latin American and Caribbean Literatures and Cultures at Colorado State University. His works include *Poética de la Frialdad: La Narrativa de Virgilio Piñera* (1997), *Arqueología de las sombras: La narrativa de Marcio Veloz Maggiolo* (2002), *Autorretratos* (2002), *Memorias del último cielo* (2002), and *Café Insomnia* (2003). He is working on a book on the representations of Rafael Leónidas Trujillo's dictatorship in Dominican literature. JULIA ALVAREZ.

Isabel Valiela is an assistant professor of Spanish at Gettysburg College where she teaches the course "Bridging the Borders: Latina and Latin American Women Writers" in the Women's Studies Program. She has a Ph.D. from Duke University. Her research interests are in the field of Women's Studies, and more specifically, Latino and Latina literature. Her most recent publication appeared in the book *Encompassing Gender: Integrating International Studies and Women's Studies* (2002). TOMÁS RIVERA.

Santiago R. Vaquera-Vásquez is a senior lecturer in the Department of Spanish, Italian, and Portuguese at the Pennsylvania State University. His published works have appeared in *Tinta*, *Los universitarios* and *El país* as well as in major anthologies on contemporary literature such as *Líneas aéreas* (1998) and *Se habla español, voces latinas en USA* (2000). He is editing his first novel, *Una chava de ojos tristes.* JUAN FELIPE HERRERA.

Diana L. Vélez is an associate professor of Latin American literature at the University of Iowa. She earned her Ph.D at Columbia University. Focused primarily on Puerto Rico, she has published widely in literary criticism and literary translation. Her book *Reclaiming Medusa* contains her translations of texts by five Puerto Rican women writers. She has also published studies on the work of Luis Rafaél Sánchez and on Argentine and Spanish women writers. PEDRO PIETRI.

Guillermina Walas is an assistant professor of Spanish at Eastern Washington University. Originally from Argentina, she received her Ph.D. from the University of Pittsburgh in 1999. She has published *Entre dos Américas. Narrativas de Latinas en los '90s* (2000) and several articles on Latin American women writers, autobiography, *testimonio,* and U.S. Latino and Latina issues. MARJORIE AGOSÍN.

Alan West-Durán is an assistant professor of modern languages at Northeastern University. He has two books of essays, *Tropics of History: Cuba Imagined* (1997) and *African-Caribbeans: A Reference Guide* (2003); and two collections of poetry—*Dar nombres a la lluvia/Finding Voices in the Rain* (1995), which won the Latino Literature Prize in Poetry (1996), and *El tejido de Asterión o las máscaras del logos* (2000). He has translated Alejo Carpentier's *Music in Cuba* (2001), and Rosario Ferré's *Language Duel* (2002). CROSSING BORDERS, CREATIVE DISORDERS: LATINO IDENTITIES AND WRITING.

R. Joyce Zamora Lausch received her doctoral degree in May 2003 from Arizona State University, where she teaches literature in the departments of Chicana and Chicano Studies and English. She is a coeditor of *New Bones: Contemporary Black Writers in America* (2001). DEMETRIA MARTÍNEZ.

Chicana Feminist Criticism

DEBRA A. CASTILLO

Until very recently, scholars working in Chicana studies have had to pay their dues to the establishment by first pursuing a research specialization in a non-U.S. hispanophone literature (for example, Tey Diana Rebolledo and Norma Alarcón both did Ph.D. dissertations on Mexican poet and feminist Rosario Castellanos, and Elizabeth Ordóñez studied women from Spain) or in a canonical U.S. English area of study. Others, like Gloria Anzaldúa, have intentionally eschewed the traditional academic credentialing process. Thus, unlike the current, younger generation of thinkers, the women who entered the profession in the 1970s and 1980s, founding the Chicano Studies programs and establishing journals and presses, had to do much of their most important early work outside (and often with resistance from) the institutional channels, and without either recognition or reward. The consequences of this academic myopia on the part of the dominant culture are manifold. Until astonishingly recently, anglophone Chicana literature has been institutionally homeless, perceived as marginal or second rate, and thus not respected within English Department circles. Hispanophone Chicana literature has been seen as culturally contaminated, written in "bad Spanish," and certainly not appropriate for (Latin) American literature courses. Critics who write on such works have therefore been marginalized as well,

and have been continually on the defensive, having to define and redefine their field of interest, justify it to the academic community as a valid and exciting area of study, and then, finally, begin to lay the groundwork of serious analysis. These are severe handicaps for any field, and help explain the strong anti-institutional thread and oppositional rhetoric in much of the most well-known Chicana feminist thought.

The Mexican literary establishment has, unfortunately, been similarly reluctant to take into account the contributions and potentiality of a dialogue between Mexican and Chicana scholars. In fact, one of the strongest criticisms made regarding the III Border Seminar, "Mujer y literatura Mexicana y Chicana: Culturas en contacto," which took place in Tijuana, Mexico, in May 1989, addressed the lack of comparative analysis among Mexican and Chicana women. Alarcón, discussing one of the uncomfortable confrontations at that event in her article "Cognitive Desires: An Allegory of/for Chicana Critics," warns of an increasingly vast distance between Mexicans and Chicanas, precisely at the point in which contact and exchange could be most fruitful. "We became spectators to a textual performative that claimed to incorporate us. . . . Thus Chicanas were placed in a negative position whereby if they had wanted to speak it would have been to note their exclusion from an event that supposedly included them in the

1

conference's goals" (*Chicana (W)rites: On Word and Film,* pp. 191–192). Obvious but often unspoken class and race differences lie at the bottom of much of this distance, Alarcón finds, as the Mexican women are whiter and higher class than their browner, working-class origin Chicana counterparts.

Curiously enough, in recent years one could almost say that the situation has been reversed, and that Chicana feminist thinkers and writers are now the pre-eminent figures in the field, far surpassing in influence their male counterparts. And the field itself has more than confirmed its intellectual force, with strong institutional advocates in the U.S., Europe, Australia, and Asia. Even in Mexico, where resistance to *pochos* (acculturated Chicanas) has often been high, Chicana writers' works are now widely available in Spanish translation, and prominent social critics like Elena Poniatowska and Carlos Monsiváis have spoken and written extensively about the real and potential contribution of vital Chicana thinking to the Mexican imaginary. This high degree of recognition is particularly true of the strong generation of women writers forged in the crucible of a double resistance: on the one hand, an early lack of academic respect for their work; on the other, the disapproval of the male leadership of the oppositional Chicano movement. These women are the most cited of the feminist critics and their efforts have provided the groundwork for the field of Chicana studies as a whole; thus, they are also the focus of this article. Norma Alarcón, Gloria Anzaldúa, Ana Castillo, Cherríe Moraga, and Chela Sandoval must be taken into account in any evaluation of the status of Chicana feminist thought. More forcefully, one should argue that these women need to be included in any evaluation of Chicano thought in general, and into any evaluation of contemporary U.S. thought.

As Norma Alarcón notes in one of her essays, "Since the emergence of Chicana critics can be traced no further back than about 1965, applying the name retroactively is a reconstruction of a chosen gene(an)alogy, much like calling Sor Juan Inés de la Cruz a Modern Woman" ("Cognitive Desires," pp. 186–187). In tracing this genealogy, today's scholars necessarily recognize their debts to activists that include Rosaura Sánchez, Linda Apodaca, Martha Cotera, Mary Helen Alvarado, Sonia López, Mary Lou Espinosa, Ana Nieto Gómez, Francisca Flores, and Marta Vidal. Yet, because much of these women's work is directly activist rather than presented in traditional scholarly formats, and because it tended to be published in journals and small magazines of limited circulation like the *Revista Chicana-Riqueña* (now *Americas Review*), *El Grito, ChismeArte,* or *La Cosecha,* their writings have only recently begun to receive the attention due them. Fortunately, through the publication of recent anthologies like Alma Garcia's *Chicana Feminist Thought,* crucial works by these foremothers is now more widely available.

Fundamentally then, Chicana feminist theory and criticism as a body of analysis is of relatively recent vintage, and, like Alarcón, most scholars point to the activist days of the 1960s as the starting point for this academic field of study. Armando Rendón's *The Chicano Manifesto,* often seen as a defining statement for the Chicano movement in general, dates from 1971, and a contemporary perusal of this historic document reminds today's readers of the often bitter conflicts between male leaders who frequently rejected the legitimacy of Chicana struggles and women activists who saw the profound contradictions in a political struggle that left women behind. Rendón evokes heroic figures like the Mexican Revolutionary generals Emiliano Zapata and Pancho Villa as models for contemporary political praxis and as models of a virile leadership. At the heart of Rendón's document is a strong statement that identifies machismo as a positive ideology and as the symbolic organizing principle for Chicano family life. This combination of revolutionary rhetoric and traditional family values leaves very little space for independent and powerful women who reject the traditional supportive roles of wife and mother as their only proper sphere of involvement. Tellingly, the movement leaders evince a considerable suspicion of and nervousness about the potential participation of their Chicana counterparts.

Thus, in Rendón's famous document, the Chicano activist represents a (male) political force for positive change; as Angie Chabram-Dernersesian writes in her essay "I Throw Punches for My Race, but I Don't Want to Be a Man: Writing Us—Chica-nos (Girl, Us)/Chicanas—into the Movement Script," "he grounds his symbolic treatment of machismo in a specific male body, equating macho with Chicano, a term generalized to embrace the nationalist objective" (*Cultural Studies: A Critical Reader,* p. 83). The Chicana, on the other hand, has "thus been removed from full-scale participation in the Chicano movement as fully embodied, fully empowered U.S. Mexican female subjects. They are not only engendered under machismo but their gender is disfigured at the symbolic level under malinchismo" ("I Throw Punches for My Race," p. 83). On a more mundane level, as Adelaida del Castillo recalls in "Mexican Women in Organization," even when women provided the major organizing force for local movements, they were forced to defer to a male figurehead as the visible representative of their group—this was a lose-lose situation: "Commonly women in leadership were labeled unfeminine or deviant. . . . When a woman leader had a compañero, he was frequently taunted or reprimanded by the other men for failure to keep her under his control" (*Mexican Women in the United States,* pp. 8–9).

It is not surprising, thus, that Chicana activists rejected this exclusionary discourse, along with the male domination of the political movement, and their relegation to traditional roles in the *familia.* Cherríe Moraga says it succinctly in *The Last Generation:*

> For a generation, nationalist leaders used a kind of "selective memory," drawing exclusively from those aspects of Mexican and Native cultures that

served the interests of male heterosexuals. At times, they took the worse of Mexican machismo and Aztec warrior bravado, combined it with some of the most oppressive male-conceived idealizations of "traditional" Mexican womanhood and called that cultural integrity.

> (pp. 156–157)

Similarly, Aida Hurtado critiques the 1960s movement for its lack of sensitivity to gender issues—this is in fact one of the three "blasphemies" explored in her 1996 book *The Color of Privilege: Three Blasphemies on Race and Feminism.* In her "Manifestación tardía" (Belated manifesto), Margarita Cota-Cárdenas argues passionately for rethinking militancy as derived from the Chicano movement frame, and for writing women more definitively into the movement script as full partners, as *hermanas* (sisters), as Chicanas, as *mujeres* (women) in the full sense of the term. She notes that it is not sufficient to replace the "o" at the end of "Chicano" with the letter "a"; instead, activist Chicanas need to imagine new social relations, new subjectivities, and new strategies of interaction. Cota-Cárdenas's reflection, published in 1980, anticipates the work of her fellow Chicana activists and scholars during the blossoming of Chicana scholarship in the 1980s and 1990s.

From a more contemporary perspective, we know that these Chicanas, formed in the crucible of movement politics, and often reviled as *malinchistas* (a slur referring to the mistress and translator of Spanish conquerer Hernán Cortés meaning race traitor) and *vendidas* (sell outs), by their male counterparts, have been crucial in setting the groundwork for a specifically Chicana feminism, for re-evaluating the symbolic structures of Malinche and Guadalupe, and for claiming for themselves a source of pride in coming from a long line of *vendidas.* La Chicana, then, in the more developed sense anticipated by Cota-Cárdenas, becomes an important concept for helping think through these new subjectivities. At the same time, says Tey Diana Rebolledo in her 1995 book *Women Singing in the Snow,* the problem for Chicanas is specifically how to imagine these new subjectivities given a long history of silence:

> The problems and multiple answers to "Who am I? How do I see myself, How am I seen by others?" are thus constantly being refigured and repositioned, so the issue of "identity" in feminist work is one that will not go away. On a wider scale . . . it is not only a question of the individual processes of "subject positioning" but also one of ideological processes that are fully implicated in social formations of the individual and the group.
>
> (p. 97)

Chicana feminists have traditionally focused on two large areas of inquiry where the political and the personal intersect: the *familia* (especially studies of expected gender roles), and the institution (social, political, religious, linguistic, academic). The Chicana's family in particular has been the focus of social, scientific, and literary studies, essays, autoethnographies, novels, stories, poems, plays, critical analysis, and sui generis mixed forms. In a nutshell, the basic concept of the typical *familia* would be as follows: The *familia* structures itself around a self-sacrificing mother, whose power resides in her absolute control over her children as well as in the moral authority that derives from her unending suffering. The good father is neither faithful to his wife nor particularly available to his children, but he does support his family economically and observes a certain amount of discretion in his outside affairs. In the best of cases, the father is a background influence in the family, while day-to-day household decisions are made by the mother. The bad father, on the other hand, is often violent, is irresponsible with his money, drinks to excess, and also allows his wife and children to know about his philandering (this adds to the wife's suffering and thus increases her moral capital). The Chicano son is privileged and petted, a spoiled being that will grow up into a man neither to be trusted nor depended upon. He will, however, revere his mother, though he is unlikely to show respect for any other woman. The protofeminist daughter, compelled throughout childhood to serve the men in her *familia*, begins to question this traditional order and asserts her right to explore alternative family dynamics and sexual partnerships with women as well as with men.

In their analyses of the various levels of institutional culture, Chicana critics have addressed questions of politics and ideology at every level from local to global. They have explored the implications of pockets of the third world in the first, rethinking, for example, girl gangs and *maquiladora* (assembly plant) industries. They have re-evaluated and re-valorized traditional spiritual and healing practices, looking to *curanderismo* (folkhealing), *brujería* (witchcraft), and Mexican native customs for their inspiration. They have argued in favor of the full richness of Chicana linguistic expression in English, Spanish, Spanglish, and Caló. They have spoken forcefully about the shoehorning of Chicana scholarly work into an academic system that was never structured to accommodate them. Above all, these critics have explored a feminocentric writing and thinking process that interrupts the long, patriarchal monologue and contests the institutional prejudices against alternative forms of argument. At the same time, many of these women are acutely conscious of the institutional stakes in their own status as token minorities. In 1985 Carmen Tafolla warned: "Don't play 'will the Real Chicana Please Stand Up?' Much as we have heard different groups compete for 'charter membership' in the Most Oppressed Club, Deep in the Barrio Bar, Pachuca of the Year Award, Mujer Sufrida ranks, and Double Minority Bingo, we must admit that membership dues must be continuously paid and advertised" (*To Split A Human: Mitos, machos, y la mujer Chicana*, p. 175).

GLORIA ANZALDÚA

According to Rebolledo, "after Gloria Anzaldúa published *Borderlands/The New Mestiza* in 1987, Chicanas breathed a sigh of relief because the tensions, the conflict, the shiftings were finally articulated. And Anzaldúa not only defined what Chicanas had been feeling for some time, but she presented it in a positive way" (*Women Singing in the Snow,* p. 103). Strikingly, her book is both hermeneutical and performative, and its ideologically charged discourse of self-enactment electrified the Chicana community. Critics have made Gloria Anzaldúa *the* representative scholar of the U.S.–Mexican border, and no respectable work on border theory can avoid engagement with her absolutely central text. *Borderlands/La Frontera* is the mega-bestseller of Chicana theorizing, and Anzaldúa's work is read, cited, and debated in a wide range of contexts, making her one of the most quoted scholars in the United States of any ethnicity. Success brings its own challenges, of course. Anzaldúa writes about being tired of being "repeatedly tokeni[zed]" (*Making Face, Making Soul: Haciendo caras,* p. xvi) as one of the same half dozen women continually called upon as a resource, and thus drained of energy that would allow her to continue her own literary and political work.

Anzaldúa's *Borderlands* in many senses is a continuation of her lifelong task of building a woman of color feminism that is theoretical, empirical, and personal at the same time. In this project, what she calls "the new mestiza"—a mestiza being a woman of mixed European and American Indian ancestry—emerges through consciousness-raising, in the evolution of an oppositional perspective. Gloria Anzaldúa is critical of United States authoritarianism, and in her writings she challenges what she sees as the hegemony of dominant-culture U.S. discourse. For this author, theory and lived experience cannot be divided, and work best when they speak coterminously, as a coherent and embodied knowledge set. Ultimately, her goal is alliance building. Hence, while she knows that her work is much discussed among scholars and critics (and agrees that for her part she finds abstract theoretical language seductive), she makes a special effort to reach out to nonacademics. Likewise, she emphasizes support for the work

of women of color in general, including those who do not yet know they are writers, and she is particularly concerned by a too-common tendency among women of color to suppress each other's voices. She writes: "Nothing scares the Chicana more than a quasi Chicana; nothing disturbs a Mexican more than an acculturated Chicana; nothing agitates a Chicana more than a Latina who lumps her with the norteamericanas. It is easier to retreat to the safety of difference, behind racial, cultural, and class borders" (*Making Face, Making Soul,* p. 145). These are precisely the borders she wants to break down. Speaking of her anthology, Anzaldúa says she is "acutely conscious of the politics of address. *Haciendo caras* addresses a feminist readership of all ethnicities and both genders—yes, men too. Contrary to the norm, it does not address itself *primarily* to whites, but invites them to 'listen in' to women-of-color talking to each other and, in some instances, to and 'against' white people" (p. xviii). Later in the same text she adds, "mujeres-de-color speak and write not just against traditional white ways and texts but against a prevailing mode of being, against a white frame of reference" (p. xxii). This white frame of reference also includes pressure to write and speak in standard English rather than to use code-switching or Spanish. For this reason, Anzaldúa eschews familiar, dominant culture forms of theorizing, and peppers her language with key words and phrases in her own Tex–Mex Spanish. An engagement with the borders of language in all their senses is among Anzaldúa's most persistent images; she is, we recall, a poet as well as a theorist.

To address the inequities she sees from other grounds—from an alternative perspective—she draws heavily from indigenous myth, leading up to a celebration of the indigenous part of her mestiza heritage. In another move, she describes a symbolic equivalence between the border and her body. In a much quoted poetic passage in *Borderlands,* for instance, she describes the geopolitical line as "una herida abierta" (an open wound), a:

1.950 mile-long open wound

. . . .

running down the length of my body,
staking fence rods in my flesh,

. . . .

me raja me raja.

(pp. 2–3)

In Anzaldúa's work the border functions primarily as a metaphor, in that the border space as a geopolitical region converges with discourses of ethnicity, class, language, gender, and sexual preference.

Borderlands/La Frontera consists of two parts, each with seven chapters. The first part, entitled "Atravesando fronteras/Crossing Borders," is the most frequently read and discussed part of the book; it consists of a sui generis mix of historical, personal, and poetic reflections leading up to a passionate call to a Chicana self-empowerment. The second half, entitled "Un agitado viento/Ehécatl, the Wind" rearticulates her theoretical positions in even more lyric form, privileging politically charged poetry. Drawing on one of Anzaldúa's principal metaphors, critics have sometimes described this book as serpentine. Certainly it does not offer an argument in the traditional, Western form, but rather proposes something closer to a spiritual journey, and one that frequently reflects upon Nahua/Aztec goddesses whose names and attributes contain the word for serpent, "coatl." Anzaldúa's trip begins in Aztlán, the mythic Aztec homeland, offering a capsule history of south Texas from the original peopling of the Americas to her own family's sharecropper history. Here, *Borderlands'* perspective closely approximates the everyday life of the primary cultures of the valley of Texas. In this part of her book, Anzaldúa articulates a cultural and social wall between white Americans and Mexican Americans. She describes how the Texan brand of capitalism has made its mark by dispossessing the valley's inhabitants who seem, from an Anglo perspective, strange and stubborn persons. At the same time, and as is typical in Anzaldúa, the Anglo perspective is itself distanced and mediated, seen through the eyes of the oppressed who then reinterpret it to contest oppression.

In U.S. dominant culture terms, says Anzaldúa, "Borders are set up to define places that are safe and unsafe, to distinguish *us* from *them*" (*Borderlands/La Frontera*, p. 3). Clearly, in this projection, U.S. dominant culture is the normative "us"; the unsettling "them" consists of "the prohibited and the forbidden. . . . the squint-eyed, the perverse, the queer, the troublesome, the mongrel, the mulato, the half-breed, the half-dead; in short, those who cross over, pass over, or go through the confines of the 'normal'" (p. 3). It is a land distinguished by its tension, its ambivalence, its danger, and the overwhelming, constant presence of violence and death.

In subsequent chapters she explores her own oppression as a Chicana and a lesbian, and then in chapters 3–7 articulates the growth of her political and feminist consciousness, rejecting the patriarchal Aztlán for what she calls the Coatlicue state, responding to a feminist consciousness that demands new myths and new symbols. On her way to this conclusion, she rethinks such crucial culture figures as the Virgin of Guadalupe with respect to the Aztec goddess Coatlopeuh, "she who has dominion over serpents" (p. 29), and argues passionately that all Chicanos, and more urgently, all Chicanas, need to overcome the linguistic oppression that has limited the possibilities for expression to devalorized and stumbling tongues. The culminating chapter of this section of the book, the most closely read and most influential, is the final chapter of this first part: "La concienca de la mestiza/Towards a New Consciousness."

Anzaldúa's recuperation of this space begins with the myth of Aztlán, the mythical homeland of the Aztecs, a nomadic tribe that left the southwest in the twelfth century and eventually wandered south to the area of central Mexico, where they established the empire that was conquered by Hernán Cortés in the early sixteenth century. Spanish, *mestizo* (mixed blood), and indigenous conquerors then traveled back northwards in a journey of conquest to the border area: "this constituted a return to the place of origin, Aztlán, thus making Chicanos originally and secondarily indigenous to the southwest" (p. 5). Anglo *Tejanos* (Texans) brought a second conquest force to the area, and with the victory over Mexican forces in 1848 established the current borderline with the Treaty of Guadalupe–Hidalgo. While the rights of Mexican citizens were guaranteed by that treaty, the actuality of subsequent events was a shameful history of swindles and outright theft, leaving the Mexican Chicana inhabitants of the region dispossessed and feeling alien in their own land. Meanwhile, on the other side of this artificially constructed political boundary, poverty-stricken Mexicans dreamed of a better life for themselves and their families on the U.S. side of the border, and faced the dangers of illegal crossing and the humiliation of their treatment by the INS and the employers on the other side. This, says Anzaldúa, is "what Reagan calls a frontline, a war zone. The convergence has created a shock culture, a third country, a closed country" (p. 11). The entire weight of her intellectual, personal, and spiritual journey in this book is to provide a counternarrative to this story of betrayal and loss, to this culture of violence and spiritual devastation. "Don't give me your tenets and your laws," she writes. "So don't give me your lukewarm gods. What I want is an accounting with all three cultures—white, Mexican, Indian. I want the freedom to carve and chisel my own face, to staunch the bleeding with ashes, to fashion my own gods out of my entrails" (p. 22).

Because she lives in more than one culture, the new mestiza has to process conflicting messages, and she develops what Anzaldúa describes as "a tolerance for contradictions, a tolerance for ambiguity" (p. 79). The clash of cultures strengthens her tolerance and provides her with the tools to achieve a pluralistic consciousness greater than the sum of its parts. Ultimately, Anzaldúa's is a utopic project:

> The work of the mestiza consciousness is to break down the subject-object duality that keeps her a prisoner and to show in the flesh and through the images of her work how duality is transcended. . . . A massive uprooting of dualistic thinking in the individual and collective consciousness is the beginning of a long struggle, but one that could, in our best hopes, bring us to the end of rape, of violence, of war.
>
> (p. 80)

In keeping with the goddess imagery and the undertow of feminist spirituality that runs through the whole book, Anzaldúa adds: "La mestiza has gone from being the sacrificial goat to becoming the officiating priestess at the crossroads" (p. 80). Instead of rebellion and revolution in the old, death-seeking sense, in this project an evolution, "an inevitable unfolding" defines "the quickening serpent movement" (p. 81).

The new mestiza must not only officiate over these changes in herself, but, as is the function of priestesses in any spiritual practice, assist others in coming to the same crossroads. As a feminist, her task is to reinterpret patriarchal history and create a new story that privileges feminocentric, health-giving imagery. Thus, Coatlicue, the indigenous mother goddess, replaces the Spanish hybrid Virgin of Guadalupe, and the patriarchal nation-state of Aztlán gives way to the feminist Coatlicue state. This feminist project of shaping new myths with political and social resonance is most fully articulated in the central chapters of the first part of the book. In this section she first discusses the importance of the Coatlicue state as a key image in her nonlineal, serpentine form of thinking, then develops her argument about the legitimacy and expressiveness of Chicano Spanish, and argues forcefully for the role of the writer/artist in advancing this project. For the white person there is also an important task in this process: "Admit that Mexico is your double, that she exists in the shadow of this country, that we are irrevocably tied to her. Gringo, accept the doppleganger in your psyche. By taking back your collective shadow the intracultural split will heal" (p. 86).

Anzaldúa speaks from the interstices of U.S. dominant culture and she has self-authorized her hybrid discourse in the social construction of difference. Nevertheless, upon becoming the authorized and canonized voice of that difference, she is ineluctably allied to the practices of political and economic power on an international level, even given the fact that—ironically—her writing and her performative actions resist such practices. Her fertile concept of the mestiza consciousness has been exceptionally influential, and as a consequence she is frequently quoted as the premier thinker/theorist on border issues, sometimes in ways quite distant from her original project.

A typical example is Walter Mignolo's influential article, "Posoccidentalismo: el argumento desde América Latina," (Postoccidentalism: The argument from Latin America), the Spanish version of what would become one of the key points in his later book, *Local Histories/Global Designs: Coloniality, Subaltern Knowledges, and Border Thinking* (2000). In this project, the metaphor of the border serves a crucial role. Mignolo recurs to the old Sarmientian opposition of civilization and barbarism and, tying it to an excursus on Anzaldúa, in "Posoccidentalismo" he calls for the revindication of

> la fuerza de la frontera que crea la posibilidad de la barbarie en negarse a sí misma como barbarie-en-la-otredad; de revelar la barbarie-en-la-mismidad que la categoría de civilización ocultó; y de generar un nuevo espacio de reflexión que mantiene y trasciende el concepto moderno de razón.
>
> (*Cuadernos americanos*, p. 157)

the force of the border which creates the possibility for barbarism to deny itself as barbarism-in-otherness; to reveal the barbarism-in-the-self that the category of civilization occulted; and to generate a new space of reflection that maintains and transcends the modern concept of reason.

This is a considerable distance from Anzaldúa's Shadow Beast and Coatlicue state, especially in its complete lack of attention to Anzaldúa's strong feminist message, yet throughout his argument, as well as in the later book, Anzaldúa is credited as the guiding consciousness in Mignolo's formulation of the concept of a (genderless) border epistemology.

If the feminized border is insufficiently actualized as a conceptual tool in works like those of Mignolo, Anzaldúa poses another kind of problem for the work of other well-known border thinkers, where the concept of the borderlands can be too easily recuperated into a certain type of cultural nationalist discourse. David Johnson and Scott Michaelsen ask: "Of what use, finally, are concepts like 'culture' and 'identity' if their invocation, even in so-called multicultural contexts, is also exclusive, colonial, intolerant?" (*Border Theory: The Limits of Cultural Politics,* p. 29). On the U.S. side, the contributors to Johnson and Michaelsen's border theory volume quite rightly question, as the editors note, "the *value* of the border, both as cultural indicator and as a conceptual tool," finding "the identity politics of border studies' most prominent instantiations naive and wanting in quite similar ways" (pp. 29, 31). Benjamin Alire Saenz trenchantly argues this point from another perspective in his critique of Anzaldúa's canonical text, *Borderlands/La Frontera,* which he sees as a dangerously escapist romanticization of indigenous cultures, offering little of practical value to today's urban Chicanas.

Another critique is that *Borderlands/La Frontera,* despite its multiple crossings of cultural and gender borders—from ethnicity to feminisms, from the academic realm to the world of blue-collar labor—tends to essentialize relations between Mexico and the U.S.–Mexican border. Scholars like María-Socorro Tabuenca Córdoba have noted that Anzaldúa's transnational commentary strangely omits any concrete reference to the Mexican side of the border despite continually evoking its metaphorical presence. Her third country between the two nations, the binational borderlands, is still a metaphorical country defined and narrated from a first world perspective. Even her primary indigenous imagery is drawn not from the northern Mexico/southwestern U.S. indigenous nations, but, tellingly, from the central Mexican imaginary, invoking the Aztec imperial power (which, in pre-Columbian times, as in the present, has had tremendously strained relations with the north). By defining her referents solely in terms of an outcast status in the United States, Anzaldúa's famous analysis does not take into account the many other othernesses related to a border existence; her "us" is limited to U.S. minorities; her "them" is U.S. dominant culture. Tabuenca Córdoba reminds her readers that Mexican border dwellers are also "us" and "them" with respect to their Chicana counterparts; they can in some sense be considered the "other" of both dominant and U.S. resistance discourses. It is in no wise the same, however, to belong to an official minority within the U.S. as it is in Mexico.

CHERRÍE MORAGA

Californian Cherríe Moraga is a frequent collaborator with Gloría Anzaldúa, and their work together is often spoken of as reflecting the most important axis of Chicana feminist, and especially Chicana lesbian thought. She is well known as the coeditor of crucial volumes of women-of-color writing, and is a prize-winning playwright and poet as well as a theorist and essayist. Her theoretical work—from the 1983 *Loving in the War Years: Lo que nunca pasó por sus labios* (What never passed through her lips), which still remains fresh and pertinent, to her 1993 *The Last Generation*—comprises a continuum of uncompromisingly political and social theorizing and poeticizing. Displaying a similar genre-bending style as Anzaldúa, she combines poetry with political autobiography and more abstract meditations. Also like Anzaldúa she focuses much of her attention on reevaluating her own experience as a Chicana

lesbian brought up in a repressive subculture, one that in its turn is the object of oppression by the dominant society. While Anzaldúa comes from an experience of an obviously mixed race background (she is *la prieta*—dark of skin), Moraga, by contrast, can pass as white (*la güera*—fair of skin). Thus for Moraga, in contrast to Anzaldúa, the struggle often shapes itself symbolically as an effort to come to terms with her ability to pass, and her fear of passing.

Loving in the War Years fundamentally concerns itself with the search for her brown mother and all that search implies: the acknowledgment of her lesbian identity, the yearning for her lost mother tongue, the desire for her mother's culture (and her mother's body), the worry about being accepted as a *mestiza*. As the subtitle of the book suggests, the central image for all of these issues is that of the mouth, and of the silencing of the Chicana's voice (*lo que nunca pasó por sus labios*). In *Loving in the War Years* Moraga critiques fellow Chicana feminists who ignore the contributions of the women's movement, and she decries homophobia wherever it manifests itself: in the Chicano movement, among fellow feminist colleagues, and in Chicano culture in general. Thus, for example, she points out the damage done when sexist Chicano men put down assertive women by accusing them of lesbianism (similar charges on the part of Latin American men have poisoned relations with their activist colleagues), and she highlights the even worse damage suffered when the Chicana leader's response is merely to deny the accusation. Such responses, she notes, "make no value judgment on the inherent homophobia in such a divisive tactic. Without comment, her statement reinforces the idea that lesbianism is not only a white thing, but an insult to be avoided at all costs" (p. 32). Moraga is always attentive to these complex crossings of race and gender politics and the implicit hierarchies of value that they imperfectly uncover. She notes: "It is far easier for the Chicana to criticize white women who on the face of things could never be *familia*, than to take issue with or complain, as it were, to a brother, uncle, father" (pp. 106–107), and she points out the irony of Chicana critics who see no conflict in citing white men like Marx and Engels but ferociously attack fellow Chicanas who find something useful to build upon in feminist theory authored by white women.

In her introduction to her 1993 collection of essays, autobiographical meditations, and poems, *The Last Generation,* Moraga describes the project as "a prayer [written] at a time when I no longer remember how to pray" (p. 1). In keeping with the metaphor of the book as prayer, she frequently evokes language that reminds the reader of its rich religious underpinning. She calls it, for example, a "prophecy" and speaks of "resurrection"; she describes the elegiac quality in terms of the Aztec tradition of "floricanto." There is a particular urgency to this text, a sense of imminent loss. This loss is mostly defined in terms of a gradual abandonment of Mexican culture and traditions:

> I write it against time, out of a sense of urgency that Chicanos are a disappearing tribe, out of sense of this disappearance in my own *familia.* . . . My tíos' children have not taught their own children to be Mexicans. They have become "Americans." And we're all supposed to quietly accept this passing, this slow and painless death of a *cultura.* . . . But I do not accept it.
>
> (p. 2)

In a larger sense, though, the loss is planetary, as Moraga links the fading of Chicano and Native American cultures to the dominant culture's indifference to the environment. The work is divided into five sections, which as a group give a good sense of the book's overall argument: "New Mexican Confessions," "War Cry," "La fuerza femenina," "The Breakdown of the Bicultural Mind," and "The Last Generation."

Much of the book concerns itself with a parsing out of Moraga's own struggles as a light-skinned lesbian Chicana. Born of a Mexican mother and a poor white father, Moraga grew up in a family that prized acculturation; her own turn to the Mexican half of her heritage seemed a betrayal to those family expectations, and coming out as a lesbian seemed strangely to confirm her rebelliousness, as if the terms "Chicana" and "lesbian" somehow support and describe each other by definition. While Moraga can (and at certain periods of her life, did) pass for white, her emotional and intellectual commitment in her adult years has been to her Chicano heritage, and she notes that she holds the customs of her mother's family more dearly because she exercised that choice: "Had I been a full-blood Mexican, I sometimes wonder whether I would have struggled so hard to stay a part of la raza" (p. 127). And yet, this decision is not entirely comprehensible even to her Mexican mother. Moraga's lovely poem, "Credo," begins "frente al altar de mi madre," and in this meeting of mothers, the poetic persona comments: "*Tenemos el mismo problem* / the one says to the other / sin saber the meaning" (p. 65). Here, it is precisely the split across two cultures, two languages, two spiritual systems that causes words to splinter into a poignant incomprehensibility. As Moraga says elsewhere in this volume, naming her pain: "I am always hungry and always shamed by my hunger for the Mexican woman I miss in myself" (p. 121). At the same time, "Credo," the Latin word for "I believe," also echoes with the resonances of the Roman Catholic tradition of her Mexican mother. It is an expression of faith anchored in "this templo / my body" (p. 66).

Like the other Chicana theorists discussed in this article, Moraga also mines Aztec myth for its symbolic system. "Credo," ultimately, is not a Christian poem, but one much closer to the *floricanto* tradition. Moraga also derives her central metaphorical image from one of the goddesses in the Aztec pantheon, in this case, the moon goddess Coyolxauhqui, daughter of Coatlicue and sister of the murderous younger war god Huitzilopochtli. In the myth Huitzilopochtli puts down the rebellion of his older sister, chops her into bits and throws her dismembered body from the top of the pyramid. In Moraga's eloquent description: "Breast splits from chest splits from hip splits from thigh from knee from arm from foot. Coyolxauhqui is banished to the darkness and becomes the moon, *la diosa de la luna*. In my own art, I am writing that wound" (p. 73). She adds a bit later: "Huitzilopotchli is not my god. And although I revere his mother, Coatlicue, Diosa de la Muerte y La Vida, I do not pray to her. I pray to the daughter, La Hija Rebelde. She who has been banished, the mutilated sister who transforms herself into the moon. She is la fuerza femenina" (p. 74). The image of Coyolxauhqui helps Moraga define her own fragmented self, split across competing allegiances of *familia* and family, her two cultures and two bloods. This recognition of fragmentation and a rebellious search for wholeness defines not only her autobiography, but also her writing in general. Moraga notes that all her work focuses on disfigured women and broken men and that her hope is to find, or construct, a whole woman, a free citizen.

Continuing the indigenous metaphor, Moraga ends this book with a piece called "Codex Xerí," which she describes as a "Chicana codex. I offer it as a closing prayer for the last generation" (*The Last Generation*, p. 184). This poem in prose serves as what she calls a record of remembering and a demand for retribution in the name of all dispossessed and fragmented peoples. Her text reminds the reader of the long, slow struggle: "The Chicano codex es una peregrinación [is a pilgrimage] to an América unwritten" (p. 187). And it ends on a positive, or at least rebellious, note. In the face of the dissolution that Moraga elsewhere in the book pessimistically sees as given, in this final chapter she inscribes a challenge: "A Mechicana glyph. Con Safos" (p. 188).

"Queer Aztlán: the Re-formation of Chicano Tribe" is the longest and most directly political of the writings in the volume. In this essay, Moraga reminds her reader of the background to the Chicano movement of 1968 and her own disillusionment with movement politics. She comments that because of the off-putting heterosexism and narrowness in the movement's nationalist agenda, she came to her own real politicization not with the movement, which left her out, but the recognition of her lesbianism. Thus, while Moraga mourns to some degree the dissolution of active Chicano movement, she also recognizes that it belongs to a historical moment that is now past and that even at its best it was problematic and insufficiently progressive. Moraga's own proposal involves revitalized and more inclusive, more progressive movement that she calls in this essay "queer Aztlán." Her discussion of this project begins with a critique of "El Plan Espiritual de Aztlán" by Chicana feminists and gay men, urging that "men have to give up their subscription to male superiority" (p. 161). In contrast with the heterosexist Aztlán of the "Plan espiritual," Moraga suggests that queer Aztlán would be the spiritual homeland for Chicanos that would embrace all of its people.

Moraga's queer Aztlán also extends its embrace to all native peoples of the Americas, in a more than metaphorical sense. Thus, while like her Chicana feminist colleagues Moraga makes use of Aztec mythology to help develop a contesting and non-Western, feminist spiritual practice, she is also aware that the Aztec myth, however spiritually relevant, misses the point to some degree for the real, living people of indigenous heritage in the southwest. She defines a longing to return to indigenous roots that has been a hallmark of Chicana theorizing, but also reminds her reader that this longing is often paired with a lack of knowledge about native cultures. Chicanas, she argues, are mostly of southwestern origin, and thus have a "verifiable genealogy" (p. 166) in Apache, Yaqui, Tarahumara, Navajo and other border nations. One of her most urgent calls to action requires Chicanas to find ways of constructing a community that will connect them to the indigenous nations that share their physical geographies "in order to find concrete solutions for the myriad problems confronting us, from the toxic dump sites in our neighborhoods to rape" (p. 166). Here, Moraga brings the book back to one of her most crucial bottom-line considerations. If, on one level, she theorizes about the fragmented self and a longing for wholeness, on the other she is pragmatically committed to a concrete political agenda revolving around land-based struggles, environmental issues, and the effects of NAFTA.

NORMA ALARCÓN

Among Norma Alarcón's most striking services to the intellectual community has been her apparently unconditional willingness to give of herself as an editor of Third Woman Press and as a participant in colloquia, conferences, symposia, and so forth. She has taken part in a truly mind-boggling number of such activities, and has won considerable visibility in the field as a strong, articulate, and inspirational spokesperson for Chicana studies. At the same time, her work represents one of the most theoretically sophisticated approaches in the field. She is best known for a series of articles that bring together U.S. and European theory, especially 1980s so-called high theory and French Feminist theory, and in her analyses she reinscribes these works into the context of Chicana theorizing. Some of her work is necessarily introductory—introducing and surveying a field that was only beginning to impinge upon the consciousness of the establishment—other essays explore in much more abstract and sophisticated ways the theoretical issues that derive from the specificity of Chicana cultural experience. These pieces have helped open up new approaches and have served as the starting point for other related work that is re-imagining and rethinking not only Chicana and Chicano writing, but also to some extent Mexican literary studies as well.

In all her works, Norma Alarcón has been specifically concerned with developing an ideologically responsible theory of culture and of subjectivity that would help define the particularity of the Chicana feminist subject in contradistinction to both the U.S. dominant culture feminist (or more straightforwardly, what is often defined as the kind of feminism that speaks only to white, middle-class women) and, to a lesser extent, the Mexican feminist movement. The way to this new subjectivity, in the first instance, comes through consciousness-raising, and is inspired by such crucial works as *This Bridge Called My Back.* She notes in her essay on that important book that naming one's experience is one first step to a feminist consciousness, but it is not enough. In much of her work she takes on the hard task of a meticulous exploration of the next step—a nuanced and complex philosophical and cultural analysis.

In her 1992 essay, "Cognitive Desires: An Allegory of/for Chicana Critics," she speaks to the invention of the Chicana—what Alarcón calls her "gene(an)alogy" (p. 187)—playing on the Chicana's yearning for roots and on her recognition that this desired history "could only take shape through this fabulous construction," an analogy which is also a history, which is also a fable (*Chicana (W)rites,* p. 187). While this genealogy is based in the feminine line, Alarcón makes thoughtful use of a wide range of thinkers and philosophers to establish her points. In this essay, for example, Alarcón uses Jean-François Lyotard's notion of the "différend," and Gayatri Spivak's understanding of the subaltern to help her think through the location of the Chicana critic with respect to her intellectual cohort. "My contention," she writes, "is that heretofore the Chicana critic has not taken account of her insider/outsider/insider status with respect to multiple discourse structures. . . . To pursue the nexus of intersectionality of the multiple discourse structures . . . is in a sense to come to terms with the modes through which her disappearance is constantly promoted" (p. 187). At stake in this theoretical question is the issue of how and under what circumstances the subaltern speaks. This question, suggests Alarcón, defines the struggle for both actual and imaginary histories; and histories, she argues, determine position within culture and the political economy.

As Alarcón acutely notes with respect to the Mexican/Chicano studies conference scenario that frames this commentary, texts and other cultural products can cross borders much more easily than people, and individuals are much more tightly bound up in political and nationally defined identities than are their works. In the section entitled "Speaking in Tongues: Cursing the Academy," Alarcón offers a fiery indictment of academic politics that all too often take the institutionalized prerogative "to decide where we belong, which may foreclose almost all possibilities for self-propelled inquiry on the part of Chicanas" (p. 193). She describes three options Chicana critics have exercised in the past for cutting through the double bind that alternately views the Chicana scholar as a wonderful resource and as a narcissistically obsessed minority: (1) the "Richard Rodríguez" option of denying his relationship to his ethnic group while simultaneously affirming it in an oversimplified but coherent story; (2) the orthodox Marxist option of appealing to the generic class struggle; and (3) the resource option often decried as essentializing. In response to these unsatisfactory choices, Alarcón proposes subjects-in-process "who construct provisional (self-determining) 'identities' that subsume a network of discursive and signifying practices and experiences imbricated in the historical *and* imaginary shifting national borders of Mexico and the United States" (p. 198). Alarcón here is very close to the kind of proposal made by Argentine-American philosopher María Lugones when she posits that love (and acceptance of plurality) is central to women-of-color feminisms. For Lugones, Latinas express this love in learning to travel among many different social and psychic worlds, inhabiting more than one mental space at the same time.

One of the places that Alarcón mines for these historical/imaginary identities is Mexican myth.

Her much reprinted article "De la literatura feminista de la chicana: Una revisión a través de Malintzin, o Malintzin: Devolver la carne al objeto" is an excellent case in point. In this essay, Alarcón reviews the historical documents describing the original indigenous translator for Hernán Cortés; explores the traditional and highly negative uses of the term *malinchista* in Mexican and Chicano popular culture; and, finally, in her most important contribution, re-evaluates the relevance of this figure in a reimagined, positive framework as an important symbolic image in Chicana feminist writing. Similarly, her more recent article, "Chicana Feminism: In the Tracks of 'The' Native Woman," highlights the reappropriation of a symbolic structure designed around the abstract native Mexican woman, drawing heavily from texts like the *Mitología nahuátl* for inspiration from figures like the Nahua/Aztec goddesses Coatlicue, Cihuacoátl, and Ixtacihuátl. The point, says Alarcón, is not to pretend to recover a lost origin, or a true essence, but rather to define a spiritual kinship with the indigenous part of the Chicana's mestiza heritage; it too is a gene(an)alogy rather than a conventional history or family tree. This claim represents, thus, a pivotal psychic, cultural, and political project. Alarcón compares this project to the U.S. dominant culture concept of the melting pot as an ideological structure and as a "regulative psychobiography" (p. 379). In the melting pot, it is whiteness rather than *mestizaje* that defines the outcome; for the Chicana, the figures of the goddesses, along with other powerful women like Guadalupe, Malinche, and La Llorona, counter U.S. dominant culture models. At the same time and on another level, they also provide a resistant corrective to Mexican dominant culture with its persistent downplaying of the figure of the feminine. Thus, the continuum of meanings constructed in such symbolic gene(an)alogies allows the Chicana to bring the triad of race/class/gender into fruitful discussion, and also opens up "negotiating points . . . to enable 'Chicanas' to grasp their 'I' and 'We' in order to make effective political interventions" (*Living Chicana Theory,* p. 379). Overall, Alarcón's work may sometimes seem very dense and difficult, and perhaps overly reliant on European philosophical structures that in other terms, and on sound ideological ground, she will reject or decry. Nevertheless, she represents some of the best and most powerful abstract thought in the field.

CHELA SANDOVAL

Chela Sandoval also has been thinking through the theoretical implications involved in questions of how to understand women-of-color feminisms in the U.S. context, and this questioning has led to her most important work—densely argued theoretical pieces (her 2000 book, *Methodology of the Oppressed,* offers the most important example, as well as a welcome synthesis of her earlier theoretical work, all of which has led directly to this project) and brief passionate manifestos (such as the frequently reprinted 1981 report on the National Women's Studies Association conference in Oakland). There are several persistent foci of interest in Chela Sandoval's work. Like Alarcón, she is profoundly interested in the complex imbrication of national discourse and literary-theoretical representations, and is especially concerned with the creation and theoretical elaboration of what she calls a "differential" or "oppositional" consciousness among the communities she designates as "U.S. third world feminist critics." She is deeply committed to laying out the history and current strategies of such practices in a rational and coherent form and for this reason her work is frequently structured around well-considered sets of numbered points. Unsurprisingly, her favored vocabulary includes words like "map," "system," "methodology," and "technology," all of which point toward a particularly synthetic structure of mind.

The guiding spirits of Sandoval's *Methodology of the Oppressed* are Jameson, Barthes, and Fanon, and to a lesser extent, her colleagues like Ruth Frankenberg and mentors such as Hayden White and Donna Haraway at the University of California-Santa Cruz (surprisingly, not Paolo Freire, despite the homage to the influential Brazilian thinker in her title). The "methodology" of the title can take various forms—womanism, nomadic consciousness, the mobilization of "love" as a critical category—all of which serve as techniques for the marginalized person to resist and respond to dominant culture practices. The author moves with confidence among some of the most difficult and prickly theorists on the Anglo-French scene. She indicates early in the introduction that she intends this project as an "archeological" analysis of theory, one in which she is as interested in revealing the theorists' unstated hopes and desires as she is in parsing often obscure prose. The body of the book offers fine and trenchant readings of Jameson, Fanon, and Barthes, especially in terms of the unhappy set of cultural and personal circumstances that ultimately prevent these fine thinkers from superseding the paradoxes of their irremediable insertion in the dominant culture. By rereading these classic texts from the point of view of a post-deconstructionist theory of the oppressed, Sandoval rejuvenates these works and offers a fresh and original perspective on them. If she sometimes overstates her case—as in her repeated statement that theory superstar and ultrapopular thinker Roland Barthes "was left alone, abandoned, and in despair" because of his inability to enact a methodology of the repressed—such lapses fade into insignificance alongside the magnitude of this book's achievement and the passion of its argument.

A quite different aspect of Sandoval's work surfaces in the report on the NWSA conference that she wrote while serving as secretary for the National Third World Women's Alliance. "Feminism and Racism: A Report on the 1981 National Women's Studies Association Conference," like Alarcón's commentary on the 1989 Tijuana conference, describes not only the dynamics of a particular event, but, more importantly, it signals a crucial turning point in Chicana/feminist/third world women's thinking. It is for this reason, more than for its unique historical interest, that the essay has been so frequently reprinted. Sandoval begins her article by echoing Audre Lorde's question, "Do the women of the Academy really *want* to confront racism?" (*Making Face, Making Soul,* p. 56) and anticipates her conclusion by noting, sadly, that the academy apparently preferred no confrontations at all, creating a watered-down version of a liberatory rhetoric instead of opportunities for dialogue. Instead of rich discussion, Sandoval observes a "flamboyant disguise of over-abundance" that created a shopping mall effect (p. 58). At the same time, she says, the very structure of the conference made it "too easy for us to identify who our friends and who our enemies might be. Though empowered as a unity of women of color, the cost is that we find it easy to objectify the occupants of every other category" (p. 65). Finally, she concludes, "through the compassionate inclusion of our differences and the self-conscious understanding that each difference is valid in its context, we are awakened to a new realm of methodological, theoretical, political, and feminist activity" (p. 67), with the potential to reshape the academic field of women's studies. Unfortunately, concrete efforts in that direction met with institutional resistance on the part of some of the white women, and antagonism in both groups. While this antagonism could perhaps be explained away as an unfortunate side effect of a specific organizational mistake, the conclusions Sandoval draws and the implications for institutional theory building have been found valid and important in discussions of the dynamics of women's studies programs as well as other programmatic, departmental, and curricular initiatives.

Alarcón and Sandoval both highlight the slippages in Chicana representations, and Tey Diana Rebolledo, among others, has observed how typical, and how problematic, is this theoretical move: "While Chicana writers were trying to seize their own voices and become speaking subjects, they were at the same time 'decentered' and tended to dissolve into the collective and political. . . . Unable to completely unify or ally with one group, Chicanas felt themselves pulled and pushed (and often rejected) by the various representations" (*Women Singing in the Snow,* p. 102). This is an equivocal positioning at best, since, as José Esteban Muñoz reminds us, all too frequently the "discourses of essentialism and constructivism short circuit" (*Disidentifications: Queers of Color and the Performance of Politics,* p. 6). For minority subjects, the effort to resist dominant ideology is fraught with peril and, in these writers, often expressed in prose that seems fiendishly complex.

ANA CASTILLO

Like the writings of her colleagues and collaborators Gloria Anzaldúa and Cherríe Moraga, Ana Castillo's *Massacre of the Dreamers: Essays in Xicanisma* (1994) deeply influenced the U.S. third world women's movement. Ana Castillo is from Chicago, thus adding the midwestern U.S. to the map created by this essential triad of feminist thinkers, and complementing Anzaldúa's Texas-based border theory and Moraga's California. Castillo begins her book with a discussion of the roots of *machismo,* tracing it back to the preconquest Arab heritage in Spanish culture. She then explores the intersection of Roman Catholic liberation theology and feminist spirituality, in counterpoint to the male-dominated Chicano movement and its roots in a more conservative version of Catholicism, despite claims deriving from its leftist rhetoric. The next three chapters of the book, "In the Beginning There Was Eva," "La Macha: Toward an Erotic Whole Self," and "Brujas and Curanderas: A Lived Spirituality," serve as the analogous chapters to the central section of Anzaldúa's *Borderlands/La Frontera.* In this section, Castillo, like Anzaldúa, works on elaborating an alternative, feminocentric spirituality with broad implications for feminist practice. Her concept of Xicanisma implicitly contrasts with Chicanismo, which Castillo would see as overly contaminated by *machismo,* and hence unsalvageable in any real sense by the feminist of color. Thus, the Xicanista, and Xicanismo in general, serve an analogous function to Anzaldúa's Coatlicue state, though Castillo grounds her project more straightforwardly in a conception of the woman's body that is distinctly maternal. In each case, the most prized quality for the writer is a sense of community among whole, empowered women who are claiming their rights to full participation in their societies. This community naturally and essentially evolves as a spiritual one, as, says Castillo, "women's history is one of religiosity" (*Massacre of the Dreamers,* p. 145). In tracing this heritage, Castillo finds significant links among U.S. indigenous American, African (Yoruba), and Aztec customs that confirm her faith in the strength of traditional healing practices and suggest to her their relevance in a woman's path to self-empowerment. In support of this argument, Castillo confirms her credentials as the granddaughter of a *curandera,* and even offers her own recipe for an herbal bath "to cleanse the self of negative energies in the environment, to rid one of an unsettling feeling, or regularly, for chronic anxiety" (p. 160).

The heart of the project is "Un Tapiz: The Poetics of Conscientización." Significantly, Castillo calls this section a poetics rather than a theory, and the distinction is an important one. Like her colleagues Moraga and Anzaldúa, Castillo is a poet, and while this book is less of an obviously mixed-genre production than that of the other two writers, her sensibility is equally a poetic one. Like theirs, her form of argumentation accordingly builds upon a metaphorical and lyrical logic that does not match the traditional Western style of proof. Castillo writes: "The vast majority of us were taught to be afraid of a certain type of English: the language of Anglos who initiated and sustained our social and economic disenfranchisement. . . . At the same

time, we were equally intimidated by the Spanish spoken by people of middle-class or higher economic strata who came from Latin America" (p. 167). She is, then, concerned with the way language shapes reality and forms (or deforms) community. Castillo urges her Xicanista readers to face these fears and to take responsibility for their many languages—to hold themselves accountable for their use. In taking charge of the ideas they communicate, the Xicanistas "may begin to introduce unimaginable images and concepts into our poetics" (p. 170). This is what Castillo calls, finally, a "conscienticized poetics" (p. 171), using a loan-blend from the Spanish language in the absence of an adequate English word.

Castillo's "tapiz" highlights three works: Anzaldúa's *Borderlands/La Frontera,* Moraga's *Loving in the War Years,* and her own novel, *The Mixquiahuala Letters.* Castillo contrasts the former two works as follows: "Anzaldúa's spiritual affinity for Coatlicue serves as a resonant reflection of her desire for disembodiment that would free her from a tremendous physical and emotional anguish. . . . Moraga . . . contrary to Anzaldúa's *Borderlands,* reflects an acute connection with her physical self and sexuality" (p. 173). She later adds: "While Anzaldúa would have us see her physical self as indistinguishable from her spiritual image of duality, Moraga concludes the opposite, that is, she claims the spiritual through the physical" (pp. 176–177). For her own part, Castillo describes her novel as an example of "public risk-taking" and notes that "the ideological problem that the personal is political does not include a formal, theoretical solution" (p. 179). Her character, Teresa, is a subversive, insurgent, feminist woman analogous to the central figures in the narratives of her counterparts. All three women, then, in form and content of their work embody a similar ethics: "Subversion of all implied truths is necessary in order to understand the milieu of sexist politics that shape the lives of women" (p. 177). At moments like these, Castillo's urgency may make her voice seem a bit too strident, a bit too categorical, a bit too close to the twinned evils of white oppression and Chicano movement politics for which it explicitly serves as a countervoice and counternarrative.

And yet, Ana Castillo's manifesto-like conclusion to *Massacre of the Dreamers* calls for a resurrection in terms as purely lyrical as anything we have seen from any of the writers surveyed here. These words, this call to action, serve as a conclusion to this piece as well:

> What we have been permitted to be without argument in society is the compassionate, cooperative, yielding, procreator of the species, india fea, burra beast of burden of society. Viewed as ugly and common as straw. We know that we are not. Let us be alchemists for our culture and our lives and use this conditioning as our raw material to convert it into a driving force pure as gold.
>
> (p. 226)

Selected Bibliography

Alarcón, Norma. "Chicana Feminism: In the Tracks of 'The' Native Woman." In *Living Chicana Theory.* Edited by Carla Trujillo. Berkeley, Calif.: Third Woman Press, 1998. Pp. 371–382.

———. "Cognitive Desires: An Allegory of/for Chicana Critics." In *Chicana (W)rites: On Word and Film.* Edited by Maria Herrera-Sobek and Helena Maria Viramontes. Berkeley, Calif.: Third Woman Press, 1995. Pp. 185–200.

———. "De la literatura feminista de la chicana: Una revisión a través de Malintzin, o Malintzin: Devolver la carne al objeto." In *Esta puente mi espalda: Voces de mujeres tercer mundistas en los Estados Unidos.* Edited by Cherríe Moraga and Ana Castillo. San Francisco, Calif.: Ism Press, 1988. Pp. 231–241.

———. "The Theoretical Subject(s) of *This Bridge Called My Back* and Anglo-American Feminism." In *Making Face, Making Soul/Haciendo caras: Creative and Critical Perspectives by Feminists of Color.* Edited by Gloria Anzaldúa. San Francisco, Calif.: Spinsters/Aunt Lute Books, 1990. Pp. 356–369.

———. "Traddutora, Traditora: A Paradigmatic Figure of Chicana Feminism." *Cultural Critique,* vol. 13 (fall 1989): 57–87.

Alarcón, Norma, Ana Castillo, and Cherríe Moraga, eds. *Third Woman: Sexuality of Latinas.* Berkeley, Calif.: Third Woman Press, 1993.

Anzaldúa, Gloria. *Borderlands/La Frontera: The New Mestiza.* San Francisco, Calif.: Spinsters/Aunt Lute Books, 1987.

———. "En Rapport, In Opposition: Cobrando cuentas a las nuestras." In *Making Face, Making Soul/Haciendo caras: Creative and Critical Perspectives by Feminists of Color.* Edited by Gloria Anzaldúa. San Francisco, Calif.: Spinsters/Aunt Lute Books, 1990. Pp. 142–148.

———, ed. *Making Face, Making Soul/Haciendo caras: Creative and Critical Perspectives by Feminists of Color.* San Francisco, Calif.: Spinsters/Aunt Lute Books, 1990.

Castillo, Ana. *Massacre of the Dreamers: Essays on Xicanisma.* Albuquerque: University of New Mexico Press, 1994.

Castillo, Debra, and María Socorro Tabuenca Córdoba. *Border Women: Writing from La*

Frontera. Minneapolis: University of Minnesota Press, 2002.

Chabram-Dernersesian, Angie. "I Throw Punches for My Race, but I Don't Want to Be a Man: Writing Us—Chica-nos (Girl, Us)/Chicanas—into the Movement Script." In *Cultural Studies: A Critical Reader.* Edited by Lawrence Grossberg, Cary Nelson, and Paula Treichler. New York: Routledge, 1992. Pp. 81–95.

Cota-Cárdenas, Margarita. "Manifestación tardía." *La Palabra,* vol. 2, no. 2 (1980).

Del Castillo, Adelaida. "Mexican Women in Organization." In *Mexican Women in the United States.* Edited by Magdalena Mora and Adelaida del Castillo. Los Angeles: Chicano Studies Center, 1980. Pp. 7–16.

Garcia, Alma. *Chicana Feminist Thought: The Basic Historical Writings.* New York: Routledge, 1977.

Herrera-Sobek, Maria, and Helena Maria Viramontes, eds. *Chicana Creativity and Criticism: Charting New Frontiers in American Literature.* Albuquerque: University of New Mexico Press, 1996.

———. *Chicana (W)rites: On Word and Film.* Berkeley, Calif.: Third Woman Press, 1995.

Hurtado, Aida. *The Color of Privilege: Three Blasphemies on Race and Feminism.* Ann Arbor: University of Michigan Press, 1996.

———. *Voicing Chicana Feminisms: Young Women Speak Out on Sexuality and Identity.* New York: New York University Press, 2003.

Lugones, María. "Playfulness, 'World'–Traveling, and Loving Perception." In *Making Face, Making Soul/Haciendo caras: Creative and Critical Perspectives by Feminists of Color.* Edited by Gloria Anzaldúa. San Francisco, Calif.: Spinsters/Aunt Lute Books, 1990. Pp. 390–402.

Michaelsen, Scott, and David E. Johnson, eds. *Border Theory: The Limits of Cultural Politics.* Minneapolis: University of Minnesota Press, 1997.

Mignolo, Walter D. *Local Histories/Global Designs: Coloniality, Subaltern Knowledges, and Border Thinking.* Princeton, N.J.: Princeton University Press, 2000.

———. "Posoccidentalismo: El argumento desde América Latina." *Cuadernos americanos,* vol. 12, no. 67 (1998): 143–165.

Mora, Pat. *Nepantla: Essays from the Land in the Middle.* Albuquerque: University of New Mexico Press, 1993.

Moraga, Cherríe. *Giving up the Ghost: Teatro in Two Acts.* Los Angeles, Calif.: West End Press, 1986.

———. *The Last Generation.* Boston, Mass.: South End Press, 1993.

———. *Loving in the War Years: Lo que nunca pasó por sus labios.* Boston, Mass.: South End Press, 1983.

Moraga, Cherríe, and Gloria Anzaldúa, eds. *This Bridge Called My Back.* Watertown, Mass.: Persephone Press, 1981.

Moraga, Cherríe, and Ana Castillo, eds. *Esta puente mi espalda: Voces de mujeres tercer mundistas en los Estados Unidos.* San Francisco, Calif.: Ism Press, 1988.

Muñoz, José Esteban. *Disidentifications: Queers of Color and the Performance of Politics.* Minneapolis: University of Minnesota Press, 1999.

Quintana, Alvina. "Politics, Representation, and the Emergence of a Chicana Aesthetics." *Cultural Studies,* vol. 4 (1990): 72–83.

Rebolledo, Tey Diana. *Women Singing in the Snow: A Cultural Analysis of Chicana Literature.* Tucson: University of Arizona Press, 1995.

Rendón, Armando. *The Chicano Manifesto.* New York: Macmillan, 1971.

Saenz, Benjamin Alire. "In the Borderlands of Chicano Identity, There Are Only Fragments." In *Border Theory: The Limits of Cultural Politics.* Edited by Scott Michaelsen and David E. Johnson. Minneapolis: University of Minnesota Press, 1997. Pp. 68–96.

Saldívar-Hull, Sonia. *Feminism on the Border: Chicana Gender Politics and Literature.* Berkeley: University of California Press, 2000.

Sánchez, Rosaura, and Rosa Martínez Cruz. *Essays on la mujer.* Los Angeles: Chicano Studies Center Publications, University of California, 1977.

Sandoval, Chela. "Feminism and Racism: A Report on the 1981 National Women's Studies Association Conference." In *Making Face, Making Soul/Haciendo caras: Creative and Critical Perspectives by Feminists of Color.* Edited by Gloria Anzaldúa. San Francisco, Calif.: Spinsters/Aunt Lute Books, 1990. Pp. 55–71.

———. "Mestizaje as Method: Feminists-of-Color Challenge the Canon." In *Living Chicana Theory.* Edited by Carla Trujillo. Berkeley, Calif.: Third Woman Press, 1998. Pp. 352–370.

———. *Methodology of the Oppressed.* Minneapolis: University of Minnesota Press, 2000.

Tabuenca Córdoba, María-Socorro. "Viewing the Border: Perspectives from 'the Open Wound.'" *Discourse,* vol. 18, no. 1–2 (1995–1996): 146–168.

Tafolla, Carmen. *To Split a Human: Mitos, machos, y la mujer Chicana.* San Antonio, Tex.: Mexican American Cultural Center, 1985.

Trujillo, Carla, ed. *Chicana Lesbians: The Girls our Mothers Warned Us About.* Berkeley, Calif.: Third Woman Press, 1991.

———, ed. *Living Chicana Theory.* Berkeley, Calif.: Third Woman Press, 1998.

Crossing Borders, Creative Disorders: Latino Identities and Writing

ALAN WEST-DURÁN

THE EVER-GROWING field of Latino and Latina writing is reshaping U.S. literature, something that would have been inconceivable only three decades ago. Sandra Cisneros, Julia Alvarez, Oscar Hijuelos, and Rudolfo Anaya may not be household names like Selena, Sammy Sosa, Marc Anthony, or Jennifer Lopez, but they are authors being read by scores of high school and college students, as well as by a wider reading public. The Latino and Latina literary expansion is fueled by many factors, some that bode well for the evolving place of Latinos in U.S. letters, others that reflect a more problematic stance. The increasing presence of Latinos in the new demographic realities of the U.S., genuine scholarly interest, increased demand for literature written by women that has brought well-deserved attention to outstanding Latina writers, and an ever increasing Latino readership reflect positive developments. The marketing and commercial whims of the publishing industry, cashing in on the latest "ethnic" and "exotic" storytelling, betray a less positive stimulus for this expansion of Latina and Latino literature in the public eye.

To speak of Latino and Latina literature is, of course, a gross simplification. The field encompasses writers who might be born in the United States or abroad. U.S. Latina and Latino writers represent a world of diversity, and biography can help us understand these differences. For U.S.-born Latinos and Latinas, it is significant to know whether they are first-, second-, third-, or fourth-generation (or beyond). For those born abroad, it is germane to know at what age they came to the United States and why. Were their parents fleeing civil war, revolution, or political persecution, seeking better employment opportunities, or wanting to join family that was already here? Were they born in Mexico, the Caribbean, South America, or Central America? Are they mono-, bi-, or multilingual? If they speak English, do they do so with an accent? And if they speak Spanish, do they do so with an accent? Did their families live in rural communities and come here as migrant or agricultural workers, or are they from the middle class, having stayed on after attending college in the U.S.? What do they look like? Are they bronzed skin, Afro-Latin, of mixed race, white, or Asian? Are they heterosexual, gay, lesbian, bi- or transsexual? Are they Catholics, Protestants, or Jews, or do they practice syncretic religions like Regla de Ocha (Santeria), shamanism-*curanderismo,* Candomblé, or *espiritismo?*

Given this panoply of difference, what gives anyone license to group such heterogeneous populations together? Many of Latin descent do not subscribe to the term "Latino," for example. In Florida and New Mexico, the word "Hispanic" is preferred. Many refer to their nation of origin, and so call themselves "Puerto Ricans," "Colombians," or "Salvadorans." Still others use hyphenated designations, such as "Cuban-American" or "Mexican-American," to indicate their Americanness but still affirm their ethnic and cultural roots. Julia Alvarez says she is not a "Latina writer," but a writer who is Latina; she has also referred to herself as "Dominican gringa." While certainly proud of her Dominican heritage, she wants to be considered a writer first.

The social, historical, racial, ethnic, cultural, and linguistic diversity of the Latino population in the United States is reflected in a wide variety of expressive voices. Some authors are proud of their heritage, and their work is saturated with references to their ethnicity (names of characters, places, use of Spanish, elements of Latin American and Latino and Latina popular culture); others want to be part of the mainstream and play down these markers. For some, these decisions are part of an explicitly political self-identification and may be associated with activism; for others they reflect the desire to assimilate, but still with social repercussions such as opposition to affirmative action and bilingual education. Ultimately, one could ask why a Latino or Latina author could not write a novel about the interwoven lives of two brothers and two sisters who make up a Norwegian string quartet, with the entire narrative taking place in Oslo. Or why a Latina or Latino music critic could not write about Elvis

Presley or Beethoven, why a Latina or Latino travel journalist could not write about Canada, or why a Latina or Latino political scientist could not write about voting patterns in white suburban communities.

With these differences and pitfalls in mind, some common traits can be identified, albeit with great caution. Most scholars point out that there is shared heritage among Latinos: the Spanish language, Catholicism, a common Spanish colonial legacy, and certain patterns of socialization and regulation of family life, not to mention immigration to the U.S. (for many, but not all). As for certain themes that reappear in Latino and Latina literature, one could point to the immigration experience, fitting in (or not) into U.S. society, the relationship to a "home" country, the exploration of personal, cultural, and social identity, the depiction of barrio life, and the recuperation of family memory as it intersects with the sweep of history. Of course, exceptions can be offered to every one of these common traits, even if commercial interests tend to promote a homogenized Latino experience to sell more books.

Guillermo Gómez-Peña warns of the mainstream tendency to essentialize and folklorize ethnic literary expressions:

> To "be" in America, I mean in this America, is a complicated matter. You "are" in relation to the multiplicity of looks you are able to display. I am brown therefore I'm underdeveloped. I wear a mustache therefore I am Mexican. I gesticulate therefore I'm Latino. I am horny therefore I am a sexist. I experiment therefore I'm not authentic. I speak about politics therefore I'm un-American. My art is indescribable therefore I'm a performance artist.
>
> (*Dangerous Border Crossers: The Artist Talks Back,* pp. 91–92)

Gómez-Peña's warning is aimed at a strategy that tries to reduce Latinos and their culture to a few traits that can be easily catalogued and made safe for Anglo cultural consumption.

Martín Espada's poem "My Native Costume" performs a similar type of deconstruction. The poet has been invited to read at a suburban high school. The teacher asks him to wear his native (Puerto Rican) costume. Espada first replies that since he is a lawyer, his native costume is a pinstriped suit. The teacher insists, so the poet replies that maybe a *guayabera,* a shirt worn over slacks with pockets at chest and waist level that is tropically cool and practical. Except that it is February and freezing cold. The poet's solution is to wear the short-sleeved *guayabera* over a turtleneck. Triumphantly, he proclaims to the class, "Look kids, cultural adaptation." Espada's poem not only speaks to an Anglo exoticizing gaze, but also to issues of authenticity. The *guayabera* is not an indigenous piece of attire, like a Mexican *huipil,* nor is it African, either. Actually a Cuban creation from the countryside, perhaps from the eighteenth century, it became popular in Puerto Rico in the 1930s (they are also worn in Mexico and Central America), and most *guayaberas* are now made in Korea or Taiwan. Puerto Rico really has no national costume. Implicit in arguments about authenticity are notions that "traditional culture" is static and unchanging. Espada has humorously turned the whole issue of authenticity on its head.

In avoiding these homogenizing or exoticized images, we must ask, "What does a working-class Chicano Vietnam vet have in common with a middle-class, light-skinned Cuban? What commonalities are there between a dark-skinned Chicana who has lived through physical and sexual abuse and a mixed race Dominican male who is an ex-gang member, aside from an experience of violence? What does a third-generation Puerto Rican school teacher share with a Colombian landowner who has fled civil war?"

TRANSCULTURATION: SURVIVAL AS CREATIVE RESISTANCE

The complexity of personal, social, and historical experiences speaks to a fundamental issue at the heart of much Latino and Latina writing: its willingness to explore and explicitly examine cross-cultural encounters. The term "transculturation" has been used, often superficially, by many scholars. Fernando Ortiz (1881–1969), the Cuban ur-scholar who wrote extensively on Afro-Cuban culture, coined the phrase in *Cuban Counterpoint, Tobacco and Sugar* (1995) when he analyzed the historical, cultural, and economic counterpoint between tobacco and sugar, which he claimed could be the organizing image for understanding Cuba's rich sociocultural brew. Ortiz analyzed transculturation as occurring when a subjugated culture under colonialism and slavery that is able to incorporate, transform, and subtly subvert elements of the dominant culture to fashion meanings that ensure not only the survival of a culture and its people, but also their ability to thrive and create a new culture. Latinos in the U.S.—while not under conditions of colonialism or slavery—still find themselves subordinated in the social hierarchy and subjected to various forms of economic, linguistic, racial, or cultural exclusion. Transculturation can be understood as a form of historical and cultural translation. Since two cultures are meeting (or colliding), their interactions and attempts to know each other are a form of translation. Fashioning a poetics of historical understanding, transculturation is a practice of cultural creativity, a material practice that both reinscribes the past and transforms the present, a performative philosophical reasoning, and an act of social resistance (West-Durán). Transculturation can be defined as a continuous exchange between two or more cultures or cultural components that generate or create something "new and independent, although its bases, its roots, rest on preceding elements" (Morejón, p. 229). These exchanges can be peaceful or violent, but in either case they "unleash the demons of history" (Gómez-Peña, p. 47).

In the cultural encounters between Spain and the "New World," between Latin America/the Caribbean and the U.S., a history of violent conquest and creative resistance has generated communities with a unique sensitivity to the movement of politics and history in the flow of everyday lives. For the immigrant, the *contrapunteo,* or contrapuntal readings of self in dynamic, sometimes treacherously shifting contexts can be required for physical survival. In a U.S. context, transculturation makes it possible to understand Latina and Latino writing identities as complex acts of creation yielding diverse experiences that nevertheless share key commonalities.

The demons and angels of history are the product of asymmetrical power relationships, and therefore the intercultural exchange can go through a number of scenarios: colonial imposition (conquest, slavery, racialist domination), obligatory assimilation, genocide, political co-optation, passive resistance (theft, sabotage, feigning sickness, illegal trade), political subterfuge, tricksterism, and outright rebellion. From the point of view of the subjugated, the cultural response can involve mimicry, commercial exploitation, top-down appropriation, and bottom-up subversion (irony, parody, pastiche, carnival, open revolt) (Shohat and Stam, pp. 41–43). Transculturation, then, can be used to describe religious phenomena (syncretisms, such as in Regla de Ocha or Santeria), biological terms like hybridity (music like the *danzón* or salsa, food like *ajiacos, calalloos* or *sancochos*), human-genetic realities (*mestizaje* and race mixing), language (creoles, Spanglish, Tex-Mex), and healing methods (*curanderismo,* shamanism, Afro-Latin/Caribbean religions) (West-Durán).

Transculturation assumes that identity is something that is evolving constantly, often taking place over long historical periods. It is not a smooth process, nor a violence-free cultural theme park (Stam); the process can stall, be interrupted, unfold haltingly, be incomplete, or simply fail. Transculturation is characterized by displacements, dislocations, and retrenchments. It takes place in a series of different spaces as well: public and private, practical and cultural,

and leisure- and work-related. More importantly, and often forgotten in the highly theoretical discussions on identity and hybridity, transculturation also relates to material practices: to commodities, objects, the physical construction of tools, products, images, ideas, and symbols. It also includes the material dimensions of the workplace, home, school, street corner, bar, and club, the methods of transportation, and the movement from site to sight (West).

Through transculturation, Latin Americans, Caribbean peoples, and U.S. Latinos have created plural, sometimes contradictory, identities and new ways of knowing. The French literary critic and semiotician Roland Barthes (1915–1980) thought that photography might be the "impossible science of the unique being" (Barthes, p. 71). Implicit in his notion is that science need not be abstract, universalist, and reductive. Latina and Latino literature could be described as a moving, scripted image of the unique science of being Latino or Latina enacted creatively by authors as living examples of transculturation.

These border, transnational, or transculturated identities pose new questions for traditional paradigms of the immigrant experience. The Latino and Latina experience is antiassimilationist and at least bilingual, positing new definitions of what constitutes citizenship, political loyalty, and home and homeland (María Torres). For many though not all Latinos, being a U.S. citizen (which is not the same as being an American or being a "gringo") does not mean giving up one's mother tongue and cultural traditions, and breaking off completely with one's country of family origin. This rejection of the standard immigrant narrative—or in the words of Juan Gonzalez, "Speak Spanish, You're in America!" (*Harvest of Empire,* p. 206)— implies two things: multiple loyalties and a different perspective on what constitutes the difference between public, political, and private life. In the assimilationist model, the immigrant has a single home. For a recent immigrant, home is the native country; for an immigrant who has been in the U.S. for several years or a generation, home is where they currently live. The new, transculturated realities admit to several homes (or homelands). One could have an emotional home where one currently lives (Boston), several family homes, where parents, grandparents, and uncles reside (Puerto Rico, Cuba, the U.S., Portugal), political-citizenship homes (the U.S., Puerto Rico, Cuba) and several cultural homes (Puerto Rico, Cuba, the U.S., Spain, the Caribbean).

This hybridity and complexity has literary and artistic analogies. Gloria Anzaldúa's *Borderlands/La Frontera: The New Mestiza* shifts from essay, to poetry, to autobiography, to reconstruction of pre-Columbian mythology as a way of defining a border, Xicanista feminism, to political tract. In Giannina Braschi's *Yo-Yo Boing!*, the author shifts from Spanish to English to Spanglish without skipping a beat, and with no attempt to translate. As the introduction to the novel states, "Choose and lose." Latino and Latina identity and its cultural creations are not either/or propositions. Rather, they reveal an acute, nuanced, and sometimes adversarial relationship to language. Their mixing of languages and genres, their going back and forth between cultures and their questioning of both, and their effortless immersions into different milieus and systems of values benefit from being seen through the lens of transculturation.

LANGUAGE: HOMECOMING THROUGH OTHERNESS

Language is both natural, like skin, and openly defining, our portable and oral passports. Anzaldúa speaks to its power of communication and self-definition, and to its significance as a tool of legitimation:

> So, if you really want to hurt me, talk badly about my language. Ethnic identity is twin skin to linguistic identity—I am my language. Until I can take pride in my language, I cannot take pride in myself. Until I can accept as legitimate Chicano

Texas, Spanish, Tex-Mex and all the other languages I speak, I cannot accept the legitimacy of myself. Until I am free to write bilingually and to switch codes without always having to translate, while I still have to speak English or Spanish when I would rather speak Spanglish, and as long as I have to accommodate the English speakers rather than having them accommodate me, my tongue will be illegitimate.

> (quoted in Chambers, p. 76)

Even writers who would disagree with Anzaldúa, like Richard Rodriguez (who would accommodate to English speakers) or others who insist on speaking both English and Spanish correctly (thus seeking to avoid Spanglish), would find it difficult to disagree with her plea for the acceptance of linguistic complexity or how language is a legitimating agent of personal and social identity.

In his influential autobiography, *Hunger of Memory*, Rodriguez claims that academic and intellectual success can only be achieved by banishing Spanish, and that the rupture between a Spanish-speaking family world and an English-speaking school and professional world must be absolute. Yet Rodriguez's own autobiographical writings subsequent to that work suggest the complex sociopolitical and personal context within which he achieved such a radical rejection of his own and his family's cultural background. Rodriguez describes a strong color line in his family, typical of mestizo families growing up in colonial and racist societies, within which his dark-skinned "Indian" look, closely associated with his family's poverty and his father's struggles as a laborer, had to be overcome with a radical leap into all things white, Anglo-Saxon, and English speaking. More recently, Rodriguez has also disclosed the role his homosexuality played in the course of his personal life, within which his struggle with and against his ethnic identity must be understood. These dimensions of personal autobiography create the frame of reference from which to interpret Rodriguez's claim that the rejection of Spanish language and culture is necessary for academic achievement. Clearly,

25

Rodriguez has creatively and successfully mastered dilemmas of his own development with this strategy. Yet without a critical analysis of the writer's "positioned partiality," we are left to believe that one-dimensional assimilation and acculturation processes are necessary for the successful development of all Latino children. The beauty of Rodriguez's writing, and the consistency of his monolingual assimilationist belief in the dominant culture, has contributed to the belief of many educators that, to be successful, Latinos must amputate their native language and culture, even at the expense of a lifelong burden of grief (Shapiro, 1997).

Anzaldúa's remarks highlight some issues about identity in our current times. Latinos and Latin Americans, like many people around the globe, have experienced major social, economic, and political upheaval, in part due to the demands of globalization that have created global displacements of labor markets. In the last few decades, whether due to shifting labor markets, new migration patterns, new emancipatory movements or an ever-increasing commercialized culture that foments individualism, people's rootedness in a given community has been loosened, if not overturned. Identities previously seen as fixed, natural, and local are now situational, contextual, creative, changing, performative, and portable. The "baggage" we carry includes garments for all seasons, races, languages, genders, ideologies, and religions.

Language is integral to these processes. In a poem titled "Convocación de palabras" ("Convocation of Words"), Tino Villanueva reminds us that language is not made up of just words, as Roque Dalton suggests in "Poetic Art," included in *Small Hours of the Night: Selected Poems of Roque Dalton*. Villanueva's poem, originally written in Spanish, speaks to his acquisition of English and is sprinkled with words that he kept in notebooks to build up his vocabulary. Early in the poem, he refers to the shame of not understanding what is on TV and subtly mentions the racism of the school system, which expected him to be late and indecisive,

and to learn nothing. Slowly, he begins to build his vocabulary, confidence, and self. The poem ends,

> A constant effort,
> creating myself in my own image
> each time I pronounced one of them:
> *postprandial*
> *subsequently*
> and finally willing myself to write
> the fourteen letters of my name
> and over them
> the word
> *libertad.*

(Villanueva, p. 27)

Villanueva's struggle with English is embedded within the historical context of a Mexican migrant family. The poet deftly weaves the emergence of his new self and the growth of his vocabulary, an act of self-creation that is echoed in the poem itself, and yet the poem ends with a reference to his name and with the word *libertad*, as if to remind the reader that his new self must be built on his Mexican roots and on the Spanish language, not on their obliteration.

"HISTORY AS A SECOND LANGUAGE"

Poet Dionisio Martínez's expression "history as a second language," which was also the title of his 1993 book, is an apt description of a major concern of U.S. Latino and Latina writers. Whether it be a reexamination of La Malinche or the Virgin of Guadalupe by the likes of Ana Castillo or Anzaldúa, a family's response to the events of the Cuban Revolution (as in Virgil Suárez's *The Cutter*), a re-creation of the life of the Mirabal sisters in the Dominican Republic (*In the Time of the Butterflies*), the play *Zoot Suit* by Luis Váldez, which imaginatively re-creates Anglo-Chicano relations in 1940s Los Angeles, or Pedro Pietri's biting poetic satires about the dark side of the American dream for Puerto Ricans in New York (*Puerto Rican*

Obituary), Latino and Latina writers have been fascinated by the play of history in the unfolding of intimate lives.

There are myriad reasons for this: in some instances the writers themselves, or someone in their immediate family, have lived through these historic events, which some call borrowed memories. Many writers are motivated by the desire to document the untold dimension of U.S. history that has traditionally silenced minority voices, or by the need to speak out against injustice, racism, or sexism. Others feel compelled to explore their cultural roots, or examine the strengths and contradictions of the communities they grew up in. Writers growing up in the 1960s and 1970s were affected by the Chicano movement, involvement with the Young Lords, anti–Vietnam War protests, the civil rights movement, union struggles, feminist movements, and support for Latin American solidarity groups. Some were activists in one or more of these social movements. Many drew analogies between U.S. domestic and foreign policy, especially with regard to people of color.

The history of Latin America is intimately related to the United States and its Latino populations. The connections are many and complex, be they outright military conquest of territory (such as in Mexico), colonial takeover (in Puerto Rico), counterinsurgency warfare (in El Salvador, Guatemala, Nicaragua, and Colombia), CIA-engineered coups (in Guatemala and Chile), military intervention (in Cuba, Haiti, Panama, and the Dominican Republic), or the propping up of military dictatorships in Chile, Bolivia, Brazil, Argentina, El Salvador, Guatemala, and Ecuador (in the 1960s, 1970s, and 1980s).

U.S. economic involvement in Latin America is almost two centuries old, and it is not an innocent relationship, as Juan Gonzalez has pointed out:

> If Latin America had not been raped and pillaged by U.S. capital since its independence, millions of desperate workers would not now be coming here

in such numbers to reclaim a share of that wealth; and if the United States is today the world's richest nation, it is in part because of the sweat and blood of the copper workers of Chile, the tin miners of Bolivia, the fruit pickers of Guatemala and Honduras, the cane cutters of Cuba, the oil workers of Venezuela and Mexico, the pharmaceutical workers of Puerto Rico, the ranch hands of Costa Rica and Argentina, the West Indians who died building the Panama Canal, and the Panamanians who maintained it.

> (Juan Gonzalez, 2000, p. xviii)

The upshot of that economic exploitation is what Gonzalez calls the "harvest of empire." This political and economic relationship has formed the contours of a diasporic Latino community in the United States, and is clearly an integral part of U.S. history, albeit one that is often silenced, forgotten, or distortedly explained away under a benign veneer of paternal concern about "underdevelopment" and "democracy" that barely disguises imperial designs. None of this implies that Latino and Latina writing exclusively deals with issues of histories of oppression. However, to forget the historical record underlying current realities is to miss out on important contextual factors that make Latino and Latina literature what it is. This historicity offers an especially meaningful contrast to the "milk of amnesia" (in the words of Carmelita Tropicana), or ahistoricity of U.S. public life.

In the case of Chicano and Chicana literature, some of its key works blurred the distinction between literature as an aesthetic and literature as a tool for political organizing. Such would be the case with the classic "Yo Soy Joaquín/I Am Joaquín" by Rodolfo "Corky" Gonzales, a long narrative poem that both denounces oppression and racism and affirms the author's cultural heritage by defiantly ending with "I SHALL ENDURE! / I WILL ENDURE!" Gonzales's poem would often be read at rallies, was performed by street-theater groups, and was rendered into slide and film. His work, along with that of other poets such as Abelardo Delgado and Alurista (Alberto Baltazar Urista), formed a corpus of socially oriented poetry that both complemented and inspired the burgeoning Mexican American civil rights movement.

As part of the movement, Chicanos, as Mexican Americans now called themselves, indicating that they were neither "pure" Mexican nor "gringos," spoke of a mythic-spiritual homeland called Aztlán, which needed to be reclaimed. Aztlán, which was the ancestral home of the *mexicas* (or Aztecs) before they went south to found Tenochtitlán (now Mexico City), today would encompass Texas, New Mexico, Arizona, Utah, Colorado, and Arizona. It was a potent symbol of cultural origin, ethnic unity, territorial integrity, and national sovereignty, made all the more poignant since this land had been conquered by the U.S. and ceded from Mexico in the Treaty of Guadalupe Hidalgo (1848). Significantly, the cultural dimensions of Aztlán reaffirmed Chicanos' Indian background, mining the cultural, religious, and mythological treasures of pre-Columbian Mexico (Olmec, Zapotec, Maya, Toltec, Aztec, among others).

Chicano novelists like Rudolfo Anaya, Oscar Z. Acosta, and Miguel Méndez drew on Aztlán, not as nostalgic indulgence, but as affirmation of cultural identity to aid Chicanos in their current and future struggles for social, educational, and political advancement. Says Alurista:

> Anaya uses myth as a "healer," whereas Méndez sees myth as a restructuring agent, and Acosta renders myth as a revolutionary war cry. All three codify Aztlán as borderless and belonging to those who work, who toil for the wealth that, presently, others who own the means of production enjoy. Aztlán is a cry for struggle, redefinition, and self-determination; it abhors war, misery and the total annihilation of the human species in any of the novels here examined. Aztlán is positioned as an origin and the promise of human possibility for a more humane social formation.
>
> (Alurista, p. 227)

Aztlán then was not mere nostalgia stuck in the past, but a spiritual, cultural, and historical homeland to draw sustenance from in order to build a better future for La Raza.

Some writers, like Gloria Anzaldúa, drew on Aztlán but within the context of border or mestiza consciousness, a new country that is neither Mexico nor the U.S. Anzaldúa calls this border an open wound,

> where the Third World grates against the first and bleeds. And before a scab forms, it hemmorhages again, the lifeblood of two worlds merging to form a third country—a border culture. Borders are set up to define the places that are safe and unsafe, to distinguish *us* from *them*. . . . *Los atravesados* live here: the squint-eyed, the perverse, the queer, the troublesome, the mongrel, the mulato, the half-breed, the half dead; in short, those who cross over, pass over, or go through the confines of the 'normal.' Gringos in the U.S. Southwest consider the inhabitants of the borderlands transgressors, aliens—whether they possess documents or not, whether they're Chicanos, Indians or Blacks. . . . Ambivalence and unrest reside there and death is no stranger.
>
> (Anzaldúa, pp. 3–4)

Anzaldúa's words, made all the more poignant in a post-9/11 climate, poetically evoke many borders that run through Latino life, be they historical, territorial, racial, national, or sexual (preference), all fraught with danger at moments, and a potential for violence.

Although Anzaldúa's words relate to the almost 2,000-mile border between Mexico and the U.S., her words are applicable (even if with substantial refinements) to Puerto Ricans, Cubans, Salvadorans, Dominicans, and others. Similar (but not identical) to Chicanos of the Southwest, the U.S. has control over Puerto Rico's national territory. Boricuas are U.S. citizens and can freely travel between the island and the mainland U.S., the only group among Latinos in the U.S. for which that is true. On the other hand, Cubans on U.S. soil are the product of Cold War and Third World revolutionary politics that characterized a period from the end of World War II to the fall of the Berlin Wall

(1945–1989). For almost twenty years, until the late 1970s, Cubans who left the island could not return home. They were considered *gusanos* (counterrevolutionary worms), and their status with their homeland was at the opposite spectrum to that of Puerto Ricans.

And yet Puerto Ricans and Cubans, like Chicanos, were *atravesados*, in the way (stuck in between), along with all the rich associations given by Anzaldúa: mongrel, squint-eyed, troublesome. This in-betweeness is evoked in the work and *travesuras* (mischief, wit) of several authors, the junkies and street people of Miguel Piñero's plays, the eternal misfits in Pietri's poetry, the melancholic characters of Oscar Hijuelos, and Zeta Acosta's *vatos locos*. It is also poignantly expressed in the poetry of Lourdes Casal, specifically in "For Ana Veldford" from the collection *Bridges to Cuba/Puentes a Cuba* (1995):

> And still New York is my home.
> I am ferociously loyal to this acquired *patria chica*.
> Because of New York I am a foreigner anywhere else,
> . . . .
> I carry this marginality, immune to all turning back,
> too *habanera* to be *newyorkina*,
> too *newyorkina* to be
> —even to become again—
> anything else.
>
> (Casal, pp. 21–22)

Casal's poem touches on a sensitive topic for Latina and Latino writers: the relationship to homeland. Cuban authors, like Casal, had to deal with the reality of exile in not being able to go back, except for short visits. Some authors have chosen not to go back to Cuba, stung by the political fortunes dealt to them by a communist regime. For other writers, going back is a way to recharge their creative energies (aside from seeing family, of course) or to continue to explore their cultural past.

For other writers, like Abraham Rodríguez Jr., going back to Puerto Rico seems pointless. Rodríguez, author of *The Boy without a Flag: Tales of the South Bronx* (1992), is relentlessly unsentimental about the island, and sharply criticizes both those who view it nostalgically and those who live there, for letting themselves be hoodwinked into thinking they have a special relationship with the U.S. instead of living under a colonial regime. Rodríguez is equally critical of U.S. racial categorizations:

> Some Hispanics are white, some Hispanics are black, some Hispanics are even Asian. Hispanic is not a race. . . . I grew up with that idea that I'm a minority, I'm Hispanic. I threw it off. I don't need somebody else to define me. I don't need someone else to tell me what I am or what my concerns are, or the concerns of Hispanics. I'm not Hispanic.
>
> (Rodríguez, p. 143)

LATINOS AND RACE: BEYOND THE DROP, A RIVER OF CULTURES

Rodríguez's words point to a central aspect of Latino and Latina life in the United States: how Latinos and Latinas support, challenge, and redefine racial constructs that have long governed this country. The concept of *mestizaje* (race mixing) is often invoked to distinguish Latinos from the binary racial system of the United States and its one-drop rule. To simplify radically, if in the U.S. a drop of black blood made you black, in the Caribbean and Latin America it was the reverse. A drop of white blood made you white. Other factors contextualize racial definitions for Latinos as well: occupation, education, clothing, residence, surname, accent, and family. In Latin America and the Caribbean, as opposed to the situation in the United States, nationality and culture have strongly inflected views on race.

The term *mestizaje* was used as a key metaphor in José Vasconcelos's seminal essay *La raza cósmica* (1925; *The Cosmic Race*, 1997), in which he expresses pride in Mexico's and Latin America's mixture of races, claiming that after the four major racial categories (black, Asian, Indian, and white), Latin America's racial mixtures would yield a fifth, cosmic race, a synthesis of the previous four. But recently, scholars have revealed some of the Eurocentric biases of the book, showing that its celebration of miscegenation was, in effect, a celebration of whitening, an ultimate downplaying of racial and cultural difference (Marentes). In fact, Vasconcelos would be aghast at today's radical multiculturalists who emphasize ethnic, gender, racial specificity, and sexual preference.

For some Latinos *mestizaje* has meant a welcome break from the U.S.'s polarized racial history, particularly if they did not look black according to U.S. norms. But what if they did? Evelio Grillo (in *Black Cuban, Black American*) and Piri Thomas (in *Down These Mean Streets*) point out that often they were considered too black to be Hispanic, but by virtue of their Spanish, they were also too Hispanic to be black. Still, both Grillo and Thomas decided to become more identified with African American life and culture, while still holding on to their Latin heritage. Grillo, who grew up in Ybor City, Florida, speaks to both Cuban and U.S. racism. Cuban blacks lived in African American neighborhoods even if

> Black Cubans worked in factories alongside white Cubans. While my mother formed interracial friendships at work, few, if any, such friendships extended to visits in the homes. Nor did whites and blacks attend church together. Black Cubans had their one mutual benefit society and social center, La Unión Martí-Maceo. . . . I don't remember playing with a single white Cuban child.
>
> (pp. 7, 9)

What both Grillo and Thomas's work underline is some of the unexamined (and uglier) side of *mestizaje* theory: that behind its celebration of racial mixing there is a tacit, unspoken reaffirmation of whiteness as the norm. Not all of its proponents necessarily feel that way, but one needs to examine its assumptions closely and rigorously.

Although Grillo and Thomas's coming-of-age stories go back to the 1930s, 1940s, and 1950s, we should not be lulled into thinking that living in a post–Civil Rights era makes their stories seem like historical relics. A recent series in the *New York Times,* "How Race Is Lived in America," outlines the story of two recent Cuban immigrants, one black, the other white, who were best of friends in Cuba but subsequently drew apart in racially segregated Miami (Lelyveld, pp. 23–41). What makes their story both compelling and saddening is that they drew apart partially because of the more racially segregated nature of U.S. society. But what is more disturbing but also revelatory is how the racial consciousness of U.S. society allows Joel Ruiz, the African Cuban liquor store employee studying to be a physical therapist, to understand the racist nature of Cuban society retrospectively.

Gerald Torres, among others, believes that something similar to the dream of Venezuelan patriot Simón Bolívar (1783–1830), who yearned for the unity of Latin America by wanting it to be one huge country that could withstand pressure from major powers (at the time, Great Britain, France, and the U.S.), will become a reality in the U.S. among Latinos (Gerald Torres, p. 165). He believes that the exigencies of attaining political power, greater social mobility, and educational opportunity will make Latinos of different nationalities and regions (Mexico, the Caribbean, and Central and South America) work out their differences and unite to achieve common goals. However, this unity has to be created within the space of American politics, structured on a black/white racial division. This implies that Latinos identify themselves as nonwhite, or as people of color. The advantage to this is that what was previously considered nonwhite goes beyond blackness (physically and psychologically), embracing almost one-third of the population of the U.S. In addition, it makes people of color a political term, not a mere racial descriptor. Even people who are white-looking can be people of color, but this must be a conscious decision on their part.

The negative side of this new social construction is that individuals can be swayed by what Torres calls the "racial bribe." Some Latinos and Latinas opt out of being Latino or Latina and simply pass for white, but that is "a strategy for individual assimilation . . . not a strategy for political empowerment" (Gerald Torres, p. 166). Others go along with being people of color and when it is no longer convenient become white. Surveys show that many Latinos do classify themselves as white, but a majority (56 percent) would prefer to have Hispanic/Latino as a distinct racial category, and another 20 percent prefer "another option" (Pew Hispanic Center, pp. 32–33). In terms of a pan-ethnic identity, 85 percent of Latinos still feel that their individual cultures are distinct, with 14 percent identifying with a common Hispanic/Latino culture, and almost half believed that Latinos of different nationalities are not working together. Whether Torres's predictions come true or not, even the partial success of these options will begin redefining ethnic/racial politics in the U.S., as well as create new rules for democratic participation, and carve out a more inclusive polity. Latino and Latina writers, regardless of how they define themselves ethnically or racially, will play a critical role in the evolution of the political, social, and cultural definitions of race in the U.S. Given the ever-increasing complexity of these realities, artists and writers will offer more nuanced portraits that will elude the more conventional parameters of social scientists.

MIGRANCY, BORDERS, WOUNDS: DO YOU EVER ARRIVE?

Much of Latino and Latina literature seems to focus on the immigration and coming-of-age experience. This should not be surprising: in 1997, the foreign-born population of the U.S. was listed at twenty-seven million, with half of those twenty-seven million having come from Latin America. Almost two-thirds of Latinos in the U.S. are foreign born. This continuous renewal of people from home countries will make the immigration experience a central issue in the lives of Latinos into the foreseeable future. The continuous injection of home culture not only gives U.S. Latinos a renewed sense of their own heritage, but also brings newer, ever-changing elements of their home culture, thereby creating a living, more dynamic relationship to that culture rather than one based on a static image shaped by nostalgia. Many of the significant works of Latino and Latina literature are memoirs or fiction that read like memoirs. Readers who are not Latino or Latina often assume that if a work of fiction by a Latina or Latino writer takes place in a Latino neighborhood, the work must be grounded in the author's own experience. This runs the risk of assuming an "authenticity" that often tacitly or openly devalues the agency and creativity of Latino and Latina writers, since they are often only considered barrio chroniclers with an occasional literary flair. The implicit corollary of this view is that Latino and Latina writers can only write about Latino or Latina characters, themes, and places. Fortunately, many writers have refused to limit their creativity in such a fashion, and some have taken on the more absurd dimensions of U.S. identity politics. For example, in Ed Vega's *The Comeback* (1985), a zany political-psychological thriller, a Puerto Rican–Eskimo college hockey star, Armando Martínez, has an identity crisis and thinks he is Frank Garboil, an economics professor. Vega doggedly and unflinchingly examines and critiques the unexamined assumptions of what is considered ethnic literature.

Despite the moniker of the U.S. as being the land of immigrants, each immigrant wave always faces varying degrees of difficulty: resistance, racism, and sometimes outright hostility, either from the population or from the U.S. government. The Immigration and Naturalization Service was created in 1924 and, though ostensibly it was created to curb immigration from all parts of the globe, it clearly was targeted to the Mexico-U.S. border, where some 250,000 Mexicans had emigrated between 1910 and 1930. Given the xenophobic and racist climate at the time, the government was urged to look into the matter. A 1930 report by Vanderbilt University economist Roy L. Garis, prepared for John Box, a Texas congressman who was sponsoring anti-immigration legislation, warns of Mexicans arriving in such numbers that they are reconquering the Southwest, undoing the results of the U.S.–Mexican War (1846–1848), indeed threatening the foundations of "our white civilization." A few pages later, the report quotes an anonymous statement that "seems to reflect the general sentiment of those who are deeply concerned with the future welfare of this country":

> Their minds run to nothing higher than animal functions—eat, sleep, sexual debauchery. In every huddle of Mexican shacks one meets the same idleness, hordes of hungry dogs, and filthy children with faces plastered with flies, disease, lice, human filth, stench, promiscuous fornication, bastardy, lounging, apathetic peons and lazy squaws, beans, and dried chili, liquor, general squalor, and envy and hatred of the gringo. These people sleep by day and prowl by night like coyotes, stealing anything they can get their hands on, no matter how useless to them it may be. Nothing left outside is safe unless padlocked or chained down. Yet there are Americans clamoring for more of these human swine to be brought over from Mexico.
>
> (Garis, p. 436)

It would be difficult to find anywhere a more complete catalog of racist stereotypes than in the previous paragraph. Every conceivable human realm is slandered or debased: physical, spiritual, social, legal, culinary, psychological, racial, even medical.

These are Oscar Z. Acosta's "cockroach people," and with all due respect to Kafka,

Acosta's use of the image in his last novel (*The Revolt of the Cockroach People*) is a double-edged and bitterly sardonic rejoinder to the congressional report: at one level roaches have an almost infinite capacity to survive and even increase in number, and at another defiantly saying to the dominant culture, "We are ubiquitous, no matter how much you would like to be rid of us we are here in the streets, the schools, the churches, the businesses, the concert halls, everywhere."

Now, for the most part, Latin American immigrants are not facing this type of venomous behavior or attitude from Anglos, but U.S. views toward immigration remain profoundly ambivalent if not negative, and the aftereffects of 11 September 2001 show a visible hardening of attitudes. Negative perception of immigrants run from 50 percent to 70 percent, and among Latin Americans, Mexicans, and Cubans fare most negatively. Interestingly, these negative attitudes are not only immigration-related; some scholars claim that negative attitudes toward Latinos affect attitudes toward immigration (and not the other way around). Some of these attitudes are fueled by the usual concerns about jobs, use of social services, and education. But increasingly immigration is perceived as a cultural threat: a nationwide survey by the *Los Angeles Times* (in August 1996) had 42 percent of respondents replying that Latinos and Latinas were a cultural threat (30 percent said they improved U.S. culture, 18 percent said they had no effect). The so-called "threat" is perceived demographically, linguistically (the use of Spanish), and politically, with some respondents saying the disunity caused by immigration will fragment the U.S.

Latino and Latina writing profoundly humanizes the experience that is often missed in the glut of statistics or in the heated (and often inaccurate) polemics around immigration, which are often ideologically or racially motivated. Whether it be the history of four sisters as told by Julia Alvarez in *How the García Girls Lost Their Accents,* or the first-person narrative of Esmeralda Santiago's *When I Was Puerto Rican,* or José Antonio Villareal's migrant farm laborers in *Pocho,* the Latino and Latina immigration story is complex, heart wrenching, and often enraging.

Even for writers born in the U.S., the immigration experience, the relationships between home and host country, are paramount. In more recent writing, this relationship is no longer viewed as rigidly structured, that is, as a one-way process of Americanization. Unlike the European immigrant experience, the break with the motherland is never complete, but at the same time, embracing a new life in the U.S. is not always an unmitigated triumph. Rubén Martínez's words in *The Other Side: Fault Lines, Guerilla Saints, and the True Heart of Rock 'n' Roll* (1992) evoke that rich ambiguity:

> Mine is the generation that arrived too late for Che Guevara but too early for the fall of the Berlin Wall. Weaned on a blend of cultures, languages, and ideologies (Anglo/Latino, Spanish/English, individualist/collectivist), I have lived both in the North and the South over my twenty-nine years, trying to be South in the South, North in the North, South in the North and North in the South. Now, I stand at the center—watching history whirl around me as my own history fissures: my love shatters, North and South, and a rage arises from within as the ideal of existential unity crumbles. I cannot tell whether what I see is a beginning or an end. My quest for a true center, for a cultural, political and romantic home, is stripped of direction. . . . It has been, it is, in other words, a search for a one that is much more than two. Because, wherever I am now, I must be much more than two. I must be North and South in the North, and in the South.
>
> (pp. 3–5)

Martínez's observations could apply to a wide spectrum of Latinos in the U.S., be they writers or not. Family ties to the south include sending home money (in countries like El Salvador and Cuba, this constitutes one of the main sources of income), traveling home, receiving family members in the U.S., constant phone (and now Internet) contact, and keeping up on events in native countries through Spanish-language media. Martínez seems to suggest, however, that notions of home and host countries have become porous, almost nonexistent, or perhaps more accurately, multi-existent. Martínez describes what some would call a new ethnoscape created by Latinos in the U.S.

> By *ethnoscape,* I mean the landscape of persons who constitute the shifting world in which we live: tourists, immigrants, refugees, exiles, guest workers, and other moving groups and individuals constitute an essential feature of the world and appear to affect the politics of (and between) nations to a hitherto unprecedented degree. This is not to say there are no relatively stable communities and networks of kinship, friendship, work, and leisure, as well as of birth, residence, and other filial forms. But it is to say that the warp of these stabilities is everywhere shot through with the woof of human motion, as more persons and groups deal with the realties of having to move or the fantasies of wanting to move. . . . The landscapes of group identity—the ethnoscapes—around the world are no longer familiar anthropological objects, insofar as groups are no longer tightly territorialized, spatially bounded, historically unselfconscious, or culturally homogeneous.
>
> (Appadurai, pp. 33–34, 48)

THE PERSONAL AND POLITICAL POETICS OF "WRITING HOME"

Martínez's search for center and Appadurai's ethnoscape echo my own writer-scholar-translator journey to "write home," an act that re-creates not only a sense of loss, but equally creates a new home through language and art, a new complex self that is *atraversado* (traversed, in verse, in between). I have considered myself a true resident of four cities: Boston, New York, San Juan, and Havana. I was born in Cuba, from a father born in Brooklyn, whose family moved to Havana when he was eleven months old, and a mother born on the island. My maternal grandparents emigrated from Galicia, Spain, trying to make a better life in the Americas, and without knowing it, enlisted as part of the 1880–1910 demographic wave to whiten post-independence Cuba (1902). After leaving Cuba, we went to Houston, where I lost my Spanish (*perdí la lengua, me tragué la lengua*, literally "to lose one's tongue" or "swallow one's tongue"), since Texas in 1960 was a downright hostile place for people who spoke Spanish. Groups of my fellow students taunted me, called me names, physically cornered me, and said I should go back where I came from. It was my first taste of Texan and U.S. xenophobia and racism; I was a child of the revolution whose family felt betrayed by the radical course mapped out by Fidel Castro, and who landed in the house of a redneck uncle of Jim Crow Houston.

During the year we lived in Houston, the travails of fitting in were deeply haunted by the question no child could answer: Would we ever see my father again, or would he be swallowed up by the uncertain and abrupt shifts in the Cold War that were heating up into a barely avoided nuclear confrontation?

After my father joined us, my family moved three more times in as many years, first to New Orleans, which I found out many years later is a most Caribbean city. Its architecture, its rich multiracial Creole culture and music, and its street life reminded me of San Juan and Havana, and was a welcome counterpoint to the soul-annihilating climate of Houston. We then moved to Panama for a year, where I began to regain my Spanish, and finally we settled in Puerto Rico. Panama and Puerto Rico were both countries where English was overvalued, and my Spanish was a *lengua de trapo* (literally, "rag," but actually the mumbled language children speak).

In San Juan, I became both more (and less) Cuban and certainly more Puerto Rican, given the peculiar dynamics between Cubans and Puerto Ricans on the island in the 1960s and 1970s. Actually, for a while I simply spoke and acted

Puerto Rican (or even as a "gringo"), as Cubans were viewed with more hostility than North Americans. There was a reason for this: Cubans tended to be very clannish and to criticize Puerto Ricans, and they occupied an inordinately powerful role in the island's economy and media. Their Cuban-centric view of the world, which many viewed correctly as arrogant, did not help matters. But I became Spanish dominant again (*a soltar y sacar la lengua*, "let the tongue loose, stick it out").

Despite this reimmersion into a Spanish-speaking milieu, as an adolescent I began writing poetry in English. I had read only a few Latin American and Caribbean authors, and preferred Beckett to Burgos, Pound to Paz. As my social and political world expanded, I increasingly found that English, unadorned, linear, musically flatter than Spanish, could not do justice to what I yearned to speak (*darle a la lengua*). I worked with the Young Lords on the island before I went to college in New York. During those years in New York I worked with the anti–Vietnam War movement and progressive Cuban activists and wrote for the magazines *Joven Cuba* and *Areíto*. I was exposed to salsa, a lifelong passion that has influenced not only my own poetry but a wider interest in Afro-Caribbean music. After discovering the Puerto Rican poet and fiction writer Manuel Abreu, I began writing in Spanish, especially poetry, which I continue to do. As a bilingual poet with a political sensibility, I became interested in the literary translation of a Latin American poetic-political myth (Roque Dalton), as well as in translating for cases of political asylum for Central Americans, which required the poetics of persuasion. My experience in video with alternative media, and the repercussions of the Sandinista revolution, motivated me to work for the Radio Venceremos System of El Salvador, but always based in New York.

The experience of living in New York, first from 1971 to 1975, then from 1977 to 1986, brought me in touch with many Latin

Americans fleeing brutal military regimes that tortured and disappeared thousands (in Argentina, Uruguay, Chile, and Bolivia), not to mention the Central American conflicts of the 1980s. These often heart-wrenching friendships gave me both a pan–Latin American consciousness, quite in the spirit of Bolívar's dream, and also the realization that I was becoming a U.S. Latino, by virtue of being a translator and an activist, as someone who was trying to bridge the gaps between the U.S. and Latin America, as someone redefining his own identity constantly, albeit within Caribbean/Latin American/Latino parameters.

As a poet and essayist, my writing has embraced both spare verses of political denunciation and baroquely layered descriptions of San Juan and Havana. Roque Dalton, Ernesto Cardenal, Sor Juana Inés de la Cruz, and José Lezama Lima were my poetic mentors. The first was a Salvadoran revolutionary who made fun of the left, the second a Marxist mystic and Sandinista minister with a cinematic bent that was influenced by Pound, Sor Juana was a "lesbian" nun of the seventeenth century who wrote exquisite baroque poetry, and the last was a gay Cuban poet who wrote the most stunning neobaroque and erotic re-creations of family life in his novel *Paradiso*, as well as a seminal essay on Latin American and Caribbean identity, *La expresión americana*. All these poetic currents converge in a poem written by Dionisio Martínez, "Years of Vision," similar to my own aesthetic and historical concerns.

> I changed my name and taught myself not to
>   answer when you
> called me by the old familiar one.
>
> It became obvious that accidents are worth
>   repeating.
>
> Each day I woke a little closer to the sea with
>   little more
> than my cobalt blue history to keep me afloat.

> I bought a shirt to match the earth of each new
>   country I
> stumbled into—*terra cota, terra firma, terra
>   incognita.*
>
> In countries with nothing but overabundance,
>   language has the
> luxury of moving backward—*red hibiscus, dark
>   leaves.*

(Martínez 1995, p. 72)

I have lived in Boston for roughly half my adult life, where I have been more devoted to cultural issues, and in the last decade have worked as an academic, writer, music critic, and translator. As a Boston BoriCuban Latino, I inhabit a peculiar landscape, since this is a city that has both a Latino and Latina professional class and a huge population that is one of the poorest Latino populations in the nation. As a writer and academic, I often find myself trying to explain or translate (to Anglos and Latinos alike) the textures and transculturations of Latino identity and culture.

My life as writer, translator, and academic, then, embodies an ethnoscape that is becoming more common for Latinos in the U.S.: one that is carried on over vast geographical spaces, multiple languages, intricate and overlapping histories, and differing ideologies, religions, and cuisines. We are fiercely nationalistic and local, and yet carry multiple loyalties that are global; in a country obsessed with racial definition we say, "None of the above" (or "all of the above"). We are Catholics, *santeros,* and believers in shamanism in a Protestant country. Within us coexist pre-Columbian beliefs, biblical commandments, West African practices of magic, and a collectivist ethos, tested daily in a market-drenched milieu of individualism, work at the expense of family, trivialization of sex and violence, and deification of money. With our rice and beans, we might have a spring roll, along with mashed potatoes and ham. In a country where the 1960s seems as remote (and misunderstood) as ancient Egypt, we carry within us the movements of history: its voluntary and involuntary displacements, migrations, political upheavals, and exiles (the fallout of loyalties and treasons).

THE FUTURE OF LATINO AND LATINA WRITING

Latino and Latina writing will continue to thrive in the U.S. despite the whims of the U.S. publishing industry. First, the growing demographic reality of the U.S. Latino population (thirty-five to thirty-eight million) will ensure a wider Latino and Latina reading public, in addition to an equally growing Anglo readership. There is also an interest in Latin America and Spain in reading U.S. Latino and Latina literature, which has also spawned a small but growing list of translations of these authors' works into Spanish. More specifically, within the U.S. is a significant group of the Latino and Latina population that has an annual household income over $50,000 (17 percent) and an ever-growing college-educated group (over 15 percent, but for U.S.-born Latinos the figure is closer to 40 percent) with such incomes. None of this automatically ensures writers or readers, but without these numbers it would be hard to create or sustain a burgeoning group of literary talent.

What will the new writing look like? Will it be like the work of Castillo, Alfredo Vea, or Braschi, drawing on the Latin American boom as well as postmodern mentors such as Severo Sarduy, Manuel Puig, and Julio Cortázar? Will it have the gritty and unflinching tone of Abraham Rodríguez Jr. or Junot Díaz? Or the wild, absurd, and hilarious conundrums seen in the plays of Pietri? Will it have the bilingual, poetic inventiveness of Alurista, Sandra María Estévez, or Victor Hernández Cruz? Will it freely combine genres like Anzaldúa or Judith Ortiz Cofer? Will it flow with the street-wise hip-hop cadences of Willie Perdomo and Anthony Me-

dina? Will it be inflected with the political poignancy of Jack Agüeros's eloquent sonnets or the long flowing line of Jimmy Santiago Baca's distilled rage? Will it tackle issues of race with the honesty of an Esmeralda Santiago, Lorna Dee Cervantes, or Tato Laviera? Will it take on issues of identity with the verve and wit of Vega or Culture Clash? Will it take on the sexual hypocrisy, gender violence, and sexism of Latino and Latina culture like Alicia Gaspar de Alba, or Cherríe Moraga? Will it have the performative edge of Nao Bustamante, Luis Alfaro, Carmelita Tropicana, and Coco Fusco?

These questions already contain a partial answer: Latino and Latina writing will continue to be as varied, different, and protean as it is now. It will be realist, magical realist, fantastic, poetic, prosaic, political, and performative as it has always been, offering the literature of the U.S. not a variant with a "different flavor," but a truly new way of expressing and seeing the U.S., one that allows us a glimpse of deeper, emerging forces that are transforming society in ways that are powerful but still shaping themselves. The questions this literature poses are multiform, as Gómez-Peña points out:

> Multilingualism, syncretic aesthetics, border thought, and cultural pluralism are becoming common practices in the artistic and intellectual milieus of this continent, not because of matters of fashion as the dominant art world likes to think, but because of a basic political necessity. To study the history, art, and political thought of our neighboring others and to learn Spanish and other languages becomes indispensable if we want to cross borders, regain our lost "American" citizenship, and participate in the drafting of the next century's cartography.
>
> (Gómez-Peña 1993, p. 56)

Seen within a post-9/11 climate and open calls for U.S. empire, these words are an open challenge to engage and enlarge the cultural, social, and historical imaginary of the United States. Latino and Latina literature is a vibrant, defiant, and poetic enjoinder to make those imaginaries more inclusive and authentically democratic.

Selected Bibliography

Alurista. "Myth, Identity and Struggle in Three Chicano Novels: Aztlán . . . Anaya, Méndez and Acosta." In *Aztlán: Essays on the Chicano Homeland.* Edited by Rudolfo A. Anaya and Francisco A. Lomelí. Albuquerque: University of New Mexico Press, 1993.

Anzaldúa, Gloria. *Borderlands: The New Mestiza/La Frontera.* San Francisco: Spinsters/Aunt Lute, 1987.

Appadurai, Arjun. *Modernity at Large: Cultural Dimensions of Globalization.* Minneapolis: University of Minnesota Press, 1996.

Barthes, Roland. *Camera Lucida: Reflections on Photography. Translated by Richard Howard.* New York: Hill and Wang, 1981.

Braschi, Giannina. *Yo-Yo Boing!* Pittsburgh: Latin American Literary Review Press, 1998.

Casal, Lourdes. "For Ana Veldford." In *Bridges to Cuba/Puentes a Cuba.* Edited by Ruth Behar. Ann Arbor: University of Michigan Press, 1995.

Chambers, Iain. *Migrancy, Culture, Identity.* London: Routledge, 1994.

Espada, Martín. *Imagine the Angels of Bread: Poems.* New York: W. W. Norton, 1996.

Garis, Roy L. "Mexican Immigration: A Report by Roy L. Garis for the Information of Congress." *Western Hemisphere Immigration.* Committee on Immigration and Naturalization. 71st Congress, 2nd Session. Washington, D.C.: Government Printing Office, 1930.

Gómez-Peña, Guillermo. *Dangerous Border Crossers: The Artist Talks Back.* London: Routledge, 2000.

———. *Warrior for Gringostroika: Essays, Performance Texts, and Poetry.* St. Paul, Minn.: Graywolf Press, 1993.

Gonzalez, Juan. *Harvest of Empire: A History of Latinos in America.* New York: Viking, 2000.

Grillo, Evelio. *Black Cuban, Black American: A Memoir.* Houston: Arte Público Press, 2000.

Lelyveld, Joseph, ed. *How Race Is Lived in America: Pulling Together, Pulling Apart.* New York: Times Books/Henry Holt, 2001.

Marentes, Luis A. "The Prophet of Race." In *Hopscotch: A Cultural Review,* vol. 2, no. 1 (1999): 142–151

Martínez, Dionisio D. *Bad Alchemy: Poems.* New York: W. W. Norton, 1995.

———. *History as a Second Language.* Columbus: Ohio State University Press, 1993.

Martínez, Rubén. *The Other Side: Fault Lines, Guerrilla Saints, and the True Heart of Rock 'n' Roll.* New York: Verso, 1992.

Morejón, Nancy. "Race and Nation." In *AfroCuba: An Anthology of Cuban Writing on Race, Politics, and Culture.* Edited by Pedro Perez Sarduy and Jean Stubbs. Melbourne, Australia: Ocean Press, 1993.

Ortiz, Fernando. *Cuban Counterpoint, Tobacco and Sugar.* Translated by Harriet de Onís. Durham, N.C.: Duke University Press, 1995.

Pew Hispanic Center. *2002 National Survey of Latinos.* Washington, D.C.: Kaiser Family Foundation, 2002.

Rodríguez, Abraham, Jr. *The Boy without a Flag: Tales of the South Bronx.* Minneapolis: Milkweed Editions, 1992.

————. "Abraham Rodríguez Jr." In *Puerto Rican Voices in English.* Edited by Carmen Dolores Hernández. Westport, Conn.: Praeger, 1997.

Shohat, Ella, and Robert Stam. *Unthinking Eurocentrism: Multicutluralism and the Media.* London: Routledge, 1994.

Torres, Gerald. "The Legacy of Conquest and Discovery: Meditations on Ethnicity, Race, and American Politics." In *Borderless Borders: U.S. Latinos, Latin Americans, and the Paradox of Interdependence.* Edited by Frank Bonilla et al. Philadelphia: Temple University Press, 1998. Pp. 153–168.

Torres, María de los Angeles. "Transnational Political and Cultural Identities: Crossing Theoretical Borders." In *Borderless Borders: U.S. Latinos, Latin Americans, and the Paradox of Interdependence.* Edited by Frank Bonilla et al. Philadelphia: Temple University Press, 1998. Pp. 169–182.

Vasconcelos, José. *The Cosmic Race: A Bilingual Edition.* Translated by Didier T. Jaén. Baltimore: Johns Hopkins University Press, 1997.

Vega, Ed. *The Comeback.* Houston: Arte Público Press, 1985.

Villanueva, Tino. *Chronicle of My Worst Years/Crónica de mis años peores.* Translated by James Hoggard. Evanston, Ill.: TriQuarterly Books, 1994.

West, Alan. *Tropics of History: Cuba Imagined.* Westport, Conn.: Bergin & Garvey, 1997.

West-Durán, Alan. "Transculturación, traducción y saberes híbridos." *Estudios,* vol 10, no. 19: 91–105 (January–July 2002).

GENERAL BIBLIOGRAPHIES ON LATINO AND LATINA LITERATURE

Aranda, José F., and Silvio Torres Saillant, eds. *Recovering the U.S. Hispanic Literary Heritage.* Vol. 4. Houston: Arte Público Press, 2002.

Augenbraum, Harold, and Margarite Fernández Olmos, eds. *U.S. Latino Literature: A Critical Guide for Students and Teachers.* Westport, Conn.: Greenwood Press, 2000.

Flores, Juan. *Divided Borders: Essays on Puerto Rican Identity.* Houston: Arte Público Press, 1993.

Gonzales-Berry, Erlinda, and Chuck Tatum, eds. *Recovering the U.S. Hispanic Literary Heritage.* Vol. 2. Houston: Arte Público Press, 1996.

Gutiérrez, Ramón, and Genaro Padilla, eds. *Recovering the U.S. Hispanic Literary Heritage.* Vol. 1. Houston: Arte Público Press, 1993.

Habell-Pallán, Michelle, and Mary Romero, eds. *Latino/a Popular Culture.* New York: New York University Press, 2002.

Herrera-Sobek, María, and Virginia Sánchez Korrol, eds. *Recovering the U.S. Hispanic Literary Heritage.* Vol. 3. Houston: Arte Público Press, 2000.

Huerta, Jorge. *Chicano Drama: Performance, Society and Myth.* Cambridge, U.K.: Cambridge University Press, 2000.

Kanellos, Nick. *A History of Hispanic Theater in the United States: Origins to 1940.* Austin: University of Texas Press, 1990.

Lomelí, Francisco, and Carl Shirley, eds. *Chicano Writers*. Third Series. Detroit: Gale Group, 1999.

Luis, William. *Dance between Two Cultures: Latino Caribbean Literature Written in the United States*. Nashville, Tenn.: Vanderbilt University Press, 1997.

Maciel, David R., Isidro D. Ortiz, and María Herrera-Sobek, eds. *Chicano Renaissance: Contemporary Cultural Trends*. Tucson: Arizona University Press, 2000.

McCracken, Ellen. *New Latina Narrative: The Feminine Space of Postmodern Ethnicity*. Tucson: The University of Arizona Press, 1999.

Pérez-Firmat, Gustavo. *Life on the Hyphen: The Cuban-American Way*. Austin: University of Texas Press, 1994.

Pérez-Torres, Rafael. *Movements in Chicano Poetry: Against Myths, against Margins*. Cambridge, U.K.: Cambridge University Press, 1995.

Sánchez-González, Lisa. *Boricua Literature: A Literary History of the Puerto Rican Diaspora*. New York: New York University Press, 2001.

Sandoval-Sánchez, Alberto. *José Can You See? Latinos on and off Broadway*. Madison: University of Wisconsin Press, 1999.

Shapiro, Ester R. "Developmental Outcomes for Puerto Rican Adolescents Under Different Circumstances of Migration: A Risk and Resilience Developmental Approach." Boston: Mauricio Gaston Institute for Latino Public Policy, 1997. (Unpublished paper.)

Stavans, Ilan. *The Hispanic Condition*. New York: Harper Collins, 2001.

Suárez-Orozco, Marcelo M., and Mariela M. Páez, eds. *Latinos: Remaking America*. Berkeley: University of California Press, 2002.

Vázquez, Francisco H., and Rodolfo D. Torres. *Latino/a Thought: Culture, Politics, and Society*. Lanham, Md.: Rowman & Littlefield Publishers, 2003.

Zimmerman, Marc. *U.S. Latino Literature: An Essay and Annotated Bibliography*. Chicago: MARCH/Abrazo Press, 1992.

ANTHOLOGIES OF LATINO LITERATURE

Antush, John V., ed. *Nuestro New York: An Anthology of Puerto Rican Plays*. New York: Mentor-Penguin Books, 1994.

Augenbraum, Harold, and Margarite Fernández Olmos, eds. *The Latino Reader: An American Literary Tradition from 1542 to the Present*. New York: Mariner Books, 1997.

Behar, Ruth, ed. *Bridges to Cuba / Puentes a Cuba*. Ann Arbor: University of Michigan Press, 1995.

Castillo-Speed, Lillian, ed. *Latina: Women's Voices from the Borderlands,* New York: Simon & Schuster, 1995.

Cortina, Rodolfo, ed. *Cuban American Theater*. Houston: Arte Público Press, 1991.

————, ed. *Hispanic American Literature: An Anthology*. Lincolnwood, Ill.: NTC Publishing Group, 1998.

De Jesús, Joy L., ed. *Growing Up Puerto Rican*. New York: Avon Books, 1997.

Espada, Martin, ed. *El Coro: A Chorus of Latino and Latina Poetry*. Amherst: University of Massachusetts Press, 1997.

Feyder, Linda, ed. *Shattering the Myth: Plays by Hispanic Women.* Houston: Arte Público Press, 1992.

González, Ray, ed. *Currents from the Dancing River: Contemporary Latino Fiction, Nonfiction, and Poetry.* New York: Harcourt Brace, 1994.

———, ed. *Muy Macho, Latino Men Confront Their Manhood.* New York: Random House, 1996.

———, ed. *Touching the Fire: Fifteen Poets of Today's Latino Renaissance.* New York: Doubleday, 1998.

Huerta, Jorge, ed. *Necessary Theater: Six Plays about the Chicano Experience.* Houston: Arte Público Press, 1989.

The Latina Feminist Group. *Telling to Live: Latina Feminist Testimonios.* Durham, N.C.: Duke University Press, 2001.

López, Tiffany Ana. *Growing Up Chicana/o: An Anthology.* New York: Avon Books, 1993.

Poey, Delia, and Virgil Suárez, eds. *Little Havana Blues: A Cuban-American Literature Anthology.* Houston: Arte Público Press, 1996.

Sandoval-Sánchez, Alberto, and Nancy Saporta Sternbach, eds. *Puro Teatro: A Latina Anthology.* Tucson: University of Arizona Press, 2000.

Santiago, Roberto, ed. *Boricuas: Influential Puerto Rican Writings—an Anthology.* New York: One World, 1995.

Svich, Caridad, and Marrero, María Teresa, eds. *Out of the Fringe: Contemporary Latina/Latino Theatre and Performance.* New York: Theatre Communications Group, 2000.

Historical Origins of U.S. Latino Literature

HAROLD AUGENBRAUM

As the study of Latino culture grew in the last quarter of the twentieth century, an important aim was to understand its literature's position in history. Research uncovered literary and narrative work by Hispanics in the United States in archives and private collections around the country and laid to rest a general misconception that no U.S. Latino literature existed before the 1960s, when political activism created a new awareness of cultural identity. This new awareness resulted from Latino responses to groundbreaking civil rights movements among African Americans and helped inspire local political action among Chicanos, Puerto Ricans, and Dominicans, as well as among Asian Americans, gays and lesbians, and women. Scholars took these rediscoveries, identified a distinct tradition, and related the bases of Latino culture to the broader historical and cultural continuum of the United States, Europe, and South America.

As the long history of Spanish-speakers and their descendants was mapped, influences from cultures in Europe, the Americas, Africa, and Asia emerged. These influences had resulted from demographic movements caused by conquest, colonization, slavery, religious proselytizing, and economic migration that began well before the British colonization in 1607. Because Latino culture has so many influences, understanding its multifaceted nature solely through the various national cultures that comprise it is difficult. Mexican American and Chicano literature, Puerto Rican literature on the mainland, Cuban American literature, and Dominican American literature each had its own cultural production and subsequently developed its own U.S.-based literature, research, and criticism. Periodic attempts to combine these nationally based cultures into a whole—in essence to create a Latino literature—date back to the early eighteenth century. They have met with varying degrees of success, and the process has always been complicated by political ideologies.

The best starting point to examine the development of Latino literature is 1492, when four significant events occurred. In January, the Catholic Royals *(los reyes católicos),* Queen Isabella of Castile, and King Ferdinand of Aragon, whose 1469 marriage had united most of the Iberian Peninsula, finally conquered the last holdouts of the Ibero-Arab populations in Granada, called the Moors, and solidified Christian dominance of the peninsula. *La Reconquista* (The reconquest), as it was called, then provided a paradigm for Spanish conquistadors in the Americas, who often referred to the native population as Moors.

The second major development was the expulsion of the Jews from Spain, which had major negative repercussions. Under the laws of most Spanish kingdoms, Jews were not allowed to own land. Since much Spanish industry depended on land ownership (especially the raising of sheep for export-quality wool), in order to prosper, Jews had to assume positions as merchants or in the movement and manipulation of capital, particularly as bankers or as investment advisors. After their expulsion, capital reinvestment was left in inexperienced hands. Spanish banking and investment suffered from general incompetence during the colonial period, which led to overborrowing, crushing royal debt, and severe inflation during the sixteenth and seventeenth centuries, even though Spain's empire was producing great wealth.

The third major development was the publication of Antonio de Nebrija's *Grammática Castellana (Castilian Grammar)*. In presenting his grammar to Queen Isabella, Nebrija emphasized that language, in addition to religion, would become crucial in the colonization of the Americas and be the means of Spanish control. (Language has always been the instrument of empire, he wrote.) This emphasis on language has changed little throughout the centuries. Interestingly, some scholars have noted that the Aztecs had come to a similar conclusion and were already developing plans to systematize language in the Americas.

The fourth major development in 1492—and arguably the single most important event in the creation of Latino culture—was the encounter between Christopher Columbus and the native populations of the Americas. Though paradigms through which the conquistadors would filter their own endeavors already existed in the form of the story of the conquest of the Moors and medieval legends, the landing of Christopher Columbus on the island of Hispañola in 1492, his subsequent voyages throughout the Carib-

bean, and the resulting island colonization would create a new layer of models and attitudes from which the Spanish conquerors and colonizers would view the native population of the Americas, some of which Columbus himself created through his writings.

Columbus wrote several documents that leaned heavily on European influences and models. Among these were the Bible as interpreted by the Catholic Church at Rome and in Spain (the Book of Isaiah being a particular favorite), late medieval romance, folktales and legends of the Iberian Peninsula, and even ancient and medieval natural histories. Columbus's *Journals* and later Hernan Cortés's *Letters from Mexico* provided two blueprints for the conquistador experience. Their influence is especially evident in what is generally considered the first literary work to emerge from the encounter between the Spanish and the native population of North America, Alvar Nuñez Cabeza de Vaca's *La relación* (*Chronicle*), published in 1542. Intermittent voyages to the mainland of North America in the vicinity of what is now Florida, Georgia, and South Carolina had begun to extend these European influences, but until the colonization of the southern tier of North America through the expeditions of Panfilo de Narvaez (the subject of Cabeza de Vaca's *Chronicle*) and Hernán de Soto and the northward movement of the Spanish from Mexico City, they were limited to regions in Mexico, South America, and the Caribbean.

At first glance the story of Cabeza de Vaca's "adventures in the unknown interior of America," as the translator Cyclone Covey titled it, is a simple account of his experiences, but a closer inspection reveals a much more subtle and personal argument on behalf of Cabeza de Vaca himself, employing both obvious and veiled biblical motifs to contend that the expedition in which he took part was not a failure, that his heroism played a central role in his own survival and that of his three companions, and that his mystical transformation had made him into a valuable subject for the Crown. Cabeza de

Vaca's depiction of himself as a changed man initiated the literature of transformation in North America, which the hands of later immigrants from the Caribbean and Latin America would shape into a literature of both personal transformation and inscription into history. In his story, Cabeza de Vaca affords himself mystical powers derived from God and Jesus, and paints subtle portraits of himself as Job ("as naked as we had been born"), and a mystical hero who has undergone a meaningful, pre-ordained trial, emerging as a great judge and leader.

In her brilliant study of the literature of conquest of the Americas, the critic Beatriz Pastor Bodmer has argued that Cabeza de Vaca wrote against earlier established conventions, such as the medieval chivalric romance, and Columbus's and Cortés's models. Columbus's journals and Cortés's letters, according to Pastor Bodmer, represented a discourse of mythification, that is, the creation of a new mythology based on earlier models but refashioned according to current experience, whereas Cabeza de Vaca's account mythified failure. Stories of failed conquest and the dissolution of dreams would later comprise a new strain of North American Hispanic letters, from four accounts of the de Soto expedition, the most famous of them by the Gentleman of Elvas and El Inca, Garcilaso de la Vega in the sixteenth century, to late twentieth-century novels and a preponderance of immigrant and assimilationist sagas. In other words, tradition, the effect of past writings on current ones, was an early aspect of literature by Hispanics in North America. Few writings of the period contest the Spanish dominance of the literature, though native stories record the European arrival into local territories. Politically, however, the Spanish were chastised by such activists as Bartolomé de las Casas in his book *Short Account of the Destruction of the Indies.*

Among the medieval romances, legends, and myths that surely influenced Cabeza de Vaca were the Amadis of Gaul stories popular at the time and legends of the Seven Cities of Cíbola, the same type of books Miguel Saavedra de Cervantes satirized in his novel *Don Quijote,* the first part of which was published in 1605. In *Books of the Brave* (1949), Irving Leonard catalogued book sales in the Americas in the decades after Columbus, mostly deriving his information from contemporary bills of lading now in the Archivo General de Indias in Sevilla, Spain. Influenced by such works, according to Leonard, soldiers who arrived in the Americas internalized the image of the adventuring knight errant, later transforming it into one of themselves as conquistadors.

The Seven Cities of Cíbola and the related legends of the Seven Bishops and Seven Cities of Gold played a major role in expeditions to North America, especially after Cortés conquered the Aztecs and their city of gold. The legend was revived in the late nineteenth and early twentieth centuries as one of "streets paved with gold," and influenced western expansion and the romance of the frontier in American life, particularly after gold really was discovered in California in 1848. An early result of this legend was Francisco Vázquez de Coronado's 1540 expedition that may have reached as far north as what is now Kansas, led by a native who claimed to know of El Dorado, the Golden City; when the Spaniards realized that the native was leading them in circles, they killed him, an emblematic instance of tension between the local population and the expectations of immigrants.

The first great verse epic of the Spanish period in North America was Gaspar Perez de Villagrá's highly stylized *History of New Mexico,* published in 1610, which initiated the region's preeminence in southwestern literature. Like the first American performance of Farfán de los Godos's *Los moros y cristianos (Moors and Christians)* in 1598, which it describes, and like many works that followed, it focused on a successful conquest modeled on the Catholic conquest of the Moors in Iberia (an Iberian master-plot), but, like Cabeza de Vaca's chronicle of the Narváez expedition, it was written in Spain, as a retrospective by a disgraced man exiled from the Americas after being implicated in the deaths of two Spanish deserters. Hence it is both a political and personal narrative.

In the seventeenth century, chronicle and history were also written by itinerant priests, as the Catholic Church began to exert apostolic control over North American Hispanic culture and its literature. Christian legends and stories, employed as master-plots as early as Cabeza de Vaca's invocation of God and Jesus and his underlying references to the story of Job, continued to dominate the literature; missionaries began to use such models to chronicle their own lives and the lives of those among whom they lived and preached the gospel. Though this apostolic literature often had little aesthetic value, the missionaries' political, social, and cultural presence were felt throughout Spanish lands, which by the end of the eighteenth century had reached along the southern tier of the United States from the Atlantic to the Pacific, as far north as present-day South Carolina in the east and present-day southern Oregon in the west, in addition to most of the interior portions of the West. By extending their reach into these areas, missionaries helped develop an underlying Hispanic culture that survives today not only in place-names but in oral culture. Well into the twentieth century, folktales persisted, many of them seemingly appropriated directly from the Spanish highlands (see Juan B. Rael, *Cuentos Españoles*). In addition, the traditions of *corridos* (heroic ballads) and *trovos* (call-and-response poetry) also survived into the twentieth century, with the former evident in popular songs about the murdered Texas Mexican singer Selena and the *narcocorridos* (songs of drug dealers and the police) of the 1990s.

Spanish conquest and colonization also brought the slave trade to the Americas, with considerable effect on the religions of Caribbean societies and later in the United States,

particularly in the nineteenth and the twentieth centuries. African-influenced music and religion from the Yoruba region of West Africa made their way into North America through the Caribbean archipelago, and Santeria, a Cuban-based syncretic religion, grew in the U.S. when working-class Cubans and Puerto Ricans arrived in large numbers, resulting in a U.S.-based syncretism in the barrios and appearance in U.S. Latino literature in such works as Judith Ortiz Cofer's *The Line of the Sun* (1990) and Cristina García's *Dreaming in Cuban* (1991).

Because so much Native American literature of the seventeenth and eighteenth centuries was oral, its influence on Latino literature and culture is more difficult to assess, except for appearances by natives in the work of European or Creole writers. Native literature survives today in its pure form in Native American culture, though hybrid Latino culture, especially in the Southwest, emerged in the last decade of the nineteenth century in the work of Eusebio Chacón (possibly influenced by popular Mexican writers of the time), but especially in the twentieth century in the work of such writers and Rudolfo Anaya, Denise Chávez, and Ana Castillo. In *Bless Me, Ultima* (1972), Anaya employed many themes and motifs of the shamanism of the Southwest, and southwestern writers have begun to discover and use the cultures of their Native American and syncretic past.

From the late seventeenth century through the eighteenth, the fabric of the Spanish Empire frayed, its European power fading and its finances in disarray. Administrative policy continued to pretend that the empire was a single entity, but the empire was far-flung, its territories separated by geographic barriers. The two centers of political power, Mexico City and Havana, held separate spheres of influence in North America, the former in the west, the latter in the east.

By the late eighteenth century, Spain had become a second-rate European power, dominated in Europe by Britain and France and in its own colonies by many revolutionary groups. With the successful revolt of the United States of America against Great Britain as their model, Spain's American colonies began their own push toward independence. Gradually, Spain's empire in the Americas unraveled. In 1821, Mexico finally achieved its independence, after a long and bloody struggle that included events that would later make up a part of U.S. Latino culture (El Grito de Dolores). At the same time, Puerto Rican and Cuban rebels struggled for independence in the Caribbean.

EXILE LITERATURE

These independence movements would have varied effects on the Hispanic populations of the United States. In one sense, with Spain no longer the central organizing authority, the colonies (and former colonies after independence) would develop separate cultural and political paths. An empire divided along regional and cultural lines would draw these countries further apart. Puerto Rican and Cuban rebels became exiles in the northeast of the United States of America. The poet José María Heredia (1803–1836), for example, born in Santiago de Cuba (where Cabeza de Vaca had spent a short while in 1527), lived in exile in New York, New Haven, and Boston in the early 1820s. While in the U.S., Heredia composed some of his most beautiful verse, including "Niagara" (1824), a Romantic poem about nature and exile, and "Himno del desterrado" (1825; "The Exile's Hymn"). In Heredia's hands, exile is defined in terms of loss. Loss becomes internalized, a sensibility that affects all aspects of existence. In the country of exile distractions are gradually stripped away to reveal raw wounds. Despite the brief time he spent in the U.S., Heredia also helped develop Spanish-language newspapers and theater. Though he took his lead, especially in his early works, from the European Romantics, Heredia initiated an important tradition in U.S. Latino letters (the literature of exile), especially among

Cubans and Cuban Americans, that would continue later in the century with Leopoldo Turla, Miguel T. Tolón, and José Marti. In 1826, Father Felix Varela, a Roman Catholic priest born in Havana and resident in New York City, known later for his humanitarian work, published *Jicotencal,* probably the first historical novel written in the Americas, about Hernán Cortés and the conquest of Mexico.

Born in Havana in 1853, Martí lived most of his adult life in the United States, where his literary output was prodigious, but his dedication to Cuban independence made him into a political and literary hero in his native country (where the airport at Havana is named for him). He wrote for the *New York Sun,* edited *Patria* (the publication of the Cuban Revolutionary Party, which he established in 1892), translated books into Spanish, published a journal for children, and wrote essays, journalism, drama, fiction, and poetry. His most famous work, *Versos sencillos* (1891; *Simple Verses*), was written in the Catskill Mountains of New York. In 1895 Martí returned to Cuba to lead a revolutionary force; he was killed only a few weeks later. Martí's oeuvre, in both Spanish and English, provided an extraordinary catalogue of writings about U.S. literature, culture, and politics, in addition to his various defenses of Latinos resident in the U.S. He wrote articles on Ralph Waldo Emerson, Walt Whitman, Coney Island, and the Metropolitan Museum of Art, among other topics. His writings on the United States were later collected in *Martí on the U.S.A.* (1966).

The careers of Heredia and Martí demonstrate the difficulty of classifying exile writers as Latinos. Heredia lived only about two years in the United States. Though he produced some of his best work in the U.S., and the environment inspired much of that work, it was for the most part influenced by European Romantic poetry and engendered by a backward look at the island. Martí's influence on U.S. Latino letters was much greater. Critical consensus is that he was the greater poet and he lived longer in the U.S. than Heredia, becoming a vocal spokesman for Latinos in general and Cubans in particular. Still, their concerns were mainly Cuban and less so the homegrown population of the United States.

Puerto Rican exiles in the nineteenth century also migrated to New York, America's commercial center; among them was the poet and essayist Francisco Gonzalo "Pachin" Marin (1863–1897). Like many exiles from the Hispanic Caribbean, Marin was able to eke out a living by writing for the several Spanish-language newspapers in New York City. The exiles' lives were portrayed as precarious and uncomfortable, themes that continued among Puerto Rican writers on the mainland into the middle of the twentieth century through the work of Bernardo Vega and Pedro Juan Soto, and reflected worsening social conditions into the late century in the work of Miguel Piñero, Edward Rivera, and Abraham Rodriguez Jr. A few Dominican writers also lived in the United States at the time (the poet Fabio Fiallo, for example, as a diplomat), but their impact would not be felt on U.S. Latino letters until the 1970s.

The Spanish–American War (also known as the Cuban–Spanish–American War) of 1898 changed the political landscape of the Caribbean. By the end of the hostilities, Cuba had gained its independence, and Spain had ceded Puerto Rico and the Philippines to the United States. This began a long period of uneasy relationships, but also made New York City into the de facto second city of Puerto Rico. Cuban independence obviated the need for as large and active an exile community in the United States until the late 1950s, when the accession of Fidel Castro would lead to a large influx of Cubans to the United States and the growth of Cuban American culture.

Around the turn of the century it was estimated that fifteen thousand to twenty thousand Puerto Ricans lived in the United States, most in the New York metropolitan area. But in 1917, the U.S. Congress passed the Jones Act, which affirmed that Puerto Ricans were citizens of the United States, thereby initiating the extensive migration from the island to the mainland that peaked in the period after World War II and abated only very late in the century, as the island began to achieve a measure of economic self-sufficiency.

The result of this migration was the expansion of Puerto Rican culture to the mainland, again mainly in the New York metropolitan area. Such highly cultured writers as Arturo Schomburg (1874–1938), Jesús Colón (1901–1974), and Bernardo Vega (1885–1965) became political and cultural leaders, which resulted in stirring portraits of life in the small Puerto Rican community, against which ethnic discrimination was the norm. Schomburg in particular had a great deal of influence on later writers and educators, especially with regard to racial problems among African Americans and Puerto Ricans, on the island or on the mainland. Schomburg's exploration of racial identity, especially the devaluation of people of African descent in the Americas and their contributions to the American culture, opened new avenues of discussion on *latinidad* and thorny problems of ethnographic and artistic classification. His collection of materials on African American culture formed the base for The New York Public Library's Schomburg Center for Research in Black Culture.

Colón became a political leader, once running for the U.S. Senate. His *Puerto Rican in New York* (1961), a collection of short pieces about coming-of-age, educating himself, and becoming active in the labor movement, became a vital publication in leftist circles. Vega's work took an odd turn. He originally wrote his book as a novel of Puerto Rican life in New York. A friend and editor wanted him to turn it into a memoir, but Vega balked. Only after his 1965 death did *Memoirs of Bernardo Vega* appear (1977), and which parts of it are fiction is still being debated.

After the Second World War, economic migration from the island grew by tens of thousands as Puerto Rican men sought work in New York City. Wives were often left behind, and the development of a culture of young males in the city, frequently lonely and depressed, also created a fertile ground for alienation, drug use, and crime (though a number of families and a culture of Puerto Rican family life on the mainland also burgeoned during the period). As the media emphasized negative aspects of Puerto Rican culture in New York, non-Latino populations formed stereotypes of Puerto Rican society, such as those depicted in the film *West Side Story* and in the sociologist Oscar Lewis's development of the controversial theory of the culture of poverty.

Pedro Juan Soto's vivid series of short works and novels about this alienation includes *Spiks* (1956), *USMAIL* (1958), and *Ardiente suelo, fría estación* (*Burning Ground, Cold Season*, 1961). Soto, who lived in New York from 1946 to 1955, when he returned to the island, often painted a picture of New York City as a dark, hellish place in which single men prowl the streets seeking companionship. Such social and cultural bitterness is an important precursor to Piri Thomas's *Down These Mean Streets* (1967) and Miguel Piñero's *Short Eyes* (1974), though these two writers would expand the scope of Soto's work from the political to the personal, in which quests for identity and meaning play a more important role.

Another Puerto Rican writer who found the streets of New York cold and unforgiving was Julia de Burgos (1914–1953), one of the island's best lyric poets, who died on a New York City street. Much of her final collection was written in New York, including the poems "Retorno" ("Returning") and "Farewell in Welfare Island," which was written in English when she was hospitalized for alcoholism. Her final poems of despair, emanating from both personal and political sentiments, are heartbreaking in their loneliness.

LITERATURE OF THE AMERICAN SOUTHWEST

In the Southwest, cultural and literary developments also reflected political changes. In 1833,

twelve years after independence, an autonomous Mexico secularized its missions, thereby lessening Spain's religious influence in the American church, eroding the Church's power in the Southwest, and diminishing Catholic political authority. In the same year, Ramón Abréu brought a printing press from Mexico, installed it in Santa Fe, and began printing the newspaper *El Crepúsculo de la Libertad* (The dawn of liberty). By the following year, Abréu's effort had failed, but his press was acquired by Padre Antonio José Martínez, who began printing secular texts, mainly for schools. Then in 1848, the Treaty of Guadalupe Hidalgo was signed, which effectively ended the two-year-old war between Mexico and the United States and ceded what later became Texas, New Mexico, Arizona, and California to the United States of America. (Another former Spanish possession, the Louisiana Purchase, had been acquired in 1803 from Napoleon, who had himself acquired it through his conquest of Spain the previous year.) Now citizens of the United States of America, the inhabitants of these territories had had three nationalities in fewer than thirty years, without moving an inch. The *corrido* flourished under these circumstances, and hundreds evolved within the Mexican American community, especially along the Rio Grande, creating new heroes and helping to preserve a distinct identity.

By the 1850s, the Southwest had developed a thriving journalistic culture, greatly influenced by Mexican exiles fleeing repressive federal and state regimes south of the Rio Grande and inclined to publish both local and imported work. Some, like *El Clamor Público* in Los Angeles and *El Boletín Popular* in Santa Fe, New Mexico, published for several decades. Others lasted less than a year.

Despite under-capitalization and the resulting precariousness of finances, dozens of Spanish-language weeklies were printed, with the best known papers published in Los Angeles, San Francisco, and Santa Barbara in California; Mora, Las Vegas, and Albuquerque in New Mexico; and Brownsville and San Antonio in

Texas. These dailies and weeklies, in addition to reporting on breaking news, also carried literary and other cultural pieces, including feature stories on regional cuisine, Spanish and Mexican American customs, and religion. They thus preserved local culture and pockets of cultural resistance to domination by English. With a great interest in maintaining a cultural identity, newspapers and small-press documents educated Spanish-speaking populations about imperiled traditions and sometimes made an English-speaking population aware of the literacy of its Spanish-speaking neighbors.

Editors of these periodicals were often among the best-educated members of the community, and they doubled as poets, essayists, editorialists, and short-story writers. José Escobar, Manuel Salazar, and Luis Tafoya were perhaps the best writers among them. According to the critic Doris Meyer, "Neomexicano newspapers were the de facto literature of their time" (*Speaking for Themselves*, p. 18). In many cases, news articles and political literature ran side-by-side, which gave additional meaning to both. Eusebio Chacón, one of the region's great orators and scion of the territory's most prominent families, could publish "A la Patria" in *El Boletín Popular* next to the gazette of local news. Catholic religious images, cultural and political commentary, and moral and ethical guidance appeared in newspaper verse, which ranged from stylistically poor versions of Romantic European- or Mexican-style poetry, to ardent expressions of U.S. patriotism, to calls for local cultural preservation, and even to reprints of Spanish and Mexican poetry by the foremost poets of the age. Some publications focused on personal matters, such as love of spouse and family, and included homage to one's children or friends. Short fiction also appeared, focusing less on patriotism and the development of cultural identity than on changing cultural mores. Although many of these poems and stories were published anonymously, one can speculate that they were written by the newspapers' editors and staff writers. During the period of

rediscovery in the late twentieth century, many of these works were collected in anthologies, such as *Los pobladores nuevo mexicanos y su poesía 1889–1950* and *The World of Early Chicano Poetry*. Clearly, along with performance, the newspaper had become an important medium for poetry.

Full-length books by Mexican American poets may have been rare before World War II, but an early single-author collection of poetry was *Las Primicias* (1916) by Vicente J. Bernal (1888–1915). Bernal was born and grew up in New Mexico, but it seems that most of his poems were written during the years he spent at the Dubuque German College in Iowa and collected after his untimely death by his brother Luis and the Dubuque administrator and educator Robert N. McLean. Bernal wrote stories in English and poems in both Spanish and English, though most critics have preferred the poems in English. Erlinda Gonzales-Berry has noted that Bernal's poetry was filled with romantic longing, preoccupations with death, classical allusions, and a love of nature, very much like the English Romantics of the nineteenth century, which is unsurprising since the poems "To Byron," "To Tennyson," "To Burns," and "Elvira by the Stream" pay homage to that period. Bernal also translated John Greenleaf Whittier's poem "The Barefoot Boy" into Spanish, further evidence of his immersion in U.S. and European poetic culture. Curiously, though nature plays a prominent role in this poetry, New Mexico does not. This may mean that, living and studying in an institution dedicated to the education of foreigners, Bernal immersed himself in the traditions of the Euro-American culture and temporarily ignored the images of his childhood.

Another poet represented by a single volume is Felipe Maximiliano Chacón, cousin of Eusebio, whose only book-length work was titled *Obras de Felipe Maximiliano Chacón, "el Cantor Neomexicano": Poesía y Prosa* (1924). Chacón began writing poetry at a very early age, and most of these poems were written between the ages of seventeen and fifty. According to the historian Benjamin Read, by the age of fourteen Chacón had already published verse in local newspapers. His literary work is marked by genuine expertise in Spanish, a rarity at that time in the Southwest, where English-language education was dominant. In fact, in his preface to Chacón's book, Read noted that "the literary works of Felipe Maximiliano Chacón are destined to mark a distinct era in the literary history of the United States. I say a distinct era because it has produced a clearly American genius, the first to give luster to his homeland in the beautiful language of Cervantes" (p. 5).

MEMOIR, ORAL HISTORY, POLITICAL AND SOCIAL HISTORY

Memoir also played an important role in southwestern and western Hispanic literature of the time. Memoirists seemed to have a need to tell the story of their own lives, but like Cabeza de Vaca and, much later, Ernesto Galarza and Richard Rodriguez, they were often also motivated by a desire to inscribe themselves into the fabric of history. These memoirists ranged from the highly educated to the unlettered, from the obscure to the famous. Among them were New Mexico's provincial governor Miguel Antonio Otero Jr., the prominent attorney Rafael Chacon, Texas Ranger Jesse Perez, and frontier scouts Andrew Garcia and José Policarpo Rodríguez.

Memoirs also provided a look into the harsh confluence of two frontiers, Hispanic and Anglo, and into the dual personality of Mexican American culture. Their many voices were reflected in the broad range of narrative styles and structures, including oral histories (such as those collected in the 1870s by representatives of the historian Hubert Howe Bancroft), testimonials dictated and meant to be published, Jesse Perez's unlettered hunt-and-peck typescript, and Miguel Antonio Otero Jr.'s renderings into history.

In 1858, Juan Nepumuceno Seguín wrote *Personal Memoirs: From the Year 1834 to the Retreat of General Woll from the City of San Antonio in 1842*, which is a good example of the dichotomy of the Mexican American's dual or intercultural personality. Seguín was an active member of the Texas army that helped the republic achieve its independence. Yet when history was being written within decades after the signing of the Treaty of Guadalupe Hidalgo, he was omitted, as if the Spanish-speaking population had had no hand in the struggle. The need to explain motivated others, such as Manuel C. de Baca, who, in *Vicente Silva y sus cuarenta bandidos* (1895; *Vicente Silva and His Forty Bandits*) recounted the history of the pursuit and prosecution of one of the Southwest's most brutal gang leaders, including his own role in the prosecution. The role of the Indian fighter and scout also became a memoir topic. Though folklore of the United States often included scouts, mountain men, and cowboys, who were romanticized in the dime novels published by Erastus Beadle and others, the Hispanic presence in the West was rarely represented other than by its *cholos*, low-class squatters and ne'er-do-wells, or bandits. According to G. B. Winton, the editor of José Policarpo Rodríguez's extraordinary, 121-page *"The Old Guide" His Life in His Own Words* (1897) Rodríguez's memoir was dictated to the Reverend D. W. Carter, D. D., at odd times during the years from 1892 to 1897. Much of it focuses on Rodríguez's conversion from Catholicism to Protestantism. The publication in 1968 of Andrew Garcia's *Tough Trip Through Paradise*, written decades earlier, provided an autobiographical account of a Tejano's daily life as a trail-rider, cowpoke, and working man who moved north and west to explore and settle in Montana in the late nineteenth century. Jesse Perez, an unlettered former Texas Ranger (one of the few Mexican Americans to join those ranks), pecked out an extraordinary memoir of his adventures on his typewriter, an episodic, almost picaresque account discovered in a Texas archive by historian Frank Dobie in the 1930s and never published.

Writing oneself into history took a different turn among those who were witness to some of the extraordinary events of the period, as exemplified by Leonor Villegas de Magnón's *The Rebel*. Unearthed by later literary detective work, *The Rebel* has had a tortured publishing history. Unpublished when Villegas de Magnón died, the original Spanish text, "La Rebelde," was written in the late teens or early 1920s, only a few years after the events it related (the Mexican Revolution), but was not published until it appeared in serial form in *The Laredo Times* in 1961. With the outbreak of the Revolution, Villegas de Magnón had crossed the border to join the nursing corps of La Cruz Blanc (the White Cross), where her own involvement in bloody combat and witnessing of injustices to the poor radicalized her. In Mexico, she met Pancho Villa, a populist revolutionary leader notorious for his caprice in politics and with young women.

One of the most extraordinary efforts to document Mexican American culture of the nineteenth century was Hubert Howe Bancroft's oral histories. In the 1870s, Bancroft sent modestly trained oral historians out across the state to interview Spanish-speaking Californians, whose stories were often nostalgic recollections of the days before 1848, when the land-owning *californios* ruled Alta California, and depicted a world at odds with both fictional and historical accounts of the period by Anglo writers, who had often described the area as lawless or deserted. The interviewers' abilities in Spanish and the type of questions they posed may have limited the scope of the subjects' oral histories, and their accuracy is doubted by many critics and historians.

Despite these limitations, Bancroft's oral histories provide a fascinating look into Mexican American culture of the time. Among the most interesting was that of Eulalia Perez (c.1780–c.1880), recorded by Thomas Savage in 1878 and translated into English by Vivian Fisher as part of the volume *Three Memoirs of Mexican California* (1988). Some of Perez's stories involve confusions or inventions: according to Savage, she claims at one point that she is 139 years old, which would place her birth in 1738, yet elsewhere she claims that she was pregnant during the devastating earthquake of 1812, which would have made her seventy-four years old at the time, had she been born in 1738. But her positions as midwife, chief cook, concierge, and supervisor of the San Gabriel Mission provide a fascinating look into California mission culture of the time. Such *testimonios* prefigure those of Benjy Lopez and Ramon "Tianguis" Perez in the twentieth century, in both the east and the west.

One of the western frontier's most important chroniclers was Miguel Antonio Otero Jr. (1859–1944), who wrote the first of his three volumes of memoirs, *My Life on the Frontier, 1864–1882* (1935), when he was seventy-six years old, followed by two others, *My Life on the Frontier, 1882–1897* (1939), and *My Nine Years as Governor of the Territory of New Mexico, 1897–1906* (1940), which appeared when he was eighty and eighty-one, respectively. Because of his position and education, Otero's work, like that of Rafael Chacón, who was also among the educated elite, shows an important aspect of Mexican American culture that was often obscured as working-class images predominated. Rafael Chacón's literary output was limited to the unpublished "Memorias," which Genaro Padilla has called "a crucial example of the formation of autobiographical consciousness split by contending sociocultural regimes" (p. 51), and which he wrote between 1906 and 1912. It covered his youth in New Mexico, his education, the conquest of New Mexico by the Americans, the transfer of power from the Mexican to the U.S. government, the widespread abrogation of the Treaty of Guadalupe Hidalgo, his own service in the Union Army during the Civil War, his return to the Southwest, and his retirement to Colorado. Since he lived such a long life, these memoirs encompass the broad experience of Mexican Americans in New Mexico before the modern era, from the arrival of the first printing press in the Southwest through the Gadsden Purchase (1912), which completed the state's geography.

Closely related to oral history and memoir were political and social histories written by Mexican Americans, such as *A History of Alta California* by Antonio María Osio y Higuera (1800–1878) and the works of Benjamin Read. In 1832, Osio and seven other prominent citizens of Mexican California expelled California's Mexican governor and developed a government of their own based on the theories of the Enlightenment and drawn from the experiences of eighteenth-century revolutions in Europe and North America.

By the early 1850s, control of California had passed to Anglo settlers, and the dissipation of the *californio* estates had begun. Such men as Pio Pico, Mariano Guadalupe Vallejo, and Juan Bandini (grandfather of Ralph) watched as their lack of political influence and their competitors' aggressive business tactics whittled away at their holdings. Osio himself had pressed a claim for Angel Island and Point Reyes (near San Francisco), without much luck. He and his family left Alta California in 1852, returning to Mexico, where he continued to take an active role in local politics until his death in 1878.

In 1851, Osio completed a 220-page manuscript, in the form of an "account," less history than story, called "La historia de Alta California," the earliest history of the territory. He begins the story in 1815 with the death of Don José Joaquín de Arrillaga and the establishment of the new governor, Colonel Don Pablo Vicente de Solá, and ends with the takeover of Alta California by *americanos*.

FICTION

Of fiction, a few pieces have survived from the nineteenth and early twentieth centuries. Like much of the surviving poetry of the period, short fiction in particular appeared in southwestern

newspapers, while surviving novels are rarer. The work that is currently available represents widely varied approaches in style, politics, and aesthetic practice. Some writers who wrote in Spanish, for example, were interested in finding a particularly Mexican American style; others tried to mimic the prevailing Anglo style of the time, though often with a strong political message about relations between Mexican Americans and Anglos. The most prominent of these was María Amparo Ruiz de Burton (1832–1895).

Though Ruiz de Burton's first known work was a five-act comedy based on the adventures of Don Quixote, it was her novel, *Who Would Have Thought It?* (1872), published anonymously but registered under the names "H. S. Burton" and "Mrs. Henry S. Burton," that is most likely the first novel by a Mexican American, and certainly the first novel by a Mexican American written in English. *Who Would Have Thought It?* takes place immediately before, during, and after the Civil War. It tells the story of Lola, a young Mexican girl brought to live in the home of a prominent provincial Anglo family of New England, the Norvals, after the patriarch of that family had rescued her from Indian captivity during his travels in the Southwest. When first seen, Lola is wrapped in a bright red shawl, with face coated by black dye, which makes the household and neighbors refer to her as "the little black girl." As Lola's complexion gradually returns to normal, the circumstances of her mother's death and her own wealth are revealed, and she becomes the object of the household's greed, which Ruiz de Burton uses to satirize a hypocritical New England gentry and clergy.

The author name on the title page of Ruiz de Burton's second novel, *The Squatter and the Don* (1885), was "C. Loyal," which stood for Ciudadano Loyal (Loyal Citizen). Most critics have interpreted this as Ruiz de Burton's declaration of loyalty both to the exemplary goals of the United States and to the collective welfare of those Mexican Americans living in the former Mexican territories. California at the time was rife with governmental corruption, which had undermined certain provisions of the Guadalupe Hidalgo accord. The Treaty, meant to protect the interests of formerly Mexican citizens in former Mexican-controlled territories, instead undermined the patron/peon-based economy that had existed before the influx of U.S. citizens tipped the balance of power. When California became the twentieth state of the Union in 1850, loose and corrupt interpretations and lax enforcement of the law allowed representatives and judges to turn a blind eye to land-grabbing Anglo migrants who appropriated major parts of *latifundios* (large estates) from *californios*. Gradually these large areas of private property were subdivided, and the upper class *californios* were relegated to middle-class status, which in many ways destroyed the traditional, and stable, Mexican class system of the time. (The history of these losses has become part of Californian lore, and appears in such novels as John Steinbeck's *East of Eden* (1952); a good, but flawed, history of these landowners is available in Leonard Pitt's *The Decline of the Californios* (1966).)

Another major current in late nineteenth-century Mexican American fiction is represented by the two novellas of Eusebio Chacón (1870–1948), *Hijo de la tempestad (Son of the Storm)* and *Tras la tormenta la calma (The Calm After the Storm)*, both published in 1892 by El Tipográfia *El Boletín Popular*, most likely a private printing on the presses of that newspaper. Chacón's prose reflects his attempt to develop a style of fiction linked to Mexican and New Mexican traditions more than to those of his University of Notre Dame education, an effort at developing what he called "una literatura nacional," a national literature. In reviewing the two novels, his contemporary José Escobar said, "Chacón's small book, although unknown among many *nativos*, is a true jewel in our national literature." Unfortunately, no reprint or English translation of either work appeared until 1997. The themes of *Son of the Storm* are derived from local legends and superstitions, mixed with the pervasive fear of the violence of *bandoleros* in New Mexico of the late nineteenth century. The two novels were written, for example, just after the arrest and conviction of the bloodthirsty Vicente Silva and during the time of *Las Gorras Blancas* (the White Caps), a band of men who, under the guise of Mexican American nationalism and pride, committed countless crimes in the vicinity of Las Vegas.

In addition to this more literary fiction, another type that appealed more to middlebrow readers of both literary and mainstream magazines was practiced by such authors as Maria Cristina Mena (1893–1965), Isidoro Armijo (1871–1949), and Ralph Bandini (1884–1961).

Mena published eleven short stories between about 1910 and 1930, but her public reputation was also based on her literary relationships, which included her husband, the playwright and journalist Henry K. Chambers, and the British poet and novelist D. H. Lawrence, with whom she corresponded for several years and whom she visited at his Italian villa. Just before the Mexican Revolution of 1910, Mena moved to New York City, where she lived with various family friends and submitted her short stories to magazines. Most of these stories were written and published between 1913 and 1916, when she married Chambers and her publications abruptly stopped. After his death in 1935, Mena wrote children's books and dedicated herself to working with the blind, which included learning Braille and transcribing her work into that writing system.

Another type of fiction practiced at this time was folklore-inspired and would influence late twentieth-century fiction of the Southwest, especially in the work of Rudolfo Anaya and Ana Castillo. The folklorist was particularly important in the early part of the twentieth century, as mass communication began to make inroads into the Hispanic cultures of the Southwest. Aurelio and Gilberto Espinosa, Arturo L. Campa, and Aurora Lucero-White Lea (who also published under the name Aurora Lucero) played a significant part in uncovering, through interviews with older inhabitants of the region, folktales and dramatic presentations that had changed little in hundreds of years, some of them evidently related to folktales of the rural areas of Spain.

Other folklorists were also able to document a disappearing contemporary culture. Among these was Jovita González de Mireles (1904–1983), who ably gathered and retold local tales that reflected a recent past of violence and resistance to the established orders. Her 1930 article "America Invades the Border Towns" laments the changes to, and losses of, local Hispanic culture, just as her later retelling of such stories as "The Bullet-Swallower" and "The Mescal-Drinking Horse" would convey new legends that had developed on the border and re-create in English the atmosphere of Mexican American storytelling. "The Bullet-Swallower" is a romantic tale of a man who has left his upper-class environment to challenge the harshness of the west. González peppers her English with carefully chosen Spanish words, *conquistador, pelo en pecho* (hair on the chest), *jacal* (shanty), and *tequila,* adding authenticity to her tale and re-creating, through language, a Hispanic atmosphere that conveys to the English reader the narrator's exoticism.

Auroro Lucero's father was the well known associate editor of the Spanish-language weekly *La Voz del Pueblo,* published in Las Vegas, New Mexico (further evidence of the cultural influences of newspapers in the Southwest). She wrote her master's thesis at New Mexico Highlands University on "El coloquio de los pastores" ("The Dialogue of the Shepherds"), two versions of which she later included in her *Literary Folklore of the Hispanic Southwest,* and she published several pamphlets and books on New Mexico folklore, including *Folk-Dances of the Spanish Colonials of New Mexico* (1940) and *The Folklore of New Mexico* (1941), which are compilations, retellings, and critical and

structural studies. She would spend weeks at a time traveling the back roads of New Mexico talking to isolated residents and collecting stories, songs, and poetry, and ranks as an ethnographer with such southwestern folklorists as Juan B. Rael and Charles Lummis. In 1962, she adapted the folktale "Bertholdo," which featured one of the ubiquitous characters of the Southwest (also called Juan Tonto or Juan Catorce), into the children's book *Juan Bobo,* who was also popular in folktales of the Caribbean.

In the early twentieth century, some authors reacted to the politicized literature of the period by writing from a Hispanic American model, a trend that has been called by some critics—who thereby reveal their own ideological prejudices—"the Spanish Fantasy Heritage." Often exemplified by women writers whose stated purpose was to maintain traditions that had been passed down from Spanish colonists in the Americas to their Creole descendants, the Heritage movement was particularly strong in New Mexico and Arizona in the first half of the twentieth century. Lucero, in her *Literary Folklore of the Hispanic Southwest,* noted that

> the establishment of the artist colony in New Mexico at Santa Fe, Taos and Albuquerque has stimulated the production of Hispanic arts and crafts. The coming of tourists in great numbers has given impetus to New Mexico cookery (Spanish and Indian), and the excellent taste of persons of wealth from the East and elsewhere has made fashionable the reconstruction of old adobe houses and the building of new ones patterned after the old.
>
> (pp. 209–210)

Domestic traditions and a refusal to allow Spanish heritage to be lost were these women's attempt to broaden the concept of Spanish-Mexican-American culture in the Southwest, in much the same way as later critics in the Caribbean and in the northeastern United States examined African and Jewish influences on Hispanic Caribbean traditions.

The literature of heritage ran the gamut from family history and memoir to cookbooks, which feminist critics of the late twentieth century embraced as proto-feminist domestic literature, since the works often crossed the line between ethnography and autobiography. Inherent in some, however, such as *Romance of a Little Village Girl* (1955), is the romanticizing of New Mexican Spanish culture. Important because of the sex of their authors and their giving an account that was generally rejected by more politicized scholarship of the post-1960s generation, they were resurrected in the 1990s and termed "politically subversive" by the literary critic Tey Diana Rebolledo and other Latina feminist scholars. Among the better-known practitioners of this mode were Cleofas Martínez Jaramillo (1878–1956), Adelina "Nina" Otero Warren (1881–1965), and Fabiola Cabeza de Baca Gilbert (c. 1894–1991).

Jaramillo's first published work was *Cuentos del Hogar* (1939), a collection preserving folktales passed down from her mother. These cross the line between Spanish and American culture and are closely related to the folktales collected by Juan Rael. Her second book, *The Genuine New Mexico Tasty Recipes* (1939), was a collection of seventy-five dishes such as "Wild Quelites and Verdolagas" (greens) and "Rueditas" (dried green squash). Jaramillo also published *Shadows of the Past/Sombras del Pasado* (1941), an account of religious and cultural practices of northern New Mexico.

Though the publication of these books represented, for Jaramillo, an effort to document and preserve the Spanish–New Mexican way of life, they also formed a cultural backdrop to *Romance of a Little Village Girl,* Jaramillo's mix of folklore and autobiography. Jaramillo's strength was to bring the internal workings of the home into the literature along with a feminine cultural perspective and a desire to force the surrounding culture to acknowledge the culture of Spanish New Mexico.

A career in home economics led Cabeza de Baca Gilbert to write on topics in food, which then led to explorations of food preparation as a cultural signifier. Her first book, *Los Alimentos y su Preparación* (1934; *Food and Its Preparation*) was followed by *Boletín de Conservar* (1935; *Conservation Bulletin*), the two-volume *Historic Cookery* (1939), and *The Good Life* (1949). Though such works are not traditionally included in literary histories, feminist critics have embraced them as conveyors of domestic culture and manners, akin to the family memoir and an important element in the recovery of women's literature of the Southwest.

We Fed Them Cactus (1954) is probably Cabeza de Baca Gilbert's best-known work, her third in English. The change from Spanish to English most likely gave her access to a larger market than she had enjoyed when writing in her native tongue. Critics have noted that this change can also be seen as undermining Anglo-American society's image of the Hispanic woman as an illiterate peasant.

Nina Otero's *Old Spain in Our Southwest* (1936) is one of the best portrayals of the Spanish customs that survived Mexican independence from Spain in 1821 and the U.S. takeover of the region in 1848. The book is filled with many narrative voices and generally attempts to provide a broad look at the world of Spanish New Mexico, how its customs and traditions developed and continue in their various guises into the twentieth century.

HUMOR

Among the least known of the various types of literature practiced by Mexican Americans in the early twentieth century was humor, represented by the writers Julio G. Arce (1870–1926), Kaskabel (which means "rattlesnake"), and Daniel Venegas. By the teens and 1920s, Latino writers had begun to find a comic sensibility in everyday life that may have taken its inspiration from skits performed before or after the Spanish-language theatrical productions popular at the time, Mexican and Latin American newspaper *crónicas* (lightly satirical feature chronicles), and similar columns in Anglo publications such as *The Smart Set* and *Vanity Fair*. Today they might be compared to the writings of Art Buchwald, Dave Barry, and Fran Leibowitz.

Arce was born in Guadalajara, Jalisco (Mexico) in 1870, the son of a prominent surgeon, and by the age of fourteen had founded his first student newspaper. After a brief career as a pharmacist, he returned to journalism, through which he made enough enemies to be forced to flee the country. By 1915, he had settled in San Francisco, California, where he began writing the *Crónicas diabólicas (Diabolical Chronicles)*, a series of newspaper columns of commentary on the daily life of Hispanics in the United States, in the *costumbrista* (manners and customs) tradition of Mexican journalism. In them, Arce portrays himself as the fictional author Úlica. In one instance, he receives a phone call from someone who asks if he is the "inclito [illustrious] defender of the race" (p. 23), an epithet to which he reluctantly accedes. In another, he attends a Spanish class, only to find a proud group of students butchering the language under the tutelage of a "false Iberian."

A different comic vision of Mexican American life in the early part of the century was the picaresque *Las aventuras de Don Chipote; o, cuando los pericos mamen* (1928; *The Adventures of Don Chipote; or, when parrots suckle*) by Daniel Venegas (birth and death dates unknown). One of the first full-length novels written in Spanish in the United States and dealing with U.S. themes, it relates the comic story of a Mexican immigrant who, believing the many stories of "streets paved with gold," has come to the United States to pry it up. Employing *caló*, the slang of common workers, well before its critical acceptance in the late 1940s and 1950s, Venegas, who was also a playwright, depicted a subculture of flophouses, drug-dealers, pimps, and quacks who preyed on the uneducated

campesinos and *paisanos* who had emigrated from the Mexican rural areas to become urban laborers in Los Angeles. Reminiscent in tone of the adventures of Lazarillo de Tormes and Don Quixote, Venegas's narrative of pleasures and trials in the U.S. urban environment was the first novel of Chicano language and sensibility.

MID-TWENTIETH CENTURY LITERATURE

By the middle decades of the twentieth century Latino writers who would not always identify themselves with a specific Latino community had emerged. Among the best known of these were the poet William Carlos Williams (1883–1963), whose mother was Puerto Rican, and Josephina Niggli (1910–1983), who was raised in Mexico by American parents but moved to the United States as an adult.

Williams was brought into the Latino canon by the poet and critic Julio Marzan's in-depth study *The Spanish American Roots of William Carlos Williams* (1994), through which one understands the influence of the poet's mother's life in his work, especially in such poems as "To Elsie":

> Unless it be that marriage
> perhaps
> with a dash of Indian blood
> will throw up a girl so desolate

(p. 217)

and "All the Fancy Things":

> music and painting and all that
> That's all they thought of
> in Puerto Rico in the old Spanish
> days when she was a girl.

(p. 268)

What makes Williams's inclusion in a Latino tradition so extraordinary is that his family background was rarely taken into account before the 1990s, though he was deemed by many to be the quintessential American poet of the twentieth century and an heir to the all-encompassing Walt Whitman.

A well-known screenwriter and playwright in the middle of the century, Josephina Niggli (1910–1983) has not always been included in the ranks of Latina writers of the United States either. Though she was born and raised in Mexico and the Mexican American southwest, Niggli's father was from Texas and her mother from Virginia, and neither of them had Hispanic roots. The subject matter of her work is usually set into Mexican, not Mexican American, context, and she often focuses on the Anglo among the Mexicans on the southern side of the Río Bravo. Niggli published collections of poetry and prose and had several of her plays produced. In 1931, her poetry collection *Mexican Silhouettes* was published, followed by the plays *The Red Velvet Goat* (1938) and *Sunday Costs Five Pesos* (1939). In 1945 she published the novel of connected short stories *Mexican Village*, which would become her best-known work, and which Raymund Paredes has called the first literary work by a Mexican American to reach a general American audience. She also worked for several years as a staff writer in Hollywood studios, where her work was usually uncredited.

Like Pedro Juan Soto and Julia de Burgos in the east, one of the interesting transition figures in Latino letters whose influences seem to emanate from both the Mexican American and Anglo worlds (as Soto's and Burgos's do from the islands of Puerto Rico and Manhattan) is the short story writer Mario Suarez (1925–). Between 1947 and 1950, Suarez published four short stories in Southwestern magazines. The stories are all set in the Mexican American community, and their characters strongly resemble those found in the work of Julio G. Arce and John Steinbeck, especially in the latter's Monterey novels and his short stories. Like Pedro Juan Soto in the east, Suarez is a transition figure, focused squarely on the Mexican

American community without a great deal of Anglo-American involvement, yet highly influenced by Anglo writing. Only a decade after Suarez's work appeared, José Antonio Villarreal would begin to wrestle with the concept of an intercultural being who lived in (and between) two worlds, trying to navigate a line between them. He would be, in essence, a literary Latino.

The beginning of a community of Latino letters on the historic continuum of letters is difficult to pinpoint, and later even its members are difficult to identify with any certainty. Is the Cuban exile poet Heberto Padilla a Latino? The Chilean Isabel Allende? It is also difficult to decide when the contemporary period begins. In the west, consensus among scholars holds that the publication of José Antonio Villarreal's *Pocho* (1959) is the watershed event, with its principal character's burgeoning awareness of himself as a new kind of person caught between cultures marking the emergence of a third consciousness, neither Mexican nor Anglo. In the east, the separation of pre-Latino and Latino literature is even more difficult to assess, since the links between pre-Latino writers such as "Pachin" Marin, Bernardo Vega, Pedro Juan Soto, Miguel Algarín, and Miguel Piñero, and Latino writers such as Piri Thomas and Ed Rivera is evident. Ethnologists have noted that the growth of a permanent community itself, from exiles to sojourners to residents, may hold the key, but this would imply that a dividing line between pre-Latino writers and contemporary Latinos is artificial and that the concept of a continuum—though a historical and cultural continuum does indeed exist—would have to be rejected. In her article "Linguistic Utopias," the critic Mary Louise Pratt notes that "National literatures motivate what one might call a 'criticism of community,' another long-standing utopian project whose task has been to secure a national patrimony or official culture" (*The Linguistics of Writing*). If the task of criticism in U.S. Latino literature has been to create such a patrimony, to reflect the nature of an inter-culture made up of two linguistic communities, then its origins reach beyond Cabeza de Vaca and the literature of transformation, to the written literature of Europe and the oral tradition of the Americas.

Selected Bibliography

Arce, Julio G. *Crónicas diabólicas de "Jorge Ulica."* Edited by Juan Rodríguez. San Diego, Calif.: Maize, 1982.

Arellano, Anselmo F. *Los pobladores nuevo mexicanos y su poesía, 1889–1950.* Albuquerque, N.Mex.: Pajarito Publications, 1976.

Augenbraum, Harold, and Margarite Fernández Olmos. *The Latino Reader: An American Literary Tradition from 1542 to the Present.* Boston, Mass.: Houghton Mifflin, 1997.

Baca, Manuel C. de. *Vicente Silva and His Forty Bandits (1895).* Translated by Lane Kauffmann. Washington D.C.: E. McLean, 1947.

Bernal, Vicente J. *Las primicias.* Edited by Luis E. Bernal and Robert N. McLean. Dubuque, Iowa: Telegraph-Herald, 1916.

Burgos, Julia de. *Song of the Simple Truth: The Complete Poems of Julia de Burgos.* Translated by Jack Agüeros. Willimantic, Conn.: Curbstone Press, 1997.

Cabeza de Vaca, Alvar Nuñez. *Chronicle of the Narvaez Expedition.* Translated by Fanny Bandelier, revised and annotated by Harold Augenbraum. New York: Penguin, 2002.

Chacón, Eusebio. *Hijo de la tempestad* and *Tras la tormenta la calma.* Santa Fe, N.Mex.: Tipográfia *El Boletín Popular,* 1892.

Chacón, Felipe Maximiliano. *Obras de Felipe Maximiliano Chacón, "el Cantor Neomexicano": Poesía y Prosa.* Albuquerque, N.Mex.: [self-published], 1924.

Chacón, Rafael. *Legacy of Honor: The Life of Rafael Chacón, A Nineteenth Century New Mexican.* Edited by Jacqueline Dorgan Meketa. Albuquerque: University of New Mexico Press, 1986.

Colón, Jesús. *A Puerto Rican in New York and Other Sketches.* New York: Mainstream, 1961.

Columbus, Christopher. *The Journal of Christopher Columbus.* Translated by Cecil Jane. London: 1968.

Cortés, Hernan. *Letters from México.* Translated and edited by A. R. Pagden. New Haven, Conn.: Yale University Press, 1986.

Fisher, Vivian, trans. *Three Memoirs of Mexican California.* Berkeley, Calif.: Friends of the Bancroft Library, 1988.

Gilbert, Fabiola Cabeza de Baca. *The Good Life: New Mexico Traditions and Food.* Santa Fe, N.Mex.: San Vicente Foundation, 1949.

———. *Historic Cookery.* Santa Fe: Museum of New Mexico Press, 1983.

———. *We Fed Them Cactus.* Albuquerque: University of New Mexico Press, 1954.

González de Mireles, Jovita. *Dew on the Thorn.* Edited and introduced by José E. Limón. Houston, Tex.: Arte Público Press, 1997.

Gutiérrez, Ramón, and Genaro Padilla, eds. *Recovering the U.S. Hispanic Literary Heritage.* Houston: Arte Público Press, 1993.

Heredia, José María. *Selected Poems in English Translation.* Miami, Fla.: Ediciones Universal, 1970.

Herrera-Sobek, María. *Reconstructing a Chicano/a Literary Heritage: Hispanic Colonial Literature of the Southwest.* Tucson: University of Arizona Press, 1993.

El Inca, Garcilaso de la Vega [Gómez Suárez de Figueroa]. *La florida del Ynca.* 1605. Reprint, Mexico City: Fondo de Cultura Económica, n.d.

Jaramillo, Cleofas. *The Genuine New Mexico Tasty Recipes.* Santa Fe, N.Mex.: Seton Village, 1942.

———. *Romance of a Little Village Girl.* San Antonio, Tex.: Naylor, 1955.

———. *Shadows of the Past/Sombras del Pasado.* Santa Fe, N.Mex.: Seton Village, 1941.

Lea, Aurora Lucero-White. *Literary Folklore of the Hispanic Southwest.* San Antonio, Tex.: Naylor, 1953.

Leonard, Irving. *Books of the Brave.* Cambridge, Mass.: Harvard University Press, 1949.

Luis, William. *Dance Between Two Cultures: Latino Caribbean Literature Written in the United States.* Nashville, Tenn.: Vanderbilt University Press, 1997.

Martí, José. *Martí on the U.S.A.* Selected and Translated, with an Introduction by Luis A. Baralt. Carbondale: Southern Illinois University Press, 1966.

———. *Selected Writings.* Edited and translated by Esther Allen. New York: Penguin, 2002.

Marzan, Julio. *The Spanish American Roots of William Carlos Williams.* Austin: University of Texas Press, 1994.

Melendez, A. Gabriel. *So All Is Not Lost: The Poetics of Print in Nuevomexicano Communities 1834–1958.* Albuquerque: University of New Mexico Press, 1997.

Mena, María Cristina. *The Collected Stories of María Cristina Mena.* Edited and introduced by Amy Doherty. Houston, Tex.: Arte Público Press, 1997.

Meyer, Doris. *Speaking for Themselves: Neomexicano Cultural Identity and the Spanish-Language Press, 1880–1920.* Albuquerque: University of New Mexico Press, 1996.

Montes-Huidobro, Matías, ed. *El Laúd del Desterrado.* New York: Imprenta de "La Revolución," 1858. Reprint, Houston, Tex.: Arte Público Press, 1997.

Niggli, Josephina. *Mexican Village.* Chapel Hill: University of North Carolina Press, 1945.

Osio, Antonio María. *A History of Alta California.* Translated, edited, and annotated by Rose Marie Beebe and Robert M. Senkewicz. Madison: University of Wisconsin Press, 1996.

Otero, Miguel Antonio, Jr. *My Life on the Frontier, 1864–1882.* New York: Pioneers, 1935.

———. *My Life on the Frontier, 1882–1897.* Albuquerque: University of New Mexico Press, 1939.

———. *My Nine Years as Governor of the Territory of New Mexico, 1897–1906.* Albuquerque: University of New Mexico Press, 1940.

Pastor Bodmer, Beatriz. *The Armature of Conquest: Spanish Accounts of the Discovery of America, 1492–1589.* Translated by Lydia Longstreth Hunt. Stanford, Calif.: Stanford University Press, 1994.

Pérez, Jesse. "Memoirs." Typescript archived at the Barker Texas History Center, University of Texas, Austin.

Pitt, Leonard. *The Decline of the Californios: A Social History of the Spanish-Speaking Californios, 1846–1890.* Berkeley: University of California Press, 1966.

Pratt, Mary Louise. "Linguistic Utopias." Edited by Nigel Fabb et al. *The Linguistics of Writing.* Manchester: Manchester University Press, 1987. Pp. 48–66.

Rael, Juan B. *Cuentos Españoles de Colorado y Nuevo México.* Stanford, Calif.: Stanford University Press, 1957.

Rodríguez, José Policarpo. *"The Old Guide": His Life in His Own Words.* Dallas, Tex.: The Methodist Episcopal Church, 1897.

Ruiz de Burton, María Amparo. *The Squatter and the Don.* 1885. Reprint, Houston, Tex.: Arte Público Press, 1992.

———. *Who Would Have Thought It?* 1872. Reprint, Houston, Tex.: Arte Público Press, 1995.

Seguín, John N. *Personal Memoirs: From the Year 1834 to the Retreat of General Woll from the City of San Antonio in 1842.* San Antonio, Tex.: Ledger Book and Job Office, 1858.

Soto, Pedro Juan. *Spiks.* 1956. Translated and edited by Victoria Ortiz. New York: Monthly Review Press, 1973.

Stavans, Ilan. *The Hispanic Condition.* New York: HarperCollins, 1995.

Torres, Luis A. *The World of Early Chicano Poetry, 1846–1910.* Mountain View, Calif.: Floricanto Press, 1994.

Vega, Bernardo. *Memoirs of Bernardo Vega.* Edited by César Andreu Iglesias. Translated by Juan Flores. New York: Monthly Review Press, 1984.

Venegas, Daniel. *Las aventuras de Don Chipote; o, cuando los pericos mamen.* Los Angeles: El Heraldo de México, 1928. Reprint, Houston, Tex.: Arte Público Press, 1998.

Villagrá, Gaspar Pérez de. *The History of New Mexico.* Translated by Miguel Encinias, Alfred Rodríguez, and Joseph P. Sanchez. Albuquerque: University of New Mexico Press, 1992.

Villegas de Magnón, Leonor. *The Rebel.* Edited and introduced by Clara Lomas. Houston, Tex.: Arte Público Press, 1994.

Warren, Nina Otero. *Old Spain in Our Southwest.* New York: Harcourt Brace, 1936.

Williams, William Carlos. *The Collected Poems of William Carlos Williams,* vol. 1. Edited by A. Walton Litz and Christopher MacGowan. New York: New Directions, 1986.

The Latino Autobiography

SILVIO TORRES-SAILLANT

THE AUTOBIOGRAPHY, which is as problematic a genre in American writing as in any other branch of world literature, reveals particular levels of complexity in the hands of Latino authors. For the purposes of this overview, autobiography will mean the same as memoirs, testimonios, confessions, and other docu-mentary personal narratives that purport to tell the story of the self with the presumption of truth. The constituent etymological elements of the word that names the genre (auto = self; bio = life; graphy = writing) all point to areas of epistemological uncertainty. In other words, these elements seem to offer no guarantee of truth, often causing scholars to raise such questions as "What do we mean by the self *(autos)?* What do we mean by life *(bios)?* What significance do we impute to the act of writing *(graphē)*—What is the significance and the effect of transforming life, or *a* life, into a text?" (Olney 1980, p. 6). Students of the autobiographical tradition as practiced by writers from Jean-Jacques Rousseau to Malcolm X to Richard Rodriguez have insisted on highlighting the multiple layers of psychological, cultural, and ideological complexity that impinge on the literary constitution of the self (Gutman 1988, Eakin 1980). The autobiography is, in the words of Roger Rosenblatt, "the least reliable of genres" (1980, p. 169). Several scholars have followed Paul de Man's lead in denying the form the status

of a "genre or mode," conceiving it instead as "a figure of reading that occurs, to some degree, in all texts" (de Man 1979, p. 921). Consequently, some would favor Leigh Gilmore's contention that to construe the autobiography as a genre one would have to engage in "domesticating its specific weirdness" (cited in Mostern 1999, p. 46). Since autobiographers produce their texts while the life being evoked is still in progress, necessarily rely on the less than impeccable mechanism of memory, and contend with the fact that the structure of a person's lived experience will not easily accord with the contours of a literary form, their discursive task presents obstacles that many deem insurmountable.

Against the backdrop of the epistemological indeterminacy that scholars regard as inherent to the practice of writing the self, Latino autobiographers face complications stemming from the history of colonial domination that created U.S. Hispanics as a segment of the American population. As a result, these authors will rarely escape the need to superimpose the private and the public in their texts, namely the drive to represent the collective experience of their community through narrations of their own individual lives. Their texts thus play the dual roles of accounts of personal dramas and analyses of their community's predicament as it wrestles with questions of identity, citizenship, and belonging. As literary interventions, autobiographical texts invariably function as metaphors for the composite experience of the group. Writing the self thus becomes an act of collective representation. Since such writing almost invariably treads a sociopolitically and ethnically charged discursive ground where the nation and the self intersect, the intersection determined by their fractious historical background, Latino autobiographers cannot help but serve as mediating voices with the power to assist in shaping the image of their people that gains currency in the eyes of the larger society. In light of the multivalent nature and the less than solid texture of the form, the literary criticism and theory of autobiography have considered the difficulty of placing the autobiography as a genre, isolating fiction from purely biographical reportage, and establishing a firm separation between literary and non-literary instances of the form.

LATINO IDENTITY

The Latino autobiography presupposes the existence of a literary corpus bearing the same designation and a group of people to whom the name applies. A prefatory explanation, therefore, is in order. The term Latino specifically describes the Hispanic-descended segment of the U.S. population. Currently numbering over thirty-five million, the group came to form part of American society as a result of a combination of historical factors, chief among them, U.S. imperial expansion to the south and migratory flows triggered primarily by American involvement in Latin America. The 1846 invasion of Mexico that culminated in the 1848 treaty whereby the vanquished nation ceded to the victor the lands that now make up the American Southwest, and the 1898 Spanish-American war that led to the U.S. takeover of Puerto Rico as well as the establishment of a protectorate in Cuba were key among the events that gave momentum to the mobility of people north of the Rio Grande. Today Latinos are a composite of diverse realities, national experi-ences, and collective existential traumas. Before emigration from Latin America, which for each distinct group corresponded to different socio-historical and geopolitical events, no one was Latino or Hispanic but Puerto Rican, Cuban, Colombian, or Dominican, to name only some of the Latino subgroups. Once in the United States, however, they become unified in significant ways. They share the experience of being uprooted by large socioeconomic forces from their original homelands. They come from societies with a history of unequal association with the United States, a country that has influenced and sometimes even dictated political behavior in Latin America. The image of "backyard," often invoked by U.S. policy-makers to identify Latin America's geographical proximity to the United States, entails a qualitative view that construes the region not as a partner but as a subordinate.

By the 1930s, a good many Latin American nations already had ascertained, through the incursion of U.S. armed forces into their territory, the concrete inequality of their relationship with their North American neighbor. They had also become acquainted with the views that often informed these military invasions. For instance, President Theodore Roosevelt publicly decried the Cubans', Dominicans', Haitians', and Nicaraguans' conduct of their political lives. The famous "corollary to the Monroe Doctrine" in Roosevelt's annual message to Congress in 1904 hints at the U.S. sense of moral and political superiority vis-à-vis the people of Latin America. "Chronic wrongdoing or an impotence which results in a general loosening of the ties of civilized society, may in America, as elsewhere, ultimately require intervention by some civilized nation, and in the Western Hemisphere the adherence of the United States to the Monroe Doctrine may force the United States, however reluctantly, in flagrant cases of such wrongdoing or impotence, to the exercise of an international police power." (cited in Torres-Saillant 1998 pp. 139–141).

The popular view of the Spanish-speaking inhabitants of the hemisphere that prevailed in the United States during the first half of the twentieth century is reflected in a poll conducted in 1940 by the Office of Public Opinion Research. The questionnaire gave respondents nineteen adjectives with which to describe Latins. "Dark-skinned" came first, chosen by 80 percent of the respondents, followed by "quick-tempered," "emotional," "religious," "back-ward," "lazy," "ignorant," and "suspicious," chosen by 40 to 50 percent of those who answered. At the very bottom, chosen by a mere 5 percent, came "efficient," preceded by the adjectives "progressive," "generous," "brave," "honest," "intelligent," and "shrewd," none of which obtained a ranking higher than 16 percent (cited in Torres-Saillant 1998, pp. 139–141). The perceptions suggested by this list of adjectives helped shape the reception accorded to Latin Americans upon their arrival in the United States, where they came to occupy not the center but the margins of society. This marginalization has been intensified because, except for Mexicans and Puerto Ricans, the majority immigrated at a time when the country's economy was less expansive than during early waves of European immigration. The arrival in the United States of Dominicans, Cubans, Colombians, and Central Americans coincided with the virtual transformation of economic life in former industrial centers such as New York, where the service sector has become the primary area of employment. Instead of fostering integration, this arrangement has produced a widening gap between recent Latino immigrants and the mainstream of productive economic life.

New York exhibits what scholars have called a "dual city" model, where Spanish-speaking immigrants almost invariably occupy the less prosperous side of the divide, with clear implications for their sense of identity. Their political, economic, and cultural marginality relegates them to a condition of "otherness" with respect to the dominant social structure. The awareness of this otherness leads them to assert their commonality with those who share their condition, particularly when they can claim linguistic, ethnic, and historical links among the various national groups. The experience of diasporic uprooting and the sense of living outside the dominant realm of the receiving society penetrate the core of Latino identity. For, even though Mexicans, Cubans, Puerto Ricans, and Dominicans became ethnic communities in the United States through profoundly different processes, they are bound by political imperatives to see themselves as one. The feeling that they occupy a contested terrain, that they do not inherit their social space but must carve it out for themselves in the face of adversity, leads them to lift the banner of their oneness despite differences in the circumstances under which each of the distinct groups came to the United States. The language of unity functions as an instrument of survival.

LATINO LITERATURE

The foregoing scenario, which explains the emergence of a sense of community among U.S. Hispanics, provides a necessary context for understanding that they would have a distinct literary tradition. To recognize the boundaries of Latino literature, and the occurrence within it of the autobiography, perhaps it might help to draw a parallel. Readers will easily agree that African American literature is not African. Despite the shared blackness of the two authors, nobody would think of Harlem Renaissance poet Langston Hughes and Nigerian novelist Chinua Achebe as belonging in the same literary tradition. Similarly, Latino literature is neither Latin American nor Spanish. It would therefore seem inappropriate to group Chicano author Américo Paredes together with Argentinian fiction writer Jorge Luis Borges though they both have Spanish last names. The reader will encounter readily available reference sources that do precisely that. One of them undertakes to map Latino letters by surveying "a rich tapestry of Latino literary culture" from "the early poetry of Sor Juana Inés de la Cruz to the contemporary poetry of Jimmy Santiago Baca" (Magill 1994, p. v). Another chaotically skims over Latin American authors such as Alejo Carpentier, Eduardo Mallea, Laura Esquivel, and Luis Rafael Sánchez along with the likes of U.S. Hispanic authors Cristina García, Abraham Rodríguez, Luis Valdez, and Sandra Cisneros, without making the necessary distinction. A reference volume titled *Hispanic Writers,* consisting of sketches extracted from the series *Contemporary Authors,* provides information on "over 400 20th century authors representing Hispanic literature and culture" (Ryan 1991, p. vii). The sketches included range from U.S.-born (Oscar Zeta Acosta) to Latin American (Cesar Vallejo) to peninsular writers (Francisco García Lorca), exhibiting a planetary rather than a U.S.-ethnic understanding of the term Hispanic. Guided by a loose application of the terms Latino and Hispanic, encompassing cultural histories that simply do not belong together, those reference texts end up organizing the knowledge of Latino literature rather inaccurately. They proceed as if a shared Hispanic ancestry suffices to group writers together irrespective of their different cultures, histories, languages, geographies, or countries of birth, and languages.

Yet, we cannot think of nineteenth-century Dominican poet Salomé Ureña as a Latina in the way one uses the term when referring to Dominican American poet Rhina P. Espaillat. Nor can we think of the Mexican poet and playwright Rosario Castellanos as a Latina in the way we do of Mexican American poet Pat Mora. For as long as nation-states continue to exist, it will behoove readers to recognize the difference between an American writer of Latin American descent who is located in society as a member of a disempowered ethnic minority and a writer from Chile, who belongs there as a normal citizen, unencumbered by marginalized difference and ethnic constraints. Readers will simply find that their texts require different reading practices. For obvious reasons, in Latin America or the Hispanic Caribbean, Hispanic descent does not constitute a differentiated ethnic identity that merits naming. The naming of ethnicity normally occurs by reference to a normative, dominant group. Hispanic descent in the region is the norm. The misuse of the term Latina—with capital L—for a woman in Nicaragua has serious conceptual implications for our understanding of the contours of Latino identity and Latino literature. Latinos exist as a component of an ethnoracial pentagon that makes sense only in the context of U.S. history. There may be writers who, on account of their discrete circumstances, authentically occupy a sociocultural space where the dividing line between Latinos to the north and Latin Americans to the south gets considerably blurred. Nor can the earnest desire of scholars who yearn for an eventual erasure of borders be ignored. Consistent with that spirit, Roman de la Campa opens his book *Latin Americanism* (1999) with a series of questions that occupy his attention throughout the volume. One of them asks: "Are Latino texts produced in the United States directly transferable to the study of Latin American literature?" (p. 6). The question remains unanswered at the close of the book, but people concerned with a serious inquiry into Latino literature, committed simultaneously to defining and heralding the tradition that U.S. Hispanic texts have formed cannot afford to leave it unanswered. Enough data exist for scholars confidently to affirm that Latino texts are not borderless. They speak primarily to interlocutors whose ears have been tuned by the sounds of the American experience. Even in those cases when the text occurs in Spanish, as with Tomás Rivera's *...Y no se lo tragó la tierra* (1971), one can hardly think of them as "directly transferable" to Latin American literature. The Spanish of Tomás Rivera or the Spanish passages in the texts of Rudolfo Anaya or Denise Chávez, is an American, not a Latin American language.

THE FORM

The autobiography may be regarded as the most important form in Latino literature since its practice epitomizes in an exacerbated manner the main sociocultural compulsions that have fueled U.S. Hispanic writing from the outset of the tradition. Latino authors, when thinking of American literature, tend to display two dissimilar yet paradoxically complementary intents, like writers, literary scholars, and cultural critics from the other racialized minorities in the United States. They generally wish to assert their rightful place in the national corpus that bears the name of "American literature" while at the same time challenging the sociocultural framework that informs traditional notions of Americanness. They seem to demand inclusion as legitimate members of the national community while asserting their right to proudly display the trappings of their difference (Torres-Saillant 2000 p. 10). Robert Sayre persuasively argued that autobiography offers a vehicle by means of which citizens discursively travel the public sphere, assess the republic, and enter into the "House of America," which means that they partake of America as an idea and a restorative project (Sayre 1980, p. 150). While applying harmoniously to classic mainstream autobiographies like those of Benjamin Franklin and Henry Adams, the formulation needs adjustment to fit the situation of autobiographers from "communities not part of American success" (p. 162). No expression of the form exhibits a more forceful response to or coming to terms with that predicament than the Latino autobiography. Anyone approaching the U.S. Hispanic literature section of a major bookstore or any student browsing a description for a Latino literature course at a competitive college or university will most likely note the prominent place accorded to autobiographical texts. Consistent with the unstable generic constitution of the form, the selection would typically include memoirs, novels, and assorted works, all linked by their autobiographical texture, as in this list: *Down These Mean Streets* (1967) by Piri Thomas, *Pocho* (1959) by José Antonio Villareal, *The Autobiography of a Brown Buffalo* (1972) by Oscar Zeta Acosta, *Barrio Boy* (1971) by Ernesto Galarza, *Hunger of Memory* (1984) by Richard Rodriguez, *Family Installments* (1982) by Edward Rivera, *How the Garcia Girls Lost their Accents* (1994) by Julia Alvarez, *Rain of Gold* (1991) by Victor Villaseñor, *Silent Dancing* (1990) by Judith Ortiz Cófer, *When I Was Puerto Rican* (1993) by Esmeralda Santiago, and *Drown* (1996) by Junot Díaz.

Certainly some Latino authors, like the fiction writer Ed Vega, could seek to stay clear of "wholly autobiographical" work and even decry the practice of autobiography if it does not meet their criteria for linguistic sophistication and literary excellence (Augenbraum and Stavans 1993, pp. xx–xxi). But, for the most part, autobiographical writing dominates Latino literature. This no doubt has to do with the importance of the immigrant story in the cultural history of the United States. Taking the form of "ethnic autobiography," which Nicolás Kanellos in *Herencia: The Anthology of Hispanic Literature in the United States* (2002) aptly describes as "that melting pot genre par excellence," this kind of writing accords neatly with the values by which American society defines itself (Kanellos 2002, p. 11). Needless to say, not all memoirs or autobiographies buy into the assimilationist ethos. But it seems fair to assert that the cult of the individual in American society creates a favorable ambience for publicly sharing personal stories. Narratives of individual lives also tend to make the human experience more apprehensible than when presented in the collective plights of groups. When singly presented, the human experience appears graspable to the consumer, the reader, who also comes to the product assured of its value because of its inherent truth. The pull of the market, therefore, plays a meaningful role in the production of autobiographies. When the writer from a minority group has a social sensibility, the urgency to fight invisibility will easily surface. Nicholasa Mohr has recalled her desire early in her career to see her people and herself in the text: "*Nilda,* my first novel, like so many writers' first books, contains a great deal of autobiographical material . . . In American literature I, as a Puerto Rican child, did not exist . . . and I as a Puerto Rican woman do not exist" (cited in Rodriguez 1993 p. 268). Some Latino texts that set out to write the self constitute milestones, providing key resources for understanding the formation and development of particular subsections of the overall community. The *Memoirs of Bernardo Vega* (1984), an engaging account of the life of a Puerto Rican labor organizer and political activist living in New York during the first half of the twentieth century, offers invaluable data for reconstructing the early years of the Puerto Rican community in the United States. Similarly, the recently published memoir of Evelio Grillo, *Black Cuban, Black American* (2000), the personal narrative of a Cuban Tampa native who, split by the dividing force of Jim Crow lines in the South, carved for himself an identity space in the African American community, offers a wealth of knowledge about race relations among U.S. Cubans prior to the migratory flow that followed the 1959 Revolution.

Besides those texts that appear evidently autobiographical, in that the narrative "I" in the story corresponds to the name of the person writing it, several works exist which powerfully invite the reader to connect the life of the living author with the fictional life represented in the book. Readers of Villareal's *Pocho,* a story of a young man growing up in California among farm laborers, will find it compelling to identify the main character Richard Rubio's cultural ambivalence about Mexican and Anglo values with the author's own experience growing up between competing traditions. By the same token, when perusing *Drown* by Díaz, readers will find it hard to resist equating the incidents in the life of Yunior, the main character, with those in the life of the author, especially given the many points at which the two seem identical as we gather from his interviews. One could probably apply to Latino writing Roger Rosenblatt's judgment about African American texts, namely that "fiction is often so close to

autobiography in plot and theme that the study of the latter almost calls the existence of the former into question" (Rosenblatt 1980, p. 170). In some Latino books the line between the biographical and the fictional blurs so intensely, as in Rivera's *Family Installments* and *García Girls* by Alvarez, that publishers and librarians classify them as "fiction" or "autobiography" indistinctly.

MEXICAN AMERICAN PIONEERS

Autobiography has emerged to the position of prominence it currently enjoys in Latino literature as a result of the community's need to assert, protect, and encourage itself. The rise of the form corresponds to stages of collective self affirmation occurring at moments in history that vary for each of the subgroups that make up the U.S. Hispanic population. Following their different moments of insertion in given U.S. labor markets, the creation of ethnic enclaves on the margins of mainstream society, and the recognition of existing inimical structures that would ignore or silence the group's voices, Latinos begin to brandish language as a tool to insert themselves in the national discourse. The drive for the community to make its presence felt triggers the need to speak up. Since Mexican Americans became part of the U.S. population initially through an act of military conquest and political subjection, their need to speak up, which Genaro Padilla calls "discursive necessity," may have come from the very start: "The rupture of everyday life experienced by some 75,000 people who inhabited the far northern provinces of Mexico in 1846 opened a terrain of discursive necessity in which fear and resentment found language in speeches and official documents warning fellow citizens to accommodate themselves to the new regime" (Padilla 1993, p. 153). Political traumas shake the pillars of memory, forcing amnesia or accentuating the desire to remember. Thus ensues a scenario that is hospitable to testimonial utterance.

The earliest U.S. Hispanic autobiographical narratives in the Southwest—José Antonio

Menchaca's "Reminiscences" (c. 1850) and Juan Nepomuceno Seguín's *Personal Memoirs* (1858)—share a common desire to bear witness to the authors' plight as they negotiated the delicate circumstances that caused them to shift loyalties more than once. Perhaps the most ambitious attempt to mark the community's historical presence from the perspective of the observing individual subject was the five-volume compendium "Recuerdos históricos y personales tocante a la Alta California" (1975) by the land-owning Californio Mariano Guadalupe Vallejo, whose unpublished manuscript forms part of the holdings of the University of California at Berkeley's Bancroft Library. Examples of Mexican Americans who felt compelled to bear witness abound from Vallejo's time through the mid-twentieth century, with women playing a salient role at key moments. Some fifteen women of Hispanic descent notably participated in the project conducted during the late 1870s by California bookseller and historian Hubert H. Bancroft, who had numerous autobiographies transcribed from oral dictation as part of his data gathering for writing the history of the state. The stories told by several of the participants provided otherwise unavailable ethnically oriented and gender-inflected perspectives on society, culture, and politics. The documents they left, including the noteworthy personal accounts "Cosas de California" (Things Californian) by María Inocenta Avila, "Narración de una californiana" (A California woman's story) by Josefa Carrillo de Fotch, and "Recuerdos del pasado" (Memories of the past) by Felipa Osuna de Marrón, constitute invaluable glimpses at the human experience in California during a pivotal moment of cultural transition. Scholars often highlight the personal narratives of Apolinaria Lorenzana, "Memorias de la beata" (Memoirs of a pious woman), and Eulalia Pérez, "Una vieja y sus recuerdos" (An old woman and her recollections), for their meaningful portrayal of courageous women wrestling with adversarial social forces in a patriarchal milieu. Lorenzana,

who became a teacher, nurse, and supervisor of the Indian seamstresses in San Diego Mission, had come to Alta California as an orphan to serve in various homes. A witness to the Anglo takeover of California, she rose to become owner of three ranches. Pérez, for her part, served as a housekeeper in the San Gabriel Mission, where she oversaw the distribution of all stock and supervised the Indian domestic workers.

Lodged in the archives of the Bancroft Library, those autobiographical interventions by Mexican American women remain unpublished as the project that instigated their collection did not contemplate their dissemination and restricted their value to enhancing the research resources of their Anglo collector. Ironically, *The Rebel* (1994), an autobiography written in Laredo, Texas, by a participant observer who wished to stress the role of women on both sides of the border during the Mexican Revolution, did not make it to print until nearly a half century after the death of the author, though she tried hard to publish it either in Spanish or in English. Leonor Villegas de Magnón (1876–1955), author of *The Rebel,* founded in 1913 the women's nursing corps La Cruz Blanca (The White Cross), made up mostly of women from the Texas side of the border who supported the insurgent leader Venustiano Carranza in Mexico. Her legacy as an activist and as a writer poignantly affirms the fundamentally transnational texture of political and social life on the border. Born in northern Mexico of an elite family, Villegas attended Catholic school in San Antonio and Austin, Texas, and received her bachelor's degree and teaching certification in 1895 from the Academy of Mount St. Ursula in New York (Kanellos, p. 382). Her involvement in the work of the Revolution, a political movement that would bring about significant social transformation south of the border, did not imply a choice of commitment to life in Mexico over the United States. The binationality of her own family background would seem to make such a choice untenable. On the night of her own birth, her father wondered thus: "My son born in American soil. My daughter in Mexican territory, and I, a Spanish subject. Who will be more powerful, he or she?"—a question which her mother, holding the newborn daughter "in a warm embrace," settled by addressing the infant with these words: "A Mexican flag shall be yours. I will wrap it together with your brother's. His shall be an American flag, but they shall be like one to me" (Villegas 1994, p. 7). A U.S. citizen whose national loyalty would continually be questioned by Americans and Mexicans, she chose to embrace an agenda of "international social justice that" ignored juridical boundaries (Lomas 1994, p. xxxix).

In the generations that followed Villegas de Magnón, Nina Otero-Warren, author of *Old Spain and Our Southwest* (1936), Fabiola Cabeza de Baca, who published *The Good Life* (1949) and *We Fed Them Cactus* (1954), and Cleofas Jaramillo, author of *Romance of a Little Girl* (1955), stand out among the Mexican American women who had recourse to autobiographical writing to stave the field of their identity. Members of the cadre of women authors who merit mention as founding mothers of Latina letters, Otero-Warren, Cabeza de Vaca, and Jaramillo, all natives of New Mexico, satisfy their discursive necessity in a manner that accentuates the significance of class in collective constructions of identity. Evincing an aristocratic mode of representation consistent with their own upper-class origins, their texts formulate claims to cultural resistance by stressing their association with a glorious Spanish past devoid of the oppression perpetrated by the conquistadors against the indigenous population. As their evocations repress the other in the margins ("savage" Indians, "lazy" Aztecs, and simple *peones*), their "autoethnographies" participate in a process that Sonja Pérez terms "participatory resistance," meaning that they "simultaneously participated in and resisted Anglo-American domination" (2002, p. 288). On the whole, one can give these women their due credit by viewing them as subordinate writers in whose texts we can find "a textual signal of embryonic consciousness, whispers of antecedent resistance" that contributed to making possible the clearer expressions of Latino contestation that would later follow (Padilla 1993, p. 60).

Though initially criticized for its assimilationist emphasis, Villareal's *Pocho* showed a meaningful willingness to delve into the issues of identity that emerge from the clashing worldviews that Mexican Americans experienced on the eve of World War II. In that respect, it stands as a key text in the evolution of the form among Chicano authors. Galarza's *Barrio Boy*, which depicts a protagonist whose sense of identity and self-worth stems from a healthy affiliation with his community, also has a special place as an ideologically fundamental autobiographical text. Contemporary Mexican American autobiographers such as Ruben Martinez, Ruben Navarrete, Luis J. Rodriguez, John Phillip Santos, Gary Soto, and Luis Alberto Urrea add further layers of complexity to the exploration of identity and the relationship between the individual and the collective.

CUBAN AMERICAN VARIATION

The Latino subgroup with the deepest historical roots in the United States, after Mexican Americans, is the Cuban community. The 1858 publication in New York of *El laud del desterrado,* a compilation of patriotic Cuban verse by exiled poets that includes poems as early as the 1825 "Himno del desterrado" by José María Heredia, clearly illustrates the longevity of Cuban writing in this country. Suffice it to add the case of Cirilo Villaverde's *Cecilia Valdes* (1882), an abolitionist novel that has a central place in the national literary history of Cuba yet was published while the author lived as an exile in the United States, or the sizable body of work written while living in New York by José Martí, the founding father of the Cuban nation. Throughout the nineteenth century, American legislators and government officials sustained a set of undefined and ambiguous positions regarding U.S.-Cuban relations often providing a haven for rebels from the island seeking the overthrow of the Spanish colonial regime and often exhibiting solidarity to Cuba's colonial rulers. A U.S. interest in annexing Cuba to the American territory dating back to the times of Thomas Jefferson largely modulated that inconsistent policy (Montes-Huidobro 1995, pp. x–xi). The ambivalence came to an end in the mid-1890s, when the American government announced its support of the Cuban independence movement, culminating in the invasion of 1898 and the Spanish–American War that did away with the last remnants of an Iberian imperial presence in the hemisphere. Of course, the interests of Cuban independence leaders did not prevail once U.S. forces secured their defeat of Spain, which led to the American occupation of Puerto Rico, the Philippines, and other overseas territories. But in 1895, U.S. imperial interests did not fail to benefit from autobiographical writing. William Randolph Hearst, the powerful publisher of the *New York Journal,* like his competitor Joseph Pulitzer, owner of the *New York World,* favored the invasion and passionately lobbied on its behalf. Among his most successful advocacy stunts was the publicity campaign he orchestrated around the liberation of the patriot Evangelina Cossío y Cisneros, a sort of Cuban Joan of Arc whom the Spanish authorities had incarcerated in the women's prison of Las Recogidas. Hearst sent to Havana his employee Kart Decker, then one of the paper's star correspondents, with the mission to free the young damsel. The plan to rescue Evangelina, which involved a clever stratagem, proved successful, and she escaped disguised as a man, ending her fifteen-month-long imprisonment. Evangelina and her gallant American savior came to New York to a triumphant reception at Fifth Avenue with President McKinley in attendance (Fernández 2002, p. 21).

Born in 1878 in Puerto Príncipe, the capital city of Camaguey province in Cuba, Evangelina

was seventeen years of age when American gallantry brought her out of captivity. Two years later, while she enjoyed her status as media darling in New York, an autobiography signed by her came out in English. The *Story of Evangelina Cisneros* (1897), which had the backing of the Hearst publicity machine, appealed directly to American women. "This is the story of my life," says the author, adding pointedly, "American women may find it interesting" (Cossío y Cisneros 1998, p. 356). The author stresses the similarity between her birthplace and the host country ("Camaguey is said by Americans to be the Kentucky of Cuba," p. 356). Contrasting their political realities in a way that subtly invokes the geopolitical logic of the Monroe Doctrine, anticipating the thinking that generations later would construe the rest of the hemisphere as the "backyard" of the United States, Evangelina deemed it inconceivable "that some of the things which I must tell you could really happen so close to the free country of America" (Cossío y Cisneros 1998, p. 356). Since it does not seem that a Spanish version of Evangelina's story really existed, we can speculate that both her writing in English and the ideological direction of her thought received considerable input form Hearst and his staff. On the whole, Evangelina's autobiography probably deserves credit for garnering allies to the cause that promoted the invasion of Cuba, which happened the following year.

At the time of the Spanish–American War whereby Cuba became a U.S. protectorate, a numerous and vigorous émigré Cuban community thrived, especially in Florida, connected with the cigar industry. Since their presence in the United States precedes the U.S. takeover of their ancestral island, they can be said to have escaped the sociocultural traumas associated with marginalized ethnic minorities of color. Perhaps that may explain why the autobiography occurs less frequently among Cuban authors. In other words, they suffered less from the existential impact of the inimical forces that trigger the need to speak up, the discursive necessity that Mexican Americans revealed from the outset. A major work that could be listed among autobiographies, *The Goodbye Land* (1967) by Tampa native José Yglesias, lacks the markers of ethnic self-affirmation or quest evinced, for instance, by *Down These Mean Streets,* which appeared the same year. Apart from offering some initial scintillating glimpses of the author's childhood in Tampa at the start of the twentieth century, the book evokes the memory of his father, a native of the northern Spanish province of Galicia who at the age of thirteen arrived in Havana, where he learned the cigar trade and years later went to Tampa to work in the cigar factories. His father got sick with typhoid in 1920, and efforts to help him regain his health took him back to Havana, the first trip out of Tampa for the author's twenty-eight-year-old mother. From the Cuban capital his father had to go on a ship for Spain while the wife and the children returned to Tampa. Since his father died in Spain and the family never saw him again, the story tells of the author's quest to reconstruct his father's personal and family background. Already an adult, traveling with his own wife and children, the author undertakes an evocatively described and moving sentimental journey. He goes in pursuit of meaning by connecting with family roots. The pathos in the narrative comes from a personal search rather than from ethnic constraints.

The autobiographical impulse in Cuban writing is to be found in texts that are better known as fiction such as the novel *Our House in the Last World* (1983), a tale by Oscar Hijuelos that spans three generations of a Cuban family in the United States. Subscribing to "the conventional norms of an immigrant memoir," with evident fictional elements, the text has been described as the author's "first autobiographical novel" (Duany 1993, p. 171). The same scholar refers to Cristina García's *Dreaming in Cuban* (1992) as a novel that tells "the partly autobiographical story of three generations of a Cuban family," namely the children and grandchildren of Jorge and Celia del Pino (1993 p. 177). What causes

the del Pino children to come to the United States, splitting from the branch of the family that chooses to stay in the island, is the Cuban Revolution, an event that had traumatic consequences for several contemporary Cuban memoirists. Their texts range from the moving narrative of Flor Fernandez Barrios in *Blessed by Thunder* to the personal drama of a gay Cuban physician dealing with AIDS patients told by Rafael Campo in *The Desire to Heal.* In *Next Year In Cuba: A Cubano's Coming of Age in America,* Gustavo Pérez Firmat offers analytical recollections of his life, therein developing his one-and-a-half generation thesis to describe the identity of those Cubans who came to the United States around the age of twelve. Their exodus prompted by the Revolution, they were old enough to retain a cultural memory of the Cuban past but too young to share the exilic mindset of their parents. That Cuban American autobiographers seldom address racial matters in narrating their lives, an issue other Latino authors cover almost invariably, may have to do with the great hold that the trauma of the Revolution has had on their imagination. Grupo Areito in 1978 put together *Contra viento y marea,* a collection of personal testimonies by young U.S. Cubans who by then already wished to rethink their relationship with post-1959 Cuba outside the parameters set by their elders. The 1995 collection *Bridges to Cuba,* edited by Ruth Behar, retakes the intent in the context of post-Berlin Wall Cuba. Both compilations include highly engaging texts on the existential implications of the geopolitics of U.S.-Cuban relations for individuals.

Perhaps most illustrative of the way in which the Cuban American autobiography deploys its discursive necessity differently from its other Latino counterparts is a text like Pablo Medina's *Exiled Memories: A Cuban Childhood* (1990), which tells the story of the author's first twelve years, a period which ends at 5 a.m. on 1 January 1959, when his father rushed into the house and said "Batista fell!," and preparations immediately began for the family to leave for the

United States, starting their interminable exile (Medina 2002, p. 108).

The 1990 edition of Medina's autobiography concludes with the inevitability of departure and the loss of home. A second edition in 2002 adds a chapter in which the author summarizes the deaths of several older relatives and records his experience of returning for a visit to Havana in January 1999, at the age of fifty, to reconnect with his past. At the end, despite the indictment of the Cuban Revolution, what emerges is a more serene adult, one who seems to have reconciled himself to the losses inherent in growing up. What we do not get is any inkling of the life the author has lived between the loss of his world of childhood and his subsequent coming to terms with the loss. Interestingly, the omitted portion of the life is precisely the one that would yield material for ethnic autobiography. Despite the political setting in which the story is placed, the text really belongs with *The Goodbye Land* among tales of personal quest devoid of the constraints that typically fuel the Latino autobiographer's desire to bear witness.

PUERTO RICAN AUTOBIOGRAPHERS

Medina avoids the bildungsroman component that so characteristically shows up in Latino autobiographies, which are predominantly coming-of-age stories. Santiago's *When I was Puerto Rican*, which devotes the greater bulk of the volume to evoking seductively, nostalgically, and even, at times, exotically, the author's childhood years in her rustic village of Macún, with less than a third of its pages going to her growing up as an immigrant in low-income Brooklyn tenements, could perhaps compare with Medina's *Exiled Memories*. Yet they differ significantly in that Santiago's tale, more characteristic of the Latino autobiographic tradition, does not, like Medina's, seek to reconstruct a tragically lost world of comfort and solace. Rather her book recollects the transition from the discomfort of poverty in rural Puerto Rico to the discomfort of poverty in inner-city New York. What changed for her was her inevitable coming-of-age, which, with the loss of the magical schemes of thought prevalent in innocent childhood, made her less able to smile in the face of utter misery. Santiago's book, in that respect, behaves normally in relation to the texts of other U.S. Puerto Rican authors as well as the overall Latino corpus. *Almost A Woman,* the second installment of Santiago's autobiography, concentrates fully on the exploration of her American experience.

Scholars often mention Pedro Juan Labarthe's *Son of Two Nations*: *The Private Life of a Columbia Student* (1931) as an exceptional intervention culturally and ideologically. The text glorifies the cultural and social options that Puerto Ricans have enjoyed since the U.S. occupation three decades earlier. Illustrating the benefits of the colonial condition, the book recounts an immigrant success story of the kind that "Americanization makes possible and which reflects the worldview of more privileged Puerto Ricans" (Acosta Belén 1993, p. 18). Labarthe seems particularly atypical when compared with contemporaries of his such as Bernardo Vega, whose *Memorias,* though published for the first time in the 1970s and issued in English in the 1980s, was written in the 1940s, and Jesús Colón, whose 1961 collection *A Puerto Rican in New York and Other Sketches* gathered personal essays that he had published over the previous decades. Imbued with a sense of community, the two came at a young age from the countryside town of Cayey to New York City, where they became cigar workers and involved themselves in political activism on behalf of working-class constituencies. Both wrote texts of a "compelling autobiographical and testimonial nature" that at the same time serve as "invaluable historical sources" for the study of the Puerto Rican and overall Hispanic community in the city during the first half of the twentieth century (Acosta Belén 1993, p. 183).

As practiced by Esmeralda Santiago, Judith Ortiz Cófer, and others, contemporary U.S. Puerto Rican autobiography traces its social, political, and existential roots to Vega and Colón rather than to Labarthe. The reason for this genealogy is found in the socioeconomic profiles of the migratory flows that came from the island to the mainland during the first two thirds of the twentieth century, when working-class arrivants predominated. Extreme poverty and racial discrimination provide the backdrop against which Piri Thomas sets his own story in *Down These Mean Streets.* We learn about his dealing with self-hatred, gangs, drugs, crime, incarceration, and ultimate rehabilitation. The young man's inability to cope with the difficulty of negotiating the racial code of his Hispanic Caribbean household along with that of the pre-civil rights streets of New York largely accounts for the pain he endures. Issued by a major publisher and reviewed very widely in the press, the book brought considerable celebrity to the author, making him an influential figure in Latino literature. A pithy autobiographical essay by the poet and translator Jack Agüeros, a New York–born Puerto Rican whose father in 1920, at the age of sixteen, ventured to the big city as a stowaway on a steamer that shuttled from San Juan, articulates the principal cause of migration for his community. When an "environment gets hostile," meaning it presents a challenge to survival, birds migrate: "Men move for the same reason. When a Puerto Rican comes to America, he comes looking for a job. He takes the cold as one of a negative series of givens. The mad hustle, the filthy city, filthy air, filthy housing, sardine transportation, are in the series (Agüeros 1971, p. 104). Typically, when scenarios such as Agüeros describes present themselves, the parents, if fortune smiles on them, can return. Their U.S.-born children, if social marginality blocks their sense of belonging in the United States, usually have no place they can go back to. The Puerto Rican pilgrimage that Agüeros enacts in his moving autobiographical essay, which is entitled "Halfway to Dick and Jane," epitomizes the angst of the immigrant experience as it afflicts the young, when they lose their ancestral homeland without necessarily gaining a home in their birthplace. The Latino autobiography in general and its Puerto Rican segment in particular characteristically capture that predicament, whether in straightforward accounts of individual lives, in texts that explore the author's biography while deploying imaginative modes of community portrayal, or in literary exercises resembling the "testimonial novel" such as Nicholasa Mohr's *Nilda* (1973) and Edward Rivera's *Family Installments* (Flores 1993, p. 65). Although Rivera's book temptingly woos the reader to take it for a biographical account—its labeling as "memoir" on the back cover and its affixing "Memories of Growing Up Hispanic" as subtitle, for example—it also asserts its fictional texture. The story begins prior to the protagonist's birth, and his name differs from that of his author. Partly a portrait of the artist as a young man, the story captures the growing up experiences of a Puerto Rican lad who carves his individual identity as a Latino in New York without treating his Puerto Rican background with contempt nor pastoralizing the promises of the American dream. The ideological sobriety of Rivera's book, which is to be found also in the title story of the collection *The Boy without a Flag* (1992) by Abraham Rodriguez Jr., largely characterizes the overall Puerto Rican contribution to the form, a body of writing that is more substantial than this overview can aspire to survey.

THE RISE OF DOMINICAN VOICES

When Dominican American writers began to come into view as bona fide members of the Latino literary family in the 1990s, they became known primarily for the autobiographical bent of their texts. The case has elsewhere been made that it should not have taken so long for U.S. Dominican writing to attain visibility since its history is not as short as scholars of Latino literature seem to have assumed (Torres-Saillant 2000, pp. 250–251). However, though belated, the recognition did come, ushered in by the remarkable success of *How the García Girls Lost Their Accents* (1991) by Julia Alvarez. Now a staple in reading lists for courses dealing with the immigrant experience or ethnic minorities, as representing the Dominican case, the book by Alvarez so much resembled the author's life that friends and relatives recognized themselves in it and occasionally objected to their representation. As a gesture to the protagonists of the other lives that cross paths with the main character in her narrative, Alvarez produced the ingenious novel *¡Yo!* (1997), which consists of a series of appraisals in which the other people "write back," deploying their own representations of the main character.

Born in New York City to affluent immigrant parents from the Dominican Republic, Alvarez was taken to her parents' country only a few weeks after her birth. Her family lived there until 1960, when political problems would cause them again to migrate to the United States with all four daughters. Details about the writer's early childhood in the homeland of her parents appear throughout her essays, especially in "An American Childhood in the Dominican Republic," which chronicles the extent of her continuous contact with American society during the ten years of absence from her birthplace. Her maternal grandfather, a long-standing cultural attaché to the United Nations, "spoke perfect English," having graduated from an American university, and kept an apartment in New York City (1987, p. 72). His children, in turn, went to boarding schools in the United States and, especially the boys, attended top American institutions of higher education: "Cornell, Yale, Brown." Alvarez recalls that back in the Dominican Republic, her family "subscribed to American magazines, received mail-order catalogues, and joined honorary societies," while she and her three sisters, along with their numerous cousins, played with American toys (p. 80). Similarly, during her formative years, Alvarez attended the Carol Morgan School, an institution started by a diplomat's wife to serve the learning needs of the children of Americans who lived in the small Caribbean country: "we began each day by pledging allegiance to the flag of the United States, which I much preferred to the Dominican one, for it had the lovely red-and-white stripes of the awning at the ice-cream parlor" (p. 77).

Alvarez has described her early linguistic experience in the 1992 essay "My English," which now appears in her collection *Something to Declare* (1995). There we learn that her parents spoke English, first, when the children did not know enough and they wanted to keep a secret from them. Later, when all had become "a bilingual family," her parents stressed the use of English to make the children practice the language. When her parents migrated to the United States, the ten-year-old Alvarez's knowledge of English facilitated her settlement.

Alvarez offers a recollection of her feeling at the precise moment when her plane landed in New York from Santo Domingo. The author's yearning for the United States while in her parents' homeland resonates with the mood of the speaker in her autobiographical collection of poems *The Other Side/El Otro Lado* (1995). The section that gives the book its collective title is a narrative poem made up of twenty-one parts which chronicle the speaker's adventures in a quasi-mystical *over there*. She, a "so-called writer working on her two-year writing block," goes to spend a "winter's residency" at an artist colony up on a mountain in the Dominican Republic (pp. 109–110). The speaker and her American boyfriend Mike, "like two Brits / trekking through darkest Africa," hike down to the level of the common folk (p. 111). During her momentous crossing of a Dominican vale that strikes one as a heart of darkness, the speaker stops to seek the spiritual service of a Haitian vodou priest to help her make up her "divided Dominican-American mind," which she does, to stay in America.

The other Dominican American author who has gained considerable distinction, Junot Díaz, has had to speak *ad nauseam* about his personal and family lives to readers and interviewers, who tend to see his texts as transcriptions of events in his life. He has explained his relationship to autobiography thus: "I love to play with it. It's like a medium. I was saying in an interview before that, no matter how hard I try to be autobiographical, the demands of fiction transform the material. There was no possible way to be autobiographical. . . . a memoir is also a kind of fiction." (Céspedes and Torres-Saillant 2000, pp. 905–906). Still, reviews of his work and interviews invariably privilege the sociology of his background of utter poverty and living without a father at home (Stanton 1998).

Díaz has had a remarkable literary career since he first broke into print with a short fiction piece entitled "Ysrael" in the Autumn 1995 issue of *Story,* earning inclusion in *Best American Short Stories* in four different years. When his highly acclaimed collection *Drown* came out in 1996, it met with practically universal praise. While his stories might dabble in the scrutiny of contemporary Dominican history and "cross cultural experiences," David Gates, appraising *Drown* for the *New York Times Book Review,* confidently places the book "smack-dab in the middle" of the American experience. With a sharp clinical eye, Díaz delves piercingly into the Dominican chapter of the human experience, revealing a field virtually unexplored by American fiction. Set in a discrete history and geography—following the characters' whereabouts from the homeland in the Dominican Republic through their immigrant odyssey in the United States—the book unveils a contemporary yarn of misery, uprooting, and endurance. Dominicans, like any other people of the earth, harbor the greatness, the baseness, the good, the evil, the beauty, the ugliness, the brilliance, and the mediocrity of all humanity.

The last and longest of *Drown's* stories, "Negocios," reconstructs the adventures of Ramón,

the father who left his wife and children behind to try to make it in the States, from the vantage point of Yunior, the youngest son. In the host country, having survived the initial hurdles of a Herculean immigrant crossing, Ramón ends up married to Nilda, a parallel wife with whom he procreates an additional set of children. The narrator's father and mother have names that coincide with those of the author's parents, Ramón and Virtudes, and the evocation of family life loosely resembles the biographical details the author has shared with interviewers. That resemblance between people or events in their books with people or events in their lives occur also in *Geographies of Home* (1998) and *Soledad* (2001), novels authored respectively by Loida Maritza Pérez and Angie Cruz, the other Dominican American writers who have drawn discernibly from personal and family circumstances to compose their immigrant tales. Nelly Rosario's *Song of the Water Saints* (2002), a novel that links the drama of a family in New York City's Washington Heights to a historical genesis traceable to the 1916 U.S. military invasion of the Dominican Republic, is less clearly connected to the tradition of ethnic autobiography. Besides those mentioned here, Dominicans writing in the United States make up a numerous constituency, the majority producing their texts primarily in Spanish, but the autobiography does not seem to have surfaced as a prominent form in the body of work they have put out. On the whole, the biographical engagement of Dominican American fiction, like the greater Latino literary corpus to which it belongs, would seem to justify de Man's recommendation to place the distinction between fiction and autobiography in the realm of the "undecidable" (de Man 1979, p. 921).

AMORPHOUS FORM

The Chicana writer and scholar Norma Elia Cantu, herself a fine autobiographer, has drawn attention to autobiographies written in the late twentieth century by denizens of the border town of Laredo, Texas. Focusing on four such cases, she discusses *Infancia peregrina* (n.d.) by Belia Trevino, *Mis memorias* (1985) by Hilario Coronado, *Holidays and Heartstrings: Recuerdos de la casa de miel* (1995) by Norma Benavides, and *My Spanish-Speaking Left Foot* (1997) by José Cardenas. These autobiographers, none of whom appears moved by the desire for literary recognition, apparently wrote their texts strictly for the purpose of passing on accounts of what they have experienced to family and community. Humbly and unassumingly presented, their writings constitute narrative attempts to preserve the cultural memory of lives lived along the borderlands by simple folks dealing with the challenges of ordinary existence in that space where two nation-states dilute. Cantu notes that these "homemade autobiographies" do not necessarily document the exploits of one person but tend to portray "a much wider protagonist, the community," and, to discuss question of form, she quotes the following disclaimer offered by Benavides to introduce her work: "Aside from liberties of content, there are those of form and style, mood, language, and punctuation. The text fluctuates from one style to another, never adhering to any definite pattern or fixed set of rules. Also, it drifts from formal to informal, from carefree to soulful, dramatic, or even philosophical at times, or from comical to tragic. After all, isn't life itself this way?" (cited in Cantu 2001, p. 6).

Curiously, though representing herself as a "non-writer," Benavides formulates a disclaimer that goes directly to the core of the theory and practice of Latino autobiography, an eminently amorphous form which has historically embraced all of the deviations that she confesses to. The frequently cited definition of autobiography offered by Philippe Lejeune would seem hardly to apply to the occurrence of the form in the Latino literary tradition: "a retrospective prose narrative produced by a real person concerning his own existence, focusing on his individual life, in particular on the development of his personality" (Lejeune 1982, p. 193). Lejeune, of course, has concurred with others in viewing the autobiography "as a way of reading" as much as "a kind of writing," accepting its very existence as "an historically variable contractual product" (p. 220). Among Latinos the form is not circumscribed to "prose narrative" since examples abound that incorporate verse in the evocation of the protagonist's life, as Ortiz Cofer's *Silent Dancing* and Cherríe Moraga's *Loving in the War Years* would illustrate. Cantu's *Canicula: Snapshots of a Girlhood en la frontera* (1995) oscillates between the scribal and the pictorial by having the words on the page converse with family photographs in the process of weaving her story. The author provokes the reader by offering a tantalizing explanation of her use of family pictures: "although it may appear that these stories are my family's they're not precisely, and yet they are. . . . I was calling the work fictional autobiography, until a friend suggested that they really are ethnographic and so if it must fit a genre, I guess it is fictional autoethnography" (1995, p. xi). Probably merely following a sexist linguistic habit of his generation, Lejeune describes the autobiographer as a "he" writing singly about his own existence and his personality, but in Latino literature the she predominates. *Getting Home Alive* (1986), a collection of verse and prose that now figures among autobiographies by Latinas, presents us with the peculiar collaboration of two women, Aurora Levins Morales and her mother Rosario Morales, as co-authors of the volume (Torres 1998, p. 276). With *Borderlands/La Frontera: The New Mestiza*, the celebrated book by Gloria Anzaldúa that has also earned inclusion among autobiographies, we have a volume that combines poetry with speculative thought and hardly any "retrospective prose narrative" (Torres 1998). Linguistic code-switching occurs frequently in these texts, as narrators move from English into Spanish at their will. Acosta's *Autobiography of a Brown Buffalo*, a fair portion of which we receive from a hallucinating narrator with a perception altered by the effects of heavy drugs, makes the reader struggle to distinguish the real from the imagined. Finally, the best known Latino autobiographer, Richard Rodriguez, the author of *Hunger of Memory*, actually chose to structure his text as a series of essays despite the advise by his New York editor that he stress "narrative" potential of his manuscript (Rodriguez 1982, p. 7).

A more exhaustive study would have to consider the ways in which the form manifests itself in the literary production of writers of Central and South American descent since U.S.-based Colombian, Guatemalan, Nicaraguan, Peruvian, and Salvadoran communities have become increasingly visible, having already evinced a nascent presence within Latino literature. But the foregoing overview of authors from the four largest Latino subgroups would seem already to justify some preliminary generalizations. The Latino autobiography defies formal prescriptions, and therein lie its vitality and power as well as its pitfalls. Irrespective of its generically protean quality and the difficulty of guaranteeing the continuous stability of the self it contains, the form can command formidable authority to represent a particular community. Its unreliability will not preclude its ability to influence the articulation of the community's collective identity vis-à-vis the larger society. A commercially successful autobiography will far outweigh the impact of politicians and activists on the choice of frameworks that will orient the rapport between the minority community and the cultural mainstream. An autobiographical intervention can wield the power to represent an ethnic minority community even if its author's ideological orientation clashes with the overall political persuasion or cultural worldview of the group. The African American community received the autobiography of Malcolm X as an unproblematic account of a completed self with a stable moral structure and an unchanged political creed. As such, the book went into high school and college curricula. But, consistent with

the difficulty of living a life and writing an autobiography, the Malcolm of biographical fact had diverged from the Malcolm of the text by the time Alex Haley completed the book. Haley even had to struggle to keep Malcolm from going back to reinterpret, on the basis of new disappointments, statements he had dictated before but no longer believed (Eakin 1980, p. 189). Similarly, the Latino community receives representations of itself with which it may disagree without being able to arrest their power to shape society's perceptions about it. The ideology of the Latino autobiographer will always be individual, but it will have repercussions at a collective level. Each will champion a construction of identity informed by his or her individual positionality. Anzaldúa, wielding the authority of the theorist and the license of the poet, posits a new mestiza with the power to occupy multiple and disparate identity spaces simultaneously while transcending all borders. Rodriguez formulates a view of citizenship and belonging that promotes ethnoracial and cultural self-effacement. Alvarez commits herself to a structure of belonging that celebrates hybridity while safely storing the trappings of her ancestral origins under the regulatory moral and political superiority of the Anglo tradition. Unable to cope with race outside the logic spawned by U.S. history, Piri Thomas overemphasizes the place of racial considerations in his own family and ends up breaking with it. Cherríe Moraga posits the inseparability of class, gender, and ethnoracial position from sexual orientation in the articulation of social identity: "It wasn't until I acknowledged and confronted my own lesbianism in the flesh, that my heartfelt identification with and empathy for my mother's oppression—due to being poor, uneducated, and Chicana—was realized" (Moraga 1983, p. 52).

The autobiography ultimately enjoys the special privilege of placing itself beyond refutation. For even while its deployment of a particular ideological agenda may have implications for the image of the community, critics will find it hard to prove it wrong. For instance, the foes of affirmative action and bilingual education have on occasion brandished the famous autobiography written by Richard Rodriguez to make their case. Yet, the author will invariably have the option of averting criticism by reminding the "gullible reader" that, far from modeling his "life as the typical Hispanic-American life," he is himself the subject of his book: "I write about one life only. My own" (1982, p. 7). Whether the book consists of public policy opinions, speculative articulations of community identity, or poetic meditations on the dark lure of the author's ancestral homeland in Latin America, it will retain its status as a text about the self, making it inherently indisputable. Autobiographers remain the ultimate authority on their material, which is the self, even though we cannot assume them to be in command of their subject. As Georges Gusdorf once argued, the historian of the self confronts a serious difficulty: "returning to visit his own past, he takes the unity and identity of his being for granted, and he imagines himself able to merge what he was with what he has become," a difficulty not easily overcome since narrating one's past, rather than a simple recapitulation, involves a struggle to "reassemble himself in his own likeness at a certain moment of his history" (Gusdorf 1980, pp. 40, 47). Gusdorf contemplated the potential of the writing to turn back on the life and affect it as well as to take precedence over the life, once the artist has begun to live for his or her autobiography. At a time when American society shows a voracious appetite for personal stories that promise to be true, Latino authors who have established their credentials in the literary market as autobiographers will have to decide what use to make of the knowledge that all that they experience today may end up in the next volume of their autobiography. Authors such as Rodriguez and Santiago, who have cultivated the multi-volume life story, à la Maya Angelou, may confront the temptation to choreograph their daily lives so it can become usable as material for the next installment of their autobiography.

Selected Bibliography

Acosta Belén, Edna. "The Building of a community: Puerto Rican Writers and Activists in New York City (1890s–1960s)." In *Recovering the U.S. Hispanic Literary Heritage.* Vol. 1. Edited by Ramón Gutíerrez and Genaro Padilla. Houston: Arte Público Press, 1993. Pp. 179–195.

Agüeros, Jack. "Halfway to Dick and Jane: A Puerto Rican Pilgrimage." *The Immigrant Experience: The Anguish of Becoming American.* Edited by Thomas C. Wheeler. New York: Penguin Books, 1971.

Alvarez, Julia. "An American Childhood in the Dominican Republic." *The American Scholar.* 56 (1987): 71–85.

————. *The Other Side/El Otro Lado.* New York: Dutton, 1995.

————. *Something to Declare.* Chapell Hill: Algonquin Books of Chapell Hill, 1995.

Aranda, José, and Silvio Torres-Saillant, eds. *Recovering the U.S. Hispanic Literary Heritage.* Vol. 4. Houston: Arte Público Press, 2002.

Augenbraum, Harold, and Ilán Stavans, eds. *Growing Up Latino: Memoirs and Stories.* New York: Houghton Mifflin Company, 1993.

Cantu, Norma Elia. *Canicula: Snapshots of a Girlhood en la frontera.* Albuquerque: University of New Mexico Press, 1995.

———. "Whose Story Is It Anyway?: Autobiography on the Border." XXIV International Congress of the Latin American Studies Association. Washington, D.C. September 6–8, 2001.

Céspedes, Diógenes, and Silvio Torres-Saillant. "Fiction Is the Poor Man's Cinema: An Interview with Junot Díaz," *Callaloo* vol. 23, no. 3 (2000): 892–907.

Cossío y Cisneros, Evangelina. *The Story of Evangelina Cisneros.* New York: B.F. Johnson Publishing Company, 1897. Excerpt "To free Cuba." In *Hispanic American Literature.* Edited by Rodolfo Cortina. Lincolnwood, Ill.: NTC Publishing Group, 1998. Pp. 355–358.

De la Campa, Roman. *Latin Americanism.* Minneapolis: University of Minnesota Press, 1999.

De Man, Paul. "Autobiography as De-facement." *MLN Comparative Literature.* vol. 94, no. 5 (1979): 919–930.

Díaz, Junot. *Drown.* New York: Riverhead Books, 1996.

Duany, Jorge. "Neither Golden Exile nor Dirty Worm: Ethnic Identity in Recent Cuban-American Novels." *Caribbean Studies* 23 (1993): 167–183.

Eakin, Paul John. "Malcolm X and the Limits of Autobiography" In *Autobiography: Essays Theoretical and Critical.* Edited by James Olney. Princeton: Princeton University Press, 1980. Pp. 181–189.

Fernández, Alfredo A. "Crónica de una guerra anunciada: A Critical Report about the USA Press in the Spanish American War." In *Recovering the U.S. Hispanic Literary Heritage.* Vol. 4. Edited by José Aranda and Silvio Torres-Saillant, eds. Houston: Arte Público Press, 2002. Pp. 18–30.

Flores, Juan. "Puerto Rican Literature in the United States: Stages and Perspectives." In *Recovering the U.S. Hispanic Literary Heritage.* Vol. 1. Edited by Ramón Gutíerrez and Genaro Padilla. Houston: Arte Público Press, 1993. Pp. 53–88.

Gutíerrez, Ramón, and Genaro Padilla, eds. *Recovering the U.S. Hispanic Literary Heritage.* Vol. 1. Houston: Arte Público Press, 1993.

Gusdorf, Georges. "Conditions and Limits of Autobiography." Trans. by James Olney. In *Autobiography: Essays Theoretical and Critical.* Edited by James Olney. Princeton: Princeton University Press, 1980. Pp. 28–48.

Gutman, Huck. "Rousseau's *Confessions:* A Technology of the Self." *Technologies of the Self: A Seminar with Michel Foucault.* Amherst: The University of Massachusetts Press, 1988. Pp. 99–120.

Kanellos, Nicolás, ed. *Herencia: The Anthology of Hispanic Literature of the United States.* New York: Oxford University Press, 2002.

Lejeune, Philippe. "The Autobiographical Contract." *French Literary Theory: A Reader.* Edited by Tzvetan Todorov. Trans. by R. Carter. Cambridge: Cambridge University Press, 1982. Pp. 192–222.

Lomas, Clara. "Introduction: Revolutionary Women and the Alternative Press in the Borderlands." *The Rebel.* By Leonor Villegas de Magnón. Edited by Clara Lomas. Houston: Arte Público Press, 1994. Pp. xi–li.

Magill, Frank, ed. *Masterpieces of Latino Literature.* New York: Harper Collins, 1994.

Medina, Pablo. [1990]. *Exiled Memories: A Cuban Childhood.* New York: Persea Books, 2002.

Montes-Huidobro, Matías. "Prólogo." *El laud del desterrado.* Anonymous. Edited by Matías Montes Huidobro. Houston: Arte Público Press. 1995. Pp. vii–xix.

Moraga, Cherríe. *Loving in the War Years: Lo que nunca paso por sus labios.* Boston: South End Press, 1983.

Mostern, Kenneth. *Autobiography and Black Identity Politics: Racialization in Twentieth-Century America.* Cambridge: Cambridge University Press, 1999.

Olney, James. "Autobiography and the Cultural Moment: A Thematic, Historical, and Bibliographical Introduction." In *Autobiography: Essays Theoretical and Critical.* Edited by James Olney. Princeton: Princeton University Press, 1980. Pp. 3–27.

Padilla, Genaro. "Recovering Mexican-American Autobiography." *Recovering the U.S. Hispanic Literary Heritage.* Vol. 1 Edited by Ramón Gutiérrez and Genaro Padilla. Houston: Arte Público Press, 1993. Pp. 153–178.

Pérez, Sonja Z. "Auto/Ethnography and the Politics of Recovery: Narrative Anxiety in the Borderlands of Culture." In *Recovering the U.S. Hispanic Literary Heritage.* Vol. 4. Edited by José Aranda and Silvio Torres-Saillant. Houston: Arte Público Press, 2002. Pp. 277–290.

Rodriguez, Joe. "United States Hispanic Autobiography and Biography: Legend For the Future." In *Handbook of Hispanic Cultures in the United States: Literature and Art.* Edited by Nicolas Kanellos and Claudio Esteva-Fabregat. Houston: Arte Público Press, 1993. Pp. 268–290.

Rodriguez, Richard. *Hunger of Memory: The Education of Richard Rodriguez, An Autobiography.* New York: Bantam, 1982.

Rosenblatt, Roger. "Black Autobiography: Life as the Death Weapon," In *Autobiography: Essays Theoretical and Critical.* Edited by James Olney. Princeton: Princeton University Press, 1980. Pp. 169–180.

Ryan, Bryan, Edited by *Hispanic Writers: A Selection of Sketches from Contemporary Authors.* Detroit: Gale Research, 1991.

Sayre, Robert F. "Autobiography and the Making of America." In *Autobiography: Essays Theoretical and Critical.* Edited by James Olney. Princeton: Princeton University Press, 1980. Pp. 146–168.

Stanton, David. "Junot Diaz: On Home Ground." *Poets & Writers Magazine.* vol. 26, no. 4 (1998): 27–37.

Stavans, Ilán. "The Quest for a Latino Literary Tradition." *The Chronicle of Higher Education,* section 2. December 1, 2000.

Torres, Lourdes. "The Construction of the Self in U.S. Latino Autobiographies." *Women, Autobiography, Theory: A Reader.* Edited by Sidonie Smith and Julia Watson. Madison: The University of Wisconsin Press, 1998. Pp. 276–287.

Torres-Saillant, Silvio. "Before the Diaspora: Early Dominican Literature in the United States." In *Recovering the U.S. Hispanic Literary Heritage.* Vol. 3. Edited by María Herrera–Sobek and Virginia Sánchez Korrol. Houston: Arte Público Press, 2000. Pp. 250–267.

———. "Introduction: Inscribing Latinos in the National Discourse." In *Recovering the U.S. Hispanic Literary Heritage.* Vol. 4. Edited by José F. Aranda and Silvio Torres-Saillant. Houston: Arte Público Press, 2002. Pp. 1–10.

———. "Vision of Dominicanness in the United States." In *Borderless Borders: U.S. Latinos, Latin Americans, and the Paradox of Interdependence.* Edited by Frank Bonilla, et al. Philadelphia: Temple University Press, 1998. Pp. 139–152.

Villegas de Magnón, Leonor. *The Rebel.* Edited by Clara Lomas. Houston: Arte Público Press, 1994.

Performance Art and Theater

ALICIA ARRIZÓN

No ATTEMPT AT mapping U.S. Latino and Latina theater and performance art should define it in absolute terms because it ties together the histories of various ethnic groups: Mexican Americans/Chicanos, Puerto Ricans/Nuyoricans, Cuban Americans/ Cuban exiles, and Dominicans, to mention only a few. While some of the origins of Latino theatrical productions can be located in mid-nineteenth century California (San Francisco, Los Angeles, and San Diego)—with the contributions of itinerant performers touring from Mexico to the coastal cities that had been founded by the Franciscan missionaries—the contemporary foundations of U.S. Latino theater can be located in the Chicano theater movement initiated by El Teatro Campesino (The Farmworkers Theater) during the 1960s.

TEATRO CAMPESINO

If one has to trace a genealogy of U.S. Latino and Latina performance art and theater, the influence of El Teatro Campesino is of great significance. Luis Valdez, the founder of Teatro Campesino, used theater to broadcast the call for unity and social change. El Teatro Campesino was oriented toward the cultural affirmation of working-class Mexicans. In conjunction with the political Chicano movement, the theater movement began with El Te-

atro Campesino's improvised performances in the fields of the Salinas Valley to support the striking farmworkers in California. The theater company, which included members of the National Farm Workers Association (later the United Farm Workers), created satirical social skits, called *actos,* that focused on issues related to the strikes and to Chicanos in general.

The development of an active Chicano theater movement, along with the emergence of other cultural practices such as poetry and art, heightened the cultural awareness embedded in the Chicano movement at large. The following excerpt from Luis Valdez's introduction to his *Early Works,* which was published in 1990, underscores *Chicanismo,* or Chicano nationalism, as the *grito* (cry, shout) that aroused Mexican Americans in the 1960s to assert control over their own cultural survival and determination.

> The nature of Chicanismo calls for a revolutionary turn in the arts as well as in society. Chicano theater must be revolutionary in technique as well as content. It must be popular, subject to no other critics except the pueblo [people] itself; but it must also educate the pueblo toward an appreciation of *social change,* on and off the stage.
>
> (pp. 7–8)

Valdez's contributions to the development of Chicano theater are paramount; however, it is important to acknowledge that his leadership involved serious limitations for women in El Teatro Campesino and more generally for female representation in Chicano theater. Significant critical evaluation of El Teatro Campesino's evolution has reinterpreted the company's history and analyzes the gender relation at work in its productions. Yolanda Broyles-González, in the 1994 *El Teatro Campesino: Theater in the Chicano Movement*, argues that the combined effects of male domination and Chicano nationalism shaped the company's productions and even affected the documentation of its history. "The history of the company," she observes, "has been constructed as the history of the life and times of Luis Valdez. As such El Teatro Campesino history has been shaped into a male-dominated hierarchical structure that replicates oppressive dominant tendencies within society" (p. xiii). Broyles-González examines the effects of that male-centeredness, beginning with El Teatro Campesino's early *actos*. A feminist who situates her work in contemporary cultural studies, Broyles-González draws attention to the gender politics that infused El Teatro Campesino's collective system of production. While Broyles-González's gender politics presents a serious critique, it also recognizes the great contributions Luis Valdez has made, particularly in the trajectory and development of the company and more generally in the Chicano/Latino theater movement.

Valdez's contributions as director, playwright, and producer are many. His first major critical and popular victory is the Broadway production of *Zoot Suit*, which was originally created for the Mark Taper Forum in Los Angeles and funded through a 1977 Rockefeller Foundation Artist-in-Residence grant. *Zoot Suit* is a historical play that dramatizes the 1942 Sleepy Lagoon case, in which twenty-two young pachucos were unfairly convicted of criminal conspiracy in connection with the death of a Chicano named José Díaz. Valdez created El Pachuco as an archetype and the alter ego of the main protagonist, Henry Reyna, the leader of the 38th Street Gang. The historical event of the Sleepy Lagoon case becomes the driving force for the narrative, which Valdez underlines clearly: race and class discrimination against Chicanos in 1940s Los Angeles, as manifested in the dominant Anglo system of justice, the press, and law enforcement.

In addition to his contribution as a theater director and playwright, Luis Valdez became interested in film. In 1981 he directed the film version of *Zoot Suit*, which became the first Chicano feature-length Hollywood film. The film received a Golden Globe Award nomination for the Best Musical Picture. Valdez also directed *La Bamba* (1987), the story of the Mexican American rock and roll singer Ritchie Valens, who died in a plane crash with Buddy Holly in 1959. Other projects that marked Valdez's success include the adaptation of his 1983 play *Corridos: Tales of Passion and Revolution* for PBS, starring Linda Ronstadt and the ballerina Evelyn Cisneros. This production received the George Foster Peabody Award for Excellence in Television Broadcasting in 1987.

While the Chicano theater movement was mainly influenced by the farmworkers' struggles in the 1960s and by the creativeness of Luis Valdez, it was instrumental in organizing a forum for the development of Latino and Latina theater. By 1970, El Teatro Campesino had established what would come to be known as Chicano theater: a type of agitprop theater, which integrated an aestheticism reproducing some elements of the Italian Renaissance commedia dell'arte. It combined humor, satire, folklore, music, dance, and popular Mexican culture, representing a performance culture greatly influenced by the tent theaters and vaudeville companies that had toured the Southwest early in the twentieth century. The performance culture introduced by the early touring companies influenced the creation of *La gran carpa de los Rasquachi* (The big tent of the underdogs) in the early 1970s. When the play reached its best moment in 1976, the company launched an eight-country European tour. For many years the company has produced an evolving series of plays during the Christmas season. Among these are the miracle play classics of *La Virgen del Tepeyac* (The virgin of Tepeyac) and the traditional shepherds' play, *La Pastorela,* staged in the Old Mission of San Juan Bautista. Since 1975 El Teatro Campesino produces the Pastorela with the desire to preserve the folk theater tradition brought to Mexico by the Franciscan Missionaries in the sixteenth century. The Pastorela, as most Christmas medieval dramas, represents morality as the central symbolic concern. In 1991, a film version of *La Pastorela* was adapted and directed by Luis Valdez for the PBS *Great Performances* series, starring Linda Ronstadt and Paul Rodriguez. As a professional theater arts organization, El Teatro Campesino continues to evolve in the twenty-first century.

TENAZ

TENAZ (Teatro Nacional de Aztlán, or National Theater of Aztlán) is the umbrella organization of the Chicano theater movement. Aztlán is the mythical place of origin of the Aztecs and is often linked with the Mexican lost territories taken by the United States after the Mexican–American War of 1846–1848. It is the belief that this geographical space represents the point of parting of Aztec migration. Following Teatro Campesino's aesthetics of collectivity, cultural affirmation, and resistance, the emergence of community-based Latino theaters such as El Teatro de La Esperanza, Centro Su Teatro, Pregones, Puerto Rican Traveling Company, Teatro Avante, and Prometeo, just to mention a few, provided an alternative to mainstream theatrical institutions. In the 1980s, TENAZ was instrumental in the Latinization of the stage. Theater practitioners, or *teatristas,* who began their careers with El Teatro Campesino became increasingly aware of a world beyond *Chicanismo.*

TENAZ festivals contributed enormously to these changes, incorporating representative groups and individuals from Latin America as well as other U.S. Latino *teatristas.* TENAZ festivals started a tradition of including personalities or representative groups from Latin America, who offered symposiums, group theatrical presentations, and workshops. The Brazilian director and playwright Augusto Boal (author of *Theater of the Oppressed*) and the well-known Colombian director and playwright Enrique Buenaventura (director of TEC: Teatro Experimental de Cali, or Experimental Theater of Cali) were two of the most influential *teatristas* who often participated. By the 1990s the TENAZ festivals were attended by theater companies which had been influenced by Teatro Campesino and which had been together for fifteen years or more. Groups and organizations such as El Teatro de la Esperanza (Santa Barabara and San Francisco, California), the Guadalupe Cultural Arts Center (San Antonio, Texas) and the Chicago Latino Theatre Company, for example, had well-established play-development programs. According to the critic Jorge Huerta, author of the 2000 *Chicano Drama: Performance, Society and Myth,* the plays that these groups were producing during the 1990s marked changes in the groups' attempt "to reach higher levels of professionalism, even if they were not yet able to pay living wages of their artist" (p. 8).

PROFESSIONALIZATION

A significant phase in the professionalization in Latino theater was in part nourished by the Latino Theater Company in Los Angeles. Since 1985 this company has been dedicated to developing and staging award-winning productions in mainstream theaters such as the Los Angeles Theater Center (LATC) and the Mark Taper Forum. Jose Luis Valenzuela, who started as an actor and director with El Teatro de La Esperanza and is currently a professor of drama at the University of California, Los Angeles, assumed the direction of the LATC's Latino Theater Lab (LTL). In 1988, the LTL received a grant from the Ford Foundation to fund the growth of the LTL ensemble component and the production of works by commissioned playwrights as part of the LATC's regular season. In 1994 the production of *Bandido! The American Melodrama of Tiburcio Vásquez, Notorious California Bandit,* directed by Valenzuela, became one of the highest grossing productions of the year. The dramatization of Tiburco Vásquez as a Mexican American who took the law into his own hands was perhaps a big hit because it not only presents an alternative version of this historical/mythical life and death, but it significantly targets an audience that had witnessed Chicano theater evolved from the rural scene to the urban stage. The LTL changed its name to the Latino Theater Company that year in an effort to create a venue in which to develop the work of Latino *teatristas.* In 1996 the LTC became the only professional Latino group to work under an Actor's Equity Theater contract.

Also in 1996, the company produced Evelina Fernández's one-act play *How Else Am I Supposed to Know I'm Still Alive.* This play was first produced at the Plaza de la Raza in East Los Angeles as the winner of Nuevo Chicano L.A. Theaterworks contest in the summer of 1989. It deals with the experience of being female, of searching for love, of being middle aged, of wanting sex, and of women supporting each other. The author, who started her acting career in Luis Valdez's *Zoot Suit,* has commented that she wrote the play out of frustration over the absence of roles for Latinas in mainstream theater and television. She specifically wrote the play for the actresses Lupe Ontiveros and Angela Moya, "Two extremely gifted actors who are rarely given the opportunity to play leading roles" (p. 159), she writes in the introductory notes to her play in the 1996 *Contemporary Plays by Women of Color: An Anthology.* Since its first production, the play has been produced by El Centro Su Teatro in Denver, Colorado, Teatro Visión in San Jose, California, and toured nationally with El Teatro

Campesino. The play was adapted into an award-winning film through the Hispanic Film Project at Universal, starring the original cast members (Lupe Ontiveros and Angela Moya) and directed by Jose Luis Valenzuela.

The premiere of *Luminarias,* also written by Evelina Fernández and directed by Valenzuela, proved to be a major development for the LTC. In 1998, following the success of *Luminarias,* the company experimented with motion pictures by forming Sleeping Giant Productions and making *Luminarias* into a feature film. The movie was produced by Valenzuela and by company co-founder Sal Lopez and received national distribution through New Latin Pictures. The LTC has returned to its place of origin at the LATC and continues its mission of enhancing the Latino experience in the United States through dramatic literature.

Two other projects have made important contributions to the professionalization of the Latino theater: the Costa Mesa California South Coast Repertory's Hispanic Playwrights Project and the New York INTAR (International Arts Relations) Hispanic Playwrights-in-Residency Laboratory. Director and playwright José Cruz González headed the directorship of the South Coast Repertory from 1986 through 1997. Since its inception, this project was responsible for fostering and developing new plays by Latino and Latina playwrights for the American stage. The South Coast Repertory has extended its efforts to disseminate Latino theater with the publication of an anthology of seven plays by Latino and Latina writers, *Latino Plays from South Coast Repertory: Hispanic Playwrights Project Anthology* (2000). This anthology is part of its fifteenth annual Hispanic Playwrights Project and includes the work of American writers of Mexican, Cuban, Puerto Rican, and Bolivian heritage. Four of the writers are renowned (Luis Alfaro, Cherríe Moraga, José Rivera, and Octavio Solis) and three of the contributors are emerging artists (Cusi Cram, JoAnn Farías, and Rogelio Martínez). In the preface of this groundbreaking anthology, Eduardo Machado writes:

I remember fondly one night at Jerry Patch's office when he told me that South Coast Rep was beginning their Hispanic Playwrights Project and my play, ONCE REMOVED, had been chosen for that year. It was an odd occurrence in the middle of all that pristine Anglo-Saxon Americana—where Latinos could be seen lurking in the shadows of hallways, picking up dishes in restaurants or handing out tickets in parking lots. In the middle of all this clean and polish Gringoism, the "other" was about to take center stage.

(p. iv)

Machado correctly marks with irony the entrance of the Latino, or as he calls it, the "other," to a mainstream theater institution. He places the Latino and Latina artist as the "other," who historically has been on the margins, not recognized by the dominant professionals on the American stage. The question of the otherness is relevant to the mapping of Latino theater and performance art within Anglo-American theatrical spaces. The visibility of the Latino marginal other marks the relationship between "us" and "them" in relation to a system of representation inscribed in the institutionalization of culture. For Latino and Latina playwrights, directors, and performers, the process of entering certain dominant systems involves situating the self between certain relations of power and the fluidity of identity.

IDENTITY FORMATION

The whole issue of the Latino subject in theater gets more complicated when one looks at the notion of identification or identity formations and its complexities. While some may accept the notion of the Latino, others may prefer the term "Hispanic," and others may use specific, ideologically charged descriptions such as Chicano or Nuyorican. The term was appropriated by Mexican American activists who took part in the Chicano movement of the 1960s and 1970s in the U.S. Southwest and has come into widespread usage. While the term Chicano mainly refers to people of Mexican heritage (other Latino groups such as Central Americans may use it too), the term Nuyorican refers to Puerto Ricans living in New York. In some cases some writers prefer to be considered just American, reducing the identification with any nationalistic, ethnic, or ideological terms. In Machado's own words, "I think my work is American. It's in English, it's about being here, it's not about being in Havana" ("What's a Hispanic Play?" p. 39). Machado speaks clearly about the struggles of being an "American" ethnic artist and trying to be recognized as such, in and out of the mainstream. Recognized as one of the most gifted Latino playwrights, he is the author of many plays and is well known as a director, actor, and filmmaker. His works include: *The Floating Island Plays* (a four-play collection that follows four generations of a Cuban American family), *Cuba and the Night,* and *Don Juan in New York City,* as well as the film *Exiles in New York,* which opened the 1999 Santa Barbara Film Festival. His plays have been produced in London and New York, and at regional theaters all around the country. In the fall of 1999, his play *Broken Eggs* was performed by Roberto Español in Havana. The production was a significant cultural exchange between the United States and Cuba. His most recent play, *Havana is Waiting,* which received its world premiere in 2001 (under the title *When the Sea Drowns in Sand*), blends autobiography with identity politics. Inspired by his return to Cuba, Machado uses humor and drama to explore the notion of home. The play dramatizes the need to find the roots and origins of self in order to understand its complexities.

The complexity of being caught in between national borders of being both in the United States and in some ways elsewhere constitutes the struggle for cultural survival. In Latino and Latina theater, issues of cultural survival are a unifying concept in the struggle for recognition and the effort to project a public voice. In a brilliant piece, "The Show Does Go On," published in the 1989 *Breaking Boundaries: Latina Writing and Critical Readings,* the Cuban dramatist Dolores Prida captures this sense as she describes her experiences as a struggling *teatrista*.

> In the theater, we have that saying—you know the one: "The show must go on." As I said before, soon Hispanics will be the largest minority in the U.S. Our presence here promises to be a long-running engagement—despite the bad reviews we get most of the time, despite problems we may have with the lights, and the curtain and the costumes, and the enter and exit cues. Despite all that, this show will go on, and you might as well get your tickets now.
>
> (pp. 187–188)

Prida affirms the political economy implicit in Latino and Latina theater and also directly attests to the ongoing development of that theatrical tradition. She is confident that the presence of Latinos as a future demographic majority will necessarily make them more visible as minority artists. She envisions a positive future; despite all the obstacles, "the show must go on," and the Latino and Latina stage, even if it is not fully recognized now, will soon be widely acclaimed.

In addition to her numerous plays, collected in her 1991 *Beautiful Señoritas and Other Plays*, she has also written two books of poetry, *Treinta y un poemas* (Thirty-one poems) and *Women of the Hour*. She is ranked among the most important playwrights of contemporary U.S. Latino and Latina theater. She is also one of the few artists of Latin American descent to have been awarded an honorary degree from Mount Holyoke College. Considering herself a "theater worker," she stresses that her work is part of a collaborative process.

> Theater is people. Theater is teamwork. We need each other: playwright, director, designers, actors, choreographers, technicians, carpenters, composers, ticket takers, audience. We don't exist without each other.
>
> ("The Show," p. 183)

Prida conceives of her theater practice as a social forum where collaboration among directors, actors, and playwrights makes the performance a collective medium of expression.

Her experience bears out her commitment to collaboration. When Prida began working with Teatro Orilla (a collective theater group on New York's Lower East Side), she swept floors and collected tickets. Then she progressed to running the sound equipment, designing the stage lighting, and "fill[ing] out endless forms for grant money." Only after she had done all of that did Prida begin "to think [she] could write a play that would appeal to that particular audience: people who had never been to a theatre before" ("The Show," p. 183). The specific audience she has in mind is Latinos. Prida believes that theater that addresses the needs and everyday realities of Latinos will draw this community in. Theater is far more engrossing when audience members can readily relate to and identify with what they see on stage. She advocates an increased cultural awareness in the Latino community.

It is precisely this cultural awareness that characterizes the work of Latino and Latina dramatists and *teatristas* in general. In addition, this cultural awareness has contributed to locating the Latino and Latina subject in and out of the mainstream American theater. As a cause and an effect of a necessary cultural awareness, Latino theater has become, in the twenty-first century, as diverse as the multifaceted audience it targets. Dramatists such as Matías Montes Huidobro, Carlos Morton, Nilo Cruz, Pedro Monge Rafuls, Miguel Piñero, Milcha Sánchez-Scott, and Josefina López, to mention a distinctive and multigenerational group, have contributed enormously to the development of contemporary U.S. Latino and Latina theater.

While Matías Montes Huidobro is considered one of the most distinguished dramatists in the generation of Cuban playwrights who were torn apart by the impact of the Cuban Revolution, Morton belongs to a generation of Chicano writers who take their inspiration from Luis Valdez. In fact, both Valdez and Morton began their artistic careers as members of the San Francisco Mime Troupe. Whereas Huidobro is the author of approximately thirty plays, among them *Las cuatro brujas* (The four witches) and *La sal de los muertos* (The salt of the dead), Morton's work has had numerous productions, both in the United States and abroad. He is the author of *The Many Deaths of Danny Rosales and Other Plays*, *Johnny Tenorio and Other Plays*, and *Rancho Hollywood y otras obras del teatro Chicano* (Hollywood Ranch and other works of the Chicano theater). In 2003, Morton's libretto *Esperanza* (Hope), a musical drama that was adapted from the 1954 film *Salt of the Earth*, had its West Coast premiere in San Bernardino, California. The musical is based on a true story of Mexican American miners and their families in New Mexico.

While Morton's work deals directly with the Mexican American/Chicano experience, other writers, such as Cuban-born Nilo Cruz, deal with material that is heavily symbolic and lyrical. This is the case with *Anna in the Tropics*, which won the 2003 Pulitzer Prize in drama. It is set in Florida in 1930 and deals with a family of cigar makers whose lives are played out against the backdrop of the Depression. Cruz's other plays includes *Night Train to Bolina*, *A Park in Our Home*, *Dancing on Her Knees*, *Graffiti*, and *Two Sisters and a Piano*.

Cruz's compatriot, Pedro Monge Rafuls (editor of *Ollantay Theater Magazine*), represents the Latino experience in distinctive ways. In his *Noche de ronda* (Cruising at night), Monge Rafuls creates a spectrum of queer identities intertwined with different ethnicities. The subject of AIDS is represented in humorous and didactic ways. While Monge Rafuls (like Huidobro) usually writes for a Spanish-speaking audience, his monologue *Trash*, which premiered in 1995, represents the struggles of a *marielito* (anyone who departed the harbor of Mariel in Cuba to travel to the U.S. in the 1980s) who is presumed to be gay and is victimized by socio-political circumstances. At the end of the monologue, it is revealed that the protagonist, Jesús, is talking from inside a prison.

For other Latino dramatists, the subject of incarceration becomes a harsh reality that shapes their creativity. This was the case for Miguel Piñero, who in 1972 was serving a jail sentence for second-degree robbery. Two years later he became famous with the production of his first play, *Short Eyes*, a realistic portrayal of life, love, and death among prison inmates. Piñero was a remarkable poet and performer and one of the founders of the Nuyorican Poets Café. He died in 1988. Although he wrote many plays, which were often produced, *Short Eyes* remains his best. It won the New York Drama Critics Circle Award for best American play of 1973 and 1974. In 2001 the film *Piñero* (played by Benjamin Bratt) was written and directed by Leon Ichasco. It represented the chaotic true story of the author's life and works.

Since the 1980s, Latina playwright Milcha Sánchez-Scott has authored remarkable theater works. In 1980 she wrote her first play, *Latina*, commissioned by Susan Lowenberg of LA Theater Works. With humor and innovation Sánchez-Scott explores the struggles of women coming to terms with their identity (Chicana, Cubana, Guatemalan, Colombian, and so forth) as they recognize the common context of their struggle for survival in the U.S. Other plays written by Sánchez-Scott include *Dog Lady*, *El Dorado*, *Stone Wedding*, *The Old Matador*, and *Roosters*. *Roosters*, which is one of her most produced plays, was adapted into a 1995 movie starring Edward James Olmos, Sonia Braga, and María Conchita Alonso. In 2002, the work of dramatist Josefina López was also adapted into a film directed by Patricia Cordoso. Her best-known play, *Real Women Have Curves*, made it to the big screen. While the play had been produced numerous times since the late 1980s with great success, the movie received astounding accolades, including being honored at the Sundance Film Festival with the Audience Award. López, who is a self-described all-around *chingona* (a tough independent woman), has also written *Confessions of Women from East L.A*, *Simply María; or, The American Dream*, and *Unconquered Spirits*. Overall, Sánchez-Scott and López have created protagonists who offer positive and realistic models for negotiating identity inside and outside of the theater.

THE HISPANIC PLAYWRIGHTS PROJECT

Projects such as the Hispanic Playwrights Project have contributed enormously to increasing the visibility of Latino and Latina *teatristas.* In such projects, professional directors, dramaturges, and actors are given the opportunity, over several weeks, to rewrite, experiment, and ultimately have their work read or performed before a general audience. Many Latino and Latina playwrights developed their early works through the Hispanic Playwrights Project and have established a special reputation in the field. Playwrights such as Edith Villarreal, Octavio Solís, Edwin Sánchez, Oliver Mayer, and Lisa Loomer are among the writers who got their first mainstream professional experience through the project and became recognized contributors of the Latino stage in the United States. Playwrights such as Cherríe Moraga, Eduardo Machado, and José Rivera, who had already established positions in the field, were given national visibility through their involvement in the project. Both the Hispanic Playwrights Project in California and, in New York, INTAR's Hispanic Playwrights-in-Residency Laboratory served as examples of programs that helped the dissemination of Latino and Latina theater. The Hispanic Playwrights Project at South Coast Repertory and INTAR's Hispanic Playwrights-in-Residency Laboratory have as their main purpose to stimulate and develop the writing abilities and foster the visibility of Latino and Latina playwrights at the national level.

Latino and Latina theater would be unthinkable without the contributions of María Irene Fornes, who served as director of INTAR's Laboratory from 1981 to 1992. Despite her abundant productivity (she has written more than forty plays), many critics noted that she has never moved onto Broadway, staying behind in the fringe playhouses that gave her a start in the 1960s. However, one of her greatest achievements may be managing to make a living on Off-Broadway. In fact, she has earned a Playwrights USA award, Guggenheim and NEA fellowships, and eight Obies. In honor of her many contributions, New York's Signature Theater hosted a retrospective of three of her plays in 1999. This event had an awkward effect on Fornes, who acknowledged in an interview with the Art and Culture Network, "[it] makes me feel I am now on the border of mainstream—not quite in it. To be mainstream frightens me. Then people put claims on you and expect things of you. I've always liked being on the border." Being on the border for her does not necessarily mean writing about identity politics (as a Cuban and/or as a lesbian) but evoking the intricate social relationships involved in being a woman. Having been the first Latina to write a feminist play, the 1977 *Fefu and her Friends,* Fornes's dramatic works and valuable contributions have influenced other Latino and Latina playwrights.

Cherríe Moraga, for example, who studied with Fornes in 1983 and 1984, benefited tremendously from her generosity and wisdom. Moraga, who began writing *Shadow of a Man* in Fornes's workshop, ended up sending the final product to Fornes without any expectations. Fornes not only liked the play, but also offered to direct it herself at San Francisco's Eureka Theatre in 1990. In *Shadow of a Man,* Moraga depicts a family struggling under the shadow of machismo in 1960s Los Angeles. The bilingual play offered Fornes an opportunity to explore the complexities of Latino culture, which include the bicultural and bilingual techniques and sensibilities of her own cultural experience. In an interview, Fornes said that Moraga's play interested her because of its passionate characters:

> Because it deals with the relationship between men and women, in this case, passionate Chicano men and women, from the perspective of the family. It's

hard to explain. I think that all family plays, of course, are different, yet this play, to me, makes all other family plays seem the same. The play doesn't follow traditional patterns, and yet it's a classical story.

(*San Francisco Independent*, p. 2)

The presence of both Fornes and Moraga can be felt in the development of contemporary Latino and Latina theater. Their impact is by now legendary. While Fornes directs most of her own plays as well as plays by others (including classics by Calderón, Ibsen, and Chekhov, and new work by contemporary authors), Moraga's impact on Latino and Latina theater is mainly as a dramatist and taboo breaker in Chicano culture. Moraga's premiere collection of theater pieces, *Heroes and Saints and Other Plays*, brought together *Shadow of a Man, Heroes and Saints*, and her first produced play, *Giving Up the Ghost*. The collection covers ten years of work and showcases Moraga's priorities as a writer and producer of Latino and Latina theater—lesbian desire, AIDS, religion, pesticide poisoning, family, and community. Her protagonists, real or surreal, move in and out of the instability of border spaces. From the butch-in-the-raw to the head with no body, Moraga's border-crossers represent the many possibilities of hybrid cultures.

Since the production of *Giving Up the Ghost* in the mid-1980s, Moraga's gendered subjectivities in theater and in the discursive configurations of her writing as a whole demonstrate that the construction of nation, authority, history, and tradition are deeply sexualized and therefore depend upon a particular appropriation of space. Her recognition of this structure of everyday reality and her understanding of its implications are perhaps best illustrated in *The Hungry Woman: A Mexican Medea*. This Medea embodies the power and resistance of the native woman who feels a profound connection with the lost territory of Aztlán, which in her play has been recovered by the Chicano people. Nevertheless, as a Chicana lesbian, Medea is evicted, a homeless exile, because Aztlán has become a place where queer identities are perceived as decadent and harmful to the sense of group collectivity.

Since its inception in 1966, INTAR has been committed to producing Latino theatrical works. It both creates and produces original works as well as hosting plays by notable playwrights from around the country. In 2001, INTAR celebrated its thirty-fifth anniversary with a trilogy of plays collectively titled *Nuyorican Voices*. These plays were specially selected and directed by INTAR's founding artistic director, Max Ferra. They include: *Miriam's Flowers*, by Migdalia Cruz; *Giants Have Us in Their Books*, by José Rivera; and *Unmerciful Good Fortune*, by Edwin Sánchez.

The first play takes place in the South Bronx in 1975 and tells the story of a family grieving the loss of its youngest child, who was violently killed in a car accident. The second play is made up of six imaginative stories that range from the fantastic to the sobering. The third is an intriguing drama that focuses on three female characters (the defendant in a murder trial, an assistant district attorney, and her dying mother).

Migdalia Cruz, who is from the South Bronx and studied under Irene Fornes at INTAR, is best known for *Miriam's Flowers* but she has written over thirty plays, operas, and musicals, which have been produced in Canada, Mexico, Australia, and the United States in venues as diverse as the Houston Grand Opera, the Latino Chicago Theatre, and the Brooklyn Academy of Music. She has received numerous awards and commissions, including two National Endowment for the Arts fellowships, and has twice been a finalist for the Susan Smith Blackburn prize for playwrighting. Two of her plays, *The Have-Little* and *Lucy Loves Mew* were included in *The Best Women's Stage Monologues of 1991*. Her *Another Part of the House* is inspired by Federico García Lorca's classic *The House of Bernarda Alba*.

On the other hand, Rivera, who is best known for *Cloud Tectonics* and *Marisol*, has an amazing grasp of magic realism. *Adoration of the Old*

Woman, which premiered in 2002 at La Jolla Playhouse, is about a Puerto Rican family struggling with its own generational changes and the status of its country as a U.S. territory. In this play, Rivera uses politics to represent Puerto Rico's statehood debate with a romantic subplot. In an interview, Rivera acknowledged that the play's message might not resonate as much in southern California as it would in New York. Nevertheless, he suggested that the play is universal enough to appeal to everyone.

This belief in the universality of the Latino experience is also central in the dramatic works of Rivera's contemporary Edwin Sánchez, who in 1988 participated in the Eugene O'Neill Playwrights Conference with his remarkable play *Barefoot Boy with Shoes On.* This play was also selected to represent the National Playwrights Conference at the Schelykovo Playwrights Seminar in Schelykovo, Russia, in June 1999 and was produced by Primary Stages in New York as part of its 1999–2000 season. In it, Sánchez brings to the stage the struggles of three generations of Latino men living in a one-room New York apartment. The play demonstrates how dreams and nightmares collide on the margins of their lives. Sánchez's other notable productions include: *Icarus, Trafficking in Broken Hearts, Unmerciful Good Fortune,* and *Doña Flor and her Trained Dog.*

Any attempt to synthesize Latino and Latina theater and performance art into a single definition is reductionist and naïve because it is important to recognize the complexity, diversity, and historical specificity of subject formation in order to bring into sharper focus the contributions of Latino and Latina *teatristas.* In symbolic terms, in his 1999 book *José, Can You See?: Latinos on and off Broadway,* Alberto Sandoval-Sánchez describes the image of Latino and Latina theater as an "octopus with many legs." This multi-legged "creature," he suggests, rejects any homogenization of the subject. He adds:

> Latino theater always locates itself within the domain of difference, of hybridity, of monstrosity.

We can imagine this gigantic animal, "Hispanic theater," with a huge head, sitting over the U.S., moving its tentacles on a multiplicity of stages and suctioning audiences. It is this image of monstrosity that accurately captures the nature of a U.S. Latino theater that denies all categorization based on superficial resemblances such as labeling and the imposition of rigidly defined and dominant dramatic structures. This theater reveals in problematizing and destabilizing the essentialist notion of monolithic Latino experiences, identities, and ways of seeing.

(pp. 108–109)

As a native Puerto Rican now living and teaching in the United States, Sandoval-Sánchez is well aware that Latino and Latina theater takes place within the context of revision and deconstruction of dominant structures. The title of his book *José, Can You See?,* is a conflation of "no way, José" and the first line of the U.S. national anthem. As the author suggests in his introduction, the imposition of this "implied command" on a non-Anglo other (José, who embodies Latino culture in various ways) asks him to see and embrace America's dominant culture. Within this context, Sandoval-Sánchez makes clear that his exploration of Latino and Latina theater takes place within the context of a revision of Broadway's and Hollywood's negative stereotyping of the Latino body. He defines Latino and Latina theater and performance art as a phenomenon deeply rooted within cultural values and traditions that critique the repressive elements of that tradition. Latino and Latina theater practitioners take inventory of their history as a neocolonial community in the United States. Within this context, questions of identity and subject formation have been fundamental in defining Latino and Latina theater and performance art.

PERFORMANCE ART

In particular, performance art, with its focus on identity formation, enhances the cultural and political specificity of categories such as ethnicity, race, class, and sexuality. While performance art can be defined in opposition to theater convention, dismantling the textual authority of directors and playwrights, theater practice is more subjected to institutional structures. To study theater requires the involvement of the dramatic text and its stage production. Many consider performance art itself a contested cultural practice, where meaning is embedded in multiple levels of representation. This definition moves identity formation into the realm of indefinite processes unfolding in the bodily acts of the performer, the agency of production, and the spectator. It is this identity-forming and affirming aspect that has defined Latino and Latina performance art in the last fifteen years. Performance art is a hybrid form, insofar as it borrows not only from the fields of visual culture, such as theater, painting, and video art, but also from dance and music. Moreover, performance art is considered an alternative cultural practice in that it resists a representational system in which Latino and Latina identity is made a spectacle. "The term performance, and specifically the verb performing," Diana Taylor writes in "Opening Remarks," published in the 1994 *Negotiating Performance: Gender, Sexuality, and Theatricality in Latin/o America,* "allow for agency, which opens the way for resistance and oppositional spectacle." It is precisely within such oppositional spectacles that Latino/a performance artists "expose themselves" in order to subvert the enactment of power and representation.

The term performance not only stands for spectacles beyond traditional theater, it also looks at theater practice itself more critically. In its most general use, performance suggests not only conventional theater but also any number of cultural events and social processes that involve ritual, movement, and the various roles that an individual may embody in society. Furthermore, the boundless definitions of performance not only actualize the potential of human behavior, but its object embodies a reflec-

tion on culture and difference as terms that develop new critical spaces in theater and art history.

Expressed in this way, the process may sound rigorous, but when humor is used as an aesthetic form of resistance, the potential for transformation can be exposed in particular ways. For the members of Culture Clash (Rick Salinas, Herbert Siguenza, and Richard Montoya), the complexities of race relations in America are without a doubt a performative system that allows them to envision certain kinds of change. In their book, *Culture Clash: Life, Death, and Revolutionary Comedy,* they insist on the blending of Latino political consciousness with sardonic representation. The book brings together three of their most memorable performances: *The Mission* (1988), *A Bowl of Beings* (1991), and *Radio Mambo: Culture Clash Invades Miami* (1994). The book also includes a short interview with the group in which they discuss their origins, and an introduction to the plays, which was written by one of the members. While *The Mission* is about a comedy group and the kidnapping of the greatest Latino entertainer, Julio Iglesias, *Bowl of Beings* is a collection of sketches including *The Returns of Ché Guevara* and *Chicano on the Storm,* among others. *Radio Mambo* (which was commissioned by the city of Miami) is a series of sketches done in interview form, examining the social complexities of the black, Jewish, Cuban, Haitian, and white communities of Miami. In this work, as in *Radio: Bordertown* (an ethnographic performance about San Diego), the group moves beyond its members' own identities to perform multiple subjects marked by gender, race, class, and region.

It is not by chance that artists such as Luis Alfaro, Guillermo Gómez-Peña, Nao Bustamante, Laura Esparza, Coco Fusco, Josefina Baez, Marga Gómez, Carmelita Tropicana, Monica Palacios, and Elia Arce, and comedy groups such as Culture Clash (just to mention a few) have chosen to work in performance art. While Gómez-Peña has become well known for his performances of border subjects inhabiting different cultural landscapes since the creation of *Border Brujo,* Luis Alfaro's solo performances explore in poetic terms issues of sexuality and class oppression in Los Angeles. Alfaro writes plays, poetry, and short stories, and is currently one of the best Latino performance artists. A Chicano born and raised in downtown Los Angeles, he is the recipient of a MacArthur Foundation fellowship. He has been a resident artist at the Mark Taper Forum, where he co-directs (with Diane Rodriguez) the Latino Theatre Initiative. In his most acclaimed performance, *Downtown* (also in a compact disc, released in 1993), Alfaro insists on centering the queer self, criticizing and reinventing the notion of Latino/Chicano family. In addition to centering his gay identity in this piece, Alfaro narrates his working-class upbringing in the Pico-Union district, a Latino community in downtown Los Angeles. In the introduction to *Downtown,* published in a 1998 anthology of queer performances, *O Solo Homo: The New Queer Performance,* Alfaro speaks of his work:

> I call myself a gay Chicano. I create work that asks questions about identity and social power and addresses the intersections of nationality and sexuality. More than all of that, I am trying to tell the story of my people, of what it means to live in a city like Los Angeles, to give a voice to the stories that have not been heard.
>
> (p. 316)

For him, performance art is an investigation of the everyday life. His community becomes embodied in his art. Alfaro performs his body not in isolation but in connection to others who have had an impact on his life. In his 1996 *Cuerpo politizado* (Politicized body), Alfaro looks at the American consumption game as performed through his body, which feels the need to justify it.

Alfaro's work is amazing because of the way it gets disseminated in live performances, compact discs, and written form. His performances have been produced in regional theater houses such as the Mark Taper in Los Angeles, the South Coast Repertory, the Midwest Play Lab in Minneapolis, the Chicago Latino Theater, and Center for the Arts in Boston. In addition, his appearances in alternative spaces such as Highways Performance Space and Self-Help Graphics in Los Angeles, as well as in many cultural centers and universities across the United States, have contributed to the diversification of his audience to include Latino and non-Latino and gay, lesbian, and heterosexual audiences.

Like Alfaro, Gómez-Peña is also the recipient of a MacArthur Foundation fellowship. Since his arrival from Mexico City in 1978, he has investigated border culture and the impact of interculturalism and transculturation. Through performance, radio, video, poetry, and installations, he has explored the relationship between Latinos and the United States. From 1984 to 1990 he founded and participated in the Border Arts Workshop in San Diego, California. He is one of the editors of *High Performance* magazine and of the *Drama Review: The Journal of Performance Studies.* He is the author of the 1993 *Warrior for Gringostroika* and the 1996 *The New World Border,* which received the American Book Award. In his 1992 collaboration with Coco Fusco, *Two Undiscovered Amerindians Visit,* the performers put themselves on display for a few days in a large cage as "authentic" indigenous people. The project premiered in September 1992 at the Walker Art Center in Minneapolis. The performance artists took their installation to Madrid, London, Washington D.C., and Irvine, California. Dressed in a hybrid "exotic" Amerindian style, Gómez-Peña and Fusco impersonated fictional islanders from the Gulf of Mexico. The installation was an experiment that interpreted the history of the so-called discovery of the Americas. The cage performance within the installation became an important component of the project, which presented the protagonists as "undiscovered Amerindians." More recent Gómez-Peña's collaborative performances or installations with Roberto Sifuentes, James Luna, Michelle Ceballos, and others, have dealt with processes of transformation and the impact of globalization and technology. Collaborative performances such as *The Temple of Confessions, El Naftazteca: Cyber-Azteca TV for 2000 AD,* and *The Dangerous Border Game* are sophisticated experiments combining visual art, music, poetry, sound, and computer technology. Gómez-Peña's 2003 collaborative project, *Ex-Centris (A Living Diorama of Fetish-ized Others),* was part of the Living Art Development Agency's Live Culture sponsored by the Arts Council of England's Visual Arts Department and London Arts. In it, Gómez-Peña collaborated with Juan Ibarra and Michelle Ceballos (of La Pocha Nostra) and British-based artists Kazuko Hohki and Ansuman Biswas, creating an interactive museum of experimental ethnography. With sardonic humor, it explores colonial practices and representation.

FEMINIST PERFORMANCE ARTISTS

The celebration, in the early 1990s, of the so-called discovery of the Americas—which was promoted in many mainstream cultural events and public institutions—influenced the work of many performance artists, who responded sardonically to the call for celebration. For example, *Indigurrito* was Nao Bustamante's response. In this piece, the performative subject exposes herself in a provocative game of parodic exaggeration and inversion. Even the title is a transgressive referential. A blend of two common Spanish words, "Indian" and "burrito," *Indigurrito* manages to allude directly to the subject of colonization and decolonization and, amusingly, to a traditional Mexican dish. In it, Bustamante plays with words and with her body. Sometimes her improvised vocabulary makes no sense. Nevertheless, these absurd linguistic games produce suspense and hilarious repercussions as the audience reacts to and sometimes participates in her performance. At one point, Bustamante touches her crotch, where a provocative-looking device hangs from a harness attached to her pelvis. This appendage appears to be either a dildo or a vibrator; its phallic resemblance is paramount. However, when Bustamante finally reveals the hidden device, she shows the audience that it is a burrito, wrapped in aluminum foil. At one point in the performance, Bustamante holds it with one hand while she eats chips, which she pulls out from between her breasts. Suddenly she pulls out a small container of salsa. At this point, her performance becomes a comic event. Laughter (the audience's and her own) and the carnivalesque mood become part of the transgression and subversion.

While *Indigurrito* is a one-woman show, Bustamante has collaborated with Coco Fusco in a performance, *Stuff* (commissioned by London's Institute of Contemporary Art), which deals with the complexities of the female body, food, and sex. She has toured internationally with her piece *America the Beautiful,* and with the experimental dance group Osseus Labyrint in Taiwan and Hong Kong, performing *The Frigid Bride.* Her performances are characterized by the use of the body, which becomes a source of narrative and emotion. As she explains in a statement for the *San Francisco Chronicle,* her "performances communicate on the level of subconscious language, taking the spectator on a bizarre journey, cracking stereotypes by embodying them. [She disarms] the audience with a sense of vulnerability only to confront them with a startling wake up call." Some of her stories are highly provocative. For example, in one, she describes an experience in which she masturbated while playing guitar. Bustamante's expressive language generates an amusing spectacle where meaning is subverted and, of course, multiply interpreted.

The contradictions embedded in colonialism and neocolonialism have influenced the creative contributions of Latino and Latina theater practitioners and performance artists. For Bustamante's performance, it is precisely the monolithic space of the white male heterosexual—the dominant subject in power—that she subverts with innovation and wild humor. In *Indiguritto*, the process of decolonization, rendered suggestive and comic, again represents a metaphor inherent in the body's endless utterance. Sometimes the use of autobiography in performance art contributes to the process of decolonization. In general the one-woman show is aimed at bringing about just such a rupture with patriarchy and other dominant systems.

Bustamante and other Latina performance artists conceive of their performances as a means of enacting the world(s) of difference. But even more importantly, they see performance art as a feminist vehicle for liberating the inner self from what feminists call the patriarchal text. This is also an important feature in Laura Esparza's work. In addition to being a solo performance artist and director, Esparza has worked extensively in community theaters. In the early 1990s, she became the artistic director of San Francisco's community-based Teatro Misión (Mission Theater) and then became involved with San Jose's Teatro Visión (Vision Theater). In 1997, she was appointed program director for the Mexican Heritage Plaza in San Jose.

In *I DisMember the Alamo* (which also responded to the so-called discovery of the Americas and was published in the 2000 *Latinas on Stage: Practice and Theory*), Esparza departs from the official history of the 1836 confrontation at the Alamo to trace her family lineage. She makes her individual and collective identity the subject of the performance. The construction of Esparza's identity is based upon a collective whole, which transcends the limitations of dominant discourses that have declared history homogenous. She insists that the personal is the real history, and that the story of the Alamo is "herstory." She claims, "My body is the battlefield of the colonized self. The land where conquests of Spanish, and Mexican, and American have occupied my cells" (*Latinas on Stage,* pp. 87–88). Esparza invents a history as a way of performing her identity. In her version,

only "herstory" is the real story. With a *rebozo* (shawl) around her waist, Esparza ends her performance drawing diagrams with lipstick on her naked chest. She tells the audience:

> I am this:
> an india
> inside a mestiza
> inside a gringa
> inside a Chicana
> I am all of these
> and my psyche is like a road map of Texas
> traversed by borders
> with never any peace at these borders.
>
> (p. 88)

Esparza enacts the reality of her multiple selves, acknowledging the many "borders" that crisscross her identity and give it its distinctive shape. Esparza's use of transgression within transgression allows the "I" to evolve in a continuous, multidimensional process of identity (de)formation. Her body—that of the performative subject present on stage—represents the ongoing exchange between colonization and decolonization. If decolonization holds out the capability of transformation in the realms of the subjected, for Esparza—and other Latina performance artists who affirm a neocolonized position—this negotiation remains a discursive strategy of representation and self-representation.

In the works of performance artists such as Monica Palacios, Marga Gómez, and Carmelita Tropicana, self-representation is a powerful act of queer performativity because it evokes a sense of being located historically and socially. This positioning provides the basis for a sense of belonging and participating in the creative processes of a particular culture. Latinas and other women of color act upon the racialized subordination and discrimination that has been designed to silence them. When the performance artist functions as the representer of "her-self," she is simultaneously placed in a position of power as she articulates her identities through a process of self-definition. The technology of

94

self-representation allows the artist to create and sustain a metaphorical resonance of reality. This approach involves a total rethinking of the gendered self as an autobiographical subject. The performative subject cannot be constructed separately from her sexuality, race, and ethnicity.

In one of the best performances of Monica Palacios, the 1990 *Latin Lesbo Comic: A Performance about Happiness, Challenges, and Tacos*, the artist represents herself growing up as a lesbian. Her acceptance becomes crucial in her coming-out story, presenting the act of self-representation as a metaphor for visibility and empowerment. As in many other performances by Latina lesbians, the examination of sexuality deliberately constructs a space for evaluating the oppression of women in the heterosexual order. In most performances dealing with issues of sexuality, ethnic identity and racialization are equally important in the process of self-definition. Palacios refuses to accept one facet of her identity without the other. Both are equally important in her process of self-definition. Her racialized sexuality is a distinctive part of her coming-out story. She puts it this way:

> You see, I figure artists are going to save this planet. So I must continue with my plan. Weaving the lesbian side of me with the Mexican side of me. And writing about it. And talking about it. And pushing for and demanding change! BECAUSE, HEY FOLKS, IT'S TIME!
>
> (*Latinas on Stage*, p. 115)

Her performance of assumed ethnic and sexual identities transgresses patriarchal and heterosexual privileges and indicates that it is not an accident that lesbians and Latinas are often marginalized. Defiantly, *Latin Lezbo* couples the politics of identity with those of visibility.

Humor and parody are characteristic of Palacios' work. In her later performances, the 1995 *Greetings from a Queer Señorita*, the 2000 *Confessions: A Sexplosion of Tantalizing Tales*, and the 2001 *Queer Soul*, Palacios uses comedy as a tool to construct new ways of displaying and making visible the queer self in opposition to the marked heteronormativity of our society.

The same politics of representation are implicit in Marga Gomez's work. In her 1991 *Marga Gomez is Pretty, Witty, and Gay*, her 1993 *Memory Tricks*, her 1994 *Half Cuban/Half Lesbian*, and her 1995 *A Line around the Block*, Gomez deals with issues of self-representation and assimilation, as well as racism, misogyny, and homophobia as they affect her life. While in *Memory Tricks* the artist makes the subject of her performance her mother's story (she was a Puerto Rican dancer in the 1950s), in *A Line around the Block*, Gomez centers on the story of her father (a Cuban vaudeville impresario). Gomez brings the story of her parents to the stage as a way to investigate the individual and collective identity.

The reenactment of individual and collective identity is also a powerful ingredient in Carmelita Tropicana's work. In addition to being an outstanding performer, Tropicana is an excellent writer. She has brought together her performances in *I, Carmelita Tropicana: Performing between Cultures* (2000). In particular, her 1994 *Milk of Amnesia/Leche de amnesia* is a performance of resistance to a forced assimilation into Americanness. The performance brings together Alina Troyano, the Cuban writer/artist, and Carmelita Tropicana, the scandalous queer performance artist. Carmelita Tropicana is the staged identity of Alina Troyano. She began her artistic career in New York. She has become well known in the East Village performance scene, mainly in queer and feminist spaces, such as the Club Chandelier and the WOW Cafe. Tropicana is a wholly invented identity; she is a cultural icon of discursive oppositions forged through the interstices of two American nationalities, each distinct from the other, culturally and geographically. Carmelita Tropicana and Alina Troyano engage in a tête-à-tête where memory, humor, and autobiography become integrated. The narrative base is about

Tropicana's loss of memory, an amnesia she attributes to the process of acculturation.

Most critics and theorists of performance art rightfully underscore a performance's foregrounding of the personal as well as of the role of the body as text. Given this double emphasis, it is not surprising that feminist critics have overlooked the work of Latina performance artists as well as the work of other women of color in performance art.

It is precisely the interdisciplinary possibilities performance art offers that allow Josefina Baez to validate her gendered and racialized body as a trope for representation. Baez is a black performer, born in the Dominican Republic and raised in New York. She has been teaching theater and creative writing in New York's public schools since 1984 and is the founder and director of the Latinarte Theatre Troupe. Her writing has been published in *Forward Motion* magazine, *Brujula/Compass*, *Ventana Abierta*, *Vetas*, *Caribbean Connections: Moving North*, and elsewhere. Since 1996, Baez has been touring houses and apartments with her *Apartarte/Casarte* (split up/to get married) performance dialogue project. The performances are organized as social events and take place in living rooms, bathrooms, and kitchens all over New York City, in particular around Dominican immigrant communities. She explores themes of migration, marginality, identity, and the body. In another performance, *Dominicanish*, Baez employs poetry, soul music, and *kuchipudi* (a type of yoga) in an exploration of what it means to be Dominican in New York.

Baez's contemporary, Elia Arce, uses a similarly multidisciplinary approach in her work. Since 1986, she has been creating, directing, and performing solo theater works, as well as collaborations. A dual citizen of Costa Rica and the United States, Arce is based in the California desert. Her performance *First Woman on the Moon* was featured at the Los Angeles International Theatre Festival in November 2002 and was staged at the 2003 Perfo Puerto,

the first Latin American performance art festival in Chile. Arce became famous in the early 1990s with her solo performance *Stretching My Skin Until It Rips Whole,* in which she combines autobiography with the politics of representation. An excerpt of this performance has been published in *Latinas on Stage* under the title "My Grandmother Never Past Away: A Stream of Consciousness and Unconsciousness." In a biographical note on the National Performance Network Website Arce asserted that she believes that performance art as an interdisciplinary system of representation—including music, dance and puppetry—"challenges our minds, spirits, and bodies towards social justice and community self-empowerment."

Latina performance artists enter the scene of representation not as the otherwise absent or objectified other but as speaking subject, transgressive and dynamic. Their work is, and always has been, the result of a cultural *mestizaje* (the blending of the indigenous and the Hispanic worlds or other European cultures) representing the ongoing conflict inherent in different processes of transculturation. Recent publications in the field of Latina and Latino theater and performance art pay tribute to the great contributions of Latina *teatristas* in the contemporary era. Publications such as *Latinas on Stage* (2000); *Latina Performance* (1999); *Stages of Life: Transcultural Performance and Identity in U.S. Latina Theater* (2001), and *Puro teatro: A Latina Anthology* (2000) are evidence of the scholarly discussion currently taking place, providing material for research and teaching. All these publications recognize the maturity of Latinas in the American stage today.

CONCLUSION

If one looks at the success of John Leguizamo (Off-Broadway, *Mambo Mouth* and *Spic-O-Rama,* and on Broadway, *Freak*); the MacArthur Foundation fellowships awarded to the performance artists Guillermo Gómez-Peña and

Luis Alfaro; the Obie winners María Irene Fornes, José Rivera, Luis Delgado, and Leguizamo; Nilo Cruz's Pulitzer Prize; Josefina Lopez's film *Real Women Have Curves;* and the success of performance artists such as Marga

Gomez, who has appeared on HBO's *Comic Relief,* Showtime's *Latino Laugh Festival,* and Comedy Central's *Out There Special,* one can conclude that the Latino and Latina artists are visible at last.

Selected Bibliography

Alarcón, Norma. "Latina Writers in the United States." In *Spanish American Women Writers: A Bio-Bibliographical Source Book.* Edited by Diane E. Marting. Westport, Conn.: Greenwood, 1990.

Alfaro, Luis. "Downtown." In *O Solo Homo: The New Queer Performance.* Edited by Holly Hughes and David Román. New York: Grove Press, 1998.

———. *Downtown.* Lawndale, Calif.: New Alliance Records, 1993. (Spoken word.)

Alfaro, Luis, et al. *Latino Plays from South Coast Repertory: Hispanic Playwrights Project Anthology.* New York: Broadway Play Publishing, 2000. (Includes works by Luis Alfaro, Cusi Cram, Joann Farias, Rogelio Martinez, Cherríe Moraga, José Rivera, and Octavio Solis.)

Algarín, Miguel, and Lois Griffith. *Action: The Nuyorican Poets Café Theater Festival.* New York: Simon & Schuster, 1997.

Antush John V., ed. *Nuestro New York: An Anthology of Puerto Rican Plays.* New York: Mentor, 1994.

———. *Recent Puerto Rican Theater: Five Plays from New York.* Houston: Arte Público Press, 1994.

Arce, Elia. "Elia Arce," National Performance Network. Available at http://www.npnweb.org.

Arrizón, Alicia. *Latina Performance: Traversing the Stage.* Bloomington: Indiana University Press, 1999.

Arrizón, Alicia, and Lillian Manzor, eds. *Latinas on Stage: Practice and Theory.* Berkeley, Calif.: Third Woman Press, 2000.

Barber, Matthew. "María Irene Fornes: Former Student's Play Pulitzer-Nominated Writer Back in the Director's Chair." *San Francisco Independent* 35, no. 82 (November 15, 1990). Pp. 1–4.

Boehm, Mike. "Latino Playwrights Inch Slowly to Center Stage." *Los Angeles Times* (June 16, 2000).

Broyles-González, Yolanda. *El Teatro Campesino: Theater in the Chicano Movement.* Austin: University of Texas Press, 1994.

Bustamante, Nao. "Biography," *San Francisco Chronicle.* Available at http://www.sfgate.com/offbeat/naobiohtml.

——— *Indigurrito.* Performed at Highways Performance Space, Santa Monica, Calif., January 23, 1994.

Cortina, Rodolfo, and Miguel Pardo, eds. *Cuban American Theater.* Houston, Tex.: Arte Público Press, 1991.

Cruz, Migdalia. "Telling Tales" In *Telling Tales: New One-Act Plays*. Edited by Eric Lane. New York: Penguin, 1993.

Delgado, María, and Caridad Svich, eds. *Conducting a Life: Reflection on the Theatre of María Irene Fornes*. Lyme, N.H.: Smith and Kraus, 1999.

Elam, Harry J. *Taking It to the Streets: The Social Protest Theater of Luis Valdez and Amiri Baraka*. Ann Arbor: University of Michigan Press, 1997.

Ellis, Roger, ed. *Multicultural Theatre: Scenes and Monologs From New Hispanic, Asian, and African American Plays*. Colorado Springs, Colo.: Meriwether Publications, 1996.

———. *Multicultural Theatre 2: Contemporary Hispanic, Asian and African American Plays*. Colorado Springs, Colo.: Meriwether Publications, 1998.

Fernández, Evelina. "How Else Am I Supposed to Know I'm Still Alive?" In *Contemporary Plays by Women of Color: An Anthology*. Edited by Kathy A. Perkins and Roberta Uno. New York: Routledge, 1996.

Feyder, Linda, ed. *Shattering the Myth: Plays by Hispanic Women*. Houston, Tex.: Arte Público Press, 1992.

Fornes, María Irene. *María Irene Fornes / Plays*. New York: PAJ Publications, 1986.

———. "María Irene Fornes," Art and Culture Network. Available at http://www.artandculture.com/arts/artist?artistId=765.

Fusco, Coco, ed. *The Bodies That Were Not Ours: And Other Writing*. New York: Routledge, 2001.

———. *Corpus Delecti: Performance Art of the Americas*. New York: Routledge, 2000.

Fusco, Coco, and Nao Bustamante. "Stuff." *The Drama Review: The Journal of Performance Studies* 41, no. 4 (1997): 63–82.

Garza, Roberto I., ed. *Contemporary Chicano Theatre*. Notre Dame, Ind.: University of Notre Dame Press, 1976.

Glore, John. "What's a Hispanic Play? That's a Tough Question." *American Theater* 3, no. 9 (1986). Pp. 39–41. (Interview with Eduardo Machado.)

Gómez-Peña, Guillermo. "Border Brujo: A Performance Poem." *The Drama Review: The Journal of Performance Studies* 35, no. 3 (1991). Pp. 46–66.

———. *Dangerous Border Crossers: The Artist Talks Back*. New York: Routledge, 2000.

———. *El Mexterminator*. Mexico: Oceano Grupo Editorial, 2002.

———. *The New World Border: Prophecies, Poems, & Loqueras for the End of the Century*. San Francisco, Calif.: City Lights, 1996.

———. *Warrior for Gringostroika: Essays, Performance Texts, and Poetry*. St. Paul, Minn.: Graywolf Press, 1993.

González-Cruz, Luis, and Francesca M. Colecchia, eds. and trans. *Cuban Theater in the United States: A Critical Anthology*. Tempe, Ariz.: Bilingual Press, 1997.

Huerta, Jorge. *Chicano Drama: Performance, Society and Myth*. New York: Cambridge University Press, 2000.

———, ed. *Necessary Theater: Six Plays about the Chicano Experience*. Houston, Tex.: Arte Público Press, 1989.

Kanellos, Nicolás. *A History of Hispanic Theatre in the United States: Origins to 1940*. Austin: University of Texas Press, 1990.

Larson, Catherine, and Margarita Vargas, eds. *Latin American Women Dramatists: Theater, Texts, and Theories*. Bloomington: Indiana University Press, 1998.

Leguizamo, John. *Spic-O-Rama: A Dysfunctional Comedy.* New York: Bantam, 1994.

Leschin, Luisa, et al. *Latin Anonymous: Two Plays.* Houston, Tex.: Arte Público Press, 1996.

López, Josefina. *Real Women Have Curves.* Seattle, Wash.: Rain City Projects, 1988.

Machado, Eduardo. *The Floating Islands Plays.* New York: Theatre Communications Group, 1991.

Marrero, María Teresa. "Out of the Fringe?: Out of the Closet: Latina/Latino Theatre and Performance." *The Drama Review* 44, no. 3 (fall 2000). Pp. 131–153.

Montoya, Richard, Ricardo Salinas, and Herbert Siguenza. *Culture Clash: Life, Death, and Revolutionary Comedy.* New York: Theatre Communications Group, 1998.

Moraga, Cherríe. *Giving Up the Ghost: Teatro in Two Acts.* Los Angeles, Calif.: West End Press, 1986.

———. *Heroes and Saints and Other Plays.* Albuquerque, N.Mex.: West End Press, 1994.

———. *The Hungry Woman.* Albuquerque: University of New Mexico Press, 2001.

Morton, Carlos. *Johnny Tenorio and Other Plays.* Houston, Tex.: Arte Público Press, 1992.

———. *The Many Deaths of Danny Rosales and Other Plays.* Houston, Tex.: Arte Público Press, 1983.

———. *Rancho Hollywood y otras obras del teatro Chicano.* Houston, Tex.: Arte Público Press, 1999.

Najera, Rick. *The Pain of the Macho and Other Plays.* Houston, Tex.: Arte Público Press, 1992.

Osborn, Elizabeth M., ed. *On New Ground: Contemporary Hispanic-American Plays.* New York: Theatre Communications Group, 1987.

Portillo Trambley, Estela. *Sor Juana and Other Plays.* Ypsilanti, Mich.: Bilingual Press/ Editorial Bilingüe, 1986.

Prida, Dolores. *Beautiful Señoritas and Other Plays.* Houston, Tex.: Arte Público Press, 1991.

———. "Screens." In *Cuban Theater in the United States: A Critical Anthology.* Edited by Luis González Cruz and Francesca M. Colecchia. Tempe, Ariz.: Bilingual Press Review, 1992.

———. "The Show Does Go On." In *Breaking Boundaries: Latina Writing and Critical Readings.* Edited by Asunción Horno-Delgado, et al. Amherst: University of Massachusetts Press, 1989.

Ramos-García, Luis A. *The State of Latino Theater in the United States.* New York: Routledge, 2002.

Rivera, José. *José Rivera Anthology.* New York: Theatre Communications Group, 1991.

———. *Marisol and Other Plays.* New York: Theatre Communications Group, 1997.

Robinson, Marc. *The Theater of María Irene Fornes.* Baltimore Md.: Johns Hopkins University Press, 1999.

Román, David. "Latino Performance and Identity." *Aztlán* 22 no. 2 (fall 1999). Pp. 151–167.

Rosenberg, Joe, ed. *¡Aplauso!: Hispanic Children's Theater.* Houston, Tex.: Arte Público Press, 1995.

Sánchez, Edwin. *Barefoot Boy with Shoes On.* Broadway Play Publication, 2000.

———. *Icarus.* Broadway Play Publication, 1999.

———. *Plays by Edwin Sánchez,* Broadway Play Communications, 1997.

Sandoval-Sánchez, Alberto. *José, Can You See?: Latinos on and off Broadway.* Madison: University of Wisconsin Press, 1999.

Sandoval-Sánchez, Alberto, and Nancy Saporta Sternback, eds. *Puro teatro: A Latina Anthology.* Tucson: University of Arizona Press, 2000.

———. *Stages of Life: Transcultural Performance and Identity in U.S. Latina Theater.* Tucson: University of Arizona Press, 2001.

Schechner, Richard. *Between Theater and Anthropology.* Philadelphia: University of Pennsylvania Press, 1985.

Solis, Octavio. *Santos and Santos.* Santa Monica, Calif.: L.A. Theatre Works, 1997. (Sound recording.)

Svich, Caridad, and María Teresa Marrero. *Out of the Fringe: Contemporary Latina/ Latino Theatre and Performance.* New York: Theatre Communications Group, 2000.

Taylor, Diana, and Juan Villegas, eds. *Negotiating Performance: Gender, Sexuality, and Theatricality in Latin/o America.* Durham, N.C.: Duke University Press, 1994.

Troyano, Alina, with Ela Troyano and Uzi Parnes. *I, Carmelita Tropicana: Performing between Cultures.* Boston, Mass.: Beacon, 2000.

Valdez, Luis. *Early Works.* Houston, Tex.: Arte Público Press, 1990.

———. *Zoot Suit and Other Plays.* Houston, Tex.: Arte Público Press, 1992.

Yarbro-Bejarano, Yvonne. "The Female Subject in Chicano Theater: Sexuality, 'Race' and Class." In *Performing Feminism: Feminist Critical Theory and Theatre.* Edited by Sue-Ellen Case. Baltimore, Md.: Johns Hopkins University Press, 1990.

Alurista

(1947–)

FRANCISCO A. LOMELÍ

Ommonly recognized as the Chicano movement poet par excellence, Alberto Baltazar Urista Heredia, born in Mexico City on 8 August 1947, first gained considerable notoriety after 1968 using the nom de plume of Alurista, which is a combination of his names Alberto and Urista. Alurista's contributions transcend the realm of literature, with his fame starting in San Diego, California, spreading to the American Southwest, and eventually extending nationally and internationally until he achieved the informal status of poet laureate for the movement. His persona, along with those of Tomás Rivera, Rudolfo Anaya, Rodolfo "Corky" Gonzales, Ricardo Sánchez, and a few others, came to be viewed as synonymous with the early period of the Chicano Renaissance between 1965 and 1975. His role soon expanded into multiple functions, including cultural leader, community organizer, thinker, educator, and social activist. Aside from his unprecedented innovations with code-switching between Spanish and English, Alurista's other major contribution marks the rediscovery of Aztlán, a geographical, cultural, psychological, political, and symbolic entity, modeled after a mythic place in Aztec mythology with which he claimed to establish a new sense of nationhood for a social movement. Such a revelation gave renewed credence to the definition of Chicanos' reaffirmation in search for their Mexican origins and roots. He was also instrumental in the promotion of the term Chicano as a new ethnic label in the mid-1960s. His literary trajectory shows a prolific writer who has delved into a variety of genres beyond poetry, as he has produced fourteen books to date, ranging from single-authored collections to coedited volumes, a series of children's books, and an experimental novel. However, poetry is ultimately his forte and where he has made the greatest literary impact, having recited his poetry throughout the United States, Germany, Mexico, France, and Holland.

Among Alurista's works of poetry are the following: *Floricanto en Aztlán* (1971), *Cantares arrullos* (1975), *Timespace Huracán: Poems 1972–75* (1976), *A'nque: Collected Works 1976–79* (1979), *Spik in Glyph?* (1981), *Return: Poems Collected and New* (1982), *Tremble Purple* (1987), *Z Eros* (1995), and *Et Tú . . . Raza?* (1996). He also has to his credit various coedited anthologies: *El Ombligo de Aztlán: An Anthology of Chicano Student Poetry* (1972; coeditor Jorge González), *Festival de Flor y Canto: An Anthology of Chicano Literature* (1976; coeditors José Flores Peregrino and Arnold C. Vento), and *Southwest Tales in Memory of Tomás Rivera: A Contemporary Collection* (1986; coeditor Xelina Rojas-Urista). Alurista has also edited a series of nine volumes of children's books under the general title *Colección Tula y Tonán: Textos generativos* (1973). Other works include an important play titled *Dawn* (1974), a cultural-political manifesto known as "El Plan Espiritual de Aztlán" (1969), a Ph.D. dissertation in 1983 ("Oscar Z. Acosta, In Context") at the University of California at San Diego, and the experimental novel *As Our Barrio Turns . . . Who the Yoke B On?* (2000). He has also on occasion embarked on writing either critical essays on Chicano writers or foundational essays on cultural politics, such as "The Chicano Cultural Revolution" (1973). Given his multiple talents and activities, it should be noted that he was instrumental in founding a variety of community and intellectual enterprises, including the organization of a group of artists from San Diego called Toltecas de Aztlán (1970), the San Diego newspaper *La Verdad*, the Chicano Studies Center at San Diego State College (1969), the Flor y Canto Literary Festivals (USC in 1973; University of Texas at Austin in 1975; Albuquerque in 1977), the literary journal *Maize* (1977–1983), and the first national Chicano Moratorium Against the Vietnam War (1970). He has taught at Colorado College, Cal Poly in San Luis Obispo, California, San Diego State University, the University of California at Santa Barbara, and California State University, San Marcos.

The range and variety of his writings are noteworthy, but what stands out is his poetic flair for challenging linguistic conventions, proposing internal rhyme or alliterations, and, most of all, the blending of Spanish and English into virtually a new third language. Frequently, these mixtures are inflected by black English modalities as well as indigenous languages (mainly Nahuatl and Maya) with cadences from the farm worker or urban argot. In this regard he resembles a modern-day Vicente Huidobro, the Chilean poet who in the 1920s promoted a movement called *creacionismo,* which tried to create images and metaphors that could be used to supplant common reality. Alurista demonstrates signs of influence from various other sources: the Latin American Vanguard (1925–1945); the Social Realists; the Beat Generation (1952–1958); the youthful expression of the Literatura de la Onda from Mexico (1965–1970); Malcolm X and other black movement writers; pachuco aesthetics (Mexican American urban youth since the 1940s who felt estranged between both American and Mexican cultures); pre-Columbian poets (such as Netzahualcóyotl); the erotic and existentialist poetry of Octavio Paz; Japanese haikus; the hippie movement; and e. e. cummings, among others. It should be noted that he is one of the most anthologized poets in Chicano literature.

POLITICAL ACTIVISM

Born in Mexico City, Alurista moved with his family to nearby Cuernavaca where he finished elementary school. He also lived a short time as a youngster in Acapulco, but most of his early years were spent in Tijuana until migrating to San Diego, California, at the age of thirteen where he finished middle school and high school. In Cuernavaca he studied in an all-boys Jesuit seminary where he acquired an intense curiosity about philosophy and the world of ideas. Being a precocious young man, he discovered early a natural inclination toward poetry, which made him stand out among his peers. He turned such talents into an entrepreneurial business by charging small fees for writing poems for classmates for special events, such as Mother's Day, romantic declarations, exchanges of admiration, expressions of friendship, or simply verbal duels. At San Diego High School, from which he graduated in 1965, he developed into an inquisitive and restless member among his peers, itching to gain a broader view of social issues while intimating his own ethnic alienation. He decided to try a change of scenery by enrolling at Chapman College near Los Angeles. This experience galvanized a new consciousness in Alurista, and he sensed that his mission was to probe further into what it meant to be of Mexican descent in the United States. He made a critical decision by transferring to San Diego State College in 1967 where he eventually received his Bachelor of Arts in psychology in 1970. The move sparked a heightened awareness during the academic year of 1966–1967 when he first indulged in what he considered serious poetry with the intent of publishing. In the process, he was instrumental in the creation of a student group called MEChA (Movimiento Estudiantial Chicano de Aztlán— Chicano Student Movement of Aztlán), and the founding of the Mexican American Studies Department at San Diego State College in 1969. He suddenly blossomed with a boundless curiosity about history, ideas, politics, and power, emerging with a new worldview of his cultural self while acquiring a messianic intent to confront inequities. A critical event occurred around 1967 when, browsing through either *Life* or *Look* magazine, he encountered a key article that would change his outlook forever. The article contained an anthropological summary of Aztec civilization, including a detailed account on the myth of Aztlán, the homeland of the Aztecs that was north of Mexico City. He wondered if north meant as far as the American Southwest. From such a deduction, he reconnected with his Mexican past in order to better contextualize his Chicano circumstance, understanding it as an extension of Mexico being filtered through an American socialization process. By rediscovering Aztlán, the loose strands of his identity came together as one, and he acquired a new philosophy enriched by his indigenous past. As it was a core concept of his newfound philosophy, he was able to more effectively lay out the basic tenets of cultural nationalism, usually referred to as "Chicanismo," which became the grand impulse of the Chicano movement.

The burgeoning movement seemed splintered, needing a philosophical boost beyond its farm worker origins, its student walkouts, its quest for civil rights, and its urban politics. Alurista, the most widely known poet of that era, provided the movement with the ideological glue it lacked by offering the name to a symbolic nation: Aztlán. More than anyone else, he formulated a neo-indigenous rationale for reconceptualizing Chicano culture through a contemporary social agenda, including a cultural design, but, most of all, a new language. If the movement appeared reactive to its times, with Alurista it became spurred on by a wave of creativity through art and literature while reconfiguring its ethnic definition. The relative invisibility of Chicanos slowly began to wane, much like an obsolete image. Thanks to leaders such as Alurista, Cesar Chavez, Luis Valdez from California, Rodolfo "Corky" Gonzales from Colorado, Reies López Tijerina from New Mexico, and José Angel Gutiérrez from Texas, the movement became a broad-based, grassroots social phenomenon with concrete issues and concerns. The California poet soon became a pivotal cornerstone in the movement's overall impetus.

By 1968 Alurista was fast becoming a spokesman for Chicano civil rights in the San Diego area, but his reputation catapulted onto the national scene in 1969 when he presented a poetic manifesto, called El Plan Espiritual de Aztlán, at the First Chicano National Conference in Denver, Colorado (also referred to as the Chicano Youth Conference). This document outlined for the first time the basic parameters of a Chicano blueprint for an ideological framework for self-determination and liberation, an underscoring of brown pride, an indigenous affiliation, and a political program. The highly idealistic document aimed to make a declaration of autonomy vis-à-vis mainstream society, while setting out to reclaim lands stolen from the ancestors—suggesting Reies López Tijerina's land grant movement in New Mexico called *Alianza de las Mercedes*. Alurista also emphasized the formulation of a bronze continent, that is, one dominated by an indigenous presence previously repressed. He coalesced much of what Rodolfo "Corky" Gonzales had proposed in his epic poem, *Yo Soy Joaquín* (1967), except that cultural nationalism, regarded as the organizational "common denominator that all members of La Raza [our people] can agree upon" (*Aztlán: Essays on the Chicano Homeland*, 1989, p. 2), now assumed a more grounded focus as a guide for action. In a key section of the manifesto, Alurista writes: "Our struggle then must be for the control of our barrios, our campos [fields], pueblos [towns], lands, our economy, our culture, and our political life" (p. 2). Specifically, the main points delineated in the manifesto include the following: unity, economy, education, institutions, self-defense, cultural values, and political liberation. Alurista, the poet at heart, had left an indelible imprint in the new Chicano consciousness with regards to the ideological framework, the forms of action, and the specific plan for liberation. In the process he combined poetry and politics in order to inject substance and content into the movement as opposed to simply reacting to forms of oppression.

POETRY

Although he had just published his first poems in 1968, the Chicano poet became an overnight sensation nationally with the vanguard journal from Berkeley called *El Grito: A Journal of Contemporary Mexican-American Thought*, founded in 1967 by Octavio I. Romano-V. If the publication of his first poems represented a risk for the editors, given the social scientific orientation of the journal, Alurista saw it as an opportunity to almost single-handedly create a new sensibility and aesthetics while marking the resurgence of a bilingual and bicultural voice. He therefore occupied a prominent position in spearheading the Chicano literary renaissance of the late 1960s with his daring expression—filled with neologisms, Spanglish, and code-switching—but most of all with his unconventionalisms that defied both Spanish and English norms in terms of syntax,

punctuation, "high brow" literature mixed with "low brow" literature (such as Whitman with hard rock), and his particular penchant for inserting indigenous concepts and barrio motifs. He is the first to present compelling poetry that mixes various languages in a natural way, although less savory samples of such writings can be found in newspapers as far back as the mid-nineteenth century. His intent is not to necessarily show the drawbacks of such a strategy or to mock the limitations of languages. In effect, he set out to cultivate, validate, and legitimize an expression that existed unacknowledged, devoid of any formal literary representation. In the process, he discovered that mixing English and Spanish possessed its own artistic flair and raison d'être. When he blended this with indigenous elements, he contributed toward a new taste in a neo-indigenist movement, weaving together various languages and their variants (like slang and argot with a standard language), such as popular Spanish with black English, or barrio expressions with formal poetic utterances. In this sense, Alurista became a guru of Chicano poetics because, contrary to other poets—aside from Rodolfo "Corky" Gonzales—he had the plan that spoke to the largest number of Chicanos.

Alurista became the cutting-edge figure of Chicano expression that complemented the insatiable search for identity, self-determination, and cultural politics in the Chicano movement. Most of his early works were well received as groundbreaking attempts to express the Chicano's place in American society in terms of the long-standing historical marginalization. He confronted an array of social issues in his quest for justice, cultural vindication, and spiritual rebirth, but his works also explored the type of language that could best delve into questions of inequities, alienation, entitlement, recovery of the past, existential dilemmas, and especially the role of myth in the modern world. Along with Rudolfo A. Anaya in *Bless Me, Ultima* (1972) and other works, Alurista clearly led the philosophical charge to examine and understand myth for its contemporary relevance.

In his first landmark work, *Floricanto en Aztlán* (1971), which consisted of one hundred of his earliest testimonial and paradigmatic poems, Alurista collected his published poems up to 1971 and combined them with new poems. The work represents one of the most important contributions to Chicano literature in general for its thematics, its style, and the literary space it defined at the time. Both the volume of poetry and the content stirred interest unlike any other early movement collection. The work made an immediate impact for its bilingual mode, its neo-indigenous bent, and its historical-mythical messages steeped in a reconstructed system of a dual symbolism. Alurista embarks on defining the world from a Chicano perspective—its struggle in America, the contributing factors to a bilingual/bicultural culture, and elements of alienation and self-awareness. The use of Aztlán in the title called attention to a discovery of identity, and *Floricanto* (flower and song) inserted the work within Aztec poetics, alluding to a metaphor that translates as "poetry." The work became a source of inspiration for a whole new generation that sought a renewed sense of ethnicity. Foundational in its literary aspirations, the collection encompasses various steps in self-discovery while using literature to fill a void. First, a revelation about a cultural past takes place in the poem "me habló en el sueño" ("it spoke to me in a dream"), referring to the bird *tenoch* from which the Aztec capital derived its name, Tenochtitlán. Through this direct connection with pre-Columbian Mexico, the poet recovers from a long lapse in history, suggesting that the revelation has led to a new consciousness about the condition of his people, including their long suffering and quiet oppression. The sense is one of rebirth and reaffirmation in order to become active agents of change. "Tenoch" then functions much like a phoenix where something new emerges out of the ashes of an erased past. Waking up from the dream now signifies action in order to manifest the present

and prepare for a new and better tomorrow: "and we tilled our land / today we eat / dreams no more" (*Floricanto en Aztlán*, p. 11).

Floricanto en Aztlán, illustrated by the renowned artist Judith E. Hernández, contains some of the most anthologized poems in Chicano literature. Among the most unforgettable are the following titles: "when raza?" "we've played cowboys," "in the barrio sopla el viento," "must be the season of the witch," "mis ojos hinchados," and "Once, I wrote a Letter to Emiliano." These poems show the thematic range Alurista seeks, some of the key imagery and linguistic combinations, and important ideological allusions. The first poem poses a rhetorical question for change while invoking his people to rise and prepare for action now: "no verá mañana / our tomorrow es hoy" (p. l). The second one conjures up a false cowboy-Indian dichotomy found in American culture because Chicanos are both European and Indian, suggesting that if Chicanos must play cowboys, that they should be Mexican *caballeros* (gentlemen with horses). The third poem describes the anti-ecological agents destroying a Chicano environment through the symbol of the wind, except that here it assumes a double significance: this wind distributes the smells of a rotting place that contaminates the inhabitants, but it also hints at turmoil and unrest about to burst which will free "our alienated pride" (p. 16). In the fourth poem, the alienating effects of abandonment by an ambiguous symbol (witch) strike a troubling chord. The title is extracted from a 1968 hard rock song with the same title, "Must Be the Season of the Witch." The innovation here lies in the convergence of a cryptic symbol of death (witch) related to drugs with two other symbols—*bruja*, meaning either witch or sorceress, and *llorona*, or wailing woman. The symbolic dynamics between the three kinds of women emphasizes the idea of orphans who have lost the protection from their mother, consequently exposing them to exploitation and suffering. The offspring of such disenfranchised people become aware of their vulnerability, but this suffering mother figure realizes she must recover her children. The implication is one of a full circle whereby an ominous witch preys on people, but that woman figure, transformed by cultural necessity, at the end becomes one who regains a sense of needing her children. The fifth poem, "mis ojos hinchados," offers a snapshot of a history lesson on how to recover from oppression, including some of the most cited verses in Chicano poetry:

> the scars of history of my face
> and the veins of my body
> that aches
> vomita sangre
> y lloro libertad
> i do not ask for freedom
> i am freedom.

(p. 40)

Here we can readily appreciate the usage of both languages and how the author maximizes connotation, nuance, and sensorial effects by switching languages suddenly. In addition, the two languages merge rhythmically and naturally as if one. The title refers to swollen eyes from a long-standing suffering, but the poet feels an urge to pursue his own, and by extension, his people's freedom. The sixth poem, in the form of a letter written to Emiliano Zapata, the Mexican Revolution (1910–1920) leader who proposed that land should belong to those who work it, becomes a rhetorical tool to connect with such a noble hero. The poet hopes to ask for guidance and strategies on how to deal with current social problems. The writer of the letter, named Cactus Tears, suggests a metaphorical neo-indigenous voice that waits for inspiration from his hero. Therefore, *Floricanto en Aztlán* represents a major poetic tour de force of an expression and cultural symbolism that Chicanos used to create a new ethnic identity.

Alurista's next work, *Nationchild Plumaroja* (1972), continued to explore a more explicit cultural culturalism while experimenting with various forms and genres, creating numerous new terminologies, or neologisms, along the way. This collection matches his first work in terms of the one hundred poems, except that the division is quite different: five sections of twenty poems, each section bearing an Aztec motif, such as *nopal* (cactus), *xóchitl* (flower), *serpiente* (serpent), *conejo* (rabbit), and *venado* (deer). Although highly lyrical in quality, much of the poems are motivated to imitate and re-create a nativist sensibility, thus underscoring the neo-indigenous orientation. A call to action is explicit and a poetic legitimacy is implicit. The poet imagines much of his subject matter and language like a combination of fifteenth- and sixteenth-century Nahuatl and Mayan writings from Mesoamerica. Virtually everything about them feels ancient and earthy, except that Alurista inserts contemporary allusions and topics to make them more relevant. Even the form resembles a Mayan codex thanks to the use of pictographic numbers instead of resorting to traditional Arabic numbers. The work is dense and at times heavily concentrated on tone and modality more than message, often oscillating between death and social commitment. More contemplative than *Floricanto en Aztlán* and inspired by Carlos Castaneda's *The Teachings of Don Juan*, this work focuses on a renewed cosmic sense of the world, partly defying or superseding institutionalized religions and particularly Western philosophies. Francisco A. Lomelí and Donaldo W. Urioste observed in their 1976 work, *Chicano Perpectives in Literature: A Critical and Annotated Bibliography*: "That explains the metaphor-filled expression because Alurista thinks [more] in images and symbolism powered by a drum-like rhythm" (p. 18). If his first work is a kind of poetic manifesto on the potential for code-switching, this second work marks an in-depth penetration into what an indigenous expression can offer in contemporary times. In the poem "labyrinth of scarred hearts," the dilemma of finding a destiny is crucial, as is the hope of humanizing that path and journey. In other cases, reminders are sprinkled throughout to remind the Chicano reader of a purpose and mission to confront engaged priorities: "let the barrio / be a barrio, barrio, barrio / barrio and not blood sweating colonia" (*Nationchild Plumaroja,* "dusk double doors," serpiente section).

Along with his own publications, Alurista coedited a significant and groundbreaking volume, *El Ombligo de Aztlán* (1972), with Jorge González. The student poetry anthology from San Diego State University had the distinction of being the first collection of cultural nationalist writings inspired and influenced almost exclusively by Alurista. In 1973 he experimented further in a series of children's literature, titled *Colección Tula y Tonán: Textos generativos,* in which he espoused a developing cultural nationalism adapted for children. Although the series failed to have widespread success, its attempt was more important than the actual content, serving as alternative materials for teachers at a time when educational institutions were desperately seeking relevant materials for minority children.

In 1974 Alurista made a radical change by turning to theater with his work *Dawn.* In this highly allegorical work, considered by some an *auto sacramental,* a religious or sacramental play, he re-creates the Aztec myth of creation to represent how the Chicano originated. He resorts to a whole gallery of Aztec gods, such as Quetzalcóatl, the god of creation; Huitzilopochtli, the lord of war; Coatlicue, the figure for mother earth or the universe; and others. Much like in Carlos Fuentes' work, *Tiempo mexicano,* Alurista combines divine figures from Aztec mythology with new versions of contemporary gods: Pepsicóatl and Cocacóatl, warlord and warlady, respectively, referred to as "lord of imperialism racism / lady of blood money" (*Dawn,* p. 56). The creation of such contemporary characters aims to satirize the corporate side of capitalism, except that the play emphasizes a subversion of Pepsicóatl and Cocacóatl's avarice and exploitative tendencies. The latter gives birth to newborn twins, named Huehuetéotl and Mixcóatl, who mark a rebirth

and aim to overcome their parents' inhumanity and destruction. The title of *Dawn* denotes such a new beginning.

Alurista continued to develop verses filled with economy and precision within a purely lyrical quality. A short chapbook of poetry, *Cantares arrullos* (1975), reiterates many of his cultural nationalist themes and imagery, except that the focus centers on what he calls Amerindian values (indigenous or Native American). He speaks of black eagles and pyramids, Tláloc (the god of water), "flechas melodías eternas" (eternal melody spears; p. 27), and so forth. The title alludes to a lyrical lullaby or chants of deep reflections that re-create a spiritual ambience. The collection represents a pause for the poet who goes into himself as if to regroup and recharge his combative spirit, which becomes more apparent in his next work.

In *Timespace Huracán: Poems 1972–75* (1976), his third collection of one hundred poems divided into seven sections, Alurista continues to delve further into the resurrection of an Amerindian ideology while attempting to create poems of myth-building, nationhood, and solidarity. The lyrical qualities are richer, more varied, considerably experimental and even more confident in terms of purpose and tonality. Whereas his first books show signs of an uneasy defensiveness, his aesthetic outlook changes into greater affirmation, oftentimes resorting to code-switching as a natural mode of expression, but less so than in his previous works. Even the title contains a new level of neologisms where poetic messages are contained and insular. This "whirlwind" appears as an outpouring of his neo-indigenousness, except that now the focus is principally lyrical poetry that is less socially charged. The nationalist expression takes on new heights, however, by using more Spanish than ever while experimenting with form and the visual structure of the poems. Calligrams and short, rhythmic verses add vitality and dynamism. As Lomelí and Urioste have noted: "[The] book expresses the general sentiment that now is the time to anticipate the coming of a new era" (*Chicano Perspectives in Literature*, p. 18). The entire work is filled with endless innovative versifications in which the poems assume a life of their own: sometimes they resemble birds flying; other times they zigzag or create parallel poetic imagery—insinuating two poems in one; they take on forms like pyramids; and on occasion there are separate fragments of independent stanzas to give the impression of a puzzle. For example, the poem "Dogs Bark Cantos (chants)" is meant to be read downside up:

> dogs bark cantos [chants]
> oceánicos rugidos [oceanic roars]
> mares lunares [play on words between "sea" and
>   "lunar" but also "mole" or "beauty mark"]
> vientos norteños [northern winds]
> humos oscurecen [smokes darken]
>
> (*Timespace Huracán*, p. 47)

Alurista also modifies and injects new meaning into the haikus. Ultimately, the poet manages to create a sense of the neo-indigenous aesthetics that he so ardently professes. In the end he returns to the foundational topics found in *Floricanto en Aztlán*, referring to a new agenda of struggle by first establishing unity among his people in order to sustain the Amerindian nation he envisions.

Alurista's next work, *A'nque: Collected Works 1976–79* (1979), consists of twenty-four poems divided into three sections titled *canciones, cantos,* and *cuentos* (songs, chants, and short narratives). Once again the poet experiments with forms that influence the genre, oftentimes collapsing the three literary forms. He presents poetry that is intended to be either sung or read out loud in a recital. Orality, then, dominates the texts, which explains why he writes words phonetically and with the inflections of common folks. He sets out to contribute further to his Amerindian aesthetic project, but one change is notable: he focuses first on word games and second on ideological content. In other words, he becomes enamored with the infinite potential

of language, dividing words into syllables or mixing syllables into new creative combinations. Words as sound and rhythm resonate more than his social agenda, although this still plays a key role in sustaining his popularity as a poet. Alurista continues in the vein of *Timespace Huracán* through his extensive use of Spanish.

Another notable change is found in his newfound global perspective, particularly in the short narratives section. Two aspects stand out here: a poetic prose prevails more than straight prose, almost detracting from the conventional short story format; and he experiments with various accents. Orality is stretched to its limits (*a'nque* means "although" or "even though"), rendering the work a meditative, quasi-spiritual tone filled with musicality. In some cases he concentrates on melodies, internal rhyme, and, especially, onomatopoeia: "swoosh, swoosh, swoosh, clinkclinkclink" (*A'nque*, p. 54). Word games become more ingenious, sometimes even somewhat cryptic, in his short narratives: "too way out, two güey [an 'ox' but it rhymes with 'way'] out en la com pañía [one word divided into two] del mayor [oldest] to b sellin his color tv too caro [expensive], to carol? tuck'n'roll?" (p. 57). Here the author plays on the homophonic sounds of "*caro*" and "Carol" for an effect. In the process, he invents words such as "tuck'n'roll" and "shoechine" (created by combining pronunciations from English and Spanish in one word), and "wi'chu" (from the expression "what's wrong wi'chu?"). He also modifies set expressions, such as "cada loco con su dogma" ("everyone with their own dogma," thus altering the saying "cada loco con su tema" or "everyone lives in their own world"). Despite its contributions, *A'nque* became a text that few read because its focus was almost too introspective and stylistically driven, with relatively little flair.

If his previous book opened new avenues of expression for Alurista, *Spik in Glyph?* (1981) became a landmark work due to its boundless inventiveness and puns—a trend that has prevailed in his writing up through his groundbreaking novel, *As Our Barrio Turns . . . Who the Yoke B On?* (2000). Three other short collections can be grouped with *Spik in Glyph?*, *Tremble Purple* (1987), *Et Tú . . . Raza?* (1996), and *Z Eros* (1995). In between he also published *Return: Poems Collected and New* (1982). Together the five texts encompass the epitome of what most readers expect to find and enjoy in Alurista beyond *Floricanto en Aztlán,* which is still considered the classic of all his works. With these later works, Alurista's cleverness reached a point whereby he was no longer imitated as much as he was in his first three books. His followers had to sit back and watch him create a literary style. His uniqueness became unprecedented, his virtuosity unparalleled, and his linguistic pyrotechnics unmatched. He became the master of a Spanglish repertoire, thanks, in great part, to codifications and neologisms in which he combined various accents, pronunciations, dialectics, word games, and poetic efficacy with prosaic plasticity—almost to the point of creating a new language.

In *Spik in Glyph?* Alurista is more outrageous and daring, displaying cutting-edge originality, pushing Chicano poetics into a whole new realm. If the kinds of language mattered to the poet up to this point, suddenly he opts for examining language within language, oftentimes creating signifiers within words. His vanguard propensity appears to embrace new experimentations with imagery and metaphors, but he makes another significant turn in order to return to socially relevant issues. His neo-indigenousness for neo-indigenousness's sake, which prevailed in *Timespace Huracán* and *A'nque*, now becomes an exploration into social problems within and beyond Chicano culture, frequently probing into transnational issues. *Spik in Glyph?*, consisting of forty-nine very short poems—except for "borinquen" and "cratching six, plucking one"—offers a high-charged collection of poetry that indulges in constant word play and varied formats. Furthermore, Alurista abandons the Mayan pictographic numbering for the respective pages

that he used in his last two books. Instead, he plays with the names of the numbers by using words in English or Spanish, including improvised syllables that simulate or come close to the sound of a specific number, producing in effect two sounds and two words with unrelated meanings. Thus, one becomes "juan," two becomes "tú," three becomes "tree," four becomes "fi," five becomes "fi," six becomes "seex," seven becomes "se ven," nine becomes "na in," ten becomes "ten," eleven becomes "ee le ven?" twelve becomes "tú él," and "thirteen" becomes "tracy." No explanation is provided for why he stopped with the number thirteen, except for the impossibility to stretch such numbers into further word games. He crisscrosses languages freely to match sounds while proposing a clever interplay of fragments and sometimes whole words. This collection, however, becomes more English dominant, only using Spanish to enhance his word plays.

Alurista's short poems in *Spik in Glyph?* resemble haikus, but more in the sense of aphorisms. Much of his expression in the collection exploits sounds and echoes of sounds. It is perhaps more conventional to have such sonorous connections linked like a chain, but Alurista does that and more, even creating sound associations backwards. For example, in the poem titled "contra," the poet begins with a political allusion to the Contras who opposed the Sandinista government in Nicaragua in the 1980s. Then the poem goes much further, as from contra, the association quickly becomes "contraceptive" a syllable at a time, except that the individual syllables are broken into separate verses, calling greater attention to the semantics of the poem. The other reference to "viet" followed by the word "many" is indeed creative because he has insinuated "Vietnam," but turned the second part of the word backwards to create another independent. Alurista proceeds to place "d c" before "Washington"—except that here it is broken into three distinct syllables: "wash," "in," and "gton." The technique allows him to insert various semantic messages simultaneously.

By reordering words and syllables, the poet accomplishes multiple allusions, such as associating the Contras with contraceptives. The word "viet" actually resembles or echoes "yet," thus critically pointing to the fact that politicians from "thee" 1970s have reverted to tactics of "thee" 1960s:

contra
cept
ive
nasal
sprays
viet
many
around
d c
wash
in
gton
have
resettled
during
thee late
70s
into thee/60s

(*Spik in Glyph?* p. 49)

With so few words, lined vertically, the poem becomes packed with expression, connotations, and significance, consequently saying much more than in the first reading.

In another poem, called "allow," two vertical stanzas are side-by-side. It can be read one stanza at a time or across the two stanzas at the same time, providing a challenging poem of multiple readings. The ideas here become secondary to the internal "dialogue" between one stanza and the other. Alurista appears to insist that poetry is about language and all that it has to offer semantically, syntactically, and linguistically:

allow	and, if one
if thy pleasure	may add,
smiles,	thy fruit

thy roots	will, shall
to hugthee	b, c, see?
earth	the seed
and sky too	in side did
also wel	with in
come, thy	germ in
branches	ate, and enjoy
and thy	fully
fruits, blessed	agreed to
b thy	let the sun
womb	shine in

(p. 32)

The overall sense is one of ecology and praising the earth and the sky. The reverence is accentuated by the use of the older English forms "thee" and "thy." At the same time, it also reads as a prayer by referring to "blessed / b thy / womb" and "thy fruit." Ambiguity is partly at the root of understanding the meaning because it depends on how the poem is read. This requires an active reader to fill in the gaps and pause to reflect on the many messages contained.

Spik in Glyph? is indeed groundbreaking. The title alone entails a series of connotations: "spik" either alludes to "spic," a derogatory term for Latinos, or "speak." By combining the first word with the second, "in," the statement is extended to say either "spik-ing" or "speaking," or both. When the word "glyph"—denoting a symbolic figure or character incised or carved in relief—is attached to the previous two, the result is a provocative wordplay about the nature of language and communication, suggesting levels, nuances, and signification. If this were not enough, Alurista adds a question mark to the enigmatic title, thus further problematizing what he himself is proposing, consequently expanding the possibilities that much more. Besides expressing "speaking in glyph," he may also be inferring that "spics" are in "glyph," implying that these Spanglish speakers are characterized by the usage of their language(s). His focus on language in and of itself denotes a technician who deals with language as if it were a plastic that can be altered or molded. He strips set phrases and words down to their password possibilities to indicate that communication consists of smaller blocks. His expression, then, is filled with explorations into echoes of orality (verbal), as well as printed objects (textual). Together this creates an integrated interplay between performance and meaning; that is, an insistence on reading this literature to an audience (collectively), or on an individual basis (personally).

In the collection *Return: Poems Collected and New* (1982), Bilingual Press/Editorial Bilingüe reprints *Nationchild Plumaroja* in its entirety because the first printing was a rare edition. A new section, called "dawn's eye (1979–1981)," has been added to include the author's other miscellaneous writings up to 1981. The format used in the edition precedes the Chicano Classics series the press would later produce after the mid-1980s and includes a lengthy introduction by Gary D. Keller ("Alurista, Poeta-Antropólogo, and the Recuperation of the Chicano Identity") and an extensive and invaluable bibliography of works by and about Alurista compiled by Ernestina N. Eger. The latter two items contribute notably to enhance the status and importance of Alurista within Chicano letters, thereby documenting a legitimate poet whose writings had attracted considerable critical attention. The added section, "dawn's eye (1979–1981)," contains fifty-seven poems of varied lengths, style, and focus. The collection brings together a number of poems that bring to mind portions of his previous books already discussed. They are generally not as innovative as *Spik in Glyph?* although remnants of such vanguard creativity can be found, particularly in the form of short, image-driven poems that resemble haikus. The most fundamental change from other books is that the lyrical poetry in *Return* offers two distinct orientations: a fair amount of love poetry filled with nostalgia ("till i hold u in my eyes again / u remain imageless," p. 113) is included, and prosaic sections appear ("people asking me" and "sunday desperados"), which anticipate the kind of free-flowing narra-

tive which blends poetry with straight prose, as is evident later in his novel *As Our Barrio Turns . . . Who the Yoke B On?* A significant testimonial poem, "from amsterdam," figures near the end and discusses the wanderings of Chicano writers in an alien ambience such as Amsterdam. This marks one of the first times that the writer acknowledges leaving his environment to taste a foreign country, thus commenting on the reception of Chicano literature by the Dutch. The poetic voice comments, "debo estar soñando / en amsterdam" ("I must be dreaming / in Amsterdam"; p. 134). A new direction in promoting and disseminating Chicano poetry emerges at this point in time, setting the stage for the numerous international conferences and symposia in which Alurista was a focal point. These conferences were held in Germersheim, Germany (1984); Paris (1986); Barcelona (1988); Madrid (1990); Germersheim again (1992); Bourdeaux (1994); Amsterdam (1998); Vitoria, Spain (2000); and Málaga, Spain (2002). Furthermore, the relevance of the collection's title, *Return*, does not become clear until the last poem in the book. It is here that the poet realizes that such wanderings and reflections lead him to conclude the necessity to return to his roots which he can find within himself lost in the chaos of the modern world. He seems to suggest that simplicity is desirable in order to continue the "unbending revolution," but the idea is truncated and consequently left hanging.

After the publication of *Return,* Alurista experienced a temporary creative shutdown. His writings had explored extremes in style and particularly experimentation in semantic fragments. His cultural nationalism had reached a plateau and his mythifications, for some, became if not annoying, at least contrived. He recoiled into his creative bank to resurrect his reputation and status as *the* Chicano poet. In 1987 he presented *Tremble Purple*, a modest collection of seven poems which indulge in some of his stylistic predilections, but they appear mellower and less strained. The tone avoids an overwhelming rapture of Alurista puns and clever combinations, although neither does he stray away completely from them in "left just":

```
–no bombs please
an i
    4
    an i
hammer for hammer
tooth 4 tooth
```

(*Tremble Purple*, p. 21)

In the same poem he displays his ability to squeeze significance out of few sounds and words:

```
possibly correct
not, naught, nut, knot
  right
knot, nut, naught, not
  wrong
```

(p. 22)

The book also focuses on the insurrection developing in Central America, for example the Sandinista movement in Nicaragua which, for Alurista, brought to bear concerns about new Latinos coming into the social scene in the United States. His nationalism then became internationalized as he began to appreciate a larger pan-Latino agenda by referring to "transnational bargaining chips" (p. 58), and he wondered how much the world would change in the late 1980s. His geo-political concerns embraced ecology, corruption, ideological indoctrination, American dominance, and future shock considerations. Therefore, the collection served as a transition for the poet to test the pulse of the world while monitoring his immediate milieu.

With *Z Eros* (1995) and *Et Tú . . . Raza?* (1996), Alurista entered a new stage of maturity in his poetic development, producing two works that are identified as characteristic of his writings. The two resemble and complement each other in overall composition and innovation,

partly due to the proximity of their publication. They continue the author's penchant for creating titles with multiple meanings in order to provoke a central idea. In *Z Eros*, dedicated to eighty-seven women mentioned in alphabetical order, Alurista plays with the various signifiers, such as "the" (or is it "see?"); "eros," or the god of love; and "zeros," or a form of nothingness. The sixty-six poems add to his general repertoire by expanding his thematic emphases, oscillating from personal reflections about the art of writing and the importance of love and company to constant unrequited dialogues with fantasy partners. The lyrical quality of capturing experiential instances predominates with scattered social commentary. The mixture of language appears less of a rhetorical tool than in his previous works because he maintains a single language longer. Nonetheless, he is unable to avoid his trademark word plays:

```
u b u as i b i and we b we
  b history u, i, we make
    b herstory, u, i, we bake
```

(*Z Eros*, p. 9).

Lyrical echoes of desire figure prominently throughout, bringing to mind Federico García Lorca in such lines as "ven tú, que yo quiero verte"("come here because I want to see you," p. 13), or Pablo Neruda's existential poem "Walking Around" in Alurista's "walking about," which highlights nostalgia and longing for a loved one. The collection's contemplative nature reveals a poet more from within while lamenting a loss and bringing to the forefront phantoms of the life he has lost. On one occasion, he even has an internal dialogue with his grandfather in the poem "tú." Here he concentrates less on politics, economics, violence, and injustice in order to focus on "let eros, b!" (p. 63).

Et Tú . . . Raza? appears as more contestatory and at times acerbic in the subjects it explores. The forty-six poems vary considerably in composition, thematics, and tone. In contrast to

Z Eros, Alurista is less introspective about himself as he examines social issues of the 1990s: the Central American wars in Nicaragua and El Salvador, globalization, and corporatism. The title of the collection seems accusatory, wondering if his own people are contributing to such modern ills. The main innovation consists of the poems in the forms of calligraphy, that is, poems in vertical oval shapes. Within these shapes, Alurista experiments once again with the separation of syllables, an insistence on alliteration or internal rhyme, and various languages, including slangs, thus suggesting multiple readings. The following example illustrates an infinite number of word games by stretching semantics and meaning to an extreme with cryptic allusions:

> jazz i
> ficando pel
> daños arch e
> o lógicos slabs up
> on slabs epi taph
> not ions a bout death
> i la capa cid a de
> ser im per ece de roca
> si in moral sin em bargo
> carnal hue sudo y circu latorio
> meta bólico re lamp a go lu min oso
> de e ner gía ovular cáscara
> blank i llos con sal sa ran
> chera, era ché i 'ora
> pos es lama lava
> volcán y águila
> es cameando
> mon
> soon

(*Et Tú . . . Raza?* p. 12)

The collection also contains two other creative innovations: a satirical dramatic piece titled "tango malvino" with its translation ("lastango news") and seven pieces that resemble a narrative prose more than poetry in preparation for his subsequent novel.

In 2000 Alurista published a highly experimental narrative titled *As Our Barrio Turns . . . Who the Yoke B On?* Encased in the title is a mouthful of what might be considered an anti-novel—an extended narrative that deliberately goes against tradition. First, there is an attempt to return to the barrio as his focal point, except that here it acquires a slightly melodramatic tone from the soap opera *As the World Turns*. But Alurista wishes to say more. With his question in the subtitle, he tries to overtly provoke by conflating the words "yoke" and "joke." The reader can take his choice but both options are suggested. The narrator, Xandro Juárez, an alter ego for Alurista, tells his life story as a young man growing up in a cadet school in central Mexico. In this maturation story, Xandro shows how he goes from being a precocious master with words, writing poems for his friends, to becoming a leader of the Chicano movement in San Dago, a veiled reference to San Diego. Two parallel stories emerge: Xandro's militancy as an intellectual at San Dago State University and an ethnography on the local movements. The poetic novel is more about how to tell a story than what is being told. Poetry and prose intermingle with ease through extensive code-switching. In the process, an important historical period and place are recreated to provide insight into the spirit of the times where hippies mixed with political militants, and idealistic youth (existentialists, Taoists, neo-indigenous devotees favoring Native American spirituality) with cultural nationalists. The tumultuous times are represented with great detail through a series of characters surrounding Xandro, namely Ahuitzol (a theoretician), Huitzil (a visionary), Pinder (a guide or guru), and *la chiva* (the goat), the only woman of the group, who reminds them of gender considerations within the movement. While the narrative is dominated by a poetic impulse, containing poetic sections as demarcations for chapters, the work turns into a guessing game. One example is this philosophical word play that defies a Cartesian formula:

> what it is
> ain't

what it was
neither is it
what it will b
what it is
b
what it does
what's done b
just what it was
what will b b what'll do
someday
shall
when what does b what is is

(*As Our Barrio Turns . . .
Who the Yoke B On?* p. 119)

Alurista provokes logic and reasoning in order to understand the origins of things. The question emerges: Is this a documentary, a fictionalized account, or a modern codex to be deciphered? A hint of the novelistic intention might be contained in the subtitle. If so, then Alurista is challenging the reader to figure out who is who because, as the narrator points out in the original epigraph, the names have been changed to protect the guilty.

Alurista's trailblazing trajectory is indeed one endowed with achievements for his rendering of credibility and recognition to code-switching and a Spanglish aesthetics. His body of work serves as the testament of a writer who experienced a revelation and then proceeded to recapture a Chicano past as well as re-create its identity through poetic means. Another major contribution he made was to resurrect the myth of Aztlán so Chicanos would regain a sense of place and belonging in a world that otherwise seemed to marginalize them. Alurista's poetic spirit has left an indelible mark in Chicano letters by enhancing a cultural nationalism that nurtured the movement and by promoting a new language of which Chicanos could feel proud. His taste for experimentation with form, language, thematics, and flair are simply unmatched. As Guillermo Rojas in *Chicano Literature: A Reference Guide* summarizes: "Through his creativeness and sensitivity Alurista has established a poetic legacy that mirrors the struggle and the hope of the Chicanos" (p. 32).

Selected Bibliography

WORKS OF ALURISTA

Floricanto en Aztlán. Los Angeles, Calif.: University of California, Chicano Studies Center, 1971.

Nationchild Plumaroja, 1969–1972. San Diego, Calif.: Toltecas en Aztlán, Cultural de La Raza, 1972.

Colección de Tula y Tonán: Textos generativos. San Diego, Calif.: Toltecas de Aztlán, 1973.

Dawn. Berkeley: *El Grito* Year 7, Book 4: 55–84 (June–August 1974).

Cantares arrullos. Jamaica, New York: Bilingual Press, 1975.

Timespace Huracán: Poems, 1972–75. Albuquerque, N.Mex.: Pajarito Publications, 1976.

A'nque: Collected Works 1976–79. San Diego, Calif.: Maize Press, 1979.

Spik in Glyph? Houston, Tex.: Arte Público Press, 1981.

Return: Poems Collected and New. Ypsilanti, Mich.: Bilingual Press/Editorial Bilingüe, 1982.

Tremble Purple: Seven Poems. Oakland, Calif.: Unity Publications, 1987.

"El Plan Espiritual de Aztlán." In *Aztlán: Essays on the Chicano Homeland*. Edited by Rudolfo A. Anaya and Francisco A. Lomelí. Albuquerque, N.Mex.: Academia/El Norte Publications, 1989. Pp. 1–4.

Z Eros. Tempe, Ariz.: Bilingual Press/Editorial Bilingüe, 1995.

Et Tú . . . Raza? Tempe, Ariz.: Bilingual Press/Editorial Bilingüe, 1996.

As Our Barrio Turns . . . Who the Yoke B On? San Diego, Calif.: Calaca Press, 2000.

EDITED COLLECTIONS

El Ombligo de Aztlán: An Anthology of Chicano Student Poetry. Edited by Alurista and Jorge González. San Diego, Calif.: Chicano Studies Center, San Diego State University, 1971.

Festival de Flor y Canto I: An Anthology of Chicano Literature. Edited by Alurista et al. Los Angeles, Calif.: University of Southern California Press, 1976.

Southwest Tales: A Contemporary Collection. Edited by Alurista and Xelina Rojas-Urista. San Diego, Calif.: Maize Press, 1986.

CRITICAL AND BIOGRAPHICAL STUDIES

Anaya, Rudolfo A., and Francisco A. Lomelí, eds. *Aztlán: Essays on the Chicano Homeland*. Albuquerque, N.Mex.: La Academia/El Norte Publications, 1989.

Elizondo, Sergio. "Myth and Reality in Chicano Poetry." In *Latin American Literary Review* 5 no. 10 (spring–summer 1977): 23–31.

Keller, Gary. "Alurista, Poeta-Antropólogo, and the Recuperation of the Chicano Identity." In *Return: Poems Collected and New*. Ypsilanti, Mich.: Bilingual Press/ Editorial Bilingüe, 1982. Pp. xi–xlix.

Lomelí, Francisco A., with Donaldo W. Urioste. *Chicano Perspectives in Literature: A Critical and Annotated Bibliography*. Albuquerque, N.Mex.: Pajarito Publications, 1976.

———. "El concepto del barrio en tres poetas chicanos: Abelardo, Alurista y Ricardo Sánchez." *De Colores* 3 no. 4 (1977): 22–29.

Maldonado, Jesús. *Poesía Chicana: Alurista, el mero chingón*. Seattle: Centro de Estudios Chicanos, University of Washington, Monograph No. 1, 1971.

Ortego, Philip D. "Chicano Poetry: Roots and Poetry." *New Voices in American Literature: The Mexican American*. Edited by Edward Simmen. Edingburg, Tex.: Pan American University, 1971. Pp. 1–17.

Rojas, Guillermo. "Alurista (1947–)." In *Chicano Literature: A Reference Guide*. Edited by Julio A. Martínez and Francisco A. Lomelí. Westport, Conn.: Greenwood Press, 1985. Pp. 19–34.

Segade, Gustavo. "Chicano Indigenismo: Alurista and Miguel Méndez." *Xalmán* l no. 4 (spring 1977): 4–11.

Ybarra-Frausto, Tomás. "Alurista's Poetics: The Oral, the Bilingual, the Pre-Columbian." *Modern Chicano Writers*. Edited by Joseph Sommers and Tomás Ybarra-Frausto. Englewood Cliffs, N.J.: Prentice-Hall, 1979. Pp. 117–132.

INTERVIEWS

Bruce-Novoa, Juan. "Alurista." *Chicano Authors: Inquiry by Interview*. Austin: University of Texas Press, 1980. Pp. 265–287.

Lomelí, Francisco A. "Interview with Alurista." November 17, 1999. Santa Barbara, California.

Rodríguez del Pino, Salvador. "Interview with Alurista: Encuentro with Chicano Poets Series." University of California, Santa Barbara, 1977. (videotape.)

Rudolfo A. Anaya

(1937–)

MARGARITE FERNÁNDEZ OLMOS

ONE OF THE founders of the contemporary Chicano literary movement, Rudolfo A. Anaya is also one of the most celebrated, versatile, and prolific Mexican American writers, credited as a novelist, poet, essayist, short story writer, anthologist, playwright, an author of children's literature, a travel journalist, and an editor of literary journals. Anaya's most famous work, the novel *Bless Me, Ultima,* published in 1972 and subsequently translated into numerous languages, is one of very few Chicano best-sellers. Anaya, who paved the way for younger Chicano writers and continues to play a pivotal role in the development of the contemporary U.S. Latino literary tradition, is the most studied and most anthologized Mexican American author. The well-known fictional character of his first novel, Ultima, an old Mexican folk healer and witch, is now familiar to several generations of U.S. high school and college students for whom *Bless Me, Ultima* has frequently become their initial introduction to Chicano writing.

Considered the "Dean" of Chicano letters, Anaya has received numerous awards in recognition of his achievements, including the 2001 National Medal of Arts for his literary contributions to contemporary American letters and his lifelong promotion of U.S. Hispanic writers. More than any other prominent Mexican American author, Anaya has inscribed the physical and spiritual landscape of his New Mexico origins onto the terrain of contemporary U.S. literature and led others to appreciate the historical, political, linguistic, and spiritual complexities of his Chicano cultural tradition.

SOUTHWESTERN ROOTS

Throughout Anaya's fictional work, landscape is a palpable presence. Closely identifying with his geographic origins, Anaya was born on 30 October 1937 in Pastura, a small village in the eastern *llanos,* or plains, of New Mexico, a barren area for which he nonetheless has expressed an affinity and a spiritual bond, stating in his essay "Shaman of Words," "My time and place impressed the sacredness of a story into my blood. I was deeply affected by the stark beauty of the eastern New Mexico llano, land of my birth . . . The voices of los antepasados [the ancestors], the song of the river and hills, and the hum of the Earth permeate all of my work" (*Genre,* p. 18).

For Anaya nature creates an epiphany which produces profound transformations in those open to the experience. His sensitivity and his ability to respond to *la tierra* (the land) he credits to the elders of his community, who were his mentors in arriving at a consciousness and a harmonious relationship with the environment. Indeed he credits the oral tradition learned in his youth as the foundation of his skills as a storyteller. His community worked hard but sustained itself with its religious faith and the world of spirits it brought to the New World from the Iberian Peninsula, a new home it filled with its own spiritual essence. "The storyteller's gift is my inheritance. The voice of the llaneros and the Pecos Valley people filled my young ears. I can hear them now. They taught me that stories create mythic time. Stories reveal our human nature and thus become powerful tools for insight and revelation. That's why my ancestors told stories. That's why I write" (*Genre*, p. 16). Among the original settlers of the La Merced de Atrisco Spanish land grant in the Rio Grande Valley, Anaya's ancestors moved eastward into a sheep and cattle grazing area in the mid-nineteenth century. His roots, planted by the Spaniards, were nourished additionally, by the pre-Columbian cultures of the Native Americans. All of these elements appear in his writings.

Anaya's mother and father embodied contrasting cultures from within the New Mexico Hispanic community of his youth: the farmers and the ranchers. His mother, Rafaelita Mares, grew up in a farming family from the Puerto de Luna valley. Traditional people, tied to the land, they were hardworking and poor, and devout Catholics. Widowed and left with a son and daughter from her first husband, who was a *vaquero,* or cowboy, she remarried Martín Anaya, a man who also worked the sheep and cattle of the prominent ranchers of the area, and who had a daughter of his own from a previous marriage. The family would be large. Anaya had a total of three older brothers and six sisters. (Anaya's older brothers left home as adolescents to fight in World War II.) The tranquil life of the farming, settler community of the Mares was a huge departure from the free-spirited, nomadic lifestyle of the *vaquero* culture of Anaya's father. Both cultures would influence the world of the protagonist in his autobiographical first novel, *Bless Me, Ultima.*

Childhood experiences in Santa Rosa, the town to which his family moved soon after his birth, also permeate the novel: the Pecos River where Anaya continued to evolve a spiritual kinship with nature, a river that he claims haunted him with its powerful soul and its beautiful golden carp; the religious instruction of the parish priest, encouraged by his devout mother despite the skepticism of his father; the family tales of his birth assisted by a woman called La Grande (the old wise one) who was not only a midwife but a *curandera* (wise woman, folk healer, shaman) who cured with her knowledge of the sacred secrets of nature. (Clearly this figure would inspire the creation of Ultima, the character who became the namesake of his first novel.) As a baby, Anaya's mother claimed he was offered different items to attract his attention—a saddle, pencil, and paper—and Rudolfo crawled to the writing implements as his mother had hoped he would. His father's way of life was symbolically lost to this son.

Childhood experiences and family legends were complemented by other tales from the oral tradition that were common to all young Hispanic children, particularly that of the frightful wailing woman called La Llorona, the spirit of a tortured soul who was said to have murdered her own children and can still be heard crying for them in the night. Anaya credits such oral tales and legends with inspiring his storytelling instinct. These experiences and the influence of the Catholic Church—encouraged by his mother—were the focus that formed his early life; a crisis of faith in later years would distance Anaya from the Church and lead to a more personal spirituality.

Anaya attended school in Santa Rosa where he moved into an Anglo or English-speaking world, a difficult journey for a boy who had spoken Spanish exclusively until the age of six. His early years of schooling also introduced him to the realities of ethnic difference and social prejudice against Mexicans. In later years, responding to economic and social changes in the post World War II era of the early 1950s, the Anayas joined many other Hispanic families and moved to the booming city of Albuquerque, to the barrio, or neighborhood, of Barelas. There Anaya lived the typical teenager life of the era until a serious swimming accident paralyzed him for several months and required a prolonged hospital stay that changed the rhythms of the soul, altering his life forever. This experience would become the subject of his third novel, *Tortuga.*

After graduating from Albuquerque High School in 1956 and spending two unfulfilling years in business school, Anaya attended the University of New Mexico, majoring in English. He later commented that his high school and college training both shared a lamentable lack of awareness of the significance of the long and vital history of the Hispanic presence in the United States. Both neglected in particular the cultural reality of his Mexican American heritage. The solidarity of fellow Chicano students—a very few of them from his barrio—and a shared interest in art and reading sustained him throughout those years. Initial attempts at writing poetry proved unsatisfactory and while still at the university he attempted to write several novels, an experience he has described as exercises in learning to write. In 1963 Anaya graduated with a bachelor's degree in English and American literature, and in 1968 he completed a master's degree in English, with another master's degree earned four years later in guidance and counseling. In 1966 Anaya married Kansas native Patricia Lawless, and worked during this period as a high school teacher. The 1960s were productive years in many artistic respects as well, as during the early part of the 1960s Anaya began to work on the story that would eventually become his award-winning first novel.

BLESS ME, ULTIMA

In typical Anaya fashion, the author has described his inspiration for the novel as the result of a magical or spiritual encounter. In his essay "An American Chicano in King Arthur's Court" (*Old Southwest/New Southwest: Essays on a Region and Its Literature,* 1987), the metaphor of King Arthur's court with its myths and symbols serves to represent the communal memory of Anglo-Americans whose history and culture in U.S. society is associated almost exclusively with "American" identity. Although Anaya's university training had afforded him an extensive knowledge of the classics of English and North American literatures, as well as contemporary U.S. literature in English, those literary voices could not serve an artist so identified with his Hispanic/Indian/New Mexican identity.

Anaya has described the beginning of his career as a lonely time when writers like him were composing the first models of what would be Chicano literature. And although he had begun to work on the story of a young boy named Antonio Márez and his relationship with his family, Anaya found it difficult to uncover the myths, patterns and symbols of his own culture, his own artistic voice. That voice, he claims, arrived one evening thanks to Ultima's appearance. In "An American Chicano" he describes the encounter: the *curandera* "came to me one night and pointed the way. That is, she came to me from my subconscious, a guide and mentor who was to lead me into the world of my native American experience. Write what you know . . . learn who you really are" (p. 115). Thanks to this illuminating episode, Anaya discovered that the creative symbols and myths of his Hispanic and indigenous heritage were more accessible to him, resulting in a burst of creative energy. His struggle with the art of fiction writing, however, and his painstaking attention to detail, as well as his unrelenting search for a unique literary Chicano voice, led Anaya to spend seven years, from 1963 to 1970, completing *Bless Me, Ultima* after producing some seven complete drafts.

The search for a publisher proved equally daunting. First-time, unknown authors typically find the East Coast publishing world inaccessible, but the mainstream publishing world of the 1970s was even less interested in nontraditional authors, especially those who, like Anaya, incorporated the Chicano culture's distinctive bilingualism into their prose. Although for Anaya it was not unusual to flavor his novel with Spanish words and phrases in order to reflect his bilingual and bicultural reality, mainstream publishers were not yet prepared to appreciate the values of diverse writing and readership. Luckily this rejection did not diminish Anaya's faith in his novel. He submitted his work in response to a call for manuscripts he happened to notice in 1971 in the literary journal *El Grito*, one of the first such Chicano journals published in California by students, professors, and writers. The response was overwhelming. Anaya's manuscript of *Bless Me, Ultima* won the Premio Quinto Sol in 1971 as the best novel written by a Chicano; the following year the small press Quinto Sol published the work, which became an immediate success. The emergence of the novel coincided with the growth of the Chicano movement for social, economic, and political change and struck a chord in the Mexican American population. Today the novel continues to be taught in colleges and universities in Chicano and Latino studies and in other ethnic studies programs, as well as in classes on contemporary U.S. literature.

The success of the novel in part is due to its appeal to those from the Mexican American culture or those who share a similar cultural background and language and recognize much of themselves on its pages; alternatively, it also appeals to those fascinated by a culture so different from their own, yet so authentic to U.S. society. The magic and spirituality of the work distinguishes it from other coming-of-age novels and also enhances its universal significance.

Described as the quintessential Chicano bildungsroman, or coming-of-age novel, it is distinct in several features from the traditional type. Although the reader observes the main character's maturation through a series of rites of passage, the span of time in Anaya's novel—two years of the young boy's life—is much briefer than in traditional novels and, as a character from an ethnically and racially marginalized group in his society, the protagonist's adjustment and integration into the wider society is more problematic.

The main character in the ethnic bildungsroman must redefine himself from the vantage point of his own distinct cultural identity as he attempts to forge a reconciliation with the larger society. The ethnic or minority writer, however, is attempting to create alternative standards and perspectives from his or her position far from the center, on the periphery of mainstream society. In Anaya's novel the figure that will assist the young boy's growth and maturity and bring him into contact with his own Hispanic/ Indian culture (as well as with a mystical, primordial world intimately linked to his rites of passage into maturity and his growing consciousness) is the old female folk healer, Ultima, who makes Antonio her apprentice in the art of traditional healing. A fascinating character, she represents the ancient traditions that will guide the young boy to his true identity.

Bless Me, Ultima is, of course, semi-autobiographical, closely paralleling Anaya's own life: it is the story of the growing awakening of the consciousness of a young boy, Antonio Márez, growing up in a small New Mexico town during and after World War II; the protagonist's parents respect the art of folk medicine and mirror the cultural background of Anaya's—farmers and *vaqueros*; the main character and his siblings are raised in a devoutly Catholic home and move between the Spanish- and English-speaking worlds; and like Antonio, Anaya's brothers were fighting in World War II during most of his early childhood. Some of the other characters share Anaya's teen experiences as well; the swimming injury that left the author temporarily paralyzed appears in *Bless Me, Ultima* when one of Antonio's friends dies in a similar accident. As Anaya has said, however, while his writing is autobiographical, it is not necessarily true to reality; the experiences of the fictional Antonio Márez's differ from those of the author and from Mexican Americans in general in many magical and mysterious ways.

Out of respect for an old woman who, as the local folk healer, has dedicated her life to the community, Antonio Márez's father and mother have decided to provide for her in their home rather than allow her to stay alone on the solitary *llano*. Gabriel, Antonio's father, is a former *vaquero*; his mother, María, is the daughter of farmers, the Lunas. She had convinced her husband to move to the town of Guadalupe for the sake of their children's education. Their differing approaches lead to arguments about Antonio's future: Gabriel wishes the *vaquero* life for his son while the devout María hopes he will become a priest. Pleased with Ultima's arrival into their home, six-year-old Antonio dreams the scenes of his own birth. The Márez family and the Lunas had argued over the child's destiny after he was born, each seeking to take control of the afterbirth and his future by disposing of it symbolically: the Márez *vaqueros* would burn it and scatter the ashes to the winds and the Lunas would bury it in the earth. Ultima, who served as the midwife, halts the disagreement by assuming her right to bury the afterbirth, thereby reserving to herself the knowledge of Antonio's future. Indeed, Ultima's influence will be crucial in reconciling his diverse heritages and the other conflicts he will be forced to confront. In a short period of time, Antonio confronts violence and murder, tragic death, witchcraft, and supernatural phenomena, and actively participates in a ritualized healing during which he experiences a symbolic death and rebirth as a part of his spiritual and psychological maturation.

The novel follows Antonio's telling of the often dramatic experiences that force the young boy to resolve his conflicts of conscience and of doubt: he witnesses the death of a shell-shocked World War II veteran by a mob who shoots him after he kills the town sheriff, a death that leads Antonio to question sin, death, hell, and the moral choices made in the adult world; Antonio's brothers return from the war traumatized by the experience and, rather than fulfill their father's dream to move to California, leave home to follow their independent paths, perplexing the boy with their decision; a young friend takes Antonio fishing and shares the legend of the river god, a golden carp, a belief that challenges his Catholic faith; with Antonio's assistance, Ultima's powers, stronger than that of the local priest, banish a curse set on Antonio's uncle Lucas by the Trementina sisters, witches whose father, Tenorio, threatens the townspeople with their evil powers; Antonio witnesses another violent death when Tenorio, blaming Ultima for the death of one of his daughters, seeks her out to kill her but shoots the town drunk who comes to her defense; Antonio's long-anticipated experience of first Communion fails to bring the boy the enlightenment or spiritual understanding he seeks; Ultima helps a family to dispel a curse on their home by Tenorio; Antonio's friend drowns in a tragic swimming accident; and after a rest on his uncles' farm to recover from these events Antonio suffers a final blow when the murderous Tenorio chases after him with the intent to kill him but Ultima's owl—her spiritual double—saves the boy by attacking his pursuer and dying in the process, leading eventually to Ultima's death as well.

Ultima, as her name implies, represents origins and beginnings, extremes, and the extent of time and distance that Antonio will travel on his passage from innocence into awareness. As in most novels of the coming-of-age genre, however, a significant element of Antonio's development is his relationship with peers who introduce him to a world of native legend and a type of spirituality and morality outside of official, established religion, proposing an alternative religiosity and code of morality based on indigenous beliefs and a contrasting pagan deity to his family's devout Christianity. Their stories create more religious dilemmas for Antonio, adding to his already confused spirituality. Antonio confronts and partially resolves these conflicts in his dreams; what he cannot face or understand on a conscious level is deciphered in the dream world. There his doubts and uncertainties are echoed on the subconscious level and occasionally resolved there as well. Antonio's reactions to these events as expressed in his dreams are the most revealing insights into the growth and evolution of the character, providing a thematic framework of his gradual transformation. As noted earlier, Antonio's first dream is of his own birth; both his biological mother and his spiritual mother (Ultima) are present. The dreams that follow reflect concerns about family and fear of losses (of people and illusions) that prepare him for his passage into adulthood and individuality.

The quest for personal and cultural identity, the significance of Chicano tradition and myth in spirituality and healing, and the role of mentors and guides in psychological and spiritual growth and development are a few of the numerous and diverse themes of the novel. The work's density of symbolism, myth, and cultural references has also inspired a variety of critical responses. The novel's message is one of reconciliation in which conflict and imbalance find a solution in harmony and a recognition of oneness: synthesis resolves opposites and mediates differences. The protagonist needs to reconcile the seemingly irreconcilable opposites in his life presented as dichotomies, the most obvious being the clash between Antonio's father's pastoral lifestyle and his mother's farming tradition, repeated throughout the novel and underscored by their very surnames—Márez (from the Spanish word for sea, *mar*, a people of the plains, as vast as the sea) and Luna (the moon). Other conspicuous examples include the conflicts between male and female, good and evil, love and hate, town and country, a Christian

god versus the golden carp, and so forth. While the principle mediator is of course Ultima—from the first dream in which she resolves the family dispute for control of Antonio's destiny to a dream in which she reconciles the dichotomy of the waters of the sea and the moon by reminding Antonio that "the waters are one"—Antonio is also a mediator, searching for a middle ground.

Bless Me, Ultima offers ample opportunities for archetypal interpretations, particularly given Anaya's remarks on the validity of such an approach as in his observations in David Johnson and David Apodaca's 1990 interview "Myth and the Writer: A Conversation with Rudolfo Anaya:" "One way I have in looking at my own work is through a sense that I have about primal images, primal imageries. A sense that I have about the archetypal, about what we once must have known collectively" (*Rudolfo A. Anaya: Focus on Criticism*, p. 422). Archetypal principles are evident throughout the novel: the feminine principle for example—the life-affirming, intuitive, loving protector and nurturer—can be attributed to Ultima, the Good Mother/Earth Mother, and to the Virgin of Guadalupe, who is Antonio's mother's spiritual protector and appears often in his dreams, and the Terrible Mother—the frightening, emasculating, and life-threatening female figure—corresponds to La Llorona, the legendary mother-figure who destroyed her own children and threatens those of others. Other female characters are presented as contrasts. Tenorio's witch daughters are Ultima's evil counterparts; the female temptress, representing female sexuality, appears on the idealistic plane in the imaginary sirens and mermaids that lure men into dangerous waters, but also in the prostitutes that work in the town brothel, causing men to stray from their rightful path. The archetypal Shadow is illustrated most obviously in the form of evil that Tenorio embodies, but the novel also suggests that evil can reside within, as demonstrated in Antonio's dreams, in which he is forced to confront his own sinful temptations and self doubts.

An interpretation of the novel based on a Jungian approach can run the risk of leading to a static, unchanging mythical perception, one that would not correspond to Anaya's own views on mythology. According to Anaya, mythology should speak to our contemporary lives and give significance to a community rather than simply refashion or retell ancient or universal tales and patterns. In Anaya's estimation, myths can help us understand contemporary realities and conditions. A more dynamic approach to myth criticism in *Bless Me, Ultima* is described by Enrique Lamadrid in "Myth as the Cognitive Process of Popular Culture in Rudolfo Anaya's *Bless Me, Ultima:* The Dialects of Knowledge" as "an ongoing process of interpreting and mediating the contradictions in the everyday historical experience of the people" (*Rudolfo A. Anaya: Focus on Criticism,* 1990, p. 103). The role of Ultima and Antonio as mediators is to reconcile the contradictions enumerated above to arrive at harmony and synthesis and, in keeping with the original role of myth, resolve the internal schisms of their community. A myth criticism interpretation of *Bless Me, Ultima* should not ignore the fact that Anaya describes a specific culture—a particular belief system. While the character of Ultima may reflect universal principles, her responsibility of shaman/*curandera* (often indistinguishable roles) represents an actual vocation, that of a healer or spiritual leader, roles with a useful and important function in an authentic living culture. Both the *curandero* and the shaman can resort to dreams and visions for help and guidance, and both practice medicinal, magical, and spiritual arts. The curative practices of a *curandera* are intertwined with religious beliefs and respect for nature; the shaman is believed additionally to have the power to change her or his human form into that of an animal or spirit. For the traditional healer, a disruption of health is caused by disharmony and imbalance, and healing is a return to oneness and harmony with nature.

Bless Me, Ultima presents these alternative healing values, which have endured for centuries as historically relevant in our contemporary world. Anaya's novels were among the first Chicano writings to successfully incorporate a sacred mythic vision from pre-Columbian and pre-Christian traditions into contemporary fiction; these mythic qualities also led, however, to some of the most strident criticism of Anaya's first novel.

Published during a highly politicized era in U.S. history, the novel's detractors noted its lack of a bold and direct political message as it concentrated instead on myth and symbolism. Marxist critics considered that the focus of a progressive Chicano literature should emphasize the failings of capitalism and its exploitation of the working class, and denounced *Bless Me, Ultima* as being illusory and possessing an evocative vision of the past that ignored the pressing need for change in the present. Some critical readings of the novel have portrayed it as a nostalgic text that romanticizes an era with little or no relevance for a contemporary Chicano reader who is largely urban and for whom the conflicts among rural Hispanic traditions are issues of the past.

Horst Tonn disagrees. In his study "*Bless Me, Ultima:* Fictional Response to Times of Transition," he claims that *Bless Me, Ultima* can be read on another level at which "the novel constitutes a significant response to relevant issues of the community. In broad terms, these issues are identity formation, mediation of conflict, and utilization of the past for the exigencies of the present" (*Rudolfo A. Anaya: Focus on Criticism,* p. 2). In the 1960s, at the time Anaya was writing his work, U.S. society was experiencing a crisis of values similar to that portrayed in the novel in the mid-1940s. The disruptive effects of World War II on veterans and their families, and the internal migration from rural areas to the cities, have their counterpart in the social upheavals of the 1960s when Chicano movements for social change produced a corresponding questioning of cultural values and identities. Just as Antonio and Ultima function as mediators, healing a community suffering from strife and disruption, Tonn considers that "the novel itself can be said to share in and contribute to a mediation process at work in the Chicano community during the 1960s and early 1970s" (p. 5).

Juan Bruce-Novoa agrees, stating in "Learning to Read (and/in) Rudolfo Anaya's *Bless Me, Ultima*" that the novel is reflective of its era in which, in the midst of conflict and of violence, some present proposed alternative responses of "love, harmony, and the brotherhood of all creatures in a totally integrated ecology of resources. . . . *Bless Me, Ultima* belongs to the counter-culture of brotherhood based on respect for all creation" (*Teaching American Ethnic Literatures,* p. 186). For other critics the novel transcends the narrow perceptions of what has been characterized as ethnic or regionalist literature and goes beyond a strictly Mexican American experience to reflect a more universal one.

NEW MEXICO TRILOGY

Bless Me, Ultima incorporates features that are now recognized as Anaya literary hallmarks. These elements appear in the two novels that follow his first, *Heart of Aztlán* (1976) and *Tortuga* (1979)—the three works combined forming what has been called Anaya's "New Mexico trilogy"—and are present in subsequent works by the author. These elements include an emphasis on tradition, myth, spirituality, and cultural identity; the repetition of certain types of characters—shamanic figures, seers, mentors—both from the real world and from legend (La Llorona, the wailing woman of Mexican American folklore, the "Lords and Ladies of Light," for example); an affinity for dream sequences, archetypal patterns, and mystical motifs; the geographic setting of New Mexico and the U.S. Southwest; the use of symbols related to the natural world and the stress on the

need for balance and harmony with the environment. Anaya linked his first three novels with the central importance of a young male protagonist, autobiographical details, and the use of recurring characters from previous novels.

Thus in *Heart of Aztlán* one of the central characters is Jason Chávez, the minor character in *Bless Me, Ultima* of the friend who introduced Antonio to a mystical world of nature. In *Heart of Aztlán* Jason will witness the disintegration of his family as a result of their struggles in their new Albuquerque urban environment. Anaya's second novel is different in style and theme from his first, however. *Heart of Aztlán* is not a strictly coming-of-age novel as its main concern is the Chávez family, and in particular the father, Clemente, whose manhood is tested in the social exploitation and abuse he experiences in the new environment of the city's Chicano barrio The novel is fittingly dedicated to the people of the barrio of Barelas, Anaya's neighborhood as a young teenager in Albuquerque, and to all who fight for dignity and justice. Addressing the displacement of the rural Hispanic communities of New Mexico from the plains to the urban barrios, the work develops a favored Anaya theme, connecting the Chicano community's spiritual well being with its ties to the land and to myth, in this case the legendary myth of Aztlán.

In their demands for social justice in the 1960s, the Chicano community asserted the right to recover lost cultural identities and affirm the validity of Chicano historical roots in U.S. society. The heightened self-awareness of the Mexican American community was accompanied by the articulation of countervalues in contrast and opposition to Anglo culture, among them the promotion of the mythological Aztlán, believed to be the ancestral home of the Aztecs, or *mexicas*, in the U.S. Southwest (an area of the country that stretches from present-day Texas, Colorado, Utah, and California to the Rio Grande). Aztlán became a symbol of Chicano cultural origins, unity, and self-determination, in addition to being a territorial challenge, as a Chicano presence in the area prior to that of the Anglo-Americans afforded them a moral right to these lands. Considered a part of the collective Chicano history, the legend revives Native American myths and symbols rooted in Aztec lore. It states that seven tribes left their seven mountain caves in Aztlán based on a prophesy claiming the Aztecs would find in the south the site where they could establish a new civilization. They would recognize the spot by a sign: an eagle perched on a nopal cactus with a snake in its claws. That site was Tenochtitlán, present-day Mexico City.

In *Heart of Aztlán*, the ideas of displacement and change are centered on a particular family. The hostile urban environment they encounter effects a change on each individual member in various and diverse ways and results in profound consequences. The novel opens with a family in transition: Clemente Chávez, his wife Adelita, and their five children are leaving the small town of Guadalupe for Albuquerque. Clemente was forced to sell the land settled by his ancestors in order to pay his debts. The novel immediately places their plight within a wider sociohistorical context; although the Chávez family and their neighbors are part of a widespread internal migration from rural New Mexico to the urban centers of the state and as far away as California, Clemente recalls earlier events when the arrival of the *tejanos* (Texans) and the new laws imposed by Anglo settlers caused many to lose their ancestral lands much earlier. The family remains in touch with the land and their memories of it through the coffee tin that Adelita fills with the earth surrounding their rural home and carries to Albuquerque.

Heart of Aztlán is a more political novel than *Bless Me, Ultima*. Among the themes the work explores are the fragmentation of family life, moral disintegration, the loss of paternal authority, the negative influence and brutality of drugs and gang culture, the lack of employment and educational opportunities, social neglect, abuse and discrimination, and the erosion of traditional values resulting from the displace-

ment of a people. Although the novel presents these problems from the perspective of an individual family, it is clearly understood to reflect a larger collective process affecting an entire ethnic group. A central focus of the novel is the struggle for workers' rights. The Chávez family and the entire barrio are paralyzed by the oppression of their employers in the railroad industry, the corrupt unions that misrepresent them, and the indifference of the Catholic parish priest. The novel also condemns the traumatic effects of war on young, poor men who have fought for liberties abroad they do not enjoy at home, and the lack of educational and employment opportunities in general.

The solutions to these sociopolitical problems are implicit in the novel but are not exclusively political or ideological; the spiritual element found in all of Anaya's works is also presented as a solution, maintaining that true change requires spiritual growth on a personal and communal level for social struggles to succeed. Radical violent change is rejected in the novel as a futile response to the technological power and control of capitalist oppression. The novel proposes the need to heal the community and the culture with a unifying device in the myth of Aztlán, not as an actual place, but in the healing power of discovering the purpose of one's life, in spiritual union with one's people. The novel proposes the idea that change starts from within, where the answers to the community's problems must first be discovered.

While most of the novel is narrated in standard English, Roberto Cantú notes that the third person narrator on occasion adopts a pachuco discourse, the language of Chicano youths in large urban areas. Although described as a "strange, mysterious argot" (*Heart of Aztlán*, p. 10) in the first chapter of the novel, Cantú observes that pachuco eventually permeates the novel as the narrator gradually employs the language from within, identified with the characters themselves, without recourse to translation or explanation for the reader. Far from hindering the reader's appreciation, however, the use of everyday spoken idiom provides an authentic tone and flavor to the novel and reflects Anaya's sensitivity to the oral tradition and his desire for authenticity. For some critics, the use of Spanish in the work conveys an even more profound significance. For Paul Beekman Taylor, the fact that Anaya has written his novels in English to transmit his ideas regarding Chicano culture represents more than simply another contribution to the body of American letters; in his 1990 article "The Mythic Matrix of Anaya's *Heart of Aztlán*," he claims the author "validates [English] as a transmitter of Chicano lore. Anaya is, quite simply, giving the old myths a new home" (*On Strangeness*, p. 203).

The use of italics to distinguish levels of time and space in the narrative, a device used frequently in *Bless Me, Ultima* in the dream sequences, in *Heart of Aztlán* links the story to an alternative spiritual reality. Italicized segments vary in tone and rhythm from the rest of the narrative and tie the ongoing actions of the plot to an enduring, mythical past. Thus when Adelita fills the coffee can with earth from the land they are leaving, the italics passage that follows underscores an ageless indigenous myth: centuries earlier an Indian woman performed the same ritual as the people "*wandered across the new land to complete their destiny*" (*Heart of Aztlán*, p. 7). These frequent passages provide a mythical-symbolic dimension that amplifies and enriches the emotional impact of the work. Mythical motifs from *Bless Me, Ultima*, most notably the crying woman figure of La Llorona, evolve in this novel to a contemporary form, as the wailing woman here is a destroyer of Chicano males in the form of the piercing whistles of the railroad yards and the sound of police sirens. Though events in the novel may originate in ancient legends, Anaya adapts them to present-day circumstances. An italicized segment about ancient sacrificial rites follows the death of a Chicano worker in the railroad yard, for example; the eagle and serpent of the Aztec culture are reinterpreted in the call for a leader who will rise like an eagle to conquer the steel snakes of the railroad. The myths are not confined to those of the Aztecs, however, as the Llorona legend is of the Hispanic tradition, and the golden deer mentioned frequently in the work in its race across the sky combines the solar symbolism of Aztec mythos with the totemic animal of Native American Pueblo culture. In a 1989 essay entitled "Visit with Rudolfo Anaya" by Karen Kenyon, Anaya observes that his readers were surprised by his infusion of myth into his works: "Our modern impulse had been working to hide out nature as mythmaking animals. I didn't, but instead I followed my intuition, the secrets whispered in the cells, as the source of illuminations. At that source you find humanity, you find myth" (*Confluencia*, p. 126).

Critical response to Anaya's second novel was less favorable than to his first. Critics believed that his attempt to blend sociopolitical themes with mystical elements was contrived and found the work to be disjointed and less polished than *Bless Me, Ultima*, lacking the depth and meticulous prose of his earlier novel. While Marvin A. Lewis noted in his 1981 essay "Review of *Heart of Aztlán*" the novel's redeeming qualities in "its treatment of the urban experience and the problems inherent therein, as well as . . . its attempt to define the mythic dimension of the Chicano experience" (*Revista Chicano-Riqueña*, p. 74), others considered the work to be simplistic and didactic, lacking the organic unity between myth and reality, mystical message and plot development found in *Bless Me, Ultima*. Anaya himself observes in his autobiographical essay that in *Heart of Aztlán* his inclination was to follow the symbols he encountered during that period, and the concept of Aztlán became an obsession, later admitting that the work may have suffered from excess in its reliance on symbols.

During the 1970s Anaya and his wife continued to travel; at the university he started teaching in a creative writing program, and founded a statewide writers' organization, the

Rio Grande Writers Association. Anaya also served on the board of the Coordinating Council of Literary Magazines (CCLM), which brought him into contact with other well-known authors from around the United States. During those years he published translations of Southwest Hispanic folk tales (*Cuentos*, 1980) and was invited to read at the White House in 1980. He also managed to find the time to complete the third novel of the New Mexico trilogy, *Tortuga*, which is linked to the first two novels by the repetition of certain motifs; the extensive use of myth, symbolism, and dreams; and a continued message of healing and hope through the power of love.

Tortuga was inspired by Anaya's traumatic accident during his adolescent years when, while swimming with friends in an irrigation canal, he dove in, hit bottom, and fractured two vertebrae in his neck. Paralyzed instantly, he was saved from death by friends and had to undergo an agonizing process of physical therapy and healing. The anguish and fear he faced and the solutions he forged to heal a battered body and tortured psyche made their way into the novel *Tortuga*, the story of a teenager who must conquer fear and doubt in order to overcome the limitations of his physical condition. As he explains in "Shaman of Words," "I tried to put part of that time of my life into the novel *Tortuga*. I tried to describe what it means to die and go to the underworld and return. Looking back on that time of extreme suffering, I understand how I came to be a shaman of words" (p. 18).

The protagonist of *Tortuga* is a teenager who is paralyzed as the result of a tragic event (we later discover he is the character Ben Chávez from *Heart of Aztlán* and from Anaya's subsequent novel *Alburquerque*). In the first two chapters the reader is introduced to the young man who will be referred to by the nickname the other patients in the hospital have given him: "Tortuga" (turtle) is the name of the turtle-shaped mountain he observes from his hospital bed, but also a name suggested by the oppressive hips-to-head body cast that will

become his "shell" in the hospital location. Everyone that Tortuga meets during his experience—the drivers who transport the young patient to the prisonlike hospital in a converted hearse that serves as ambulance, the doctors, nurses, assistants, therapists, and particularly the other patients—will have a profound effect on the protagonist's physical and spiritual quest. Although the ambulance driver refers to Tortuga Mountain and the healing springs that run below it as magical, the young man's faith in magic "had drained out the night the paralysis came" (*Tortuga*, p. 3). The novel opens with the young man's feeling of hopelessness and alienation and will follow his journey to wellness and understanding.

Like *Bless Me, Ultima* and *Heart of Aztlán*, *Tortuga* is constructed around the motif of the mythic journey or quest and the rites of passage that lead to a more evolved consciousness. A combination of his interaction with other patients and the experience of his own dreams will lead Tortuga to wisdom and psychological evolution. Some of the patients, such as Danny, who suffers from a strange debilitating illness and is a fanatic oblivious to the pain of others, are harmful and disturbing; others, such as Mike, are helpful but unable to transcend the world of material reality, having lost faith in anything outside of himself. Critical to Tortuga's development is the patient Salomón, his mentor, shaman, or guide. Salomón is unusual, however, in that he is a disembodied voice more than a flesh-and-blood character. He communicates telepathically and in dreams, with messages like that of an oracle. Salomón's contacts with Tortuga (italicized in the text) have a healing effect on the adolescent, but Tortuga's physical recovery is linked to his spiritual progress and requires further illuminating experiences to develop. A visit to the ward where the vegetables, or children on life-sustaining devices are kept, and to the ward where patients, surrounded by ghostlike nurses, are sustained by iron lungs which remind Tortuga of strange caskets with thin skeletons horrifies him, creating doubt as to the meaning and validity of life. In another dream, Salomón anticipates Tortuga's actions and anxieties with a message repeated in one form or another throughout the novel: "*As we teach you to sing and to walk on the path of the sun the despair of the paralysis will lift, and you will make from what you've seen a new life, a new purpose*" (p. 41).

Like the wise old Solomon of the Bible, Salomón is a teacher and sage, despite the fact that he is a frail young boy who abides in the vegetable patch of severely crippled children and is completely paralyzed except for his eyes. His philosophical tenet to follow the path of the sun is a familiar one in Anaya's works; it is a solar theology of transformation in which mankind, transformed into a new sun, can shine on new worlds. His ideas reflect a belief in the oneness of all things and a search for harmony, essence, and illumination—themes which are also repeated throughout Anaya's body of work. Furthermore, although Salomón's name is associated with a biblical king, his nickname, Sol, means sun in Spanish. He illuminates Tortuga's journey from a symbolic death to a rebirth as he casts off his shell and former self. His messages instruct Tortuga at crucial moments, explain events, and prepare him for his future role. By the end of the novel, Salomón's messages have been internalized and assimilated, and Tortuga has evolved from a tortured young man to one who has considered the arguments of contrasting creeds, taken the measure of good and evil, and developed knowledge of himself and the universe.

Although the work has been compared to Thomas Mann's *The Magic Mountain* (1924) due to a similar plot and theme (the story of a young man who spends an extended time in a Swiss sanatorium and is changed radically by the experience), *Tortuga* is less ambitious and culturally specific. From the title of the novel to the names of characters, references to foods, places, and traditions described in the Spanish language, *Tortuga* is rooted in the Hispanic culture. The young woman with whom Tortuga falls in love,

Imelda, and her friend, Josefa, cure the patients with their natural folk remedies, which prove more effective than the conventional medicine of the hospital staff. When the folk and Native American traditions of healing and spirituality are compared in *Tortuga* to Anglo medical technology and institutionalized religion, the latter come up short. Although the novel's critique of mainstream medicine and religion does not necessarily call for total elimination of those traditions, it does invite the reader to consider the power of alternative approaches that are compatible and valuable. Although *Tortuga* can be compared to *The Magic Mountain* in its philosophical significance, Anaya is more focused on emotions and would convey his message through the heart. The deformity of the patients is a metaphor for the unequal value systems the protagonist has to learn to distinguish; good and bad, beautiful and ugly, must be differentiated on a level beyond outward appearances. Thus despite his love for the beautiful Ismelda, for example, Tortuga can learn to express feelings of love for the hunchbacked patient Cynthia, a valuable lesson in his moral maturity.

Although *Tortuga* follows a classic plotline of initiation and transformation where a character retreats to an isolated space, undergoes a type of initiation, apprenticeship, and ritual or ordeal in order to achieve enlightenment before his return, Juan Bruce-Novoa notes in "The Author as Communal Hero: Musil, Mann, and Anaya" that Anaya takes the classic hero figure one step further. In Anaya's novel the hero raises not only his own consciousness but that of his community as well, "in order to lead the community into a higher realm of existence, one in which the essential, transcendent order of being can be recognized and followed in everyday life" (*Rudolfo A. Anaya: Focus on Criticism*, p. 193). The protagonist fulfills his destiny as singer or narrator of their shared communal stories of human suffering and regeneration; his self-fulfillment is contingent upon his responsibility to the community.

The metaphor of illness can be extended, however. What will Tortuga's song be about? The immobility of the patients and the bureaucracy of the hospital community extend to the outside world and can be understood as a reference to the situation of the larger Hispanic community, inactive and paralyzed in the face of overwhelming social problems. Within that context, the singer as healer metaphor (in some Native American traditions healer and singer are interchangeable) can be interpreted as a call to action, to an awakening to social consciousness from a life-threatening state of unconsciousness.

MYTHOPOESIS

In "The Achievement of Rudolfo A. Anaya" (*The Magic of Words: Rudolfo A. Anaya and His Writings,* 1982), Antonio Márquez states "Mythopoesis—myth and the art of mythmaking—is the crux of Anaya's philosophical and artistic vision" (p. 45). Anaya's novels and novellas substantiate that claim. In 1984 Anaya published a novella with a title referring to a character that appears in one form or another in most of his works: *The Legend of La Llorona.* In one of many folk versions of the legend, La Llorona, as a result of a betrayal, killed her children and her spirit is forced to wander near the banks of rivers, moaning their loss and searching for her lost progeny. The wailing woman of Mexican American folklore, who has violently transgressed the role of mother, is transformed in Anaya's novels into a present-day threat of some type. In this work she is blended with another legendary female figure, La Malinche, the Indian consort/translator of the sixteenth-century Spanish conquistador, Hernán Cortés. As a counterpart to La Llorona, who many Hispanic children are cautioned against in order to control their wayward behavior, the historical Malintzin (Malinche's original indigenous name) has been reviled for centuries by Mexicans as a symbol of treachery, betrayal, and sexual transgression for her supposed role in assisting the Spaniards in the destruction of the pre-Columbian world. According to Anaya in his 1995 essay "La Llorona, el Kookóee, and Sexuality," his role as an author is "to rescue from anonymity those familiar figures of my tradition. . . . *The Legend of La Llorona* [is] a novella that describes . . . the trials and tribulations of the New World wailing woman, the Malinche of Mexico" (*The Anaya Reader,* p. 426). Anaya's novella reinterprets historical events, changing details to suit his intent to analyze the human motives behind the famous affair between the conquistador and his infamous consort, as well as the cultural impact of the encounter between the Old World and the New.

In 1522 the historical Malinche purportedly gave birth to Cortés' son but was soon married off to one of his lieutenants. In Anaya's novella, set in a mythic world of pre-Columbian society where the gods must be appeased with human sacrifices, Malinche sacrifices her own sons as warriors of a new resistance to Spanish domination. Their bodies are cast into a burning lake and their mother is transformed into the mythic wailing woman of folklore but with a new significance, proclaiming in the final chapter, "My sons were to be made slaves, and I paid for their liberation dearly. Now they are dead . . . but other sons of Mexico will rise against you and avenge this deed. The future will not forgive any of us" (*The Legend of La Llorna,* p. 89).

The same year that *The Legend of a Llorona* was published, Anaya and his wife traveled to China on a trip sponsored by a W. F. Kellogg Foundation fellowship. The trip contributed to his evolving self-definition as a New World man, which he describes in his travel journal *A Chicano in China* (1986). He has claimed in interviews that it helped him to identify more closely with that part of himself that is Native American, given the Asiatic origins of the indigenous peoples of the Americas. Indeed, throughout his collections of short stories, children's tales, plays, and numerous essays, Anaya has consistently emphasized the significance of his diverse cultural heritage.

Although most recognized for his novels, Anaya published a collection of short stories, *The Silence of the Llano,* in 1982. The critic Luis Leal considers the author's stories excellent examples of his mythical interpretation of his native land and the people who inhabit it, comparing Anaya's expression of universal themes through a Chicano perspective to that of such eminent Latin American writers as Juan Rulfo and Gabriel García Márquez: "Anaya, like them, has been able to create new versions out of old realities" ("Voices in the Wind: Anaya's Short Fiction," 1990, p. 335).

In 1987 Anaya returned again to pre-Columbian mythology with his novella *The Lord of the Dawn: The Legend of Quetzalcóatl,* presenting the foremost pre-Columbian Toltec deity as a redeemer and savior who walked among mankind bringing wisdom and art to humanity. Exploring a figure that has fascinated scholars and authors for generations, *The Lord of the Dawn* draws on different Quetzalcóatl archetypes based on mythical historic accounts of a respected leader and spiritual model. In early accounts, according to Anaya's work, the peace-loving ruler was opposed by a warrior class, representing the militarists in Toltec society, who employed the magic of evil sorcerers in order to trick the ruler and priest Ce Acatl Topiltzin Quetzalcóatl, because his opposition to human sacrifice was intolerable to them. After his symbolic death and resurrection, Quetzalcóatl is consumed by flames and his heart rises to the heavens where he becomes the morning star, thus fulfilling the famous prophesy of the return of the deity from the East to redeem the Aztec peoples one day (coinciding with the arrival of Spanish ships to Mexican shores in 1519). Anaya's novella combines various Quetzalcóatl myths, presenting him as a figure devoted to promoting peace, the arts, agriculture, and the ancient teachings, and ends fittingly with the promise of Quetzalcóatl's return. Anaya has stated that he has discovered not only creative inspiration in the Quetzalcóatl myths, but also close parallels between the present and the world of the ancient Toltecs in the struggle between militarists and men of peace, materialist instincts versus spiritual thought, and the fact that Toltec civilization fell due to is reliance on warfare and greed: "Even now, the story of the Toltecs and Quetzalcóatl speaks to us across the centuries, warning us to respect our deep and fragile relationships within nations and among nations, and our meaningful relationships to the earth" ("The Myth of Quetzalcóatl in a Contemporary Setting," p. 199).

Anaya's 1996 modern-day parable, *Jalamanta: A Message from the Desert,* can be considered the culmination of his mythic vision begun with *Bless Me, Ultima* and continued with the two novels that conclude his New Mexico trilogy; it is also an outgrowth of the two novellas mentioned above. Fashioned in the mythical tradition of his novellas, the novel's main character is an original contemporary creation, although the work is written in the tone of an earlier, ancient time. Despite great opposition and repression, Jalamanta is a spiritual leader who spreads the message of personal and communal salvation through the power of love.

The novel takes place in a period described as the end of time and in a place called the fabled Seventh City of the Fifth Sun. It is a repressive society at war with its neighbors, surrounded by outcasts who had revolted in earlier periods, among them Fatimah and Amado, the man she loves who was exiled to the desert for his challenges to official control. During Amado's absence he became known as Jalamanta, "or he who strips away the veils that blind," and gained a reputation as a prophet who preaches the search for a path of illumination to the tribes of the southern desert. The novel explores Amado's return after a thirty-year absence and his continued struggle to preach among the people against the repressive central authority.

The format and tone of Anaya's work bring to mind *The Prophet* by Kahlil Gibran for its combination of poetic parables and aphorisms and a similar philosophy. The prophet-like character also answers questions that lead to teachings on trust, love, and unity with the universe, and the novel is written in a simple, poetic, and archaic tone that recalls biblical language. The philosophical ideas evoke some of the pre-Columbian notions of cosmology expressed in *The Lord of the Dawn* and repeated in subsequent works regarding the end of an era, the age of the Fifth Sun, and the requirements to walk on the Path of the Sun. In ancient Mexican creation myths it was believed that the cosmos had undergone four cycles of creation and destruction prior to the present or fifth age. The present age is that of the Fifth Sun or the Sun of Motion, so called because it moves according to its own path. The end of the age represents, therefore, the beginning of a new era.

Jalamanta does not limit itself to pre-Columbian ideas, however. The work reflects the traditions of thought and practice associated with Buddhism and Hinduism, particularly in the essential principle of the oneness and unity of all existence and the harmony of all religions. The predominant spiritual imagery, however, is from Anaya's own personal background—Christian and Native American. *Jalamanta* evokes the Christian shepherd of souls Jesus Christ and advocates the same Golden Rule of conduct: "Love one another." Native American passions for the earth and its web of life also influence many of the novel's ideas regarding the relationship of men and women to the cosmos, to the natural world, and to the ancestors. A favorite Anaya theme regarding the power of spiritual healing based on Native American spiritual imagery also appears: the belief that the spirits of nature and the animal world are forces that can help human beings in need, and that the modes of ritual healing assisted by a shaman place psychic and even cosmic power at the shaman's disposal. While not directly related to the suspense/detective novels initiated by *Alburquerque* in 1992, *Jalamanta* nonetheless reflects the quest for truth that pervades all of Anaya's writing.

MYSTERY, DETECTIVE FICTION, AND ANAYA'S ONGOING QUEST FOR TRUTH

By the 1980s Anaya had recognized the need for a more political stance in Chicano writing and, in an interview with Rubén Martínez, argued for writing that would allow the community to determine its own cultural path and identity and not accept one imposed from above. His 1992 novel *Alburquerque* is an example of a more socially conscious approach.

The spelling of the title of Rudolofo Anaya's novel is based on a New Mexico legend. In 1880 an Anglo stationmaster reportedly dropped the "r" from the original name of the city because he could not pronounce the word (for Anaya a symbol of the emasculation of the Mexican way of life). The novel restores the city's original name of "Alburquerque" as it addresses other historical events that have left their mark on the region and continue to effect changes there. As is customary in Anaya, the author revisits several of the characters from earlier works in his fictional world and introduces new ones, several of which will be prominent in later novels. Sonny Baca, for example, a minor character in *Alburquerque*, will be the protagonist of his detective novels *Zia Summer* (1995), *Rio Grande Fall* (1996), and *Shaman Winter* (1999).

A more contemporary story with less emphasis on mystical themes and symbols and a more accessible style, *Alburquerque*, a winner of the PEN West Fiction Award, is a departure from Anaya's earlier fiction in both setting and tone, although it expresses Anaya's ongoing concerns: the preservation of communal relationships that have sustained traditional cultures for centuries, the pernicious rise of materialism, and the classic struggle between good and evil. The novel reflects a new emphasis on contemporary social issues that directly affect the U.S. Southwest region and a new literary focus on mystery and suspense. While the novel ostensibly concerns the quest of the young boxer Abrán González to find his biological father (the reader will discover González to be the coyote or ethnically mixed offspring of a Chicano father and Anglo mother—Benji and Cindy from *Heart of Aztlán*), the reader soon discovers that Abrán's personal mission is not really the main story. *Alburquerque* is a wide-reaching and complex tale of history, ambition, and greed and their effects on the people of New Mexico. A real estate development scheme to divert the Rio Grande and create a commercial atmosphere that will threaten the traditional way of life of the Hispanic and Indian communities is a subplot of the novel, which also includes the mystical scenes and characters typical of Anaya's works.

In his 1995 essay "Mythical Dimensions/ Political Reality" *(The Anaya Reader),* Anaya states, "We, the writers, cannot wait out the storm; we have to confront it. For us, the bedrock of beliefs of the old cultures provides our connection, our relationship. From that stance we must keep informing the public about the change that has come upon our land" (p. 351). The rapid economic growth of the U.S. Southwest and specifically of such urban centers as Albuquerque has produced sociopolitical consequences that concern authors like Rudolfo Anaya who feel a spiritual and cultural bond with the area. Who will control the development and benefit from it? What will happen to the natural environment and the traditional peoples of the region? *Alburquerque* confronts these issues via the story of change, growth, and eventual victory of a young man in search of his true identity, arguing for an appreciation of cultural authenticity and an understanding and respect for the past. In several interviews Anaya has referred to the contemporary dynamics of Southwest urbanization as a new model of colonialism. *Alburquerque* takes full advantage of every occasion to insert history into the narration, assuring that readers will not forget that the effects of the old models of colonialism imposed in New Mexico continue to be felt today. Anaya insists on reminding his readers

that conquest and colonization comprise the historical foundation of New Mexico reality.

In 1993 Anaya retired from his teaching post at the university, allowing him more time for his writing and the development of new fictional characters. In Anaya's 1995 novel *Zia Summer,* the author introduces a new character into the Anaya fictional cast, the handsome and daring private detective Sonny Baca (who had a previous brief appearance in *Alburquerque*), and a new Chicano detective into the tradition of U.S. Latino writing. Perhaps Anaya's most memorable character since the Ultima-Antonio pair of his first novel, Baca must solve the murder of his cousin, whose body had been drained of blood and etched with the ancient Zia sun symbol by a terrorist group. The novel contains elements of New Age cults and ancient rituals combined with political corruption and environmental activism. It also introduces another new character, Baca's nemesis, the *brujo* (sorcerer) Raven, an enemy from past lives who, like Sonny, is an old soul. Raven and Sonny are the latest shamanic-type characters in a long list of Anaya healers and visionaries.

True to his allegiance to themes relative to Chicano historical and cultural experience, Anaya has furnished his detective leading man with a unique past that rationalizes Sonny's personality and motives: a renowned ancestor based on the historical figure Elfego Baca, the celebrated sheriff of Socorro County whose fame is the stuff of legends, the theme of novels and plays, and even the basis of a 1958 Walt Disney movie, *Nine Lives of Elfego Baca.* Sonny Baca will follow the path of other Anaya fictional characters who must face a quest or task that will lead to the self knowledge required to fulfill their destiny. Baca meets that challenge in *Zia Summer* and also in the following two novels of Anaya's mystery quartet, *Rio Grande Fall* and *Shaman Winter.* Sonny resists leaving the everyday world to enter the world of dreams where his shamanic power resides, but he is assisted in his endeavors by accepting the guidance of his elders, the intuition of women, and the insight of nature itself (that of the coyote, Sonny's *nagual,* or animal double).

Despite the commercial success of his novels, and the frequent demands on his time, Anaya has never lost contact with his community. He assists young writers and is generous when responding to continuous requests for interviews, and so forth. One of many examples of his commitment to his culture and community is a gathering of children and artists he organized in Albuquerque in the summer of 1990. He proposed they create and burn an effigy of the bogeyman of Hispanic children, El Coco, or El Cucúi (Anaya spells the name phonetically in his works as Kookoóee). Although no one was quite certain what the fearful figure might look like, an ominous sixteen-foot effigy was assembled, tales were told to the children, and the creature was burned one October evening at a community gathering. The children gained much from the event, Anaya states in his essay "La Llorona, El Kookoóee, and Sexuality": "Unlike my generation's experience at school, they saw that the stories from their culture were worthy of artistic attention. As the sun set and the Kookoóee went up in flames, we realized that we had created a truly moving, communal experience. We had taken one character out of the stories or our childhood and rescued him from anonymity" (p. 428).

Anaya's recent detective fiction presents the Chicano culture as part of the modern, multicultural, scientific U.S. world, but also as a people who retain significant elements of their Hispanic and Native American heritage. Their *mestizo,* or mixed tradition, is perceived, among other things, in the religious syncretism of their belief systems and traditional healing practices, and in a profound spirituality. His writings in the 1990s do not represent a break from his former literary or philosophical concerns, however, the setting is still his beloved New Mexico, and the quest for illumination his characters must confront is the same one that has always challenged Anaya, an author for whom writing is a gift and who believes himself destined to be a shaman of words.

Selected Bibliography

WORKS OF RUDOLFO A. ANAYA

NOVELS AND SHORT STORIES

Bless Me, Ultima. Berkeley, Calif.: Quinto Sol Publications, 1972; New York: Warner Books, 1994.

Heart of Aztlán. Berkeley, Calif.: Editorial Justa, 1976.

Tortuga. Berkeley, Calif.: Editorial Justa, 1979; Albuquerque: University of New Mexico Press, 1995.

The Silence of the Llano. Berkeley, Calif.: Tonatiuh-Quinto Sol Publications, 1982. (Short stories.)

The Legend of La Llorona. Berkeley, Calif.: Tonatiuh-Quinto Sol Publications, 1984.

The Lord of the Dawn: The Legend of Quetzalcóatl. Albuquerque: University of New Mexico Press, 1987.

Alburquerque. Albuquerque: University of New Mexico Press, 1992; New York: Warner Books, 1994.

Zia Summer. New York: Warner Books, 1995.

Jalamanta: A Message from the Desert. New York: Warner Books, 1996.

Rio Grande Fall. New York: Warner Books, 1996.

Shaman Winter. New York: Warner Books, 1999.

EDITED COLLECTIONS

Voices from the Rio Grande. Edited with Jim Fisher. Albuquerque: Rio Grande Writers Association Press, 1976.

A Ceremony of Brotherhood, 1680–1980. With Simon J. Ortiz. Albuquerque: Academia Press, 1981. (Anthology of prose, poetry, and artwork.)

Cuentos Chicanos: A Short Story Anthology. Edited with Antonio Márquez. Albuquerque: University of New Mexico Press, 1984.

Voces: An Anthology of Nuevo Mexicano Writers. Albuquerque: El Norte Publications, 1987.

Aztlán: Essays on the Chicano Homeland. Edited with Francisco Lomelí. Albuquerque: Academia/El Norte Publications, 1989. Distributed by University of New Mexico Press.

Tierra: Contemporary Short Fiction of New Mexico. El Paso, Tex.: Cinco Puntos Press, 1989.

The Anaya Reader. New York: Warner Books, 1995. (Collection of essays, stories, and plays.)

ESSAYS

"The Writer's Landscape: Epiphany in Landscape." *Latin American Literary Review*, vol. 5, no. 10 (spring–summer 1977): 98–102.

"The Light Green Perspective: An Essay Concerning Multi-Cultural American Literature." In *The Journal of the Society for the Study of the Multi-Ethnic Literature of the United States* (hereafter *MELUS*), vol. 11, no. 1 (spring 1984): 27–32.

"*The Silence of the Llano*: Notes from the Author." *MELUS*, vol. 11, no. 4 (winter 1984): 47–57.

"An American Chicano in King Arthur's Court." In *Old Southwest/New Southwest: Essays on a Region and Its Literature*. Edited by Judy Nolte Lensink. Tucson, Ariz.: Tucson Public Library, 1987. Pp. 113–118.

"The Myth of Quetzalcóatl in a Contemporary Setting: Mythical Dimensions/Political Reality." *Western American Literature*, vol. 23, no. 3 (November 1988): 195–200.

"The Writer's Sense of Place: A Symposium and Commentaries." *South Dakota Review*, vol. 26, no. 4 (winter 1988): 93–120.

"Aztlán." In *The Anaya Reader*. Edited by Rudolfo A. Anaya. New York: Warner Books, 1995. Pp. 367–383.

"La Llorona, El Kookoóee, and Sexuality." In *The Anaya Reader*. Edited by Rudolfo A. Anaya. New York: Warner Books, 1995. Pp. 417–428.

"Mythical Dimensions/Political Reality." In *The Anaya Reader*. Edited by Rudolfo A. Anaya. New York: Warner Books, 1995. Pp. 345–352.

"The New World Man." In *The Anaya Reader*. Edited by Rudolfo A. Anaya. New York: Warner Books, 1995. Pp. 353–365.

"Shaman of Words." *Genre*, vol. 32, no. 2 (1999): 15–26.

TRANSLATION
Cuentos: Tales from the Hispanic Southwest, Based on Stories Originally Collected by Juan B. Rael. Edited by José Griego y Maestas. Santa Fe: Museum of New Mexico Press, 1980.

DRAMA
Who Killed Don José? Produced by La Compania Menual High School Theatre, Albuquerque, N.Mex., 1987. In *The Anaya Reader.* Edited by Rudolfo A. Anaya. New York: Warner Books, 1995. Pp. 437–493.

Matachines. Produced by La Casa Teatro, Albuquerque, N.Mex. December 1992. In *The Anaya Reader.* Edited by Rudolfo A. Anaya. New York: Warner Books, 1995. Pp. 495–553.

UNPUBLISHED DRAMA
The Season of La Llorona. Produced by El Teatro de la Compania de Albuquerque, Albuquerque, N.Mex., 1979.

The Farolitos of Christmas. Produced by La Compania Menual High School Theatre, Albuquerque, N.Mex., 1987.

Billy the Kid. Produced by La Casa Teatro, Albuquerque, N.Mex.,1997.

Angie. Produced by La Casa Teatro, Albuquerque, N.Mex., July 1998.

Ay, Compadre. Produced by La Casa Teatro, Albuquerque, N.Mex.

OTHER WORKS
The Adventures of Juan Chicaspatas. Houston, Tex.: Arte Público Press, 1985. (Epic poem.)

"Autobiography." In *Contemporary Authors Autobiography Series*, vol. 4. Detroit, Mich.: Gale Research, 1986. Pp. 15–28.

A Chicano in China. Albuquerque: University of New Mexico Press, 1986. (Travel journal.)

The Farolitos of Christmas. Illustrations by Edward Gonzales. New York: Hyperion, 1995. (Children's picture book.)

Maya's Children: The Story of La Llorona. Illustrations by Maria Baca. New York: Hyperion, 1997. (Children's picture book.)

Farolitos for Abuelo. Illustrations by Edward Gonzales. New York: Hyperion Books for Children, 1998. (Children's picture book.)

My Land Sings: Stories from the Rio Grande. Illustrations by Amy Córdova. New York: Morrow Junior Books, 1999. (Children's stories.)

Elegy on the Death of César Chávez. Illustrations by Gaspar Enriquez. El Paso, Tex.: Cinco Puntos Press, 2000. (A poem eulogizing the Mexican American labor activist Cesar Chavez.)

Roadrunner's Dance. Illustrations by David Diaz. New York: Hyperion Books for Children, 2000. (Children's picture book.)

CRITICAL AND BIOGRAPHICAL STUDIES

Bruce-Novoa, Juan. "The Author as Communal Hero: Musil, Mann, and Anaya." In *Ru-*

dolfo A. Anaya: Focus on Criticism.* Edited by Cesar A. González-T. La Jolla, Calif.: Lalo Press, 1990. Pp. 183–208.

————. "Learning to Read (and/in) Rudolfo Anaya's *Bless Me, Ultima.*" In *Teaching American Ethnic Literatures.* Edited by John R. Maitino and David R. Peck. Albuquerque: University of New Mexico Press, 1996. Pp. 179–191.

Bus, Heiner. "Individual Versus Collective Identity and the Idea of Leadership in Sherwood Anderson's *Marching Men* (1917) and Rudolfo Anaya's *Heart of Aztlán* (1976)." In *Rudolfo A. Anaya: Focus on Criticism.* Edited by César A. González-T. La Jolla, Calif.: Lalo Press, 1990. Pp. 113–131.

Calderon, Hector. "Rudolfo Anaya's *Bless Me, Ultima*: A Chicano Romance of the Southwest." *Crítica,* vol. 1 (fall 1986): 21–47.

Candelaria, Cordelia. "Rudolfo Alfonso Anaya (1937–)." In *Chicano Literature: A Reference Guide.* Edited by Julio A. Martínez and Francisco A. Lomelí. Westport, Conn.: Greenwood Press, 1985. Pp. 34–51.

————. "Rudolfo A. Anaya." In *Dictionary of Literary Biography: Chicano Writers,* vol. 82. Edited by Francisco Lomelí and Carl R. Shirley. Detroit, Mich.: Gale Research, 1989. Pp. 24–35.

Cantú, Roberto. "The Surname, the Corpus, and the Body in Rudolfo A. Anaya's Narrative Trilogy." In *Rudolfo A. Anaya: Focus on Criticism.* Edited by César A. González-T. La Jolla, Calif.: Lalo Press, 1990. Pp. 274–317.

Clark, William. "Rudolfo Anaya: 'The Chicano Worldview.'" *Publishers Weekly,* vol. 242, no. 23, June 5, 1995. Pp. 41–42.

Colby, Vineta, ed. *World Authors,* 1985–1990. New York: H. W. Wilson Co., 1995. Pp. 10–14.

Dick, Bruce, and Silvio Sirias, eds. *Conversations with Rudolfo Anaya.* Jackson: University Press of Mississippi, 1998.

Elias, Edward. "*Tortuga*: A Novel of Archetypal Structure." *Bilingual Review/La Revista Bilingüe,* vol. 9, no. 1 (January–April 1982): 82–87.

Fernández Olmos, Margarite. *Rudolfo A. Anaya: A Critical Companion.* Westport, Conn.: Greenwood Press, 1999.

Gerdes, Dick. "Cultural Values in Three Novels of New Mexico." *Bilingual Review/La Revista Bilingüe,* vol. 7, no. 3 (September–December 1980): 239–248.

Gunton, Sharon R., and Jean C. Stine, eds. "Rudolfo A(lfonso) Anaya, 1937–." In *Contemporary Literary Criticism,* vol. 23. Detroit, Mich.: Gale Research, 1983. Pp. 22–27.

Gonzalez-T., César A., ed. *Rudolfo A. Anaya: Focus on Criticism.* La Jolla, Calif.: Lalo Press, 1990.

Kenyon, Karen. "Visit with Rudolfo Anaya." *Confluencia,* vol. 5, no. 1 (fall 1989): 125–127.

Lamadrid, Enrique. "Myth as the Cognitive Process of Popular Culture in Rudolfo Anaya's *Bless Me, Ultima*: The Dialectics of Knowledge." In *Rudolfo A. Anaya: Focus on Criticism.* Edited by César A. González-T. La Jolla, Calif.: Lalo Press, 1990. Pp. 100–112.

Lattin, Vernon E. "Chaos and Evil in Anaya's Trilogy." In *Rudolfo A. Anaya: Focus on Criticism.* Edited by César A. González-T. La Jolla, Calif.: Lalo Press, 1990. Pp. 349–358.

————."The 'Horror of Darkness': Meaning and Structure in Anaya's *Bless Me, Ultima.*" *Revista Chicano-Riqueña,* vol. 6, no. 2 (spring 1978): 50–57.

————."The Quest for Mythic Vision in Contemporary Native American and Chicano Fiction." *American Literature,* vol. 50, no. 4 (1979): 625–640.

Leal, Luis. "Voices in the Wind: Anaya's Short Fiction." In *Rudolfo A. Anaya: Focus on Criticism.* Edited by César A. González-T. La Jolla, Calif.: Lalo Press, 1990. Pp. 335–348.

Lewis, Marvin A. "Review of *Heart of Aztlán.*" *Revista Chicano-Riqueña,* vol. 9, no. 3 (summer 1981): 73–75.

Márquez, Antonio. "The Achievement of Rudolfo Anaya." In *The Magic of Words: Rudolfo A. Anaya and His Writings.* Edited by Paul Vassallo. Albuquerque: University of New Mexico Press, 1982. Pp. 33–52.

Márquez, Teresa. "Works by and about Rudolfo A. Anaya." In *The Magic of Words: Rudolfo A. Anaya and His Writings.* Edited by Paul Vassallo. Albuquerque: University of New Mexico Press, 1982. Pp. 55–81.

Newkirk, Glen A. "Anaya's Archetypal Women in *Bless Me, Ultima.*" *South Dakota Review,* vol. 31, no. 1 (spring 1993): 142–150.

Rogers, Jane. "The Function of the *La Llorona* Motif in Rudolfo Anaya's *Bless Me, Ultima.*" *Latin American Literary Review,* vol. 5, no. 10 (spring–summer 1997): 64–69.

Taylor, Paul Beekman. "The Mythic Matrix of Anaya's *Heart of Aztlán.*" In *On Strangeness.* Edited by Margaret Bridges. Tübingen, Germany: G. Narr Verlag, 1990. Pp. 201–214.

Testa, Daniel. "Extensive/Intensive Dimensionality in Anaya's *Bless Me, Ultima.*" *Latin American Literary Review,* vol. 5, no. 10 (spring–summer 1977): 70–78.

Tonn, Horst. "*Bless Me, Ultima:* Fictional Response to Times of Transition." In *Rudolfo A. Anaya: Focus on Criticism.* Edited by Cesar A. González-T. La Jolla, Calif.: Lalo Press, 1990. Pp. 1–12.

Vassallo, Paul, ed. *The Magic of Words: Rudolfo A. Anaya and His Writings.* Albuquerque: University of New Mexico Press, 1982.

Wilson, Carter. "Magical Strength in the Human Heart." *Ploughshares,* vol. 4, no. 3 (June 1978): 190–197.

INTERVIEWS

Bruce-Novoa, Juan. *Chicano Authors: Inquiry by Interview.* Austin: University of Texas Press, 1980. Pp. 183–202.

Crawford, John. "Rudolfo Anaya." In *This Is About Vision: Interviews with Southwestern Writers.* Edited by William Balassi, John F. Crawford, and Annie O. Eysturoy. Albuquerque: University of New Mexico Press, 1990. Pp. 83–93.

Dick, Bruce, and Silvio Sirias, eds. *Conversations with Rudolfo Anaya.* Jackson: University Press of Mississippi, 1998. Pp. 153–160.

Gonzalez, Ray. "Songlines of the Southwest: *An Interview with Rudolfo A. Anaya.*" *Bloomsbury Review,* vol. 12, no. 5 (September–October 1993): 3, 18.

González-T., César A. "An Interview with Rudolfo A. Anaya." In *Rudolfo A. Anaya: Focus on Criticism.* Edited by César A. González-T. La Jolla, Calif.: Lalo Press, 1990. Pp. 459–470.

Johnson, David, and David Apodaca. "Myth and the Writer: A Conversation with Rudolfo Anaya." In *Rudolfo A. Anaya: Focus on Criticism*. Edited by César A. González-T. La Jolla, Calif.: Lalo Press, 1990. Pp. 414–438.

Jussawalla, Feroza F., and Reed Way Dasenbrock, eds. *Interviews with Writers of the Post-Colonial World*. Jackson: University Press of Mississippi, 1992. Pp. 244–255.

Martínez, Rubén. "Interview with Rudolfo Anaya." In *Conversations with Rudolfo Anaya*. Edited by Bruce Dick and Silvio Sirias. Jackson: University Press of Mississippi, 1998. Pp. 116–130.

Gloria Evangelina Anzaldúa
(1942–)

JUAN D. MAH Y BUSCH

SINCE THE 1980s, Gloria Anzaldúa's writing has been at the forefront of contemporary critical theory. Whether we discuss American literature or cultural studies, border theory or queer theory, feminism or postmodernism, her work is possibly the most analyzed, quoted, and debated of contemporary U.S. Latina and Latino writers. The mixed genre nature of Anzaldúa's poetic-*testimonio* style introduces literary tensions that, coupled with her intentional ambiguity, seems to imply conceptual contradictions. As a result, Anzaldúa's work gives rise to a radical diversity of interpretations, often conflicting and incompatible with one another. Therefore, an understanding of her social context, political interests, and philosophical strategies is important for any close reading and critical understanding of her work. Illuminating her literary strategies, such political and theoretical contexts provide a relative coherence to Anzaldúa's protean content. Though she relentlessly discusses a multiplicity of intersections and a plurality of differences, throughout her writings Anzaldúa grounds her anthologies, essays, poetry, *autohistorias,* and children's stories in embodied experience.

Born on 26 September 1942, Anzaldúa was raised by her parents, Amalia and Urbano, with her sister, Hilda, and her two brothers, Urbano and Oscar, on a farm near Hargill, outside of Edinburg, South Texas. She grew up with animals, land, and nature. At three months of age, Gloria Anzaldúa began to menstruate. This extraordinarily early onset of a menstrual cycle and the pain she endured for seven to ten days of each month encouraged young Anzaldúa to withdraw. As one might expect, suffering through monthly pain at such a young age was undoubtedly formative to her consciousness. Surprisingly, as she attempted to numb herself to her own pain, the suffering connected her to the discomforts, misfortunes, and struggles of the people around her. Therefore, in addition to withdrawal, her suffering paradoxically encouraged a simultaneous sense of connectedness. This confluence of seemingly incompatible qualities underwrites the themes of her literary endeavors and guides her philosophical imagination. Foreshadowing her work's compassionate sensibility, Anzaldúa's solitude coexists with sympathy, interiority with social activism. Her embodied solitude reaches outward, inspiring her notion of a consciousness embedded in social and spiritual realities.

In *Interviews/Entrevistas* (2000), a collection of interviews with Gloria Anzaldúa, she describes midnight episodes of under-the-cover reading sessions. In the working-class, yet conventionally gendered, home in which she grew up, Anzaldúa shared a bedroom with her sister Hilda. In order to avoid her sister's tattling, Anzaldúa explains that she would trade stories for secrecy. As she told Hilda stories, Anzaldúa began to express her creativity through narrative. In the role of storyteller, Anzaldúa continued a family tradition passed on most memorably through her grandmothers, a matrilineal line of creative narrators that gave shape to her reality and provided her with models for narrative subjectivities. Words maintained an introspective solitude even as she utilized language in order to share and sympathize with another person. Again, as in the case of menstrual pain, her storytelling maintained solitude and connectedness, both of which inspired Anzaldúa's more philosophical endeavors. With this twofold function of language, refining self-awareness and developing communicative solidarity, Anzaldúa continued to maintain a socially embedded solitude in the dorms at Texas Woman's University, eight hundred miles from her family; it is in this context that Anzaldúa first experienced lesbian sexuality.

Creative use of language, social solitude, and *lesbiana* sexuality continue to be the hallmarks of Anzaldúa's literary interventions in theories of liberation. It is equally significant that the material context of Anzaldúa's childhood and of her storytelling—whether her narrative content refers to physical pain, sisterly secrecy, or a border geopolitics—gave rise to Anzaldúa's oft-discussed thematics of difference and unity, alienation and synthesis, fragmentation and fluidity, themes whose collective sensibility underwrites her discussion of the embodied spirit, liberation politics, and the development of new knowledge. Through writing, Anzaldúa struggles to reconcile irreconcilable tensions. The confluence of tensions also animates her desire to liberate from unnecessary or undue suffering.

THIS BRIDGE CALLED MY BACK AND MAKING FACE, MAKING SOUL/ HACIENDO CARAS

In literature, Anzaldúa first became known as a conduit for previously unseen identities and unheard voices. In 1981 she coedited, with Cherríe Moraga, a groundbreaking anthology titled *This Bridge Called My Back: Writings by Radical Women of Color*. In her foreword to the second edition, Anzaldúa explains that with *Bridge,* "hemos comenzado a salir de las sombras" (we have begun to leave the shadows; p. v). Though women of color have been actively present throughout U.S. history, especially in resistant movements, there persists an irrational inattention given to their role as activists. The historical and political blind eye extends to their unacknowledged contributions to U.S. intellectual history. Despite this context, and largely because of it, *Bridge* has sold by the thousands, winning the Before Columbus Foundation American Book Award in 1986.

The anthology marks a watershed moment for any discipline that considers the multiethnic nature of U.S. culture and society and the complexities of late-capitalist globalism. It has become required reading for women's studies courses. In Chicana/o Studies, Chicana feminisms arguably have moved from the margins to the center of the field's development, even if their intellectual contributions continue to be undervalued and not matched with increased institutional power. The field's now commonly used suffix, "-a/o," signifies a gendered shift in its theoretical foundations. Anzaldúa's literary interventions continue to be central to this intellectual production. *Bridge* enabled the theoretical articulation of race and feminisms, as noted in Norma Alarcón's 1990 essay, "The Theoretical Subject(s) of *This Bridge Called My Back* and Anglo-American Feminism." The anthology also highlighted ways in which Chicana and other Latina feminisms had given rise to some of the field's literary traditions. The anthology's literary form expanded the notion of *testimonios.* As women wrote of their own respective experiences, the text further merged subject and object, giving rise to texts like the 2001 anthology *Telling to Live: Latina Feminist Testimonios,* collectively edited and written by The Latina Feminist Group. In her *Feminism on the Border: Chicana Gender Politics and Literature* (2000), Sonia Saldívar-Hull theorizes a "fronteriza feminism" in part through a lucid explication of Anzaldúa's work within a literary and political context of the United States and feminisms of color. (Although this is not the place, nor is there sufficient space, for a more elaborate and intricate understanding of Anzaldúa's intellectual interventions, readers should directly engage in the work of U.S. Latina feminists in order to see the rich intellectual context and extensive reach of Anzaldúa's work.)

At first glance the anthology's title, *This Bridge Called My Back,* would seem to be a harbinger of Anzaldúa's later work, signaling a continuum from bridges to borderlands. In the title, however, "bridge," like language, is not just about crossing borders. The image signifies a doubling and duplicitous social location. As much as interpersonal connections, the title *Bridge* describes a structure constructed by others and upon which those other people cross. In other words, the bridge is a structure constructed by society for men of color and Euro-Americans to use the labor of women of color. As mentioned above, this social reality of divisions of (unrecognized) labor is paralleled in academia when writings by feminists of color are used in a just-add-and-stir manner instead of as a body of knowledge that calls into question the very foundations of our understanding of subjectivity and epistemology, that is, of what it is to be a person and how that person comes to knowledge. The twofold meaning of *Bridge*—as a mechanism for connection as well as that which maintains the burden of transmission—signifies the text's purpose: through its writing, a group of "radical women of color" identify oppressions, recognize some of their significant

implications, and transform them into various modes of liberation. A socially imposed existence as a bridge becomes bridges of solidarity and a path toward new knowledge. The authors do so by naming lived experience and by developing a literary space in which liberationist desires can flourish.

Regarding its particular discursive politics, the editors explain in the preface that with the anthology they intended to "expand what 'feminist' means to us" (p. xxiii). The editors wanted the anthology to intervene in feminist thought, especially Anglo-feminisms' problematic inattention to race and class, thereby allowing women of color to maintain a raced, gendered, and classed identity. By bringing words to experience, experiences that previously were invisible and silenced within a women's movement proclaimed as unified, the collection serves as an intervention. As the editors and writers radicalize themselves through writing, putting words to feelings, the anthology attempts to radicalize their social context, including other women of color, men of color, Anglo feminists, and others. Highlighting the hallmark of Anzaldúa's work, the collection's various genres and authors—including letters, formal theory, poetry, and short fiction, written by professional writers, academics, and first-time literary artists—create a collage of perspectives, cultures, and experiences. The bridge, then, not only draws attention to unrecognized labor, but it also offers a crossing for those who contribute, for those who share a particular arrangement of experiences—primarily by, about, and for women of color. For many readers, however, bridges are readily seen as modes of connection. Though she draws on this commonsense notion, Anzaldúa's usage complicates such an understanding. In addition to shared similarities, the anthology's range of genres, types of writers, and multiplicities of experience draw attention to a diversity of differences. These differences reveal Anzaldúa's resistance to a universalized understanding of subjectivity and draw attention to the ways in which many readers are complicit with the various discourses against which the authors write.

Judging on *Bridge*'s wide circulation and numerous citations in its first ten years, Anzaldúa and Moraga were at least partially successful. The text not only illuminated hitherto unexamined intersections of sexisms, racisms, classisms, and heterosexisms, but *Bridge* also brought together a group of writers, women of color, who shared a range of experiences and a set of otherwise diverse social identities. The unseen identities have become readily visible, and the voices' echoes continue to reverberate through the halls of academia. The success has been limited, though. In 1990, nine years after *Bridge* was published, Anzaldúa began the new decade by publishing another anthology, *Making Face, Making Soul/Haciendo Caras: Creative and Critical Perspectives by Feminists of Color.*

A sequel to *Bridge, Haciendo Caras* renewed with vigilance Anzaldúa's effort to intervene in the discursive politics of feminism. From "writings by radical women of color" to "creative and critical perspectives by feminists of color," the difference between the two anthologies' respective subtitles signifies the latter's more formal theoretical focus. *Haciendo Caras* more aggressively claims the feminist title, not only signaling a political shift by the writers (*Bridge* certainly contains a radical politics), but also revealing a shift in its feminist context. *Haciendo Caras* does not abandon its predecessor's poetry, essays, and *autohistorias*; rather, it shifts from a focus on lived experience to a more self-conscious theorization of what occurred within the production of *Bridge. Bridge* and Anzaldúa's *Borderlands/La Frontera: The New Mestiza* (1987), as well as other texts published in the 1980s by women of color, forced Anglo feminist critics to deal with this body of writings, even if at times grudgingly so. To this end, *Haciendo Caras* focuses on the writers' interiority and exteriority—the title represents this figurative interface between the two realms—as well as the subversive act of "making faces," as

Anzaldúa explains in the introduction. With this move toward the center of feminist thought, in her essay "En rapport/In Opposition: Cobrando cuentas a las nuestras," Anzaldúa argues that other tensions have arisen. With the ongoing publishing explosion, women of color, according to Anzaldúa, no longer fight invisibility. They struggle against their own formation of a doctrine, a language about "the ways things should be" (p. 143). As she explains in *Borderlands,* to be static or split is to be dead. Dogmatic politics do both. They ossify understanding, thereby repressing fluidity; and such rigid politics inadvertently split women of color into two opposing categories, those who do things correctly and those who do not. *Haciendo Caras* reflects on *Bridge* and attempts to reinvigorate a philosophy of confluence into what Anzaldúa sees as a new radical feminist rigidity. Yet, these more direct theorizations are balanced by and are grounded in the living body.

Continuously traversing traditional boundaries, Anzaldúa not only edited the anthologies, but she also contributed to them. Her early essay in *Bridge,* "La Prieta," serves as a useful, early introduction to Anzaldúa's work because it demonstrates her narrative method of moving from embodied experience to social knowledge. The essay does so by bringing a materialist-realist narrative clarity to the methods of Anzaldúa's more mystical and spiritual essays found in her later work. "La Prieta" opens with an inspection of the newborn Anzaldúa's buttocks. Her Mamágrande Locha looks for a dark blotch, a common birthmark on children of color. The dark blemish is "the sign of indio, or worse, mulatto blood" (p. 198). Along with her first breaths, Anzaldúa inhaled racism against the indigenous and against other dark people; through the examination her maternal family members inscribed her body with a U.S. racial ideology. The inspection demonstrates a process discussed throughout Anzaldúa's writings: the embodied inscription of various ideological hierarchies, such as a classed race and a gendered sexuality that, for

Chicanas, constitute the politics of being born. Though we can imagine a crying baby, Anzaldúa describes only the infant's quiet; the baby welcomes conflicted maternal compassion. Since the uncoordinated infant has not even developed a voice, she inherits classed racial hierarchies of (de)gradations of dark. In order to gain protection from poverty and punishment, and without any articulate defense mechanisms, the child uncomfortably embraces women's role as transmitters of culture's racist, sexist, heterosexist, and classed repressions. The adult speaker's resistant retrospection is the only refuge from such problematic pain.

The speaker then describes the doctor's explanation for Anzaldúa's early menstruation: he declares that she is like an Eskimo. The doctor thereby racially reduces Anzaldúa's Mexican heritage to Arctic indigenousness. The doctor utilizes his knowledge of Eskimos and his presumption of a phenotypical indigenous similarity in order to mask with false certitude his inability to understand, cure, and control. Though several doctors explain to her that the pain will subside with childbirth—certainly a somewhat empty consolation for a person who is lesbian—the doctor's benevolent racism provides Anzaldúa with an opportunity to create distance between social discourse and her sense of self. The implicit shame and her body's monthly pain inspire Anzaldúa to seek her aforementioned narrative solitude. Since young Anzaldúa knew nothing of Eskimos, the tenuous racial link impelled her to read about this other indigenous race. In *Interviews/Entrevistas* Anzaldúa elaborates, explaining that the literature about Eskimos was the first positive portrayal of indigenous and dark-skinned people with which she had come in contact. As a result, although the speaker does not identify the epistemological motivations, the doctor's reference to Eskimos clearly gives rise to moments of racial revelation for Anzaldúa. She recognizes the oddity of ethnic homogenization in the name of race, and she is drawn to solidarities to which racial ignorance gives birth.

Moreover, through reading about Eskimos, Anzaldúa inadvertently experiences her first positive portrayals of being indigenous.

Young Anzaldúa begins to disassociate, however slightly, from South Texas anti-Mexican racism. The duplicitous racial signifier is not only seen as false, but it also provides literary avenues for socially engaged solitude and insightful solidarities. Then, after the doctor's reductive declaration, on the essay's next page the speaker describes another moment of liberating epiphany: Anzaldúa's father dies, "aorta bursting" as he drives a truck, and after he is thrown from it, the vehicle falls on his face. The violently bloody imagery returns us once again to the body, never allowing epiphanies and liberating moments to divorce themselves from the realities through which they emerge. Anzaldúa explains a significant shift in her sense of self due to her father's death:

> The bloodshed on the highway had robbed my adolescence from me like the blood on my diaper had robbed childhood from me. And into my hands unknowingly I took the transformation of my own being.
>
> (p. 200)

After the cruelly classed death of her father, Anzaldúa no longer holds romantic notions of an invincible patriarchal hero who will protect her. She realizes that she must develop her own agency. Rather than imagine a transcendent self, divorced from her reality, Anzaldúa's transformative agency involves vision, engagement, and intervention.

With such a complex, yet efficient, opening, Anzaldúa frames her ensuing discussion of awareness, choice, and action. The immediate racial inspection of the newborn child becomes the oft-stated maternal warnings that young Anzaldúa—like many Mexican American children—should be wary of the sun, lest she become too visibly dark in a racist United States. This is especially true for the severe modes of anti-Mexican racist oppression in Texas. Anzaldúa inverts the oppressive imagery. She describes one day when she was working in the fields as a child. She decided to replace her *gorra* with a sombrero. Though the bonnet would better protect her from the sun, young Anzaldúa disregards the common concern of darkening. Her preference extends metaphorically. Instead of clinging to gendered protections, with the sombrero's higher and flatter brim, Anzaldúa prefers to see with less obstructed vision. She chooses to sense the movement of a cool breeze breaking through the Texas heat, drying beads of sweat on her neck. Vision fosters transformation. Though the light is bright, increasing clarity diminishes her confinement. With clear vision and a cool breeze resisting labor's heat, a sense of struggle and liberation permeates Anzaldúa's poetic, autobiographical essay. The passage's poetic strength lies not only in the way she sifts through social and moral complexities, all the while maintaining metaphors of liberation and poignant examples of inchoate politics, but also in how Anzaldúa's narrative never loses a sense of realism, relentlessly portraying the intimacy and strength, laboring and wanting of her body.

Though it has no reference to politics, since she frames the scene with the racial inspection, when Anzaldúa replaces the *gorra* with the sombrero the gesture is deeply political. The young laborer literally changes her gendered hats. Anzaldúa does not leave her politics implicit, however. She encourages her reader to extend the politically charged image metaphorically to more creative and spiritual realms. In the following paragraph the speaker explains that the cool breeze becomes a hurricane, a tempest that instigates an uncontrollable flood of images released through the writing process. The author puts words around the images in order to sift through her experiences. Anzaldúa's words are immediate and self-reflective. She relentlessly pushes intimacy toward insight. Her courage, however, does not lack compassion. Despite the essay's incisiveness, the speaker deliberates being hard on her mother, her family,

and her community, however she defines the latter. In short, she frets over discussing not only those who create oppressive social and cultural institutions, but also those who maintain such institutions. As cultural transmitters, women contribute to the bridge-like construction of their own existence; as women interested in a better life, they must cross those bridges. The bridge image demonstrates the trodden-over, unrecognized labor of women of color. It also signifies potential solidarities. With this early essay, Anzaldúa provides her readers with a blueprint for reading her most sustained work.

BORDERLANDS/LA FRONTERA: THE NEW MESTIZA

In 1987 Gloria Anzaldúa published *Borderlands/La Frontera: The New Mestiza*. If *Bridge* introduces her as a Marxist and mystical third-world lesbian feminist, *Borderlands* establishes Anzaldúa as a poetic intellectual. The textual politics, personal content, and literary genre combine to describe and demonstrate Anzaldúa's entwined notions of subjectivity and epistemology. For example, she opens her fourth chapter with visually fluid text not only to describe but also to illustrate the Coatlicue state, Anzaldúa's concept of self-development and knowledge formation:

> protean being
> dark dumb windowless no moon glides
> across the stone the nightsky alone alone
> no lights just mirrorwalls obsidian smoky in the
>   mirror she sees a woman with four heads the
>   heads
> turning round and round spokes of a wheel her
>   neck
> is an axle she stares at each face each wishes the
>   other not there
>
> (p. 41)

The passage describes a person looking into a mirror. With a fluid sense of self, the reflection refracts back at the viewer. The glance is a critical pause in order to apprehend an image of reality as well as a creative pause through which the person re-imagines herself. The passage reveals at least two aspects of *Borderlands*. It reemphasizes Anzaldúa's effort to merge object and subject and it contains references to Latina indigenousness.

As form gives shape to content, *Borderlands* brings together personal experience and indigenous iconography, social history and family stories, weaving a new *testimonio*-like literary genre that can be thought of as a braid, *una trenza* representative of its maternal indigenousness. As Sonia Saldívar-Hull acknowledges in her introduction to the second edition of *Borderlands*, Anzaldúa best describes the text's visually fluid, mixed genre when she calls it "autohistoria." The autohistoria moves beyond traditional literary genres, utilizing a visual narrative that blends diction and imagery in order to unite the artist's soul with the soul of the community. The testimonio-like genre's sensibility is more collective than conventional autobiography and more personal than traditional history, a *testimonio* that narrates a cultural history. Politically problematic and philosophically productive, Anzaldúa's visual narrative elicits a literary image that demonstrates the vexed standpoint of postcolonial feminists of color. As a result, the literary term *autohistoria* does not fully capture the various discourses within the vast theoretical reach of Anzaldúa's narrative. In addition to a cultural-historical *testimonio, Borderlands* is also a political geography, a feminist (of color) manifesto, and a study of social linguistics. *Borderlands'* discursive range lends itself to countless reprintings in various contexts, establishing the book's *mestizaje* narrative as one of the more popular in U.S. Chicana and Chicano literature.

Though many passages and chapters are reproduced as self-contained essays, *Borderlands'* fifth chapter, "How to Tame a Wild Tongue," is possibly the most reprinted piece of Anzaldúa's corpus. Within a Latina American context, it addresses a topic common in postcolonial studies: language. Whereas Anzaldúa describes language in her youth as a literary refuge, a creative and critical space within which she refines knowledge, in "Wild Tongue" she elaborates on language's fraught relationship with liberation. In order to avoid suffering Anzaldúa decides not only to identify language's hierarchical games, but she also reconfigures social discourses by playing with a word or phrase's malleability. Like so many of Anzaldúa's concepts, she resists static theories of language and dogmatic stratagems, preferring a creative understanding of narrative production.

The chapter's title is ironic because, of course, Anzaldúa is not interested in writing a manual on how to tame a wild tongue. She writes about how particular tongues have been silenced historically; and, significantly, she writes about how to strengthen a Chicana's wild tongue. The chapter opens with a dentist's words: as he cleans her teeth, the dentist announces a frustration with Anzaldúa's stubborn tongue. According to him, its defiance needs to be controlled. Though the example does not reverberate with a lived politics in the same way that the image of Anzaldúa donning a sombrero does, the anecdote nonetheless illustrates a common social structure: if a young woman lacks self-control, a deferential silence to male authority, her voice should be controlled, in a word, repressed. Anzaldúa abruptly punctuates the story with a quote by Ray Gwyn Smith that stands as an independent paragraph. In it Smith identifies language as a site of struggle, questioning the significance of worded violence and comparing it to the trauma of war. After the quote Anzaldúa shifts to anecdotes that enable her to theorize more directly the politics of language. The speaker recalls her elementary school's punishment for speaking Spanish, or even for merely correcting the teacher on her surname's pronunciation. The story exemplifies institutional linguistic racism. A school, the place where a child identifies intelligence, teaches Mexican American children that the language they speak marks them as inadequate. The institution's linguistic hierarchy extends to higher education. In Edinburg, at the University of Texas–Pan American, Anzaldúa explains that all Chicana and Chicano students were required to take speech classes. Even within the English language, an accent that does not correspond to the predominant Euro-American dialect is subject to recriminations. This is one example of a socially imposed split that Anzaldúa illuminates: a Mexican American child must choose between her cultural identity and her intellectual identity. The education system's institutional racism represses Mexican American students, limiting their access to recognition as scholars. Such socially split subjectivities and their social consequences are central to Anzaldúa's work.

From a context of struggle between national languages, one that extends historically from the United States' war with Mexico, in "Wild Tongue" Anzaldúa shifts culturally inward to the gendered repressions within Mexican Spanish. She discusses, for instance, the word *nosotras,* with an "-as" ending, which is a first-person plural pronoun from Puerto Rican Spanish that is gendered female. In Mexican Spanish the collective word *nosotros* (we) always is gendered male. Anzaldúa juxtaposes the two words in order to explain another way in which Mexican American women are further split, this time through the gendering of language: women who speak Mexican Spanish reduce themselves, however slightly, to the masculine plural. Because of their mutually exclusive definitions, Chicanas are made to choose between an ethnic identity and a feminist identity. However, while the example illuminates culturally specific gender repression, it also demonstrates diversity of languages within Spanish. If we recognize differences between Mexican and Puerto Rican Spanish, then what other qualities of a language become significant? How is language a historical product of the colonial process? Should we define a linguistic system by national borders or by the qualities that the language produces? In general, how does language function? Specifically for Anzaldúa, how can language function for liberation?

With this narrative movement from the dentist's repression to a linguistic colonialism and a sexist anti-colonial nationalism, Anzaldúa loosens our understanding of standard languages. This is important for her ensuing discussion of language politics, which begins with a listing of the various forms of Chicana and Chicano Spanish.

1. Standard English
2. Working class and slang English
3. Standard Spanish
4. Standard Mexican Spanish
5. North Mexican Spanish dialect
6. Chicano Spanish (Texas, New Mexico, Arizona and California have regional variations)
7. Tex-Mex
8. *Pachuco* (called *caló*)

(p. 55)

In the list, Anzaldúa numbers each dialect, as if to grant it sociolinguistic status as an official language. She legitimizes that which professional scholars and academic institutions diminish. By naming the various systems and relevant discourses, Anzaldúa validates not only the various languages but also the experiences described by their respective words. Moreover, through her trans-Latina adoption of Puerto Rican Spanish, Anzaldúa is politically playful. As she recognizes language's creative aspect, Anzaldúa also allows herself to create language, a sort of narrative transculturalism that attempts to foster awareness. The object continues to become subject.

Though a writer strives to reach readers, especially a writer with Anzaldúa's politics of the marginalized and philosophy of confluence, a wide-ranging readership also poses several problems, especially for a text of minority literature that approaches canonical status in multicultural America. Out of context, such readings can disembody and deracinate

Borderlands' passages. Juxtaposed with "La Prieta," "How To Tame a Wild Tongue" feels more sedate. It is a sensible discussion of experience-based sociolinguistics and the politics of language. In it, Anzaldúa theorizes linguistic *mestizaje,* the politics of language, and the constitutive nature of language as well as its repressive productions. Since these concepts, generally speaking, regard psychological over-determination, hybridity, and language—issues of identity and knowledge that all people presumably share—there is a tendency for readers to prematurely universalize Anzaldúa's work. The fragmented reprinting of Anzaldúa's book encourages this inclination to reduce concepts to generic categories of the universal. The universalizing tendency draws attention to certain concepts and obfuscates others, narrowing Anzaldúa's poetic insights.

Making matters worse for readers, in addition to a range of social discourses, Anzaldúa simultaneously employs her various literary genres. Therefore, she derives a literary accessibility from an interplay among anecdote, myth, and politics. Her mix of genres extends to her content. Anzaldúa makes a reasonable argument against rationalism, spiritualizes materialism, and materializes spirituality. As a result of her multiple mixtures, readers tend to diminish her philosophical underpinnings, categorizing her narrative within the reader's pre-established concerns. Consequently, the same qualities that are praised in Anzaldúa's writing also besiege it with criticism. Critics say that she is too much of this, not enough of that. A classical Marxist may argue against her spirituality: she is not sufficiently materialist. New Age readers may avoid her aggressive politics: she is too abrasive. Even when generous, such readings that attempt to compartmentalize *Borderlands* inadvertently split Anzaldúa's narrative, this time in the name of resistant politics or alternative literatures. The sheer multiplicity and diversity of social discourses that her work addresses makes difficult any effort at a coherent, unifying analysis of Anzaldúa's work.

Though Anzaldúa's narrative resists simple unity, there are recurring thematic threads that bring together her various concepts. Anzaldúa often discusses a border-crossing imperative. As mentioned above, since everyone crosses psychological boundaries in everyday experience, Anzaldúa's imperative seems to address a primarily universal quality of human existence. Such a generalization about what it means to be human at once individualizes and universalizes subjectivity: everyone is the same in that they are radically distinct individuals. This sort of reading underestimates the resistant nature of Chicana and Chicano narrative. Individualist universalisms do not tend to the messy specificity of social realities—certainly not from the perspective of the oppressed and the marginalized for which crossing is often forced, a dangerous path that reveals a person's social vulnerability. Anzaldúa grounds her ethic of crossing in her experiences of oppression and social marginalization. She writes from her perspective as an anti-heterosexist Chicana, an anti-racist feminist, an anti-sexist Marxist, and an anti-capitalist *lesbiana.* This is not a universal identity. It is an entwined identity that, like her literary genre, is a complex, dialogic unity—what Anzaldúa refers to as "completa," or a sense of wholeness that includes fragmentation.

Politically, the simultaneous multiplicity of oppositional identities subverts a tendency toward a narrowly oppositional, reactionary stance. Anzaldúa explicitly avoids such forms of politics, what she calls the "counterstance." Yet, her politics are indeed resistant, transgressive, and intentionally oppositional in multifarious ways. Therefore, though it occurs in the everyday, her imperative is not a weak or diffused sense of border crossing. For Anzaldúa, becoming familiar with the unknown, in a word, learning, is about the development of personal and social awareness through struggle. Therein lies what Sonia Saldívar-Hull refers to in her introduction as a "New Mestiza hermeneutics" and a "feminista Chicana epistemology," the formation of new meanings and the knowledge they yield. With her recognition of Anzaldúa's *autohistoria*, Saldívar-Hull extrapolates a set of theories that regard Anzaldúa's epistemological methodology, her process for developing awareness. After all, *Borderlands'* movement from *la frontera* to the New Mestiza is not narrowly physical. The shift ultimately concerns awareness and its role in a person's ability to act. That is, it regards consciousness.

Borderlands braids various narratives, allowing its content to build a conceptual palimpsest. This, again, is overlooked by decontextualized readings that can misread Anzaldúa's use of historical and cosmological imagery that otherwise may seem straightforward and self-contained. For if she purposefully orders her chapters and rigorously tends to certain grounding concepts like the body, struggle, and identity, one may ask why she opens *Borderlands* with "The Homeland, Aztlán/El otro México," a chapter that situates Anzaldúa's project in relation to the metaphor of Aztlán, a Chicano nationalist homeland. For a Chicana lesbian feminist, such a historically masculinist metaphor would seem to stand in harsh contrast to the rest of Anzaldúa's project. As Anzaldúa points out, the term "Aztecs" means "people of Aztlán" (p. 4). In American (think continent not country) Indian legend, Aztlán mythologizes a return migration.

Anzaldúa opens *Borderlands* with a chapter on Aztlán for at least two reasons. First, her discussion of Aztlán realigns our historical paradigm in various ways. Anzaldúa's prominent use of Aztlán slows time, complicating a nationalist history with a more cosmic or geological sense of time. She paces her narrative with the historical rhythms that underwrite each moment. Since Mexicano nationalism parallels the birth of Anglo-American nationalism, the slower historical pace makes time more spacious and reveals the United States as an imperialist presence in the Southwest, as the region is now called. Aztlán introduces the indigenous, thereby drawing attention not only to a postcolonial loss, alienation, and dispersal but also to a

cultural tenacity that survives colonialism and imperialism. In addition to a slower, more spacious historical paradigm, Anzaldúa's Aztlán converges paradigms. The indigenous imagery draws parallels between the precolonial and the postcolonial periods in Chicana and Chicano cultural history. By naming the region Aztlán, Anzaldúa recalls the legendary return migration: a linear history coincides with a cyclic notion of time. Progressive liberation coincides with mythic cultural memory. Therefore, a careful reader must approach *Borderlands* less as a strictly linear, (anti)colonial project than as a palimpsest, a conceptual layering.

Furthermore, with imagery of Aztlán Anzaldúa situates her history within the standpoint of the marginalized, the overlooked, and the invisible: Mexicanas, Mexicanos, and queer people of the Southwest. Though contemporary media tends to focus on Latino immigration, seemingly reinforced by Anzaldúa's use of Aztlán, it mischaracterizes Chicana and Chicano cultural history. While certainly indigenous Mexicanas and Mexicanos fled the region before and during the U.S. war with Mexico, in South Texas there have always been Mexicanas and Mexicanos, that unique mix of Spanish and Indian people, or what is referred to as mestiza, the Mexican concept of racial mixtures. Why would Anzaldúa use a metaphor of return even though she describes herself as being from South Texas? How can one return to a homeland that she has never left? This ambiguity, like so much of her work, suggests that while Anzaldúa is deeply concerned with the material reality of Chicana and Chicano politics, and while she takes seriously Indian cosmologies, *Borderlands* regards something else. Since the metaphor highlights a return migration to a region the speaker has not left—and a place that does not materially exist—Anzaldúa's Aztlán emphasizes the role of awareness. It is the speaker's return to an uncomfortable comfort, a discomfort utilized for the development of critical awareness.

In addition to paradigmatic shifts, the image serves as a conceptually fertile materialist metaphor. Anzaldúa utilizes the image of Aztlán in order to introduce her methodology for consciousness. The image of a homeland identifies a particular place, a Chicano nationalist narrative, a realigned history, and a creative component, all of which, when united in a complex metaphor, affect the paradigm through which we understand the world—in a word, our awareness. The literary device works to bring together materiality and creativity. Metaphor juxtaposes one object's identity to that of another object. In a poem, love may become a rose, which makes the state of love seem more tangible. The metaphor brings together two objects, love and roses, so that we momentarily look at love differently. We diminish the significance of transitory identities in order to highlight the qualities shared by the two objects.

The same is true for more elaborate social metaphors. For instance, in her essay "La Prieta," the doctor reduces Anzaldúa's identity, as well as her early menstruation, within a racial metaphor that he oddly makes medicinal. Through his homogenous notion of indigenousness, the doctor compares two otherwise dissimilar identities, a young Tejana Chicana with Alaskan Eskimos. When the metaphor is undone and seen for what it is, a form of racial ignorance that produces an inadvertent racism, the doctor's declaration is laughable; but within the context of Anzaldúa's *autohistoria* we never lose sense of the body and the ways in which we live according to these metaphors. Metaphors release a creative, or spiritual, image—oppressive, liberatory, or playful—we then live according to that to which our attention is drawn. In Anzaldúa's opening, I refer to Aztlán as a materialist metaphor because of the way in which it reveals connections and relations among various domains, yet remains relentlessly grounded in the existence of a concrete natural place. Anzaldúa draws attention to qualities that collectively serve as the New Mestiza consciousness and she intends to affect how we perceive

by expanding our historical view, by realigning our point of view, and by discarding strict notions of objectivity. Anzaldúa's Aztlán, then, can be seen as a counter metaphor. Anzaldúa avoids direct realism, preferring a metaphorical flourish that can release the imagination from narrow materialism and other conventional doctrines. Therefore, her poetic *testimonio,* as a genre, crosses a philosophical divide that Anzaldúa openly resists.

Many scholars find fault with Anzaldúa's poetic politics. Against the claim that Anzaldúa's spirituality is too ungrounded, I propose that when read in conjunction with Anzaldúa's larger project, each poetic gesture becomes an experiential vocabulary of the body, and it should be read as a materialist metaphor. The difficulty in much of Anzaldúa's work is the way in which metaphor merges domains. With Aztlán as a materialist metaphor, Anzaldúa more readily moves between the social and the personal, the cultural and the political, the philosophical and the poetic, the spiritual and the material. Each realm merges, or collides, within the imagination while the reader simultaneously maintains recognition of the respective identities involved in the image. Grounded in the concrete, these metaphors of pain, suffering, and desire reach beyond the material images that they contain, as do all metaphors. Such liminal spaces of a creative and critical consciousness are the spirit to which Anzaldúa refers.

A potentially more fatal critique argues that Anzaldúa's use of Aztec iconography romanticizes the indigenous, overlooking not only the Mexican role in Catholic missionary conquests but also neglecting the lived realities of present-day American Indians. When a writer professes a radical politics, poetic license is constrained by the narrative's stated values. While there may be some merit to this argument, the critique is also problematic. Without an indigenous cultural history, Chicanas and Chicanos are nothing more than Spanish Americans, more similar to a Hispanic consciousness. Along with language, the loss of cultural memory is a primary colonial strategy. Anzaldúa counters this with a creative indigenism. Thus, as a postcolonial Chicana feminist, the question should not be whether or not Anzaldúa is culturally justified, but a question of poetic excess. Philosophically, her indigenous iconography realigns paradigms in politically significant ways. Her imagery enables her philosophical *pirámide* and narrative *trenza*.

In *Borderlands* form and content both contribute to Anzaldúa's method for developing awareness. The concept that Anzaldúa later calls *conocimiento* is an understanding that inspires action. The New Mestiza consciousness is the product of such understandings. She explains how an antagonistic existence is still dependent on that which she struggles against. Anzaldúa explains how relations of power lock oppressor and oppressed into reductive violence. Anzaldúa's emphasis, therefore, is in the recognition of such binaries in order to move beyond them:

> A counterstance [is] a step towards liberation from cultural domination. But it is not a way of life. At some point, on our way to a new consciousness, we will have to leave the opposite bank, the split between the two mortal combatants somehow healed so that we are on both shores at once and, at once, see through serpent and eagle eyes. Or perhaps we will decide to disengage from the dominant culture, write it off altogether as a lost cause, and cross the border into a wholly new and separate territory. Or we might go another route. The possibilities are numerous once we decide to act and not react.
>
> (pp. 78–79)

It is significant that while Anzaldúa identifies oppositional engagement as a necessary state, as well as necessary for crossing to a new territory, she privileges the territory, not the crossings. The book's title, after all, is not "borders" but "borderlands." Her usage of indigenous imagery reinforces a standpoint of critical integration. Anzaldúa implicitly writes within a realm that is reminiscent of Latina American indigeneity and a godlike union between the air-borne eagle and an intimately grounded serpent. While "the counterstance [is] a step towards liberation from cultural domination," it is not a way of life. In the text, Anzaldúa adamantly distinguishes between rupture and the new consciousness. The distinction is made more apparent by her use of two interrelated, yet independent, metaphors: Coatlicue and the New Mestiza. One signifies her method and the other represents the more liberating state of consciousness.

The Náhuatl image of the goddess Coatlicue (*coatl* denotes "serpent," *cue* denotes "skirt") entwines the imagery of birth and light. "Coatlicue da luz a todo y a todo devora" (p. 46). In Spanish "da luz" (to give light) figuratively means to give birth. Anzaldúa's language, "da luz a todo," metaphorically binds the process of birth with the giving of light, or knowledge; rebirth extends to the evolution of consciousness, an ongoing development of awareness. As in birth, when an infant departs from the mother's body, the goddess personifies the political and epistemic demands for discursive rupture. Within the context of Anzaldúa's methodology, Coatlicue is the source of life and death. She devours all things. Characterized by serpents, whether it is through her serpent skirt, or at times through her two serpent heads, Coatlicue signifies the grounded nature of human life and, as a goddess, the image maintains a sense of dispersal and transformation. As Coatlicue ruptures certain notions of life, she unites others. All the while, like the serpent whose body embraces land, she is always grounded in the materiality of human reality. Just as the goddess is that which devours and gives (ongoing re-)birth, Anzaldúa unites rupture and integration. The Coatlicue state is a method of perception in which the agent perceives the sociocultural oppression and gives birth to the more liberating: "Coatlicue is a rupture in our everyday world" (p. 46). The rupture exists in contrast to the social splitting of Chicana subjectivity, a split that ranges from capitalist privilege and sexism to discursive categories like race, class, and gender. Pulled by the various demands of diverse social identities, there seems to be no place for a Chicana *lesbiana* standpoint to feel at home. In this sense, like looking in obsidian mirrorwalls, rupture is a prayer-like pause in which the person inhabits a process that yields insight. Entwining the body and knowledge, this process of devouring and giving birth/light produces the New Mestiza.

Anzaldúa demonstrates the relationship between Coatlicue and the New Mestiza by once again discussing a phenomenology of split subjectivities and how social discourses produce it. This is why Anzaldúa discusses shame. Moral emotions reveal a tension between a person's desire and her belief system. It also binds embodied knowledge to the sensation of troubling, internally incompatible emotion. When Anzaldúa describes undoing this tension through a creative use of language she enacts what Saldívar-Hull calls "mestizaje hermeneutics." This relationship between awareness and experience found within meaning is the focus of several chapters, including "Entering Into the Serpent." Throughout the book, references to Tonantzin recall "Entering Into the Serpent," in which Anzaldúa describes discursive silences that divide Chicanas into three categories of meaning, la Virgen, la puta, or La Llorona (the Virgin Mary, the prostitute, and a ghost woman of Mexican legend). Either virgin, whore, or mother, the words give narrow meaning to female experience, especially in relation to sexual desire. In language, the words reductively represent socially imposed, sexist notions of what a woman should be. Since a woman either is or is not a virgin, is or is not mother, the language once again encourages a split between a Chicana's sexuality and her cultural belief systems—the social formation of a personal shame.

Language expresses the meaning of experience produced by culture and social circumstance. The production of the in-

voluntary, enforced silences that Anzaldúa describes give rise to the social split of Chicana subjectivity.

> There are many defense strategies that the self uses to escape the agony of inadequacy and I have used all of them. I have split from and disowned those parts of myself that others rejected. I have used rage to drive others away and to insulate myself against exposure. I have reciprocated with contempt for those who have roused shame in me. I have internalized rage and contempt, one part of the self (the accusatory, persecutory, judgmental) using defense strategies against another part of the self (the object of contempt). As a person, I, as a people, we, Chicanos, blame ourselves, hate ourselves, terrorize ourselves. Most of this goes on unconsciously; we only know that we are hurting, we suspect that there is something "wrong" with us, something fundamentally "wrong."
>
> (p. 45)

Anzaldúa then explains that there are two responses to the shame produced: compulsive adherence to distractions, or "seeing," and the development of consciousness. Chicana experience (which includes social words' discursive significance that split a person's sense of self) coupled with *mestizaje* hermeneutics—the formation of a meaning that liberates awareness—transforms a split subjectivity into a New Mestiza.

Like the protean subject looking into, and through, the obsidian mirrorwalls, Anzaldúa reintroduces the notion of conscious reflection on not-always-conscious experience as well as that which is less conscious or repressed. "To see" unites experience and reflection. Her analysis of Chicana emotions exemplifies this process of perception. She quotes from Gershen Kaufman's *Shame: The Power of Caring*, a text she credits for much of her understanding of the emotion: "Shame is a wound felt from the inside, dividing us both from ourselves and from one another" (p. 42). She resists such division. Instead of focusing on the moral question of right and wrong, Anzaldúa discusses shame in a more therapeutic context of an ethics of self-care. Speaking to this sort of ethical epistemology, feminist philosophers of emotion have shown how emotion is not simply something inside of a person, something that bubbles up without reason; rather, emotions are socially formed and potentially yield knowledge. While emotions have a cognitive component, the moral emotions are unique because they reveal an explicit dissonance between an internalized social expectation and the agent's desire. If the agent identifies the sensation of shame or guilt and pursues a more whole perception of this sensation, she can often observe the moral belief system as well as the repressed desire. With new awareness, a person can then choose to transform either the desire or the belief. As many Chicana feminists have pointed out, the experience of sexuality is probably one of the more significant examples, one in which the social belief systems are hypocritical and unevenly repressive. As a consequence, Anzaldúa brings together her discussion of shame and discursive splits in sexuality with a discussion of *lesbiana* sexuality. However, Anzaldúa is not content with merely seeing oppression.

Grounded in actual experience, *mestizaje* hermeneutics is the development of meaning that produces more liberatory perception. It is enabled by what Anzaldúa calls "la facultad." *La facultad* is a person's capacity for perceiving. Specifically, for Chicanas, years of layered oppressions, social contradictions, and repressed desire have refined the perceptive faculty. "Pain makes us acutely anxious to avoid more of it, so we hone that radar. It's a kind of survival tactic that people, caught between the worlds, unknowingly cultivate. It is latent in all of us" (p. 39). Anzaldúa explains:

> *La facultad* is the capacity to see in surface phenomena the meaning of deeper realities, to see the deep structure below the surface. It is an instant "sensing," a quick perception arrived at without conscious reasoning. It is an acute awareness mediated by the part of the psyche that does not speak, that communicates in images and symbols which are the faces of feelings, that is,

behind which feelings reside/hide. The one possessing this sensitivity is excruciatingly alive to the world.

> (p. 38)

Later in the text she elaborates on the relation between fear and a deeper sensing. Fear may be the product of compulsive habituation. Anzaldúa's deeper sensing is a more genuine and holistic awareness, and as such it maintains its plasticity. It is knowledge that is in the moment. It tends to the moment as well as to an understanding of the moment's context, its layered nature.

With the struggle against fear caused by oppression, *la facultad* is the capacity to see socially constructed systems of belief as well as to explore a deeper sense of self. Moving through the Coatlicue state depends on *la facultad*. Rather than a split or rupture from the social, the Coatlicue state is the ability to see through the splits and ruptures within fear, guilt, or shame. While each emotion unites social expectations and personal desire, to see them is to achieve a new kind of awareness. The agent can then choose to pursue desire in the face of oppression. In so doing, she would bring together her more liberatory perception as she decides how to act. In place of the shameful split, through critical, reflective union of the Coatlicue state, the New Mestiza creates a more harmonious balance between action and desire.

In addition to immediate, socially imposed splits, Anzaldúa also identifies Western intellectual history and its effects on postcolonial *lesbianas* of color. In particular, she draws attention to a Cartesian divide that, though it gives rise to modern philosophy, splits the mind from the body and the individual from the social. She declares that, "this dichotomy is the root of all violence" (p. 37). For this reason, Anzaldúa concludes her explanation of the Coatlicue state by describing a complex union:

> And suddenly I feel everything rushing to a center, a nucleus. All the lost pieces of myself come flying

from the deserts and the mountains and the valleys, magnetized toward that center. *Completa.*

Something pulsates in my body, a luminous thin thing that grows thicker every day. Its presence never leaves me. I am never alone. That which abides: my vigilance, my thousand sleepless serpent eyes blinking in the night, forever open. And I am not afraid.

(p. 51)

In addition to the social belief systems, there is the reality of the mestiza body, its desires and experiences. Holistic and ephemeral, her sense of *completa* is grounded in concrete experience.

Because of split subjectivities, *mestizaje* hermeneutics develop a sense of *completa*. It is this awareness of a critical and open sense of wholeness that characterizes the New Mestiza. It is a standpoint of integration, of synthesis. In order to circumvent the historical weight of Western terms like unity and completeness, Anzaldúa situates *Borderlands* within a different intellectual history. Though Spanish is also a colonial language, Anzaldúa already has diversified it in an earlier chapter, infusing it with creative, postcolonial resistance. This is especially true when she uses it in the English-speaking, U.S. context. The indigenous imagery realigns a reader's philosophical understanding. Her project is not within the discursive terrain of Anglo-America—although it runs up against it—hers is within an experiential and indigenous cartography of Latina liberation. It is inclusive of, yet more than, an oppositional or differential consciousness. The New Mestiza is to have a sense of *completa,* discursively open-ended without sacrificing political stability and a sense of wholeness. This mestiza wholeness is open-ended as well as *completa.* The New Mestiza maintains flexibility. As Anzaldúa states, comparing consciousness of the oppressed to a borderland, "Rigidity means death" (p. 79). And with this flexibility of perception, grounded in experience and a deeper sense of self, the New Mestiza achieves, "a more whole perspective" (p. 79). It is a method in which the agent sees

through that which melts into air; she is then able to reflect on that which is more solid—on desire and on her real social relations.

BORDERLANDS POETRY

Borderlands has two sections. The above development of a method for seeing—or what Anzaldúa calls the New Mestiza consciousness—constitutes the first section, "Atravesando Fronteras/Crossing Borders." Section Two, "Un Agitado Viento/Ehécatl, The Wind," is a collection of poetry that describes that which the speaker actually sees, from her social standpoint and with her political perspective. Since Anzaldúa relentlessly entwines form and content, and since she illuminates a notion of *completa,* her two sections' delineation between *autohistoria* and poetry may seem too severely formalist, oddly contrary to her literary, political, spiritual, and epistemological projects. It is not genre, however, that distinguishes the two textual halves; it is function. They do not privilege distinct forms but a shared sensibility. These poems are not just fragments. They are snapshots, a collection of moments situated within the book's larger developments. In this sense, the poetry demonstrates the complex unity that constitutes Anzaldúa's fragmented and open sense of *completa.*

Anzaldúa significantly frames the poetry with her discussion of the New Mestiza consciousness. She therefore explains how readers should understand the poetry, a pedagogical process inherent to the text that is evident in the way Anzaldúa scales down her Spanish-English translations. From the New Mestiza's earlier discussion of socio-philosophical complexities, at the end of each poem she now defines the Spanish in a simpler, more straightforward linguistic manner. Three poems demonstrate particularly well the continuity between the two sections. "Letting go" not only discusses a process that simultaneously develops awareness and enables an ethics, but it also depicts the tenacity with which the oppressed must take on such a task. "Cihuatlyotl, Woman Alone" utilizes a protean form in order to lucidly discuss, with an appropriately tense sensibility, ways in which the speaker negotiates the formation of her sense of self with her commitments to culture despite its sexist and heterosexist conventions.

The poem that most explicitly parallels the cultural specificity and the epistemological imperative of Anzaldúa's New Mestiza is "To live in the borderlands means you." Like the entire text's metaphorical style, the poem maintains cultural specificity while addressing every reader, delivering the cultural analysis along with a transcultural social ethics. Anzaldúa's other poems relay a similar sensibility, with possibly more abandon than the prose. For instance, the first poem, "White-wing Season," opens with a discussion of gun-carrying white men. The first line's colonial hostility contextualizes the speaker's ensuing resistance. The poem's imagery echoes the *autohistoria*'s third-eye serpent and ends with a description of a stormy sky that is interchangeably red and black, recalling the earlier chapter "Tlilli, Tlapalli: The Path of the Red and Black Ink," which describes a literary imagination that illuminates deeper, underlying structures. Throughout the section, Anzaldúa writes compassionately about women's labor, undocumented migrants, racial conflict, and lesbian love. The poems describe tension between egalitarian hopes and society, sexual desires and culture.

As in the book's opening Aztlán imagery, the speaker maintains a physical sense, as well as a more elusive figurative sense, of lived experience. Recalling her layered materialist metaphors, Anzaldúa's concrete reality grounds poetic exploration. The metaphorical aspect forces readers to reach and thereby enables a critical awareness to flourish. The narrative prose poem "Cervicide" demonstrates this most explicitly. At the most immediate level, the poem describes the speaker's attempt to save her father from the game warden by killing a deer that has become a family friend. The end-of-the-poem definitions, however, reveal a second meaning. Anzaldúa explains that in archetypal symbolism a deer signifies a woman's self. The poem's title doubles, then, as a parallel description of women's conflicted position in an oppressed culture, for often they are made to choose among various incompatible loves: their fathers, cultural survival, and their gendered sense of self. The personal becomes representative of a social structure; the poem's statement is generalizable in its specificity to a particular population. Although *Borderlands'* poetry is discussed with less detail in this essay, this does not diminish the section's significance. Rather, it encourages the reader to engage in the second section to discover the poetry's more phenomenological function in light of the first section's more methodological process.

Even though Anzaldúa's writing continues to evolve, the social themes, narrative sensibility, and political strategies found in *This Bridge Called My Back* and *Borderlands/La Frontera* establish a common set of themes that exist throughout her work. In addition to *Interviews/ Entrevistas*, a collection of interviews edited by AnaLouise Keating, after her famous *autohistoria* Anzaldúa published two children's books and a third anthology. These more recent texts shift toward describing a more explicit value scheme and the corresponding epistemological framework.

CHILDREN'S LITERATURE

In 1993 Anzaldúa published *Friends from the Other Side/Amigos del otro lado*, illustrated by Consuelo Méndez. Her form changes but Anzaldúa's interests remain constant. On a pale crayon blue sky, bordered by drawings of penciled mesquite, soft desert, and a blossoming cactus, the first page of text introduces Prietita, the story's protagonist, through an autobiographical paragraph. In it Anzaldúa describes life growing up in South Texas, along the Rio Grande River, which serves as the Mexican-U.S. border. She discusses a common occurrence that she saw as a child: Mexican women and their children crossing over (to the United States) in search of work and the racism with which they were greeted. Three social discourses collide: class and gender motivate a migration despite the hostilities of racism. Her opening demonstrates the return migration to a homeland that does not want them. As in her previous work, Anzaldúa grounds the story in her personal experience, even giving the protagonist her own childhood nickname, Prietita, thereby reminding readers of her early essay by the same title. As in her essay, the children's book attempts to reinvent the name, transforming it from a derogatory racial term to an idealized young Chicana.

The book's narrator tells the story of young Prietita, who meets a poor and undocumented boy named Joaquín. Significantly, the narrator names the boy before she describes him, giving him a sense of personhood before he is submitted to social codes. After a brief interaction, Joaquín leaves Prietita; but then Prietita hears her cousin, Teté, tease Joaquín. Anzaldúa even allows the story's bully to appear human by making that character a family member connected to the protagonist. Anzaldúa refuses to other. After Prietita steps in to stop her cousin from bullying the boy, she befriends him. She then meets Joaquín's mother and, by taking both of them to a *curandera*'s house, eventually saves them from *la migra,* an I.N.S. agent who is Chicano (the narrator again refuses to other). The children's book privileges a Chicana sensibility, including Spanish character names, a Southwest ecology and geography, and dual language text. In addition to muted crayon colors, Méndez uses pencil to illustrate the story with great detail. Through such elements as a lizard's attentive eye and individual spines of a cactus, she furnishes texture to the Southwest sky, desert trees, and character's skin. On some pages, illustrating house decor or a board game, Méndez

superimposes actual images of religious postcards and *Lotería* boards, a popular bingo-like game. The artwork feels like something a child may experience in rural South Texas.

In 1995 Anzaldúa published *Prietita and the Ghost Woman/Prietita y La Llorana,* illustrated by Christina Gonzalez. This story is once again told by an omniscient narrator from the perspective of young Prietita. Since her mother is sick, Prietita consults a *curandera,* who is teaching Prietita the medicinal qualities of herbs. However, the *curandera* informs Prietita that she is out of the rue needed to cure her mother. The story's first tension, her mother's illness, propels Prietita to search for rue in a forest known to be dangerous. After she silently communicates with various animals, infusing the narrative with a sense of myth and naturalism, she encounters Llorona, the ghost woman of Mexican legends who children are told to fear. This meeting introduces a second tension to the story. Turning the legend on its head, however, and as an adult reader might expect, instead of frightening Prietita, Llorona helps her find the rue as well as her way out of the forest. Gonzalez's artwork shifts from the penciled realism of *Friends* to broader strokes and bolder colors appropriate for *Llorona*'s more mythic storyline. Prietita's hair is thickly black, long and ubiquitous. There is also a clearer delineation between text and artwork, at least in part to allow the text to be more visible among the darker and bolder colors. Whereas *Friends* paints a working-class sensibility through broken fences, torn clothes, and shacks, the *Llorona* text is bordered predominantly by images of the characters. Also, whereas the first book cleanly delineates between standard Spanish and standard English, *Llorona* introduces (and translates) terms from South Texas Spanish into the more standard English text.

In a literary form that overtly attempts to give shape to the next generation's consciousness, Anzaldúa's value scheme, which is reminiscent of *Bridge* and *Borderlands,* is clear. In both children's books, there is an implicit valuation of respect for elders, especially female figures like Joaquín's mother and the *curanderas*. Even Llorona protects Prietita when she is lost in the woods, offering safety to the young Chicana. Both stories equate growth, a central theme in children's literature, with learning knowledge that is often ignored, what Anzaldúa refers to as *desconocimientos*. For instance, after Prietita helps Joaquín and his mother, in the last line of *Friends* the *curandera* tells Prietita, "It's time for you to learn. You are ready now." After facing the forest and finding the rue, the *curandera* then declares to Prietita in the last line of *Llorona*, "You have grown up this night." In both stories the protagonist is willing to engage with the unfamiliar and remains open to that which her friends and family fear. Not only are the fears revealed to be unfounded, but Prietita also learns something that enables her to help her friend and her mother. Whether Prietita is now ready to learn or already has learned, both narratives' transitions hinge on Prietita's willingness to inhabit Anzaldúa's valorization of *nepantla* and *desconocimiento,* key concepts in Anzaldúa's third anthology. The moral values are apparent: respecting cultural wisdom even when it remains socially unsanctioned, engaging *nepantlerismo* and *desconocimiento,* and humanistically connecting with other people and living creatures. The children's books demonstrate a scheme of values Anzaldúa more directly theorizes in her anthologies and *autohistorias.*

THIS BRIDGE WE CALL HOME

In 2002 Anzaldúa coedited with AnaLouise Keating *This Bridge We Call Home: Radical Visions for Transformation.* Her contribution to this work is somewhat controversial for at least two reasons. First, the anthology is so inclusive that it tends to diminish the other anthologies' aggressive attention to the invisible and the unheard specificity of women of color. *Home*'s textual politics privilege coalitions. Yet, experiential complexity remains. Second, in her essay "Now let us shift . . . ; the path of conocimiento . . . inner work, public acts" Anzaldúa is perhaps too clear about her project. The messiness of everyday experience may be reduced to schematics. Because Anzaldúa's literary corpus gives rise to a conceptual palimpsest, there may be a tendency to overlook the work as something that already has been read. This is not the case.

In the essay Anzaldúa develops a specialized language in order to describe seven stages for transformation of awareness. She no longer discusses awareness in general terms like "critical" or "creative," though those qualities are inherent to it. She names the process *conocimiento,* which is an understanding of that which is unfamiliar or ignored, *desconocimiento.* The seven stages move through fear, *nepantla* (an in-between space), overwhelming sense of chaos, a desire to act, the formation of meaning, testing new knowledge, and, upon realizing the failure of a conventional paradigm, shifting realities. Learning is a progression. Anzaldúa mitigates this pedagogical linearity with a parallel indigenous process. Recalling indigenous spirituality, Anzaldúa associates each stage of *conocimiento* with a prayerful direction: south, west, north, east, below, above, and the person's center. Anzaldúa associates this development of consciousness with an interwoven, transcultural spirituality. The Latina American spiritual indigenism extends to Christianity (the seven sacraments), Buddhism (the seven chakras), and West African deities like Yemaya.

From what was previously the protean Coatlicue state, Anzaldúa develops a tight schematic approach to the development of consciousness. It may make Anzaldúa's reader uncomfortable, feeling as though the epistemological system is too clean in order to allow for spontaneity, the messiness of life, and the existence of the impossible. Yet Anzaldúa is clear that even though it is schematic, the process is not a systematic doctrine. Linear progress is coupled with pauses, returns, and denials. However, if one chooses the path of *conocimiento,* then by (Anzaldúa's) definition the person chooses to reject compulsive habits of denial. She or he chooses to engage with *desconocimiento.* The transformation of consciousness, its various states of awareness, impels the person to move continuously between *conocimiento* and *desconocimiento.* However, even though the essay's narrative is smooth, adopting a more standard English, the specialized Spanish terms suggest that the language is an esoteric spiritualist language. The essay undoubtedly will be read as excessively romantic, too spiritualist.

The romantic-spiritualist critique implies that Anzaldúa's writing has become too detached from concrete, lived reality. That is a misreading. Anzaldúa repeatedly defines *conocimiento* as an engaged-in-the-world form of knowledge upon which a person must act.

> Conocimiento comes from opening all your senses, consciously inhabiting your body and decoding its symptoms—that persistent scalp itch, not caused by lice or dry skin, may be a thought trying to snare your attention.
>
> (p. 542)

We may say that her concept is tautological, since her definition of *conocimiento* conveniently fits her scheme of things, but we cannot say that it is detached. The healing imperative that she describes, la Coyolxauqui, involves a person's gaze inward as well as outward. This is why she opens the essay by describing with snake imagery our perception as we walk across a field: "You swallow air, your primal senses flare open. From the middle of your forehead, a reptilian eye blinds, surveys the terrain" (p. 540). While the reptilian perception recalls Buddhist notions of a third eye, Anzaldúa describes the intuition, coupled with the healing imperative, as an inward and outward vision, the personal and the political that are central to feminism. Moreover, there is a long, rich tradition of philosophers who conceive of a union between doing good, feeling healthy, and the good life.

Though she insists that her indigenous iconography circumvents the judgmental nature of those classical moralist doctrines, Anzaldúa utilizes a similar union of one's personhood and justice. Her theory of the self is in a deeply symbiotic relationship with the social and natural world.

Her reader still may be uncomfortable, though. If there is an insight latent within the romanticist critique of her schematic development of awareness it is that Anzaldúa may draw too strong of a parallel between her own perception and the transformation of her social context. Her shifts of consciousness include becoming a well-known professional writer, which is not true for every Chicana lesbian in South Texas. If consciousness is engaged in the world and shaped by that world, how can Anzaldúa speak beyond the "I"? In contrast to her earlier essays, Anzaldúa strikingly switches the pronoun from which she speaks. The first-person of "La Prieta" becomes second- and third-person pronouns. The linguistic shift may overidentify the speaker's perception with the reader's. Thus, she claims that "we" are caught in "profound transformations and shifts in perception" (p. 541). Since the anthology, unlike its two predecessors, includes men and white women, Buddhists and Africanists, as well as other writers with different identities, Anzaldúa's shift from a complex "I" to an overbearing "you" and a holistic, at times reductive, "we" may feel contrived, unreal. But then maybe Anzaldúa attempts to reach for that which is not yet real. To mend this contradiction she claims that the contemporary world, within a "crack of change between millennia" (p. 541), is so radically transformed that we need entirely new ways of seeing. Though we may need a new way of seeing, collective consciousness, relations of power, and materiality have not changed as dramatically as she suggests. This is a common error in historical periodization of the postmodern. Anzaldúa acknowledges as much when she cites the continuing existence of Anglo feminist racisms.

Along with creative and resistant qualities, culture can confine and constrict.

The reader may remain uncomfortable with Anzaldúa's shift away from a less organized process to an organized scheme. Anzaldúa intends to discomfort her readers. Within the healing imperative, the Coyolxauqui impulse, Anzaldúa's process of *conocimiento* requires engagement with the uncomfortable; and it involves the un-othering of other people. A readerly discomfort is intentional. Indeed, it is the first step in her scheme for developing consciousness. It is the shadow that the reading body casts downward on the ground. A person can deny it. He or she can choose to turn a back to the shadow, blinding him- or herself in the sun; or the reader can confront that which he or she as of yet has not. Moving between *conocimiento* and *desconocimiento,* that *nepantlera* in-between, a person chases shadows. Like rainbows, she never quite catches a shadow, never fully grasps it, but in seeking it she sees differently. She shifts her mode of perception. The ignored becomes more familiar. The subject person un-others the object, which often times is oneself.

Guided by her twofold project of liberation and awareness, Anzaldúa continues to write and to act according to her *des/conocimientos.* She continues to cross borders, relentlessly demanding the same of her readers. As she writes, crossing and recrossing bridges, remaking homes, Anzaldúa undoubtedly will continue to make more fertile the borderlands that we all inhabit.

Selected Bibliography

WORKS OF GLORIA EVANGELINA ANZALDÚA

ESSAYS, INTERVIEWS, POETRY, AND SHORT FICTION
"El Paisano Is a Bird of Good Omen" In *Cuentos: Stories by Latinas.* Edited by Alma Gómez, Cherríe Moraga, and Mariana Romo-Carmona. New York: Kitchen Table, Women of Color Press, 1983.

Borderlands/La Frontera: The New Mestiza. San Francisco: Spinsters/Aunt Lute, 1987.

"To(o) Queer the Writer." In *Inversions: Writing by Dykes, Queers and Lesbians.* Edited by Betsy Warland. Vancouver: Press Gang Publishers, 1991.

Interviews/Entrevistas: Gloria E. Anzaldúa. Edited by AnaLouise Keating. New York: Routledge, 2000.

ANTHOLOGIES
This Bridge Called My Back: Writings by Radical Women of Color. Edited by Gloria Anzaldúa and Cherríe Moraga. Watertown, Mass.: Persephone Press, 1981.

Making Face, Making Soul/Haciendo Caras: Creative and Critical Perspectives by Feminists of Color. Edited by Gloria Anzaldúa. San Francisco: Aunt Lute Foundation Books, 1990.

This Bridge We Call Home: Radical Visions for Transformation. Edited by Gloria Anzaldúa and AnaLouise Keating. New York: Routledge, 2002.

CHILDREN'S BOOKS
Friends from the Other Side/Amigos del otro lado. Illustrated by Consuelo Méndez. San Francisco, Calif.: Children's Book Press, 1993.

Prietita and the Ghost Woman/Prietita y La Llorona. Illustrated by Christina Gonzalez. San Francisco, Calif.: Children's Book Press, 1995.

SECONDARY WORKS

Alarcón, Norma. "Anzaldúa's Frontera: Inscribing Gynetics." In *Displacement, Diaspora, and Geographies of Identity.* Edited by Smadar Lavie and Ted Swedenburg. Durham: Duke University Press, 1996. Pp. 35–58.

———. "The Theoretical Subject(s) of *This Bridge Called My Back* and Anglo-American Feminism." In *Making Face, Making Soul/Haciendo Caras: Creative and Critical Perspectives by Feminists of Color.* Edited by Gloria Anzaldúa. San Francisco: Aunt Lute Foundation Books, 1990. Pp. 356–369.

Brady, Mary Pat. "Intermarginalia: Chicana/a Spatiality and Sexuality in the Work of Gloria Anzaldúa and Terri de la Peña." In her *Extinct Lands, Temporal Geographies: Chicana Literature and the Urgency of Space.* Durham: Duke University Press, 2002. Pp. 83–110.

Calderón, Héctor. "Literatura fronteriza tejana: El compromiso con la historia en Américo Paredes, Rolando Hinojosa y Gloria Anzaldúa." *Mester* 22–23, no. 1–2. (fall 1993–spring 1994): 41–61.

Espinoza, Dionne. "Women of Color and Identity Politics: Translating Theory, Haciendo Teoría." In *Other Sisterhoods: Literary Theory and U.S. Women of Color.* Edited by Sandra Kumamoto Stanley. Urbana: University of Illinois Press, 1998. Pp. 44–62.

Kaufman, Gershen. *Shame: The Power of Caring.* Cambridge, Mass.: Schenkman Publishing Company, 1980.

The Latina Feminist Group. *Telling to Live: Latina Feminist Testimonios.* Durham, N.C.: Duke University Press, 2001.

Mignolo, Walter D. "Linguistic Maps, Literary Geographies, and Cultural Landscapes: Languages, Languaging and (Trans)Nationalism." In *The Places of History: Regionalism Revisited in Latin America.* Edited by Doris Sommer. Durham, N.C.: Duke University Press, 1999. Pp. 49–65.

Moraga, Cherríe. "Algo secretamente amado." In *Third Woman: The Sexuality of Latinas* 4 (1989): 151–156.

Saldívar-Hull, Sonia. Introduction to *Borderlands/La Frontera: The New Mestiza,* by Gloria Anzaldúa. 2d ed. San Francisco: Aunt Lute Books, 1999. Pp. 1–15.

———. "Mestiza Consciousness and Politics: Gloria Anzaldúa's *Borderlands/La Frontera.*" In her *Feminism on the Border: Chicana Gender Politics and Literature.* Berkeley: University of California Press, 2000. Pp. 59–80.

Sandoval, Chéla. "Mestizaje as Method: Feminists-of-Color Challenge the Canon." In *Living Chicana Theory.* Edited by Carla Trujillo. Berkeley, Calif.: Third Woman Press, 1998. Pp. 352–370.

Tabuenca, Córdoba, and María Socorro. "Teoría y creación en la prosa de Gloria Anzaldúa." In *Las formas de nuestras voces: Chicana and Mexicana Writers in Mexico.* Edited by Clarie Joysmith. Mexico City: Universidad Nacional Autónoma de México, Centro de Investigaciones sobre América del Norte, 1995. Pp. 153–165.

Yarbro-Bejarano, Yvonne. "Gloria Anzaldúa's *Borderlands/La Frontera*: Cultural Studies, 'Difference,' and the Non-Unitary Subject." *Cultural Critique* 28 (fall 1994): 5–28.

———. "The Lesbian Body in Latina Cultural Production." In *¿Entiendes?: Queer Readings, Hispanic Writings.* Edited by Emilie L. Bergmann and Paul Julian Smith. Durham, N.C.: Duke University Press, 1995. Pp. 181–197.

Jimmy Santiago Baca
(1952–)

B. V. OLGUÍN

JIMMY SANTIAGO BACA'S writing career, like his turbulent life, is distinguished for defying the odds: he has transformed himself from an illiterate petty drug dealer into an internationally renowned author; gained economic inde-pendence in the otherwise unprofitable genre of poetry; cultivated a largely non-Latino audience despite his preoccupation with a gritty Mexican American, or Chicano, underclass experience; and, despite having learned to read and write at the late age of twenty-one, had his writings and personal papers purchased by Stanford University for permanent archiving in its distinguished authors collection. Accordingly, Bill Moyers, producer of the widely acclaimed anthology *The Language of Life: A Festival of Poets* (1995), recognizes Baca as a "leading voice" among contemporary American poets, and has included him in this groundbreaking collection of renowned authors alongside Gary Snyder, Adrienne Rich, Robert Bly, David Mura, Claribel Alegría, and Carolyn Forché, among other luminaries.

It must be noted that such phenomenal success by a Latino author is no longer as anomalous as it might have been a decade ago. Writers such as Oscar Hijuelos, Sandra Cisneros, and Gary Soto, to name but a few, have begun to be incorporated into the American literature canon and are frequently taught in secondary school and university courses. Authors such as Julia Alvarez also have their works regularly translated into languages other than English. However, unlike working-class authors such as Soto and Cisneros and upper-class authors such as Alvarez and Alegría, Baca represents the still-neglected voice of the Chicano underclass, especially the Chicano prisoner, or *Pinto*. Yet what distinguishes Baca's success from these and other Latino writers—and from most writers in general—are the distances he has traveled and challenges he has overcome in his life and writing career.

Baca (who uses his nickname "Jimmy," which is the Anglicized diminutive version of his Spanish name, "Santiago") was born in Sante Fe and grew up in the small rural town of Estancia, New Mexico, in 1952. In his memoir, *A Place to Stand: The Making of a Poet* (2001), Baca recalls that his mother, Cecilia, was from a family of Spanish descent that relished their light skin and looked down upon Indians and mestizo (mixed-blood) Mexicans and Mexican Americans. Because his mother "was fair-skinned, green-eyed, and black-haired," he writes, she was expected "to marry a well-off gringo with a big ranch" (p. 10). However, she fell in love with Damacio Baca, who was born to poor, racially-mixed Indian and Mexican parents. (Baca's paternal great-grandmother was said to be of Apache heritage.) These contentious in-group racial dynamics, and his father's chronic alcoholism, presaged the collapse of his parents' marriage. The ultimate disintegration of Baca's nuclear family occurred when Baca was still a small child. His mother abandoned Jimmy, his brother Mieyo, and his sister Martina to marry an overtly racist Anglo man with whom she had been having an extramarital affair. (This man would later murder her, upon learning of her plans to divorce him.) His father, who had fallen deeper into his alcohol dependency, was virtually absent from his children's lives. Jimmy and his siblings subsequently were sent to live with their paternal grandparents in their hometown village.

Yet the worst for the young Jimmy and his siblings was yet to come. Upon the death of Baca's paternal grandfather in 1959, he and his brother were further traumatized when they were sent to an orphanage in Albuquerque. Baca was just seven years old. This was his first experience with institutionalization. His orphanage ordeal—which is described in Dickensian detail throughout his corpus—was subsequently followed by a stint in a juvenile home and frequent sojourns in local jails, interspersed with aimless intermittent travels across the southwestern U.S. At the age of twenty-one, Baca was convicted of drug possession and sentenced to five years in the Florence Penitentiary in Arizona, a maximum security prison. He served the full five years. In his collection of essays, *Working in the Dark: Reflections of a Poet of the Barrio* (1992), Baca recalls that he taught himself to write by phonetically sounding out words from a textbook he had stolen from a prison official, in a scene reminiscent of Malcolm X's famous example. With practice, he eventually developed enough competency to compose letters and ultimately poems. The difficulties arising from his extremely limited literacy skills were compounded by the daily distractions of bloody fights with other convicts, an alleged contract on his life by the brutal Mexican Mafia prison gang, guard brutality, and frequent trips to isolation. He also endured a brief stay in the prison's mental ward, during which he was forcefully medicated with powerful mind-numbing psychotropic drugs.

By Baca's own admission, his early poetry was naïve and sentimental. However, these early efforts at creative writing were nonetheless accomplished enough to be published in some of the nation's most renowned literary journals, including *The Greenfield Review, The Sun,* and *Mother Jones.* In fact, Baca's literary promise was immediately recognized by journal editors and established writers, such as Joseph Bruchac and Denise Levertov, as well as mainstream publishers and literary critics. Having already published a series of individual poems while in prison, Baca premiered his first full-length collection of poems, *Immigrants in Our Own Land* (1979), shortly after his release. This collection immediately received nationwide acclaim and was subsequently reprinted in 1990 with the addition of selected early poems. After his debut collection, Baca also published smaller chapbooks, *Swords of Darkness* (1981), *What's Happening* (1982), and *Poems Taken from My Yard* (1986), all of which examined his prison experiences and post-prison struggles to reintegrate into society. His second full-length collection of poetry, *Martín & Meditations on the South Valley* (1987), a two-part lyric mock-epic that included an introduction by the renowned American poet Denise Levertov, received the American Book Award in 1988. Baca has since published several other collections of poetry: *Black Mesa Poems* (1989), *Healing Earthquakes: A Love Story in Poems* (2001), *Set This Book on Fire!* (2001), and *C-Train (Dream Boy's Story); and Thirteen Mexicans* (2002). Moreover, he has produced two screenplays, one of which was made into the Hollywood prison film *Bound by Honor* (previously titled *Blood In, Blood Out;* 1993). He has complemented this creative writing with creative nonfiction that includes the aforementioned collection of essays, *Working in the*

Dark: Reflections of a Poet of the Barrio, and the memoir *A Place to Stand: The Making of a Poet* (2001). As a writer now recognized by the mainstream literary establishment, Baca's work has been featured in foundational American literature anthologies, such as Bill Moyer's aforementioned groundbreaking collection of preeminent American poets. Along with the American Book Award, Baca has received the Pushcart Prize (1988), the Hispanic Heritage Award (1989), the Southwest Book Award (1993), and the lucrative International Prize (2001). More recently, as a self-proclaimed "poet of the barrio," in 2003 Baca received a Ph.D. in literature from the University of New Mexico with the goal of further sharing his underclass experiences and insights with people across cultures, classes, and countries.

JIMMY SANTIAGO BACA AND AMERICAN PRISON LITERATURE

Baca's almost archetypal rise from poverty to prison to literary fame is extraordinary yet not uncommon. Indeed, Chicano literature is replete with autobiographical accounts of poverty and personal trauma that lead to political transformations that have been facilitated by writing. As a writer who first learned to read and write while in prison, Baca also has several other important precursors among America's prison authors. The most famous of these American prison-educated writers, of course, is Malcolm X. Renowned for transcribing the entire dictionary, Malcolm X recast the old literary trope that linked writing with self-discovery to explore the nation's atrocious history of race relations, namely slavery and its legacy of modern racism. By thus modeling the link between history, politics, and personal empowerment, Malcolm X inspired legions of racial minority writers, as well as prisoners of all races. H. Bruce Franklin notes that prisoner writers are foundational to the evolution of American literature in general. Moreover, he argues that many of the greatest American writ-

ers, such as Herman Melville, were in fact shaped by their experiences or observations of bondage, whether slavery, indentured servitude, or more modern forms of incarceration in jails and penitentiaries. Through his extensive research, Franklin persuasively asserts that American literature was born of bondage. Moreover, he lists no less than three hundred texts by prisoner authors in an annotated bibliography. Baca is one of several Latino authors who appear in Franklin's bibliography, which also includes Chicano authors Raul Salinas and Ricardo Sánchez (who have also had their personal papers archived by Stanford University). Baca underscores his prisoner author genealogy in his collection of essays, *Working in the Dark,* in which he states: "I was born a poet one noon, gazing at weeds and creosoted grass at the base of a telephone pole outside my grilled cell window. The words I wrote then sailed me out of myself, and I was transported and metamorphosed into the images they made. . . . Writing bridged my divided life of prisoner and free man" (p. 11).

The centrality of Baca's prison experience in his writing career is further underscored in his repeated attempts to explicate life behind bars through different genres, from poetry to essay, memoir, and even film. His writings on prison inevitably confront the brutality of prisoner life and, in doing so, foreground a poetic that distinguishes his entire corpus. His signature poetic is especially evident in his poem "The Sun on Those," which opens his inaugural collection, *Immigrants in Our Own Land* (1979):

> The sun on those green palm
> tress, lining
> the entry road to prison. Stiff rows of husky-
> scaled bark,
> with a tuft of green looping blades on top, sword
> twirling
> in wind, always erect and disciplined, legallike.
>
> (p. 1)

Here, Baca juxtaposes the loss of freedom and attendant loss of legal rights—or rather, his civic death—to the lively free-flying trees, birds, and other flora and fauna. The dissonance in the poem arises from Baca's juxtaposition of images of pastoral tranquility and fertility with cell-block screams, bucketfuls of blood, broken ribs, cutoff fingers caught in the doors of cages, and "dead men thrown to the hoofed mud / like chewed corn husks." His father, he recalls, used to plant trees to protect crops, adding, "All that / he owned was those trees." The poem ends with an epiphanic crescendo that foregrounds the younger Baca's emergent pantheistic sensibility:

> I was not his only son. And when
>
> they captured me through the turn of my days,
>   one was still
>
> free, greening more, spreading wide in wind,
>   sheltering crows,
>
> and mourning our imprisonment, rejoicing our
>   endurance, ever
>
> plunging its roots deeper into the face of progress
>   and land-
>
> grabbers. Fences mean nothing to the trees.
>
> Walls and fences cannot take me away from who I
>   am, and I
>
> Know, as the tree knows, where I come from,
>   who is my father.

(p. 1)

This theme of transcendence is in fact common in prisoner literature. However, Baca adds nuances to it with a historical critique of the dispossession of Native Americans. Furthermore, and perhaps even more importantly, he also attempts to transcend the chauvinistic nationalist pantheism that distinguishes—and ultimately undermines—Chilean poet Pablo Neruda's *Canto General* (1950) and Walt Whitman's *Leaves of Grass* (1892). For Baca, the land—Mother Earth—cannot be reduced to competing claims to nationhood. Instead, it is a palimpsest, or a conglomeration of all that has existed in a given place over time. Of this epiphany, he would later write:

> One day, looking up from my journal to stare absentmindedly at the cell wall, I experienced a revelation. In the wall—in the sand and mortar and stones and iron and trowel sweeps—were the life experiences and sweat of my people. It contained a mural of my people's toil, their aspirations, their pain and workmanship. I imagined my grandfather's hand smoothing out the concrete. I saw my Uncle Santiago stepping out of his truck, laughing, and I could hear him talking in his good-natured way to his friends.
>
> The iron that made the bars came from a mill in Silver City; the workers who had built the mill came from little villages on the plains. The dirt that mixed with the cement, before it was scooped up and trucked and delivered to make this wall, had been prairie soil where families camped and a woman had lain and gave birth to a child.
>
> (*A Place to Stand*, pp. 238–239)

This lyrical pantheistic progression of previous communions with the land later climaxes with his own recognition that the dust on his cell floor ultimately is also connected to the beloved earth of his hometown of Estancia a few hundred miles away.

The huge corpus of writings by Chicano convicts and ex-convicts, who also are known as *Pintos*, has fueled productive critical debates about whether a unique "Pinto poetic" exists. Baca's work is crucial to this dialogue. Some critics, such as Raul Villa, argue that Latino prisoner writing can be understood as resistance literature similar to the vitriolic and lamenting Mexican *corrido*, or folk ballad form. Other critics, including Cordelia Candelaria, claim that no unique Pinto poetic exists. Candelaria argues that the themes and imagery of the most renowned Pinto poets situate them as "Movement poets," that is, poets who were part of the Chicano Civil Rights Movement of the 1960s and 1970s. Yet other critics, such as Rafael Pérez-Torres, propose that even as there may be common features to Pinto writings in general, most contemporary Pinto writers, such as Baca, are too eclectic to be confined within a single poetic. Baca's concerns, Pérez-Torres notes, not only include the bravado and tales of horror common to most prisoner writings, but also involve broader poignant meditative laments about human suffering. When viewed in its entirety, it becomes clear that while Baca's writing always explores his past imprisonment, his experimentation with various themes as well as genres has enabled him to explore much broader metaphysical concerns as well.

JIMMY SANTIAGO BACA AND THE CHICANO PICARESQUE

While Baca's writing is clearly informed by his personal experiences of poverty and trauma, and his efforts at recuperation, his work also may be further seen to be deploying the traditional genre of the picaresque to mold his experience into a didactic form of art. Originally written by Catholic monks in medieval Europe, the picaresque genre emerged as a moral allegory designed to warn parishioners against deviation from church doctrine. The protagonist of the picaresque, or *pícaro,* is always a rustic underclass antihero. He usually is an orphan who experiences horrible misadventures, including imprisonment, bondage, and even famine, throughout his travels. Though the anonymous monks presented this figure through humor, it served as a warning to the wayward reader. Significantly, the *pícaro* eventually realizes the error of his ways, repents and reintegrates into society, and eventually learns to accept his subordinate status in life. The Chicano picaresque draws upon but ultimately departs from the traditional model. It, too, involves the similar theme of movement—both lateral (geographic) and vertical (moral)—but differs in its conclusion. Chicano picaresque tales by authors such as Tomás Rivera and Helena María Viramontes, for example, always end with a critique of institutions, especially those that acquiesce to the suffering of the working classes. In their works, the Chicano *pícaro* becomes a proto-revolutionary underclass hero. Baca's corpus is consistent with this subgenre of Latino writing.

As with all picaresque tales, Baca's writings feature a Chicano protagonist who is preoccupied with geographic place and social space. That is, he attempts to reexamine his past experiences in order to understand his present condition and future possibilities. For instance, in *Martín & Meditations on the South Valley,* his two-part collection of poems, Baca presents a thinly veiled autobiographical character, "Martín," who recounts in a first-person voice his movement from trauma to redemption. In the first poem of *Martín,* the picaresque journey begins in the land of "Pinos Wells," a fictional substitute for Estancia, Baca's beloved utopian birthplace:

> Blackened sheds rust
> in diablito barbs.
> In barn rafters cobwebs
> hang intricate as tablecloths
> grandma crocheted for parlors
> of wealthy Estancia ranchers.
> Now she spins silken spider eggs.
>
> My mind circles warm ashes of memories,
> the dark edged images of my history.
>
> (p. 3)

The land is now abandoned and all that is left are the narrator's nostalgic memories of fertile lands being produced by sturdy farmers and teenage vitality displayed nightly at the local hamburger joint. Martín's utopian past, we quickly learn, was replaced by a life of wandering from town to town and state to state that the author, Baca, casts as an archetypal schism. Poem I continues:

> Months after I headed West
> on I-40,
> in my battered Karmen Ghia.
> Desperate for a new start,
> sundown in my face,
> I spoke with Earth—
>> I have been lost from you Mother Earth.
>> No longer
>> does your language of rain wear away my
> thoughts,

nor your language of fresh morning air
wear away my face,
nor your language of roots and blossoms
wear away my bones.

(p. 7)

The poem ends with the pledge "But when I return, I will become your child again," thereby commencing the quest motif central to all picaresque tales.

In this collection, the quest is for a home, both real and metaphorical. For instance, in the second part of the collection, *Meditations on the South Valley,* Baca's picaresque hero Martín survives the orphanage and subsequent traumas of drug addiction and incarceration only to have his home—along with ten years worth of poems—burn down. The balance of the tale involves his attempts to rebuild his home atop the ashes of the past. Poem XXVII begins:

We started on the house.
At first there was the black mass
of garbage—
loading burned rubbish
en la truckita.

(p. 96)

The actual construction of the new home involves the felling of an ancient tree, an act that illuminates the painful realities of the life cycle and also recalls the pantheism in Baca's earlier poems. Martín understands this cycle through the labor of his hands, where he and a collective of other outcasts rebuild atop the remnants of the older foundation, plank by plank. The narrator describes his new home as "my finest poem" (p. 98). He arrives at an epiphany in the last two stanzas of Poem XXVIII:

My house burned
and we re-built it.
I felt hurt, yes . . .
and grieved with the shovel of ashes,
the ashes heaped on the truck,
and drove it to the dump with a numb sense of
     duty

I had to do,
full of loss and grief, and joy
that I was able to create
another house,
a child in its own image.
I gave birth to a house.
It came, cried from my hands, sweated from my
     body,
ached from my gut and back. I was stripped down
     to the essential
force in my life—create a better world, a better
     me,
out of love. I became a child of the house,
and it showed me
the freedom of a new beginning.

(pp. 99–100)

Unlike the traditional picaresque tale, Baca's *picaro* thus refuses to accept his misfortune and subordination as natural consequences of his actions or as preordained by a divine power. Instead, he re-creates the past through his own hands in order to reshape his present and ultimately his future—all in the same place.

PLACE, SPACE, AND RACE

Baca's exploration of geographic place and social space inevitably explores the racialized trope of land. Since the immigration of Europeans to the Americas, race relations in the southwestern U.S. have persisted in a state of chronic tension punctuated by atrocities committed by whites against Native Americans. This theme of a European American racism has been a feature of Chicano literature since its inception in the mid-eighteenth century, which is not surprising since Chicanos were constituted as a people upon the U.S. occupation of one-half of Mexico's national territory at the end of the U.S.-Mexico War in 1848. By rehearsing the trope of a turbulently contested land, Baca thus aligns himself with Chicano literature's historical and political focus on racial conflict. In much of his highly autobiographical work, Baca invokes the controversial figure of the tragic mestizo along with related misogynist analogues such as La Malinche, who was Hernán Cortes's Indian translator and the mother of his children. He subsequently presents scenarios whereby racially-mixed characters, as well as characters who attempt to cross the racial divide through interracial marriage or friendship, are doomed to failure. By doing so, Baca is engaging not only the personal trauma of his particular family history—most notably his mother's abandonment of her dark-skinned children and her apparent attempt to "pass" as white by marrying an Anglo—but also the historical trauma of European and then American colonization in the lands of his indigenous ancestors, which indelibly marks the Native American and Chicano experience in general.

In his memoir, *A Place to Stand,* Baca signals the significance of place and space not only in the title but also in his discussion of his family home in Estancia, which roughly translates into "the place." He recalls, for instance, how he first found refuge and reverie under his family's meager wood-frame shack:

> I often bellied into the crawl space under our shack to be alone in my own world. I felt safe in this peaceful refuge. The air was moist and smelled like apples withering in a gunnysack in the cellar at my Uncle Max's ranch in Willard. A stray dog might be waiting when I entered. Happy to see me, he would roll on the cool earth, panting, his tail wagging, and lick my face. After playing with him, I'd lie on the dirt and close my eyes and float out of my skin into stories my grandfather, Pedro Baca, told me—about those of our people who rode horses across the night prairie on raiding parties, wearing cloth over their heads, as they burned outsiders' barns, cut fences, and poisoned wells, trying to expel the gringo intruders and recover the land stolen from our people.
>
> (p. 7)

This refuge was interrupted one day as he witnessed, through a gap in the floorboard, his mother having a sexual affair with the Anglo man who would later marry and then murder her. She not only was marked for having

betrayed her family's rule against marrying a poor half-Indian Mexican, but also was condemned by her son, who repeatedly recalls her other betrayals—her abandonment of her children and subsequent marriage to a racist white man who once instructed the young Baca that he should aspire to leave behind his Mexicanness. This racial schism is further exemplified in Baca's comparisons of the rural Mexican neighborhood of his birth to the largely white suburbs to which his mother fled with her new white husband. In *Martín & Meditations on the South Valley,* as well as in his other writings, the barrio is described as utopian and the suburbs as stifling as a prison. This dichotomy of place and space thus stands as a touchstone in Baca's writing.

Baca's mapping of the racial binaries that structure the experience for America's indigenous-descent population—and all Americans for that matter—also emerges in the literary representations of his life on the road and in prison. Symptomatically, Baca's incarceration was facilitated by his Italian American drug-dealing partner, who cooperated with prosecutors in order to receive a reduced sentence. (This same white friend is revealed to have been a traitor even before his arrest, when Baca discovers that he had had an affair with Baca's fiancée.) To further accentuate the racial divide, Baca recalls in his memoir how, as a favor for another old friend, he once saved this man from an assassination contract placed by the Mexican Mafia, only to become the new target of the prison assassination plot. Instead of gratitude, the Anglo friend for whom he performed this favor eventually, for his own survival, gravitated towards the Aryan Nations prison gang in the racially stratified penitentiary. In a prison encounter, this man purportedly tells Baca: "You're leaving soon, aren't you. I shot that FBI and saved your life and you're getting out while I've got a shitload of more years. . . . I'm glad, because if you weren't I'd probably have to kill you" (p. 252). Despite Baca's retort that the racial segregation and animosity that structures the social order of the American penitentiary is "bullshit!" Baca cannot dismiss the realities of discrimination and segregation in prison and out. In Baca's literary landscape, past racial injustices not only are reflected in the eclectic, if not beautiful, colonial architecture that he notices throughout his travels in the southwest, but also in hostile neocolonial interpersonal relationships. This persistent dialectic between *mestizaje* and segregation compounds the historical tragedy that Baca reveals as the archetypal U.S. experience.

Significantly, in recent interviews, Baca has attempted to distance himself from what he calls his past "racial hatreds." In his most recent writings, he offers a symbolic resolution to the historical segregation that undergirds American colonialism, slavery, and racism by challenging the "melting pot" myth of American democracy that demands homogenization and deracination or self-denial. He thus responds to the implicit charge that his critique of racism somehow implies "racial hatred." Moreover, he presents a historicist alternative that puts the burden on White America to make amends for persistent racial animosities and atrocities. In charting his own development and understanding of the racial divides that still haunt the U.S., Baca recalls in the conclusion to his memoir how he once wandered into a Catholic church near his birthplace soon after relocating to his native New Mexico. He was surprised to find one entire side of the church occupied by Native Americans and the other side by regular parishioners. He ultimately realized that he had stumbled upon a special mass decreed by the pope, in which the church asked for forgiveness from the indigenous people for its brutal colonization efforts over the past five hundred years. In a crescendo characteristic of the pantheistic tone in Baca's writing, he imagines himself at his own baptism, and begins to cry: "And suddenly I began to forgive them for what they had done or had not done. I forgave myself for all my mistakes and for all I had done to hurt others. I forgave the world for how it had treated

us" (p. 264). As he leaves the church, a soft rain begins to fall and the bells chime as he thinks to himself that he is "truly free at last" (p. 264), which invokes Martin Luther King Jr.'s famous speech on racial tolerance. By presenting the still-resonant history of the European and American "conquests" of Native America along with the possibility of rapprochement between the two cultures in the southwest that merge in the mestizo, Baca offers us a means to hold both the critique of continued oppression and the hope of ultimate justice in one imaginative space.

WRITING AS TROPE

This attempt to revise earlier characterizations of race conflicts ultimately introduces yet another significant theme in Baca's writing: writing as a trope, or rather, a metaphor that gains ever more complex meanings each time it appears. Baca foregrounds the link between writing as revision and revision as personal redemption in the service of human solidarity in his earliest poems from prison. For instance, in the poem "I Am Sure of It," which is included in his first anthology, *Immigrants in Our Own Land,* the poet's autobiographical poetic persona is shaken from his cellblock solitude by a guard who calls out his prison identification number, "32581," as he leaves a letter between the bars. The second stanza reads in its entirety:

> It's from a magazine I sent three poems to.
> On the envelope in bold black letters,
>   it's rubber-stamped, FUNDS RECEIVED. . .
>   AMOUNT $10.
> I open the letter and read the first paragraph.
> They usually don't pay for poems, they say,
> but wanted to send a little money in this case,
> to help me out. My poems were beautiful,
> and would be published soon.
>
> (p. 10)

The letter, money, and positive appraisal of his writing come as a complete shock to the novice poet of the poem, who only began writing poetry a few years before. The poem continues:

> Holding this letter in my hand,
> standing in the middle of my cell,
> in my boxer shorts, it's now, times like this,
> rapt in my own unutterable surprise, I wonder
>   about people.
>
> (p. 10)

This sense of wonderment unleashes broader meditations on the simple lives of imprisoned convicts like himself and eventually leads to broader reflections on human ontology: that is, the reason for our existence. The title of this poem ultimately foregrounds the epiphany the author expresses at the end of the composition, which he states in the staccato rhythm and passionate voice that defines his early verse: "This is life / even in prison, respecting each other, helping each other, / close or far away, it doesn't matter, I am sure of it" (p. 11). It has been a long road to his arrival at this realization, and his writing has been the catalyst for it.

But Baca also recognizes that writing also involves profound ironies and contradictions. In an interview in the *Progressive Magazine* in January 2003, Baca noted that he feels uneasy about receiving awards for writing about his own personal tragedies. He even decries the ills of success, along with the damage that is done to writers who achieve widespread acclaim and economic success. This critique must be seen as ironic given that Baca, in fact, fits this profile. Indeed, Baca's work reveals a preoccupation with revisiting old traumas and writing about them, sometimes verbatim but oftentimes from a new perspective in which facts are rearranged. This is the case with his discussions about his mother's death, which is framed as a murder in *A Place to Stand* and as either a suicide or the result of her "trying to be white" in *Martín & Meditations on the South Valley* (p. 75). His recollections about his incarceration also involve apparent discrepancies. But these inconsistencies and rhetorical embellishments do not necessarily reveal inconsistencies or "lies." Rather, they reveal that writing has always involved a mediated retelling of facts. Like many prisoner writers and many Latino authors, Baca's writing is as concerned with self-discovery and his personal rearticulation onto a collective past as it is with providing an exemplary model for others to follow. Because of its didactic intent, the retelling of the experience thus is sometimes more important than the actual experience. In this enterprise, the reconstruction of the past becomes as essential as the construction of a future. Indeed, it becomes the condition for imagining that new future. Similar to the medieval picaresque hero's ultimate displacement by the Renaissance era notion of the self-made man of letters, Baca's autobiographical picaresque persona also is remade and redeemed at each retelling.

Selected Bibliography

WORKS OF JIMMY SANTIAGO BACA

POETRY

Rockbottom 6 (co-authored with Mike Finely and Lawrence Perry Spingarn). Santa Barbara, Calif.: Mudborn Press, 1978.

Immigrants in Our Own Land: Poems. Baton Rouge: Louisiana State University Press, 1979.

Swords of Darkness. San Jose, Calif.: Mango Publications, 1981.

What's Happening. Willimantic, Conn.: Curbstone Press, 1982.

Poems Taken from My Yard. Fulton, Mo.: Timberline Press, 1986.

Martín & Meditations on the South Valley. New York: New Directions, 1987.

Black Mesa Poems. New York: New Directions, 1989.

Immigrants in Our Own Land and Selected Early Poems. New York: New Directions, 1990.

Healing Earthquakes: A Love Story in Poems. New York: Grove Press, 2001.

Set This Book on Fire! Mena, Ariz.: Cedar Hill Publications, 2001.

C-Train (Dream Boy's Story); and Thirteen Mexicans. New York: Grove Press, 2002.

PROSE

Working in the Dark: Reflections of a Poet of the Barrio. Santa Fe: Red Crane Books, 1992.

A Place to Stand: The Making of a Poet. New York: Grove Press, 2001.

OTHER

Bound by Honor (screenplay; also known as *Blood In, Blood Out*). Hollywood Pictures, 1993.

Moyers, Bill, ed. *The Language of Life: A Festival of Poets. Part 6: Swirl Like a Leaf—Jimmy Santiago Baca, Robert Bly and Marilyn Chin* (audio and video series). Public Affairs Television and David Grubin Productions, 1995.

Drake, James. *Que linda la brisa: Photographs by James Drake.* (Poetry by Benjamin Alire Sáenz and Jimmy Santiago Baca.) Seattle: University of Washington Press, 2000.

SECONDARY WORKS

CRITICAL AND BIOGRAPHICAL STUDIES

Davis, Philip J. "Searching Anaya, Saenz, Fuentes and Baca for a Common, Cultural Center." *Confluencia: Revista hispánica de cultura y literatura* 11, no. 2 (spring 1996): 137–167.

Grandjeat, Yves-Charles. "Errance et transfert chez Jimmy Santiago Baca." In *Multilinguisme et multiculturalisme en Amérique du Nord: Espace seuils limités.* Edited by Jean Béranger, Jean Cazemajou, Jean-Michel Lacroix, and Pierre Spriet. Bordeaux, France: PU de Bordeaux, Centre de Recherches sur l'Amérique Anglophone, 1990. Pp. 113–124.

Olivares, Julian. "Two Contemporary Chicano Verse Chronicles: The Poetry of Jimmy Santiago Baca and Tino Villanueva." *The Americas Review* 16, nos. 3–4 (fall/winter 1988): 214–231.

INTERVIEWS

Crawford, John and Annie O. Eysturoy. "Jimmy Santiago Baca." *This Is about Vision: Interviews with Southwestern Writers.* Edited by William Balassi, John F. Crawford, and Annie O. Eysturoy. Albuquerque: University of New Mexico Press, 1990. Pp. 181–193.

Keene, John. "'Poetry is What We Speak to Each Other': An Interview with Jimmy Santiago Baca." *Callaloo* 17, no. 1 (winter 1994): 33–51.

Melendez, Gabriel. "Carrying the Magic of His People's Heart: An Interview with Jimmy Santiago Baca." *The Americas Review* 19, nos. 3–4 (winter 1991): 64–86.

Stahura, Barbara. "Jimmy Santiago Baca." *The Progressive,* January 2003.

BOOK REVIEWS

McKenna, Teresa. "*Immigrants in Our Own Land:* A Chicano Literature Review and Pedagogical Assessment." *ADE Bulletin* 91 (winter 1988): 30–38.

GENERAL STUDIES

Candelaria, Cordelia. *Chicano Poetry: A Critical Introduction.* Westport, Conn.: Greenwood Press, 1986.

Franklin, H. Bruce. *Prison Literature in America: The Victim as Criminal and Artist.* Expanded edition. New York: Oxford University Press, 1989.

Pérez-Torres, Rafael. *Movements in Chicano Poetry: Against Myths, Against Margins.* Cambridge: Cambridge University Press, 1995.

INTERNET SITES

Nelson, Cary, ed. *An Online Journal and Multimedia Companion to Anthology of Modern American Poetry.* http://www.english.uiuc.edu/maps/ (accessed June 12, 2003).

Ana Castillo
(1953–)

DEBRA A. CASTILLO

CHICAGO-BORN WRITER and activist Ana Castillo has been called by Mexican American writer Ilan Stavans "the most daring and experimental of Latino novelists." While it is true that in some of her works, especially the earlier novels, the prose style can be challenging, Castillo's body of work overall is sustained by a strong commitment to her readers, and her works center on traditional concepts like spirituality and romantic love. Likewise, while a fiercely rebellious side to her work is evident in the themes she chooses, in both poetry and prose she frequently uses familiar stereotypes and flirts with the edges of cliché. Cliché, she seems to tell us, once it is properly explored in a conscientious manner, exposes the most profoundly held of society's beliefs, the ones that tend to pass unquestioned, the ones that are most revelatory of prejudice in all its forms, the ones that serve as the glue that holds communities in check and—at the same time—keeps families together. Her persistent themes, thus, include love, motherhood, spirituality—particularly with their Mexican American variants: the Latin Lover, the Mexican mother, the Virgin Mary—and their darker counterparts: sexual dysfunction, crippled *familias,* wounded bodies and spirits. Deliberately confounding expectations about content, style, and genre,

Castillo—passionately and, in her most recent works, with an increasingly finely-evolved sense of humor—demonstrates the continuing valence of what has often been dismissed as a hackneyed second-wave feminist lemma: "The personal is the political." Writing, for Castillo, is an expression of aesthetic creativity, and it is also a way of reaching out to a wide readership while at the same time addressing the price paid for having been persistently marginalized from dominant society in more than one cultural setting. It is her way of acknowledging the force of cliché and stereotype but not succumbing to their seductions.

The wonderful short story "Subtitles," in her 1996 collection *Loverboys: Stories,* offers a collection of many of these playfully polished, ironically revelatory clichés. "i have lived my life in a foreign film," the narrative opens. "Black and white mostly. Fassbinderish, i think" (p. 166). Later in the story the narrator adds:

My dark fingers, rimmed with gold, reach up to my collarbone to rub the Virgen de Guadalupe/Tonantzin talisman medal. . . . i have cultivated a disturbing but sensuous foreign accent like Ingrid Bergman's. i don't always wear huipiles from Chichicastenango, Xela, or Mitla. i usually show off spandex pants . . . or a silk raincoat or Djuna Barnes red lipstick and wide-brimmed hat or Marlene Dietrich waves or Katherine Hepburn shoulders or a Greta Garbo cleft and i don't mean on the chin. It is so hard to be original.

(pp. 167–168)

In this passage, the narrator's range of popular cultural referents range from traditional Mexican to Hollywood cliché. A little later, alluding to one of her favored Aztec goddess images, she adds: "i am Coatlicue. But no, not then, not yet. Then i was only a neophyte stone fertility filth-eating goddess" (p. 174). Here, whimsically, we have a compressed set of some of Castillo's favorite obsessions: a spiritual axis defined by Coatlicue and Guadalupe, the pressures on a brown woman in a society defined by black and white, the self-parodying ethnic authenticity of *huipiles* paired with spandex, the cool outsiderness that covers the pain of rejection, a confessional tone that slips between self-exoticizing and self-indulgent.

In a brief autobiographical meditation in *Hungry Mind Review* in the fall of 1992, Castillo describes herself as "a brown girl from a lower working class background." She continues:

We lived upstairs from our racist Italian landlords who had close ties to the Mafia. . . . My mother spoke very little English. She is dark and could not "pass" like my father did sometimes. He was often taken for Italian and at some point in his life changed the spelling of his surname to Costello. The rest of us "Mexicans" in my family kept the name Castillo.

(p. 12)

In *Massacre of the Dreamers: Essays on Xicanisma* she adds, "I am a brown woman, from the Mexican side of town—torn between the Chicago obrero roots of my upbringing and my egocentric tendency toward creative expressions" (p. 1), and later: "I am commonly perceived as a foreigner everywhere I go, including in the United States and in Mexico. . . . I am neither black nor white. . . . And by U.S. standards and according to some North American Native Americans, I cannot make of-ficial claim to being india" (p. 21). Further on in this same essay, she comments on her estrangement from familiar expectations about her cultural alliances: "While I have more in common with a Mexican man than with a white woman, I have much more in common with an Algerian woman than I do with a Mexican man" (p. 23). In this self-description, Ana Castillo clearly lays out the most salient elements of her background, defining herself against a racialized and sexist context that is differently calibrated, but at the same time equally marginalizing and oppressive, in both her ancestral homeland of Mexico and the United States. She also hints at her own transnational feminist alliances in commenting that she feels closer to Algerian women than to Mexican men or U.S. white women, and she suggests a personal and political commitment to women's concerns in a global sense.

This persistent bringing home of the political to the level of individual practice and of the daily stresses of a woman's life is entirely consistent with Castillo's background, training, and lifework. Castillo's formative years were the heady times of the emerging Chicana feminist movement in the activist 1970s, and, along with collaborators and colleagues like Norma Alarcón, Gloria Anzaldúa, and Cherríe Moraga, Ana Castillo has been instrumental in shaping the agenda of a Chicana consciousness separate and distinct from the masculinist/*machista* tendencies of the 1960s–1970s Chicano movement. She joined the Chicano movement at seventeen, demonstrating an early commitment to activism and also an early allergy to easy solutions to complex social quandaries. Like many Chicanas of her generational cohort, she was made at first uneasy, and then outraged, by Movement politics that labeled as *vendidas* (sellouts) the early feminists who questioned the Causa's entrenched masculinist bias. This outrage only sharpened her critical eye and voice.

One of the tangible signs of this commitment is her work as a cofounder of the literary journal and academic press *Third Woman,* and as contributing editor to the journal *Humanizarte*. Her contributions to scholarly projects have also included coediting books like the landmark *The Sexuality of Latinas*, editing and co-translating for a Spanish-speaking audience the classic woman-of-color anthology *This Bridge Called My Back: Writings by Radical Women of Color* (first published in English, in 1981), and, most recently, editing a collection of stories, poems, and personal meditations on the Virgin of Guadalupe, Mexico's most celebrated spiritual figure.

Castillo was born on 15 June 1953. Her early education took place in her home city, Chicago. She began her postsecondary education while she was working on activist causes and beginning to make her mark as a poet. She attended Chicago City College for two years, and then transferred to Northwestern University, where she graduated in 1975 with a B.A. in art and a minor in secondary education. During her years as an undergraduate, Castillo already saw the need for coalition-building among the many Latino and Latina ethnicities beyond those of her own Chicano and Chicana background, and she was active in organizing the Association of Latino Brotherhood of Artists. After graduating from college, Castillo taught briefly in Sonoma County, California, at Santa Rosa Junior College, before returning to Chicago in 1977 as writer-in-residence for the Illinois Arts Council. In 1979 she decided to pursue a social science M.A. in Latin American and Caribbean Studies at the University of Chicago. She then returned to California for several years, teaching at various community colleges and working on several creative projects. A dissertation fellowship in the Chicano Studies Department at the University of California in Santa Barbara in 1989–1990 gave her some breathing space to work on *Massacre of the Dreamers,* and in 1991 she received a Ph.D. in American Studies from the University of Bremen, in Germany. She currently teaches in the English Department at DePaul University in Chicago, where she lives with

her son, Marcel Ramón Herrera (born in Evanston, Illinois, on 21 September 1983).

Castillo's nonfiction serves as an excellent point of entry to her body of work as a whole. *Massacre of the Dreamers* (1994) is an angry, polemical book, deeply imbued with the struggles and language of the U.S. third-world women's movement of the 1970s. Castillo has described her thinking in this book as "akin to archaeologists," in that it involves uncovering and exploring her indigenous imaginary and her roots as a woman of color in an unforgiving environment. At the same time, Castillo expresses dissatisfaction with existing academic models; both archeology and anthropology, she finds, tend to privilege the dominant society's scientific observer at the expense of the native/indigenous subject (who becomes merely the object of research and receives none of the recognition or rewards). Furthermore, their supposedly objective scientific perspective, argues Castillo, imperfectly hides an extreme bias: while supposedly universal, the narrative perspective is tacitly assumed to be white and male, as is the readership. Thus, like white feminists who have to read against the grain, between the lines, to find traces of themselves in the male-authored texts of the Western classical tradition, so too Castillo, with a more urgent emphasis, argues that she must read herself into the Western tradition from an even greater degree of alienation. She says of women of color like herself, "We exist in the void, en ausencia, and surface rarely, usually in stereotype" (p. 5). Thus the racist, sexist image is often the only recognized presence of women of color in dominant understandings; ironically, for Castillo to forward her own agenda she must not only fill in the void of women's voices but also speak to and about the only existing image in the current social context: the stereotype.

Massacre has an entirely different agenda from the dominant-culture books that Castillo finds so unfulfilling, and she opens her analysis with a strong statement of her position: "Within the confines of these pages, 'I' and the mestiza /

Mexic Amerindian woman's identity becomes universal. It is to that woman to whom I first and foremost address my thoughts" (p. 1). Implicitly, then, the white reader, male or female, who reads this book will inevitably experience a sense of alienation analogous to that which Castillo and fellow Chicana feminists suffer upon reading dominant culture texts. Western society, in this book, belongs to the margins, though it is necessarily a foil to the project that Castillo promotes. The volume, accordingly, is full of programmatic, manifesto-like statements that deliberately confront the dominant paradigm: "Subversion of all implied truths is necessary in order to understand the milieu of sexist politics that shape the lives of women" (pp. 176–177); "It is an absolute impossibility in this society to reversely sexually objectify heterosexual men, just as it is impossible for a poor person of color to be a racist" (p. 127). Castillo rarely argues points such as these. Taken as axiomatic, they define a passionately held political agenda: with her or against her, she sweeps the reader along with the force of her expression.

In this loosely connected body of essays, Castillo explores the ramifications of a concept she calls "Xicanisma," a term she coins to describe the position of Chicana feminists with respect to a U.S. struggle against racism and sexism that too often has been limited by a misleading and dichotomous black/white paradigm, a national civil rights agenda that almost entirely ignores brown people except as an afterthought or a footnote. She describes Xicanisma as "the sense of *familia* that exists among women who identify themselves as Chicanas throughout the United States and that crosses the U.S./Mexican border" (p. 46). Implicitly, she argues for the universal applicability of this model, along parallel lines to the white male model that has been for so long the invisible standard in the United States. The book is highly polemical in its sociopolitical stands; nevertheless, for Castillo, Xicanisma at its core is not based on polemics. Rather, it transcends conflict and proposes itself

as a politically aware, holistic way to understand the relation of the self to the world, without the "us-them" dichotomy that Castillo ascribes to Western sociopolitical establishments. In principle, then, an Algerian woman can be a Xicanista; the model is not limited to women of Mexican ancestry.

Massacre is not fundamentally an academic study, though it shares some of the qualities of a scholarly book. On the one hand, Castillo is concerned with addressing a wide spectrum of interested readers, and would for that reason reject the specialized language typical of much of the scholarly production in the academic world. At the same time, she specifically eschews the standards of evidence and proof typical of that format when she warns her reader up front that "Characteristically, as a poet I am opinionated and rely on my hunches" (p. 1). Instead of obscure references and abstruse argumentation, she offers something like an autoethnography of her own coming to political consciousness (she uses the more succinct Spanish term *concientización*). In this meditation, she evokes along the way a broad sweep of cultural practices including pre-Columbian indigenous and Spanish-Arab influences on Chicano and Chicana culture, explored in general terms, and commentary on recent events such as the 1986 strike against a Watsonville, California, canning and frozen food company by its Mexican American women workers. In this respect, her work is very much aligned with the earlier projects of her fellow Chicana activists Gloria Anzaldúa and Cherríe Moraga, whose *Borderlands: The New Mestiza/La frontera* (1987) and *Loving in the War Years: Lo que nunca pasó por sus labios* (1983), respectively, serve as important reference points in this book as well. Like these other members of her cohort, Castillo derives her authority from personal experience and from having her finger on the pulse of popular culture in her community. Like their work, *Massacre* combines autobiographical elements and what Castillo called "concientized" meditations in a sui generis form. In this respect Castillo's work is informed as well by the highly influential Brazilian thinker, Paulo Freire, whose seminal *Pedagogy of the Oppressed* has been an important point of reference for progressive thinkers since the mid-twentieth century. Consciousness-raising, *concientización,* involves reflection on lived experience so as to create a knowledge base for grounding political action. At the same time, while Anzaldúa, for instance, does without the baggage of academic verification or historical citations much more readily than Castillo, Castillo's book seeks a middle ground, frequently anchoring her analyses in a wide-ranging body of footnote references to source material while retaining an accessible style.

Castillo is particularly interested in questions of a female-grounded spirituality; thus, in *Massacre* her remarks on the white male establishment and on Chicano/Mexican machismo serve not so much as stand-alone studies, but more importantly as an opening into her discussion of women's liberation theology. In her commentary on this aspect of women's lives, she ranges among syncretic religious practices such as the veneration of hybrid saints/gods, popular spirituality as reflected in *curanderismo,* and Native American and African-derived religions. The most important focus, however, is her discussion of the Virgin of Guadalupe. Castillo summarizes the familiar Mexica genealogy of Coatlicue-Tonantzin-Virgin Mary (in her miraculous visitation to recently converted Nahua Juan Diego on the hill of Tepeyac). She reminds us of the Virgin of Guadalupe's preeminent role in Mexican culture and society, before developing her central argument about the particular relevance of this figure for the Xicanista. Says Castillo, "The Xicanista combines the traditional view of the Christian god with goddess worship to give her a source of inner strength" (p. 101). Her own Xicanista reverence for this figure derives from the earth-goddess's sexuality, a startling and unconventional variation on an old Mexican tradition.

It is not surprising, thus, that Castillo returns to the Virgin of Guadalupe three years later in *Goddess of the Americas/La diosa de las Américas: Writings on the Virgin of Guadalupe* (1997), a volume she edited. Castillo's editorial hand is very light in this volume; a brief introduction, and a first-person narrative called "Extraordinarily Woman" complete her own contributions. In this story, the narrator's *abuelita,* an able *curandera,* heals a child with a life-threatening *susto* (traumatic shock) by engaging in a complicated ritual that includes a Virgin of Guadalupe candle as one of its key elements. While in this narrative the role of the Virgin is incidental, the volume as a whole offers a multifaceted set of poems, stories, personal narratives, and essays that reflect on this much-beloved figure, from perspectives ranging from respectful to raucous. And, of course, the guiding spirit of this anthology is Ana Castillo, who brings these disparate elements together through her own inspired sense of their place in this nearly five-century-long conversation about the Indian Virgin. Throughout this volume, as in *Massacre,* the Virgin's origins as a pre-Columbian goddess are brought to the fore, as is Castillo's inclination to see her as an earthy variation on spirituality (Sandra Cisneros's contribution, "Guadalupe the Sex Goddess," is a case in point). This is clearly not a nostalgic volume, nor a conventionally hagiographic one; yet its deep, if sometimes troubled, spiritual impulse is very evident. In an interview with Samuel Baker after the work's publication, Castillo shows how much she delights in its iconoclasm. She tells Baker that one of her goals "is to get an encyclical from the church . . . to ban the book" (p. 60). Here, of course, in a backhanded way, Castillo inserts her book into a long Roman Catholic tradition, playing with stereotype, but with a twist.

The same qualities that define Castillo's polemical prose help offer keys to understanding her poetry as well. Like her prose, much of her poetry provides a vehicle for social protest. In her first books, as she said later, she explicitly takes on a critique of how women were "demeaned, misunderstood, objectified, and excluded by the politic of those men with whom I had aligned myself on the basis of our mutual subjugation as Latinos in the United States" (*Massacre,* p. 121). In later works, the social critique remains, but gentled, with more of an emphasis on celebrating women's strength, especially in her elaborations of erotic parables and poignant lyrical forms. There is in all these works a persistent outspokenness about the wrongs perpetrated against the immigrant, the inner-city urban dweller, the disenfranchised woman in a globalized economy. At the same time, Castillo offers in each of her books a strong sampling of poems that present her variations on the more traditional lyric theme of romantic love. And in *My Father Was a Toltec* (1988), Castillo especially displays her bilingual abilities. More than one-third of the poems in that volume, including such exemplary lyrics as "Lamento de Coatlicue," "La heredera," "Encuentros," and "Todo me recuerda tu ausencia," are written wholly in Spanish (seventeen are in Spanish; twenty-nine are in English).

Castillo's most recent poetic volume is *I Ask the Impossible: Poems* (2001). The title poem in this collection is a beautiful example of one of the important strands in Castillo's work and takes the form of a pure, timeless lyric:

> I ask the impossible: love me forever.
> Love me when all desire is gone.
> Love me with the single-mindedness of a monk.
>
> . . . .
>
> Love me withered as you loved me new.
>
> Love me as if *I* were forever—
> and I will make the impossible
> a simple act,
> by loving you, loving you as I do.
>
> (p. 3)

At the same time, while highly recognizable in sentiment, the lyric impulse in this poem is slightly skewed from the traditional celebration of the lover's body and spirit. Here, Castillo celebrates a timeless love, but prefaces her lyric by forthrightly stating its impossibility. As the lyric progresses, the poetic voice literally takes on the challenge of limning a long-standing relationship—the inevitable effects of aging that wrinkle the body and that put a limit on naïve promises of eternal affection. And yet the poem ends triumphantly, with an achievement of this impossible dream of loving someone forever.

The lovely title poem of her earlier volume *Women Are Not Roses* (1984) had already established a similar antilyric dynamic: "Women have no / beginning / only continual / flows," the poet says in her most tender of love poems. "Women are not / roses / they are not oceans / or stars" (p. 7). Here the poet succinctly pulls together some of the most familiar and clichéd images from sentimental love poems from Bécquer to Neruda—the comparison of women to roses, oceans, stars—and delicately negates these sentimental favorites. The repetition of the negatives "no" and "not" establish this poem as an admonishment to that Hallmark cards–type tradition of romantic poetry. At the same time, the poem offers no alternative lyric motifs, so that the unstated complicity of knowledge among women about what they are *not* does not and cannot spill over into the lyric itself to replace the roses, oceans, and stars with other, more radical imagery. Here, as is typical in Castillo's work, the stereotype is questioned, but not erased.

Frequently, Castillo's poetry foregrounds the difficult challenges that face women in a sexist world. In *Women's* "El ser mujer," the adolescent poetic voice asks, "Mami, dime por favor, si puedes: / Must I be a woman now?" (p. 54). A later poem in the same volume, "Euthanasia," is about abortion, focusing on a bitter and accusatory mourning for the dead child. In the even more powerful Spanish-language poem "Traficante, Too," from *My Father Was a Toltec: Poems,* Castillo returns to this theme. A young woman, condemned for being sexually active, sees a doctor secretly for an abortion and, at the end of the poem, unable to face her circumstances, locks herself in a bathroom "donde una / pícara navaja jugó / con las muñecas / hasta la hora / de cenar" (*My Father Was a Toltec: Poems*, p. 37). The horror of this poem lies in the double meaning of "muñecas" in Spanish; it can be read equally as "dolls" or "wrists," evoking the tragedy of a young woman, barely out of childhood, who should be playing with dolls and instead is cutting her wrists in despair.

Survivors in this world need to become strong in a different way from the strength-through-abnegation that stereotypically defines Chicana/*mexicana* motherhood. It is no wonder that the poet of "Ixtacihuatl died in vain" states, "Hard are the women of my family, / hard on the mothers who've died on us / . . . / hard on all except sacred husbands" (p. 34). In the same volume, the poem "Wyoming Crossing Thoughts" forcefully decries these Marianist traditions: the poetic voice here is a woman who affirms that she will never marry a Mexican, never act like a traditional self-sacrificing wife. Instead, this poem ends with a strong affirmation of independence, of loving her chosen man in her own way in her own time, of following the rhythms of *her* desire rather than his. This open assertion of her right to her sexuality may be paired with an uncommon metaphorical violence that, despite all its murderousness, remains deeply sensual: "drive an obsidian blade / through his heart, / lick up the blood" (p. 39).

Coatlicue, Ixtacihuatl, and the obsidian blade all point to a Mexican-indigenous body of referents, and, indeed, Castillo's work in both prose and poetry is enriched throughout by a range of metaphors and allusions drawn from a pre-Columbian (specifically from the Nahua, or Aztec) past. At the same time, Castillo is aware that this body of referents, too, can turn into a cliché, especially for decultured Mexican Americans who have only a casual and decontextualized relationship to their indigenous heritage. The title poem of *My Father Was a Toltec* is a case in point. The reference to "Toltec" in this poem is to a street gang rather than to a proud Mexican indigenous nation, and the poet's naming of that absent indigenous heritage only serves to poignantly signal its loss. The father is a warrior, but of a particularly modern and debased sort. He does not wear a breastplate, but rather an "emblemed jacket" that has been split by a blade in the back in a turf battle (p. 3).

Many of Castillo's poems have to do with the dysfunction of Chicano families ruled by a double standard that allows sexual freedom to men while tightly restricting a woman's right to express her sexuality. "Saturdays," for example, ends, "That's why he married her, a Mexican / woman, like his mother, not like / they were in Chicago, not like / the one he was going out to meet" (p. 6). Castillo does not unilaterally condemn the men for their *machista* attitudes, though; that would be far too simple. One of the best poems in *My Father Was a Toltec*, "Daddy with Chesterfields in a Rolled up Sleeve," explores these difficult family dynamics in a narrative format, highlighting both the love and bitterness, the admiration and the rejection, of a girl-child who is growing into adolescence with an ever clearer sense of the difficult and selfish road her father walks.

Beginning with her earliest poems, Castillo has maintained a strong thread of social commentary and denunciation. Thus, in *Women* there are poems like "Napa, California," which is dedicated to Cesar Chavez and focuses on the issues surrounding grape pickers. Her poem "1975" also aims for social resonance, and the repeated line "talking proletarian talks" also reminds the reader that Castillo overtly intends her poetry for a wide, working-class audience. *Toltec* features straightforward political statements, in poems like "A Christmas Gift for the President of the United States, Chicano Poets, and a Marxist or Two I've Known in My Time," "In My Country," and "We Would Like You to Know," which includes the admonition:

We do not all carry
zip guns, hot pistols,
steal cars.
We do know how
to defend ourselves.

(p. 67)

I Ask the Impossible's "Women Don't Riot" also highlights the role of social poetry: this is a powerful political poem constructed around a list of negative actions: what women do not do, implicitly contrasting them with their militaristic and malcontent male counterparts. Women, says Castillo, do not riot, revolt, or run rampant through the streets, nor do they rise up in arms, storm cities, take over the press, form a battalion, or even speak the official language. They do not dare to hope for justice, or to desire a TV or the things they see on TV. This long list of negatives eventually resolves in a powerful questioning of the social order:

Quietly, instead, one and each takes the offense,
rejection, bureaucratic dismissal, disease
that should not have been, insult,
shove, blow to the head,
a knife at her throat.
She won't fight, she won't even scream—
taught as she's been
to be brought down as if by surprise.
She'll die like an ant beneath a passing heel.
Today it was her. Next time who.

(*I Ask the Impossible,* pp. 59–60)

This is a striking and powerful indictment, and indexes well Castillo's rage at the continuing victimization of women at all levels, ranging from inequality in the workplace to sexual abuse and murder. Like other poems cited earlier, Castillo typically uses negative phrasing to make her points: focusing her lyric on strong but denied images of what is *not*. It is a pattern that emerges throughout her poems in the last quarter century: define the lyric territory, hedge it around with negatives, and then open up a small space for a woman's revelatory and redeeming knowledge. As she suggests doing in *Massacre of the Dreamers,* Castillo first constructs a frame within which she can imagine women's absence; only then can she begin the more positive work of defining the relationships that give strength and power.

In *Massacre of the Dreamers,* Castillo describes her objective in writing her first novel, *The Mixquiahuala Letters* (1986): "The principal thematic concern is that of relationships or connections, with all their seemingly irreconcilable complexities: woman with man, woman with woman, woman as daughter, woman as mother, woman with religion, woman with Chicano/mexicano culture, mestiza with Anglo society" (p. 179). As the title suggests, this is an epistolary novel, and it consists of forty numbered letters sent by a Mexican American woman named Teresa to her friend Alicia over an undetermined period of time. The letters are of varying length, and some of them include "Teresa's" poetry, including poems previously or subsequently published under Ana Castillo's name in other books. The novel does not include Alicia's potential letters in response, so the conversation between the two women is an implicit one, filtered through Teresa's memory only and putting the reader in the position of playing Alicia's role as interlocutor and desired recipient. Perhaps because of its first-person narrative voice, the novel has often been taken to be autobiographical, an issue Castillo addresses at least in part in her essay "Yes, Dear Critic, There Really Is an Alicia."

Castillo further complicates the novel by dedicating it to Argentine novelist Julio Cortázar, whose novel *Rayuela* (1963; *Hopscotch,* 1966) famously sent that author's readers scurrying through the book, jumping some chapters, skipping others, in accordance with the author's "table of instructions." In a similar manner, Castillo begins her book with a note: "Dear Reader: It is the author's duty to alert the reader that this is not a book to be read in the usual sequence," and she proposes four reading options: "for the conformist," "for the cynic," "for the quixotic," and "for the reader committed to nothing but short fiction." In the first three options, significant portions of the novel will go unread, and the novel concludes differently as well for each option, creating an interesting reading effect for the person who chooses them. As with Cortázar's earlier text, the reader is presented with a puzzle of sorts, but in Castillo's case, the interpretative stakes are already predetermined by the labels, except for the case of the undefined reader who chooses to think of this book as a novel, reading it from beginning to end—which is, of course, the most conventional reading of all.

The central image defining this novel derives from a long-ago summer-school weekend spent in a pre-Columbian Mexican village named Mixquiahuala. Teresa writes Alicia, with apparent approbation, "For years afterward you enjoyed telling people that i was from Mixquiahuala," and, as the title of the book suggests, that once-seen and now mythic town represents less an actual place than the state of mind that pervades these letters. This poetically reinvented pre-Columbian town represents for Teresa a spiritual homeland. "There was a definite call to find a place to satisfy my yearning spirit," she writes, "i chose Mexico" (p. 46). Nevertheless, Mexico functions as a spirit home only from the U.S. side of the border; once she actually begins to live in that country she discovers that it is antagonistic to her sense of self. She recalls to Alicia, "i'd had enough of the country where relationships were never clear and straightforward but a tangle of contradictions and hypocrisies," and she captures her frustration in a poem: "This was her last night / in the homeland / of spiritual devastation" (pp. 54–55). Says Castillo of this book, "As Teresa evolves as a feminist, she is placed in the dangerous position of being viewed as a traitor to the male-dominated Chicano Movement" (*Massacre*, p. 178); Teresa also finds herself in physical danger when she escapes to Mexico, hoping for an alternative. *The Mixquiahuala Letters* is Castillo's most studied novel, and it is frequently adopted as a textbook in literature courses across the country. Along with her second novel, *Sapogonia: (An Anti-Romance in 3/8 Meter)* (1990), these two works are the technically more challenging works of Castillo's narratives; they are also the novels that were published first by small presses. Interestingly enough, her more recent works, all published by mainstream presses (Norton and Random House), are more accessible to her readers, and they also display a sunnier quality. While the concern with feminist social issues remains, the later works are by far more relaxed, giving evidence of a quirky sense of humor and a willingness to allow for the potential of a happy ending.

In *The Mixquiahuala Letters,* the vision is much darker. Teresa looks to Mexico to cure the discomfort she feels with the markers of her U.S. identity. In the United States, she is made to feel an outsider, with the copper skin and fuller body type that marks her racial heritage, the slight accent that betrays her cultural background, the often angry reactions that betray her efforts to resist the traditions of her family's economic class. Teresa suffers the scars of a divided self that drives her to foreground those specific features, but she knows that this idealized land, while intimately hers in dreams, belongs to her only in dreams. Her own words distance her from Mixquiahuala when she is awake. Likewise, when she travels in Mexico only one part of her divided self is coming home; the rest of her visits an exotic and unfamiliar land. She too, like the people in her fantasy town, is of mixed blood, but she has not grown up in the out-of-the-way provincial village of her dreams, where copper-colored skin is the norm. Her skin color is racialized and defined by her U.S. reality in a way alien to that half-imagined utopian town. Her color is, as she says, "exotic," her origin, even to herself, "indiscernible."

Neither Alicia nor Teresa find in Mexico any alternative to the conflicts resulting from their situation in the United States, although distance and exoticism provide them with a space to imagine an idealized other world. From the U.S. side of the border, Mexico seduces as the *tabula rasa* upon which they might rewrite their pasts, and that familiar-but-alien other provides a more malleable form for this self-imagining than the resistant molds of their own country. Thus, to the extent that Mexico confirms her fictional image, including her dream of a seductive exoticism, Teresa loves it and its people; to the extent that it insists on deviating from her dream, on confirming a stubborn incomprehensibility—or worse, a matter-of-fact counterstereotype, she rejects it utterly. Again and again, in each visit to Mexico, Teresa's dream of finding a simple, exotic homeland fragments. Each encounter is wounding, and each wound reconfirms her divided self. Castillo's epistolary novel does not attempt to resolve the tension of this double vision. Instead, the strained theatricality remains highlighted in the text in the epistolary format and in the instructions for reading the text, pointing directly at the heart of Teresa's confused longing, her double and distanced misreadings of two cultures' typical tropes.

Early in the novel, the narrator asks why "so many of our ideals were stamped out like cigarette butts when we believed in them so furiously" and answers her own question: "Perhaps we were not furious enough" (p. 16). Certainly the protagonists in this novel suffer as a result of their efforts to redefine themselves and their lives outside of conventional cultural expectations, whether dominant Mexican, dominant U.S., provincial Mexican, or Chicano and Chicana. Furiously, they declare their independence and their right to a relationship of equality with the men they choose as husbands and lovers. It is a fury worn down in the relentlessness of everyday life. Like infants, the men in these women's lives suck dry their wives and lovers. Teresa writes: "A woman takes care of the man she has made her life with . . . as if he were her only child, as if he had come from her womb. . . . There isn't a woman who doesn't understand this deathtrap" (p. 112). And yet, of course, Teresa herself repeatedly falls into it. She

reminds Alicia, who is grieving over the suicide of her lover, "Abdel was a weak man, Alicia, and he had already sucked you dry of more than what a child can demand of its mother," for unlike a child, a man remains dependent on the woman-mother figure (p. 129).

Teresa decides to go elsewhere for her earthly paradise, to travel to Mexico to reinvent herself and recover her past, to seek an alternative present, to dream a Mixquiahualan future. There, in that utopian realm, she imagines that she achieves real self-sufficiency. Yet when Teresa steps back from her dreams and into the contemporary reality of the Mexico she has visited on various occasions with her friend, she finds no real alternative to the dilemma. Mexico rejects the young women even more firmly than does the patriarchal United States. It is not even that they are seen as legitimate prey for the Mexican men they encounter (although they are) but that they go through the country unacknowledged and unaccounted for. Despite their longing to belong to an alternative reality, Mexico refuses to recognize them, and, as Teresa notes, snips them out of the societal pattern. They are anomalies. Insofar as they exist at all in Mexican consciousness, they exist as exotic creatures, outside normal laws: "We would have hoped for respect as human beings, but the only respect granted a woman is that which a gentleman bestows upon the lady. Clearly, we were no ladies. What was our greatest transgression? We traveled alone" (p. 59).

Not only did they travel alone; they did so in what is practically the uniform of U.S. tourists. In one encounter, when the women hitch a ride with a trio of heavily armed men, the men ask Teresa and Alicia if they are from the United States. Teresa says: "i tried to laugh, as if the suggestion was ludicrous. How could they possibly think that? Couldn't they see by our color that we weren't gringas? It's the blue jeans, one said, as if stating a statistical fact" (p. 63). What is fascinating about this scene is that two clichés about the United States are played off against each other. The U.S. women of color assume that they can "pass" as non-U.S. by virtue of their race; underlying their presumption is a hurtful and deeply inbred feeling that the "typical American" (ugly or not) is necessarily white. Under that assumption, they do not fit in the United States, and thus it is both shocking and distressing for them to be immediately identified with a rejecting and rejected nationality in the country to which they wish to escape. The Mexican soldiers recognize the women despite their native Spanish by clichéd cultural markers the women don't care to disguise: their independence (traveling together without a man for protection) and their clothes (the cliché that all and only U.S. women wear blue jeans). The jeans that are so ubiquitous as to seem an invisible and unmarked class-dissolving fact of life for young people in the U.S. become, in their chosen dreamland, a marker of an exotic and vulnerable femininity for the Mexican men. Pointedly, Teresa and Alicia meet very few Mexican women, except in dreams, and in dreams those women are motherly *mestizas* who work the fields and care for their children in provincial homes. They are not blue-jean–clad adventurers. In fact, they look and act uncomfortably like Teresa's own mother and aunts in unromantic Chicago.

The way they see themselves and the way they imagine future relationships are both affected by the scars of past failures, literally as well as figuratively. In fact, with Teresa and Alicia, Castillo begins the tradition of scarred, wounded, or handicapped heroines that have become the hallmark of her narrative. In this novel, as in her poem "Euthanasia," Castillo uses the aborted child as her narrative frame. Teresa and Alicia have both had abortions, and for both the lost child represents a crisis event that is unresolved or irreconcilable, but at the same time both incomplete and unforgettable. Teresa describes both abortions at considerable length because these difficult and painful experiences of "having life sucked out from between [their] legs" (pp. 109–110) are strongly defining elements of the context in which these women

see themselves. In Alicia's case, a borrowed welfare card results in involuntary sterilization, so in her case there is no way back into the redemptive potential of childbearing. For Teresa the end of the novel and the sign of her new-found self-confidence is her decision to bring her son Vittorio to term when she once again finds herself with child by another faithless lover. Nevertheless, for the reader who defies all the authorial instructions and reads the novel straight through, from beginning to end, the conclusion to the book is stark, offering potential hope for the future with baby Vittorio in letter thirty-nine, but taking away that dream in letter forty with its violent replay of Abdel's committing suicide, shooting himself in the head.

What saves this novel, and makes it interesting, is that Teresa does not rest on the clichés she constantly evokes. Mixquiahuala (in some ways like Xicanisma) eventually becomes the tool she uses to attack her own prejudices: her hatred of middle-class Chicano "brothers" with their intermittent and hypocritical commitment to barrio causes; her resentment toward white women; her intransigent romanticism about Mexico. It is, of course, the friendship with Alicia that contributes most to this reevaluation. At the same time, their very differences—of race, temperament, and background—bring them together, making them mirrors for each other and for their own self-reflection. Alicia and Teresa reserve their sharpest weapons for each other, as well as their most thoughtful and loving exchanges: "Each time we've parted it has been abruptly. We picked, picked, picked at each other's cerebrum and when we didn't elicit the desired behavior, the confirmation of allegiance, we reproached the other with threatening vengeance. . . . We begged for the other's visit and again the battle resumed. We needled, stabbed, manipulated, cut and through it all we loved, driven to see the other improved in her own reflection" (p. 23). Teresa calls their intense relationship "a love affair" (p. 39), although of a particular, non-sexualized kind: "we were experts at exchanging empathy for heart-rending confusion known only to lovers, but you and I had never been lovers" (p. 121). This love affair between the two women is different from any relationship they share with their various male lovers.

In many ways, Mixquiahuala is an earlier version of the country that Castillo identifies in her second novel as "Sapogonia," which she describes in that novel as "a distinct place in the Americas where all mestizos reside, regardless of nationality, individual racial composition, or legal residential status—or perhaps, because of all these." Castillo goes on: "Sapogonia (like the Sapogón/a) is not identified by modern boundaries" (*Sapogonia*, p. 6); it is, then, a place both spiritual and physical that recognizes and celebrates the overlapping of two realities, two myths, two cultures, two ways of living and dreaming, two different political and economic modes of perceiving the world. In fact, Teresa and Alicia make a brief cameo appearance in this second novel. About halfway through *Sapogonia*, Pastora, the Sapogonian heroine, "made her way to the apartment of the woman named Alicia. . . . Her friend in Chicago, Teresa, had given her Alicia's address" (p. 147). Alicia attends Pastora's performance in the Village, but unlike the earlier incarnation of the character in *The Mixquiahuala Letters*, she turns down alcohol, waves away cigarette smoke, and tells Pastora she's tired and wants to go home to eat when Pastora and her friends invite her to a party in Soho.

Sapogonia is the most pitiless and intimidating of Castillo's works. Told in first and third person, from a shifting set of viewpoints, the novel focuses on two native Sapogonians, Máximo Madrigal and Pastora Velásquez Aké, whose obviously symbolic names foreground for the reader that these are larger-than-life types, not rounded, believable characters. Since this is a romance, or an anti-romance, of course the two become lovers, but they are sexual partners of a particularly violent and obsessive sort. Their on-again, off-again affair involves the dream of mutual annihilation, and while they do not always live together, they remain constant in their obsession. At one point the narrator notes that their coexistence is "certain as death" (p. 111). The two are supremely well matched: "Each was a prima donna, a matador, fearless with the kind of bravado inherent in those whose motives are heightened in the face of danger before a crowd. . . . They were each sources of destruction for the other" (p. 110).

The word "matador" provides a clue to students of popular culture for a parallel work against which to read this unusual and difficult novel. Spanish director and scriptwriter Pedro Almodóvar, in his 1986 film *Matador*, also focuses on such a lethal attraction between two splendid egoists. The film tells the story of a retired bullfighter, Diego Montes, who has a profound need to continue killing. His dream, finally realized at the end of the movie, is to make love to a woman and kill her and himself at the moment of orgasm. Castillo herself refers in her novel to another erotic classic, Nagisa Oshima's 1976 Japanese film *In the Realm of the Senses*, and she has her protagonists come back again and again to that film's climactic scene. In the final chapter of the novel (before the epilogue), in a passage written from Máximo's perspective, the narrator asks: "Had she seen *In the Realm of the Senses*? How would she feel, knowing as she tightened the sash around my neck, that she was receiving the last of my energies, my semen surging into her body, hoping against mortality as I gasped my last breath?" (p. 305). This is sexual obsession at its most disturbing and cruel.

The novel also begins with a climax of sorts: "In one thrust his clenched fist holding the scissors from her sewing table comes down to pierce the hollow spot between the lumps of nippled flesh. Her eyes open and are on him. Her face is wild as she inhales with the thrust and exhales when he pulls the scissors out" (p. 8). This graphic scene is repeated again and again in the novel as Pastora and Máximo come together.

The stab wound is a figurative "[puncture] through to her soul" (p. 17), as well as a literal wound.

Pastora is an ambiguously attractive and repulsive figure, a narrative version of Castillo's poetic femme fatale who drives her lovers to erotic extremes and laughingly buries an obsidian knife in their hearts. Pastora, like all Castillo heroines, has an abortion early on in the novel and she is still bleeding "the final vestiges of the fetus she had eliminated" (p. 23) the night she meets Máximo. His first impression of Pastora, on catching her eye is: "Was it possible to castrate a man with a glance? She had looked up at me and at once chewed my existence and spit me out" (p. 25). To some extent, she creates Madrigal as her necessary counterpart, and he, for his part, invents her: "It was Máximo alone who concocted Pastora and he did not ever want to know the formula. . . . There was no other way. Pastora was celluloid, the chanteuse of the silver screen of silent films, and larger than life." She is, finally, identified with the earth goddess Coatlicue, who demands blood in war and gives blood in menstruation (pp. 311–312).

No character is exempt from this violent sexuality, but only Máximo and Pastora meet it with godlike fierceness and godlike creative powers. For Perla, who also loves Pastora, "desire was like an unhealable wound open to the world" (p. 21). Máximo and Pastora, however, are artists (a sculptor and a musician, respectively). Of course they inevitably end up together. Of course their passion feeds their art. They live in a constant state of arousal and vengeance, using murderous sex fantasies as a way to recharge their creativity. They incidentally create a son between them, but the son is merely a plot point, a footnote to their fixation on each other. As in *Matador* and *In the Realm of the Senses*, the protagonists' world is essentially a closed one involving only the two of them. Sapogonia, in the final analysis, is less the land of the downtrodden indigenous peoples of the Americas than it is the land of their still-powerful and bloodthirsty gods.

In her most recent novels, Castillo, like her fellow writers in the much applauded "Latina Boom" of the 1990s—Sandra Cisneros, Julia Alvarez, Denise Chávez—has had to come to terms with mainstream success. Too often Latina artists and writers have found to their dismay that their works are being appreciated for their "exotic" Latin American charm, the radical edge ignored in favor of an aestheticized and chic marginality. At the same time, larger sales and wider access open up the possibility of communicating a political and social message to a wider audience, of redefining the mainstream. Castillo's midcareer body of texts, including *So Far from God: A Novel* (1993), *Loverboys*, and *Peel My Love Like an Onion: A Novel* (1999), have all been published to critical acclaim by major presses. June Juffer asks the question that has often haunted these works, and in stated or unstated form is the charge against which Castillo, like Cisneros and Alvarez, must repeatedly defend herself: "Yet what happens when the roads lead you to W. W. Norton, *USA Weekend* and Barnes and Noble? Have you then lost your soul?" As Juffer reminds us, one of the stories from *Loverboys* celebrates the small bookstore and the importance of "alternative press publications that inform you about what's going on with the majority of the population when you sure don't hear it from the mass media" (*Loverboys*, p. 12). Ironically, as Juffer notes, "another story from *Loverboys*, 'Juan in a Million,' was featured in *USA Weekend*, with a distribution of 40 million."

Castillo's third novel, *So Far from God* is set in an unincorporated village named Tome near Chimayó in New Mexico. It tells the story of matriarch Sofía and her four daughters: the portentously named Esperanza, Caridad, Fe, and the baby of the family, who is known only as La Loca. The tone of this novel is set from its opening pages. *So Far from God* begins with the death of the three-year-old baby, who at her funeral sits up, talks, and floats to the ceiling, endowed ever after with miraculous powers. The novel that follows is a blend of folk spirituality, local color, magical realism so overdone as to seem convincingly parodic, and quirky characterizations. It is, in fact, this recapturing of New Mexican Hispano spirituality that has most interested the critics of this novel and that has served as the main focus of literary studies on it. Here again, Castillo's spiritual side departs from traditional Catholic doctrine, as is immediately evident in her irreverent play on the names Fe, Esperanza, and Caridad (Faith, Hope, and Charity).

Esperanza, the least interesting and unusual of the daughters, disappears from the novel after a few chapters, to serve as a TV journalist reporting on a U.S. war in the Middle East, where she is kidnapped and killed. Fe, "La Gritona," is rejected by her first fiancé, goes on to a ho-hum career in ACME, marries, gets pregnant, and dies of a cancer caused by chemical exposure at work. The other women in the family have more extraordinary destinies. Caridad, after sleeping around with men she meets in bars and suffering through three abortions, all of which are performed rather magically by her sister La Loca, is found one day mutilated and left for dead by the side of the road. With La Loca's help, she manages to miraculously restore herself to full health and beauty, with the odd side effect that ever after she is blessed with the ability to see the future. As a natural extension of these powers, she dedicates herself to honing her talents as a *curandera* (some of the *remedios* she learns from her centenarian mentor are included in the text for our delectation). La Loca is a multitalented woman; she speaks with ectoplasmic spirits including La Llorona, trains horses, cooks magnificently (samples of recipes are included), and performs miracles. Eventually, she finds herself mysteriously ill with AIDS, and despite the best in both *curanderismo* and pyschic surgery, dies a second time. Matriarch Sofía, meanwhile, finds in herself a talent for leadership and becomes the unofficial mayor of her village and in later years the founder of MOMAS (Mothers of Martyrs and Saints).

The novel's setting is the arid beauty of the New Mexican desert, and Castillo eloquently captures the feel and flavors of small town Hispano life in the rural backwaters of the state. There is also some of Castillo's trademark social commentary in this novel. For instance, Sofía's neighbors, under her leadership, form a group in Tome called "Los Ganados y Lana Cooperative," a clear homage to the well-known, successful, real-world, grass-roots–based New Mexico cooperative Ganados del Valle. Furthermore, Castillo hints at the racial dimension of environmental devastation as reflected in the way the infamous NIMBY (not in my back yard) agitation usually means that ethnic minorities bear the brunt of toxic exposure.

There are many other small pleasures in this novel—the New Mexican *santero* who relaxes with Charles Bronson videos, and the story of Domingo and Sofía's courtship—but overall *So Far from God* treads a thin line between ironic citation and affectionate homage. Too often it slips over the edge. This is, after all, Castillo's first work to appear from a major publishing house. Much of the language reads like an overdone in-joke against a mainstream public that looks to U.S. Latinas for exotic Latin American–style magic realism and that has until very recently been reluctant to allow a full range of writing from such recognizably ethnic writers. Whether out of conscious parody or editorial marketing pressures, this book offers downmarket magic realism in its most straightforward form. Parallels with other books that have captured the dominant-culture imagination are almost too obvious. Gabriel García Márquez, in the mega-international bestseller *Cien años de soledad* (1967; *One Hundred Years of Solitude,* 1970), has Remedios la Bella; Castillo has La Loca; Sofía is an updated Ursula Buendía; Francisco el Penitente wanders through the novel like a hapless José Arcadio. The *remedios* and recipes seem drawn directly from Laura Esquivel's equally famous book, the phenomenal 1989 best-seller *Como agua para chocolate* (*Like Water for Chocolate: A Novel in Monthly*

Installments, with Recipes, Romances, and Home Remedies, 1992). *So Far from God* is, finally, a moderately entertaining but too extravagantly imaged narrative.

Much more interesting is Castillo's *Peel My Love Like an Onion,* which returns to a more tempered and balanced narrative form. This diary-like novel follows the adventures of an unusual heroine from her adolescence to her forties. It tells of the ups and downs in Carmen la Coja's life, from her early and disabling bout with polio, through her career as a professional flamenco dancer despite her handicap, and ending with her success as a singer and recording artist. Carmen profoundly identifies with Frida Kahlo, who is mentioned several times throughout this novel as an example of another exceptional woman who was able to achieve astonishing artistic heights despite a crippling injury, and the reader is surely intended to see Carmen as a strong, creative woman in that vein. Spice is added to the novel by Carmen's two lovers: the older and married Agustín, and the passionate and talented young Manolo. In her travels, Carmen meets a good many other interesting men as well, including *Sapogonia*'s Máximo Madrigal, who makes a cameo appearance. Máximo praises Carmen's dancing, plays piano for her one evening in a Sapogón restaurant, and becomes her lover for a summer during one of Agustín's periodic absences to visit his Romany wife in Spain. All three of these wildly attractive and sexy men leave Carmen at the low point in her career, when dancing becomes impossible for her and the polio returns to further disable her. At this emotional and economic low, Carmen is forced to sew in a Korean sweatshop ("a page right out of Dickens" [p. 123]) until the place is raided by the Immigration and Naturalization Service, and then to make pizzas at the airport Domino's for minimum wage. All three men appear again at the end of the novel, when Carmen makes a name for herself as a successful flamenco singer. In an apparently unrelated move, the three men renew their affairs with her.

The novel wears its melodramatic roots self-consciously; it is, after all, fundamentally a romantic tale of the trials and tribulations of passion from the perspective of an abandoned woman. Despite Carmen's status as childless, crippled, never having been married, and working long hours at a soul-draining, exhausting job, she never evokes or asks for pity. Likewise, her relationships with the men in her life are completely healthy and natural. Carmen defines what she feels for the two main lovers as a deep and abiding love, or maybe an obsession, or at least a strong lust, and she is highly aware, in hindsight at least, of the way hormonal changes come to be defined in flowery emotion. As Carmen says on the first page of the novel: "When you are in love no single metaphor is enough. No metaphor appears just a tad clichéd. . . . Love . . . is riddled with clichés" (pp. 1–2). Carmen's knowledge does not prevent her from falling into this emotional minefield; for example, her teacher and seventeen-year lover Agustín "became as essential to my life as the sun that rises each morning" (p. 23). The melodrama of these sentiments is tempered by realism. As Carmen knows, both Agustín and Manolo are faithful only to their Romany traditions, in that they feel no compelling need to be either honest or faithful with a non-Romany lover: "Gajo. Gaji. That probably means you. And in the end, it meant me, too" (p. 31). In the relationship with Agustín, the line that is crossed is his immediate instinct to buy the first ticket back to Spain when Carmen becomes pregnant (she loses the child). Carmen does not remain inconsolable for long; his abandonment opens the way for Agustín's godson and fellow dancer Manolo, a knife-carrying bad boy oozing wicked sensuality.

As literary scholar Ivelisse Rodríguez says, in this novel

> Carmen is in love in every cliché way possible, first with one man, Agustín, and then with a second, Manolo. But Castillo plays with clichés by often pointing them out, and busting them open. Women, Castillo suggests, are fed notions of what

love is and with these notions are taught to wait and suffer. . . . We are taught to love in clichés.

The end of the novel, however, is entirely unexpected. Carmen triumphs over the clichés, earns a successful and fulfilling life on her own terms, and as a mature, independent woman is able to accept back into her life both of her lovers—changing entirely the script for the familiar happily-ever-after ending of fairy tales and series romance. Says Rodríguez: "Castillo presents us with a woman that waits but changes the end to the myth, and oft times reality, of the waiting woman by stripping love of its clichés." In Carmen's own words: "My two lovers were not gods or real men. They just thought they were" (p. 140). Carmen's most astringent observation is precisely this: that real men take responsibility for their actions. However, that type of male human being has never entered the orbit of either Carmen's or her mother's life, nor the lives of most of the women they know. And so Carmen deals with this reality without covering it up: "You just have to face the music pay the piper dance to the beat of your own drum and keep in mind that clichés aside all is fair in love and war" (p. 197).

The men in Carmen's life never become any more responsible, but as an older and wiser woman she no longer expects anything from them, and she also learns that ignoring them, letting them go, is the most perfect aphrodisiac of all, confirming her desirability. "I was no longer obsessing over Manolo," she says at the end of the novel. "I had waited for him to show up for five years and for five years had thought of nothing but being with him again. But since we made love in the back office it had all stopped. My heart was at peace. . . . Sometimes when Manolo calls I say, Okay, you can come see me. . . . Sure, come over! I also say to Agustín on other nights when he calls" (pp. 212–213). For Carmen, if "real men" are not part of her life, then learning to be a real woman—meaning a strong and independent individual—is a top priority: "like Kahlo, Benítez, Kali, I'm not afraid. No matter what you do, when you are first a woman it means you cannot ever be afraid" (p. 186).

Recently Castillo has been dipping into children's literature. In 2000 she published a book for elementary school children, *My Daughter, My Son, the Eagle, the Dove: An Aztec Chant (Mi hija, mi hijo, el aguila, la paloma: Un canto Azteca, 2000).* The book features a chant based on Aztec traditions that mark rites of passage with specific admonitions, and it has separate sections for a son and a daughter. In another genre, the most highly visible poem of *I Ask the Impossible,* "El Chicle," also speaks to many age groups. This poem first appeared as part of the Poetry in Motion series on the subways and buses of the Chicago Transit Authority and the Metropolitan Transit Authority of New York City. In the best sense, this poem belongs to the great and under-recognized genre of children's literature, and it has some of the delightful unexpectedness of the "On Top of Old Smokey" parody "On Top of Spaghetti," which details the adventures of a hapless lost meatball. In Castillo's poem, the narrator's son accidentally loses his gum while laughing, and it gets stuck in his mother's hair. She has to clip out *el chicle,* which,

> after I clipped it,
> flew in the air,
> on the back
> of a dragonfly
> that dipped in the creek
> and was snapped
> fast by a turtle
> that reached high
> and swam deep.
>
> (p. 4)

"El Chicle" shows Castillo's fantasy at its absurd and clever best, and together these recent projects suggest new directions for a talented artist who is still continually reinventing herself. Ana Castillo's work has evolved from the darker and more overtly political work of her earlier publications, to a turn toward a lighter, if equally committed style in her more mature writings.

Selected Bibliography

WORKS OF ANA CASTILLO

POETRY

Otro Canto. Chicago: Alternative Publications, 1977.

Women Are Not Roses. Houston: Arte Público Press, 1984.

My Father Was a Toltec: Poems. Albuquerque, N.Mex.: West End Press, 1988.

My Father Was a Toltec and Selected Poems, 1973–1988. New York: W. W. Norton, 1995.

I Ask the Impossible: Poems. New York: Anchor Books, 2001.

The Invitation. Berkeley, Calif.: Third Woman Press, 1979.

PROSE

The Mixquiahuala Letters. Binghamton, N.Y.: Bilingual Press, 1986. (Novel.)

Sapogonia: An Anti-Romance in 3/8 Meter. Tempe, Ariz.: Bilingual Press. (Novel.)

So Far from God: A Novel. New York: W. W. Norton, 1993. (Novel.)

Massacre of the Dreamers: Essays on Xicanisma. Albuquerque: University of New Mexico Press, 1994. (Essays.)

Loverboys: Stories. New York: W. W. Norton, 1996. (Short stories.)

Máscaras. Berkeley, Calif.: Third Woman Press, 1997.

Peel My Love Like an Onion: A Novel. New York: Doubleday, 1999. (Novel.)

My Daughter, My Son, the Eagle, the Dove: An Aztec Chant / Mi hija, mi hijo, el aguila, la paloma: Un canto Azteca. Illustrated by Susan Guevara. New York: Dutton Books, 2000. (A children/young adults coming-of-age story.)

"Yes, Dear Critic, There Really Is an Alicia." In *Máscaras.* Edited by Lucha Corpi. Berkeley, Calif.: Third Woman Press, 1997.

EDITED VOLUMES

This Bridge Called My Back: Writings by Radical Women of Color/Esta puente, mi espalda: Voces de mujeres tercermundistas en los Estados Unidos. Edited by Cherríe Moraga and Ana Castillo. Translated by Ana Castillo and Norma Alarcón. San Francisco: ISM Press, 1988. (Essays.)

The Sexuality of Latinas. Edited with Norma Alarcón and Cherríe Moraga. Berkeley: Third Woman Press, 1993. (Essays.)

Neueste Chicano-Lyrik. Edited with Heiner Bus. Bamberg: Universitätsbibliothek Bamberg, 1994.

Goddess of the Americas/La diosa de las Américas: Writings on the Virgin of Guadalupe. New York: Riverhead Books, 1996. (Essays.)

SOUND

Castillo, Ana. The author reads from her works on December 2, 1994, in the Recording Laboratory, studio A, Library of Congress, Washington, D.C., for the Archive of Hispanic Literature on Tape.

SECONDARY SOURCES

INTERVIEWS

"American Fear." *Hungry Mind Review* (fall 1992): 12.

Baker, Samuel. "Ana Castillo: The Protest Poet Goes Mainstream." *Publishers Weekly* 243, no. 33 (August 12, 1996): 59–60.

Brady, Thomas. "An Artist Drawn to Write Poetry of Protest." *Philadelphia Inquirer,* April 12, 1998.

Calzada, Susana Urra. "Ana Castillo: La Voz de la Mujer Chicana." *FoxNews.com* (Fox en Español), February 25, 2000.

Fernández de la Reguera, Tanit. "El vuelo de las brujas: Celebran 'Las bellas brujas' el Día de Muertos." *¡EXITO!* (November 5, 1998): 41.

Garza, Melita Marie. "After Years of Self-Imposed Exile, Latina Writer Ana Castillo Returns to Chicago." *Chicago Tribune,* November 26, 1996, North Sports final edition, Tempo, p. 1.

Grimshaw, Heather, and Jana Siciliano. "Interview." *BookReporter.com,* November 12, 1999.

March, Dido. "Entre dos mundos: Ana Castillo explora la compleja identidad chicana." *¡EXITO!* May 20, 1999, p. 13.

Milligan, Bryce. "Interview with Ana Castillo." *South Central Review: The Journal of the South Central Modern Language Association* 16, no. 1 (spring 1999): 19–29.

Robinson, Alice. "Chicano Poet Speaks of Civil Rights." *The Michigan Daily,* February 17, 1997.

Romero, Simon. "Interview." *NuCity* 18 (June–July 1993).

Saeta, Elsa. "A MELUS Interview: Ana Castillo." *MELUS* 22, no. 3 (fall 1997): 133.

Seyda, Barbara. "Massacre of the Dreamers: An Interview with Ana Castillo." *Sojourner* 20, no. 9 (May 1995): 16–17.

Shea, Renee H. "Ana Castillo: No Silence for This Dreamer." *Poets & Writers* (March/April 2000): 32.

"Universally Speaking; Ana Castillo's Writings Reach Out to Mainstream Audience." *Austin American-Statesman,* November 24, 1996, Lifestyle, p. E8.

Vázquez, Sonia. "Múltiples facetas del talento femenino." *La Raza,* Festival Sor Juana, 1999.

PAPERS

Castillo, Ana. *Papers.* 1973–1990. University of California, Santa Barbara. 7 linear ft. (16 boxes): ill. Organized into five series:

Series I. Personal and biographical information, 1974–1990.

Series II. Correspondence with poets and writers, 1973–1990.

Series III. Correspondence and contracts with publishers, 1977–1990.

Series IV. Writings published and unpublished, 1973–1990.

Series V. Silkscreens and offset poster, 1977–1982.

(Three subseries of Series I closed until 2038 or ten years after the donor's death, whichever occurs first.)

CRITICAL STUDIES

Alarcón, Norma. "The Sardonic Powers of the Erotic in the Work of Ana Castillo." In *Breaking Boundaries: Latina Writing and Critical Readings.* Edited by Asunción Horno Delgado et al. Amherst: University of Massachusetts Press, 1989.

Bennett, Tanya Long. "No Country to Call Home: A Study of Castillo's *Mixquiahuala Letters*." *Style* 30, no. 3 (fall 1996): 462–478.

Bower, Anne L. *Epistolary Responses: The Letter in Twentieth-Century American Fiction and Criticism,* University of Indiana Press, 1996.

Bus, Heiner. "'I Too Was of the Small Corner of the World': The Cross-Cultural Experience in Ana Castillo's *The Mixquiahuala Letters* (1986)." *Americas Review: A Review of Hispanic Literature and Art of the USA* 21, no. 3–4 (fall–winter 1993): 128–138.

Caputi, Jane. "Review of Goddess of the Americas." *The Women's Review of Books* 14, no. 8 (May 1997): 16.

Carr, Irene Campos. "*The Mixquiahuala Letters*." *Belles Lettres: A Review of Books by Women* 8, no. 3 (spring 1993): 19.

———. "*So Far from God*." *Belles Lettres: A Review of Books by Women* 9, no. 1 (fall 1993): 52.

Castillo, Debra A. "Borderliners: Federico Campbell and Ana Castillo." In *Reconfigured Spheres: Feminist Explorations of Literary Space.* Edited by Margaret R. Higonnet and Joan Templeton. Amherst: University of Massachusetts Press, 1994. Pp. 147–170.

Chávez-Silverman, Susana. "Chicana Outlaws: Turning Our (Brown) Backs on La Ley Del Papá(cito)." *Revista Canaria de Estudios Ingleses* 37 (November 1998): 69–87.

Cook, Barbara J. "La Llorona and a Call for Environmental Justice in the Borderlands: Ana Castillo's *So Far from God*." *Northwest Review* 39, no. 2 (2001): 124–133.

Cooper, Janet. "A Two-Headed Freak and a Bad Wife Search for Home: Border Crossing in *Nisei Daughter* and *The Mixquiahuala Letters*." In *Literature and Ethnicity in the Cultural Borderlands.* Edited by Jesús Benito and Anna María Manzanas. Amsterdam: Rodopi, 2002.

Curiel, Barbara Brinson. "Heteroglossia in Ana Castillo's *The Mixquiahuala Letters.*" *Discurso: Revista de Estudios Iberoamericanos* 7, no. 1 (1990): 11–23.

Delgadillo, Theresa. "Forms of Chicana Feminist Resistance: Hybrid Spirituality in Ana Castillo's *So Far From God*." *MFS: Modern Fiction Studies* 44, no. 4 (winter 1998): 888–916.

Dubrava, Patricia. "Ana Castillo: Impressions of a Xicana Dreamer: A Profile." *Bloomsbury Review* 15, no. 6 (November–December 1995): 5, 13.

Elenes, C. Alejandra. "Chicana Feminist Narratives and the Politics of the Self." *Frontiers: A Journal of Women's Studies* 21, no. 3 (2000): 105–123.

Espin, Olivia M. "*Third Woman: The Sexuality of Latinas.*" *The Journal of Sex Research* 27, no. 1 (February 1990): 143.

Evenson, Brian. "Review of Loverboys." *The Review of Contemporary Fiction* 17, no. 1 (spring 1997): 201.

Gillman, Laura, and Stacey M. Floyd-Thomas. "Con un pie a cada lado/With a Foot in Each Place: Mestizaje as Transnational Feminisms in Ana Castillo's *So Far from God*." *Meridians: Feminism, Race, Transnationalism* 2, no. 1 (2001): 158–175.

Gomez-Vega, Ibis. "Debunking Myths: The Hero's Role in Ana Castillo's *Sapogonia*." *The Americas Review: A Review of Hispanic Literature and Art* 22, nos. 1–2 (spring–summer 1994): 244–258.

Gonzales-Berry, Erlinda. "*The* (Subversive) *Mixquiahuala Letters*: An Antidote for Self-Hate." In *L'Ici et ailleurs.* Edited by Jean Beranger and Jean Cazemajou. Press Universitaire de Bordeaux: Centre de Recherches sur l'Amérique Anglophone, 1991. Pp. 227–240.

Hampton, Janet Jones. "Ana Castillo pinta con palabras." *Américas* 52, no. 1 (January–February 2000): 48–53.

Her Heritage: A Biographical Encyclopedia of Famous American Women, CD-ROM, Pilgrim New Media, 1996.

Juffer, Jane. "On Ana Castillo's Poetry." http://www.english.uiuc.edu/maps/poets/a_f/castillo/about.htm (December 12, 2002).

Lanza, Carmela. "Hearing Voices: Women and Home and Ana Castillo's *So Far from God.*" *MELUS* 23, no. 1 (spring 1998): 65–79.

———. "'A New Meeting with the Sacred': Ana Castillo's So Far from God." *RLA: Romance Languages Annual* 10, no. 2 (1998): 658–663.

Manríquez, B. J. "Ana Castillo's *So Far from God*: Intimations of the Absurd." *College Literature* 29, no. 2 (spring 2002): 37–49.

———. "Doing Rhetorical Analysis: *Sapogonia,* The Rhetoric of Irony." *Genre: Forms of Discourse and Culture* 32, no. 1–2 (spring–summer 1999): 53–72.

Marzan, Julio, and Ron Padgett. "Other Poetic Models." *Teachers & Writers* 28, no. 3 (January–February 1997): 8–11.

Mejía, Jaime Armin. "Review of *So Far From God.*" *Southwest American Literature* 19, no. 1 (fall 1993): 94.

"*My Father Was a Toltec and Selected Poems.*" *The Literary Review* 41, no. 1 (fall 1997): 137.

Pérez, Domino Renee. "Crossing Mythological Borders: Revisioning La Llorona in Contemporary Fiction." *Proteus: A Journal of Ideas* 16, no. 1 (spring 1999): 49–54.

Platt, Kamala. "Ecocritical Chicana Literature: Ana Castillo's 'Virtual Realism.'" *Isle: Interdisciplinary Studies in Literature and Environment* 3, no. 1 (summer 1996): 67–96.

Quintana, Alvina E. "Ana Castillo's *The Mixquiahula Letters*: The Novelist as Ethnographer." In *Criticism in the Borderlands: Studies in Chicano Literature, Culture, and Ideology.* Edited by Hector Calderon and Jose David Saldivar. Durham, N.C.: Duke University Press, 1991.

Racz, Gregory J. "Two Bilingual Spanish-English Collections." *Literary Review: An International Journal of Contemporary Writing* 41, no. 1 (fall 1997): 137–141.

Ricard, Serge, ed. *Etats-Unis/Mexique: Fascinations et répulsions réciproques.* Paris: Harmattan, 1996.

Rodríguez, Ivelisse. "Killing Buddha, Killing Myths: Ana Castillo's *Peel My Love Like an Onion.*" *Gráfico,* http://www.latnn.com/grafico/books/articles/books010200.htm (accessed April 16, 2003).

Rueda Esquibel, Catriona. "Memories of Girlhood: Chicana Lesbian Fictions." *Signs: Journal of Women in Culture and Society* 23, no. 3 (spring 1998): 644–681.

Saeta, Elsa. "Ana Castillo's *Sapogonia*: Narrative Point of View as a Study in Perception." *Confluencia: Revista Hispanica de Cultura y Literatura* 10, no. 1 (fall 1994): 67–72.

Sanchez, Alberto Sandoval. "Breaking the Silence, Dismantling Taboos: Latino Novels on AIDS (Gay and Lesbian Literature Since World War II: History and Memory)." *Journal of Homosexuality* 34, no. 3–4 (March 1998): 155–175.

Sanchez, Rosaura. "Review of *Massacre of the Dreamers.*" *American Literary History* 9, no. 2 (summer 1997): 350.

Sauer, Michelle M. "'Saint-Making' in Ana Castillo's *So Far from God*: Medieval Mysticism as Precedent for an Authoritative Chicana Spirituality." *Mester* 29 (2000): 72–91.

Shea, Maureen E. "Latin American Women and the Oral Tradition: Giving Voice to the Voiceless." *Critique: Studies in Contemporary Fiction* 34, no. 3 (spring 1993): 139–154.

Socolovsky, Maya. "Borrowed Homes, Homesickness, and Memory in Ana Castillo's *Sapogonia*." *Aztlán: A Journal of Chicano Studies* 24, no. 2 (fall 1999): 73–94.

Stavans, Ilan. "The New Latino: A Literary Renaissance." *Bloomsbury Review* (March/April 1993): 1, 7.

Toyosato, Mayumi. "Grounding Self and Action: Land, Community, and Survival in *I, Rigoberta Menchú, No Telephone to Heaven*, and *So Far from God*." *Hispanic Journal* 19, no. 2 (fall 1998): 295–311.

Walter, Roland. "The Cultural Politics of Dislocation and Relocation in the Novels of Ana Castillo." *MELUS* 23, no. 1 (spring 1998): 81–97.

Yarbro-Bejarano, Yvonne. "The Multiple Subject in the Writing of Ana Castillo." *The Americas Review: A Review of Hispanic Literature and Art of the USA* 20, no. 1 (spring 1992): 65–72.

OTHER WORKS

Anzaldúa, Gloria. *Borderlands: The New Mestiza/La frontera.* San Francisco, Calif.: Spinsters/Aunt Lute, 1987.

Esquivel, Laura. *Como agua para chocolate: Novela de entregas mensuales con recetas, amores, y remedios caseros.* New York: Doubleday, 1993.

Freire, Paul. *Pedagogy of the Oppressed.* Translated by Myra Bergman Ramos. Revised 20th anniversary edition. New York: Continuum, 1993.

García Márquez, Gabriel. *Cien años de soledad.* Buenos Aires: Editorial Sudamericana, 1969.

Moraga, Cherríe. *Loving in the War Years: Lo que nunca pasó por sus labios.* Boston: South End Press, 1983.

Lorna Dee Cervantes

(1954–)

AMANDA NOLACEA HARRIS-FONSECA

Lines from Lorna Dee Cervantes's poetry have become pervasive and characteristic in Chicana literary and critical texts. Her first book, *Emplumada* (1981), which won the 1982 American Book Award from the Before Columbus Foundation, addresses themes intrinsic to feminism and to the Chicano movement. Adela de la Torre and Beatríz M. Pesquera's now-classic anthology of Chicana criticism, *Building with Our Hands: New Directions in Chicana Studies,* borrows its title from the closing stanza of what is probably Cervantes's most cited poem. The adoption of "building with our hands" by Pesquera and de la Torre, when read in the context of Cervantes's poem, suggests the construction of a matriarchally defined field of studies involving the history and culture of Chicanas and Chicanos. Her second book, *From the Cables of Genocide: Poems on Love and Hunger* (1991), received the Paterson Poetry Prize, the 1993 Latino Literature Prize, and a National Book Award nomination. The poetry in this collection, markedly denser and less idealistic than that in *Emplumada,* furthers the themes of the first book in drawing on the matriarchal family and woman-specific concepts of the world in her development of the topics of survival, loss, disillusionment, and the coexistence of beauty and the abject.

The critical-theoretical trends of the women's movement (roughly from the late 1960s to the mid-1980s) deconstruct linear concepts of history, previously unchallenged Western concepts that have excluded women and assumed a universal cultural experience. Feminist theories and strategies of this period refuse linear temporality and retrospectively construct the first wave by identifying their predecessors, thus designating the women's movement as the second wave of feminism. Tey Diana Rebolledo explains in "The Writer as Translator of Foreign Mail/Male; or, The Writer as Malinche" that the emphasis on foremothers in Chicana writers' construction of identity bridges the alienating effect of entering into written discourse as a Chicana woman. Chicana writers, explains Rebolledo, draw upon ancestors such as Malinche as pioneers for women's participation in the construction of history and culture, and particularly in the negotiation of a non-antithetical identity as Chicanas and writers. Julia Kristeva explains in her 1997 essay "Women's Time" that second-wave feminism conceptualizes time as cyclical and thereby links female subjectivity to the maternal and eternal—a concept that, unlike linear temporality, allows for simultaneous and varied experiences of history.

Cervantes develops the cyclical concept of time through her use of matriarchal genealogy. She dedicates her second book to her intellectual foremothers: the American poet Sylvia Plath, the Mexican artist Frida Kahlo, and the South American poet and songwriter Violeta Parra. Many Chicana authors of the seventies and eighties address identity as women, Chicanas, and writers through allusions to and allegories of historical foremothers, and through female archetypes that highlight lineage, and thus an entitlement to the traditions of empowering female-centered discourse. (For archetypal theory in Chicana criticism, see María Herrera-Sobek's introduction and Tey Diana Rebolledo's 1995 *Women Singing in the Snow: A Cultural Analysis of Chicana Literature*, chapters 3, 4, and 8.) The focus on historical public women and matriarchal female archetypes (as opposed to the patriarchal female archetypes such as virgin and whore) draws a line of ancestry for women writers that does not concede to men the monopoly over written and public intellectual discourse—a purpose that emerges clearly in the tension that *Emplumada* develops between access to education through men and loyalty to women. Cervantes's consistent employment of the Native American grandmother archetype echoes second-wave Anglo-European feminism's assertion of precedent as a strategy for negotiating a space in the male-dominated discourse. Sandra Gilbert and Susan Gubar theorize this trend as a manifestation of the women's "anxiety of authorship." Their theory, however, addresses only gender-based lack of access to language, ignoring other social factors that Chicana feminism cannot avoid. While the poem clearly addresses gender-based oppression within the Chicano community, it also uses ethnically specific lineage. Very much in line with the trends of the Chicano movement, Cervantes emphasizes Native American ancestry and family ties. Like the issue of social immobility that frames the whole poem, the grandmother archetype connotes ethnicity and gender at once.

Chicana feminists (along with feminists of color and third-world feminism in general) of the second wave go beyond gender as the major sociocultural factor in inequality. The prevailing message of feminists of color from the late sixties to the present is that no complete revolution exists if it does not liberate everyone. To the primarily white, middle-class, heterosexual second-wavers, feminists of color demand that class-, race-, and ethnicity-based inequality among women (and in society generally) be a part of the feminist struggle; to the nationalists and ethnic activists they demand recognition of women's oppression (and ethnic female subjectivity) within the ethnic movements. This theme is explicitly laid out in Cervantes's "Para un revolucionario" (1975, For a revolutionary), originally published in *Revista Chicano-Riqueña*, which demands gender equality within the Chicano struggle. After describing the gender segregation in the movement, the relegation of women to child rearing, cooking, and service work contributions, Cervantes reminds her Chicano (male) counterpart, "I too am raza" (p. 74). The struggle for freedom from oppressive structures described in Cervantes's poetry encompasses gender-based inequality within the ethnic community as well as class-, race-, and ethnicity-based inequality in the larger world of Chicanos in the United States.

CERVANTES AND CHICANA FEMINISM

"Beneath the Shadow of the Freeway," from *Emplumada*, sets the framework of Cervantes's oeuvre and textualizes the major concepts of second-wave feminism as well as the themes of class, race, and ethnicity specific to Chicana feminism of the eighties.

> and in time, I plant geraniums.
> I tie up my hair into loose braids,
> and trust only what I have built
> with my own hands.

> (p. 14)

This final stanza exemplifies the connection to the land and ethnicity, and the quest for self-determination that the 1969 "Plan Espiritual de Aztlán" and the 1970 "Plan de Santa Bárbara" claim as integral tenets of the Chicano movement. The poem constructs a female, gender-specific self: the braiding of the hair (which connotes indigenous heritage) and the planting of geraniums are tasks performed by a woman—unlike the two plans, much of the classic Chicano literature, and Armando Rendón's *Chicano Manifesto,* for example, which construct a universal Chicano community through masculinity. In Cervantes the connection to the land, to ethnicity as symbolized in the braiding of the hair, and the construction of a Chicana subjectivity have everything to do with cyclical, matrilineal concepts of self and the relationship of the self to the surrounding cultures, moving in concentric circles—first the woman-centered community, then Chicano culture, then the United States.

The poem opens with a description of the social and geographical setting in which this matriarchal and matrilineal family lives: between "Sal Si Puedes" and "Los Altos" (literally, between "Get Out If You Can" and "The Heights"), fixed under the shadow of mobility symbolized in the freeway of the poem's title. The poet, speaking from the third generation of a woman-centered family, draws an initial connection between immobility and women's connection to land:

> I watched it [the freeway] from my porch
> unwinding. Every day at dusk
> as Grandma watered geraniums
> the shadow of the freeway lengthened.
>
> (p. 11)

She highlights immobility in the juxtaposition of the freeway, which literally overshadows the house, and the images of earth, pointing to both gender and ethnic issues. The Chicano movement has traditionally tied closeness to nature and native heritage to the entitlement to Aztlán, the Aztec homeland, which encompasses California and the southwest. Two classic Chi-

cano novels, Tomás Rivera's *. . . Y no se lo tragó la tierra* and Rudolfo Anaya's *Bless Me, Última,* as well as the activism of the United Farm Workers, speak to the pervasive rhetoric of Aztlán and the reclaiming of land as liberation. Ironically, the same connection to the land that enables the argument for social equality (and sometimes Chicano autonomy) becomes a source of oppression—usually due to the capitalist exploitation of workers and native communities (see Tomás Rivera). Similarly, feminism looks to the connection to mother earth and non-Western philosophies as empowerment. Cervantes marks both of these connections through the grandmother's relationship to the hills of Santa Barbara and the potted plants, and signals the irony of immobility in the shadow of the hovering freeway. She picks up the theme of land dispossession and displacement later in the collection, for example in "Poem for a Young White Man," "Poema Para los Californios Muertos" (Poem for the dead Californians), and "From Where We Sit."

Establishing the setting of the family's story in the first stanza is part of the narrative style that both Marta Sánchez, in her 1985 *Contemporary Chicana Poetry,* and Deborah Madsen, in her 2000 *Understanding Contemporary Chicana Literature,* identify as characteristic of Cervantes's poetry. Cervantes's narrative, however, highlights a more cyclical than traditionally linear concept of history. The cyclical structure of the poem (observable in many of the poems of *Emplumada,* including "Uncle's First Rabbit"), beginning with the grandmother watering geraniums and ending with the poet planting geraniums, exemplifies the rejection of linear temporality characteristic of second-wave feminism.

The second section of "Beneath the Shadow of the Freeway," composed of two stanzas, positions the poet within her family. "We are a woman family," she states, and goes on to explain the role of grandmother as the "innocent Queen," the role of mother as the "Warrior" who wants to be a princess, and the role of self as "Scribe: Translator of Foreign Mail" (p. 11).

The third section of "Beneath the Shadow of the Freeway" introduces the bird-and-feather motif that recurs throughout Cervantes's two books of poetry and that informs the name of the first book. As the author explains in the epigraph of *Emplumada,* the feathers connote molting, symbolic rebirth, and liberation from the past, as well as writing, "pen flourish." Given the theme of cyclical patriarchal violence and social immobility over generations, the dual signification of the word "*emplumada*" ties writing directly to liberation. The grandmother is the first figure to introduce birds into the book. She frames the poet's interpretation of the birds, making them carriers of omens and ideals. The seagulls warn of coming storms, and the mockingbirds represent an ideal in their mating practices, in direct contrast to the absent men of the poem: "They don't leave their families" (p. 12), and they sing for their nesting wives. The grandmother serves here again as a figure connecting the poet to nature and feminism. Cervantes evokes ethnic inequality through the image of seabirds begging from tourists in "From Where We Sit: Corpus Christi," and she signals contrast and the coexistence of life and death or beauty and abjection in various poems in both collections through the image of diving and flying seabirds. The black crows appear as scavengers, as death, and as liberation from the recurring cycles of violence and immobility. In "Crow," the poet clearly projects herself into the female crow that flies out from a pine tree to bask in the sun and change color. "I saw myself," states the poet, after observing the crow. She then goes on to outline the process of liberation based on the tools and education that women gave her "before men came" (p. 19). The feathers of the book's title also appear in the title of last poem, which presents the image of two hummingbirds "stuck to each other, / arcing their bodies in grim determination / to find what is good" (p. 66). The observer in this poem characterizes the two birds mating at summer's

end as "warriors / distancing themselves from history," able to resist the passage of the seasons and to "contain the wind" (p. 66). Again, the birds allegorize an ideal that encircles the entire book, from title to last poem—transcendence, romantic union, and liberation. (These ideals appear impossible later, in Cervantes's second book of poetry, *From the Cables of Genocide: Poems on Love and Hunger,* which emphasizes the loss of ideals and the conceptualization of the world as simultaneously beautiful and abject, pointing always to the loss of a male partner's love.)

The third section of "Beneath the Shadow of the Freeway" ends with the grandmother's strategy for survival: "She believes in myths and birds. / She trusts only what she builds / with her own hands" (p. 12). The fourth section fleshes out the contrast between the ideal quality of birds and the practical reality of domestic violence and neglect introduced implicitly by the mockingbirds of the third section. Here we read that the grandmother built her own house after escaping twenty-five years of violence at the hands of her husband, and we read of the mother's rejection of the grandmother as a "soft," culpable victim. The fifth section narrates the mother's relationship with an abusive husband, revealing another dimension of the family cycle. During the quarreling between the mother and her partner, the grandmother stitches a quilt from the recycled material of her husband's suits. The patchwork is "singing / of mockingbirds" (p. 13)—the birds that never leave their nesting wives. Only when deconstructed and re-created by the hands of the grandmother can any vestige of men's participation in the family result in shelter or comfort. Using the house as a metaphor for the family structure and the community, Cervantes presents the matriarchal community as the only trustworthy structure. The physical construction of home and blankets by the matriarch also points to the dismantling of patriarchy and the construction of an alternative, woman-determined structure of community, family, and heritage. Thus the title of the book Pesquera and de la Torre edited, *Building with Our Hands.*

Section six opens with the mother's voice warning the daughter about being too soft and being abused for it, as well as the internalized message from the grandmother's generation, "don't count on nobody" (p. 13). The daughter ignores what the grandmother tells her, implicitly blaming her mother for her own abandonment, and stating about men, "If you're good to them / they'll be good to you back." The author then pans out to the freeway backdrop in the beginning of summer to describe how she enters into the cycle of romance, heterosexual structures, and structural revision. She sleeps every night beside a "gentle man" to the tune of fidelity symbolized in "the hymn of mockingbirds" (p. 14) and inevitably realizes that she cannot trust any structure but the ones that she builds in the self-affirming tradition of the grandmother: "Every night I sleep with a gentle man / to the hymn of mockingbirds, / and in time, I plant geraniums" (p. 14). The mid-sentence transition between finding an exception to the rule of male absence and reverting to the ways of the grandmother marks the transition from believing in romance as something unrelated to structures that oppress women to recognizing that patriarchal structures cannot be trusted. (In *From the Cables of Genocide,* she will push the theme of disillusionment in the male-female family structure further and deal primarily with the reconceptualization of the world from the perspective of the loss of love as an ideal.)

EMPLUMADA: VIOLENCE AGAINST WOMEN, EDUCATION, AND COMMUNITY, DISPLACEMENT, AND DEATH

The opening poem of *Emplumada,* "Uncle's First Rabbit," establishes several themes that appear in the collection. The poem connects the violence of hunting to the grandfather's domestic violence and the uncle's fighting in war to the abuse of his own wife. Here violence is phallic, related to the use of guns and rifles—the word "first" in the title implies the beginning of a cycle, and killing with a hunting rifle is an initiation into the violence embedded in generational cycles that the uncle cannot escape in childhood or adulthood. The poem is about an uncle, not a father, who consciously attempts to break the cycle and who

> had dreamed of running,
> shouldering the rifle to town,
> selling it,
> and taking the next train out.
>
> (p. 3)

The determinism of the cycles make the uncle's efforts to stop the violence pointless. Even when he goes to war, "taking / the bastard's last bloodline / with him" (p. 4), he is unable to die, and comes back only to beat his own wife. As an old man, he reveals that he lives to watch his wife die, and that he has not had sex with her for thirty years. That the poet is not the daughter but the niece of the man in the poem attests to his strategy for breaking the cycle of violence, which is suggested in the uncle's stopping of the patrilineal bloodline: he broke it by not procreating, since he could not escape.

Critics have addressed this poem as a rite of passage and an example of how the author connects patriarchy to political and domestic violence. But considering it in relation to the cyclical nature of the rest of the book, in relation to the parallel generational cycle of the women in "Beneath the Shadow of the Freeway," and in contrast to the female rite of passage allows for a reading of the author's construction of gender. While "Beneath the Shadow of the Freeway" follows the matriarchal line, "Uncle's First Rabbit" follows the patriarchal. The recurring generational motifs in the patrilineal poem are guns, trucks, and trains—all phallic, all related to violence or movement or both, and all synthetic. The train is the only symbol that the character does not want to get rid of, because it offers the potential for escape. In the matrilineal poem, the recurring motifs that tie together the generations are the geraniums and the braided hair. Both are organic and preserve continuity in the family; both grow and are nurtured by the characters in the poem; neither connotes movement, escape, or violence. In both poems, physical mobility, in the form of the train and the freeway, follows a predetermined track and is just out of reach for the protagonists.

"Uncle's First Rabbit" also stands in contrast to "Lots: I" and "Lots: II" in its approach to the loss of innocence in the context of violence between men and women. But while the loss of innocence in "Uncle's First Rabbit" comes from the perpetration of violence, the "Lots" poems construct the process through overcoming victimization. "Lots: I," subtitled "The Ally," narrates the story of a girl "only two years / more than a child" (p. 8), in the third person. The violence suggests sexual assault, as it is set on a "bed of shrubs." The male antagonist, who is more than likely the ironic "ally" of the subtitle, evokes the young woman's voice with his knife:

> But it was the glint
> of steel at her throat
> that cut through
> to her voice.
>
> (p. 8)

After the voice is revealed in this incident, the protagonist ceases to be "silent and still," deciding to live

> arrogantly,
> having wrestled
> her death
> and won.
>
> (p. 8)

The following poem, "Lots: II," subtitled "Herself," begins with a shift in perspective: "I picked myself up" (p. 9). The girl forgets her previous self and notices her body for the first time. She describes her "used skin" glistening, her "first diamond" (p. 9). This unexpected image in the aftermath of abuse signals abuse as a source of strength, something that can create beauty and a hardness with which to confront life as an adult woman. Strangely, this narrative of a woman's coming-of-age is a contrast to the dominant male narrative of a boy triumphantly having a first sexual experience. It also is a contrast to the uncle's coming-of-age, which results from acting out violence for the first time—not from receiving it. Problematic in positing heterosexual violence as a source of female maturity, the "Lots" poems describe a phase of feminism that employs a dialectic between male and female in identity development. The book explores the possibility of same-sex identity development in several poems, always circumscribed by the heterosexual and patriarchal surroundings.

"The Anthill," which immediately precedes "Lots," describes an effort at same-sex identification in a schoolyard. The innocent play of the two girls in the poem leads them to investigate an anthill, and the ants take on the proportions of heterosexist protectors of patriarchal dogmas. The "army" of ants defends its missals (Catholic mass books) while the two girls kick in the nest to uncover the queen and "Recover / The soft white packets / Of her young" (p. 7). Like the protagonist in "Uncle's First Rabbit" who attempts to end the patriarchal violence in his life by refusing to procreate, the girls of this poem steal the generations to come from the patriarchy, which has metamorphosed into the army of ants that protects religion.

Most of the poems that explore same-sex relationships deal with education. Generally, Cervantes portrays the relationship to education as male-identified. "Caribou Girl," "For Edward Long," "Beneath the Shadow of the Freeway," "For Virginia Chavez," and "Crow" highlight the tension between woman-identified knowledge and male-identified education, which is usually symbolized by books. "Beneath the Shadow of the Freeway" privileges women-centered knowledge and cultural heritage, but it also positions the poet as a liaison between the world of writing and the world of women—a position implying that the two worlds do not occupy the same space. When the poet characterizes two generations of her family as innocent queen and fearless woman warrior, she states that she could not decide between those two roles, so she "turned to books, those staunch, upright men. / I became Scribe: Translator of Foreign Mail" (p. 11). "For Edward Long" also posits a man as the source of book learning. Long, who is simultaneously grandfather, father, and man, teaches the poet how to read the poetry of Robert Louis Stevenson and how to write verse.

"For Virginia Chavez" contrasts female experience and books as hard-to-reconcile sources of knowledge. This poem, however, narrates disillusionment with phallic knowledge. Also a narration of the journey from childhood to womanhood, "For Virginia Chavez" recollects the way two girls rejected boys and believed they could steal the power of language from them ("Their wordless tongues we stole / and tasted the power") and then

> utter
> the rules, mark the lines
> and cross them ourselves—we two
> women using our fists, we thought
> our wits, our tunnels.
>
> (p. 16)

The narrative lends itself to a psychoanalytical reading from the perspective of feminism's critique of the Freudian concept of phallocentric language, as is found in the work of Julia Kristeva or Luce Irigary. The past tense marks the inevitable end to the idealism of the same-sex relationship, which appropriates phallic tools for its own purposes. Later, the poet compares

Virginia Chavez's knowledge about love, which she acquired from sexual encounters with men, to her own readings of "Lord Byron, Donne, / and the Brownings" (p. 17). Virginia's pregnancy and the poet's processing of the loss of innocence lead her to say,

> you cried
> when you read that poem I wrote you,
> something about our "waning moons"
> and the child in me
> I let die that summer.
>
> (p. 17)

The metaphorical dead child (innocence lost as textualized in the poem she alludes to), juxtaposed to the child in fourteen-year-old Chavez's belly, points to the difference between knowledge that is acquired intellectually and personal experience. The poem concludes with a description of Virginia's face after a beating, presumably by a man. Chavez and her poet-friend link arms and retreat together in an effort to ignore the major rift between them: "my diploma and the bare bulb / that always lit your bookless room" (p. 18). In contrast, "Crow" looks to "the words women gave me" as a source of liberation. Directly following "Virginia Chavez," "Crow" marks a lesson she has learned about not relying on male-centered power.

Many critics draw upon Cervantes's biography in interpreting her poetry. Doing so would make Cervantes herself the poetic voice that struggles with her relationship to education and community. She received her B.A. at San Jose State University and did her graduate studies at the University of California, Santa Cruz, where she received her Ph.D. in philosophy and aesthetics in 1979, the same year she was awarded a National Endowment for the Arts grant. Cervantes is associate professor of English at the University of Colorado, Boulder, where she teaches graduate and undergraduate creative writing workshops as well as poetry, poetics,

Chicano and indigenous literature, multicultural writing, contemporary women's literature, cross-cultural American literature, and the literature of exile. Her awards and honors include National Endowment for the Arts fellowships and a Pushcart Prize. Cervantes has maintained an academic relationship to the Chicano community through her involvement in Chicana/Chicano and women-specific publications. As founder and editor of literary journals such as *Mango* and *Red Dirt,* a cross-cultural poetry journal, Cervantes has been a leader in the Chicana/Chicano literary movement.

In addition to presenting a gendered relationship to education, Cervantes presents education in light of class and ethnicity. "To My Brother" looks at education as a means of escape from poverty. In "Cannery Town in August," she writes about the poet's role as a voice writing on behalf of the silent, "dumbed" (p. 6), working poor. Such a position, however, distances the poet from the community. "Visions of Mexico While at a Writing Symposium in Port Townsend, Washington" also addresses the often antithetical relationship between community on one hand and writing and education on the other. The poem describes an uneasy relationship with language for both men and women: "I come from a long line of eloquent illiterates / whose history reveals what words don't say" (p. 45). Mexicans, Chicanos, and Chicanas in this poem use gestures and song in lieu of language. The poet finds language, particularly written language, in the north: "I come north / to gather my feathers / for quills" (p. 47).

The sense of displacement brought on by separation from community is described in "Visions" and takes on specifically ethnic tones in the relationship to the Spanish language and dispossession from the land. The loss of Spanish becomes symbolic of displacement in "Refugee Ship" and the parallel "Barco de refugiados," Cervantes's only poem written solely in Spanish. Cervantes's use of bilingualism has drawn critical attention (see Ada Savin) as being

symbolic of her culture. The two poems, the second a Spanish version of the first, explain the irony of the poet's discomfort with Spanish, given her "bronzed skin, black hair" (p, 41). The resulting lack of belonging comes across in the metaphor of a refugee ship that never docks. The Spanish version demonstrates limited knowledge of grammar and syntax. Her apologetic tone fits the content, in which the poet discloses that she is an orphan from her Spanish surname (p. 40). "Oaxaca, 1974" takes place in Mexico, where the poet cannot understand the language and encounters difficulty as a dark-skinned *pocha* (an Americanized, U.S.-raised Latina) with a Hispanic name. Imagining that Mexico rejects her, spitting at her or calling her a whore ("Esputa" [p. 44]), and that old women whisper in corners as she passes, the narrator exclaims: "I did not ask to be brought up tonta! [ignorant] / My name hangs about me like a loose tooth" (p. 44).

"Four Portraits of Fire" discusses the massacre of Native Americans, again using bird metaphors and drawing attention to the concept of an internal colony, which became a rallying point for the Chicano movement. "Four Portraits," "Starfish," and "In January" explore death, a topic that Cervantes returns to in some depth in the second collection.

FROM THE CABLES OF GENOCIDE: POEMS ON LOVE AND HUNGER

In contrast to the last third of *Emplumada,* which discusses young love and the early phases of love and companionship with a man, *From the Cables of Genocide: Poems on Love and Hunger* looks at love as loss and decay. While many themes of the first book reappear in the second, the development of the topics of death and love stand out. The author's approach to these matures markedly in the second book, where she develops a world vision that is holistically beautiful and abject.

The poems of the second collection pick up on the seascape imagery and romantic optimism of the previous book, and the metaphorical imagery is dense and often paradoxical in its union of the beautiful and the abject, of love and either loss or decay. The aesthetic of this collection often connotes the surreal, and the agility of the language stands out in contrast to the language of the first collection. Here the poet unexpectedly changes the direction of a poem, stanza, or line by changing the end of a common phrase, image, or rhythm, confounding the reader's expectations. In "The Poet Is Served Her Papers," for example: "My broke blood is sorrel, is a lone / mare, is cashing in her buffalo chips" (p. 19). Counting wins and losses, "cashing in your chips," turns into summing up hardened feces, old waste material. The author highlights disappointment and other unexpected outcomes by employing idiomatic phrases to set the readers' expectations for the outcome of a line or thought and then changing it.

In accordance with the title of the collection, food (particularly fruit and fish) in its abundance, absence, and decay serves as a metaphor for what meets one's needs. The first of the book's three sections, "From the Cables of Genocide," sets a tone of disillusionment, of uncertainty about the future in a world where love (contrary to the optimism of the first book) does not last, of emotional need, and of the investment of writing, all to the setting of divorce. The inability of heterosexual love to last forever fits uncannily with the cyclical themes of the first collection and does not surprise. In "The Poet Is Served Her Papers" (presumably divorce papers), love and writing are put into opposition; the first is optimistic yet transient, the second a permanent testimony to the failure of the first.

So tell me about fever dreams,
about the bad checks we scrawl

with our mouths, about destiny
missing last bus to oblivion.

(p. 19)

The poet compares a finite bank account and the written check that overestimates its content to a kiss, or a promise of everlasting commitment. The poem goes on to speak of the emotional need to believe in love and romance after already concluding otherwise, stating, "I want to tell lies / to the world and believe it" (p. 19).

As she does in the first collection, the poet looks to writing for transcendence but realizes that such an over-determination of the labor is also idealistic and unrealistic. In the last stanza of the first poem, "Drawings: For John Who Said to Write about True Love," the poet states, "Someday, I said, I can write us both from this mess. But the key / stall outs from under me when I spell your name" (p. 15). Later, the memories of love and romance appear as predators on the poet's strategy for survival—writing. "But I write, and wait for the book to sell, for I know / nothing comes of it but the past with its widening teeth, / with its meat breath baited at my neck" (p. 15).

"Persona Ingrata," "Santa Cruz," "Valentine," and "Raisins" (from the second section), present love in decay and decomposition. Memories of beaches in "Santa Cruz" fill with flies and worms. The yellow of the sun on the Pacific horizon "crusts at your insides" in "Persona Ingrata" (p. 17). The object of love in the poet's dreams even turns into virtual decay, "a / decayed holo / gram" in "Valentine" (p. 24). The second section, "On Love and Hunger," employs rotting food in its description of sexual love gone sour. "Raisins," full of conflicting imagery of sex as rotten food that the poet uses to gratefully stave off starvation, concludes with a comparison of the lover and dehydrated fruit in the sun, while the poet tastes the hunger, "my spit, sweet as acid, damp as rot" (p. 29).

Critics have described the simultaneity of beauty and ugliness characteristic of this second collection as tense and conflictive. Images of spit, blood, urine, dandruff, sewers, rot, flies, and dead animals couple with images of feasts, seabirds, oceanscapes, romantic encounters, and sunsets. The third poem of the collection, "Levee: Letter to No One," however, presents a holistic panorama of beauty and abjection in coexistence, through the filter of a solitary woman at a sewer repository. The poem opens with the poet observing a woman who looks like her mother, crying on the edge of the pier. The woman wears a hairdo full of promise: a "nest-egg." The poet describes the mother-woman's tears as urine-like as she swings her legs girlishly above the "sewer spew" (p. 18). The woman, object of the poet's contemplation, is at once mother and child, pregnant and abject. (The poem lends itself to a Kristevian reading of the abject mother as counter-identity; see *Powers of Horror.*) The poet then describes the paradoxical beauty of the setting by projecting her perspective onto the woman's, asking if she is able to notice the beauty of birds, egrets, and herons among the waves of wastewater. After laying out the scenery in questions about the woman's ability to see, the poet cuts through the setting with the "slice" of a diving bird, an image that ties together separate horizontal planes of sea and air—ugly, fishless waters and bird-filled skies. Once the bird has marked the natural connection between the two seemingly separate spaces, the poem states:

Only symmetry harbors loss,
only the fusion of difference
can be wrenched apart, divorced
or distanced from its source.

(p. 18)

Again, the author plays on the reader's expectations of symmetry and harmony, concluding that such an expectation only leads to loss and implying that each side of an apparently symmetrical structure can exist on its own only in view of its original fusion with other elements.

Assuming symmetry and severability, then, erases the wholeness and falsely attributes equal proportions to the parts. The whole, Cervantes might agree, is greater than the sum of its parts. The poem suggests a holistic view of the world (and the book), which does not consider beauty to be in conflict with ugliness. The poem pans out as the poet leaves the reservoir, a "depository bank, for piss / and beauty's flush" (p. 18). Immediately preceding the poem "The Poet Is Served Her Papers," which begins with the metaphor of the bad check, "Levee" draws a connection between the bank that holds everything, from urine to immaculate white birds, and the unrealistic optimism of commitment.

In addition to the death of love ("Death Song," "Colorado Blvd.," "Hotel," "Le Petit Mal") and the death of dispossessed pre-Anglo-American cultures ("Flatirons," "Pleiades from the Cables of Genocide"), the second collection, and particularly its third section, addresses new love as it connects to death. Most of the poems are dedicated to Jay, a hunter and romantic companion. Jay's hunting and killing ("Buckshot") sits uncomfortably with the poet's use of bird and animal metaphors for massacred native cultures. In "Shooting the Wren," the poet ties the feathers of the game bird directly to genocide and fashions them into adornments that she wears: "Your trophies bear witness to gunfire in the / numbed trees . . . / . . . while I fashion / these feathers into the fragile art of my tribe" (p. 69). The last section pairs the poet's resolve to survive and get over divorce ("On the Last Anniversary," for example) with the companionship and mutual encouragement for survival she finds with Jay, the bearer of death and food ("Continental Divide"). Images of death and food (the game that he kills) always accompany Jay: "What you kill / I will pray for, what you let live / we will praise, ignore it, and eat" (p. 69). In direct contrast to the emphasis on meals not shared with the former lover/

spouse ("My Dinner with Your Memory," for example), the descriptions of the new love abound with eating and sharing. Death, in this sense, translates into life.

Selected Bibliography

WORKS OF LORNA DEE CERVANTES

Emplumada. Pittsburgh: University of Pittsburgh Press, 1981.

From the Cables of Genocide: Poems on Love and Hunger. Arte Público Press, 1991.

"Para un revolucionario." In *Chicana Feminist Thought: The Basic Historical Writings.* Edited by Alma García. New York: Routledge, 1997. Pp. 76–77.

Herrera-Sobek, María. *The Mexican Corrido: A Feminist Analysis.* Bloomington: Indiana University Press, 1990.

Kristeva, Julia. *The Powers of Horror: An Essay on Abjection.* Translated by Leon Roudiez. New York: Columbia University Press. 1982.

———. "Women's Time." In *Feminisms: An Anthology of Literary Theory and Criticism.* Edited by Robyn R. Worhol and Diane Price Herndl, 2d edition. New Brunswick, N.J.: Rutgers University Press, 1997. Pp. 860–879.

Pesquera, Beatriz, and Adela de la Torre, eds. *Building with Our Hands: New Directions in Chicana Studies.* Berkeley: University of California Press, 1993.

Rebolledo, Tey Diana. *Women Singing in the Snow: A Cultural Analysis of Chicana Literature.* Tucson: University of Arizona Press, 1995.

ANTHOLOGIES INCLUDING CERVANTES

Annas, Pamela J., and Robert C. Rosen, eds. *Literature and Society: An Introduction to Fiction, Poetry, Drama, Non-Fiction.* Englewood Cliffs, N.J.: Prentice Hall, 1994.

Creating Community in a Changing World. McGraw-Hill, 1999.

Deming, Alison Hawthorne, ed. *Poetry of the American West: A Columbia Anthology.* New York: Columbia University Press, 1996.

Flores, Lauro, ed. *The Floating Borderlands: Twenty-Five Years of U.S. Hispanic Literature.* Seattle: University of Washington Press, 1998.

García, Alma M., ed. *Chicana Feminist Thought: The Basic Historical Writings.* New York: Routledge, 1997.

Gilbert, Sandra M., and Susan Gubar. *The Norton Anthology of Literature by Women: The Traditions of English*, 2d edition. New York: W. W. Norton, 1996.

Gillan, Maria Mazzioti, and Jennifer Gillan. *Unsettling America: An Anthology of Contemporary Multicultural Poetry.* New York: Penguin, 1994.

Gonzalez, Ray. *Touching the Fire: Fifteen Poets of Today's Latino Renaissance.* New York: Anchor, 1998.

Herrera-Sobek, María, and Helena María Viramontes. *Chicana Creativity and Criticism*, rev. ed. Albuquerque: University of New Mexico Press, 1996.

Howe, Florence, ed. *No More Masks! An Anthology of Twentieth-Century Women Poets*, rev. ed. New York: HarperPerennial, 1993.

In Other World: Literature by Latinas of the United States. Houston: Arte Público Press, 1994.

Kanellos, Nicolás. *The Hispanic Literary Companion.* Detroit: Visible Ink, 1997.

Lauter, Paul, et al. *The Heath Anthology of American Literature, Vol. II.* Boston: Houghton Mifflin, 1998.

Madison, Soyini, ed. *The Woman That I Am: The Literature and Culture of Contemporary Women of Color.* New York: St. Martins, 1994.

McKenna, Teresa. *Migrant Song: Politics and Process in Contemporary Chicano Literature.* Austin: University of Texas Press, 1997.

The Norton Anthology of American Literature, Vol. 2. New York: W. W. Norton, 1998.

Ochester, Ed, and Peter Oresick, eds. *The Pittsburgh Book of Contemporary American Poetry.* Pittsburgh: University of Pittsburgh Press, 1993.

Oresick, Peter, and Nicholas Coles, eds. *Working Classics: Poems on Industrial Life.* Urbana: University of Illinois Press, 1990.

Phillips, J. J., et al., eds. *The Before Columbus Foundation Poetry Anthology: Selections from the American Book Awards, 1980–1990.* New York: W. W. Norton, 1992.

Power Poetics: Women and Literature, 1945 to the Present. Twayne/Macmillan, 1993.

Repp, John, ed. *How We Live Now: Contemporary Multicultural Literature.* Boston: St. Martin's Press, 1992.

Rebolledo, Tey Diana, and Eliana S. Rivero, eds. *Infinite Divisions: An Anthology of Chicana Literature.* Tucson: University of Arizona Press, 1993.

Sotto Il Quinto Sole. Passigli Edizioni, 1990.

Vendler, Helen. *Poems, Poets, Poetry: An Introduction and Anthology.* Boston: Bedford Books, 1997.

SECONDARY WORKS

Baym, Nina, ed. *The Norton Anthology of American Literature.* New York: W. W. Norton, 1998.

Bruce-Novoa, Juan. "Bernice Zamora and Lorna Dee Cervantes." *Revista lberoamericana* 51, nos. 132, 133 (July–December 1985): 565–573.

Buck, Claire, ed. *The Bloomsbury Guide to Women's Literature.* New York: Prentice Hall, 1992.

Candelaria, Cordelia. *Chicano Poetry: A Critical Introduction.* Westport, Conn.: Greenwood Press, 1986.

Cota Cardenas, Margarita. "The Faith of Activists: Barrios, Cities, and the Chicana Feminist Response." *Frontiers* 14, no. 2 (1994): 51–80.

Crawford, John F. "Notes toward a New Multicultural Criticism: Three Works by Women of Color." In *A Gift of Tongues: Critical Challenges in Contemporary American Poetry.* Edited by Marie Harris and Kathleen Aguero. Athens: University of Georgia Press, 1987. Pp. 155–195.

Gillan, María Mazziotti, and Jennifer Gillan, eds. *Unsettling America: An Anthology of Contemporary Multicultural Poetry.* New York: Penguin, 1994.

Gonzalez, Ray, ed. *After Aztlán: Latino Poets of the Nineties.* Boston: Godine, 1993.

Madsen, Deborah L. *Understanding Contemporary Chicana Literature.* Columbia: University of South Carolina Press, 2000.

McKenna, Teresa. "'An Utterance More Pure Than Word': Gender and the Corrido Tradition in Two Contemporary Chicano Poems." In *Feminist Measures: Soundings in Poetry and Theory.* Edited by Lynn Keller and Cristanne Miller. Ann Arbor: University of Michigan Press, 1994. Pp. 184–207.

Monda, Bernadette. "Interview with Lorna Dee Cervantes." *Third Woman* 2, no. 1 (1984): 103–107.

Ordonez, Elizabeth J. "Webs and Interrogations: Postmodernism, Gender, and Ethnicity in the Poetry of Cervantes and Cisneros." In *Chicana (W)rites: On Word and Film.* Edited by María Herrera Sobek and Helena María Viramontes. Berkeley, Calif.: Third Woman Press, 1995. Pp. 171–183.

Rebolledo, Tey Diana. "Soothing Restless Serpents: The Dreaded Creation and Other Inspirations in Chicana Poetry." *Third Woman* 2, no.1 (1984): 83–102.

———. "Tradition and Mythology: Signatures of Landscape in Chicana Poetry." In *The Desert Is No Lady: Southwestern Landscapes in Women's Writing and Art.* Edited by Vera Norwood and Janice Monk. New Haven, Conn.: Yale University Press, 1987. Pp. 96–124.

———. *Women Singing in the Snow: A Cultural Analysis of Chicana Literature.* Tucson: University of Arizona Press, 1995.

Sanchez, Marta Ester. *Contemporary Chicana Poetry: A Critical Approach to Emerging Literature.* Berkeley: University of California Press, 1985.

Savin, Ada. "Bilingualism and Dialogism: Another Reading of Lorna Dee Cervantes' Poetry." In *An Other Tongue: Nation and Ethnicity in the Linguistic Borderlands.* Edited by Alfred Arteaga. Durham, N.C.: Duke University Press, 1994. Pp. 215–223.

———. "Lorna Dee Cervantes' Dialogic Imagination." *Annales du Centre de recherches sur l'Amérique anglophone* 18 (1993): 269–277.

Seator, Lynette. "*Emplumada*: Chicana Rites-of-Passage." *MELUS* 11 (summer 1984): 23–38

Wallace, Patricia. "Divided Loyalties: Literal and Literary in the Poetry of Lorna Dee Cervantes, Cathy Song, and Rita Dove." *MELUS* 18 (fall 1993): 3–19.

Yarbro-Bejerano, Yvonne. "Chicana Literature from a Chicana Feminist Perspective." *Chicana Creativity and Criticism: Charting New Frontiers in American Literature.* Edited by María Herrera-Sobek and Helena María Viramontes. Special Issue, *Americas Review* 15. nos. 3, 4 (fall–winter 1987): 39–45.

Denise Chávez

(1948–)

TEY DIANA REBOLLEDO

IN "WORDS OF WISDOM" (1987), an essay written for *New Mexico Magazine,* Denise Chávez tries to define what elements constitute a New Mexican or regional writer. She includes the following six characteristics: (1) the writer should be influenced by the oral tradition, be it Hispano, Native American, or other—in other words, the writer should be a *cuentista;* (2) the writings should exhibit a spirituality that is not necessarily religion, but a balance of healing wholeness; (3) the writer should seek links to his or her ancestors; (4) there should be a connection to the land that surrounds him or her; (5) the writer should exhibit a bilinguality or trilinguality; and (6) there should be the performative value of the storyteller. In sum, the writer should be one "whose world is grounded in the multifaceted, multicultural universe that is New Mexico, storytellers whose concept of time pays homage to the past while celebrating the present" (p. 73). Clearly Denise Chávez exhibits these characteristics in their many complexities.

Denise Chávez was born in Las Cruces, New Mexico, on 15 August 1948 and still lives in the house in which she was born. Moreover, she writes in the very room in which she was born. Over the years she has also acquired the house in which her father lived, several houses away, and other property in her neighborhood. The land, her neighborhood, and her sense of connection to family, history, and culture in this southern New Mexico town has been an important facet in her life and has also greatly influenced her writing. As she says: "I see myself as a writer who is very deeply rooted in the community" (Ikas, *Chicana Ways,* p. 53).

Denise Chávez is the daughter of Epifanio Ernesto Chávez (E. E. or "Chano" Chávez), a lawyer, one of the few Hispanos in his time to earn a law degree. As Chávez states: "During the Depression he went to Georgetown University in Washington, D.C., to get a law degree. It was really unheard of in those days that a Mexican American would leave a town like this, a dusty little town, to get a degree and become a lawyer" (Ikas, *Chicana Ways,* p. 49). Because her father had been punished for speaking Spanish as a child, he suppressed his native language.

Her mother, Delfina Rede Faver, was a schoolteacher from west Texas who had been widowed. She taught school for forty-two years in West Texas and then in Las Cruces. She was one of the first Spanish-speaking graduates of Sul Ross State University in Texas and came from a long line of teachers. She had studied in Mexico, even taking classes from the famous painter Diego Rivera. A strong advocate of Spanish and bilingual education, she was an important cultural influence on Chávez, always challenging her children to look up words and to read. Denise has a younger sister, Margo Chávez-Charles, and an older sister, Faride Conway, a child from Delfina's previous marriage.

In an interview with Annie Eysturoy, Chávez tells us that she grew up in a religious family with traditional folk culture, such as folk plays like "Los pastores," and community events, such as Las Posadas, generally produced at Christmas time. But although religion was an important part of her childhood, she was also skeptical about organized religion (*This Is about Vision,* p. 160). She went to a Catholic high school, Madonna High, where she was one of twelve members of the graduating class, who called themselves "The Apostolettes." Her devotion to spirituality and her analysis of the importance of religion in the everyday life of women who grew up in the Catholic tradition is paramount in her writing. She does not view the influence of the Catholic Church upon the lives of women uncritically, however; in her writing she demonstrates the stifling effect strict adherence to religious ideals can have on women, and the necessity at times to break away from those practices.

This family history has strongly influenced Chávez's writing, as she says: "My father divorced us when I was ten years old, so I basically grew up in a house of women, and I think that has probably affected my writing quite a bit" (Eysturoy, *This Is about Vision,* p. 159). Although her father was not constantly around, at the same time he was not totally absent. He was an alcoholic, and she took on the responsibility of looking after him in his old age.

Because her mother was a teacher and worked, and since her father was absent as a responsible parent in her life, Denise and her sister Margo grew up surrounded by maids and workers who helped in the house. Chávez often honors these women and men in her writing,

underscoring the importance of these workers who grow to be more than just workers: they become family friends and lifelong *comadres*. In particular, many of her works honor the hard work and devotion of maids, such as the character of Chata in *Face of an Angel* and the protagonists of the play "Hecho en México," a theater piece on maids where the Spanish translates as "Made in Mexico," or the English play on words, "Maid in Mexico" (p. 160). In *Literature and Landscape,* Chávez writes: "I like, more than like, love to write about the people of this world, the compadres and comadres I have grown up with, the maids I have loved, who've taken care of me, taught me the language of love, the handymen who left their indelible mark of kindness in my heart" (p. 18).

Chávez received her Bachelor of Arts degree in drama from New Mexico State University in 1971 and her master of fine arts from Trinity University in San Antonio, Texas, in 1974. In 1984 she received a second M.A. degree, in creative writing, from the University of New Mexico. New Mexican writer Rudolfo Anaya was one of her teachers and became an important mentor for her. Chávez has taught at various schools and universities, including Northern New Mexico Community College, the American School in Paris, the University of Houston, and New Mexico State University. Since 1994 she has written full time, although she is involved in various community activities, such as directing workshops on writing "Family Stories" and serving as the artistic director of the Border Book Festival in Las Cruces, which she established in 1994. She has written three major novels, numerous short stories, more than thirty-five plays, and many essays in both the academic and the popular press. Until recently she was writing a column in a local newspaper, *The Ink,* titled "La Vecindad." This allowed her to write short sketches on topics of interest to her and also to the community.

Chávez has been working on a book titled *The King and Queen of Comezón* for many years. It is a tale about an immigration officer on the U.S.-Mexico border. Because she lives near the border, the issues that affect both sides of the border are of great concern to her. The word *comezón* means itch, but it also means a longing that can never be satisfied. Much of Chávez's writing deals with absences, losses, lacks, and desires that are not fulfilled. But her writing also deals with the ways in which people are able to overcome that lack of satisfaction. In an interview with Stacey Hearn, she describes this as the "ni modo" philosophy: *ni modo* means "'that's too bad' but you have to keep living life the best you can" (*Desert Exposure*, p. 1). She continues to read from her work and perform her plays, in particular *Women in the State of Grace*. *Women in the State of Grace* is an unpublished play written in two parts. It is a series of vignettes with each vignette capable of being interchanged with other vignettes in the play. This flexibility allows Chávez to select sections as the moment arises.

Her work has received much recognition and many honors. She has received grants from the New Mexico Arts Division, the National Endowment for the Arts, the Rockefeller Foundation, the Lannan Foundation, and the Lila Wallace–Readers' Digest Fund. She also received the 1995 Governor's Award in Literature, and *Face of an Angel* earned the American Book Award, the Mesilla Valley Author of the Year Award, and the Premio Aztlán. She is married to photographer and sculptor Daniel Zolinsky and lives in Las Cruces, New Mexico.

WRITING AND SHARING THE HEAT

When Denise Chávez writes about writing, she describes it in terms of heat, rain, and dust. She likes to comment that her mother's family came from a town called "El Polvo," the dust. Living in Las Cruces, New Mexico, a place where the heat can be almost unbearable, where it soaks up your very body and soul, one appreciates the

coolness and relief rain brings. For her, writing is connected to the landscape, the mountains, and the desert. In *Literature and Landscape*, she says, "To understand me is to know this land I love" (p. 18). Thus she calls her essay on writing "Heat and Rain." In this essay, Chávez explains that on her way to becoming a writer she wrote diaries—diaries that upon reading them today emphasize both sad and elated days of her life. She sees that, as a child in these diaries and in her endless practicing of writing the alphabet, she was teaching herself to write efficiently and with fluidity. She was also a voracious reader and lover of popular culture. In the middle of two languages, Spanish and English, she created a third space for herself using both languages. The voice of her mother was Spanish, that of her father was English. When she was a child, she created her own language "as a defense" (p. 31).

Chávez writes in English with Spanish words interspersed. However, she notes in an interview with Ikas that "the underpinnings of the works, the basis, has to do with that linguistic ability to be able to go back and forth in English and Spanish if I choose. Thus I am able to say things in English and also throw in a Spanish word or phrase, or to deal with concepts in Spanish that are very different from English" (*Chicana Ways*, p. 50). She speaks Spanish in her daily life but also notes how English and Spanish mutually influence each other. As she says, "Every language just has its own power" (p. 51).

She was influenced in her writing by authors from Spanish, Latin American, and American literature such as Federico García Lorca, Thomas Wolfe, Eugene O'Neill, Lillian Hellman, Juan Rulfo, Gabriel García Márquez, Edward Albee, Fyodor Dostoyevsky, Bernard Malamud, and Isaac Bashevis Singer—writers who deal with voice and character. The Chicano author Rudolfo Anaya has also been an important literary influence and mentor.

From her father and mother and her large extended family she inherited spirit, curiosity, practicality, and compassion. She also learned to listen, and to listen carefully, and to write what she hears: voices, intonation, inflection, mood, timbre, and pitch. She writes characters, stating that her training in theater has helped sharpen her characterization. And her adeptness in portraying these characters has grown over the years and through the course of her novels, short stories, and dramas. In this essay on writing, Chávez states clearly that she writes for the common person, for alternative groups, "for the poor, the forgotten" (p. 32).

In 1986 she published *The Last of the Menu Girls* with Arte Público Press, then a small Chicano press which published many new writers. The structure of *The Last of the Menu Girls* puzzled many readers because they could not determine if it was a novel or a series of short stories. Many other Chicano and Chicana writers were playing with similar structures, utilizing short stories and linking them to a longer narrative form, writing novellas and mixing poetry, essays, and narrative: for example, Sandra Cisneros in *The House on Mango Street* (1984), Margarita Cota-Cárdenas in *Puppet* (1985), and Gloria Anzaldúa in *Borderlands/La frontera: La nueva mestiza* (1987). Renato Rosaldo has commented that, following Mary Louise Pratt's analysis of the short story, this particular short story cycle allows for marginalized groups to experiment and for the development of "alternative visions." He finds that Chávez's experimentation allows her to "cross over" into different voices, narrators, and ancestry (*Criticism in the Borderlands*, p. 89). Alvina Quintana, in her book *Home Girls*, contends that the important contribution that Chávez makes to literature in this text is not just that she "reconfigures Chicana silence and invisibility into recognition and empowerment" but also that she emphasizes "domestic orality," thus showing that even if women's voices are not inscribed into print writing this does not mean that they do not have ideas or creativity, or that they are silent.

At first glance, Chávez's *Last of the Menu Girls* appears to be a series of short stories, each one a self-contained narrative, or what Chávez calls "scenes." However, the central protagonist is Rocío Esquivel, a young woman whose growing-up story this is. In the first and title story, "The Last of the Menu Girls," we see Rocío as an aide at Altavista Memorial Hospital. Although she dislikes hospitals, while recounting the lives of the patients she serves, she begins to detail their lives. Even as she fills out the employment form, her mind jumps back and forth to her family and community experiences. Her employment at the hospital begins as just a job, but when she leaves at the end of the summer to enter college, it has become more than a job. Her experiences with people sick or being healed, rude and indifferent and needy, have affected her and made her a different person. The needs of people have sucked her in until she can no longer remain indifferent to them. Outside of work she reads patients' charts and studies a medical book so she can better understand their illnesses.

The stories continue; in "Willow Game," Rocío reminisces about her neighborhood while she was growing up, but particularly about her neighbors Ricky and Randy, two boys with, it turns out, severe physiological problems. Randy takes his anger out on a willow tree, one of those trees that in childhood are magic, territorial landmarks. He cuts off the branches of the tree until it dies. In a moment of understanding, the young Rocío realizes that the pain he carried around was vented on the tree: a tree that can never really be replanted.

"Shooting Stars," the third story in the book, details her visits as a child and then adolescent to her family in Texas. She looks to the many different women of her family and the friends she meets there for a role model, but none of them fit what she is looking for. Perhaps it is because, as Eysturoy suggests, what is lacking is "the authenticity of a self-defined identity, the affirmation of selfhood Rocío is searching for" (p. 122). Thus she will have to find her role model deep within herself, choose her own destiny, and fulfill her own dreams.

In the fourth story, "Evening in Paris," Rocío examines the problematic relationship she has with her mother. Anxious to please her, she buys a bottle of *Evening in Paris* perfume, a special gift for her mother. On Christmas Day, explored in detail by Chávez, her mother opens the gift, unimpressed. As Rocío explains, hurt by her mother's indifference: "Later it seemed to me that perhaps Mother had thought the *Evening in Paris* had been given to her by one of her students" (p. 74). This indifference is one of the indications that there is something missing in Rocío's life. She says: "As usual, I felt unfulfilled, empty, without the right words, gifts, feelings for those whose lives crowded around me and who called themselves my family " (pp. 74–75).

In "The Closet," the fifth story, Chávez explores the secret heart of the house, the different centers where lurks all that which is not brought out to life. The closets have special meaning for Rocío because she was actually born in one of them, "a closet full of shoes, old clothes" (p. 84). Her mother's closets, where old photographs of her mother's first husband, home movies, and other memories were stored, beckon to Rocío as she tries to understand her mother's dreams and desires. But in the house are also the medicine closet, Rocío's closet, the hall closet, her older sister's closet, and the living room closet. Each closet holds its memories and secrets, inscribed in the material physicality of objects—an umbrella, a prom dress, shoes—and the smells associated with them.

Because she wants to discover and understand the mysteries that closets hold, she also has the necessity of creating closets of her own. And so as a child she imagines the gray closet and the blue closet. These are not stagnant, imaginary spaces but ones that change as the child has need for change. They represent the hopeful and the sad spaces of a child's life. As she tries to explain these spaces to her younger sister, Mercy, her sister asks, "Rocío, Rocío, if that's *your* room, *what's mine?*" Rocío answers, "I don't know, Mercy, everybody has their *own* rooms, their *own* house" (p. 93).

The next story, "Space Is a Solid," details the most difficult episode in Rocío's life as she leaves her community and family and becomes a teacher. She is alienated from family and friends, even her name is shortened to Miss E. This story is different from the other narratives in the book as different voices carry the narration: Kari Lee (a little girl in Rocío's drama class), Rocío herself, the Wembleys (Kari Lee's parents), Nita (Kari Lee's mother), and Loundon (Rocío's friend). Seen from different perspectives, we note Rocío's struggles in a world where she is not nourished or supported. She is alienated from the world surrounding her and especially from herself. In this environment she becomes ill, suffering from what one person calls "a nervous breakdown." Clearly she is depressed, as she is tired all the time. Yet even in this sad situation, she has one friend, her little student Kari Lee.

In the final story, "Compadre," Rocío has returned home and is known as a writer. Yet the story describes her childhood and her mother's relationship to Regino Suárez, a man who works for her and who is her *compadre*; that is, she is the *madrina* or godmother to one of Regino's daughters. Being a *compadre* or *comadre* in Mexicano culture involves giving and receiving mutual help and sustenance. It carries obligations that are strong and profound. For example, Regino comes whenever Nieves, Rocío's mother, needs him for anything, but it is also Nieves's obligation to help out her *compadre* when he needs help. Regino is not necessarily the most gifted worker; nevertheless, Nieves supports him and pays him for work, even if it is not well done. As she explains to Rocío, "I'm bound by the higher laws of compadrazgo, having to do with the spiritual well-being and development of one of God's creatures" (p. 168). Nieves is also a bit bound by self-interest. Having no husband to do the work of maintaining her property, it helps that her *compadre* is a handyman and can fix the things around the house.

Throughout the narrative, Rocío resists getting close to Regino and his family, yet we see the passing of his life as he involves himself with another woman (known in Rocío's house as "La Puta," the prostitute), returns to his wife, has his wife leave to live with one of their children in Montana, and is left to live on his own. At the end of the story, Rocío sits down for the first time to eat with Regino, a symbolic act that emphasizes her growing up, her coming into her own self, and her understanding and compassion for her family and those that live around them. It is in this final paragraph that we learn she has become a writer, that she understands who she is and where she comes from. She has become complete, filled with family and the nourishment of tamales.

As a child, all Rocío wanted was a room of her own, a place to read and to think, but family and community life intruded on her space constantly. She is, as various critics have pointed out, "unformed," in an amorphous state of being. She receives things, ideas, sensations. But throughout the narrative, Chávez feels that Rocío moves "from self-absorption and selfishness toward a more caring stance" (Mehaffy and Keating, *Aztlán*, p. 144). At the end of *The Last of the Menu Girls*, Rocío is a writer, nourished by her mother, who tells her: "I say, Rocío, just write about this little street of ours, it's only one block long, but there's so many stories. Too many stories!" (p. 190). Later her mother decides that it would be enough to write only about the house. "Why not just write about 325? That's our house! Write about 325 and that will take the rest of your life. Believe me, Rocío, *at least the rest of your life*." The many houses we inhabit, both from the outside and from interior spaces like the closets, are truly the subjects of this narrative.

As Rudolfo Anaya says in his introduction to the book:

> Denise's novel reflects her particular sense of place, revealing the depths of the world of women and the flavor of southern New Mexico. The central metaphor of the novel is the home. The family, the known neighborhood and the role of women in

this context are Denise's concern as a writer. Her eye for detail is sharp; the interior monologues of her characters are revealing; and Denise's long training as a dramatist serves her well in creating intriguing plot and dialogue. In short, all the strengths of a writer are here.

Mehaffy and Keating agree, writing that the frameworks of her narratives are based on dramatic performance (anyone who has heard Chávez read from her work would agree with this); thus there are many forms of dialogue between characters as well as chapters and sections which "require a different and shifting relation between a reader and the text" (*Aztlán*, p. 128).

In her chapter on this novel, "The Last of the Menu Girls: Learning from the Women," Eysturoy writes that the border, bicultural and bilingual, is the setting for Rocío to examine her "relationship to her environment, look for role models, and examine the lives of the women around her in search of her own identity, her own self" (p. 113). Eysturoy argues in her book, *Daughters of Self-Creation*, that Chicana writers have had to create their own growing-up stories and re-create the genre because they have no role models for the genre as their lives are outside the general pattern of the bildungsroman, or growing-up story. She believes that Chicana writers like Chávez, Sandra Cisneros, Isabella Ríos, and Estela Portillo Trambley have had to look to themselves and to other Chicana writers for a way to establish an authentic Chicana sense of self and self-identity for their characters. Of particular interest in Eysturoy's analysis of *The Last of the Menu Girls* is her description of the meaning of the closets in Rocío's home. We have already seen how the house is a central metaphor in this narrative, and how Rocío begins her examination of self with her job outside the home at the hospital. Eysturoy demonstrates that for Rocío, as she tries to understand her mother and her mother's dreams and desires, the closets of her home "correspond to the interior, secret life of her mother that forms part of Rocío's memories and shapes her own concept of self" (pp. 115–116). It is in these closets that Rocío pieces together her mother's life. However, at the same time that she needs to connect with her mother, it is also necessary that she distance herself from her mother if she is to grow into her own person. As a child she created her own imaginary closets as a private space for herself, but as a growing young woman she needs to create her own house and to separate herself from her mother's house.

AnaLouise Keating, in "Towards a New Politics of Representation?" finds *The Last of the Menu Girls* an elusive text because of its fragmented scenes, its lack of resolution for Rocío's desires and longings, and her inability to articulate her experiences. Keating finds the solution to the critic's dilemma by emphasizing that it is precisely the loss and absences in Rocío's desires that she needs to accept. Keating sees this as a representation of the internal split, or divided self, that many Chicanas experience. Moreover, this absence becomes a "form of connection" (*We Who Love to Be Astonished*, p. 80) among Chicanas/Latinas as a whole as they have had the same experiences.

The Last of the Menu Girls is a first novel whose style and experimentation will be developed more fully in later novels. Here in the early stages we see techniques that Chávez utilizes more fully later on. Among these are her characterization of the chaos and instability—yet also nobility—in the lives of poor people; the interior monologues of characters who are trying to find solutions to their problem; the complex interrelationships among family members; and the love/hate aspects of adolescents toward their parents and their family. And finally we experience the acceptance of the complexity (both absence and loss as well as fulfillment) of human lives. Missing in this particular text are the humor and terrific exaggeration that will become a staple of her writing later on. However, *The Last of the Menu Girls* is

a fine first narration, and a fine growing-up story/bildungsroman.

Her second novel, *Face of an Angel* (1994), is a text with a complicated and experimental form that has left readers puzzling as to how to read it. Because the narrative about the life of the heroine, Soveida Dosamantes, is interspersed with several other narratives, the book circles the narrative at the same time that it is elaborating it and opening it up. The main narrative details the life of Soveida, her family, her friends, her loves, and the people she works with at a restaurant, El Farol, in a small desert town in southern New Mexico. The book has been called a family saga, and it has all the characteristics of a saga, as Chávez explores the details and secrets of a vast family network. But it is also a saga of friends and friendships, of the lives of people Soveida works with, and it is filled with eccentric characters, sad and happy stories, domestic details, and day-to-day (but often strange) life in a small town. Because it is such a complicated narrative, it is impossible to enumerate every aspect of the book in the short space given here. However, some of the central themes in the book include the importance of the work of women and service workers, as well as how women are able to assert themselves in taking control of their lives and seizing their subjectivity—that is, becoming the subject and not the object of their lives and stories. It is also about identity, the meaning of a sense of place, masks and reality, and, of course, coming of age. It is also about the importance of the telling of the stories. At the beginning of the novel, Soveida's grandmother tells her:

> Soveida, you like to read. What you're reading is the story of the world. Everyone has a story, your mamá has a story, your daddy has a story, even you have a story to tell. Tell it while you can, while you have the strength, because when you get to my age, the telling gets harder.
>
> (p. 4)

Soveida accepts the challenge, saying: "I speak for them now. Mother. Father. Brother. Sister.

Cousin. Uncle. Aunt. Husband. Lover. Their memories are mine. That sweet telling mine" (p. 4).

This is mainly a woman's world, although men and their relationships to the women in the story filter in and out. It is the story of how women are strong and how they sustain each other that is of most importance. As Soveida states, "The stories begin with the men and always end with the women; that's the way it is in our family" (p. 11). Thus she details the everyday life, love, pleasures, agonies, and small and large hurts of the women who surround her and her family and friends in particular: her mother, Dolores; her father, Luardo; her ex-mother-in-law, Lourdes Torres; the maid, Chata Vialpando; the restaurant owner, Larry Larragoite; and an enormous cast of restaurant workers, cousins, and friends.

The novel begins by telling us Soveida was named after a young woman who died in a car accident that Dolores read about in the obituary column. Soveida, at the time of the narrative, is working as a waitress at a Mexican restaurant, El Farol, and during the course of the story marries twice, the first time to Ivan Eloy Torres, who leaves her for "La Virgie," a woman untouched by life's anxieties or by morality, who "would take a woman into seeming confidence, then turn around and sleep with either her boyfriend or her husband" (p. 189). Her second husband is Veryl Beron, a sad and troubled man who kills himself the night of their six-month wedding anniversary.

Recovering from this last tragedy, Soveida decides to take a night class and chooses one in Chicano Studies, "Folklore and Tradition in Chicano/Chicana Society—a Look at the Ni Modo Philosophy." She becomes involved with the teacher of the class and with his family, finally falling in love with his brother Tizio, who is married. For some time Soveida has wanted to have a child, but she was disappointed in this by both her husbands. As the narrative continues, Soveida's father Luardo dies, and later

Oralia Milcantos, her mother's companion, dies. Larry Larragoite has a heart attack, and one of the longtime waitresses at the restaurant decides to retire. Soveida cuts back her hours so she can go to school; the saga of El Farol and the community surrounding it is coming to an end. Soveida discovers she is pregnant but she decides to be a single parent and to go back to school full time. As Soveida tells Tirzio: "I need to be settled. Peaceful. Not only for myself. I'm expecting a baby, Tirzio. I haven't told you because I wanted to be complete in myself" (p. 455).

The land and her family nourish and sustain her in her decision; after telling Tirzio, Soveida sits in her yard and awaits the fruit of her life—one that comes both from her body and from her mind:

> The yard was still, except for the growing song of the cicadas. Thunder rumbled in the distance, and lightning cracked the sky behind the Lagrimas. I could smell rain. I would sit outside and await its approach. Surely it would come and nourish the yellow and blue desert flowers in the sand, the white yucca flowers by the side of the winding road, the ocotillo's red-tipped tendrils waving to the seemingly empty sky, the nopal's sweet, blood-red fruit.
>
> (p. 457)

THE STRUCTURE OF THE NOVEL

Face of an Angel has nine principal chapters, each of which is signaled by the picture of a *milagro*, or amulet of protection. These chapters are: Angels (ear); Archangels (a person kneeling); Principalities (foot); Powers (hand); Virtues (heart); Dominations (eye); Thrones (leg); Cherubim (face); and Seraphim (house). These chapters follow the order of angels in Catholic iconography, from the lowest to the highest orders. The *milagros* are important because the stories in the chapters are loosely organized by their symbols. Thus in Angels (ear) the story begins and we are told why the story is being told. Likewise in the last chapter, Seraphim (house), Soveida comes into her own and finds her place, and in Virtues (heart) the stories are about loves won and lost.

In addition to the principal narrative, several other narratives within the narratives weave in and out of the text. One of these narratives is "The Book of Service," a book that Soveida is writing about how to be a good waitress. This book, nevertheless, is a how-to manual on life in general. The "Book of Service" is composed of fourteen sections: The Service Creed, Hands, Voice, Costume, Talks with Dedea #1: Los que se presentaron, The Waitress Fugue, Bras and Girdles, The Tip Checklist (or How to Get a Good Tip), Talks with Dedea #2: The New Waitress, Shoes, Order, Meditations on Hair, The Waitress's Face, and The Passing of the Waitress Torch. As can be seen, many of these sections have to do with the presentation of the waitress. But even as realistic expectations on appearance are detailed, the narrative suddenly shifts to discourses on the meaning of life and the meaning of work. For example, in "Meditations on Hair," when the weekend cook Eloisa Ortiz is asked her opinion on hair, she states: "I like a man with a smooth chest. Oh, that kinda hair! Hair has nothing to do with it. A bald woman can still make good enchiladas. Huevos rancheros red, side of beans and rice. Whose order is this, anyway?" (p. 391). In another section, "Bras and Girdles," the advice is to wear comfortable shoes and undergarments. Soveida then writes: "Pray that when you are a waitress you are relatively young. Pray that your outfit is not too juvenile. Ever see an old woman in a red, puffy miniskirt, bird legs swaddled in tights, sagging bosom accented by white lace? . . . If you are a waitress, you have to live hard, drink hard, love hard. There is no other way" (p. 289). By these examples you notice the shift from the physical presentation of self, to comments about life, to humor. These constantly shifting registers enliven the narrative while at the same time opening up our perspective about what it means to be a waitress, to serve people.

Another minor narrative in the text is a diary that Soveida wrote when she was twelve. Titled "Saint or Sinner," it parallels the main narration of *Face of an Angel* as she asks the important question: who am I? "I try to make others understand me. And yet, no matter how hard I try, I am still a mystery to myself" (p. 76). Yet other texts are two papers that Soveida has written for a Chicano Studies class she is taking. In the first paper, "An Oral History of the Elderly Chicano Community," Soveida elaborates the life of Oralia Milcantos, her grandmother's maid. On this paper she receives a B for content and a C– for presentation. Her professor, J. V. Velásquez, with whom she later has an affair, has written that she is too emotional and caught up with the subject. Her paper is not analytical enough. In her second paper, "Mothers, Teach Your Sons," Soveida comments that Hispano males have been defeated through the process of assimilation and history; they have thus also oppressed and abused their women. But these women are survivors and need to teach gentleness and love to the men they live with and nourish. On this paper the professor gives her a C for content and a C– for presentation, stating, "Your scholarship leaves much to be desired" (p. 321). Of course, this is precisely because he is one of those males she is writing about and he is unable to accept this version of history. In addition, it is precisely Soveida's passion and compassion, her aligning herself with the subject of her writing, that makes her the sensitive human being that she is. It is also those qualities that will enable her not only to survive, but also to bloom in the end.

In *Face of an Angel* we live, breathe, and smell the life in the restaurant where Soveida works, El Farol. Chávez is an expert in evoking the small and poignant details of everyday life. Her descriptions bring to life working-class people and their jobs. As she tells us in an interview with Kevane and Heredia, "I wanted my readers to feel the heat, to smell the enchiladas in El Farol Restaurant and to feel the restless energy that surrounds you in such a place" (p. 40).

Loving Pedro Infante (2001), Chávez's third novel, has not received much scholarly attention. Like *Face of an Angel,* it is a monumental work of epic proportions, although the heroines of the novel, Teresina "La Tere" Avila and Irma "La Wirma" Granados, are not necessarily epic heroines. In fact, they more closely resemble the heroines of "romance" novels who are nevertheless mired in the details of everyday life, although they long for more. Thus they are connected to the world of Mexican movies of the Golden Age (1930s–1940s), and to the larger-than-life hero of these movies, actor Pedro Infante.

Who was Pedro Infante? He was an immensely popular and handsome matinee idol in Mexican films who died in an airplane crash at the age of forty. He personified the perfect Mexican hero with all his traits, good and bad. By turns, he was dashing, gentlemanly and courteous, brave, funny, a womanizer, and a loving husband, father, and son. After his untimely death, numerous "Pedro sightings" occurred, as his fans did not believe he was dead. The novel is divided into five sections, each the title of an Infante film: (1) La Vida no vale nada (Life Is Not Worth Anything); (2) Ansiedad (Anxiety); (3) El Inocente (The Innocent); (4) Dicen que soy mujeriego (They Say I Am a Womanizer); and (5) ¡Viva mi desgracia! (Long Live My Disgrace!). Within each section, the subsections have titles that also sound like romantic movies, but these sections refer instead to the melodramatic disasters or events in the lives of Tere, her family, and friends.

Tere is a teacher's aide in Cabritoville Elementary School. Cabritoville is a small town in southern New Mexico where everyone knows everyone else—and everyone else's business. In her thirties, she is unmarried and calls herself the big "p," which stands variously for *puta* (prostitute), *pendeja* (stupid), or *piojos* (head lice). It could also refer to Pedro. Her best friend is Irma, with whom she shares not only the Pedro-athons but also Friday and Saturday nights at La Tempestad, the local bar, as well as the ups and downs of her life.

Tere and Irma are Pedro Infante fans, and they belong to the Pedro Infante Club de Admiradores Norteamericano #256, a fan club that watches Pedro Infante movies in the El Colón theater on Thursday nights, meets regularly to discuss Pedro movies (and to relate them to the events in their own community and world), and has Pedro-athons. The members of the Fan Club are relatives and friends and mostly women, although there is one male member, Ubaldo, who is gay. The main narrator of the novel is Tere, and during the course of the narration she describes the multiple roles that Pedro has played in the movies as well as what she knows about his personal life, as reported in fan magazines and interviews. She underscores Infante's roles in the movies by separating his personal life and his on-screen life (Pedro as Pablo, Pedro as Juan). Pedro Infante is seen as an actor and man who can do no wrong. As Tere tells us, "Pedro was the type of man who took care of all the women in his life, from Doña Refugio [his mother] to María Luisa [his wife] to all of his mistresses" (p. 5). Tere looks to find an ideal man, like Pedro, in her life, but instead she falls in love with a married man, Lucio Valadez, who treats her badly. Her own life is not like that of a large-screen heroine, but rather the mishap-filled life of a *telenovela* character. It is exaggerated, seamy, and going nowhere. Chávez not only utilizes Pedro Infante movies to mirror and undermine the concept of the hero, but she also analyzes the role of "romance" in women's lives.

As Tere and her friend Irma discuss the plots and turns of Infante movies, they are also constantly comparing the movies, and Pedro's role in them, to the realities of their own lives. These comparisons and contrasts often speak directly to us and to Mexicana and Chicana women everywhere. Chávez underscores that the role of women in contemporary life has not changed much from the time of Pedro's movies.

Book reviewer Pari Noskin Taichert, not understanding the role of oral tradition and the place of exaggeration in telling stories, criticized *Loving Pedro Infante* for how it "stretch[es] the truth." Chávez deliberately plays with the structure of those melodramatic Mexican films in order to emphasize the melodramatic aspects of Tere's life. Taichert also criticized "how easily her [Chicana] women identify totally with their Mexican sisters," saying that the women in Chávez's novel were not like any New Mexican women she knew. In this novel Chávez is exploring a border identity; Cabritoville (sounding very much like Las Cruces) is only forty miles from the border. As Chávez's essay about the north and south of New Mexico explains, people living near the border have much more affinity with the other side than their northern neighbors.

Loving Pedro Infante is both a tragic novel and an extremely humorous one. The tragedy centers, once again, around the *ni modo* philosophy. The desires and longings of Tere, Irma, Ubaldo, and other members of the Fan Club for a life filled with love and with meaning are aptly contrasted against the romantic films of Pedro Infante. In the films, there is always a resolution, while the lives of the Fan Club members are always changing and have no resolution. To be complete vis-à-vis a romantic love is not necessarily the life of the Fan Club members. Irma marries an older man, Tere finally breaks off with Lucio, and Ubaldo disappears: not your usual happy ending. But in the end, Irma and Tere resolve their differences over Irma's marriage: after all, their relationship is central to the novel and to their lives. They are lifelong friends as were La Lucy and La Ethel. And finally, as in many of Chávez's novels, it is the land and the community that sustains them. Through the discussion of the movies, Tere is able to work through the predictable narration to forge a meaning for herself, where a man doesn't always control the ending. As she tells us, to understand a people you have to understand their dreams. In *Loving Pedro In-fante* we come to understand Tere, her community, her dreams, and her aspirations: in short, what her life is all about. In this novel Chávez explores the nature of real love, as opposed to the illusion of love, a big-screen celluloid love.

Perhaps the most important tool in Chávez's later novels is the use of humor. Whatever the subject, sad, trite, taboo, or philosophical, Chávez's humor always sparks an understanding of the plight of human beings. Several texts that are set apart from the main narrative emphasize this. One is a list that Tere makes, comparing herself to her *tocaya*, namesake, the Spanish Saint Teresa de Avila. Titled "Ways Mi Tocaya and I Are Alike and Not Alike," the comparisons between saint and sinner create a comic dysfunction. In addition, the use of colloquial language further emphasizes the differences between the two women. For example, on her list she says that Teresa de Avila was a mystic, but she, Tere, "can't see anything worth shit, literally and metaphorically" (p. 69). In addition, there are several sets of the minutes of the Pedro Infante Fan Club (Tere is the secretary), and these minutes vacillate between sounding like official, formal discourse on the one hand, and giving intimate trivial details of the occurrences at the meeting. These shifting discourses and languages set the stage for hilarious contrasts. Thus in the minutes we find:

> Irma Granados introduced her new puppy, who goes by the name of Pedrito. He's a mix between a chihuahua and a French poodle. He was officially voted the club mascot, 12–0. After we all said hello to him, Irma showed us how smart he is. She told him to get his snuggy-wuggy and he went out of the room and came back with a little blanket. Then she said get your boney-woney and he came back with his bone. The same thing for the bally-wally and the little blue birdy-wirdy.
>
> (p. 240)

The shifting of linguistic registers is a very successful strategy in this novel as it leaves the reader laughing at the moment of crying.

Another source of humor is the poking of fun at the human body and its functions, sexuality, and other taboo subjects. One section is called "Pink Eye," which would lead us to think of an eye disease that often occurs in children. However, the subject here is Tere's diaphragm, "el demonio/the demon," which she has left in the motel room after an encounter with Lucio and which she has to retrieve, thus subjecting herself to the humiliation of the desk clerk knowing that she has been sleeping with Lucio. Although the situation in itself is not that funny, it is Tere's description of her diaphragm and her feelings about it that makes the reader laugh. It is not a subject that should be talked (or written) about publicly, and so we laugh, if a bit nervously.

In *Face of an Angel,* Chávez also uses the body as a vehicle for humor. For example, Chapter 4 is titled "Are You Wearing a Bra?" This chapter deals with all the difficulties women have with body image, but focuses specifically on breasts. Chávez contrasts the idea that society works to hide women's breasts while at the same time specifically targeting them in a sexual way. Soveida tells us that her mother Dolores is a large-breasted woman (wearing a size 40D brassiere). Her breasts function as a double signifier: on the one hand they attract men, in particular her husband Luardo, and on the other hand they often cause Dolores physical pain as "the straps cut into her shoulders, leaving reddened, indented areas. She was prone to headaches, as well as back and neck problems. Sleep was a dilemma. Dolores could never rest on her chest or sides. From the age of twelve, she slept fully on her back, without a pillow" (p. 19). Here Chávez represents the physical pain, as well as the psychological inhibitions that large-breasted women suffer.

Chávez is not content to let the matter rest, however. Later in the novel she brings on another character, Lourdes Torres, Soveida's mother-in-law, who has even larger breasts than Dolores, but who also has a completely different attitude toward them. Indeed, Lourdes has a dif-

ferent attitude toward everything physical, and as a mother-in-law, she is a ripe object for ridicule. Seen through the eyes of Soveida, Lourdes becomes a caricature of female vanity. To begin, we are told her hobby is shopping and her "pastime" applying makeup. Here Chávez exaggerates the obsession of many Mexican women, who spend money and time to appear exquisitely made up. As Chávez remarks, "Italian women have nothing over them." The description of Lourdes's applying makeup is worthy of a comedy routine.

> Lourdes Torres eagerly constructed herself daily. She began each morning by steaming her face over a pan of boiling hot water and chamomile tea. This was followed by a gentle scrub with a mild soap called Las Tres Marías that she bought from a little shop near the old cathedral in Juárez. The owner, María Leyba, concocted the soap herself in the back room. After her morning scrub, Lourdes applied a face cream that she bought from the same shop, and let her face rest fifteen minutes while she tweezed, plucked, squeezed, pinched, rubbed and removed anything that needed to be dealt with. Then the real artistry began as she applied various shades of makeup base to her face, to lengthen, highlight, cover up and generally make more attractive what was already there. This was followed by adding the powdered rouge in varying shades to bring the rose to bloom. An eyelash curler helped train the disconcerting Indian eyelashes upward. Black Cleopatra eyeliner winged outward as if in salute. A careful and deliberate mascara application came next. This was repeated fifteen times. The lips were then lined in black eyebrow pencil and filled in with a lip brush with four alternating shades of lipstick and blotted with powder. The whole process took about thirty minutes.

> (p. 176)

Chávez's technique here is to minutely describe, exaggerate, and lengthen the process most women go to in applying makeup. The point of view of the narrator is skillfully switched to that of Lourdes as she assesses her state of beauty and becomes objectified in the process. The contrast between Lourdes's assessment of what she accomplishes with her makeup routine and that of other women is emphasized by the fact that most women think Lourdes looks like a clown.

Immediately after the description of Lourdes's makeup process and her day spent shopping, however, we are reminded that Lourdes also possesses two enormous breasts (magnificent ones in her opinion), which she calls "Mi atracción." Her chest of drawers is full of lace brassieres of all colors, as Lourdes understands that men are attracted by female breasts. For Soveida, Lourdes is a larger-than-life exaggeration of a woman, "a cartoon image of Mexican womanhood" (p. 178). Chávez has captured, in the image of Lourdes, one of the stereotypes of Mexican cultural life. She does not ridicule her out of cruelty; rather, she celebrates her eccentricities and in the process makes us laugh. In many ways, Lourdes is a very touching character, blind as to how she appears to others, but strong and positive in her own way.

THEATER

In addition to her reputation as a novelist, Denise Chávez is also known as a prolific playwright. She studied drama and has written and acted in plays. She characterizes her quirky and dramatic characters in her narratives as a side effect of her dramatic training. She has written over thirty-five plays, and many of them have been produced. Among these, her "Novena narrativas y ofrendas Nuevomexicanas," also titled "Women in the State of Grace," and "Hecho en Mexico," are perhaps her most widely known. In addition to her own creative work, she selected the plays to be included in *Shattering the Myth: Plays by Hispanic Women* (1992). This anthology includes plays by Latina playwrights Cherríe Moraga, Migdalia Cruz, Caridad Svich, Josefina López, Edit Villarreal, and Diana Sáenz. In the foreword to the plays, the editor Linda Feyder states that the plays question traditions deeply rooted in Latino family culture and explore and reinvent those traditions for a new identity. One could say the same of Chávez's plays: they present and analyze traditions in Chicano/Mexicano culture that sustain Chicanas in their endeavors and their survival, as well as customs that inhibit growth and prohibit experimentation and freedom. As other Latina writers address the methods and strategies by which women survive and prosper, so does Chávez explore the reevaluation of female relationships within the family. Taking strength from the survival techniques of their mothers, grandmothers, aunts, family friends, and *comadres,* the new generation of Chicanas also uses the female gathering of voice and herself as the subject of her own narrations to gain power and strength to become their own true selves. And although Chávez understands and expounds on what it is to serve others, as in *Face of an Angel,* it is never a selfless serving; instead, it is one that is not egotistical, but which also reserves space for oneself.

"Novena Narrativas" is a play with nine women characters: nine being the nine days of prayer that make up a novena in the Catholic church. The players, who appear one by one, are, in order of appearance: María Isabel Gonzáles, the main narrator of the play; Jesusita Rael, the store owner and a spinster; Esperanza Gonzáles, the wife of a Vietnam veteran; Minda Mirabal, a foster child; Magdalena Telles, the mother of seven children; Tomasa Pacheco, a nursing home resident; Juana Martínez, a factory worker; Pauline Mendoza, a teenager; and Corrine "La Cory" Delgado, a bag lady. The centerpiece in the play is an altar with a clay figure of the nursing Madonna at its center. The play is performed by one actress, although it could also be performed by many actresses. The player takes out her props and costumes one by one and transforms herself into the different characters in front of the audience. The multiple voices of the women range from a young girl of seven to a woman of seventy-eight. The creative one, the writer Isabel, comments that while the women on the surface seem different from her, there is something familiar about all of them: they remind her of her mother, grandmother, sister, other female family members, and yes, of herself. This harks back to the theme that women are united in a long chain of patience, survival, and love.

Jesusita, who never married although she had her chance, as she tells us, is a charitable woman who has a young foster child and who is very devout, "too busy with God to be worrying about people" (p. 90). But she does worry about people and is a kind person. Then enters Esperanza, who prays that the Virgin will take care of her loved ones, especially her husband José and other Vietnam veterans whose lives have been ruined by their experiences in the war. Minda is the seven-year-old who invents an imaginary friend, a complete opposite of herself, to get away from the tragedy of her life: a father who sexually molests her. She prays for a real mother. Magdalena is a middle-aged woman who has made a promise to the Virgin to go on a pilgrimage as thanks for petitions received. She has no job, and a recently returned no-good husband, but she has faith. Tomasa is a seventy-eight-year-old woman who has cancer, is forgetful, and resides in a nursing home. However, she remembers the Virgin on Esperanza's altar. Juana is a worker in a pantyhose factory. She is a hard worker who knows the healing arts. She recognizes that the Virgin is a mestiza virgin, a comfort to women like her, with Indian heritage. Pauline is a fourteen-year-old girl who cannot read and is a rebel. Isabel has gone to her school and has inspired her to be an artist. Another character, Corrine, "La Cory," is a bag lady: she is a survivor taking the good with the bad. The play ends with Isabel, who says, "Each of our lives is a song, or a prayer, like a novena" (p. 100). When life gets difficult for these women, they pray and they dream. The message in the play is clear: we need to accept and help each other and to hope for each other.

Because of the different perspectives of these women and what little we know of their lives, this play is quite successful. There are funny moments and sad moments, but the central focus is hope and survival. By juxtaposing the different characters against each other and by seeing how they help each other in little things, such as encouraging a little girl who cannot read to be an artist, or by taking communion to a friend, life becomes more manageable. Alvina Quintana, in her book *Home Girls,* analyzes this play through the spectrum of orality. She sees that Chávez uses ritual (the prayers) and the unity among the women to deal with the gender and cultural predicament in which minority women often find themselves. They are subjugated both by the men in their families and by a surrounding culture that does not allow them the freedom to be themselves; nevertheless, these women are united by culture, religious ritual, and tradition. For Quintana the *Narrativas,* in documenting the domestic problems these women face, show how contemporary Chicanas are able to fashion their own identity by combining their cultural traditions with modern life. She sees that Chávez seeks to unite the body and the spirit (p. 101).

Many of Chávez's unpublished plays continue to be works in progress, waiting to be written down. Because the plays may change in collaboration with the actors or because of the success or failure of a particular scene, when performed, the plays are not completely finished. At times, ideas that surface in a play may find their completion in her narratives.

OTHER WRITINGS

Descansos is a book that includes essays by Chávez and two other well-known New Mexican writers, Rudolfo Anaya and Juan Estevan Arellano. *Descansos,* or marked resting places, are crosses, rocks, or other memorials that mark the death of a person. These line the highways, roads, and paths of the countryside and are constant reminders of the fragility of life. The book is accompanied by black-and-white photographs of different kinds of *descansos,* evoking both memory and ironic contrast.

As Chávez has commented: "I have been struck by the devotion and love that goes into erecting those white crosses and plastic flower memorials and by their strange incongruity to the place and the moment" (p. 142). For Chávez the book was a "call from the ancestors." Thus her essay is named "Meditations on Death."

In "Death by the Road," the first section of the essay, Chávez reminds us that the *descanso* forms the physical emblem of that which is gone; it is remembrance, belief. As the physical mementos—the cross, the plastic flowers—begin to disintegrate, the only remaining indication of the memory is the energy field of the *descanso.* The energy field is also one of death, and Chávez wonders if, as a curandera friend has told her, death follows a "pulling in" in winter and a "letting out" in spring. Crosses, particularly on long, clear stretches of road, are particularly problematic. She feels the pull of a *descanso* instinctively, even before she sees one. These *descansos,* however, do not make her afraid. Instead she feels wonder and love.

"Fotosías" is a series of poems about different people and their *descansos.* For Tony Gonzales, death is seen as a woman, erotically luring him to his grave. Another poem/*descanso* speaks of a mother, Rufina, another of Ronnie Ralston, whose death came after he was sent to the penitentiary, destroying his mother's hopes for him when he graduated from college. And while death is sadness, it is also linked with life. Life-death: the death date on a *descanso* could be the date of someone's birth.

The final section of *Descansos* is "El Camino/ The Road," a play in verse. Evoking a journey both contemporary and past, it begins with observations by Joe the bus driver, who comments on the sights he sees as he drives and wonders what people dream. He evokes his Spanish ancestors and notes the crosses left by early travelers and settlers. The town of Cruz Blanca is a testament to those crosses. There had been a set of crosses there, but the governor had them removed, fearing they would scare travel-

ers. The town took the name of the only cross left. In earlier times it was believed that if you were killed on the side of the road, you were condemned to wander the road forever. A later *descanso* remembers Charlie, who died after he came back from Vietnam, sick with drugs and desperation. Finally there is a commentary on the Spanish word *ya,* which means ready, enough, or yes. As Chávez comments: "Anyone can use this word—reprimanding parents, overtaxed listeners, prophetic analyzers of the world situation choosing to end their words with a period. Ya. That's it. Basta! Se acabó—it's done. That's it. Ended. Finished. Ya. A word like death" (p. 180). The meditations in *Descansos* link death and life, memory, remembrance, and the consciousness that we too will take that long journey.

Chávez has written a number of short essays for *New Mexico Magazine* which have explored regional topics of interest to readers of the magazine. In "Our Lady of Guadalupe" (1986) she writes that the image of Guadalupe encompasses the belief that understanding is possible between people of different cultures, races, and traditions and is at the heart of reconciliation.

"My North, Your South or My South, Your North" (1992) tries to discern the characteristics that distinguish the different regions of New Mexico from one another. In her description we find there are cultural characteristics including attitudes and language (Spanish) that can be distinguished. She comments that northerners form closer communities and are more together, while southerners like more space and privacy. Language differences are accentuated, as the word for bread pudding in the north is *sopa,* in the south *capirotada;* the word for the fires on Christmas Eve in the north is *farolitos,* in the south *luminaries.* The word for post office in the north is *estufeta,* in the south *correo,* while the world for friend or pal in the north is *Mano/ Mana,* in the south *compa.* These words create geographic difference and linguistic diversity at the same time.

"Scenes of Home" (1996) is her homage to chile, its preparation, its workers (those unsung heroes who plant and pick it), and her patron saint of chile, Dr. Fabian García, the man who created the Sandía chile pepper. She combines the emotional sense of home and all of its requisite meanings, connecting it to the vibrancy and physicality of chile. She says, "Chile is my legacy, so is the hot pungency of this southern land, the miles of earth tilled and seeded, yielding crops valuable and cherished" (p. 37). She enlarges this concept while at the same time bringing it back to its smallest element: "Home is this place of hard-won earth, a place forged out of heat and little rain, this land that has allowed me my little heaven on this earth: red enchiladas with an egg, beans and rice" (p. 37). In these essays, Chávez captures what for her is the essence of life in New Mexico.

"Crossing Bitter Creek: Meditations on the Colorado River" is an essay written when a group of fifteen women writers went down the river on separate trips from April to October of 1997. These trips were documented in a series of essays published in *Writing Down the River: Into the Heart of the Grand Canyon* (1998). Although Chávez has a strong connection to water and to the land, she acknowledges she is a desert woman. Voicing her fears, she writes: "There is a sense of the ludicrous in the scenario: A woman with a fear of heights and rapidly moving water, enclosed spaces, and small planes, a woman with bad knees (not a camper, who thinks that camping out is room service at the Holiday Inn), a desert woman who has no wool socks, no long johns, no rain suit, agrees to run the rapids on the Colorado River for a week then take a helicopter up to the rim to catch a small propeller plane to catch another plane to go back home" (p. 109). Facing her fear of the water, she understands that the trip will only be successful if she can abandon herself to the water and let go, sage advice from a cousin. But this trip also reminds her of journey to death and to life. The name "Bitter Creek" reminds her of

descansos: all those people throughout history who died alongside the river. The days pass with wonder and anguish. Chávez says, "I am overwhelmed by the smallness and fragility of our raft in this vast space" (p. 114). The raft and the river become symbols of our passage through life. The river allows her to meditate not only about nature but about the nature of the world. Reaching the heart of the canyon, her fears put behind her, she relaxes, "beginning to understand the river's flow" (p. 119).

As Denise Chávez has said: "My writing is a mirror into my culture. Also, my writing has a deeper message of healing, harmony and of people trying to find a better way" (Ikas, *Chicana Ways*, p. 58). And she also sees herself as a voice for women. She is a writer who uses ritual, traditions, and culture to more deeply examine how women are affected and what they can do to empower their lives. As Davis-Undiano has said, "Whether dealing with the girl who brings menus to hospital rooms or a waitress in a diner, Chávez is interested. She cannot save these women from their fates, and does not try, but she never withdraws her interest and sympathy" (*Hispanic Magazine*, p. 2). Her writing is complicated and profound, often difficult to read because of its experimental nature. Chávez has stated that going back is going forward. Speaking with Eysturoy, she said:

> You never understand a situation or experience a relationship when you are in the midst of it; you have to step back from it and look again, and that may be a matter of going back in time, or analyzing what that experience did to you. I will use an example: I mentioned my parents were divorced, and recently I found a diary. There was a book coming out of Smith College in which I have written a chapter about my origins as a writer, and that chapter has some excerpts from this diary. It wasn't until I worked on that chapter last year that I realized I was able to see myself as that ten year old going through a major life change. So you go back and you go forward.

> (*This Is about Vision*, p. 161)

She is connected to family, ancestors, community, land, and heritage. Through her extensive writing, essays, narrative, and theater, she has provided a kaleidoscope of Hispano/Mexicano life on the New Mexican/Mexican border, but a kaleidoscope that is also universal.

Selected Bibliography

WORKS OF DENISE CHÁVEZ

ESSAYS

"Our Lady of Guadalupe." *New Mexico Magazine,* December 1986, 55–63.

"Words of Wisdom," *New Mexico Magazine,* December 1987, 73–78.

"Denise Chávez." In *Literature and Landscape: Writers of the Southwest.* Compiled by Cynthia Farah. El Paso: Texas Western Press, University of Texas at El Paso, 1988. Pp. 18–19.

"Heat and Rain (Testimonio)." In *Breaking Boundaries: Latina Writing and Critical Readings.* Edited by Asunción Horno-Delgado. Amherst: University of Massachusetts Press, 1989. Pp. 27–32.

"My North, Your South or My South, Your North." *New Mexico Magazine,* July 1992, 86–91.

Anaya, Rudolfo, Juan Estevan Arellano, and Denise Chávez. *Descansos: An Interrupted Journey: Tres Voces.* Albuquerque: Academia/El Norte Publications, 1995.

"Scenes of Home and a Dream in Green." *New Mexico Magazine,* February/March 1996, 32–37.

"Crossing Bitter Creek: Meditations on the Colorado River." In *Writing Down the River: Into the Heart of the Grand Canyon.* Edited by Kathleen Jo Ryan. Flagstaff, Ariz.: Northland Publishing Company, 1998.

NOVELS

The Last of the Menu Girls. Houston: Arte Público Press, 1986.

Face of an Angel. New York: Farrar, Straus, and Giroux, 1994.

Loving Pedro Infante. New York: Farrar, Straus, and Giroux, 2001.

PUBLISHED PLAYS

"Novena narrativas y ofrendas Nuevomexicanas." In *Chicana Creativity and Criticism: Charting New Frontiers in American Literature.* Edited by María Herrera-Sobek and Helena María Viramontes. Houston: Arte Público Press, 1988. *The Americas Review,* 15 nos. 3–4 (fall–winter 1987): 85–100.

"Plaza." In *New Mexico Plays.* Edited by David Richard Jones. Albuquerque: University of New Mexico Press, 1989. Pp. 79–106.

"The Flying Tortilla Man." In *Mexican American Literature.* Edited by Charles Tatum. Orlando, Fla.: Harcourt, Brace, Janovich, 1990.

Shattering the Myth: Plays by Hispanic Women. Selected by Chávez and edited by Linda Feyder. Houston: Arte Público Press, 1992.

UNPUBLISHED PLAYS

Novitiates. Produced by Dallas Theater Center, Dallas, Tex., 1971.

Elevators. Produced in Santa Fe, N.Mex., 1972.

The Mask of November. Produced in Espanola, N.Mex., 1977.

Adobe Rabbit. Produced in Taos, N.Mex., 1979.

Nacimiento. Produced in Albuquerque, N.Mex., 1979.

Santa Fe Charm. Produced in Santa Fe, N.Mex., 1980.

Sí, Hay Posada. Produced in Albuquerque, N.Mex., 1980.

An Evening of Theatre. 1981.

How Junior Got Throwed in the Joint. Produced in Santa Fe, N.Mex., 1981.

El Santero de Córdova. Produced in Albuquerque, N.Mex., 1981.

Hecho en México. Produced in Santa Fe, N.Mex., 1982.

The Green Madonna. Produced in Santa Fe, N.Mex., 1982.

La Morenita. Produced in Las Cruces, N.Mex., 1983.

Francís. Produced in Las Cruces, N.Mex., 1983.

Plaza. Produced in Albuquerque, N.Mex., 1984.

Plague-Time. 1985.

Novena Narrativas. Produced in Taos, N.Mex., 1986.

The Step. Produced by the Museum of Fine Arts, Houston, Tex., 1987.

Language of Vision. Produced in Albuquerque, N.Mex., 1987.

Women in the State of Grace. Produced in Grinnell, Iowa, 1989.

CHILDREN'S LITERATURE

The Woman Who Knew the Language of the Animals. Boston: Houghton Mifflin, 1992.

SHORT STORIES

"Grand Slam." In *Voces: An Anthology of Nuevo Mexicano Writers.* Edited by Rudolfo
   A. Anaya. Albuquerque: El Norte Publications, 1987. Pp. 187–191.

SECONDARY WORKS

INTERVIEWS

Davis-Undiano, Robert Con. "Author Denise Chávez." *Hispanic Magazine,* http://
   www.hispaniconline.com/magazine/2001/apr/Features/cultura.html (accessed April
   16, 2003).

Eysturoy, Annie O. "Denise Chávez." In *This Is about Vision: Interviews with
   Southwestern Writers.* Edited by Balassi, William, John F. Crawford, and Annie O.
   Eysturoy. Albuquerque: University of New Mexico Press, 1990. Pp. 157–169.

Hearn, Stacy. "Interview with Denise Chávez." *Desert Exposure,* http://www.zianet.com/
   desertx/mar98/chavez.html (accessed April 16, 2003).

Ikas, Karin Rosa. *Chicana Ways: Conversations with Ten Chicana Writers.* Reno:
   University of Nevada Press, 2001.

Kevane, Bridget, and Juanita Heredia, eds. *Latina Self-Portraits. Interviews with
   Contemporary Women Writers.* Albuquerque: University of New Mexico Press, 2000.

Mehaffy, Marilyn, and AnaLouise Keating. "Carrying the Message: Denise Chávez on the Politics of Chicana Becoming." *Aztlán* 26, no. 1 (spring 2001): 127.

CRITICISM

Eysturoy, Annie O. *Daughters of Self-Creation: The Contemporary Chicana Novel.* Albuquerque: University of New Mexico Press, 1996.

Keating, AnaLouise, "Towards a New Politics of Representation? Absence and Desire in Denise Chávez's *The Last of the Menu Girls.*" In *We Who Love to Be Astonished: Experimental Women's Writing and Performance Poetics.* Edited by Laura Hinton and Cynthia Hogue. Tuscaloosa: The University of Alabama Press, 2002.

Quintana, Alvina E. "Orality, Tradition, and Culture: Denise Chávez's Novena Narratives and *The Last of the Menu Girls.*" *Home Girls: Chicana Literary Voices.* Philadelphia: Temple University Press, 1996. Pp. 93–111.

Rebolledo, Tey Diana. "The Tools in the Toolbox: Representing Work in Chicana Writing." *Genre* 32, no. 172 (1999): 41–52.

Rosaldo, Renato. "Fables of the Fallen Guy." In *Criticism in the Borderlands: Studies in Chicano Literature, Culture, and Ideology.* Edited by Héctor Calderón and José David Saldívar. Durham, N.C.: Duke University Press, 1991. Pp. 84–93.

Taichert, Pari Noskin. "For Good or Ill, a Reeling 'Pedro Infante' Stretches Truth." *The Albuquerque Tribune*, August 16, 2002, p. c2.

Sandra Cisneros
(1954–)

ELLEN MCCRACKEN

THE SELF-CONSCIOUS girl from Chicago who moved from flat to flat and school to school attained only C's and D's on her fifth-grade report card in 1964. By 1992, however, she had achieved such literary renown that magazines and advertisers scrambled to make money from her image and words. On the heels of the successful launch of a book of fiction for which she had received a six-figure advance, she turned down an invitation to pose for an Annie Leibovitz ad for Gap clothing, remaining faithful to the principles that had guided her artistic production from the start: she rejected the lucrative advertising contract and the prestigious photo shoot because in her view Gap Inc. did not adequately support Latino communities. While Sandra Cisneros's literary talent connected with an audience hungry for multicultural themes in the 1990s, her personal and professional commitment to her community kept the relationship between writer and public honest. The "ugly duckling" (as she referred to herself in interviews) who as a child was embarrassed by her glasses from Sears and her poorly cut hair could become the glamorous swan of multicultural literary marketing circles thirty years later while refusing to compromise her social conscience or her commitment to her community.

THE FIRST FIVE DECADES

Born in Chicago on 20 December 1954, Sandra Cisneros had two older brothers and four younger ones, her only sister having died as a child. She felt marginalized by gender in the family as the only girl, the one who had to sleep in the living room or with her brothers in a shared double bed and who could only find privacy in the bathroom. (Her early poem "Mexican Hat Dance" recounts her seeking refuge in the bathroom after accidentally stepping on one of her mother's favorite Lucha Villa records while practicing the Mexican dance around it: "Come out of that bathroom. / No, I'm never coming out!" [p. 9]). Poverty and cultural hybridity further marginalized her. Her father, Alfredo Cisneros del Moral, had been born in Mexico to a middle-class family, but he squandered his only year at Mexico's National Autonomous University and then joined the U.S. Army, where he served during World War II and received help in becoming a U.S. citizen. After the war he stopped in Chicago on a whim and met Sandra's mother, Elvira Cordero Anguiano, at a dance. Cordero's father had come to Flagstaff, Arizona, during the 1910s to escape the violence of the Mexican Revolution and worked his way north to Chicago as a railroad laborer. Cisneros's household was one of linguistic hybridity in which she spoke English to her mother, who had grown up in Chicago, and Spanish to her father, who had come to the United States and its dominant language later in life. Further, during several summers her father moved the family back to Mexico to spend time with his relatives.

With seven children to support and only his pay as an upholsterer, Alfredo Cisneros moved his family from one cramped flat to another until he was finally able in 1966 to buy a small old house at 1525 North Campbell Street in a Puerto Rican, Ukrainian, and Polish neighborhood called West Town. During her elementary-school years, after returning to the United States from summers in Mexico, Sandra would find herself in still another rented apartment and starting a new Catholic school. Poverty and cultural hybridity burdened her as a child.

Cisneros spoke on several occasions about the experience of feeling marginalized at school. In a 1991 presentation at Mount Holyoke College in Massachusetts, she noted that "the nuns treated some of us better than others." In an interview, she referred to the nuns at St. Callistus school as "majestic at making one feel little" (Sagel, *Publishers Weekly*, p. 74). Stories such as "A Rice Sandwich," "The House on Mango Street," and "Eleven" describe episodes of humiliation that children experience at the hands of nuns and lay teachers. Nonetheless, she was able to escape through library books and fell in love with reading; even as a child, she enjoyed mentally retelling herself scenes of her life as if she were a fictional subject. She redevelops this early writing strategy in her 1984 book *The House on Mango Street*: "I make a story for my life, for each step my brown shoe takes. I say, 'And so she trudged up the wooden stairs, her sad brown shoes taking her to the house she never liked'" (p. 101). Later she found support for her creative writing at Josephinum, her Catholic all-girls high school in Wicker Park, where she edited the literary magazine and published several of her poems in it. In

Cisneros's sophomore year, a dynamic English teacher taught the work of contemporary poets and asked students to write poetry about the Vietnam War and ecological themes.

Cisneros entered Loyola University of Chicago in 1972 and earned a degree in English. Despite the burgeoning Chicano movement and the publication of early poetry, essays, and fiction of the movement by small presses in the mid-1970s, Cisneros found herself the only Mexican-American English major at the university and she read primarily white male authors in her classes. In her junior year she enrolled in a creative writing course and finally began to view herself as a writer. She wrote poems about homeless people and alcoholics who slept in the park and the public library. After graduation she entered the prestigious University of Iowa Writers' Workshop, where she earned a master's degree in creative writing in 1978. Again she felt marginalized, not only because of the rigor of the program but also because of her economically disadvantaged background. She was recovering from an affair with a married older man, one of her college professors, whose writing she had tried to imitate as an undergraduate. Her first poems at Iowa were unsuccessful attempts to write about the relationship. She recounts that in a seminar discussion of the French theorist Gaston Bachelard's *The Poetics of Space*, other students talked about their vacation homes on the Cape or in the Berkshires, while all she could refer to was a rundown house in Chicago. She realized at that moment, however, that here was precisely what made her unique and what she needed to write about. She transformed her economic and ethnic marginalization into a positive tool of identity. "It was not until this moment when I separated myself, when I considered myself truly distinct, that my writing acquired a voice," Cisneros noted in a 1990 interview with Pilar E. Rodríguez Aranda (p. 65). By the beginning of her second year at Iowa, her poems about the neighborhoods she lived in as a youth were well received in class. During vacations when she returned home, she became involved with the Chicago literary group Movimiento Artístico Chicano, or MARCH, and did some poetry readings with them. During the Iowa graduate seminar, she began to conceive of the stories that would form her first book of fiction, *The House on Mango Street*. Influenced by Vladimir Nabokov, she tried to capture children's voices in these short pieces. She worked on the stories off and on from ages twenty-two to twenty-eight and published them two years later. Her main literary project at Iowa, however, was her master's thesis, a group of poems titled "My Wicked Wicked Ways."

Cisneros returned to Chicago after earning her master's degree, accepting a job teaching and counseling at the Latino Youth Alternative High School for dropouts. The street language and some of the tragic lives of the students she worked with found their way into the stories she was writing that would become *The House on Mango Street*. She saw poetry in their street slang, at the same time that she was troubled by the contrast between her own successful life and theirs. Her writing became inspired by wanting to change these students' lives by telling some of their stories and suggesting an alternative path for them in her fiction. But Cisneros was also frustrated by how little time she had for writing because of her demanding job and her work with MARCH, where she organized poetry readings and writing classes in poor Latino neighborhoods. In December 1980 she took a new job as a recruiter at Loyola University. That year, *Bad Boys*, her first chapbook of poetry, was published by a small Chicano press in San José, California. In 1982 she was awarded her first National Endowment for the Arts Fellowship, which enabled her to work full-time on her creative writing for two years. At the same time, the Chicano publisher and editor Nicolás Kanellos, who had published her short story "Chanclas" in the *Revista Chicano-Riqueña*, asked Cisneros to submit her other stories in this vein

for publication as a book. With the fellowship money, she worked on these stories and her poetry in Provincetown, Massachusetts, and in various locations in Europe. In 1984 this first book of fiction was published, and she moved to San Antonio, Texas, to work as literary director for the Guadalupe Cultural Arts Center.

Settling in the vibrant city of San Antonio nourished Cisneros's work. The strong presence of Latinos there made her feel closely connected to her Latin American roots, an insider and not a stranger. The varieties of Spanish she heard had a dynamic effect on her writing, as did the deeply rooted Chicano and Latino traditions of the city. In 1985 she won the Before Columbus Foundation's American Book Award and a Dobie Paisano Fellowship, which supported her financially for six months of writing. In 1987 she taught at California State University at Chico, and later that year published her first book-length volume of poetry, *My Wicked Wicked Ways*. Cisneros was awarded a second NEA Fellowship and finally got up the courage to call the New York literary agent Susan Bergholz, who had been trying to contact Cisneros for four years. Cisneros sent her only thirty-nine pages of a new volume of stories *(Woman Hollering Creek and Other Stories)*, yet Bergholz was able to sell the not-yet-written book to Random House for a large advance amounting to what established authors might garner. Cisneros was about to become the first Chicana writing about Chicano themes to publish a book with a mainstream press. She remarked in 1989, as she was finishing the manuscript, that she felt tremendous pressure as a member of a minority community who had been awarded this prestigious contract; she worried that if the book were not a success, literary arbiters would assume that Chicanos simply could not write well.

It is important to place this key accomplishment in its historical context. The so-called boom of Latina fiction that Cisneros's publishing contract initiated did not emerge spontaneously or accidentally. The Chicano movement of the late 1960s and the 1970s militantly struggled to give voice and identity to minorities whose culture the myth of the American melting pot once tried to efface. A few women published poetry, short stories, and political essays early in the movement, and some longer works of fiction by Chicanas appeared in the 1970s. However, the majority of literary texts published in this period were by men. Cisneros offered several explanations for this. The early writers, such as Tomás Rivera, Rudolfo Anaya, and Rolando Hinojosa, were teaching at universities, while it took longer for the women to fight social prejudices and find the financial resources even to enter universities and receive degrees. Cisneros also argued that patriarchal privilege gave men confidence to write and spared them from either-or decisions that women were forced to confront, such as choosing between writing or marriage and children. Although Cisneros had earned a master's degree, it never occurred to her in the late 1970s that she might seek a university teaching position that would afford her more time to write.

Nonetheless, throughout the 1980s an emerging group of Latinas—among them Cisneros, Ana Castillo, Denise Chávez, Judith Ortiz Cofer, Nicholasa Mohr, Sheila Ortiz-Taylor, Carmen de Monteflores, and Helena María Viramontes—published fiction with small regional presses. Writers such as these contested the masculinist blind spots of earlier movement politics and culture. Little by little, they began to come together across geographic distances to support and critique one another's work. In *Something to Declare*, Dominican American writer Julia Alvarez spoke of how publication of *The House on Mango Street* in 1984 helped her to feel part of a community of writers in the tradition of previous groups such as the Black Mountain Poets or the Lost Generation.

Larger social pressures also catalyzed the boom in publication of fiction by Latina women. As militant movements continued to demand an end to the myth of the melting pot, corporations and institutions sought ways to pacify, limit, and even profit from the social unrest. Universities established departments of ethnic studies, and one by one mainstream publishing houses—many owned by large media conglomerates—offered book contracts to selected Latina writers in the late 1980s and 1990s, aware that there was now a large audience of minority and non-minority readers interested in ethnic fiction.

Cisneros's lucrative advance contract in 1987 also allowed Random House to reissue her first book, *The House on Mango Street,* and this involved difficult negotiations with Arte Público Press, the original publisher. When the new book, *Woman Hollering Creek and Other Stories,* appeared in 1991, it won the $35,000 Lannan Literary Award for Fiction. Cisneros also signed another large advance contract with Turtle Bay Books (a subsidiary of Random House) for a new volume of poetry, *Loose Woman: Poems,* which was published in 1994. Turtle Bay had reissued *My Wicked Wicked Ways* in 1992. That year Cisneros began working on her magnum opus, the novel *Caramelo,* signing a six-figure advance contract with Knopf (also owned by Random House) for the book, which was nine years in the making. In 1995 she received her most significant award of the decade, a MacArthur Foundation Fellowship, or "genius grant," for $225,000.

Awards, advances, royalties, and large speaking fees enabled Cisneros not only to support herself but in 1991 to fulfill the dream of buying her own house: a 1903 Victorian in the King William district of San Antonio. In June 1997 she ran afoul of the city's Historic and Design Review Commission when it charged that the periwinkle purple she had painted her house was not historically appropriate for the neighborhood. Cisneros argued to the contrary:

> The issue is bigger than my house. The issue is about historical inclusion. . . . Purple is historic to us. It only goes back a thousand years or so to the pyramids. It is present in the Nahua codices, book of the Aztecs, as is turquoise, the color I used for

my house trim; the former color signifying royalty, the latter, water and rain.

(www.accd.edu/sac/english/
mcquien/htmlfils/kingwill.htm)

CNN, the *New York Times,* the *Los Angeles Times,* and the Associated Press all reported on the controversy, with much of the coverage being collected in the 2001 book *In Context: Participating in Cultural Conversations.* Skeptics accused Cisneros of trying to sell books, but many of her neighbors tied purple ribbons on their trees in support of her. Finally, after two years the dispute was settled when the commission inspected a sample of the paint and agreed it had faded enough to be acceptable.

In the nine months preceding the controversy, Cisneros had undergone another ordeal: her father's illness and death from cancer. In 1997, for the feast of the Day of the Dead (2 November, a day in which Mexicans bring offerings of food, mementos, and flowers to the graves of their dead), she composed a literary *ofrenda* for him that was published in the *Los Angeles Times,* "An Offering to the Power of Language." Her father's irreplaceable gift to her, Cisneros explains, was the powerful, affectionate Spanish language that ties her to her ancestors and her people's long traditions. The Spanish language represents "another way of seeing" (a term the Russian formalists early in the twentieth century regarded as the primary characteristic of all art); her offering, or *ofrenda,* to honor her father in the year of his death and to honor all immigrants who come to a new country, "dragging their beloved homeland with them in their language," consisted of beautiful yet ordinary things through which her father still spoke to her, such as marigold flowers or the opening notes of an Agustín Lara bolero.

In another essay, "Only Daughter," Cisneros recounts her sadness that her father could not read her writing because it was in English and because he preferred mass culture: "My father represents . . . the public majority. A public who is disinterested in reading, and yet one whom I am writing about and for, and privately trying to

woo" (p. 256). In 1989 she brought him a Spanish translation of a story she had written about Tepeyac, the *colonia* in Mexico City where he had been raised. He stopped watching a Pedro Infante movie on Galavisión to read the story, laughing in the right places, reading lines out loud, and asking about certain characters he recognized. To her extreme gratification, he then asked where he could get extra copies for the relatives. Both the language of the story and the cultural representation of his childhood barrio afforded him a pleasurable aesthetic experience. Cisneros worked to achieve a similar effect in her long novel *Caramelo,* published simultaneously in English and Spanish editions in 2002 to reach both U.S. linguistic communities with the story of her father and his family's life on both sides of the border.

In 1994, Random House's Vintage imprint published *La casa en Mango Street,* Cisneros's 1984 book translated into Spanish by the noted Mexican writer Elena Poniatowska, with the assistance of Juan Antonio Asencio. Especially noteworthy is that the prolific author made room in her overburdened schedule to take on the translation. Such a gift of time and talent from one of Mexico's foremost contemporary writers was a stamp of approval and support for this most talented Chicana writer. Further, the launching of this Spanish translation in the United States marked the beginning of an important new publishing phenomenon, the drive by mainstream presses to market books to Spanish-speaking immigrants and Spanish-dominant bilingual speakers in the United States. U.S. publishers even began issuing Latin American works in Spanish before their English translations were available. An important element of this new trend was the simultaneous release of Cisneros's novel *Caramelo* in separate English and Spanish hardcover editions in 2002.

POETRY: BAD, WICKED, AND LOOSE

During her years of shy self-consciousness in elementary school, Sandra Cisneros became a fascinated observer of the speech, voices, and customs of others. She enjoyed the sound of words and experimented with various sounds in her youthful poetry, and after her initial embarrassment she found pleasure in hearing herself read her poems aloud in high school. One of her professors at Loyola University encouraged her to continue writing poetry and to pursue a graduate degree. Nonetheless, it appears that she had little contact with the poetry of the burgeoning Chicano movement at the time.

At the height of the Chicano movement in the early 1970s, a handful of Chicana poets were beginning to make their mark. Among them, Lorna Dee Cervantes taught herself printing and founded a small press and literary magazine, *Mango,* which published from 1976–1980. At the time, Cisneros was working at the Latino Youth Alternative High School in Chicago and giving poetry readings in coffee houses. She was selected by the Poetry Society of America and the Chicago Transit Authority to display one of her poems with those of other famous poets on the buses and subways of Chicago. The well-known Chicano writer Gary Soto phoned Cisneros after reading a manuscript she had given to Cervantes, and together with Cervantes published a chapbook of her poetry at Mango Publications in 1980.

Titled *Bad Boys,* the small pamphlet included seven of Cisneros's poems from her master's thesis submitted in 1978 to the University of Iowa Writers' Workshop. Among the "bad boys" of these poems are the barrio boys who aggressively stare at the young girls playing on the back porch "where rats hid under" in "Velorio" (p. 3); the fifty-four-year-old mama's boy of "Joe," who likes go-go dancers and spends hours in the garage with "naked lady pictures" before he dies in an auto accident (p. 16); the father who tells his children to lie about their disabled brother hidden at home ("Arturo Burro"); the drunken father who punches his wife's belly and, when she refuses to let him in, kicks the door and throws a rock through the window ("South Sangamon"); the "doctor" at

Traficante's Drugs who treats the child's infected hand by banging a medical volume on the wound to open it ("Traficante"); and the father-to-be who buys flowers for the pregnant girl in a blue dress who has been sent away to the nuns, but who doesn't notice she needs a seat on the bus or is hungry for some of the food he can't finish ("The Blue Dress"). Sometimes the young girls in these poems function as "bad boys" by engaging in small transgressions such as touching a baby's corpse at a *velorio* (a wake) or enjoying hot dogs at a store instead of going home for lunch as they are supposed to. In this first publication of her early poems, Cisneros begins to represent the diverse ethnic people of her Chicago barrio through the optic of a critical feminist consciousness. This aesthetic strategy functions as a point of departure for much of her subsequent writing. With this 1980 chapbook, Cisneros joined the ranks of other early Chicana poets, such as Lucha Corpi, Alma Villaneuva, Bernice Zamora, and Ana Castillo, who began to publish in the mid-1970s.

Cisneros expanded her master's thesis for publication as her first major volume of poetry in 1987. Some of the poems were published earlier in magazines such as *Nuestro, Revista Chicano-Riqueña, Spoon River Quarterly,* and *Third Woman.* The sixty poems in the 1987 volume *My Wicked Wicked Ways* emphasize women's sexual autonomy, pleasure, and pride, among other themes. Right from the front cover, Cisneros presents herself photographically as a "wicked" subject, parodying film-star vamps such as Rita Hayworth, who she argues were the only role models she had for powerful women when she was growing up. In the black-and-white photo, she sits cross-legged in cowboy boots, leaning forward in a black, low-cut evening dress and smiling impishly at viewers. Her lips, sections of her gold hoop earrings, and the wine glass are tinted bright red to match the book's title. Cisneros noted that even the lettering on the cover is intended to re-create this period of the movies. She argued: "The cover is of a woman appropriating her own sexuality. In some ways that's also why it's wicked: the scene is trespassing that boundary by saying: 'I defy you. I'm going to tell my own story'" (Rodríguez Aranda, *Americas Review,* p. 68) Combining incongruous visual signs, Cisneros entices readers to engage with the diverse images in the poems they are about to read that recode women's "wickedness."

In "His Story," the poetic persona and character of Sandra Cisneros defies her father's warnings about other doomed women in the family: a great aunt who was sinfully beautiful, a cousin who was a prostitute, a great-grandmother who died through voodoo. Trapped by what her father perceives to be her unlucky fate, the only daughter leaves home to pursue a writing career, while the six brothers remain at home as she should have done. The poem "Six Brothers" revisits the Grimm fairy tale about a girl who rescues her brothers from their transformation into swans by weaving thistle shirts for them. Because she omits one sleeve, the youngest brother comes back with a swan's wing instead of an arm; Cisneros compares him to one of her own brothers who, along with her, fails to keep the family name clean according to their father's traditional standards. In "The Poet Reflects on Her Solitary Fate," Cisneros argues that her destiny, now that she has left her family, is to write poetry.

Other female figures in the poems proudly express their sexuality. In "I the Woman," the speaker is a "temporary thing" for her illicit partner, leaving behind a "live wildness" remembered in an earring dropped in the car and black smoke in his mouth (p. 30). The waitress in "Something Crazy" looks back on the pleasure she felt as a young woman when the regular customer with the blue hat would turn to look at her as he left each day; the "something crazy" she experienced as the object of his gaze represents the "kind of thing you look for all your life," she says (p. 32). The poetic voice in "Ass" experiments playfully with various euphemisms for this area of the lover's body which has enraptured the speaker "since mine

eyes did first espy that paradise of symmetry" (p. 53). Read through the heterosexual dominant, this poem refers to female/male sexual attraction, but it is simultaneously open to homosexual readings. Nonetheless, on another occasion Cisneros anchors her authorial intention by foregrounding her own heterosexuality with respect to this image: "For all the things that I argue about men, they have such *bonitas nalgas* [pretty asses]. I can't help it. I've never looked twice at a woman's *nalgas* like I do at men's" (Rodríguez Aranda, *Americas Review,* p. 71). The central section of poems in the volume recounts European experiences. In "December 24th, Paris—Notre-Dame," for example, the poetic voice has recovered from thoughts of suicide at year's end. Instead of passersby finding in the Seine "a body here— / unraveled like a poem, / dissolved like wafer . . . I go out into the street once more. / The wrists so full of living. / The heart begging once again" (p. 46). "Fishing Calamari by Moon" expresses the poet's sympathy for all the world's underdogs, symbolized by the bulls killed in bullfights and the freshly caught calamari whose "skins turn black as sorrow" once they are taken from the water (p. 60).

The last section of *My Wicked Wicked Ways* contains twenty poems denominated "The Rodrigo Poems" and a final one in Spanish that Cisneros wrote in Mexico. The poetic sequence begins with a poem imagining a woman's perspective when her partner does not come home (perhaps one of Rodrigo's ex-wives)—the point where the story begins, according to Cisneros. Successive poems discuss the ups and downs of the relationship with Rodrigo—his departures and returns, the sexual attraction to him, and the woman's sense of self, which remains intact despite the tumultuous relationship. The closing poem, "Tantas Cosas Asustan, Tantas" (So many things terrify, so many) is distinctive because it is the only one entirely in Spanish. Cisneros said she wrote it while living with her friend Norma Alarcón in San Cristobal de las Casas in Chiapas, Mexico. At the time, she was thinking and dreaming in Spanish, so the poem worked its way out in that language and she found it impossible to translate. Because Cisneros is an English-dominant bilingual speaker, the Spanish poem is less sophisticated than her others. She returns to the volume's central issue of rejecting traditional expectations for women: "Cual es peor? / Estar siempre sola, / o estar con alguien para siempre." (Which is worse? To be alone forever, or to be with someone forever.)

Turtle Bay republished *My Wicked Wicked Ways* in November 1992 with a new prefatory poem that Cisneros had finished in Hydra, Greece, on 11 June of that year. In the new poem, she recounts her sins of the "girl grief decade" in which these poems were written (p. ix). She tells of the pain of forging an artistic path on her own, with no track laid out for her as for other privileged writers, and of the loneliness of living on her own, trying to make her way. Her first "felony" was taking up with poetry while the rice figuratively burned and her mother warned she'd never marry. A second transgression was to break with the life her father planned: "Winched the door with poetry and fled" (p. x). During these years she looked for love ("Played at mistress / Tattooed an ass") and did her share of drinking (p. xi). The "wicked" poems that follow are "my colicky kids / who fussed and kept / me up the wicked nights," key elements of her identity at the time of this new publication just as they were when she wrote them (p. xii).

Cisneros's third volume of poetry, *Loose Woman: Poems* (1994), represents a new phase in her poetic creation. *My Wicked Wicked Ways* was more controlled, like classical music and ballet, Cisneros said, while *Loose Woman* involves a freer, more colloquial poetic voice similar to jazz. After having dealt with controlling institutions such as the Iowa workshop and the Roman Catholic Church in the 1987 volume, she could treat nontraditional subjects more freely in the new book. The title refers both to the Spanish term *"poemas sueltos,"* or uncol-

lected poems eventually brought together in a volume, and to the sexually transgressive undertone of the phrase in English. Cisneros notes that everything about the book is loose, from its lines to its subjects. In "Down There," for example, Cisneros catalogues the often crass subjects of poetry written by men, including John Updike's "Cunts" about a woman's bloody tampon. Following and transcending this model, she devotes the second half of the poem to an aesthetic, down-to-earth reappropriation of menstruation from a woman's perspective: "Gelatinous. Steamy / and lovely to the light to look at / like a good glass of burgundy. Suddenly / I'm artist each month. . . . In fact, / I'd like to dab my fingers / in my inkwell / and write a poem across the wall" (pp. 83–84). In a splendid inversion of men's prerogative to address any subject no matter how off-color, Cisneros's poem represents a woman speaking for herself on subjects she chooses in order to please herself, whether taboo or not. The euphemism "down there" of the title is belied by the bold, confident speech of the poem itself.

In "You Bring Out the Mexican in Me," Cisneros plays on the Catholic ritual of the litany, in which repeated praiseworthy titles are invoked in praying to saints and other religious figures. Here the poetic persona of Cisneros is herself the object of this adulatory language, which describes in line after line characteristics of Mexican culture that her lover brings out in her, such as "the Dolores del Río in me," "The tidal wave of recession in me," and "The Agustín Lara hopeless romantic in me" (pp. 4–5). The modified ritualistic incantations praise the poet's ethnic self that the lover helps to validate. Here, instead of the religious supplicant praising the dozens of titles of the Blessed Virgin in asking repeatedly for intercession, the Chicana poet valorizes herself through the aspects of her Mexicanicity that the U.S. melting pot has traditionally undervalued. Cisneros also associates love with alternative notions of religion in the poems "Love Poem for a Non-Believer" and "With Lorenzo at the Center of the Universe, el

Zócalo, Mexico City." In "A Man in My Bed Like Cracker Crumbs," she recounts praying to La Virgen de la Soledad (Our Lady of Solitude) in the morning and sitting down to begin writing "because she's answered me" by giving Cisneros the solitude she needs in order to write. Cisneros presents an alternative model for the godmother and baptism in "Arturito the Amazing Baby Olmec Who Is Mine by Way of Water," a poem written for her nephew's baptism in February 1993. As a godmother who "dislikes kids and Catholics," Cisneros offers her nephew three positive spiritual role models for his life: Emiliano Zapata, who protects those weaker than himself; Gandhi because "he knew the power of the powerless"; and Mother Teresa, who found wealth in giving herself to others (p. 99).

Cisneros pays homage to the Mexican artist Frida Kahlo in two poems that focus on the vital role of poetry in her own life. In "Unos Cuantos Piquetitos" ("A Few Small Nips"), also the title of Kahlo's 1935 painting that depicts a woman brutally stabbed dozens of times by her drunken boyfriend, Cisneros suggests that her poems are the potential sites of life-threatening wounds on her body—"the bull's eye of my heart," (p. 59) her jugular, wrists, and womb. Her answer to the image of the victimized woman in Kahlo's painting is to publicly expose her vulnerability by publishing poems that represent both the bull's eye and the "sigh" of her heart. (Elsewhere Cisneros has noted that writing poetry is like becoming naked in public, exposing the terrifying center of oneself to public view.) In "*Los Desnudos*: A Triptych," Cisneros remakes the nude woman in Francisco de Goya's painting *The Naked Maja* with an anatomically specific portrait of one of her lovers in the first panel; in the second she portrays a man whom she has borrowed from another woman, who like Frida Kahlo will accuse her of betraying a sister. Cisneros argues, in response, that poetry is her husband and is as jealous as her lover's wife; her lover should not try to "pluck me to fidelity" (p. 88). She again uses the metaphor of poetry as her

husband in "I Let Him Take Me": "Husband, love, my life— / Poem" (p. 11). Finally, in the poem "Loose Woman," Cisneros redefines the role of the woman poet as one who will "strike terror among the men," who is "foot-loose, / loose-tongued /, let-loose, / woman-on-the-loose, / loose woman"—a woman free from subservience to men (pp. 114–115).

POETIC PROSE: THE TWO LIVES OF A BOOK

Having sold over two million copies to date in fifty-six printings, simple yet profound *House on Mango Street* is widely read in schools from junior high through university and even doctoral studies. Although its first publisher, Arte Público, marketed the book as children's literature, its aesthetic and intellectual profundity belies this classification. The wide distribution and marketing network of the larger publisher Random House, in combination with the growing national interest in multiculturalism in the 1990s, gave the book an immense increase in sales from 1991 onward. The book, in effect, has had two lives to date: its first seven years, in which its launch by Arte Público in 1984 helped to inaugurate the long-awaited entrance of women fiction writers into the Chicano literary renaissance, and its second publication by Random House in 1991, after which it rapidly reached a vast national and international readership. Although the book was not well known and was difficult to obtain in its first stage, it quickly entered the literary canon once it was distributed more widely in the decade of flowering multiculturalism of the 1990s.

Cisneros wrote *The House on Mango Street* in stages between 1977 and 1982. Begun the very night she experienced the turning point in her graduate writing seminar in Iowa, the book evolved over the years as she worked on it part-time, piece by piece. Influenced by the concise form of Jorge Luis Borges's *Dreamtigers*, she tried to produce stories that were a cross between poetry and fiction, "compact and lyrical and ending with a reverberation" ("Do You Know Me?" p. 78). In the same essay, she terms the stories "lazy poems," texts that could have been developed into poems but remained stories, hovering between the two genres. Indeed, "The Three Sisters," "Beautiful & Cruel," and "A House of My Own" were originally poems or drafts of poems. (Compare, for example, "The Three Sisters" with the poem "Velorio.") Cisneros wanted to write a nonlinear narrative that could be opened to any section and be understood. While each of the forty-four stories in the collection stands on its own, they relate to one another as well. In the manner of books such as Sherwood Anderson's *Winesburg, Ohio* (1919), Tomás Rivera's *. . . Y no se lo tragó la tierra/And the Earth Did Not Devour Him* (1971), Pedro Juan Soto's *Spiks* (1956; English translation, 1973), and Gloria Naylor's *The Women of Brewster Place* (1983), Cisneros's volume combines the intense effect of the short story with the longer discursiveness of the novel, forming a hybrid genre midway between the two forms of fiction. Cisneros's book engages in a double genre hybridity by combining the effects of poetry and fiction along with forms of the novel and the short story.

Another of her intentions, after the revelation in the Iowa Writers' Workshop that she had something different to write about, was to present a more realistic portrait of the Latino barrio than that offered by the children's television program *Sesame Street*. She noted that poor neighborhoods lose their charm after dark or when the garbage isn't picked up, that rats abound and people get shot. But her portrait of the barrio would also differ from the accounts many men had written: "I was writing about it in the most real sense that I knew, as a person walking those neighborhoods with a vagina. I saw it a lot differently than all those 'chingones' that are writing all those bullshit pieces about their barrios" (Rodríguez Aranda, *Americas Review,* p. 69). Her unromanticized images of the barrio offer a woman's critical perspective or

rereading of events remembered from childhood and adolescence.

The first stories, written in Iowa, function as memoirs and try to record characters that she remembered from the barrio: "The Earl of Tennessee," "The House on Mango Street" "Louis His Cousin & His Other Cousin," "Meme Ortiz," "Marin," "Edna's Ruthie," "Sire," and "Gil's Furniture Bought & Sold." Then, when she was working at the alternative high school in Chicago, she wrote about the students she met, hoping to help to change their lives through her writing. These stories include "Alicia Who Sees Mice," "Sally," "What Sally Said," "Darius & the Clouds," "The Family of Little Feet," "A Rice Sandwich," and "The First Job." Cisneros's aunt inspired "There Was an Old Woman She Had So Many Children She Didn't Know What to Do." After receiving her first NEA grant and moving to Provincetown, she edited with help from a friend from the Iowa Writers' Workshop stories such as "My Name," "Hips," "Elenita, Cards, Palm, Water," "Laughter," "Our Good Day," "Four Skinny Trees," and "Bums in the Attic." Finally finishing "Mango Says Goodbye Sometimes," "The Monkey Garden," and "Red Clowns" on a Greek island on 30 November 1982, she sent the manuscript to her publisher.

In 1976, in the first issue of the literary magazine *Mango,* editor and publisher Lorna Dee Cervantes told readers, "Aquí, we want to sprout mangos from the tops of your heads while we sing you fine songs." She was alluding to a poem by Víctor Hernández Cruz in which a Puerto Rican who has come to New York singing fine songs drops the strange seeds he has brought with him out his window so that they land on people below. One falls on a policeman's head, from which a beautiful green mango tree begins to sprout within a few months. In addition to alluding to North Mango Avenue in Chicago, Cisneros paid homage to Cervantes's important magazine and small press, the publisher of Cisneros's own *Bad Boys,* by choosing this name "Mango" for the street in the

Chicago barrio that is the center of her book. She no doubt hoped that the hybrid poetic prose pieces in the collection would sprout figurative mangoes in the heads of her readers, following Cervantes's and Hernández Cruz's image.

The mangoes that sprout in *The House on Mango Street* are not simply pieces of pleasant tropical fruit. The central image of the house in the book is both a literal lack in the past and present, and a figurative image connected to self-fulfillment through writing in the future. In each time period, the house is intimately connected to narrative or other forms of writing. While the family moves from one inadequate flat to another, their mother tells her children bedtime stories about the perfect white house with trees and a large lawn that they will someday buy. The book's protagonist, Esperanza Cordero, recounts how her school principal and another nun humiliate her on two separate occasions by asking her to tell them exactly which dilapidated flat she lived in. Only when imagined in the future does the image of the house become positive, as Cisneros suggests that it is the prerequisite for a woman to be able to write: "Not a flat. Not an apartment in back. Not a man's house. Not a daddy's. A house all my own. . . . Only a house quiet as snow, a space for myself to go, clean as paper before the poem" (p. 100). Cisneros also communalizes her future imagined house, thinking against the grain of American individualism and the notion of private property. She imagines that she will invite bums to live in the attic of her future house, and that their creaking noises upstairs will replace the sound of rats in previous dwellings. Another immigrant family in the neighborhood tries to "tropicalize" their apartment by painting the interior walls pink to match the picture of their house in their homeland. Despite wearing brightly colored clothes, listening to Spanish-language radio, and repainting the walls, the family's mother still finds the dwelling a prison because she speaks only Spanish and cannot adjust to life in the United States.

Other mangoes that Cisneros wishes to grow in readers' heads center on the theme of women's victimization under patriarchy and their resistance to it. Several young girls in the book are gradually introduced into the realm of adult female sexuality in frightening or violent ways that sometimes masquerade as exciting fun and flattery. When playfully parading in the neighborhood streets in high heels one day, Esperanza and her young friends at first enjoy their new liminal status between childhood and adult womanhood. The corner grocer tries to police their game, which is overlaid with sexuality, and warns them that this play is dangerous, but a bum on the street offers one of the girls a dollar for a kiss, almost entrapping her in a kind of proto-prostitution. On another occasion, an old man forces a kiss on Esperanza at her first day of work, after leading her to believe he would befriend her and ease her anxiety at the new workplace. Near the end of the book, Esperanza's sexual initiation comes through rape at a carnival, brutally destroying the romantic illusions about sex gleaned from a girlfriend. A cycle of stories within the larger collection focuses on Esperanza's friend Sally, whose father frequently beats her in his efforts to control her sexuality. One day Esperanza senses imminent physical danger for her friend, who is playing a sexual game with a gang of boys in a rundown neighborhood park. While the young Esperanza is not able to articulate the nature of the danger (gang rape), she is so traumatized that she imagines ways to kill herself. Sally's ostensibly fun game with the boys only superficially disguises patriarchal violence that even the young Esperanza can see. The pattern of patriarchal victimization in Sally's life continues after she runs away to marry a marshmallow salesman before eighth grade and becomes trapped in a violent marriage.

In contrast, figures such as Esperanza's mother (Elvira Codero), Minerva, and Alicia present alternatives to female victimization. Mrs. Cordero (the real maiden name of Cisneros's mother) tells Esperanza about her own childhood foolishness in dropping out of school because she was ashamed of her clothes. As the story reveals details of her intelligence and talents, she tells her daughter sarcastically, "I was a smart cookie then" (p. 84). Minerva, whose husband has left her with two children, transcends patriarchal oppression by writing poems late at night on pieces of paper. Although she folds them up to hide them, she eventually reads them to Esperanza, who reciprocates with her own poems. Art, Cisneros suggests, is one powerful means of combating women's victimization. Alicia puts herself through school with great sacrifice while doing double duty as substitute mother in her family. She inspires Esperanza in one conversation at the end by urging her to work to make their barrio better since people can't simply sit back and expect the mayor to do it. At the end, Esperanza vows to return to the barrio in the future to help the others who are unable to leave as she is. Already the book in our hands is one means of doing this. The distinctive characters whose stories the "wise child" narrator recounts offer an unromantic yet appreciative portrait of an urban immigrant community in the Midwest that promotes understanding in the best sense of diversity and multiculturalism.

THE GROUNDBREAKING COLLECTION OF STORIES

In the pathbreaking 1991 *Woman Hollering Creek and Other Stories,* Cisneros captures the voices of a myriad of Latino characters predominantly from Texas. As the mainstream publishing industry's first work of fiction by a Chicana writing about her culture, the volume has more than lived up to the industry's expectations. Winning several awards including the PEN Center USA West Award for fiction and the Lannan Foundation Literary Award, the book established Cisneros as one of the foremost talents in contemporary American fiction. With innovative technical experiments in voice, narration, and themes, the twenty-two stories

aesthetically reconfigure Latino ethnicity for various sectors of the reading public that differ in ethnicity, gender, age, and income. The book's wide appeal results both from the contemporary interest in multiculturalism and from Cisneros's postmodern narrative style with its multiple points of entry for diverse readers.

The seven stories of the opening section focus on girlhood memories, serving as a literary bridge between *Mango Street* and the new book, and between Chicago and Texas. Cisneros inserts herself autobiographically into the text by the use of her maternal grandmother's family name, Anguiano, and her paternal grandfather's exact address in Mexico City—La Fortuna, number 12—just as she had used her mother's maiden name, Cordero, for the protagonist of *The House on Mango Street.* The figure of the dear childhood friend Lucy mentioned in *Bad Boys, My Wicked Wicked Ways,* and *Mango Street* now is given the last name "Anguiano" to suggest that she is a part of the family, like the sister Cisneros never had to grow up with. In fact the narrator wishes to be part of Lucy's family, hoping that by sitting in the midday sun she will make her skin as dark as her friend's, and that Lucy's eight sisters could also be hers. The story not only conveys class, race, and ethnic difference to readers who had less poverty-stricken childhoods, it also allows many points of identification for readers who created transitory utopian communities of their own through childhood play. Many readers can also identify with the young girl's wise ruminations on birthdays in the following story, "Eleven," and perhaps have even had similar run-ins with mistaken, authoritarian teachers like Mrs. Price. But Rachel, another childhood friend who appears in Cisneros's previous three books, here also faces racial discrimination, as the teacher insists without foundation that a dirty old red sweater must be hers and makes her put it on. By giving the narrator of the story a friend's name instead of her own, Cisneros invites us to join her in remembering similar events we witnessed in childhood where one classmate was publicly humiliated and broke down sobbing, now with more information and experience to understand what these victims might really have undergone.

Along with memories of famous Mexican movies that her parents took the family to see and the milieu of her grandparents' life in Mexico City, Cisneros also focuses her memories on an emblematic image of U.S. mass culture—the Barbie doll, from which few girls can escape no matter what their ethnicity. With deft postmodernist experimentation that recycles and parodies the advertising jingles that overcode the Barbie doll, Cisneros interjects the reality of poverty to explain that some children are less equal than others in attaining this gendered version of the American Dream. Just as girls learn much later that they can only be imperfect copies of the Barbie doll, so do the Chicago barrio girls in the story "Barbie-Q" learn that they must be content to play with damaged versions of American ideal femininity—the Barbie dolls sold in a fire sale.

In the second section of the book, a single pair of stories recounts dangerous sexual initiation experiences of young girls. "One Holy Night" tells of an eighth grader in the Chicago barrio who is impregnated by the thirty-seven-year-old Chato; he says he is the descendant of Mayan kings, but in fact he has killed eleven girls in the past seven years. Cisneros fictively imagines the young victim's version of the events, allowing readers a more realistic understanding of a person who would otherwise only be one of the statistics of young Latinas' pregnancies. In the second story, "Mi *Tocaya*," Patricia, a younger-than-usual high school girl who wears rhinestone earrings and glitter high heels with her Catholic school uniform, disappears from her repressive home. After a body is found and declared to be her, she rises from the dead three days later and returns home. Realistic readers suspect she has either run away from sexual abuse or become the victim of it after running away.

The last and lengthiest section of the book primarily tells stories of adult women's love relationships. Cleófilas, a Mexican immigrant whose husband beats her in "Woman Hollering Creek," tries to emotionally escape her situation through *telenovelas* (Latino soap operas) and romance novels. With the help of a health care worker and a character who seems to be a stand-in for Cisneros herself, she begins to learn that she must transform herself from the image of the crying woman, or La Llorona, to that of the empowered, shouting woman—La Gritona, the name of a local creek. In an interview with Feroza Jussawalla and Reed Ray Dasenbrock, Cisneros noted that she herself was part of this true story. Readers can infer that the Chicana who helps Cleófilas to escape the abusive marriage is a subtle allusion to Cisneros; for instance, the character drives a pickup truck, and Cisneros would use the second half of her advance for the book to buy one—bright red—for herself. In "Eyes of Zapata" Cisneros returns to the time of the Mexican Revolution to retell history through the eyes of Inés, a woman with supernatural powers who bore Emiliano Zapata two children. By fictionally recreating Inés's version of events, Cisneros deconstructs the famous male hero of both Mexico and the Chicano movement, arguing for women's rightful place in that history. Inés is the flip side of Cleófilas in the sense that she remains empowered rather than victimized when mistreated by a strong male figure.

In three of the stories in this section, Chicana visual artists offer distinct paths of women's strength in the face of adversity. Ultimately Cisneros takes a degree of critical distance from the artist Clemencia in "Never Marry a Mexican," naming her ironically to underscore her egregious failure to forgive and grant clemency. Cisneros implies that Clemencia's revenge in seducing her young art student—the son of the lover who has rejected her—is misguided, but Cisneros nonetheless reveals the protagonist's complexity and strength. Chayo, however, in "Little Miracles, Kept Promises" and Lupe in

"*Bien* Pretty" both represent Cisneros herself—artists whose paths the writer validates approvingly. At the end of "Little Miracles," the typeface reverts to that used for the book's other stories, subtly alerting the reader to associate Chayo's interior monologue with the author herself. Fighting the resistance of her family to her art, Chayo cuts her hair against their wishes, reconfigures the image of the Virgin of Guadalupe, and leaves her braid of hair at the Virgin's shrine. Cisneros herself promised to make a pilgrimage of thanksgiving to the same shrine when she successfully completed the book *Woman Hollering Creek.* Similarly, Cisneros signals that the character Lupe in "*Bien* Pretty" is like herself in many ways by having her live at a house on East Guenther Street in San Antonio, eat at Torres Taco Haven (a Cisneros favorite), and work long hours at an arts center, as Cisneros did when she moved to San Antonio. When the man Lupe has fallen in love with leaves her abruptly to return to his wife and children in Mexico, she seeks consolation in Mexican cultural artifacts such as magic powders, herbs, mass culture, and nightspots. She most successfully transcends her pain, however, by her artistic vision—an epiphanic moment on the roof of her house at sunset with thousands of *urracas,* or grackles, flying beneath the stars. By revisioning the ordinary and communicating this scene to readers, Lupe creates her own art to replace the boyfriend's poems, which she has burned. She overcomes adversity through the aesthetic.

Every story in *Woman Hollering Creek* experiments with one or more distinct narrative voices and discursive patterns that are often humorously rearranged to evoke auditory pleasure. Whether it is the love poem in "Tin Tan Tan," with its Spanish syntax that Lupe saved from the incinerator and that "sounds goofy" (p. 161) in English, or the parody of the advertising circular for "La Cucaracha Apachurrada Pest Control" (the squashed cockroach) in the tandem story "*Bien* Pretty," Cisneros recaptures and estranges multiple varieties of ordinary speech to represent a myriad of Latinos in San Antonio. The testimonial voices in "Little Miracles, Kept Promises," and its prelude story invoking her grandmother's name, "Anguiano Religious Articles Rosaries Statues . . . ," fictionally re-create the deepest needs, hopes, and prayers of Latinos who leave ex-votos at San Fernando Cathedral in San Antonio and other shrines. Arnulfo Contreras writes to the Virgencita de Guadalupe:

> I promise to walk to your shrine on my knees the very first day I get back, I swear, if you will only get the Tortillería la Casa de la Masa to pay me the $253.72 they owe me for two weeks' work. I put in 67½ hours that first week and 79 hours the second, and I don't have anything to show for it yet.
>
> (p. 120)

A gay man leaves a message written in code to ask that his lover be protected overseas. Barbara Ybañez asks San Antonio de Padua to please send her a man "who isn't a pain in the nalgas" (p. 117) and whose mother didn't ruin him "with too much chichi" (breastfeeding; p. 118). Intercalating humor and pathos in this experimental story and throughout the book, Cisneros presents pleasurable reading spaces for the diverse audiences who continue to buy the book long after its original publication.

POSTMODERN EPIC: *CARAMELO*

After two decades of publishing concise, finely crafted shorter works, Cisneros released a superb 440-page novel in September 2002. The result of years of disciplined work, *Caramelo* combines the carefully honed language of Cisneros's poems and short stories with the discursive length and vision of an epic saga. On one level *Caramelo* is an expansion of Cisneros's earlier stories "Mericans" and "Tepeyac" about her paternal grandparents in Mexico City in *Woman Hollering Creek,* and of "Papa Who Wakes Up Tired in the Dark" from *Mango Street.* Now these snapshot narratives of her grandparents and father are extended into longer biographical texts and intertwined with the stories of three generations of the family on both sides of the border. Wishing to pay tribute to her father and the immigrant generation he was part of, Cisneros discovered that his story was interconnected with many others. Narrative tributaries and imbricated layers continued to evolve as she combined fiction, family lore, and historical research to imaginatively re-create the milieu of her father's generation. The multiple, complicated layers of the story and the sense that her audience is not well versed in the history and customs of Mexico and Mexican Americans led Cisneros to innovative narrative techniques such as lengthy footnotes in most chapters and even footnotes to footnotes.

The story of the Reyes clan is the excavation project of Celaya Reyes, who attempts to uncover the repressed secrets of both her family and the larger historical master narrative. The "awful grandmother" from "Mericans" (*Woman Hollering Creek,* p. 17)—now given the dignity of a name, Soledad Reyes—is a contradictory figure who takes a hand in telling the involved story of her life. The stories of Celaya's father, grandparents, and mother are situated within both the broad sweep and the everyday minutiae of Mexican and U.S. history. Cisneros recounts poignant scenes of the father, Inocencio Reyes, soaking his hands in bowls of water while eating dinner after working all day as an upholsterer, and being asked in an immigration raid to prove his citizenship after he risked his life for the United States during World War II. Strong political and humanist images such as these are woven together with forgotten mass cultural figures such as the Spanish ventriloquist Wenceslao Moreno, who appeared on *The Ed Sullivan Show* and who meets Inocencio in a Chicago police station's holding tank. Although Celaya promises her dying father that she will not reveal the family secrets he has told her, she is compelled to tell the family story (truthfully or fictitiously) in the novel *Caramelo.*

Although the extensive use of footnotes implies the documentation and accuracy of facts, Cisneros playfully uses this scholarly technique for other reasons and even to destabilize the idea of truth and accuracy. The footnotes in the novel perform such functions as expanding the narrative, parodying scholarly erudition, offering ethnographic explanations of Mexican customs and traditions, providing linguistic translations, presenting an opinion about or a revision of history, and even humorously addressing the reader. In postmodernist fashion, Cisneros breaks down the borders between genres by merging this technique of scholarly documentation with fiction. This breakdown is central to the novel's desire to call into question the distinction between fact and fiction.

One of the central epistemological issues of the novel is the destabilization of the fixed dichotomy of truth and lies, or history as opposed to fiction. From the outset Cisneros disrupts these comfortable distinctions, telling readers that the book is "puro cuento," or pure invention: "The truth, these stories are nothing but story. . . . I have invented what I do not know and exaggerated what I do to continue the family tradition of telling healthy lies. If, in the course of my inventing, I have inadvertently stumbled on the truth, *perdónenme.*" Cisneros celebrates the postmodern erosion of the border between fact and fiction, and its questioning of fixed notions of the truth.

Twelve years earlier, in an interview with Rodríguez Aranda, Cisneros found the stable distinction between truth and lies useful to explain the difference between poetry and fiction: "Poetry is the art of telling the truth, and fiction is the art of lying. The scariest thing to me is writing poetry, because you're looking at yourself *desnuda* [naked]. You're always looking at the part of you that you don't show anybody. . . . And that center, that terrifying center is a poem" (p. 75). Now, after the postmodern debates of the 1990s, Cisneros questions this distinction. Audiences who read *Caramelo* can never be certain if they are reading facts about Cisneros and her family or imaginative inventions. Playfully insisting that we remain in this uncertain liminal space, Cisneros protects the members of her family from the exposure of their private life to the public, yet at the same time reveals and preserves their story for posterity. She invites readers to question the ostensible objectivity and truth of historical documents by coming to terms with the subjectivity and fictionality of such records. By the same token, we can often learn more about people in a given historical period from imaginative fictional narratives about them that are not overwhelmed and constrained by accurately telling every known detail. Cisneros blends fact and fiction throughout the novel not only to destabilize these categories but also to render an effectively more accurate narrative about her father's generation.

The postmodern notion that all representation is a simulacrum or copy of reality, the accuracy of which must be questioned, imbues the novel, beginning on the front cover and in the opening pages. The image of the smiling young woman in Edward Weston's 1926 photograph *Rose, Mexico* on the cover alludes as well to the way the grandmother, Soledad, might have looked in that time period. The novel attempts to tell what a photograph cannot—the complicated story of the long life of the "awful grandmother," a term belied by the beautiful image on the front cover and ultimately shown to be part of a complicated constellation of good and bad elements. Similarly, the first chapter visually describes a souvenir photograph taken when the children were young and visiting Acapulco. The narrator corrects the ostensibly accurate image of the past by noting that she herself has been left out of the photo, like the photographer himself. What is to follow, the chapter suggests, is the untold story that the Acapulco photograph fails to tell, in which the author herself becomes a key character. Already on the first page Cisneros foreshadows the hidden family secret revealed at the end as if the book were a *telenovela*: "Here is Father squinting the same squint I always make when I'm photographed" (p. 3). The foreshadowing advances to prolepsis on page 78, and finally to revelation on page 404.

Among the numerous postmodern strategies of the novel is the narrator's dialogue with the character representing her grandmother, Soledad, who participates in the telling of her story and sometimes complains about the way it is told. In chapter twenty-five the power relationship briefly changes and Soledad temporarily takes over the telling of her own story. Reminding readers that they are reading a fictive construct, not an unmediated version of reality, the narrator Celaya accepts a certain degree of participation from her character but insists on her own ultimate control of the narrative. Beginning with her childhood memories of her extended family's long summer drives to Mexico in a nationalistic caravan of red, white, and green cars, Celaya digs back into her family's history in an attempt to recapture the country she is homesick for but which in fact never really existed—"A country I invented. Like all emigrants caught between here and there" (p. 434). Named after a Mexican city, Celaya weaves thousands of elements of Mexican culture and history in the *caramelo* colored *rebozo*/story, the final unfinished knots of which are tied by the characters' tales. The double figure of Celaya/Cisneros is an ethnographer of her communities on both sides of the border, frequently presenting the images of ethnicity she deploys in telling the story as spectacles. Examples include tropicalized language experiments using false or invented cognates ("*Estás* 'deprimed'?" or "What a barbarity!" pp. 238, 256) and the outsider ethnographer's description:

Little girls in Sunday dresses like lace bells, like umbrellas, like parachutes, the more lace and frou-frou the better. Houses painted purple, electric blue, tiger orange, aquamarine. . . . Above doorways, faded wreaths from an anniversary or a death till the wind and rain erase them. A woman in an apron scrubbing the sidewalk in front of her house with a pink plastic broom and a bright green bucket filled with suds.

(p. 18)

The *rebozo* of *caramelo* color that Cisneros figuratively constructs through writing the novel is also sweet-tasting like the candy that the title word simultaneously refers to. As the magnum opus of a twenty-five-year writing career, *Caramelo* brings together aesthetic nuances, postmodern experimentation, pleasurable images of ethnicity, linguistic play, humor, and new points of entry into history to create a compelling family saga that offers readers many sites of identification. The novel marks Cisneros's definitive entry into the U.S.' literary canon.

FUTURE PROJECTS AND THE CHANGING BOOK INDUSTRY

Throughout her career, Cisneros has directed her artistic talents to diverse projects such as organizing a book fair and a prison inmates' show through the Guadalupe Cultural Arts Center; adapting two of her stories for the stage production "Milagritos," which she directed, wrote, and performed in; publishing a children's book, *Hairs/Pelitos,* based on one of her stories; writing a travel article about San Antonio for the *New York Times* and a controversial article for *Ms.* magazine, "Guadalupe: the Sex Goddess"; and volunteering many hours in her community. In an interview with Robert Birnbaum in 2002, she spoke of future projects that would continue this diversity of cultural expression. For example, she envisioned an adaptation of *Caramelo* as a *telenovela,* a Latino soap opera that would reach a wide international audience. Her next literary project she said she planned to undertake was *Infinito,* a book of erotic vignettes based on small ideas she began to write down while working on *Caramelo.* Similar in form to Eduardo Galeano's *Book of Embraces,* Cisneros's volume would include her own drawings and focus on small erotic moments that were not overtly sexual but instead would take one to another spiritual dimension, a level she found missing from most books of erotica.

Cisneros has been critical of the more conservative turn and nervousness in the contemporary book industry, a marked change from the time of exuberance and risk-taking in the early 1990s. With an occasional spectacular exception, publishers have begun offering smaller advances and only contracting books that are sure to sell well. Early in 2003 the head of Random House Trade Group—Cisneros's publisher and a division known for its high-quality literature—was dismissed, reportedly because profits for the year before had been $2 million instead of the target of $6 million. Random House's owner, Bertelsmann, merged the company with Bertelsmann's mass-market group, Ballantine Books, and named Ballantine's president and publisher as the new head. These changes created much concern among publishing executives, editors, and writers who feared that Random House's tradition of high quality literature would now be compromised. Although Cisneros's relationship with Random House may change because of the reorganization, her successful and principled literary career will not be suppressed. Readers can expect many more fine literary works from Cisneros, one of the foremost voices of contemporary American literature.

Selected Bibliography

WORKS OF SANDRA CISNEROS

NOVELS

The House on Mango Street. Houston: Arte Público Press, 1984; New York: Random House, 1991.

Woman Hollering Creek and Other Stories. New York: Random House, 1991.

Hairs/Pelitos. New York: Alfred A. Knopf, 1994.

Caramelo; or, Puro Cuento. New York: Alfred A. Knopf, 2002.

SHORT STORIES

"Woman Hollering Creek." *Los Angeles Times Magazine,* July 1, 1990, p. 14.

"Divine Providence." In *New Chicano Writing.* Vol. 1. Edited by Charles M. Tatum. Tucson: University of Arizona Press, 1992, pp. 76–78.

"Dirt." *Grand Street,* 15, no. 1 (summer 1996): 122–125.

SPANISH-LANGUAGE TRANSLATIONS OF FICTION

La casa en Mango Street. Translated by Elena Poniatowska. New York: Vintage Español, 1994.

El arroyo de la llorona y otros cuentos. Translated by Liliana Valenzuela. New York: Vintage Español, 1996.

Caramelo; o, Puro cuento. Translated by Liliana Valenzuela. New York: Knopf, 2002.

POETRY

Bad Boys. San Jose, Calif.: Mango Publications, 1980.

My Wicked Wicked Ways. Bloomington, Ind.: Third Woman Press, 1987. Revised, New York: Turtle Bay Books, 1992.

Loose Woman: Poems. New York: Alfred A. Knopf, 1994.

"Still-Life with Potatoes, Pearls, Raw Meat, Rhinestones, Lard and Horse Hooves." *New Yorker,* May 23, 1994, pp. 68–69.

"Tango for the Broom" and "It Occurs to Me I Am the Creative/Destructive Goddess Coatlicue." *Massachusetts Review* 36, no. 4 (winter 1995): 598–599.

ESSAYS

"An Offering to the Power of Language." *Los Angeles Times,* October 26, 1997, section M, pp. 1, 6.

"Do You Know Me? I Wrote *The House on Mango Street.*" *Americas Review* 15, no. 1 (spring 1987): 77–79.

"Ghosts and Voices: Writing from Obsession." *Americas Review* 15, no. 1 (spring 1987): 69–73.

"Guadalupe the Sex Goddess: Unearthing the Racy Past of Mexico's Most Famous Virgin." *Ms.,* July–August 1996, pp. 43–46.

"Mexico's Day of the Dead: ¡Vivan los muertos!" *Elle,* October 1991, p. 194.

"Notes to a Younger Writer." *Americas Review* 15, no. 1 (spring 1987): 74–76.

"Only Daughter." *Glamour,* November 1990, pp. 256–258.

"The Tejano Soul of San Antonio." *The Sophisticated Traveler (New York Times Magazine),* May 17, 1992.

"Cactus Flowers: In Search of Tejana Feminist Poetry." *Third Woman* 3, nos. 1–2 (1986): 73–80.

"Los Tejanos: Testimony to the Silenced." *Texas Humanist,* November–December 1984, pp. 11–12.

OTHER

Loose Woman. Read by the author. New York: Random House Audio Publishing, 1994. Audio recording.

Woman Hollering Creek and Other Stories and The House on Mango Street. Read by the author. New York: Random House Audio Publishing, 1992. Audio recording.

Vecinos/Neighbors. Sandra Cisneros interview with Lillian Santiago and reading at Mount Holyoke College, South Hadley, Mass., April 1991. Video recording.

SECONDARY WORKS

Alvarez, Julia. "So Much Depends." In *Something to Declare.* New York: Plume, 1998. Pp. 163–170 .

Birnbaum, Robert. "Interview with Sandra Cisneros." December 4, 2002, http://www.identitytheory.com. Pp. 1–12

Caldwell, Gail. "El Norte, the Hard Way." *Boston Globe,* September 22, 2002, sec. D, p. 6.

Ciabattari, Jane. "Tell Us Something, Anything, Even If It's a Lie." *Los Angeles Times Book Review,* September 29, 2002, p. 16.

Di Leo, Michael. "La Boom." *Mother Jones,* October 1989, p. 15.

Feldman, Ann Merle, Nancy Downs, and Ellen McManus, eds. "Case Study: On Painting a House Purple." In *In Context: Participating in Cultural Conversations.* New York: Addison Wesley Longman, 2001. Pp. 300–326.

Ganz, Robin. "Sandra Cisneros: Border Crossings and Beyond." *MELUS* 19, no. 1 (spring 1994): 19–29.

Grobman, Laurie. "The Cultural Past and Artistic Creation in Sandra Cisneros's *The House on Mango Street* and Judith Ortiz Cofer's *Silent Dancing.*" *Confluencia: Revista Hispánica de Cultura y Literatura* 11, no. 1 (fall 1995): 42–49.

Gutierrez Spencer, Laura. "Fairy Tales and Opera: The Fate of the Heroine in the Work of Sandra Cisneros." In *Speaking the Other Self: American Women Writers.* Edited by Jeanne Campbell Reesman. Athens: University of Georgia Press, 1997. Pp. 278–287.

Hayslett, Francesca. "Latina Writers." *Elle,* August 1991, pp. 106–108.

Jussawalla, Feroza, and Reed Way Dasenbrock. "Sandra Cisneros." In *Interviews with Writers of the Post-Colonial World.* Jackson: University Press of Mississippi, 1992. Pp. 286–306.

Kaup, Monika. "The Architecture of Ethnicity in Chicano Literature." *American Literature* 69, no. 2 (June 1997): 361–397.

Kevane, Bridget, and Juanita Heredia. "A Home in the Heart: An Interview with Sandra Cisneros." In *Latina Self-Portraits: Interviews with Contemporary Women Writers.* Edited by Kevane and Heredia. Albuquerque: University of New Mexico Press, 2000. Pp. 45–57.

Kuribayashi, Tomoko. "The Chicana Girl Writes Her Way In and Out: Space and Bilingualism in Sandra Cisneros's *The House on Mango Street.*" In *Creating Safe Space: Violence and Women's Writing.* Edited by Kuribayashi and Julie Tharp. Albany: State University of New York Press, 1998. Pp. 165–177.

Leal, Luis. "Sandra Cisneros: From Mango Street to Tepeyac." In *No Longer Voiceless.* San Diego: Marín Publications, 1995. Pp. 127–134.

McCracken, Ellen. "Sandra Cisneros' *The House on Mango Street:* Community-Oriented Introspection and the Demystification of Patriarchal Violence." In *Breaking Boundaries: Latina Writing and Critical Readings.* Edited by Asunción Horno-Delgado et al. Amherst: University of Massachusetts Press, 1989. Pp. 62–71.

———. "Latina Narrative and the Politics of Signification: Articulation, Antagonism, and Populist Rupture." *Crítica* 2, no. 2 (fall 1990): 202–207.

———. *New Latina Narrative: The Feminine Space of Postmodern Ethnicity.* Tucson: University of Arizona Press, 1999.

———. "Toward a Comparative Text Grammar of Visual and Verbal Semiosis: Material Religious Culture and Chicana Fiction." In *Semiotics Around the World: Synthesis in Diversity.* Edited by Irmengard Rauch and Gerald F. Carr. Berlin: Mouton de Gruyter, 1997. Pp. 717–720.

Mena, Jennifer. "A Story Woven from the Heart." *Los Angeles Times,* September 13, 2002, sec. E, p. 1.

Mirriam-Goldberg, Caryn. *Sandra Cisneros: Latina Writer and Activist.* Berkeley Heights, N.J.: Enslow, 1998.

Morales, Alejandro: "The Deterritorialization of Esperanza Cordero: A Paraesthetic Inquiry." In *Gender, Self, and Society: Proceedings of the IV International Conference on the Hispanic Cultures of the United States.* Edited by Renate von Bardeleben. Frankfurt am Main: Peter Lang, 1993. Pp. 227–235.

Mullen, Harryette. "'A Silence between Us Like a Language': The Untranslatability of Experience in Sandra Cisneros's *Woman Hollering Creek.*" *MELUS* 21, no. 2 (summer 1996): 3–20.

Nathan, Debbie. "Can Sandra Survive San Antonio?—Can San Anto Survive Her?" *San Antonio Current,* October 7–13, 1999, pp. 12–21.

Navarro, Mireya. "Telling a Tale of Immigrants Whose Stories Go Untold." *New York Times,* November 12, 2002, sec. B, pp. 1, 7.

Olivares, Julian. "Sandra Cisneros: *The House on Mango Street* and the Poetics of Space." *Americas Review* 15, nos. 3–4 (fall–winter 1987): 160–170.

Prescott, Peter S., and Karen Springen. "Seven for Summer." *Newsweek,* June 3, 1991, p. 60.

Rodríguez Aranda, Pilar E. "On the Solitary Fate of Being Mexican, Female, Wicked, and Thirty-Three: An Interview with Writer Sandra Cisneros." *Americas Review* 18, no. 1 (spring 1990): 64–80.

Rutten, Tim. "Furor over Ouster of Random House Publisher." *Los Angeles Times,* January 17, 2003, sec. A, p. 13.

Sagel, Jim. "Sandra Cisneros." *Publishers Weekly,* March 29, 1991, p. 74.

Saldívar, Ramón. *Chicano Narrative: The Dialectics of Difference.* Madison: University of Wisconsin Press, 1990.

Saldívar-Hull, Sonia. *Feminism on the Border: Chicana Gender Politics and Literature.* Berkeley: University of California Press, 2000.

Sayers, Valerie. "Traveling with Cousin Elvis." *New York Times,* September 29, 2002, sec. 7, p. 24.

Shea, Renee H. "Truth, Lies, and Memory: A Profile of Sandra Cisneros." *Poets & Writers Magazine,* September–October 2002, pp. 31–36.

Silva, Elda. "Cisneros's Newest Work Was an Epic Task, One That Honors Her Immigrant Father." *San Antonio Express-News,* September 22, 2002.

Stavans, Ilan. "Familia Faces." *Nation,* February 10, 2003. Pp. 30–34.

Tabor, Mary B. W. "A Solo Traveler in Two Worlds." *New York Times,* January 7, 1993, sec. B, p. 2.

Thomson, Jeff. "'What Is Called Heaven': Identity in Sandra Cisneros's *Woman Hollering Creek.*" *Studies in Short Fiction* 31 (summer 1994): 415–424.

Valdés, María Elena de. "The Critical Reception of Sandra Cisneros's *The House on Mango Street.*" In *Gender, Self, and Society: Proceedings of the IV International Conference on the Hispanic Cultures of the United States.* Edited by Renate von Bardeleben. Frankfurt am Main: Peter Lang, 1993. Pp. 287–300.

Lucha Corpi
(1945–)

TEY DIANA REBOLLEDO

MARRIAGE, IMMIGRATION, and divorce. Politics, history, racism, and injustice. Silence and voice. The struggles of women to survive and to find themselves. Mythology, legends, and family stories. Violence against women and family abuse. Dreams and nightmares. Beauty and music. The natural landscape. These are the subjects around which Lucha Corpi structures her novels and her poetry.

Lucha Corpi is a poet, novelist, and editor who was born in Mexico and lived and studied there until she was nineteen years old. At that age, in 1965, she married and went to California. She learned English, enrolled in college, and was involved in the intensely political Third World Student Movement at the University of California, Berkeley, and in the beginnings of the Chicano Movement in the 1960s. She has written three books of poetry: *Fireflight* (1976), *Palabras de mediodía/Noon Words* (1980, 2001), and *Variaciones sobre una tempestad/Variations on a Storm* (1990). She has also authored one novel, *Delia's Song* (1989), as well as four detective novels: *Eulogy for a Brown Angel* (1992), *Cactus Blood* (1995), *Black Widow's Wardrobe* (1999), and *Crimson Moon* (2004). She has also written a children's book, *Where Fireflies Dance/ Ahí, donde bailan los luciérnagas* (1997), and has

edited a book of essays by Chicana and Latina authors, *Máscaras* (1997). Her involvement with the Chicano movements of the 1960s and 1970s was also an introduction into writing, although her mother told her that she had always been a poet. She is widely published in anthologies, journals, and magazines. She has received numerous literary awards, including a Fellowship from the National Endowment for the Arts and the PEN Oakland Josephine Miles Literary Prize in Fiction. She helped create the Centro Chicano de Escritores (the Chicano Writers Center) and is a member of Sisters in Crime, a feminist mystery novel organization.

In addition to her writing, Lucha Corpi works as a teacher in the Oakland Public Schools. She has taught English as a Second Language, mostly to adults, since 1973. Speaking about her multiple professional roles, she said in an interview with Mireya Pérez-Erdélyi: "En realidad la maestra en mí es la persona mas equilibrada que hay, mas integrada, pues toma de las otras dos. La escritora es muy retraída, muy de estar sola, muy solitaria. No es una persona social. La persona social en mí es otra persona y esa persona siempre defiende a la otra" (In reality the teacher in me is the most stable person, she is more integrated, since she takes from the other two. The writer is very retiring, very much wanting to be alone; she is very solitary. She is not a social person. The social person in me is another persona, and that persona always defends the other one; *Americas Review*, p. 82). Moreover, she feels that as a teacher in the Oakland public schools, with students from many different countries, she functions as a mediator between cultures.

Lucha Corpi was born 14 April 1945, in a small Mexican town, Jáltipan, in the state of Veracruz. Her father, Miguel Angel Corpi, was a *telegrafista*, a telegraph operator, a self-educated man who even taught himself Morse code. He eventually became a supervisor of telegraph operators. Later on, when microwave communications supplanted the telegraph, he also taught himself that technology. Her mother, Victoria Constantino de Corpi, gave birth to eight children: six boys and two girls. Her mother was also a poet; she wrote her poems, which were classical in meter and rhyme, on pieces of butcher paper. An enterprising woman with a great deal of energy, she supplemented the family income by raising chickens. Lucha and her younger sister were known as "las hijas de la pollera" (the daughters of the woman who raises chickens), Corpi said during a phone interview. Both parents were adamant that their children should receive a good education, the girls as well as the boys. In an interview with Karin Ikas, Corpi stated that her father believed in educating the girls because "when you educate a man you educate an individual, but when you educate a woman, you educate a whole family" (*Chicana Ways*, p. 74). Yet her parents were still strong believers in more traditional roles for women. Corpi wanted to be an astronomer or a doctor, and most of her training in Mexico was in the sciences. These careers were not considered totally suitable for a woman. She was therefore encouraged by her parents to become a dentist. She could not see herself as a dentist; she said to Ikas, "I knew I was going to go crazy if I ever became a dentist" (*Chicana Ways*, p. 75).

At the same time, her father had a tremendous love of music, which Lucha inherited. As she tells us in "Voces/Voices":

Mi padre me enseñó a cantar
mi madre a hilar versos
y de mi abuela aprendí
que se llega a la verdad
también por el silencio

Hay tantas voces en mí
tantas voces que bajan
a beber de mis sueños
en noches de invierno.

My father taught me to sing
my mother to spin verses
and from my grandmother I learned
that truth can be found
through silence as well

There are so many voices in me
so many voices going down
to drink at dreams' edge
on winter nights.

(*Variaciones sobre una tempestad*, pp. 90–91)

She met Guillermo Hernández at the age of sixteen, married him several years later, and came with him to the United States. Corpi always credits Hernández with introducing her to literature and philosophy, although even in her early childhood she loved to read and was attracted to adventure tales. Later she studied comparative literature at Berkeley, graduating in 1975. In 1979 she received an M.A. from San Francisco State.

At twenty-four, her marriage was coming to an end and she was about to get a divorce. She had a child, Arturo, in 1967 and was facing life as a single mother of a young child. This was the impetus to start writing. She began writing poetry to "articulate all the ambivalence, all the contradictions, all the sorrow and pain carried within me" (Ikas, *Chicana Ways*, p. 71). She also wrote a short story, "Tres mujeres/Three

Women," which she characterizes as an autobiographical allegory. In this story there are three women: Guadalupe, Amerina, and Justina. As Corpi comments, the three women are the choices she had to make. She could return to Mexico with her child, but as a divorced woman life would be difficult. Moreover, she could not go back to living with her family. She could continue living in the United States, but she did not feel entirely comfortable there. Finally, she could stay in California and work for equality and justice. She chose the latter. Corpi believes her life revolves in cycles of seven years, with important events taking place during that time frame. In 1994 she married Carlos Medina Gonzales, a high school teacher. They live in Oakland.

Because Corpi lived through the exciting and turbulent times of the late 1960s and the 1970s, these events often constitute the central historical emphasis in her novels. In his analysis of her detective novels, Ralph Rodríguez comments that most Chicano and Chicana novels that deal with the shaping of Chicano and Chicana identity have what he calls "a mythic memory," consisting of three historical and cultural moments important to Chicanos and Chicanas. These are: (1) the history or cultural legacy of pre-Columbian America; (2) the Mexican Revolution; and (3) the Chicana and Chicano Movement. He argues that these elements are present in Corpi's novels, although not all simultaneously. It is clear that the historical and cultural backgrounds of all of Corpi's narratives fall into one of these areas and that social and political elements important to Chicanos are often detailed in her books. One Web site has stated that in her mystery novels, "the political commentary and Chicano symbolism seem equally, if not more important than the mystery itself" ("Voices," p. 5). Rodríguez agrees, commenting that because Corpi fears that what was accomplished during the Chicano Movement will be forgotten, and that the history of the movement will be erased, she reinforces the memory of the movement by writing about it.

For Rodríguez the value of Corpi's work comes about because she questions the monolithic entity that was constructed of Chicano identity in the early years of the movement. She attempts to create and represent a cultural unit that would make an intellectual and artistic space for Mexican Americans, a discursive unity that was constructed as male, migrant, or working-class poor. Clearly Corpi's subversion of this unity adds women, and strong women at that, who are not migrants, although they can be immigrants. Rodríguez emphasizes that Corpi creates fluidity between the moment of the Chicano Movement and the present as she questions the goals by moving back and forth in time. This cultural history is certainly central to her work, but there are other themes and issues that are also central: those of gender, sexuality, and space. Corpi writes about the contradictions, ambivalences, and marginalizations that occur when one exists between two spaces, whether they be the physical spaces of Mexico and the United States, the space between the Spanish and English languages, or psychological and spiritual spaces. These she interrogates, analyzes, and sometimes resolves in writing.

ON WRITING

In 1994 an encounter took place between Chicana writers and Mexican women writers in Mexico City. Lucha Corpi was among the writers present in the dialogue. First the writers were asked to present a formal paper about writing, its challenges, and its representation in their work. Then they were asked to answer several questions in a colloquium, and finally they were interviewed by Claire Joysmith, the organizer of the event, as to their reaction to the encounter. This is especially interesting in terms of Lucha Corpi because she was born in Mexico, was perhaps the most fluent in Spanish of all the Chicana writers, and because she identified as a Chicana writer and not as a Mexican writer. In her paper, Corpi placed emphasis on the meaning and importance of language for her writing.

She began writing poetry primarily in Spanish, and most of her poems have been translated into English by Catherine Rodríguez-Nieto. However, her narratives were all written in English. When asked for one single metaphor that would describe Chicana and Chicano literature, she decided, after thinking about it for some years, that the metaphor would be the mouth of a river: "El lugar al que confluyen y en el que se mezclan dos masas líquidas" (the place where two liquid masses come together and mix; "Contracorrientes," p. 94). For Corpi, language and its use are essential in this mixing. She underscored that people often don't understand Chicano literature, with its mixing of two languages, and felt that she had to defend Chicano Spanish against purists of the language. As she stated, because she was born in Mexico, she was considered a Mexican writer. It soon became clear, however, that she was a Chicana writer because she defended the right of Chicano writers to write in their own Spanish—a Spanish that some Mexicans considered degenerated and deformed ("defendía el derecho de las autoras y los autores Chicanos de expresarse en su español propio, un español que algunos de los conferencistas mexicanos tachaban de degenerado y deforme"; "Contracorrientes," p. 96).

For Corpi, writers who employ both languages often are living on the margins: writing in Spanish makes it hard to get published. Because she began writing in Spanish and then gradually in English, she received conflicting advice about the language of her writing as well as about the content of her writing. In addition, when she began to publish detective novels, she was told that because it was a popular genre, she was in danger of ruining her literary reputation ("ponía en peligro mi buena reputación literaria"; "Contracorrientes," p. 96). Spanish is the language of her poetry, because

> Este es el lenguaje en el cual aprendí de mi madre y de mi abuela a sentir y expresar el sentimiento. Es la voz a la que debe ser fiel, de la misma manera que debo serle fiel a las voces de mis personajes que llegan a contarme sus experiencias en inglés.

> Traicionar mi voz poética, o traicionar a mis personajes sería equivalente a descarnarme el corazón, a cortarme la lengua de tajo y andar por el mundo sin mas abrigo que la camiza de fuerza.

This is the language in which I learned from my mother and my grandmother to feel and to express feelings. It is the voice I must be loyal to, in the same way that I need to be loyal to the voices of my characters that come to tell me their experiences in English. To betray my poetic voice or to betray my characters would be the same as tearing out my heart or cutting out my tongue and walking throughout the world without any more covering than a straight jacket.

("Contracorrientes," p. 97)

For Corpi the complexity of language use also encompasses the levels of reality expressed in and by language. The languages she uses are familiar but at the same time foreign and strange ("Contracorrientes," p. 93).

Later in the colloquia, when asked about subversion as a literary strategy for writing, Corpi spoke about "hanging the doll." As a child, she hated playing with dolls, although her parents insisted that she do so. They were concerned because she was a tomboy and preferred to read. Her parents worried that she would not be a good wife and mother if she didn't play with dolls. Corpi would often read sitting in a big tree, but her mother insisted she take her doll with her. She soon tired of taking the doll up and down with her, so she created a rope from tree limbs, tied the rope around the doll's neck and hauled her up and down. One day her mother saw her with the doll hanging from its noose and, of course, reached the wrong conclusion.

Years later, her mother was reassured when she saw that Corpi was indeed a warm and loving mother. One can see that Corpi always felt that she had to challenge the status quo. She characterizes her life as the cord that slides between one culture and another, one country and another, one language and another ("la cuerda floja, aquella barda que caminamos, que yo camino entre un país y otro, una cultura y otra, un lenguaje y otro"; Joysmith, *Las formas de nuestras voces,* p. 222). Thus for her, hanging the doll is her metaphor for subversion as well as for survival.

As a writer, Corpi has had many influences: Federico García Lorca, Santa Teresa de Avila, the early Latin American women writers (such as Sor Juana Inés de la Cruz, Alfonsina Storni, Juana de Ibarbourou, Delmira Agustini, and Gabriela Mistral—all strong women who wrote about the condition of women), and the Mexican poet and essayist Octavio Paz. Although she writes about political and social events, such as domestic abuse and violence against women, particularly in the context of Mexican and Chicano culture, Corpi says she never intended to be a political writer. Yet the events about which she writes are often centered around political and social conflict.

POETRY

Corpi's introduction to poetry was through music. As stated before, she was especially influenced by her father's love of music and singing. Her first published poetry was in *Fireflight: Three Latin American Poets* (1976). She was one of three women included in this slender volume. The other two were Elsie Alvarado de Ricord from Panama and Concha Michel from Mexico. Although the three women didn't know each other, they were published together because the translator knew them and liked their work. At this early stage in her career, Corpi was known as a Latin American, not a Chicana, poet.

There are thirteen poems in *Fireflight,* poems that speak to her childhood in Mexico, her personal anguishes, a poem to her son Arturo, and her Marina poems. Several of the poems would be included in her next collection, *Palabras de mediodía/Noon Words.* The poems open with an *ars poetica,* a poem about writing titled "Como la semilla en espera/Like the Seed that Waits." In it the seed waits, hoping to bloom,

just as inspiration needs nurturing. The second poem, "Mexico," explores the nostalgia she feels for her childhood home; as she says in her introduction to her poetry, "My childhood was a rush of dense green, full of the smell of mango blossoms and the clean petticoats of Indian women" (p. 43). Her poetry goes on to explore a brief trajectory of emotions and despair. "Puente de cristal/The Crystal Bridge" is perhaps the most despairing poem, as it describes the plight of two people who cross a bridge that can never be crossed again.

In "Nuestros mundos/Our Worlds," she writes to her son, who that morning has given her a piece of bread, nourishment for both body and soul, and comments on how well he understands her: "Me conoces sin decirlo / Y a veces te sorprendo" (You know me without having to say it / And sometimes I surprise you; pp. 56–57). In this poem she ever so subtly comments on the political situation of the times, her son reminding her that she must not shop at Safeway. This refers to the Chicano boycott of the Safeway grocery store chain because they were selling lettuce and grapes, which were being boycotted by the United Farm Workers of America in order to ensure better pay and working conditions for the grape and lettuce pickers.

In the Marina poems, perhaps the most well-known poems of this volume, Corpi explores the meaning of this enigmatic woman. Moreover, Marina/Malinche continues to be an important symbol for Corpi, as she also reappears constantly in her novels and is a central part of the narrative in *Black Widow's Wardrobe.* Malinche/Marina was the native woman given to the Spanish conqueror Hernán Cortés when he arrived in Mexico. She served as his translator, as she knew various languages including Maya and Nahuatl (the language of the Aztecs); she was also taken as Cortés's mistress. For many years, she was vilified by Mexicans and condemned as a traitor who betrayed her people. Malinche was a Nahuatl speaker who had been sold twice as a slave and was the victim of family and historical circumstances. She is the personification of the native Indian woman who was "conquered" by the European male and made subordinate to the Europeans. Malinche also gave birth to a son by Cortés, Martín, and therefore for Chicanas she symbolically represents the mother of a new race, the mestizo, even though she was not actually the mother of the first mestizo born in the New World. Her native name was Malinche; her Catholic baptismal name was Marina. Her two names represent the Indian heritage on the one hand, and her integration into Spanish culture on the other.

For many years the figure of Malinche/Marina has been a problematic one for Chicana writers. They too are daughters of mixed cultures; they too deal with multiple languages and translations; and they too deal with various cultural spaces. For these women writers, to label a woman a traitor who had been sold and given into slavery is to blame the victim. This problematic cultural symbol has had various representations in Chicana literature as the writers struggle to understand her, to explain her, and to redeem her. This is particularly telling for Lucha Corpi, who, when asked by Barbara Brinson-Piñeda if she identified with Marina, answered:

> Yes. They say that Marina was even from the town where I'm from. . . . Another identification with Marina was the matter of her son. With my divorce there was the question of whether my son would live with my ex-husband or with me. For the first time I was confronted with the possibility of my son growing up away from me. . . . Martín Cortés, Marina's son by Hernán Cortés, was taken from her as a baby and raised in Spain. When he came back she wasn't his mother, she was the Indian woman his father had raped.
>
> (*Prisma*, p. 6)

In *Fireflight* she says, "These poems were written by way of vindication" (p. 77).

The poem has four sections: I. Marina Mother; II. Marina Virgin; III. The Devil's Daughter; and IV. She (Marina Distant). In the

first section, Corpi describes how Marina was sold, desecrated, and denied by her tribe and her son. Juxtaposing both Christian and pre-Columbian images, Corpi represents both the lineage of Marina (her name was inscribed on the bark of a tree) and her reputation as a mystic associated with knowledge and tradition. In Section II, Marina becomes a Christian who loves both Christ and Cortés, washing away her sins and hiding her spirit and soul in the earth of her country, planting it as a seed to be nurtured in future generations. In the third section, Marina dies, "her mystic pulsing / silenced," (p. 81), but the seed remains. In the fourth and last section, a flower or a child emerges, "crossing the bridge at daybreak, / her hands full of earth and sun" (p. 83), suggesting that this child is the inheritor of the tradition, knowledge, mysticism, and understanding of Malinche.

As she began to write these poems, Corpi tells us, "little by little the eagerness settled into rhythm, intimate rhyme, music and I began to explore the uses of poetry. It was then that I found Marina, whose image, both tragic and glorious, has walked ever since through the corridors of my life" (*Fireflight*, p. 43).

Her book *Palabras de mediodía/Noon Words* was first published in 1980 and later reissued in 2001. Carrying a foreword by the Mexican writer Juan José Arreola, with whom she studied, *Palabras* contains more than forty poems, six reprinted from *Fireflight*. The book follows a trajectory, narrating a journey into oneself. This journey is one that explores nostalgia for home, the poet's entrance into language, the role of the domestic, the meaning of her child, the sadness of a love that does not function, the death of a moment which engenders the birth of the next, a series of romances and poems about women, the construction of the poet as a subject who speaks out in public, and finally the coming into her own of the poet. This trajectory is self-searching and spiritual but not sentimental. It is fluid and seeking, although the answers may not be found. In "Paradoja/Paradox," for example, we have examples of people searching and finding not what they search for, but something else that is quite lovely. In these poems, images are central. In "Solario" and "Solario Nocturno," Corpi contrasts the lush countryside of her early childhood in Veracruz with the enclosed and oppressive town of San Luis, where she moved when she was nine. In "Solario" she details some moments in her childhood when she discovered the "salty freedom / of restless water" and the water carrier who taught her to swear. This was an expression of coming into taboo language, although she was punished for this transgression by having her mouth washed out with soap. She writes, "Me podó la selva / de la lengua / con navaja de lejía" ([they] pruned the jungle / on my tongue / with the razor / of laundry soap; pp. 18–19). It was nevertheless a taste of linguistic freedom. Later, she tells us, language was denied her: "As an adult it was not soap they used but repression, punishment" (Carabi, *Truthtellers of the Times*, p. 27). This repression is demonstrated in "Solario Nocturno": the description of the town is one that is gray, enclosed, repressive. The people were judgmental as they mocked her accent; as she says, "I frequently suffered the mockery of the San Luis people, who found my speech was amusing" (Carabi, *Truthtellers of the Times*, p. 26). She describes the patios of the houses as closed, the windows protected with bars, and continues: "It was like moving to another country; it was a tremendous cultural shock." There, she discovered the meaning of silence for oneself, and silence for others.

While the poems are too numerous to write about individually here, there are some that are especially significant in her poetic development. The role that domestic life plays in women's lives is one important theme. Several poems take up this subject: "De mi casa/My House," "Labor de retazos/Patchwork," "Receta de invierno/Recipe for Winter," and "Protocolo de verduras/The Protocol of Vegetables." She says that these poems describe her reality.

My house is my laboratory, set apart from the rest of the world, and when my son was small I spent most of my time there. I often wrote poems while doing housework. I always had pencils and paper throughout the house: in the laundry, in the dining room, in the kitchen. While I do housework my mind is free to write. When something comes to mind, I run to jot it down and then continue with my work.

(Carabi, *Truthtellers of the Times*, p. 25)

In an article on the poetry of Lucha Corpi, Cida Chase argues that many of Corpi's poems are not socially or politically directed, citing those of domestic or abstract content. Certainly many of Corpi's poems do not have a direct social content. Chase compares Corpi's domestic poems that have vegetables as symbols to those of Chilean Pablo Neruda and Spaniard Ramón Gómez de la Serna, in that they also use domestic symbols such as vegetables in their poetry (pp. 276–277). However, it seems that the context of Corpi's poems is different; while she ennobles the vegetables and women's work, she also recognizes that domestic duties can hinder the work of the poet.

Several poems discuss the connection she has with her son, such as "Nuestros Mundos/Our Worlds" in the previous section. In "Carta a Arturo/Letter to Arturo," she writes a letter to her son when he is away. We see that nature is out of control, as is her life because her son is not with her.

In the middle of the volume we find a series of poems, many of them "romances" or ballads that deal with the situation of women. Also included are her Marina poems and a poem to Emily Dickinson. Forming the center of the book, they are feminist poems that speak to the condition of women, the way in which culture and society undermine them, and how women overcome the obstacles against them. For example, in "Romance Negro/Dark Romance," Corpi talks about the socialization of women and the way in which family and society accept the violent rape of a woman. As she says, her poetry is indirect, based on images, but it has a base that is political and human. This poem also incorporates a very sensual edge, which Corpi often expresses in her poems. In "Romance Negro," for example, there is a line about the flavor of vanilla: "Hay sabor de vainilla / en el aire dominical" (A flavor of vanilla drifts / on the Sunday air; pp. 126–127). Corpi tells us that "the flavor of vanilla seeped into the poem because, while I was writing, someone was baking a cake, and the odor of vanilla filtered through the open window. When you're in the creative process, a certain vulnerability emerges, and you open to all possibilities. Our lives are at skin's surface, and it feels like we're walking in the open air" (Carabi, *Truthtellers of the Times*, p. 24).

One of the strongest poems in this book is "Mariachi indocumentado/Underground Mariachi." It tells of a group of mariachi musicians who have been suddenly deported to Mexico, leaving behind their instruments. The instruments are personified, demonstrating their poignant loneliness.

> El guitarrón de vientre redondeado
> Cuelga
> torpemente de la pared
> sus doce cuerdas enmudecidas
>
> The barrel-belly guitar
> awkwardly
> hangs from the wall
> its twelve strings mute
>
> (pp. 76–77)

However, upon hearing the story, a wise old man tells the poet that the musicians will be back and they will have an underground mariachi band, "sweet music of the revolution."

Throughout the book, the poet has struggled with the difficulties of being a woman, the search for self, and for the ability to find a voice that is at once genuine and public. This journey towards the self comes together in a poem titled "Conciliación/Conciliation," in which the lyric voice begins to reconcile all the doubts and ambivalences she feels and gathers strength and courage to go out into the streets: "Soy yo quien sale a entrar / al cauce de las calles / y al lecho grande del día" (I am the one who is going out / to enter the current of the streets / and the great bed of the day; pp. 156–157).

Corpi's third collection of poems is *Variaciones sobre una tempestad/Variations on a Storm* (1990). This book consists of two sections, "Márgenes/Boundaries" and "Ciudad en la Niebla/City in the Mist," which is about the San Francisco–Oakland area. The sections are preceded by a poem, "Fuga/Fugue." In this poem the influence that music has on her poetry is evident, as even the stanzas on the page are placed in the form of a fugue. In "Márgenes/Boundaries," she once again evokes the image of writing poetry and the difficulty of putting pain and grief into language: "dolor que no ha / aprendido / a ser palabra" (pain that has not learned / to be a word; pp. 16–17). In the next poem, "Dos/Two," she describes the word as living behind her worktable. In other poems she details images of grief, frustration, and rage— "heridas que nunca cierran" (wounds that never close; pp. 30–31)—and the role of memory in reinforcing that grief. Power and consolation comes in the form of writing: grief can be expressed in words, and put away on paper. But the ink on the page looks like blood spilled: "Y ya alguien exige venganza" (and someone cries out for vengeance; pp. 44–45). Yet she begins to reconcile her anger by writing until she reaches a place where there are small comforts and understandings: "Tal vez / este breve instante de conciencia / este poema / pequeña brecha en la tormenta / es todo lo que me fuera destinado" (It may be / that this moment of awareness / this poem / this small break in the storm / is all I was meant to have; pp. 56–57).

The second section of the book is "Ciudad en la Niebla/City in the Mist." The images in these poems recount the nature and people of a city where fog and rain shape the landscape. The rain is a nourishing element; it can be quiet, it can be endless, but the speaker wants more, a bolt of lightning. The rain reminds her of a time it rained so hard that the speaker, her two-year-old son, and the cat climbed into the bathtub to pretend it was an ark. The memory eases her mind and makes her smile. In the final poem of the book, "Sonata a dos voces/Sonata in Two Voices," the speaker chronicles the daily tasks that prevent dreams from being realized. In the poem's second part, "Adagio," she realizes that she cannot speak or sing. Life continues in its daily pace while in El Salvador and Africa children die and there is death. Only a friendly hand and heart reaching out can put aside the realities of life, as she says: "Porque / a fin de cuentas / solamente el amor nos salva" (because / when all is said and done / only love will save us; pp. 96–97). A beautifully lyric book, *Variaciones sobre una tempestad* is richly constructed and hauntingly powerful, even in its brevity.

NARRATIVE

Delia's Song (1989) is Corpi's first novel and recounts the struggles and history of Delia Treviño during the years of the Chicano Civil Rights movement in Berkeley during the 1960s and 1970s. Delia is a student at Berkeley during the Third World Student Movement, which was an attempt on the part of minority students at Berkeley to establish a Third World College. A coalition of minority student groups called the Third World Liberation Front was formed; the participants were the Afro-American Student Union, the Mexican-American Student Confederation, and the Asian-American Political Alliance. Other goals of the coalition were that Third World people would not only control and direct the College but that they would be appointed to positions of power at the university, including faculty in every department with proportionate employment at all levels throughout the university system. These were the demands made by the students in January of 1969. These demands were similar to ones being asserted by students at other universities

and were part of the political and social agitation fermented against the background of the Vietnam War. In the case of Berkeley, the students staged strikes that not only triggered opposition by the university administration but also police brutality and suspicion among the participants themselves. An Ethnic Studies Department was finally created by the university, but it was a department without sufficient financial support. Although the Third World Student Movement was unable to accomplish all it desired, it nevertheless made inroads into the public consciousness about the marginalization of minority students within the university, and it achieved the establishment of departments of ethnic studies and a larger percentage of minority students at the university. This, then, is the cultural, historical, and political backdrop of *Delia's Song*.

The novel is a bildungsroman (a growing up story) as well as a coming-of-age-as-a-writer story. It is divided into three sections: (1) the story of Delia and her friends as young students during the Third World Student Movement, including their struggles, dreams, and eventual dispersement; (2) Delia's family history and stories, and her entering into a period of despondency and despair; and (3) Delia's struggle against silence and repression, her meeting with Jeff Morones, a young man she had known in Berkeley, and her coming into self-knowledge and the acknowledgement of herself as a writer. It is also a very experimental novel, with a narrative sequence of events told in third person and dialogue, as well as a stream-of-consciousness narrative that represents Delia's dreams, nightmares, and thoughts.

Delia's Song is framed by a Day of the Dead Party given by Delia's friend Mattie Johnson, a professor at Berkeley, which Delia attends masquerading as Santa Teresa de Avila, a Spanish nun known for her mystic trances and her writings. The theme of the party is to dress as a writer that one admires. Thus the characters at this party symbolize writers who have influenced Corpi and whose significance is important: among noted European writers such as Charles Baudelaire, George Sand, Virginia Woolf, and Ezra Pound are mixed important Latin American writers such as Sor Juana Inés de la Cruz and Delmira Agustini, and—perhaps even more important to this novel—Chicano authors who were beginning to be important at the time, such as José Montoya, a poet and artist, and Luis Valdez, a dramatist. Delia, on her way to the party, bumps into a man dressed as James Joyce, with whom she later has a brief sexual interlude. Interspersed with the story of the party is the story of the Third World Student Movement. Jeanne Armstrong has noted that from the first, Corpi "makes it emphatically clear that personal lives and political issues are interwoven" (*Demythologizing the Romance of Conquest*, p. 85).

The characters of Santa Teresa and James Joyce not only function as a framing device for the novel, but also symbolically as Delia, who has been silenced and repressed by not only society at large but also by her own internalization of culture, struggles to find herself spiritually as well as intellectually. In the dream and thought sequences in the narrative, which are visually separated from the rest of the text by the use of italics, we have a Joycean stream of consciousness which is further emphasized in the beginning by quotes from Joyce's *Ulysses* in the voice of Molly Bloom: "*And first I put my arms around him yes and drew him down to me so he could feel my breasts all perfume yes and his heart was going like mad and yes I said yes I will yes*" (p. 12). These words resonate throughout the novel, as not only does Corpi present Delia as a sexual woman who must face her physical needs and express them, but also as one who must also learn to express her losses and sorrows. This she does through her dreams and nightmares, which represent the puzzle she must solve in a symbolic manner, and as she unravels their meaning, she is able to write down and understand their significance. As Armstrong points out, James Joyce countered the stereotype of Irish women by presenting Molly

Bloom as a sexual being. Corpi likewise counters the stereotype of Mexican women by writing Delia's needs and, in particular, Delia's writing about those needs, thereby placing them in the public domain. Conditioned by Catholicism and society's repression of women, Delia suffers from multiple oppressions: those of race, class, and gender. Armstrong says:

> It is difficult for a woman such as Delia to obtain a sense of self, the autonomy to choose what she wants rather than what others want for her, when she is pressured by familial and political expectations. Since Delia's oppression is both external and internalized, she struggles to change the society she inhabits as well as change herself by resisting the internalized scripts that have been directing her life.
>
> (*Demythologizing the Romance of Conquest*, p. 94)

Thus the importance of her relationship with the character of James Joyce (whose real name is Roger) is one of Delia's making a choice, to do what she chooses for once. The longing for that choice is finally resolved at the end of the novel, when she once again meets with Roger and realizes that she is already making choices that do not revolve around him, but about coming into her own self and in the writing of a novel.

The voice in *Delia's Song* is a young voice, involved in the passions and concerns of the political and historical moment. In the retelling of that moment there is a consciousness that the students are participating in a large event. As Delia thinks: "*We're going to re-write history I didn't even know enough of the wrong history to learn the right one. . . . All of us were such romantics I was nineteen and knew nothing*" (p. 24). Later, when she begins to write her novel, the voice is a more reflexive one. She writes to remember what happened and to make sure that the events are inscribed into history because, as she thinks, "*We were there but no one knew us*" (p. 9). While the students were unable to accomplish all of their aims, nevertheless some gains were made. Mattie comments: "'Le temps perdu. . . . They were exhilarating times, weren't they? All of you were amazing. Just think. You were only a rag-tag bunch, yet you were able to shake down one of the most powerful educational institutions in the country. That's a story to be told.' Mattie paused. 'The story you must write'" (p. 78).

Ironically it is precisely because of the Movement that Delia begins to write, because she is made the secretary for the group and begins to chronicle their actions. Suffering from a sense of loss and mourning (her two brothers have died, one from drugs and one in the war in Vietnam), ignored by the mother with whom she desires to have a closer relationship, Delia has troubling nightmares she doesn't understand. She thinks she is going mad. There are two incidents in her life which begin to free her from her oppression. In one incident, Fernando, a lover who has begun to control her life in a violent and oppressive way, strikes her. At that moment Delia feels "as if all the sadness and pain she had suffered through the years had turned into an uncontrollable rage" (p. 64). She picks up the first heavy object at hand and hits him with it. The object turns out, symbolically, to be the unabridged dictionary of the Spanish language. Then, in one particularly frightening dream she sees a man she intuitively recognizes coming towards her with a knife. She opens her mouth, stretching her tongue out as far as she can and allows him to cut her tongue out. She tells us: "I watch my blood pouring out black as ink. It turns red when it hits the floor" (p. 116). This dream frightens her because of her passivity: "I let him maim me. He took away my tongue. My tongue! The very instrument of voice" (p. 127).

At this point, her friend Mattie suggests she write her nightmares down in order to control the powerful emotions that are emerging through them. This becomes another source of her writing. Finally, she begins to write poetry and her novel in order to understand herself and the moment in history. Mattie, who functions as Delia's fairy godmother (along with her Aunt Marta), suggests that she give in to her artistic passions:

You descend, slowly at first, cautiously. You move unrestrained through the water, free. Your heart responds to the tempo of the current. It pulls you in, sucks you into a liquid abyss. Thoughts lie incomplete somewhere in your mind. Fear rushes out of your body with every breath. And all your pores open to the inebriating essence of the depths. You feel the hand pulling you toward the surface and you fight it. You've become one with the sea. Nothing else matters.

(p. 79)

Later, as Delia works on her novel, the therapeutic nature of her writing is gone; instead, writing has become a necessity for her: "Writing seemed as natural a need as eating or breathing and Delia could no longer envision her life without it" (p. 130).

In the second section of the novel, Delia's Aunt Marta tells her stories about her ancestors, telling her that her great-grandmother was a skilled silversmith as well as a storyteller, her grandmother was a curandera, her grandfather a grain broker, and so forth. Delia understands the importance of these family stories, just as she comes to understand the meaning of silence. The silence she feared so has become a friend, for it is through silence that she writes: "Silence, my oldest enemy, my dearest friend. I surrendered my tongue to you once, freely, and I learned your secret. I learned to write" (p. 150). At the end of the novel, when Delia has come into her own, Marta tells her she looks like her great-grandmother Asunción, "'The Storyteller.' *The weaver of words The weaver of silver threads The writer The silversmith*" (p. 181). Moreover, she has allowed other people to read her novel (her aunt Marta and her lover Jeff), thus overcoming the silence she has suffered from all her life, because "she had never been able to talk back to anyone, even when anger made her head throb. Her parents had taught her that keeping still in the face of argument was better" (p. 16).

As critics have pointed out, one of the techniques Corpi uses in this novel will be repeated in her subsequent detective novels, that of slipping back and forth in time in order to preserve the original events while at the same time questioning them. And while she was very experimental in *Delia's Song,* shifting between stream of consciousness and straight narrative, she experiments in her subsequent novels with different techniques.

DETECTIVE FICTION

In an essay, "La página roja/The Crime Page," Corpi tells us that she was an early reader and that when she was around seven years of age, her father had a cornea operation. Since it left him unable to read, he asked her to read from the newspaper. While the regional newspaper had news and even a cultural page with poetry and stories from regional and local writers, it also had a crime page—*La página roja* (the red page). As Corpi says:

> The red page contained news not only about murders but also about brawls in the zona roja (the red district), white slavery, and illegal gambling. My father allowed me to select reading from any page, except, of course, *La página roja.* To make sure I wasn't even tempted, every evening he pulled out the red page, folded it and put it in his shirt pocket to dispose of it later. But I always managed to find *La página roja* and eagerly read it.
>
> (p. 1)

This was the beginning of her interest in crime and in mysteries. Ultimately she became more interested in cases involving "duplicity and premeditation." Her mother, aunts, and other family friends would sit around and discuss crimes that had happened, commenting on the cleverness or stupidity of the perpetrators. After one particularly convoluted and complicated case, her grandmother asked, "Who was the real criminal?" and then added, "There is no justice in the world." Corpi tells us, "I never had the chance to let my grandmother know that I often write to bring about justice, even if poetic" (p. 5).

The first detective novel in her Gloria Damasco series is *Eulogy for a Brown Angel* (1992). This was followed by *Cactus Blood* (1995) and *Black Widow's Wardrobe* (1999). The same cast of characters appears in all three novels, and although the narrative plots are different, similar concerns about history, culture, and society are apparent in all three novels. As stated before, a historical backdrop important to Chicano culture is featured in each novel. In *Eulogy for a Brown Angel* it is the National Chicano Moratorium of 1970, which protested the intervention of the United States in southeast Asia and the induction of hundreds of Chicanos into the armed forces. It is also about the death of Ruben Salazar, a Chicano journalist who was mistakenly shot by police in Los Angeles. In *Cactus Blood* it is the boycott against table grapes and the struggles of the United Farm Workers for better living conditions and against pesticides. And in *Black Widow's Wardrobe,* it is the story of Malinche Tenepal, the mistress of Hernán Cortés, the Spanish conqueror of Mexico. Also backgrounding these novels is early California Hispano history. Thus Corpi details the early days of California, when the California Hispanos controlled large parcels of land that were later lost.

Gloria Damasco, a speech therapist turned investigator, is the detective. She is married to medical doctor Darío Damasco in the first novel and has a daughter, Tania. Her husband dies in the first novel and Gloria later falls in love with a private investigator, Justin Escobar, with whom she enters into a partnership. Her mother, Pita Vélez, and her mother's best friend, Nina Contreras, also are featured in the novels, becoming her investigative assistants in the third novel. Chicano poets, artists, and publishers also form part of the community, and they are often named in the books along with the titles of their works and a discussion about the importance of Chicano cultural life. The Day of the Dead (2 November), an important Mexican tradition that has been brought to the United States, is an important event in these narratives, signifying as it does remembrance of those who have died, as well as cultural unity. When a child dies in *Eulogy,* Gloria and her friend find him on Marigold Street. Marigolds are the traditional flowers for the dead and are put on graves in Mexico on the Day of the Dead.

As in most mystery novels, quite a few people die through violence or through other means. In addition, Gloria Damasco is a detective with a "dark gift"; she has visions or nightmares or dreams that often signal that something is going to happen. While she cannot always decipher the dreams, they often do predict the action in the narratives. Gloria struggles to control her dreams and understand them, but at the same time she is uncomfortable about talking about them to others. As she tells us: "I purposely didn't mention any of my 'flying' experiences. I suppose I felt embarrassed since I had always sought rational explanations for anything that happened to me, using intuition to support reason rather than the other way around" (*Eulogy for a Brown Angel,* p. 30).

Chicanos of all classes and social strata appear in these narratives, from gang members (Mando) to upper-class professionals (Michael Cisneros, a lawyer) in *Eulogy,* as well as the aforementioned writers and artists. Moreover, the plight of immigrants from other Latin American countries is also mentioned in the series: a political refugee from Guatemala, a Mexican immigrant. Many of the villains are powerful men who abuse their wives and children, do not respect family values, and have no social conscience at all. Thus there is a Spaniard in *Black Widow's Wardrobe* who is also a drug dealer and a thief of pre-Columbian artifacts from Mexico, and in *Eulogy* Paul Cisneros hates his adopted brother Michael enough to kill his son and leave him with excrement in his mouth; Paul is also a corporate boss who is trying to take over his brother's corporation.

What distinguishes Corpi's detective fiction from traditional mysteries is precisely her emphasis on Chicano cultural history and

cultural memory. As Adrienne Gosselin says, "Lucha Corpi's Chicana detective asks different questions of detective fiction in order to reconstruct theories about culture and society" (*Multicultural Detective Fiction,* p. 7). Gosselin is echoed by Tim Libretti, who comments that these novels are a critique of "dominant cultural and legalistic conceptions of crime and injustice," introducing new ideas "informed by an historical perspective of the racial experience in the U.S." (*Multicultural Detective Fiction,* p. 61). Thus, Corpi is looking at the more widespread socioeconomic and historical causes of these injustices. Libretti also asserts that popular detective fiction is one genre that ethnic writers have turned to in order to discuss these issues in a political way. He points out that Corpi's technique in *Eulogy of a Brown Angel* is one of returning to the original historical moment (the Chicano Moratorium) in order to question that moment and to "recover the political history and impulses of the 1960s and early 1970s" (*Multicultural Detective Fiction,* p. 72). Corpi also does this in *Black Widow's Wardrobe* when she recovers the plight of Malinche and her historical memory, thus "making the solution of the crime the discovery of history itself" (p. 77).

Eulogy for a Brown Angel is a mystery that spans two separate time periods. In the first, 1970, Gloria Damasco and her friend Lydia find the body of a small child on Marigold Street in Los Angeles during the Chicano Moratorium. They meet a mysterious teenager, Mondo, who has partially seen the murderer and who hands them a clipping about the land holdings of the Peralta family, an old California founding family. Later Mondo is found murdered. The detective on the case, Matt Kenyon, is ill, Gloria realizes. For Gloria he represents the traditional detective: "He took his personal and moral concerns for granted, for in the solution of a crime, justice was somehow served and goodness always prevailed. But goodness, like justice, was only a relative notion, depending on who interpreted or administered it" (p. 61). Thus from the beginning Corpi undermines the monolithic concept of justice as well as goodness.

Later in the novel, which is full of its share of suspects and red herrings, Corpi introduces the theme of music, in this case *Madame Butterfly*, both the songs from the opera as well as the themes. In Puccini's opera, a woman believes her lover loves her, even when he abandons her and leaves for the United States, leaving her pregnant. When he eventually returns to Japan with his new wife, he takes away her son, and Madame Butterfly kills herself. In the novel this theme will be tied to the relationships of the Cisneros family, which includes the parents of the young murder victim.

Damasco continues on her search, even though she is accused of being a traitor, in the words of journalist (and conspirator) Joel Galeano when he says, "You too, Gloria. *Traidoras, Todas*" (p. 85). These words are in reference to Malintzín, La Malinche, the mistress of Hernán Cortés, who was accused of being a traitor to the country, a subject that Corpi will take up with a vengeance in *Black Widow's Wardrobe*. With no solution to the murder in sight, Gloria becomes increasingly stressed. Her husband, Darío, convinces her to put aside her detecting for her own good and the happiness of the family. Gloria does so until after her husband's death eighteen years later, in 1988.

During the second part of the novel, Gloria uncovers the anger Paul Cisneros has held towards his brother Michael; he is in love with Michael's wife Lillian, but Lillian has become despondent over the death of her child, knowing that she is partly to blame for his death. In her grief she takes on symbolically the attributes of La Llorona, the weeping woman of Mexican/Chicano mythology who searches for her lost children. After Gloria and her partner discover that Paul has killed the child, Justin kills him in a final confrontation, but not before Paul kills Luisa Cortez, Gloria's friend, with a bullet intended for Gloria. We discover that the dead child is Paul's son from the relationship he had with Lillian, his brother's wife.

Cactus Blood, the second novel in the series, uses as its historical focal point the United Farm Workers movement and the Chicano struggle to achieve living wages and decent working conditions for those agricultural workers who picked grapes and strawberries, as well as lettuce. This narrative begins with a dream in which Gloria Damasco sees a woman impaled on a cactus: "That's when I saw her. The woman. Naked. Her arms stretched up, tied to the fleshy leaves. Her legs together, bound to the stem. A slumping female Christ with a prickly-pear cactus cross on her back, shrouded in blood, bathed in amber moonlight" (p. 11). This grisly dream continues the literary technique of Corpi's other novels, in which dreams foreshadow and anticipate later events. In this mystery, Gloria investigates the suspicious death of her friend Sonny Mares, a political activist. The book is dedicated to Cesar Chavez, the founder of the United Farm Workers union. Not only are grapes found in Sonny's refrigerator, but also a videotape of the farmworkers' strike of 1973 is playing. Libretti writes that in this novel there is a desire to return to the "innocence" of the hope and agitation of the 1970s, when Chicanos believed the world could be changed. As Gloria says:

> I knew I was wallowing in wistfulness, wishing that things were the way they used to be in the late sixties and early seventies.
>
> Intellectually, I realized it was foolish to long for the most oppressive and repressive time we, as Chicanos, had experienced. But I had the feeling I didn't miss the activism as much as the innocence that had underscored our political zeal and the newness of our commitment.
>
> (p. 21)

Interestingly enough, these feelings are also registered in *Delia's Song*.

A central character in this novel is farmworker Carlota Navarro, an immigrant from

Mexico who has suffered all the tragedies and discrimination that many farmworkers experienced. She was brought illegally into the country as a maid for a wealthy doctor, raped by him, and contaminated by a lethal pesticide, Devil's Blood, as she ran through the fields to get away. Carlota has brought a cactus with her as a symbol of her native land. She is a friend of Josie Baldomar, married to Phillipe Hazlitt. Later in the novel, Remmi Stephens, the daughter of the man who raped Carlota, is found impaled on a huge cactus in Sonora. She is the lover of Phillipe, who was killed by Josie after she discovered his infidelity. The story of the struggles of Carlota emphasizes the injustices experienced by many Chicanos, particularly the women. Ill from the consequences of the pesticide poisoning, Carlota escapes to Mexico to die.

As part of the complicated plot, Sonny and his friend Art Bello had promised to help another friend, Ramón Caballos, blow up a tank containing the deadly pesticide. At the last minute Sonny and Art refuse to help, but Ramón carries out the task, which is captured on the videotape. Later Sonny and Art testify against Ramón because they do not want to put the United Farm Workers union in jeopardy. It is an action they will regret the rest of their lives.

In the end, the investigators discover that Sonny has not been murdered; rather he killed himself, probably because of his political failure. Thus once again solving the mystery is indeed the introduction into the history of the Chicano movement. The cactus, emblematic of the Chicano struggle, is reborn as a leaf and will be planted at the grave of Gloria's friend Luisa. The novel also ends with a historical event, the devastating earthquake in San Francisco and Oakland of 17 October 1989. For Libretti, the importance of this novel is not in the solving of the mystery, for as he points out, Damasco was never trying to solve the murder of Philippe, but the death of Sonny. It is rather the meditations on the past and the importance and remembrance of their political commitments

that agitate the characters. Thus Gloria is reminded of the necessity for political involvement through the character of Carlota, others by the events that have taken place around the actions of Sonny, Art, and Ramón. Libretti argues that it is

> a recognition that the conditions of internal colonization persist in the 1990s and that the Third World Movement of the 1960s and early 1970s provide fruitful models of resistance. In the terms in which the novel defines justice, as the end of racial, class, and sexual oppression and exploitation, the quest for justice is just beginning. Apprehending the criminal means overhauling a social and economic system that is itself criminal through and through.
>
> (*Multicultural Detective Fiction*, p. 80)

In *Black Widow's Wardrobe*, the third novel in the series, Gloria has now become a partner, in love as well as in business, with Justin. The novel begins with one of Gloria's nightmares, in which she sees a woman burning. This nightmare is reminiscent of those experienced in the other two detective novels, but also recalls the dreams in *Delia's Song. Black Widow's Wardrobe* begins on 2 November, the Day of the Dead, in San Francisco, where a procession of those who want to honor the dead, as well as artists and writers dressed as skeletons and other figures, is taking place. Gloria sees a woman dressed in white, carrying a photo and a bouquet of marigolds; she looks like "a tragic Aztec Princess" (p. 3). Two men Gloria thinks look like conquistadors try to run her down. Corpi introduces ambiguity in this novel, an ambiguity that continues until the very end. Where the woman was stabbed, no blood is to be found, and Gloria's mother comments, "Maybe she's not of this world, after all" (p. 9). She discovers that the woman is the mysterious Licia Román Lecuona, who has killed her violent and abusive husband, Peter Percy Lecuona, the descendent of a Spanish count. Having been sent to prison for the murder of her husband, Licia was recently released. Moreover, we discover that Licia believes in reincarnation and thinks that she is the reincarnation of Malintzin Tenepal, Cortés's mistress and translator. This tale is also one of mystery and discovery, with the focus on the history of Malintzin or Malinche. Sending her mother, Pita, and her mother's friend, Nina, to research this historic figure, Gloria unearths her history from its negative past. As Gloria tells us: "Malinche—even as young as she was when she met Cortés—had been a complex woman" (p. 85). It turns out that Licia, pregnant when she killed her husband, gave birth to twins but was told they were dead. Her brother-in-law wanted the children for his own, and raised them. Licia discovers that her in-laws lied to her; moreover her son, Martín, now grown, knows she is his mother but also knows Licia killed his father, without knowing that his father abused her. In addition, his uncle is involved in the drug trade and in stealing and selling pre-Columbian artifacts. The Lecuonas flee to Mexico with Licia's children, and Licia follows. Gloria and another detective follow them and after a series of adventures find them. We discover that Licia's assailant in San Francisco was her son Martín, egged on by his uncle. In the end both Martín and his uncle are killed. Inés, the daughter, is not returned to the mother she has never known; instead she goes with her adopted mother, and everyone thinks that Licia commits suicide. She is constantly compared to Malinche: "Like Malinche, Licia married a Spaniard, who not only didn't love her, but mistreated her and was unfaithful to her. She had a son named Martín, who hated her" (p. 190). The tragedy of Malinche is relived in contemporary Licia; theirs is the tragedy of abused women who suffer domestic violence today. At the end of the novel, Corpi blurs the lines of reality and dream as her nightmare at the beginning of the novel becomes reality, and Licia's house burns down after neighbors have seen a woman in white who looks like Licia enter it. Gloria remarks, "No human remains were recovered at the site that once was Black Widows' dwelling" (p. 193).

Corpi's fourth mystery novel, titled *Crimson Moon*, is forthcoming. In this novel, Gloria Damasco is no longer the central detective, and Corpi experiments with different voices. Ralph Rodríguez writes that Lucha Corpi's detective series constitute a "new cultural aesthetic in Chicana/o letters" (p. 118). This aesthetic places emphasis on the fluidity of meaning and perceptions of the Chicano Movement that is not monolithic, but rather unfixed. As Corpi in her various novels goes back and forth between the years and events of the Chicano Movement to the present day, the significance of those years is questioned and takes on new meanings. He concludes that for Corpi the Chicano Movement was not a unified monolithic event, but one which is remembered and reconstructed in different ways, through memory and a shifting cultural identity. Corpi also emphasizes that we must remember the accomplishments of the past in order to shape the future.

CHILDREN'S LITERATURE

In 1999 Corpi published *Where Fireflies Dance/ Ahí, donde bailan las luciérnagas*. Once again in this book she emphasizes Mexican culture, music, and family stories. The tale is about two children, Lucha and Víctor, who visit a house believed to be haunted. In this house, according to the villagers, lived a Mexican revolutionary named Juan Sebastián. When Juan Sebastián left to join Emiliano Zapata in the Mexican Revolution, he left a note telling his mother he was going to seek his destiny. The brother and sister find a photograph of Juan Sebastián playing his guitar and singing. They hear music and at first believe that the ghost of Juan Sebastián is coming for them, but the music is, in reality, coming from the nearby cantina, Cuatro Cañas. Although they are told never to go into the cantina, the children peek inside and see a jukebox, the first they have ever seen. They then save their money and when someone goes inside, they ask him to play their favorite songs. This continues until one night their mother discovers them at the bar. Made to stay at home, their grandmother tells them the story of Juan Sebastián. When their father comes home from work, he sings songs to the children.

The narrator of the story, Lucha, says: "Over the years I never forgot the story of Juan Sebastián. One day, like him, I also left town to find what I was born to do. . . . I traveled north, carrying in me the memory of the fireflies, dancing in the night air. . . . One day I began to write stories, and I knew I had found my destiny." Thus this children's story summarizes many of the themes that Corpi utilizes in both her poetry and her novels.

Lucha Corpi is a writer who incorporates politics, social conditions, history, and the situation of women in her poetry and novels. While in her poetry she is not as overtly political as she is in her narratives, the cultural and social context in which she writes is still evident. The role of memory and identity are foremost in her writing, as is the agency of her own voice. While her initial disappointments and struggles when she came to the United States at the age of nineteen, and then her struggles at the age of twenty-four, have impacted her writing (these are ages repeated in significant number in her writing), she nevertheless has created vital and creative spaces for both her poetic and narrative voices in two languages, enriched by many cultures. In terms of her female characters, in an interview with Mireya Pérez-Erdélyi, Corpi states that in her narratives most of the women are strong. Corpi says: "In that they show something of me. Apart from that they don't have anything of me. My characters have their own destiny and their own strength" (*Americas Review,* p. 79). The idea of finding or making your own destiny is central to her writing. There must be time for introspection, for silence, and for words. And there must be time for love.

Selected Bibliography

WORKS OF LUCHA CORPI

POETRY
Fireflight: Three Latin American Poets. Berkeley, Calif.: Oyez, 1976.
Palabras de mediodía/Noon Words. Translated by Catherine Rodríguez-Nieto. Introduction by Juan José Arreola. Houston: Arte Público Press, 1980. Second edition, introduction by Tey Diana Rebolledo, 2001.
Variaciones sobre una tempestad/Variations on a Storm. Translation by Catherine Rodríguez-Nieto. Berkeley, Calif.: Third Woman Press, 1990.

FICTION
"Tres mujeres," *De Colores* 3, no. 3 (1977): 74–89.
Delia's Song. Houston: Arte Público Press, 1989.
Cactus Blood. Houston: Arte Público Press, 1995.
Eulogy for a Brown Angel. Houston: Arte Público Press, 1992.
Black Widow's Wardrobe. Houston: Arte Público Press, 1999.
Crimson Moon. Houston: Arte Público Press, Forthcoming, 2004.

OTHER
"La página roja." Unpublished essay.

"Contracorrientes: El estuario lingüístico de las escritora chicana." In *Las formas de nuestras voces: Chicana and Mexicana Writers in Mexico*. Edited by Claire Joysmith. Berkeley, Calif.: Third Woman Press, 1995. Pp. 91–97.

Editor. *Máscaras.* Berkeley, Calif.: Third Woman Press, 1997.

Where Fireflies Dance/Ahí, donde bailan las luciérnagas. San Francisco: Children's Book Press, 1997.

COLLECTIONS

Lucha Corpi Papers. California Ethnic and Multicultural Archives, Special Collections. Donald C. Davidson Library. University of California, Santa Barbara.

SECONDARY WORKS

INTERVIEWS

Brinson-Piñeda, Barbara. "Poets on Poetry. Dialogue with Lucha Corpi." *Prisma.* 1, no. 1 (spring 1979): 4–9.

Carabi, Angels. "Lucha Corpi." In *Truthtellers of the Times: Interviews with Contemporary Women Poets.* Edited by Janet Palmer Mullaney. Ann Arbor: University of Michigan Press, 1998. Pp. 23–31.

Pérez-Erdélyi, Mireya. "Entrevista con Lucha Corpi: Poeta Chicana." *Americas Review* 17, no. 1 (spring 1989): 72–82.

CRITICISM

Armstrong, Jeanne. *Demythologizing the Romance of Conquest.* Westport, Conn.: Greenwood Press, 2000.

Chase, Cida S. "Temática e imágenes prevalentes en Lucha Corpi." In *Mujer y literatura mexicana y chicana: Culturas en contacto II.* Mexico D.F./Tijuana: El Colegio de México/El Colegio de la Frontera Norte, 1990. Pp. 273–280.

Gosselin, Adrienne Johnson. "Multicultural Detective Fiction: Murder with a Message." In *Multicultural Detective Fiction: Murder from the "Other" Side.* Edited by Adrienne Johnson Gosselin. New York: Garland Publishing, 1999. Pp. 3–14.

Ikas, Karen Rosa. *Chicana Ways: Conversations with Ten Chicana Writers.* Reno: University of Nevada Press, 2002. Pp. 67–89.

Joysmith, Claire, ed. *Las formas de nuestras voces: Chicana and Mexicana Writers in Mexico.* Berkeley, Calif.: Third Woman Press, 1995.

Libretti, Tim. "Lucha Corpi and the Politics of Detective Fiction. In *Multicultural Detective Fiction. Murder from the "Other" Side.* Edited by Adrienne Johnson Gosselin. New York: Garland Publishing, 1999. Pp. 61–81.

Rebolledo, Tey Diana. *Women Singing in the Snow: A Cultural Analysis of Chicana Literature.* Tucson: University of Arizona Press, 1995.

Rodríguez, Ralph E. "Cultural Memory and Chicanidad: Detecting History, Past and Present in Lucha Corpi's Gloria Damasco Series." *Contemporary Literature* 43, no. 1 (spring 2002): 138–170.

Sánchez, Marta. *Contemporary Chicana Poetry: A Critical Approach to an Emerging Literature.* Berkeley, Calif.: University of California Press, 1985.

"Voices from the Gaps: Women Writers of Color." University of Minnesota: http://voices.cla.umn.edu, 2002. P. 5.

Alicia Gaspar de Alba
(1958–)

SILVIA SPITTA

THOUGH SHE INITIALLY made her mark as a poet, Alicia Gaspar de Alba has become one of the most prolific and versatile Latina writers working in the U.S. today, publishing not only poetry *(Beggar on the Córdoba Bridge)*, but short fiction *(The Mystery of Survival and Other Stories)*, a historical novel translated into Spanish and German *(Sor Juana's Second Dream)*, art criticism *(Chicano Art Inside/Outside the Master's House: Cultural Politics and the CARA Exhibition)*, and essays. She has also edited a collection of essays titled *Velvet Barrios: Popular Culture & Chicano/a Sexualities*. Forthcoming projects include a completed novel on the murders of over three hundred women in Juárez *(The Factor/Desert Blood)* and a second collection of poetry that includes personal essays.

Anthologized in important poetry collections such as *Floricanto Sí* (1998), the poems of *Beggar on the Córdoba Bridge,* with which Gaspar de Alba made her name, recall her childhood in El Paso, Texas, and reflect on the complexities of border life. Not coincidentally, the poem with which *Beggar on the Córdoba Bridge* opens is entitled "La frontera." The border is a border/ woman, a winding river, a woman whose blood flows on both sides of the border, "leaking sangre / y sueños" ("La fontera," p. 5), a lover on whose borders *lloronas* weep as they search for their drowned children. This difficult border is also alluded to in the short autobiography that prefaces the collection as published in the anthology *Three Times a Woman* (1989), in which Gaspar de Alba describes the difficulty of being the first Chicana in a family of Mexicans; the first to have grown up on this side of the Río Grande; the first to have gone to a Catholic nuns' school where any kind of behavior considered deviant—such as "biting your nails or scratching your crotch"—was beaten out of her with a ruler that "flattened your fingers" (p. 3); the first to have moved from a Mexican American part of town full of Vargases, Olivers, and Garcías to the east side and an Anglo-American community of Schreibners, Hayses, and Petersons; and the first to attend a white high school where she acquired a reputation as "a jock, a women's libber, and a journalist" (p. 3). All these experiences coincided with the death of her grandfather and the publication of her first short story.

In an essay appearing in *The Latino/a Condition: A Critical Reader* (1998), Gaspar de Alba describes her childhood in terms of "cultural schizophrenia," defined as signifying "the presence of mutually contradictory or antagonistic parts or qualities . . . in any group whose racial, religious, or social components are a hybrid . . . of two or more fundamentally opposite cultures" (p. 227). This culturally schizophrenic condition arose due to the conflicting demands between public and private space on the border. At home, her family, having been forced to move to the United States (one assumes for financial reasons) but rejecting that culture, forbade her to speak English, while at school she was punished if she spoke Spanish. Indeed, during her childhood the border did not yet exist as a place with its own identity—an identity as a third space that it is now fast acquiring thanks to the proliferation of border literature, art, theory, aesthetics, politics, and ecology. It was seen in purely negative terms. By extension, the border dweller was also a purely negative being: "Neither place validated the idea of the Mexican-American," Gaspar de Alba writes in the tellingly entitled essay "Literary Wetback," which appeared in the 1993 publication *Infinite Divisions: An Anthology of Chicana Literature* (p. 289). As we learn later, neither place, nor indeed neither culture at large, validates the lesbian that she became. At sixteen, like every Eve, she writes in the preface to *Bridge,* she dated a white man whom she married three years later only to divorce him shortly thereafter.

How to express her in-betweenness became the issue for Gaspar de Alba. In college, she took a fiction classes with James Ragan at the University of El Paso, and it was then that she discovered her poetic talent. Ragan helped her affirm the Mexican American roots of her imagination, art, and lifelong interests. She earned her bachelor of arts in English in 1980 and wrote *Beggar* as her master's thesis.

Rejected by mainstream publishers, and also feeling rejected by a Mexican lover, Alicia Gaspar de Alba left El Paso; she received a CIC Minorities Fellowship and went on to pursue graduate work in American studies at the University of Iowa and the University of New Mexico. A Chicana Dissertation Fellowship at the University of California, Santa Barbara, supported her in writing her thesis. In 1987, at the time she was writing the autobiographical preface to *Beggar on the Córdoba Bridge* for inclusion in *Three Times a Woman,* she had won the Massachusetts Artists Fellowship in poetry, moved to Boston, and was living a few miles from yet another bridge—this time the Longfellow Bridge. She also worked for National Braille Press translating children's books into braille—thereby experiencing an altogether different and important lesson in bilingualism—and taught freshman composition at the University of Massachusetts, Boston. After doing coursework at the University of Iowa, she took a four-year break from academia and then earned her Ph.D. in 1994 at the University of New Mexico at Albuquerque. At that point her poems had been anthologized and published in English journals such as *Revista Chicano-Riqueña; Imagine: International Chicano Poetry Journal; Iowa Journal of Literary Studies; Common Lives/ Lesbian Lives;* and *Puerto del sol,* among others. Her short stories in Spanish were published in *Palabra nueva: Cuentos chicanos* (1984 and 1985 editions). *The Mystery of Survival and Other Stories,* her first collection of short fiction, was published in Bilingual Press and won the Premio Aztlán in 1994. Coupling her vocation as a writer with academic life, she continued to teach and is currently an associate professor of Chicano and Chicana studies and English at the University of California, Los Angeles.

Gaspar de Alba's own experiences parallel her description of the border as a wound. The representation of her life in the poems of *Beggar,* and later in *The Mystery of Survival and Other Stories* (1993), allows the reader to discern an obsessive pattern: all her writings revolve around, stem from, bite into, cry, try to fathom, describe, and denounce the sexual abuse of the girl that the narrator once was. "War Cry," one of the first poems in *Beggars,* reads:

I was three. I remember the word
he called my mother: Cabrona. Her back
a tombstone to his digging.

The blood of her newborn child
still fresh inside her, the wound
a color of ripe figs.
When he passed above me, his hand
tucked in the blanket.

(*Three Times a Woman*, p. 11)

"Making Tortillas," one of the poems towards the end of the collection, describes the erotic encounter of two women—an encounter that will surpass the love of men and serve as leitmotif in Gaspar de Alba's works and life:

Pressed between the palms,
clap-clap
        thin yellow moons—
clap-clap
        still moist, heavy still
        from last night's soaking
clap-clap
        slowly start finding their shape
clap-clap
. . . .
Tortilleras, we are called,
grinders of maíz, makers, bakers,
slow lovers of women.
The secret is starting from scratch.

(*Three Times a Woman*, pp. 44–45).

The poem "Beggar on the Córdoba Bridge," which gives the collection its title, again posits a form of wisdom transmitted from woman to woman:

I want to keep you, old woman
Knit your bones
in red wool, wear your eye
teeth around my neck—
amulets filled with sage.

You could teach me
the way of the gypsy:
. . . .
How to take bread or fish
from the mouths of dogs,
travel bridges that are pure light,

. . . .
From you, I could learn to read
the cracked, brown palm
of the Río Grande.

(*Three Times a Woman*, p. 13)

The bilingual collection *The Mystery of Survival and Other Stories* (1993) followed shortly upon the heels of *Beggar on the Córdoba Bridge*. The stories which comprise the volume have been often anthologized in important collections such as Ray González's *Mirrors Beneath the Earth: Short Fiction by Chicano Writers* (1992) and Lillian Castillo-Speed's *Latina: Women's Voices from the Borderlands* (1995), or translated from the Spanish in Ray González's *Currents from the Dancing River: Contemporary Latino Fiction, Nonfiction, and Poetry* (1994). All the stories deal with the complexites of Chicano transcultural life in the U.S. With titles such as "El pavo," "American Citizen, 1921," "Los derechos de la Malinche," "The Piñata Dream," and "Facing the Mariachis," the stories tell of Chicano poverty, discrimination of Latinos by the mainstream, marginalization, and racism. They also tell of the subjugation of daughters to violent, *macho* fathers, lesbian love, pilgrimages to Chicano holy sites such as Chimayó, and the delicate balance the protagonists have to tread in order to make a life in the U.S. The stories are narrated in English or Spanish, or by switching between both languages.

The story "The Mystery of Survival," which gives the book its title, revolves around the motif of the sexually abused girl for whom the world is a war zone. The story serves as a tribute to her faculty for surviving episodes like the one that is immediately described:

"When my mother left me in the Colonia La Gran María, I was ten years old and I hated men. My stepfather had once told me that women were like the earth, and that men could mine them and take anything they wanted. Girls, he said, especially ones like me who talked back and disobeyed, had to be dealt with in a special way. . . . My mother had gone to the orphanage with food and some of my old clothes.

"I'm not a woman," I cried, terrified, staring down at the thing sticking out of his pants.

(p. 9)

This same Malinche-like motif of the girl sexually abused by a male parental figure and abandoned by a mother who sends her away either to an orphanage, a convent, or to be taken care of by relatives, will be repeated in Gaspar de Alba's historical novel, *Sor Juana's Second Dream*. A lengthy novel, *Sor Juana* details the day-to-day occurrences as well as the tediousness and aggressiveness of convent life in seventeenth-century Mexico during the time of the Inquisition. Fighting, resisting, and critiquing the double standard to which women at the time were subjected, Sor Juana (1648–1695) wrote "Hombres necios" ("You Men"), which remains one of her most famous poems and which is mentioned numerous times by different characters in the novel.

Gaspar de Alba writes her novelized biography of Sor Juana from what can be gleaned from the nun's own writings and from what critics have constructed over the centuries. The novel parallels Maria Luisa Bemberg's approach in her film about Sor Juana, *Yo, la peor de todas* (*I, the Worst of All*, 1990). Like *Yo, la peor de todas,* and like Gaspar de Alba's poetry and short stories, the novel focuses on the nun's alleged lesbianism. In the novel, Sor Juana's uncle sexually accosts her during a lunch break on their way to Mexico City, where her mother was sending her to join Doña Isabel's wealthy sister and brother-in-law. In this totally fabricated version of events, her uncle masturbates in front of her and exhibits his genitalia, Medusa-like. The young girl responds in horror and disgust, as do all the other girls in Gaspar de Alba's fiction.

As in *Beggar on the Córdoba Bridge,* where Alicia Gaspar de Alba often speaks from within the rhythm and form of religious prayers, in *Sor Juana* she uses this form of ventriloquism

extensively, quoting from the nun's poems. Letting Sor Juana speak through her poems, quoted faithfully in the novel, helps Gaspar de Alba knit the account of the nun's life together and also interweaves their voices (the seventeenth-century nun and the contemporary Chicana writer) so that at times both those voices and their lives become indistinguishable. The novel engages intertextually with Sor Juana's famous letter "The Poet's Answer to the Most Illustrious Sister Filotea de la Cruz," as well as important selections from Octavio Paz's *Sor Juana; or, the Traps of Faith.* "Hombres necios," while never quoted in full, is often mentioned by different characters, including Sor Juana herself, who recites parts of it to the Condesa. Structurally, *Sor Juana's Second Dream* also interweaves fictional diary entries, letters, and the last poem written by Gaspar de Alba herself. The story is told through these different literary genres, a third person focused on Sor Juana's point of view (used to narrate the more public and known aspects of Sor Juana's life), and a first person (diaries, letters) which reveals Sor Juana's subjectivity. These alternating narrative voices recount Sor Juana's daily routine in the convent in great detail. The poem with which the novel ends, "Litany in the Subjunctive," however, is Alicia Gaspar de Alba's and *not* Sor Juana's as the reader has come to expect. This sudden change in the direction of the ventriloquism makes the reader wonder whether Sor Juana could possibly have written *such* sexually explicit poetry. The realization that if she really was a lesbian she had to disguise her desire in a style so baroque that it has awed generations of readers proves to be a performative strategy of the text: while unveiling Sor Juana, the novel points to the nun's self-veiling as a strategy of survival.

Sor Juana's Second Dream begins and ends with newly arrived Spanish archbishop Aguiar y Seijas, his demand for a "confession" of Sor Juana's sins, and the public humiliation and punishment that will ultimately—and very shortly thereafter—result in the nun's death.

Aguiar y Seijas was known for his extreme misogyny; allegedly he could not tolerate the presence of women around him. A character describes him as "a devotee of Saint James who despises women with the same ferocity with which the saint persecuted Moors" (*Sor Juana's Second Dream*, p. 202). The Catholic Church's misogyny and the intrusion of the Inquisition into all matters private and public serve both as the backdrop to Sor Juana's life in the Jeronymite convent in Mexico City and as the measure of the immensity of her rebellion and success.

Gaspar de Alba's novel traces—and at times seems to reproduce—daily routine in one of the most wealthy and prestigious convents in Mexico. The rhythm of the novel suggests the sound of tolling bells, a sound that dominated Sor Juana's life. Gaspar de Alba describes Sor Juana's numerous scientific experiments and her enlightened fight against the superstition and misogyny of the times. Amid the novel's and the nun's sea of words, Sor Juana's cooking and her possessions stand out: the delicious foods she made; her luxurious quarters; her immense collection of books (said to be the greatest in the New World in her time); her scientific instruments (telescope, microscope, astrolabe, and many others); as well as the numerous precious gifts given to her by her patrons. It is as if these things, more than anything else, made her spiritual trajectory so dubious in the church's eyes, and therefore they get taken away from her repeatedly.

Nina Scott once remarked that everyone constructs his or her own Sor Juana, and Alicia Gaspar de Alba corroborates this observation when she explains in the postscript to the novel that she spent almost a decade researching and writing the first published "English-language novel" about the nun's life, "this incredible woman, the first feminist of the Americas, tenth muse of Mexico, great-great-great, hundredfold-great-grandmother of my Mexican heritage" (*Sor Juana's Second Dream*, p. 459). Interestingly, with this book, Alicia Gaspar de Alba shakes off the negative genealogy of La Ma-linche under which she had conceived her earlier works and instead adopts the most outstanding female writer of the Americas as her model and her muse. In this respect she follows the current feminist trend of searching for and regaining forgotten or neglected women writers as models and as an inspiration for the present. Alongside this recuperation of Sor Juana for Chicana feminism, Alicia Gaspar de Alba also consistently and explicitly "outs"—or perhaps better said, "uncloisters"—the nun throughout the novel.

Rumors of Sor Juana's alleged homosexuality, fed by the nun's celebratory poems—often (mis)read as love poems—addressed to the vicereine Maria Luisa and other members of the court, and her assertion that she had begged her mother to let her attend the University of Mexico dressed as a man, has been a matter of titillating debate for numerous years. Gaspar de Alba focuses on and highlights the sexual relationship between Sor Juana and Maria Luisa, as well as that of Sor Juana and one of her assistants, Concepción. Sor Juana's outing as a lesbian revolves around two key scenes in the novel. The first occurs when Sor Juana disregards convent policy and, upon her return from her hometown after her mother's death, decides to spend the night with the viceroy and vicereine at their temporary lodgings as they get ready to depart Mexico. While there, she gets drunk with the viceroy and spends the night debating and talking with him. At dawn, when she turns in, she finds the vicereine in her bed waiting for her, impatient with her tardiness. "'Sshh!' La Condesa covered Juana's mouth with warm fingers. They smelled of rose water. 'Kiss me, Juana.'" This greeting opens upon a scene of explicit lesbian lovemaking: "Their hips were grinding hard now" (p. 308).

This scene is repeated in public when the couple pays a final visit to Sor Juana shortly before their return to Spain, and the viceroy kisses her foot while the vicereine kisses her on the lips. While the first scene is witnessed by Belilla (Sor Juana's niece and assistant) when she walks in to wake Sor Juana in the palace and finds both women naked and holding each other in the early morning, the second is witnessed by nuns sent to spy on Sor Juana and is reported in the following scandalous way:

> "And what did Don Tomás do?"
> "He picked up Sor Juana's foot and kissed the sole of her shoe."
> "This is no jest, Sister! You might be impugning a good man."
> "It's what I saw Your Reverence. Like I said, I'm not inventing things."
> "I've always known there was something sinful in that friendship. But for Don
> Tomás to be involved! Who could believe such a thing? The Viceroy of New Spain kissing the sole of a nun's shoe!"
> "Looking on as his wife kisses the lips of another woman"
>
> (p. 369)

Kinky, if not somewhat pornographic, these scenes appropriate Sor Juana not only for Chicana writers but also particularly for Chicana *lesbian* writers. As such they say more about our time and about Alicia Gaspar de Alba than about Sor Juana. Indeed, the focus on the homoerotic relationship between the two women somewhat eclipses what was most important historically about the relationship between them: namely, the fact that, as Nina Scott points out, Maria Luisa de Paredes, upon her return to Spain and within a year, managed to publish Sor Juana's works. That is, one woman published the works of another in the 1600s. And perhaps what is even more important: a Spanish woman belonging to the royalty published the works of an illegitimately born nun in the colonies. Indeed, both vicereines took Sor Juana under their wing, protecting and promoting her, awed by her scholarship. While the focus on Sor Juana's lesbianism overshadows the fact that both vicereines were devoted and important patronesses of the arts, the highlighting of the nun's lesbianism has the unintended effect of showing that Sor Juana's *knowledge* proved

extremely seductive—sexually and intellectually—to *both* men and women. Moreover, Sor Juana's knowledge derived not only from her alternative sexual orientation, but also in response to a colonial epistemology that attempted to erase the native, indigenous culture—a culture that she never tired of affirming and writing into her life's work. This "alter-Native" pursuit of knowledge—to deploy and translate the neologism Gaspar de Alba later used to analyze Chicano art—would position Sor Juana as one of the first truly *American* intellectuals.

The relevance of the novel's title, *Sor Juana's Second Dream*, becomes clear with the final poem, titled "Litany in the Subjunctive." The poem, written by Gaspar de Alba, articulates the author's lesbian desire as if Sor Juana had spoken that desire herself. Indeed, the *second* dream is the possibility of lesbian sexual liberation and the freedom to openly voice homoerotic love and desire:

> If I could rub myself
> along your calf,
> feel your knee
> break the waters of my shame;
>
> If I could lay my cheek
> against the tender sinews
> of your thigh,
> smell the damp
> cotton that Athena
> never wore, her blood
> tracks steaming in the snow;
>
> If I could forget
> the devil and the priest
> who guard my eyes
> with pitchfork and with host;
>
> If I could taste
> the bread, the blood, the salt
> between your legs
> as I taste mine;
>
> If I could turn myself
> into a bee and free

this soul, whose bars
webbed across your window
would be vain, that black
cloth, that rosary, that crucifix—
nothing could save you
from my sting.

(p. 457)

Sor Juana's "second dream" brings us full circle to the representation of the Río Grande as a wound between two countries. Like the Río Grande/Río Bravo, her "alter-Native" stance turns Sor Juana into a border figure, opening up a third space between genders and representations and stinging us with her desire. As Gaspar de Alba concludes:

There are many whom Sor Juana has visited in our time. Several of us, interestingly, are *fronterizas* from the El Paso-Juárez/Texas-Mexico border: the artist, Martha Arat; fellow writers, Estela Portilla-Trambley and Pat Mora, and me. Tell my story, Sor Juana says, you who can tell it in a language less veiled, you who have no Inquisition guarding your eyes and tongue.

(p. 460)

As such, the second dream that follows Sor Juana's most important, arcane, and difficult publication, her *Primero sueño* (a reflection on knowledge and freedom), claims for itself the status of being the underbelly, the unveiled disclosure of homoerotic desire. Gaspar de Alba not only parallels her work to that of Sor Juana, but also situates her own novel alongside other efforts to uncloister Sor Juana, such as Bemberg's film, and in opposition to homophobic works that further cloister her, such as Octavio Paz's. *Sor Juana's Second Dream,* which took nine years to research and write, showcases Alicia Gaspar de Alba's graceful interweaving of fictional work with academic research. She has bridged the purely creative side of her work with essays devoted to literary, artistic, and cultural analysis. This bridge is not only apparent in the novel, but also in the introduction and imaginary "interview" of Sor Juana, "The Politics of Location of the Tenth Muse of America: An Interview with Sor Juana Inés de la Cruz." This "interview" reflects on the research that went into the novel and clearly articulates Gaspar de Alba's intention of wresting Sor Juana away from Octavio Paz's homophobic—if illuminating—appropriation of the writer in his massive *Sor Juana; or, the Traps of Faith.* If *Sor Juana's Second Dream* merges fiction with research, "The Politics of Location of the Tenth Muse" becomes progressively less "critical," ending with the purely imaginary interview, which weaves together several of Sor Juana's poems in lieu of answers to the interviewer. In this way it destabilizes academic generic categories even as it depends on these categories to create the fictional dialogue. Again focusing on Sor Juana's sexuality, this essay also elaborates on her cultural *mestizaje*—on her Americanness—much more than is done by the novel. Thereby recontextualized, Sor Juana is made to articulate a desire that remained veiled in her time. In this essay, "Hombres necios" is finally quoted:

"*Hombres necios que acusáis*
a la mujer sin razón,
sin ver que sois la ocasión
de lo mismo que culpáis:
"si con ansia sin igual
solicitais su desdén,
¿por qué queréis que obren bien
si las incitáis al mal?"

(*Living Chicana Theory,* p. 156)

You Men
Silly, you men—so very adept
at wrongly faulting womankind,
not seeing you're alone to blame
for faults you plant in woman's mind.

After you've won by urgent plea
the right to tarnish her good name,
you still expect her to behave—
you, that coaxed her into shame.

Finally, any discussion of *Sor Juana's Second Dream* would perhaps be incomplete without pointing to the uneasy coexistence of the two voices and the linguistic and cultural registers that Gaspar de Alba tries to merge. Readers who know Sor Juana's works approach *Sor Juana's Second Dream* expecting the same dazzling erudition, complexity, and style—and if not *that* then at least a literary experiment commensurate with her ability—only to find that Gaspar de Alba's narrative voice is very contemporary and much simpler. Gaspar de Alba saw no need to display her erudition the way Sor Juana felt she must. This disjunction in linguistic and cultural registers and expectations inadvertently unveils Sor Juana in a different, far more complex way than her sexual outing would suggest. In fact, *Sor Juana's Second Dream*'s outing, unveiling, disrobing of the nun only shows the reader how necessary—if not imperative—it was for Sor Juana to veil herself, to hide behind the stunning quetzal feather headdress that the vicereine allegedly gave her. In fact, the reader comes to realize that Sor Juana's sexuality would be an insignificant question and of no importance had her writings not awed her audience so much and for so long.

It seems clear upon studying all Alicia Gaspar de Alba's works that her academic and lifelong goal, like that of Gloria Anzaldúa, Guillermo Gómez-Peña, and others, is to mix genres in the same way that the border mixes identities, languages, cultures, and aesthetics. Thus, Sor Juana is wrested away from an elite form of Hispanism, and she is Chicanoized. Conversely, in her academic works, particularly in her book-length analysis of the groundbreaking CARA (Chicano Art: Resistance and Affirmation, 1965–1985) UCLA 1990 Wight Art Gallery exhibition, Gaspar de Alba tries to contextualize Chicano art that has made it into the halls of "high" art. In the introduction to the volume, she reflects that CARA made it possible for her to reject her family's traditional *Hispanismo,* as well as the U.S. school system and *its* agenda of assimilation and Americanization. More specifi-

cally: Chicano art—as "popular" art—in the museum, a site of "high" art, and her study devoted to the famous CARA exhibition allowed her to theorize and negotiate Chicanismo as an in-between form of being in the world. Furthermore, this in-betweenness is viewed in positive and creative, rather than negative, terms. Reminding her readers of the two bridges that have literally and figuratively defined her life, in "Literary Wetback" Gaspar de Alba describes the first bridge as that between her identity and writing: "a symbolic border" that she crosses "at will, without a green card, without la migra or el coyote" (p. 292). The second bridge is the invisible bridge "between the marginal and the mainstream literary worlds" (p. 292). If "cultural schizophrenia" characterizes border identities, it is not a paralyzing condition.

Chicano Art Inside/Outside the Master's House: Cultural Politics and the CARA Exhibition (1998) is a book supported—ironically—by a grant from the National Endowment for the Humanities, an institution that under the direction of Lynne Cheney saw itself at the forefront of the right-wing struggle against multiculturalism and gay and lesbian issues, and which, among many other acts of overt or covert censorship, refused to fund the CARA exhibition that the book analyzes. Gaspar de Alba's illuminating study traces the debates around multiculturalism of this period as it tries to contextualize Chicano art in general, and the art exhibited by CARA in particular.

Though she studied Chicano literature in college, Gaspar de Alba nevertheless found that when confronted with the exhibition, her knowledge was insufficient:

Despite all the knowledge I had gained on the road to becoming "Doctor" Gaspar de Alba, I knew relatively little of the political history and cultural production of Chicano/as. Standing in the CARA exhibit, surrounded by this history and this material culture, I understood that in order to really "see" Chicano and Chicana art, I would have to make the exhibition the focus of an extended study.

(*Chicano Art*, p. xiv)

She was drawn to revisit the exhibition so many times it became "home" for her—and it is the structure of a house that she then uses to trace her route through the exhibition and as a frame for the individual chapters of her book. Transformed by CARA, she uses the Spanish word "*conscientización*" to describe the epiphany, the consciousness-raising that it brought about to her understanding of her own work as well as that of fellow Chicanos. Her main question in the book is an extension of her own personal position vis-à-vis CARA, which made her realize how little she knew about Chicano art despite being a Chicana writer. If the art displayed called for a contextualization that she lacked, what would a common viewer of the exhibit see? Moreover, what would a biased Anglo-American see? Would they see "folklore?" Indeed, she asks, what does it mean for Chicano art, an art that had either been invisible, marginalized consistently, or dismissed by the label "folklore," to enter the museum and the space of "high" art? Could it be understood at all? Or would it be simply folklorized and rendered quaint once again? Epigraphed by Audre Lorde's oft-quoted and illuminating saying from *Sister/Outsider,* "The master's tools will not dismantle the master's house" (*Chicano Art*, p. xvii). Gaspar de Alba's initial response to these queries was negative, hence the imperative to situate the works within the politics and times of the Chicano movement of the 60s and 70s. She realized that it was CARA's intention

to open the doors of the master's house—the hitherto exclusionary space of the mainstream museum—to remodel the interior *al estilo Chicano* and create an environment where Chicano/a art could be the vehicle for dialogue and reflection. For the thousands of Raza across the country who had never felt addressed or represented in an art museum until CARA, the exhibition signified a

personal and collective victory. They, too, were home for the first time in a public space.

(p. xv)

This moving epiphany—the finding of a "home" for Chicanos through CARA—made it imperative for her to begin repositioning Chicano art as an "*alter-Native* art"—an art that both belongs to the U.S. yet is different from U.S. mainstream culture. As Gaspar de Alba writes: "Chicano/a culture is an *alter-Native* culture within the United States, both alien and indigenous to the landbase known as the 'West'" (p. xvi). Despite the fact that the exhibition was "read" through the lens of multiculturalism, it was an immensely successful cultural event. In the same way that it transformed Gaspar de Alba herself, it also transformed myriads of people across the United States.

Indeed, it would be accurate to say that many Chicano artists who now are quite well-known and respected gained their visibility thanks to the CARA exhibit. Carmen Lomas Garza, Amalia Mesa Bains, Ester Hernández, Rupert García, Gronk, Willie Herrón, and many others showcased in CARA have since become familiar to many people both in and outside academia. Likewise, icons of the Chicano movement, such as the United Farm Workers banner, Ester Hernández's "Sun Mad Raisins," the Virgin of Guadalupe, and many other Mexican American symbols are fast becoming household items, whether they be mere fetishes of alterity in Anglo homes or as part of household Latino altars all over this country. And while multiculturalism itself has spawned intense dialogues, and been fiercely attacked for its ethnographic ethnocentrism, the art exhibited at the CARA exhibition, much like Sor Juana's writings, is so *good* that it will survive anachronistic debates.

Likewise, and viewed as a whole, Alicia Gaspar de Alba's works are fast constituting a coherent *oeuvre* which, in its attempt to Chicanoize the U.S. and Latin American literary and artistic canons is creating, along with other Latino critics, an important new border corpus situated at the heart of current, contestatory attempts aimed at expanding and redefining the American imaginary.

Selected Bibliography

WORKS OF ALICIA GASPAR DE ALBA

NOVELS AND SHORT STORIES

The Mystery of Survival and Other Stories. Tempe, Ariz.: Bilingual Press/Editorial Bilingüe, 1993.

"Malinche's Rights" (translated from the Spanish). In *Currents From the Dancing River: Contemporary Latino Fiction, Nonfiction, and Poetry.* Edited by Ray González. New York: Harcourt Brace, 1994.

Sor Juana's Second Dream. Albuquerque: The University of New Mexico Press, 1999.

The Factory/Desert Blood (forthcoming).

SELECTED POETRY

Three Times a Woman: Chicana Poetry / Alicia Gaspar de Alba, María Herrera-Sobek, Demetria Martínez. Tempe, Ariz.: Bilingual Review/Press, 1989.

"After 21 Years, a Postcard from My Father." In *The Floating Borderlands: Twenty-five Years of U.S. Hispanic Literature.* Edited by Juan Flores. Seattle: University of Washington Press, 1998.

La Llorona on the Longfellow Bridge: Poetry y otras movidas, 1985–2001 (forthcoming, Arte Público Press, fall 2003).

CRITICAL WORKS

"Literary Wetback." In *Infinite Divisions: An Anthology of Chicana Literature.* Edited by Tey Diana Rebolledo and Eliana S. Rivero. Tucson: The University of Arizona Press, 1993.

"The Alter-Native Grain: Theorizing Chicano/a Popular Culture." In *Culture and Difference: Critical Perspectives on the Bicultural Experience in the United States.* Edited by Antonia Darder. Westport, Conn.: Bergin and Garvey, 1995.

"Born in East L.A.: An Exercise in Cultural Schizophrenia." In *The Latino/a Condition: A Critical Reader.* Edited by Richard Delgado and Jean Stefancic. New York: New York University Press, 1998.

Chicano Art Inside/Outside the Master's House: Cultural Politics and the CARA Exhibition. Austin: University of Texas Press, 1998.

"The Politics of Location of the Tenth Muse of America: An Interview with Sor Juana Inés de la Cruz." In *Living Chicana Theory.* Edited by Carla Trujillo. Berkeley, Calif.: Third Woman Press, 1998.

"Response to Frances R. Aparicio: The Chicana/Latina Dyad, or Identity and Perception," *Latino Studies* vol. 1, no. 1 (2003): 106–114.

Velvet Barrios: Popular Culture & Chicana/o Sexualities, Edited by Alicia Gaspar de Alba. New York: Palgrave Macmillan, 2003.

CRITICAL AND BIOGRAPHICAL STUDIES

Andouard-Labarthe, Elyette. "L'Ailleurs des chicanas." In *L'ici et l'ailleurs: Multilinguisme et multiculturalisme en Amérique du Nord.* Edited by Jean Beranger. Bordeaux: Presses de l'Université de Bordeaux, 1991.

Castillo, Debra A., and Tabuenca Córdoba, María Socorro. *Border Women: Writing from la Frontera.* Minneapolis: University of Minnesota Press, 2002.

Chávez Silverman, Susana. "Chicanas in Love: Sandra Cisneros Talking Back and Alicia Gaspar de Alba 'Giving Back the Wor(l)d." *Chasqui: Revista de literatura latinoamericana* 27, no. 1 (May 1998): 33–46.

———. "Memory Tricks: Re-Calling and Testimony in the Poetry of Alicia Gaspar de Alba." *Rocky Mountain Review of Language and Literature* 53, no. 1 (spring 1999): 67–81.

Keller, Esther, and Birgit Rohrig. "Marina–La Malinche: Verrat, Missbrauch und Empowerment in zwei Chicana-Texten." In *La Malinche: Übersetzung, Interkulturalität und Geschlecht.* Edited by Carlos Rincón. Berlin: Edition Tranvia: W. Frey, 2001.

Poot Herrera, Sara, and Elena Urrutia. "*Y diversa de mí misma, entre vuestras plumas ando.*" *Homenaje internacional a Sor Juana Inés de la Cruz.* México: El Colegio de México, 1991.

Scott, Nina M. "Los poemas a la condesa de Paredes." In *Y diversa de mí misma entre vuestras plumas ando: Homenage Internacional a Sor Juana Inés de la Cruz.* Edited by Sara Poot Herrera. Mexico: El Colegio de Mexico, 1993. Pp. 159–170.

Juan Felipe Herrera
(1948–)

SANTIAGO R. VAQUERA-VÁSQUEZ

JUAN FELIPE HERRERA is a writer whose poetic voice is marked by wandering and rootedness. His work is a study in contrast. His poetry straddles two generations: that of the Chicano movement of the 1960s and that of the post-Chicano generation of the 1990s. He is a poet who was both a witness and an architect of the flowering of Chicano culture in the late 1960s and 1970s: he participated in poetry festivals, founded theatrical troupes, and later directed the Centro Cultural de la Raza, the Chicano cultural center in the Logan Park neighborhood of San Diego. Yet his most active period of publishing activity were the years after 1993. He had fourteen books published between 1993 and mid-2003, compared with four in the period between 1974 and 1989. He has received numerous honors, including grants from the California Arts Council (1974, 1977, 1983, and 1987), awards from the National Endowment for the Arts (1980 and 1985), the Chicano Literary Prize from the University of California, Irvine (1979 and 1985), the El Paso Chicano Poetry Prize from the University of Texas (1985), the Breadloaf Fellowship in Poetry (1990), the University of California, Berkeley, Regent's Fellowship (1997), the Smithsonian Children's Book of the Year (2000), and the Americas Award (2000). His work is highly respected and has been an influence on contemporary Chicano poets, yet, to date, there are relatively few critical studies dedicated to the work of this multifaceted and prolific artist.

For his use of poetry as a weapon for undermining binary oppositions and fixed cultural identities through an interrogation of citizenship, home, and nation, Juan Felipe Herrera is a border *brujo*. His expressionistic work evokes a migrant sensibility in its ability to cross multiple borders, including those of language, genre, and geography.

BIOGRAPHY

In "Train Notes," the introduction to his 1994 collection of writings *Night Train to Tuxtla*, Juan Felipe Herrera points out that he inherited his love of writing and performance from his mother, who would recite poetry out loud or dance in their living room. From his father he learned a philosophy of travel: "My father had the quixotic belief that moving changed one's body cells and kept the world fresh" (p. ix). These two ideals from his parents, poetry and travel, filled his life and affected his career as a poet, artist, teacher, and traveler. As a child of

Mexican immigrant parents, his cultural identity and his themes are as much rooted in place and space as enforced by movement.

Herrera was born on 27 December 1948 in Fowler, California, to Felipe Emilio Herrera and María de la Luz "Lucha" Quintana de Herrera. He was the only child of this migrant working couple. His father, from a small village in Chihuahua, Mexico, migrated north to the United States when he was fifteen. He worked first as a ranch hand and later as a farmworker. Felipe Herrera passed away when his son was sixteen. Juan Felipe Herrera's mother, Luz Quintana, came from a large family of nine, from a working-class district of Mexico City. She passed away in 1986. In order to travel to the United States, one of her brothers had petitioned the president of Mexico to allow his brothers and him to leave the country to join the U.S. Army. The strategy worked, and the brothers arrived in El Paso, Texas, in 1920. A year and a half later, the whole family was reunited in that border city. While there, Lucha came close to joining a Mexican theater troupe, "Los Pirrines," but did not do so due to pressures from her family, who felt vaudeville was not becoming of a young woman. The love of theater and music stayed with her, however, and she passed this on to her son.

It was in El Paso where his parents met and married. From Texas they moved to California, following the seasonal-crops circuit. The movement from place to place continued for the first years of the poet's young life. The sense of transition brought about by the constant moves, as well as the music his mother sang, would later become a continual theme in the young poet's artistic expression. In 1956, when Juan Felipe Herrera was eight, his family finally settled down in San Diego, ushering in a sense of stability despite living in a region marked by migration like the U.S./Mexican border. Lauro Flores, the Chicano critic who has worked most with Herrera's writing, points out that the San Diego years can be divided into two periods: "First he lived in Barrio Logan, an old Chicano com-

munity, until he was about to enter junior high school; then he moved near downtown" (*Dictionary of Literary Biography*, p. 138).

Though the move was within the same city, the transition from a rooted Chicano neighborhood like Barrio Logan to the downtown area of San Diego left a profound mark that affected his creative expression. As Herrera recalls:

> I used to spend a lot of time alone downtown . . . in Market Street, in La Placita, in the movie houses, near the Cine Azteca, the Casino Theatre, the Savoy Theatre, the Moon Cafe. . . . I used to spend day after day in the Greyhound bus depot, looking for things in the lockers, playing the pinball machines, taking photos for twenty-five cents . . . there, in *qüaino* [wino] land. . . . It was a strange scene. I was more used to the Logan atmosphere, which was more festive, more of a family neighborhood. But this was not a neighborhood, it was the phantasmagoria of downtown San Diego in the early 60's.
>
> (Flores, *Dictionary of Literary Biography*, p. 138)

Moving from a neighborhood with strong ties to family and community, Herrera found himself wandering within a downtown area in transition. The types of spaces that he frequented are places of movement, places where people meet and pass others. These are places that would also figure later in his poetry.

Herrera graduated from San Diego High School in 1967. From there he went on to attend UCLA, where he actively participated in the formation of a Chicano studies program. In spite of his interest in music and art, he chose to major in sociology. In 1972 Herrera obtained a B.A. degree in social anthropology. Although he did not pursue a degree in the arts, his creative interests remained prevalent. In 1970 he received a Chicano Studies grant from UCLA to film and record indigenous theatrical expression in three different communities in Mexico: the Huichol; the Mayans, specifically the communities living in the Lacandon rain forest of Chiapas; and the Totonac. It was a pivotal experience that would also mark another line in his creative expression:

the indigenous cultures of the Americas. In 1971 he founded the Chicano theater troupe Teatro Tolteca, modeled on the Teatro Campesino.

After graduating from UCLA, Herrera returned to San Diego, where he began to work with the Centro Cultural de la Raza (which was known at the time as the Centro Cultural Toltecas en Aztlán). His first position was in the photography department, but he rose up to become the Center's director. It was during this period that he published his first book, *Rebozos of Love / We Have Woven / Sudor de pueblos / On Our Back* (1974).

The book is influenced by Herrera's studies of indigenous cultural practices. The poems are conceived as woven texts that, taken together, form a tapestry, a shawl, a rebozo of love. As such, it is also an experimental work, in that it has neither a real beginning nor an end. It has no pagination, the poems are without titles, and the cover is a poem whose first verse has been adopted as the book title:

Rebozos of love
we have woven
sudor de pueblos
on our back
[shawls of love
we have woven
sweat of peoples
on our back]

The poems are also presented as "chants," linking them into an oral poetic tradition. These poem-chants are performances aimed at connecting with a larger indigenous shared collective. There is a sense of creation and intent towards a unification of Chicano identity. As Flores states, "Through his chants he is invoking and designing at the same time the vision of a Chicano people, the vision of a flourishing human group" (*Dictionary of Literary Biography*, p. 140).

As a document, *Rebozos* participates in an integral part of the *Movimiento Chicano* (Chicano movement): the assertion of a Chicano cultural identity with links to an indigenous past. The period in which the book is written, the late 1960s and early 1970s, is one of great importance for the Chicano communities in the southwest as they seek out their own political and cultural voice within the context of the United States. Cultural-nationalist perspectives that recovered cultural models to synthesize Chicano identity also dominate this stage of the movement. The recovery, or romanticizing, of pre-Columbian indigenous cultures, in particular Aztec, is offered up as justification for the Chicano presence in the United States. One of the leading symbols from that period is that of Aztlán, the mythical birthplace of the Aztecs and the land to which prophecies stated they would return. By proclaiming the southwestern United States as Aztlán, the architects of the movement created a direct link that transcended generations and justified the Chicano presence in the United States: Aztlán was the Chicano homeland. Herrera's chants in *Rebozos* are representative of this political and cultural move.

In 1977 Herrera entered the graduate program in anthropology at Stanford University. He completed his master's degree in social anthropology in 1980 and began, four years later, to write his doctoral dissertation. It was a project that he subsequently abandoned.

At the time, Herrera was working on a second collection of poems in Spanish. Titled *Akrílika* and mostly completed by 1981, it was not published until 1989. His second published collection was instead *Exiles of Desire*, first published in 1983. Whereas indigenous imagery predominated in *Rebozos,* in *Exiles* (as in *Akrílika*), Herrera focuses on urban imagery. Also, where in *Rebozos* there is a sense of affirmation and a calling for unity, *Exiles* focuses on more dystopian elements. The urban environment is presented as dehumanizing, where the individual is lost, exiled from the collective through a process of depersonalization brought about by progress. The urban rhythms that he performs expose themselves as fault lines affecting the Chicano urban community as the book advances through the different sections, titled "Exiles of Desire," "Tripitas," and "Photo-Poem of the Chicano Moratorium 1980 / L.A." In the Photo-Poem section, Herrera offers up poems meant to be "viewed" as photographs. By aligning the poem to the photograph, Herrera encases the moment, lifting it out of a historical progression and framing it. Photography here serves a number of functions. One, it works as a framing device, through the capturing of a specific, decisive moment. In this way the photograph functions as a carrier of historical memory. Second, it serves to reclaim the past, not by restoring what has been lost, but to attest to a moment that existed. In a sense, it reclaims the past and also brings it into the present as an object that verifies a person, a moment, a period.

In the final section of *Exiles*, "Mission Street Manifesto," Herrera offers a counterpoint to urban dehumanization. The poems from this section offer a hopeful call for rising up against global corporate culture. In the final poem, which gives title to this section of the book, Herrera returns to a collective voice, appealing for freedom against the tyranny of social evils. As a counter to the use of photography as a poetic vehicle, he returns to oral performance, in tune with musical rhythms. This poem, and the book in general, is a manifesto at once experimental and evoking Chicano movement poetry in its call for collective social action.

During this time period, Herrera worked at a number of positions, offering poetry workshops in the San Francisco schools, teaching in Intercultural Studies at DeAnza Community College, and teaching performance and creative-writing workshops at the New College of California. Meanwhile, he was composing poems that would eventually be published in his third collection, *Facegames: Poems* (1987). In 1988 Herrera entered the Iowa Writers Workshop to pursue an MFA, which he completed two years later. During his time in Iowa, *Akrílika* was published.

As previously noted, *Akrílika* was Herrera's second project, though it was not published until 1989. The experimentation that he had begun in *Rebozos* was continued with this collection of poems written in Spanish, and the collection was organized as if the poems were pictures at an exhibition. The book is broken up into six sections: "Exhibiciones" ("Exhibits"); "Galería" ("Gallery"); "Terciopelo" ("Velvet"); "Amarillo" ("Yellow"); "América" ("America"); "Eras" ("Era"); and "Kosmetik" ("Cosmetic"). Each section is a movement through a gallery of poems presented as paintings. Juxtaposing the visual with the written, Herrera asks us to envision the poem as an object represented. Indeed the problems of representation are a constant theme in his work. In particular, there is the representation not only of the poet, but also of the language that the poet uses. That the book is conceived in Spanish, at a time when many of the Chicano movement writers had moved into English, is telling. It is also worth pointing out that the Spanish that the poet employs is nonstandard, with orthographic changes such as *akrílica* instead of acrílica, or *kaos* instead of caos, or the use of such neologisms as *rimasmoradas* (violetrhymes). These are also lexical features that figure in his later poetry. Though he is employing Spanish, it is not standard. Infiltrated with English, his *Spanglish* is that of the urban Chicano communities in the United States: a hybrid language meant to convey a contemporary urban reality.

In the opening, "Nota sobre las exhibiciones" ("A Note on the Exhibits"), the only poem in the "Exhibiciones" section, he writes:

El dibujo corta, quizá mutila. La poesía mutila, quizás destruye. Estas no son páginas, son sólo astillas akrílicas en las manos.

(p. 4)

The sketch cuts, mutilates maybe. Poetry mutilates, perhaps destroys. These are not pages, just acrylic splinters in your hands.

In declaring this position, Herrera asks the reader/viewer to envision a poetic act as an act of not only creation but also destruction. Relying on painting as the visual medium for this book, he also asks the reader to focus on the distortive quality of pictorial representation: the painter, like the poet, must choose details carefully because of the impossibility of capturing everything.

The second section, "Galería," consists of seven poems, five of which describe a different artistic medium or genre: watercolor, portrait, acrylic, serigraph, and mural. This section, like the first, further sets up the reader as a participant viewing a series of artistic representations at a gallery. Four of the poems include dimensions in their titles to give the reader/viewer an idea of artworks' size. In the third section, "Terciopelo," Herrera offers up eleven poems in which the overarching imagery is that of texture: velvet, silk, sand, rock, and glass. One poem, "Quentino" ("Quentin"), is presented as a letter to an imprisoned Nicaraguan. This poem structures three out of the five texts from the fourth section, "Amarillo." As the title suggests, this section focuses on tonal variations. Though the color itself often symbolizes hope and happiness, at the same time it can also symbolize decay and deceit. This second meaning is closer to the tone of the poems in this section. The aforementioned cycle of poems on Quentino include journal fragments, a commentary on the journal, and a reworking of the earlier poem "Quentino." The other two poems from the section, "El cuarto amarillo" ("The Yellow Room") and "Ella quiere el anillo como aquél quiere el traje de la cicatriz / pero" ("She Wants the Ring Like He Wants the Suit of Scars / But"), complete a trajectory that leads from viewing a gallery exhibition to different artistic mediums and finally tonal varieties in a pictorial work. In other words, as viewers we have been led beyond a simple passive relationship with an artistic exhibition to a deeper understanding of what lies beyond the surface of the work.

The fifth section, "América," takes us into different subject matter. In particular, the poems from this section focus on urban imagery. The centerpiece of this section, and one of the neural centers of the work, is "Noche verde nuclear / Coreo-poema en dos láminas" ("Nuclear Green Night / Choreo-Poem in 2 Scenes"). The poem, presented as a theatrical piece, offers up an urban postapocalyptic representation, in which there are only four survivors after a nuclear war. Up to this poem, *Akrílica* has moved in a cycle that begins in darkness, with the poem "Eklipse / Acuarela 41 x 80 / San Francisco" ("Eclipse / Watercolor 41 x 80 / San Francisco") in the "Galería" section, and proceeds in a downward spiral through death, in the "Quentino" cycle, to the inevitable destruction of life in "Noche verde nuclear." The poem following this piece, "Es la tierra" ("Earth Chorus"), is a call to the Earth to fight against the tyranny of those who wield power over others. In the sixth section, "Eras," the three poems step back to focus on a pair of lovers. It is a brief respite following the dark themes that precede this section, before leading into the final section of the book, "Kosmetik." The five poems of this section offer broad strokes over the larger canvas that is *Akrílica*. The poem "Gráfika" is offered as a collage, or a cut-and-paste composition, in which Herrera incorporates fragments of poems from friends of his. The poem retraces themes that have been covered within the book, synthesizing urban with autobiographic imagery, as well as with events from political conflict zones, in particular Central America. This cut-and-paste structure, mirroring the overall book, ends with a series of letters and numbers and random words, as the poem returns to another type of apocalypse, the dismemberment of language as representation. And once again, as in the "Eras" section, the book steps back with a final poem-prose piece, "Para siempre, Maga" ("Forever, Maga"), which concludes with the undermining of borders to create a space for two lovers.

"Para siempre, Maga," is another of the nerve centers in the book, as it touches upon issues of national cultural identities and how they are fragmented by borders. The narrator, Steve, always frequents the same bookstore in Tijuana to visit with "Maga," to talk and be with her. He tells her stories of border crossers, asks for books from Joaquín Mortiz or Seix Barral, or from Tijuana's Centro Cultural de la Raza, and writes poetry to her.

Steve tries to become "Mexican" by speaking on Mexican themes. Maga responds with scorn. She laughs at the poetry of "Esteves" and at his concern for the poor in Mexico. She states, "¿Qué te importan los ilegales? ¿Qué sabes tú de los polleros y su gula? ¿Acaso conoces a las putas y sus escenarios de esclavitud?"(What do you care about illegals? What do you know about the *coyotes* and their greed? And now you know about the whores and their situations of enslavement? p. 158) Her harshest criticism is aimed at his Chicano identity:

> Vienes de San Diego con tu ristra Chicana; bola de pochos altaneros. Y compran libros de Miguel León-Portilla, Garibay y Octavio Paz. Los compran como compran el pan de *La Tapatía*. Idólatras. A poco crees que a Don Octavio Paz le importa a lo que llamas "El movimiento chicano"? Fanfarronadas. Tú y tus tales chicanos—hasta con X se la hechan, xicanos—caen como santos paracaidistas y dan sus conferencias y presentan sus paneles *para el Pueblo*. ¿A ver pues, cuál pueblo fue a escucharlos? solamente esas liguillas de macicitos adolescentes. Babosadas.
>
> (p. 160)

> You come from San Diego with your Chicano line; bunch of self-important *pochos*. And then they buy books by Miguel León Portilla, Garibay and Octavio Paz. They buy them as they buy bread from *La Tapatía*. Idolizers. Do you really believe that don Octavio Paz gives a damn about what you call "The Chicano Movement?" Absurdities. You and your so-called Chicanos—they even write it with an X, Xicanos—coming down like some holy paratroopers to give your conferences and present your panels *for the People*. All right now, what people came to hear you? Just those gangs of immature teen Clowns!

This lengthy attack is aimed at undermining the basis of Steve's Chicano identity. Maga cares nothing for his idealization of indigenous Mexico. With this, the text attacks a Chicanismo built upon an illusory nostalgia, a misreading of pre-Columbian Mexican myths, that fails to take into account current Mexican border culture. But her arguments fall on deaf ears. For another voice enters the bookstore, a woman looking for her husband Steve, whom she finds reading a magazine. This woman speaks to him as if to a child, in condescending tones. She exposes Steve as a dreamer fantasizing over a picture of a Spanish actress, Magdalena Murillo.

However, this does not faze him either: Steve is too far gone into the fantasy. He promises to take Maga to the border, to show her

> las transparentes multitudes marchando hacia sus cajas sagradas de perfectos deseos y perfectas memorias. . . . Al fin estaremos juntos. Ven amor. Quedaremos escritos en la cumbre de algún precipicio que nadie divisará; uno sobre el otro, como una X mayúscula sobra la tierra del Sur. Brillante. Para siempre. Para siempre, Maga.
>
> (pp. 162–164)

> the transparent multitudes marching to their sacred coffins of perfect desire and perfect memory. . . . We will finally be together. Come, my love. We will leave our mark on the tip of a precipice that no one will see: one on top of the other, a capital X over the south. Brilliant. Forever. Forever, Maga.

By attacking Steve's sense of identity, both Maga and his wife cause him to retreat and cross a border. The promise of "Para siempre, Maga" is the promise of the border as a zone of safety: once the couple crosses it, they will be together. The image of the cross (X) takes significance in the story, for not only will Steve and Maga cross a border but they will also "cross" it out. But the border space that Herrera invokes is not the United States or Mexico: it is an amalgamation of the two, an impossibility that can only be made possible in an interior space. We see the reclamation of an identity that lies for Herrera in an inward journey breaking away from the Chicano and Mexicano patriarchal cultures into a Mestizo identity implicated in a constant journey between borders.

The poetic structure of *Akrílica*, as the poetic voice of Herrera, owes a debt to beat poetry, as well as to other contemporary Chicano poets, as he acknowledges in "Gráfika." At the same time, one could note links to the avant-garde work of the Chilean poet Vicente Huidobro, who once stated that a poet was like a small God, more like a creator and not simply a medium for representing reality. In particular, *Akrílica* could be likened to Huidobro's monumental poem "Altazor" (1931). The poem, in part a distillation of Huidobro's theory of *creacionismo* (creationism), presents a downward movement that concludes in its final canto with the destruction of language represented as a seemingly irrational series of letters and words. Creationism, as proposed by Huidobro, is above all an aesthetic theory that aims to negate a past poetic history by offering an image of the poet as, above all, a creator.

To arrive at this renovation of poetic language, a destruction of the past is also needed. *Akrílica*, as a poetic manifesto, accomplishes this through its strict refusal to obey language or poetic genre. The book opposes the ideology of oppression through the invention and use of a language that refuses assimilation to any dominant cultural norms: Spanglish, which becomes a revolutionary language. The poems, in turn, are presented as paintings; some can be read as prose, others are intersected by competing dialogues. There is also the spiraling structure downward to two acts of destruction, a nuclear one in "Noche verde nuclear" and a poetic one in "Gráfika." Whereas Huidobro concludes his work with a random arrangement of letters, Herrera offers up what lies beyond the destruction of language. As in "Para siempre, Maga," that space beyond is the one where the lovers meet and cross out borders, opening up a site for creative renovations.

Another salient feature of the work is in the title itself. Acrylic as a medium is a twentieth-century invention, first marketed as a paint that could be mixed with oil paints in the 1950s. Its prominence came in the 1960s, however, with the invention of water-based acrylics. Artists like Andy Warhol, Robert Motherwell, and David Hockney experimented with the new medium, which offered the option of being either painted on thick in impasto style, mimicking oil paint, or being watered down like watercolor. It was a new medium, bridging two traditional ones—oil and watercolor. As such, it was also a revolutionary medium in that it allowed painters to expand their forms of creative expression by allowing them to break away from the histories of oil and watercolor painting. In a sense, it allowed painters to invent a new history. Within this context, we can begin to trace a general outline of the project of *Akrílica* as a work that calls for a new poetry of social action and a renovation of Chicano cultural identity.

It is in *Rebozos, Exiles,* and *Akrílica* that Herrera lays down the poetic bases that he will continue to explore in later books. Questions of representation and the power of poetic expression are put forth in these early works. Throughout, he pushes for a poetic language that teaches resistance and liberation.

Upon completion of his MFA in 1990, Herrera joined the Chicano and Latin American Studies faculty at the California State University, Fresno. It is a position that he still maintains, and since 2001 he has served as chair of his department.

After his return to California, Herrera published an astonishing fourteen books: *Memoria(s) from an Exile's Notebook of the Future* (1993); *The Roots of a Thousand Embraces: Dialogues* (1994); *Night Train to Tuxtla* (1994); *Calling the Doves / El canto a las palomas* (1995); *Love after the Riots* (1996); *Mayan Drifter: Chicano Poet in the Lowlands of America* (1997); *Border-Crosser with a Lamborghini Dream: Poems* (1999); *Lotería Cards and*

Fortune Poems: A Book of Lives (1999); *Crash-BoomLove: A Novel in Verse* (1999); *The Upside Down Boy / El niño de cabeza* (2000); *Thunder-weavers / Tejedoras de rayos* (2000); *Giraffe on Fire* (2001); *Grandma & Me at the Flea / Los meros meros remateros* (2002); and *Notebooks of a Chile Verde Smuggler* (2002). The books range from collections of poetry to works dedicated to children and young adults.

This increase in publication activity coincides with the increase in Latino publications by major publishing houses, spearheaded by such Chicana women as Sandra Cisneros and Ana Castillo. This Latino "renaissance" continued throughout the 1990s with the publications of such writers as Junot Díaz, Julia Alvarez, Cristina García, and Martín Espada. The mid- to late 1990s also brought about a generational shift in Chicano cultural identity, as a generation of writers who were born in the 1960s began to publish and question the founding principles of the Chicano movement. As products of that movement, this generation, still unnamed, continued pushing the boundaries of Chicano cultural expression through such writers, performance artists, filmmakers, and musicians as Lalo López, Rubén Martínez, Michele Serros, Yxta Maya Murray, Culture Clash, Robert Rodriguez, Lysa Flores, Luis Alfaro, and Guillermo Gómez Peña. Herrera, as participant in the Chicano movement, and as teacher to the later generation, is very much a bridge between these two generations, as his poetry shifts from the Native Americanist strain of the movement in *Rebozos* to the poetic renovations and touches of humor in *Night Train to Tuxtla.*

Coinciding with the rise in interest in Latino cultural production, the Latino communities have also paradoxically become more divided. Herrera attributes this to the fact that contemporary writers, unlike those of the late 1960s and the 1970s, do not travel:

One thing that has retreated amidst this techno-lit is the idea of "the writer on the road." In the past we were all doing the Kerouac shuffle. That is how we connected with each other and shared and learned our work. . . . Things were created back then because many writers physically moved their bodies and made things happen at other sites with other writers.

(p. 20)

For him, the writers of the Chicano generation traveled because of a need to connect with other poets and artists. Contemporary Latino writers, due to the easier access to publication venues, the creation of communities in localized regions, and the advent of e-mail and the Internet, do not have the same need for physical travel.

Herrera's 1994 collection of poetry, *Night Train to Tuxtla*, reflects on this issue of travel and of wandering, while at the same time focusing on themes of representation and political expression. Composed of five sections, "Listening to Santana," "Night Train to Tuxtla," "These Words Are Synonymous, Now," "On the Day of the Dead, Mr. Emptiness Sings of Love," and "Letter to the Hungry Students of Berlin," the book moves across a landscape constantly in change.

The eight poems from the first section, "Listening to Santana," focus on the 1970s and the Chicano movement. The poetic verses are electric guitar riffs aimed directly at the heart of the readers. At the same time, the rhythm Herrera establishes sets down a groove that travels the length of the section.

In "Rolling to Taos on an Aztec Mustang," he writes about a drive through the southwestern United States with a troupe of Aztec dancers. The geography the poem routes moves from Tijuana to Austin, Texas, for the second Floricanto Festival. The festivals were events where Chicanos got together to perform and to meet other Chicanos from different regions. They were fundamental in fostering the spirit of collectivity and community. Passing through El Paso, Herrera recalls his personal history:

When we passed El Paso
in Mario Aguilar's white Mustang,

288

I thought of my mother, Lucha,
who grew up in el Segundo Varrio.

I thought of la *calle* Kansas,
la Stanton,
Paisano Drive
la Overland,
la Segunda,
la Tercera,
la Poplar—

the streets were fragments
of an incomplete story I carried.

(p. 27)

Arriving in Austin, the troupe members participate in the event and watch other performers, including poets RaulrSalinas and Veronica Cunningham, writers Miguel Méndez, Tomás Rivera, and Oscar "Zeta" Acosta, and playwright Teresa Palomo Acosta. From there Herrera and crew drive to New Mexico to dance in the towns of Peñasco and Taos. Herrera effectively captures the spirit of a community willing to physically move for their cause, doing the Kerouac shuffle. At the time, through the direct references to the people he meets and the places he passes through, the poem adds another dimension to the geography that he maps. By writing about this period and these places, he lifts them out of the past to maintain them in the present.

Two of the titles from this section, "How to Do the Merengue in the End Zone" and "M.O.C.O.S. (Mexicans or Chicanos or Something)," are references to works by the Chicano comedy troupe Culture Clash. These references also demonstrate another element of Herrera's poetry: his frequent use of humor as a counter to dark themes or as a way to illustrate a point. In this particular case, these references also act as a bridge to more contemporary Chicano cultural production and to one of the main characteristics of this generation: the use of irony.

The second section, "Night Train to Tuxtla," travels geographically and temporally, expand-ing out from the California Chicano scene of the 1970s to the conflict zones in Latin America in the 1980s. The fifth text, "Memoria(s) from an Exile's Notebook of the Future," published earlier as a separate chapbook, expands the geography to encompass conflict zones from around the globe and throughout history. The exile here comes to represent a collective history of exile and wandering. In the third section, "These Words Are Synonymous, Now," Herrera returns to the urban imagery of southern California. The three poems from this section also take place in the 1990s, generally pushing the book forward to the contemporary scene. The fourth section, "On the Day of the Dead, Mr. Emptiness Sings of Love," contains fifteen poems that radiate outward from the previous section. That is, they expand to include urban images as well as focus on the plight of the indigenous and the poor in Latin America.

The opening poem, "Norteamérica, I Am Your Scar," situates itself in the border, echoing Gloria Anzaldúa's famed commentary on the U.S./Mexican border as an open wound that bleeds. The border is a scar that marks all those who cross it. It is a call to subvert the systems of domination, in a move similar to "Para siempre, Maga" from his previous work, *Akrílica*. The poetic voice is collective, rather than individual as in the poems from "Listening to Santana." This collective voice demands to be seen and recognized—witnessed. In the poem "The Sea during Springtime," a similar process of recognition takes place, though not from the perspective of a collective voice. Here it is an individual, the poet, who invokes his family history. In a type of almanac of the dead, Herrera writes his family into the present, so that they are not lost in the past. The overarching theme of this section of *Night Train to Tuxtla* is an invocation to remember one's past, to bear witness to who one is. In the final section, "Letter to the Hungry Students of Berlin," Herrera directs his attention to Europe, in particular Germany after the fall of the Berlin wall. The poem opens with a reference to the sky above, the same sky shared by all. Including references to diverse geographic areas and different historical epochs, Herrera maps out a space for the "hungry" students to reach out and create their new society.

In 1995 Herrera published *Calling the Doves/El canto de las palomas,* his first foray into children's literature. Though he was unsure at first about writing for children, it was a logical progression for this artist, activist, and teacher. The book is a recollection of his migrant-worker childhood, and a celebration of that life and that of his parents. The book won a number of awards, including the Ezra Jack Keats award, and was listed as a Smithsonian Notable Book for Children. Subsequent children's and young-adults books have continued to refer to his childhood and have included CrashBoom-Love, which won the Americas Award, *The Upside Down Boy/El niño de cabeza,* and *Grandma & Me at the Flea/Los meros meros remat.*

Mayan Drifter: Chicano Poet in the Lowlands of America was published in 1997. It is a lyrical ethnographic account of a trip that he conducted to the Lacandon region of southern Mexico between December 1992 and mid-January 1993, before the start of the Zapatista revolution in 1994. The roots of the work lie in Herrera's first voyage to the Mayan lowlands in 1970, when he was an undergraduate anthropology student at UCLA, traveling in Mexico documenting different forms of indigenous cultural expression. While this work is ethnographic in nature, it is not strictly a sociological document. It could be called personal ethnography, as the book itself is in part an ethnography of the conditions of the Mayans living in the jungle of Chiapas and in part a personal narrative. Through poetry, drama, and ethnographic observations, Herrera guides the reader through history, memory, and place, juxtaposing the life of the Maya and reflections on his own life as a traveler.

The first two chapters, "Gathering a Mayan Repertoire" and "Welcome to El Prospero," are the most "ethnographic," in that they offer an objective analysis about the region and its Mayan communities. This objectivity is interjected with his self-aware subjective commentary, the result being an objective commentary aware that the hand that guides it is itself subjective. As he travels through the region, he remembers his own life as he makes connections between his migrant autobiography and the path that has brought him back to Chiapas after thirty years. He also questions his own motives for wanting to make the journey again, and questions his own seeking of "authentic" experiences. He realizes the cultural baggage that he is carrying distorts his own intentions.

He writes about the people that he meets on his journey and the different roles that they play in the unfolding drama that is Chiapas and its history. These include anthropology students from Mexico City; the Na Bolom research center, dedicated to working with the communities of the Lacandon rain forest of Chiapas; the people Herrera calls the "traveling men" who have passed through the Mayan regions, including Fray Diego de Landa, Frans Blom, William Coe, and himself; and the Ladinos and the Mayan indigenous communities. And there are always the tricks of memory. The Mayans he carries with him in his memory have changed: some are workers with trucks and other trappings of consumer culture, such as big-screen televisions and indoor plumbing; others sell their culture to the tourists passing through, either as guides into the jungle or through the vending of objects like arrows. The Na Bolom research center that he also remembers has become by the early 1990s a resort hotel staffed by the indigenous, open to ecotourists who take tours into the jungle, wanting to get a feel for "authentic" Mayan life. All the while, he tries to shake the feeling that he too is some kind of cultural imperialist.

One of the justifications for his trip is to seek out an old friend, K'ayum. The search is problematic because, as Herrera admits, the only information he has on this person is a name. Arriving in a village he thinks may be the right one, he stays with the family of K'ayum, who is away. When he returns, Herrera discovers that he found the wrong person, that the K'ayum he seeks is not the one he finds. This discovery serves as a metaphor for the book: drifting opens paths for self-discovery. The chance meeting with K'ayum is not entirely new; Herrera had met this man briefly on his trip thirty years before. Given this previous encounter, K'ayum graciously opens his house to this visitor from the Chicano borderlands. During his stay, Herrera travels with his new friend and his family, all the while making note of the pace of development in southern Mexico. Roads have been built into the jungle, allowing the transport of goods from the city to flow into the communities. Leaving Chiapas, he reflects on the changes to the communities and the changes to himself.

Chapter four, "Jaguar Hotel," is a two-act play set in an old hotel in a remote area of southern Mexico. The characters are a compendium of the individuals that Herrera has met in his travels and reflect a cross-section of contemporary Latino and indigenous identities. They include Canek, a young Mayan male influenced by urban culture, wearing rubber sandals and carrying a Walkman; Chan Ma'ax Viejo, father of Canek and a village elder, carrier of the collective history of his community; Lionel, a middle-aged Chicano professor who has bought into the middle class; Margarita, a Chicana activist; and Oscar, a Mexican anthropology student. Against the backdrop of presidential speeches about plans for the modernization of Chiapas, the uprising of the Zapatistas, as well as an invasion by the Mexican army to quell the insurgency, the characters act out a play marked by discussions about the effects of globalization on an indigenous community that is itself undergoing a state of transition.

Chapter five, "Anahuak Vortex," is a poem centered in the Mexican vortex: Mexico City. Rising out of this center, Herrera gives voice to those who would fight against the government policies of the PRI, the political party that ruled

Mexico for seventy-two years, whose political might shut down protest movements in the late 1960s and 1970s and whose neoliberal policies in the 1980s and 1990s widened the gap between rich and poor. The poem criticizes the bloody history of the PRI: the massacre of Tlatelolco, in which the government ordered the military to fire upon a peaceful political protest on 2 October 1968; the secret war against insurgents in the state of Guerrero in the 1970s; and the military repression of the Mayans and the indigenous communities in the 1990s. Herrera denounces this history and the politics of globalization as he evokes the indigenous communities oppressed and left drifting by this Anahuac vortex.

In the fifth chapter, "Mayan Drifter," he writes a letter to K'ayum Ma'ax, reflecting on the state of Mexico following the assassination of Luis Donaldo Colosio in Tijuana. Though Colosio was the political candidate for the PRI and the man who would have been president, in the months prior to the election the belief had been formed that he was going to be a genuine reformer. He was perceived as having separated from the neoliberal economic policies of his predecessor, Carlos Salinas de Gortari, and at the same time breaking with his presidency. Colosio was assassinated while campaigning in the northern Mexican border city of Tijuana, in the area of Lomas Taurinas. The shockwave was felt throughout the country. The PRI nominated Ernesto Zedillo as its candidate, and he was expected to continue the policies of Salinas de Gortari. In the days following the election of Zedillo, the economy suffered a major downturn, almost bankrupting the nation, and on 1 January 1994, the day the North American Free Trade Agreement (NAFTA) took effect, the Zapatistas in Chiapas rose up against the government. Herrera writes about this recent history and how he has heard that K'ayum and the rest of his village have fled the Zapatistas, possibly because of the privileged position the village had with the government. As he writes, he seeks his own place against the drama unfolding in Mexico. At the same time, he writes of the drifting of Mexico, drifting into violence by political assassinations and drifting into hope by an indigenous revolution. The letter ends with Herrera offering flowers for Tijuana and for Chiapas, flowers in the form of a book that reflects his own journey across the borders.

The work is part autobiography, as he reflects on his own personal history; part meditation on self and representation as he strives to find ways to talk about the Mayas without falling back on the discourse of the anthropologist; part analysis of place where ancient rural communities meet with contemporary urban dwellers, where cultures meet and press together; and part a reflection on the impact of neoliberal policies in southern Mexico, on NAFTA and on the impact of globalization on marginalized cultures.

On the reception of the book, Herrera has said:

> Many young students have contacted me about *Mayan Drifter* and its theme of a Chicano going back with questions of ancestry. Many people want to learn about their culture with a real "ahistorical" attitude. . . . History has been used as a "junkie" treasure of places, names, and famous events people throw around freely. These same people are not willing to find a new perspective by exploring their own origins—right in their own backyard.
>
> (González, p. 19)

This is a central element to the work of Herrera: the seeking of roots through an exploration of their own origins. In his drifting across borders and regions, Herrera has explored ideas of identity formation and the changes one undergoes in constructing one's identity. In particular, his search has led him to consider the idea of nation. *Mayan Drifter* synthesizes this search as what America means, how best to represent it, and, above all, how to speak of the marginalized and oppressed in America. His idea of America is not simply the United States, but rather a space that includes the continents of North and South America. To write about this

notion of America, he travels to Mexico, to its southern border. It is on borders that questions of nation are focalized, and since Chiapas is the poorest state in Mexico and had been undergoing political turmoil for years, and given Herrera's previous contacts there, it is a logical place for him to travel to address these issues as well as to seek out his own place in relation to these types of struggles.

Mayan Drifter, like much of Herrera's work, is situated in a border zone. In "The Third Conversation," one of the two sections of the introductory chapter "American Preludes," he writes:

> Juan was well aware that when he talked of Mexico, he was actually talking about Latin America. . . . As soon as he mentioned Latin America, he would slip; he knew this. The rhetoric would falter and soon enough he would end up referring to Malaysia or the Philippines; each landscape was interchangeable, Third World borders seemed to be illusory—the border work was more like an Escher pattern superimposed throughout various zones of exploitation throughout the globe.
>
> (p. 11)

Training his writing to zones of conflict, as he has done in other works, Herrera offers a voice to those who have been left without one or who have been marginalized by structures of power: the Mayans in southern Mexico; the Mexican American migrant communities in the southwestern United States; workers in Brazil and Asia; and Chicanos living in the barrios of California. The border zones that make up his work intersect and collide and are regions where people live and cross on a daily basis.

In 1999 Herrera published *Border-Crosser with a Lamborghini Dream*, a book that looks back upon the twentieth century with rage. One reviewer stated:

> Anyone who thinks high art and performance poetry don't mix should re-read "Howl" and then pick up Herrera's latest, following 1994's *Night*

Train to Tuxtla. Wryly drawing on our expectations of "ethnic" poetry, . . . Herrera performs the rare trick of simultaneously speaking from a self-aware, culturally marginalized perspective, while refusing to limit his poetic horizons.

(*Publishers Weekly* 1999, p. 91)

The reference to Allen Ginsberg's "Howl" is not casual. The opening poem in the book, "Punk Half Panther," is Herrera's own *grito* (howl) to the end of the century. Whereas the beat-generation poetry flowed to the rhythms of jazz, this poem shakes to the twin sounds of hip-hop and punk rock, the thunderous beats of post-1994-riots Los Angeles. It is a brilliant opening salvo, full of tension. The poem opens at night and moves forward, kicking into overdrive, tracing a geography that progresses from urban Los Angeles to Cuba, Thailand, and Africa, radiating outward and encompassing late-twentieth-century oppression to cast it aside, to move beyond and cross into another space.

The second section, "Blood on the Wheel," contains eighteen poems with the word "blood" in their titles. These are darker and harder-edged than other poems that Herrera has written. With a tough and jagged tone, they focus on death and destruction in a world awash in blood. They are responses to power, how it is given, received, and suffered. In the third section, "My Rice Queen," Herrera steps back from the jagged verse of the previous section, constructing poems filtered through an aesthetic, borderized language. A number of poems from this section are also constructed around an alternative alphabet, which Herrera has called a "webback affabet": "P is for ask me once again;" "X is for fancy tacos sold w/ Mayan Rebellion." This illegal alphabet carries within it the border-crossing nature of this book. The fourth section, "Broadway Indian," is a poem that Herrera defines as a *canto* (chant) divided into nine subsets. As in *Rebozos*, Herrera continues to experiment with the poetic form. In this particular case, the words flow to a different rhythm than that found in "Punk Half Panther." Literally, the words flow across and down the page, the surface of the book becoming an integral part of the representation of the poem. The canto is dedicated to the indigenous communities of north-central Mexico (the Huichol, Cora, and Tepehuano). The fifth section, which brings closure to the book, is titled "We Are All Saying the Same Thing." Each poem in this section speaks to different geographical regions, traveling across a landscape of oppression.

It has been said that the twentieth century was the century of migration, with massive movements of communities across borders, oceans, and countries. It could also be seen as the century of space, of geography, as French philosopher Michel Foucault predicted. Places are connected by the different migrations. *Border-Crosser* explores this notion, as it explores ways of being in the world. These are not linear poems; they cut across time and space, superimposing multiple places on one another in a dense pattern. Ultimately, the book is also about being an active participant in a society.

In 2002 Herrera published *Notebooks of a Chile Verde Smuggler*. It is his poetic autobiography, tracing his life, his work, and his role as teacher, scholar, and activist. It is not ordered chronologically, at least not in what one could consider chronology. Rather, it follows a spatial-temporal path, one that moves forward and back. As such, it is his most personal work to date.

It consists of five "books," each one corresponding to a different aspect of his work. The first, "Hard Curas on 'C' Street," refers to the address in San Diego where he grew up. The title poem is a memory from the 1950s of having a toe infection cured by his mother, the hard way. She used an old Gillette razor and a pan of hot, salted water. The second poem, "Limpia for Walking into Clear Campos," moves forward to the early 1990s, when Herrera was teaching at creative workshops at the University of Southern Illinois, Carbondale, for a year. The text is a chant for relaxing, for moving across an icy landscape. He repeats the refrain "I drop my burdens" as a structural meter, a coda that relaxes him further and further so that he will float over the ice. Once the stage is set, the hard *cura* (cure) sets in. The third poem, "Immigrant Fortune Teller Machine," is written in an Afro-Latin voice ("trow out all that razz / matazz affabet") that tells the poet to let go, to step back inside himself and remember his past.

The first book sets the stage for the interior voyage that takes place in the second and third books. "Chile Con Karma," the second book, is the most extensive of the five. Consisting of poems, journal fragments, and "Undelivered Letters to Victor," the book is an accounting of his life, work, and the people he has encountered. The "Victor" of the "Undelivered Letters" is National Book Award–winning writer Victor Martínez. Like Rilke's "Letters to a Young Poet," these letters offer an insight into Herrera's relationships with other writers. He writes about the Chicano movement, the opening up of the publishing houses to Chicano writers, the meaning of America, and the seeking of roots by the younger generation through the recovery of such images as Aztlán. As in "Para siempre, Maga," he questions this last theme, wondering if things ever really change. In such poems as "Chican Literature 100," "How to Enroll in a Chicano Studies Class," and "How to Be a Warrior for the Aztlán Liberation Army (ALA)," he puts into question the idea of fixed cultural identities by ironically undermining the idea of Chicano studies. In this way, he aligns his work with the work of such younger-generation Chicano performers and writers as Culture Clash, Lalo López, and Michelle Serros. These are artists who have moved beyond the nationalist stance of the early *Movimiento* to reconfigure notions of Chicanismo for a generation born after the movement.

It needs to be pointed out that Herrera is not against Chicano identities, but rather that he questions constructing an identity through a simple fetishizing of the old as an authentic experience. He champions and recognizes those who would learn from the movement to become community organizers and activists while remaining cognizant of the changes within the society, as in "La Marlene Grew Up in the Movimiento."

Book Three, "On the Other Side of Puccinni's," bridges the second and fourth books. Consisting of two poems, one of them dedicated to the memory of José Antonio Burciaga, they come from a transitional period in Herrera's writing career, marked by his second trip south to Chiapas, the publication of *Night Train to Tuxtla,* and the passing away of Burciaga in 1996. The death of this Chicano poet, artist, and essayist is noted in one of Herrera's "Undelivered Letters to Victor" as an "end of an era" (*Notebooks,* p. 134). The death of Burciaga is one of the deaths that weighs upon him, like the death of his father and mother. These deaths he keeps present, close to him. From his father, he received the need for travel; from his mother, the love of music and poetry; from Burciaga, a love of laughter and irony. These structure Book Four, "Hispanopoly: The Upwardly Mobile Identity Game Show." In this book, Herrera trains his eye on contemporary Latino identity and its commodification. Employing the structure of a game show hosted by Sancho, referred to as the "stereotypical sellout," and his sidekick, Wanna B. White, the contestants vie for prizes, including a "2003 two-tone Chevy-con-Bush Slowrider" and one hundred kilos of PRI cigars, as well as a round trip for two to the Chiapas rain forest, with lodging at the PEMEX Motel. Incorrect responses by the contestants means deportation by the *Migra* (border patrol). Exchanges include:

WANNA B: "Mucho Fashion," Sancho. Please identify the following new fashion trend, pende-jos: "Beef-flavored non-cholesterol polyester campesino-print handkerchief, also comes in plaid pork and two-tone menudo."

(*Notebooks,* p. 161)

The text plots an ironic course in a game show whose aim is to "gain your true identity through the acquisition of someone else's property, usually lower than you" (p. 161). In texts employing the same type of topical cutting-edge humor found in the work of Culture Clash or in *Pocho* magazine, Herrera dismantles Latino cultural stereotypes through parody. For the younger generation, and as used by Herrera here, parody functions as a distancing strategy from the previous generation, while also imbuing it with new meanings. The final book, "How to Make a Chile Verde Smuggler," is a summation of the previous books.

Humor plays a strong role in *Notebooks,* as in poems like "Fuzzy Equations":

> Humility + oppression + a Virgin – territory = Latin America
> Democracy + annihilation by color x 12 = Education
> . . . .
> Two kilos of corn tortillas x roped luggage boxes = Latin promo
> Hard-core Chicana writer ÷ hard-core Latino writer = Fried race.

(p. 74)

This ironic perspective, tinged with sadness, is a liberating force. Subverting the notion of poem as an aesthetic, subjective object, he presents a poem at its most objective: a set of mathematical equations. The equations all seem random, but their finality exposes a "truth." At the same time, his "fuzzy" math asks the reader to consider the meanings behind the equations.

In another poem, "Don't Worry, Baby," he offers a list of things that worry him:

> I worry about exotic birds learning too much English
> I worry about Sub-Comandante Marcos getting acne under the ski mask
> . . . .
> I worry about tourists who think maids are natural
> . . . .
> I worry about the return of folk singers
> . . . .
> I worry about Spielberg's next ethnic movie

> I worry about New Age music repeating itself
> . . . .
> I worry about Mexicans digging their stereotypes
> . . . .
> I worry about children with careers
> . . . .
> I worry about blues without color
> . . . .
> I worry about high school cafeterias as artillery ranges
> I worry about what I am saying
> I worry about people who say "Don't worry, Baby."

(pp. 26–29)

Again, this presentation, humorous on the surface, exposes certain awful points about contemporary society. Each worry carries with it a cultural weight that bears down on the poet.

As Herrera's most recent publication, *Notebooks* offers his statement on Chicano cultural identity from the *Movimiento* to the post-Chicano generation of the late 1990s. In reference to whether political poetry can wake people to action yet still remain relevant, he says:

> That is a stinging question because we have to assume there is a difference between poetry, political action, and people. . . . We live in a post-Einstein world where consciousness explodes and implodes and there are black holes everywhere. We don't even see these black holes where many conflicts are being born. The act of writing poetry is the very act of being and living—the very act of spirit.
> (González, p. 20)

Notebooks is a continuation of this response. While not structured chronologically, it moves as memory does; in leaps and bounds. Traveling across the landscape of his life, Herrera offers a book that is as searching as *Mayan Drifter.*

WANDERING POETICS

Emergent cultural identities make use of hybrid strategies as oppositional forms of resistance—

295

or subversion—to dominant, national cultures. We can look at the Chicano movement as one such cultural identity that employs hybridity in the construction of a self-identity, fusing together issues of politics, gender, and home in the creation of Aztlán and later the Borderlands. The work of Juan Felipe Herrera positions itself between national borders and questions not just the concept of America but also that of Chicano writing.

Herrera plots out geographies on maps that are unwritten. There are a number of binary oppositions in his work: urban/rural, Chicano/ post-Chicano, American/Latin American, roots/ migrancy. But he does not simply invoke them to maintain their structures. Using poetry as a tool for destruction and creation, he moves beyond binary oppositions to deconstruct them and expose the false hierarchies that formed them. He draws new maps upon the old.

One of the most common metaphors in Herrera's work is that of wandering. Wandering can be expressed through diverse means. In relationship to Herrera's writing, it is most often related to liminality, to being in in-between places. Liminality as an expression of wandering implies a transitional structuring—the way that *Notebooks* is not presented chronologically or the manner in which *Mayan Drifter* is presented, not just as a sociological document but also as a poetic statement, and an autobiographical inquiry.

Border culture wanders in the sense that being in the space between countries produces a mixture of hybrid cultural effects, including bilingualism and sampling, as in cut and paste. These are employed as devices for creating distance between different traditions while at the same time evoking them. Belonging to various regions, Herrera's border texts employ such hybrid narrative strategies that refer back to liminal, marginalized communities. That is to say, hybrid strategies such as these open up an interstitial space in the world and allow for multiple possibilities of being. This intervening space transforms the myth of a single temporal order (be it "Modernity," "Progress," or "United States") into multiple orders and histories.

At the heart of this type of wandering culture is the construction of an identity out of a migrant space, for borders are never fixed, never certain, never stable. To stand on the border is to be in the beyond and inhabit multiple spaces at once. The migrant who moves through the space of the borderlands is deterritorialized and transformed by the push and pull of national cultures.

In the borderlands, wandering becomes a central issue in the discussion of place. The border dweller develops a sense of place by relating to the surrounding landscape. This relation implies a mediation between the self and the "other"; it is a dialogical ethics that is constructed in the approach to the "other." This approach in relation to a text takes place on different levels: the approach of the reader to the page, the approach of the writer to the characters, the approach of the characters to others, and so on, in a complex dialogue of shifting relations.

CONCLUSIONS

Responding to a question by Ray González about the state of contemporary Chicano poetry in relation to the creative expression during the Chicano movement, Herrera notes that one of the main differences is that the contemporary poets are becoming far more localized. This is distinct from the Chicano-generation poets, who would travel from place to place, doing the "Kerouac shuffle" and adding a physical element to the notion of the generation as a *Movimiento*. This movement through space helped bridge the Chicano communities in the southwest and aided in the further strengthening of the movement as a support group separated by geography but united by creative expression. Contemporary Chicano poetry has lost this sense of travel and has chosen instead to build local literary scenes where the support group is connected in place and expression. He states:

> They create at home. There is a danger in staying home all the time. [The extended Chicano *movimiento* community] is now eroded, and we have the literary *movimiento* in multifaceted groups staying at home all over the country.
>
> (González, p. 19)

In the early 1990s, Lauro Flores noted the dearth of critical studies on the work of Juan Felipe Herrera. Unfortunately, this still remains the case, in spite of the strength and vitality of his poetry. In *Mayan Drifter,* Herrera cites a line of verse from another Chicano poet, Benjamín Alire Saénz, who writes, "I want to write an American poem." Juan Felipe Herrera has written an American poem, situated in the juncture between the United States and Mexico, uniting the continent.

Selected Bibliography

WORKS OF JUAN FELIPE HERRERA

POETRY

Rebozos of Love/We Have Woven/Sudor de Pueblos/On Our Back. San Diego, Calif.: Toltecas en Axtlan, 1974.

Exiles of Desire. Houston: Arte Público Press, 1985.

Facegames: Poems. San Francisco: As Is/So & So Press, 1987.

Akrílica. Translated by Stephen Kessler and Sesshu Foster, with Dolores Bravo, Magaly Fernandez, and the author. Santa Cruz, Calif.: Alcatraz Editions, 1989.

Memoria(s) from an Exile's Notebook of the Future. Santa Monica, Calif.: Santa Monica College Press, 1993.

Night Train to Tuxtla. Tucson: University of Arizona Press, 1994.

The Roots of a Thousand Embraces: Dialogues. San Francisco: Manic D. Press, 1994.

Love after the Riots. Willimantic, Conn.: Curbstone Press, 1996.

Border-Crosser with a Lamborghini Dream: Poems. Tucson: University of Arizona Press, 1999.

Loteria Cards and Fortune Poems: A Book of Lives. San Francisco: City Lights Books, 1999.

Thunderweavers/Tejedoras de rayos. Tucson: University of Arizona Press, 2000.

Giraffe on Fire. Tucson: University of Arizona Press, 2001.

Grandma & Me at the Flea/Los meros meros remateros. San Francisco: Children's Books Press, 2002.

Notebooks of a Chile Verde Smuggler. Tucson: University of Arizona Press, 2002.

OTHER WORKS

Calling the Doves/El canto a las palomas. San Francisco: Children's Book Press, 1995.

Mayan Drifter: Chicano Poet in the Lowlands of America. Philadelphia: Temple University Press, 1997.

Laughing Out Loud, I Fly: Poems in English and Spanish. New York: HarperCollins, 1998.

CrashBoomLove: A Novel in Verse. Albuquerque: University of New Mexico Press, 1999.

The Upside Down Boy/El niño de cabeza. San Francisco: Children's Book Press, 2000.

SECONDARY WORKS

CRITICAL AND BIOGRAPHICAL STUDIES

Cruz, Víctor Hernández. "Introduction." In Herrera's *Facegames.* Berkeley: As Is/ So & So, 1987. Pp. i–ii.

Flores, Lauro H. "Auto-referencialidad y subversión: Observaciones (con) textuales en torno a la poesía de Juan Felipe Herrera." *Crítica* 2 (summer 1990): 172–181.

———. "Juan Felipe Herrera." In *Dictionary of Literary Biography,* vol. 2. Edited by Francisco A. Lomelí and Carl R. Shirley. Detroit: Gale Group, 1992. Pp. 137–145.

Héctor Mario Cavallari, "La muerte y el deseo: Notas sobre la poesía de Juan Felipe Herrera," *Palabra* 4–5 (spring–fall 1983): 97–106.

Lomelí, Francisco A., and Donaldo W. Urioste. *Chicano Perspectives in Literature: A Critical and Annotated Bibliography.* Albuquerque: Pajarito, 1976. Pp. 26–27.

BOOK REVIEWS

Ayres, Annie. Review of *Calling the Doves. Booklist,* January 1, 1996, p. 823.

Bradburn, Frances. Review of *CrashBoomLove. Booklist,* February 1, 2000, p. 1018.

Nelson, Cyns. Review of *The Upside Down Boy. Bloomsbury Review* 20 (March–April 2000): 20.

Olszewski, Lawrence. Review of *Love after the Riots. Library Journal* 121 (April 1, 1996): 84.

Ratner, Rochelle. Review of *Border-Crosser with a Lamborghini Dream. Library Journal* 124 (January 1999): 103.

———. Review of *Night Train to Tuxtla. Library Journal* 119 (August 1994): 86.

Redburn, Maria. Review of *Calling the Doves. School Library Journal* (December 1995): 97.

Review of *Border-Crosser with a Lamborghini Dream. Publishers Weekly,* January 25, 1999, p. 91.

Review of *Mayan Drifter. Publishers Weekly,* January 6, 1997, p. 57.

Review of *Thunderweavers. Publishers Weekly,* March 6, 2000, p. 107.

Trevino, Rose Zertuche. Review of *Calling the Doves. School Library Journal* 42 (February 1996): 128.

Whalin, Kathleen. Review of *Laughing Out Loud, I Fly. School Library Journal* 144 (May 1998): 156.

INTERVIEWS

Foster, Sesshu. "From Logan to the Mission: Riding North through Chicano Literary History with Juan Felipe Herrera." *Americas Review* 17 (fall–winter 1989): 68–87.

González, Ray. "Poetry Marauder: An Interview with Juan Felipe Herrera." *The Bloomsbury Review* 20, no. 2 (March–April 2000): 19–20.

Rolando Hinojosa
(1929–)

ROSAURA SÁNCHEZ

ROLANDO HINOJOSA IS widely known for his chronicle of the Texas Valley—el "cronicón del condado de Belken" (*Claros varones de Belken/Fair Gentlemen of Belken County*, p. 131)—which configures twentieth-century events, social types, cultural practices, and conflicts in an area north of the Rio Grande, an imaginary local space linked to national, transnational, and international spaces. It is this sociogeographical imagination that provides readers a historical and spatial view of life in a fictitious southern Texas county, where violence as well as camaraderie is an everyday affair. For purposes of this study of Hinojosa's body of work, what the author has termed his "Klail City Death Trip Series" will be considered collectively as a macrotext, although each of his ten novels can stand on its own. Hinojosa's novels, often classified strictly within Chicano and Chicana letters, are rightfully part of a larger national U.S. literary canon.

Rolando Hinojosa was born on 21 January 1929, in Mercedes, Texas. His ancestors came to the Rio Grande Valley with José de Escandón's Spanish colonization project in the mid-eighteenth century. One of the earliest settlements organized by Escandón was the Lugar de Mier settlement (later Tamaulipas), established in 1753 on the south side of the Rio Grande,

where the Hinojosa family first settled. In subsequent years, settlers would receive individual grants, and some would move north of the Rio Grande. Among them were two Hinojosas who received land grants: J. J. Hinojosa, who received the Llano Grande grant (25.5 leagues) in 1790, and Vicente de Hinojosa, who received the Las Mesteñas grant (35 leagues) in 1794. Hinojosa's Rio Grande Valley roots are thus of long standing, and it is this deeply rooted knowledge of the area that he brings to bear in his novels.

Hinojosa's father, Manuel Guzmán Hinojosa, to whom his two police mysteries are dedicated, was a policeman. Like a character of the same name in his novels, don Manuel participated in the Mexican Revolution. The author's mother, Carrie Effie Smith, came to the Valley as an infant, the daughter of a family allied to the Confederacy during the Civil War. Both of Hinojosa's parents were bilingual and bicultural, but he grew up in a community that was primarily Spanish-speaking. At the age of seventeen he enlisted in the army. He was later placed on reserve and in 1949 was recalled and served in Japan and Korea in 1950. After his tour of duty he attended the University of Texas at Austin, where he earned his B.S. in 1953. A variety of jobs in civil service and business followed before he returned to academia and earned his M.A. from New Mexico Highlands University in 1962 and his Ph.D. from the University of Illinois in 1969. Since then he has been a university professor, with appointments at several universities, including the University of Illinois, Trinity University, Texas A & I (Kingsville), the University of Minnesota, and the University of Texas at Austin. Rolando Hinojosa holds the Ellen Clayton Garwood Chair and is a professor in the English department at the University of Texas at Austin.

Hinojosa's fiction received its first major public recognition in 1972, when he was awarded the Third Annual Premio Quinto Sol for his work *Estampas del valle y otras obras (The Valley)*. In 1976 he won the prestigious Latin American Premio Casa de las Américas award for his novel *Generaciones y semblanzas (Klail City)*. Hinojosa is one of the most prolific writers in Chicano and Chicana literature, having published ten novels, three of them in both Spanish and English versions. His body of work has earned recognition throughout the nation and abroad. His novels have appeared in both English and Spanish, and two have also been translated into German. Hinojosa is not only a novelist but a short-story writer, poet, and literary critic as well, whose works have appeared in a variety of journals and anthologies. Hinojosa is also known for his translations, not only of his own work but of the novel of another key figure in Chicano and Chicana literature, Tomás Rivera.

In his construction of the fictitious Belken County, Hinojosa has produced a plurigeneric macrotext with a multinarrative perspective that allows for the construction of a broad consciousness of history, one dating back to the late eighteenth century and extending up to the decade of the 1980s in southern Texas. Yet its focus on the local—the Texas Valley—is, as previously noted, inextricably linked to both national and transnational spaces; in fact, the macronovel narrates the national and transna-tional through the local. The local is thus the lens through which numerous social conflicts, national and transnational in scope, are viewed. As Hinojosa's character Echevarría notes: "Según me cuentan Rafa y Jehú, el mundo afuera del Valle se parece a éste. . . . Yo iría más allá: no sólo se parece, lo es" (Rafa and Jehú tell me that life outside of the Valley is similar to life here. . . . I'd go further and say that not only is it similar, it's one and the same; *Claros varones de Belken*, p. 211). It is a site that includes spaces of marginality and domination, wherein a variety of responses to economic, political, and cultural domination, from resistance to acquiescence, are configured. For Hinojosa's characters the Valley is, first and foremost, "home," a part of Texas, "that slice of hell, heaven, purgatory and land of our Fathers" (*Korean Love Songs from Klail City Death Trip*, p. 53), the site also from which to try to make sense of local, global, and transnational military conflicts. All the sociospatial locations in the novels share one thing in common: they are the sites of change, loss, and death.

Perhaps the best way to approach the work of Rolando Hinojosa is through a spatial-temporal perspective: temporal because his narratives, though focused on twentieth-century events, reveal sedimentation of previous periods and modes of production in the Rio Grande Valley, and spatial because it is both the transformation of space and the dislocation of the characters that figure centrally in this complex novel. At the historical level, earlier displacement within the social order also occurs without geographical movement, as military, political, and economic forces in the nineteenth century reconfigure Mexican Texas as United States territory. Once the local is penetrated by Anglo settlers and a capitalist mode of production, earlier social relations begin to break down and what is constructed as a close-knit community—despite its internal conflicts—faces external pressures that eventually lead to loss of land, forcing workers into the migrant circuit that will take them from the Valley to the Midwest—to work in the fields of Michigan, Illinois, and Minnesota—and back again. The novels capture and configure the characters' particular sense of situatedness as well as their displacement within the Texas Valley and their inevitable acquiescence to modernization. The local is thus characterized by its complex and contradictory nature.

The major contradictions in the novel series are economic and political; social antagonisms are particularly evident in the first two novels, as residents express their resentment and their sense of powerlessness. Time-space is at the same time hierarchical and binary, with clearly drawn lines between the two communities and with Texano-Mexicanos (hereafter also Mexicanos) subordinated to Anglos. Even poor Anglos coming into the Valley have a good chance of doing well, like the family of the banker Noddy Perkins. Although the novels do not narrate a change in social stratification per se, they do document a collective consciousness of what has been lost and what is changing before their eyes, as Klail City evolves from a small rural community into a heterogeneous site, with all the tensions and complexities that characterize modern U.S. cities along the U.S.-Mexican border. The decentering and marginalization of the Mexicanos, despite being the majority population in the Texas Valley, is never overcome, but toward the end of the twentieth century, as seen in *Ask a Policeman*, time-space has become multidimensional and while still hierarchical, some of the outsiders—the main characters of the "Klail City Death Trip Series"—have become insiders and occupy positions of power. Clearly, upward mobility and assimilation have relocated these characters within the dominant order.

The multidimensional spatiality of Hinojosa's macronovel is built on a fragmented structure that permits constant shifts in time and space, from local to national and international spaces, from Belken County to the midst of battle scenes in Korea, along the 38th parallel. The novels are further marked by ruptures and gaps that often are never fully explained in subsequent texts. There are thus periods in the

life of Jehú Malacara, for example, that are referenced in passing but never narrated, such as his life as a chaplain's assistant during the Korean War, about which we know little. And yet amidst the discontinuity there is continuity as well, with particular events and moments revisited, often with additional or even contradictory information added, given the multiple narrative perspectives, in subsequent texts. The life of Viola Barragán, for example, is alluded to or narrated in several of the narratives, as is the death of Rafa Buenrostro's father, "El Quieto."

Among the macrotext's other distinctive features is its heteroglossic and intergeneric organization, with the use of a variety of discourses that include correspondence, journal entries, sketches, notes, dialogues, interviews, court depositions, and witness testimonies. The richness of Hinojosa's novels is most notable in his narrative styles, which vary from irascible to sardonic, from humorous to all-out *choteo* or jiving, from serious to plaintive. Through his intimate knowledge and feel for language, Hinojosa is able to suggest the rhythm and style of local speech in its various inflections, ranging from the conversation of *comadres* to the jiving at a cantina, and even particular styles, like that of the local Spanish-language radio disc jockey, as in the case of Enedino Broca López in *Generaciones y semblanzas* (p. 151). Humor is clearly a major strategy in the novels, serving, for example, to ward off nostalgia and an idealization of the past, or to deal with sensitive issues, the painfulness of which is displaced or undermined, although never totally disguised, through pungent scorn or male derisive discourses. What is always striking in Hinojosa's work is the degree to which the content is the form, the particular sardonic delivery of the characters' lives, pains, and joys.

Like the Valley, the characters—both Mexicanos and Anglos—that inhabit Hinojosa's novels are for the most part bilingual. *Estampas del valle y otras obras*, *Generaciones y semblanzas*, and *Claros varones de Belken* were written in Spanish and translated into English, but *Mi querido Rafa (Dear Rafe)* is a bilingual text, with Jehú's letters evidencing a good deal of code-switching. The others—*Korean Love Songs, Rites and Witnesses, Partners in Crime, Becky and Her Friends,* and *Ask a Policeman*—have all been published in English, but even here there are always shifts to Spanish for particular terms or greetings. Hinojosa has also published his own English versions of three novels: *The Valley, Klail City,* and *Dear Rafe,* and a Spanish version of *Becky and Her Friends, Los amigos de Becky.* From the start this distinctive bilingual cross-border locus of his work undoubtedly foreshadowed subsequent Latino and Latina cultural production.

In his novels Hinojosa deploys a range of distinct narrators, including not only the primary narrators—Rafa Buenrostro, Jehú Malacara, Esteban Echevarría, Pedro Galindo, and "the listener"—but also a panoply of Klail City residents, all of whom allow for a multifaceted macronovel. Whether narrating through sketches and notes, addressing other characters through letters, or interviewing Klail City residents, these narrators provide a variety of perspectives in the novels. For example, the numerous testimonials given by informants interviewed by Galindo and "the listener"—especially in *Rites and Witnesses, Mi querido Rafa,* and *Becky and Her Friends*—refract contradictory views on events and individuals, by both Mexicanos and Anglos. Nevertheless, there is an overriding perspective shared by Rafa, Jehú, Viola Barragán, Echevarría, and Galindo that pervades the entire novel series. The multiple narrators and informants also serve to provide the contours of the multidimensional sites encompassed within the local through comments and gossip that recall past events and shed light on the past of particular individuals within Klail City or Belken County. These narrators also intercalate entire stories in their narrations. For example, in *Claros varones,* P. Galindo, in musing over what a reserved but determined person can accomplish, recalls the story of how Ignacio Loera got back at his wife Rita, who was

having an affair with the car dealer Moisés Guevara. In this volume Galindo likewise provides his own version of what happened to Tomás Imás when a snake bit him, an account that is much more interesting than Jehú's in *Generaciones y semblanzas,* and introduces not only a new space, the cotton fields, but also an entirely new aspect of local culture: cures for "el susto."

The first two volumes of this macrotext deal primarily with the Mexicano communities in the Texas Valley (and sometimes follow Valley migrants on the road to Michigan, Iowa, or other parts of the Midwest in search of work), and although it is evident that the Anglos are in control of the economy and the political dimension of the County, it is the everyday life of the Mexicano community in Klail City, with its intragroup conflicts, that is central to these novels. The Anglo and Mexicano communities are segregated, or as Echevarría puts it: "Los bolillos y la raza (cada quien en su lugar y por su lado)" (the Anglos and the Mexicanos [each one in its place and doing its own thing]; *Generaciones y semblanzas,* p. 61). If the earlier novels highlight a history of interethnic conflicts and discrimination against the Mexicanos, however, the later novels will portray a willingness among a portion of the Mexicano community to incorporate itself into the dominant Anglo social structure. The macronovel does not lament this accommodation; instead it suggests that what really matters to Valley residents is cultural identity. Thus those who know who they are and what they are ("sabíamos quiénes éramos y qué éramos" [*Generaciones,* p. 67])—that is, those with a strong cultural identity—can make demands and get what they want.

Changes at the local level are foregrounded throughout the macrotext. As Echevarría points out, toward the end of his life: "Desaparece el Valle, gentes. . . . Los bolillos con sus propiedades, sus bancos y contratos" (The Valley's disappearing, folks. . . . The Anglos [are there] with their properties, their banks, and their contracts; *Claros varones de Belken,* p. 207). Characters suggest that what once was a valley where a number of Mexicano families owned land has now become an area where it is the Anglos who own the land and the ranches where the Mexicano townspeople work. Historically, only a few of the Mexicano families were able to retain their lands, some by allying with the Anglos; yet others, like the Buenrostros, through long-term resistance to dispossession, are able to hang on to their land. In time, and more specifically by the decades of the 1960s and 1970s, some Mexicanos begin to acquire land through purchase, even while others continue to sell theirs. In the novels the Buenrostros are represented as an exceptional family, and in that sense idealized, one that gives land away to other Valley families.

As might be expected, the issue of land is central to the families, but the novels do not focus on life on the ranches nor on sites of production, not in the Valley nor even in the Midwest, where migrants from the Valley work. While social spaces are fundamental sites in Hinojosa, what is mapped in these novels is not, then, defined by the actual physical characteristics of the Texas Valley. In fact, only in *Claros varones de Belken* does Rafa Buenrostro provide a short description of the mixed Valley landscape (fertile valley along the Rio Grande River surrounded by semidesert) and the region's diverse vegetation and agricultural production—citrus, melons, watermelons, strawberries, as well as cotton, onions, cabbage, and so forth (p. 171). Clearly what is central to these various texts is lived or imagined space, cultural spaces wherein social relations of kinship and friendship determine survival. It is the practice of everyday life and its ongoing construction in the midst of loss, as well as change, that characterizes the novels.

The overarching cultural conception of space is figured through sociocultural practices—the principal one being conversation and gossip, with and without malice—and the recording of events by various narrators. One of the main spheres of these sociocultural practices is the cantina or bar. The cantina operates as a hetero-topia of sorts in Hinojosa's work, where through the interpersonal contacts and relationships of male residents, both of older and younger Klail men, readers gain access to the town's history, the background of various residents, and the conflicts between the principal Mexicano families. The cantina brings together prostitutes and family men, the police officer and drunkards, gamblers and craftsmen, the bank cashier and the local police inspector, the teacher and the pharmacist—a variety of social types within the Mexicano community. It is at the cantina that we also gain insight into the various relations between households, defined by marriage, *compadrazgo,* friendship, and kinship, for in Klail City a number of families are closely related.

The local itself is, however, varied and diversified and in the earlier novels defined primarily by public spaces, which include not only the previously mentioned bars and cantinas but other sites, such as gaming houses, the cemetery, the whorehouses, the parks and plazas, the circus tent, the street and roads, the sidewalks and benches, the open fields, the flat-bed trucks, the outsides of homes in town and ranches, and their front gardens and fences. Progressively, as we move beyond the voices of Valley old-timers and Jehú's and Rafa's sketches, with P. Galindo and "the listener" we begin to enter people's homes and sometimes offices, as in the case of Viola Barragán, where the interviewer is asked to sit and have tea, lemonade, or lunch. Only then do domestic spaces begin to appear as well in the recollections of Rafa, as he recalls the Vielma household, where as a child he had dinner once a week. The local domestic spaces will become more heterogeneous when we enter the homes of the wealthy, for example the Klail-Blanchard-and-Cooke Ranch, with its swimming pool and fancy dining room, and of the middle class, including the home of Becky Escobar. The public spheres also become progressively modernized and include larger stores, pharmacies, the savings and loans, banks, car dealerships, and in the detective narratives, state offices, police stations, yacht club centers, fishing boats, pawn shops, and hospitals. By then the local has expanded to include the transnational border area as well.

Transnational spaces are actually evident from the first volume, *Estampas del valle,* where through don Víctor Peláez's 1920 letters from Papantla, Veracruz, and Mexico City, readers are relocated to Mexico during the period of the Mexican Revolution. Like don Víctor, a number of Texano-Mexicanos born north of the Rio Grande would fight in the Mexican Revolution, including don Manuel Guzmán (the local—and only—Mexicano policeman), Braulio Tapia, and Evaristo Garrido, whose participation is also recorded in *Estampas.* An account of don Manuel's role in the Mexican Revolution is intercalated with letters from his wife in *Generaciones y semblanzas.* The Texanos' participation lends credence to the notion of an imaginary greater-Mexico that extends beyond the Rio Grande, but the reality of the incoming Anglos eager to take over don Manuel's land while he is away makes only too clear that, however imaginary, the state line is determinant, as is the relative weakness of the native Texano-Mexicanos vis-à-vis the Anglos.

Throughout the novel, the local is viewed through a historical lens. Key to this historical perspective is the character Esteban Echevarría, born around 1872, who provides the historical framing that enables us to acquire a sense of the continuity and discontinuity in the Texas Valley (*Rites and Witnesses,* p. 109). Already an old man in his eighties when he dies in 1959 or 1960, he has witnessed the major twentieth-century changes in the Texas Valley and managed to preserve a sense of history. A native of Bascom, Texas, and not a member of one of the founding Klail City families, he will nevertheless be the link to previous generations, having known four generations of Buenrostros. Through Echevarría the novel creates a consciousness of the decades before the 1940s, a period that includes the Mexican Revolution and the Seditionists' insurrection in Texas in 1915 against the state and its

Rangers, the infamous *rinches.* Echevarría is thus the voice of memory and its conservator:

> Ha sobrevivido a todos los de su edad y ahora es el único que todavía se acuerda de cómo era el Valle. De cómo fue y de cómo era el Valle antes de que vinieran los bolillos a montón, y el ejército, el gobierno estatal y sus rinches, el papelaje y todo el desmadre que arrambló con tierras y familias; con el desprendimiento personal y el honor de haber sido lo que fuimos.
>
> (*Claros varones de Belken,* p. 129)

He has survived all those of his generation and now is the only one that still remembers what the Valley was like. What it was and used to be before the Anglos came, by the many, before the army, the state government and the Rangers, the paper work and all the shit that swept over the land and families, and devastated our pride and honor in being what we had been.

With the U.S.-Mexican War troops in 1846, there came many who chose to stay in Texas after the war. Among the U.S. soldiers settling in the area was Captain Rufus T. Klail, founder of Klail City. As the number of Anglo settlers grew, it became increasingly difficult for the Mexicanos to retain their land. Echevarría, for example, recalled that many of the old families were ready to fight to retain their land—los Vilches, los Garrido, los Malacara, los Buenrostro—even if it meant an armed struggle against the *rinches,* the Texas Rangers. The novel recounts how, faced with Anglo incursions, at one point the families got together first at the Toluca Ranch, owned by the Vilches, and later at the El Carmen Ranch, owned by the Buenrostros, to assess and confront their collective situation. That struggle for the land continued through the period of the Seditionists in the early part of the twentieth century, when Texano-Mexicanos took up arms against the Rangers (*Estampas del valle,* p. 128). This attempt to defend their land was not supported by all the Mexicanos, some of whom, like the Leguizamón family, allied with the Anglos. In the end, the Rangers, the land laws, the droughts, the poverty, and pressure from the Anglo landowners all conspired to deprive them of their lands. Only a few, such as los Buenrostro, los Villalón, los Vilches, los Farías, and a few others, were able to hold on to their lands.

With Echevarría goes the memory of the past, one that Rafa, Galindo, and Jehú have taken great pains to record. When Echevarría dies by the old mesquite tree planted by his own father—"un árbol aguantador como la raza" (a sturdy and lasting tree like the raza, *Claros varones de Belken*, p. 221)—he is fittingly buried by his friend Rafa in the Cemetery of the Four Founding Families on the Carmen Ranch. Echevarría's death signals the end of a period that inspires nostalgia in the older residents of Klail City and marks the beginning of a new period, one of accommodation and integration in the Texas Valley. This new period begins around 1960, with Jehú's hiring at the KBC Bank, but is preceded by what is constructed as a major uprooting of the main characters with their relocation to the battlefront in Korea. Twelve years after Echevarría's death, there are numerous changes among his friends and in Klail City. It is another, wholly transformed *Valle* that ensues.

The two main characters in Hinojosa's macronovel are Rafa Buenrostro and Jehú Malacara, distant cousins and the best of friends. Although initially set up as opposites, as their last names ("Buen rostro" = good face; "Mala cara" = bad face) would indicate, they are in fact doubles, spitting images of each other except for their dispositions. While Rafa is said to be reserved, like his father, Jehú is more extroverted, with a sardonic sense of humor but, like his cousin, never totally frank. Both are orphaned at a young age: Jehú at nine and Rafa at eight; both lose the women that they either marry (Conce Guerrero, Rafa's first wife) or plan to marry (Olivia San Esteban, Jehú's fiancée) to accidents. Both relate to old and young alike, treat poor and rich without distinctions, and are close friends of Echevarría. It falls to Rafa and Jehú to live the changes that their old friend perceives are taking place. And, like

Echevarría and Galindo, Jehú and Rafa are both concerned with "making memory," recording events and the lives of those who populate their Klail City. Their sketches and notes reconstruct conversations and their own childhood, adolescence, youth, and adulthood, and through the contrastive trajectories of their lives portray another generation's lived experience of life in the Valley.

The picaresque childhood of Jehú Malacara is reconstructed in *Estampas del valle* and *Generaciones y semblanzas*. As in the Spanish picaresque genre that these texts recall, Jehú will go from place to place and from mentor to mentor, in the process giving readers a look at a variety of sites within the Mexicano community, such as the cemetery, the open road, the plaza, the gaming house, the circus, the goat ranch, and so forth. Orphaned at an early age, Jehú lives first with don Victor Peláez, who works a one-tent circus in the area; upon Victor's death, Jehú moves on to work as an altar boy with don Pedro Zamudio, the local priest, while also working at don Javier Leguizamón's store. Having neglected his chores to go swimming, Jehú will escape from the priest's anticipated wrath by running off with a young evangelical missionary, Tomás Imás, who is on the road selling bibles and preaching. When the preacher loses a leg and moves on to Jonesville, Jehú becomes a card dealer at "El Oasis," a gaming house owned by his uncle Andrés Malacara, and later decides to leave town to become a goat herder at don Celso Villalón's ranch. It will be don Manuel, the policeman, who will put a temporary stop to Jehú's rambling by having him come live with his family so that he can return to school, where he will again team up with the character that functions as his alter ego, Rafa.

Rafa's adolescence is likewise recorded in these various sketches, notes, and dialogues. After the death of his mother from dengue fever, he and his brothers Israel and Aaron are raised by his aunt Matilde Buenrostro, his father's sister. Except for very brief references to writing her from Korea in *The Useless Servants* and to her care of them in *Claros varones,* there are no sketches of her or other references to her in the macronovel. As a teenager and after the death of his father, Rafa works at *El Chorreao*'s cantina, "Aquí Me Quedo," serving beer and coffee; later, after high school, Rafa joins the Army, returning to Klail City on reserve status. His plans to study at Jonesville College and his marriage to Conce Guerrero are very briefly recorded; her drowning with her parents on an outing one Easter Sunday after only ten months of marriage is again briefly mentioned in *Claros varones.* Shortly thereafter Rafa, Jehú, Joey Vielma, Chale Villalón, and other Valley young men are called up as the Korean War breaks out. It is upon Rafa's return from Korea, and after Echevarría's death, as previously noted, that things begin to change dramatically in the Valley. By then Jehú and Rafa have finished their studies at the university at Austin and returned home. That more is known about Rafa's military service in Korea and his journal writing during the war than about his years at the university, narrated briefly in *Claros varones,* would seem to indicate that coming into contact with this international space was a transformative and highly significant period in the life of the main character. When next the novel focuses on Rafa, he has become a police detective in Klail, after studying law and becoming an attorney.

Through the fragmented structure of Hinojosa's macronovel, we are able to piece together this new period of change and modernization in Klail City, enabling social mobility for several local residents, who move into spheres and particular professions previously off-limits to Mexicanos. Before moving on to other jobs or additional studies, for example, Rafa and Jehú become high school teachers, the first Mexicano teachers at their former high school. Jehú soon leaves that job to work at the local savings and loan, and with Viola Barragán's strong recommendation is then hired at the Klail City National Bank, owned by the Klail-Blanchard-Cooke corporation. In a city where Mexicanos are divided into Ranch Mexicans, who live on the KBC Ranch, and non-Ranch Mexicans, who live and work elsewhere, "Ranch" can only refer to the KBC Ranch owned by the Klail, Blanchard, and Cooke families, who, given their intermarriage, function as one family and are the largest landholders in the area.

It is Jehú's career at the bank that offers the macronovel the entrée to explore the spaces of the ruling class in Klail City and the social contradictions that have been suggested throughout the novels but are now made more explicit; these will be viewed through the eyes of Jehú and Galindo, who interviews a number of Klail City citizens to trace the transformations that are taking place in the last half of the twentieth century. The learned P. Galindo, who has been a migrant worker, assistant truck driver, and writer, is a major narrator within Hinojosa's macronovel; he will die of cancer, but little else is known about his personal life, except that everyone knows him and is willing to talk to him about what they think has happened in their city.

Hinojosa's novels recount significantly that by 1959, around the time of Echevarría's death, the KBC—the Klail-Blanchard-Cooke corporation—not only owns the better part of the Valley lands, but through the First National Bank also controls the economy of Klail City, as well as Belken County politics. Hinojosa's novels document the private and public spaces within which the KBC families move and how they operate. The KBC's dirty laundry is aired through accounts of alcoholism and sexual abuse of the hired help, in this case a thirteen-year-old Guatemalan girl working at the KBC Ranch. At a public level, however, the three families, headed by Rufus Klail Junior, who is married to Anna Faye Blanchard, function not only as a closely held family corporation but as a political machine as well, with the connections to pull strings at several levels. Their chief strategist is the banker Noddy (Arnold-Norberto) Perkins, from a working-class family (Jehú deridingly calls them "fruit tramps") that came to the Valley at the beginning of the twentieth century; a man with a good head for business and bilingual, Perkins married into the wealthy KBC clan. As Blanche Cooke's husband, he is also the father of Sammie Jo Perkins, who in the 1970s will marry Rafa Buenrostro. Blanche's brother E. B. (Everett Blanchard) Cooke is the bank cashier and also the secretary-treasurer for the KBC Corporation, which is involved not only in ranching but in the oil industry as well.

Access into the inner sanctum of this financial and political machine is limited, more so of course for Mexicanos, but when Jehú is hired at the KBC Bank as head of loans despite the opposition of Fredericka Cooke, he learns a great deal about the inner workings of the family business and soon finds himself right in the middle of things. It is through Jehú's letters and notes that the novel explores how politics work in the Valley and how, for example, Noddy Perkins manipulates local politics and commissioner elections, as well as state and federal elections. Events evolve with Perkins's selection of Ira Escobar, Leguizamón's nephew, as future candidate for commissioner to force out the Anglo incumbent, the liberal Roger Terry. The KBC's ulterior motive is complicated. The election for commissioner is thus an excellent example of the type of political-economic and cultural intrigues involving the KBC family, and points to the source of their power. Not only is the KBC interested in manipulating and blackmailing the liberal Terry (through dirty tricks like harassing his wife with reckless driving tickets, having the printing of his political leaflets delayed, and having his clients drop or threaten to drop his legal services), but Noddy Perkins also wants to get back at Terry for helping several Mexicanos acquire lands in Ellis County. The plan is even more devious, however, for the KBC is interested in urging Terry (once he loses the election and is totally beholden to the KBC for a loan to run as an Independent) to be the write-in candidate for Congress, to depose current Congressman Hap Bayliss, whom they want to get rid of after finding out that he is the gay lover of Sidney, Sammie Jo Perkins's husband. Jehú, of course, becomes privy to all these "family" machinations by virtue of his position at the bank.

The novels go on to detail how the selection of Ira Escobar was meant to please Leguizamón, who is thought to carry some weight in the Mexicano community. Unaware of his role, however, Ira begins to act self-important and believes himself on his way to the top. To ensure Escobar's acknowledgment of his total dependence on the KBC, Noddy Perkins makes his move. Suddenly Ira's election looks uncertain, as he begins to receive calls from sponsors saying they are leaving him for the Independent candidate, Terry. Panicking, Ira calls Noddy, who is unavailable, of course. His dozens of calls lead Noddy to perceive that Ira better knows his place in the scheme of things. The humorous description of Ira's total subordination is sarcastically recorded by Jehú:

> Noddy lo sentó y entonces le explicó, en esa voz, ce por be cómo corría el agua en Belken; que quién se encargaba de las compuertas; que quién era el señor aguador; que quién decidía a cuáles acequias se les daba agua y a cuáles no; y cuánta agua y también cuándo; y etceterit y etceterot. Así. Noddy habla de agua pero hasta el más lerdo sabe perfectamente de *qué* se está hablando.
>
> (*Mi querido Rafa*, p. 38)

> Noddy sat him down and explained, in that voice of his, in precise terms, how water ran in Belken, who was in charge of opening the water gates, who was in charge of letting the waters flow, who decided what irrigation ditches received water and which didn't and how much water and also when, etc., etc. Just like that, Noddy goes on and on about water but even the dumbest fool knows perfectly well what he's talking about.

To make sure that Escobar does in fact win, Perkins recruits his sister and daughter to help in making Ira and his wife look acceptable among the local well-to-do. This requires making Becky Escobar a member of the KC Women's Club, despite Anglo women's disapproval. Conniving is Noddy Perkins's specialty and though not a blood member of the KBC family (he married into it), he is the power and brains behind that capitalist enterprise, although the titular head is Junior Klail (Rufus T. Klail V).

Hinojosa's novels, by highlighting the schemes of the KBC corporation and Noddy Perkins's role as power broker, make plain that Mexicanos are, for the most part, cut out of the power structure. The political manipulation of the sort detailed above allows them to decide who represents the area at a local, state, and national level, for the KBC's interests have to be represented at every level. Its interests are of course capitalist interests, and increasingly those of finance capital. As Jehú discovers, the KBC is not simply interested in acquiring land; it now plays on a bigger field. Among the various things the KBC "worked" were federal funds, or more specifically, G.I. Bill funds for training veterans, which could be tapped for schools established by the KBC, although under other names. The creation (after Fredericka's death) of the Fredericka Cooke Institute, a tax-exempt organization under the Tax Code, also allowed it to buy land without paying taxes. The scheme involved having the Institute buy land owned by another corporation by having that corporation convey its stock to the Institute, liquidating the old corporation, and then creating a new corporation, its lands to be leased to the original owner under a five-year lease. In the end the KBC corporation received $1.5 million, with the entire operation turned over to the ostensibly nonprofit Cooke Institute. As Jehú notes: "The KBC didn't have to put it to the Mexicanos anymore; they now went after bigger game; the U.S. Treasury, for one. It wasn't the evasion of taxes; it was their avoidance" (*Rites and Witnesses*, p. 54).

The Klail City First National Bank is involved in a number of other deals in order to avoid paying taxes. For example, it acquires land without declaring it as a purchase; instead, the money is given to the owner as a loan, which the seller will receive in deferred payments and is payable in twenty years. In the meantime the money lies in the bank and the land is subdivided by the bank and rented out, in part to the original owner as well, who in turn can continue to get his share of government inducements—that is, ironically, money for not planting sugar cane. "Everyone" profits from machinations like these and for twenty years the bank is not the legal owner and does not have to pay taxes.

Jehú learns the "business" of banking fast, but there are aspects of dealing with the KBC and Noddy that do not appeal to him. Nevertheless, he uses his position at the bank to facilitate loans to a number of Mexicanos who use the money to recover land. One day, however, he too finds himself subjected to Noddy's scheming. He is invited to dinner at 8:00 p.m. at the KBC Ranch, unaware that dinner has been served already; a number of people are there, including Ira Escobar and his wife Becky, and after Jehú walks in Noddy says point blank: "Jehú, I recommend that you resign as loan officer" (*Mi querido Rafa*, p. 45). Understanding that he has been set up, Jehú turns around and walks out without saying a word, subverting Noddy's staging of his public humiliation.

Jehú counters by devising a plan of his own to keep his position at the bank. He not only knows all too much about the KBC's inner workings, but he also has bedded Becky Escobar and even Perkins's daughter, Sammie Jo. Jehú's strategy is to return to the bank on the day after the Armistice Day Holiday, also a bank holiday, and ask to be reassigned to the savings and loan, also owned by the KBC, where he had worked previously, but Noddy says matters are "out of [his] hands" (*Mi querido Rafa*, p. 46). Jehú turns things around by confronting Noddy and making it seem as if his firing is due to his "tussles with Becky" and his denying that he was involved with Sammie Jo. By treating it all as a light affair with Becky, Jehú is able to undo his firing, for the moment. He sees the writing on the wall nonetheless and ultimately decides to leave the bank on his own after a couple of months.

Scandal and speculation occupy their own space in Klail City, where rumors are rampant. Why did Jehú, then chief loan officer at the Klail City National Bank, suddenly leave the bank in 1962 and spend the next three years in graduate school at the university in Austin? Above we have one take, but the macronovel provides others. Galindo will investigate the widespread speculation in Klail City as to the reason for Jehú's relocation, with the Leguizamón adherents suggesting that he was fired, that he must have stolen money, and so forth. But as Jehú often notes, in a self-deprecatory style: "La raza es medio cabrona cuando quiere, and I'm fresh out of brotherly love" (La raza can be downright merciless . . . ; *Mi querido Rafa,* p. 41).

Three years later, in 1965, Jehú returns to Klail City and to the KBC bank. We learn that he returned to work while his fiancée, the pharmacist Olivia San Esteban, went to medical school in Galveston. About a year later, Ollie is killed in a car accident. When we next see him, in *Partners in Crime* in 1972, Jehú is thirty-six years old, and now vice president of the KBC Bank (p. 157). Five years later he is still at the Bank and now married to Becky Escobar, his former lover, by then divorced from Ira and now a wholly transformed Becky, learning Spanish and working as an independent businesswoman for the powerful Viola Barragán. Noddy and Jehú have come to an "understanding," and the bank's plotting and manipulation of individuals for its political and economic gain is no longer troublesome to Jehú. As long as his own personal principles are not challenged, Jehú is satisfied with his job and convinces himself that he is helpful to Mexicanos by facilitating loans, and so forth. The socially upwardly mobile Jehú has accommodated, although he continues to visit community cantinas as before and to use Spanish. The Bank space itself is now also presented as accessible space, in good part because of Jehú's presence there. But if Jehú has changed, so have others around him. This will become clear when, in the second detective

mystery, Rafa, who by then is married to Sammie Jo Perkins, receives a request unthinkable ten years before: while in the hospital, Noddy Perkins asks to be buried among Mexicanos in the Old Families cemetery by the Carmen Ranch when he dies (*Ask a Policeman,* p. 19). The local has changed as well, for even as Rafa agrees to his request, he reminds Noddy that by then the cemetery is a state-designated landmark, under state care.

What now seems like a reconciled, happy, bicultural, bilingual, integrated Texas Valley community is of course not really the case, as the novels make clear, although the last three novels do toe that fine line between idealist constructions and critical realist configurations. In *Ask a Policeman,* local spaces expand into national spaces, as the visiting congressman from North Dakota makes clear at the U.S. Immigration Office on the Mexican border: "Welcome to the hub of activity where we who serve are proud to hold off the hordes of hardened criminals and thus protect the citizenry from Mexican banditry" (*Ask a Policeman,* p. 33). The discrimination and exploitation is faced now not only by native Texano-Mexicanos but also by the incoming Mexican immigrant workers, in such a way that the problems of the Valley residents are dispersed throughout the country, where Mexican workers arrive to perform agricultural, service, food processing, and sweatshop work and are subject to criminalization and hate.

Hinojosa's macronovel, as previously indicated, is populated with numerous characters, most of whom are male and appear only briefly; some, like Rafa and Jehú, are core characters. Aside from these two, there are a number of characters that stand out. One of these is don Orfalindo Buitureyra, who as a young pharmacist poisoned a Mexican military surgeon, Viola Barragán's first husband. As a cuckolded husband himself and secretly in love with Viola, Buitureyra periodically goes to the cantina "Aquí Me Quedo" on a drinking binge, dancing and singing by himself. What is clear is that the major characters in Hinojosa's novels are for the most part men, as the texts are dominated by masculinist spaces, whether these be sites of warfare in Korea or the local cantina, where older men like Echevarría sit, drink, and recall earlier times and comment on past looks of women. In this masculinist world, comments on women are sexist; women are at best tangential and always sexualized, as when Jehú refers to Becky; his comments have to do with her body and her skills in bed: "She doesn't rank among the best; lo que ofrece es la conocida furia mexicana" (what she offers is the famous Mexican female fury; *Mi querido Rafa*, p. 40). Hinojosa's female characters are for the most part presented from a masculine perspective.

The macronovel, however, breaks out of this masculinist gendering of Valley space through its incorporation of the ethnographer, the investigating P. Galindo, and later "the listener," whose interviews of Valley residents, both Mexican and Anglo, both male and female, provide a polycentric view of the area and allow for an examination of a variety of problems from a wider perspective. Issues of fathers' sexual abuse of daughters (as in the case of Elvira Navarrete), sexual and economic liberation (as in the case of Viola Barragán), women's independence (as in the case of Becky), women's opinion of divorce (as in the case of Reina Campoy), and women's independence from the Church (as in the case of Julia Ortegón) now appear. There are also interviews with conservative women, like Nora Salamanca and Elvira Navarrete, who feel that having a leading family husband, like Ira Escobar, even if a fool, is preferable to being married to an unknown quantity like Jehú. Or as Lucas Barrón, El Chorreao, pointedly notes: women are often just as *machistas* as men (*Becky and Her Friends*, p. 97).

Strong female characters like Olivia San Esteban disappear or are killed off a bit too fast from the macronovel, and we know very little, for example, about the attorney Angela Vielma, who dropped out of school at an early age after she found teachers had nothing to teach her, began working for a lawyer, and eventually returned to school to earn her law degree; unmarried, she has chosen to live with another woman, Delfina, Rafa's sister-in-law (Conce's sister). The two strongest female characters in the novel series, however, are Viola Barragán and Becky Escobar. Viola is an anomalous character, a world traveler who first marries a Mexican surgeon, then a German Consul in Mexico who later is assigned to Asia and Africa, where they are imprisoned during World War II. After the war Viola and Karl-Heinz return to Germany and later relocate to South Africa, where he is the manager of a Volkswagen plant. His death will take Viola back to Germany and eventually back to the Texas Valley, where she arrives with some capital and an enterprising spirit, ready to engage in business. Her protégée Becky, daughter of Viola's best friend Elvira Navarrete, makes her initial appearance in the macronovel as an empty-headed snob, a young woman who marries into the Leguizamón family to please her mother. Later she wakes up to assess what she has become, rejecting Ira and becoming personally and financially independent; a working woman who operates outside the traditionally female domestic realm, she develops her business talents as she becomes Viola Barragán's business assistant. A short while later she marries the "quasi-widowed" Jehú, joining the ranks of the macronovel's middle class, the assimilated and upwardly mobile Mexicano petty bourgeoisie with intimate links to the Anglo power structure.

There is another gendered space that marks Hinojosa's macronovel: the space of male violence. We see it not only in the Texas Rangers' lynching of Mexicanos—the ranch hands from the Galvestón Ranch are shot and dropped off at the Buenrostro El Carmen Ranch (*Rites and Witnesses*, pp. 88, 109, 110)—but in numerous other instances as well. The insurrection of the Mexicano Sediciosos of 1915–1917 would come about specifically in response to *rinche* attacks and in turn fall under attack by state violence in the form of the Army, Texas National Guard, and Rangers (*Rites and Witnesses*, p. 86; *Estam-*

pas del valle, p. 128). In some cases the violence represented is intragroup, with rivalries going back generations. Rafa is about eight years old (fourteen in one version) when his father, Jesús Buenrostro, el "Quieto," who resisted the takeover of El Carmen Ranch by Anglos, is murdered. Everything points to the Leguizamón family, who at different times both opposed and supported the Anglo takeover of Mexicano lands. A month later (the accounts vary), Jesús Buenrostro's brother, Julián, will follow the two hired killers to Mexico, kill them there, cross the river again, and look for the man who ordered the killing: Alejandro Leguizamón, whose head will be bashed in front of the Sacred Heart Church.

There are also individual cases of violence configured in the novel, such as Baldemar Cordero's killing of Ernesto Támez in the cantina "Aquí Me Quedo." Violence is not limited to intragroup spaces but is shown to be pervasive. In 1946, Ambrose Mora, a veteran of World War II, is killed (by Sheriff's Deputy Van Meers, in *Generaciones y semblanzas*) by Ranger Choche Markham (in *Rites and Witnesses*). In the early part of the century, Markham had been one of the lynching *rinches* and already then was working (as official "muscle") for the KBC families and would continue to be in their pay as late as 1959, much like Sheriff Big Foot Parkinson, who from the 1940s, when first elected, continued to be useful to the KBC well into the 1970s. The long delay in bringing Markham to trial, and more importantly the ultimate innocent verdict, point to the Mexicanos' lack of political clout, denounced and underscored throughout Hinojosa's novels.

That violence of different orders is pervasive in the novels has been pointed out, but here I would like to stress that, given its fragmented structure, the novel's juxtapositions of particular spaces and events are especially meaningful; we find different periods of violence intentionally juxtaposed throughout the works. For example, witness accounts of the lynching of Mexicanos are intercalated in *Rites and Witnesses* with

dialogues from the Korean Front, where Rafa is wounded and his two best friends, as well as several of his Army Division buddies, are killed. In another example from the same novel, an Anglo's comment on Mexicans as lazy, unambitious, hard-drinking people is followed by a scene in Korea between Rafa and a buddy who visits him while he lies wounded in a hospital; it is then that he learns of Villalón's death. These juxtapositions point to a number of well-known facts: the disproportionate number of ethnic minority soldiers who served and died in Korea and Vietnam, and at the same time, the racism in the U.S., where they continued to be seen as second-class citizens.

U.S. military service is in the background of several of the characters in Hinojosa's novels. Don Genaro Castañeda, a house painter, served in World War I; Israel Buenrostro and other Klail Mexicanos were in World War II; Rafa and Jehú in Korea, along with others such as Cayo Díaz and Tony Balderas, both of whom died in battle. Rafa's war experiences and the loss of his best friends, Joey Vielma and Chale Villalón, are documented in detail in four texts: *Mi querido Rafa, Korean Love Songs, Rites and Witnesses,* and *The Useless Servants.* These texts document the social bonding between soldiers, the conflicts between officers and soldiers, the racial interaction and friction among soldiers, and the class affinity of poor working-class whites and Valley Mexicanos. The destruction of civilian life, like blowing up the bridge on the River Naktong while it is full of Korean refugees (*The Useless Servants,* p. 35), the gruesome nature of the reification of dead soldiers when they become mere corpses to be fished out of the river for their tags and subsequently sent down the river again, the stress and battle fatigue that incapacitate soldiers and cause them to crack up and commit suicide or run away, the daily routine of setting up and loading the guns, the R and R periods in Japan, the deserter who stays behind, and especially the loss of buddies from back home are all part of the barbarity of war portrayed in these texts. The novels also introduce new characters, some of whom make Rafa's life difficult, like Texan Captain Bracken, and others of whom become his friends, like Hatalski, Frazier, and Rusty. *The Useless Servants* is, however, a different type of narrative. It is a daily and sometimes weekly battlefield journal that provides in abbreviated shorthand style entries on battles, wounded, dead, attacks, advances, retreats, nights and days under bombardment, and the daily toil of staying alive, keeping warm, changing socks, eating canned rations that Rafa comes to detest, and trying to get some sleep. Here too readers learn of Rafa's own hospitalization after a rocket blast kills Joey and two of his division buddies. *Korean Love Songs* is striking for its experimentation at the level of genre, offering a new narrative style, for these are prose poems interspersed with dialogue that document the pain, the male bonding, the friendships made and lost with death all around, and the psychological scars that will last beyond the war, as well as the camaraderie of the Valley boys in Japan while on R & R. *Korean Love Songs*'s plaintive style offers a poignant and painful analysis of the reification of soldiers and their use and misuse as instruments of death:

> It comes down to this: we're pieces of equipment
> To be counted and signed for.
> On occasion some of us break down,
> And those parts which can't be salvaged
> Are replaced with other GI parts, that's all.
>
> (p. 50)

In the final analysis, as Rafa asks, rhetorically and knowing full the answer, "Who cares?" (p. 51), certainly not the government ("I work for the State"; p. 51) that sent him there.

In the midst of this violence on a global scale, the Klail City soldiers are also forced to come to grips with their particular status in a larger frame. Not only are they subject to the same kind of discrimination, especially from officers on the war front, but they also come in contact with other working-class soldiers, white soldiers, who come from similar situations and suffer the same sense of dislocation. This violence will inevitably produce strategies for coping, as is clear in the case of Sonny Ruiz, who goes AWOL and ends up in Japan, where he "goes native"—that is, deserts. And Rafa helps him out by testifying before the Board of Inquiry (*Korean Love Songs*) that as far as he knows, Corporal Ruiz is dead, so that his mother Tina, back in Klail City, will be entitled to government compensation and assistance. The soldiers on the battlefield harbor no particular resentment against the Koreans or Chinese troops, but like "useless servants" merely obey and fire their weapons to keep from being killed; the same cannot be said, however, back home, where the Mexicanos have to struggle daily on the Texas Valley battlefield—"that slice of hell, heaven, / Purgatory and land of our Fathers" (*Korean Love Songs*, p. 53)—in full social interaction with their oppressors.

Violence is by definition also the driving force of Hinojosa's two police mysteries: *Partners in Crime* and *Ask a Policeman*. Both situate Rafa Buenrostro, the attorney turned policeman and then detective, in the Belken County Homicide Squad. In the first detective narrative, *Partners in Crime*, set in 1972, Rafa is lieutenant of detectives after having served six years on the force. In the second narrative, *Ask a Policeman*, set five years later, Rafa is the chief inspector of the Belken County Homicide Department and has been married to Sammie Jo Perkins for the last four years.

It bears noting here that Hinojosa's police mysteries are not in the vein of the traditional detective novel, where there is a rational, often upper-class investigator who through his intellectual acumen, à la Sherlock Holmes, proceeds by logical deduction to discover who did what, or at least how and perhaps why. Hinojosa's police narratives are unlike the traditional "whodunit," but neither are they in the "hardboiled" detective fiction tradition, à la Raymond Chandler, where the detective is more likely to be a loner, a cynical, chain-smoking detective addicted to whisky and, of course, women, whose language is a vernacular and peppered with as much slang and four-letter words as the criminal element he moves in. Nor are Hinojosa's novels like the hard-boiled detective fiction of Mexican writer Paco Ignacio Taibo, where the detective is politically committed and the criminal perpetrator is often the state and corporate capital. No, Hinojosa's novels are marked by a police homicide team that solves crimes on the basis of its collective investigations. The ensemble, the team, includes Rafa Buenrostro, Sam Dorson, Peter Hauer, Ike Cantú, and others, assisted by various laboratory technicians, and it depends on a spirit of cooperation and on the input of various informants in order to figure out a case.

In Hinojosa's detective fictions, the problem is the corrupt individual, often a predator in more ways than one, like Felipe Segundo Gómez or the two sadistic sons of Lee Gómez. Searching for the rotten apple or the lifetime criminal often implies going up against other law agencies. Bureaucratic ineptitude or interagency rivalry, with the local county police competing with the FBI or Immigration Service for hard data or jurisdiction, serves to complicate and often thwart an investigation. Still, it is often the personal touch, like Inspector Buenrostro's letter to the prison system requesting the early release of the dying Enrique Salinas, alias "el Camarón," that will later in the novel facilitate putting a criminal family out of business.

The border configuration of the Texas Valley further complicates not only the law's jurisdiction but the spatial play available to criminals. In both detective novels, these geographical considerations call for transnational cooperation, as the crimes often involve cross-border drug trafficking, money laundering, contraband of weapons, hired assassins who cross the border to do the deed, car stealing across the border, and the evasion of capture by crossing the border. For this reason the Homicide Squad is in frequent contact with the head of the Public Order in Barrones (that is, Matamoros); in one

novel *(Partners in Crime),* however, the Director of Barrones's Public Order, Captain Lee (Lisandro) Gómez-Solís, is in fact the corrupt mastermind behind the drug trafficking and a string of murders. In the second novel, and after Lee Gómez's indictment, a new Director of Public Order in Barrones is appointed by the governor of Tamaulipas: a woman, Lu Cetina, who is viewed as an honest cop ready to clean house, who will help her cross-border partners by facilitating investigations and sharing the data, resulting in the arrest of various suspects. The fact that Cetina, like the nefarious Lee Gómez, has studied and spent part of her life in the United States points to the permeability of the two systems.

Given the macronovel's focus on change, the configuration of the border itself is also seen to have undergone change. At one level it is no longer the porous border of the past, when no imaginary line separated one nation-state from another; the post-1924 border and its ever increasing militarization have generated apprehension and expectation, especially on the part of the undocumented nationals who cross the border daily. Yet as *Ask a Policeman* characters comment, the lives, cultures, and economies of both sides are inextricably intertwined: "Many came to shop and spend American dollars, and more came to earn their dollars as maids, store clerks, gardeners, painters, carpenters, janitors, and still others to serve as pick-up day laborers paid for work done on the spot" (p. 32). The Valley, while recognized as one of the poorest areas in the country, is a gateway for all sorts of transactions that indicate that Belken County is no longer an area of small isolated rural communities; its border location across from a large Mexican city now has accelerated time and converted the transnational into a local and everyday reality.

In the macronovel's mapping of life in the Texas Valley, as much in the detective fiction as in his other novels, Hinojosa's grounding in the local does not leave out the global, the national, or the transnational, because, as the author's body of work demonstrates so well, all of these spaces are interconnected; they overlap, with traces of the past always in the present, and with the outside world always impinging upon and in effect constituting the local. In his "Klail City Death Trip Series," Hinojosa has created a world of unique characters whose everyday lives constitute the cultural history of particular sec-

tors of the Texas Valley. Narrated in that particular sardonic style of his, Hinojosa's Klail City chronicle makes clear that the history of the Valley, and perhaps all history, is collective and multifaceted and its narration calls for experimentation with form. And finally, what is most important is its recording, constructing and reconstructing memory, lest it disappear without a trace.

Selected Bibliography

WORKS OF ROLANDO HINOJOSA

NOVELS

Estampas del valle y otras obras. Berkeley: Quinto Sol Publications, 1973. English-language version published as *The Valley.* Ypsilanti, Mich.: Bilingual Press, 1983.

Klail City y sus alrededores. Havana: Casa de las Américas, 1976. Bilingual edition, with translation by Rosaura Sánchez, published as *Generaciones y semblanzas.* Berkeley: Justa Publications, 1977. English-language version by the author published as *Klail City.* Houston: Arte Público Press, 1987. Spanish language reprint published as *El condado de Belken–Klail City.* Tempe, Ariz.: Editorial Bilingüe, 1994.

Korean Love Songs from Klail City Death Trip. Berkeley: Justa Publications, 1978.

Mi querido Rafa. Houston: Arte Público Press, 1981. Revised English-language version published as *Dear Rafe.* Houston: Arte Público Press, 1985.

Rites and Witnesses. Houston: Arte Público Press, 1982.

Partners in Crime. Houston: Arte Público Press, 1985.

Claros varones de Belken/Fair Gentlemen of Belken County. English translation by Julia Cruz. Tempe, Ariz.: Editorial Bilingüe, 1986.

Becky and Her Friends. Houston: Arte Público Press, 1990. Spanish-language version published as *Los amigos de Becky.* Houston: Arte Público Press, 1991.

The Useless Servants. Houston: Arte Público Press, 1993.

Ask a Policeman. Houston: Arte Público Press, 1998.

PROSE

"One of Those Things." Translated by José R. Reyna. In *El Espejo/The Mirror: Selected Mexican-American Literature.* Edited by Octavio Romano and Herminio Ríos. Berkeley: Tonatiuh/Quinto Sol International, 1969.

"Por esas cosas que pasan." *El Grito* 5, no. 3 (spring 1972): 26–36.

"The Mexican American Devil's Dictionary, I." *El Grito* 6, no. 3 (spring 1973): 41–53.

"E pluribus vitae." *Revista Chicano Riqueña* 1, no. 2 (1973). Reprinted in *Flor y Canto: An Anthology of Chicano Literature,* 1975.

"Voces del barrio." *El Grito* 6, no. 4 (summer 1973): 3–8.

"Cosas de familia." *Caracol,* September 1975.

"Seis," *Caracol,* October 1975.

"El Maistro. Tía Panchita." In *Chicano Voices: An Anthology of Chicano Literature.* Edited by Carlota Cárdenas de Dwyer. Boston: Houghton Mifflin, 1975.

"Epigmenio Salazar. Enedino Broca López." *Hispamérica* 4, nos. 11–12 (1975).

"Don Marcial de Anda. Apple Core! Baltimore!" *Mester* 5, no. 2 (1975).

"Don Orfalindo Buitureyra. Un poco de todo." *Revista Chicano Riqueña* 4, no. 2 (1976).

"From the Mexican American Devil's Dictionary, II." *Revista Chicano Riqueña* 4, no. 2 (fall 1976): 45–46.

"Marcando Tiempo. Los Támez." In *Festival de Floricanto: An Anthology of Chicano Literature.* Edited by Alurista, et al. 1976.

"Rayando el sol. El hermano Imás." In *El Quetzal Emplumece: An Anthology of Chicano Literature.* Edited by Carmela Montalvo, et al. San Antonio, Tex.: Mexican American Cultural Center, 1976.

"Con el pie en el estribo." *Bilingual Review/La Revista Bilingüe* 3, no. 1 (January–April 1976): 64–65. Reprinted in *Mosaicos de la vida.* Edited by Francisco Jiménez. New York: Harcourt, Brace, Jovanovich, 1981.

"El sepulturero." *El cuento: Revista de imaginación* (Mexico City), no. 76 (1977).

"Vidas chicanas." *Tejidos: A Bilingual Journal for the Stimulation of Chicano Creativity and Criticism* 4, no. 1 (1977).

"A Foot in the Stirrup" and "Echevarría Has the Floor: a. Choche Markham; b. Doña Sóstenes; c. All in the Family." Translated by Fausto Avendaño. *Latin American Literary Review* 5, no. 10 (1977).

"Choche Markham." In *Mestizo: An Anthology of Chicano Literature,* 1978.

"Al pozo con Bruno Cano." In *Alcanzando.* Edited by de la Vega & Parr. Gin and Co, 1978.

"Claros varones de Belken: seis trozos." *Plural* (Mexico City), no. 96 (1979).

"El hermano Imás." In *La Semana de Bellas Artes.* Mexico City: n.p., 1979. Reprinted as "Brother Imás." *Southwest Review* 71, no. 4 (fall 1986).

"Feliz cumpleaños, E.U.A.." *La Palabra* 1, no. 1 (spring 1979): 54–56. Reprinted in *Mosaicos de la Vida.* Edited by Francisco Jiménez. New York: Harcourt, Brace, Jovanovich, 1981.

"Penthouse Views." In *Requisa treinta y dos.* Edited by Rosaura Sánchez. La Jolla, Calif: Chicano Research Publications, 1979.

Generaciones, Notas y Brechas. Generations, Notes and Trails. (compilation of previously published prose). Translated by Fausto Avendaño. n.p.: Casa, 1980.

"Spanish Majors." In *Cuentos Chicanos.* Edited by Rudolfo A. Anaya and Antonio Márquez. Albuquerque: New America, University of New Mexico, 1980.

"P. Galindo I y II." In *Hispanics in the United States.* Edited by Gary D. Keller and Francisco Jiménez. Ypsilanti, Mich.: Bilingual Press, 1980.

"The Witnesses. The Rites." *Revista Chicano Riqueña* 8, no. 3 (1980).

"Los revolucionarios." In *Chicanos: Antología histórica y literaria.* Edited by Tino Villanueva. Mexico City: Fondo de Cultura Económica, 1980.

"The Witness I and II" (fragments). *Revista Río Bravo* 1, no. 3 (1981).

"Conversations on a Hill I and II." *Mester* 10, nos. 1–2 (1981): 93–97. Reprinted in *Riversedge. Second Chicano Collection.* Pan American University, 1982.

"Don Manuel." *Discovery* 7, no. 3 (spring 1983).

"Out of Many Lives." *Dallas Times Herald,* March 20, 1983, sec. A, p. 36.

"The Gulf Oil Can Santa Claus. A Texas Christmas." In *Pressworks.* Edited by J. E. Weems. 1983.

"Sunday Mornings." *Pax: Journal of Art, Science and Philosophy* 3, nos. 1–2 (1986). Reprinted as "Remembrance of My Father." Southwest Airlines *Spirit,* June 1986.

"Braulio Tapia." In *Adventures in American Literature, Pegasus Edition.* Edited by Francis Hodgins, Kenneth Silverman, et al. New York: Harcourt Brace Jovanovich, 1989.

"The Rites." In *The Faber Book of Contemporary Latin American Short Stories.* Edited by Nick Caistor. Boston: Faber & Faber, 1989.

"Sometimes It Just Happens That Way." In *The Heath Anthology of American Literature,* vol. l. Edited by Paul Lauter, et al. Lexington, Mass.: Heath, 1989.

"Un poco de todo." In *Saga de México.* Edited by Seymour Menton and María Herrera-Sobek. Tempe, Ariz.: Editorial Bilingüe, 1992.

"A Spring Break." In *New Chicano/a Writing.* Edited by Charles Tatum. Tucson: University of Arizona Press, 1993.

"Otra vez la muerte." *Los universitarios* (Universidad Autónoma de Mexico, Tercera Epoca). No. 46 (1993).

"Coming Home I and II." In *Short Fiction by Hispanic U.S. Writers.* Edited by Nicolás Kanellos. Houston: Arte Público Press, 1993.

POETRY
"Retratos para el abuelo; Pepe Vielma; el Muerto; Los fundadores." *Caracol* 5, no. 3 (1977).

"Native Son Home from Asia." *Maize* 1, no. 3 (1978).

"Fit for Duty." *Flor y Canto en Minnesota,* 1978.

"Old Friends." *Canto al Pueblo: An Anthology of Experiences,* 1978.

"Night Burial Details. Boston John McCreedy Drinks with Certain Lewd Men of the Baser Sort." *Bilingual Review/La Revista Bilingüe* 5, nos. 1–2 (1978).

"Brodkey's Replacement." *Riversedge* 2, no. 2 (1978).

"Poems by Rolando Hinojosa: Eigth Army at the Chongchon. A Matter of Supplies." *Latin American Literary Review* 8, no. 13 (1978).

"Above All, the Waste." *The New Mexican Independent* 84, no. 6 (October 12, 1979).

"Incoming. Until Further Orders." *Revista Chicano Riqueña* 7, no. 4 (1979).

"Crossing the Line." *Revista Chicano Riqueña* 7, no. 4 (1979).

"Retaguardia en noviembre. Which Means the 219th Isn't Doing Well at All." *Maize* 4 (spring–summer 1981).

"The Eighth Army at the Chongchon," "Rear Guard Action I," and "Above All the Waste." In *Mexican American Literature.* Edited by Charles Tatum. New York: Harcourt Brace Jovanovich, 1990.

OTHER WORKS

"A Voice of One's Own," "The Sense of Place," "Crossing the Line: The Construction of a Poem," and "Chicano Literature: An American Literature with a Difference." In *The Rolando Hinojosa Reader: Essays Historical and Critical.* Edited by José David Saldívar. Houston: Arte Público Press, 1984.

"*I Am Joaquín.* The Relationship between the Text and the Film." In *Chicano Cinema.* Edited by Gary Keller. Binghamton, N.Y.: Bilingual Review/Press, 1985.

Rivera, Tomás. *This Migrant Earth.* Translated by Rolando Hinojosa. Houston: Arte Público Press, 1985.

SECONDARY WORKS

INTERVIEWS

Bruce-Novoa, John D. "Interview of Rolando Hinojosa." *Latin American Literary Review* 5, no. 10 (spring-summer, 1977): 103–114. Reprinted in *Chicano Authors: Inquiry by Interview.* Edited by John D. Bruce-Novoa. Austin: University of Texas Press, 1980. Pp. 49–65.

Saldívar, José David. "Our Southwest: An Interview with Rolando Hinojosa." In *The Rolando Hinojosa Reader. Essays Historical and Critical.* Edited by José David Saldívar. Houston: Arte Público Press, 1985.

CRITICAL AND BIBLIOGRAPHICAL STUDIES

Akers, John C. "From Translation to Rewriting: Rolando Hinojosa's *The Valley.*" In *The Americas Review* 21, no. 1 (spring 1993).

Bruce-Novoa, Juan. "Who's Killing Whom in Belken County: Rolando Hinojosa's Narrative Production." In *Monographic Review/Revista Monográfica* 3: 1–2 (1987).

Calderón, Hector. "Texas Border Literature: Cultural Transformation and Historical Reflection in the Works of Américo Paredes, Rolando Hinojosa and Gloria Anzaldúa." *Dispositio* 16, no. 41 (1991): 13–27. Spanish-language version published as "Literatura fronteriza tejana: el compromiso con la historia en Américo Paredes, Rolando Hinojosa y Gloria Anzaldúa." *Mester* 22–23 (1993–1994): 41–61.

Cota-Cárdenas, Margarita, "Mi Querido Rafa and Irony: A Structural Study," in *Revista Chicano-Riqueña* 12 (fall–winter 1984): 3–4.

Espadas, Elizabeth, "Bridging the Gap: Rolando Hinojosa's Writings in Their Latin American Dimension." *Maclas: Latin American Essays* 1 (1987): 7–15.

Espadas, Juan, and Arvilla Payne-Jackson. "Estampas del Valle: One Life of the Klail City Death Trip Series." *Maclas: Latin American Essays* 8 (1994): 63–75.

Flores, Lauro. "Narrative Strategies in Rolando Hinojosa's Rites and Witnesses." *Revista Chicano-Riqueña* 12: 3–4 (fall–winter 1984).

Martín-Rodríguez, Manuel M. "La muerte como indicador histórico y social en *Estampas del Valle* de Rolando Hinojosa." In *National Association for Chicano Studies.* Boulder, Colo.: 1989.

———. "Rolando Hinojosa y su 'Klail City Death Trip Series: Una novela del lector," *The Americas Review* 21, no. 2 (summer 1993).

Saldívar, José David, ed. *The Rolando Hinojosa Reader: Essays Historical and Critical.* Houston: Arte Público Press, 1985.

Torres, Hector. "Discourse and Plot in Rolando Hinojosa's *The Valley*: Narrativity and the Recovery of Chicano Heritage." *Confluencia-Revista Hispánica de Cultura y Literatura* 2, no. 1 (fall 1986).

Sánchez, Rosaura. "From Heterogeneity to Contradiction: Hinojosa's Novel." *Revista Chicano-Riqueña* 12 (fall–winter 1984): 3–4.

Graciela Limón

(1938–)

FLORA M. GONZÁLEZ

WITH SIX NOVELS in the late 1980s and 1990s, Graciela Limón makes a valuable contribution to the renaissance of Chicana works. Her novels express her commitment to Latina activism as it pertains to U.S. involvement with Mexico and Central American countries, and the political and human consequences of that involvement. Like other Chicana writers such as Ana Castillo, Limón gives voice to women caught in the maelstrom of civil wars, as in El Salvador, and represents the changing roles of women as they and their families migrate from their homelands to find better political and economic futures in the United States. One of Limón's most marked contributions to Chicana literature records this North-South legacy particularly as it has affected the lives of women. She reaches out to her readers through the literary adaptation of narrative modes found in melodrama and other forms of popular literature, as well as in investigative reporting, testimonial literature, and academic research. Her fiction reflects her autobiography inasmuch as she is one of three children, having been born on 2 August 1938, in Los Angeles, to Mexican immigrants, Jesús Limón and Altagracia Gómez Limón, both members of the working class.

On the occasion of her retirement after thirty-five years of teaching at Loyola Marymount University in Los Angeles, Limón stated that, after years of writing as a scholar for journals and conferences, she looked forward to dedicating her time to writing fiction about the political struggles of Latin Americans and Latinos. Limón received her B.A. in peninsular Spanish literature from Marymount College in 1965, her M.A. in the same from the Universidad de las Américas, Mexico City, in 1968, and her Ph.D. in Latin American twentieth-century literature from the University of California, Los Angeles, in 1975. She gained critical acclaim in 1993 with the publication of *In Search of Bernabé,* which received the American Book Award and the 1994 Before Columbus Foundation American Book Award. She has published four other novels, *The Memories of Ana Calderón* (1994); *Song of the Hummingbird* (1996), an earlier version of which was published as *María de Belén: The Autobiography of an Indian Woman* (1990); *The Day of the Moon* (1999); and *Erased Faces* (2001). *In Search of Bernabé* resulted from her having served in the 1990 delegation that investigated the assassination of six Jesuit priests in El Salvador in 1989. The priests, a female employee, and her daughter were killed violently, pointing to the abuses of the Salvadoran military. Here as in her other novels, Limón combines activism and literature.

Her novels reflect the commitment of a Chicana writer in the last decade of the twentieth century, for whom the fate of indigenous people and mestizos, people of mixed Spanish and Indian ancestry, living and working across the borders of the United States, Mexico, and Central America, matters. Their lives as migrant laborers and survivors of overwhelming political upheavals are rooted in the economic and political interdependence between north and south, which trap them on a level where mere survival is the best they can hope for. In her novels, the female protagonists always endeavor to reveal their stories in the context of a historical and mythical past that allows them to engage in multiple forms of resistance. In *Song of the Hummingbird, The Day of the Moon,* and *Erased Faces,* the fate of women is mythically linked to what Norma Alarcón, in "Chicana Feminism in the Tracks of 'The' Native Woman," called "the evocation of indigenous figures" (p. 67), thus allowing for a consciousness and an understanding of contemporary reality that is rooted in cultural recollection.

It is not surprising, then, that Graciela Limón should write within the genre of testimonial literature, in which the voice and story of one character evoke that of an entire community. Testimonial fiction is modeled after the genre of *testimonio,* in which a member of the intelligentsia engages the testimony of a member of society who would otherwise remain voiceless. Classic examples of *testimonio* involve the interviewing, by journalists, ethnographers, and writers, of a member of a voiceless minority, such as the indigenous women Rigoberta Menchú (Guatemala) and Domitila Barrios (Bolivia), who as witnesses and activists for their communities tell of their individual and collective realities with the intent of advancing their cause in the international arena. The *testimonio* assumes a collaboration between a witness who divulges an unknown story and a member of an international community who then edits and publishes the testimony. In most cases, the person who gives testimony has categorized her-

or himself as a representative, yet distinguishable, member of the group. In her first novel, *María de Belén: The Autobiography of an Indian Woman,* Limón fictionalizes the testimonial relationship between a former Mexican princess, Lady Huitzitzilin (Hummingbird), who is known in colonial Mexico as doña María de Belén, and the scribe Sor Tiburcia Solares, who records her personal and collective version of the conquest of Mexico.

Limón has written two versions of this story, *María de Belén* and later *Song of the Hummingbird,* tracing her transition from academic writer to fiction writer. *María de Belén* fictionalizes the *testimonio* relationship and superimposes on it the story of a graduate student who has been handed a manuscript that was bought in a market by her former Mexican professor—a manuscript that she then translates into English and publishes with all the academic paratextual matter: translator's notes, an introduction, footnotes, a glossary of indigenous and colonial terms, and a bibliography. Preceding the fictionalized academic format comes the author's note, written by Limón, which clarifies that "The story of Doña María de Belén is a novel, and to read it otherwise would be a departure from the author's intention" (p. xv). Limón gives us a fictional autobiography of an academic who after many years in the teaching profession receives a box with the manuscript she had left behind in her Mexico City apartment. With this novel, Limón expresses a Chicana concern about being colonized by academic language and failing to communicate with those illiterate in academese. At the same time, the writer acknowledges the necessity of using theory to analyze past histories and categories such as race, class, gender, and ethnicity in order to clarify past and present experience.

In the prologue, through the fictionalized professor, Natalia Roldán, Limón gives herself permission to embark on a fictional task, which, at least in this first version, still retains traces of the academic endeavor: to find a significant manuscript, to translate it for a wider audience, and then to publish it with all the markers of the academic world. The translator's note reproduces the prototype introduction of a *testimonio,* in which the person who publishes the testimony makes evident the editing process of the manuscript, a process that wishes to both respect the voice of the original Lady Huitzitzilin and to facilitate the understanding of her story by "shortening the lengthy sentences typical of sixteenth century Spanish prose" (p. 11). Mediating between the story told and the scribe who records it are a series of letters from a reverend mother who has commissioned the scribal work from one of her nuns with the intent of not losing the alternative historical record which only a former lady of the Mexicas can provide. (The use of the word "Mexica" instead of "Aztec" denotes respect for the multiplicity of ethnic groups that made up the Aztec empire.) In this sense, the reverend mother acts as a mirror image of the author, for whom the recovery of a noble woman's story at the moment of the arrival of Cortés and the fall of the Aztec empire constitutes a form of witnessing an irrevocable past.

Throughout the novel, the teller establishes a hierarchy in which Lady Huitzitzilin, who is of noble origin and the teller of a momentous history, reverses the societal order so that an indigenous woman stands above the scribe who will make her words resound on the written page: "Yes, my people were kings and princes— and yours? Who were your ancestors, Little Sister?" (p. 34). Her story is meant to place women at the heart of history by virtue of their toil and suffering. What is most radical about her narrative, however, is her revisionist interpretation of the fall of the Mexica empire, which she ascribes to the rulers' refusal to abide by the god Quetzalcóatl's predictions.

If throughout most of the novel, Lady Huitzitzilin's narration coincides with what most chroniclers of the Mexican colonial past have recorded (which is acknowledged in the endnotes), she differs in her interpretation of Quetzalcóatl's significance as a peacemaker:

"Lord Feathered Serpent preached moderation and understanding, and above all, he insisted that our advancement need not depend upon rage or violence or war or upon all its trappings of quilted armor, helmets, insignias, and the other displays men love to flaunt and preen" (p. 39). With this statement, the noblewoman offers an alternative version of Mexican history, the colonial version of which emphasizes the Mexica rulers' adoration of Huitzilopochtli, god of war and conquest, to whom blood sacrifices were offered. She even goes on to establish a relationship between women and the Lord Feathered Serpent. "Quetzalcóatl was all things, he was life and death, fire and water, animal and human, but most important, he was both man and woman" (p. 38). Through her emphasis on Quetzalcóatl, whose gentle nature she highlights, Lady Huitzitzilin repositions women at the center of her people's history, before those who favored Huitzilopochtli and enforced the banishment of the god Quetzalcóatl.

When in 1996 Graciela Limón published *Song of the Hummingbird,* she presented the story of Hummingbird (Huitzitzilin) as told to Father Benito Lara. He records what he hears and is eventually deeply affected by her words. In the author's note, Limón stresses the importance of the story because it differs from official versions of the fall of the Aztec empire, because it is told by an indigenous woman, because Lady Huitzitzilin was a participant in and a witness to that history, and because that history had been silenced and must now be heard. The author's note reinforces the desire of testimonial literature to underline the plural nature of true historical accounts. Here the academic mediations have all but disappeared and only the figure of Father Benito as listener remains. And whereas in *María de Belén* the relationship between Lady Huitzitzilin and the Little Sister is a confrontational one, in *Song of the Hummingbird* the relationship between teller and scribe highlights the transformation of the priest's concept of Mexican history.

Huitzitzilin begins as a young girl of privilege who falls in love with her cousin Zintle, a future ruler. She is forced to marry a much older, prestigious lord in her cousin's court, is battered by her husband because she is not a virgin at the time of her marriage, and is witness to the entrance of Cortés into Tenochtitlán and to the fall of the empire. Finally, she is forced to flee the great city back to her place of origin. She is a woman who must abide by the patriarchy that rules her life, beginning with her father, who arranges her marriage to a man she cannot love. Her narration emphasizes the many losses she encounters throughout her life, including that of her son, begotten by her cousin Zintle, and later of the children she has with a Spanish captain. These children are torn from her once Captain Ovando realizes that his official wife cannot bear children. Her mestizo children are sent to Spain to receive a colonial education. Like the mythical figure of La Llorona, the wailing woman who has drowned her children so that they will not be enslaved by the Spanish and forever looks for them, Huitzitzilin travels to Barcelona in search of them. She finds that her son has died of European diseases and her daughter has become a Spanish lady and rejected her mother because of her indigenous origins. Paradigmatic of her many losses is the loss of her name, Huitzitzilin, meaning beautiful hummingbird, since after colonization she must take the Christian name María de Belén. When Father Benito insists on knowing her Christian name rather than her indigenous name, she replies by emphasizing that with the arrival of the Spanish she has been robbed of her name and of much more: "You mean you have to make sure that I have been robbed of everything, even my name" (p. 62).

Limón's restoration of proper names to her characters underlines her description of herself as a Chicana writer. Her novels, and this one in particular, respond, as Alarcón says, to her acceptance of a Chicana critical agenda "for dismantling historical conjunctures of crisis, confusion, political and ideological conflict, and

contradictions of the simultaneous effects of having 'no names,' having 'many names,' not 'know[ing] her names,' and being someone else's 'dreamwork'" (p. 65). *Song of the Hummingbird* dismantles the colonial version of the fall of the Aztec empire and addresses the effects of women's nameless condition in both Aztec and Hispanic societies.

In order to respond to this namelessness, Limón creates female characters who survive the overwhelming effects of patriarchy by resisting and talking back. In *Song of the Hummingbird*, this resistance is played out in the relationship between Huitzitzilin and Father Benito. At the beginning of the novel, Huitzitzilin is eighty-five and living in a convent, where she insists that she is about to die. She asks for confession. Her most important mode of resistance entails turning that confession into an act of witnessing both her life and that of the Mexica people. Parallel to her narration/confession, the novel presents the Indian woman in lyrical communication with her ancestors through songs in her native tongue. Limón's protagonist thus speaks out on behalf of Indian women with the intent of divulging information not yet recorded in any of the colonial chronicles. Huitzitzilin's audience comprises both members of the conquering class and her ancestors, who need to hear a woman's version of their own history. As soon as Father Benito realizes that she intends to narrate more than her sins, he consents to listen out of curiosity, always careful to separate the narrative of her people's customs from that of her sinful personal life, which includes lying with a man before wedlock, aborting her first child so that he would not be enslaved by the conquerors, and killing the father of her mestizo children for having sent them to Spain. The first he will record for posterity, the last he will forgive as the Church mandates.

Song of the Hummingbird employs a narrative strategy that couples the oral narrative of Huitzitzilin's life with dialogues that show the slow transformation of Father Benito. At first he feels repulsed by what he hears, then slowly he begins to gain an understanding of alternative ways of looking at history. Ultimately, he becomes sympathetic enough with that history to rescue it as a "missing chronicle" (p. 174). When Huitzitzilin narrates the arrival of the Spanish in Tenochtitlán and through her eyes Father Benito witnesses the devastation wrought by European diseases, he begins to see the conquest as the natives have. As in *María de Belén,* where the Little Sister asks the Reverend Mother to dismiss her from her task of listening to the old woman, in this later version of the tale Father Benito consults his superior, Father Anselmo, whenever he needs guidance about the religious doubts that Huitzitzilin's narration raises for him. As in the first novel, the superior advises Father Benito not to be ensnared by the imaginative tales that the Indian woman weaves. Throughout *Song of the Hummingbird,* the priest confesses to being captivated by "the Indian woman's revelations and their unexpected, abrupt tangents" (p. 31). Tangents, illustrated in fanciful descriptions of ritualistic dances, Father Anselmo suggests, point to the reason why they are not already being recorded in the Seville Archives: they represent a false rendition of history. At times Father Benito loses patience with Huitzitzilin—for example, when she concentrates on the loss of her children and her desire to recover them from the hands of their father, Captain Ovando. Father Benito considers such matters unimportant, not historical, while the Indian woman questions what constitutes historical material. Huitzitzilin resists women's lack of centrality in historical records, just as Graciela Limón does.

Ultimately, Father Benito's desire "to capture it all," and "to write a chronicle of the same magnitude as those written by Fathers Sahagún and De las Casas" (p. 93) propels him to continue listening. By the end of her tale, Father Benito stands in awe of the woman's determination to recover her children and of her insistence that he listen and record her hummingbird song. The act of listening and recording an otherwise forgotten tale brings to the priest, and to the reader of Limón's novel, a consciousness and an understanding of an Indian woman's life seen "through her eyes in its wholeness and not in fragments" (p. 217).

Besides creating female protagonists whose voices reposition the role of women in colonial historical accounts, Gloria Limón engages the mythical figure of La Llorona, who has antecedents in two contradictory pre-Columbian figures, one who emphasizes the destructive mother (Cihuacoatl), the other a fertility goddess who gives life (Coatlopeuh). These two figures originally coincided in Coatlicue, who, as Ana María Carbonell writes in "From Llorona to Gritona: Coatlicue in Feminist Tales by Viramontes and Cisneros," "encourages resistance by pitting the desire for survival against the act of destruction" (Carbonell, p. 56). Whatever negative qualities La Llorona personifies are seen as imposed by the violence perpetrated on her and her children by the destructive forces of war and colonization. In Chicana feminist imaginary, La Llorona becomes an appropriate image for indigenous Mexican and Central American women. These women fled across borders, running from repressive governments, particularly during the 1980s in Central America. They experienced the devastation of internal strife in their countries, often coupled with the disappearance or uprooting of their children. Ironically, large numbers of immigrants marched north to the United States, the country that supported the military governments that made their migrations necessary.

Luz Delcano, the female protagonist of *In Search of Bernabé* (1993) personifies La Llorona's search, having lost both of her male children. The first, Lucio Delcano, offspring of the rape of Luz by her grandfather don Lucio Delcano, was taken away from her by the Delcano family to be raised as the child of an upper-class family. He goes on to become the head of the death squads in El Salvador, a man obsessed with having been abandoned by his mother and bound to take revenge on his mother by killing her other son, Bernabé. Bernabé was on his way to becoming a priest at the time of the assassination of Archbishop Romero. Caught in the terror and the confusion that followed the April 14 massacre, when the military slaughtered the mourners at Romero's funeral, Bernabé finds himself the leader of the crowds trying to flee the country by crossing the Sumpul River. He thus incurs the rage of his brother Lucio, who has to exterminate him as a leader of the opposition. Through the character of Luz Delcano and her two sons, Limón represents the political turmoil of a Central American nation at war, as well as the consequences of that political turmoil.

Luz Delcano, seeking Bernabé, travels by bus in the company of Arturo. Arturo is fleeing political persecution for having dared to work for the betterment of the poor. During long bus rides, first to Mexico City, then to Los Angeles a year later, Luz and Arturo share their stories and their hopes of finding a life free from violence. They find jobs and work toward solidarity with other Central American immigrants in the church-run Casa Andrade, and Luz begins to look upon Arturo as her son. But because of the political connections between El Salvador and the United States, persecution follows Arturo to his supposed safe haven. When masked assassins break into the small apartment they share in Los Angeles and kill him, Luz responds as a mother: "Momentarily stunned out of her mind, Luz let out a lament, a mournful cradle song for a dead son" (p. 85). In this scene, Luz Delcano becomes the prototype of the suffering mother, a modern-day La Llorona, whose lamentations resound across national borders. The scene anticipates the violence that her true son Bernabé will experience in El Salvador soon afterward, a scene she does not witness but which she intuits when she finds his body in a garbage heap. On her way back to her country after being deported, she anticipates the grief which will permeate her life: "A growing distance between her body and spirit took hold of her, as if her soul were drifting away from

pain, uniting itself to Arturo and to Bernabé" (p. 88). Luz survives the tragedy of losing her son through both emotional alienation and her desire to be united with the dead. In the conjoining of Arturo and Bernabé as victims of political violence, she becomes the mythical figure of the suffering mother in the midst of Central America's civil strife.

Parallel to the plot of Luz Delcano's search for Bernabé stands the strained friendship of two other characters in the novel. They are two Americans, Father Hugh and the contraband arms salesman Augie Sinclair. The latter supplies Lucio Delcano with the ammunition that makes possible the terror in El Salvador, while Father Hugh supplies the respectability of a college professor/priest whose university invests in the construction company Augie purports to own. Through these two characters, a connection is made between U.S. economic interests and El Salvador's civil war. Limón ties together the two main plots of the novel through Luz Delcano's confession to Father Hugh when they find refuge in the cathedral during the guerrilla offensive of 1989. As she does in *Song of the Hummingbird*, Limón utilizes the narrative device of a confession so that her characters may bear witness to political turmoil. Luz's confession begins with her stating her name and the fact that she's a sinner, then she blames Salvadorans' sinful nature for the violence they must all endure. Father Hugh responds with a more cynical interpretation: "Señora, you're wrong! Those people out there are being slaughtered, not because of their sins but because of the greediness and cruelty of others" (p. 99). Through the use of the confessional dialogue, Limón records Luz's life of suffering, the contradictions of Father Hugh's life as a college professor/priest driven by his desire for recognition in the academy, and a running commentary on the complexity of the civil war in El Salvador. In addition to the two voices in the confessional, the narrative records Father Hugh's conflict with Augie's voice, which haunts the priest and accuses him of being a hypocrite: "*Hugh, you're a god-damn hypocrite! Cut the crap, and stop pointing the finger at others. Go on! Tell her about your own greed. Why don't you fess up to your own sins?"* (p. 99). By exploiting the multiple voices described by theorist Mikhail Bakhtin as, in Ana Patricia Rodríguez's paraphrase, the "historically situated, social plural language" of novels or narratives of contact ("Refugees of the South: Central Americans in the U.S. Latino Imaginary," p. 406), Limón foregrounds the intersection of cultural and political involvement due to north-south economic and subversive alliances.

In addition to the many voices of the characters, the novel is flanked by journalistic accounts of the events depicted. The first, from *Time Magazine,* 14 April 1980, describes the massacre that took place the day Romero was buried. The second, from the *Los Angeles Times,* 17 January 1992, depicts the joyful celebration of the peace treaty and then ends with the words of a woman whose missing son was returned to her dead. Between these two journalistic accounts stand the fictionalization of events and the development of characters based on the real lives of mothers and sons on either side of the political conflict. To reinforce the ties between the fictional representation and the actual witnessing of events, the novel ends with a statement about the flood of refugees to the north and Luz Delcano's survival as she found refuge in a small village away from the capital. Beginning with the prologue and continuing with epigraphs at the beginning of each section of the novel, quotations appear from both Genesis and the Book of Daniel to underscore the mythical dimensions of the events and the suffering depicted. The quotation from the Book of Daniel in the prologue ends with a statement about the daughters of Israel who "were too frightened to resist" (p. 406). This connects to the novel's portrayal of women whose lives only replicate the figure of La Llorona, who feels helpless against the overwhelming forces of history. While Luz's act of witnessing can be construed as a form of resistance, the fact that

she does it through the act of confession and not through more any political outlet reflects the lack of agency some Central American women faced in the decade of the 1980s. Only in her subsequent novels, such as *Erased Faces,* does Limón find, in the Chiapas uprisings of the 1990s, a way to represent the military involvement of women.

Before giving full agency to women through their participation in political events, Limón wrote two novels depicting the repression endured by women within the patriarchally constructed family unit: *The Memories of Ana Calderón* (1994) and *The Day of the Moon* (1999). The first vacillates between the first person narration of Ana Calderón and a third person omniscient narrator. As she did in her previous novels, Limón writes about migration from the south to the north. In this instance, a widowed father, fleeing abject poverty in a Mexican fishing village, travels north with his children, to be exploited in the agricultural fields of California. The oldest daughter, Ana, sees going north as a way of fulfilling her dream of becoming a dancer. Her expectations are dashed when she is forced to become the surrogate mother to her younger siblings, all girls except for the youngest. From her birth, Ana carries the stigma of being a first girl child who is believed responsible for having "done something bad to my mother's womb" (p. 11). Two boys are born to the family, and both die. Her father's hatred of Ana for not being a boy, and for poisoning her mother's womb, drives Ana to prove herself a worthy "son" throughout her life. The birth of a brother ten years later, on the date of her own birth, constitutes the beginning of life for Ana. It is as if her brother had given birth to her: "I've always thought that my life really began on the day that my little brother, César, was born" (p. 11). On that day, seeing her mother suffering birth pains, she feels certain that she will never want children. Yet on the day that her first menstrual flow marks her as a woman, she realizes that her dreams are but a fantasy and that she might soon become like all the women in the tomato fields beside her, wasted by childbearing and back-breaking work. As the first of six girls and one boy, Ana Calderón, as both a girl and a woman, carries the weight of a patriarchal family, which both represses her dreams and demands that she thwart her femininity and reject her family and culture in order to eventually pursue a successful career as a businesswoman.

The Memories of Ana Calderón records the life of a young migrant worker in the United States, who through education, hard work, and separation from family and Mexican culture fulfills the American dream. Her accomplishments result from escaping the brutal treatment she receives from her father, Rodolfo, her sister Alejandra, and her sister's husband, Octavio. While still a hard-working student, Ana falls in love with Octavio, the orphaned boy her family in Mexico has adopted and raised. Throughout their early years, the younger sister Alejandra has hoped to marry Octavio. But when Ana and Octavio attended school together, a romance develops and Ana becomes pregnant. Ana assumes that Octavio will ask her father for her hand in marriage, but Octavio fears Rodolfo too much to acknowledge his transgression. Eventually, Octavio marries Alejandra, to the father's satisfaction. In almost Dickensian style, Ana survives the physical and psychological abuse her father metes out once he realizes she is pregnant, as well as that of Octavio, who eventually wants to raise his own son and kidnaps the boy. Ana survives these tragedies, first through the help of a Japanese neighbor, doña Hiroko, who takes her in when she becomes pregnant, and later through the help of a farming couple, Amy and Franklin, who welcome her as a farmworker and help her raise her son, Ismael. During her stay with this family, Ana finds comfort in the Protestant religion and begins to develop the entrepreneurial skills that will lead her to become an extremely successful businesswoman. For the first half of the novel, Ana's life is a series of abuses that she survives only as a result of her intelligence, her perseverance, and

the loving support she receives from people increasingly distant from her own culture. Amy and Franklin, in particular, represent for Ana a new, much healthier model of a nuclear family, a family that loves her and that she can love.

The novel displays a deterministic bent: the curse of paternalism pursues the female protagonist even when she seems to find fulfillment away from her family. Just about the time when Ana finds peace in her life, Octavio enters it again, demanding custody of his son. Ana reacts to the kidnapping by attempting to kill him and again loses control of her life. She must now serve a two-year jail sentence, and the child is forever lost to her when he is adopted by a wealthy family in San Francisco. Once out of jail, she becomes a labor organizer for women doing piecework at the Ezra Feurmann and Son clothing factory. Her organizational skills impress her boss, and she joins management once she has improved working conditions in the factory. Ezra encourages Ana to pursue an education while still working and becomes the father Rodolfo could have never been. After Ana inherits Ezra's estate, she turns the business into a high-fashion company.

At this juncture in the novel, Ana has fulfilled the American dream of becoming successful through education and hard work. Her obsession with work is caused by the hatred she still holds for her father, a hatred that fuels her ambition but makes it impossible for her to risk intimacy with anyone. At forty-five she is still beautiful and wealthy; however, she has never been able to find her son. When she does fall in love, it is with a young man from San Francisco whom she has employed and who turns out to be her actual son (now called Terrance Wren). They have an affair, he is killed in a plane accident, and when she attends his funeral she finds Octavio there—the only person in the family who has known the whereabouts of their son. As a voice from the patriarchal past she thought she had left behind, Octavio curses her just as her father had done many years before: "Oh, you dirty, filthy woman! You slept with him! You! His mother! You actually did that with him! And you poisoned him too, didn't you? Just like all the others, you killed him with your poison! Not even God will forgive you this time! Pig! Go blow your brains out! That's what you should do! You bit. . . ." (p. 191). At this point in the narrative, the novel effects a reversal of the Oedipal tragedy, but without the force of its classic counterpart.

Throughout the story, Ana's character responds to a patriarchal determinism that marks women as cursed from the time of their birth (the girl-child who poisoned her mother's womb) and in their roles as destructive mothers (the successful woman who kills her son with her own poison). Although Ana is capable of surviving multiple tragedies, she does so at the expense of her emotions and culture. Paternalistic curses dominate her existence almost to the point of not allowing her to find redemption. If there is anything redeeming to be found, it comes at the end of the novel, when Ana rejects the stereotype of the suffering Mexican woman—that is, the penitent who gets down on her bleeding knees to ask forgiveness for her multiple sins. Her thoughts return to the evenings of bible reading with Amy and Franklin. She finds meaning in her own life through a comparison with the biblical Hagar, mother of Ishmael, whose distress ruled her life, but whose life, like Ana's own, was filled with love as well as with loss. This gives Ana the strength to continue. Even though this moment of recognition seems a bit forced, it nonetheless depicts a woman's liberation from paternalistic cultural constraints. It is unfortunate that in order to release her character from those constraints, Limón felt compelled to have the character reject her culture completely and adopt the Protestant work ethic of her adopted country.

The force of machismo surfaces in the character of Flavio Betancourt in Limón's next novel, *The Day of the Moon* (1999). This character reflects the complexity of the societal forces that drive men to feel inferior because of their mestizo heritage and so to abuse the

women in their lives. In her 1990 "La conciencia de la mestiza: Towards a New Consciousness," Gloria Anzaldúa writes:

> "Machismo" is an adaptation to oppression and poverty and low self-esteem. . . . In the Gringo world, the Chicano suffers from excessive humility and self-effacement, shame of self and self-deprecation. Around Latinos he suffers from a sense of language inadequacy and its accompanying discomfort; with Native Americans he suffers from a racial amnesia which ignores our common blood, and from guilt because the Spanish part of him took their land and oppressed them. He has an excessive compensatory hubris when around Mexicans from the other side. It overlays a deep sense of racial shame.
>
> (p. 382)

Flavio Betancourt lives out most of his adult life in Chihuahua, in his Hacienda Miraflores, and dies in Los Angeles. His despicable machismo stems from his inability to accept that his father Edmundo, who is from Spain, died in poverty in Mexico, and that his mother, a nameless Indian woman from Jalisco, was treated like a servant in her own home. As an adult, he cannot reconcile himself to the fact that he forced himself onto his wife to have their daughter Isadora because his wife, Velia Carmelita, and his sister Brígida were lovers under his own roof. He is forced to leave Mexico with his grandchildren, sister, and servant Ursula Santiago after he puts his only daughter in an insane asylum because she has had a child with Jerónimo Santiago, a Rarámuri Indian and the son of his own *capataz* (foreman) at the hacienda. According to Ursula Santiago, Jerónimo's aunt, who has served in the Betancourt household her entire life, Flavio "lived to strike back" (p. 143). Incapable of accepting his mestizo inheritance, Flavio focuses on the white skin and blue eyes that he and Brígida inherited their father. He refuses to accept, as well, that his father was a hard-working grocer and could not give his children the status in society that Flavio wanted. A consummate gambler, Flavio won the hacienda from his former *padrón* (boss), don Anastasio, and became a rich man practically overnight. Even though during his youth he joined the forces of the Mexican Revolution under Pancho Villa, his life is defined by the values of the white landed elite that the Revolution fought so hard to abolish. The novel begins with Flavio's near-death, then recollects his entire life. In this respect, Limón's novel depicts the failures of the Mexican Revolution through the life of a male protagonist whose life revolves around the values of machismo. *The Day of the Moon* stands as a feminist contestation of novels such as *Pedro Páramo,* by Juan Rulfo, and *The Death of Artemio Cruz,* by Carlos Fuentes.

The Day of the Moon takes the structure of several life narratives, the first about Flavio Betancourt, the other four about the women who surround him and whose lives he seeks to annul: Isadora Betancourt (his daughter), Ursula Santiago (his servant), Brígida Betancourt (his sister), and Alondra Santiago (his granddaughter). In the first section of the novel, the reader learns about his life, about his disillusionment with his wife and his desire to mold his daughter according to his own patriarchal values. During his participation in the Mexican Revolution, his daughter Isadora is raised by his *capataz* and his wife, both Rarámuri Indians. When he returns to the hacienda, he tries to inculcate in her the values of a loyal and obedient daughter and wife who must marry within her own class and race. But his daughter, who until then has accepted the values of the Rarámuri, consistently questions his teachings. The four sections that follow divulge the secrets that Flavio imposes on his family. At the end of the novel, when all secrets are fully revealed, the last female in the family line, Alondra Santiago, accepts her heritage with pride. But final disclosure does not take place until after the death of the patriarch.

The last four sections allow the women in the family to counteract the silence Flavio imposes according to the measure in which they are able to dismiss his power and their fear of him. His daughter tries to speak but finds she is too drugged in the insane asylum to do so. Ursula, his servant, divulges information to Alondra through Rarámuri legends. Brígida, his sister, tells the family history to César and Alondra, Flavio's legitimate and illegitimate grandchildren respectively, from her deranged perspective. She assumes the role of a madwoman in order to divulge the family secrets and not be punished or exiled from the family by her brother. Alondra, his grandchild, is left to ask Ursula about her hidden origins and to look for them in documents and photographs that Brígida and Flavio leave behind after their deaths. The sections on Isadora Betancourt, Ursula Santiago, and Brígida Betancourt are built around the relationships between women and children. In the section on Isadora Betancourt, for example, Limón creates dialogues between Isadora as a child and her supposedly deranged aunt Brígida. Through her aunt's photographs, which are arranged in her room like a story, Isadora learns that her grandmother was an Indian. Isadora also learns about the loving relationship between her mother Velia Carmelita and her Aunt Brígida, a relationship whose nature she does not fully understand. The lesson her aunt teaches her, however, is about forbidden loves: the love of women for other women and love across racial lines.

The section about Ursula Santiago stages conversations in a theatrical sense between Alondra and her supposed grandmother Ursula. Given the grandmother's invisible status as a servant and an indigenous woman, her story allows Alondra to witness scenes that other members of the family were not allowed to see. Ursula was sworn to secrecy regarding Alondra's parents (Isadora and Jerónimo), and she agreed so that she could be close to Alondra. By guarding secrets, Ursula has been able to keep her promise to Isadora to care for her son César by her upper-class husband and her daughter Alondra by the Indian love of her life. So that Alondra does not grow up without a heritage, Ursula tells her the Rarámuri legend of Xipe Totec, the goddess of healing and life. According to Ursula, she was Alondra's mother and her father was a famous Rarámuri long-distance runner.

The section on Brígida Betancourt involves storytelling sessions through which the aunt informs the two children about good and bad daughters, implicitly referring to Isadora, the children's mother. The paradox, which the children do not understand, is that because of Flavio's mandate, one child, César, was born out of the legitimate union of their mother with the son of a landowner. The other, Alondra, was born out of the illegitimate union between their mother and the Rarámuri Indian. Unlike her mother, Alondra is brown and does not wish to be. She wants to be white, like the good mother Isadora. Ursula provides her with a different model, her Rarámuri ancestry. The deranged aunt keeps repeating "Mi hermano Flavio tuvo dos hijas, una buena y la otra mala" (My brother Flavio had two daughters, one good, the other bad; p. 165). On her deathbed, Brígida finally divulges to Alondra that she's the child of the bad mother, and that revelation sets Alondra on the track of documents hidden by her grandfather, and that lead her to the asylum where her mother died. Once she acquires the missing information, she's capable of setting out on a new life. The novel ends with Alondra writing a letter to her brother and expressing a desire to stay in Mexico to discover more about her past. In "The Historical Night of Desire: Recovering 'Queer' Community in Graciela Limón's *The Day of the Moon*," the critic María DeGuzmán contends that "Alondra's function as the L.A.-based young reader-writer figure qualifies her . . . as a representative of both Chicana readers and writers" (p. 56).

Thus, through the conscious resistance of women who question and investigate their pasts, the novel traces the difficult task of erasing the legacy of paternalism. Women's resistance is grounded in the necessity of knowing about the past as constructed by patriarchal secrets and mandates in order to live more fully in the present. The feminist agenda proposed by Chicana theorists such as Gloria Anzaldúa is that solidarity among women allows them to resist and comes from feminine bonds across boundaries of class, sexual definition, languages, and Spanish and indigenous ethnicities. Graciela Limón fictionalizes it well in this novel.

If in *The Day of the Moon* Limón depicts solidarity among women in their personal lives, in *Erased Faces* (2001) she records solidarity among women in their political lives. In *Erased Faces*, Adriana Mora, a U.S. Latina photojournalist, wishes to create a photo-history of indigenous women of Lacandona, and Juana Galván, an indigenous woman from that area, has joined the Zapatista movement in the jungle. Because Adriana has earned the trust of the villagers along the perimeter of the jungle, Juana Galván comes to recruit her to record their revolutionary actions as photographic images and in writing. Limón wrote *Erased Faces* after having visited Chiapas in 1999, in the aftermath of the Zapatista insurrection. The novel is dedicated to those who died in the massacre in Acteal, Chiapas, in 1997. Before the acknowledgments, the author quotes from a communiqué by Subcomandante Insurgente Marcos in 1996: "She meets with her face erased, and her name hidden. With her come thousands of women. More and more arrive. Dozens, hundreds, thousands, millions of women who remember all over the world that there is much to be done and remember that there is still much to fight for" (p. vii). Even though, on the same page, Limón reminds us that *Erased Faces* is a work of fiction, with Marcos's communiqué she alerts the reader to the novel's political context. Within this context, she focuses on the liberation of women in one of the poorest, most rural provinces of Mexico. Women join the ranks of the movement in large numbers to attain the freedom to choose their husbands, to determine the number of children they will have, and to lessen the burden of heavy labor in the fields, in the markets, and at home. In a loose interpretation of the genre of *testimonio*, Limón brings together a photojournalist and a revolutionary activist to divulge the women's version of the Zapatista movement.

Linking past lives to present and future, Limón structures her novel around the Lacandona belief that "we repeat ourselves" (p. 21). The scar on Adriana's left arm, put there by a foster mother's abuse, for example, mirrors the scar of a Mexica woman, a maternal ancestor who witnessed the death of the last of the Mexica kings. This scene in turn recalls a scene recorded by Limón in *Song of the Hummingbird*. Adriana remembers her ancestral past through a series of nightmares that are interpreted for her by Chan K'in, aged Lacandón shaman and reader of dreams. In her recurrent dream, she sees herself as a woman running through the jungle, fleeing from dogs. She runs along with many others. Suddenly she stops as if she had lost something and desperately begins to dig for it in the mud. When she awakens, Adriana experiences a great sense of loss. Chan K'in links her dream to her ancestor's history and suggests that in the present she is repeating her ancestor's life. Her ancestor had traveled from Chiapas and witnessed the repression of the Mexica people, as well as the desperate desire of her people to take their lives so as not to be enslaved by the Spaniards. The modern-day journalist repeats her ancestor's life by witnessing the economic and political repression of the Lacandón by modern-day Mexicans. Adriana's future, Chan K'in says, holds the experience of a great loss, which is foretold by the dream. Although Adriana wonders what object the woman in the dream desperately seeks, Chan K'in predicts that her experience of loss will involve a person, not an object. That person will be Juana Galván.

Erased Faces makes the lives of three characters converge in the massacre in Acteal, with the characters recollecting their lives so that their destinies coincide in the Zapatista movement. Adriana, Juana, and another insurgent, Orlando Flores, return to their past through dreams and recollections to discover for the reader a childhood of violence in the case of Adriana, an arranged marriage to a violent man

in the case of Juana, and a youth wasted working in the mahogany forests in the case of Orlando. When they come together in the jungle, both Juana and Orlando have become leaders in the insurrection, while Adriana has been enlisted to record the movement's history.

The three characters recollect their past lives so that they may rectify injustices committed against them. When Adriana was four, she awoke to find that her mother had killed her father and then had taken her own life. In her dreams she returns to that scene to ask her mother why she killed herself and abandoned her. Her mother responds that she could not endure life with Adrian's father, but the answer does not satisfy Adriana, who wants to know why a mother would abandon her child. In dreams that allow her to evaluate her past, Adriana eventually forgives her mother. Juana, however, finds it hard to forgive her father for having sold her into marriage for the price of a mule. When, after having left her husband, she confronts her father, he demands that she honor his wishes and return to her husband, Cruz Ochoa. Juana has incurred Cruz's rage because she miscarried three children in the span of four years. He beat her with a sharp rock, leaving a scar above her left eyebrow. Her scar mirrors the scar of an ancestor who helped build the Cathedral of San Cristóbal de las Casas, hauling stones on her back up a ravine. When Juana becomes a leader in the army, she takes the name Teniente Insurgente Isabel, losing her name and face in order to give faces to her people. Likewise, Orlando Flores's real name is hidden once he flees to the jungle. As Quintín Osuna, he was a servant in the household of the ruthless owner of mahogany forests, Don Absolón, and befriended Absolón's son Rufino. When the father found out, he chastised Quintín for not knowing his place and sentenced him to work in the mahogany forests, pushing the oxen that dragged the cut wood so that neither animals nor workers would sink into the mud of the jungle. Quintín survives this dangerous work only because of the friendship of fellow worker Aquiles Rendón. When on one occasion Aquiles is about to be swallowed by the mud, Quintín goes to his rescue. The overseer tries to shoot Quintín for daring to step out of his position and kills Aquiles instead. Quintín decapitates the overseer with his machete and flees, to become Orlando Flores.

Erased Faces reproduces in fictional terms the coming of age of indigenous leaders made famous by the testimony of the Maya Quiché woman Rigoberta Menchú. Throughout their brief time together, Orlando, Juana, and Adriana transform themselves. Juana and Orlando become literate in Spanish and train themselves in guerrilla tactics. Juana also becomes excellent at recruiting people to the cause, and Orlando becomes an eloquent speaker. As is true in Menchú's testimony, the hardship and oppression endured by individuals represent the experience of the many. Recording the difficult lives of these characters as children, young people, and then adults becomes imperative in narrative terms so as to establish the necessity of the insurrection. Limón records, as well, the involvement of the Catholic Church in trying to quell the anger of the indigenous crowds, who want to be led by church leaders against their oppressors, as they were by Bartolomé de Las Casas in colonial times. Las Casas was a Dominican priest who attacked the exploitation of the indigenous peoples by the Spaniards, alleging that they were children of God and could not be enslaved. He visited the city of Chiapas in 1544. This time, however, the hierarchy shrinks away from the defense of the indigenous populations.

A quite unusual element in the fictionalization of revolutionary leaders is Limón's introduction of an erotic relationship between Juana and Adriana—a relationship that, according to the Lacandón concept of repeating lives, is predictable. Even in revolutionary times, such relationships are forbidden, and the *manflora* (lesbian) pays with her life. When the insurrection fails, Orlando is summarily shot by military

forces at the Plaza of Ocosingo, Juana is persecuted and killed for being a homosexual, and Adriana lives to publish the images and record the lives of the two fallen heroes.

When considered as a group, Graciela Limón's novels reflect an adherence to the Chicana mandate of what Norma Alarcon calls "dismantling historical conjunctures of crisis" (p. 65). Limón focuses on the time of the Spanish conquest, the Mexican revolution, and peasant and working-class insurrections in the late twentieth century as conjunctures of crisis. She does so because, during times of social and political upheaval, people, and particularly women, occupy new spaces that allow them to redefine their identities in terms of race, class, gender, and sexuality. In several of Limón's novels, particularly in *Song of the Hummingbird, In Search of Bernabé,* and *Erased Faces,* the present and the future harken back to ancestral times, whether of biblical or of American indigenous origins, pointing to heroic figures whose valor and perseverance can serve as examples for present-day struggles. The reinterpretation of figures such as La Llorona brings out the contested nature inherent in mythical figures, who are seen by the patriarchy as destructive forces. Limón foregrounds the act of witnessing as a primary form of resistance so that official historical accounts may not silence or erase alternative female voices, which are usually omitted. Through characters such as Lady Huitzitzilin, Luz Delcano, Alondra Santiago, and Adriana Mora, Limón emphasizes the relevance of women's participation in history. These characters define their own lives and the lives of other women as heroes in the battlefields of domesticity, motherhood, and the social and political arenas. In *The Day of the Moon,* female characters work in solidarity through intergenerational communication to counteract the silences and mandates of patriarchy. In *Erased Faces,* they occupy the ranks of the militant, working toward social and political change. They bear witness to the devastating effects of patriarchy within and across cultures and provide alternative interpretations of history that make radical changes possible.

Exploiting the multivocal possibilities of the novel as genre, Limón engages fictional, mythical, testimonial, journalistic, and academic discourses to reflect her own commitment as a Chicana writer to practice activism in word and deed. Her reworking of her first published novel, *María de Belén: The Autobiography of an Indian Woman*, into *Song of the Hummingbird* reflects her own rite of passage from academic writer to novelist. While in the first she still clings to the academic enterprise, with its emphasis on institutionally sanctioned ways of telling a story, by the time she writes the second she has liberated herself, and in fictional terms transformed her scribe, Father Benito, into the character who personifies her own new task as a writer of fiction. Starting with *In Search of Bernabé* and continuing through *Erased Faces*, Limón excels in the art of witnessing the possibilities of mestiza women's potential in the Americas.

Selected Bibliography

WORKS OF GRACIELA LIMÓN

NOVELS

María de Belén: The Autobiography of an Indian Woman. New York: Vantage Press, 1990.

In Search of Bernabé. Houston: Arte Público Press, 1993.

The Memories of Ana Calderón. Houston: Arte Público Press, 1994.

Song of the Hummingbird. Houston: Arte Público Press, 1996.

The Day of the Moon. Houston: Arte Público Press, 1999.

Erased Faces. Houston: Arte Público Press, 2001.

TRANSLATIONS

En busca de Bernabé. Translated by Miguel Angel Aparicio. Houston: Arte Público Press, 1997.

CRITICAL AND BIOGRAPHICAL STUDIES

Alarcón, Norma. "Chicana Feminism in the Tracks of 'The' Native Woman." In *Between Woman and Nation: Nationalisms, Transnational Feminisms, and the State.* Edited by Caren Kaplan, Norma Alarcón, and Minoo Moallem. Durham: Duke University Press, 1999. Pp. 63–71.

Anzaldúa, Gloria. "Haciendo caras, una entrada." In *Making Face, Making Soul/Haciendo caras: Creative and Critical Perspectives by Feminists of Color.* Edited by Gloria Anzaldúa. San Francisco: Aunt Lute Books, 1990. Pp. xv–xxviii.

———. "La conciencia de la mestiza: Towards a New Consciousness." In *Making Face, Making Soul/Haciendo caras: Creative and Critical Perspectives by Feminists of Color.* Edited by Gloria Anzaldúa. San Francisco: Aunt Lute Books, 1990. Pp. 377–389.

Carbonell, Ana María. "From Llorona to Gritona: Coatlicue in Feminist Tales by Vira-montes and Cisneros." *MELUS* 24 no. 2 (summer 1999): 53–74.

DeGuzmán, María. "The Historical Night of Desire: Recovering 'Queer' Community in Graciela Limón's *The Day of the Moon.*" (2000) Available at http://epsilon3.georgetown.edu/~coventrm/asa2000/panel6/deguzman.html.

McCracken, Ellen. "Graciela Limón." In *Chicano Writers*. Third Series. Francisco A. Lomelí and Carl L. Shirley, eds. Detroit: Gale Group, 1999. Pp. 127–132.

Rodríguez, Ana Patricia. "Refugees of the South: Central Americans in the U.S. Latino Imaginary." *American Literature* 73, no. 2 (June 2001): 387–412.

Sommer, Doris. "'Not Just a Personal Story': Women's Testimonios and the Plural Self." In *Life/Lines: Theorizing Women's Autobiography*. Edited by Bella Brodzki and Celeste Schenck. Ithaca, New York: Cornell University Press, 1988. Pp. 107–130.

Demetria Martínez
(1960–)

R. JOYCE ZAMORA LAUSCH

Demetria Martínez couples her literary art with her political activism, engaging in a fight for human rights and social justice that is simultaneously of the page and for the people. As Martínez integrates the power of faith as political force, the images, spirituality, and doctrine of Catholicism pervade her work. As she speaks her *Nuevo Mexicana* (New Mexican) subjectivity and collective voice, Martínez steeps her poetry, fiction, and essay in the landscapes of the southwest and Latin America, their peoples, and their histories. Martínez also refuses the divide between the personal and the political, infusing her writing with a Chicana perspective on love, sexuality, and self-exploration. As a woman, Chicana, committed political activist, journalist, novelist, and poet, Martínez's accomplishments voice revolution and adamant repudiation of silence.

Born to Ted and Dolores Jaramillo Martínez and raised in Albuquerque, New Mexico, Demetria Martínez's commitment to social activism is partially motivated by the example and influence of family members. While her mother was a kindergarten teacher and her father was the first Chicano elected to the Albuquerque school board, her grandmother and aunt also held local public offices. Additionally, her grandmother exemplified the inherent tie between religion and the word, sharing with Martínez the poetry of the Bible, particularly the Psalms, and encouraging Martínez to practice an intellectual spirituality through the influential testament of her own daily practice of religious devotion. Martínez's grandfather's *corridos* (ballads), in their combination of poetic and journalistic function, also helped set the precedent for her creative work.

Educated in Albuquerque public schools, Martínez went on to receive her undergraduate degree from Princeton University's Woodrow Wilson School of Public and International Affairs. While studying national and world affairs, Martínez enrolled in poetry workshops under the tutelage of such poets as Maxine Kumin, Ted Weiss, and Stanley Kunitz. Absorbed by the intersection of politics and religion, Martínez was a Wilson Scholar as a Princeton senior and studied religious social ethics with Dr. Gibson Winter at the Princeton Theological Seminary. She completed internships with the *Albuquerque News* and *Time* before graduating in 1982.

Martínez returned to Albuquerque after her graduation from Princeton, living at Sagrada Art Studios for six years and concentrating on her poetry. A poetic drama and product of this focused time, "Only Say the Word," was first performed at the Albuquerque Museum, then adapted and performed in Spanish at Arizona United Farm Workers meetings, and was later published in Martínez's first poetry collection, *Turning* (1989).

During this same time frame, Martínez became a correspondent and freelance writer for the progressive and independent weekly *National Catholic Reporter* in 1985 and, in 1986, a religion writer for the *Albuquerque Journal.* Her work as a reporter and columnist led her to write both journalistically and poetically about the plight of Salvadoran refugees and to be an activist for the cause of sanctuary—immigration in defiance of U.S. immigration laws with political exigency as motive.

In 1988 Martínez and Lutheran minister Glen Remer-Themert were indicted on charges related to their December 1986 smuggling across the Mexico-U.S. border of two pregnant Salvadoran women refugees in search of asylum. Her poem "Nativity: For Two Salvadoran Women" was utilized by government prosecutors as evidence of alleged violation of immigration laws. The incriminating poem speaks the political irony of yuletide reverence in contrast to war's inhumanity: "In my country, we sing of a baby in a manger, finance death squads" (*Three Times a Woman,* p. 133). Carrying the possible consequence of a twenty-five year prison sentence and $1.25 million in fines for Martínez, the first reporter to be prosecuted in connection with the sanctuary movement, the case was tried in Albuquerque in July and August of 1988. Martínez was fully acquitted on grounds of her First Amendment rights to research the sanctuary movement as part of her profession as journalist. Her codefendant was also fully vindicated. Even before her acquittal, Martínez remained dedicated to the sanctuary movement, reading at the Kimo Theater in Albuquerque with Allen Ginsberg for a Sanctuary Defense Committee benefit.

Moving from Albuquerque to Tuscon, Martínez resided in the Arizona desert for a decade,

where she continued her work as a monthly columnist for the *National Catholic Reporter* and became involved with the Arizona Border Rights Project/*Derechos Humanos,* an organization that concentrates on the militarization of the U.S.-Mexico border and on documenting abuses committed by the U.S. Border Patrol. She also worked directly with the Southern Arizona People's Law Center, an organization dedicated predominantly to civil rights–related cases and to providing the poor with legal services.

While her pen crosses boundaries of genre, Martínez is a poet at heart, her lyricism permeating her written work. Indeed, Martínez began writing poetry at a very young age as a mechanism for confronting and transcending depression. The author of three collections of poetry, Martínez and the voice and quality of her poetry were recognized from her high school days forward. She received a Southwest High School Creative Writing Award from New Mexico State University for two poems, "Stained" and "Ode to My Hair," in the spring of 1978 and began entering poetry contests and publishing poetry in literary journals in 1984. She was the winner in poetry of the 1987–1988 fourteenth annual Chicano Literary Contest sponsored by the University of California at Irvine, and in 1989 her first collection of poetry *Turning* was published.

Published by Bilingual Press/Editorial Bilingüe, Martínez's *Turning* is featured in *Three Times a Woman* (1989), a compilation of Martínez's poetry and the poetry of two other renowned Chicana poets, Alicia Gaspar de Alba and María Herrera-Sobek. The linking of her poetry with Herrera-Sobek's and Gaspar de Alba's establishes thematic and imagistic dialogue between their works and invites examination of Chicana poetry as a yet emergent and distinct literary tradition.

Martínez dedicates *Turning* to her maternal and paternal grandparents and follows this dedication with a poetic epigraph that stands as metonym for the collection as a whole. Within the epigraph, Martínez unites the voices central to her collection and defines the function of poetry and her role as poet:

> *Refugees at the border*
> *of a century.*
> *The Río Grande, neck-high tonight.*
> *Men, guns. Thunder.*
>
> *The dangers are new but fear, familiar.*
> *The old ones told us:*
> *To find the eye of the storm*
> *we must walk where lightning falls.*
>
> *'Indocumentados.'*
> *Hunger, our one proof of origin.*
>
> *Although we cry out,*
> *we are not dying.*
>
> *Too dark to see now.*
> *Follow my voice.*
>
> (*Three Times a Woman,* p. 104)

Within these stanzas, Martínez parallels time and borders through environment and war; hers is a refugee voice, *una voz indocumentada* (an undocumented/unsanctioned voice) afraid of the "new dangers," of wars between and within nations. Both sheltered and battered by environment, she speaks through the universal experiences of hunger and survival, informed by ancestors; and she also speaks as guide, illuminating darkness through poetry.

Martínez's poetry is built upon the tradition of Latin American poetry, which asserts that poetry does not belong to the individual poet but to the people. Indeed, in a 2002 Tucson Weekly interview with James Reel titled "Between the Sheets: Demetria Martínez's Greatest Love Affair Is with Language," Martínez captures the connection between individual poet and audience when she asserts that poetry is "a window into the collective soul" (Reel, *Tucson Review*). She also speaks of

the dynamic between poetry and journalism that embeds the duality of individual and collective voice in her written work: "Reporting keeps you looking, and the great thing about poetry is it keeps you honest—you can't be authentic if you deny what you're feeling" (Reel, *Tucson Review*). Thus, the poetry of *Turning* employs a blurring of genre characteristic of this union of personal and collective voice. As U.S. and international human rights are a central subject matter, many of *Turning's* poems are precisely poetic journalism.

Within the five sections of her first published volume of poetry, Martínez establishes themes and images that remain central to her literary production across genres. Her poems are peopled with women and family members. The overarching themes are of love and politics through the eyes of a young Chicana feminist poet discovering and practicing voice with both freedom and trepidation. The tropes of birth, mothering, and maligned womanhood are central to the collection. The central image of the first poem of the collection's initial section, "To Keep Back the Cold," for example, is a five-year-old girl, Elena, warming a brown egg, believing that she has the power to bring life from the cold, unfertilized orb she has rescued from its refrigerated carton. The magic that persists in her child's faithful vision, despite the nay-saying of her mother, results in "a brown egg . . . throbbing / In the cup of her hand" (*Three Times a Woman,* p. 105), and it is this magic Martínez wishes to hold onto, must hold onto, in and through her poetry. The cold shell of the egg is a thin barrier to the life-giving faith of a child, and as Elena's magic sets the tone for the collection her example is also reminiscent of the Christian teaching of a child leading the masses.

The second and title poem of the first section is set against a backdrop of winter freeze, which does not distinguish by socioeconomic class in wreaking its havoc. The final lines of the poem convey frustration, questions without answers or borders:

Against whom do we revolt
for such sorrows as a baby
frozen in a manger?
I will not sing of it,
I will not sing.
Feel ashes storm into your eyes,
you will burn
with questions of continents,
you will turn and ache
all nights forever, longing
to keep back the cold.

(p. 108)

The metaphor of a frozen Christ-child both humanizes him, connecting the material to the spiritual, and represents the seeming futility of religious succor in adversity, both natural and human-induced, even as faith, the "longing" (p. 108), must prevail.

The third poem returns to the familiar and familial and maintains the trope of birth and the images of both inclement weather and Elena's egg as Martínez celebrates the premature arrival of her goddaughter, "illegitimate as Jesus" (p. 109):

Little raisin, you lay in a glass manger
ten days . . . .
. . . .
. . . . .When the timer
rang we lifted you out and wondered,
will there be room for you at the inn
when the winds blow and your cradle falls?

(p. 109)

This child is a miracle and must weather the storms with her magic. In this poem, as in "To Keep Back the Cold" and "Hail Mary," Martínez revises the biblical, humanizing the archetypal to link the ancient to the contemporary. The initial poems set the tone for those that follow, poems which are laden with moments of suffering—a Juárez woman raped and laboring for less than minimum wage to make ends meet—and moments of grace, such as a Puerto Rican waitress offering a moment of respect to an impoverished black man at a breakfast counter.

The poems of *Turning* dominantly exemplify Martínez's commitment to the dispossessed and disenfranchised of the U.S. and of Latin America. Her participation in the sanctuary movement figures centrally, particularly in the second of *Turning*'s five sections, "Border Wars: 1985." In "Prologue: Salvadoran Woman's Lament," the speaker articulates feelings of love and loss as she considers the fate of her lover and his inevitable North American exile:

When he finds a Woman
to take the war out of him,

she will make love to a man
and a monster,

she will rise from the bed,
grenades ticking in her.

(p. 117)

While the themes of birth and hope remain in this section, the voice is angrier, more fed up with the utter inhumanity that accompanies both the war in El Salvador and the parallel war of immigration policy and enforcement within the U.S. To underscore these inhumanities, Martínez introduces several poems within "Border Wars: 1985" with quotations of ultraconservative opinion of immigration, immigrants, and those who strive to aid them in their journeys. A balance of male and female voices, the voice of these poems shifts from war-wounded immigrant to enraged U.S. activist. The poems convey how immigration is more compelled than chosen. For example, in "Angelo's Story" the brother of a murdered Salvadoran flees to the U.S. after cutting his brother down from a lamppost, while in "Orlando's Story/The War Persists," a young man, fearing for his own life, flees after his mother and sister are murdered, only to experience the same paralyzing fear and nightmare once in the U.S. "North American Woman's Lament (for Orlando)" articulates the conflict of a U.S. woman attempting to love and to understand a man for whom peace does not exist, despite immigration. The voice that will become Mary/María, one of the protagonists in Martínez's novel *MotherTongue,* expresses guilt in her U.S.-privileged complicity and also hope that from solidarity and love something productive may be born:

> Your rib throbs
> at my palm, the rib
> they fractured with a rifle,
> the rib, that if taken into the body
> of America might make us new,
> a country where mercy and nobility
> reside, where the bones we have broken
> teach us strength.
>
> (*Three Times a Woman,* p. 123)

Through intricate weaving of voice, the poems of *Turning* are intimately personal and globally political. Significantly, Martínez employs a distinct crossover between her works of poetry, fiction, and prose, as, for example, she claims the voice of "North American Woman's Lament" for *MotherTongue's* Mary/María and attributes the poem "Prologue: Salvadoran Woman's Lament" to José Luis's disappeared *novia* (girlfriend), Ana.

The poems of the third section, "Love Notes," are sensual and intimate, yet the consequences of war wound and challenge the love to rawness. Images of the loss visible in brutal and bloody death illuminate the fragility and contingency of love and life. Each titled by month, the poems of "Love Notes" illustrate the embrace of love and the ways human beings hold on to each other for survival and in faith, in spite of life's tenuousness.

The theme of the fourth and title section of *Turning* is dialogue. This section contains the powerful and renowned words of "Nativity: For Two Salvadoran Women, 1986–1987," which figured so prominently into the 1988 trial and features the voices of the Salvadoran women and the reporter in conversation. "Blessed the

Hungry" creates a stanzaic dialogue between an older woman and a younger woman who have become lovers and who negotiate joy and shame, the older woman speaking from a position of years, experience, a husband and family, and belonging, and the younger speaking from a position of liberated celebration of the love they have experienced, love she believes is "light" and "a sign / an act of piety" (p. 138). Martínez speaks the theme of the section through the simple diction of "Bare Necessities":

> Laboriously, joyfully
> we come
>
> to truth together
> or not at all.
>
> (p. 138)

These poems address women's independence, and women in solidarity and communion. The poems feature personal agency, the difficult and painful choices women make for their own survival and to see themselves clearly and with love.

Martínez ultimately embodies the theme of the communion and sanctuary in conversation in *Turning's* final section, "Only Say the Word," which is composed of the single piece "A Poem for Three Women's Voices." Here Martínez describes the timelessness of the setting of the Santuario de Chimayó and the powerful healing capacity of its soil. The poem features the voices of a Guatemalan Indian woman who calls for Christ to intervene in war and alleviate the suffering of her people, a North American school teacher who questions Christ's and her own ability to make a positive difference, and a Chimayó native who understands the healing capacity of prayer, faith, and the *tierra bendita* (blessed earth) of the sanctuary. "At a time when I had no faith left, / The only thing left was faith" (p. 154), the Chimayó native says as she recognizes the weariness of the other two women praying in the sanctuary and offers them a place in her home, an offering of solidarity and compassion.

With her voice repressed by the trauma of her 1988 trial, Martínez faithfully waited for poetic revelation, which arrived in 1992. Martínez writes in the afterword of her second volume of poetry, *Breathing Between the Lines* (1997), of listening to Sandra Cisneros read from *Woman Hollering Creek,* and of hearing the initial lines of *MotherTongue* (1994) in her head: "His nation chewed him up and spat him out like a piñon shell and when he emerged from an airplane one late afternoon I knew I would one day make love with him" (*Breathing Between the Lines,* p. 59). These lines were both revelation and motivation to write what she describes as a "long poem in disguise" (p. 60). *Mother-Tongue* was published in 1994 by Bilingual Press and won the 1994 Western States Book Award for Fiction. Republication in 1996 by Ballantine Books and in Spanish translation by Editorial Seix Barral increased the novel's accessibility for its intended audiences.

MotherTongue is narrated through the retrospective voice of an Albuquerque-residing *Nuevo Mexicana,* Mary/María, who at age nineteen enters into a relationship with a Salvadoran political refugee, José Luis. Driven by depression and the desire to escape the doldrums of her life, Mary initially falls in love with the idea of love rather than with the material entity of the physically, emotionally, and psychologically war-wounded José Luis Romero, a man with a name adopted upon entrance into the U.S. Mary/María, who lost her mother to cancer and was abandoned by her father early in life, feels lost and alone and longs for a life other than her own. Not particularly politically active nor in touch with her own Mexican heritage, Mary/María is directionless and uninspired, while José Luis is wracked by nightmares of the torture he endured at the hands of the military as a vocal insurrectionist against Salvadoran military tactics, including the assassination of a local priest teaching liberation theology to his congregation, gunned down as he was delivering the mass of communion. Brought together by Mary's godmother,

Soledad, an activist directly involved in the sanctuary movement, Mary/María's initial ignorance and disinterest fade as she and José Luis interact and, against the odds, attraction grows into a love that produces a child. In the final section of the novel, José Luis Jr. and Mary/María travel to El Salvador in search of the father and lover who, unable to adjust to U.S. life with so much left undone in his own country of El Salvador, abandoned them.

Martínez artfully generates a love story between two complicated individuals, one searching for herself and longing to escape into the sunset and the other torn between exile (and its accompanying yearning for home) and genuine love for María. Martínez also imbues *MotherTongue* with the historical richness of Albuquerque as the setting. A city she knows and loves, the Albuquerque Martínez inscribes is textured by her respect for the timelessness of the city's past. Her description is poetic, a product of Martínez's mornings spent writing in Old Town Albuquerque.

Martínez's *MotherTongue* is an extremely artful tapestry of intertextuality, as she weaves into the texture of the novel the lexis of women's lives—recipes, letters, poems, journal entries, grocery lists, descriptions of photographs and postcards—and includes these documents of the everyday alongside newspaper accounts of the war in El Salvador and fragments of José Luis's *testimonio* (testimony).

In a particularly powerful passage, Mary/María self-reflexively speaks of the intertextual composition of the tale she weaves from memory and remnants of experience:

Soledad died many years ago, but I have her letters. He [José Luis], too, is dead, but I have a tape recording of a speech he gave, the newspaper accounts of it, some love poems. El Salvador is rising from the dead, but my folder of newspaper clippings tells the story of the years when union members disappeared and nuns were ordered off buses at gunpoint, a country with its hands tied behind its back, crying, *stop, stop.* These and a few journal entries are all I have left to fasten my story to reality. Everything else is remembering. Or dis-remembering. Either way, I am ready to go back. To create a man out of blanks who can never wound me.

(MotherTongue, p. 8)

Martínez imbues Mary/María's voice with exemplary poetic diction.

The articles she includes emphasize the U.S. role in supplying arms to the government-supported military, which routinely "disap-peared" Salvadoran insurrectionists and guerilla forces and their families. Nurtured by her godmother, Soledad, Mary includes her letters and recipes as items in the scrapbook of memory she revisits in order to reconstruct the story of her encounter, falling in love with José Luis, and the subsequent growth inspired by her relation-ship with him. José Luis is a poet himself, and his poems converse within the novel with poems by Pablo Neruda and Claribel Alegría, as well as with the poetic journal entries of Mary/María. As Mary/María narrates the text through retrospect, she defies linear narrative through narrative intrusion, a questioning of her own memory and the possibility of constructing truth through a reconstruction of the past. The past, present, and future collide as Mary/María looks back on her nineteen-year-old self and her relationship with José Luis through her thirty-eight-year-old eyes and the lens of motherhood, and as José Luis Jr.—their son, who has not known his father—embarks on his own journey toward self-discovery, cultural heritage, and a love of his own, a Salvadoran woman. Martínez writes fiction as a poet, lyrically and with a sense of purposeful diction and metaphor and a consciousness of how parts fit together from sentence to paragraph to chapter.

MotherTongue was followed by the publica-tion of Martínez's second collection of poetry, *Breathing Between the Lines,* in 1997. Her first post-trial collection of poetry, Martínez speaks of the trial in the afterword to the collection as "a poet's nightmare, in which words, so full of liberating possibilities, were twisted and used against me" (p. 58). Through two epigraphs, one a quoted verse from the Book of Ezekiel in which God promises "breath" for the "bones," and the other a verse by Native American poet Joy Harjo that conveys that the "most danger-ous ones" are those "who escape / after the last hurt is turned inward," Martínez sets the tone of *Breathing Between the Lines.* The two section divisions, "Code Talkers" and "First Words," and the autobiographical afterword that traces Martínez's development as a writer speak the volume's focal point of language as breath of life and resistance.

In the first poem of the volume, "Untitled," Martínez searches for language adequate to experience, conveying the way that language evades truths:

> For sixteen years
> I have ransacked
> the universe
> . . . .
> looking for a way
> to say how it was.
>
> Because we have
> no word for light
> we live in shadows.

(p. 3)

Martínez writes about the limits of language because language does not reach far enough to, as she writes in "Milagros," "storm heaven" (p. 5) or bring gods to earth. Yet even as language is a barrier, it also has the potential to unite across boundaries, to document truths that some would prefer not to hear. Words travel across continents and imposed silences, and a vigil of words evidence activism and faith in love for the speakers of "Night" and "The Dress That Daisy Gave Me." A dominant image in these poems and in "Code Talkers" is the telephone, a mechanism that joins voices when distance separates bodies. Poems are love made manifest, as the speaker of "Before You" boldly states: "Where you go, these words / go" (p. 11).

In several poems Martínez focuses particularly on Spanish as a second language for both the speaker and a North Vietnamese friend/beloved; both fill in the gaps with "stars" (p. 11) that represent both the limited capacity of language and the persistence of gaps representative of distances, spaces in experience that cannot be shared through language. In the penultimate poem of the section, "Fragmentos/Fragments," Martínez the speaker seeks to know herself in Spanish versus the more familiar self she knows in English. A second set of dominant images is of *la comida* (food), the salty and the sweet of "Everywoman," the staples of "Squash, beans, / chiles, corn" in "History" (p. 15) and the cross-cultural joining of "pinto beans on jasmine rice" of the final poem "Las Mañanitas" (p. 29). The tongue unites language and taste, both linked to hungers. The seeds of growing things with potential to satiate hunger are the same as the seeds that words represent in filling the hunger for communication and communion. Finally, the idea of music as wordless language is also a repeated motif: "six notes of Vietnamese" in "Night" (p. 7), a "six-toned wood flute" in "Translation from the Vietnamese" (p. 21), and the mariachis, rooster's crow, and rising sun "like an orchestra warming up" of the final poem "Las Manañitas" (p. 29). The lines and stanzas of these poems are short, clipped like the dots and dashes of code, and dense, each character, including spaces, deliberate.

The second section, "First Words," begins with an untitled poem. Spoken in a poet's voice, this poem documents the acts of love and courage embedded in writing. Overall, the speakers in this section are searching for authentic voice, not the colonizing "proper" English alluded to in "Imperialism" or the American "smooth talk" discussed in "Wanted" (p. 37). A poem patterned, as Martínez notes, after Allen Ginsberg's poem "America," "Wanted" is addressed directly to a personified America and functions as a call to repentance:

America I don't want progress I want redemption
Cut the shit we could be lovers again don't hang
     up
America I'm your dark side embrace me and be
     saved.

(p. 38)

Martínez emphasizes the perpetual state of struggle, the necessity of revolution, and the connectedness of humanity. The voice of the poem is genuine, raggedly angry.

Most notably in "Rally," Martínez links activism and writing, and simultaneously echoes *Turning* and *Breathing Between the Lines* through repetition of the central images of those earlier poems:

hearing you, my shoulders ache
remembering when they were wings
I would speak too, but my truths emerge silently
in typos: Chiapaz, the z breaking out *peace.*
. . . .
if a poem is not itself love it is noise
. . . .
the hard work is the wait, the endless breathing
upon the brown egg held in our hands,
warming a world as breakable
as a rib at the end of a rifle butt
passing the egg from hand to hand to hand
until the *quetzal's* wings open
like cathedral doors

I have no proof
this day will come, all I can give you
is a sign, all I know is what
I have seen in my poems.

(pp. 41–42)

Martínez engages the voice of public activist and poet, but often follows that voice directly with the vulnerable and intimate voice of heartbreak and healing, in poems such as "Meantimes," "Discovering America," "Only So Long," and the concluding poem of the section, "First Things," which implies hope through preparation for renewed flight of the soul.

Martínez's most recent collection of poetry, *The Devil's Workshop,* was published in 2002.

While the poems in this volume are not divided into thematic sections, Martínez continues to explore themes familiar to her writing: human rights and political failures; the complicated dynamic of both the potential and possible consequences of romantic love and sexual politics; the omnipresence and endurance of spirituality as the fire of the soul; and the necessity of a nurturing relationship with the self as fuel for the work of social transformation. Her imagery is both blatantly political and of the body, sensual. She invites the reader in by observing herself and the world around her with keenness and compassion.

As if in direct conversation with "First Words," the last section of *Breathing Between the Lines*, the first poem of *The Devil's Workshop* is titled "Last Words" and witnesses the reality of the renewed flight she forecasts and hopes against hope for in the final poem of *Breathing Between the Lines*. The speaker voices mystification and wonder at the faith that has allowed her to fly: "Tell me how—after the winds / Severed a wing—I flew on . . . then landed" (p. 3). The initial poem articulates the focus on healing.

Several of the poems, including the title poem, are addressed to an ex-lover, the source of the idleness of the title. Voice shifts in "Deposition," "Interlude," and "Lessons" range from anger to pity and accusation to refusal to place blame solely on him, while "Her Ghost" represents the sadness of love's death, as while reading the paper the speaker and lover cerebrally discuss current events around their own emptiness:

Our
Moment
Died
In the dark
Without even a line.

(p. 47)

Martínez also writes of the consequence of personal conflict and heartbreak for the poet, particularly in "Through a Needle's Eye":

Should your spirit return, you will know it
By the words that smolder
In your belly: tend the fire, count
On nothing except the alphabet.
Throw it like dice, fifty-fifty chance
The right word will come up.
This gamble is no game, this crack
At salvation, this making poetry
Out of what you nearly destroyed.

(pp. 53–54)

Meditating on relationship from interior spaces, Martínez echoes the legal lingo of divorce. "Class Action" is the follow-up to "Deposition," a letting go: "The redwood you hear falling / In the forest is you" (p. 61). The speaker in this series also conveys the range of healing that evidences self-embrace, including the sweet revenge of embracing another man in "You Didn't Believe Me" and the timid celebration of sexuality typically forbidden in writing in "At a Kentucky Derby Party, Tucson Arizona."

However, the poems are also more broadly reflective, a taking stock after heartbreak and disappointment in multiple realms, public and private. Some are poems of a woman looking back on her younger self with greater wisdom. The speaker in "Rear Views," for example, conveys a sense of acceptance and an awareness of limitations: "I'm older now, in no / Rush to arrive" (p. 91). This voice is a perspective beyond the arrogance and security of youth, when loneliness and more questions than answers prevail. In other poems, such as "Loneliness" and "Another White Man Goes Numb," Martínez repeats the assertion of women's intuitive knowledge of each other and their shared experiences. In the more intimate poems "Blessing Poem," "Birth Song," and "La Promesa," Martínez celebrates the births of family members Benjamin Theodore and David Demetrio and the hours of life of baby girl Sonia, gifting each with poetic legacy. In "La Promesa," written for Sonia, Martínez repeats the image of peace, the eye of the storm that must constantly be sought through the struggle for justice.

The lines of the poems in *The Devil's Workshop* are descriptive and lyrical, some composed of sentences that reach for the right margin while other lines hug the left with two-word lines and concise stanzas. For example, "Another Way to End a Relationship" embeds the ending of a relationship in a single image with a tough and unyielding voice:

> If you can't pull it up
> By the roots,
> Take it out
> Of the sun, stop
> Watering it.
>
> (p. 67)

The images in this poem, and the poems of the collection as a whole, are of the everyday. The majority of Martínez's poems are brief, capturing a single moment, a thought, and sending it outward, beyond the page, to ripple on the reader's tongue and in their mind.

In poems such as "News Footage: Kosovo Refugee Woman," "Upon Waking"—written for Amadou Diallo—and "Not by the Gun but by the Grant Application," Martínez reminds readers that she is always paying attention to the world around her; her poems are anything but self-absorbed as she reaches out with activist tongue and pen to add her voice to the struggle for human rights and justice.

Demetria Martínez's voice reaches with force and felicity across the genres of poetry, fiction, and essay. Her ability to create a vibrant and potent dynamic between the breadth and passion of journalistic vision and her poet's heart, sense of rhythm, and imagistic diction is unparalleled. She is simultaneously an activist for social justice and a woman unafraid to visit the most intimate and vulnerable flesh of human relationship and emotion. Readers are blessed by her art, both intellectually and spiritually.

Martínez keeps a traditional altar in her home, reads other New Mexican poets, Native American poets, Chicano and Chicana poets, feminist poets, and practices the martial art of kung fu to gain strength and energy to keep her voice alive and compelling. She has taught creative writing courses and workshops at several universities and colloquiums in the U.S. and abroad. She continues to lecture and read from her works widely and is on the board of directors for Curbstone Publishing Company, a company committed to publishing creative works with strong political-social emphasis and to promoting literacy.

Selected Bibliography

WORKS OF DEMETRIA MARTÍNEZ

NOVEL
MotherTongue. Tempe, Ariz.: Bilingual Press/Editorial Bilingüe, 1994.

POETRY
Three Times a Woman: Chicana Poetry. With Alicia Gaspar de Alba and María Herrera-Sobek. Tempe, Ariz.: Bilingual Press/Editorial Bilingüe, 1989.
Breathing Between the Lines. Tucson, Ariz.: University of Arizona Press, 1997.
The Devil's Workshop. Tucson, Ariz.: University of Arizona Press, 2002.

SHORT FICTION
"Mark." In *New World: Young Latino Writers.* Edited by Ilan Stavans. New York: Delta Publishing, 1997.

"From *Mexican Rubies.*" *Colorado Review* 27, no. 2 (summer 2000): 77–80.

COLUMNS FOR *THE NATIONAL CATHOLIC REPORTER*

"Abortion in Latin America Is a Matter of Desperation." October 13, 1989.

"I Won't Forget the Night My Grandma Lucy Died." December 13, 1996.

"Talk with the Animals and Learn about Life." February 21, 1997.

"Amid Economic Mirage, Homeless Speak Truth." March 20, 1998.

"No Matter What Theorists Say, Art and Politics *Must* Mix." May 28, 1999.

"Latinos Need to Know Their Rights." July 16, 1999.

"Progressives Need to Break the Silence That Follows the Hype." September 3, 1999.

"Segregation in Catholic Intellectual Life." December 3, 1999.

"Violence Against Women—A Cause for Pro-Life Activists." April 21, 2000.

"Tally of Dead Rises on Mexican Border." June 30, 2000.

"Brown Paper and a Candle." September 8, 2000.

"Overcoming a Ratzinger Moment at Mass." January 5, 2001.

"Chavez's Charity." January 19, 2001.

"Downloading the Mysteries." March 30, 2001.

"Coming to Grips with the Fact of Passing On." October 26, 2001.

"American Flag Belongs to Dissenters, Too." February 8, 2002.

"Bush's War Brings Uncertain Times for Peacemakers." April 19, 2002.

"On Exhibit, Found Objects Mark Border Crossers' Treacherous Passage." August 2, 2002.

"Men Key to Ending War against Women." September 20, 2002.

"Tune the Ear Untwist the Tongue and Make a Latino Connection." April 25, 2003.

CRITICAL AND BIOGRAPHICAL STUDIES

Castillo, Debra A. "Barbed Wire Words: Demetria Martínez's *MotherTongue.*" *Intertexts* 1, no. 1 (1997): 8–24.

Gutierrez-Muhs, Gabriella Favela. *Subjectifying Entities/Emerging Subjectivities in Chicana Literature through the Literary Production of Demetria Martínez and Norma Elia Cantú: Madres, comadres, madrinas, nina madres, tias, abuelas y solteronas.* Dissertation Abstracts International, Section A: The Humanities and Social Sciences 61, no. 9 (2001): 3566.

Martínez, Elizabeth Coonrod. "*Nuevas voces salvadorenas: Sandra Benítez y Demetria Martínez.*" In *Reflexiones: Ensayos sobre escritoras hispanoamericanas contemporáneas.* Edited by Priscilla Gac-Artigas. Fair Haven, N.J.: Nuevo Espacio, 2002. Pp. 109–119.

Pérez, Daniel G. "La internalización de la voz narrativa chicana en el trabajo de Demetria Martínez." *Escritura: Revista de Teoría y Critica Literarias* 18 nos. 35–36 (1993): 133–140.

INTERVIEWS

Ikas, Karin Rosa. *Chicana Ways: Conversations with Ten Chicana Writers.* Edited by Karin Rosa Ikas. Reno: University of Nevada Press, 2002. Pp. 113–125.

Iversen, Kristen. "Poetry, Politics & the Drama of the Unseen: An Interview with Demetria Martínez." *Bloomsbury Review* 18, no. 2 (March/April 1998): 11–12.

Manolis, Argie J. "The Writer as Witness: An Interview with Demetria Martínez." *Hayden's Ferry Review* 24 (spring/summer 1999): 37–51.

Reel, James. "Between the Sheets: Demetria Martínez's Greatest Love Affiar Is with Language." *Tucson Weekly,* Feburary 14–February 20, 2002. Available at http://www.tucsonweekly.com/tw/2002-02-14/review.html (accessed June 17, 2003).

WEB SITE
http://www.DemetriaMartínez.com (accessed May 9, 2003).

Pat Mora
(1942–)

MARÍA HERRERA-SOBEK

Perhaps the best description of the essence of Pat Mora can be found in some words she wrote herself:

Desert women know
about survival.
Fierce heat and cold
have burned and thickened
our skin.

(*Chants,* p. 80)

The lines from Mora's frequently quoted poem "Desert Women" aptly describe this brilliant U.S.-Mexican border poet, essayist, novelist, and author of children's books. Born Patricia Estella Mora in 1942 in the town of El Paso, Texas, she grew up bilingual, bicultural, and binational because El Paso and Juárez, Mexico, are twin cities—a stone's throw from each other. Her poem "Legal Alien" perfectly encapsulates the psychological ease and unease of growing up in such a fluid state of identity formation:

Bi-lingual, Bi-cultural,
able to slip from "How's life?"
to *"me'stan volviendo loca,"*
able to sit in a paneled office
drafting memos in smooth English,
able to order in fluent Spanish

at a Mexican restaurant,
American but hyphenated,
viewed by Anglos as perhaps exotic,
perhaps inferior, definitely different,
viewed by Mexicans as alien,
(their eyes say, "You may speak
Spanish but you're not like me")
an American to Mexicans
a Mexican to Americans
a handy token
sliding back and forth
between the fringes of both worlds
by smiling
by masking the discomfort
of being pre-judged
Bi-laterally.

(*Chants,* p. 52)

Mora's personal family migration narrative adheres to the millions of other immigrant stories told and retold since the 1848 U.S.-Mexican War transformed northern Mexico into the American Southwest (encompassing the present states of Texas, Arizona, Colorado, Utah, New Mexico, California, and Nevada) and in this manner instituting "La Frontera"—the border that Gloria Anzaldúa describes as a place "where the Third World grates against the first and bleeds" (*Borderlands/La Frontera,* p. 3). The fluidity and permeability of the border induced Mexican immigrant workers to pour into the territory newly acquired by the United States, where they worked on the railroads and highways being built, the irrigation projects being constructed, and the immense agricultural lands being planted with fruits, vegetables, cotton, and so forth. They came to labor in the cattle industry, to erect the infrastructure for the emerging cities, towns, suburbs, and industrial and business complexes. Mexican brown arms built in the past and continue building the United States's Southwest, Northwest, and Midwest, and the multibillion-dollar industries existing there today.

The Mexican Revolution (1910–1917) further stimulated migration into the United States, and it was precisely during this chaotic period that Pat Mora's maternal grandfather, Eduardo Luis Delgado, a circuit judge in the town of Cusihuiriachic in the northern state of Chihuahua, left Mexico and settled in El Paso, Texas, where he met and married Sotero Amelia Landavazo, his second wife. Their daughter, Estela Delgado, was born in El Paso in 1916 and wed Raúl Antonio Mora in 1939. Estela and Raúl settled in the Texas border town and raised their three daughters, Pat, Cecilia Teresa, Stella Anne, and one son, Roy Antonio. Mora's fictionalized autobiography, *House of Houses,* describes the harrowing experience her grandfather and his young daughters from his first marriage encountered in crossing the border (the river known as the Rio Bravo in Mexico and the Rio Grande in the United States) during the tumultuous years of the Mexican Revolution: "The Delgado sisters clutch one another's hands, can't cry out their fear as the carriage bobs. Since they can't swim they'd normally be terrified hearing the small waves slap against the doors, fearing the carriage will sink or tip, and they'll be gasping their last breath." (p. 32).

After Raúl Antonio Mora and Estela Delgado marry, the young husband continues to work for Riggs Optical Company, where he "grinds, cuts and mounts lenses" (*House of Houses,* p. 190). In 1949 he opens his own optical company,

which he names United Optical. It is a family business where the wife and children and several relatives help make the business thrive. However, in 1964 Mr. Mora is no longer able to sustain the business and the family moves to Santa Monica, California, where they begin a new optical business. Pat is married by this time and does not move with the rest of the family but stays in El Paso. Pat's mother generally took care of the four children but at the same time worked as the main bookkeeper for the optical business. Later, in Santa Monica, she also earned extra money working as a teacher's aide for bilingual classes, and freelanced as a translator for UCLA's Institute for Social Science Research.

Mora graduated from Texas Western College (now the University of Texas, El Paso) with a bachelor's degree and later earned a master's degree from UTEP. She worked as a university administrator at UTEP before devoting herself full-time to her creative writing. Mora has received numerous awards and honors, including a Kellogg National Fellowship (1986); a Premio Aztlán for her novel *House of Houses* (1997); the Carruthers Chair–Distinguished Visiting Professor at the University of New Mexico for fall 1999; and a Civitella Ranieri Fellowship (Umbria, Italy) in 2003. She also has been the recipient of a National Endowment for the Arts fellowship.

Mora's literary production includes five collections of poetry—*Chants* (1984), *Borders* (1986), *Communion* (1991), *Agua Santa/Holy Water* (1995), and *Aunt Carmen's Book of Practical Saints* (1997)—a novel, *House of Houses* (1997), the collection of essays *Nepantla: Essays from the Land in the Middle* (1993); and twenty-three children's books. This essay examines through feminist and border theories the articulations of place, race, class, and gender in Mora's creative work. It explores how Mora charts, maps, the geographies of place— principally the desert and the border—and how these geographic spaces are cleverly interwoven within issues of race, gender, and class. Her work does all of this within a poetic aesthetic and lyrical sensibility that brilliantly fuse politics with art.

Mora's biography is fundamental in the structuring of her literary universe. Her inspiration, themes, and subject matter stem from her lived experiences as well as the narratives recounted by her close relatives: her mother, grandmother, father, aunts, and uncles. Her cultural production, then, tends to veer toward the autobiographical. Mora's work, however, is not just straight autobiographical material, since in her skilled and talented hands the raw autobiographical subject matter is transformed into a finely crafted work of art. In this sense Mora resembles/is a shaman who, through the conjuring up of memory, remakes the real world that surrounded her into sculpted pieces of art; the rituals she performs transform the remembered facts into delicately crafted jewels—each piece a shiny work of exquisitely fashioned art. Her first book of poems, *Chants* (1984), is indicative of this shamanistic endeavor since the title readily points to the sacred task the poet is embarking upon. The book is not just a collection of words but instead, as the title indicates, of *Chants*; the vocable is intimately connected to the sacred because chants are frequently associated with sacred words and phrases used to conjure up the transcendental, the spiritual, the stratosphere located beyond reality. The poet embarks on a spiritual journey, and the reader, through the title, is forewarned of the sacredness of the words enclosed within the pages of the book. The first poem of the collection, "Bribe," sets the stage. It presents the poetic persona describing how a Native American woman performs her rites as a shaman, *curandera*, folk healer, witch—used here in the positive sense. The woman makes an offering to the desert at the dawn of day. She knows how to please the desert, the land, the wind, the elements, the birds, the sun, water, and so on. In an analogous manner to the Native American woman who knows how to cajole the animate and inanimate world into rendering their gifts of

life to humans, the poet's voice learns from these wise shamans and, following their example, offers her gifts of pen and paper to the desert land in hopes of securing future fruits—the poems that will spring forth, that will be born from the seemingly empty, sterile, inhospitable El Paso desert land.

The poetic persona's incantations and offerings to the desert are evidently successful since the book of poems will contain several entries directly related to this dry, sandy terrain. The second poem in *Chants*, "Unrefined," is a fine example of these desert gifts rendered to the poet and the manner in which the landscape serves as a tremendous fount of inspiration. "The desert is no lady," the poem proclaims, describing a being who shouts out loud and hikes up her skirts to dance—"Her unveiled lust fascinates the sun" (p. 8).

Here the desert is personified as a woman—one who is aggressive, violent, sensual, loud. The poem evidences Mora's feminist leanings, since the poetic text structures an image of a woman who is far from typical stereotypes, particularly of Chicana women; that is, as being passive, voiceless, submissive, asexual, with no will or mind of their own. Mora turns the stereotypes of passivity and invisibility, both characteristics attributed to the desert and to Chicanas, and portrays a more authentic side of both: a being who is alive and kicking. "Unrefined" is a fine example of Mora's poetry—well-chosen metaphors and images that encapsulate a strong message subtly crafted and perhaps not visible to the undiscerning reader.

In her highly perceptive article "Tradition and Mythology: Signatures of Landscape in Chicana Literature," Tey Diana Rebolledo rightly points to Mora's frequent personification of the desert and to her use of the desert landscape as what Teresa McKenna would call an "informing female principle" (p. 118). In addition, Mora's poetry is characterized by a surprising sensuality. It often breaks the stereotype of an asexual Chicana who submits passively to her macho husband or lover—a man who supposedly takes her when and where he pleases, without regard to her own sensual desires. Mora's poem "Mielvirgen" (Honeyvirgin) deconstructs this stereotype by projecting a totally different image of sensuality vis-à-vis Chicanas:

> In the slow afternoon heat she sits
> in the shade watching the bees,
> remembering sweet evenings
> of dipping her fingers into warm
> honey, smoothing it on his lips,
> licking it slowly with her tongue,
> hearing him laugh
> then breathe harder
> slowly unbuttoning her
> blouse, rubbing his
> tongue on her sweet skin,
> lips, honey, breasts.

(p. 45)

"Mielvirgen" presents the reader with a poetic voice describing the sensual activity of a woman. Here it is not the male who is the agent, the subject of the poem: it is a woman in charge of her sexuality, enjoying her body and her sensual feelings. Mora is again demolishing stereotypes and presents a woman with agency taking pleasure in sex and being very much the active partner in this erotic encounter.

Her second book, *Borders* (1986), is described by its jacket as a collection of poems exploring "borders—political, cultural, social, emotional—that divide people, forming their individual identities while also challenging the very concept of society. As a poet who brings two cultures, two traditions, two languages and nations together, Mora holds a positive, a sane position on an otherwise divisive topic." The last poem in *Chants,* "Legal Alien," provides a foreshadowing of the route taken by her second book. *Borders,* indeed, continues the desert and border themes so wonderfully and skillfully constructed in *Chants.* It is inevitable that the land, the desert terrain, the border will exert a strong hold on all of Mora's writings. *Borders* includes the splendid poem "Desert Women," a

few lines from which were quoted at the beginning of this essay:

> Desert women know
> about survival.
> Fierce heat and cold
> have burned and thickened
> our skin. Like cactus
> we've learned to hoard,
> to sprout deep roots,
> to seem asleep, yet wake
> at the scent of softness
> in the air, to hide
> pain and loss by silence,
> no branches wail
> or whisper our sad songs
> safe behind our thorns.
>
> Don't be deceived.
> When we bloom, we stun.

(p. 80)

The poem reiterates the image of desert women as survivors—an image that Mora desires to etch in the reader's mind. Women are not frail but, like the desert, are deceptive in their power. However, in *Borders* Mora veers toward a more socially engaged stance in the sense of underscoring in her poetry the plight of the downtrodden, the disposed, the exploited, the oppressed. Her poems are lyrical weapons advocating social justice for the poor; the poet in effect offers a voice for the voiceless. Mora's poems are populated with everyday people: the maid, the farmworker, the Native American, immigrants and the elderly, and so forth. For example, in the poem "Tomás Rivera" she pays homage to the Chicano writer and activist by narrating the story of Rivera's rise from a farmworker to an educated individual (and eventually chancellor of the University of California at Riverside, although this is not in the poem). Rivera came from a migrant working family from Crystal City, Texas; and the poem describes how he travels through Iowa, Michigan, and Minnesota, picking crops along the way, feeling the sting of discrimination from the prejudiced people he encountered along the migrant route—one that only keeps the family in poverty in spite of backbreaking work. Tomás's love of books and learning eventually rescues him from this world of unrelenting poverty and overt racism; his legacy is not only his books and essays but also the fact that he never forgets his people and always works toward improving their condition.

Mora's concern for the hardships experienced by working-class people is evident in "The Grateful Minority":

Why the smile, Ofelia?
Ofelia who?
Why the smile at lysol days
scrubbing washbowls, mop—
mopping bathrooms for people
who don't even know your name.
Ofelia who?
Dirty work you'll do again tomorrow,
mirrors you've polished twenty-five years.

(p. 22)

The poem pays homage to the maids not only toiling daily to clean our houses, hotels, restaurants, and businesses but doing so with a warm smile. The poetic voice chastises those who ignore these anonymous, hardworking women, often invisible and nameless to hegemonic society. This is a social protest poem that does not necessarily present the workers as victims but as survivors, as women who have so much inner strength that they are able to bypass the inequities of life and still smile and whistle while they labor.

The poem that follows "The Grateful Minority" is titled "Echoes" and in an analogous manner presents the cold-hearted harshness of those who employ Mexican maids to do their dirty work:

I sipped white wine
with the women in cool dresses
and sculptured nails shimmering
in the May heat as our children
whacked the piñata whirling

in the desert wind, candy
and colored paper tossed carelessly.

(p. 23)

The poetic persona recounts how Magdalena, the maid, interacts with the children and is busy working during the party. It narrates how the maid is invisible to her employers, who do not seem to care about the amount of work given to the servant:

Again and again I hear:
        just drop the cups and plates
        on the grass. My maid
        will pick them up.
Again and again I feel
        my silence, the party whirring round me.

(p. 23)

The poetic voice yearns to scream at the offending, insensitive employer and in fact through her poem does exactly that.

Poetry with a social message has normally not been perceived as meritorious by those holding fast to canonical edicts of the past. However, the 1960s civil rights movements and social revolutions challenged what is canonical and what is not and introduced a new way of evaluating works of art. Chicano and Chicana literature—together with women's, African American, Asian American, Native American, gay and lesbian, and other literatures emanating from the less privileged—successfully emerged from the margins and took their rightful place at the universities and mainstream publishing houses. Pat Mora's work speaks to the mind as well as to the heart. It is aesthetically pleasing, rich in imagery, and at the same time socially relevant.

Mora's poems in *Borders* touch upon other subjects, such as family relations and religious connections (or nonconnections, to be more exact). "To Big Mary from an Ex-Catholic" provides a glimpse of the religious introspection and conflicts the poetic persona seems to have vis-à-vis estrangement from the Catholic Church:

Will you kick me in the teeth?
Will your foot spike so fast
from under your blue robe
no one will see
but I will bleed?

My fault. I stopped the bribes
hoarded soft petals
didn't lay them at your feet
didn't speak to you at all.

If some day in a dark church
I wait for a nod, smile, wink,
will you just smash your foot
into my mouth?

(p. 77)

The poem not only expresses her supposed remorse for neglecting the Virgin Mary but does so in a humorous manner. It follows the path many Chicana visual artists—Yolanda M. Lopez, Rosa M., Ester Hernández, and Alma López, to name a few—have taken in reconceptualizing the Virgin of Guadalupe in ways that have scandalized some of the more conservative faithful. Yolanda M. López portrayed the Virgin of Guadalupe in the guise of her grandmother, her mother (as a seamstress), and also herself as a jogger. She painted the Virgin in midankle-length dress and midsize heels, no longer confined to her pedestal but free to walk out and about. Asked why she trimmed the Virgin's dress, the artist answered, "The Virgin looked like her dress impeded her movements; I wanted to liberate her" (personal communication, January 2000). Likewise, Alma López portrayed the Virgin of Guadalupe wearing a bikini made of roses. In a similar manner, Pat Mora has reconceptualized the normally passive Virgin Mary and imagined her as a powerful woman capable of negative emotions such as anger, someone willing to use violence if provoked. This new vision is absolutely original, since Mary is generally portrayed as being a loving, forgiving, passive, perfect mother. In this sense Mora is providing Chicanas with a new role model: an active and powerful woman who possesses agency and subjectivity.

Chants and *Borders* were followed in 1991 by another chapbook, *Communion.* It exhibits the pattern established in the first two books vis-à-vis subject matter and worldview. The desert once again appears as a privileged geographic space that stimulates the poetic imagination and sprouts lyrical word structures. It is the desert landscape—viewed as arid and dead by the unknowing eye, but in reality rich in rhythms, smells, plants, changing temperatures, stark outlines, and bright moonlit nights—that continues to predominate in Mora's lyrical discourse. In the poem "My Word-House," Mora builds a solid structure erected upon the hot, shifting sands of the desert. Her structure is adorned with a rich tapestry of words that conjures up a cool, green, soothing oasis rising as if it were a mirage amid the blistering, sun-scorched sand. Inhabiting this house of words are the poetic persona's family and particularly the different generations of its women, with whom she evidences a strong emotional attachment:

The walls grow of the desert
naturally, like *agave, nopal,* yucca.
Vines, winds, and strangers enter large, bare
rooms with ease, no private entrances, no secret
     locks,
Just rough *álamo* slabs framing windows and
     doors.

(p. 86)

Women sprout and bloom like desert flowers in the springtime across Mora's poetic landscape, and she pays homage to these exceptional beings who have nurtured her throughout her life. A splendid example is her poem "Strong Women":

Some women hold me when I need to dream,
rock, rocked my first red anger through the night.
Strong women teach me courage to esteem,

to stand alone, like cactus, persevere
when cold frowns bit my bones and doubts incite.

Some women hold me when I need to dream.

They walk beside me on dark paths I fear,
guide with gold lanterns: stories they recite.
Strong women teach me courage to esteem.

(p. 90)

Mora evidences a feminist perspective throughout her literary production. Her concern for gender issues and commitment to human rights led the poet to indict abusive patriarchal systems wherever she traveled. During a trip to Pakistan, she had a series of jarring experiences regarding women's status in that country. The fact that Pakistani women were not allowed to appear in public uncovered with bare skin showing unnerved her and led her to seriously question that harsh reality. Through her poetry, Mora brought to task the oppressive patriarchal system extant in Pakistan and critiqued the subordinate position women occupied in it. The poem "Veiled" clearly delineates Mora's feminist concerns and challenges the women to rid themselves of the oppressive conditions under which they exist:

If before the *mullah's* morning call,
we tiptoe through the village
gather *burqas* that shroud
even the eyes,
heavy, dark, like storm clouds

if we rush to the river
float the black and brown
garments on soft waves,
close our eyes, listen

will the water loosen
laughter trapped inside those threads,
will light songs rise
and swirl with the morning mist.

(p. 34)

"Veiled" is one of several poems based on her reactions to traveling throughout Pakistan with her husband. Her poetic voice, however, subtly "veils" the strong message inscribed in the lyrical images she structures of women ripping their veils from their faces and throwing them in the river. Although the outcome is not certain, the poem definitely invites the women to try.

The poem "The Eye of Texas" further explores the subject of oppression, but this time Mora does it through a brilliant metaphor: a one-eyed bull, representative of the blindness Texas has toward its minorities and the environment. The title mocks the famous Texas song "The Eyes of Texas Are upon You" by transforming the plural eyes into one eye, that of a Cyclops who blindly tramples nature and everyone not white:

The Eye of Texas
                    is white
as sun-bleached bone,
its one eye, a star
between two long horns,
was once two new eyes
that stared at one another until
the young bull could see only itself
reflected in those huge, soft mirrors
that grew together, hardened, a scar white

as its hoofs that trample deserts,
valleys, fields, shores, country roads,
the bull pausing to raise its
thick neck, its one white eye to the unseen
sky and bellow louder than the combined cries
of *coyotes,* wolves, mountain lions,
bellowing a dark, bitter smoke
then charging on, crushing cotton, onions,
hierbabuena, trampling toys and children
in narrow dirt streets of the Rio Grande Valley,
deaf to the cries of old Mexican voices.

(p. 63)

The poem is a harsh indictment of Texas—of the blatant racism sometimes found there and the disregard its elite has for ecological systems; the poet does this through the use of an all-encompassing metaphor—the one-eyed bull—a very apropos symbol, since Texas privileges its longhorn cattle.

In 1993 the poet veered away from her lyrical writings to produce *Nepantla: Essays from the*

Land in the Middle, a collection dealing with life in general but more specifically with the Chicano and Chicana experience. Teresa McKenna perceptively characterizes the essays as challenging "official versions of culture, gender, and sexuality" (p. 146). The word *nepantla* is taken from Nahuatl (the language the Aztecs spoke and still speak today) and means "place in the middle." In her first essay, "Bienvenidos," she explains why she is publishing the collection of essays (some of which she wrote for conferences and speaking engagements). At the time she began to assemble and write some of the articles for the collection, Mora was in Cincinnati and feeling terribly out of place. In this Midwestern city she began to experience a burning desire to explore issues related to her identity, since upon finding herself in the middle of the United States she felt the discomfort of never quite being fully accepted by Anglo American society, "the slight frown from someone that wordlessly asks, What is someone like her doing here?" (p. 6). A number of essays focus on issues of being away from the border—her native land and the border culture she misses.

Other essays in the *Nepantla* collection explore family relationships such as her close ties with her aunt Ignacia Delgado, who is better known in Mora's writings as Lobo (wolf). "Remembering Lobo" centers on her warm relationship with this aunt, who lived in Mora's parents' house as an extended member of the family. Lobo lived to the ripe age of ninety-four and exerted a great influence on the poet; her presence is felt in every book Mora has written. Several essays in the collection explore issues of cultural differences, since the poet has traveled to many parts of the world, including Pakistan, the Dominican Republic, Guatemala, and Cuba. In these essays, issues of poverty in other parts of the world as contrasted with American wealth are expounded upon. In her profoundly thoughtful essay "University: A Mirage," she writes, "Like many Latin American writers, I believe that the writer also has a responsibility to struggle against injustice in this unjust world"

(p. 169). Pat Mora's work is indeed committed and socially engaged, with this brilliant writer advocating for a better world, not just for Chicanos and Chicanas but for all humanity.

Mora returned to her first love, poetry, with the excellent collection *Agua Santa/Holy Water* (1995). Containing a series of poems about water, the book is divided into six sections: "Old Sea," "Rivers," "Descent," "Where We Were Born," "What Falls from the Sky," and "Wondrous Wetness." The entire collection pays homage to women, be they family members, historical figures, mythic goddesses, sacred icons, or plain, ordinary women. Some of her poems describe personal family members such as Lobo (see "Ofrenda for Lobo"), her wonderful maiden aunt. Others focus on historical women, such as Frida Kahlo in the poem titled "Dear Frida." The stanzas narrate this famous Mexican visual artist's love and obsession for Diego Rivera, her husband, and at the same time pay homage to her amazing talent.

Other poems in the collection base their structural framework and content on mythic figures and Mesoamerican goddesses such as Coatlicue, Ixtabay, and La Llorona, and Catholic sacred figures such as the Virgin of Guadalupe. Some of her poems are tinged with a strong dose of humor, as for example the poem "Coatlicue's Rules: Advice from an Aztec Goddess," where the divine mother complains, "There's something wrong in this world / if a woman isn't safe even when she sweeps." She's recalling the story of how she was impregnated by a speck of dust while doing housework. The result was the birth of Huitzilopochtli, the god of war and the sun, and the rebellion of Coatlicue's daughter, the moon goddess Coyolxauhqui, who united in battle her four hundred brothers and sisters, the stars, against their mother for getting pregnant. The birth of Huitzilopochtli and the dismemberment of Coyolxauhqui have been interpreted by Cherríe Moraga and other feminist scholars as the defeat of matriarchy and the rise of patriarchy in Aztec society (*The Last Generation,* pp. 73–76).

Equally humorous is "Malinche's Tips: Pique from Mexico's Mother":

Tip 1: In an unfriendly country,
wear a mask.
You will see more.

I hear your sticks-and-stones:
Whore, traidora, slut.
What happened to mother?

My reputación
precedes me. I come
from a long line of women
much maligned,
hija de Eva,
rumors of gardens,
crushed flowery scent
heavy as sprawling, tangled
branches, scarlet breeze
velvetmoist with petals,
piel, fruitflesh, ripe
tempting tongue,
sweet juice of
words, plural hiss
of languagessssss.

(p. 64)

The poem's referents are Malinche and Eve, the two women blamed for losing paradise: Eve is blamed for losing the Garden of Eden, Malinche for losing the Aztec Empire. Feminist scholars such as Adelaida del Castillo and Norma Alarcón have revisioned Malinche's role in the Spanish conquest and argued against placing the blame on Malinche for the defeat of the Aztecs. The collection *Agua Santa/Holy Water*, therefore, addresses feminist issues of patriarchal domination and oppression; it deconstructs master narratives indicting women as traitors, whores, bad mothers, and so forth. Mora's poetic voice seeks to rewrite these patriarchal narratives and turn them upside down with a strong sense of humor and *picardía*. The poems present the voices of women fighting back and telling their own stories. Mora's women, whether mythic goddesses or mortals of flesh and blood, are depicted with agency; as subjects who challenge (his)story and desire to replace male master narratives with (her)stories.

Mora followed the publication of *Agua Santa/Holy Water* with her autobiographical novel *House of Houses* in 1997. In this novel Mora weaves a rich tapestry of family history, anecdotes, jokes, legends, songs, folk speech (including proverbs), food recipes, folk beliefs, children's games and songs, and personal experience narratives. The author derives the title from a Latin phrase she found inscribed in a book of natural history: *Ut rosa flos florum, sic est domus ista domorum* (as the rose is the flower of flowers, so is this the house of houses; p. 4). The phrase "house of houses" is an apt title for the book, since the author returns to the memory of her childhood house in El Paso where she grew up and begins to reinhabit it with her words; in this manner she builds the structure, adobe upon adobe, room by room, and slowly populates the house with the familiar faces of her childhood, both dead and alive. Her relatives join her in constructing the "house of houses," which is the family history.

Mora begins her book with an introduction in which she explains the nature of the work and the meaning of the title. Thereafter she offers twelve chapters, each one bearing the title of a month of the year: "*Enero friolero*/Chilly January," "*Febrero loco*/Crazy February," "*Marzo airoso*/ Windy March," and so forth. Most of the months are characterized by a folk saying, or *dicho*, that aptly describes the "nature" of each month according to folk wisdom: for example, "*Abril lluvioso*/Rainy April"; April is characterized as "*floreado y hermoso*" (flowery and beautiful). Other months are linked with well-known folk proverbs not necessarily related to anything characterizing the month. Each chapter basically focuses on a family member, and the reader is provided with biographical data and the personal adventures or misadventures in the life of that relative. Thus, Chapter 1 features her aunt Ignacia Delgado, or Lobo, and her family saga of emigrating to the United States, as well as the tremendous role she played in the narrator's life. Chapter 2 focuses on Sotero Amelia Landavazo, nicknamed Mamande (grandmother), and her biography. The chapter tells of her birth in the state of Guerrero, Mexico, to Refugio Rochín de Barroso and to a Spanish sea captain, Juan Domingo Landavazo, who is from the Basque city of Bilbao in Spain. The Mexican Revolution forces her family to flee to the United States, and it is in El Paso, Texas, that she marries Eduardo Luis Delgado, nicknamed "Papande" (grandfather) and also born in Mexico. The author's mother, Estela Delgado, and her brothers and sisters are born in the United States from the marriage of Eduardo and Sotero Amelia Landavazo.

In Chapter 3 the narrative centers on the paternal side of the author's family, the Moras. We read of how Lázaro Mora is a well-established tailor born in 1880 in Jiménez, Chihuahua, Mexico. Lázaro marries Natividad Pérez, and out of this marriage the author's father, Raul Antonio Mora, is born in the city of Chihuahua in Mexico. Again, although the family is prosperous they are forced to emigrate to the United States to escape the ravages of war. There Raul Antonio Mora marries Estela Delgado in El Paso, Texas, in 1939. At the beginning of the novel, the author provides a genealogical chart to help the reader unravel the intricacies of family relationships and track the names of great-grandparents, grandparents, parents, great aunts, uncles, and aunts.

The family saga is written in an aesthetically pleasing, poetical style. In fact, many of the chapters contain poems either written by the author herself or obtained from other sources. The desert plays an important part in the development of the family history, since it is from the desert imagery that much of the poetic language will spring forth. The desert landscape and its vegetation will serve as a splendid backdrop for each chapter written.

House of Houses incorporates much of her Catholic upbringing. Mora's relatives, particularly the women, are devoted Catholics, and the author is raised with much of the Catholic belief systems, both orthodox and popular. Her aunts are a fount of folk beliefs, and it is from this fount that the poetry collection *Aunt Carmen's Book of Practical Saints* (1997) is derived. The faithful believe that each of the saints has a particular function, a specialty: Saint Anthony is well known for finding lost objects and for finding young women boyfriends, Saint Jude is known as the saint who is able to do the impossible, Saint Isidro's specialty is agriculture; and so forth. The poetic voice in "Prayer to the Saints/Oración a los Santos" directs her invocation to a whole roster of them:

> At sixteen I began to pray to you, old friends,
>   for a handsome man who would never stray,
>   Devoutly, I'd say,
> Saint Peter the Apostle,
>   please grant me this miracle,
> Saint Raphael, the Archangel,
>   remove every obstacle,
> San José, dear father,
>   may he frown at liquor,
> Saint Clare,
>   for Mother, could he be a millionaire,
> Saint John Nepomuk,
>   my few faults may he overlook,
> Santa María Magdalena,
>   que a veces me sirva mi cena.
>
>   (p. 11)

Mora's feminist concerns nevertheless pervade many of the poems. In "Santa Rita," an abused wife triumphs over her monstrous, cruel husband; furthermore, Santa Rita is linked to the poetic persona's abused neighbor. The saint becomes somewhat of a role model, since she left her husband and entered a convent even though she was no longer a virgin. According to legend, Santa Rita demonstrated her saintliness through having one of Jesus's thorns stuck on her forehead. The intended feminist message is to leave your abusive husband and follow your heart's desire.

In addition to her poetry collections, essays, and novel, this talented Chicana writer also wrote about a score of children's books, among them Pablo's *Tree, The Rainbow Tulip,* and *The Desert Is My Mother/El desierto es mi madre.* These children's books continue to focus on the desert landscape and on family traditions, family stories, and Mora's relatives. For example, *The Rainbow Tulip* is based on a personal experience her mother had in elementary school. For a school performance her mother was asked to represent a tulip. Not being aware that tulips only come in one color, the little girl requested her aunt to sew a multicolor skirt. When she went to school everyone stared and the child felt very self-conscious. However, her relatives and the teacher made her feel very special, so all turned out well. The moral of the story is that sometimes it is painful to be different but that love conquers all. Other stories concentrate on the flora, fauna, and landscape of the desert, while still others focus on Native American myths and legends. With more than twenty of the books, Mora was considered the leading Latina writer of children's books. Hers are poetically written, many of them in a bilingual format or with translated versions, and encompass Mexican and Latino cultural information, encoding didactic information regarding the importance of animals and natural surroundings.

CONCLUSION

Pat Mora's essays, novel, poetry, and children's books take us on a journey—a journey of extraordinary lyrical beauty as well as profound understanding of the human condition. Her poetry and other writings, while lyrically immersed in the stunning landscape of the desert and the highly enriching experience of living on the U.S.-Mexican border area, is permeated with a deep sense of commitment towards social justice. Her poetic voice challenges the structures of power and politics that promote prejudice, discrimination, oppression, and exploitation. Her poetic voice falls within the Chicano and Chicana literary tradition dating back to the second half of the nineteenth century after the U.S.-Mexican War and resonates with both a sense of resistance and affirmation—resistance towards those political institutions that seek to economically and socially oppress and exploit the Chicano and Chicana population and other marginal groups; reaffirmation for a cultural identity (Mexican) deemed to be rich and powerful in the spiritual realm.

While Mora's works are infused with a sense of place, her commitment to in-depth explorations of racial stratifications, class structures, and gender politics transforms her poetry and other writings from mere lyrical excursions into powerful weapons that give voice to the voiceless. The poet in Mora never lets her forget the aesthetic dimensions of her work of art. She is, nevertheless, able to conflate poetry and politics and transforms her "word house," as she calls her poetry (and her fiction), into "cultural acts of resistance." Mora's poetics in the final analysis is a "word house" that seeks to include all humanity within its walls of love and understanding; a "word house" that is filled with harmony and peace and, following an ecological paradigm, is able to encompass a multicolored world.

Selected Bibliography
WORKS OF PAT MORA

POETRY
Chants. Houston: Arte Público Press, 1984.

Borders. Houston: Arte Público Press, 1986.

Communion. Houston: Arte Público Press, 1991.

Agua Santa/Holy Water. Boston: Beacon Press, 1995.

Aunt Carmen's Book of Practical Saints. Boston: Beacon Press, 1997.

PROSE

Nepantla: Essays from the Land in the Middle. Albuquerque: University of New Mexico Press, 1993.

House of Houses. Boston: Beacon Press, 1997.

"Foreword" to *The Earth Moves at Midnight and Other Poems* by Murray Bodo. Cincinnati: St. Anthony Messenger Press, 2003. Pp. xi–xiii.

CHILDREN'S BOOKS:

A Birthday Basket for Tía. Illustrated by Cecily Lang. New York: Macmillan, 1992.

The Desert Is My Mother/El desierto es mi madre. Illustrated by Daniel Lechón. Houston: Arte Público Press, Piñata Books, 1994.

Listen to the Desert/Oye al desierto. Illustrated by Francisco X. Mora. New York: Clarion Books, 1994.

Agua, Agua, Agua. Parsippany, N.J.: Good Year Books, 1993; Scott, Foresman and Company, 1994.

Pablo's Tree. Illustrated by Cecily Lang. New York: Macmillan, 1994.

The Gift of the Poinsettia/El regalo de la flor de Nochebuena. With Charles Ramirez Berg. Illustrated by Daniel Lechón. Houston: Arte Público Press, Piñata Books, 1995.

Confetti: Poems for Children. Illustrated by Enrique O. Sánchez. New York: Lee and Low Books, 1996.

Uno, Dos, Tres/One, Two, Three. Illustrated by Barbara Lavallee. New York: Clarion Books, 1996.

Tomás and the Library Lady. Illustrated by Raul Colón. New York: Alfred A. Knopf, 1997.

Tomás y la señora de la biblioteca. Translated by Amy Prince. Illustrated by Raul Colón. New York: Dragonfly Books, 1997.

This Big Sky. Illustrated by Steve Jenkins. New York: Scholastic, 1998.

Delicious Hulabaloo/Pachanga Deliciosa. Illustrated by Francisco X. Mora. Houston: Arte Público Press, Piñata Books, 1998.

The Rainbow Tulip. Illustrated by Elizabeth Sayles. New York: Penguin Group, Viking, 1999.

My Own True Name: New and Selected Poems for Young Adults, 1984–1999. Illustrated by Anthony Accardo. Houston: Arte Público Press, Piñata Books, 2000.

La noche que se cayó la luna: Mito Maya. Illustrated by Domi. Toronto: Groundwood Books, 2000.

The Night the Moon Fell: A Maya Myth Retold. Illustrated by Domi. Toronto: Douglas & McIntyre, 2000.

The Race of Toad and Deer. Illustrated by Domi. Toronto: Douglas & McIntyre, 2001.

La carrera del sapo y el venado. Illustrated by Domi. Toronto: Groundwood Books, 2001.

The Bakery Lady/La señora de la panadería. Illustrated by Pablo Torrecilla. Houston: Arte Público Press, Piñata Books, 2001.

Love to Mamá: A Tribute to Mothers. Edited by Pat Mora. Illustrated by Paula S. Barragán M. New York: Lee & Low Books, 2001.

A Library for Juana: The World of Sor Juana Inés/Una biblioteca para Juana: El mundo de Sor Juana Inés. Illustrated by Beatriz Vidal. New York: Alfred A. Knopf, 2002.

María Paints the Hills. Illustrated by María Hesch. Santa Fe: Museum of New Mexico Press, 2002.

SECONDARY WORKS

Alarcón, Norma. "Chicana's Feminist Literature: A Re-vision through Malintzín; or, Malintzin: Putting Flesh Back on the Object." In *This Bridge Called My Back: Writings by Radical Women of Color* 2d ed. Edited by Cherríe Moraga and Gloria Anzaldúa. New York: Kitchen Table-Women of Color Press, 1983. Pp. 182–190.

———. "Traddutora, Traditora: A Paradigmatic Figure of Chicana Feminism." *Cultural Critique* 13 (fall 1989): 57–87.

Anzaldúa, Gloria. *Borderlands/La Frontera: The New Mestiza.* San Francisco: Spinsters/Aunt Lute, 1987.

Del Castillo, Adelaida R. "Malintzín Tenépal: A Preliminary Look into a New Perspective." In *Essays on la Mujer.* Edited by Rosaura Sánchez and Rosa Martínez Cruz. Los Angeles: Chicano Studies Center Publications, University of California, 1980. Pp. 124–149.

Moraga, Cherríe. *The Last Generation.* Boston: South End Press, 1993.

McKenna, Teresa. *Migrant Song: Politics and Process in Contemporary Chicano Literature.* Austin: University of Texas Press, 1997.

Prignano, Mary. "Pat Mora." http://web.nmsu.edu/~tomlynch/swlit.mora.html. Accessed July 24, 2003.

Rebolledo, Tey Diana. "Tradition and Mythology: Signatures of Landscape in Chicana Literature." In *The Desert Is No Lady: Southwestern Landscapes in Women's Writing and Art.* Edited by Vera Norwood and Janice Monk. New Haven, Conn.: Yale University Press, 1987. Pp. 98–124.

Cherríe Moraga
(1952–)

DEBRA J. BLAKE

HERRÍE MORAGA'S WORK is at once incisive, intrepid, lyrical, and spiritual. Although these terms suggest ironic, even incongruous, meanings, collectively they describe the qualities she inscribes in every work she writes. Her works reveal a postmodern ethnic sensibility of rupture, disturbance, uncertainty, and diverse racial, cultural, and sexual contexts. The juxtaposition of expressions of contemporary popular culture with elements of ancient Native rituals represents her mestiza (racially and cultured mixed) consciousness. In form as well as content, her works reflect postmodernist ethnic practice through the interweaving of multiple languages, including Spanish, English, Chicano vernacular, and Quiché Maya, into her character's dialogues and her own narrative writings. Revaluing oral tradition and inserting nonlinear writing are fundamental elements of her work, stemming from Native and Mexican storytelling cultures. In addition, she breaks down genre boundaries by weaving poetry, journal entries, dreams, and essays into all of her works.

Moraga's writings convey a lesbian feminist and woman-of-color consciousness rarely portrayed in literature before the publication of the early anthologies she edited and her own multi-genre collections. Her works disturb mainstream views of the U.S. melting pot, the American Dream, and the nuclear Christian family. Instead, she advocates alternative belief systems originating in Native identity and spirituality, Chicana lesbian sexuality and family, and a Chicano homeland based on tolerance of difference.

Moraga brought new energy and vision to U.S. feminist thought and to Chicano studies by insisting on the inclusion of women of color and lesbians. She contributed bold and insightful analyses and creative works to American studies and American literature. Her writings push the boundaries of art and political activism, expanding the tradition of the Teatro Campesino (Farmworkers' Theater) begun by Luís Valdez during the Chicano civil rights movement. Throughout her career as an editor, poet, essayist, educator, and award-winning playwright, Moraga has contributed to late-twentieth-century discussions of what constitutes literature, difference, nationalism, and social justice in the United States.

EARLY INFLUENCES: LA FAMILIA AND INTERSECTING OPPRESSIONS

Moraga's life experiences fertilize the themes and styles of her writing. Growing up in Chicano communities adjacent to Los Angeles (Whittier, South Pasadena, and San Gabriel), Moraga became familiar with the storytelling skill of Mexican oral tradition. *Cuentos,* stories told by female family members around the kitchen table, still influence her writing today. Significantly, the young Moraga learned storytelling techniques by listening rather than by reading.

Moraga, born 25 September 1952, is the child of a mixed-race marriage, Chicana and Anglo. Her mother, Elvira Moraga, was born in Santa Paula, California, in 1914, to parents from the Sonora desert. Her father, Joseph Lawrence, was born in San Francisco in 1926 to a French Canadian father and Missouri mother. As a child, Moraga received mixed messages about which culture was important and valued. On the one hand, Chicano culture permeated her home with the daily presence of her mother's extended family members, who spoke Spanish and English. On the other hand, Moraga's mother encouraged the children to speak English and pursue white, middle-class values.

After high school, Moraga attended a progressive private college near Los Angeles, where her exposure to dedicated artists both intrigued and frightened her. Despite a fascination with the arts, Moraga chose the practical route expected by her parents. She graduated with a B.A. in English education in 1974 and began teaching at a private high school in Los Angeles. At the same time, she enrolled in a writing class sponsored by the Los Angeles Women's Building and became passionate about writing. The passion for writing released through the course coincided with an acknowledgement of her desire for women: during this time she came out as a lesbian. She expressed her passion in lesbian love poems, and her work took on a new vibrancy.

In 1977 Moraga quit her teaching job to commit a year to writing, living on unemployment and part-time work. She also moved to the San Francisco Bay area so that she could be more openly lesbian, in a city apart from her family. During this time, she expanded her reading list, focusing on writings by white lesbian authors such as Radclyffe Hall's *The Well of Loneliness* and the works of Djuna Barnes. In the course of working and living as a lesbian in 1970s San Francisco, where gay activism was in full swing, Moraga discovered the bond between literary writing and political activism. She was introduced to Judy Grahn's working-class lesbian poetry, and from it gained insight to imbue her own work not only with a lesbian consciousness, but also with race and class awareness. She met with Grahn, who further inspired her to write from the voices she knew best—those of her Chicana relatives telling stories in a fusion of Spanish and English around her mother's kitchen table.

From her year of committed writing, she decided to pursue a master's degree at San Francisco State University, which combined creative writing with the study of feminist literature. In the master's degree courses, Moraga met other writers who were women of color and was approached by Gloria Anzaldúa to edit a collection of writings by women of color that could serve as testimony to their life experiences and as a resource for feminist courses, where previously no such collection had existed. *This Bridge Called My Back: Writings by Radical Women of Color,* a book that changed the face and scope of U.S. feminist studies, was the result of their inspiration and effort. The book manuscript served as Moraga's thesis for the master's degree she earned in 1980, and it was first published in 1981 by Persephone Press.

In putting together the collection, Moraga and Anzaldúa opened dialogue among women of color about their common experiences of racism and oppression and the power of working together. The collection confronted white feminists and scholars with the inadequacy and harm of a feminism that did not include a diversity of voices and lacked an understanding of how women of color experience intersecting oppressions of race, class, culture, and gender.

This Bridge Called My Back also raised concerns about and advanced new understandings of women's sexuality and heterosexism, both of which were taboo subjects in the national feminist agenda. This collection brought new vision and vitality to the largely white, middle-class, second-wave feminist movement. Republished in 1983 by Kitchen Table: Women of Color Press, of which Moraga was a cofounder, *This Bridge Called My Back* gave voice to the silences and frustrations of women of color and celebrated the significance of being a black, Chicana, Latina, Asian American, or Native woman. Just as importantly, it established the feminist identity and political coalition denoted by "women of color," and the radical politics of working to end all oppressions, which function together as an interlocking system rather than as isolated concerns. In 1986 *This Bridge Called My Back* received the Before Columbus Foundation American Book Award. In 1988 it was rewritten and republished by Moraga and Ana Castillo as *Esta puente, mi espalda: Voces de mujeres tercermundistas en los Estados Unidos* to address a Latin American feminist audience.

The title proposes the possibility of women of color working together to bridge their differences and overcome the suspicion and doubt that often undermined potential alliances. In addition, it alludes to the amount of work that women of color do within the family, culture, and society to serve others. This concept connects with another idea that Moraga called "experience in the flesh," which challenges theoretical conceptions of the lives of women of color and replaces them with real experiences. Moraga later refined this concept and called it "theory in the flesh," paradoxically linking the rational with the sensational. *This Bridge Called My Back* has been used extensively in women's studies courses and has sold over eighty thousand copies.

From the experience of editing this collection, Moraga forged her own identity and radical politics as a woman of color, a Chicana lesbian writer, and a creative activist, self-conceptions that motivate and undergird all of her writings. Moraga articulates this philosophy in one of the poems published in *This Bridge Called My Back*. "The Welder" contrasts alchemy, the medieval chemical science of discovery, with welding, which bonds elements together and creates new forms. The speaker of the poem declares herself a welder, who effects change in the white heat of inspiration and desire, the welder's torch. She does not need magic; rather, she avows the self-empowerment she experiences through creative work and the power that exists in art to work for change.

> I am the welder.
> I understand the capacity of heat
> to change the shape of things.
> I am suited to work
> within the realm of sparks
> out of control.
>
> I am the welder.
> I am taking the power
> into my own hands.
>
> (p. 220)

A second poem published in *This Bridge Called My Back*, "For the Color of My Mother," traces Moraga's recognition that her route to creative activism was inspired by her rising awareness of the struggles of lesbians and women of color. In particular, the poem portrays the necessity for the next generation to speak out and say what their mothers and the older generation of women had not been able to utter.

In the first lines, the speaker represents taking a political stance and creating poetic work as acts of resistance, a resistance her mother could not speak: "*I am a white girl gone brown to the blood color of my mother / speaking for her through the unnamed part of the mouth / the wide-arched muzzle of brown women*" (p. 12). In these lines, the speaker makes public the political position she has decided to take. She will not assimilate as white by taking the socially easier route of identifying with her father's Anglo bloodline; rather, she declares herself a woman of color who fights for the rights of Chicanas and others who have experienced oppression. Furthermore, the speaker links this activism with being a lesbian, as implied by the metaphor "wide-arched muzzle," which suggests that the female labia as well as the lips are involved in the enunciation of taboo love and other desires. The second stanza of the poem portrays the speaker's childhood pain of a split lip, suggesting the split identity of the daughter of a Chicana and Anglo. The pain from the split is vocalized as a howl that reverberates through the hospital, in contrast to the silences the mother keeps when she is forced to submit to the will of white people, when she performs hard labor, or when she fears being raped.

> at five, her mouth
> pressed into a seam
> a fine blue child's line drawn across her face
> her mouth, pressed into mouthing english
> mouthing yes yes yes
> mouthing stoop lift carry . . .
>
> at fourteen, her mouth
> painted, the ends drawn up
> the mole in the corner colored in darker larger
>   mouthing yes
> she praying no no no.
>
>   (p. 13)

The poem ends with a healing ceremony that brings the speaker together with other "dark women," who acknowledge and understand the mother's pain and the daughter's mission to voice it.

> touching each carved feature
>   swollen eyes and mouth
> they understand the explosion the splitting
> open   contained within the fixed expression
> they cradle her silence
>   nodding to me.
>
>   (p. 13)

Moraga's consciousness of internalized racism and repression of desire is explained in an essay in *This Bridge Called My Back,* "La Güera" (light skinned woman). The essay details, as the title suggests, Moraga's identification as light-skinned, and the epiphany that led her to understand the privileges light skin gave her. As she relates in the essay, her awakening to experiences of discrimination as a lesbian, and the subsequent recognition of her mother's similar experiences as a woman of color, came when she "lifted the lid to [her] lesbianism" (p. 28). For Moraga, being silenced and oppressed as a lesbian forced her to confront how her light skin had saved her from being oppressed as a person of color while she was growing up. Her mother's stories of manual labor, poverty, and inadequate schooling resonated as examples of a brown person's experience. Just as importantly, she recognized that her mother had insisted that the children speak English to save them from such situations. "It was through my mother's desire to protect her children from poverty and illiteracy that we became 'anglocized'; the more effectively we could pass in the white world, the better guaranteed our future" (p. 28).

The final step Moraga takes to achieve awareness is to face the "nightmare" she discovered within: that she was both oppressor and oppressed. She realized she had internalized racism, the idea that white middle-class thinking represented everyone, and homophobia, "my own hatred of myself for being queer" (p. 32). The internalized racism and heterosexism caused dual harm: "I have internalized a racism and classism, where the object of oppression is not only someone *outside* my skin, but the someone *inside* my skin" (p. 30). In identifying the "someone *inside,*" she faced her own denial of Chicana and Native ancestry and lesbianism. In identifying the "someone *outside,*" she faced the fear and reality that as a light-skinned person she had participated in the subordination of people of color, lesbians and gays, and working-class people. *Beyond* her personal introspection, the essay provides a paradigm that encourages readers to "look at the nightmare within us" and face their own fears.

When Persephone Press went bankrupt, Moraga was determined to reclaim the rights to *This Bridge Called My Back* and republish it. These efforts and the founding of Kitchen Table: Women of Color Press led to her move to the northeast—first Boston, then New York—and to the publication of another anthology in 1983, *Cuentos: Stories by Latinas,* which she edited with Alma Gómez and Mariana Romo-Carmona. *Cuentos* also broke new ground with its novel focus on the experiences of first-generation Latinas in the United States who considered themselves feminists. With Latina feminism as the underlying theme, the editors also incorporated works that represented Latina sexuality, especially lesbian sexuality. In addition, the editors insisted that language is a fundamental element of Latina experience and representation. Contributors' works were printed in Spanish, English, and a mixture of the two.

Moraga's contribution to the collection included the short story "Pesadilla" (Nightmare) which represents the inner struggle of Cecilia, the Chicana protagonist, with race and sexuality in her relationship with her black partner, Deborah. "Pesadilla" portrays Cecilia's struggle to accept herself as a lesbian woman of color or choose the safety of whiteness and pass as white and heterosexual. The story reveals how the protagonist brings to the relationship her own racism and homophobia, a theme Moraga examines further in *Loving in the War Years.*

While editing *Cuentos,* Moraga pursued her own writing and published still another book in 1983. *Loving in the War Years: Lo que nunca pasó por sus labios* (What never passed her lips) is a compilation of poems, essays, dreams, and journal entries written between 1976 and 1983. The poem "For the Color of My Mother" and the prose pieces "La Güera" and "Pesadilla," published in the earlier anthologies, were included in *Loving in the War Years,* along with new material. As a whole, the collection expresses Moraga's difficult personal voyage to Chicana lesbianism and feminism and the problems of religion and sexuality she confronted within herself and within Chicano culture. The writings in the collection are connected to each other through the use of an autobiographical character variably named "Cecilia," "Ceci," "Cher'ann," and "Cherríe," which, along with the inclusion of various genres, signifies a postmodern ethnic sensibility that challenges hierarchies of genre and the idealized individual "I" (white, male, and heterosexual) that governs traditional autobiographies. Moraga's varied autobiographical identities trace the growth and development of a young Chicana who grapples with cultural and societal mores that repress lesbian and female sexuality, idealize maleness, and encourage assimilation to white, middle-class values.

The book begins with poems written in the late 1970s that express the struggles of lesbians coming out and the dangers of repressing their desire. "Voices of the Fallers" relates the despair and hopelessness many lesbians experience along with the exhilaration of falling in love. The poem suggests a variety of interpretations for the metaphor of falling: falling for fantasy, falling into depression, falling in love, falling from grace, falling to one's death. Based on actual incidents of a lesbian who fell to her death and another who pushed her lover's child over a cliff, the poem communicates the sense of loss of self (and others) due to the shame of loving women, and simultaneously the release from inhibitions that accompanies falling in love. The poem begins with the image of a girl being carried away, swept off her feet by the proverbial white, winged horse. Moraga ironically subverts the heterosexual fantasy of the heroic man on a white horse rescuing a woman and carrying her off to wedded bliss. She replaces this image with a lesbian horseback liberation fantasy.

> You were born queer with the dream
> of flying
> from an attic with a trap
> door   opening
> to a girl who could

handle a white horse
with wings   riding her away.

(p. 1)

However, the fantasy repeatedly gives way to the reality of young women who experience rejection and isolation rather than happiness ever after: "*I'm falling / can't you see / I'm falling?*" One girl falls to her death, literally (from a cliff) or metaphorically (by stifling her sexual desires). The speaker concludes that "it is / this end / I fear," the silence and deprivation of withholding desire and passion (p. 6). "Waking / to the danger / of falling / again / falling / in love the dream" (p. 6).

Loving in the War Years established Moraga as a Chicana lesbian writer and Chicana feminist who boldly confronted sexism and heterosexism within Chicano culture and Catholic religion and envisioned the creative force of female desire. The collected works express how she came to understand the relationship between the repression of female sexuality taught by the Catholic Church and the devaluing of women reinforced by Chicano cultural practices. One essay raised questions about the white, middle-class feminist movement's treatment of women of color and its limited definition of feminism. However, the focus of the book is inward, on Chicano culture, religion, and community, and Moraga confronts the enemy within, even within herself.

When *Loving in the War Years* was published, Moraga had not yet recovered the Aztec goddesses whom she would later refigure as powerful, sexual female divines. At this point, she felt deeply that Chicano culture and institutionalized Catholicism did not serve her own or other Chicanas' emotional, physical, or spiritual needs and desires. She also recognized that taboo subjects within Chicano culture had to be reckoned with as much as the racism and sexism of the dominant culture. Yet she sensed just as much the risk in speaking out. In the introduction, she writes, "On some level, you have to be willing to lose it all to write—to risk telling the truth that no one may want to hear, even you" (p. v).

For Moraga, the right to passion became far more important than the fear of loss, because "the right to passion" refers to the development of the self as a whole human being (p. 136). It also implies self-determination, the right of women to choose whom they love, how they love, and what they want to do with their lives. The subtitle of the book and title of the final section, "Lo que nunca pasó por sus labios" (What never passed her lips) refers to both the powerlessness of women to speak and the wordless expression of female desire that is nonetheless "utterly / utterly / heard" (p. 149). As she explains in an interview with Norma Alarcón, delving into her desires released the passion to write about what had been unnameable. Before she came out as a lesbian, her poetry was stilted and formal, as she tried to write around her secrets. When she allowed her lesbianism to surface, she found her voice, which came from the heart.

Loving in the War Years became a vital text in the development of a Chicana lesbian and woman-of-color feminism. In particular, the essay "A Long Line of *Vendidas*" contributed an analysis of the pervasive conceptions within Chicano and U.S. cultures that regulate Chicanas' sexuality and gender roles. Moraga chose the essay title, which refers to female betrayers or sellouts, partly for its association with the historical Native woman Malintzin Tenepal (La Malinche), who was given to the Spanish conqueror Hernán Cortés and became his interpreter, adviser, and sexual interest. La Malinche is considered the mother of the mestizo (mixed) race, Native and Spanish, due to the child she bore with Cortés. Yet over the centuries she lacked esteem; rather, like the Christian Eve, La Malinche became negatively mythologized as the woman who betrayed her people by aiding the Spaniards and who sold them out by sleeping with the white man. Instead of being designated the revered mother, as was the Catholic Virgin Mary, La Malinche became known as "la vendida" (sellout) and "la chingada" (the violated one). These terms made her, and by association all Chicana or Mexican women, passive objects serving and pleasing others rather than actively determining their own life paths and pleasures.

As Moraga argues, this conception of female gender roles contributed to a heterosexual and hierarchical emphasis on putting men first as the primary function of women. In consequence, women betray each other continually to retain the affection of men. Even so, they are suspected by the male-dominated culture of disloyalty, because every woman has the potential to transgress with another Chicano or a white man. In addition, Chicanos and Mexicans, like many cultures of color, have experienced attempted genocide. Because of this, race helps determine female sexuality and gender roles. Moraga notes that the preservation and reproduction of the race through the institution of the family is "infused into the blood" (p. 110). "And so we fight back, we think, with our families. . . . We believe the more severely we protect the sex roles within the family, the stronger we will be as a unit in opposition to the anglo threat" (p. 110). In contrast, Moraga states that this limited conception of family as hierarchical is the weakest aspect of the culture. She argues against a patriarchal conception of family, and for a conception of family in terms of emotional bonds within and between sexes and generations.

Most of all, Moraga maintains that lesbianism and emotionally committed male homosexuality serve as the greatest challenge to the hierarchy within the family by the fact that the male is no longer served by the female. Moraga points out that women who take control of their own sexual destiny are considered "Malinchistas" because they enable genocide by refusing to have children. Whether heterosexual or lesbian, like Malinche, they are betrayers for pursuing their own desires and interests. However, Moraga turns the concept of betrayal around, noting that a culture's refusal to look at its own weaknesses is itself an act of betrayal, in particular, betrayal of self-determining women who are denigrated or driven into silence and isolation.

Moraga understands sexuality as the source of both oppression and liberation for women. In allowing herself to express and accept desire, Moraga maintains that she is reborn in the process of speaking. In the epilogue to "A Long Line of *Vendidas*," she includes a short poem that metaphorically describes the power of desire, speech, and writing to create or birth oneself. The poem, "La Mujer Que Viene de la Boca" (The woman who came out of her mouth), again draws on the metaphors of lips and mouths for female desire and self-creation.

> There resides in her, as in me, a woman far greater
>   than
> our bodies
> can inhabit
> So I stay
> and take what I can
> in thick drops
> like oil that leaks
> from the cave of anger
> wrestling between her legs.
>
> (pp. 140–141)

The metaphorical nourishment of the "thick drops," which implies placenta-like matter, provides sustenance for the speaker and her lover and nurtures the rebirth of both of them.

> *And there is a woman coming out of her mouth.*
> *Hay una mujer que viene de la boca.*
>
> (p. 142)

For Moraga, passion, and in particular the love of women, is the force that sparks female liberation and the recognition of a self-determining female subject.

Living in the northeast, far from childhood influences, she was able to express more freely in writing her concerns about the strict Mexican Catholic environment in which she was raised.

In the culturally and racially diverse atmosphere of New York City, she also began to appreciate the uniqueness of Chicano culture and its contributions to her sense of self.

Having dealt with intensely personal themes in *Loving in the War Years*, Moraga decided to focus on fictional personas in her next writings. In the interview with Norma Alarcón, Moraga says that she began writing the characters in her journal, not thinking about a play. As the writing progressed she realized this was one piece that "needed to be oral, wanted to be spoken, heard" (p. 134). *Giving Up the Ghost*, a two-act play written mainly in poetic monologues, was the result. The development of *Giving Up the Ghost* was sponsored in part by the Minneapolis Broadcloth Series and presented as a staged reading at the feminist theater At the Foot of the Mountain, in Minneapolis in 1984. That same year, Moraga was chosen to participate at INTAR's Hispanic Playwrights-in-Residency Laboratory in New York City, based on the script of *Giving Up the Ghost*. The residency was directed by the lesbian Cuban playwright María Irene Fornés, who produces her own sensitive feminist dramas exploring women's laborious lives. Fornés encouraged Moraga to draw on a poetic aesthetics when writing drama, which affirmed for Moraga her place in theater as a poet-playwright.

Giving Up the Ghost examines the relationship between two women, one heterosexual and one lesbian, and the sexual and cultural demons that haunt their interactions and their existence. In this play Moraga expands on the themes presented in "A Long Line of *Vendidas*," showing how cultural taboos against female desire, both heterosexual and lesbian, enter and affect women's psyches and relationships.

With the character of Marisa, a Chicana lesbian in her twenties, Moraga explores the damage caused by sexual abuse, confining gender roles, and repression of lesbian sexuality. Marisa functions as the dual of a separate character, Corky, Marisa's younger pachuca self.

Corky is a street-savvy teenage Chicana who poses as a boy, having learned early that boys have more freedom than girls; furthermore, boys can pursue girls and get their attention. Corky recalls fantasizing when she was young that she and a male friend captured women and forced them to strip. From Corky's perspective then, as "big 'n' tough 'n' a dude," she viewed the pursued woman as an animal, or an object that did not suffer pain. However, as Corky grows into a teenager, she recognizes that this view of women is false. "I never could / quite / pull it off / always knew I was a girl / deep down inside" (p. 8). Further, Corky recognizes her vulnerability in these fantasies and the resistance she would enact if boys or men tried to violate her: "I knew / always knew / I was an animal that kicked back." Along with Marisa, Corky concludes: "Cuz it hurt," suggesting the sexual abuse she has experienced yet repressed (p. 8).

As a young woman, Marisa carries Corky's scars and anger. "I never wanted to be a man, only wanted a woman to want me that bad" (p. 8). The ghosts that revisit Marisa throughout the play include the repressed memories of the rape, memories of rejection by a lover whom she had told about the rape, and desire for acceptance as a lesbian and for a woman who will love her. The play imagines the possibility that Marisa may be able to give up the ghosts through her relationship with Amalia.

Amalia, a heterosexual Native Mexican artist, one generation older than Marisa, is haunted by the ghost of a man who represents Mexico, a land her Native people were forced to leave when, as a teenager, she migrated to the United States. In the character of Amalia, Moraga introduces a sense of Native identity and spirituality that provides solace for the characters. The cultural heritage the characters rely on emanates from a pre-Aztec spiritual conception of La Tierra (the sacred earth). Amalia draws on this collective memory of the precolonial past, remembering the words of an Aztec earth mother goddess whose stone-sculpted representation carved in the precolonial era was unearthed in Mexico City in the 1970s: "Regresaré, Ella nos recuerda. Regresaré, nos promete. [I will return, She reminds us. I will return, She promises.] Nothing remains buried forever. Not even memory. Especially not memory" (p. 25).

Amalia's words portend Marisa's subsequent unearthing of the memory of being raped. The play suggests that Marisa's revelation, aided by Amalia's love, enables her to recover an intact, grounded sense of self. Marisa also recognizes that their relationship helped Amalia recover her Native self. After Amalia is gone, Marisa remembers the spiritual nature of their lovemaking and the transformation it wrought in Amalia. "I'd look up at her face, kinda grey from being indoors with all those books of hers, and I'd see it change, turn this real deep color of brown and olive. . . . I'd think . . . *I could save your life*" (pp. 34–35). Amalia's temporary recovery of her Native Mexican self cannot completely save her or their relationship (p. 24). In the end, she cannot overcome societal expectations of heterosexual love and the loss of her native land.

However, Marisa is saved by Amalia as she learns to accept her lesbian self apart from cultural norms. And she learns how to survive as a Chicana lesbian, even without Amalia, by creating family through relationships with people who appreciate and value her. She says, "It's like making familia from scratch / each time all over again . . . / with strangers, if I must. / If I must I will" (p. 35). The line "making familia from scratch" resonates as both reality and a means of survival for individuals who are not accepted by their families or communities. The term has been used extensively by scholars to discuss the ways in which lesbians, feminists, women of color, and other displaced people have formed new meanings of "family" outside the conventional nuclear family.

Giving Up the Ghost opened the door for discussion of Chicana lesbian sexuality within the Chicano community. The production of the play on the West Coast broke twenty years of silence in the Chicano artistic movement about female desire. Only once before in 1981 had the topic of homosexuality and desire been broached publicly, when Edgar Poma's play *Reúnion* was produced in San Francisco's Mission District.

Giving Up the Ghost was published by West End Press in Los Angeles in 1986. Full-scale productions of the play were presented in Seattle in 1987 and in San Francisco in 1989. A revised script based on the San Francisco production was published in the collection *Heroes and Saints & Other Plays* in 1994, and serves as the basis for this analysis.

During the INTAR residency, in addition to further development of *Giving Up the Ghost*, Moraga began work on two other plays, *Shadow of a Man* and a musical drama. The residency provided an opportunity to write and collaborate with actors and directors, a process that stimulated Moraga to consider playwriting as a genre that could reach many Chicanos who would not read her books. During this time, she also realized that she needed explicitly Chicano feedback, which the other playwright residents, who were primarily Cuban and Puerto Rican, could not provide. In order to immerse herself in Chicano culture, she returned to California at the end of 1985.

Moraga took up residency in the San Francisco Bay area and in 1986 began teaching part-time as a writing instructor at the University of California, Berkeley. She also became associated with a newly formed production company and theater, Brava! For Women in the Arts, that specializes in premiering new works by women of color and lesbian playwrights. As Moraga tells Mary Pat Brady in an interview, she felt very fortunate that Brava! offered her a space where she could work on the writings with actors and be assured of good opening performances. In addition, she noted, Brava! cultivates a broad audience for her plays by promoting them to Chicano and Latino populations and staging them in the Mission District of San Francisco, where many immigrants live. Moraga admits that her relatives never read any of her books, but when she began staging plays, they all wanted to see them. From this, she infers that her plays have a greater political effect than poetry or prose. Drama also provides an avenue for Moraga to work poetry into the common tongue, presenting it as oral tradition and reflecting the multilingual quality of Chicano lives.

After several staged readings in 1989, *Shadow of a Man* premiered in San Francisco in 1990, produced by Brava! and the Eureka Theatre Company. Fornés directed the play and designed the set. *Shadow of a Man* received a Fund for New American Plays Award and major support from the Rockefeller Foundation. Following in the tradition of Moraga's first play treating sexual taboos, *Shadow of a Man* takes up the theme of male homosexuality and again focuses on the damage caused when people are forced to keep their desires secret. The title is ambiguous, suggesting different understandings of the play. The first relates to the character, Manuel Rodriguez, who has become a shadow of his former self, abusing his body with alcohol and shutting himself off from his wife, Hortensia, because he loves his best friend, a man. In this interpretation, Manuel is not only a shadow to himself— "How did I let myself disappear like that. I became nothing, a ghost"—but also to his wife— "His heart is as closed as [a fist]. I can't make him open up to me" (pp. 69, 63). Manuel not only refuses to open up, but worse, violently vents his rage at having to suppress his gay desires, physically abusing Hortensia when she tries to reach out to him.

On a second level, Manuel's love interest and *compadre* (close friend) represents the shadow of his beloved, Conrado, to whom Manuel cannot express his desire. Manuel is unwilling to come out as gay, and Conrado haunts him until he is consumed by the idea of the man and begins to skip work, drink heavily, and cry frequently.

A third level of thinking about the meaning of "Shadow" concerns Hortensia, who is troubled by the shadow of the man she married. She tells her sister that she cannot live without a man. Manuel has become nothing more than a shadow figure in their relationship, yet she holds onto the hope that he will return. In desperation, she nearly kills her youngest child to gain Manuel back. This scenario invokes the legends of the Mexican La Llorona (the Wailing Woman) and the Greek tragic figure Medea, both of which Moraga writes into the play *The Hungry Woman: A Mexican Medea,* developed in the mid-1990s.

On a fourth level, "Shadow" relates to the absent son, Rigo, who has abandoned the family and Chicano culture to marry a white woman. Manuel cannot understand how his son could be the kind of man who takes orders from a woman. As in her earlier works, Moraga explores how Chicano culture's limiting gender roles cause harm even for men. In *Shadow of a Man,* she tackles the issue of machismo as a damaging concept for men. The shadow of Rigo as a boy troubles Manuel as he struggles to understand what he perceives as his son's rejection of him. He blames himself for being weak and not setting the proper example for his son. Manuel is haunted not only by the idea of his son, but also by the cultural idea of a strong, controlling man. This culturally embedded concept of masculinity impairs his ability to love himself or express his desires as a gay man.

Unlike *Giving Up the Ghost,* which anticipates a future for female desire, *Shadow of a Man* does not offer hope for a gay Chicano stuck in conventional ways of thinking about men's roles. Manuel commits suicide rather than challenge cultural norms. However, the play does suggest possibilities for the Rodriguez women as they support each other throughout the family's difficulties. At the end of the play, the youngest child sees herself in the mirror as a lesbian, a sign that barriers can be broken down and that the next generation can move beyond cultural expectations.

MID-CAREER—INTERWEAVING THE PERSONAL AND GLOBAL

While working on these plays, Moraga continued writing poetry and essays; however, the content of her works moved from the personal to include larger issues of injustice in the nation and world. Her multigenre collection of poems and essays, *The Last Generation*, published in 1992, shows the development of an increasingly politicized worldview and her return to the essay to express her disillusionment with U.S. involvement in international affairs and, concurrently, her vision of a more equitable world. The book's two linked themes express concern over the loss of Mexican culture represented by the imminent deaths of her Mexican relatives and the global events that reinforce Anglo dominance and destruction of other cultures and their lands. In the introduction, she reflects on the passing of the elder generation and the declining use of Spanish by the young. "My tio's children have not taught their children to be Mexicans. They have become 'Americans'" (p. 2). She also acknowledges herself as the last generation, attending to the role she plays as a Chicana writer. "I am the last generation put on this planet to remember and record" (p. 9).

Moraga merges the personal with the global by discussing the effect of particular events on people of color, including the loss of the Sandinista election in Nicaragua in 1990, the international celebrations of the 500th anniversary of Columbus's discovery of the New World, the Gulf War, Native peoples' campaigns for sovereignty, the AIDS epidemic, and the United States' refusal to sign environmental accords at the Earth Summit in Brazil. With these things occurring as the 2000 millennium approached, "the last generation" assumes significance beyond Moraga's familial concerns, to include the quality of life on the planet and the question of humankind's survival. Moraga sees her mission as exposing the dangers of materialism and profit and serving as prophet of the future effects of global imperialism. As a prophet, she also creates a model of a utopian space and defines her writing as a form of activism that raises awareness and regenerates a worldview in which the individual belongs to the global community. *The Last Generation*, then, is both an extended lament and a revival. It looks to the future by heeding the past.

The Last Generation also elaborates Moraga's recovery of the Native goddesses, gods, and cultural practices she calls "México Antigua," which figured in her future plays. In these writings, she excavates Mexico's precolonial past and the prewarrior Aztec state, situating her idealized model in civilizations such as that of Teotihuacán, which preceded the Aztec and emphasized community over dynastic rule, cyclical time over linear, and had numerous female deities in its pantheon (Miller and Taube, p. 18). In taking this step, she also begins to develop the *mestizaje* (culturally mixed—Mexican Catholic and Mexican indigenous) belief system that pervades the plays she produces in the 1990s.

Moraga's most far-reaching vision in *The Last Generation* takes form in the essay "Queer Aztlán: The Re-formation of Chicano Tribe." She imagines a metaphysical or actual nation called "Queer Aztlán," which recovers Chicano and Native Mexican land and is "[a] Chicano homeland that could embrace *all* its people, including its jotería ['queer' folk]" (p. 147). She conceptualizes Queer Aztlán as a place of tolerance for difference, founded in an actual land space within the U.S. Southwest. This place that Chicanos and Chicanas could call their homeland would maintain the governing power of a sovereign nation working for the good of mestizos (mixed-race peoples). Similar to the goals of "El Plan de Aztlán," formulated by the Chicano Nationalists in the late 1960s, Moraga's vision of Queer Aztlán is of a self-governing community that cultivates economic sustainability, cultural expression, and land reclamation for its people. Queer Aztlán retains the radical, revolutionary thinking of El Plan de Aztlán, without its biases.

In naming her imaginary homeland, Moraga borrows from both Chicano Nationalism and Queer Nation, the gay and lesbian movement of the 1970s and 1980s that failed to represent the concerns of people of color. "Aztlán" is the Aztec term for the unknown creation place from which Aztec peoples of Mexico originated. During the Chicano civil rights movement of the late 1960s and 1970s, Aztlán was configured as the U.S. Southwest (once part of Mexico and originally Native lands) and symbolically claimed as the Chicano homeland. The naming of Aztlán as the Chicano homeland emphasizes the origin of Chicanos as Native peoples, which many Mexicans and Mexican Americans deny in order to assimilate. Despite its attention to race and class discrimination, El Plan de Aztlán upheld the hierarchy of heterosexual men as leaders of the state and family. Moraga casts off the heterosexual and male-dominated perspective of the civil rights movement and imagines Aztlán as a place of tolerance and safety.

For Moraga, Queer Aztlán is both a symbolic concept of home and a political vision that revives the activist era of the 1960s and 1970s from a broader perspective. "Chicanos are an occupied nation within a nation, and women and women's sexuality are occupied within Chicano nation. . . . The nationalism I seek . . . decolonizes the brown and female body as it decolonizes the brown and female earth" (p. 150). Moraga configures cultural nationalism as an anticolonial, antiracist, antiheterosexist effort. With Queer Aztlán, she conceptualizes a late-twentieth-century political perspective, a new civil rights movement working toward sexual, racial, and land-based sovereignty for Chicano communities.

A fundamental concept to Moraga's Queer Aztlán is the recovery of female power and desire. In the essay "En busca de la fuerza femenina" (In search of female power), Moraga turned to pre-Aztec stories of the female goddesses as strong, powerful women. In her search, she realized that the Mexica Aztec, who ruled before the Spanish conquest, had devalued the goddesses, elevating the male war gods to justify their conquest of neighboring city-states. She relates the fall of one such goddess, the powerful

earth mother goddess Coyolxauhqui, who is defeated and dismembered by her brother, Huiztlilopotchli, the war god. Moraga reads the Coyolxauhqui story as an appropriate metaphor for the devaluation of female sexuality and power in contemporary times. "In my art, I am writing that wound. That moment when brother is born and sister mutilated by his envy" (p. 73). Further, Moraga finds in Coyolxauhqui the inspiration for her activism. "She is la fuerza femenina, our attempt to pick up the fragments of our dismembered womanhood and reconstitute ourselves" (p. 74). Coyolxauhqui represents not only female power, but also a spirituality that reveals the divine element within women. With this writing, Moraga establishes her spiritual, philosophical, and political base in ancient female power.

Along with the rewriting of Mexica Aztec goddess stories, Moraga finds a way to reconcile with Catholicism. In *Loving in the War Years*, she criticized the representation of the Catholic Virgin Mary (Guadalupe) as a bodiless, desireless, and submissive female god. In recovering the power of the Aztec goddesses, she also recovered Guadalupe as an acceptable symbol of female power. In addition, the recovery of the Catholic Virgin brought her closer to understanding the working-class Chicana and Mexican regard for Mary as a source of inspiration, support, and liberation from oppression. This view of the Mexican Virgin, called popular religiosity, honors her as a force for the people apart from the meanings the Catholic Church has given her. Moraga portrays this popular religiosity in the poem "Our Lady of the Cannery Workers," based on a reported sighting of the Virgin Mary in Watsonville, California, in 1992 and the appearance of her image in a nearby tree.

Moraga weaves two counter-discourses into the poem to reveal the speaker's beliefs. The first discourse represents a belief in the Aztec earth mother goddess, Tonantzín, whom pilgrims come to worship and to whom, as a sequoia tree ("Sequoia Virgen"), the speaker brings flowers

(p. 144). The second is the Catholic discourse of women who visit the image of Mary in the tree (or in the basilica in Tepeyac), murmuring ritualized Catholic blessings: "*Ahora, ¿la ves? / Si. / Dios te salve / María*" ("Now, do you see it? / Yes. / God save you / Mary"; pp. 142–143). The poem works against this strictly Catholic view of Mary by suggesting that there is at least one person who rejects the Catholic doctrine and instead practices Native spirituality. The poem further suggests that the Catholic Virgin and the Aztec goddess can be interwoven into a new form of spirituality that represents the speaker's beliefs. Imagining the Virgin in her own image, the speaker thinks of her not as a cannery worker but as a painter, a creative force, and a lesbian sexual being. This image of the Catholic Virgin enables Moraga to rehabilitate the Virgin as a viable female model for contemporary Chicanas, a woman of passion and an activist force that seeds (in the form of the sequoia tree) a more tolerant world.

Another theme that Moraga explores passionately is what it means to be a literary citizen. In the essay "Art in América con Acento," she poses the question in relation to the U.S.'s self-interested responses to world events. "*I am Latina, born and raised in the United States. I am a writer. What is my responsibility in this?*" (pp. 52–53). In answer, she defines her allegiance outside U.S. nationalism, positioning herself as a Native person aligned with other indigenous peoples in the world. Rather than identifying as a "Republican 'Hispanic' loyal to the United States," she chooses to act as an insurgent who works for the "creation of a force of 'disloyal' americanos who subscribe to a multicultural, multilingual, radical re-structuring of América" (p. 56). Similar to the position Moraga outlined in *Loving in the War Years*, when she chose to identify as a woman of color rather than as white, in "Art in América con Accento" she also refuses to assimilate to mainstream U.S. ideologies. "I call myself a Chicana writer. . . . To be a Chicana is not merely to name one's racial/cultural identity, but also to name a politic" (p.

56). For Moraga, "*art is political,*" and her writing is the means by which she serves as an activist (p. 59).

In keeping with these politics, Moraga has chosen to publish her works through small, progressive, not-for-profit presses, rather than large, corporate, New York–based publishing houses. She fears that current and future generations of Chicano writers "will look solely to the Northeast for recognition" and create writings that satisfy assimilated Anglo American audiences (p. 60). She challenges Chicano writers on the politics of their writing, insisting that recognition of the Native past is essential for future survival: "Without the memory of our once-freedom, how do we imagine a future?" (p. 60). Moraga views her writing not only as an aesthetic expression, but also as a way to convey alternative visions of human existence. Subverting the singular national identification "American," Moraga creates a more inclusive, borderless identity for herself. She declares: "I am an American writer in the original sense of the word, an Américan *con acento*" (p. 62). In this example, she emphasizes the power of language to work for change by illustrating how stressing one syllable of a word can alter its meaning and signify a different way of thinking about everything.

In *The Last Generation*, Moraga also publicly reckons with the racism and classism of both sides of her heritage. The autobiographical poem "I Was Not Supposed to Remember" challenges the melting pot concept that encourages individuals to forget their ancestry in order to meld into a successful, generic Americanness. She confronts the Mexican racism that neglects and denies its Nativeness and disavows the first recorded rape of a Native woman, La Malinche, by the Spanish conqueror, Hernán Cortés.

I was not supposed to remember being she
the daughter of some other Indian some body
   some where
an orphaned child somewhere somebody's

cast off half-breed I wasn't
supposed to remember the original rape.

(p. 98)

Furthermore, she delves into her father's French Canadian and Missouri American past to acknowledge his parentage by a distinguished French Canadian father, who ignored his family and distanced himself from the legacy of his mother's poor white family.

Claiming both neglected histories, the speaker names herself and claims her whole being.

I, thoroughly hybrid
mongrel/mexicanyaqui/oakie girl.
"Yaquioakie" holds all the world.

(p. 99)

"Yaquioakie" identifies Moraga as a Native Mexican and a poor white American, an identity that she believes encompasses the inhabitants of the Americas. By claiming to be a Yaqui, she draws attention to the Native Mexicans who successfully resisted the Aztec and Spanish conquests and the Mexican government's attempted genocide. In doing so, she emphasizes that the Yaqui people are living beings who have retained their distinct beliefs and practices. By claiming to be an Oakie, Moraga points out the alternative history of white people who did not achieve the American Dream. Playing on the word "okie," literally referring to a person from Oklahoma and often extended to include people from Missouri and Arkansas, she uses the slang term for poor whites who struggled to survive during the Depression and Dust Bowl, often by migrating west.

Moraga explores this history further in the essay "The Breakdown of the Bicultural Mind," writing about "my working-class aunt," who was maligned by her Mexican relatives. By naming her aunt, Moraga acknowledges her aunt's experiences of hardship and gives value to her life. "My aunt's name is Barbara and I am here to make peace with her in the white women I love, in the white woman I am" (p. 125). Ironi-cally, she recounts how the poor white relatives on her father's side of the family were alienated and denigrated by the Mexican relatives on her mother's side. This mindset resembles the denigration of Native ancestry by Mexican culture. The essay's title challenges the romanticized U.S. melting pot and debunks the idea that all whites can achieve the American Dream. Likewise it challenges the Mexican concept that Indians were conquered and are a people of the past, rather than contemporary living beings.

Her next writing, the play *Heart of the Earth: A Popul Vuh Story,* illustrates that Native practices remain a vital part of many people's lives. The *Popul Vuh* is a complex creation story of the Quiché Maya who live in southern Mexico and Guatemala, which Moraga condensed and rewrote to deliver contemporary messages. In *Heart of the Earth,* Moraga comments on racism when the dark-skinned goddess, Ixquic, escapes persecution by the white ghosts of the underworld. She includes allusions to the AIDS epidemic, represents the characters' longing for home, and mocks the Twins' obsession with sports. Moraga also creates strong female characters who counter the male-dominated view of *Popul Vuh.* Ixquic flees from the subjugation of her father, Patriarchal Pus, and the goddess Ixmucane mocks the efforts of her husband, the god Ixpiyacoc, who is unsuccessfully attempting to create acceptable human beings. In the end, Ixmucane originates human beings by fashioning them from corn, water, and oil, which are the fundamental elements of *masa,* the corn tortilla that is a staple Mayan food. *Heart of the Earth* exhibits a postmodern ethnic sensibility that challenges assimilated European playwriting models by presenting a mixture of peoples, languages, and cultural practices. *Heart of the Earth* infuses the stage with Spanish, English, and Quiché and other Mayan tongues, and with vernacular common to Chicanos such as Spanglish, southwestern Chicano speech, and urban U.S street language. The teenaged characters, the Twins, provide comic relief by slipping into *cholo* and pachuco speech and actions representing the urban youth scene. Cultural practices such as games also represent ancient and contemporary cultures. The ballgame the Twins play retains the structure of the traditional pre-Columbian game but adds contemporary soccer and basketball moves. To contribute to the mythical and comic sense of the play, Moraga collaborated with puppeteer Ralph Lee in the design and direction of the fantastical characters. *Heart of the Earth: A Popul Vuh Story* was commissioned by INTAR's Hispanic American Art Center and premiered in 1994 at The Public Theatre, New York City, in conjunction with the Jim Henson Foundation's International Festival of Puppet Theatre. It was also produced at The John F. Kennedy Center for the Performing Arts in Washington, D.C., in 1997.

When Moraga turned forty in 1992 after writing *The Last Generation*, she decided to have a child. Aided by her lesbian partner and a sperm donor she had chosen, Moraga conceived a child in the early months of 1993. During gestation and after her son's premature birth, Moraga recorded her thoughts and experiences in a journal, which she expanded and published in 1997. *Waiting in the Wings: Portrait of a Queer Motherhood* documents her emotional and physical changes, the baby's four-month struggle to survive after being born three months premature, and Moraga's struggle to reawaken the writing spirit again and then to find time to create with the demands of motherhood, being a partner, and earning a living. *Waiting in the Wings* is the story of the survival of a preterm baby, the survival of a writer, and the survival of a lesbian love relationship. Like *The Last Generation*, it is also a story of the fear of loss, by death or other separation. Just as significantly, it is a story of Chicana and Chicano experience. Rafael Angel's birth and survival symbolizes the rebirth and difficult lives of Chicanas and Chicanos in the United States, and the creation of a new definition of family for Chicana lesbians and Chicano gay men.

Waiting in the Wings chronicles how Rafael's father, Pablo, a gay Mexican who initially thought of himself only as a sperm donor, became an integral part of Rafael's life. The memoir also reveals Moraga's desire to preserve Chicano culture and family by infusing them into Rafael's life. Moraga's desire to raise Rafael within Chicano culture also produced tensions within her relationship, because she could not name her partner, a white woman, unequivocally as Pablo's legal guardian if she were to die. Responding to the sense of loss of family and culture she wrote about in *The Last Generation*, the Chicana family she creates in *Waiting in the Wings* seeks to continue the legacy of her parent's generation, with a lesbian difference.

SETTLING INTO DRAMA: A FOCUS ON PLAYWRITING

Having returned to the essay form in *The Last Generation* out of a sense of the "political urgency of the times" and to autobiographical prose in *Waiting in the Wings* to spark her creativity, Moraga nonetheless continued writing plays. She wrote with anger and revolutionary fervor about global injustices in her essays "En busca de la fuerza femenina" and "Queer Aztlán: the Re-formation of Chicano Tribe" and in dramas that depicted actual oppressions experienced by Chicanos. Four plays, *Heroes and Saints* (1994), *Watsonville: Some Place Not Here* (2000, 2002), *The Hungry Woman: A Mexican Medea* (2000, 2001), and *Circle in the Dirt: El Pueblo de East Palo Alto* (2002), cultivate on stage the social and political activism Moraga advocates in her prose writings. These plays interweave social problems such as labor and land rights, with family and cultural concerns. For example, the next play Moraga wrote, *Heroes and Saints,* forces the audience to confront the hard working conditions of farm laborers, the harm caused by their exposure to deadly pesticides, and the callous greed of the corporations that profit from the crops they harvest. Interwoven into this social critique is the story of a young woman born without a body—appearing onstage as a head—because of her mother's exposure to pesticides, who fights to be recognized as a whole human being, intelligent, sexual, and capable.

The play is based on the discovery of cancer clusters among the population of the San Joaquin Valley of California, linked to pesticide poisoning of farmworkers in the grape fields. In the town of McFarland, during 1978–1988, a disproportionate number of children were born with birth defects or diagnosed with cancer. Moraga's character Cerezita de Valle, whose name means "little cherry of the valley" and plays on Moraga's own name, Cherríe, represents the children who were most affected by the poisoning. Rather than make Cere a helpless victim, Moraga defies disability stereotypes and portrays her as an intelligent, perceptive, and active character. She is, however, confined physically by Dolores, her mother, who views her as an innocent child rather than as a gifted, sensitive young woman. Nonetheless, Cerezita's character leads a subversive movement that protests children's deaths from cancer, a comment on her capability as a person with disabilities and on her awareness of the local political situation.

The play also provides a commentary on masculine gender roles, which ironically Dolores reinforces in speaking about her absent husband and in her interactions with her gay son. She tells her son, Mario, that he needs to marry a woman to become a man. When he insists that he can't separate his body from his heart, she tells him, "You lower yourself into half a man" (p. 124). As a counter-argument to Dolores's reinforcement of traditional masculinity, the neighbor, Don Gilberto, defines a new concept of manhood. Don Gilberto, who admits he cannot have children, creates a masculine model through emotional commitment rather than biological performance. "A real man tiene brazos [has arms]. Nos llaman braceros [We are called manual laborers] because we work and love with our arms. Because we aint afraid to lift

a sack of potatoes, to defend our children, to put our arms around la waifa at night" (p. 121).

The play also comments on the Catholic Church, which does little to change the circumstances of working-class and oppressed peoples. Father Juan, a mixed-blood Chicano who was born in the valley, returns to help the people. Yet Cere teaches Father Juan about liberation theology, the radical Latin American Catholic doctrine that encourages priests to lead the people in their fight for liberation. Juan insists that his body is asleep underneath the vestments and that "Once ordained, you've given up volition" (p. 115). In other words, he claims that he has no choice, no free will, to act for himself or the people. By the end of the play, Cere has converted him into an activist, and he enters the poisoned fields with her to burn them.

Another theme of the play is the right to passion of those society deems passionless: priests and people with disabilities. After they have become friends, Cere asks Father Juan to make love to her so she can feel as if she has a body. Juan betrays her in a rape-like scene that conveys his denial of his own body and passions. Addressing his embodied self in comparison to hers, Cere tells him that he is "a waste of a body" (p. 144).

Finally, the play enacts the themes of Aztec spirituality joined with revolutionary conviction that Moraga articulated in *The Last Generation*. Cerezita appears to her mother as the Mexican Catholic Virgin of Guadalupe and inspires the community to take action against the owners of the grape fields. In a passionate call to remember the ancient land and the goddess of the earth, Cere as Guadalupe galvanizes the community (p. 148). As in other writings, Moraga brings together popular religiosity and Aztec spirituality to inspire revolution. As the Virgin Mary, Cere vocalizes the liberal Catholic spirit of liberation theology, and as an earth mother goddess, she reminds them of Native spirituality, the "red memory" of "Madre Tierra. Madre Sagrada. Madre . . . Libertad." (Mother Earth,

Sacred Mother, Mother Freedom.) "The radiant red mother . . . rising" (p. 148). Then she leads the community to set the fields afire as corporate helicopters begin to shoot them from above. The play portrays the revitalization of the radical civil rights movement Moraga proposes in *The Last Generation,* taking on capitalism, racism, sexism, and heterosexism to create a more equitable living environment.

Heroes and Saints was commissioned by José Luis Valenzuela's Latino Lab in Los Angeles in 1989. It premiered 4 April 1992 at El Teatro Mísíon, produced by Brava! For Women in the Arts. *Heroes and Saints* won numerous awards, including the prestigious Pen West Award for Drama in 1992 and the Will Glickman Prize for Best Play of 1992, as well as a Drama-Logue award and a Critics Circle award. It was published in 1994 as the title play of a collection of three plays.

In her next play, *Watsonville: Some Place Not Here,* Moraga continues the themes of Chicana radical activism and its interrelationship with Native spirituality. The plot revolves around three actual events in Watsonville: cannery strikes in 1985–1987, a major earthquake in 1989, and the appearance of the Virgin of Guadalupe on an oak tree in a park near Watsonville in 1992. Moraga fictionalizes the chronology by conflating the dates of the three events and shifting the action into the late 1990s. The play also features several characters that appeared in *Heroes and Saints,* including Cere's mother, Dolores, the activist, Amparo, and Juan Cunningham, formerly Father Juan. Cerezita, killed during the revolution that burned down the fields in *Heroes and Saints,* appears throughout *Watsonville* in the image on the tree of the Virgin Goddess, Guadalupe (Tonantzin).

The play depicts the extended strike by the cannery workers, primarily Mexican women, which comes to crisis when a national anti-immigrant law is passed. This scenario responds to a series of propositions that were passed in California and other states in the 1990s targeting immigrants and youths. In *Watsonville,* Moraga expands these measures to the entire country with the passing of a national law that denies undocumented immigrants and their children education, medical care, legal representation, and other social services. She states in the foreword that such laws were passed "I believe, by the aging whiteman's collective fear of this unacknowledged but increasingly evident re-Indianization of [California]" (p. vii).

Moraga's writing of the play resists the law's emphasis on Anglo assimilation. Before creating *Watsonville,* she conducted interviews with female cannery workers following the labor strikes of 1985–1987, and the language of the play reflects the fluent Spanish many of the women spoke. In addition, she portrays a swelling rebirth of Native consciousness and spirituality among the striking cannery workers. The play also includes the local history of the Ohlones, Native people who lived in the Watsonville area before the Spanish and U.S. conquests. Moraga integrates their religious beliefs, based on the worship of native oak trees, by depicting a grove of aging oaks as the spiritual site that inspires the cannery workers to strike. In one of these trees, the Virgin Goddess's image appears. Moraga emphasizes Chicanos' connection to the land and to understanding themselves as Native peoples, when Dolores explains the meaning of the Virgin's appearance. "La Virgen 'sta con nosotros. [The Virgin is with us.] . . . Like that holy tree, tan fuerte [so strong], tan viejo [so old], tan sagrado [so sacred], ustedes tienen raíces [all of you have roots] that spread all the way to México. . . . Seguimos siendo americanos [We will continue to be Americans] whether we got papeles (papers) or not" (p. 98). With these words, Dolores asserts Native peoples' sovereignty over the land and citizenship of it as indigenous people.

To portray the gravity of the anti-immigration laws, Moraga shows how they rely on divisive tactics to conquer. In *Watsonville,* one member of the strike committee, Chente, wants to settle the strike by accepting a contract that leaves out the undocumented workers. He is portrayed as a *vendido,* a sellout to the cannery owners, and a betrayer of his people. This development pits second- and third-generation Americans against recent immigrants who entered the country illegally and signals variations of a nativism that privileges those born in the U.S. or naturalized, and xenophobia. Moraga chooses to portray hope for the betterment of the community in the collective action the workers take at the end of the play; however, she documents a threat to a unified community that splits people apart along nationalistic lines and prevents the formation of coalitions against injustice.

Through Juan's character, Moraga also continues the critique she began in *Heroes and Saints* of the indifference of the Catholic Church to working-class and oppressed peoples' concerns and spiritual needs. Juan tries to persuade local church authorities that the apparition of Mary on the tree should be averred by the church to show support for striking workers. In a meeting with a church official, he cites several biblical passages that validate Dolores's vision. He also challenges the church's view of the Virgin Mary as a long-suffering woman, and its teaching women to endure their husband's transgressions. Instead, he refigures the Virgin as an activist who wants to help the poor, not the rich. He says the biblical passage portrays "an angry woman, sir. Not some passive, long-suffering santa" (pp. 71–72). Here Moraga takes the Catholic Virgin one step further in recreating her as a feminist model, a strong and powerful woman, for Chicanas and Mexicanas. Moraga makes the Virgin into an active symbol of resistance, a fighter who represents and inspires the women workers in the play.

In contrast to the violent protest that ends *Heroes and Saints,* in *Watsonville* Moraga depicts nonviolent protests reminiscent of Cesar Chavez's leadership of the United Farm Workers Union strikes against grape growers in the 1970s and 1980s. Dolores and other female workers participate in hunger strikes to protest the cannery corporation's refusal to offer the workers a fair contract. The workers reject the discriminatory contract the company offers and follow Dolores on their knees in a pilgrimage to the sacred tree. Dolores's leadership of the strikers in the play also honors UFW vice president, Dolores Huerta, the chief negotiator for the UFW in settling labor contracts. Moraga's emphasis on the character Dolores as the strike leader recognizes Huerta's considerable leadership contributions to the UFW. In Moraga's *Watsonville,* Moraga reinforces the idea that collective community action based in Native spirituality will bring about change. As the workers venerate their mestiza (Native and Catholic) shrine, the rest of Watsonville is leveled by a major earthquake that Dolores had predicted. The canneries and townspeople are destroyed and the ten thousand workers praying at the shrine are the only survivors.

Watsonville: Some Place Not Here is Moraga's second play to receive the Fund for New American Plays Award, this time as a project of the John F. Kennedy Center for the Performing Arts. The play was originally commissioned and developed by the new Brava Theatre Center of San Francisco, where its world premiere was held in May 1996. With *Watsonville,* Moraga's work became known to a wider, bicoastal audience when it was performed at the John F. Kennedy Center for the Performing Arts in Washington, D.C., in February 1996. In addition, the play received support from several major grant agencies, including Theatre Communications Group's National Theatre Resident Artist Residency Program, which is the national organization of the American Theater. The play was republished, along with *Circle in the Dirt: El Pueblo de East Palo Alto,* in 2002.

The third play that personifies Moraga's visions of a revitalized civil rights movement is set in a futuristic place, an imagined homeland utopia, like Queer Aztlán, achieved by a Chicano uprising against the U.S. and then lost to women and queers by the reinstatement of male leadership and heterosexual values. Although *The Hungry Woman: A Mexican Medea* does not focus on actual occurrences, as do *Heroes and Saints* and *Watsonville*, many of the struggles of Chicanas, lesbians, and Native peoples remain the same. However, Moraga also adds complexity to the plot by mirroring her consciousness of motherhood and the angst of separation from or loss of her child.

The Hungry Woman combines two stories, the Greek tragic myth of Medea and the Mexican legend of La Llorona (the Wailing Woman). Moraga rewrites both stories of infanticide from a lesbian feminist perspective, representing the power imbalances that remain between women and men, white people and people of color, heterosexuals and lesbians. In addition, the repression of female desire in the Medea and Llorona myths is interwoven with an Aztec creation myth of the hungry woman, providing the title of the play and the idea that women's bodies are the originators and sustainers of life and the Earth. In the Aztec creation myth, the hungry woman, whose insatiable appetite instigates the gods to feed her, creates the world from her body. Her myth embodies what Moraga calls "la fuerza femenina" (female power), yet it also represents female desire as unfulfilled.

Euripides' *Medea* and the legend of La Llorona both relate similar stories: a woman kills her children because her husband or lover has betrayed her with another woman. However, Euripides' play, unlike some of the contemporary renditions of Medea's story, also focuses on Medea's autochthonous claim to the land and Jason's greed for the land and the status he would have obtained through possession of their children. This storyline suggests that Medea, and all women by association, are merely the vessel by means of which men obtain status and wealth.

In *The Hungry Woman*, Moraga contemporizes the story to the imagined, liberated nation, Aztlán, which requires residents to have a certain proportion of Native ancestry to own land. Taking the characters' names from the Greek story to reveal the continuation of sexism and imperialism from ancient to contemporary times, Moraga examines how Jasón, a poet and leading figure in Aztlán, requires possession of Medea or their son in order to further his economic and political ambitions. Jasón does not have enough Native blood to claim a right to land in Aztlán, and he attempts to take their son, who will give him that right, away from her.

In addition, *The Hungry Woman* contemplates the inability of a lesbian, Native woman to live freely and safely in Aztlán. Medea, a *curandera* (healer) and midwife, is a leader in the Chicano revolt, fighting for her right to land and freedom as a Chicana and lesbian. Following the masculinist counter-revolution, she is exiled from Aztlán, and the play begins as she resides in the wasteland border region of Phoenix, between Gringolandia (the United States) and Aztlán (Mechicano country). She has been confined to a prison psychiatric hospital, where her memories of the love she experienced with Luna, and her hope that the female spirit lives on in her son, torture and sustain her.

Moraga rewrites the traditional interpretation of Medea and La Llorona's acts of infanticide as revenge, configuring them instead from a feminist perspective as a necessary sacrifice to save the child from harm. In *The Hungry Woman*, Medea's killing of her son can be read as a means of saving him from the militaristic, masculine role he would be forced to assume if he lived with his father in Aztlán. This violent, hierarchical role contrasts with the equitable practices and beliefs she has taught him in exile. Medea's nonviolent sacrifice of her son in a Native ritual with other women also calls into question whether infanticide actually occurs. Whether in spirit or in actuality, the play portrays her son as returning to take her home, either to the Aztlán he has converted to an egalitarian nation as he promised earlier in the play or to the cosmic Aztlán she has created in recovering female goddesses.

Moraga's rewriting also conveys Medea's right to choose lesbianism, rather than submit to forced heterosexuality (rape) as Jasón's mistress. In Moraga's version, Medea or La Llorona defies the female role model of long-suffering woman and fights back.

Again, as in *The Last Generation,* the significance of Moraga's vision relies on the metaphysical and geographical space of Aztlán that is defined by being Native. For Chicanas and Chicanos this means remembering their Native ancestry. While Native ancestry serves as a powerful force in this play, for Moraga the recovered past must also associate female power and desire with Nativeness and cultural nationalism.

The Hungry Woman: A Mexican Medea was commissioned by the Berkeley Repertory Theatre, where a staged reading was held in 1995. Other staged readings have been held in Los Angeles, San Francisco, and San Antonio. The play was developed at the Brava Theater Center of San Francisco and sponsored by the Theater Communications Group National Theater Artist Residency Program. The script was published in an anthology in 2000 and republished in 2001, along with *Heart of the Earth: A Popul Vuh Story.*

Moraga's next published play, *Circle in the Dirt: El Pueblo de East Palo Alto (2002),* moves from a concern with creating Chicano community to an emphasis on the creation of communities among peoples of color. *Circle in the Dirt* depicts a section of East Palo Alto where Chicanos live with African Americans, Japanese Americans, Anglo-Americans, and immigrants from Vietnam, Samoa, and Mexico. Moraga provides a history of how peoples of color and poor whites became ghettoized in East Palo Alto in the past and how gentrification is destroying their community in the play's present. In addition, she portrays the internalized racism that keeps individuals and peoples from standing up

for their right to high-quality education and depicts the stereotypes that keep the various racial-ethnic groups from joining together to protest the destruction of their apartment complex. Moraga represents the need for communities to come together like a circle in the dirt to preserve their histories and secure their futures. *Circle in the Dirt* was originally commissioned by the Committee for the Black Performing Arts of Stanford University. It premiered at the Cesar Chavez Academy in East Palo Alto and at the Nitery Theatre at Stanford University in 1995.

Moraga's writings, too, have come full circle over the past twenty years. From emphasizing the power of coalition and common experience in her first edited anthology, *This Bridge Called My Back,* in 1981 and 1983, she returned to this theme with the publication of *Circle in the Dirt* in 2002. At the beginning of a new century, her messages resonate worldwide. The recurring themes threading through all of Moraga's works, which encourage the characters and readers to make "familia from scratch" and create communities dedicated to resistance and renewal, reveal her concern not only with the survival of individuals, peoples, and cultures, but with the quality of their survival. For Moraga, sustaining people, culture, and land on both the personal and global level are key elements in surviving the next century. From a literary perspective, Moraga's numerous and varied contributions played a major role in late-twentieth-century reconsiderations of the experiences and creative capacities of Chicanas and Latinas, women of color, and lesbians and gays, and in the development of a postmodern racial-ethnic vision. The issues her works raise regarding expressions of women's "right to passion," labor and land rights, Native identity and sovereignty, and international human rights hold immense future significance as we define ideals and artistic endeavors of the twenty-first century. Moraga is the recipient of a National Endowment for the Arts Theatre Playwrights Fellowship and is the

Artist-in-Residence in the Departments of Drama and Spanish and Portuguese at Stanford University. She lives in Oakland, California, with her lover and their children.

Selected Bibliography

WORKS OF CHERRÍE MORAGA

MULTI-GENRE WORKS

Loving in the War Years: Lo que nunca pasó por sus labios. Boston: South End Press, 1983.

The Last Generation. Boston: South End Press, 1993.

Waiting in the Wings: Portrait of a Queer Motherhood. Ithaca, N.Y.: Firebrand Books, 1997.

Loving in the War Years: Lo que nunca pasó por sus labios. Expanded edition. Cambridge, Mass.: South End Press, 2000.

PLAYS

Giving Up the Ghost. Los Angeles: West End Press, 1986.

"Shadow of a Man." In *Shattering the Myth: Plays by Hispanic Women.* Selected by Denise Chávez. Edited by Linda Feyder. Houston: Arte Público Press, 1992.

Heroes and Saints & Other Plays. Albuquerque: West End Press, 1994. (Contains *Giving Up the Ghost, Shadow of a Man,* and *Heroes and Saints.*)

"Heart of the Earth: A Popul Vuh Story." In *Puro Teatro: A Latina Anthology.* Alberto Sandoval-Sánchez and Nancy Saporta Sternback, eds. Tucson: University of Arizona Press, 2000.

"The Hungry Woman: A Mexican Medea." In *Out of the Fringe: Contemporary Latina/ Latino Theatre and Performance.* Caridad Svich and Maria Teresa Marrero, eds. New York: Theatre Communications Group; St. Paul, Minn.: Distributed by Consortium Book Sales, 2000

"Watsonville: Some Place Not Here." *Latino Plays from South Coast Repertory: Hispanic Playwrights Project Anthology.* New York: Broadway Play Publishing, 2000.

The Hungry Woman. Albuquerque: West End Press, 2001. (Contains *The Hungry Woman: A Mexican Medea* and *Heart of the Earth: A Popul Vuh Story,* with a useful Afterword by Irma Mayorga.)

Watsonville/Circle in the Dirt. Albuquerque, N.Mex.: West End Press, 2002. (Contains *Watsonville: Some Place Not Here* and *Circle in the Dirt: El Pueblo de East Palo Alto.*)

CO-EDITED WORKS

This Bridge Called My Back: Writings by Radical Women of Color. With Gloria Anzaldúa. New York: Kitchen Table Press, 1981, 1983.

Cuentos: Stories by Latinas. With Alma Gómez and Mariana Roma-Carmona. New York: Kitchen Table Press, 1983.

Esta puente, mi espalda: Voces de mujeres tercermundistas en los Estados Unidos. With Ana Castillo. ISM Press. 1988 Revised, bilingual edition of *This Bridge Called My Back.*

The Sexuality of Latinas. With Norma Alarcón and Ana Castillo. Berkeley: Third Woman Press.

We Are the Young Magicians. With Ruth Forman. Barnard New Women Poets' Series. Boston: Beacon Press, 1991.

Lenguas Sueltas: Poemas; Anthology of Seventeen Chicano Latino Poets. With Elba R. Sánchez and Francisco X. Alarcón. Santa Cruz, Calif.: Moving Parts Press, 1994.

CRITICAL AND BIOGRAPHICAL STUDIES

Alarcón, Norma. "Interview with Cherríe Moraga." *Third Woman* 3, nos. 1–2 (1986): 126–134.

Blake, Debra J. "Unsettling Identities: Transitive Subjectivity in Cherríe Moraga's *Loving in the War Years.*" *a/b: Auto/Biography Studies* 12 no. 1 (June 1997): 71–89.

Brady, Mary Pat. "Coming Home: Interview with Cherríe Moraga." Parts 1 and 2. *Mester* 22, no. 2; 23 no. 1 (fall 1993–spring 1994)

Ikas, Karin Rosa. "Cherríe Moraga: Poet, Playwright, Essayist, and Educator." *Chicana Ways: Conversations with Ten Chicana Writers.* Reno: University of Nevada Press, 2002.

Miller, Mary, and Karl Taube. *The Gods and Symbols of Ancient Mexico and the Maya: An Illustrated Dictionary of Mesoamerican Religion.* London: Thames and Hudson, 1993.

Yarbro-Bejarano, Yvonne. "Cherríe Moraga's *Giving Up the Ghost*: The Representation of Female Desire." *Third Woman* 3 nos. 1–2 (1986): 113–120.

———. "Cherrie Moraga." In *Chicano Writers: First Series.* Edited by Francisco A. Lomelí and Carl R. Shirley. Detroit: Gale Research, 1989.

Alejandro Morales
(1944–)

JAVIER DURÁN

THE NOVELIST, short-story writer, and essayist Alejandro Morales is one of the most accomplished Chicano writers of his generation. An active protagonist in Chicano letters since the 1970s, Morales, who began teaching Chicano and Latino literature at the University of California in Irvine in 1974, was the first Chicano author to publish in Mexico a novel written in Spanish.

Born in Montebello, California, on 14 October 1944, Morales is the descendant of Mexican immigrants who came to the area in the early years of the twentieth century. The migrant experience or the final stage of a pilgrimage—the act of rooting oneself in a particular space—is vital to Morales's works. Morales's narratives develop strong ties and a deep commitment to places and spaces that the author sees as fundamental roots of community and individual identity. Some critics consider Morales a "borderlands" writer. Perhaps only in a general way can Morales be considered a border author, because the scope of border representation in his works goes beyond the geographical demarcations of the U.S.-Mexico frontier. Rather, it would be more accurate to say that his works oscillate between four major themes: history, genealogies, borders, and heterotopias.

The son of Juana Contreras Ramíriz and Delfino Morales Martínez, Alejandro Morales was the first member of his family to have been born in a hospital, a fact that, according to his mother, explains his personality and his inclination for writing: "Sin mi permiso [Without my permission] they made you part of an experiment. Por eso estás tan [That is why you are so] messed up!" ("Dynamic Identities in Heterotopia," p. 14). Morales's parents lived in Simons, the old site of a brick factory and the same barrio that would later become a narrative space for his fourth novel, *The Brick People* (1988).

Morales, who grew up in a working-class environment, was part of a happy family unit, and he always felt supported by his relatives. This favorable situation seemed to contrast sharply with the world surrounding him in Montebello, where it was not rare to find "many sad, lonely, sick, addicted people" ("Dynamic Identities in Heterotopia," p. 17). These visions are the first literary pretexts in Morales's work. Anger, despair, confusion, helplessness, and a chronic acceptance of the status quo are representative of the intense feelings evoked in his first writings.

THE BEGINNINGS: OLD BARRIO, NEW FACES ON THE EDGE

After graduating from Montebello High School in 1963, Morales attended East Los Angeles College, where he received an associate in arts degree. Later he attended California State College, Los Angeles, where he graduated with a bachelor's degree in 1967. That same year he married Rohde Teaze with whom he parented two children: Gregory Stewart and Alessandra Pilar. In 1969 Morales left Southern California to enroll in Rutgers University. He received a master's degree in 1971 and a doctoral degree in Latin American Literature in 1975. Morales has been the recipient of numerous awards, including Ford Foundation, ITT International, and Mellon Foundation fellowships. He has also served as an essayist, critic, and book reviewer for the *Los Angeles Times.*

In 1975 Morales finished writing his first novel, *Caras viejas y vino nuevo* (translated into English by Max Martinez as *Old Faces and New Wine* and by Francisco A. Lomelí as *Barrio on the Edge,* a bilingual edition and the title that will be used in the remainder of this essay). *Barrio on the Edge,* which originally was written in colloquial Spanish, represents a vision of urban Chicano life in the barrios of the American Southwest. After a number of failed efforts to publish the novel in the United States, including a rejection from Quinto Sol, the only Chicano press of stature at the time, Morales traveled to Mexico City in search of other publishers. Most major presses in Mexico found Morales's work too exotic. After a series of disappointments and rejections, he persisted and decided, on his last week in the city, to contact Mexico's three major editorial houses: Fondo de Cultura Economica, Siglo XXI, and Joaquin Mortiz. Finally, Joaquín Díez Canedo, the editor of Joaquin Mortiz, took a chance and decided to publish *Barrio on the Edge.*

Once in print, the work received mixed reviews. Some critics in Mexico continued reading *Barrio on the Edge* as an exotic text that depicted a surreal world very distant from Mexican reality (See Fernando Diez de Urdanivia, Evodio Escalante, and Oscar Wong). Chicano critics were likewise unenthusiastic about Morales's first novel. The novel's crude, realistic style, its complicated language, and its experimental techniques seemed to deviate from the existing Chicano models developed during the 1960s and early 1970s. Morales's barrio life was seen by some as a terrible way to represent Chicano culture. In fact, it was seen by some as precisely the type of representation that should not be portrayed in Chicano cultural artifacts because it reproduced stereotypes that other artists and writers were trying to shed. As the author explains in an essay titled "Dynamic Identities in Heterotopia": "It was written in a convoluted Spanish that offered a vision, de un mundo torcido [of a twisted world], for which the Mexican American community was not ready" (p. 17).

In his 1986 essay "State of Siege in Alejandro Morales' *Old Faces and New Wine,*" Lomelí placed Alejandro Morales within what he called the "isolated generation" of Chicano literature, along with Ron Arias and Isabella Ríos. Lomelí differentiated this group from the more canonical and established group of authors belonging to the Quinto Sol generation, such as Tomás Rivera, Rudolfo Anaya, Rolando Hinojosa, and Miguel Mendez. For Lomelí, the isolated generation uses location as the essential medium to examine specific themes (p. 186). The barrio thus becomes the privileged narrative space in which Morales develops a fictional, but incisive, and yet subtle critique of moral decay and economic inequality in Chicano communities.

Barrio on the Edge can also be read as an X-ray of the lives of many Chicanos and Chicanas at the time of the civil rights movement. Although the novel was not enthusiastically welcomed at the time, it is important to point to its relevance in terms of the social and cultural issues that arose at a time when the political stature of the Chicano community began to acquire significant political and symbolic resources.

During the 1970s, several Chicano scholars begin questioning the social and economic mechanisms that prevailed around Chicano communities. In particular, scholars focused on barrio dynamics in order to understand issues of inequality facing the communities. At the same time, dependency theory emerged as a viable way to scientifically explain the marginal conditions of Third World countries, including those in Latin America. Within this framework, dependency theory focused on the effects of asymmetric relations of production based on colonial or neocolonial models. International scholars, such as the Pablo Gonzalez Casanova, Celso Furtado, and Andre Gunder Frank, pointed to several socioeconomic structures that reproduced conditions of exploitation and marginality. Chicano scholars, including Mario Barrera and Tomas Almaguer, began comparing these variables and applying some of the ideas of the dependency theory model to explain the marginal situation of the Chicano communities. One consequence was the notion of the barrio as an internal colony. In this model, racial prejudice becomes encapsulated in a series of practices that translate into a system of economic oppression that seems to emulate colonial treatment of subjugated populations such as the case of apartheid in South Africa.

In a significant scene of *Barrio on the Edge*, Julián, a young man who lives a dissolute life, is attempting to recover from a drinking spree in a bathroom. On the wall of the bathroom is a 1968 calendar. This dating connects spatial boundaries to a historical timeline. By 1968 many of the challenges undertaken by the Chicano movement were still very much in progress. Many of these events took place in rural areas of California, Colorado, and Texas, including Cesar Chavez's unionist struggle. By the time the agenda of the Chicano movement became urban, many of the major problems faced by Chicanos were still being fought on a local or regional

scale. In fact, some communities did not actively participate in the Chicano movement until the early or mid-1970s. Still, the novel addresses indirectly issues such as the high participation of Latinos in the Vietnam War. The text refers several times to the "war heroes" who roam the barrio's streets, just looking to survive a local war where the enemy is not a foreign country, but their own socioeconomic situation, a theme amply developed in the writings of the Chicano author Charley Trujillo in his 1990 book *Soldados: Chicanos in Viet Nam*.

Social inequality becomes a paramount aspect of spatial representation in *Barrio on the Edge*. Moreover, the sense of confusion that permeates the text also gives rise to a persisting topic in Chicano narrative: the search for identity. If the Quinto Sol generation resorted to folkloric visions, migration, rural spaces, the Mexican Revolution, and the search for Aztlán as sources of identity, in Morales's first novel the search for identity begins in the very same neighborhood where Chicanos reside.

Barrio on the Edge underscores the connection between language and identity at a time when both factors were sometimes overlooked. In addition, the text frees itself from political and ideological ties to language use by giving emphasis to the linguistic limitations and extensions of a younger generation of Chicanos. Many young Chicanos in the early 1970s found themselves caught in between the language issues of the time; they grew up aware of the prejudice and social dangers of using Spanish and, at the same time, the need to communicate with an older generation comprised mostly of monolingual Spanish speakers. This communication breakdown fuels the generation gap and contributes to the lack of dialogue that dominates the social environment in the novel. Perhaps the author's awareness of this issue is one of the reasons that Morales decided to write the novel in Spanish: "It was during my elementary school years that I recall learning how to read in Spanish. My father, who read *La Opinión* from front to back, sat me at his side and gave me the comics." Language connects Morales with his ancestry, yet he is well aware of the importance of using English as well: "It was in those last years of high school that two important events happened: first, I discovered that the educational system had transformed me into an English-dominant individual; second, I started to write with the intent of wanting people to read and enjoy my work" ("Dynamic Identities in Heterotopia," p. 15). Ironically, Morales's first novel is written in Spanish. This act marks Morales's stand on his view of identity construction. The Chicano identity is comprised of a multiplicity of factors, including language and a strong sense of place. Spanish and English are fundamental markers of this identity as well as the hybrid linguistic and artistic constructions in between, such as slang and "Spanglish," which in the early 1970s were setting the future of Chicano representation.

Barrio on the Edge is a text constructed around binary oppositions, contrasts, and contradictions. If language is an important part of its discourse, the same can be said for silence. This silence is incorporated into the narration through the use of ellipses and fractured sentences that offer the reader a sense of incompletion. Morales developed mysticism in the text, according to Lomelí, to present infrahuman conditions. The people who populate Morales's first novel are their own worst enemies. They have adopted violence as a way of life and have assimilated alcohol and drugs as vehicles to reach a banal transcendentalism. Sexual desire also becomes a force that creates conditions of exploitation and subjugation (Lomelí, "Rereading Alejandro Morales's *Caras viejas y vino nuevo,*" p. 55). This mysticism of the dispossessed, along with the violence, the drugs, and the overall decay of the barrio, dictates the extreme conditions under which the main characters Mateo and Julián struggle to survive.

The characterization of a not-so-imagined world (the author admits basing many of his characters on real people surrounding the environment where he grew up) is impregnated

with binaries and resentment. Lomelí has suggested that *Barrio on the Edge* could be considered a Chicano *Notes from the Underground* (1864), but perhaps Morales's characters are closer to Raskolnikov than to the sordid underground narrator. If Fyodor Dostoyevsky's first-person narrator in *White Nights* (1848) distances himself from any sense of guilt by assuming abjection as a way of life, Morales's narrative subjects equally and unassumingly travel through life carrying resentment as a vital force that makes them continue their journey at the expense of others.

Mateo as the barrio's intrahistoric hero clashes with Julián, the apparent antihero. Yet Julián and Mateo share essential values that somehow keep them tied to a common ground. Both share some positive traits that offer them the possibility of escaping the barrio. Julián is a gifted athlete whose baseball skills could enable him to attend college somewhere. Mateo, on the other hand, is an avid reader and writer who eventually does go to college on the East Coast. Neither of the characters, however, is allowed to transcend his fatal destiny: Julián dies in an accident at the presumed beginning of the novel, and Mateo dies rather unexpectedly of leukemia at what might be considered the end of the novel. Both times of death are illusory, because the narrative does not adhere to a chronological, linear development, but rather to a constant flashback that reminds the reader of a videotape continually being rewound, back and forth. This effect creates a long shot of memories and images that transcends the individual stories being remembered by different characters and assembled by a narrative voice that is many times associated with Mateo.

Barrio on the Edge is not an easy novel to read. It demands from the reader patience and a high degree of openness. It is anchored in the 1960s, yet Morales's novel depicts events that are very much relevant in the twenty-first century. While it is true that the novel's representation of women is rather stereotyped, denunciation of violence and abuse against women permeates the text. Moreover, some of the sexually explicit passages of the novel, while offensive to some at the time of the book's publication, could no longer be considered pornographic, given the extremes that sexual representation has been taking in more recent years. Despite the above and the chronic shyness of the author to read the novel in public, *Barrio on the Edge* has become a classic of Chicano literature that reminds us of the trials and tribulations of several generations of Latinos who have fought hard to survive harsh economic and social conditions in order to dignify their past and their future.

THE VOICELESS TRUTH OR THE *DEATH OF AN ANGLO*

La verdad sin voz (1979; *Death of an Anglo*, 1988) represents a serious effort to expand the horizons of Chicano literature in the late 1970s. According to the author: "This novel was born on a New Jersey winter night. . . . A fellow graduate student handed me a magazine article entitled, 'Death of an Anglo' dated July 27, 1970. My friend said: 'Read this. It's a novel!' I saved the article for the correct time for me to start writing the novel" ("Dynamic Identities in Heterotopia," p. 18). Years later, while teaching at the University of California at Irvine, Morales wrote the text in the middle of a busy semester. The basic plot deals with the story of Michael Logan, an Anglo doctor who opens a clinic in an impoverished Mexican American neighborhood in Mathis, Texas. Logan manages to antagonize the dominant Anglo establishment by providing free medical care for the Mexican American population. By providing this service, Logan breaks unwritten segregation customs that rule the social relations in this southern town. The novel documents Logan's personal tragedy and the ongoing tensions produced by racial and social prejudices. Moreover, the text offers a narrative space to include a subplot in which a Chicano professor deals with the tribulations of academic life at a time when Latino interests

were not properly represented in mainstream academic circles.

Published in Spanish in Mexico, again by Joaquin Mortiz, Morales's second novel establishes a dialogue between two generations of hemispheric writers. On the one hand, Morales's text derives its title and begins with a quote from the Mexican writer José Revueltas (1914–1976). This notion of "la verdad sin voz" (the voiceless truth) is a motif that guides the strong social protest that permeates the text. Not by coincidence, Morales chose to quote Revueltas, a legendary figure of dissent in twentieth-century Mexican culture and politics. A committed and dynamic communist, Revueltas was also a self-taught intellectual and an accomplished writer who won a national literature prize in 1943 with his second novel *El luto humano* (translated into English first as *The Stone Knife* in 1947 and later as *Human Mourning* in 1990). Revueltas was sent to prison several times due to his political activities. He symbolizes several epochs of Mexico's leftist politics beginning in the 1930s.

During the 1968 student movement, Revueltas supported the student protests at the Universidad Nacional Autónoma de México and joined in the struggle. Accused by the Mexican government of being a leading figure of the movement, he was arrested in 1968. He remained in prison at the infamous Black Palace of Lecumberri until 1971. Revueltas later became a popular figure for many young Mexican Americans participating in the Chicano movement when he traveled to several California universities to lecture during the early 1970s. It is not an exaggeration to say that his presence and his writings inspired a whole new generation of Chicanos attending universities in California, including Alejandro Morales. Many critics consider critical realism and the grotesque trademarks of Revueltas's novels. Morales infuses these literary techniques in his novels to create an atmosphere of extenuation where justice seems a distant objective for many of the characters.

A second important hemispherical connection can be established with the narratives of William Faulkner and the Mexican author Juan Rulfo. In Morales's fictional space of Mathis, many of the characteristics of the American South as portrayed by Faulkner are present. The Spanish saying "Pueblo chico, infierno grande" (Small town, big hell) is a fitting description for the Mathis shown in *Death of an Anglo*. If Faulkner created Yoknapatawpha County and Rulfo created Comala from lived experiences, Morales re-created Mathis from a prudent distance.

Death of an Anglo documents the poor living conditions of Mexican Americans in South Texas as a result of years of domination by Anglo elites. Logan, the idealistic doctor, attempts to break the social inertia of Mathis by proposing the creation of a clinic that will benefit mostly the poor Mexican population of the region. This deed, however, angers the town's Anglo leaders and their Mexican American political bosses, those in charge of maintaining the status quo among their own. Logan thus crosses the line and becomes a political scapegoat, reflecting the twisted local issues and tensions emerging from years of unequal economic conditions.

Morales's novel is a creative work—"Relying exclusively on my emotions and imagination, I wrote about the characters, events, and tragic results"—yet he has stated several times that he was astonished by the closeness of his literary creation in *Death of an Anglo* and the story of Michael Logan ("Dynamic Identities in Heterotopia," p. 19). Morales has claimed that the novel inspired a series of hauntings, or coincidences, that placed him several times in uncomfortable positions. Despite several opportunities to do so, Morales declined to visit Mathis, Texas. It was not until several years later that Morales decided to see for himself the real space that he re-created in his novel. Once in town, he had the opportunity to speak to a number of people in town about Logan's case and about the story. Most people corroborated his fictional version of the events. Moreover, he met several people

who looked and acted very much like his fictional characters. In the final analysis, Logan was a victim of the political forces that controlled both sides of the border, due to his idealism, his commitment to the Mexican American community, and his human shortcomings (alcoholism and sexual promiscuity).

Death of an Anglo not only criticizes the corruption on the American side of the border. It also censures Mexico and its political system as well as the consequences that such a system has created for the Mexican people, all of which seems in tune with the presence of Revueltas's dissenting thought in the novel. In a series of indirect statements, the novel depicts particular events of modern Mexican history to denounce the institutional violence and convoluted political machinery that the PRI (Institutional Revolutionary Party) led government managed to run during more than sixty years as a way to control its citizenry. The 1968 Tlatelolco student massacre in Mexico City, the guerrilla movements of the 1970s, the implications of drug trafficking, and the enormous amount of power ascribed to the nation's president are also addressed in the text.

A third narrative strand in *Death of an Anglo* deals with the story of a Chicano faculty member teaching in a South Texas college. Professor Morenito's struggle to survive academia is an important leitmotiv in the novel. Logan and Morenito are joined by destiny when Logan moves to Mathis. They become neighbors and friends. Morenito becomes then a sort of archivist who records Logan's ordeal. The power of writing is the sustaining force that drives Morenito through his battle against the academic establishment where he feels rejected. Some critics have pointed to Morenito as a possible alter ego of Morales because in the last scene Morenito, feeling angry, sits at his typewriter and begins writing the novel *La verdad sin voz* (the voiceless truth). The author, however, has rejected this idea, attributing any similarities between the novel and his life to the hauntings discussed earlier: "To my astonishment just about all of my colleagues [at UC Irvine], save a few, mistakenly recognized themselves in the novel's professor caricatures. They accused me of writing about them, of listening in on their most intimate conversations in the most private places" ("Dynamic Identities in Heterotopia," p. 19). Rather than serving as an indictment of the author, these hauntings prove the power of Morales's imagination and his ability to narrate and connect fiction and reality in new and direct ways.

A CHALLENGE IN PARADISE: *RETO EN EL PARAÍSO* OR THE REWRITING OF HISTORY

Morales's third published work, *Reto en el paraíso* (Challenge in paradise), is his first novel published in the United States. It was not until 1983 that his wish—"Ojalá que se llegue el día que no tenga que salir de mi país para publicar una novela en español" (I hope the day arrives when I will not have to leave my country to publish a novel in Spanish; p. 7)—became reality. A bilingual novel that endeavors to rewrite history through a wide range of narrative strategies, *Reto en el paraíso* is a 381-page historical tour de force. The underlying strength of the novel is its careful archival research; Morales investigated primary sources for several years in order to collect archival data as well as oral histories from California informants. *Reto en el paraíso*'s spatial coordinates gravitate around the history of the James Irvine family ranch in Southern California, the actual site of the city of Irvine, home of the University of California campus where Morales has spent much of his adult life. The text develops valuable insights that renegotiate the official history of the region by highlighting the role of Hispanic culture in the creation of a historical record, which is many times overshadowed by the dominant Anglo discourses. To accomplish this Morales organized a research project involving local area students. Moreover, the author conducted archival work in several important California libraries, including the Bancroft and the Huntington.

Reto en el paraíso uses the motif of the lost manuscript to create a sense of originality. In a 1989 essay, the critic Marvin A. Lewis succinctly points to the connections between fiction and history that this narrative device invokes:

> Morales in his acknowledgments gives credit to Father Felisberto Imondi Bianca, who gave him permission to read the manuscript "Reto en el paraíso" which was penned by Antonio Francisco Coronel and discovered by Bianca in Monte de Carmela church in Simons, California. The novelist is supposedly told by the priest that he is reading probably the most important novel of the many written by the Mexicans who lost California. Whether or not such a manuscript exists, it becomes apparent that there are elements of the historical novel incorporated in the work to the extent that it places the multiple characters in a clearly defined historical framework and interprets their reactions to a concrete set of circumstances. *Reto en el paraíso* interprets the impact of the transition from landowners to the landless upon the descendants of Don Ignacio and Doña Francisca Coronel: Antonio Francisco Coronel, Manuel Damián Coronel and Refugio Coronel.
>
> (p. 1,816)

As suggested by the critic Luis Leal in his 1995 essay "Historia y ficción en la narrativa de Alejandro Morales," *Reto en el paraíso* complicates nineteenth-century representations of Hispanics living in California, who many times were viewed as lawless and rebellious (pp. 36–37). The depiction of the Mexican as a bandit emerges from this turbulent time in California history following the military conquest, occupation, and eventual annexation of these territories by the United States. Morales's novel creates a counterdiscourse that challenges these assumptions. Perhaps it is no coincidence that the title strongly refers to this; "reto" means challenge in English, and this book is a challenge indeed to tell the history of those erased from the official records in the books written by the California

Anglo conquerors. Dennis Berreyesa Coronel, the novel's main character, becomes then the depository of California's Hispanic memory. Dennis also represents contemporary Chicano identity—a mix of traditions, history, language, and experiences. Moreover, Dennis's anxiety about his past represents a type of "hunger of memory" inscribed in Chicano literature, as Richard Rodríguez suggests in the title of his autobiography

Published by Bilingual Press, *Reto en el paraíso* is a truly bilingual text in which the use of English and Spanish is not artificially mediated. Rather, both languages flow according to the particular characters who use them. Hispanic characters tend to speak in Spanish, and Anglo characters in English. Modern Chicano characters, such as Dennis, use both languages and their respective variations, reflecting contemporary identity politics in Southern California. The subject of language is also addressed through a woman character, Rosario Cecilia Revueltas, who links the figure of the Mexican militant writer José Revueltas to Morales's writing project, in part because she represents many of the essential values of Chicanismo, including a sense of pride for maintaining the Spanish language.

The novel resorts to a number of narrative strategies, such as interior monologues, discourse fragmentation, and intertextuality. It also incorporates elements from the fantastic and magical realism. Photography also becomes an important strategy to link the two main historical strands of the text. Dennis's grandmother gives him two photographs attributed to his great-great-granduncle Antonio Francisco Coronel, but Dennis discovers that the photographs, rather than illuminating the past, tend to blur it. The images do not seem to correspond to any plausible reality. In fact, the image of the presumed early *californios* playing guitar and posing in a folkloristic attitude seems to irritate Dennis: "It's a fucking photographic fabrication, a misrepresentation that distorts our history. In effect, Don Antonio is rendered a

senile clown who likes to play the guitar to pretty women and who lives in the past. He's not at all a danger to the dominant society" (p. 308). The second photograph receives the same treatment because for Dennis:

> It's a fake like the other picture. The man is surrounded by unkept broken objects. The truth of the image is that it represents a photograph of a broken old man, certainly not a powerful Spanish Don, which was the original intention of the photograph. Both photographs are images of lies, and I can't accept lies. Abuelita gave them to me, I'll keep them for her. When I return, she may be a butterfly, a hummingbird. She is wise and beautiful.
>
> (p. 310)

Dennis looks at both photographs while he flies to Mexico in search of some answers to his identity questions. Unlike its portrayal in *Death of an Anglo*, Mexico in this novel is depicted in a more favorable light. Moreover, the relationship of the characters to Mexico takes a different direction, because it is the ancient past and grandiose cultural tradition rather than politics that is highlighted in this novel, perhaps to counterbalance the inevitable advancement of modernity that preoccupies the narrator through the text. Mexico's premodern characteristics are emphasized, giving place to an idealized vision of this country.

Reto en el paraíso ends with a scene that prefigures Morales's next novel. The scene likely takes place during the 1930s, because the Los Angeles–San Diego highway is opened and thousands of Mexicans are being deported to Mexico as a result of tensions brought about by the economic hardship of the Great Depression. The Berreyesa Coronel family moves to Simons, the place where Mexicans could find employment in the brick factory. The city of Montebello and its Simons Mexican community represent the possibility of paradise in the harsh times of the Depression. This paradise will face a number of challenges or "retos" in Morales's following novel, a powerful exercise in personal and collective memory.

THE BRICK PEOPLE AND THE POSSIBILITY OF FAMILY REDEMPTION

In *The Brick People,* Morales offers a literary return to his own historical roots. By drawing parallelisms between history, myth, and space, Morales connects his own personal genealogy to the region's historical record. Whereas in *Reto en el paraíso* the Coronel and the Lifford families are the historical actors who mediate the link between past and present, in *The Brick People* Morales's mother's oral account of her journey north is the narrative base of the novel. As in *Death of Anglo,* Morales pays homage explicitly to the figure of José Revueltas by using his last name as the fictional surname of his protagonists. In *The Brick People* the Revueltas family migrates from Mexico to Simons, the site of the brick factory founded by Walter Robey Simons and his family and a place that later represented, in part, the Mexican labor paradise in Southern California at the end of the nineteenth century. The novel follows a chronological line that ends in the 1950s.

The Brick People is Morales's first novel written entirely in English. In a 1995 interview with José Gurpegui that was published in a special edition of *Bilingual Review,* the author claimed: "I wanted to broaden my audience, my readership . . . so I started to write in English. I also went to Arte Público, and they published my last two books in English. I think that was the main thing, trying to have everybody read my books. That is not to say that I am not going to write in Spanish" (p. 8). In addition, *The Brick People* follows a more traditional, linear narrative development than Morales's previous works; it is less experimental and fragmentary than his first three novels.

Throughout the course of this work, Morales's characters develop a sense of awareness of their place in the roles that have been as-

signed to them. This in turn makes the characters poetic entities within the scope of the general plot of the novel. Morales therefore follows an important principle of historically grounded narratives, because what is important in historical novels is not the telling of great historical events but rather the poetic awakening of the human beings who participated in those events.

The novel begins with the journey of Rosendo Guerrero, a Mexican laborer who escapes Mexico during the harsh times of the Porfirio Díaz regime to seek a better life in the north: "He kept advancing on the Flint Knife of the Northern axis of the ancient Aztec coordinates his parents had taught him. . . . Traveling through pure blackness for seven years, Rosendo followed the brilliantly sharp Flint Knife that opened a path to the North" (p. 7).

As the story develops, Rosendo becomes the bridge between Simons and Quiseo de Abasolo, a small Mexican town located in the state of Guanajuato and the origin of most of Simons's eventual Mexican labor force. Rosendo escapes from a semifeudal system that has practically enslaved a great deal of Mexico's population. He carries with him not only a strong will to survive, but also a profound knowledge of the earth and its products: he is an expert adobe brickmaker.

In addition to revealing Rosendo's adventure, the theme of pilgrimage serves as a poetic catalyst that allows for the incorporation of symbolic elements in the novel: "Rosendo arrived in Los Angeles to realize that most of his young adult life had been spent journeying to a place that he knew nothing about. He had followed a directional mandala that his parents had inculcated in his psyche" (p. 7). This pilgrimage north represents a symbolic return to Aztlán, the land of Rosendo's indigenous ancestors. In a 1981 essay titled "In Search of Aztlán," Luis Leal suggested that Aztlán has two meanings: first, it represents the geographic region known today as the southwestern part of the United

States, composed of the territory that Mexico ceded in 1848 with the Treaty of Guadalupe Hidalgo; second, and more important, Aztlán symbolizes the spiritual union of the Chicanos, something that is carried in the heart, no matter where they may live or where they may find themselves (p. 18). The return to Aztlán, or at least the possibility of recovering this mythical place, insinuates a new position in Morales's worldview—a type of coming to terms with his own local history.

Once established in the north, Rosendo transmits his knowledge of the land to Walter Simons, the young and progressive boss of a construction company in the area surrounding Los Angeles. Walter dreams of running an orderly and harmonious community of Mexican workers who are happy and productive: "He would give them a school, a church, a clinic, everything, and create a paradise in which his workers would depend totally on him, so much so that the rising unrest in Mexico would not affect him or his people. They would never leave, he thought" (pp. 64–65).

Walter travels to Mexico during the regime of Porfirio Díaz, or the Porfiriato, in order to find out for himself what the Mexicans and Mexico are really like. He travels throughout various regions of the country at the invitation of William Randolph Hearst (who appears as a character in the novel) and witnesses the impoverished conditions in which millions of men and women live. Walter studies the Mexican hacienda system so that he can modify it to meet his own needs in California. According to Walter, the Mexicans have a great capacity for surviving and adapting to anything if they are treated well, and if they are given basic accommodations they might become the ideal workforce. The Anglo businessman takes advantage of his friendship with Rosendo Guerrero (whom he names supervisor of the brickyard) in order to lure hundreds of immigrants from Guanajuato, who want refuge from the horrible repression of President Díaz's special police force, the infamous Rurales.

As a result, Simons, California, becomes an overwhelmingly Mexican community. In an effort to adopt the methods used by the Mexican haciendas, the brick company establishes a general store, an equivalent of the Mexican "tienda de raya," and all of the employees are required to shop there. Buying on credit is instituted, and one of Walter's Mexican confidants, a cruel and ambitious man named Gonzalo Pedroza, is made the sheriff. Certainly the company's economic high point occurs after the San Francisco earthquake of 1905, when the company receives contracts to reconstruct that city. It is at this time when the beginnings of the town and the Chicano community are manifested.

Another historical aspect in *The Brick People* is the intermittent appearance of historical figures acting as participants in the narration. The reader finds in the novel a number of historical figures—including William Randolph Hearst, Porfirio Díaz, Charles Lindbergh, Pancho Villa, General John Joseph Pershing, and Theodore Roosevelt—who intervene in one way or another, according to the period in question. The reader also finds a number of characters in the novel, including members of the Revueltas and Simons families, who assume traits of representation in order to validate their life experiences. When these characters are less abstract, their true and realistic representation is stronger. These characters succeed in establishing a multiplicity of interactions that contrast other individuals or protagonists in the work and thereby incorporate so-called historical reality in the narration. This does not mean that *The Brick People* is an entirely realistic text, but rather the historic element is interwoven in the characterization in order to create an ambience of narrative credibility. It is in this way that the novel containing historical elements is able to prove through poetic means its existence, the very nature of the circumstances, and the historical figures.

Another theme in the novel worth noting is the function of myths and legends as ties between history and narration. Legends and myths function as a bridge between the historical present (the character's reality at that precise moment in the narrative) and a cultural tradition or past (the stories and beliefs that manifest themselves through unusual events). That bridge between the characters' historical present and their cultural tradition integrates the vision of history of the dominant class and the dominated class alike. On the other hand, and following the above, Rosaura Sanchez, in her 1987 article "Postmodernism and Chicano Literature," offers an interesting discussion about the role of history in postmodern Chicano narrative. She notes that the use of "meta-narratives" and what she calls "burlesque realism" have begun to appear in some works by Chicano writers: "Burlesque realism, à la García Márquez, is now beginning to appear, as to have 'magical' elements, in the Carpentier mode of the 'marvellous real,' common in the works of Rudolfo Anaya, Genaro González, and Alejandro Morales, in which female characters blessed with supernatural powers are portrayed" (p. 9). Consequently, those supernatural elements are included in the cultural traditions that are handed down orally from generation to generation as parts of an unofficial history.

In *The Brick People* the bridge between history and myth is best portrayed by the cockroach as the symbol of the Mexican people. In the novel, according to a regional legend, doña Eulalia Perez de Guillen, an early *californio* woman, made a pact with the land and on her property, under an oak tree, buried her family upon their deaths. Nevertheless, her house and other holdings were destroyed by a group of Anglos who wanted her land. Doña Eulalia was swallowed up by a hole in the earth on her own land. Some time later, neighbors found her clothes in a hole, and upon entering to look for her body, they found thousands of brown insects like a plague on the area. That same land was bought by the Simons family for their business operations.

Members of the Simons family die strange and tragic deaths, where the presence of brown insects is inevitable. One of Walter Simons's nephews is asphyxiated by an incredible number of insects that pour from his mouth and nose in a never-ending stream. Walter's father dies from choking on a huge insect that becomes lodged in his throat. His mother dies of asphyxiation as well, by choking on some brown rice. Her head turns 180 degrees, and they have to bury her that way, as it is impossible to return it to its original position. Joseph, Walter's brother, goes insane: "Ever since 1929, when Joseph claimed to have seen millions of brown insects rise from a pit in a field near his home and devour a family of street people, his mind had slipped slowly into itself until his words and actions became inside out, absurd" (p. 185). Joseph finally dies from a fall. Thousands of brown insects are found on his body, and he is buried with them.

The comparison of the insects (cockroaches) to Mexicans becomes more obvious as the Anglos come to see Mexicans as actual cockroaches. This becomes explicit in the narration when Kaila Morrison, a prominent Anglo sociologist who follows Charles Darwin's theory of biological determinism, visits the Simons family to interview them about their Mexican paradise. During one conversation, Edith Simons confesses: "Mexicans, like cockroaches, are extremely adaptable. They will survive anything. Many may perish but there will always be survivors to propagate the race. They are just like cockroaches" (p. 126).

The Chicano author Oscar Zeta Acosta also used the cockroach as a symbol of the Mexican in his 1973 novella *The Revolt of the Cockroach People*. However, Morales uses cockroach symbolism supernaturally to subvert an ideological framework imposed by the dominant society. Curiously, the cockroaches always take the lives of the bosses and always by tragic and inexplicable means. One can see then how this image creates a pattern of cultural unity, which in any other way would mean not only economic and social, but also cultural submission on the part of the Mexicans. With the revolt of the insects, symbolizing the Mexican, the narration expresses a subversive quality that brings dignity to the figure of the Mexican from a symbolic perspective.

Morales's personal view of history involves a strong connection with his family history: "I am my grandparents, my parents, my aunts and uncles, my brothers and sisters, and my cousins. They are my nation that slowly changes. To recover them in history is my goal. In remembering and writing stories rich with truths and fictions, I accomplish their salvation and my own" ("Dynamic Identities in Heterotopia," p. 15). This vision is transformed in his next work by extending the notion of fictional genealogy, using again the Revueltas family through several generations and over the course of three hundred years.

THE RAG DOLL PLAGUES AND THE BORDERS OF IMAGINATION

The Rag Doll Plagues, Morales's second novel written entirely in English, was published in 1992. In its manuscript form, Morales tentatively titled *The Rag Doll Plagues* "The Ancient Tear" (Leal, "Historia y ficción en la narrativa de Alejandro Morales," p. 41). The choice of this first title becomes apparent given that all three sections end with the narrator Gregorio, or Gregory Revueltas, shedding a tear due to his parting with the past and embracing of the newly found present and the forthcoming future. The idea of the ancient tear expressed by the original title is best described in the novel's final paragraph, where the narrator reaches closure regarding his personal and professional life: "I am no longer me. I am transfigured into all those that have gone before me: my progenitors, my hopeful ever-surviving race. From the deepest part of my being there rushes to the surface of my almond shaped eyes an ancient tear" (p. 200).

Alejandro Morales's futuristic positioning of the region often designated as Aztlán is sup-

planted by the borderland—the metaphoric border that symbolizes "the divisions and limits of culture, language, food, traditions, influence, and power" as well as "fear, desire, love and hatred" ("Dynamic Identities in Heterotopia," p. 23). Spanning over three hundred years of past, present, and future history, Morales's representation of the border in *The Rag Doll Plagues* is characterized by the encounter between culturally different worlds, often resulting in horrific devastations manifested in the form of incurable disease and ecological destruction.

The Rag Doll Plagues's three sections all take place in different times and geographic areas—from the Colonial Spanish rule of Mexico through Southern California and Mexico City in the 1980s to the futuristic reconfigured Los Angeles-to-Mexico City area known as the LAMEX corridor at the end of the twenty-first century. In all three timeframes, tensions emerge through the coming together of different cultures. In the futuristic section, the text centers on the LAMEX corridor, a geo-political entity that prefigures and goes beyond post-NAFTA North America and, according to critic Manuel M. Martín-Rodríguez in the article "Deterritorialization and Heterotopia: Chicano/a Literature in the Zone," a place in which "the colonial and the postcolonial, the center and the periphery, the inherited and the created culture, are brought together" (p. 395)

In part, this junction is due to the virtual vanishing in this third and final section of the novel of the geographic boundary between the United States and Mexico. As Gregory Revueltas, the narrator, protagonist, and descendant of the narrators in the previous sections states, "About twenty years after the turn of the century, the border became stabilized and eventually abolished" (p. 151). In his 2000 article "Border Real, Border Metaphor: Altering Boundaries in Miguel Méndez and Alejandro Morales," the critic José Pablo Villalobos comments on this erasure, arguing that this eradication, triggered by political and economic stability between the two countries, also de-emphasizes the location of the pre-LAMEX border region and its people. Morales thus replaces the present geographical border by remapping the region and reemphasizing the importance of the axis cities of Mexico City and Los Angeles in his text (p. 135).

This border defacement is obvious when the narrator describes the surrounding areas of his home: "The house is only minutes from two computer travelways that run from Los Angeles to Mexico City. One follows the Pacific Coast and the other travels through the desert, right to the center of Mexico directly to its heart, ancient Tenochtitlan, the name under which the Aztecs ruled nearly six hundred years ago, today Mexico City, the capital" (pp. 133–134). The focus on these core areas at the expense of the real borderlands is a constant reflected in the LAMEX Health Corridor, whose headquarters are located simultaneously in Los Angeles and Mexico City.

The text focuses on these core cities, reinforcing the importance of such places in today's world. The Mexican capital is described as a "cultural hub, where the talented people of the world congregated," and the narrator is quick to resort to foundational myths that help to falsely define the totality of the Mexican experience:

> Ancient times and cultures issued forth from deep within the soul of the Mexican earth. It was a past ignored, but felt deeply, an ancient fervor that ran through the mind, heart and blood of Mexico. Since the time of Tenochtitlan to today's Mexico City, the Mexicans continually carried their historical ghosts dangling from their modern ritualistic necklaces.
>
> (p. 162)

As the center of the world for the Mexican people, Mexico City "functioned like the Los Angeles to San Diego area, as a political, economic and cultural core" (p. 162).

Mexico City as the center of Mexicanness is a delicate topic among contemporary Chicano writers. Take for instance the border author Luis Urrea's comments about the topic in his 1998 autobiographic text *Nobody's Son: Notes from an American Life*:

> The last time I was interviewed by the Mexican press, I was in Mexico City, the self-appointed home of all true Mexicans. I was startled to find out that I was not a true Mexican. I was a number of things: I was an American, I was "just" a Chicano, I was a norteño (which, in Mexico City, is like saying you're of the Mongol horde). I was lauded for speaking Spanish "just like" a Mexican, or chided for having what amounted to a cowboy accent. That I was born in Tijuana didn't matter a bit: Tijuana, I was informed, is a no-man's land. Mexicans don't come from Tijuana. Tijuanans come from Tijuana. That I was an American citizen was apparently a faux pas. That I wrote in English was an insult. That I was blue-eyed, however, allowed me to pass for Mexican high society.
>
> (pp. 10–11)

Urrea's comments confuse the idea of Mexico as a loving, caring nation. Villalobos likewise comments on Morales's preoccupation to locate "real Mexicanness" within essentialist and traditional parameters:

> Although usage of "the Mexican people" appears to encompass all Mexicans, the text constantly utilizes this centralizing denominator for all when in reality it simply rejects the peripheral, other Mexican. This false synecdoche first becomes apparent when Los Angeles is hit by a plague that threatens to decimate the population. While it is true that "Most of the casualties are Euroanglo and Japanese. . . . Only those Mexicans born in [the U.S. die]" and "Not one from Mexico City."
>
> (p. 135)

Mexican blood eventually proves to be an antidote for the plague. However, only the blood from a Mexico City Mexican (MCM) contains the proper mutations that endow it with curative properties. When the people of Los Angeles realize the healing nature of the MCM's blood, the population of people from Mexico City triples in a matter of weeks: "They came with their identification documents, birth certificates and letters of residence, certifying that they were born and had lived in Mexico City or in the surrounding area all their life. These people from ancient Tenochtitlan were in demand" (p. 194). MCMs then become targets for domestication. They are treated as expensive pets and prompted to procreate with others of excellent pedigree because of their blood's worth: "Millions of MCMs signed contracts of blood enslavement" (p. 195).

Irony permeates the text when the narrator notes: "In a matter of time Mexican blood would run in all the population of the LAMEX corridor. Mexican blood would gain control of the land it lost two hundred and fifty years ago" (p. 195). The novel suggests a demographic reconquest of Mexico's lost territories. Moreover, the novel also points to the foundational myths regarding the Chicano nation as established in "El Plan Espiritual de Aztlán" (1969), where Aztlán, situated in the American Southwest, is established as the land "from whence came our forefathers," thus becoming a symbol for Chicano history, culture, identity, and more importantly destiny. The Aztlán-Tenochtitlan connection joins centers of power in past and present time, projecting the fictional possibility that in the future the LAMEX axis of power in geographic space will indeed prevail.

The Rag Doll Plagues, as Villalobos has astutely observed, effaces the geo-political border and its subject. Morales's text appears to give primacy to the Aztlán myth, a contention that contradicts current trends in Chicano studies concerning recent postnationalist appreciations of the border as metaphor, particularly in the works of Gloria Anzaldúa. In both cases, the joining of these entities clearly displaces into oblivion the peripheral in-between border regions and their border dwellers.

Some critics have commented on the utopian aspects of some of Morales's recent works. The Mexican writer Carlos Monsiváis has stated that the twentieth century's fin de siècle utopian thought has come to safeguard the idea of legitimate causes that entail, in whatever order of things, the transformation of the world. This is the deep rationale of today's utopian language, whose demiurgic strength is modestly concentrated in the mere possibility of its existence. According to Monsiváis, utopia may be defined as the freedom to dream, in which the stimuli and pleasurable fantasy alike occupy the spaces of the oppressive inertia of everyday life. If in everyday speech the utopian is associated with what is unrealizable (for example, "What you are saying is frankly utopian!"), utopia still signifies the will to create, on the basis of everyday behavior, images of another reality. In the midst of the declared end of all utopias, the point has been reached where the most voluntary of gestures is considered a utopian prefiguration ("Millenarisms in Mexico," p. 141). On the other hand, at the end of the twentieth century, Mexico City also has been represented as postapocalyptic space. However, in Mexico the specter of apocalypse is tainted by a sense of popular festivity in which chaos seems to prevail. Despite all the negative living conditions, few people leave Mexico City, perhaps because there is nowhere else to go in Mexico, but also because—as Monsiváis tells us—it is a secular city after all, and very few take seriously the predicted end of the world. For many, Mexico City's major charm is precisely its (true or false) apocalyptic condition. Despite literary prophecies, as depicted in Carlos Fuentes's novel *Cristóbal nonato* for example, the spirit and the overall attitudes of the *capitalinos* is optimistic. In practice, optimism wins out. In the last instance, the advantages seem greater than the horrors, and the result is Mexico, the postapocalyptic city. The worst has already happened— the monstrous population whose growth nothing can stop, the 1985 earthquake, crime and violence as a way of life, increasing levels of pollution, and economic hardship. Nevertheless, the city functions in a way the majority cannot explain, while everyone takes from the resulting chaos the visual and vital rewards they need and that, in a way, compensate for whatever makes life unlivable. Love and hate come together in the vitality of a city that produces spectacles as it goes along, something like a continuous dystopia of the present.

Yet it seems as though contemporary Chicano narratives such as Morales's have attempted to go against this tendency of discrediting utopia precisely because they want to open alternative spaces to the ethically and sociably demandable. Morales's next novel moves on to the thematic mechanisms and narrative strategies used by this Chicano author to renegotiate representation of borders, memory, and national imageries, looking for possibilities to escape reality. This apparent distancing from the real produces critical processes that allow for a reevaluation of utopia, particularly Chicano utopian spaces, and its relation with apocalypse, not so much in its intentions, but rather in the consequences created by the articulation of language.

WAITING TO HAPPEN OR THE IMPOSSIBILITY OF RETURN

Waiting to Happen, Alejandro Morales's 2001 novel, is the first part of what the author has called the Heterotopian Trilogy. Morales uses Michel Foucault's notion of heterotopia to explain the new realities of the borderlands region. Basically, for Morales, heterotopia is an idea that attempts to bring order and understanding to a space accommodating a wealth of displacement among different entities, peoples, and cultures ("Dynamic Identities in Heterotopia," p. 23). For him this notion explains contemporary border cultures.

Lomelí succinctly summarized the book when he wrote for its cover:

Morales has once again broken new ground with another tour de force, consequently expanding the Chicano novelistic space. Blending various narrative modalities (part detective novel, part prophesy and future shock, part historical chronicle, part fictional biography, part reportage, part myth, and part novel of metempsychosis), he offers a double view of Mexico and the U.S. from their past and their future. He shows how these two cultures merge, clash, and reconcile, or at least learn to deal with their differences. In the process a persistent past reappears through a modern 'ilusa,' J. I. Cruz, protected by the cyclops Endriago, who we gradually and surprisingly come to realize possesses qualities and traits of the famous poetic muse of the seventeenth century, Sor Juana Ines de la Cruz. At this point the novel takes on new layers of meaning and intertextuality.

This is a complex work of plotlines characterized by oscillations and changes in opposite directions. Reading this provocative work is at times equivalent to crossing a two-way street where seductive characters and dangerous situations criss-cross in unexpected ways. *Waiting to Happen* intimates a perplexing, apocalyptic future while shuffling characters of historical resonance with fictional and mythic elements, which adds to the virtuosity of the narrator's views of a new world order.

Yet Morales takes the core of the action back to Mexico in a transnational displacement that involves a number of binational characters and events. *Waiting to Happen* is the story of an Ivy League–educated Chicana named J. I. Cruz and her life experiences in Mexico and the United States. Cruz, whose full name is Juana Ines Cruz, like the famous seventeenth-century Mexican poet, becomes involved in a series of events that depict the state of U.S.-Mexico relations during the 1990s.

In this novel Morales revisits the strategy of blurring fact and fiction. In the book's acknowledgements section, for example, the author expresses gratitude to a number of people and institutions, including the protagonist, J. I. Cruz herself, whom, according to the note, the author met in Southern California. Fact and fiction are therefore blended from the very start of this narrative saga that explores the depth of corruption, deceit, and impunity in Mexican and U.S. high power circles. If Morales's previous works only touch U.S.-Mexico relations in a tangential way,

Waiting to Happen penetrates beyond the front lines occupied by the press and the media of both nations. In between there is a network of American and Mexican characters who craft what is called the AmerMex collaboration from the underground. Current issues—such as energy production and distribution, the environment, drug trafficking networks including the involvement of high-ranking officials and business people, and the unofficial nets that attempt to uncover these dealings—are central to the novel.

On the other hand, there is a determination in the handling of cultural icons and images that sometimes obstructs the development of some of the characters. The twentieth-century Mexican painters Frida Kahlo and Diego Rivera become guiding motifs, the continued presence of the mythical ancient indigenous past, sort of a new "haunting" that seems to appear in Morales's texts. In addition, the overtones of excessive or singular spirituality and the relationship of some characters to religion and to the church are sometimes variables that deviate from the context of a detective-like narration that breaks with these premises. Another significant element of the text is the role of excessive violence attributed to Mexico and to the Mexicans. There are a high number of killings, tortures, and deaths, many of them by-products of an institutionalized violence that the text critiques.

One wonders if a reader not familiar with the long list of names and characters that appear in the novel will be prompted to search for who they are. On one level, *Waiting to Happen* seems at first directed solely to academics and intellectuals, who are familiar with each other on both sides of the border. And yet, far from being a shortcoming, the novel transcends its local tone to appeal to a broader readership that may be wondering why Frida and Diego are so important to J. I. Cruz and not to other Mexicans involved in the plot.

If Morales's previous historical novels followed a more or less traditional path, *Waiting to Happen* deviates from this strategy, and fragmentation becomes its trademark. Throughout the novel, there are numerous headlines and divisions that announce what will be featured in the following section. Fragmentation also occurs at the subject and discourse levels, truly making the text part of the postmodern zeitgeist. There are multiple narrative perspectives in the novel that offer several levels of inter- and intratextuality mixed with other discourses to produce a polyphonic effect that enriches the narration.

There are three main themes that *Waiting to Happen* recovers from Morales's previous works. This does not necessarily mean that the author has recycled them, but rather that he has reworked them to construct a nexus between his preoccupations and current events. First, Morales continues to explore historical relations and the intrinsic connections between past and present. If some of his previous works focused on historical events through a few individuals, this text involves a wide range of characters, both fictional and nonfictional. Many of these people are from the world of culture and literature, including Carlos Fuentes, Elena Poniatowska, Carlos Monsiváis, Jacobo Zabludowsky, and Juan Jose Arreola.

Second, Morales uses transnational spaces to locate the action of the novel. Again, there is an expansion from the barrios of Southern California to the globalized village that the world has become. The LAMEX corridor of *The Rag Doll Plagues* has opened to encompass the hemisphere. Mexico now faces the possibility of becoming integrated in more ways than one to the United States. It also faces the risk of becoming a nuclear power involved with the unwanted development of nuclear weapons. Fear of this development emanates not only from environmental groups in Mexico but also from political forces in the United States.

The third theme deals with the connections the text establishes with ancient Mexican imagery through the mystic process that J. I.

Cruz experiences. If in *Barrio on the Edge* mysticism was a coded term used to explain the unavoidable dependence of the barrio people on drugs and alcohol, in this text mysticism follows a more traditional pattern. It becomes the mechanism under which the Mexican people will attempt to break free from the institutionalized corruption that has surrounded them for five hundred years. J. I. Cruz becomes a contemporary *ilusa* whose power will illuminate the path to freedom and to a better future. Morales's essentialized and idealistic version of Mexico's future leaves out the possibility that the real Mexican people can achieve a democratic society on their own. His work suggests that they need a divine intervention, a miracle embodied in a Chicana woman who like a postmodern Guadalupe will guide her subjects to another state, a Nepantla where liberation from the oppressor is always possible, provided that nuclear energy remains out of the picture. Morales's fantastic denouement rivals any of the best endings of the 1990s television series *The X-Files*. J. I. Cruz awakens from her *ilusa* state to recover and come back to normality. In this condition, she is ready to return to California and join her sweetheart, a Jewish college professor who waits for her. After all, no Chicana seems to be ready to liberate Mexico or herself from the faith that a place like Aztlán(dia) has prepared for the inhabitants. It is then no coincidence that the novel's last scene takes place in, of all places, Orange County's John Wayne Airport, a safe terrain away from the dystopic realities encountered south of the border. Mexico and the Mexicans and the corruption and violence of the novel are left behind and probably forgotten. J. I. Cruz and her American love embrace and promise to be happy forever and ever. A happy ending? Perhaps.

CONCLUSION

Alejandro Morales continues to write fiction narrating the past, present, and future of Chicano culture. He continues to be committed to representing Latinidad beyond the narrow scopes of the barrios and the media, providing opportunities for readers across the globe to learn from his fiction. Morales is very generous with his time. When he is not engaged in writing, he lectures, attends conferences, and gives public readings of his work for all types of audiences. He works closely with college students and with several writing projects in elementary, junior high, and high schools in Southern California. His novels have become representative of several developments in the field during the last three decades. A pioneer of Latino literature written in Spanish and published abroad, Morales continues to be, without a doubt, a guiding literary force, and his works will continue to inspire present and future generations of Latinos and Latinas.

Selected Bibliography

WORKS OF ALEJANDRO MORALES

BOOKS
Caras viejas y vino nuevo. Mexico: Editorial Joaquin Mortiz, 1975.

La verdad sin voz. Mexico: Editorial Joaquin Mortiz, 1979.

Reto en el paraíso. Ypsilanti, Mich.: Bilingual Press/Editorial Bilingüe, 1983. Reprint, Mexico: Grijalbo, 1993.

The Brick People. Houston: Arte Público Press, 1988.

The Rag Doll Plagues. Houston: Arte Público Press, 1992.

Waiting to Happen. San Jose, Calif.: Chusma House Publications, 2001.

TRANSLATIONS

Old Faces and New Wine. Translated by Max Martinez. San Diego, Calif.: Maize Press, 1981. Translation of *Caras viejas y vino nuevo.*

Death of an Anglo. Translated by Judith Ginsberg. Tempe, Ariz.: Bilingual Press/ Editorial Bilingüe, 1988. Translation of *La verdad sin voz.*

Barrio on the Edge. Translated by Francisco A. Lomelí. Tempe, Ariz.: Bilingual Press/ Editorial Bilingüe, 1998. Translation of *Caras viejas y vino muevo.*

SHORT STORIES

"Cara de caballo." *The Americas Review* 14, no. 1 (spring 1986): 19–22.

"The Curing Woman." *The Americas Review* 14, no. 1 (spring 1986): 23–27.

"Salió de la casa por la puerta de atras." In *Literatura fronteriza: Antología del Primer Festival San Diego–Tijuana, mayo 1981.* San Diego, Calif.: Maize Press, 1982. Pp. 110– 113.

EXCERPTS

"Caras viejas y vino nuevo." *Sighs and Songs of Aztlán: A New Anthology of Chicano Literature.* Edited by F. E. Albi and Jesus G. Nieto. Bakersfield, Calif.: Universal Press, 1975. Pp. 151–160.

"Death of an Anglo." *De Colores* 4, nos. 1–2 (1978): 136–142. Excerpt from *La verdad sin voz.*

"Reto en el paraíso." *La Opinión* 22 (December 14, 1980): 11–12, 15.

ESSAY

"Dynamic Identities in Heterotopia" In *Alejandro Morales: Fiction Past, Present, Future Perfect.* Edited by José Antonio Gurpegui. Tempe, Ariz.: Bilingual Press/Editorial Bilingüe, 1996. Pp. 14–27.

SECONDARY SOURCES

CRITICAL AND BIOGRAPHICAL STUDIES

Akers, John C. "Fragmentation in the Chicano Novel: Literary Technique and Cultural Identity." *Revista Chicano-Riqueña* 13, nos. 3–4 (1985): 124–127.

Alarcón, Francisco X. "Califas es una novela, el arte narrativo de Alejandro Morales." Parts 1 and 2. *La Opinión,* June 5, 1983, pp. 6–7; *La Opinión,* June 12, 1983, pp. 6–7.

Batiste, Victor N. "A Kaleidoscope on Many Levels: A Review Article of *Reto en el paraíso.*" *Revista Chicano-Riqueña* 13, no. 1 (spring 1985): 91–94.

Benavides, Ricardo F. "Estirpe y estigma en una novela chicana." *Chasqui* 6, no. 1 (November 1976): 84–93.

Bentley-Adler, Colleen. "Crossing Cultures: Morales' Novels Reflect the Dilemma of Dual Ethnicities." *UCI Journal* 8, no. 3 (January–February 1989): 7.

Bottalico, Michele. "Illness in Alejandro Morales's *The Rag Doll Plagues.*" *Cuadernos de Literatura Inglesa y Norteamericana* 5, no. 1–2 (November 2002): 64–73.

Bustamante, Nuria. "Permanencia y cambio en *Caras viejas y vino nuevo.*" *Confluencia: Revista Hispanica de Cultura y Literatura* 1, no. 2 (spring 1986): 61–65.

Diez de Urdanivia, Fernando. "Alejandro Morales y la narrativa chicana: El escritor y su mundo." *El Día* (Mexico), August 1, 1976, p. 15.

Elías, Eduardo. "La evolución narrativa de Alejandro Morales a través de sus textos." *Explicación de Textos Literarios* 15, no. 2 (1986–1987): 92–102.

Escalante, Evodio. "Escrito en chicano." *Siempre!* March 31, 1976, p. ix.

Garcia, Mario T. "History, Literature, and the Chicano Working-Class Novel: A Critical Review of Alejandro Morales's *The Brick People.*" *Crítica: A Journal of Critical Essays* 2, no. 2 (fall 1990): 188–201.

Ginsberg, Judith. "*La verdad sin voz*: Elegy and Reparation." *Americas Review* 14, no. 2 (summer 1986): 78–83.

Gonzales-Berry, Erlinda. "*Caras viejas y vino nuevo*: Journey through a Disintegrating Barrio." In *Contemporary Chicano Fiction: A Critical Survey.* Edited by Vernon E. Lattin. Binghamton, N.Y.: Bilingual Press/Editorial Bilingüe, 1986. Pp. 289–298.

———. "Doctor, Writer, Warrior Chief." *Bilingual Review/La Revista Bilingüe* 9, no. 3 (September–December 1982): 276–279. Review of *La verdad sin voz.*

———. "Morales, Alejandro." In *Chicano Literature: A Reference Guide.* Edited by Julio A. Martínez and Francisco A. Lomelí. Westport, Conn.: Greenwood Press, 1985. Pp. 299–309.

González, María. "*Caras viejas y vino nuevo*: Análisis temático y estructural." *Tinta* 1, no. 1 (May 1981): 15–18.

Grandjeat, Yves-Charles. "L'ici est l'ailleurs: *Reto en el paraíso,* d'Alejandro Morales." In *L'ici est l'ailleurs: Annales du Centre de Recherches sur l'Amérique Anglophone,* vol. 16. Edited by Jean Beranger, et al. Talence Cedex, France: PU de Bordeau–Centre de Recherches sur l'Amérique Anglophone, 1991. Pp. 203–215.

Grandjeat, Yves-Charles, and Alfonso Rodríguez. "Interview with Chicano Writer Alejandro Morales." *Confluencia: Revista Hispanica de Cultura y Literatura* 7, no. 1 (fall 1991): 109–114.

Gurpegui, José Antonio. "Alejandro Morales: Fiction Past, Present, Future Perfect." *Bilingual Review/La Revista Bilingüe* 20, no. 3 (September–December 1995): 1–114.

———. "Implicaciones existenciales del uso del español en las novelas de Alejandro Morales." *Bilingual Review/La Revista Bilingüe* 20, no. 3 (September–December 1995): 43–51.

———. "Interview with Alejandro Morales." *Bilingual Review/La Revista Bilingüe* 20, no. 3 (September–December 1995): 5–13.

———. "*Tortilla Flat* de Steinbeck y *Caras viejas y vino nuevo* de Alejandro Morales: Dos perspectivas de una misma realidad." *REDEN (Revista Española de Estudios Norteamericanos)* 3 (spring 1990): 73–84.

Gutierrez-Jones, Carl. "'Rancho Mexicana, USA' under Siege." In his *Rethinking the Borderlands: Between Chicano Culture and Legal Discourse.* Berkeley: University of California Press, 1995. Pp. 80–89.

Herrera-Sobek, María. "Barrio Life in the Fifties and Sixties." *Latin American Literary Review* 5, no. 10 (spring–summer 1977): 148–150.

———. "Epidemics, Epistemophilia, and Racism: Ecological Literary Criticism and *The Rag Doll Plagues.*" *Bilingual Review/La Revista Bilingüe* 20, no. 3 (September–December 1995): 99–108.

Kanellos, Nicolás. "Alejandro Morales (1944–)." In *The Hispanic American Almanac: A Reference Work on Hispanics in the United States.* Edited by Nicolás Kanellos. Detroit: Gale Research, 1993. Pp. 454–455.

Kaup, Monika. "From Hacienda to Brick Factory: The Architecture of the Machine and Chicano Collective Memory in Alejandro Morales's *The Brick People.*" In *U.S. Latino Literatures and Cultures: Transnational Perspectives.* Edited by Francisco A. Lomelí and Karin Ikas. Heidelberg, Germany: Carl Winter Universitätsverlag, 2000. Pp. 160–170.

Lattin, Vernon E. Review of *Death of an Anglo. Confluencia: Revista Hispanica de Cultura y Literatura* 4, no. 1 (fall 1988): 163–165.

Leal, Luis. "Historia y ficción en la narrativa de Alejandro Morales." *Bilingual Review/La Revista Bilingüe* 20, no. 3 (September–December 1995): 31–42.

———. "In Search of Aztlan." *Denver Quarterly* 16, no. 3 (fall 1981): 16–22.

Lewis, Marvin A. "Alejandro Morales." In *Dictionary of Literary Biography,* vol. 82. Chicano Writers, First Series. Edited by Francisco A. Lomelí and Carl R. Shirley. Detroit: Gale Research, 1989. Pp. 178–183.

Libretti, Tim. "Forgetting Identity, Recovering Politics: Rethinking Chicana/o Nationalism, Identity Politics, and Resistance to Racism in Alejandro Morales's *Death of an Anglo.*" *Post Identity* 1, no. 1 (fall 1997): 66–93.

Lomelí, Francisco A. "Hard-Core Barro Revisited: Violence, Sex, Drugs, and Videotape in a Chicano Glass Darkly." In *Barrio on the Edge,* by Alejandro Morales. Translated by Francisco A. Lomelí. Tempe, Ariz.: Bilingual Press/Editorial Bilingüe, 1998. Pp. 1–21. Introduction to Lomelí's translation of *Caras viejas y vino nuevo.*

———. "Rereading Alejandro Morales's *Caras viejas y vino nuevo*: Violence, Sex, Drugs, and Videotape in a Chicano Glass Darkly." *Bilingual Review/La Revista Bilingüe* 20, no. 3 (September–December 1995): 52–60.

———. "State of Siege in Alejandro Morales' *Old Faces and New Wine.*" In *Missions in Conflict: Essays on U.S.-Mexican Relations and Chicano Culture.* Edited by Renate von Bardeleben, Dietrich Briesemeister, and Juan Bruce-Novoa. Tübingen, Germany: G. Narr, 1986. Pp. 185–194.

López-Lozano, Miguel. "The Politics of Blood: Miscegenation and Phobias of Contagion in Alejandro Morales's *The Rag Doll Plagues.*" *Aztlán: A Journal of Chicano Studies* 28, no. 1 (spring 2003): 39–73.

Mariscal, George. "Alejandro Morales in Utopia." *Confluencia: Revista Hispanica de Cultura y Literatura* 2, no. 1 (fall 1986): 78–83.

Martín-Rodríguez, Manuel M. "Deterritorialization and Heterotopia: Chicano/a Literature in the Zone." In *Actes du VIe Congrès européen sur les cultures d'Amérique latine aux États-Unis: Confrontations et métissages.* Edited by Elyette Benjamin-Labarthe, Yves-Charles Grandjeat, and Christian Lerat. Bordeaux, France: Maison des Pays Ibériques, 1995. Pp. 391–398.

———. "The Global Border: Transnationalism and Cultural Hybridism in Alejandro Morales's *The Rag Doll Plagues.*" *Bilingual Review/La Revista Bilingüe* 20, no. 3 (September–December 1995): 86–98.

———. "El sentimiento de culpa en *Reto en el paraíso* de Alejandro Morales." *The Americas Review* 15, no. 1 (spring 1987): 89–97.

———. "El tema de la culpa en cuatro novelistas chicanos." *Hispanic Journal* 10, no. 1 (fall 1988): 133–142.

Márquez, Antonio C. "The Use and Abuse of History in Alejandro Morales's *The Brick People* and *The Rag Doll Plagues*." *Bilingual Review/La Revista Bilingüe* 20, no. 3 (September–December 1995): 76–85.

McLellan, Dennis. "In *Rag Doll,* the Plague's the Thing." *Los Angeles Times,* February 14, 1992, p. E3.

Monleón, José. "Dos novelas de Alejandro Morales." *Maize: Notebooks of Xicano Art and Literature* 4, nos. 1–2 (fall–winter 1980–1981): 6–8.

———."Entrevista con Alejandro Morales." *Maize: Notebooks of Xicano Art and Literature* 4, nos. 1– 2 (fall–winter 1980–1981): 9–20.

Monsiváis, Carlos. "Millenarisms in Mexico: From Cabona to Chiapas." In *Mexican postcards.* Edited, translated, and introduced by John Kraniauskas. London; New York: Verso, 1997.

Muñoz, Willie O. "*Caras viejas y vino nuevo,* la tragedia de los barrios." *Aztlán: A Journal of Chicano Studies* 15, no. 1 (spring 1984): 163–177.

Newman, María. "He Does It All for Love of Written Word." *Los Angeles Times,* September 26, 1991, p. 5.

Nieto, Margarita. "Chicano History Brick by Brick." *Los Angeles Times,* September 18, 1988, p. 3.

"Nueva novela chicana en español." *Defensa: Boletín de la Liga Nacional Defensora del Idioma Español* 4–5 (November 1976): 8–9.

Rodriguez del Pino, Salvador. "Interview with Alejandro Morales." *Encuentro with Chicano Writers Series.* Santa Barbara: Center for Chicano Studies, University of California, 1977. Video recording.

———."La novel a chicana de los setenta comentada por sus escritores y criticos." In *The Identification and Analysis of Chicano Literature.* Edited by Francisco Jiménez. New York: Bilingual Press/Editorial Bilingüe, 1979. Pp. 153–160.

———. *La novela chicana escrita en español: Cinco autores comprometidos.* Ypsilanti, Mich.: Bilingual Press/Editorial Bilingüe, 1982. Pp. 65–89.

Rosales, Jesús. "El cronotopo del encuentro en *Reto en el paraíso* de Alejandro Morales." *Bilingual Review/La Revista Bilingüe* 20, no. 3 (September–December 1995): 61–75.

———. *La narrativa de Alejandro Morales: Encuentro, historia y compromiso social.* N.Y.: Peter Lang, 1999.

Sanchez, Rosaura. "Postmodernism and Chicano Literature." *Aztlán: A Journal of Chicano Studies* 18, no. 2 (fall 1987): 1–14.

Shirley, Carl R., and Paula W. Shirley. *Understanding Chicano Literature.* Columbia: University of South Carolina Press, 1988. Pp. 117–121.

Somoza, Oscar U. "Choque e interacción en *La verdad sin voz* de Alejandro Morales." In *Contemporary Chicano Fiction: A Critical Survey.* Edited by Vernon E. Lattin. Binghamton: Bilingual Press/Editorial Bilingüe, 1986. Pp. 299–305.

Tatum, Charles M. *Chicano Literature.* Boston: Twayne, 1982. Pp. 126–128.

———. *A Selected and Annotated Bibliography of Chicano Studies.* Lawrence: University of Kansas Press, 1976.

Villalobos, José Pablo. "Border Real, Border Metaphor: Altering Boundaries in Miguel Méndez and Alejandro Morales." *Arizona Journal of Hispanic Cultural Studies* 4 (2000): 131–140.

Waldron, John V. "Uncovering History in the 'Post Modern Condition': (Re)Writing the Past, (Re)Righting Ourselves in Alejandro Morales' *The Brick People*." *Confluencia: Revista Hispánica de Cultura y Literatura* 7, no. 2 (spring 1992): 99–106.

Wong, Oscar. "Caras vemos . . . Chicanos no sabemos." *Vida universitaria* (Monterey, Mexico) 1299, June 2, 1976, p. 18.

John Rechy

(1931–)

PATRICK O'CONNOR

ALTHOUGH HIS FIRST published novel's opening scene takes place during the second-generation Mexican American pro-tagonist's childhood in the American southwest, neither John Rechy nor his contemporaries of the 1960s who founded the Aztlán movement would probably have considered the work to be Chicano or U.S. Latino fiction. Indeed, for the first twenty years of his career, Rechy's writing fit smoothly into quite a different canonical subgenre, just then being founded: transgressive or taboo fiction, associated primarily with the Evergreen Review and Grove Press and affiliated with writers like the Surrealists and Jean Genet in Europe, and the Beat writers, Gore Vidal, and Norman Mailer in the United States. Like Genet (in his novels) and Jack Kerouac, Rechy tantalized the reader with the promise of crossing the boundary between fiction and nonfiction; like Genet and Burroughs, Rechy chose to examine homosexual subcultures, although often with an essayistic, almost documentary precision. Rechy's subculture changed out from under him—in part, due to his own writings—and his novels of the 1980s until the present show a more deliberate attempt to continue his search for identity with and through his Chicano heritage.

As this essay reviews the writings of this prolific, evolving writer, attention will be paid to *lo latino* in Rechy's gay fiction, as well as what is gay or queer in his pursuit of his Chicano roots, and his extension of U.S. Latino literary traditions. What becomes clear is that Rechy's transgressive contributions to both worlds, the world of the gay literary tradition and the world of the Latino literary tradition, develop strands in American literature connected to the American Gothic impulse—the brooding masculine and the vulnerable feminine, in dark spaces haunted by grotesque and extreme figures who encounter uncanny doubles of themselves—and the American confessional or documentary impulse—in which truth claims are made and personal experience, however contrarian or sordid, is defiantly validated.

TRANSGRESSIONS IN THE CITY OF THE NIGHT: THE GOTHIC AND THE DOCUMENTARY

Charles Casillo's 2002 biography, *Outlaw*, confirms what most readers of *City of Night* (1963), *Numbers* (1967), *This Day's Death* (1969), *The Sexual Outlaw* (1977), and *Rushes* (1979) would like to think, namely that Rechy's protagonists are barely fictionalized versions of himself. His paternal grandfather was Scottish, the personal physician to Mexican dictator Porfirio Díaz, and his paternal grandmother a light-skinned Spaniard. His father was an orchestra conductor and composer whose career was ruined by the Mexican Revolution, which forced the family to emigrate to El Paso, Texas. Rechy's mother was, according to family lore, "the most beautiful woman in Chihuahua" (Casillo, p. 13) but was still ridiculed by her color-conscious mother-in-law. John, nonathletic but handsome and the youngest of six children, was abused and bullied by his elderly alcoholic father, whose menial jobs during the Depression were the source of obvious unhappiness. Anger toward his father (as well as occasional attempts to placate him, including a sex game in which the child bounced on his father's and his father's friends' laps for nickels) are suggested as the root cause of the main protagonist's narcissism and need to become a hustler in *City of Night*.

Rechy's books, and the Casillo biography, share the mid-century psychoanalytic paradigm elaborated on by Mexican essayist and poet Octavio Paz: *machismo* is a refusal to open oneself, a defensive stance against the world, a mix of anger at the contempt that one's father feels for one's mother and, on other levels, an imitation of that contempt. It is true that Rechy was very close to his mother and sisters and as an adult had many straight women friends. But it is also true that, after completing college and a stint in the army, he understood masculinity—as Paz and other theorists of *machismo* such as Tomás Almaguer do—as a pose of invulnerability. Rechy made conscious use of this pose by spending much of the next four years on the streets, in New York, Los Angeles, Chicago, and New Orleans, gathering the raw material for *City of Night*.

City of Night follows the unnamed first-person protagonist through the various hustler bars and dirty streets of late 1950s urban America. Rechy and his character engage in identity politics, so to speak, but the identities are understood as external—three social roles that men play, organized around the fiction of masculine power. The hustlers or trade are men who sell their bodies, but only in the active position and always withholding reciprocation or affection. The clients or johns often make the mistake of falling in love with the men they rent even as they maintain a social position in the real world. And the queens and queers, some prostitutes and some not, are social outcasts who identify with the female position, wear as much feminine clothing and make-up as the restrictive laws of the 1950s would allow, and while looking for a "real man" often settle for co-dependent relationships with the trade. (The novel ends in New Orleans during Mardi Gras because then the laws against transvestism are lifted for the entire city.) *City of Night* acknowledges the existence of two other categories: the masculine homosexuals looking for love and a long-term partner (the protagonist is offered such a love three times in the book, turning it down each time), and the furtive men cruising for sex with each other in parks, public toilets, and movie theaters, a scene in which the hustlers take no interest. The world of trade, johns, and queens is the world of *City of Night*.

The form of *City of Night* is no doubt as important to the book's success as its honesty. Shortish vignettes, written in a tough-guy poetic prose, are each titled "City of Night" and give the narrator's biographical itinerary—a childhood in Texas mourning the death of a beloved dog; then New York; Los Angeles; the beaches of Los Angeles; brief vignettes in San Francisco and Chicago; and finally New Orleans. Surface differences in these different cities give way to a more general similarity. The narrator lives in many cities, but always finds *the* City of Night wherever he is. These short vignettes serve as a sort of backdrop for chapters organized around various individuals, inhabitants of the underground of importance to the narrator's life. Three apiece in each of the novel's four parts, some are johns, some are fellow trade, two are highly differing drag queens, and one is the woman owner of a New Orleans bar.

Rechy experiments somewhat with the form of these chapters, telling the story of the downfall of the straight-appearing actor Lance as if it were a sort of Greek tragedy with a chorus of gossipy queens, for instance, or staging the last of the chapters as a postcoital debate on the worth of a genuine relationship, while the streets of New Orleans outside prepare for an orgy. His chapter vignettes about his fellow hustlers—Pete in New York, the first to offer him something like vulnerability and love, Chuck and Skipper in Los Angeles, who were both lured to Los Angeles by something in the air of American culture—are just as vivid even though their tones and narration are not strongly different from that of the "City of Night" interchapters. Certainly the most vivid of these chapters are the self-dramatizing figures, such as the grotesquely fat and ugly client The Professor, who compares beautiful young men to "lost angels," a metaphor that Rechy would elaborate on throughout his career. The Professor's metaphoric use of religious imagery leads quite naturally to a sort of reverse theology:

> I can conceive of no more beautiful world than one ruled by the emotions—what a lovely world! One would not push through the subway, thinking one might crush someone lovely. . . . But then, child, the world is All Wrong. You see, it is backwards. How much more logical, for example, had we been brought up on the idea that God is evil?
>
> (*City of Night*, p. 70)

The Los Angeles drag queen Miss Destiny was so accurately, and positively, captured as she planned her dream wedding with one or another young man to whom she took a fancy that the real person Rechy based the character on was interviewed by the gay newspaper *The Advocate* and would occasionally call Rechy up with some prospective conquest so that he could verify that she was, indeed, the "heroine" of a novel. Among the titles Rechy considered for the novel

were *The Fabulous Wedding of Miss Destiny* and *Hey, World,* the catchphrase brayed by the aggressive, bitter, muscular drag queen Chi-Chi in New Orleans, who wielded a cigarette holder like a weapon and was as unhappy in his/her masculine body as Miss Destiny was happy in his/her effeminate one.

City of Night, like much of Rechy's fiction, is balanced between two impulses, the documentary and the Gothic. In this first book the Gothic will mostly appear in the form of grotesques and a love of melodrama, although—as in much Gothic, from its origins in the eighteenth century and especially in Poe—a theory of masks and a tilt towards parody sometimes taints the melodrama. In his documentary honesty, Rechy's protagonist, and Rechy himself in interviews, acknowledges that he never had to hustle full-time to survive on the streets, but at intervals took various jobs to support himself and rented apartments away from the hustling district to preserve a distance from that scene, which enabled him to write. This distance is thematized in *City of Night.* First, Rechy underlines that the trade is not supposed to have anything to do with books, but more than once his mask slips when he shows enthusiasm for literature to one of his johns. More importantly, this distance is the supposed unreachable interior protected by the mask of the hustler's aloofness. The last of the novel's three offers of a relationship is precipitated when a young man, possibly a client, overhears Rechy with two other potential clients, in a moment when the combination of pre–Mardi Gras drugs and noise wears down his façade and his mask slips:

> Minutes later, my own mask began to crumble. . . . Incongruously, like this: out of nowhere, surprising myself by the sounds of my words, I blurted to those two [clients]: "I want to tell you something before we leave. Im not at all the way you think I am. Im not like you want me to be, the way I tried to look and act for you: not unconcerned, nor easygoing—not tough: no, not

at all. . . . Like you, like everyone else, Im Scared, cold, cold terrified."

(p. 369)

Rechy would abandon the systematic elimination of some apostrophes but preserved other orthographical tricks throughout his work, especially strategic capitalization. Even though the narrator rejects the man who eavesdrops on this confession and offers him the chance for true love, the novel returns at its very end to the image of a little boy furious at God for the death of his beloved dog, and Gothic will always give way to existential honesty: we live in a world of masks because of a fear of the emptiness within. In the end the paradoxes of *City of Night* are less about a seemingly straight man receiving money to perform technically gay sex acts than about a milieu that reinforces solitude by means of (rigorously conventional) intimate bodily acts.

How might one relate *lo latino* to Rechy's transgressive/gay fiction? When he declared his affiliation to U.S. Latino literature, Rechy frequently attributed parts of his aesthetic to his Catholic, especially Mexican Catholic, upbringing. In his books during this period, such influences bear a marked resemblance to the novels of Genet, especially *Our Lady of the Flowers, A Thief's Journal,* and *Miracle of the Rose.* The working-class posture of the hustler approaches the classic definition of Latin *machismo*— although such a posture could be inhabited by, say, Italian American Marlon Brando playing a Polish American Stanley Kowalski; working-class machismo is not limited only to Latinos in the mid-century United States. Sometimes the ethnicity of Rechy's protagonist is not marked at all, as Johnny Rio's is not throughout *Numbers.* The equation of working-class or lumpen masculinity with Latin ethnicity is mentioned explicitly by some writers of this era, like Edmund White and Paul Rogers. But perhaps rather than looking towards the stereotype of Latin masculinity, we should look towards a stereotype of Latin "femininity," the Latin drag queen.

Part three of *City of Night* extends part two's Los Angeles tales to Venice Beach and in the chapter titled "Someone," the narrator befriends a closeted married man. This unnamed married man's desirability is supported by the props of the straight world, yet his normality also makes him vulnerable to a certain kind of demand:

I always came [to the beaches] with the intention of meeting someone. But then I would see a screaming fairy—and suddenly I'd be ashamed. It's very strange—but I couldnt bear to look into his eyes, afraid, I guess, that he'd look back at me with recognition.

(p. 240)

Recognition and the look become exactly the issue the next day, in a beachfront gay bar where only one patron flagrantly violates the various legally enforced laws of decorum:

The jukebox is rocking, sounds monotonous but exciting: African-drumming, jungle-moaning. . . . From somewhere, lured by the jungle sex-sounds—a dark Latin queen rushed frenziedly onto the small clearing of the dancefloor: beach-hat with lurid dyed feathers, red-polka-dotted loose-sleeved blouse tied at her stomach. . . . Dark body gleaming, thin and sinewy, she twists, grinds—lips parted, teeth gnashed. In convulsed, savagely rhythmic movements, accompanied by guttural groans, she writhes the reptile's body. . . .More than a dance, it has been a demand for Recognition of her mutilated sex.

I look at the man, and his eyes are staring down at the table.

Face shiny with perspiration, eyes almost demented: wide-blackcentered—the queen removes her hat and passes it along the crowd, collecting money . . . subtly choosing those from whom she will *demand* recognition—and she is carrying it all off Triumphantly: her woman-act so exaggerated, so distorted, so uncompromisingly brutal in its implied judgment, that this crowd [is] hypnotized by her.

(pp. 247–248)

Of course the queen chooses to demand recognition from the closeted married man, and Rechy maintains the tension of the stare between queen and closet case for three more pages. As in this scene, the narrator's hustling is superficially about money but really about a demand for "recognition," by means of an orchestration of extravagantly gendered signs, in his case of masculinity, and in the queen's case of femininity. The "implied judgment" is double: the queen judges that she and the gay-but-straight-appearing audience share a "mutilated sex," only that she is more honest in flaunting it. The text has underlined the confrontation of straight and queer, masculine and effeminate. Also there, but *not* underlined, is the Anglo-Latin confrontation which the Chicano narrator seems compelled to present as such, with the African-rhythmic music and the queen's stereotypically Carmen Miranda dress, but equally compelled to forgo comment on. Miss Destiny at the beginning of the book and Chi-Chi at the end are given their own chapters, but this unnamed Latin queen presents her demand to the equally anonymous Someone without receiving a chapter for herself and is all the more unsettling for that unofficial status.

FURTHER EXPLORATIONS INTO THE NIGHT: RECHY'S NOVELS, 1967–1979

City of Night was a financial and, for the most part, critical success (the cadre of transgressive fiction writers of the day—Vidal, Mailer, Baldwin—praised it, although Rechy never forgave gay novelist Alfred Chester for a venomous review in *The New York Review of Books,* titled "Fruit Salad"). *Numbers* (1967) could easily be seen as the novel's sequel. A character much like Miss Destiny comes up to Johnny Rio and remarks about the publicity Pershing Square has received from the book, and no-college, no-literary-ambition Johnny takes time off from his obsessive cruising of Griffith Park to dine with a group of gay novelists and their lovers (based on evenings Rechy spent with Christopher Isherwood), who discuss, among other things, novels based on fact and Sontag's essays on camp. These self-referential gestures break up a text that is otherwise organized around the documenting and questioning of obsessive-compulsive behavior.

Johnny, now prosperous in El Paso, returns to Los Angeles, where he used to hustle, and gets quickly drawn into the cruising scene of Griffith Park. From the novel's beginning, where Johnny counts the dead birds on the highway and the moths that splat on his windshield in Phoenix, repetition is associated with counting (reps in body-building, rosary beads used in one's childhood, and the priest in the confessional asking how many times you'd committed a sin) and with death. Even though many of the encounters are described quite vividly, they too are reduced to "numbers" (the phrase '60s queens used to describe a handsome man, "That's a cute number," also appears throughout). Johnny's superstitious behavior is also related to death or loss of control. He is soothed by the constant presence of an old black preacher woman who repeats, "We all doomed" (p. 39), and he is anxious on the days he cannot find her; he gives private names to parts of the park, claims that he is participating in a ritual, and returns to the toilets in the Park's Observatory regularly to look at himself in the mirror; and eventually, he is so horrified by his inability to stop cruising in the Park that he superstitiously decides that he has to make it with thirty men before he leaves to return to El Paso. His counting begins in earnest, and he makes his quota in time to return to the house of the older gay novelist friend. One of the other guests, an actor obsessed by Johnny's tales of cruising, abandons his own lover to have sex with Johnny. While it seems at first that this proves that Johnny has moved on from cruising to making it—in Johnny's own words earlier that night—"only with people with identity—men *or* women—people I know, not people without names—not just 'numbers'" (*City of Night,* p. 235), Johnny nevertheless returns to the park the next day. The legitimacy of sexual desire and the search for pleasure, despite its meaninglessness, is affirmed at the end, much as the Rechy character refuses to renounce hustling in favor of relationships at the end of *City of Night*.

If there is a *literary* problem with the portrayal of hustling as an affirmation of the value of meaningless pleasure, it is that such a pursuit does not support a narrative (beyond the pleasures of pornography: the same Grove Press that published Rechy was also publishing translations of the works of Sade, a comparison to which this essay will return). The four books that follow *Numbers* are generically quite different from each other and arguably could stand as four different attempts by Rechy to write himself out of the corner that the sporadic, barely narrative act of anonymous cruising could afford him. The first three are novels; the fourth, as it says in the subtitle, is "a documentary."

The first of the novels published, *This Day's Death* (1969), is the most autobiographical and was repudiated in an essayistic part of *The Sexual Outlaw* as well as in Rechy's 1995 interview with Debra Castillo. The novel's protagonist's mother is suffering from increasingly graver bouts of an undefined illness in El Paso, while he must keep returning to Los Angeles to stand trial for an arrest for public sex in Griffith Park. Jim Girard has led a basically heterosexual life up until the arrest, but the character is clearly Rechy once again, and there is absolutely no distance between the arrest in the novel and Rechy's own arrest in the park—at least as Rechy recounts it in *The Sexual Outlaw* and again to Casillo. Rechy presumably repudiated the novel because Girard's hostility toward his mother's illness is too unpleasant for him to reread, given that Rechy's mother died so soon afterwards, in 1970. In the same interview in which he repudiates the book, however, Rechy draws attention to his inventive portrait of the Mexican woman who appears on their doorstep to be a companion for Mrs. Girard.

Lucía, a small Mexican woman in her forties, is at first evaluated by Girard for her potential in the unspoken three-sided war between himself,

his mother, and his mother's illness, yet Lucía is just too strange to be considered merely a pawn. She appears dressed in "an unconscious parody of modishness . . . a child playing adult; but: a crazy child, playing too realistically" (*This Day's Death*, pp. 87–88). As a Mexican woman, Lucía apparently can have a relationship to death that Jim cannot, especially because she is crazy: "'I cried in my mother's womb. . . . If a child cries in its mother's womb, it can feel things others can't,' she reminds him of the Mexican superstition" (p. 90). The triangulated war of mother, son, and illness is now joined by a "Mexican" acceptance of death and of superstition: "And when I was a child, they took me to kiss a dying man, so he would go easily, without pain, into death" (p. 90). All this within ten minutes of her arrival into the house. Overly made up, fond of shiny trinkets, with a pathetic nomadic past that includes a stint as a naïve scab during a farmworkers' strike, and given to brilliantly poetic non sequiturs, Lucía provides the theatricality in the novel's domestic scenes that complements the nontheatrical dramatic conflict between tired mother and frustrated son, and she provides the Gothic element to contrast with the documentary element of the scenes in the Los Angeles courtroom and Griffith Park: "She continued to make up prayers: 'One in the sacred house . . . the fifth house . . . The shadow of the cross on Calvary. . . . Jesus passed through here too, weighted by his heavy cross. . . . My own Calvary—but here there's a tree like the Garden of Eden—though even the Garden of Eden was invaded by a snake,' she said" (p. 158). The imagery of Lucía's broodings obliquely echoes the imagery of the entrapping police in Griffith Park. Yet Lucía also has fits of depression and irrational behavior; nevertheless, she keeps herself together until Jim's business in Los Angeles is resolved, and, unwilling to burden her new family with her old madness, leaves in the middle of the night on the novel's next-to-last page: "Finally had she felt outside? She seemed at that moment to be one of those people doomed never to feel—to know—she's loved" (pp. 252–253). Lucía's departure returns the novel to the mother-son relationship in its isolation, a claustrophobic situation in which strategies for coping with mortality—Jim's own and his mother's—must be internalized, not externalized in the tenderly grotesque incarnation of a Chicano's Mexican background.

Every gay man should write at least one baroque-decadent-camp book; Rechy published *The Vampires* in 1971, inspired, he says, by a visit in the late 1950s to a mansion on an island of a rich man with a convoluted erotic past who invited him there after reading the early chapters of what would become *City of Night*. Some of the mind games played in the novel are related to experiences Rechy later had with a psychoanalyst acquaintance who never demonstrated that he actually desired Rechy. (Throughout his career Rechy parlayed his nonfiction-like style and his erotic thematics into a blurring of the author-reader relationship with the hustler-client relationship: he offers us an image of what we desire, and we pay for it. And in practice some of his early readers actually became, or wanted to become, his clients.) *The Vampires* has a gaudy cast of twenty-seven characters, organized around two demoniacal characters, the mansion's owner, Richard, and an ageless bejeweled woman, Malissa. Both of them stage psychodramas in order to corrupt innocence. Richard has corrupted the innocence of his three ex-wives and ex-mistress, and his two sons and his illegitimate twins are on hand, too; Malissa brings an entourage of a masochistic older man, a body builder, a drag queen in mourning, a hustler, and a circus midget. A lesbian with a bullwhip, a beautiful woman famed for her virginity, a young priest, and a hustler with his own brand of rubbers also appear among the guests. Rechy likes to claim that he was influenced by Poe and by the old Sunday comic strip *Terry and the Pirates,* and the novel's broad characterization and melodrama have much of the energy and lurid colors of a good comic book.

As with other writers of decadence in overly conventional societies, such as Laclos and at times Balzac, the social world is considered a battlefield, and much time is spent in tracking the shifting alliances. At times the ex-wives and mistress (and the lesbian with the bullwhip) form an alliance against Richard, yet at times each ex-wife also betrays the others to be loyal to the fleeting happiness she felt with him; likewise, at times Malissa's entourage jockey against each other for her favor, yet at other times they try to goad each other to get some independence from her. Sometimes Richard and his gorgeous, sexually initiated fourteen-year-old son seem to be competing with each other; other times they are clearly in cahoots. Richard proposes two games to the guests, first, a game of confessions, and then a series of improvised theater scenes in which "the blind queen seeks the prince that will return to her her sight" (p. 216). Rechy seems quite fond of most of his female characters—although none of the queens gets her prince. The difference between Malissa and Richard as corrupters, however, is that Malissa enjoys cruelty for its own sake and corrupts purity for the pleasure of it. Richard, it turns out near the end, feels saddened and melancholy every time his victims succumb to his traps and prove to have only had an illusory purity or to have lost their innocence. While it would be hard to argue that the novel treats these themes profoundly, Rechy does indeed employ the Gothic trick of expressing ambivalence through double characters (Richard and Malissa) to examine the relationship between desire, cruelty, and the meaning (or meaninglessness) of the universe. These themes were rediscovered in Sade by French philosophers in the 1960s and can be seen as constants in his work since the appearance of "Neal" in the S&M chapter of *City of Night*. Still, it would probably be incorrect to attribute French or philosophical roots to *The Vampires*. We might, however, consider Ilan Stavans's praise of *rascuache*, a garish kitschiness characteristic of U.S.-Mexican border culture, in his *Riddle of Cantinflas.* Though cut off from its populist Latino roots, *The Vampires* is nevertheless potentially a variation on the *rascuache* aesthetic.

Surely it is no accident that in all three of Rechy's novels of this intermediate period the theme of confession figures prominently (and is visible but subordinated in the first two novels as well). Everything that Michel Foucault said in his introduction to *The History of Sexuality* about internalizing Counter-Reformation Catholic invocations to confess, and the way that sexuality (especially homosexuality) has become *the* key to one's identity in post-Enlightenment modernity, seems to be absolutely true for Rechy's novels in this period. Confession is a recurring motif in *The Fourth Angel* (1972), in which sixteen-year-old Jerry is recruited by three other alienated teens who assuage their boredom together and, egged on by their girl leader Shell, attempt to harden themselves so that they will never cry again. Jerry, like Rechy himself, is mourning the recent loss of his mother and has locked the door of her room and preserved it as a sort of shrine. As in *The Vampires,* then, the hustler pose of desirelessness is as likely to be claimed by a female character as by a male character, and while tripping on acid or mescaline Shell is as much returned to the unbounded—if illusory—camaraderie and joy of childhood as the boys are. As in *The Vampires,* the novel's early scenes involve confessions and interrogations, the teens interrogating first each other and then a gay man they lure from a nearby bar; Jerry is appalled by their cruelty but often joins in their violence. The characters are constantly strategizing, forming alliances of two against two or three against one. The two other boys are a tall, thin, dark-haired white boy named Cob, who challenges Shell unsuccessfully for the leadership of the group and sees Jerry as a rival for Shell, and a Chicano named Manny, well-meaning but easily confused. All four characters have secrets connected to their parents, or their sexuality, or both, just as Foucault would have predicted, and

the novel seems reminiscent of earlier adolescent protest stories like the film *Rebel without a Cause,* and later ones such as *Less Than Zero* and *Kids.* However, this novel also tries to reconcile the language of existential loneliness in Rechy, his repudiation of the Catholic God, and the meaninglessness of the universe with the promise of utopia, community, and Escape (always capitalized in these three novels) characteristic of drug trips and the hippie revolution. Jerry has first a good acid trip and then a bad acid trip, and the hope that he gets from the first trip ("even the severed branch can grow new roots" [p. 87]) is dashed by the paranoia and emptiness he experiences in the second trip. It is the combination of the two that gives him the strength to return to his house and open the locked empty room where his mother died.

Two of these three novels are quite clearly fictional; the spacey symbolism around Miss Lucía in *This Day's Death* also adds an air of fictitiousness to that otherwise mostly nonfictional tale. Rechy's 1977 *The Sexual Outlaw: A Documentary* aspires, obviously, to be treated as nonfiction, and the minute-by-minute chronicle of a sex cruiser's weekend is interrupted by mini-essays, interviews, and other nonfictional devices. This is Rechy's first chance to weigh in on the changes in the gay community since the 1969 Stonewall riots in New York birthed the contemporary gay rights movement, and there are passing allusions to gay pride parades and the radical years of the Gay Liberation Front giving way to more middle-class institutions like *The Advocate,* as well as a familiarity with phrases like "coming out of the closet." The Rechy character no longer expresses interest in sex with women, and will reciprocate intimately with attractive men in pretty much any way short of being penetrated anally. Its most dramatic episode is his recounting of the "cleaning up" of the gay part of Griffith Park by a massive police action (documented in the nonfiction parts of the novel as occurring in 1973); the vice squad was airbrushed out of *Numbers* but figured promi-nently in *This Day's*

Death. Since *The Sexual Outlaw* emphasizes the outlaw status of all homosexuals, but especially of those having consensual public sex, it naturally emphasizes the continued presence of the law in gay life.

When translated into English, Foucault's *The History of Sexuality* called positions like Rechy's "the repressive hypothesis," meaning Rechy thinks that desire is natural, or that one's sexuality is at any rate an outcome of family dynamics, and that the only way the larger society affects it is in its attempts to repress it. At best, homosexuality under a regime of repression produces defiance, and the rhetoric of *The Sexual Outlaw* gets quite inflammatory at times. From the beginning, the language describing cruising invokes a military crusade: "You have an untested insurrectionary power that can bring down the straight world. . . . Promiscuity, like the priesthood, involves total commitment and sacrifice" (*The Sexual Outlaw,* pp. 31–32). And while much of Rechy's pre-AIDS boosterism could be considered unfortunate, queer theorists of public sex like Michael Warner (*The Trouble with Normal,* 2000) are in total agreement with the end of the section "The Gay Threat":

An acceptance of homosexuality—including, importantly, its tendency towards promiscuity—would result in a traumatic questioning of what, in the extreme, becomes oppressive in the heterosexual norm.

Why one wife? One husband? Why not lovers?

Why marriage?

Why sex with only one person?

Why *not* open sex? (Even the mere knowledge of it threatens, since gay promiscuity is invisible to all but the participants and the voyeuristic cops.)

Why *only* relationships?

Why, necessarily, children?

The heterosexual would thus be questioning, not heterosexuality itself, but the stagnant conformity of much of his tribal society.

(*The Sexual Outlaw,* pp. 205–206)

Rechy's demands for freedom are not couched in Foucaultian language, but they are consonant with much of Foucault's hopes.

However, the corollary of the repressive hypothesis, especially in the Freudian version, is a belief that society's univocal hatred of the homosexual is often internalized as self-hatred. This may or may not be so, but Rechy is so convinced of it that it becomes the only explanation he accepts for sadomasochism, the phenomenon that shadows his displays of masculinity and 1970s gay liberation. The energy of the last third of *The Sexual Outlaw,* when he turns from lecturing the straight community to lecturing his own, is focused in a full-barrel attack on S&M. Of course it should be as legal as any other consensual sexual behavior, he insists (and he describes in outraged detail the time and money spent on busting a gay bathhouse's "slave auction" in April 1976), but he nevertheless believes that it is an expression of self-hatred, especially in its imitation of the police, in a way unlike, say, hustling, cruising, or transvestism. Generous toward drag queens and honest about his own vanity, narcissism, and the limits of his sexual pursuits, Rechy seems to think that he has experienced sadomasochism from the inside because he has been tempted into playing the sadist's role from time to time and judges the scene from that level of experience alone.

Yet *The Sexual Outlaw* is most honest, in the tragic-existential mode of his previous books, in emphasizing that his "outlaw" stance is accompanied by a "saboteur" (pp. 47, 71) who reminds the audience that even successful evenings of cruising do not assuage the fear of aging, the panic of rejection, or the meaninglessness of human experience. The chronicle ends when the Rechy character, nauseated by the orgy he thought he would enjoy and then misjudging various hustling and cruising opportunities —including constant offers of heavy sex—sees the hated dawn arise and hears the sounds of the straight workaday world.

Rechy seems to be aware that there was still more to be said, and said in narrative terms, about leather sex and the cult of masculinity, as he closes the cycle of his "hustler pose" fiction with his 1979 novel *Rushes,* which recounts a single evening in a hard-core sex-and-cruising bar. Here his dissatisfaction with the directions that gay culture has taken in the 1970s coincides with his awareness that he has gotten too old for this particular scene: although he cheats, as who of us would not, by making his protagonist Endore some ten years younger than Rechy's forty-eight, an unattractive friend, Don, broods about his age throughout the novel. The novel coordinates, with some success, allusions to the Catholic mass (Tom-of-Finland-like pornographic cartoons on the wall function like the Stations of the Cross; the leatherman character Chas proposes a "baptism" of the first-timer Robert) with the evening's plot and characters. Endore, a well-known columnist for a gay newspaper, is at the heavy-sex bar Rushes with leatherman Chas—who celebrates the macho, femme-hating milieu—and their friends Don and the younger Bill. Although there are no longer any vice squads ruining New York's bars, there is violence in the air, as queer-bashers drive through the meat-packing district's streets regularly. The bar is invaded by other types: two rich slumming intellectuals, Martin and (gasp! a woman!) Lyndy, and then by two prostitutes, one a black woman and one in drag as Rechy underlines the gynophobia as well as the racism of the New York gay community of the late 1970s. Hovering outside is Tim, a hustler and sometime gay-basher, and the brother of first-timer Robert. Hovering within the bar is the man that Endore is considering as the best candidate for a long-term lover, a recent conquest named Michael. Will Endore make the effort to try to win Michael back? Will he try to compete with leatherman Chas for first-timer Robert? What do Robert's attractions tell us about the future of the gay community? Following a pattern we have seen in Rechy's previous novels, Endore rejects both the long-term love and the innocent love, loves that he nevertheless approves of, and ends the evening in The Rack, the hardcore sex club next to the Rushes (even Lyndy's connections cannot get her into there), where crucifixion rituals fulfill the Catholic

imagery lying beneath the novel. Endore repeats the characterization of S&M sex as self-hatred, and the man crucified becomes both himself and Chas, with Endore becoming both the one who whips and the one who is whipped, while Robert—or someone who looks like Robert—is murdered outside the bar by gay-bashers.

STOPPING THE CLOCK IN LOS ANGELES: *BODIES AND SOULS* AND *THE COMING OF THE NIGHT*

In some important sense, time seems to stop for Rechy's oeuvre here, in the late decadent summers. Although Endore does not choose to pursue Michael, Rechy himself decides on a long-term lover at this time, and three of his extended narratives of the next twenty years, *Bodies and Souls* (1983), *Marilyn's Daughter* (1988), and *The Coming of the Night* (1999), all return to this last moment before the awareness of AIDS, although each for different reasons. *Bodies and Souls* had difficulties in being published; *Marilyn's Daughter* has as its protagonist an eighteen-year-old girl who, she is led to believe, might be Marilyn Monroe's illegitimate daughter, hence born in 1962. Only *The Coming of the Night* fully admits its historical status, although only towards its end, as shall be seen. Neither of the other novels from this period, *Amalia Gómez* and *Our Lady of Babylon,* have gay protagonists. In that sense all of Rechy's novels of the last twenty years turn away, each in its own way, from documenting the life of the gay community in the age of AIDS.

Instead, *Bodies and Souls* takes as its topic a different sort of community of loners and dreamers: the city of Los Angeles elevated to the protagonist of the novel through accumulated vignettes much like the ones Rechy employed to describe his "city of night." Rechy's decision to retire versions of himself as the main protagonist of his novels shifts the interaction of the Gothic and the documentary impulses in his writing for the rest of his career. Rechy sweated for three years over *Bodies and Souls,* which he feels was underrated at the time; one of the first moves he made upon winning the PEN-West Writer's Lifetime Award was to get a corrected and shipshape version of this novel back into print. The novel tries to bring melodrama into the structure of *City of Night* and the social dynamics of *The Fourth Angel.* Three teenagers are shown in a short first chapter spraying the freeways of Los Angeles with gunfire from a semiautomatic weapon, and, in chapters titled "Lost Angels," the novel tells of the ten days that brought them to this scene, with fourteen more chapters focused around individual denizens of Los Angeles, all converging on those same freeways. The structure is reminiscent of Robert Altman's film *Nashville* before it, and Paul Michael Anderson's film *Magnolia* after it (especially in the repeated theme of apocalypse); however, most of the individual chapters are told in somewhat experimental fashion and are not tightly interrelated among themselves. Also, the cinematic intertexts for the book are explicitly not recent films but rather the obsessive memories of old Hollywood movies held by two of the three teenagers, Lisa and Jesse.

The intent would seem to be to give a sociologically representative sample of Los Angeles life in order to define the city of lost angels, but Rechy is drawn to those Los Angelenos who brood about the topics he's always brooded about, to wit, bodies and souls, and the fourteen characters include a Chicano punk runaway, a porn actress, a body-building competitor, two young street hustlers, a gay Chippendale's dancer invited to preside over a charity "slave auction"—oh, and a handsome gay writing professor whose students adore him and whose colleagues envy him for his dramatic lectures mixing writing and existential philosophy. Rechy happily includes himself among the Los Angeleno narcissists searching for transcendence through the body, not despite it. The three teenagers, unfortunately, are not, in this author's opinion, sufficiently "embodied":

the two normal ones are refugees from middle America, picked up on their way to California in an indigo Cadillac by the obsessed and quiet Orin, who in effect forbids the trio from having sex. Like aimless tourists (indeed they keep bumping into the same husband and wife), the three of them see famous places in Los Angeles associated with death, while Orin slowly lets the others in on his goal of pledging fealty and his inheritance to a televangelist Sister Woman if she can prove that her apocalyptic language is a mark of true prophecy. The novel deliberately permits Sister Woman to fail, so that Orin's rifle turned on the freeway is a tragic accident, not a message from God.

The novel's move out of first-person perspective into a third-person perspective should have been a triumph of the documentary over the Gothic, but Rechy hates the forces of authority and conformity—here presented in a hanging judge who dominates his family, a court psychiatrist writing in officialese excusing a homicidal policeman, and a sexually voracious TV anchorwoman—and descends to satire and other nondocumentary tones of voice. Los Angelenos uninterested in bodies and souls and apocalypses do not appear on Rechy's radar in 1983; it is not surprising that his defense of the novel, in a 2001 preface, emphasizes that he has gone "beneath the maligned façades of characters often dismissed as 'stereotypes' (which, no matter how derided, do exist, thrillingly alive, often revealing themselves to be archetypes)" (*Bodies and Souls,* p. x). The refusal to distinguish between stereotypes and archetypes is, it could be argued, the way that a Gothic imagination convinces itself it is producing a documentary reality around the melodrama that it prefers. In the end, *Bodies and Souls* is closer to *The Vampires* than it is to *The Sexual Outlaw* or *City of Night,* but it should be interesting for that very reason, as an examination of how far realism can accommodate melodrama if it claims to be at the service of an ironic admission that God is dead and therefore everything literary is lawful.

Jumping ahead sixteen years later, in 1999 Rechy published *The Coming of the Night,* also about Los Angeles and told through a series of vignettes, also set in the very early 1980s, and stylistically and thematically differing not at all from *Rushes* and *Bodies and Souls.* On a single day in the summer of 1981 made feverish by Los Angeles's Santa Ana winds, a diverse group of stereotypical men pursue extreme sex, all ending up together in a West Hollywood abandoned park. The large cast includes a gorgeous youngster who wants to celebrate with hot, lusty sex and the leatherman who arranges the orgy for him in a shack near the park. Other determined cruisers include a suicidal gay porn star, a small-endowed body builder, and a black man frustrated by the compromises he makes with his white sex partners' racist desires. Some are almost inadvertent participants: a first-timer; a young man just dumped by his lover; an older opera queen; and a handsome young priest looking for a Latino hustler named Angel with the same naked Christ tattoo that the character Manny got at the beginning of *Bodies and Souls.* We also follow three gay-bashers (one of them Latino), and of course the Rechy character, "Clint," who remembers in flashbacks to New York the scenes of heavy leathersex temptation taken almost verbatim from *Rushes.* Clint and the leatherman repeat the standoff between Endore and Chas in *Rushes,* too, after they successfully fight off the gay-bashers with the help of the black man and, surprisingly, the opera queen (the characters with historical memories of oppression rescue the more innocent ones); Clint and the leatherman are also the only ones who have heard rumors about "a strange illness. Something mysterious, something new, something terrible" (p. 238). Clint nevertheless respects the young orgiast's need for extreme sex and has sex with him, then leaves. In a symbolic crucifixion that also supposedly prefigures the plague years to come, when the leatherman has even more extreme penetrative sex with the young man he accidentally causes so much bleeding that he too leaves in horror; then the priest arrives and finds his naked Christ clinging spread-eagled to the wall.

There is something to be said for the novel's orchestration of plot through a repeating series of vignettes throughout the day and especially for the novel's shifts of tone, not between documentary and Gothic (until the end), but between documentary and camp social satire. Until he arrives at the park, the porn star has spent the day filming a command performance in a rich man's mansion, giving Rechy the opportunity (somewhat anachronistically) to send up gay porn director Chi Chi La Rue and his entourage, Joey Stefano, Zak Spears, et al. Many of the characters who attain some level of heroism or self-awareness at the end of the book were treated ironically earlier on, especially through the scenarios playing out in their heads which are interrupted by rude realities. Nevertheless, as the book that was Rechy's only direct response to the devastating crisis of AIDS after sixteen years of writing novels that avoid the sex scenes and promiscuity he had so aggressively praised (with existentialist caveats) in the 1960s and 1970s, *The Coming of the Night* seems not only a disappointment but a significant one. It seems to say that the fatalism which he saw, but also endorsed, in gay cruising somehow caused time to stop in 1981, and that any activism, grieving, or new personality types that may have arisen in the intervening two decades did not evolve out of the emotions and activities that Rechy had been chronicling, and could not also understand the doomed appeal of sexual ecstasy in a time of plague.

VIRGIN, MOTHER, WHORE: RECHY'S FEMININE FICTIONS, 1988–1996

This is not at all to say that Rechy's novels of the 1980s and 1990s lack interest—far from it. The last of the three, *Our Lady of Babylon* (1996), is ambitious but on the whole bad. Set in eighteenth-century France and possessing a verbal tone Rechy never gets right, the novel is a series of conversations between a sympathetic Oprah-like interlocutor and a woman who claims to embody the essence of, and to have retained the memory of, all the women in myth and history who have been accused of whoring and blamed for the fall of mankind. Extremely brief inclusions of the story of Malinche and Xtabay contribute to the Lady's many narratives, but these two American stories do not shift the center of gravity from Greek mythology (especially the story of Jason and Medea) and most notably the Bible (Eve, Salomé, Mary Magdalene, and the Whore of Babylon from Revelations), in which Rechy's usual accusations against God the Father and his equivalence of free will with sexual desire figure prominently. Most heavy-handed when trying hardest to be light, the novel includes some tales that are revised in interesting ways—deliberate anachronisms are introduced into the relations between Jesus, Judas, and Mary Magdalene to compare their revolution with the sexual revolution of the 1960s, and the portrayal of Jesus's mother Mary in this context is especially delicate—but the general effect is of an author congratulating himself on being daring and trying to deflect all other criticism as conformist or prudish.

An earlier novel is much more successful in catching a certain kind of feminine voice, and also more successful in describing the effect of sex and fantasy in American history. *Marilyn's Daughter* (1988) is quite serious in its attempt to combine bildungsroman, glamour gossip, and psychodrama as it tells the tale of young Normalyn Morgan from Gibson, Texas, who has reason to believe that her real mother is Marilyn Monroe, and her real father possibly one of the Kennedy brothers. Normalyn travels to California to find out her true identity, constantly being manipulated by a variety of characters who parcel out information to her in glittering flashbacks. Normalyn has been brought up by (also Rechy's invention) Enid Morgan, one of Marilyn Monroe's oldest friends from their days in California orphanages

together; a variety of other Texas types are sketched in during the opening chapters, including the crusading young Latino lawyer Ted Gonzales who tries to atone for having at first participated in, but also then halted, a gang rape of Normalyn when she was sixteen. In California, Normalyn quickly comes upon an old woman in Long Beach who not only provides the first flashback into Marilyn Monroe's life, but also a sort of moral center for judging the other characters, insofar as she may be the same Alberta Holland who refused to testify against other Hollywood actors for their leftist connections during the red scares. Normalyn enters Los Angeles proper and ends up sharing an apartment with a black transsexual, Troja, who does a "black Marilyn" impersonation, and her aging body builder and cocaine-addicted boyfriend, Kirk. This will be her base of operations for most of the rest of the novel.

Perhaps unintentionally, the structure of the novel's relationships bears similarities with the psychodrama of *The Vampires*. The two-entourages there were organized around a purely evil female character and a tragically evil male character. The Malissa and Richard figures here are the once powerful gossip columnist Mildred Meadows and the once reputable journalist and liberal political consultant David Lange. They make their own contributions to the Marilyn Monroe story at significant moments but also send Normalyn to various other characters who fill in other parts of the story. Rechy's most sustained (melo)dramatic invention in this novel is a group of teenagers called the Dead Movie Stars, who have captured public attention by dressing up as dead movie stars and conducting autocratic "auditions" to add to their ranks in the decayed San Simeon mansion built by William Randolph Hearst. (*Citizen Kane* and its series of narrations about a famous dead man is a narrative intertext, as are *The Wizard of Oz* and the great multivoice narrative experiments of the nineteenth century, with Dickens and Emily Brontë named explicitly.) The leader of the Dead Movie Actors, a girl named Lady Star, tries to goad Normalyn into presenting herself as a candidate to "become" their Marilyn Monroe. Mildred Meadows has arranged for a different Monroe candidate to perform the most scandalous parts of Rechy's reconstruction of Monroe's life—her liaisons with John and then with Robert Kennedy—for the benefit of the Dead Movie Stars and Normalyn as part of the candidate's audition.

The candidate, Lady Star, and Meadows all play with Normalyn's mind mostly for the pleasure of exercising power for its own sake; David Lange is aiming to reconstruct the truth in order to expiate his own participation in the events that led to Marilyn's suicide. But there are plots behind plots, and here the genders reverse moral valences: Meadows was in those days herself being manipulated by J. Edgar Hoover (and possibly, the text suggests, by people who assassinated the Kennedys), and David is still being judged not just by Alberta Holland but by her lifelong friend Teresa del Pilar, a leftist refugee from the Spanish Civil War. Besides the Alberta-Teresa relationship, thrust quite far into the novel's historical background, we see much of the warm relationship between Marilyn and Enid. Rechy's portrayal of these female friendships is more Gothic than realistic, in the sense that they serve as doubles for each other (Enid literally disguises herself as Marilyn at strategic moments in the plot). Marilyn is constantly hounded by "the darkness within," memories of her mother's and grandmother's madness, and Enid and Marilyn try to exorcise this darkness in the orphanage by changing Norma Jeane's name to Marilyn. Indeed Marilyn's suicide is attributed not just to madness but also to a last-ditch attempt to safeguard her daughter from the scandal about to break on her and the Kennedys' heads. On learning of all these old scandals, Normalyn refuses to publicly accept the mantle of Marilyn's daughter, preferring to live her own life. David Lange commits suicide, and Normalyn, who has learned her identity and gained strength from the revela-tions and from her true friends, visits Marilyn Monroe's gravestone before getting on with her life and a handsome film student Michael she has met along the way.

1980 Los Angeles still seems like a very white city, especially in its obsession with recreating the Hollywood past. One of the Dead Movie Actors' real names is Rosa Mendoza, and some of the people Normalyn encounters on the street are Mexicans, but this story is not about them, and they can be excluded . . . or *almost* excluded. Ted Gonzales follows Normalyn to Los Angeles and offers himself to her after showing her his new workplace in East L.A., a model of progressive liberalism in its immigrant-rights law and political organizing. Ted Gonzales has taken on the mantle of the 1960s pursuit of justice, just as Marilyn (once married to Arthur Miller, remember) and her fellow orphan/actress Enid rebel against 1950s Hollywood conservatism and take on the mantle of Alberta and Teresa del Pilar's 1930s search for justice. Normalyn's in-ability fully to forgive Ted is, to this author's mind, a sort of inside allusion to Ted Kennedy's cowardice at Chappaquiddick, permanently disqualifying him from the presidency while not tarnishing the liberal ideals he continued to work for. And although Marilyn Monroe is hardly William Randolph Hearst in terms of her importance to the political currents of American history, Rechy, like Welles in *Citizen Kane,* is concerned with the relationship between celebrity and politics, between myth-making and truth-telling, and between poetic justice and social justice. One repeated aesthetic misjudg-ment in the novel is Rechy's recourse to an exclamation-heavy, mass-market, pulp-novel style in order to portray Normalyn's naïveté (a misstep reminiscent of the intolerable voice of Esther Summerson in Dickens's *Bleak House*) but also in order to re-create Marilyn's way of thinking, and in order to portray the Dead Movie Stars' performances of their idols. One can compare this project to the more successful rewriting of *The Wizard of Oz* in Geoff Ryman's *Was,* a novel that is far less dependent on plot and skullduggery and that incorporates the age of AIDS directly into the project. Rechy has frequently claimed that he uses stereotypes and stereotypical language because they exist in real life, but it also seems that he prefers the more exteriorized of the authors of the Great Tradition, such as Poe, Brontë, and Dickens, instead of the more subtle modernists like James and Conrad, out of a genuine preference for self-dramatization, let nuance be damned.

Of the three novels organized around a woman figure, the last one that this essay will examine is, in many ways, the most important, *The Miraculous Day of Amalia Gómez* (1991). If Latino/Catholic archetypes for women are limited to three, that of virgin, mother, and whore, Marilyn's daughter would seem to be the virgin, Our Lady of Babylon the whore, and Amalia Gómez, a twice-divorced maid and occasional sweatshop worker, raising two teenagers in the seedier part of Hollywood while mourning the death in prison of her eldest, would be the mother. The novel is told entirely from her point of view, as *Marilyn's Daughter* was told entirely from Normalyn's point of view, although the third-person narrator strategically inserts information that extends Amalia's point of view, often for significant dramatic effect. For instance, the first chapter ends with Amalia wondering exactly why she flirted with a stranger in the bar the night before:

> And that's why she said yes to him when he asked to join her, because—
>
> Because—
>
> Because he had given her a gardenia, the color of the pearl-white wedding dress she had never worn because at fifteen she had already aborted one child by a man who raped her and whom she was forced to marry.
>
> (*The Miraculous Day of Amalia Gómez*, p. 11)

Such a narrative tone indicates an omniscient narrator lurking just behind the character, hovering protectively, outraged at the horrible life that Amalia and women like her have had to endure.

Yet the motives of the omniscient narrator who accompanies Amalia shift over the course of the day. (And indeed, the ideas of the virgin, the mother, and the whore shift around in these three novels. Marilyn Monroe is simultaneously virgin and whore for her fans, and Rechy adds the idea that she is a loving mother separated from her child. Among other unjustly accused "whores," Our Lady of Babylon channels Medea, who murders her children.) As long as the novel's flashbacks remain in El Paso, the narration seems wholly sympathetic to Amalia, especially in the ways in which she is bullied by her own oppressive mother, Teresa, which are symbolized by the large statue of the Mater Dolorosa that Teresa insists upon (versus Amalia's own preference for Our Lady of Guadalupe). Yet step-by-step we are led to see the various levels of denial at work in Amalia's protestations, especially in the face of her constant need to confess: as an adolescent she found a defrocked priest who was willing to talk in such a way that she could convince herself that God would forgive divorcées. In church on her miraculous day she tries to get the priest to declare that she was not at fault (in one of the novel's few directly comic scenes, this priest elicits details from her in order to masturbate in the confessional booth), and she enters a pair of spiritualists' consultation room and pays them to change the first, negative opinions they have of the behavior to which she confesses.

The novel's flashbacks thicken and slow the first two-thirds of the novel; Rechy wants us to be with Amalia as she gets a generally positive view of the Aztlán movement and the zoot suit riots from older figures in the Los Angeles community, but he positions her more complexly between two other characters, Rosario and Milagros, during her sweatshop years. Rosario, who believes in trying to organize labor and who hides people from the *migra* (immigration police), is the more obviously sympathetic figure; but while at first Amalia and Rosario make fun of Milagros, who is apolitical and always chattering over the plots of Mexican soap operas or *telenovelas,* these very same *telenovelas* provide Amalia later with material with which to think over her situation, and Milagros turns out to be more of a friend to Rosario than Amalia had been led to believe. Nevertheless, one feels a generational difference between Rechy's ironic acceptance of such melodramatic and sexually conservative *telenovela* storytelling modes and the enthusiastic camp use of them in Ana Castillo's *So Far from God*—among other Latinas' rethinking of the romance genre—or the camp use of Hollywood scandal sheets in *Marilyn's Daughter.* Perhaps this is because Hollywood's 1950s sexual conservatism is so much more clearly outdated than the reigning stereotypes of Mexican American propriety. By the time the flashbacks become recollections of what happened the night before with the attractive man named Angel who claims to be a Nicaraguan refugee, the narrative technique is openly ironic, and we are encouraged to see Amalia's self-delusions clearly.

If emphasis is given here to the narrator's ability to criticize Amalia implicitly while still portraying her sympathetically, it is because otherwise stylistically the novel breaks little new ground for Rechy. Yet this in and of itself is surprising. The novel is unexpectedly successful at recreating "the Rechy character" as a mid-forties Mexican American divorced mother of three. Amalia too doubts God and engages in superstitious behavior while claiming that she isn't superstitious. She as well needs to defend herself, in her own mind and to her own mother, against charges of sexual misbehavior—in her case, self-induced abortion, divorce, and (the night before the day of the novel) allowing a man to seduce her away from her live-in lover and her ordinary habits. She also, on that night, discovers that the man she has gone home with has a degrading sexual scenario in mind (in which she is supposed to play the masochistic role, as opposed to all the Rechy heroes who are begged to play a sadist's role), and when she rejects him he criticizes her for being too old.

Rechy also plunders from his previous Los Angeles fiction to describe Amalia's family and milieu. Amalia's first son, Manny, is a rewriting, with very few details changed, of the first character vignette, "Manny," in *Bodies and Souls,* and the personality of that Manny is an expansion of the character of the same name in *The Fourth Angel.* In all these Manny characters, the rejection by the mother, although sometimes only temporary, fuels the son's bad behavior and self-destructive impulses. While Rechy's creation of Gloria, Amalia's daughter and a member of a girls' gang, is new, Amalia's other son, Juan, is gay and hustling on the same streets that Rechy himself did. Amalia's walk through the poor parts of Hollywood is reminiscent of the old black woman's walk through Watts in *Bodies and Souls,* and the same tourists who were the inadvertent catalysts for the apocalypse in *Bodies and Souls* have a cameo reappearance in this novel, too. What is new about Gloria and Juan, however, is that they are unashamed of their sexual promiscuity and their resorting to violence in order to defend themselves in the crack-infested turf wars and police harassment of late 1980s Los Angeles, and on the whole Rechy thinks that this is a good thing.

All flashbacks cleared away, the novel ends with crisp speed in a sudden confrontation between Amalia and her two children, and she is forced to face ugly truths about her live-in lover Raynaldo, Gloria, Juan, and most of all herself: after various shouts of *puta* (whore), *puto* (gay whore), and *maricón* (faggot) between the three family members, Gloria screams at her, "You have *not* been a good mother!" and the narrative continues, "Amalia's heart died" (p. 188). The novel does not end there, however. Rechy concludes the novel with a genuinely original scene for him: unlike the many recidivist male characters, who reach their anagnorises in the penultimate scene yet defiantly return to their transgressive behavior in the final scene, Amalia uses her desolation to throw her exploitative live-in lover out of the house. Then, still reeling from the psychodrama at home, she performs a heroic act of self-defense while staggering around one of Hollywood's shopping malls, an act that combines elements of Rosario's politics, Amalia's stubborn faith in the Virgin despite all, and a streak of self-protectiveness that had been beneath much of her seemingly *abnegada* (submissive) behavior, but which she can now accept as part of herself.

If *Our Lady of Babylon* is supposed to reveal that, on the mythic level, no whore is ever really a whore, and if *Marilyn's Daughter* is supposed to reveal that the virgin-whore could also have been a loving (if absentee) mother, then *The Miraculous Day of Amalia Gómez* reveals that with the right sort of intervention the long-suffering mother, who had to deny engaging in various "whorish" survival strategies, can turn the stereotypes of motherhood around without continuing to play the psychodrama games that her own mother used in order to cripple her. In this loving but ironic mode, Rechy finally makes an important critique of his documentary, confessional impulses by showing that strategies of denial can persist even for people who are repeatedly driven to confess. Rechy's only concession to his enduring taste for the Gothic is that these extreme (but not implausible) events should all happen to a single family in a single day.

CONCLUSION: CANONICAL LONER

Casillo's 2002 biography concludes that *City of Night* will probably remain Rechy's best-remembered contribution to American and gay literature. While one might agree, this leaves open the question—will *City of Night* also be recognized as a contribution to U.S. Latino fiction, or will that status only be awarded to *The Miraculous Day of Amalia Gómez*?

On the one hand, one would like to think that any of Rechy's novels could be considered Latino literature, and both Juan Bruce-Novoa and Ricardo Ortiz have decided to use Rechy's earlier gay novels for comparisons with

homosexuality in other Chicano fiction. Canonicity is not quite as elastic as other thought experiments, however. To treat, say, *Bodies and Souls,* which has some but not all gay characters, as a contribution to gay literature is simply easier than to treat *The Vampires,* with no Latino characters, as a contribution to Latino literature, although in its heterodox Catholicism and its ebullient cartoonish characterization it shares some aspects of U.S. Latino *rascuache* border-culture tackiness. Still, canons are actual practical matters of reading lists and library shelves, and who would teach *The Vampires* rather than *Amalia Gómez* in a course on Latino literature? Hopefully the first part of this essay has suggested how to present *City of Night,* at least, as a contribution to a course on Latino literature, including the ambivalence that the John Rechy of 1963 felt toward overlapping his double identity: he embodies *machista* hustler without ambiguity, yet the abject Latino queen has an unsettling power that is not fully reflected in the structure of the book's chapters.

More relevantly, it has been argued throughout that Rechy's contribution to the gay literary tradition, and to the Latino literary tradition, has in each case involved adapting pre-existing elements in the American literary canon: the Gothic, from Hawthorne and especially Poe; and the documentary or confessional, in American nonfiction genres like journalism and the Beat roman-à-clef, although there is no doubt a streak of American Protestantism underneath it as well. One can look toward France to see how homosexuality can be incorporated into these genres, how Jean Genet—more than Burroughs or Ginsberg—served as a model for Rechy's homosexualization of the (French-Canadian Catholic) Kerouac mode, and how Foucault's ideas on transgression and confession in sexuality describe what is at stake in their postures. To say that Rechy is an original, and that he portrayed himself as a loner, is not to say that he wrote alone, nor should he be read alone. His great theme of loneliness in the midst of the most physically intimate acts certainly can remind us of the paradoxes of a community or a canon of the excluded, and of belonging to two worlds at once, often affected by the same forces while only the affected is aware of them both at the same time. Rechy is central to the canon of mid-century American literature because, as a loner, he is central to the canon of mid-century gay literature. As a writer at that crossroads, he offers one of the many different ways to connect the canon of Latino literature to mid-century American literature, however ambivalent he, as a loner, would feel about that role.

Selected Bibliography

WORKS OF JOHN RECHY

NOVELS AND DOCUMENTARY NOVELS

City of Night. New York: Grove Press, 1963. The 1984 re-edition has a new foreword.

Numbers. New York: Grove Press, 1967.

This Day's Death. New York: Grove Press, 1969.

The Vampires. New York: Grove Press, 1971.

The Fourth Angel. New York: Viking, 1972. Grove Press reprint, 1983.

The Sexual Outlaw: A Documentary: A Non-Fiction Account, with Commentary, of Three Days and Nights in the Sexual Underground. New York: Grove Press, 1977. The 1984 re-edition has a new foreword.

Rushes. New York: Grove Press, 1979.

Bodies and Souls. New York: Carroll and Graf, 1983. The 2001 Grove Press edition has a new foreword.

Marilyn's Daughter. New York: Carroll and Graf, 1988.

The Miraculous Day of Amalia Gómez. New York: Arcade Publications, 1991. The 2001 Grove Press edition has a new foreword.

Our Lady of Babylon. New York: Arcade, 1996.

The Coming of the Night. New York: Grove Press, 1999.

The Life and Adventures of Lyle Clemens. New York: Grove Press, 2003.

PLAYS

Momma as She Became—Not as She Was. In *Collision Course.* Edward Parone, compiler. New York: Vintage Books, 1968.

Tigers Wild. A stage version of *The Fourth Angel.* Produced by Playhouse 91. New York City, October 1986. Also staged in Los Angeles under the name *The Fourth Angel.*

ARTICLES

"El Paso del Norte." *Evergeen Review* 2, no. 6 (1958): 127–140.

"Jim Crow Wears a Sombrero." *Nation* 20 (October 1960).

"No Mañanas for Today's Chicanos." *Saturday Review,* 14 (March 1970).

"On Being a Grove Press Author." *The Review of Contemporary Fiction,* 10, no. 3 (fall 1990): 137–142.

"El Paso del Norte—1991." *Review: Latin American Literature and Arts,* July–December 1991.

SECONDARY SOURCES

Almaguer, Tomás. "Chicano Men: A Cartography of Homosexual Identity and Behavior." In *The Lesbian and Gay Studies Reader.* Edited by Henry Abelove, Michèle Aina Barale, and David M. Halperin. New York: Routledge, 1993. Pp. 255–273.

Bredbeck, Gregory W. "John Rechy (1934–)." In *Contemporary Gay American Novelists: A Bio-Bibliographical Critical Sourcebook.* Edited by Emmanuel S. Nelson. Westport, Conn.: Greenwood. 1993. Pp. 340–351. According to Casillo, Rechy has only recently stopped lying about the year he was born, unless he is lying now.

Bruce-Novoa, Juan. "Homosexuality and the Chicano Novel." In *Homosexual Themes in Literary Studies.* Edited by Wayne R. Dynes and Stephen Donaldson. New York and London: Garland, 1992. Pp. 33–41. A reprint of a 1986 article, this essay compares Rechy with Villareal, Ortiz Taylor, Acosta, Salas, and Islas. One of the earliest essays I've seen to treat Rechy, fully conscious of the way his writing questions the canon, as a Chicano writer.

Casillo, Charles. *Outlaw: The Lives and Careers of John Rechy.* Los Angeles: Advocate Books, 2002. Very much an authorized biography by one of Rechy's former writing students. Despite the title, the theme of the book's analysis is narcissism, treated neutrally or even positively.

Castillo, Debra. "Interview: John Rechy." *Diacritics: A Review of Contemporary Criticism,* vol. 25, no. 1 (spring 1995): 113–212. Most of Rechy's opinions on sex are unchanged since his 1977 *Sexual Outlaw;* Rechy's answers about his Chicano heritage (in the context of *Amalia Gómez*) are therefore more interesting.

Foucault, Michel. *The History of Sexuality: An Introduction: Volume One.* Translated by Robert Hurley. New York: Pantheon Books, 1978 (orig., 1976).

Ortiz, Ricardo. "Sexuality Degree Zero: Pleasure and Power in the Novels of John Rechy, Arturo Islas, and Michael Nava." In *Critical Essays: Gay and Lesbian Writers of Color.* Edited by Emmanuel S. Nelson. New York: Haworth Press, 1993. Pp. 111–126. A crisp reading of Rechy's *Numbers* in the context of Roland Barthes's *The Pleasure of the Text*—the essay's further comparisons to other Latino writers in effect demonstrates how difficult it is to find common ground with Rechy.

Paz, Octavio. *The Labyrinth of Solitude: Life and Thought in Mexico.* Translated by Lysander Kemp. New York: Grove Press, 1962, c1961 (orig. 1949).

Pérez-Torres, Rafael. "The Ambiguous Outlaw: John Rechy and Complicitous Homo-textuality." In *Fictions of Masculinity: Crossing Cultures, Crossing Sexualities.* Edited by Peter F. Murphy. New York: New York University Press, 1994. Pp. 204–225. One of the few attempts to take the ideas of queer theory and apply them to Rechy's oeuvre (Ricardo Ortiz's essay on Jim Morrison and Rechy in Patricia Julianna Smith, ed., *The Queer Sixties,* would be another).

Stavans, Ilan. *The Riddle of Cantinflas: Essays on Hispanic Popular Culture.* Albuquerque: University of New Mexico Press, 1998.

Tomás Rivera
(1935–1984)

ISABEL VALIELA

Tomás Rivera, Chicano educator and writer, left a profound mark on the Chicano literary heritage. His many roles in life, as a migrant worker, novelist, poet, short-story writer, essayist, professor, and administrator, produced a deeply felt existence grounded in the Chicano collective experience. Tomás Rivera could have easily fit into a rags-to-riches success story, had he not remained, in his life and his work, passionately committed to the people with whom he shared his first twenty years: the Chicano migrant farmworker community and the wider Chicano population. The trajectory of his life from young farmworker to president of the University of California at Riverside is only the surface of a complex man who understood the importance of the individual search for community, and the need to express that search in the collective voice of the people. Even in his most intimate literary production, his poetry, his voice reflects the individual's longing to find meaning beyond himself. His poem "Another Me" reflects this essential characteristic of his outlook:

There must be
there has to be
another me.

For how would I know,
why would I want to know?

There must be
there has to be
another me

Our children
am I in them or
they in me?

I was the leaf
that I know.

(*The Searchers*, p. 42)

This poem is one example of Rivera's concept of the *other* in his creative process. In the introductory remarks of his essay "Chicano Literature: Fiesta of the Living," he explains: "For me the literary experience is one of total communion, an awesome awareness of the 'other,' of one's potential self. I have come to recognize my 'other' in Chicano literature" (*Tomás Rivera: The Complete Works*, p. 338). He finds his other in the collective experience of *la Raza Chicana*, but understands this search for communion as a characteristic of all literature. Rivera was a man in love with words and their power, and this led him to appreciate the universal qualities of literature:

When I began my formal education and learned to read, I saw man manifested in so many words and with such evocative imagery that I came to expect that miracles, heroics, love and all human experience could be contained in words. I have found this to be the case in Walt Whitman, Hemingway, Shakespeare, Azuela, Cela, in Sábato, Machado, Guillén, Lorca. Even in the worst writings I have found an exact, pure desire to transform what is isolated in the mind into an external form. To perceive what people have done through this process and to come to realize that one's own family group or clan is not represented in literature is a serious and saddening realization.

(*Tomás Rivera: The Complete Works*, pp. 338–339)

This lack of literary representation of the Chicano experience in the United States, particularly with regard to the life of migrant workers, convinced Rivera that it was up to him to contribute his literary talents toward a full, dignified, and humanized portrayal of his people.

Rivera's appreciation for world literature and his discovery of the need to give literary form to the Chicano experience fueled his creative activity and led to his involvement with the Chicano literary movement. He contributed as poet, novelist, short-story writer, and essayist. Many of his essays originated at conferences in literary circles. It is useful to notice the titles of these critical essays, because they reveal Rivera's main passions and preoccupations. His *Complete Works* contains "Into the Labyrinth: The Chicano in Literature"; "Chicano Literature: Fiesta of the Living"; "Remembering, Discovery and Volition"; "Critical Approaches to Chicano Literature and Its Dynamic Intimacy"; "On Chicano Literature"; "The Great Plains as Refuge in Chicano Literature"; "Chicano Literature: The Establishment of Community"; and "Richard Rodríguez's *Hunger of Memory* as Humanistic Antithesis." These essays contain some of the main themes that he will develop in his fiction and poetry: memory, the labyrinth, community, and the creative act of writing about, and recreating, the Chicano experience.

Tomás Rivera is best known for his only published novel, *. . . And the Earth Did Not Devour Him* (*. . . Y no se lo tragó la tierra*). It won the first Annual Quinto Sol Literary Award in 1970 and was subsequently published as a Quinto Sol Book in 1971. Rivera wrote the novel in Spanish, but it was published as a bilingual edition translated into English by Herminio Ríos C. in collaboration with the author and with the assistance of Octavio I. Romano V. The English title of this first edition was rendered as *. . . And the Earth Did Not Part*. Winning the first Quinto Sol Award marks a significant moment in the history of Chicano literature, one that echoes the social changes of the time and a growing self-consciousness and pride in the Chicano population of the Southwest. In 1987 Arte Público Press published a new bilingual edition translated into English by Evangelina Vigil-Piñón titled *. . . And the Earth Did Not Devour Him*. This work is now in its third edition and is quite faithful to the linguistic nuances of the original Spanish text. Rolando Hinojosa, Rivera's friend and collaborator, created another unique rendition of this novel, with the title of *This Migrant Earth: Rolando Hinojosa's Rendition in English of Tomás Rivera's . . . Y no se lo tragó la tierra*. This work respects the structure of Rivera's novel, but takes considerable linguistic liberties in the translation.

. . . And the Earth Did Not Devour Him is a coming-of-age novel about a young Chicano migrant worker from Texas, set during the 1940s and 1950s. It came out during the height of the Chicano movement of the 1960s and 1970s and is considered a landmark in Chicano literary history. It brought a strong and authentic voice to the growing list of young Chicano writers and has been appreciated by a widening audience. Many of the events narrated in the book are based on Rivera's own life as a migrant worker during his early years. In this novel he fulfills his objective of giving form and voice to the Chicano migrant worker's experience, recreating through literature a part of United States history that had been widely ignored. Riv-

era explains his conception of the novel, and the reasons for writing it:

In . . . *Tierra* . . . I wrote about the migrant worker in [the] ten year period [1945–1955]. . . . I began to see that my role . . . would be to document that period of time, but giving it some kind of spiritual strength or spiritual history. . . . I felt that I had to document the migrant worker para siempre [forever], para que no se olvidara ese espíritu tan fuerte de resistir y continuar under the worst of conditions [so that their spirit of resistance and willingness to endure should not be forgotten], because they were worse than slaves. El esclavo es una inversión [A slave is an investment] so you protect him to keep him working. A migrant worker? You owe him nothing. If he came to you, you gave him work and then you just told him to leave. No investment. If he got sick, you got rid of him; you didn't have to take care of him. It was bad, labor camps and all that.

(Bruce-Novoa, quoted in *Tomás Rivera: The Complete Works*, pp. 26, 429)

Rivera clearly saw that his task in writing this novel was to expose to the world the injustices faced by migrant workers, their hardships, and also the great spiritual strength they show in surviving and resisting defeat in life. It is no coincidence that his young protagonist has no name, since his experience encompasses the collective experience of his people.

LIFE, EDUCATION, AND PROFESSIONAL CAREER

Tomás Rivera was born in Crystal City, Texas, on 22 December 1935. Both branches of his family were deeply rooted in the Texas migrant work experience. His parents were Florencio Rivera Martínez and Josefa Hernández Gutiérrez; both had migrated to Texas from Mexico as children. His father was ten years old when his family, fleeing the turbulence of the Mexican Revolution, moved to northern Mexico, and from there moved to Texas five years later. In Texas, Florencio worked on the railroad, an occupation that led to other moves to California, the midwest, and west Texas. He married Josefa after the two met in Crystal City, Texas. Josefa's father, Apolonio Hernández, had been an officer in the Mexican army and a union organizer in the mines of Northern Mexico. Fleeing reprisals for these activities, he had settled in Crystal City. He had realized that the agricultural work in his area was not sufficient to sustain his family, and soon had begun his migrant labor experience. Apolonio took his family to California, the Midwest, and back to Crystal City, a pattern of life he would follow until his death.

Tomás spent his formative years sharing this migratory existence with his family and its surrounding community. In spite of the instability implied in the migrant life, there was a set cycle to their existence. The family would follow the migrant stream leaving Crystal City in mid-April, heading north to Michigan and Minnesota to look for farm work, and would return to Texas in the beginning of November. As a child, Rivera had to make up much of his schoolwork upon returning to Crystal City, since he was unable to attend school while on the road with his family. Rivera alternated between migrant work and school throughout his primary and secondary school years. He graduated from high school in 1954. Once he entered a junior college, he could only be with his family during the summer months. He received a B.S. in English education in 1958 from Southwest Texas State University. After this he taught English and Spanish at various high schools and eventually returned to Southwest Texas State to pursue a master's degree in education, which he completed in 1964. He began graduate studies again in 1966, receiving a Ph.D. in Spanish literature from the University of Oklahoma in 1969. This rapid transit through various degree programs preceded a similarly rapid professional ascent in higher education. He began as associate professor of Spanish at Sam Houston State University in 1969. In 1971 he became professor of Spanish and director of the Foreign Language Department at the University of Texas in San Antonio. Here he took his first administrative post in 1976 as vice president for administration. He became executive vice president of the University of Texas at El Paso in 1978. Only one year after this move, he went on to the University of California, Riverside, as Chancellor. He held this post for five years until his sudden death of a heart attack at the age of forty-eight, on 16 May 1984, in Fontana, California. He left behind his wife Concepción Garza and three children, Ileana, Irasema, and Javier.

TOMÁS RIVERA, WRITER

The speed with which Tomás Rivera moved from one professional position to another tells of a passion for the educational endeavor, both in the classroom and in the administrative offices. His literary and academic careers were simultaneous, and his demanding schedule as an educator and administrator limited his literary productivity. By the end of his life he had written one novel, . . . *And the Earth Did Not Devour Him,* seven short stories, a chapbook of poems called *Always and Other Poems,* thirteen additional unpublished poems, and eight critical essays. Some of his poems, and an essay on "Richard Rodriguez's *Hunger of Memory* as Humanistic Antithesis," were published posthumously. Julián Olivares, one of Rivera's best friends and a literary collaborator, edited most of his posthumous collections, including *The Harvest: Short Stories by Tomás Rivera* and *The Searchers,* a collection of Rivera's poetry. In 1992 *Tomás Rivera: The Complete Works* was published by Arte Público Press, under the editorial supervision of Olivares. At the time of his death, Rivera was working on a novel that was to be called *The People's Mansion (La casa grande del pueblo),* but attempts to find segments of this literary project were mostly unfruitful. Some of Rivera's short stories, such as "El Pete Fonseca," were originally intended to be included in . . . *And the Earth Did Not Devour Him,* but in the interest of aesthetic unity in structure and tone, were published

separately. "La cosecha" ("The Harvest") and "Zoo Island" were unpublished until they appeared in *The Harvest.* He also wrote other short stories such as "In Search of Borges," "The Salamanders," and "Inside the Window." This last story is the only one known to have been planned as part of *The People's Mansion (Tomás Rivera: The Complete Works,* Olivera, p. 28,).

THE VOICES OF MIGRANT FARMWORKERS

It is not possible to separate the name of this writer from the most prominent theme of his literary work: the Chicano migrant worker. The bulk of his literary production revolves around this figure. Rivera writes about what he knows, gathering literary resources from the well of personal experience. In his essay "The Great Plains as Refuge in Chicano Literature," he explains that "literature is a personal endeavor—whether you write it or read it" (*Tomás Rivera: The Complete Works,* p. 384). The authenticity with which he approached literature, coupled with his strong educational background in the literature of both the Hispanic and the English-speaking world, provided the substance and sensitivity that are the most perceptible mark one detects upon reading any of his work, be it his novel, short stories, poetry, or essays. All of his work is imbued with a remarkable charisma grounded in his unique combination of humble roots, broad literary knowledge, and genuine love of people. When he writes about the community of migrant workers, he excels both at authentically recreating their particular speech and manners and at illuminating their universal human qualities.

Rivera's knowledge of Chicano speech patterns, particularly those of the farmworkers with whom he grew up, coupled with his extensive knowledge of the oral tradition in literature, produced dialogues that are the markers of his literary style. Specifically, his knowledge of popular traditions in Spanish literature, as well as the Mexican tradition of *corridos* and other popular forms, complemented his writer's desire to reproduce the memory of his own people's experiences through a literary rendition of their oral expression. In both his poetry and prose, there is a strong and authentic oral voice that seems to speak directly from experience. Rivera gives new form to this experience by a process of recovery of memory. In his essay "Remembering, Discovery, and Volition," he traces the process by which he accomplishes this recovery. He writes:

> I will discuss remembering first. I refer to the method of narrating which the people used. That is to say, I recall what they remembered and the manner in which they told it. There was always a way of compressing and exciting the sensibilities with a minimum of words. New events were also being constantly added. Needless to say, this is what the oral tradition is all about. Although many of the workers were illiterate, the narrative system predominated. There was always someone who knew the traditional stories—*el gigante moro, el negrito güerín*, etc. Then there were always those who acted out movies, told about different parts of the world and about Aladdin and his magic lamp. An oral literature was, in this way, developed in migrant camps. . . . The past and the future were concretized . . . as inner sensitivity that can be learned through creative and imaginative sensibilities. Remembering, each time abetted by imagination, was able to project this inner sensitivity.
>
> (*Tomás Rivera: The Complete Works*, pp. 366–367)

A typical rendition of his oral style can be found in the many dialogues of . . . *And the Earth Did Not Devour Him*. In the vignette called "Los niños no se aguantaron" ["The Children Couldn't Wait"], the boss of a migrant camp shoots a child who is attempting to get water to drink. The narrator tells what happened, followed by a dialogue between unnamed migrant workers who were at the scene. The original Spanish narrative is included here to showcase the authenticity of Mexican speech:

> Lo que pensó hacer y lo que hizo fueron dos cosas. Le disparó un tiro para asustarlo; pero ya al apretar el gatillo vio al niño con el agujero en la cabeza. Ni saltó como los venados, sólo se quedó en el agua como un trapo sucio y el agua empezó a empaparse de sangre.
>
> —Dicen que el viejo casi se volvió loco.
>
> —Usted cree?
>
> —Sí, ya perdió el rancho. Le entró muy duro a la bebida. Y luego cuando lo juzgaron y que salió libre dicen que se dejó caer de un árbol porque quería matarse.
>
> —Pero no se mató, ¿verdad?
>
> —Pos no.
>
> —Ahí está.
>
> —No crea compadre, a mí se me hace que sí se volvió loco. Usted lo ha visto como anda ahora. Parece limosnero.
>
> —Sí, pero es que ya no tiene dinero.
>
> —Pos sí.
>
> (. . . *Y no se lo tragó la tierra*, pp. 10–11)

What he set out to do and what he did were two different things. He shot at him once to scare him but when he pulled the trigger he saw the boy with a hole in his head. And the child didn't even jump like a deer does. He just stayed in the water like a dirty rag and the water began to turn bloody.

> "They say that the old man almost went crazy."
>
> "You think so?"
>
> "Yes, he's already lost the ranch. He hit the bottle pretty hard. And then after they tried him and he got off free, they say he jumped off a tree 'cause he wanted to kill himself."
>
> "But he didn't kill himself, did he?"
>
> "Well, no."
>
> "Well, there you have it."
>
> "Well, I'll tell you, compadre, I think he did go crazy. You've seen the likes of him nowadays. He looks like a beggar."
>
> "Sure, but that's 'cause he doesn't have any more money."
>
> "Well . . . that's true."
>
> (. . . *And the Earth Did Not Devour Him*, pp. 86–87)

These dialogues represent what the witnesses to the events are thinking and discussing, revealing, in very few words exchanged, significant realities—for example, the reality of a justice system that exonerates someone for killing a migrant child whose only crime was to seek drinking water. The question of the killer's sanity is taken up as a factor in his downward spiraling life, only to be discarded by the explanatory reference to his lack of money. Rivera masterfully maneuvers the art of understatement, making the silences speak, such as the thoughtful final line: "Pos sí" ["Well . . . that's true"]. The overall effect is one of revealed contemplation, the thought processes and sensitivities of the people who experience these events. This dialogue illustrates Rivera's observation of the way people told stories, compressing them into a minimum of words, while at the same time creating a sense of heightened excitement stemming from the understated meanings that are communicated.

NARRATIVE TECHNIQUE

. . . And the Earth Did Not Devour Him is a showcase of Rivera's mastery of narrative devices. Not only does he endow his dialogues with authentic voices, but he also structures his narrative to show a multidimensional perspective, inclusive of the many collective voices that live in the fragmented memory of the protagonist. The effect is equivalent to the stream of consciousness in writers such as William Faulkner or James Joyce, but with a very distinctive Chicano voice. Interestingly, Faulkner and Joyce also felt a need to communicate through literature in the language of their own specific communities.

Rivera's novel has a complex narrative structure, with voices that are constantly switching. This enhances the collective character of the story. The short dialogues interjected into the protagonist's monologues represent memories that linger in his mind. These interjections present contrasting perspectives of the same situations. An example of this is found in the

vignette called "Primera comunión" ("First Communion"), when we see the protagonist struggling with his conscience because he had witnessed a couple making love in the laundromat. In this excerpt there is the narrative voice of the older protagonist remembering the incident followed by an internal monologue, in the present tense, of the same, but younger, protagonist struggling with his own conscience and not knowing what to do. This is followed by the older narrator remembering how he felt toward all the adults at his communion party, followed by a dialogue between the adults at the party, who are totally unaware of his turmoil and making comments about his behavior. The entire episode merits quoting because of the seamless manner in which these various narrative voices seem to weave into each other:

> Pero ya no me podía quitar de la cabeza lo que había visto. Pensé entonces que esos serían los pecados que hacíamos con las manos en el cuerpo. Pero no se me quitaba de la vista aquella mujer y aquel hombre en el piso. Cuando empezaron a venir los demás compañeros les iba a decir pero pensé mejor decirles después de que comulgaran. Me sentía más y más como que yo había cometido el pecado del cuerpo.
>
> —Ya ni modo. Pero no puedo decirles a los otros, si no van a pecar como yo. Mejor no voy a comulgar. Mejor no me confieso. No puedo ahora que sé, no puedo. Pero ¿Qué dirán mi papá y mi mamá si no comulgo, y mi padrino, ni modo de dejarlo plantado. Tengo que confesar lo que vi. Me dan ganas de ir otra vez. A lo mejor están en el piso todavía. Ni modo, voy a tener que echar mentiras. ¿A lo mejor se me olvida de aquí a cuando me confiese? ¿A lo mejor no vi nada? ¿Y que no hubiera visto nada?
>
> Recuerdo que cuando me fui a confesar y que me preguntó el padre por los pecados, le dije solamente que doscientos y de todos. Me quedé con el pecado de carne. Al regresar a casa con mi padrino se me hacía todo cambiado, como que estaba y no estaba en el mismo lugar. Todo me parecía más pequeño y menos importante. Cuando vi a papá y a mamá me los imaginé en el piso. Empecé a ver a todos los mayores como desnudos y ya se me

hacían las caras hasta torcidas y hasta los oía reir o gemir aunque ni se estuvieran riendo. Luego me imaginé al padre y a la monjita por el piso. Casi ni pude comer el pan dulce ni tomarme el chocolate y nomás acabé y recuerdo que salí corriendo de la casa. Parecía sentirme como que me ahogaba.

—Y éste qué tiene? ¡Qué atenciones!

—Ándele, déjelo, compadre, no se apure por mí, yo tengo los míos. Estos chicos, todo lo que piensan es en jugar todo el tiempo. Déjelo, que se divierta, hoy es su primera comunión.

—Sí, sí, compadre, si yo no digo que no jueguen. Pero tienen que aprender a ser más atentos. Tienen que tener más respeto a los grandes, a sus mayores, contimás a su padrino.

—No, pos, eso sí.

Recuerdo que me fui rumbo al monte. Levanté unas piedras y se las tiré a unos nopales. Luego quebré unas botellas. Me trepé a un árbol y allí me quedé mucho rato hasta que me cansé de pensar.

(. . . *Y no se lo tragó la tierra,* pp. 40–41)

I couldn't get my mind off of what I had seen. I realized then that maybe those were the sins that we committed with our hands. But I couldn't forget the sight of that woman and that man lying on the floor. When my friends started arriving I was going to tell them but then I thought it would be better to tell them after communion. More and more I was feeling like I was the one who had committed a sin of the flesh.

"There's nothing I can do now. But I can't tell the others 'cause they'll sin like me. I better not go to communion. Better that I don't go to confession. I can't now that I know, I can't. But what will Mom and Dad say if I don't go to communion? And my padrino, I can't leave him there waiting. I have to confess what I saw. I feel like going back. Maybe they're still there on the floor. No choice, I'm gonna have to lie. What if I forget it between now and confession? Maybe I didn't see anything? And if I hadn't seen anything?"

I remember that when I went to confess and the priest asked for my sins, all I told him was two-hundred and of all kinds. I did not confess the sin of the flesh.

On returning to the house with my godfather, everything seemed changed, like I was and yet wasn't in the same place. Everything seemed smaller and less important. When I saw my Dad and my Mother, I imagined them on the floor. I started seeing all of the grown-ups naked and their faces even looked distorted, and I could even hear them laughing and moaning, even though they weren't even laughing. Then I started imagining the priest and the nun on the floor. I couldn't hardly eat any of the sweet bread or drink the chocolate. As soon as I finished, I recall running out of the house. It felt like I couldn't breathe.

"So, what's the matter with him? Such manners!"

"Ah, compadre, let him be. You don't have to be concerned on my account. I have my own. These young ones, all they can think about is playing. Let him have a good time, it's the day of his first communion."

"Sure, compadre, I'm not saying they shouldn't play. But they have to learn to be more courteous. They have to show more respect toward adults, their elders, and all the more for their padrino."

"Ah, well, that's true."

I remember I headed toward the thicket. I picked up some rocks and threw them at the cactus. Then I broke some bottles. I climbed a tree and stayed there a long time until I got tired of thinking.

(. . . *And the Earth Did Not Devour Him,*
pp. 116–117)

All this narrative multiplicity transforms the narrative voice into a richly inhabited territory where we can look deeply into the lives of migrant workers. At the same time, we follow the individual child's consciousness through the interplay between his first-person narrative voice that remembers, the first-person present tense monologues as he lives the events of the "Lost Year," and the third-person narrative that oversees the events through much of the book. These narrative layers have the effect of merging the individual and collective identities, while at the same time involving the reader very deeply in the relationship of all the voices. Critic William Penn likens the effect of Rivera's multiple voices to a conversation in a parlor, where people come and go. He says, "Imagine that the parlor is the United States enduring all the pressures that 'border narratives' implies" ("A Whole Lot of Talking Going On," p. 190). Penn likens the experience of reading such scenes to overhearing the Mexican voice of resistance "as though we stood just outside the window of the parlor of Chicano cultural conversation" (p. 193). This excerpt from "Primera comunión" shows that Rivera was well aware of modern literary techniques and knew how to use them to reveal the multiple dimensions of relationship within the migrant farmworker community. But as Penn points out, it also opens a space for the unfolding of Chicano culture through a rich dialogue full of the nuances of daily life and the cultural elements that participate in it. Moreover, Rivera's technique of incorporating a narrator who remembers and relives scenes from the past also reveals that he had a profound knowledge of the workings of the mind, and the many ways in which memory reconstructs the significant events of the past. The reader, at the beginning of the novel, is just as disoriented as the protagonist, and because of Rivera's keen literary mastery of psychological processes, he is able to follow the adolescent through the labyrinth of his memory and make the same connections that eventually lead to his recovery from the "lost year."

SEARCHING, MEMORY, AND THE LABYRINTH

Searching is a theme that appears in much of Rivera's work, and its importance is evident in the titles of some of his poems. His epic poem is called "The Searchers," and a poem he wrote after visiting a class at middle school is called "Searching at Leal Middle School." In . . . *And the Earth Did Not Devour Him,* the theme is embedded in the experience of migrant workers, who are always on the move, searching for work and a better life. As explained by Julián Olivares in his introduction to *The Searchers*, a collection of Rivera's poetry, this theme can be interpreted on many levels. On a material level, it can simply be the search for economic improvement. On a social level, it can be the search for a place in society, a community that is identifiable and recognized by the larger society. It can also be the search for justice. On a spiritual level, it can be the search for the meaning of one's life. Rivera finds all of these levels of searching in the life of a migrant worker. Essentially, searching is linked to remembering; as Rivera states, "Anyone who seeks to discover his inner being by remembering will find the will to invent himself continually as desirous of loving all mankind" (*Tomás Rivera: The Complete Works,* p. 370). The same meaning is echoed in the final lines of his epic poem "The Searchers":

We were not alone
murmuring novenas,
los rosarios, each night,
los rosarios we hoped
would bring joy and lasting peace
for Kiko
killed and buried in Italy in 1943
or
when we gathered each night
before bed
and waited
for the nightly sound
of the familiar cough
and the sweet
pan dulce
that it brought
warm milk
pan dulce
opened the evening door
or
when we walked
all over Minnesota
looking for work
no one seemed to care
we did not expect them to care

We were not alone
after many centuries
How could we be alone

We searched together
We were seekers
We are searchers
and we will continue
to search
because our eyes
still have
the passion of prophecy.

(The Searchers, pp. 62–63)

Here past, present, and future are joined in the act of searching. More importantly, this temporal fusion speaks of human connectedness. Rivera finds the essence of human community in the repetition of the act of searching through the centuries. Instead of the isolated individual farmworker seeking work in a world that largely ignores him, Rivera presents the migrant worker experience in the plural "we," and adds that the same experience has been repeated through history, thus enhancing its collective quality. The use of the refrain "We are not alone" enhances even further the idea of carrying on an ancient tradition of searching. The passion of prophecy is in their eyes because they know their history, and this knowledge gives them the strength to go forward. Moreover, even though he speaks from the particular experience of the Chicano migrant worker, Rivera always points to the universal human essence of such experiences. In this poem, he achieves the inclusion of the Chicano experience in the universal human experience, contributing to the enrichment of the world's literary epic tradition.

In the same manner in which Rivera's theme of searching is linked to the process of remembering, the labyrinth weaves itself into the thematic tapestry of his works. Rivera sees the search as an act of discovery, and the existential plane through which one passes in this process of discovery is a labyrinth. Nowhere in his work is this more evident that in his novel, *. . . And the Earth Did Not Devour Him.* The young protagonist's path toward adulthood has all the tortuousness of a labyrinth. Rivera masterfully structures the novel into an achro-nologically ordered series of vignettes representing snatches of memory of the "Lost Year," all framed by the first and last segments, titled respectively "The Lost Year" and "Under the House," which take place in the protagonist's present moment, as he tries to gather in his memory the events of the past year. Within these bits of dialogues and memories representing various voices of fellow travelers and his own voice, the protagonist eventually manages to discover the source of his true identity: his community. While he is hiding under the house, thinking, he makes the following discovery:

—Quisiera ver a toda esa gente junta. Y luego si tuviera unos brazos bien grandes los podría abrazar a todos. Quisiera poder platicar con todos otra vez, pero que todos estuvieran juntos. Pero eso apenas en un sueño. Aquí sí que está suave porque puedo pensar en lo que yo quiera. Apenas estando uno solo puede juntar a todos. Yo creo que es lo que necesitaba más que todo. Necesitaba esconderme para poder comprender muchas cosas. De aquí en adelante todo lo que tengo que hacer es venirme aquí, en lo oscuro, y pensar en ellos. Y tengo tanto en que pensar y me faltan tantos años. Yo creo que hoy quería recordar este año pasado. Y es nomás uno. Tendré que venir aquí para recordar los demás.

(. . . Y no se lo tragó la tierra, p. 75)

I would like to see all of the people together. And then, if I had great big arms, I could embrace them all. I wish I could talk to all of them again, but all of them together. But that, only in a dream. I like it right here because I can think about anything I please. Only by being alone can you bring everybody together. That's what I needed to do, hide, so that I could come to understand a lot of things. . . . I think today what I wanted to do was recall this past year. And that's just one year. I'll have to come here to recall all of the other years.

(. . . And the Earth Did Not Devour Him, p. 151)

He realizes that in reality "se dio cuenta de que . . . no había perdido nada. Había encontrado. Encontrar y reencontrar y juntar" *(. . . Y no se lo tragó la tierra,* p. 75) ["he hadn't lost anything. He had made a discovery. To discover and rediscover and piece things together . . ." (. . . *And the Earth Did Not Devour Him*, p. 152)]. He comes out from under the house into the daylight, symbolically walking away from the dark labyrinth of the "Lost Year."

> Y le dio más gusto. Luego cuando llegó a la casa se fue al árbol que estaba en el solar. Se subió. En el horizonte encontró una palma y se imaginó que ahí estaba alguien trepado viéndolo a 'l. Y hasta levantó el brazo y lo movió para atrás y para adelante para que viera que él sabía que estaba allí.
>
> (. . . *Y no se lo tragó la tierra*, p. 75)

He was thrilled. When he got home he went straight to the tree that was in the yard. He climbed it. He saw a palm tree on the horizon. He imagined someone perched on top, gazing across at him. He even raised one arm and waved it back and forth so that the other could see that he knew he was there.

(. . . *And the Earth Did Not Devour Him*, p. 152)

This final scene echoes in imagery what Rivera says about the labyrinth in his essay "Into the Labyrinth: The Chicano in Literature":

> A labyrinth is a man-made maze for the purpose of testing and for the purpose of observing. Mainly, it is to observe if someone is capable of searching and finding his way to the center or the entrance. . . . For it is a vicarious notion of humanity, or man, to attempt to search for the other, "alter ego," in order to comprehend himself better.
>
> (*Tomás Rivera: The Complete Works*, p. 325).

When the protagonist of this novel discovers his other "self," he is ready to integrate socially with his community because he sees himself in it, here symbolically represented by a mirror image of himself waving from another tree. In his analysis of this scene, Julián Olivares attributes the appearance of this other youngster waving at him to the collective consciousness that he has just discovered within himself. It is at this point that he becomes one with his people

and he can begin to move away from his sense of isolation (*Tomás Rivera: The Complete Works*, p. 23).

HUNGER FOR COMMUNITY

In Rivera's essay "Chicano Literature 1970–1979: The Establishment of Community," he praises Rolando Hinojosa-Smith, a close friend and fellow Chicano writer, for defining community as "place, values, personal relationships, and conversation [*lugar, modales, relaciones personales, conversación*]" (*Tomás Rivera: The Complete Works*, p. 401). Indeed, these key words sum up Rivera's conceptualization of community in his literary work. The idea of community is explored in this essay, and reveals Rivera's deep preoccupation with this theme, particularly because he saw in Chicanos a need for community:

> Chicano literature as it began to flourish in the 50's and 60's revealed a basic hunger for community (*hambre por una comunidad*). Here was a group of kindred people forming a nation of sorts, loosely connected politically and economically and educationally but with strong ties and affinities through its folklore and popular wisdom. Also there were strong ties through varying degrees of understanding of its historical precedence and a strong tie because of language. Yet the political and social organizations of the Chicanos were weak within and existed within sophisticated North American and Mexican societies that really had not cared about the development of the group itself.
>
> (*Tomás Rivera: The Complete Works*, pp. 398–399)

Rivera's consciousness of the Chicano movement's need for community led him to write works that revealed how they struggled for a sense of community in the midst of mobility and exclusion from mainstream society. In his short story "Zoo Island," the children of a migrant camp decide to conduct a census of their camp's inhabitants, only to find out that there were more people there than in their town. As

José, the fifteen-year-old protagonist, goes around asking people if they can be counted, much is revealed about how they feel as a community. His father is resentful of the way white people drive by the farm where they are working and laugh at their humble living quarters, making them feel like monkeys in a zoo park. As the children count one by one the inhabitants of the camp, they begin to feel empowered by the positive comments of the adults. Even old don Simon, who has a reputation for violent behavior, commends the children: "Bueno, si vieran que me gusta lo que andan haciendo ustedes. Al contarse uno, uno empieza todo. Así sabe uno que no sólo está sino que es" (*The Harvest*, p. 57) ["Well, you know, I kinda like what ya'all are doing. By counting yourself, you begin everything. That way you know you're not only here but that you're alive." (p. 119)] It is the sense of belonging to an identifiable community that makes José shout for joy every morning when he sees the sign he put up at the farm gate: "Zoo Island, Pop. 88 1/2." The "1/2" indicates that one of the pregnant women in the camp has given birth. The simple act and process of counting has the effect of establishing a sense of community. We can come back to the key words that define community in Rivera's eyes: place, values, personal relationships, conversation.

THE CHILD'S EYE VIEW

Rivera often uses the child's eye view as a narrative device in order to imbue his work with a sense of discovery. He speaks about the child's perspective in his essay "Remembering, Discovery, Volition":

I deliberately use in my work young characters or children for the most part. There is no doubt that the greatest and purest discovery is that in which a child becomes aware of himself as a person. And what does a child appreciate most if not quality, logic, a realistic story told in the tradition which has been handed down throughout the centuries. A child is naturally inclined toward mysticism,

but at the same time, demands a consistent reality. Thus, the child in migrant work becomes aware of an inner sensitivity and a way of narrating, in his own language or dialect.
(*Tomás Rivera: The Complete Works*, p. 367)

Rivera sees the Chicano child as a vehicle for expressing universal concerns: the question of justice, purpose of life, suffering, and love. Nowhere is this more evident than in the protagonist of . . . *And the Earth Did Not Devour Him*, particularly when he challenges his mother's passive acceptance of life as it is:

— Ya me canso de pensar. ¿Por qué? ¿Por qué usted? ¿Por qué papá? ¿Por qué mi tío? ¿Por qué mi tía? ¿Por qué sus niños? ¿Dígame usted por qué? ¿Por qué nosotros nomás enterrados en la tierra como animales sin ningunas esperanzas de nada? Sabe que las únicas esperanzas son las de venir para acá cada año. Y como usted misma dice, hasta que se muere, descansa. Yo creo que así se sintieron mi tío y mi tía, y así se sentirá papá.

—Así es, m'ijo. Sólo la muerte nos trae el descanso a nosotros.

—Pero, ¿por qué a nosotros?

—Pues dicen que . . .

—No me diga nada. Ya sé lo que me va a decir—que los pobres van al cielo.
(. . . *Y no se lo tragó la tierra*, pp. 33–34)

"I'm so tired of thinking about it. Why? Why you? Why Dad? Why my uncle? Why my aunt? Why their kids? Tell me, Mother, why? Why us burrowed in the dirt like animals with no hope for anything? You know the only hope we have is coming out here every year. And like you yourself say, only death brings rest . . ."

"I think that's how it is m'hijo. Only death brings us rest."

"But why us?"

"Well, they say that . . ."

"Don't say it. I know what you are going to tell me—that the poor go to heaven."
(. . . *And the Earth Did Not Devour Him*, pp. 109–110)

This novel shows children as victims, along with the rest of the community of migrant workers.

435

However, unlike the adults who are resigned to their fate, the protagonist rebels against this fate with his insistent questioning. When the father becomes dangerously ill with sunstroke, it is the children who go out to the field to work. It is important to note the different attitude of the children in the field, as opposed to the adults. The children tell each other not to go on working if the sun gets too hot. While strategizing about how they are going to tackle the hottest hours of the day in the field, they say:

—Ahí nos va a tocar lo mero bueno del calor. Nomás toman bastante agua cada rato; no le hace que se enoje el viejo. No se vayan a enfermar. Y si ya no se aguantan me dicen luego luego ¿eh? Nos vamos para la casa. Ya vieron lo que le pasó a papá por andar aguantando. El sol se lo puede comer a uno.

(*. . . Y no se lo tragó la tierra,* p. 34)

That's where the hottest part of the day will catch us. Just drink plenty of water every little while. It don't matter if the boss gets mad. Just don't get sick. And if you can't go on, tell me right away, all right? We'll go home. Y'all saw what happened to Dad when he pushed himself too hard. The sun has no mercy, it can eat you alive.

(*. . . And the Earth Did Not Devour Him,* p. 110)

This scene is in sharp contrast to a previous scene in the field, where we see the adults talking with the children:

—Tengo mucha sed, papá. ¿Ya mero viene el viejo?

—Yo creo que sí. ¿Ya no te aguantas?

—Pos, no sé. Ya siento muy reseca la garganta. ¿Usted cree que ya mero viene? ¿Voy al tanque?

—No. Espérate un ratito más. Ya oíste lo que dijo.

(*. . . Y no se lo tragó la tierra,* p. 10)

"I'm very thirsty, Dad. Is the boss gonna be here soon?"

"I think so. You can't wait any longer?"

"Well, I don't know. My throat already feels real dry. Do you think he's almost gonna be here? Should I go to the tank?"

"No, wait just a little longer. You already heard what he said."

(*. . . And the Earth Did Not Devour Him,* p. 86)

The children are closer to the truth of situations, wanting to make sense out of life, and wanting their life to be sensible. In the preceding quote, the children need to drink water to quench their thirst, and their thirst is presented in the dialogue as an urgent reality. The parents, though sympathetic, are coerced into submission by the boss and forced to become the intermediaries between their children's needs and the boss's rules. In like manner, the protagonist's mother, a devout Catholic, is an intermediary between her son's need to know the answers to his questions and her religion's pressure to accept their state in life, promising heaven to the poor. In both cases, the children suffer the consequences of the oppressive environment at work, as well as those elements that are oppressive within their own culture.

EDUCATOR, WRITER, SEARCHER

The scope of Tomás Rivera's interests could be seen in the poem he wrote after visiting a middle school classroom where he met Chicano children. The poem, "Searching at Leal Middle School," reveals his love for the give-and-take of teacher and students, and of his enthusiasm for the educational as well as for the creative process. He describes the students in metonymic terms:

At first I saw only
the backs of black hair heads
Cabezas de pelo negro, negro era
Cabezas de pelo negro
brillante, de brillo, brillo era
and as
I went to the front of the room
to face them
I saw their limitless eyes
ojos sin límites
ojos oscuros

ojos sonrientes
juguetones
—¿Y éste?

We talked of thinking
of inventing ourselves
of love for others
of love to be
of searching
for ourselves

It was a good day for searching
Yet I became lost in my past
I saw myself and became
each one for an instant
and grasped for a second
the curious blink.

(*The Searchers*, pp. 67–68)

The code-switching from English to Spanish, which is more prevalent in his poetry than in his prose, here plays an important role in demonstrating Rivera's complex identity. Spanish establishes his connection to the students through ethnicity (dark hair and eyes), but also expresses a memory-triggering image of himself as a migrant child. Spanish is also the language he uses in engaging in conversation with the children—"¿Y éste?" This last question in Spanish indicates the playfulness of the exchange. It is equivalent to "And who is this?" and probably refers to one particular student that caught his attention. The English dominates the narrative voice of the poem ("We talked of thinking.") It is in this language that he communicates the ultimate significance of this encounter: discovering oneself in others. The overall effect of the poem is that it captures the uniqueness of both the external and internal qualities of this particular encounter, lending significance to what would otherwise be a routine visit to a middle school classroom. The capacity to lend significance to everyday human exchanges is vintage Tomás Rivera.

When Tomás Rivera died, it sent a ripple of shock and sadness through the southwest and through all Chicano circles. But his passing left a legacy of projects created in his name and promoting those objectives that were a significant part of his life. In the spring of 1985, the University of California, Riverside, General Library was renamed the "Tomás Rivera Library," and there his wife Concepción placed her husband's papers in a collection called the Tomás Rivera Archives (*Tomás Rivera, 1935–1984: The Man and his Work*, p. 150). He also inspired the Tomás Rivera Policy Institute, founded in 1985 to advance research and critical thinking on issues affecting the Latino community. His influence in education led to the creation of the Tomás Rivera Center, established to promote student success in the academic system. These are only some of the many projects founded after his death. But perhaps the most poignant reminders of what he meant to so many people were the poems and *corridos* written at the time of his death. The following lines from "Corrido de Tomás Rivera" by Héctor P. Márquez are a fitting ending for this essay about a man who was probably the most beloved Chicano of the twentieth century:

Día diez y seis de mayo
la gente se estremeció
pues llegó mala noticia
Tomás Rivera murió.

¿La tierra se lo tragó?
¡La tierra se lo ha tragado!
Sus hazañas vivirán
y nunca será olvidado.

Lejos de Texas andaba
distante su pueblo natal,
llora este pueblo que amaba
llora su madre cabal.

Mucho bien hizo este hombre
a quien tantos conocían
se lució primero en Texas
californios lo aplaudían.

Hizo mucho por su raza
buen maestro y profesor,

fue profesionista astuto,
líder, poeta, y asesor.

Fue primero entre los buenos
un ejemplo para todos,
puente entre los dos países
con los listos codo a codo.

¿Quién olvidará sus cuentos
de los niños quemaditos,
del pícaro Pete Fonseca
Laíto y Bone los malditos;

de los que quieren "llegar"
más no saben cómo y cuándo
del que perdió un año entero
del que al diablo anda buscando?

¿Quién olvidará sus versos,
versos del limón partido,
los que con su clara voz
cantó al público cumplido?

Siempre tuvo bien presente
su deber a la enseñanza
preparar a nuestra gente
sin perder esa esperanza.

La tierra se lo tragó
La tierra se lo ha tragado.
Sus hazañas vivirán
y nunca será olvidado.

(*Tomás Rivera, 1935–1984: The Man and His Work*,
p. 88)

On May sixteenth
the people were deeply moved
bad news had just arrived
Tomás Rivera died.

Did the earth swallow him?
The earth has swallowed him!
But his deeds will live on
and he'll never be forgotten.

He was far away from Texas
distant from his native town,

this town that loved him is crying
his mother cries as well.

Many a good deed was done by this man
who was known by so many
first he excelled in Texas
Californians applauded him.

He did a lot for his people
a good teacher and professor,
he was an astute professional,
leader, poet, and advisor.

He was first among the good
an example for all,
a bridge between the two countries
shoulder to shoulder with the brightest.

Who can forget his stories
of the children who were burned
of the scoundrel Pete Fonseca
Laíto and Bone, so wicked;

of the ones who want to "arrive"
but don't know how or when
of the one who lost an entire year
of the one who's searching for the devil.

Who can forget his poems
poems about a sliced lemon,
the ones that with his clear voice
he sang to a trusted audience?

He always kept in mind
his duty to education
to prepare our people
without losing any hope.

The earth swallowed him
The earth has swallowed him.
But his deeds will live on
and he'll never be forgotten.

This corrido and many others like it, plus numerous eulogies, letters, and poems written shortly after his death, are testimonies to Tomás Rivera's legacy of involvement with the Chicano community. The lives he touched have also expressed themselves in multiple ways, some artistically, some through social action. Rivera's great love for his people, which was the driving force behind all his endeavors, binds all these facets together to inspire others.

Selected Bibliography

WORKS OF TOMÁS RIVERA

NOVEL

. . . Y no se lo tragó la tierra / . . . And the Earth Did Not Devour Him. Translated by Evangelina Vigil-Piñón. Houston: Arte Público Press, 1995.

SHORT STORIES

The Harvest: Short Stories by Tomás Rivera. Edited by Julián Olivares. Bilingual edition. Houston: Arte Público Press, 1989.

POETRY

The Searchers: Collected Poetry. Edited by Julián Olivares. Houston: Arte Público Press, 1990.

COMPLETE WORKS

Tomás Rivera: The Complete Works. Edited by Julián Olivares. Houston: Arte Público Press, 1992.

FILM BASED ON HIS NOVEL

. . . And the Earth Did Not Swallow Him. Produced by Paul Espinosa. Written and directed by Severo Pérez. American Playhouse Theatrical Films presents a production of KPBS and Severo Pérez Films, 1997.

SECONDARY WORKS

CRITICAL AND BIOGRAPHICAL STUDIES

Bruce-Novoa, Juan. *Chicano Authors: Inquiry by Interview.* Austin: University of Texas Press, 1980.

Calderón, Héctor, and José David Saldívar, eds. *Criticism in the Borderlands: Studies in Chicano Literature, Culture, and Ideology.* Durham, N.C.: Duke University Press, 1991.

Davis-Undiano, Robert Con. "Chicanos Read Lacan: Tomás Rivera on 'Authorship.'" In *Literature and Psychology* 47, no. 4 (2001): 38–59.

Fredericksen, Brooke. "Cuandos lleguemos/When We Arrive: The Paradox of Migration in Tómas Rivera's '. . .Y no se lo tragó la tierra." In *Bilingual Review/La Revista Bilingüe* 19, no. 2 (May–August 1994): 142–150.

Hinojosa-Smith, Rolando. "On the 30th Anniversary of Tomás Rivera's *. . . Y no se lo tragó la tierra.*" *World Literature Today* 75, no. 1 (winter 2001): 82–85.

Lattin, Vernon E., Rolando Hinojosa, and Gary D. Keller, eds. *Tomás Rivera, 1935–1984: The Man and His Work.* Tempe, Ariz.: Bilingual Review/Press, 1988. (Especially useful are Santiago Daydí-Tolson's "Ritual and Religion in Tomás Rivera's Work," Luis Leal's "Remembering Tomás Rivera," Alfonso Rodríguez's "Tomás Rivera: The Creation of the Chicano Experience in Fiction," and Teresa B. Rodríguez's "Nociones sobre el arte narrativo en . . . *Y no se lo tragó la tierra* de Tomás Rivera.")

Martín-Flores, Mario. ". . .Y no se lo tragó la tierra: Cruzamientos multidirecionales entre oralidad y modernidad." In *Double Crossings/EntreCruzamientos.* Fair Haven, N.J.: Nuevo Espacio, 2001.

Morales, Alejandro. "La tradición oral como estructura en la cultura postmoderna." In *Nuevo Texto Crítico* 3, no. 1 (1990): 153–158.

———. ". . .Y no se lo tragó la tierra: Orality as Structure in Postmodern Culture." In *Discurso: Revista de Estudios Iberoamericanos* 7, no. 1 (1990): 67–79.

Olivares, Julián. "'La cosecha' y 'Zoo Island' de Tomás Rivera: Apuntes sobre la formación de . . . *Y no se lo tragó la tierra.*" In *Hispania: A Journal Devoted to the Teaching of Spanish and Portuguese* 74, no. 1 (March 1991): 57–65.

———. "Los índices primitivos de . . . Y no se lo tragó la tierra y cuatro inéditas." In *A Journal of Critical Essays* (University of California, San Diego) 2, no. 2 (fall 1990): 208–222.

Penn, William. "A Whole Lot of Talking Going On." *Cimarron Review* 121 (October 1997): 189–200.

Saldívar, José David. "Texas Border Narratives as Cultural Critique," Working Paper Series No. 19. Stanford, Calif.: Stanford Center for Chicano Research, April 1987.

Sanchez Manzano, María Jesús. "Character and Protagonist in . . . And the Earth Did Not Part." In *Revista Española de Estudios Norteamericanos* 7, no. 11 (1996): 43–50.

Sommers, Joseph, and Tomás Ybarra-Frausto, eds. *Modern Chicano Writers: A Collection of Critical Essays.* Englewood Cliffs, N.J.: Prentice Hall, 1979. (Contains Joseph Sommers's "Interpreting Tomás Rivera," Daniel Testa's "Narrative Technique and Human Experience in Tomás Rivera," and Ralph Grajeda's "Tomás Rivera's Appropriation of the Chicano Past.")

Luis J. Rodriguez
(1954–)

B. V. OLGUÍN

AT A TIME when a growing number of Latino authors have parlayed their stories about poverty-stricken characters into highly lucrative writing careers, Texas-born and Los Angeles–raised Chicano author Luis J. Rodriguez has used his literary fame to mount an aggressive grassroots crusade aimed at empowering the poor and other outcasts. Renowned in the U.S., Latin America, and Europe for his raw and brutally honest testimonial, *Always Running: La Vida Loca— Gang Days in L.A.* (1993), Rodriguez has eschewed the accoutrements of literary fame in favor of a life of service to the masses of people living on the margins of society. After all, their story also is his story. Drawing upon his own life experiences as a gang member, drug addict, high-school dropout, homeless person, prisoner, factory worker, truck driver, carpenter, pipe fitter, and steel worker, Rodriguez has chronicled these lives in a broad corpus of literary works. He has published numerous books in several genres and also has been featured in various literary videos and audio programs. In addition to his prolific literary production, Rodriguez also has designed grassroots therapeutic creative writing workshops and related counseling and mentoring programs at a variety of venues, such as youth detention facilities, maximum security prisons, homeless shelters, farmworker labor camps, union halls, Indian reservations, and low-income neighborhood centers. In each context, he has sought to use personal stories of pain, struggle, and survival to assist workshop participants in developing individual and collective strategies for empowerment.

Having experienced firsthand the failure of established educational and governmental institutions to serve racial minorities and special-needs populations, Rodriguez instead relies on the wisdom of his underclass constituents. In the introduction to his collection of policy-oriented essays, *Hearts and Hands: Creating Community in Violent Times* (2001), he observes:

From the segmented and conflicted class structure in our society, a new social class is emerging. Excluded from the technologically driven economy, this class is also politically, socially, and culturally ostracized. They are the exiled, the alienated, the abandoned, the demonized. Included are those on welfare, the homeless, prisoners, migrant workers, urban and rural poor (of all races, including the working poor), the indigenous and the undocumented, but also former managers, professionals, teachers, artists, and intellectuals who have been unable to make a transition through the recent societal changes. They are the ones capitalism can no longer effectively exploit, and therefore value—the locked out as well as the locked down.

As the core culture becomes increasingly materialist and profit oriented, it also becomes mean-spirited, intolerant, and devoid of a regenerative spirit. So, where do we turn when the center of the culture becomes hollow? As many others have poignantly remarked, to the margins, to the so-called periphery where everything is struggling and alive, to the "outcasts" and outlawed. Just as the extremities of the body energize the heart, so, too, do the peripheries of a culture revitalize its heart.

(p. 18)

In contrast to the conventional notion that the "fine arts" pertain only to cultural elites, Rodriguez adds in the preface to his 1998 collection of poetry, *Trochemoche,* that "artists are not a special kind of person; every person is a special kind of artist" (p. 1). Accordingly, Rodriguez seeks to facilitate change from below by cultivating the artistic talents and political voices of the periphery. Rodriguez thus exemplifies what Italian theorist Antonio Gramsci has dubbed the "organic intellectual." Whereas a "traditional intellectual" oftentimes is co-opted to serve powerful interests and preserve the status quo, organic intellectuals are distinguished for utilizing their skills and resources to empower society's downtrodden to transform society along more egalitarian principles. As a former member of various population segments that have been denied access to institutions of power, Rodriguez therefore deliberately and defiantly blurs the line between literature and politics. For him, the former is not so much at the service of the latter; instead, they inform and complement each other.

Rodriguez's populist philosophy of art is inalienably grounded in his own turbulent life history. He was born in El Paso, Texas, on 9 July 1954, after his father frantically drove his laboring wife across the border from his home in Ciudad Juárez, Mexico. Rodriguez's father, a highly educated but underpaid teacher in Mexico, apparently was determined to provide

better economic opportunities in the U.S. for his growing family and believed that his son's U.S. citizenship could facilitate this goal. As it turned out, Rodriguez's tumultuous birth episode presaged an even more turbulent life on the run once his family relocated to the U.S. While growing up in low-income neighborhoods in Los Angeles and surrounding municipalities, Rodriguez became involved with gangs and drug abuse at an early age. With the 1965 Watts Riot as a backdrop, Rodriguez formed his own "clica," or gang, in his neighborhood in east Los Angeles when he was just eleven years old. He later was inducted into "Thee Animal Tribe," and a larger, established gang "Las Lomas," which controlled his new neighborhood in South San Gabriel. This experience involved more drug abuse, and also included horrific episodes of violence that involved shootouts with fully automatic weapons. Rodriguez dropped out of high school at fifteen and subsequently gravitated between homelessness, jail, and life on the street as a hard-core gang member. However, after the deaths of over two dozen friends and several near-death experiences of his own—including an assassination attempt by his own "homeboys," who rejected Rodriguez's attempts to make peace between warring gangs—Rodriguez was ready for a change. With the help of grassroots community activists associated with the Bienvenidos (Welcome) Community Center, he eventually returned to school at the age of sixteen and weaned himself away from "la vida loca," or "the crazy life." In Michael Schwartz's biography, *Luis Rodriguez: Writer, Community Leader, and Political Activist* (1997), Rodriguez recalls that "there were a few guys at the Center that I looked up to. . . . They could influence me without judging me or telling me what to do. They were just there. They listened, and if I was wrong about something, before they would say anything, they would get me to think" (pp. 31–32). This experience had a lasting impression on Rodriguez. It not only saved his life, but transformed his entire approach to living: after graduating from high school, he resolved to commit himself to a life of community service.

Rodriguez eventually became involved in grassroots community organizing and arts projects in the greater Los Angeles area. In 1970 he participated in the infamous National Chicano Moratorium on 29 August, which at the time was the largest Chicano rally against the U.S. war in Vietnam. Rodriguez was one of several hundred protesters arrested by the L.A. County Sheriff's Department, who violently disbanded the rally in an operation that directly resulted in the suspicious deaths of two rally participants as well as an innocent bystander. Throughout this period of activism, Rodriguez continued to write, even as he alternately worked at the St. Regis Paper Company, Bethlehem Steel, and an assortment of construction and low-wage service-sector jobs. However, having previously received an Honorable Mention Award from the prestigious Quinto Sol Prize for Literature—a prize that helped foster the writing careers of noted Chicano authors Rolando Hinojosa and Rudolfo Anaya, among others—Rodriguez eventually tired of the dangerous factory work that had resulted in several co-worker deaths. He decided to pursue a writing career full-time and began attending the Barrio Writers Workshop in East Los Angeles. In an interview with Michael Silverblatt in the Lannan Literary Video Series profile dedicated to Rodriguez, the author recalls:

> I walked into the Barrio Writers Workshop in East L.A., where I met people just like me; people who wanted to write. [We] had no schooling, had no resources, but yet we wanted to do it. One was a guy who spent seventeen years in prison and twenty years as a heroin addict and gave it all up for poetry, so I knew this was the place for me.
>
> (1993, n.p.)

Rodriguez eventually began working for the *East Side Sun*, a Chicano community newspaper, and later *The San Bernardino Sun*, a daily newspaper. In 1985 he moved to Chicago to pursue his new career as editor of *The People's Tribune*, a nationwide revolutionary newspaper. He also was a frequent contributor to *The Nation* and a freelance contributor to other mainstream publications, such as the *U.S. News and World Report*, the *Chicago Tribune*, and the *Los Angeles Times*.

In 1989 Rodriguez received a grant for community-based literature that enabled him to found Tía Chucha Press, a grassroots publishing house that published his first book of poetry, *Poems across the Pavement* (1989). This enterprise was named after his flamboyant *tía*, or aunt, Jesusa, whom he recalls as a family storyteller and musician. According to Rodriguez, the mission of Tía Chucha Press is to feature previously silenced voices and long-ignored realities that are overlooked by mainstream presses. As such, Tía Chucha Press is reminiscent of grassroots Chicano publishing ventures founded by other Chicano authors. These include Raul Salinas's Red Salmon Press, whose name alludes to the author's recovery of the native roots of Chicano identity, and also Charley Trujillo's Chusma House, which is named after a popular Chicano slang term for "riff raff" that also refers to the galley slaves of the ancient Roman Empire. Tía Chucha Press has published several books and is now the publishing arm of Chicago's Guild Complex, an internationally renowned cross-cultural literary center that Rodriguez helped found. Shortly after Rodriguez's return to Los Angeles in 2000, this venture evolved into Tía Chucha Café Cultural in Sylmar, north of Los Angeles. Its motto, which is inscribed over the performance stage, reads "Where Art and Minds Meet . . . for a Change." In an 8 January 2002 interview with Tom Nolan in the online journal *Bookselling This Week*, Rodriguez reiterates that this venture was not designed to make money. Instead, "We saw it as something that was needed, to help educate the community on the need for books, as well as computers. I think it fulfills a big void in the community." He adds elsewhere that this cultural center "has a revolutionary purpose" (Biggers, *Bloomsbury Review*, p. 12). The bookstore has become host to a polyphony of readers, artists, musicians, and activists and has received nationwide recognition for its commitment to community-based arts and activism. Tía Chucha Café Cultural was even featured in "Realidades," the special television profiles that follow each episode of Gregory Nava's Chicano family serial, *American Family,* which airs weekly on select stations of the Public Broadcasting Service (PBS).

Rodriguez's broad interests in the arts and community service are reflected in his eclectic blend of genres and styles in his own writing. Following the title of his 1998 collection of poetry, *Trochemoche,* which means "helterskelter," or "without boundaries," he has published books across the genre spectrum and has appeared in numerous anthologies, recordings, and videos. Following his first collection, *Poems across the Pavement,* which won the San Francisco State University Poetry Center Book Award, Rodriguez published another collection, *The Concrete River* (1991), which received the PEN Josephine Miles Award. He followed his best-selling testimonial, *Always Running*—a recipient of the Carl Sandburg Award for Nonfiction—with a children's book, *America Is Her Name* (1998), and an illustrated juvenile novella, *It Doesn't Have to Be This Way* (1999). The latter text explores alternatives to violent gang life. He has expanded his repertoire with the publication of a collection of short stories, *The Republic of East L.A.* (2002), as well as the aforementioned collection of policy-oriented essays, *Hearts and Hands: Creating Community in Violent Times,* which addresses the complex history of gangs alongside critical analyses of contemporary trends in law enforcement and criminal justice. His writings have been included in a range of anthologies, including the groundbreaking *Outlaw Bible of American Poetry* (1999) and the prestigious recorded anthology by Rhino Records, *In Their Own Voices: A Century of Recorded Poetry* (1996). In this anthology, Rodriguez's poetry appears alongside the works of such noted American poets as Walt Whitman, Langston Hughes, Sylvia Plath, and Adrienne Rich. Rodriguez also is featured in *East Side Stories: Gang Life in East L.A.,* a photojournalism exposé jointly authored by Joseph Rodriguez and Rubén Martínez (1996). Many of Rodriguez's poems are bilingual and all his creative prose has been published into Spanish. This distinguished publication record, along with his consistent commitment to community-based literary and service-learning projects, has earned Rodriguez numerous awards. In addition to the accolades mentioned above, he has received the Lannan Fellowship in Poetry, the Lila Wallace–Reader's Digest Writers Award, the National Association for Poetry Therapy Public Service Award, and the Paterson Young Adult Book Award. Rodriguez has even been recognized by the Dalai Lama as one of the world's fifty "Unsung Heroes of Compassion" for his efforts to bring peace between warring urban gangs (Biggers, *Bloomsbury Review,* p. 12).

CHICANO TESTIMONIAL

Rodriguez's international recognition for his writing and related antiviolence activism illuminates an important issue central to his life and work: that the drug abuse and gang warfare currently plaguing American cities must be understood both as a local and global phenomenon. There are many causes that influence drug abuse and violence, and his writings consistently challenge us to avoid simplistic answers that revolve around the vilification, persecution, and mass incarceration of minority youth. Instead, he immediately notes that social groupings like gangs are neither unique nor inherently bad, since many initially were formed for the mutual aid of their members—the same rationale that undergirds the formation of fraternities, labor unions, and even country clubs. Indeed, like elite private clubs and high society organizations that are limited to a select homogeneous clientele of wealthy suburban whites, urban minority gangs also are determined by the economic conditions of their members. And like country clubs, gangs also serve to protect the interests and promote greater economic opportunities for their members. However, Rodriguez notes that these urban working-class clubs become destructive when legitimate economic and political avenues are closed to their members. They are reduced to relying on elicit underground economies, or worse: out of frustration, gang members myopically fight against similarly disenfranchised members of their social strata over control of a symbolic territory that they do not even own. They become both the victims of economic segregation and the victimizers of other members in their subordinated class. Rodriguez also reiterates that there is a historical dimension to the phenomenon of gang violence. Like many social historians, Rodriguez notes how narcotics abuse did not become a widespread problem until after the Watts Rebellion in 1965, and suggests that local and federal law enforcement agencies at the very least tolerated drug abuse, eventually stunting and redirecting the political activism of the era. Indeed, in his study of Los Angeles, *City of Quartz: Excavating the Future in Los Angeles* (1990), historian Mike Davis notes that armed gang warfare emerged in the wake of government repression and dismantling of community activist groups such as the Black Panthers, which offered free breakfast programs, among other benefits, to the urban minority poor. Rodriguez concurs with this historicist interpretation of American urban minority gangs and, more importantly, uses his own personal experience to explicate and intervene in the destructive process. Gang warfare, he notes, is a symptom of greater ills: racial and class oppression.

Rodriguez's didactic blend of personal experience with political analysis is the hallmark of the relatively new literary genre known as *testimonio,* or testimonial narrative. According to testimonial scholars John Beverley, Georg Guggleberger, and Barbara Harlow, this genre involves a first-person account of the personal and political evolution of its protagonist, yet it distinguishes itself from related genres such as the autobiography, memoir, and bourgeois novel in significant ways. Whereas these latter genres present an individualist hero who ultimately triumphs over adversity to become a full-fledged member of society, the testimonial narrative presents an underclass antihero who experiences societal injustice firsthand and resolves to fight the status quo. Whether they are miners, farmworkers, union activists, or guerrilla insurgents, these protagonists and their struggle are distinguished by their ordinariness. Above all, testimonial discourse is a dramatization of a character's attempt to unite with others for political empowerment. The testimonial text that features this ordinary person's struggle to overcome extraordinary adversity also refuses to offer an easy resolution. Even after the end of the testimonial, the struggle against injustice continues. Indeed, the testimonial text serves as a blueprint for its readers to follow in their own sites of struggle throughout the world: that is, the ordinariness of the protagonist, and the minute chronicle of their successes and failures, become touchstones for readers interested in learning how to wage a successful populist struggle in their own specific venue. With roots in the medieval picaresque and the modern proletarian novel, the testimonial reached its apex during the Latin American insurgencies of the 1960s onwards, in which many guerrilla fighters from Cuba, Argentina, Nicaragua, El Salvador, Guatemala, and Mexico wrote didactic and practice-oriented narratives designed to chronicle, critique, and extend their revolutionary struggle. Significantly, even as mainstream publishing houses continue to privilege the individualism and conservative cultural politics of some minority writers, like that which Richard Rodriguez promotes in his autobiography, *Hunger of Memory: The Education of Richard Rodriguez* (1982), the testimonial genre has become an important touchstone for more provocative Latino authors such as Cherríe Moraga, Rubén Martínez, Alejandro Murguía, and Gloria Anzaldúa, all of whom detail their painful transformations into populist activists in their respective testimonials.

Similar to these Latino authors, Luis Rodriguez's testimonial is distinguished for its attempts to extend the terrain of class struggle to the urban barrio. In *La Vida Loca,* he chronicles his personal growth from a self-centered, violent gang member to a self-critical and politically insightful member committed to community development. Thus, rather than provide an overbearing treatise on the dangers of gang life, he dramatizes specific episodes in order to illustrate the realities of this life so the reader can draw their own conclusions. For instance, he allows the reader to "view" the destructiveness of gang life by depicting the initiation rituals, which involve horrible beatings by the very members of an initiate's new gang "family." In another scene, Rodriguez features the violent and exploitative misogyny that also accompanies gang life. He describes another initiation episode as follows:

> I looked over to one side where I thought I heard a girl's muffled voice. There seemed to be a figure on top of somebody, going up and down on a body laid out on the ground, moaning with every motion.
>
> Gregorio [a member of Thee Animal Tribe] eyed me. Just staring. Finally he spoke: "She's being initiated into the Tribe."
>
> Then he laughed.
>
> (p. 54)

This understated yet chilling description of the brutal realities of gang life, however, is not designed to titillate readers. Instead, it serves to demystify the glamour of gangs and explicate its degradation of its own members by featuring the destruction of real people since, after all, the testimonial is based on fact and lived experiences.

BEYOND GANXPLOITATION

Rodriguez's testimonial text also follows the testimonial convention of reflection, candid self-critique, and theoretical analysis of the objective structural conditions that undergird individual and group dynamics. Indeed, Rodriguez's verité portrayal of violence, drug abuse, and human denigration serves to explicate the need for both a personal and political transformation. It also offers alternatives to gang life, even though some readers have mistaken the graphic depictions in his writings as a glorification of this violence. In fact, this kind of misreading of *Always Running* has also accompanied the related literary and cinematic genre known as "ganxploitation" (or, gang exploitation). The proliferation of minority gang sagas, such as Piri Thomas's *Down These Mean Streets* (1967), and similar feature films, including Michael Pressman's *Boulevard Nights* (1979), Edward James Olmos's *American Me* (1992), and Albert and Allen Hughes's *Menace II Society* (1993), led some media and law enforcement outlets to criticize these texts and films as dangerous promoters of violence. Accordingly, all these texts and films—including *Always Running*—have been banned at one time or another in school districts throughout the nation. However, these critics failed to recognize that these texts and films actually contested mainstream crime sagas that relied on minorities to serve as villains. As such, these texts functioned similarly to another misnamed and misunderstood genre, known as "Blaxploitation." Similar to Blaxploitation classics like *Superfly* (1972) and *Foxy Brown* (1974), minority-produced gang stories like Rodriguez's testimonial focus on the minority underclass experience not for the purpose of glorifying violence but to levy a political critique in the form of an underclass minority villain-cum-hero who fights against the forces of oppression. While Hollywood "ganxploitation" films such as Dennis Hopper's *Colors* (1988) blatantly vilify minority youth, many minority-produced "gang" profiles in literature and film use the horrors of gang life to critique the political and economic contexts that give rise to the poverty that leads to frustration, rage, and misguided uses of violence. In truth, they are *anti-*

ganxploitation texts. Instead of pathologizing urban minority youth for participating in gangs, Rodriguez's stories, like those of his predecessors Puerto Rican Piri Thomas and Chicano Floyd Salas, offer gritty tales to accentuate the need for and extent of their character's political transformation. Moreover, in her study, *Gang Nation: Delinquent Citizens in Puerto Rican, Chicano, and Chicana Narratives* (2002), Monica Brown identifies how Latino urban gangs assert "an alternative citizenship in a counternation" that emerges in opposition to the official state that has actively marginalized and persecuted urban minority youth (p. xxiii).

Significantly, Rodriguez recalls in *Always Running* that his own transformation from petty gang member to internationalist revolutionary was facilitated by outside intervention by community activists, thereby stressing the need for collective action. This is a point he repeatedly reiterates. For instance, in an interview on the PBS Special Series "Borders Talk," Rodriguez stresses that

> there were three major contributors to my "turnaround." One, I had help. There were a couple of teachers, a home-school coordinator, and a community organizer who saw some potential in me and tried to get me to see the resources, internal and external, that I had to reach that potential. Two, I found an art. First it was visual art (I painted ten murals from age seventeen–eighteen even when I was heavily involved in the gang and in drugs). I also wrote vignettes and poems that eventually were sent to a contest in Berkeley for which I won honorable mention and $250. Thirdly, I got tired. At age eighteen, I was facing a six-year prison sentence. I was using heroin, and I had already lost twenty-five friends to the madness of street violence, crime and drugs. Something in me had matured. If not, I would not have made the turn.
>
> (n.p.)

Rodriguez's personal and political transformation is dramatized in his testimonial in an exchange between him and members of an alternative "gang"—a revolutionary study group—with which he was involved during the final period of his street-gang life:

> "It's also time you understood whites aren't the enemy," Chente said. Take that 'tradition,' all that energy extended against each other—what a waste!"
>
> . . .
>
> "You don't have to be a genius to figure out what's in front of you," Chente said. "Yet this is the hardest thing to do precisely because what we see is not always expressing what's beneath it."
>
> "But all we know is *this* life," I questioned. "You can't change that!"
>
> "Luis, change is what we're all about," Chente offered. "Change is constant, stagnation is relative. But change follows laws of development, a process that, if appreciated, sets the conditions by which people make their own history."
>
> "What we're here to do is transform the way people have been accustomed to living," Sergio said. "The first step is removing the shackles on our minds."
>
> (*Always Running*, pp. 184–185)

The episode ends with Rodriguez's epiphany:

> The collective explained how workers of all colors and nationalities, linked by hunger and the same system of exploitation, have no country; their interests as a class respect no borders. To me, this was an unconquerable idea.
>
> I also learned there was no shame in being a janitor or a garment worker; I never looked at Mama and Dad with disdain again.
>
> (p. 185)

Elsewhere he adds, "The group aimed to train a corps of leaders. Unlike others in the Chicano Movement who strove to *enter* the American capitalist system, it prepared for a fundamental reorganization of society" (p. 184). This exchange thus illustrates how the key to *Always Running* is not violence, but the promotion of a collective sense of identity, one that involves taking responsibility for one's own life as well as the well-being of others, especially those less fortunate.

For Rodriguez, responsibility also requires coming to terms with one's own past, especially the hurt caused to others. This is crucial to his philosophy of healing and repairing lives in the wake of trauma and clearly distances his text from misinformed notions fostered by the mainstream ganxploitation genre. This issue is illustrated in a poignant scene towards the end of *Always Running* where Rodriguez is confronted by a former enemy upon his visit to L.A. years after he had left gang life to rebuild a new life for himself as a journalist and writer. Upon his return for a family *quinceañera* (a fifteen-year-old's coming-out debutante celebration), Rodriguez is confronted by "Chava," a former enemy gang leader who had been stabbed and brutally beaten on the head with an iron rim from an automobile tire:

"Look what you did to me. Somebody has to pay for this!" Chava repeats. He's so disturbed, I can see him pulling out a knife and stabbing me just to salve his pain. I look at the guys next to me, and they strike me as too young and inexperienced to act. I keep talking.

Rodriguez, who is completely shocked and surprised at the encounter, can only respond:

"There's some things to fight for, some things to die for—but not this. Chava, you're alive. I feel for you, man, but you're alive. Don't waste the rest of your days with this hate. What's revenge? What can you get by getting to me? I'm the least of your enemies. It's time to let go, it's time to go on with your life."

The scene ends with a tentative though cathartic crescendo:

Chava begins to shudder, to utter something, a guttural sound rising to his throat, a hideous moan. I think he's trying to cry, but it's hard to tell. I don't know what to do, so I pull him close to me. He twists away, the dudes to the side look lost, not knowing their next move, unprepared for what follows. I again pull at Chava, and hold him. He breaks down, a flood of fermented rage seeping out of every pore.

"If I thought my life could cleanse you of the hurt, of the memory, I would open up my shirt and let you take it from me. But it won't—we're too much the same now, Chava. Let it all out, man. . . let it out."

(p. 245, ellipsis in original)

Rodriguez's old enemy limps away, and the shaken Rodriguez is forced to recognize that his new life must inevitably confront the hurts he helped cause in his past life. As many scholars have noted, there is no closure in the testimonial text; rather, there is an ongoing urgent need for intervention and transformation of traumatic and exploitative situations. Dramatic scenes like the one above give a human face to this political imperative.

Rodriguez's sense of responsibility and atonement also is illustrated in his poem "Meeting the Animal in Washington Square Park," which opens his 1998 collection *Trochemoche*. This poem recounts an unlikely meeting between the author and a member of an enemy gang during a walk in Manhattan after a poetry reading:

I looked closer. It had to be him. It was—Animal!
From East L.A. World heavyweight contender,
the only Chicano from L.A. ever ranked
in the top ten of the division. The one who
went toe-to-toe with Leon Spinks and even
made Muhammad Ali look the other way.
Animal! I yelled. "Who the fuck are you?" he
    asked,
a quart of beer in his grasp, eyes squinting.
My name's Louie—from East L.A. He
    brightened. "East L.A.!
Here in Washington Square Park? man, we
    everywhere!"
The proverbial "what part of East L.A.?" came
    next.
But I gave him a shock. From La Gerahty, I said.
That's the mortal enemy of the Big Hazard
gang of the Ramona Gardens Housing Projects.
"I should kill you," Animal replied. If we were in
L.A., I suppose you would—but we in New York
    City, man.
"I should kill you anyway."

Instead he thrust out his hand with the beer and
    offered
me a drink.

                                        (p. 7, lines 13–31)

The tension of the encounter is replaced with a gesture of peace, and the poem ends with a lyric expression of what can be described as Rodriguez's *ars poetica,* or philosophy of art:

I told him how I was now a poet,
doing a reading at City College, and he didn't
    wince
or looked surprised. Seemed natural. Sure. A poet
from East L.A. That's the way it should be. Poet
and boxer. Drinking beer. Among the homeless,
the tourists and acrobats. Mortal enemies.
When I told him I had to leave, he said "go then,"
but soon shook my hand, East L.A. style, and
    walked off.
"Maybe, someday, you'll do a poem about me,
    eh?"
Sure, Animal, that sounds great.
Someday, I'll do a poem about you.

                                        (p. 8, lines 37–47)

Animal's friendly challenge to Rodriguez is taken to heart and comes to serve as a metaphor for his new life as a writer. Indeed, Rodriguez eventually does write a poem about Animal that expresses the author's sadness at seeing this once proud virile boxer and gang member reduced to homelessness as an alcoholic exiled from his hometown. Moreover, part of Rodriguez's new mission is to tell the stories of these tragic barrio lives.

REVISING CHICANO MASCULINITY

Rodriguez's testimonial and other writings also addresses the issue of manhood, which is a central feature of his revision of the ganxploitation genre. Following his testimonial narrative, which explores masculinist violence and the misogyny that accompanies it, and drawing

upon his poetic paeans about once-proud warriors who were felled by gang violence and drug abuse, Rodriguez's short stories and illustrated juvenile novella, *It Doesn't Have to Be This Way: A Barrio Story,* propose alternative models of manhood. In his story "Shadows," for instance, Rodriguez explores the subject of substance abuse by focusing on the damage it causes one young family. Rudy, the young Chicano protagonist who is unable to break the cycle of alcoholism that he in part inherited from a grandfather, ultimately destroys his family and threatens the future of his own son. The story ends with Rudy's decline in a pathos-laden scene that is designed to inform readers about the science of alcoholism as well as the extremely difficult challenge of overcoming the disease. The implication in this and other stories in *The Republic of East L.A.* is that manhood sometimes involves acknowledging that one needs assistance in overcoming life's challenges.

While the traditional notion of "manhood" usually is wrought with problematic presumptions, Rodriguez turns conventional sexist notions on their side. Similar to his dedication in *Hearts and Hands,* which creates a neologism in order to celebrate "peace warriors," Rodriguez instead seeks to promote a model of manhood that is not predicated on misogyny or violence. Accordingly, this juvenile story, which is bilingual and published in easily accessible large print alongside graphic watercolor illustrations, explores the early flirtations with gangs by a young Mexican American boy from a single-parent household who is named Ramón, also called "Monchi" by friends and family. Mirroring part of Rodriguez's own experiences, the gang initially validates the young boy's need to belong and feel respected. But the gang quickly gets embroiled in violence, which results in the shooting of an innocent bystander: Monchi's twelve-year-old female cousin, who is nicknamed "Dreamer." As the family awaits news of Dreamer's condition in the hospital waiting room, Monchi's uncle refuses to blame him for the incident and instead models an alternative. The child narrator notes:

> I felt so bad. I thought my whole family must hate me. In the waiting room, I hung my head and prayed that Dreamer would be okay. But Tío Rogelio put his arm around me. "It doesn't have to be this way, *m'ijo*," he said. "I know you want to be a man, but you have to decide what kind of man you want to be."
>
> It seemed like we waited forever. Then the doctor came out and told us that Dreamer was going to live.
>
> (p. 27)

Monchi's transformation has begun.

The climax in the story comes when Monchi's fellow gang members invite him to participate in an attack to avenge the shooting of Dreamer, which has rendered her a paraplegic. But Monchi has taken his surrogate father's lesson to heart: "Dreamer looked up at me to see what I'd do. I thought for a long time. Tío Rogelio's words came into my head. Then I heard myself say, 'It doesn't have to be this way'" (p. 28). Monchi, who grew up without a biological father present, is saved by his uncle—a surrogate father—from the violent cycle that Rodriguez has explicated in chilling detail throughout his writings. Rodriguez thus reappropriates the ganxploitation genre to introduce a new type of role model, one who exhibits his strength of character by preserving a positive outlook on life despite the tragedy that has befallen his family and, more importantly, by redefining one of the notions about masculinity that sometimes influences young boys to participate in gang violence. The resolution of the story comes in the form of a compliment—and validation—for Monchi's refusal to participate in *la vida loca*:

> "That was a brave thing," [Tío Rogelio] said. "I have a lot of respect for you." Nobody ever said that to me before. It made me feel real good.

> Then he said, "We can make good things happen, *m'ijo*, if we all work together."
> I liked the sound of that.
>
> (p. 31)

Monchi, Rodriguez implies in this rather telegraphic yet nonetheless effective juvenile work, is on his way to becoming a "real man."

Manhood, and the related challenges of fatherhood, are constant themes in Rodriguez's didactic writing. Significantly, Rodriguez not only provides alternative models of manhood for youth but also models alternatives for adults as well. In his testimonial, as well as related poems and interviews, for instance, Rodriguez recalls the traumatic degeneration of his relationship with his own father, who became senile and incommunicative after years of frustration at his inability to find employment as a teacher. He also includes discussions about his own failures as a father. Rodriguez frequently recalls how his own son, from whom he had been absent after a divorce from his first wife, also joined a gang and eventually was imprisoned in a maximum security penitentiary for assault. His testimonial, he adds, was initially written to explore his painful past relationship with his son in order to construct a new, positive one. Rodriguez shares these painful episodes in his life not for the purpose of denigrating his family but to present scenarios that are recognizable to his urban working-class readership. Moreover, he uses these failures to illuminate the need for surrogate fathers and positive male role models. That is, he shifts the attention to adults, whom he notes share as much responsibility for the problems of young people as the youth themselves. Indeed, in the introduction to *Hearts and Hands*, he links national traumas such as the Columbine High School massacre with daily urban gang warfare to identify a failure of the adult leaders. He asks: "What can we do? How can we get off this continually accelerating merry-go-round?" (p. 13). He offers his book of personal essays, profiles, and social analysis to the adults responsible for creating the conditions that lead to such tragedies:

A major purpose of this book is to attempt a deeper inquiry into these issues, to engage people in an ongoing dialogue about why young people seem to be more brutal, more willing to take it to the limit, more intent on resolving issues with a total and desperate finality. This is not so much about the right "answers" as it is about the right arguments. It's time to make sense of the senselessness.

(p. 13)

His life and work is offered up as a model of a socially conscious and responsible adult male. Indeed, Rodriguez, who recently has re-established contact with his family's indigenous roots, has become a respected elder among Native Americans and Latinos. His present role as an elder was prophetically foreshadowed in the poem "The Calling," which appears in his first collection of poetry, *Poems across the Pavement:*

The calling came to me
while I languished
in my room; while I
whittled away my youth
in jail cells
and damp barrio fields.

It brought me to life,
out of captivity,
in a street-scarred
and tattooed place
I called body.

(p. 38, lines 1–11)

The poem continues with Rodriguez's characteristic revision of conventional masculinist terms like "war" and "soldier":

It called me to war;
to be writer,
to be scientist
and march with the soldiers
of change.

(lines 34–38)

The poem ends, "Somehow, unexpected, / I was called" (lines 45–46). Luis Rodriguez's subsequent life's work as an artist activist is testament to his ability to rise to the challenging yet honored status of elder. He is a peace warrior.

Selected Bibliography

WORKS OF LUIS J. RODRIGUEZ

POETRY

Poems across the Pavement. Chicago: Tía Chucha Press, 1989.

The Concrete River. Willimantic, Conn.: Curbstone Press, 1991.

Trochemoche. Willimantic, Conn.: Curbstone Press, 1998.

PROSE

Always Running: La Vida Loca—Gang Days in L.A. (memoir). Willimantic, Conn.: Curbstone Press, 1993. Spanish translation by Ricardo Aguilar Melantzón and Ana Brewington published as *La vida loca: El testimonio de un pandillero en Los Angeles.* 1996.

Hearts and Hands: Creating Community in Violent Times (essays). New York: Seven Stories Press, 2001.

The Republic of East L.A.: Stories. New York: Rayo/HarperCollins, 2002. Spanish edition as *La república de East L.A.: Cuentos.* 2003.

CHILDREN'S LITERATURE

America Is Her Name. Illustrated by Carlos Vázquez. Willimantic, Conn.: Curbstone Press, 1998. Spanish translation as *La llaman América.* Translated by Tino Villanueva. 1998.

It Doesn't Have to Be This Way: A Barrio Story. Illustrated by Daniel Galvez. San Francisco: Children's Book Press, 1999.

SELECTED ANTHOLOGIES

The Outlaw Bible of American Poetry. Edited by Alan Kaufman. New York: Thunder's Mouth Press, 1999.

Bum Rush the Page: A Def Poetry Jam. Edited by Tony Medina and Louis Reyes Rivera. New York: Three Rivers Press, 2001.

AUDIOVISUAL AND MULTIMEDIA

Lannon Literary Videos: Luis J. Rodriguez (Profile #31) (videocassette). Lannon Foundation, 1992.

In Their Own Voices: A Century of Recorded Poetry (audiocassette). Rhino/Word Beat Records, 1996.

Making Peace: Youth Struggling for Survival (Profile #2) (videocassette). Moira Productions/Films for the Humanities and Sciences, 1996.

La vida loca: El testimonio de un pandillero en Los Angeles (Spanish audiocassette). AudioLibros del Mundo, 1998.

East Side Stories: Gang Life in East L.A. (photoessay). Photographs by Joseph Rodriguez, essay by Rubén Martínez, interview with Luis Rodriguez. New York: PowerHouse Books, 1998.

My Name's Not Rodriguez: Original Music and Poems by Luis Rodriguez (Audio CD). Dos Manos/Rock a Mole Music, 2002.

SECONDARY WORKS

BIOGRAPHIES AND INTERVIEWS

Biggers, Jeff. "Compassion and Community: An Interview with Luis J. Rodriguez." *Bloomsbury Review* 23, no. 3 (May/June 2003): 5, 12.

Schwartz, Michael. *Luis Rodriguez: Writer, Community Leader, Political Activist.* Austin, Tex.: Steck-Vaughn, 1997.

GENERAL STUDIES

Beverley, John. "The Margin at the Center: On Testimonio." In *The Real Thing: Testimonial Discourse and Latin America.* Edited by Georg M. Gugelberger. Durham, N.C.: Duke University Press, 1996. Pp. 23–41.

Brown, Monica. *Gang Nation: Delinquent Citizens in Puerto Rican, Chicano, and Chicana Narratives.* Minneapolis: University of Minnesota Press, 2002.

Davis, Mike. *City of Quartz: Excavating the Future in Los Angeles.* New York: Verso, 1990.

Harlow, Barbara. "Testimonio and Survival: Roque Dalton's Miguel Mármol." In *The Real Thing: Testimonial Discourse and Latin America.* Edited by Georg M. Gugelberger. Durham, N.C.: Duke University Press, 1996. Pp. 70–83.

INTERNET

Nolan, Tom. "Author Luis J. Rodriguez Opens Community Bookstore in L.A." *Bookselling This Week.* http://news.bookweb.org/features/88.html (accessed July 3, 2003).

Rodriguez, Luis J. "Border Talk." *POV: Border Talk.* http://www.pbs.org/pov/pov2002/borders/talk/dialogue003_lr.html (accessed July 3, 2003).

Rodriguez, Luis J. http://www.luisjrodriguez.com (accessed July 3, 2003).

Richard Rodriguez
(1944–)

ROLANDO J. ROMERO

RICHARD RODRIGUEZ GOES so much against the Chicano nationalist trend that we would almost have to classify him as the leader in a postnationalist movement. Rodriguez's Chicano predecessors defined orality as the primary critical mode of Chicano expression. Orality and experience are determined by the metaphysics of presence, and they lurk behind the classical myth regarding the construction of Chicano culture. Américo Paredes, for example, writes in his introduction to the now classic *"With His Pistol in His Hand," a Border Ballad and Its Hero:*

> To the memory of my father,
> who rode a raid or two with
> Catarino Garza;
> and to all those old men
> who sat around on summer nights,
> in the days when there was
> a chaparral, smoking their
> cornhusk cigarettes and *talking*
> *in low, gentle voices about*
> *violent things;*
> *while I listened*"

(emphasis added)

Similarly, Ernesto Galarza writes:

> *Barrio Boy* began as anecdotes *I told* my family about Jalcocotán, the mountain village in western Mexico where I was born. Among this limited public (my wife, Mae, and daughters, Karla and Eli Lu) my thumbnail sketches became best sellers. *Hearing myself tell them* over and over I began to agree with my captive audience that they were not only interesting, but possibly good.

(p. 1; emphasis added)

Rodriguez stands apart because writing describes his central preoccupation: as a craft, as a concept, as a philosophical construct. This writing is not defined by poststructuralism (as *écriture* metaphysics of presence, as posited by Ferdinand de Saussure's *Cours de linguistique générale,* Jacques Derrida's *Of Grammatology,* or Paul de Man's *Blindness and Insight*) but by Writing Studies (practicality, description, rhetoric, Freshman English, composition).

Rodriguez was born on 31 July 1944 in San Francisco, to Leopoldo and Victoria. He attended parochial schools for twelve years and went to college at Stanford University, where he earned a degree in English in 1967. In 1969 he graduated from Columbia University with a master's degree in philosophy and began doctorate work in Renaissance literature at Berkeley in 1970, where he taught as a graduate student for about two years. When looking for a permanent teaching position, he did not accept a position despite numerous offers from schools, deciding to become a writer instead.

BROWN: TOWARD A CHICANO EPISTEMOLOGY

Many critics call Richard Rodriguez a stylist because of his staccato syntax, his purported detachment from the subject of inquiry, his preoccupation with irony, and so on. Rodriguez is steeped in questions of identity as posited in the field of American Studies, as evidenced by his penchant for classic writers such as Alexis de Tocqueville, Richard Wright, James Baldwin, and others. He is only a reluctant practitioner of ethnic discourse, and his books *Hunger of Memory: The Education of Richard Rodriguez* (1982), *Days of Obligation: An Argument with My Mexican Father* (1992), and *Brown: The Last Discovery of America* (2002) can almost be taken as glimpses of a parade of topical issues: affirmative action and the Bakke decision of the 1970s; homosexuality, AIDS, and the Church in the 1980s; ethnic discourse in the 1990s; globalization and terrorism in the new century. With every book, he edges closer and closer to the field of Chicano/Latino Studies, though he approaches the field as a broadside, as a smear, as a counterpoint, as a slap in the face. ("Why am I here?" "Why was I invited?" But are not the arguments that negate the field what dominant culture would disseminate? More Shelby Steele than Cornel West, more Martin Luther King than Malcolm X, more Gandhi than Zapata.) He writes:

> I remain at best ambivalent about those Hispanic anthologies where I end up; about those anthologies where I end up the Hispanic; about shelves at the bookstore where I look for myself and find myself.
>
> (p. 26)

Well, what's the difference? I do not see myself as a writer in the world's eye, much less a white writer, much less a Hispanic writer; much less "a writer" in the 92nd Street Y sense. I'd rather be Madonna. Really, I would.

(pp. 39–40)

He became the Chicano most widely read outside Chicano circles, appearing regularly with his essays on "The NewsHour with Jim Lehrer" and National Public Radio. A biographical item with Pacific News Service listed him as a contributing editor to *Harper's Magazine, U.S. News and World Report,* and the opinion section of the *Los Angeles Times.* His journalism appeared in the *New York Times,* the *Wall Street Journal, Time,* and others. The appearances of his books turned into publishing events, with each succeeding text more important and widely anticipated than the last.

When *Hunger of Memory* first appeared, it was reviewed favorably in the *New York Times Book Review, Newsweek, American Scholar, Time, College English,* and *People Magazine.* Gerald Grant and several other authors consider Rodriguez's book a classic. Michael Davitt Bell compared the book to "Benjamin Franklin's *Autobiography;* Frederick Douglass's *Narrative; The Education of Henry Adams;* Jane Addams's *Twenty* [sic] *Years at Hull-House;* or Richard Wright's *Black Boy* and its posthumous sequel, *American Hunger*" (p. 38). Paul Zweig, reviewing the book for the *New York Times,* wrote that *Hunger of Memory* stands "in an honorable tradition that includes Wordsworth's *Prelude* and Proust's *Remembrance of Things Past*" (p. 26). John W. Donohue wrote in his review that *Hunger of Memory* "will still be read a century from now" (p. 404).

Rodriguez presents Chicano culture as an elegy, a fact that explains his popularity: "I eulogize a literature that is suffused with brown, with allusion, irony, paradox—ha!—pleasure" (p. xi). Lacking the affirmation of culture (bilingualism, biculturalism) that would demand concomitant public policies, he blends into the mainstream background that encourages anything but acculturation. It is in the context of Chicano cultural archaeology that his comments on Caliban can be read as a metaphor ("Ah, you taught me language") of colonialism; not in the pointing-finger mode of Roberto Fernández Retamar but in a white man's burden way:

> I cannot imagine myself a writer, I cannot imagine myself writing these words, without the example of African slaves stealing the English language, learning to read against the law, then transforming the English language into the American tongue, transforming me, rescuing me, with a coruscating nonchalance.
>
> (p. 31)

The calibanic mode in Rodriguez deceives, arrests, lures into a resolution that is nothing but an agreement with the status quo, with the English Only movement that circulated his book, with the troves of affirmative action detractors who believe there is but one way of participating in American culture.

Rodriguez is also one of the few authors who has questioned the idea of an east-to-west migration and who proposes a new geographical map that also takes into account the south-to-north migration from Latin America and the west-to-east migration of Asian cultures. His map points to the "you are here" of confluence and not of hierarchies:

> I think we are just now beginning to discern an anti-narrative—the American detective story told from west to east, against manifest destiny, against the early Protestant point of view, against the Knickerbocker Club, old Ivy, the assurances of New England divines.
>
> (p. 172)

Anglocentric constructions of U.S. culture argue that civilization progressed from east to west, from Europe to the Pacific edge of California, from feudalism to late capitalism. This idea is best epitomized in the director Ridley Scott's film *Blade Runner,* which uses as a background the philosophy of William Blake. Rodriguez would make the trip in the opposite direction, from west to east, and he thus textualizes it in the chapter titled "Gone West" in *Brown*: "That summer I was still young enough to call the last summer of my youth, I drove cross-country with three college friends. From the freeway on-ramp at Thirtieth and J Streets in Sacramento to the Lincoln Tunnel. . . . Or bust" (p. 169). The title of the chapter really stands for the subject that Rodriguez will deconstruct, the notion that culture moved from the east with the phrase "Gone West." Rodriguez points out that there is much WASP nostalgia in the construction of the West: tepees, Indians, cowboys, open range, freedom, individualism, ruggedness:

> The Atlantic myth of Genesis worked so powerfully on the first non-native imaginations that future generations of Americans retained the assumption of innocence—a remarkably resilient psychic cherry. Every generation of Americans since has had to reenact the loss of our innocence.
>
> . . .
>
> The east-west dialectic in American history reasserted man's license to dominate Nature—the right endeavor of innocence. Railroad tracks binding the continent are vestigial stitches of the smoke-belching Judeo-Christian engine, Primacy o' Man. Having achieved the Pacific Coast, settlers turned to regret the loss of Nature. That is where the West begins.
>
> (pp. 187–188)

Rodriguez, as the author who questions California's articulation in the U.S. imagination ("Poor Richard," a tongue in cheek reference to both himself and Richard Nixon; Ronald Reagan in the chapter entitled "Hispanic"; Asian Americans), may ultimately be considered the multicultural California writer. But, as Rodriguez points out, California as the West also stands as a symbol of progress, of innovation, of innocence. Thus, what happens in the state foregrounds what will happen across the nation: "Proposition 13, LSD, skateboards, silicon chips, Malibu Buddhism. California, the laboratory; New York, the patent office" (p. 174).

Whereas in other books Rodriguez hints at his homosexuality (the "Mr. Secrets" chapter of *Hunger of Memory* or the "Late Victorians" chapter in *Days of Obligation,* for example), in *Brown* he actually comes out:

Most bookstores have replaced disciplinary categories with racial or sexual identification. In either case I must be shelved Brown. The most important theme of my writing now is impurity. My mestizo boast: As a queer Catholic Indian Spaniard at home in a temperate Chinese city in a fading blond state in a post-Protestant nation, I live up to my sixteenth-century birth.

(p. 35)

His coming out in other parts of the book is less overt. His sexuality, like his outings in Sacramento, was "secretive" (pp. 14, 16). "Brown," he writes, "is the color most people in the United States associate with Latin America. . . . Apart from stool sample, there is no browner smear in the American imagination." (p. xii).

It is also Richard Rodriguez's sexuality that explains his reading of buddy films or TV programs as erotic. On *The Defiant Ones:* "Two convicts—Sidney Poitier and Tony Curtis—were shackled to each other. The movie did not occur to me racially or politically but erotically" (p. 5). In reference to the mixed couples (Tonto and the Lone Ranger, for example), he sees less race than eroticism, gay desire, a fantasy of gay communion: "The word race encourages me to remember the influence of eroticism on history" (p. xv).

Brown is the book's metaphor for impurity, for *mestizaje,* for "stool sample," perhaps for motherhood—"Brown is a bit of a cave in my memory" (p. 7)—but also for Brown epistemology, a Brown way of understanding the world:

Eve's apple, or what was left of it, quickly browned.

. . . When Eve looked again, she saw a brown crust had formed over the part where she had eaten and invited Adam's lip. It was then she threw the thing away from her. Thenceforward (the first Thenceforward), brown informed everything she touched.

(p. 40–41)

In my opinion the book is saved because of Rodriguez's boldness in exploration, both of traditional Chicano cultural nationalism and of sexuality. His ability to be brutally honest in his introspection has earned him the ridicule of the culture that considers him nothing more than a critical punching bag.

DAYS OF OBLIGATION: WRITING AND CATHOLICISM

Rodriguez's *Days of Obligation,* his first collection of essays since the publication of *Hunger of Memory,* intertwines issues of cultural identity so closely with questions of writing and Catholicism that analysis of any one of these terms (for example, the Catholic definition of sin) will invariably involve the others. The author's preoccupation (if not obsession) with religion is signaled by the very phrase "days of obligation," which according to the book's jacket, "are feast days of such importance to the life of the church that the faithful are required to attend them physically by going to mass."

Rodriguez, like many Chicano authors, equates Catholicism with ethnic identity, drawing on the myth of the December 1531 appearance of the Virgin of Guadalupe to an Indian peasant, Juan Diego ("India"). Thus, for Rodriguez, Chicano Catholicism is mediated through race as well as ethnicity. The book's subtitle—"An Argument with My Mexican Father"—suggests that the "days of obligation" also involve a confrontation, a forced introspection of the author himself through the eyes of his Mexican father, whom Rodriguez turns into a figure for Mexican culture. The theme of death (explored in the chapters "The Head of Joaquín Murrieta," "In Athens Once," and "Late Victorians") consequently encompasses not only the metaphorical death of Mexican culture in the United States but also the death of Catholicism suggested by the rise of Protestantism in the Latino communities of Latin America and the United States ("The Latin American Novel"). The author believes, for example, that "Mexico's history was death" (p. 21). Walking into a church where he finds a South American shaman "crosslegged on a dais," he asks himself, "Now, who is the truer Indian in this picture? Me . . . me on my way to the Queen's Theatre? Or that guy on the altar with a Ph.D. in death?" (p. 10).

Tension between the natural and the artificial can be read in the triad religion-ethnicity-writing. The Catholic religion has always made a distinction between body and spirit. Should the reader be surprised that since Catholicism equates sin with the artificial, Rodriguez equates homosexuality with artificiality? Homosexuality, observed through the author's religious eyes, thus turns into the sin of the artificial: "Homosexuals," Rodriguez writes, "have made a covenant against nature. Homosexual survival lay in artifice, in plumage, in lampshades, sonnets, musical comedy, couture, syntax, religious ceremony, opera, lacquer irony" (p. 32). Rodriguez apparently believes that homosexuality allows gays to withdraw from nature, from the spirit, and leads them to embrace the artificial, the cultural, the untrue. Thus, for Rodriguez, AIDS becomes God's way of reclaiming homosexuals, of forcing them to be in touch with their "natural" side (the patients' bedpans, the innumerable trips to the hospital, the gradual deterioration of the body) and to face death. Understandably, the response to the essay, when originally published in *Harper's,* was not positive.

As with most of Rodriguez's work, *Days of Obligation* does not establish the boundaries between experience and writing. His book is permeated with what seem like heavy doses of ironic detachment. Thus the reader will find it difficult to unequivocally categorize the book either within the established rules of literary genres—the picaresque and the pastoral come to mind—or as the typical ethnic text based on the author's experience. Rodriguez asks:

How shall I present the argument between comedy and tragedy, this tension that describes my life? Shall I start with the boy's chapter, then move toward more "mature" tragic conclusions? . . . No,

I will present this life in reverse. After all, the journey my parents took from Mexico to America was a journey from an ancient culture to a youthful one—backwards in time. In their path I similarly move, if only to honor their passage to California.

(pp. xvii–xviii)

The author thus transforms his parents' physical/geographical journey into a textual one, thereby allowing himself—the tragic "mature" man—to drink from the rhetorical fountain of youth in order to recapture his innocence and return to paradise and communion.

Rodriguez's travels, read in the context of his compositional intentions, affect how we understand his voyage to his parents' village, to Mexico City, to the California missions, to Sacramento in search of the head of Joaquín Murrieta. His journey begins with an epigraph from Alvar Núñez Cabeza de Vaca, the quintessential traveler of the American southwest who, shipwrecked off the coast of Florida in 1528, transformed a physical journey of reunion with his fellow countrymen into one of the understanding of alterity. The physical journey in classical literature has always entailed a degree of personal understanding and spiritual renewal; from the classic picaresque novel to the writings of the beat generation, travel serves as a metaphor for an inner journey into the dark recesses of the self. It is always, nonetheless, a romantic journey with no guarantee of self-renewal or self-awareness. In Rodriguez's case, it is unclear whether his travels signal religious pilgrimage, ethnic atonement of the Chicano prodigal son who returns to his parents' culture in the wake of the self-hatred expressed in his *Hunger of Memory,* or simply the recreation of the hero's classical voyage whose return home is fraught with perils and enticements designed to lure the hero away from his ethnic destination. It is also unclear whether Rodriguez wishes to simply present himself as the hero of classical tragedy whose sin (his romantic obsession with Chicano cultural identity) is inextricably tied to the strength that makes him endure (this obsession, after all, made him famous). Furthermore, it is unclear whether Rodriguez wants his reader to understand his feelings of guilt and loneliness in the tradition of classical tragedy in which the sulking hero is selected because of his greatness (who, after all, can endure such an eternal ethnic conflict?). Oh, Mexico, Mexico, wherefore art thou? The hero's voyage also finds in pilgrimage its religious counterpart. As Mircea Eliade has noted, the pilgrim's arduous voyage is fraught with peril because it signals a passage from man to god.

Whether consciously or unconsciously, Rodriguez equates ethnic death with the fear of AIDS. Derrida's critique of logocentrism has equated the spirit with orality. Juan Eduardo Cirlot's *Dictionary of Symbols* associates the head with the spirit. Is there any question then, why, in attempting to write about the Chicano icon Joaquín Murrieta (whose head has never been buried), Rodriguez uncannily also looks for the spirit, the logos itself? Might there not also be some significance in the fact that Freudian psychoanalysis has seen decapitation as fear of castration?

Although a little less obvious, the binarisms so clearly present in *Hunger of Memory* also operate in *Days of Obligation*. To Rodriguez, America represents the future (life), while Mexico represents the past (death). America finds her metaphor in the efficient waitress who, in one clean sweep, erases the past of the previous diner to make room for the new one. America has no memory; she does not accept newcomers who cling to their past. America demands a clean slate, a new beginning, according to Rodriguez. Ethnicity, on the other hand, has become lost in its own past, in its own justification. Mexicans who become U.S. citizens, like Rodriguez's father, simply disappear into America. Memory, Rodriguez believes, will take revenge on their children, hounding them; therein lies the hunger. Memory will make slaves of these American children. The children of immigrants leave behind Mexico, the past, home, and what is intensely the private ("For

the Mexican, the past is firmly held within") in order to find their future in America.

Ethnicity has quite literally lost its own head (to wit, the essay on Joaquín Murrieta):

> Christopherson is well known to Sacramento legislators. For years he has worked to exonerate the name of Joaquín Murrieta ("The man was never tried"). Christopherson has lobbied to remove Historical Marker 344, which identifies the Arroyo Cantua as the site of the death of "the notorious bandit, Joaquín Murrieta." On May 2, 1983, an earthquake hit the nearby town of Coalinga. The quake's epicenter was directly beneath state marker 344 (God's bull's-eye?)
>
> (p. 143)

Rodriguez speaks of Mexicans without Mexico—Cesar Chavez, the leader of the United Farm Workers, "became a quixotic figure; Gandhi without an India" (p. 68). Rodriguez's metaphor for the cities of Tijuana and San Diego is a hearse separated from its mourners by rush-hour traffic. In his rhetoric there is always a lack, a gap, a void, a vacuum. Readers may thus well be in the position to remind this Brown Orpheus that his mythical counterpart was also not allowed to look back.

HUNGER OF MEMORY: SPANISH, ENGLISH, AND THE QUESTION OF LITERACY

Hunger of Memory: The Education of Richard Rodriguez has been highly praised. The book, which analyzes Chicano ethnicity and issues of acculturation, is one of the few texts that have broken the barriers between the Chicano culture and the American culture at large. Although other Chicano authors have done well in the literary mainstream (John Rechy, for example, whose writings focus on issues of homosexuality), their texts do not specifically analyze the issue of Chicano identity as Richard Rodriguez's book does. My intention in this section is to deconstruct the terms "Spanish" and "English" that appear throughout *Hunger of Memory*. In my opinion, the two terms serve as the foundation for Rodriguez's argumentation. Additionally, it is my position that the controversial nature of the book stems from the textual ambivalence Rodriguez reveals toward issues of literacy as a function of Spanish-English bilingualism and Chicano identity. In my opinion both the dominant and the Chicano cultures, from different ends of the spectrum, share in this ambivalence. Thus my analysis of *Hunger of Memory* will also allow me to explain the favorable reception of the book by the dominant culture and the unfavorable reception by Chicano critics.

The Spanish and English languages serve as the foundation upon which Rodriguez grounds his reasoning. His arguments regarding the usage of Spanish and English sound strangely familiar especially in light of the studies concerning the differences between oral and written language. It is apparent that Rodriguez associates the Spanish language with orality, and English with writing and consequently with literacy.

When the author refers to the Spanish language he mentions an oral emission (family members "would *say* something") and an aural reception ("I'd wait to *hear* her voice return to *soft-sounding* Spanish," his brothers and sisters tell him to *listen* to the language that makes him belong) (pp. 16, 17). Spanish is soft sounding, embracing, and it is the language of closeness and joyful return. Furthermore, in the pastoral tradition, Rodriguez associates the Spanish language with youth and innocence, a "golden age." Spanish also bonds the household, the family, and by extension the Chicano community. Spanish in the text is also labeled as a private language.

Unfortunately, Rodriguez also thinks that Spanish is a source of alienation from the dominant culture. The very language that unites a group separates the group from society at large: "Spanish speakers . . . seemed related to me, for I

sensed that we shared—through our language—the experience of feeling apart from *los gringos*" (pp. 15–16). Thus, from the very beginning Rodriguez considers the speaking of Spanish a barrier to fully participating in society. Written Spanish in *Hunger of Memory* is hardly ever mentioned, although Rodriguez does state that sometimes his mother and father would receive letters from relatives in Mexico. It is only later, as an adult, that he reads the Spanish writer Federico García Lorca and the Colombian writer Gabriel García Márquez.

In opposition to the soft, private, and intimate sound of Spanish, Rodriguez considers English hard, high-sounding, and painful. But mainly the author associates English with written language, a fact that did not escape the critics. John W. Donohue, for example, wrote that *Hunger of Memory* is a pleasure to read because it was actually "*written*—not just poured off the top of the author's head or chattered out of a typewriter or into a tape recorder" (p. 403; emphasis Donohue's). English, Rodriguez insists throughout the book, is a public language. The word "public" is therefore almost a synonym for English. Rodriguez also associates the word "public" with the written language: written words are "intrinsically *public*," writing makes possible a "*public* identity" (pp. 180, 181; emphasis added). Thus, English and writing become equivalent through their common bond with the word "public." It's no surprise Rodriguez equates English and writing, since for the United States, English is the language of education, of high culture. High culture in the form of books is manifested in writing. As opposed to language that is emitted orally and perceived as sound, written language is emitted graphically and perceived visually. Its reception is not accompanied by sound—it is silent. Silence for the author becomes more acute when exercising his profession as a writer: doing research at the British Museum or writing in his San Francisco apartment. Silence thus emerges as a metaphor for the lack of communication, of isolation and solitude. The word "silence" permeates the work. Tomás Rivera sees the whole book as dealing with silence: "*Hunger of Memory* establishes its tone through patterns based on the ideas of silence and the centrality of language—silence versus non-silence, silence and active language, silence and culture, silence and intelligence" (p. 6).

Once the author makes these connections between writing and solitude, he blames the acquisition of English for his alienation. In one of the most quoted passages of the book, Richard points to the precise moment of his rude awakening. The nuns ask Richard's parents to speak English for the benefit of their children. His parents, unable to speak English well, agree to use that language when speaking to their children. In a moment of revelation, upon hearing his parents speaking Spanish and switching to English for the benefit of their child, Rodriguez feels rebuffed:

> Those *gringo* sounds they uttered startled me. Pushed me away. In that moment of trivial misunderstanding and profound insight, I felt my throat twisted by unsounded grief. I turned quickly and left the room. But I had no place to escape to with Spanish.
>
> (pp. 21–22)

Rodriguez associates the use of Spanish by the family so closely with identity that he blames the introduction of English to the household with the weakening of the family. He very clearly states that "Americanization," and with it the gradual acquisition of English, was accompanied by a gradual separation from his parents (p. 23). He also very clearly states that, having learned "public" language, "it would never again be easy for me to hear intimate family voices" (p. 28). Rodriguez's separation from the family by extension separates him from his ethnic community.

Ironically, it is not the acquisition of English that causes his alienation. English allows Rodriguez to establish ties to another community. In English he addresses this "public, this Other" (p. 187). But Richard is not able to reestablish communication with his Spanish-speaking relatives because he loses the ability to speak Spanish. His relatives call him "*pocho*" (they would have us believe that he has been touched by evil, he speaks the language of the outside) they make fun of him because he cannot address them but with a few elementary words in his native tongue. Rodriguez is unable to perceive that the acquisition of English allows him to communicate with more people and thus extend his community. He believes that English and Spanish are mutually incompatible and that the learning of English, as the nuns' request to his parents shows, can only come about with the unlearning of Spanish.

The characteristics associated with the oral and written languages in classical discourse, as detailed in Jacques Derrida's *Of Grammatology*, are also associated with Spanish and English in *Hunger of Memory*. As Derrida has pointed out, classical discourse privileges the voice by assuming that its relationship with the mind is unmediated. Spoken words are the symbols of mental experience and "mirror things by natural resemblance" (p. 11). According to Derrida, "The order of natural and universal signification . . . would be produced as spoken language" (p. 11).

Since Rodriguez associates orality with his native language, it is in Spanish that the "natural and universal signification" is produced in Rodriguez's text. The author feels his sense of belonging that filters through the Spanish language. The full meaning of the words uttered in Spanish is impossible to translate. One time when the boy is playing with a nonspeaker of Spanish, his grandmother calls him and tells him something. His friend asks Rodriguez to translate, and he realizes he cannot convey the total meaning of the words; their apparent meaning goes beyond signification. The feelings conveyed in Spanish are intimate and private. This intimacy he cannot express nor share, especially in English. Spanish is the "natural" state. In his Spanish-speaking arcadia, Rodriguez does not analyze the language, he hears it and feels secure; inside, he belongs. Words in Spanish convey more than a message; words in Spanish evidence his ties with his relatives and the Mexican community where he belongs.

Once Richard learns to write (English) he enters what is an unnatural state in classical discourse. Jacques Derrida writes: "The sign is always a sign of the Fall. Absence always relates to distancing from God" (p. 283). Ousted because of writing, Rodriguez needs logic and reason to find his way to the heart. Writing now allows him to put things in perspective. "By finding public [English] words to describe one's feelings, one can describe oneself to oneself," he writes (p. 187). Now he needs the written English language to understand what he feels, whereas before his feelings were conveyed directly in Spanish, without needing the written language as mediator. Rodriguez writes that English has provided "freedom from the intimate" ("Literature," p. 15).

In the type of discourse that privileges the voice, the written sign is viewed as a supplement. This is also clear in *Hunger of Memory*, where English becomes the supplement of Spanish. The supplementary nature of English explains why Rodriguez thinks of writing as being secondary, less important: "Writing . . . was an activity I thought of as a kind of report, evidence of learning. . . . Writing was performed after the fact; it was not the exciting experience of learning itself" (p. 181).

Additionally, English becomes Rodriguez's *pharmakon*. The *pharmakon*, according to Derrida, is a sort of medicine: "this philter, which acts as both remedy and poison" ("Plato's Pharmacy," p. 70). It operates through seduction and "makes one stray from one's general, natural, habitual paths and laws" (p. 70). Derrida equates it with writing because in Plato's *Phaedrus* the title character leads Socrates out of the city to find a peaceful spot where they can discuss the written text Phaedrus carries with him. In Derrida's eyes, the text becomes a lure. The *pharmakon* is a remedy, a recipe, a poison, a drug, a philter, that leads astray (p. 71). As a medicine or remedy, the pharmakon has the power to cure, but if not used properly—if applied to a healthy body, or applied in the wrong doses—it can kill. This pharmakon is both good and bad; it is both life and death.

Since English represents writing in *Hunger of Memory*, it becomes Rodriguez's *pharmakon*. The English language has the ability to lure, cure, and kill. Richard is lured out of his arcadia by the English written books that his teachers present to him. English also is the bearer of high culture; it is the medicine that the nuns make Richard's parents administer to their children at home in order to "cure" them of the disease (Spanish) that does not allow them to participate in society. Within the nice equations that Rodriguez has established, eliminating Spanish implies eliminating speech, and classical discourse associates speech with life. It is very telling that the magazine Rodriguez remembers his grandmother reading is *Life en Español* (p. 37).

In *Hunger of Memory*, Spanish represents life, English represents death. Silence, as we said, is a consequence of writing, and Rodriguez equates writing with the English language. Rodriguez establishes this relationship upon the death of his grandmother. Carlos R. Hortas points out that Richard's grandmother always "spoke lovingly to him in Spanish (she knew no English)." Hortas goes on to quote Rodriguez's description of his grandmother's funeral:

> Her face appeared calm—but distant and unyielding to love. It was not the face I remembered seeing most often. It was the face she made in public when the clerk at Safeway asked her some question and I would have to respond. It was her public face the mortician had designed with his dubious art.
>
> (p. 40)

"The public face is cold, the public face is a mask of death," Hortas writes (p. 357). Although Richard's grandmother spoke no

English, Rodriguez himself seems to believe that the mask of death, the public mask, is also an English mask.

But how can we explain the fact that although his grandmother spoke Spanish, which is associated with life, she winds up dead? The author has pointed out in "Literature and the Nonliterate" that:

> In Charles Dickens, Mrs. Gaskell, and Harriet Beecher Stowe, the characters who speak with accents are the characters who will end up dead, who will end up badly. The lower class characters who survive are always those daughters and sons who manage somehow to get an education, who manage to speak the impeccable language of their masters.
>
> (p. 10)

If the Spanish language kills and the English language represents death, then Spanish is somewhat equivalent to original sin: it begins life but eventually leads to death. It is thus a disease, which only the *pharmakon* baptism can cure. By Rodriguez's own lament regarding his loss of the Spanish language, we can only assume that the nuns recommended too high a dosage of the English *pharmakon*. Rodriguez's impeccable usage of the English language also guaranteed his survival. Rodriguez stayed very much alive, as his success and the favorable reception of his book showed.

The notion of classical discourse as a function of Spanish and English also extends to Rodriguez's philosophy regarding the pastoral. Although *Hunger of Memory* is considered an autobiography because it deals with Rodriguez's life, in its construction the text borrows heavily from the pastoral. As it is generally known, the pastoral "imitates rural life, usually the life of an imaginary Golden Age, in which the loves of shepherds and shepherdesses play a prominent part." (Congleton, p. 603). Rodriguez titles the introduction to his text "Middle-Class Pastoral," and additionally he acknowledges that his book is "a kind of pastoral" in which he plays a "shepherd" (*Hunger*, p. 6).

Rodriguez experienced the pastoral in his youth. An old woman's voice, "like so many of the Spanish voices I'd hear in public, recalled the *golden age* of my youth" (p. 26; emphasis added). Innocence, togetherness, intimacy, nature—all the positive qualities are thus associated with this golden age and the speaking of Spanish. In that brief era, Richard is not aware of the problems that plague society. As a child he does not react when he is called a "greaser" or "pancho."

English draws Richard out of his arcadia. As an adult, he culturally separates from his family, his home, and his community. English, the language of "high" culture, of the public, of the outside, is now Rodriguez's language. Richard is an avid reader; his ousting from Eden and fall from grace are caused by his tasting the apple of culture. Richard feels that he mortally sinned when he separated himself from Spanish, the language of his parents, the language that conveyed the intimate feelings of the family. The English language that gave him culture also, as his lament shows, caused his isolation. Rodriguez complains about the solitude and alienation he feels in the academic profession. He writes that he "yearned for that time when I had not been so alone" (p. 71). *Hunger of Memory* is a strange pastoral, since Richard mourns the loss not of a loved one, but of the Spanish language.

The literal meaning of Rodriguez's isolation and loss of innocence, played against the traditional pastoral backdrop, highlights the self-reflexivity of the text, which contributes to its parodical nature. Wayne C. Booth writes that in parody, the reader, after rejecting the surface meaning, reconstructs it to find another "incongruous and 'higher' meaning" (p. 72). Renato Poggioli has also stated that the pastoral is meant to be artificial and untrue: "The bucolic dream has no other reality than that of imagination and art" (p. 2). In the pastoral, class and wealth are bestowed upon characters merely to point out the irrelevance of material possessions and the importance of spiritual ones. The reader is not supposed to take seriously the lord's departure from the city to live among the shepherds. Consequently, all the "Spanish angst" of *Hunger of Memory* could be nothing more than a literary trope if read in this framework (p. 190). In the context of the pastoral, Rodriguez's stance against his Chicano culture could be interpreted by the reader as having exactly the opposite meaning. If *Hunger* is read as a pastoral in which the writer relies heavily on his personal experiences, the Spanish-language arcadia is held up as an ideal while English represents the language of the innocent shepherds who do not know that such a mythical place even exists. Since Rodriguez considers his text a "middle class pastoral," the innocent, naive shepherds are not the members of the Chicano community but the members of the middle class. Ironically, the political right has praised the book because of its supposed advocacy of English monolingualism, although in its pastoral mythification of the Spanish language the text would seem to advocate bilingualism. Thus the "message" of the text really contradicts the assertions made by the political right in its praising of the book.

The ambivalence of *Hunger of Memory* toward the issue of literacy as a function of Spanish and English is then carried forward to the notion of race and ethnicity. By pondering the question of the Spanish language with respect to the acquisition of literacy, Rodriguez also questions ethnicity and racial identity as a function of the Spanish language. He will later equate the Spanish language with race. He first learns to pray in Spanish and accompanies his family to the Church of Our Lady of Guadalupe. The Virgin of Guadalupe—the "Mexican Mary," as Rodriguez calls her—was an Indian maiden, "dark just like me," he adds (p. 85).

It almost goes without saying that if English is the language of the public, of the Other, the face of this Other is white. The gringo language is English. In the gringo church, Mary was a "serene white lady" (p. 86). Richard was supposed to pretend that the shy Mexican Mary and the European Mary were one and the same. This association between "race" and language is extremely naive, but ironically it also reflects the widely held perception in the United States that the Latin American population is homogeneously Indian or mestizo. With respect to Rodriguez, associating the Spanish language with race presents psychological problems that lie beyond the scope of a literary analysis. Associating the Spanish language so closely with his Indian body and the English language with the white Other explains why once Rodriguez acquires English and becomes aware of his linguistic separation from his ethnic community, he tries to shave off his dark skin. He believes that the English language goes hand in hand with a light complexion. Obviously, acquiring a new language is much easier than acquiring a new color of skin.

All the contradictions present in *Hunger of Memory* stem from the very basic assumptions of what language (Spanish or English) means with respect to literacy, identity, and "race." We find, for example, that although Rodriguez states that the Chicano culture should be monolingual, he presents his household as an Eden held together by the usage of the Spanish language. Rodriguez presents Spanish as the ultimate sign of life, and yet it also leads to death. He states that the key to participation in society is education, and yet—though he does not state this point—traditional education must become a curse that alienates Chicanos from their ethnic community, because it leaves out their own culture. Rodriguez writes that the whole issue of minorities is a myth, and yet his family heritage is Mexican, the author spoke Spanish before he spoke English, and he lived in a society where he was labeled according to "race." The nonexistence of linguistic and racial minorities implies the nonexistence of majorities, and yet Rodriguez does not address his book to the "reader" but to the "gringo reader." In his book, Rodriguez attempts to show that he is not "Chicano," and yet he uses what critics have labeled as "stylistic ethnic identity markers," or brief switches to Spanish that serve to confirm his

Chicano ethnicity. (See the work of John J. Gumperz and Eduardo Hérnandez Chávez, and of Rodolfo Jacobson.) Since Rodriguez does not address a Chicano bilingual public, most of the Spanish words he uses are either cognates (like *católico* or *Estados Unidos*) or words that are easily recognized by the non-Spanish speaker ("gringo," "macho," and "sombrero"). In truly bilingual code-switching, speakers choose the words and phrases in either language depending on the ability to convey an added level of meaning, nuances that only one language or the other can express. When a speaker uses a word in Spanish, there is no need to translate its meaning, since the listener already knows what the word means. If Rodriguez feels that his English-reading public will find his Spanish words difficult to understand, he translates: "*fuerte*, 'strong'" (p. 128). Rodriguez could have easily avoided the use of ethnic markers in the writing of his text had he so wished. These ethnic markers also allow him to authorize his discourse before the dominant culture.

By any measure, we have to conclude that Richard Rodriguez's literary preoccupations stem from his own experiences as a Chicano. Although some critics, Tzvetan Todorov being the most prominent among them, negate the role of "race" in literature, Roland Barthes has shown in his *Writing Degree Zero* that writing is determined by the social and historical circumstances in which it is produced. Although in writing one can choose to skirt personal experiences, it is unlikely that those experiences will not be represented in the text. Rodriguez's book, for example, explores Chicano issues and preoccupations: bilingualism, Mexican and Chicano culture, affirmative action. One of his articles appearing in *Harper's* is titled "Across the Borders of History" and analyzes the cultural and economic differences between Mexico's Tijuana and California's San Diego. Another one of his essays, "Mexico's Children," specifically analyzes the role the children of Mexico—that is, the Chicanos—play in the United States. Many of his articles, while exploring the nature of Mexican culture in the United States, invariably turn into a cultural analysis of the American Southwest. To Richard Rodriguez, obviously the Southwest represents the point of juncture between Mexican and U.S. society. His literary search of these themes represents, in a sense, a quest for his own identity as reflected in these two cultures. Although the choice of subject might be dictated by the assignments of the magazines for which Rodriguez publishes, Roland Barthes states in his *Writing Degree Zero* that writing, once produced, is a Pandora's box that unleashes both the conscious and subconscious preoccupations of the author.

Like most ethnic literature, Rodriguez's texts are romantically narcissistic. Although *Hunger of Memory* is in the first person, it often mentions his name, speaking about him in the third person as though trying to project his Self on the Other. His need for reflecting his image on the mirror of the dominant culture is evidenced in his binary argumentation: public and private, English and Spanish, Chicano and gringo, Mexico and United States. Abdul R. JanMohamed has called this practice the "manichean allegory," which he associates with colonialist literature: "diverse yet interchangeable oppositions between white and black, good and evil, superiority and inferiority, civilization and savagery, intelligence and emotion, rationality and sensuality, self and Other, subject and object" (p. 82). Rodriguez does not base his search for identity on the Self, but on the Self as a function of the Other: "The [gringo] reader became my excuse, my reason for writing" (*Hunger*, p. 187).

Rodriguez himself acknowledges his entering into what Juan Bruce-Novoa has called the Chicano space, the limbo that lies somewhere between the American and the Mexican culture, between the United States and Mexico, between an English and a Spanish Department. Rodriguez feels that he is not part of U.S. culture because of his skin, his heritage, his preoccupations. And yet, he says, the bilingual Chicano also scorns him. Rodriguez does not belong in academia, but neither does he belong with his Spanish-speaking family. The fact that Rodriguez falls somewhere between the two cultures is evidenced by some of the titles of the reviews: "The Child of Two Cultures" (Zweig), "Between Two Worlds" (Donohue), "Ricardo/Richard" (Seidner Adler). The reviewer for the *Christian Century* states that the book presents "a marginalized child living between Hispanic and Anglo worlds" (p. 580). The hybrid nature of Rodriguez's book is also evidenced by the title and subtitle: *Hunger of Memory: The Education of Richard Rodriguez* alludes to both Richard Wright's *American Hunger* and Henry Adams's *The Education of Henry Adams* (Bell, p. 38).

The "American" book of Richard Rodriguez also uses many images typical of literature produced in a dominant context. He speaks of Caliban, he refers to English as the language of the Other. Even though he writes extremely well, he considers himself a parvenu to the English language. The culture that English represents does not rightfully belong to him; he feels he has stolen the books of the dominant culture. His use of a word like "master" would, in his own binary argumentation, suggest "slave."

With any other text, the reader can withdraw to what Maurice Blanchot has called the "space of literature." There race, identity, ethnicity, and nationality do not exist. *Hunger of Memory,* though, does not allow the reader to withdraw to this literary utopia. The use of ethnic markers reminds the reader that the author is Mexican. He also very specifically reminds the readers that they are not. Those readers who do not belong in Rodriguez's "Other" category are thus placed in the position of Peeping Toms, voyeurs, and made to feel like the gardener or the maid, the people with no voice in those California houses in which Richard Rodriguez feels so comfortable as a guest.

We can only conclude that the reception to *Hunger of Memory* was thus a function of eth-

nicity. "Gringos" read his book, according to the articles appearing in *Newsweek* and the *Nation,* "not because Richard Rodriguez can talk about Shakespeare and the pastoral, but because he is a Mexican-American" (*Nation* p. 599, Strouse p. 74). "As a final irony," Susan Seidner Adler writes, "it was only because of his background that his views gained him a certain celebrity and made him much sought-after on the lecture circuits" (p. 83).

When we take into account the contradictory nature of *Hunger of Memory,* we cannot help but question the favorable reception the book had. Given that all literature reflects an ideology, we can only assume that the dominant culture has seen its values reflected in the book. The text, for example, appeals to British literature and completely ignores Hispanic culture: Rodriguez quotes Shakespeare in his pastoral, but Miguel de Cervantes and Luis de Góngora—the Spanish authors that serious critics of the pastoral would not dare leave out—are not present.

The values of the dominant culture are also reflected in the question of silence. Rodriguez's silence extends beyond the preoccupation with isolation and lack of communication that is associated with writing. In becoming educated and learning to write (English), Rodriguez has also learned to silence his Hispanic voice, his opinions, and his inner feelings. Tomás Rivera writes that the "author indicates that Spanish was and is his personal voice. But it is an inactive passive voice that became neutered, sterile, and finally silent—dead" (p. 6). Rodriguez is an orphan in his English-language book: "I do not give voice to my parents by writing about their lives. . . . My parents do not truly speak on my pages" (p. 186). Because Rodriguez is addressing an English-speaking public, the Spanish-speaking community is not represented in his book. Since he is also avowedly a "cultural orphan," he represents no threat to the dominant culture and can be adopted by the philanthropic reader.

Many reviewers of the book also pick up on the question of Rodriguez's guilt. He says he felt guilty because he had "somehow committed a sin of betrayal by learning English" and disassociating himself from his family (p. 30). Some reviewers thus saw *Hunger of Memory* as a mea culpa and an attempt by the author to exorcize his guilt, although one has to wonder if the guilt that Rodriguez talks about is not also shared by the dominant culture. Charles V. Willie writes that the dominant culture should be concerned about the fact that our present educational system persuades minorities to "renounce the language and culture of their childhood and youth, as Rodriguez has done" (p. 41). He further states that the dominant culture should be concerned about an educational system that "does to minorities what our system has done to Richard Rodriguez" (p. 41).

To merely point the finger at the dominant culture because of its acceptance of the book is to ignore the fact that many critics, such as George Yúdice and Ramón Saldívar, use the text as an excuse to advance preestablished ethnic and political points of view. Yúdice for example, analyzes Rodriguez's text from the perspective of postmodernism and presents Rodriguez as a linguistic Gregorio Cortez who defies the dominant culture with the only means available to him. Yúdice believes that the text is ironic since it manages to inscribe issues of ethnicity in a text that is meant for consumers with an anti-ethnic stance. He thus presents Rodriguez as a postmodern rebel who stands up to the dominant culture by speaking along the "lines of escape" (p. 217) that the dominant culture provides.

Ramón Saldívar, on the other hand, faults Rodriguez for making an issue of his individuality, in the process separating himself from the collective unconsciousness of the Chicanos. Saldívar chooses to analyze *Hunger of Memory* in opposition to *Barrio Boy* by Ernesto Galarza. Galarza's book has all the elements associated with widely held conceptions of Chicano narrative. *Barrio Boy* is the typical book in which the rhetorical nature of the composition serves as a metaphor for states of cultural and ethnic awareness. The protagonist in Galarza's book is born in Jalcocotán in the state of Nayarit, Mexico, and the novel focuses on his trip north to the United States. As the boy travels physically he also travels ethnically: he goes from being "Mexican" to being one of the "*chicanos,* the name by which we called an unskilled worker born in Mexico and just arrived in the United States" (Galarza, p. 200). From being "Chicano," the protagonist then becomes a *pocho* (discolored or pale): "Turning *pocho* was a half-step toward turning American" (Galarza, p. 207). Saldívar concludes that *Hunger of Memory* has had a better reception than *Barrio Boy* because of "our tendency to disguise the force of ideology behind the mask of aesthetics" (p. 33). It is obvious that for Saldívar *Barrio Boy* is more politically and ethnically correct than *Hunger of Memory*. Reading Saldívar, it is unclear whether he disagrees with the textual or the biographical Rodriguez (although he probably disagrees with both). Furthermore, Saldívar seems to have fallen victim to the liberal intelligentsia who perceive Chicanos only as informants and not as producers of culture in the "high, courtly" vein of Rodriguez (*Hunger,* p. 6).

Politicians have also misused *Hunger of Memory*. The book plays right into the perception of the political right that Spanish is a hindrance to participation in public life. *Hunger of Memory* also caters to the perception of the dominant culture that literacy can only come about through English, an attitude brought out by the resistance to bilingual education. George Yúdice, for example, credits the book with the passage of Proposition 61, which made English the official language of California.

The drawbacks Richard Rodriguez attributes to Spanish and English are easily understood in terms of the differences between the oral and the written languages. Rodriguez thinks that the speaking of Spanish hinders participation in the social, economic, and political arena. He also blames English for his sense of alienation from his peers and his separation from the Spanish-speaking community. It is no secret that society emphasizes the written at the expense of the oral. It is also true that reading and writing are solitary enterprises that contribute to a sense of alienation. When Rodriguez writes that people should learn English, he is merely stating that people should learn to write. And writing leads to reasoning, to exteriorization of ideas, to logic. By means of the written language, one becomes educated, and as we know, education provides the key to fully participating in society. Society alienates those people who cannot read or write, regardless of the language they speak. Education engenders power, a power that Rodriguez wrongly associates with a public English identity.

Hunger of Memory suffers from all the phono-logocentric assumptions for which Jacques Derrida criticizes Jean-Jacques Rousseau, Claude Lévi-Strauss, and Ferdinand de Saussure in his *Of Grammatology*. In establishing his dichotomy of Spanish/English, public/private, speech/writing, Rodriguez forgets that Spanish also has a written counterpart, and that the same feelings of alienation from one's own ethnic and social group can be experienced if one becomes educated in Spanish. This is an all too clear reality for those Chicanos who are educated in Spanish Departments instead of English Departments in the United States. The Spanish writer Federico García Lorca, the Colombian writer Gabriel García Márquez, and the Mexican writer Juan García Ponce are as alien to barrio culture as William Shakespeare, Henry Adams, and William Faulkner.

It is a sad commentary on the condition of American Studies that the book that has managed to open up the dialogue between two different cultures is one whose internal logic is based on the dominant group's prejudiced assumptions regarding Chicano culture. As Ramón Saldívar has pointed out, the reasons for reading *Hunger of Memory* ("it is well written," "it is an honest and courageous book") sound as mere excuses for the presentation of values that mirror those of the dominant culture. *Hunger of Memory* should be viewed as an indictment of a society that does not allow Chicanos to represent their culture, their values, and ultimately, their own literature. If there is one lesson to be learned from the favorable reception that *Hunger of Memory* found outside the Chicano community, it is that reading, like writing, is never innocent.

Selected Bibliography

WORKS OF RICHARD RODRIGUEZ

BOOKS

Hunger of Memory: The Education of Richard Rodriguez. Boston: David R. Godine, 1982.

Days of Obligation: An Argument with My Mexican Father. New York: Viking, 1992.

Brown: The Last Discovery of America. New York: Viking, 2002.

ESSAYS

"Mexico's Children." *American Scholar* 55 (spring 1986): 161–177.

"Across the Borders of History: Tijuana and San Diego Exchange Futures." *Harper's Magazine*, March 1987, pp. 42–53.

"Literature and the Nonliterate." *Literature of the Oppressed* 1, no. 1 (fall 1987) : 6–19.

SECONDARY WORKS

Alarcón, Norma. "Tropology of Hunger: The 'Miseducation' of Richard Rodriguez." *The Ethnic Canon: Histories, Institutions, and Interventions.* Edited by David Palumbo-Liu. Minneapolis: University of Minnesota Press, 1995. Pp. 140–152.

Antón-Pacheco Sánchez, Luisa. "En torno a la identidad cultural: *Hunger of Memory* y *Days of Obligation* de Richard Rodriguez." *Revista canaria de estudios ingleses* 32–33 (1996): 183–191.

Bell, Michael Davitt. "Fitting into a Tradition of Autobiography." Review of *Hunger of Memory. Change* 14, no. 7 (October 1982): 36, 38–39.

Blom, Gerdien. "Divine Individual, Cultural Identities: Post-Identitarian Representations and Two Chicana/o Texts." *Thamyris* 4, no. 2 (1992): 295–324.

Breiger, Marek. "Richard Rodriguez." In *Updating the Literary West.* Fort Worth, Texas: Western Literature Association, in association with Texas Christian University Press, 1997. Pp. 394–400.

Browdy de Hernandez, Jennifer. "Postcolonial Blues: Ambivalence and Alienation in the Autobiographies of Richard Rodriguez and V. S. Naipaul." *A/B: Auto/Biography Studies* 12, no. 2 (fall 1997): 151–165.

Bruce-Novoa, Juan. "Rechy and Rodriguez: Double Crossing the Public/Private Line." In *Double Crossings/EntreCruzamientos.* Edited by Martín Flores and Carlos von Son. Fair Haven, N.J.: Nuevo Espacio, 2001. Pp. 15–34.

Brunet, Elena. Review of *Hunger of Memory. Nation* 234, no. 19 (May 15, 1982): 599.

Candelaria, Cordelia Chavez. "Hang-Up of Memory: Another View of Growing Up Chicano." *American Book Review* 5, no. 2 (May–June 1983): 4.

Castro, Juan E. de. "Richard Rodriguez in 'Borderland': The Ambiguity of Hybridity." *Aztlán* 26, no. 1 (2001): 101–126.

Cazemajou, Jean. "*Hunger of Memory* (1982) de Richard Rodriguez: La parole et le Verbe." In *Le facteur religieux en Amérique du Nord, V: Religion et groupes ethniques au Canada et aux Etats-Unis.* Edited by Jean Beranger and Pierre Guillaume. Talence: Maison des Sciences de l'Homme d'Aquitaine, 1984. Pp. 147–165.

Crowley, Paul S. J. "An Ancient Catholic: An Interview with Richard Rodriguez." In *Catholic Lives, Contemporary America.* Edited by Thomas J. Ferraro. Durham, N.C.: Duke University Press, 1997. Pp. 259–265.

Danahay, Martin A. "Breaking the Silence: Symbolic Violence and the Teaching of Contemporary 'Ethnic' Autobiography." *College Literature* 18, no. 3 (1991): 64–79.

———. "Richard Rodriguez's Poetics of Manhood." In *Fictions of Masculinity: Crossing Cultures, Crossing Sexualities.* Edited by Peter F. Murphy. New York: New York University Press, 1994. Pp. 290–307.

Decker, Jeffrey Louis. "Mr. Secrets: Richard Rodriguez Flees the House of Memory." *Transition* 61 (1993): 124–133.

Delden, Maarten van. "Crossing the Great Divide: Rewritings of the U.S.-Mexican Encounter in Walter Abish and Richard Rodriguez." *Studies in Twentieth Century Literature* 25, no. 1 (winter 2001): 118–139.

Donohue, John W. "Between Two Worlds." Review of *Hunger of Memory. America* 146, no. 20 (May 22, 1982): 403–404.

Durczak, Jerzy. "Multicultural Autobiography and Language: Richard Rodriguez and Eva Hoffman." *Crossing Borders: American Literature and Other Artistic Media.* Edited by Jadwiga Maszewska. Peoria: Spoon River, 1992. Pp. 19–30.

Fine, Laura. "Claiming Personas and Rejecting Other-Imposed Identities: Self-Writing as Self-Righting in the Autobiographies of Richard Rodriguez." *Biography* 19, no. 2 (spring 1996): 119–136.

Flores, Lauro. "Chicano Autobiography: Culture, Ideology, and the Self." *Americas Review* 18, no. 2 (summer 1990): 80–91.

Fogelquist, Jim. "Ethnicity, Sexuality, and Identity in the Autobiographies of Richard Rodriguez." In *Double Crossings/EntreCruzamientos.* Edited by Mario Martín Flores and Carlos von Son. Fair Haven, N.J.: Nuevo Espacio, 2001. Pp. 35–65.

Foster, David William. "Other and Difference in Richard Rodriguez's Hunger of Memory." *Postcolonial and Queer Theories: Intersections and Essays.* Edited by John C. Hawley. Westport, Conn.: Greenwood Press, 2001. Pp. 139–153.

Grant, Gerald. Review of *Hunger of Memory. Teachers College Record* 85, no. 3 (spring 1984): 525–530.

Gregorio, Eduardo de. "Language and Male Identity Construction in the Cultural Borderlands: Richard Rodriguez's *Hunger of Memory.*" In *Literature and Ethnicity in the Cultural Borderlands.* Edited by Jesús Benito and Ana María Manzanas. Amsterdam: Rodopi, 2002. Pp. 127–134.

Guajardo, Paul. *Chicano Controversy: Oscar Acosta and Richard Rodriguez.* New York: Peter Lang, 2002.

———. "Identity Extremes: The Autobiographical Impulse of Oscar Acosta and Richard Rodriguez." *DAI* 57, no. 2 (1996): 680A.

Hogue, W. Lawrence. "An Unresolved Modern Experience: Richard Rodriguez's *Hunger of Memory.*" *Americas Review* 20, no. 1 (spring 1992): 52–64.

Hortas, Carlos R. "*Review of* Hunger of Memory." *Harvard Educational Review* 53, no. 3 (August 1983): 355–359.

Limón, José E., ed. "Richard Rodriguez: Public Intellectual." *Texas Studies in Literature and Language* 40, no. 4 (winter 1998): 389–459.

Márquez, Antonio C. "Richard Rodriguez's *Hunger of Memory* and New Perspectives on Ethnic Autobiography." In *Teaching American Ethnic Literatures: Nineteen Essays.* Edited by John R. Maitino and David R. Peck. Albuquerque: University of New Mexico Press, 1996. Pp. 237–254.

———. "Richard Rodriguez's *Hunger of Memory* and the Poetics of Experience." *Arizona Quarterly* 40, no. 2 (summer 1984): 130–141.

McNamara, Kevin R. "A Finer Grain: Richard Rodriguez's *Days of Obligation.*" *Arizona Quarterly* 53, no. 1 (spring 1997): 103–122.

Pérez Firmat, Gustavo. "Richard Rodriguez and the Art of Abstraction." *Colby Quarterly* 32, no. 4 (December 1996): 255–266.

Perry, Carolyn Elaine. "The Augustinian Confessional Tradition Transformed in *Black Boy* and *Hunger of Memory.*" *DAI* 62, no. 5 (2001): 1826.

Review of *Hunger of Memory. Christian Century,* May 12, 1982, p. 580.

Rivera, Tomás. "Richard Rodriguez's *Hunger of Memory* as Humanistic Antithesis." *MELUS* 11, no. 4 (winter 1984): 5–12.

Robinson, Louie García. "Me, Myself, and I." *San Francisco Review of Books* 19, nos. 4–5 (October–November 1994): 9–10.

Rodriguez, Randy A. "Aesthetics of Transgression in the Writings of Richard Rodriguez." *DAI* 60, no. 8 (2000): 2987.

———. "A Conversation with Richard Rodriguez." *JASAT* 27 (1996): 35–50.

————. "Richard Rodriguez Reconsidered: Queering the Sissy (Ethnic) Subject." *Texas Studies in Literature and Language* 40, no. 4 (winter 1998): 396–423.

Romero, Rolando J. "Spanish and English: The Question of Literacy in *Hunger of Memory*." *Confluencia* 6, no. 2 (1991): 89–100.

Rose, Shirley K. "Metaphors and Myths of Cross-Cultural Literacy: Autobiographical Narratives by Maxine Hong Kingston, Richard Rodriguez, and Malcolm X." *MELUS* 14, no. 1 (spring 1987): 3–15.

Rowe, Paul Lee. "Reading Richard Rodriguez's *Hunger of Memory*: A Dialogic Review of the Criticism from the Perspective of Working Class Academic." *DAI* 58, no. 11 (1998): 4274.

Saldívar, Ramon. "Ideologies of the Self: Chicano Autobiography." *Diacritics* 15, no. 3 (fall 1985): 25–34.

Sánchez, Rosaura. "Calculated Musings: Richard Rodriguez's Metaphysics of Difference." In *The Ethnic Canon: Histories, Institutions, and Interventions.* Edited by David Palumbo-Liu. Minneapolis: University of Minnesota Press, 1995. Pp. 153–173.

Savin, Ada. "La memoire de la rupture: Richard Rodriguez de *Hunger of Memory* à *Days of Obligation*." *Annales du centre de recherches sur l'Amérique anglophone* 20, no. 237 (1995): 131–141.

————. "Langue, identité et altérité dans *Hunger of Memory* de Richard Rodriguez." *L'altérité dans la littérature et la culture du monde anglophone.* Le Mans: Université du Maine, 1993. Pp. 229–234.

Schilt, Paige. "Anti-Pastoral and Guilty Vision in Richard Rodriguez's *Days of Obligation*." *Texas Studies in Literature and Language* 40, no. 4 (winter 1998): 424–441.

Schubnell, Matthias. "Lost in Translation: Complications of Bilingualism in the Memoirs of Eva Hoffman and Richard Rodriguez." *Trans* 13 (2002). Available at http://www.inst.at/trans/13Nr/schubnell13.htm.

Sedore, Timothy S. "'American Opera': An Interview with Richard Rodriguez." *South Carolina Review* 35, no. 1 (2002): 5–16.

————. "'Born at the Destination': An Interview with Richard Rodriguez." *New England Review: Middlebury Series* 22, no. 3 (summer 2001): 26–37.

————. "Violating the Boundaries: An Interview with Richard Rodriguez." *Michigan Quarterly Review* 38, no. 3 (summer 1999): 425–446.

Seidner Adler, Susan. "Ricardo/Richard." Review of *Hunger of Memory. Commentary,* July 1982, pp. 82–84.

Shuter, Bill. "The Confessions of Richard Rodriguez." *Cross Currents* 45, no. 1 (spring 1995): 95–105.

Staten, Henry. "Ethnic Authenticity, Class, and Autobiography: The Case of *Hunger of Memory*." *PMLA* 113, no. 1 (January 1998): 103–116.

Stavans, Ilan. "La identidad de Richard Rodriguez." *Torre* 10, no. 38 (1996): 203–208.

Strouse, Jean. "A Victim of Two Cultures." *Newsweek,* March 15, 1982, p. 74.

Tilden, Norma. "Word Made Flesh: Richard Rodriguez's 'Late Victorians' as Nativity Story." *Texas Studies in Literature and Language* 40, no. 4 (1998): 442–459.

Veeser, H. Aram. "'You're Not Just Telling Us What We Wanna Hear, Are You, Boy?'" *Poetics/Politics: Radical Aesthetics for the Classroom.* Edited by Amitava Kumar. New York: St. Martin's Press, 1999. Pp. 71–81.

Velasco, Juan. "Los laberintos de la mexicanidad: La construcción de la identidad en la autobiografia chicana contemporánea." *DAI* 56, no. 9 (1996): 3587A.

Villanueva-Collado, Alfredo. "Growing Up Hispanic: Discourse and Ideology in *Hunger of Memory* and *Family Installments.*" *Americas Review* 16, nos. 3–4 (1998): 75–90.

Waxman, Barbara Frey. "Feeding the 'Hunger of Memory' and an Appetite for the Future: The Ethnic 'Storied' Self and the American Authored Self in Ethnic Autobiography." In *Cross-Addressing: Resistance Literature and Cultural Borders.* Edited by John C. Hawley. Albany: State University of New York Press, 1996. Pp. 207–219.

Willie, Charles V. "First Learning Unchallenged and Untested." Review of *Hunger of Memory. Change* 14, no. 7 (October 1982): 37, 40–41.

Wolfe, Gregory. "A Conversation with Richard Rodriguez." *Image* 34 (2002): 53–68.

Yúdice, George. "Marginality and the Ethics of Survival." In *Universal Abandon?: The Politics of Postmodernism.* Edited by Andrew Ross. Minneapolis: University of Minnesota Press, 1988. Pp. 214–236.

Zweig, Paul. "The Child of Two Cultures." *The New York Times Book Review,* April 5, 1982, p. 1.

OTHER WORKS

Barthes, Roland. *Writing Degree Zero.* Translated by Annette Lavers and Colin Smith. London: Jonathan Cape, 1984.

Blanchot, Maurice. *The Space of Literature.* Translated by Ann Smock. Lincoln: University of Nebraska Press, 1982.

Booth, Wayne C. *A Rhetoric of Irony.* Chicago: University of Chicago Press, 1974.

Bruce-Novoa, Juan. "Deslinde del espacio literario Chicano." *Aztlán* 11, no. 2 (fall 1980): 323–338.

———. "The Space of Chicano Literature." In *The Chicano Literary World.* Las Vegas: New Mexico Highlands University, 1975. Pp. 22–51. Reprinted in *De Colores* 1, no. 4: 22–42.

Congleton, J. E. "Pastoral." In *Princeton Encyclopedia of Poetry and Poetics.* Princeton: Princeton University Press, 1974. Pp. 603–604

Derrida, Jacques. *Of Grammatology.* Translated by Gayatri Chakravorty Spivak. Baltimore: Johns Hopkins University Press, 1976.

———. "Plato's Pharmacy." In *Dissemination.* Translated by Barbara Johnson. Chicago: University of Chicago Press, 1981. Pp. 61–172.

Gumperz, John J., and Eduardo Hernandez Chávez. "Cognitive Aspects of Bilingual Communication." In *El lenguaje de los Chicanos: Regional and Social Characteristics Used by Mexican Americans.* Edited by Eduardo Hernandez Chávez and others. Arlington, Va.: Center for Applied Linguistics, 1975. Pp. 154–163.

Hassan, Ihab. "The Literature of Silence." In *The Postmodern Turn: Essays in Postmodern Theory and Culture.* Ohio: Ohio State University Press, 1987. Pp. 3–22.

Jacobson, Rodolfo. "The Social Implications of Intra-sentential Code-Switching." In *New Directions in Chicano Scholarship.* Edited by Ricardo Romo and Raymund Paredes. La Jolla: Chicano Studies Program, 1978. Pp. 227–256.

Padilla, Genaro. "The Recovery of Nineteenth-Century Chicano Autobiography." In *European Perspectives on Hispanic Literature of the United States.* Edited by Genviève Fabre. Houston: Arte Público Press, 1988. Pp. 44–54.

Paredes, Américo. *"With His Pistol in His Hand," A Border Ballad and Its Hero.* Austin: University of Texas Press, 1958.

Poggioli, Renato. *The Oaten Flute: Essays on Pastoral Poetry and the Pastoral Ideal.* Cambridge, Mass.: Harvard University Press, 1975.

Todorov, Tzevan. "'Race,' Writing, and Culture." Translated by Loulou Mack. In *"Race," Writing, and Difference.* Edited by Henry Louis Gates Jr. Chicago: Chicago University Press, 1986. Pp. 370–380.

Gary Soto

(1952–)

CHARLES TATUM

BORN IN FRESNO, California, on 12 April 1952 to parents of Mexican descent, Gary Soto overcame a childhood of poverty, loneliness, and alienation to become one of the finest and most versatile writers of his generation, an award-winning poet as well as a highly recognized prose writer and author of juvenile fiction, nonfiction, and poetry. His father, Manuel Soto, and his mother, Angie Treviño, met and married in Fresno in 1947, when they were both eighteen. Neither finished high school. Together they parented three young children—Gary, his older brother Rick, and his younger sister Debra—until Manuel's untimely death from an industrial accident when Gary was barely five years old. As Gary Soto describes it, a silence seemed to engulf the family as they struggled to cope with the sudden tragedy and sense of loss. It was not until many years later, when he was in the midst of a successful writing career, that Soto would begin to deal with that silence and the unexpressed pain he had felt with his father's sudden passing. He expresses in many poems and nonfiction prose pieces the delayed grief and longing for his father, particularly during the difficult years of his childhood and adolescence.

Realizing that she could not support her young family on the meager income she could earn working in the agricultural fields or in Fresno's factories, Soto's mother soon remarried. Soto's stepfather, who also brought small children to the marriage, was a heavy drinker who worked at mind-numbing jobs in a Fresno book-packing plant. Soto recounts the anguish he suffered as a child who had lost his father and who suddenly was forced to adapt to a life with a stepfather who treated him and his two siblings with a mixture of indifference and anger.

As Soto has said, he was a poor student throughout all of his elementary and junior high school years and barely graduated from high school in 1970 (Buckley, *Quarterly West,* p. 150). Instead of going the route of most of his Chicano classmates, however, who either joined the military or took low-paying local jobs, he enrolled at Fresno City College, where he decided to seek a major in geography. It was while browsing through the library's poetry section that he happened upon the anthology *The New American Poetry,* which included the poetry of Edward Field, Gregory Corso, Kenneth Koch, Allen Ginsberg, and Lawrence Ferlinghetti. "I thought wow, wow, wow. I wanted to do this thing" (Lee, *Ploughshares,* p. 189).

This random discovery of some of the most exciting and innovative contemporary American poetry was decisive in Soto's beginning to write poetry as a process of self-discovery. An Edward Field poem, "Unwanted," had a particularly strong impact on him. As he stated in an unpublished interview with Don Lee in 1988, he saw in this poem that his own sense of keen alienation was not unique but in fact was part of the general human condition: "It was . . . a human pain." Soto apparently recognized at this crucial juncture that poetry specifically and written language generally have the power to transform a uniquely subjective and personal experience into one that is shared broadly by humankind. He soon transferred to California State University (CSU), Fresno, to embark on his formal study of literature.

Soto began an intellectual and artistic journey of hard work and self-discipline that would result in his graduating from CSU, Fresno, magna cum laude in 1974. Crucial to his development as a poet was the mentoring he received from the critically acclaimed American poet Philip Levine, a creative writing professor who was helpful in teaching him that, in Soto's words, "subject and craft have to go hand in hand. . . . They have to mingle together" (Torres, *Reference Guide to American Literature*, p. 778). Soto said in the 1988 interview that Levine was a "constant master of the nuts and bolts of how to read a poem—how to analyze and how to critique a poem." Also crucial to Soto's development as a poet was the group of young Chicano and non-Chicano poets who were either fellow students or living in Fresno: Leonard Adame, Omar Salinas, Ernesto Trejo, and Jon Veinberg. This group would eventually become known as the Fresno Poets.

Soto married Carolyn Oda in May 1975. She is a Japanese American whose parents came from a working-class background similar to Soto's. Soon after, Soto began his postgraduate studies in the creative writing program at the University of California, Irvine. He earned a master of fine arts (M.F.A.) in creative writing in 1976, and after spending a year as a visiting writer at San Diego State University he accepted a faculty position as an assistant professor in the Depart-ment of English at the University of California, Berkeley. He was promoted to associate professor of English and Ethnic Studies in 1985 but then chose to leave a full-time academic position to devote more time to his writing. He served as a part-time senior lecturer in the Department of English until 1991, when he resigned his position and left the university. In his essay "Who Is Your Reader?" published in *The Effects of Knut Hamsun on a Fresno Kid* in 2000, Soto refers pointedly to his discontent with academic politics, problems, and pretentiousness: "I'm alerting the reader that I don't teach, having taken to heart that country-western favorite, 'Take this Job and Shove It'" (pp. 199–200).

Contributing to his disaffection with university life was his realization that few Chicanos taught literature in the University of California system, or elsewhere in the country, which meant there was correspondingly little appreciation for Chicano literature. In the same essay, he states: "You need more than wine to overcome these dismal figures. So much for affirmative action, and so much for the documentation of my work or the work of other Chicanos who are creating literary history" (p. 204).

Yet despite his strongly held negative opinion of academic life, Soto has held several short-term academic appointments, including a prestigious appointment as Distinguished Professor of Creative Writing at the University of California, Riverside, for several years; as Elliston Poet at the University of Cincinnati in 1988; and as the Martin Luther King/Cesar Chavez/Rosa Parks Visiting Professor of English at Wayne State University in 1990. He currently lives with his wife in the San Francisco Bay Area. Gary and Carolyn Soto have one daughter, Mariko Heidi, born in 1980.

Soto has won numerous national and international literary awards and fellowships, including the *Nation*/Discovery prize, 1975; the United States Award from the International Poetry Forum, 1976, for his first book of poetry,

The Elements of San Joaquin; the Bess Hokin Prize from *Poetry,* 1978; a Pulitzer Prize nomination, 1978; a Guggenheim Fellowship, 1979; several National Endowment for the Arts fellowships; the Levinson Award from *Poetry,* 1984; an American Book Award, 1985, for *Living up the Street;* a California Arts Council Fellowship, 1989; a Beatty Award from the California Library Association, 1991; a Reading Magic Award from *Parenting* magazine for *Baseball in April and Other Stories,* 1991; The George C. Stone Center Recognition of Merit from the Claremont Graduate School, 1993, for *Baseball in April and Other Stories;* a Carnegie Medal, 1993, for *The Pool Party;* a Literature Award from the Hispanic Heritage Foundation, 1999; an Author-Illustrator Civil Rights Award from the National Education Association, 1999; a Book Award from PEN Center West, 1999, for *Petty Crimes;* a Silver Medal from the Commonwealth Club of California; and the Tomás Rivera Prize. His *New and Selected Poems* was a finalist for both the National Book Award and the *Los Angeles Times* book prize in 1995.

Soto is a prolific writer of poetry and both fiction and nonfiction prose. He has continued to publish on a regular basis since the appearance of his first book of poetry, *The Elements of San Joaquin,* in 1977, but the frequency of his publications seemed to accelerate considerably after he resigned from the University of California in 1991. He has enjoyed critical acclaim, principally for his poetry but also for his books for young-adult readers and his nonfiction prose for adults. He has also published a handful of long essays collected in his 2000 book *The Effects of Knut Hamsum on a Fresno Boy.* Reviewer Alan Cheuse called him "one of the finest natural talents to emerge" (*New York Times Book Review,* p. 18) from his generation of writers.

POETRY

Even as he was finishing his M.F.A., Soto's individual poems were being published in prestigious journals and magazines, including the *Nation,* the *New Yorker, Partisan Review,* and *Poetry.* In June 1976 he submitted a book-length manuscript to the International Poetry Forum, where it was selected from 1,200 entries for the U.S. Award, which carried a prize of $2,000 and publication by the University of Pittsburgh Press. *The Elements of San Joaquin* was published in 1977 by this highly regarded academic press.

The Elements of San Joaquin is perhaps Soto's signature book of poetry, at least until the publication, in 1995, of *New and Selected Poems.* *The Elements* is divided into three parts: the first section, consisting of six poems, in which Soto presents images of Fresno in the 1950s; the second and longest section, consisting of twenty poems, in which he focuses on the hard-scrub life in the agricultural fields of the San Joaquin Valley; and the third section, in which he draws on his memories of childhood. As the critic José Varela Ibarra points out in the 1985 *Chicano Literature: A Reference Guide,* the three "spaces" function as the "elements" of his memory and "contain images full of affective reverberations that such memories from younger days usually carry" (p. 276). The "elements" also refer to one of the most basic conceptions of the word: earth, air, fire, and water. Within the context of the world Soto recreates from memory, these elements are essential to the Fresno cityscapes, the agricultural landscapes, and the fragments of a childhood existence affected deeply by the surrounding factories, streets, and fields populated by recently arrived immigrant Mexicans and Asians and by the more established Mexican Americans, Asian Americans, and Okies, all of whom came to Fresno in search of jobs to support their families.

In his 1987 "Review Essay: Recent Changes in Chicano Writing," Raymond A. Paredes perceptively characterizes Soto's tone in the first section of the book as one of clinical detachment "born of an inurement to suffering" (pp. 106–107). He highlights the violence, loneliness, and degradation that are constants in the lives of the characters that form the nuclei of the poems: an exploited worker who endlessly cleans the filthy restrooms in a grimy factory; a rapist; a neglected and faceless man dying in a county hospital ward; a purse snatcher; a raped woman; and a drug pusher. These alternating roles of victimizer and victim are played out in a kind of labyrinth of despair with no exit. The poet remains passive in both this and the other two sections of the book, as though he were powerless to intervene or in any way alter the process of what Patricia de la Fuentes, in her 1983 essay "Ambiguity in the Poetry of Gary Soto," calls the "inexorable destruction of human ties" (p. 2). In his 1982 *Chicano Poetry: A Response to Chaos*, Bruce-Novoa finds that "there is no reassuring idealism or even optimism in Soto" (p. 185). He compares *The Elements* to T. S. Eliot's *The Wasteland.* Patricia de la Fuentes seems to agree, attributing to Soto an "apocalyptic vision" (p. 35) of the universe, but she still finds some relief in faintly affirmative contrapuntal images, as in the case of the wind that whistles through many poems in all three sections of the book. Soto has the wind leveling, destroying, laying waste, and obliterating city streets, abandoned lots, and infertile fields, yet at the same time the wind also caresses and soothes.

In the second section, which gives the book its title, Soto gazes outward from Fresno's poor neighborhoods of factory, and farmworkers to the agricultural fields and rural areas that surround the city. Once again, he presents contrapuntally the great beauty of nature and the misery of the workers and their families that it cradles. Dirt, wind, and heat all conspire to wear down and defeat the farmworkers' bodies and spirits as they participate in a never-ending cycle of backbreaking work in the fields and packing sheds, saving money out of their painfully low wages in order to see them through the bleak and desperate periods of the off-season.

The third section of the book is more directly autobiographical than the first two, as Soto draws on, again in contrapuntal fashion, the positive and negative memories of his childhood. The more varied colors of the third section—red, pink, white, silver, orange, yellow, as opposed to the grays and muted greens that dominate the first two sections—provide a more nuanced prism of childhood and adolescent loneliness.

The Elements reflects most directly Soto's personal pain and anguish over growing up poor, fatherless, and alienated, but the book also peels back for the reader—especially the reader who might be ignorant or only superficially familiar with contemporary Chicano history—the multiple layers of deprivation and the dead-end existences of the lower economic class in general and Mexican Americans, Asian Americans, and poor whites in particular. In *Chicano Poetry: A Response to Chaos*, Bruce-Novoa writes of this aspect of *The Elements* that Soto has "Chicanized *The Waste Land*" (p. 207).

Several critics have observed that Soto shows stylistic affinities with the Fresno School, who came under the heavy influence of Philip Levine. This is very pronounced in *The Elements* in terms of the predominance of short lines, a simple and direct vocabulary, and an enumeration of small objects that have little symbolic value but serve to build a situation. Soto learned well from Levine how to enjamb a flat statement with another flat statement several times in the same poem while building toward a powerfully evocative ending. Soto's diction in this and in later books of poetry is idiomatic.

Soto published his second book of poetry, *Tale of Sunlight*, in 1978. Like his first book, it is divided into three sections. The first section is dominated by poems about Molina, a fictional character who has been described as Soto's childhood alter ego. The Molina poems are counterbalanced by the Manuel Zaragoza poems of the third section. Manuel, a cantina owner in Taxco, Mexico, has led a tragic life but finds some solace in magical butterflies that flit in and out of the drudgery of daily life. Several critics have observed that the magical butterflies are a tribute to the Colombian writer Gabriel García Márquez, the Nobel Laureate to whom Soto dedicates "How an Uncle Became Gray," a poem in the third section of the book. Soto contrasts Molina's childlike dreamland world to Manuel's fantasy world, which borders on magical realism. Between the first and third sections are a series of seemingly miscellaneous poems threaded together by a motif of the poet's journey from childhood to adulthood, not only in a literal temporal sense but also psychologically.

Soto departs, in this second book, from the rural and city settings of *The Elements,* all of which were associated with the socioeconomic circumstances of a Chicano childhood. The geographical and spatial aspect of the second book is much expanded to include Mexico and Latin America: Taxco, Panama, Colombia, Peru, Brazil, and the Orinoco River. The streets of Fresno are left behind as Soto's persona Molina ventures forth from his old backyard to begin a kind of magical tour. Through Soto's alter ego, the reader is able to experience the more-than-commonplace aspects of lands that perhaps the poet has begun to discover from his readings of García Márquez's *One Hundred Years of Solitude* (published in Spanish in 1967) and other Latin American magical realists whose works were becoming increasing popular in the United States in the 1970s. The squalor and violence of *The Elements* gives way to a world of wonderment as Molina, as a kind of Midas, is endowed with the power to transform plain objects. A colorful rain of butterflies and toads replaces the gray fog and dreary downpours of the San Joaquin Valley.

Social criticism is not lacking in *Tale,* but Soto expresses it more subtly and it is more generalized than in *The Elements.* Examples are the short poem "The Point" and the longer poem "The Street." In the latter Soto refers explicitly to the lower classes: "The poor are unshuffled cards of leaves / Recorded by wind, turned over on a wish / To reveal their true suits. / They never win" (p. 23). The plight of the poor in Fresno and the San Joaquin Valley of *The Elements* now becomes the travails of a less specific yet more universal lower class. *Tale* has more political overtones than *The Elements,* but it would be inaccurate to describe it as overtly political. It was clearly not Soto's intent to raise his poetry to a level of explicit political discourse, nor has this ever been a characteristic of his writing. Like almost all of his poetry and prose, it is shot through with a sense of the writer's political and social awareness and commitment but always conveyed in an artistically subtle way.

Critical reception of *Tales* was generally positive, even enthusiastic. Writing in *Poetry* in 1980, the critic Alan Williamson describes Soto as maybe "the most exciting poet of poverty in America to emerge since James Wright and Philip Levine" (p. 348).

In *Where Sparrows Work Hard* (1981), Soto continues to render poetically the lives of the poor and downtrodden who, like the common and unnoticed birds of the title, struggle endlessly to survive in a world of physical hardship imposed by their social class and economic status. For the first time in his poetry, Soto contrasts their travails with those of the more privileged, whose lives of affluence and consumption the poor only glimpse as vague and blurred images on a television, as in the poem, "TV in Black and White." The lives of the factory and seasonal agricultural workers are bound together by elements more important than comfort and self-indulgence: friendships, family loyalties, and the commonality of hard work contribute to their perseverance in a world beset by elemental issues of survival. Soto does not romanticize this struggle or the people who are caught in it. The reader finds plenty of down-and-out characters in *Where Sparrows Work Hard,* including alcoholics, transients, and petty criminals. At the same time, as a reviewer writing anonymously in *Booklist* observed, Soto describes with artistic integrity, pride, and wit the dangerous jobs, family links, friendships, and "other ties that bind or digress into the dreams, fantasies and seemingly hopeless aspirations of those who want to reach beyond 'getting by'" (p. 78).

The poet view of the human condition—especially the social conditions of the poor—borders on fatalism but grants at least some of his characters a dignity that allows them to pull back from an abyss of complete despair. Not all reviewers and critics felt any of the characters pulled back from despair, however. For example, in a review in the July–August 1982 *American Book Review,* Carlos Zamora characterizes *Where Sparrows Work Hard* as "a journey of exploration through the subterranean, labyrinthine, infernal world of the human soul, where everything gives evidence of a cosmic devastation" (p. 4). He goes on to describe Soto's world as a "ravaged and doomed globe" and anticipates that Chicano readers will object that his poetry is not in keeping with the affirmative tone of the 1960s and early 1970s Chicano poetry of, for example, Rodolfo "Corky" Gonzales, Alurista, and Abelardo. Zamora suggests that at least some socially committed readers might conclude that Soto views the degradation of man as having metaphysical rather than social root causes. His view is dark but not without hope, for many who inhabit his poems learn to seek and find solace and dignity even in bleakness and despair. In the volume's concluding poem, "Salt," two children are sent out to hunt for food for a penniless family: "The day / Was clear, and what the wind turned over / We took in our hands and imagined it bread. / We broke this wish in halves, and ate" (p. 65).

Soto did not publish another book of poetry for four years; *Black Hair* appeared in 1985. In it the poet seems to have matured, becoming more confident in his command of poetic diction, which turns more abstract, and in his more philosophical exploration of themes such as childhood, relationships, and death. He returns specifically to his own father's death but now, in contrast to *Where Sparrows Work Hard,* he seems to have established some emotional distance from this childhood loss. Rather than focusing on the emptiness he experienced as a child, he places his father's fatal accident within the broader context of the human condition, as in, for example, "The Plum's Heart." The mutability of life itself, which can be, in one instant, joyful, reassuring and deeply comforting, only to turn to tragedy, profound sadness, and despair in the next, runs through the entire volume. But Soto has established some distance from the latter feelings and considers them more abstractly.

Some poems focus on small triumphs of growing up, maturing, marrying, and having children, while others explore the transitory nature of our existence. "Oranges" is a good example of the former. A boy of twelve takes a girl on his first date to a drugstore to buy a treat. This mundane setting is the occasion of his entry into an unknown world, not only of changing sentiments toward the opposite sex but also of learning to trust others. Short of money to buy his date a ten-cent chocolate, the adolescent places one of two oranges he is carrying in his pocket on the counter along with his only nickel. The saleswoman responds to his unspoken plea: "When I looked up, / The lady's eyes met mine, / And held them, knowing / Very well what it was all / About" (p. 8).

In the last poem in this volume, Soto brings the reader full circle to a consideration of the transitory nature of life and the inevitability of our common destiny even as we go about the daily routines in which we find satisfaction and pleasure. "Between Words" reminds us that we can eat, sleep, love, show affection, desire, and appreciate beauty, but death awaits us:

Remember the blossoms
In rain, because in the end
Not even the ants
Will care who we were
When they climb our faces
To undo our smiles.

(p. 78)

Soto did not publish another book of poetry for five years and then he published two in rapid succession: *Who Will Know Us?* in 1990 and

Home Course in Religion in 1991. Both volumes share with *Black Hair* what Héctor Torres, in a 1988 essay in *Crítica: A Journal of Critical Essays,* called a sharing of discursive space between "a quiet unease" and "an equally strong sense of triumph and joy" (p. 178). Torres also notes that Soto opened a new current in his poetry in *Who Will Know Us?*: a panoramic view of California. Common images of a working people's California are distributed throughout his poems. The agricultural fields of the San Joaquin Valley that were dominant in his earlier poetry are again present but so are roadside cafes and diners, pets, cemeteries, trains in the distance, perfect houses behind white picket fences, small rural towns, radios blaring on lazy summer afternoons, and feeding time at the local zoo. Soto's broad consideration of the landscape and his focused view of what occupies its common space is not in any sense idyllic, nostalgic, or idealized. For example, in the title poem, "Who Will Know Us?" the poetic persona looks out the window of a moving train on the way to visit his father's grave. He ruminates about other journeys to foreign destinations as he observes the passing images: "This is my country, white with no words, / House of silence, horse that won't budge. / . . . / I have nothing / Good to say" (p. 18).

Soto also returns in these two volumes to the absent father and again tries to deal with the loss of a key childhood figure whose name is still not spoken in the family. He struggles with the futility of somehow resurrecting a memory of him. In "Another Time," from *Who Will Know Us?* he associates one of the places—his own childhood house—with the father's absence. In "Fall and Spring," from *Home Course in Religion,* Soto deals with the family silence that ensued after his father's death. It is not until his senior year in high school that he is able to utter words about that tragedy. In a conversation with Scott, a good friend whose father is also dead, Soto says:

> I ran sand through my fingers.
> I told him that when my father died

> My uncle heard gravel crunch in the path
> That ran along our house, and rock was one of
> The things God told us to look out for.
> The two of us ran a mile of sand
> Through our fingers.

> (p. 33)

Soto offers just a glimpse of the feelings buried beneath the poet's own deep layers of silence, but it is nevertheless a moment when he allows himself to speak the unspeakable. In the same collection, in poems such as "The Music at Home," "Best Years," "The Box Fan," and "Spelling Words at the Table," Soto evokes his deep anger associated with his stepfather, who seemed to care little for his stepchildren or their mother.

In *Home Course in Religion,* as the title suggests, Soto addresses the topic of religion more explicitly and more frequently than in any previous book of poetry. In "Pink Hands" and "Some Mysteries," he alludes to having been born Catholic; to going to Catholic school, where his teachers were members of a religious order; to the sacraments of confession, mass, and so on. He expresses nostalgia for some of the trappings of his religion, including school uniforms, meatless Fridays (a Catholic practice until about 1965), the mysterious and distant figure of the Pope, and even cities and countries he associated with being Catholic. He reflects on how the Catholic Church has changed: the abandonment of the Latin mass, the closing of the Catholic school he attended, the institution of adult retreats, the faithful—and even priests and nuns—running in races. But this should not be mistaken for regret for the diminished importance of Catholic dogma; it is rather nostalgia for the things that comforted him as he made the difficult passage from childhood to adolescence to young adulthood.

New and Selected Poems, published in 1995, brought Soto well-deserved national recognition. It consists mainly of selections from his previously published books and was selected as a finalist for the National Book Award. Only the last section, "Super-Eight Movies," contains new poems. Reviewers and critics responded positively to the volume, perhaps reading his earlier poetry for the first time because of the attention that was focused on Soto as a finalist for a prestigious award.

The new poems resonate with Soto's earlier poetry, foregrounding some of the same themes. One of the most interesting is "Old House in My Fortieth Year," in which the speaker, a man of forty, reflects in a thinly veiled autobiographical voice about the self-acceptance and psychological comfort that come with maturation: "I'm home in these bones, / This flesh with its laughter and fatherly scent, / Flesh held up by a frayed belt on its last hole." He knows that his life could have taken a different path: "One error, and I'm the man pushing a cart. / Another error, and I march a long row of cotton / Or beets. . . . / And by fortune, I'm now at home in this body" (p. 169).

In his next book of poetry, *Junior College,* published in 1997, Soto alternates between serious, even somber, retrospective poems and lighter, humorous poems that capture a young man's introduction to post-high school education. An example of the former is "Dear Journal," in which the speaker finds himself in junior college still plagued by the self-doubt, sadness, and anguish that have persisted throughout his childhood and adolescence. Even the transition from high school to the new challenges and stimuli of a junior college campus seems unable to cure these lingering feelings.

Soto draws a stark contrast between the abstract intellectualism of his course material and the lived experiences of the poor. In "The History of Science," he mocks the Russian philosopher Nicholas Fedorovich Fedorov, a believer in the potential of science to improve human well-being; Federov died before the unleashing of the unspeakable horrors of modernity's perverse use of science:

You have not seen Oakland at night,
The screams and coughing and palpitating hearts.

You're in your grave, thin as twigs,
And you missed some of the best wars
And the best stories of war.

(p. 41)

In "Some History," Soto contrasts a young man's wonder at the marvelous foreign lands and historical events depicted in his junior college history textbook with his more mature, better informed, and cynical view of the Aztecs' bloody wars, Genghis Khan's marauding and brutality, Germany's warmongering and extermination of Europe's Jews, the complicity of the French Catholic Church in colonialist genocide, and the bombing of Nagasaki. He ends the poem by contrasting a historian's idealized view of ancient peoples to the young student's own material condition.

Other poems strike a lighter tone as a young man makes his way in aimless fashion through the intellectual maze and confusion of introductory junior college courses. Soto mocks a survey course on the great ancient philosophers—Aristotle, Socrates, the skeptics: "I was Pyrrho and Rick was Sextus, / Both of us skeptical about getting good jobs" (p. 45). His and his brother's raging hormones constantly distract them from their studies as they become acutely aware of an attractive young women in their philosophy class. Women's short pants distract him from Ptolemy, Gutenberg, the Spartans, and Romans in "Western Civilization." In "Everything Twice," Soto chides his biology teacher, who habitually comes to class drunk and repeats his boring lectures.

A Natural Man was published in 1999. It picks up on some of the subject matter from *Junior College,* loops back to some of themes of his earlier poetry, and opens up the perspective of the poet in his mid-forties, who is beginning to reflect in a more focused way than before on life's mysteries, including death itself. The poems dealing with these serious themes are counterbalanced by some of a lighter nature that take us back to Soto's childhood, adolescence, and young adulthood (e.g., "Seventh Grade Shoes," "Werewolf Friends," "Werewolf Tendencies,"

"Get Out of Town," "The Weight of Diapers," "A Young Man's Belief in Dark Moods," "The Cottages of Divisadero," and "Meat and Potatoes"). Soto seems to be even less certain about the existence of God and an afterlife than before. For example, in "Late Confession," he contrasts his current beliefs with his ten-year-old faith in what his religious mentors taught him about angels and Jesus. Now these innocent beliefs are much more uncertain, and there is little to separate life and death except nothingness.

NONFICTION PROSE FOR THE ADULT READER

Soto published ten collections of poetry between 1977 and 1999. This prodigious and consistent production of poetry is all the more remarkable when we consider that for most of this period he was also publishing fiction and nonfiction prose for both young readers and adults. He has published four books of nonfiction prose for adult readers: *Living up the Street: Narrative Recollections* (1985); *Small Faces* (1986); *Lesser Evils: Ten Quartets* (1988); and *The Effects of Knut Hamsun on a Fresno Boy: Recollections and Short Essays* (2000).

Living up the Street earned Soto an American Book Award. Its publication marked not so much a turning point in Soto's writing career as a full exploration of the possibilities of a genre other than poetry. At a symposium held at the University of New Mexico in 1988, Soto spoke on some of his reasons for devoting more artistic energy to nonfiction prose than he had in the past. He said that for him prose offered a "great expanse . . . more territory, more frontier." He also said he believed that the essayist must remain closer to the facts of social reality and leave behind a "certain poetic verbiage" to write in "plain, direct, unadorned syntax" (Torres, *Crítica: A Journal of Critical Essays,* p. 40). Torres comments that Soto seems fully aware of the "rhetorical power of the descriptive scene painted in conversational prose" (p. 40). He

blends conversational syntax with poetic image to make incisive social commentary in a way that is nonconfrontational but effectively draws in the unsuspecting reader. This aptly describes all of Soto's nonfiction.

In a 1996 interview with Patricia Murphy, Soto comments on the role of memory in both his poetry and nonfiction prose: "I suspect that some people do have the ability to recall details from childhood, vividly, mind you. For years I enjoyed that prospect of looking back and seeing details, actually pieces of language" (p. 30). In the preface to *The Effects of Knut Hamsun on a Fresno Boy,* Soto expands on the importance that his ability to recall details plays in his creative process: "For me, streets have mattered. When I am ready to write, ready to sit down, usually at the kitchen table but also in bed, I conjure up inside my head an image of our old street in south Fresno, where, at the beginning of the 1960s, house after house was torn down in the name of 'urban renewal'" (p. ix). In the same preface, he recalls that even in late childhood he was conscious of this ability to notice and then recall details that focus on some of the aspects of growing up on Braly Street in a run-down section of Fresno and later on Van Ness and other streets in a more prosperous working-class part of town.

> The other Fresno streets also mattered, streets with names like Thomas and Grant, leading to simple family homes where sprinklers twirled on lawns and cooking smells wafted from open windows. I played every kind of game on these front lawns, and at night chewed stalks of grass under the immense window of the night sky. . . . I picked up so much of the arrangement of the world, both the large and the small that even to this day I can see a broken RC Cola bottle and recall my contemplating whether the bottle was full, half-full or empty when it fell to the ground. This might be described as wonderment, I suppose.
>
> (pp. ix–x)

Soto's early penchant for noticing and recording details and his ability later—sometimes many years later—to recall details and conjure up whole scenes are essential in providing the material for his nonfiction. Soto uses this material in a richly evocative way to foreground the full range of emotions and complex relationships of not only his childhood and adolescence but also his adult years. Soto uses the recollection of details to reveal the sharp edges of growing up poor in a fatherless home as well as to let the reader glimpse the strategies he developed early in life to cope with this angst.

In *Living up the Street,* there is no nostalgia for poverty, the trappings of poverty, or loneliness, but rather a purposefulness in giving concrete form to his complex relationship to the objects that seemed to help him maintain an emotional equilibrium in very difficult material and psychological circumstances. He does so by creating the illusion of what the German critic Heiner Bus, in a 1988 article in the *Americas Review,* calls Soto's "sophisticated spontaneity" (p. 188).

In the first essay, "Being Mean," Soto recounts how he and his two siblings, Rick and Debra, developed a "a streak of orneriness" (p. 5) in order to survive with some pride intact in a neighborhood in the shadows of factories that wore down and dehumanized both the Soto family and the other families on Braly Street. Readers might pass over the children's toughness and self-protectiveness as simply a phase of childhood, but we should be aware that Soto often makes social commentary unobtrusively. Meanness and fighting have become a self-protective shield to ward off the real violence that adults in these stories perpetrate against children.

Soto developed other coping mechanisms as a child to fend off the violence of poverty and the blows of other external forces that had a devastating impact on his life. In "Looking for Work," Soto tries desperately to imitate the life he sees on *Father Knows Best,* a popular 1950s television program that depicted the comfortable, uncomplicated lives of an idealized middle-class, white American family. He sets out to

bring his own family into line with the routines and practices of this television family by first trying to persuade his siblings to come to the table with their shoes on and to dress for dinner. In a vain attempt to escape the banal routines of his own impoverished childhood, he also sets out one summer to gain the middle-class comforts.

Leave It to Beaver, another popular 1950s television program that idealized life on the other side of the tracks, also heightens Soto's sense of inadequacy and desire to live differently:

This was the summer when I spent the mornings in front of the television that showed the comfortable lives of white kids. There were no beatings, no rifts in the family. They wore bright clothes; toys tumbled from their closets. They hopped into bed with kisses and woke to glasses of fresh orange juice, and to a father sitting before his morning coffee while the mother buttered his toast. They hurried through the day making friends and gobs of money, returning home to a warmly lit living room, and then dinner.

(p. 34)

In addition to childhood recollections, *Living up the Street* includes stories and vignettes from adolescence and young adulthood. In "One Last Time," he recalls working in the agricultural fields that surrounded Fresno. At fifteen, he and his siblings would occasionally accompany their mother to cut and pick grapes, thankful that they were not forced to toil season after season to supplement their family's meager income. They work for only short periods to earn spending money and to buy their school clothes.

In *Living up the Street,* Soto touches lightly on the slow and painful process of detaching himself from the emotional torture of living in a family plagued by marital strife and physical want. In "Black Hair," Soto runs away from home at seventeen in what he recalls as an important step in his own maturation and sense of self-worth. He leaves Fresno and hitchhikes to Glendale, in the Los Angeles area, where after several days of surviving by his wits and sleeping in shelters fashioned out of cardboard, he finds a job in a tire reprocessing factory. The pay is poor and the work is physically taxing and dirty, but Soto sees significance in this job as a young man's first step toward self-sufficiency.

Soto continued the practice of assembling a wide range of autobiographical short prose pieces in *Small Faces* (1986) and *Lesser Evils* (1988). Most of these are short essays, vignettes, reflections, and meditations; together they weave a richly textured tapestry of growing up Chicano in Fresno and of childhood, adolescent, and young adult triumphs, joys, and hurts.

Small Faces is characterized by the same rich thematic mix found in *Living up the Street,* but Soto seems to have changed his compositional strategy to include more sharply defined positive depictions of love, marriage, friendship, and fatherhood, which alternate with decidedly dark pieces about loss, disillusionment, death, and nothingness. The latter pieces stand in stark contrast to the book's cover, which depicts multiple happy-faced images of Soto, his wife Carolyn, and their daughter Mariko. Soto conveys a strong sense of self-embattlement and inner conflict. He carries on a constant internal dialogue, questioning why he should feel a deep-seated angst about his life even as his material circumstances (a loving and supportive wife, an adoring daughter, a deep dedication to parenthood, and economic stability) should make him happy.

He refers explicitly to this inner battle in a 1998 essay, "Getting It Done," which appeared in *The Effects of Knut Hamsun on a Fresno Boy.* He reveals that for several years a darkness enshrouded every aspect of his emotional and physical being. Persistent depression boils to the surface particularly during long sleepless nights, overwhelming any sense of well-being:

> Now I will lie here and sleep and when I wake I will be better. I repeated this every night for three years, repeating to myself that I was asleep, while in truth my eyes were closed and rolling about

behind the lids. I felt paralyzed, listless. . . . The cement weight of insomnia left me slow of mind and body. I had a difficult time concentrating as I ghosted through my days, showing my teeth in theatrical attempts to appear jolly.

> (p. 188)

In this same essay, Soto writes about beginning to write feverishly in an ultimately failed attempt to cure himself of his depression. Many of the short prose pieces in *Small Faces* reflect this process in what he identifies in "Getting It Done" as writing about "the best things in my life, namely my wife and daughter" (p. 191) in an attempt to get better. In stories such as "Secrets," "First Love," "The Man on the Floor," and "Going Back," Soto recounts settling into the first years of marriage with its comforting routines, satisfactions, sexual desire, marital love, then fatherhood, but in other selections, such as "Pulling a Cart," he raises doubts about a couple's ability to sustain over time a vital relationship of mutual support, commitment, and affection. He remembers from his youth feeling sadness for a man and a woman pulling a cart down the street in his neighborhood in search of objects to resell. This sadness turns to dismay years later as they come to represent the ebb and flow of connectedness in their marriage:

> I won't be like them, I thought then, twenty years ago when I was a little man with a pretty date. Now I wonder. My wife is not centered on that cart; our daughter is not trailing us, vacant-eyed and hungry. No one is gawking; no one is pointing out our sadness when we take walks in the evening. But some days I feel as if I'm pulling a cart. . . . We're making our way up this street, then that street. It's an effort that seems to take us no closer to what we want. The days end. . . . We never arrive.

> (*The Effects of Knut Hamsun,* p. 116)

This negative view of marriage—his marriage—is representative of the trend in *Small Faces* toward a more distressed view of aspects of his life, which he tries to overcome by reminding himself of the signs of hope that can lead him away from a precipice of despair. In "Moving Around," he questions how friendship, marriage, and fatherhood can be sufficient in the face of life's blows and ultimate disappointment: "Perhaps there's a dissatisfaction I swallow like spit each morning but won't admit: my wife is my love, my daughter is my love, and all that hurts from childhood is healed over. Is there more that this? Is there more than family and family's good-hearted friends?" (p. 32). He chides himself for doubting the affirmative answer to his own questions; nevertheless, the questions and doubts persist. Significantly, Soto chooses to end *Small Faces* with a glimpse of death and nothingness, which have shown their faces earlier in the book as the writer's nagging companions: "Today we want an indirect life: we want to talk, to think about our fate, that blackness, that grave that will rain dirt on our faces and run a root through an ear until we can really hear" (p. 125).

Soto begins *Lesser Evils,* published just two years after *Small Faces,* on the same dark note. In the first essay, "Between Points," he says, "I can't get over how some are dying while others are being born" (p. 7), ending in a similar somber fashion:

> Today I don't feel good about being where I am, aged thirty-four, and a bright childhood gone and the mad-gray years ahead of me. The earth knows how to dismantle flesh bone by bone and keep us in the ground. The sea is no help: it will wash the dead over and over without rest, if by chance we should die by water. The ones I love dearly will die, and our end, east or west, is a stone that won't roll back.

> (p. 9)

In *Lesser Evils* and to a lesser extent in his other collections of nonfiction, Soto uses what can be described as a distancing technique to mitigate or even negate the powerfully menacing thoughts that invade his introspective moments. This technique often takes the form of a comment that would strike the reader as flippant or

even humorous if it were not for the thoughts that have preceded or followed it. The ending of "Scary" is illustrative of this technique: "I like it when I'm alone. It gives me time to think. My life is half over, my wife's life is half over. The world is going to roll over and sink like a freighter. There's nothing like scaring yourself to round out the day" (p. 35).

The Effects of Knut Hamsun on a Fresno Boy, published in 2000, consists mainly of the work previously published in *Small Faces* and *Lesser Evils.* However, the volume also includes four more recent essays—"The Childhood Worries, or Why I Became a Writer," "The Effects of Knut Hamsun on a Fresno Boy," "Getting It Done," and "Who Is Your Reader?"—which are substantially longer and more developed than the essays in the two previous books. They are similarly autobiographical and illuminate aspects of Soto's personal and creative process. In "The Childhood Worries, or Why I Became a Writer," Soto shares with the reader his childhood obsession with disease and his fear that he would suffer the same fate as family members and neighbors who were afflicted with horrible, often fatal, diseases. Soto contrasts the assiduous efforts of a six-year-old to avoid germs with the suddenness of his father's death from a freak accident. He recalls that the family's silence following his father's death left him with a sea of unaddressed anger and grief, which he was left on his own to work out as best a young child could:

> I had discovered how I could make a huge noise. In the empty bedroom, the one my father and mother would have used, I spent hours with fistfuls of marbles. I bounced them off the baseboard, a ricocheting clatter that I imagined were soldiers getting their fill of death. The clatter of noise busied my mind with something like hate.

> (p. 171)

The second part of the essay's title, "Why I Became a Writer," signals that working out the confusion of his father's death would be a lifelong process. It should be emphasized, however, that as important as Manuel Soto's death is in Gary Soto's poetry and prose, it is only one of several themes that reoccur throughout his work.

The essay "The Effects of Knut Hamsun on a Fresno Boy" focuses on Soto's tentative steps to become a serious writer. Employing a self-mocking tone, Soto describes the long hours he spent at his writing desk trying to give form to a short story that will generate a healthy publication fee to help support him and his young bride. He imagines himself, like Knut Hamsun, the twentieth-century Norwegian-born writer and Nobel Laureate, "stirring the water for something good to happen" (p. 182), only to discover and finally accept that he is a far better poet than prose writer.

In "Getting It Done," Soto deals explicitly with his struggle with depression during adulthood. This is only glimpsed in his shorter nonfiction pieces and poetry. This difficult period in his life coincides with his disaffection with and abandonment of academic life, his fear of losing his sixteen-year-old daughter to a fatal accident, and the unleashing of compulsive behavior, including what he describes as writing "furiously, albeit not brilliantly" (p. 190). Corresponding to the gravity of the subject matter, this is perhaps Soto's most serious essay, in which his usual flippant, self-mocking tone is absent.

The Effects of Knut Hamsun on a Fresno Kid ends with the essay "Who Is Your Reader?" which explores the questions about readership that every successful writer eventually addresses. How would relatives, friends, fellow poets, and critics respond to his first book of poetry as well as to what he would publish subsequently? Soto's sardonic tone is captured in the following phrase: "Readership. The agony of writing is a terror in itself, but to build an audience once a book is published?" (p. 199). Ultimately, Soto decides that his most loyal and responsive readership consists of the thousands of elementary, middle-grade, high school, and college students, and their teachers, who come

to his readings and buy his books. He concludes: "My business is to make readers from non-readers" (p. 204).

JUVENILE LITERATURE

In 1990 Soto turned his attention to writing fiction and nonfiction for young readers from elementary through high school age. He has been both prolific and highly successful in this, while at the same time continuing to publish poetry. One of his first works for young readers, *Baseball in April and Other Stories,* garnered two awards, the American Library Association's Best Book for Young Adults designation and the Beatty Award. In this and much of his other subsequently published fiction and nonfiction for young readers, he explores the pain of growing up, infatuation, love, friendship, family, success, and failure. One strength of these works is his ability to portray the dilemma of adolescents who find themselves in a sometimes cruel world in which racial and ethnic discrimination are still prevalent. He takes on social issues directly, but at the same time he avoids following an overtly political agenda or falling into a strident tone.

Many of the qualities of Soto's writing for adult readers are found in his almost thirty publications for young readers. His narrative is precise, as he gives great attention to the details and small objects that surround his characters' lives. However, missing from these publications are the somber tone and darkness that characterize much of his poetry and prose for adults. He balances humor, playfulness, and references to both the joys and difficulties of growing up Chicano in the barrios of Fresno and other California cities.

Soto continues energetically to publish poetry as well as fiction and nonfiction prose for adults and young readers. He also maintains a busy schedule, giving talks, lectures, readings, and conducting workshops throughout the United States, but particularly in California and the southwest. His readers and his audiences are fortunate to be exposed to a most inventive and creative word artist, who reveals a part of himself and his view of the world, but always in an inviting and accessible manner.

Selected Bibliography

WORKS OF GARY SOTO

POETRY

The Elements of San Joaquin. Pittsburgh: University of Pittsburgh Press, 1977.

The Tale of Sunlight. Pittsburgh: University of Pittsburgh Press, 1978.

Father Is a Pillow Tied to a Broom. Pittsburgh: Slow Loris, 1980.

Where Sparrows Work Hard. Pittsburgh: University of Pittsburgh Press, 1981.

Black Hair. Pittsburgh: University of Pittsburgh Press, 1985.

Who Will Know Us? San Francisco: Chronicle Books, 1990.

Home Course in Religion. San Francisco: Chronicle Books, 1991.

Gary Soto: New and Selected Poems. San Francisco: Chronicle Books, 1995.

Junior College. San Francisco: Chronicle Books, 1997.

A Natural Man. San Francisco: Chronicle Books, 1999.

NONFICTION PROSE

Living up the Street: Narrative Recollections. San Francisco: Strawberry Hill, 1985.

Small Faces. Houston: Arte Público Press, 1986.

Lesser Evils: Ten Quartets. Houston: Arte Público Press, 1988.

The Effects of Knut Hamsun on a Fresno Boy: Recollections and Short Essays. New York: Persea Books, 2000.

JUVENILE PROSE FICTION (PARTIAL LIST)

The Cat's Meow. San Francisco: Strawberry Hill Press, 1987.

Baseball in April and Other Stories. San Diego, Calif.: Harcourt, 1990.

Taking Sides. San Diego, Calif.: Harcourt, 1992.

Pacific Crossing. San Diego, Calif.: Harcourt, 1992.

Local News: A Collection of Stories. New York: Scholastic, 1993.

The Pool Party. New York: Delacorte, 1993.

Too Many Tamales. New York: Putnam, 1993.

Crazy Weekend. New York: Scholastic, 1994.

Jesse. San Diego, Calif.: Harcourt, 1994.

Boys at Work. New York: Delacorte Press, 1995.

Chato's Kitchen. New York: Putman, 1995.

Summer on Wheels. New York: Scholastic, 1995.

Off and Running. New York: Delacorte, 1996.

Old Man and His Door. New York: Putman, 1996.

Buried Onions. San Diego, Calif.: Harcourt Brace and Company, 1997.

Snapshots from the Wedding. New York: Putnam, 1997.

Big Bushy Mustache. New York: Knopf, 1998.

Chato and the Party Animals. New York: Putman, 1998.

Petty Crimes. San Diego, Calif.: Harcourt, 1998.

My Little Car. New York: Putman, 2000.

If the Shoe Fits. New York: Putnam, 2002.

JUVENILE NONFICTION, POETRY, AND PLAYS
A Fire in My Hands: A Book of Poems. New York: Scholastic, 1990.

A Summer Life. Hanover, N.H.: University Press of New England, 1990.

Neighborhood Odes. San Diego, Calif.: Harcourt, 1992.

Canto Familiar/Familiar Song. San Diego, Calif.: Harcourt, 1995.

Novio Boy: A Play. San Diego, Calif.: Harcourt, 1997.

Nerdlandia: A Play. New York: Paper Star, 1999.

Jesse De La Cruz: Profile of a United Farm Worker. New York: Persea Books, 2000.

Fearless Fernie: Hanging Out with Fernie and Me. New York: Putnam, 2002.

ADULT PROSE FICTION
Nickel and Dime. Albuquerque: University of New Mexico Press, 2000.

Poetry Lover. Albuquerque: University of New Mexico Press, 2001.

Amnesia in a Republican County. Albuquerque: University of New Mexico Press, 2003.

BOOKS EDITED BY GARY SOTO
California Childhood: Recollections and Stories of the Golden State. Berkeley: Creative Arts Books, 1988.

Pieces of the Heart: New Chicano Fiction. San Francisco: Chronicle Books, 1993.

SECONDARY WORKS

CRITICAL WORKS
Booklist 78: 280 (October 15, 1981). Review of *Where Sparrows Work Hard.*

Bruce-Novoa, Juan. *Chicano Poetry: A Response to Chaos.* Austin: University of Texas Press, 1982. Pp. 185–211.

Buckley, Christopher. "Where Can You Go? An Interview with Gary Soto." *Quarterly West* (autumn–winter 1998–1999): 149–156.

Bus, Heiner. "Sophisticated Spontaneity: The Art of Life in Gary Soto." *The Americas Review* 16 (1988): 188–197.

Cheuse, Alan. "The Voice of Chicano." *New York Times Book Review.* October 11, 1981, pp. 18, 36–37.

Cooley, Peter. "I Can Hear You Now." *Parnasus* 8 (fall–winter 1979): 297–311.

de la Fuentes, Patricia. "Ambiguity in the Poetry of Gary Soto." *Revista Chicano-Riqueña* 11 (summer 1983): 34–39.

————. "Entropy in the Poetry of Gary Soto: The Dialectics of Violence." *Revista Chicano-Riqueña* 5 (autumn 1987): 111–120.

————. "Mutability and Stasis: Images of Time in Gary Soto's *Black Hair*." *Revista Chicano-Riqueña* 17 (spring 1989): 100–107.

D'Evelyn, Tom. "Soto's Poetry: Unpretentious Language of the Heart." *Christian Science Monitor* 77 (March 6, 1985): 19.

Edwards, Ronald. "Gary Soto." In *Writers of Multicultural Fiction for Young Adults: A Bio-Critical Sourcebook.* Edited by Daphne Kutzer. Westport, Conn.: Greenwood Press, 1996.

Erben, Rudolf. "Popular Culture, Mass Media, and Chicano Identity in Gary Soto's *Living up the Street* and *Small Faces.*" *MELUS* 17 (fall 1991–1992): 43–52.

Ganz, Robin. "Gary Soto." In *Updating the Literary West.* Fort Worth: Texas Christian University Press, 1997. Pp. 426–433.

González Echevarría, Roberto. "Giving Up North of the Border." *New York Times Book Review* 45 (August 20, 1990).

Lee, Don. "About Gary Soto." *Ploughshares* 21 (spring 1995): 188–192.

Murphy, Patricia. "Inventing Lunacy: An Interview with Gary Soto." *Hayden's Ferry Review* 18 (1996): 29–37.

Olivares, Julian. "The Streets of Gary Soto." *Latin American Literary Review* 18 (January–June 1990): 32–49.

Paredes, Raymond. "Review Essay: Recent Chicano Writing." *Rocky Mountain Review of Language and Literature* 41 (1987): 124–128.

Pérez-Torres, Rafael. *Movements in Chicano Poetry: Against Myths, against Margins.* New York: Cambridge University Press, 1995. Pp. 263–270.

Shelton, Pamela L. "Gary Soto: Overview." In *Twentieth-Century Young Adult Writers.* Edited by Laura Standley Berger. Detroit: St. James Press, 1994. Pp. 213–218.

Torres, Héctor. "Genre-Shifting, Political Discourses, and the Dialectics of Narrative Syntax in Gary Soto's *Living up the Street.*" *Crítica: A Journal of Critical Essays* 2 (1988): 39–57.

————. "Gary Soto." *Dictionary of Literary Biography, Volume 82, Chicano Writers.* Edited by Francisco A. Lomelí and Carl R. Shirley. Detroit: Gale Research, 1989. Pp. 246–252.

————. "Gary Soto: Overview." In *Reference Guide to American Literature,* 3d ed. Edited by Jim Kamp. Detroit: St. James Press, 1994. Pp. 173–179.

Trejo, Ernesto. "Interview of Gary Soto." *Revista Chicano-Riqueña* 11 (summer 1983): 25–33.

Varela Ibarra, José. "Soto, Gary." In *Chicano Literature: A Reference Guide.* Edited by Julio A. Martínez and Francisco A. Lomelí. Westport, Conn.: Greenwood Press, 1985. Pp. 375–384.

Williamson, Alan. "In a Middle Style." *Poetry* 135 (March 1980): 348–354.

Zamora, Carlos. "A Review of *Where Sparrows Work Hard.*" *American Book Review* 4 (July–August 1982): 11.

Luis Valdez

(1940–)

KIRSTEN F. NIGRO

W HEN IN 1965 a young Luis Miguel Valdez traveled to Delano, California, to join *la huelga,* the farmworkers' strike led by the union organizer Cesar Chavez, he was returning to his roots and to a life he knew well. The second of ten children, Luis Valdez was born in Delano and had grown up in a family of migrant workers. His parents, Francisco and Armida Valdez, had always been on the move, following the harvests in central California. Luis joined his parents in their peripatetic ways, and like all children of migrant workers, he was constantly uprooted, forced by circumstances to attend many different schools. Despite these disruptions, Valdez was a good student, and when his family finally settled in San Jose, California, he went on to graduate from high school and win a scholarship to attend San Jose State College in 1960. As an English major, Valdez showed great talent as a playwright. His interest in drama had begun at the age of twelve, when he staged puppet plays for family and friends. At San Jose State College, his professors encouraged this interest, and his first effort at playwriting, the 1961 one-act play *The Theft,* won first prize in a regional writing contest. This early success was soon followed by *The Shrunken Head of Pancho Villa,* which was staged by his college drama department in 1963.

After his graduation in 1964, Valdez went to Cuba at a time when Castro's revolution could still capture the imagination of young political activists. Upon his return to the United States, he spent a year with the San Francisco Mime Troupe, which was gaining national recognition for its politically committed theater. While touring with the group in 1965, news of the strike in Delano and of the accompanying grape boycott reached Valdez and he went home to help unionize farmworkers, whose plight Valdez had lived firsthand. He founded El Teatro Campesino (the farmworkers theater) as a way of entertaining and educating farmworkers and galvanizing them into political action. From that moment on, *la huelga* and Chicano culture would never be the same.

With the creation of El Teatro Campesino, Valdez accomplished many things, the foremost of which was creating a tool for political action. But his theater can also be considered a watershed in the renaissance of Chicano, or Mexican American culture. When what is now the American southwest belonged to Spain, and then later to a newly independent Mexico, pockets of creative activity grew and important literary and artistic traditions were established— albeit slowly, given the area's isolation from the centers of culture. Spanish-speaking theater in what is now the United States has a long and rich history, dating back to the 1600s. While this tradition was until recently unknown not only to the majority, English-speaking population in the United States but to Mexican Americans as well, the Chicano movement of the 1960s and 1970s had as one of its primary missions making its people aware and proud of their rich artistic heritage.

A NEW THEATER FORM IS BORN: THE *ACTOS*

El Teatro Campesino tapped into this heritage, and in the first stages of Valdez's work he owed much to the Mexican *teatro de carpa,* tent theater that acted as a kind of traveling newspaper during the Mexican Revolution (1910–1920), performing satiric skits about contemporary political events. The comedian Cantinflas came from this tradition and in his early, pre-Hollywood career was known for his biting political satire, broad humor, and zany antics. Echoes of Cantinflas, as well as of other similar comedic traditions, including the commedia dell'arte of Renaissance Italy, can easily be distinguished in the *actos,* a theater form developed by Valdez in his collaboration with the farmworkers. Short, often improvisational and slapstick pieces, the *actos* have an unselfconsciously didactic purpose and political punch. Their first concern is social change; artistic perfection is a distant second. In his *Early Works,* published in 1990, Valdez described them in the following way: "Actos: Inspire the audience to social action. Illuminate specific points about social problems. Satirize the opposition. Show or hint at a solution. Express what people are feeling" (p. 12). Valdez adds that although the theater has always done this, what makes the *acto* different is its lack of concern with a psychological or individual vision. Rather, its vision is social and collective, a trait the *acto* shares with the *lehrstücke,* or learning pieces of the German playwright Bertolt

Brecht (1898–1956), who also used the theater to educate and agitate workers to rebel against the status quo.

The *acto* was born along with El Teatro Campesino when Valdez first met with the Delano strikers, in 1965. At union headquarters, he asked volunteers to show him what had happened that day during the strike. He hung placards around their necks identifying them as *huelguistas* (strikers) or *esquiroles* (strikebreakers, or scabs). Other farmworkers shouted out that they wanted to play a role too. As Jorge Huerta, the noted scholar of Chicano theater, describes the events of that evening in his 1982 *Chicano Theater: Themes and Forms,* Valdez had brought a pig-like mask that the farmworkers immediately identified with the *patroncito,* the boss or grower. One of them put the mask on, snorting pig noises, and the other volunteers improvised a dramatic situation around their real situation. The audience's reaction was wildly enthusiastic and empowering. The villains were overpowered by the good guys, and the *huelguistas* were inspired to continue with their struggle. Some of them were also inspired to join Valdez's theater project and became the core cast for El Teatro Campesino. When not on the picket line, they were performing *actos* to encourage fellow *huelguistas* who were.

The 1965 *Las dos caras del patroncito* (The two faces of the boss) is the result of that first night at union headquarters. An allegory in which the boss and a farmworker trade roles, the mask is pivotal for two reasons. First, it defines the character, so when the farmworker has it on, he assumes all the piggish and mean-spirited qualities of the boss. Without it, the boss is powerless, and at one point, when the farmworker-as-*patroncito* cuts his salary, the boss-as-farmworker even admits that the strike is necessary, that no one can live on the pittance that farmworkers are paid. When the boss's armed guard mistakes him for the farmworker and begins to drag him away, the real *patroncito* calls out for help: "Somebody help me! Where's those damn union organizers? Where's César Chávez? Help! Huelga! Huelgaaaaa" (*Early Works*, p. 27). The farmworker takes off the mask and tells the audience that he does not want all the material things he had when he was the boss. He is giving everything back to him, except for the cigar.

All the ingredients associated with *acto* are in this piece: the exaggeratedly drawn characters; the obvious struggle between good and evil; the direct message, the immediacy of the subject matter; the use of masks and placards hung around actors' necks indicating who they are as generic characters; the satiric tone and farcical, even clownish, acting style. The staging needs were simple, in part because of the need to disband quickly during performances when faced with unfriendly authorities, such as the private guards hired to patrol the picket lines, and also because the fields themselves were the backdrop for the *acto*. The guerilla tactics of El Teatro Campesino, its hit-and-run performances staged on flatbed trucks right on the edge of strike lines, had antecedents in Brecht's German workers' theater in the 1930s. But what was happening in Delano, California, had no precedents: it was politically and theatrically groundbreaking, capturing the imagination of all involved. Neither the Chicano civil rights movement nor the development of contemporary Chicano arts can be fully appreciated without understanding what El Teatro Campesino and its *actos* were all about.

The second important *acto* to come from *la huelga* was the 1966 *Quinta temporada* (The fifth season). It introduces another character of great importance in the daily reality of farmworkers: the contractor, also known as the *coyote*. This much-hated person is the intermediary between the worker and the boss. He is the one who rounds up cheap stoop labor and brings the workers to the fields in overheated, crowded, unsafe buses. One of Chavez's demands was the formation of a union hiring, which would eliminate the odious *coyote*. In *Quinta temporada*, the contractor is a greedy and dishonest person who hires an eager farmworker only to pay him poorly and then rob what he can from his meager salary. In this *acto*, Valdez and his worker-actors created something like the medieval morality plays, with metonymic characters who each stood for the whole of his or her group: Campesino, Don Coyote, Patrón, Winter, Summer, Fall, Spring, the Unions, the Churches, La Raza (The Race, a collective term used by Chicano's to refer to their shared cultural and Spanish heritage). While *Quinta temporada* follows the paradigm of other *actos*, certain aspects stand out as particularly creative. The first is the treatment of the four seasons. For farmworkers, summer is the fullest season for work, followed by fall, with its late harvests. Winter is the time farmworkers dread, when work dries up and they suffer the greatest economic deprivation. In spring, work begins to pick up and they anticipate the abundant summer crops. Whatever the season, however, the farmworker is never assured of steady work, given the vagaries of nature, such as early and late frosts, storms, drought, excessive rain, and blistering heat. In a stroke of creative genius, an actor wearing an ordinary work shirt and khaki hat performs the seasons. When he appears as Summer, he is abundantly covered with play money. As Fall, he has begun to lose some of his paper bills, and as Winter, he rumbles onto the stage, his money tree all dried up, demanding money for the rent, heating, and electric bills. Having robbed the workers, the Patrón and Don Coyote have no problem paying Winter and go off gleefully to their seaside vacations. The poor *campesino* is left behind to "eat *frijoles*," or beans (*Early Works*, p. 34). Spring enters skipping and singing a happy tune. She is a happy little girl who fights off Winter and tells the worker to stand up for his rights. At first he is surprised that he has any rights, but he decides to follow Spring's advice. When Summer comes around again and Don Coyote goes to round up his crew, Campesino demands a signed contract. When none is forthcoming, he and the other workers go on strike. The summer crop is lost.

Fall and Winter come and go, and the strike continues. Don Coyote finds himself deeper and deeper in trouble with the boss, and the worker is hungrier and hungrier, having run out of money to buy food. Just as he is about to give in to the contractor's demands, Spring returns, dressed as The Churches, bringing with her food and aid for the strikers. Summer comes back, this time dressed as The Unions, offering encouragement and support. Fall reenters dressed as La Raza and tells the strikers to not lose faith. Following the yearly cycle, Winter comes rumbling in again, ferocious and demanding money. This time, however, with the help of The Unions, The Churches, and La Raza, the strikers do not give in. When Winter asks who has money, they all point to Patrón, who, when faced with losing all his profits to Winter, finally signs the contract. At this point, Winter takes the placard off his neck. Underneath is another placard identifying him as the *quinta temporada*, the fifth season: the one of social justice. At the mere sound of these words, Don Coyote trembles with fear. Winter kicks him off stage and as in all the *actos*, good triumphs over evil, making for a happy and hopeful resolution.

The highly theatrical and effective presentation of the seasons in *Quinta temporada* is matched by the creative pantomime that shows Don Coyote stealing from the worker and handing the money over to the boss. When Summer first enters, flush with paper money,

> The FARMWORKER attacks the [sic] Summer, and begins to pick as many dollar bills as his hands can grab. These he stuffs into his back pockets. DON COYOTE immediately takes his place behind the FARMWORKER and extracts the money from his back pockets and hands it over to the PATRON, who has taken his place behind the contractor. This exchange continues until SUMMER exits.
>
> (pp. 30–31)

Words here could not match the immediacy and clearness achieved with these actions. The audience sees in this brief pantomime the chain of greed and dishonest behavior that has forced the strike. The humor may be broad and obvious, but it is exactly what was needed in those heady days of Cesar Chavez's young farmworkers union and of Luis Valdez's nascent Teatro Campesino.

Although still very much committed to the cause, in 1967 Valdez decided that it was time to work independently and to branch out in other theatrical directions. He moved El Teatro Campesino to Del Rey, California, and while they still continued to experiment with the *acto* form, they also began exploring new themes and building new audiences. Paralleling Chavez's rural labor movement, the late 1960s also saw much social unrest within the urban Chicano community, especially among young people. Along with other minority groups, including African Americans and American Indians, urban Chicanos demanded their civil and economic rights as U.S. citizens and sought to establish a distinctive identity. Many of them began to call themselves "Chicanos" (from "Mechicano," the Aztec pronunciation of "Mexicano"), as opposed to the hyphenated term "Mexican-American," which carried with it negative connotations of being acculturated—that is, totally absorbed into and even selling out to the majority culture. During this period, El Teatro Campesino performed various new *actos* that touched on these themes. The 1969 *Yo no saco nada de la escuela* (I don't get nothing out of school), for example, is a scathing, although still humorous, critique of the deficient education given to inner-city minorities, including Chicanos. *The Militants* (1969) and *Huelguistas* (1970) are very brief pieces dealing with the strike and the growing militancy among some in the Chicano movement. *La conquista de Mexico (A Puppet Show)*, which premiered in 1968, seems to have more in common with Valdez's very first play, *The Shrunken Head of Pancho Villa*. Both are concerned with the need for Chicanos to know and accept where they come from culturally, and both are nonrealistic, with puppets in one play and one headless and one bodiless character in the other. The outstanding piece from this period, however, is the 1967 *Los vendidos* (The sellouts), a brilliant critique of assimilation that continues to be one of the most enduring of the *actos* and is still staged by many Chicano theater groups.

Set in Honest Sancho's Used Mexican Lot and Mexican Curio Shop, *Los vendidos* is a spoof on the way Anglos (white Americans) stereotype Mexicans and on how some Mexican Americans try to be Anglos. One day the totally acculturated Miss Jiménez (she pronounces it Jim-enez, with an English J) comes to the shop hoping to buy a Mexican type, suitable for work in the governor's administration. She needs someone suave, debonair, and dark—but not too dark. Honest Sancho, a former *coyote,* shows her the four models he has on display. The first is the standard farmworker model, who is durable, friendly, versatile, and economical. Initially, Miss Jim-enez is impressed, but she rejects him when she learns that he has been programmed to go on strike and that he does not speak English. She asks for someone more sophisticated and Honest Sancho quickly shows her his urban model, Johnny Pachuco, who is built to survive city life. He dresses like a city slicker, he knife-fights, and he knows how to dance. Best of all, he is bilingual. But when Miss Jim-enez learns that he has the habit of getting arrested, she rejects him too. The third model, the *revolucionario* (revolutionary), is attractive. He is well built, rides horses, and leads revolutions, and he is adept at yelling "*Viva* Villa!" (long live Villa). But she rejects him too: he was born in Mexico and the governor wants someone made in the U.S.A. The final model is a Mexican American, a very clean-cut young man. He is utterly charming, patriotic, and very good at sitting on political committees. Very taken with this model, Miss Jim-enez is about to buy him (although she thinks she is being charged way too much) when his program malfunctions. He turns into a Chicano militant, whose cries of "*Viva la huelga!*" and "*Viva La Raza!*" incite the other three models to rebellion, and as they advance towards

Miss Jim-enez, she runs away, terrified. In a surprise ending, it turns out that the models are actually real people; the robot is the not-so-Honest Sancho.

In a piece like *Los vendidos*, Valdez criticizes values and behaviors that affect Chicanos and have political consequences. Other *actos* dealt with larger political issues, like the Vietnam War. During the same period that Cesar Chavez was fighting agribusiness in California, many young Chicanos were fighting for their country in Southeast Asia. In a war that was fought disproportionately by minorities, Chicano casualties were disproportionate to all others in Vietnam. The National Chicano Moratorium was held in August 1970 in Los Angeles to protest the war, and what started as a peaceful demonstration attended by thousands ended in violence provoked by police and aggravated by some of the protesters. Vietnam had come home to Chicanos in a tragic and dramatic way. That same year, El Teatro Campesino performed *Vietnam campesino* at the annual Thanksgiving dinner at the Guadalupe Church in Delano, which was held for union and strike supporters. This *acto* was meant as a wake-up call, alerting them to the fact that too many of their young men were dying in the war and that they were being forced to kill people who were *campesinos* as well, people not so very different from them. Valdez was a strong and vocal opponent of the war, and this is the first in a series of *actos* that criticize U.S. foreign policy. The characters are again the generic types of previous *actos,* but with a few notable additions, such as General Defense, El Draft, and Vietnamese Man and Woman. The story is set in the military-agricultural complex run by Butt Anglo (who parallels Patroncito of earlier pieces), his son Little Butt, and General Defense. The three are presented with broad satiric strokes and are the objects of derision. Butt Anglo (whose name obviously makes him the butt of jokes and also alludes to his stupidity) is upset because his farmworkers are now protesting against the war: "Why are you yelling at me about the war in

Vietnam? I'm just a poor grower." General Defense is annoyed that he has to listen to protests about the strike: "Wait a minute, wait a minute! Why are you yelling at me about that farm labor strike? I'm a general" (*Early Works*, p. 99). While these men are clearly meant to be played as buffoons, they also have a more sinister side, which is seen in their collusion to benefit from the war. They agree to the following: the military will provide a new pest control, courtesy of Dow Chemical, and the grower will send the troops $1 million worth of lettuce picked by scabs. The pesticide (the same one that was being dropped over the jungles of Vietnam) will cut down on the need for labor, freeing more Mexican Americans to go to war, and the men in Vietnam can smoke lettuce (an allusion to the fact that smoking marijuana was widespread among our troops in Southeast Asia).

Vietnam campesino is full of such references to the war, many of which audiences today might not catch. However, the basic story line—a young man is drafted and killed in war—still resonates. So does the creative performance style. For example, El Draft appears as a thin male figure wearing a death mask and draped in an American flag worn like the funeral shroud that covers the caskets of fallen troops. Miming the use of a fishing pole, El Draft hooks a young *campesino* and throws him off stage (meaning, into the army). He then points a finger at Little Butt, only to be told sternly by General Defense that he is to single out minorities. The young draftee's assignment is to burn the shack of some Vietnamese peasants, represented by a paper cutout, which he at first mistakes for his parents' humble house. As he is being congratulated for a job well done, he is shot dead by one of the two Vietnamese seated on one side of the stage, opposite the young soldier's parents on the other side of the stage. The bereaved parents at first react with anger and hatred, but they end by realizing that the enemy has also lost sons, that in their shared grief and exploitation they have much in common—so much so that the

Vietnamese even end by joining the forces of Aztlán, the mythical homeland of the Chicanos. The play closes with the image of them all with clenched fists raised in the air, the sign of defiance used by Chicanos in their quest for what was then called Brown Power.

In hindsight, this closing image seems idealistic, if not naive, for there never was any real solidarity between these two groups. They were worlds apart in more than the literal sense. Symbolically, however, the image impresses for what it says about what the world could be: one of people united in their quest for justice. What has not lost any of its luster, however, is the brilliant and very simple way that *Vietnam campesino* makes use of stage effects. One of the most outstanding examples of this is when Little Butt bombs the lettuce fields with a toy plane. The sound of a whirring engine is heard as he dives down over imaginary fields, releasing pesticides from a baby powder container. Equally creative is the moment when he drops contaminated lettuces over an imaginary Vietnam:

(LITTLE BUTT stretches out his arms like wings. Drumroll. The GENERAL and BUTT ANGLO place the two lettuces in his hands. Then retrieving a black cloth each from backstage, they lay these over LITTLE BUTT'S arms. He looks like a deadly bird.)

(. . . With a scream of engines, backstage noises LITTLE BUTT flies into position and zeroes in for the kill. He drops a lettuce bomb on the male campesino and then on the Vietnamese. He swings around and comes back for the women, covering their faces with a black cloth each. . . . The women cough and choke underneath the black cloths. All die.)

(*Early Works*, p. 118)

The first of three *actos* dealing with the Vietnam War, *Vietnam campesino* inevitably moves from the comedic to the serious. In *Soldado razo* (The buck private), however, comedy makes way for tragedy. First staged in April 1971, at the Chicano War Moratorium in Fresno, California,

Soldado razo also makes fuller use of the elements from Mexican folklore that were hinted at in prior pieces. The death mask in *Vietnam campesino* is here developed into the death figure associated with the *calacas,* or skeletons that are part of Mexican Day of the Dead celebrations and which were popularized in art by the nineteenth-century lithographer José Guadalupe Posada. Death, or La Muerte, is the major character in this *acto* and serves as a narrator who, very much in the manner of Bertolt Brecht's theater, starts off by announcing that the play will end with the death of Johnny, the young Chicano who has volunteered for service in Vietnam. In this way, audience attention is drawn not so much to what will happen as to why and how it will happen. This is also the first *acto* to flesh out its characters, and although it is still very short, *Soldado razo* manages to give a real sense of depth to the story. On the eve of Johnny's departure to Vietnam, La Muerte enters, singing a famous song from the Mexican revolution about a *soldado razo* who heads for the war, leaving behind his family and his beloved. So many of these revolutionary soldiers were called "Juan" (John) that the name was used in other well-known *corridos,* or ballads, from the Mexican Revolution. With these references to Mexican history and popular culture, Valdez makes Johnny into a kind of Everyman and the symbol of all the Chicano Juans who were dying in Vietnam. On that fateful eve, we see Johnny eat his last supper with his family and Cecilia, to whom he has just proposed marriage. While the mother is worried and tearful about his departure, his father is proud that his son is finally a man, going off to war to kill the enemy. Johnny's younger brother wishes he could go too. Johnny has signed up because he wants to show his willingness to die for his country, and although he has fleeting visions of being killed, he brushes them aside. With the exception of the mother, the other family members are all influenced by notions of *machismo,* a worldview in which men are supposed to be tough and manhood is proven on the battlefield or with other violent activities. Cecilia has fallen victim to this kind of thinking as well and evaluates Johnny's worth by how good he looks in uniform.

Unlike *Vietnam campesino,* this *acto* points its finger not only at the war-makers and profit-seekers, but also at values within the Chicano community that Valdez feels blind Chicanos to reality. La Muerte here is a ventriloquist for the playwright, offering commentary and critiques of what the other characters say or think.

> MUERTE: This, of course, is Johnny's novia. Fine, eh? . . . Oh, he proposed tonight y todo and she accepted, but she doesn't know what's ahead. Listen to what she's thinking. (CECILIA *moves her mouth.*) "When we get married I hope Johnny still has his uniform. We'd look so good together. Me in a wedding gown and him like that. Chihuahua, I wish we were getting married tomorrow!"
>
> (*Early Works,* pp. 125–126)

Throughout *Soldado razo,* La Muerte has similar insights into the characters' misguided beliefs and the folly of their hopes and dreams. With these insights, Valdez hopes to make his Chicano audience see how they are also implicated in events at home and abroad.

Yet La Muerte is not the only character who sees things clearly. So does Johnny, although it is too late for him. He writes to his mother that he has seen and done things in Vietnam that both shame and sicken him, like killing entire villages, including women and young children. He tells her that he dreamed he had entered a hooch (a peasant hut), shooting his M-16 on orders to kill the three people in there. After he did, he looked at them and saw that they were his own family. As he says out loud what he is writing, his mother reacts as she reads the letter. Just as he is about to ask her to tell his friends what it is really like in Vietnam, La Muerte shoots him in the head. Off and on throughout the play, La Muerte has powdered Johnny's face white in anticipation of this final moment.

This chilling ending is achieved with an economy of theatrical means that is the hallmark of El Teatro Campesino's *actos*: characters on an almost empty stage with a minimum of props and dramatic sound effects. In the third of Valdez's Vietnam texts, the 1967 *Dark Root of a Scream,* the scenic needs become far more complex, despite its being quite brief. First produced in Fresno, it takes place during the wake for Quetzalcóatl Gonzales, nicknamed El Indio, who has died in Vietnam. The set is pyramidal, with two points at the base: the first a living room where the wake takes place and the other a street corner where three *vatos* (street dudes) talk about Indio. The dead Chicano's coffin is placed at the apex of the pyramid. The pyramid itself changes its composition as it rises, starting with "iron and the hard steel of modern civilization—guns, knives, automobile parts; others reveal a less violent, more spiritual origin—molcajetes [Mexican stone mortars], rebozos [shawls], crucifixes, etc." (quoted in Jorge Huerta's 1982 *Chicano Theater: Themes and Forms,* p. 97). The top of the pyramid is made of indigenous materials, such as jade, conchs, and feathered serpent heads. The lighting is an important element, with the pyramid's base in the light and the apex in darkness. Huerta notes that in a 1971 production light undulated from one side of the base to the other as the dialogue shifted from one space to another.

As in the other two Vietnam texts, the stress here is on the tragic waste of young Chicano life in the war. Working backwards in time, the shifting dialogue re-creates the relationship between Indio and his three buddies, Gato (cat), Lizard, and Conejo (rabbit), whose sister Dalia had been Indio's girlfriend. The conversations blend into each other, with one side answering questions or reacting to comments made on the other of the pyramid. A topic of conversation on both sides is Indio's given name—Quetzalcóatl, after the Mayan God known as the Plumed Serpent. The priest at the wake, who is not Mexican American, cannot understand why anyone would have such a name, and Lizard, betraying his racism and ignorance, can only associate indigenous people with Hollywood westerns. Gato expresses disdain for his dead friend when he learns that at one point Indio, who was active as a social leader in the Chicano community, had briefly considered dodging the draft. The three friends finally decide to attend the wake, where the only true mourner is Indio's mother, who has lost her three sons in three different wars: World War II, Korea, and Vietnam. Earlier in the play she saw blood oozing from the flag covering Indio's casket and thought her son was still alive. This incident is picked up again after the three *vatos* disrupt the service. The priest runs to get the police, with Lizard following at his heels. The tensions build up to such a pitch that the mother lets out a loud scream and Lizard returns, dressed in the priest's cassock. When he notices Indio's mother and girlfriend on top of the pyramid, he too sees the blood dripping from the flag. He is about to open the casket when the mother shoves him aside to do it herself. Lizard removes an Aztec headdress and cloak from the casket and, putting them on like an Aztec priest, he reaches in again and pulls out Indio's bleeding heart. The play closes abruptly, with the image of this heart pulsating and emitting light as the stage goes dark.

FROM THE *ACTO* TO THE *MITO*

Dark Root of a Scream is different theatrically from the other pieces in the Vietnam trilogy and marks a transition from the *acto* to another dramatic form, which Valdez called a *mito,* or myth. Although Valdez had always been interested in the history and mythology of his ancestors, and had already used some motifs from ancient Mexican mythology, in this particular play he begins to give them prominence. With Quetzalcóatl Rodríguez, the Indio, Valdez creates a hybrid character that conflates Chicano and indigenous identities. Quetzalcóatl, the Plumed Serpent of Mayan cosmology, was reputedly the gentle god of peace. In one version of his life story, he was tricked into seeing his own image in a mirror, and in another he was tricked into getting drunk and sleeping with his sister. Both versions portray Quetzalcóatl as the victim of a deception that led him to break strong taboos in his culture. The penalty was exile, and as he departed to the east he promised that one day he would return. His story is well-known in accounts of the conquest of Mexico, as it was calculated that he would return at exactly the same time that the Spanish *conquistadores,* or conquerors, arrived. Mistaking Hernán Cortés for Quetzalcóatl, the emperor Moctezuma did not resist the Spanish entry into Tenochtitlán, the Aztec capital and the present-day Mexico City.

Valdez adapts the figure of Quetzalcóatl to his own purposes in *Dark Root of a Scream,* and while recent scholarship disproves the popular notion that the Mayans did not practice human sacrifice, Valdez chooses to portray them as a peaceful people. However, he does see Quetzalcóatl as a sacrificial victim and retains the myth's central motif of betrayal. His Quetzalcóatl is symbolically sacrificed at the altar of racism and misguided politics. Gato and Lizard betray him as well when they speak ill of him and turn his wake into a brawl. Interestingly, they are also the ones who betray the gentle side of the Quetzalcóatl motif. When Lizard holds Indio's bloody heart up high, he evokes the fearsome image of human sacrifice as practiced by the more warlike Aztecs, whose adoration of the bloodthirsty war god Huitzilopochtli supposedly distinguished them from the Mayans' traditional devotion to the Plumed Serpent. With this image, however, Valdez also indirectly refers to Jesus, who was also betrayed and whose *corazón sangrante,* or bloody heart, is an important element in Catholic iconography.

The fusing of imagery from various cultures and time frames at the end of *Dark Root of a Scream* creates a theatrically powerful moment, but it also confuses the play's intent. It is not altogether clear whether Valdez means to confirm or negate the role of Aztec mythology in the lives of present-day Chicanos. Quetzalcóatl seems to return in the fallen Chicano warrior, but the forces of bloody sacrifice and Aztec ritual are what reign at the top of the pyramid. Or does the association with Jesus cancel out this image? Valdez received strong criticism for various reasons as he developed his *mitos,* but one reason was his sometimes muddled fusion of pre-Colombian cosmogony, about which more will be said later in this essay. What is important to stress at this point is that with *Dark Root of a Scream* Valdez begins a new phase in his artistic career. Discouraged by the violence of the 1970 Chicano War Moratorium and the failure of street politics to significantly change the Chicano's situation, he gradually began to stress the need for a deep spirituality and a common belief system that could unite Chicanos in a common purpose. He found this in the Mayan concept of *in lak'ech,* which loosely translated means "you are my other self," an idea not terribly different from the Christian injunction to "do unto others as you would have them do unto you." Valdez felt it was time to leave hatred behind, because hatred would come back, snakelike, to bite the haters. In his extended 1971 poem/manifesto *Pensamiento serpentino* [Serpentine Thought]: *A Chicano Approach to the Theatre of Reality,* Valdez explains that as a colonized people Chicanos must look for their roots in the ancient texts and customs of the Mesoamerican people. He believes that they must "Mexicanize" themselves, become "neo-Mayans" in order to truly understand who they are and love themselves, their culture, their language, and their brown skin color. He exhorts Chicanos to love God and to love themselves: "As Chicanos / As Neo Mayas / we must re-identify / with that center and proceed / outward with love and strength / AMOR Y FUERZA [love and strength] / and undying dedication to justice" (*Early Works,* pp. 176–177). Written at a time when the Chicano movement was suffering from serious internal factionalism and external pressures, *Pensamiento serpentino* was a rallying call for Chicanos to unite in love, to learn about and embrace their indigenous *mitos,* and to travel the spiritual road in search of peace and liberation. In this particular context, the adjective "serpentine" is associated with the Plumed Serpent Quetzalcóatl. Valdez is in turn clearly linking him with Jesus Christ: "La visión de Quetzalcóatl / era como la visión de Jesucristo" (Quetzalcóatl's vision / was like Jesus's vision; p. 196).

As he did with the *actos* before them, Valdez used the *mitos* to educate his audiences about contemporary issues. His first fully developed *mito* is the 1970 *Bernabé,* the first of El Teatro Campesino's texts to be written by Valdez alone. It tells the story of a mentally retarded farm-worker who is in love with "Mother Earth," and although the action takes places in a specific place—a tiny rural settlement in the San Joaquin Valley—the stage directions indicate that the set must be abstract in order to reflect a blend of myth and reality. This space is meant to be seen through the eyes of Bernabé, who is touched with a "cosmic madness" (*Early Works,* p. 134). The world he sees and lives in is intimately connected to the earth, moon, sun, and stars, "for he is a man who draws his full human worth not from the tragicomic daily reality of men, but from the collective, mythical universality of Mankind" (p. 135). Treated like a village idiot, Bernabé lives under the tight control of his domineering and intolerant mother. Others in town make fun of him and local growers see him only as easy and cheap stoop labor. Bernabé speaks of being in love with a woman who is out in the fields and the hills. She is beautiful and loves the rain. He says that her name is La Tierra (the earth) and that he is going to marry her. This kind of talk elicits only laughs from Torres, a local businessman, and some sympathy from Bernabé's cousin, who decides that what Bernabé really needs is a visit to the local whorehouse, where he can lose his virginity to a real woman. The visit proves traumatic and Bernabé retreats, distraught, to a hole in the ground near his house, where he can find solace, symbolically consummating his relationship with his beloved by masturbating and wetting the ground with his seed.

There is a full moon on the hot summer night of Bernabé's traumatic encounter with the prostitute. As he pulls off the planks that cover his hiding place, there is a bright light in the sky and music is heard. At this point, the action combines the real with the mythical, the material with the spiritual, the explicable with the inexplicable, as La Luna (the moon) appears, dressed like a 1940s pachuco and smoking marijuana. Like any true zoot suiter, La Luna is hip and streetwise. He knows that Bernabé loves his sister La Tierra and wants to make sure his intentions are serious, for she wants a relationship that lasts forever. La Luna calls his sister to come and she appears, dressed like a *soldadera* (a soldier woman of the type who accompanied the troops during the Mexican Revolution). She challenges Bernabé to prove his love for her, to be true to her, and if necessary to kill to protect her. Too many men have used and abused her, but she knows that Bernabé's love is pure and constant. As dawn approaches, El Sol (the sun) appears as Tonatiuyh, the Aztec sun god, and, impressed that Bernabé has dared to face him, he gives his daughter permission to marry Bernabé. El Sol recognizes that Bernabé is a poor Chicano who never has had any land of his own and that for that reason he understands that power is to be found not in owning land but in respecting it. He tells Bernabé that in dying for La Tierra he will attain eternity, as have the stars. When La Tierra turns to look at Bernabé, her face has become a death mask. The following morning, Bernabé is found dead, buried in the earth. Consoling Bernabé's distraught mother, his uncle says that this was God's will, at which there is the sound of drums and flutes. Bernabé and La Tierra appear in the sky "in a cosmic embrace. He is naked, wearing only a loincloth. She is Coatlicue, Mother Earth, the Aztec Goddess of Life, Death, and Rebirth" (p. 167).

As he did in *Dark Root of a Scream,* Valdez blends the contemporary with the ancient. By choosing two popular twentieth-century Chicano icons—the pachuco and the *soldadera*—and conflating them with Aztec deities, he is able to make important connections between the past and the present. The result, however, is a uniquely Valdezian cosmogony, in which the playwright changes the gender of certain deities, their lineages, and even their symbolism, adapting them to his own theatrical purposes. To quote Jorge Huerta: "With few experts among his audiences to challenge him on Aztec mythology, Valdez could adjust mythical relationships as he wished. By making La Tierra and La Luna symbols recognizable to Chicano audiences, the playwright gives the spectators historical and political reference points even as he fuses these with icons that have little meaning beyond the so-called 'Aztec calendar'" (*Chicano Drama,* pp. 41–42). For Valdez, the important issue in a play like *Bernabé* is not historical accuracy or total adherence to the myths he works with, but the creation of a character who could embody the belief in *in lak'ech,* someone who lives by the codes of love and who recognizes himself in others.

In 1971, El Teatro Campesino made its final move, to the small, rural town of San Juan Bautista, south of San Francisco. With a 1968 Obie Award for "demonstrating the politics of survival" and numerous national and international tours under their belt, Valdez and his troupe had gained wide recognition and respect. Always seeking to stretch the limits of his craft, in the early 1970s Valdez began to explore the use of music and dance in the *mitos,* and in June 1973 El Teatro Campesino produced its first full-length collaborative play, *La gran carpa de los rasquachis* (The big tent of the underdogs) at the fourth annual festival of Chicano Theater held in San Jose, California. Playing to an audience of some two thousand people, *La gran carpa* was an instant success and would become part of the group's repertoire at home and abroad until 1978, with a successful revival

in 2002. All of El Teatro Campesino's prior work converges in this piece: the humor and political satire of the *actos* and of Mexican tent theater; the broad acting style of the commedia dell'arte; the spiritual and religious themes of the *mitos;* and the constant use of song, most particularly the Mexican *corrido,* or ballad. With an economy of props and sets—a burlap backdrop, a shipping crate, hats, a rope, small pillows—*La gran carpa* tells the tale of Jesús Pelado Rasquachi's journey across the border and the indignities and injustices he suffers as a farmworker. "*Pelado*" and "*rasquachi*" are popular Mexican terms for an underdog, a low-life, someone uncouth or uneducated. By combining these terms with the name Jesús, Valdez creates an emblematic character of the sacrificial poor. Indeed, Jesús Pelado Rasquachi dies in a welfare office when he is forced to say he is a "welfare bum," the ultimate outcast in the eyes of social and political conservatives of that time.

The play continues with the tale of his two sons, one of whom is a money-obsessed drug dealer and the other a corrupt and power-obsessed politician. The pusher has the politician killed and the police kill the drug dealer, a situation that Valdez creates to show the dangers of Chicanos losing their moral compass and turning against each other. The final sequence of the play is called the "Salvation of our People," and Quetzacóatl appears, but as in the legend he is tricked into getting drunk and must go into exile. In his absence, the other characters fall victim to all kinds of carnal and moral temptations but are saved by the Virgin of Guadalupe, patron Saint of Mexico and of the poor. She is joined by Quetzalcóatl/Jesus and the play closes with the recitation of the Mayan phrase *in lak'ech,* accompanied by the indigenous song "Mano poderosa" (Powerful hand).

According to Jorge Huerta, the opening-night crowd reacted with spontaneous and enthusiastic applause. The beauty of the images, especially of the Virgin of Guadalupe; the ritualistic, almost sacramental, nature of the play; the lively *corridos,* guitar music, and sounds of the Aztec conch; and the humorous characters and energy of the actors all combined to make for a thrilling and unique theater experience. But as Huerta also notes, many Chicano activists grumbled about the new direction that Valdez's work was taking. Some militants felt that in moving toward the spiritual and the mythic he was not addressing the pressing problems of the here and now, and that the solutions he offered (like divine intervention) were a cop-out. There was concern that *La gran carpa* supported the very church that was oppressing Chicanos, and some people were puzzled by Valdez's embrace of a Maya/Aztec world that was so distant from the Chicano experience.

The controversy reached a head in 1974 during the fifth Chicano Theater Festival, when El Teatro Campesino performed *Baile de los gigantes* (Dance of the giants) at the pyramids of Teotihuacán on the outskirts of Mexico City on the night of the summer solstice. This highly ritualized and participatory performance was adapted from the sacred texts of the Maya-Quiché, the *Popul Vuh,* and tells the story of the creation of the moon and the sun. The festival, under the banner of "One continent, one culture, for a free theater, and for liberation," was attended by many radical groups from throughout Latin America, some of which were openly hostile to Valdez's myth-making and to his faith in the cathartic power of ritualized events.

In answer to his critics, Valdez defended himself by saying that, like the times, his theater had evolved, and while still political, it was more concerned with a politics of the spirit and of the heart:

> We do not feel that this is in any way inconsistent with our Chicanismo. Ask La Raza. They will tell you. Our people believe in the Creador, hermanismo [creator; brotherhood]. The great spirit . . .they are all manifestations of the same Cosmic force. Man is a spiritual animal. Man in his heart contains the divine spark. What we intellectuals struggle to grasp with our minds, La Raza más humilde [most humble and poor] has always known through sheer faith alone."

(as quoted by Roy Eric Xavier, "Politics and Chicano Culture: Luis Valdez and El Teatro Campesino, 1964–1990," p. 188)

Valdez continued working with his *mitos* and in 1974 produced *El fin del mundo* (The end of the world) for the traditional celebration of the Day of the Dead on 1 and 2 November. In 1976 he adapted *La gran carpa* for National Educational Television, with the new title *El corrido* (The ballad). Christmas pageants and pieces dealing with religious themes and the Virgin of Guadalupe have become part of El Teatro Campesino's permanent repertoire—testimony to the lasting influence of the *mitos* on its work and philosophy.

MOVING TOWARDS THE MAINSTREAM: *ZOOT SUIT* AND ITS CONSEQUENCES

In Luis Valdez's artistic trajectory, the year 1978 is pivotal, for it marks the opening of his highly successful *Zoot Suit* at a mainstream venue, the Mark Taper Forum in Los Angeles. Valdez was commissioned by the Taper's artistic director to write a play about the Sleepy Lagoon trial and the zoot suit riots that took place in Los Angeles in 1943. The result was a musical drama that Valdez said was unlike any of his previous work; he called it "an American play." Based on extensive research in trial transcripts, letters, defense papers, and newspaper articles, *Zoot Suit* deals with the trial of members of a pachuco gang, who were arrested on trumped-up charges of having committed a murder in the Sleepy Lagoon Reservoir area of Los Angeles. While they are ultimately set free, with the help of a generous Anglo lawyer and a dedicated Jewish political organizer, their ordeal lays bare the rampant racism and anti-Mexican feelings in wartime Los Angles, which came to a head in violent riots between sailors and pachucos.

In order to condense the voluminous material he had researched, Valdez chose to blend many of the real people involved into a more manageable number of stage characters (the play contains around forty characters, with many actors playing double roles). To avoid a strictly naturalistic approach, he divided the play into two acts, with brief scenes that take place in an abstract and symbolic setting. In addition, Valdez created a mythical character—El Pachuco— who narrates, comments on, and at times even participates in the action. The very first moment of *Zoot Suit* is decisive in letting the audience know what kind of play it is about to see. A giant facsimile of the Los Angeles *Herald Express,* dated 3 June 1943, serves as a backdrop. The headline reads: "Zoot-Suiter Hordes Invade Los Angeles. US Navy and Marines Are Called In" (*Zoot Suit and Other Plays,* p. 24). Behind the backdrop are a series of black drapes, casting eerie shadows. On them hang the outlines of pachucos. Duke Ellington music plays and El Pachuco emerges from a slit he cuts through the backdrop with a switchblade.

HE adjusts his clothing, meticulously fussing with his collar, suspenders, cuffs. HE tends to his hair, combing back every strand into a long luxurious ducktail, with infinite loving pains. Then HE reaches into the slit and pulls out his coat and hat. HE dons them. His fantastic costume is complete. It is a zoot suit. HE is transformed into the very image of the pachuco myth, from his pork-pie hat to the tip of his four-foot watch chain. Now HE turns to the audience. His three-soled shoes with metal taps click-clack as HE proudly, slovenly, defiantly makes his way downstage. HE stops and assumes a pachuco stance.

(p. 25)

One could not ask for a more provocative and theatrical first moment for a performance. Played to the hilt by Edward James Olmos in the original 1978 production, El Pachuco became a legendary character in the history of Chicano theater. The part transformed Olmos from a lounge singer into one of the most prolific and recognizable of Chicano actors. El Pachuco is the major presence in *Zoot Suit,* an all-knowing and ever-present narrator, *corrido*

singer, and devil's advocate to the other major character, Henry Reyna. With his tough-guy pose and colorful pachuco language, which combines and rhymes slang in Spanish and English, he is clearly meant to be larger than life, a Chicano myth. He comments on the discrimination suffered by pachucos and other Mexican Americans, and like a trickster he tries to confuse Henry and sometimes even needle him into violent behavior. In many ways he is an on-stage director, choreographing and blocking the action. At other times he assumes the role of playwright; at the end of the play, he and some of the other characters write three possible endings to Henry's life after he gets out of jail: he continues a life of crime and winds up in jail again; he enlists for the Korean War and is killed; he marries his sweetheart and has five children who go to the university and become proud Chicanos. Not surprisingly, El Pachuco has the last word in the play: "Henry Reyna . . . El pachuco . . . The man. . . the myth . . . still lives" (p. 94).

Zoot Suit broke attendance records at the Mark Taper Forum for twelve weeks. Its success was such that in 1979 it was invited to play on Broadway. Unfortunately, pre-opening advertising was spotty and opening night reviews were less than glowing. The play closed after only five weeks. Valdez returned to Los Angeles and *Zoot Suit* opened at the Aquarius Theatre in Hollywood, where it had a year's run, playing to full houses. In 1981 Valdez adapted it to the wide screen for Universal Pictures, and although it did not become a major box-office success, it had and continues to have considerable success on the independent circuit. The play garnered Valdez his fourth Los Angeles Drama Critics Award, and the film was nominated for a Golden Globe. In 1982 it won best picture award in the Cartagena, Colombia, Film Festival. The play's 2003 revival in San Juan Bautista was a runaway success.

With *Zoot Suit,* Valdez's career turned in a new direction. Some critics have seen this as the beginning of the end of El Teatro Campesino as a collaborative family and the beginning of Valdez's commercialization (Yolanda Broyles-González, for example, in her 1994 *El Teatro Campesino: Theater in the Chicano Movement*). Others have disagreed, arguing that Valdez needed space to continue growing as an artist, and that by the 1980s Chicano audiences were sophisticated and demanding enough to expect theater that went beyond transparent and immediate political goals (for example, Huerta, in his 1994 "Looking for the Magic," in *Negotiating Performance: Gender, Sexuality and Theatricality in Latin/o America*). The center of controversy once again, Valdez defended himself well, as he had before, stressing his continued commitment to his people on a political, spiritual, and artistic level. He argued that Chicano artists had to reach a wider audience if they were to be heard and taken seriously. He also noted that turning a profit was not necessarily a bad thing: the revenue from *Zoot Suit*, the play, and the movie, allowed El Teatro Campesino to buy a permanent theater space, a converted warehouse which also functions as a cultural center, a recording studio, and an arts laboratory. The first of the new playhouse productions was the 1982 *Corridos: Tales of Passion and Revolution*, an adaptation of his earlier *El corrido*. A loosely structured musical, the new version mixed narration, song, and brief dramatic scenes to tell the histories of the men and women popularized by the Mexican ballad. The production won eleven Bay Area critics awards, including one for best musical. Its 1987 television adaptation for the Public Broadcasting Service was honored with the prestigious George Foster Peabody Award for Excellence in Television Broadcasting.

That same year Valdez had another success with the release of his film *La Bamba*, which was a great box-office, if not always a critical, success. *La Bamba* deals with the brief life of the 1950s rock and roll singer Ricardo Valenzuela, known as Ritchie Valens, the son of migrant farmworkers, who was the first Mexican American to break into the pop music business.

The film tells about the joys of his success and of the prejudices he encountered along the way. At the age of seventeen, Valenzuela died in a plane crash in 1959 while on tour with Holly. In 1994, Valdez's new, Chicano version of *The Cisco Kid*, starring Jimmy Smits and Cheech Marin, aired on the TNT television network.

AFTER *ZOOT SUIT*

His work with film did not mean that Valdez abandoned the stage. His 1981 *Bandido! The American Melodrama of Tiburcio Vasquez, Notorious California Bandit* shares with *Zoot Suit* the mythologizing of a figure from Chicano history, in this case a so-called bandit who was the last person to be legally hung in California. Alternating between the realistic stage setting of a jailhouse and a space that acts as a bar and a gilded melodrama stage, *Bandido!* contains a play-within-the-play about a Mexican Robin Hood who has been maligned and stereotyped in Anglo tellings, which reduce him to a dirty and mercenary Mexican outlaw. To set the record straight, Valdez plays with the melodrama form, which was popular during the wild days of the Old West, when plays about the "villainous" Tiburcio Vasquez were actually presented, and with Hollywood clichés about Mexicans in general. In Valdez's version, Vasquez is a revolutionary, a leader of the oppressed, and would-be liberator of Mexican California. In short, he is a *mito*.

A recurrent goal in Valdez's work has been to undo the damage that stereotyping has done to Chicanos, and he does this for Tiburcio. This same kind of biting humor is also evident in his 1986 *I Don't Have to Show You No Stinking Badges!* co-produced by El Teatro Campesino and the Los Angeles Theatre Center. The title is taken from the 1948 John Houston film, *The Treasure of the Sierra Madre*, with Humphrey Bogart. In one scene, Bogart and his fellow gold-seekers run into a group of dirty and shifty-eyed Mexicans who claim to be the law. When asked to show their badges, one of them smiles a toothy smile and in heavily accented English, says, "I don't have to show you any stinking badges." The moment summarizes how the film industry has stereotyped Mexicans, lumping them together as poor, dirty "banditos (sic)." While the Mexican Americans in Valdez's play are solidly middle class, living a life with few traces of their heritage, they are beholden to Hollywood's images of them. Buddy Villa and his wife Conny are movie extras who lead a comfortable life, willingly accepting stereotypical roles as maids and gardeners. Their son, Sonny, arrives one night to announce that he has dropped out of Harvard to pursue a career in Hollywood based on breaking the rules and not playing the stereotype. This throws the family into crisis and Buddy promises not to let their situation comedy turn into some kind of soap opera. In Act II, Valdez's play takes on a weird, almost surreal aspect, which helps explain the stage setting: the interior of a suburban home built circa 1985, that "sits within the confines of a TV studio" (*Zoot Suit and Other Plays,* p. 157), set up for a live audience, which consists of the people watching *I Don't Have to Show You No Stinking Badges!* As in *Bandido!,* this is a play-within-a-play—or play-within-a-sitcom. From its realistic beginnings, the play morphs into something else, as the Villa family become a cast of dysfunctional sitcom characters. Sony is directing: "QUIET ON THE SET . . . ! ROLLING . . . SPEED . . . SLATE! HOMEBOY HOME MOVIE, SCENE FOUR, TAKE TWO. ACTION!" (p. 187). The characters-as-actors-in-the-sitcom are outrageous stereotypes of Mexicans, among them Buddy as the bandit from *Treasure of the Sierra Madre.* The entire dialogue becomes a series of in-jokes and references to Hollywood films: for example, Mel Brooks's *Blazing Saddles* is re-titled *Blazing Frijoles* [beans]. Sonny becomes a *cholo* (street dude) and robs a local "crap-in-the-box," playing the role that is expected of a Mexican American: a criminal, not a student from Harvard Law School. Later he reappears as a Green

Beret from the Vietnam War and threatens his parents with a gun. The line between reality and playacting has gotten so blurred that Buddy tries to put an end to it. Just when it seems that Sonny will indeed shoot him, there is a blackout, followed by another scene: "A STAGEHAND walks onstage, takes the gun from SONNY and begins to clear props" (p. 209). Sonny complains that the director has not respected his script and asks if he can at least write a spectacular ending. To the sounds of the flute and drums, a flashing object descends from the heavens and lands in the Villas' patio. Sonny comes down the stairs with his girlfriend and announces that he has decided to go back to Harvard. As in all sitcoms, all's well that ends well. The two young lovers take off in a flying saucer shaped like a Mexican sombrero while the parents kiss and say good night, just as they would in any respectable 1950s sitcom.

A highly entertaining and creative play, *I Don't Have to Show You No Stinking Badges!* continued to explore one of the themes that have preoccupied Valdez since the early days of his career: the dangers that threaten the well-being and self-image of Mexican Americans. If in the *actos* the critique was of clear and immediate social injustices, here it was of something subtler but equally destructive: mass media images of Mexican Americans that turn them into people to be laughed at or to be afraid of and that make it easy to dismiss them as insignificant or inferior. In his 2000 play, *The Mummified Deer,* Valdez continued to explore these themes and again fused reality and imagination, the historical and the mythic, much as he did in his *mitos.* The play takes place in 1969, around the hospital bed of Mama Chu, a 114-year-old Yaqui Indian who suffers from extreme abdominal pain because she has a mummified fetus lodged in her womb. Inspired by a newspaper article, *The Mummified Deer* is structured around flashbacks that reconstruct Mama Chu's life. As she lies dying, her memories allow her to come to peace with her traumatic past, and as Mama Chu's children and grandchildren put together the pieces of her personal puzzle they begin to understand the mysteries in and of their own lives.

Intrigued and obsessed with the image of the mummified fetus, Valdez used it to explore issues of Chicano identity and of his own identity as a descendant of Yaqui Indians. Known as a particularly fierce tribe, the Yaqui of Northern Mexico were not easily subdued, either by the Spaniards or by the Mexicans. The dictator Porfirio Díaz (1830–1915) was especially brutal with the Yaqui, and in the play we learn that Mama Chu witnessed a massacre of her people and was among the survivors who were relocated and enslaved by the Díaz government. She was pregnant with her dead husband's child and prayed that it not be born, since all that awaited it was pain and suffering. Her wish was granted but resulted in the mummified fetus she carried for the rest of her life. She has repressed the memory of all this, and also of her Yaqui heritage. But as death nears, she has a vision in which a Yaqui deer dancer named Cajame appears to her. A highly symbolic ritual for the Yaqui, the deer dance is performed during the Easter season and celebrates the cycles of death and resurrection. Cajame is named after a Yaqui warrior who had fiercely resisted Díaz. He is the catalyst that allows for Mama Chu to remember. He is also the mummified fetus she finally expels from her womb, and once he is outside of her she is freed of her past and can embrace her Indian self. She dies, but only to rise again, symbolically, as in Cajame's deer dance. As is true of all Valdez's plays, the intention is that audience members will share in this sense of rebirth and take pride in their identity as Chicanos.

Luis Valdez has been called the father of Chicano drama. He has been the inspiration for many young Chicano theater artists and El Teatro Campesino continues to be considered the premiere Chicano theater ensemble. While Valdez is not as active in it as he once was, his is still a major influence on the troupe, which now counts among its members many of his immediate relatives. When Valdez returned home to Delano back in 1965, little could he have imagined the long, sometimes difficult and controversial, but always rewarding road that he was to travel. All along the way he has championed his people and respected his craft. He has become not only a key Chicano artist but a significant figure in any history of modern American theater. He continues to win recognition for his work, including the Governor's Award of the California Arts Council in 1990. In 1994 he received the Águila Azteca (Aztec Eagle) award, one of the highest decorations the Mexican government gives to citizens of other countries. In 2002 Valdez and El Teatro Campesino won the Carey McWilliams Award, named after the social activist and former editor of the *Nation* magazine. These all honor Valdez and his troupe for their artistic achievements as well as their commitment to social justice. Few people in the American theater can boast such honors over such a long career on the stage.

Selected Bibliography

WORKS OF LUIS VALDEZ

PUBLISHED PLAYS

The Shrunken Head of Pancho Villa. Produced at San José State College, 1964. In *Necessary Theater: Six Plays about the Chicano Experience.* Edited by Jorge Huerta. Houston: Arte Público Press, 1986. Pp. 153–207.

Las dos caras del patroncito. Produced by On the Picket Line. Delano, Calif., 1965. In *Actos.* Edited by Luis Valdez. San Juan Bautista, Calif.: Cucaracha Press, 1971. Pp. 7–19; and in *Early Works.* Edited by Luis Valdez, with an introduction by Tony Curiel. Houston: Arte Público Press, 1990. Pp. 17–27.

Quinta temporada. Produced by Filipino Union Hall. Delano, Calif., 1966. In *Actos.* Edited by Luis Valdez. San Juan Bautista, Calif.: Cucaracha Press, 1971. Pp. 20–34; and in *Guerrilla Street Theater.* Edited by Henry Lesnick. New York: Bard Books, 1973. Pp. 197–212; and in *Early Works.* Edited by Luis Valdez. With an introduction by Tony Curiel. Arte Público Press, 1990. Pp. 28–39.

Los vendidos. Produced by Brown Beret Junta. Elysian Park, East Los Angeles, 1967. In *Contemporary Chicano Theatre.* Edited by Roberto J. Garza. Notre Dame: Notre Dame University Press, 1976. Pp. 15-28; and *Early Works.* Edited by Luis Valdez, with an introduction by Tony Curiel. Houston: Arte Público Press, 1990.

La conquista de Mexico (A Puppet Show). Produced by El Centro Campesino Cultural. Del Rey, Calif., 1968. In *Actos.* Edited by Luis Valdez. San Juan Bautista, Calif.: Cucaracha Press, 1971. Pp. 40–52; and in *Early Works.* Edited by Luis Valdez, with an introduction by Tony Curiel. Houston: Arte Público Press, 1990.

The Militants, 1969. In *Actos.* Edited by Luis Valdez. San Juan Bautista, Calif.: Cucaracha Press, 1971. Pp. 95–98; and in *Early Works.* Edited by Luis Valdez, with an introduction by Tony Curiel. Houston: Arte Público Press, 1990. Pp. 91–94.

No saco nada de la escuela. Produced by Centro Cultural Mexicano. Fresno, Calif., 1969. In *Actos.* Edited by Luis Valdez. San Juan Bautista, Calif.: Cucaracha Press, 1971. Pp. 66–94; and in *Early Works.* Edited by Luis Valdez, with an introduction by Tony Curiel. Houston: Arte Público Press, 1990. Pp. 66–90.

Bernabé. Produced by Teatro Campesino. San Juan Bautista, Calif., 1970. In *Contemporary Chicano Theatre.* Edited by Roberto J. Garza. Notre Dame: Notre Dame University Press, 1976. Pp. 30–58; and in *Early Works.* Edited by Luis Valdez, with an introduction by Tony Curiel. Houston: Arte Público Press, 1990. Pp. 134–167.

Huelguistas, 1970. In *Early Works.* Edited by Luis Valdez, with an introduction by Tony Curiel. Houston: Arte Público Press, 1990. Pp. 95–97.

Vietnam campesino. Produced by Guadalupe Church. Delano, Calif., 1970. In *Early Works.* Edited by Luis Valdez, with an introduction by Tony Curiel. Houston: Arte Público Press, 1990. Pp. 98–120.

Dark Root of a Scream. Produced by Centro Cultural Mexicano. Fresno, Calif., 1971. In *From the Barrio: A Chicano Anthology.* Edited by Omar Salinas and Lilian Faderman. San Francisco: Canfield Press, 1973. Pp. 79–89.

Soldado razo. Produced by Chicano Vietnam War Moratorium. Fresno, Calif., 1971. In *Early Works.* Edited by Luis Valdez, with an introduction by Tony Curiel. Houston: Arte Público Press, 1990. Pp. 121–133.

Zoot Suit. Produced by Mark Taper Forum. Los Angeles, Calif., 1979. In *Zoot Suit and Other Plays.* Edited by Luis Valdez, with an introduction by Jorge Huerta. Houston: Arte Público Press, 1992. Pp. 23–94.

Bandido! The American Melodrama of Tiburcio Vásquez, Notorious California Bandit. Produced by Teatro Campesino, San Juan Bautista, Calif., 1981. In *Zoot Suit and Other Plays.* Edited by Luis Valdez, with an introduction by Jorge Huerta. Houston: Arte Público Press, 1992. Pp. 99–153.

I Don't Have to Show You No Stinking Badges. Produced by Los Angeles Theater Center. Los Angeles, Calif., 1986. In *Zoot Suit and Other Plays.* Edited by Luis Valdez, with an introduction by Jorge Huerta. Houston: Arte Público Press, 1992. Pp. 156–214.

UNPUBLISHED PLAYS
Theft, 1961. Unproduced.

La gran carpa de los rasquachi. Produced by Teatro Campesino. San Juan Baustista, Calif., 1971.

El fin del mundo. Produced by Teatro Campesino. San Juan Baustista, Calif., 1972.

La virgen de Tepeyac. Produced by Teatro Campesino. San Juan Baustista, Calif., 1972.

El baile de los gigantes. Produced in Teotihuacán, Mexico, 1974.

Corridos: Tales of Passion and Revolution. Produced by Teatro Campesino. San Juan Baustista, Calif., 1981.

The Mummified Deer. Produced by San Diego Repertory Theater. San Diego, Calif., 2000.

COLLECTED WORKS
Actos. Edited by Luis Valdez. San Juan Bautista, Calif.: Cucaracha Press, 1971. Contains *La conquista de México: A Puppet Play, Las dos caras del patroncito, The Militants,* and *No saco nada de la escuela.*

Early Works. Edited by Luis Valdez, with an introduction by Tony Curiel. Houston: Arte Público Press, 1990. Contains "Notes on Chicano Theatre," "The Actos," *Las dos caras del patroncito, Quinta temporada, Los vendidos, La conquista de Mexico: A Puppet Play, No saco nada de la escuela, The Militants, Huelguistas, Vietnam campesino, Soldado razo, Bernabé,* and *Pensamiento serpentino.*

Zoot Suit and Other Plays. Edited by Luis Valdez, with an introduction by Jorge Huerta. Houston: Arte Público Press, 1992. Contains *Zoot Suit, Bandido! The American Melodrama of Tiburcio Vásquez, Notorious California Bandit,* and *I Don't Have to Show You No Stinking Badges.*

FILMS AND TELEVISION PRODUCTION
Zoot Suit. Universal Studios, 1981.

Corridos: Tales of Passion and Revolution. KQED Public Television and El Teatro Campesino, 1987.

La Bamba. Columbia Pictures, 1987.

The Cisco Kid. Turner Network Television, 1994.

SECONDARY SOURCES

CRITICAL STUDIES
Benardo, Margot L. "The Political Geography of the *Teatro Campesino* and the Construction of a Political Body." *Gestos. Teoría y práctica del teatro hispánico* 13 (April 1998): 117–126.

Broyles-González, Yolanda. *El Teatro Campesino: Theater in the Chicano Movement.* Austin: University of Texas Press, 1994.

———. "What Price 'Mainstream?' Luis Valdez's *Corridos* on Stage and Film." *Cultural Studies,* 4 (October 1990): 281–293.

———. "Women in El Teatro Campesino: ¿Apoco estaba Molacha la Virgen de Guadalupe?" In *Chicana Voices: Intersections of Class, Race and Gender.* Edited by Teresa Córdova, et al. Albuquerque: University of New Mexico Press, 1993. Pp. 162–187.

Davis, Ron G., and Betty Diamond. "*Zoot Suit*: From the Barrio to Broadway," *Ideologies and Literature* 3 (January–March 1981): 124–133.

Elam, Harry J. *Taking It to the Streets. The Social Protest Theater of Luis Valdez and Amiri Baraka.* Ann Arbor: University of Michigan Press, 1997.

Flores, Arturo. *El Teatro Campesino de Luis Valdez (1965–1980).* Madrid, Editorial Pliegos, 1990.

Huerta, Jorge. *Chicano Drama. Performance, Society and Myth.* New York: Cambridge University Press, 2000.

———. *Chicano Theater: Themes and Forms.* Ypsilanti, Mich.: Bilingual Press, 1982.

———. "Feathers, Flutes and Drama: Images of the Native American in Chicano Drama." Paper presented at the twenty-third Native American Workshop: Ritual and Performance. Trinity College, Dublin. March, 2002.

———. "Looking for the Magic. Chicanos into the Mainstream." In *Negotiating Performance: Gender, Sexuality and Theatricality in Latin/o America.* Edited by Diana Taylor and Juan Villegas. Durham, N.C.: Duke University Press, 1994. Pp. 37–48.

———. *Necessary Theater: Six Plays about the Chicano Experience.* Houston: Arte Público Press, 1989.

Kanellos, Nicolás. *Mexican American Theatre: Then and Now.* Houston: Arte Público Press, 1989.

Morton, Carlos. "La Serpiente Sheds Its Skin—The Teatro Campesino." *Drama Review* 18 (December 1974): 71–75.

Rossini, Jon. "*Bandido!:* Melodrama, Stereotypes and the Construction of Ethnicity." *Gestos: Teoría y práctica del teatro hispánico* 13 (April 1998): 127–140.

Shank, Theodore. "A Return to Mayan and Aztec Roots." *Drama Review* 18 (December 1974): 56–70.

Worthen, W. B. "Staging América: The Subject of History in Chicano/a Theatre." *Theatre Journal,* 40 (May 1997): 101–120.

Xavier, Roy Eric. "Politics and Chicano Culture: Luis Valdez and El Teatro Campesino, 1964–1990." In *Chicano Politics and Society in the Late Twentieth Century.* Edited by David Montejano. Austin: University of Texas Press, 1999. Pp. 175–200.

Yarbro-Bejarano, Yvonne. "From 'Acto' to 'Mito': A Critical Appraisal of the Teatro Campesino." In *Modern Chicano Writers: A Collection of Critical Essays.* Edited by Joseph Sommers and Tomás Ybarra-Frausto. Englewood Cliffs, N.J.: Prentice Hall, 1979. Pp. 176–185.

Alfredo Véa Jr.
(1950–)

ROBERTO CANTÚ

ALFREDO VÉA is a criminal defense attorney who has been in private practice in San Francisco, California, since 1986. With the publication of his first novel, *La Maravilla* (1993), Véa turned his attention to themes that have defined Chicano literature since the 1970s, such as migrant labor in agricultural fields, the impact of Americanization on ethnic youth, and the Vietnam War, to name only a few; however, far from being only a thematic core in his narrative, these experiences mark central biographical stages in Véa's life. His novels are also known for their formal experimentation with narrative displacement, point of view, and poetic diction, formal levels that were virtually unexplored, with few exceptions, in previous Chicano novels and autobiographies. Thus, the aesthetic tensions between personal background, storytelling, and narrative craft have placed Véa at the forefront of what is new and artistically challenging in current novel-writing and reading. Véa is a "luminous writer," observed Randall Holdridge. "His language is colorful and allusive, and he has the rare skill to match elegant syntax to the complementary expression of his thought" (*Tucson Weekly,* p. 2).

Véa's emphasis on literary innovation is no less important than his exceptional productivity in a six-year interval, as displayed in the publica-tion of *The Silver Cloud Café* (1996) and *Gods Go Begging* (1999), novels that completed a narrative trilogy woven with the threads of a literary autobiography, allusions to plays, poetry, and essays by authors stemming from different literary traditions (Aristophanes, Dylan Thomas, and Octavio Paz, to name a few), and a representation of America—that is to say, the United States—that is both historically focused and discerning in its critical vision. The convergence of biographical and aesthetic elements in Véa's novels, consequently, can be interpreted as an author's assumed kinship to other world writers, claiming an affiliation for Chicano literature beyond the conventional minority classification. In an interview with Jeff Biggers, Véa questioned the attitude of readers who view the dominant culture's art as the only legitimate expression; Mexican people in the United States, Véa argues, "have artists in their midst to compete with any artists on earth. As Irish literature has surpassed its English overlords, so Chicano literature will rise to the fore much as Irish and African writing have done" *(Weekly Wire).* Véa's novels are required reading in universities and high schools in the United States and have been translated into several languages, including French, German, and Italian.

Alfredo Véa was born on 28 June 1950 in Buckeye Road, formerly an unincorporated desert site but long since absorbed by the sprawling city of Phoenix, Arizona. Véa's mother, of Yaqui and Spanish ancestry, was thirteen years old when she married; shortly after Alfredo's birth, her husband left the household and never returned. At age nineteen, the single mother decided to leave Buckeye Road in search of better opportunities in California's agricultural fields, at the time of a postwar bonanza made possible by the Bracero Program (1942–1964) and where Cesar Chavez would soon roam from one ranch to the next, trying to organize a Farm Workers Union. The six-year-old Alfredo remained with his maternal grandparents for approximately four years, a brief time span that he considers a decisive influence on his development both as a person and as a writer. Véa's mother would return annually to Buckeye Road to visit, only to leave once again to various agricultural camps near California's San Joaquin Valley.

His early years in the company of his grandparents were a constant exposure to differing notions of spirituality, two ancient faiths and rituals that met, according to Véa, in the manzanita and cactus of the desert. Véa recalls that although both grandparents "were ostensibly Catholic, their beliefs had an undercurrent of magic and mysticism that flowed from the Moors and the Gypsies of Spain and from the Río Yaqui and the ancient Olmecs of Mexico. My days with my grandparents were filled with spirits. The nights were filled with ghosts" (María Teresa Márquez, unpublished interview, 1995). These memories are retold in Véa's novels in passages that remind the reader of a Gothic literary tradition, or of Latin America's aesthetic of magical realism, where the supernatural is often a generic code for satire and the literary imagination.

Véa spoke Spanish with his grandparents and began learning English when listening to his grandmother's favorite singers: Sarah Vaughan, the Ink Spots, and Dinah Washington. His grandmother's love of jazz, particularly the expressions of Duke Ellington, Count Basie, and Louis Armstrong, forms an integral part of Véa's novels. Contrary to American conformity and commercial standardization, Véa sees in jazz the true American ethos of spontaneity and creativity; in other words, the aesthetic significance of a national transcendent wilderness. In *Gods Go Begging,* a drifting chaplain on the Mekong River surrenders to the pull of the delta's stream and meditates on his discomfort: "The opposite of comfort is wilderness. Was this another way of saying that everything turns on jazz?" (p. 198). This question finds its answer in the affirmative on the novel's last line (p. 320), hence closing the narrative trilogy with a grandmother's favorite music as a metaphor for an immigrant's true vision of America.

Véa left Buckeye Road when he was ten years old, following his mother to the seasonal farm work that dotted the labor circuits of California, particularly around the Stockton area. Memories of this departure are key elements in the thematic structure of *La Maravilla,* illustrated by the grandparents' preparation of the young grandson for the harsh realities of the world and, at the novel's conclusion, with the image of a deserting Oldsmobile and a grandmother running next to it, giving last-minute advice to her grandson and warning him of a future unavoidable experience: the Vietnam War. The four years in the company of both grandparents turn—perhaps in Véa's life, but unquestionably for Beto in *La Maravilla*—into a psychological foundation that compensated for the absent father and mother. After reading what appears to be a discernible sketch of Véa's biography in his narrative trilogy, one soon begins to suspect that such a sketch contains its own subtle and stylized self-fashioning, and that consequently it should not be taken as a reliable record of an authorial life. Reflecting on his own past, Véa admits that to "go back to retrieve a memory and write it down, three minutes of memory can be hours of writing to actually capture the flavor of the thing." Véa adds: "I didn't know for years that what happened to me out on the desert with my grandfather was interesting in any way because it was all I had. And then people started asking me, 'Where did you grow up?' 'Well, I grew up in a squatter community next door to old Cadillacs filled with old men and a bus full of transvestites.' And people would say, 'Wow.' And I started saying, 'Wow.' My grandmother would just ravage me with baptisms. I might have been drowned" (Porter, *Hayden's Ferry Review*, p. 85).

A fictionalized representation of Véa's mother appears in *La Maravilla* and in *The Silver Cloud Café,* first as Lola, second as Lilly, but constantly as the embodiment of American ideals ("The best thing to learn is the value of a dollar," *La Maravilla*, p. 294), or of female beauty ("the prettiest woman in the valley," *The Silver Cloud Café,* p. 131). Véa's depiction of a Mexican American mother such as Lola/Lilly suggests an association with Chicana feminist protagonists who, like Teresa or Alicia in Ana Castillo's novel *The Mixquiahuala Letters* (1986), interpret female sexuality as a form of liberation from patriarchal domination. "It was in these camps," Véa recalls, "that my mother met the fathers of my brothers" (María Teresa Márquez, unpublished interview, 1995). It was also in these same camps where the author met bracero friends whose kindness and affection would, in retrospect, make up for the nuclear family he never had.

While in Brawley, California, he learned from Mexican braceros how to fist-fight; later in Stockton, Filipino braceros taught him how to read and write. These Filipino friends are remembered as the ones who gave him his second set of encyclopedias, a source of reading and learning that could be identified as the origin of both a liberating literacy and his writing. "I'm writing for all these poor people in my life whom I love," Véa told John Boudreau, "all those farm workers, Hindus, Koreans, Filipinos, everybody—so they finally have one of their own who has the discipline and energy to say who they are" (*Los Angeles Times,* p. 2). In addi-

tion to his Mexican and Filipino friends, Véa met French Canadian braceros in the northern California fields. Building on what he learned from these friends, Véa studied French at Livermore High School in Alameda County, California. Years later, in a speech for La Raza Centro Legal (published under the title "Caliban and Prospero No More"), Véa identified himself as Mexican-Yaqui-Filipino-American, knowing by then that personal identity need not be based on family or ethnic lineage. Véa responded in a similar vein to a question regarding his cultural background: "I'm Mexican, Yaqui and Filipino. But lineage isn't the totality of anybody's cultural background. I grew up the first few years of my life with Indians on the reservation, and black people from the dust bowl, and a lot of Irish and Okies. So I think those are my cultural background, too" (Porter, *Hayden's Ferry Review,* p. 81).

While still a teenager in high school, Véa was entrusted with the care of his younger siblings. He worked and studied and soon bought his first home thanks to his high school teacher, Mr. Jack Beery, who cosigned in order for Alfredo to qualify for the home loan. Véa remembers his high school report cards and the straight A's he consistently earned (personal communication, March 19, 2003). Véa dedicated *La Maravilla* to the memory of his Irish-German teacher and friend ("the best high school teacher there ever was") who, according to John Boudreau, "had instructed Véa and his brothers in everything from academics to how to use a fork and knife" (*Los Angeles Times,* p. 2). Mr. Beery died in 1992, one year before the publication of *La Maravilla.*

Véa enrolled at the University of California, Berkeley, and began his undergraduate studies, taking a leave of absence in 1967 due to financial pressures. He was picking brussels sprouts in Arizona, he recalls, when he received a letter notifying him that he was being drafted by the Army. His first reaction was to oppose the draft as a conscientious objector (CO); in fact, he went to court but lost his case because he did not believe in a supreme being. Véa got drafted into military service in 1967 and soon found himself in Vietnam in the midst of the 1968 Tet Offensive. "They didn't give me CO status," Véa revealed to María Teresa Márquez, "but they stuck me in radio school and then I ended up being shot at anyway" (unpublished interview, 1995). Before being drafted, Véa drove on his motorcycle to the heartland of the eight Yaqui pueblos in Sonora, Mexico, spending time in Ciudad Obregón, Potam, and Cokoim (ancient Yaqui for modern-day Cócorit). To be sure, Véa was not traveling as a tourist; on the contrary, he was going back to his grandfather's homeland before going to war. His grandfather had died in 1964; his grandmother's death took place in 1967, shortly after Véa's entry in the Vietnam War.

In Vietnam, Véa was active as an RTO (Radio Telephone Operator), working with portable radio communications in the demilitarized zone and carrying radios for an infantry unit. "In order to survive," Véa told Boudreau, "you can kill an entire family, including the children; you are given the license, the uniform and every weapon under the sun. You could get away with anything, and that's when you find out who you are. You realize that kindness and gentility are acts of will. You have to choose a side" (*Los Angeles Times*, p. 2). The last three sentences sum up the cognitive nucleus in Véa's narrative trilogy, particularly in regard to characters who undergo a process of self-knowledge, or who, far from being concerned only with their own interests, choose a side that is always with the underdog. Véa returned home knowing that Vietnam had become crucial in his life: "I never again," Véa tells Márquez, "had any respect for tall white men with gray hair telling me everything was going to work just fine. It gave me a real belief, I think, in myself, because that was all that was left of me." Although *La Maravilla* touches briefly on Vietnam—for instance, one finds allusions to this war in the novel's prologue, and to Beto's mournful homecoming as a war veteran in chapter 15—

such a war has become an integral part of Chicano literature. Joe Rodríguez's novel, *The Odd-splayer* (1989), and Ruben Quintero's brief memoir share with Véa's Vietnam narrative a similar vision of the dehumanizing nature of the Vietnam War and, by implication, of any other war.

Véa worked temporarily as a truck driver and as a forklift operator shortly after being discharged from the Army in 1969. One year later, Véa moved to France, where he lived in Paris for one year in an Armenian hotel close to the Louvre. To make a living, he worked as a janitor; he read widely and spent countless hours at the museum. His janitorial work allowed him to muse over memories of his French Canadian bracero friends and his French classes in high school, and to recall the backbreaking jobs of his youth as a California farm laborer. Along with these memories, he remembered a set of encyclopedias and the kindness of Filipino friends who introduced literacy into his world during their evenings after work. He recalls them with gratitude, insisting that it was they "who demanded that I not live a life in the fields. I remember so many of them, tired and dusty, sitting down next to me at the bunkhouse table, tapping their brown foreheads with a gnarled index finger and saying to me: 'use this'" (Biggers, *Weekly Wire*, p. 2). Véa returned to the United States in 1971, speaking fluent French and with his mind made up to complete what the Arizona fields and the Vietnam War had kept him away from: a university education.

Véa attended UC Berkeley from 1971 to 1975, majoring in English and physics. To earn a living he worked as a construction worker and later as a carnival mechanic doing repairs on the Tilt-A-Whirl and the Mad Mouse. After earning a B.A. in English and in physics, Véa entered the Law School at UC Berkeley, where he received his law degree in 1978. Véa immediately volunteered to work for the United Farm Workers and, in 1979, for the Centro Legal de la Raza. In 1980, Véa moved to the San Francisco Public Defender's Office, where he worked as a public defender until he left in 1986. He has been in private practice since then, specializing mostly in homicide and death penalty cases.

In 1989, while on a death penalty case in Modesto, California, a judge told him he was not aware they made Mexican lawyers in the United States; this remark opened the floodgates of memory of a forgotten youth as a poor Mexican American in nearby farms. Véa rented a trailer for the duration of the trial, sat next to his computer, and began writing *La Maravilla.* "I began to write about ancestry," Véa remembers, "about archetypes that were not European, about forms that persist. I began with the most remarkable image in my possession: the image of my grandmother, in a mourning dress, playing her upright piano in front of her cardboard house" (Márquez, unpublished interview, 1995). Véa adds that he wrote *La Maravilla* "in a way that an English reader could read it and understand what it felt like to have a childhood in Spanish"; more importantly, he wanted his novel to be "an argument that cultural maintenance and cultural difference, and especially language, are the engines of society."

La Maravilla is composed of a textual sequence that spreads through a prologue and sixteen chapters, narrated by an omniscient voice that weaves various anecdotal threads with unexpected flashbacks—the grandfather's peyote-induced visions, Josephina's visual memories of her birthplace in Granada, Spain, and fast-forwards to visual anticipations of people's future—and the embedded stories of three widows in love with a deceased husband or lover. At the center stage of the narrative drama, the reader encounters the development of a Mexican American youth—Beto—as the novel's fable of cultural transition in the United States. Beto's own vision corresponds to his Yaqui initiation, which is told as a story of psychic splitting that turns Beto into two entities, as it were: one human, the other animal (a hawk, hence a Yaqui totemic bird), thus

recapturing Native Indian conceptions of the *nagual* or zoomorphic twin of the sorcerer.

La Maravilla's internal organization is a narrative amalgam that includes stories of forbidden interracial love (African/Anglo American, Spanish/Yaqui, and American/Irish), and tales of a boy's education in the wilderness of the Arizona desert under the care of a folk healer and a sorcerer. This first novel by Véa would seem to be deliberately constructed on a city dump awaiting the cleansing fires and the new life forms that shall rise from its own ashes. This metaphor of rebirth has its concrete example in one of the novel's memorable characters, Harold, a Jewish survivor of Nazi concentration camps whose thoughts are paraphrased by the omniscient narrator: "It all seemed a dream, now. Stored in the small bank in his soul where the most profound moments are kept, he is burned then re-created anew and flawless. Yes, Phoenix was appropriate" (p. 202).

What sets Véa's novel apart from the work of other Chicano writers is his ability to interweave, in a manner of speaking, echoes and traces of varied literary works—for example, by Dylan Thomas, Andrew Marvell, and Octavio Paz—into the fabric of his tapestry-like narrative, with different literary traditions somehow achieving a composition that is thematically related and rich in resonances. In terms of the novel's neo-Romantic vision of love, *La Maravilla* stresses its transgressive quality, thus challenging social ideas of racial or ethnic segregation. The recurring references to the poetry of Andrew Marvell, particularly to the poem "To His Coy Mistress"—with its emphasis on carnal love and the dread of the grave—count among the many textual allusions to a *carpe diem* thematic undercurrent throughout the novel, achieving its best articulation in the form of an argument that contains its own syllogism of seduction in Marvell's poem ("Had we but world enough . . . But at my back . . . Now therefore"). These transgressive loves in American society fulfill their representation in characters who—because of their Native

American, Asian, African, or European backgrounds—constitute in Véa's novel a symbolic construct of the world through their unified diversity. Nonetheless, much like in Marvell's poem—with its reference to instant fires in every pore, and its initial counterfeit patience expressed through the verse "Till the conversion of the Jews"—the characters in *La Maravilla* are drawn into unexpected associations throughout one's reading, based on a "rhetoric of fire" that encourages interconnections between Nazi crematoria, human guilt, a "Phoenix" city, the mythical fires of purification, and the biblical ashes of rebirth. The presence of Jewish characters in Véa's novels is significant, as they are representatives of a nation that has experienced extreme forms of racism and exile; other Jewish characters include Stuart (with constantly interchanging surnames), in *The Silver Cloud Café,* and the Chaplain, a Mexican Sephardic Jew from the state of Chihuahua who turns into one of the leading characters in *Gods Go Begging.* "The most important places in our history," according to Véa, "are those places where the idea of life is contemplated, whether it be Auschwitz or a single poet sitting in a room trying to tear apart a moment and share it with another human being. The rest of it is chaff" (Porter, *Hayden's Ferry Review,* p. 91).

La Maravilla contains several chapters in which Véa seems to be experimenting, almost re-creating and playing, with narrative forms; examples are the chapters titled "Spilt Children" (chapter 10) and "The Whisper of the Lizard" (chapter 12), both narrated either in the language of dreams or with a rhetorical imagery that is both visual and suggestive of discourses of initiation. For instance, in chapter 12 Beto's ingestion of peyote tea serves as a ceremonial threshold for his entry into a Yaqui heritage; prior to his imagined metamorphosis as a hawk, Beto is told by his grandfather:

> I will give you a sight of your own blood so that someday years from now you will not be made anxious by wrong questions and you will not look for answers in the wrong place. You don't need to see no psychiatrist, Beto. Never. *Nunca.* You just need to look into yourself and beyond, past yourself. . . . Remember, you are not white, and if someday you find yourself asking a white man's questions, the answer will not be there for you.
>
> (pp. 217–218)

Reviews of *La Maravilla* were laudatory and not limited to ethnic critical perspectives. Some reviewers, like Sam Harrison, judged Véa's novel "sometimes brilliant, sometimes frustrating, always rich and extravagant." Along with Véa's "fascinating cultural information," Harrison found the novel's "random jumping from present to past to future" all too demanding, for it is either "ultimately frustrating" or "preachy and out of context" (*Washington Post,* p. 2). A contrasting opinion was expressed by Carolyn See, who considered *La Maravilla* "beautifully written; it's thematically vital for our times" (*Los Angeles Times,* p. 2). John Boudreau, on the other hand, considered the *marvel*—in the sense of "miracle"—of *La Maravilla*'s publication in light of Véa's past: "Teachers told him he would never attend college because he came from the fields" (*Los Angeles Times,* p. 2).

Of the courses Véa took at UC Berkeley, those on poetry are remembered as crucial in the cultivation of his love of literature, especially his early readings of Theodore Roethke, T. S. Eliot, Dylan Thomas (whose poem, "A Process in the Weather of the Heart" serves as *La Maravilla*'s epigraph), William Butler Yeats, and the poetry and essays of Octavio Paz. Among the novelists, he loves (his chosen word) Herman Melville, Fyodor Dostoyevsky, William Faulkner, Gabriel García Márquez, Alejo Carpentier, and Carlos Fuentes, among others. Of Chicano writers he only remembers Rudolfo Anaya's *Bless Me, Ultima;* he adds *Hunger of Memory* to the list and underscores the point that he wrote *La Maravilla* "as a response to Richard Rodríguez's book which I think is a pathetic work" (Márquez, unpublished interview, 1995).

Véa's views on literature and art would seem to bridge the critical aims of Chicano literature with the aesthetic manifestos of avant-garde movements; for instance, Véa asserts that "the essence of art is dissent. You have to dissent from a normal way of speaking and thinking and from other art. . . . You have to leap out of the mundane. . . . Storytelling is the best thing we do, but we're stuck with stupid stories" (Porter, *Hayden's Ferry Review,* pp. 82, 83). When Véa submitted the manuscript of his second novel to his editor, the response was troubling: *The Silver Cloud Café* was considered "too complicated, it's not like anything she's ever read"; nonetheless, he adds, "that's the kind of thing that needs to be written. She wants me to write something a little bit more marketable" (Márquez, unpublished interview, 1995).

With the publication of *The Silver Cloud Café,* it became evident to Véa's readers that the author's creative well had not run dry after his first novel, nor that the second would be a repetition or weak variant of *La Maravilla.* Both novels are connected through the main character and by narrative design. *The Silver Cloud Café* returns (in chapters 6–7) to the point where *La Maravilla* ends (chapter 16): Beto (now known as Zeferino del Campo), in the back seat of an Oldsmobile, is dragged by his mother against his will and leaves his grandmother behind in the desert dust of Buckeye Road. The structural connection between these two novels thus achieves a formal innovation thanks to its non-linear sequence: it takes place in the middle of *The Silver Cloud Café,* suggesting an unconscious center that determines the narrative's stratified organization (read as a geological metaphor for memory), and the protagonist's fulfilled recollection, or moment of recognition, at the end of the novel.

In *The Silver Cloud Café,* however, Véa mounts a global setting—the Philippines, Spain, Mexico, the United States—in a narrative that moves backward and forward in time and space, now populated by characters from different parts of the world who more by fate than circumstance meet in San Francisco. Admittedly, the Buckeye Road in *La Maravilla* could always be read as an allegory of the United States, therefore as the underside or nightmare that represents a world through its multinational population: Chicanos, African Americans, Okies, Chinese, and Yaqui Indians, among others. Nonetheless, the historical range of the second novel is broader and more confident in its rhetorical force of expression, which stems as a hybrid of two generic traditions, the Gothic and magic realism. For example, the opening paragraph in chapter 2 reveals the San Francisco cityscape as one of squalor and homelessness, covered by a gloom that is described as ghostly and apocalyptic:

> On Polk Street the wide expanses of grass in front of City Hall were glutted with the colored bedding and the scattered litter of the homeless. Squads of squalid men gathered here and there, limping and groaning like lost detachments of a decimated regiment. Like living ghosts, they haunted the corners and curbs of the city, carving out cold cloisters and hidden catacombs in the full light of day.
>
> (p. 17)

An everyday metropolitan world is transformed and made strange through a rhetorical passage that combines alliteration (*scattered litter, squads of squalid men, corners, curbs, carving, cold, catacombs*), Gothic imagery (*living ghosts, haunted corners, cloisters, catacombs*), and the point of view of a war veteran (*like lost detachments of a decimated regiment*). This passage illustrates both the style and perspective that govern the layered and nonlinear narrative in *The Silver Cloud Café,* one that is evidently congruent with the telling of a story that unites the heterogeneous destinies of several characters born in various parts of a decaying and violent world; nonetheless, more than the *what,* it is the *how* that becomes significant in the quoted passage. In her essay on the contemporary Gothic, Lucie Armitt defines magic realism as "a disruptive, foreign, fantastic narrative style that fractures the flow of an otherwise realist text."

She then makes the following association: "What we find in magic realism (particularly at the dark end of its spectrum where it meets the Gothic) is a double edged *frisson* which oscillates around the disturbing aspects of the everyday" (*A Companion to the Gothic,* p. 306). Future studies on Véa's narrative will find in this generic juncture the possibilities for productive readings of his constant aesthetic leaps ("You have to leap out of the mundane" [Véa in Porter, *Hayden's Ferry Review,* p. 82]).

For the time being, such instances of the Gothic and magic realism must be read in Véa's novels as variants of a Romantic tradition that values imagination, instinct, the unconscious, and the apotheosis of artistic expression. Contrary to the conventional view of Romanticism as a specific period in European art history, it could be argued that it is expressive of all human cultures at different points in their development. This transhistorical and transnational interpretation of Romanticism is proposed by Stanley Cavell, who includes writers and philosophers such as Henry David Thoreau, Ralph Waldo Emerson, Ludwig Wittgenstein, and Martin Heidegger as members of a Romantic tradition that is defined by Nature, God, and humanity. As an illustration of this truly global sensibility, Cavell cites Emerson's expression of *human doubleness:* "I am God in nature; I am a weed by the wall" (quoted in Cavell, p. 32). In a similar vein, Véa's novels reclaim a literary tradition which, Romantic in its mode of perception and expression, finds one of its voices in Walt Whitman: "The greatest poet hardly knows pettiness or triviality. If he breathes into any thing that was before thought small it dilates with the grandeur and life of the universe" (Walt Whitman, *Leaves of Grass,* p. 9). Features of this doubleness in human life (divine and yet mortal), and of the double-coded expression in the novel (that is to say, the poetry that redeems a commonplace world), are integral to Véa's narrative, and specifically to *The Silver Cloud Café.*

For example, the initial section in *The Silver Cloud Café* is written in italics, suggesting in its poetic diction a "heavenly" dimension that contrasts with the mundane realities to which the reader is about to be introduced. The initial two paragraphs read as follows:

In the deep El Greco darkness between a small Mexican cantina and a drawbridge that straddled two worlds, there was the long stretch and uncurling and the slow, white unfurling of glowing wings as twin narcissus rose from the bramble. Los angeles [sic] se estaban yendo. The angels were leaving. Two world-weary beings of light were packing their bags and speaking softly in auras of glimmering glissando.

The pair were perpetual brothers, or perhaps they were sisters, or perhaps both. But they were certainly unlike poor mortal siblings who are held together for those fleeting instants of childhood, then are forever separated by adulthood, reuniting now and again to glance backward at a common womb. These two would possess for all time the sexless breasts of fledglings, the secret language of twins, the murmurs of sleepless children gazing eternally at the same immutable wallpaper.

(p. 1)

In terms of its narrative function, the image of two angels returning to their celestial origin appears in various parts of the novel (chapter 1, pp. 1–2, 15–16; chapter 4, p. 76; chapter 5, p. 92; chapter 7, p. 167; and chapter 12, pp. 303–305), as a structuring device that shapes the novel's plot construction (the murder mystery) as well as the novel's conclusion, namely: Teodoro's and Radiant Ruby's married life ("Beneath the tender and hallowed care of heavenly wings of feathered air," p. 343). At the level of style, this overture-like opening alludes to (and plays with) the language of poetry used when addressing "divine" matters (with a stress on alliteration: *uncurling, unfurling of glowing wings, glimmering glissando*). At the anecdotal level, a second reading of the novel would disclose the truth behind this opening scene. Both paragraphs are a veiled reference to the deaths that take place between the Silver Cloud Café (Father

Humberto) and under the drawbridge (Bambino Reyes), hence a tacit explanation of the novel's mystery: who killed Bambino, and what relation, if any, did Father Humberto's suicide have with Bambino's murder? In other words, the ultimate solution to these two deaths is (re)vealed in the novel's beginning.

Organized according to metaphors of archaeology, architecture, or cosmic levels, *The Silver Cloud Café* weaves itself in a narrative pattern of remembrances, multistoried houses of pleasure, and a Catholic vision of sin, exile, and penance. The novel narrates the "cure" of a Vietnam veteran (Zeferino del Campo) who is now a practicing criminal defense attorney in San Francisco. The cure is not presented in the conventional setting of a Vietnam veteran's clinical case study (i.e., the psychiatric case), but as a *return to the past* that is prompted by an encounter with a long-forgotten friend—Teodoro Teofilo Cabiri (aka Ted for Short)—who sparks Zeferino's memory and process of recollection. The governing plot, as a result, displays a protagonist in intermittent situations in which memory and progressive recall replace both the analyst and the psychoanalytic couch, thus congruent in principle with Beto's lesson in *La Maravilla*: "You don't need to see no psychiatrist, Beto. Never. *Nunca.* You just need to look into yourself and beyond, past yourself. Let them have the psychiatrists" (p. 217). Zeferino's forgetfulness can be rationalized as necessary in order to repress the pain and psychic impact of a lived war, but it alludes also to a process of Americanization that depends on an immigrant's dissolution of ties or self-estrangement from a traditional culture. As a Chicano Vietnam veteran, both variants of forgetfulness apply. At the novel's conclusion (therefore at the culminating moment of Zeferino's fulfilled memory, which one can read as his cure or moment of healing), Teodoro Teofilo Cabiri gives meaning to the sense of homelessness in the United States, both in immigrants and in native-born:

When you leave your homeland like I did, you leave wondering who you will be in the new country. Everything that I was, was given to me by my Islands. Here in America I was nothing . . . less than nothing. What a surprise it was for me when I found out that people here deny their past. Each person here believes that he has succeeded on his own, without help from anyone. I asked myself, why is this? How is this possible? Everyone knows that even the strongest man rides on his grandmother's back. After years I realized the answer. If you don't share a past or a culture, you don't have to share your labor or your earnings or your future.

(p. 337)

The novel's thematic patterns of homelessness, combat narratives, and the pairings or "twinning" of characters thus turn into effective formal devices in the construction of a plot and the several subplots that compose *The Silver Cloud Café*, a novel that requires that one read it more than once. For our present purposes, the novel's governing themes of exile, war, and doubles can be registered on origins that are cosmic, historical, and local, illustrated in the novel's references to the "fabled war in heaven" (p. 62), the Cristero Rebellion in Mexico, the Vietnam War, and the final encounter of the doppelgänger characters in San Francisco. As a result, characters with different birthplaces—such as Father Humberto (Mexico), Bambino Reyes (Philippines), Faustino (Philippines), and Zeferino del Campo (Arizona)—converge in the city of San Francisco to take part in another form of cure: the resolution of a protracted vendetta in which Bambino is the vengeful agent and Zeferino, Faustino, and Teodoro are the targeted victims. The oath of revenge is expressed as follows:

His twin brother's howl would be heard over the fields, discordant, pared of joy, awakening even the heedless termites sleeping beneath the bunkhouse floors. . . . The cloven furies below would stand to applaud this grief, hail it with blue lips lined with white lime. They would raise a coal-and-pitch clamor for revenge in Simon Ditto's ear. Shaking shattered shankbones, they would sing their motley malediction. They would demand that all life be soured for all time, despoiled by the embrace of the irreversible oath of vendetta.

(p. 191)

The twinning in *The Silver Cloud Café* serves the purpose of pairing a wide range of oppositions, such as Christ/Satan, Faustino/Bambino, and Miguel Agustin/Humberto, among others. Most of these doubles are united by a combat background or a past murder, as is the case with Humberto (kills a teacher during the Cristero Rebellion in Mexico, 1927–1929), Miguel Govea (takes part in Father Humberto's *first* execution), Zeferino (Vietnam veteran), and Faustino (World War II veteran, with remorseful memories of the execution of a young Japanese soldier). One of the characters, Miguel Govea, makes a remark that one could read as an example of this novel's antiwar views: "In the end, every uniform murders the one who wears it" (p. 7).

Beyond the plot and subplots that compose the many narrative levels of *The Silver Cloud Café,* one also encounters, as previously in *La Maravilla,* references to the work of various authors, such as Constantine Cavafy (p. 263, introduced as the imaginary lover of the gay Faustino), E. M. Forster (p. 264), Johann Wolfgang von Goethe (to *Faust,* p. 270), and Rainer Maria Rilke (p. 298); to painters, such as José Clemente Orozco (pp. 54, 328), Hieronymus Bosch (p. 182), and Marc Chagall (p. 182); and to music: "The Tennessee Waltz" (p. 278), Johnny Cash (p. 280), and the Tarascan song from Michoacan, Mexico, "Corazón de Bronce" (p. 309).

Three years after the publication of *The Silver Cloud Café,* Véa published the third and final part of the trilogy: *Gods Go Begging* (1999). In an interview with Jeff Biggers, Véa disclosed the origin and meaning of the title: "The title of the book comes from an 18th century ballet in which two servants are ridiculed as they serve aristocrats at a feast. In the end, the servants remove their disguises and show themselves to be gods." Véa then reveals the thematic core of his narrative trilogy: "All three books do this: celebrate the forgotten; illuminate the unseen" (*Weekly Wire,* p. 2).

Gods Go Begging is also structured in a nonlinear format, with a stress on a narrative language that shuns naïve realism. The novel contains an expressed cognitive mission that is proposed through a well-defined idea of literacy and of the role books play in the everyday life of his characters, as well as his readers. As a result, *Gods Go Begging* suggests an indivisible connection between *craft* and *critique,* thus challenging critical positions that consider the mixing of politics with literature as artistic suicide.

The chronological and narrative scaffolding of *Gods Go Begging* finds its design, much like that of *The Silver Cloud Café,* in the trope of *remembrance,* therefore narrated in the form of an adult's flashbacks, resulting in (1) four chapters corresponding to 1967, the year relating to the war in Vietnam (chapters 4, 5, 6, and 9); (2) one chapter for 1978 (chapter 11), situated in Alexandria, Louisiana; and (3) nine chapters for 1996 (chapters 1, 2, 3, 7, 8, 10, 12, 13, 14), dramatizing the life of Jesse Pasadoble (formerly Beto and Zeferino in previous novels) as a criminal defense attorney in San Francisco. The three places—California, Louisiana, Vietnam—become the sites of three chronological clusters in the novel (1996, 1978, 1967, respectively), and to the lives of several characters across time and space, suggesting therefore an international interdependence and a shared destiny.

The reading sequence in *Gods Go Begging* thus simulates the act of remembrance and time fulfilled, flowing on a temporal stream that begins in the narrative present (1996, chapters 1–3), then is followed by a flashback to 1967 (chapters 4–6), and—other than one chapter devoted to 1978 (chapter 11)—concludes with a return to the present of the narrative, that is, to 1996 (chapters 10, 12–14). Each temporal unit is given meaning within a folk-based or literate tradition of sorts, underscoring the importance of cognition in any reading activity. Interpreted in this manner, *Gods Go Begging* combines both narrative craft and critique in three storytelling variants on the themes of fear, war, and desire, each corresponding to the chronological clusters represented by 1967, 1978, and 1996, respectively. These storytelling variants are presented in the discursive form of "supposing" (1967); through intertextual links with antiwar texts, such as *Lysistrata* by Aristophanes (chapter 11, 1978); or with Robert Frost's poem "Fire and Ice" as a subtext in the chapters corresponding to the year 1996.

In *Gods Go Begging,* the game of supposing and Véa's appropriation of an ancient literary tradition of antiwar sentiment, as expressed in Aristophanes' play, are only two of the forms that illustrate the imaginative range found in Véa's novels. Véa's characters apparently engage in the game of supposing so as to forget about war and the possibility of death. Moreover, since most of these soldiers derive from impoverished and ethnic backgrounds—for instance, Mexican American, Shoshone Indian, African American—the game of supposing turns into a critical response to an official Anglo American history of U.S. conquest of allegedly backward peoples during its westward expansion. As is usual in Véa's novels, the omniscient narrator plays an important discursive function, with observations that run as follows:

> America had fully expected to win without suffering, without loss. The boys on the hill knew differently. The American Dream—the two-bedroom house with a white picket fence—had always been built on a graveyard. It had always been built at the expense of the Huron Nation, at the expense of the bison, and at the expense of the Vietnamese. It had always been built on a hill.
>
> (p. 197)

The hidden connection between American soldiers in Vietnam and a play by Aristophanes is thus cleverly established in a shared antiwar sentiment and in the impulse to "dream" awake.

As Alan H. Sommerstein observes in his introduction to a selection of Aristophanes' plays, *Lysistrata* is "a dream about peace, conceived at a time when Athens was going through the blackest, most desperate crisis she had known since the Persian War" (p. 177). In *Gods Go Begging,* the game of supposing is played as follows: "Let's you and me talk about a different kind of world. You might call it philosophizing, but with these boys, it's called supposing. Let's suppose this. Let's suppose that" (p. 99). The supposing game unfolds in a critical and humorous manner, as told by the Chicano soldier Jesse Pasadoble:

> Just imagine what would have happened if Hernán Cortez and his men had been blown far off course and landed on Plymouth Rock instead of Veracruz. On the other hand, imagine that the pilgrims had been blown south by a terrific gale and the *Mayflower* had run aground in the Yucatán peninsula.
>
> (p. 113)

This story of supposing unfolds as a hilarious and satirical version of U.S. history, generating a different kind of world: jazz would have been born in Morocco, Anglo Americans would now live off the coast of Yucatan in a "huge self-mortification theme park" (p. 116) called the *Island of the Dullards,* and today North America would be Russian-Indian and French-Indian. A character who is new to this game of supposing feels suddenly drawn into it, and for a moment forgets "about the war that raged around him" (p. 117). Contrasting with the satirical humor in the game of supposing, the battlefield is described through horticultural metaphors that would be understood by a Mexican farm worker in the San Joaquin Valley: that is, with metaphors of a dark harvest, horrendous agricultural fields, and wasted human seed destroyed before its time.

> In one place, a ragged patch of hair follicles and skin soiled the stigma and stamens of a weeping blue blossom, repelling bee after bee. In another,

scores of red seeds had erupted from human bodies, bursting violently through the drabness of cloth and skin—seed of stomach, seed of lung, hopeless grains set onto the wind. Everywhere, shell casings littered the garden like brazen chaff.

(p. 88)

The metaphors of wasted seed and sterile soils/wombs because of a war turn into a rhetorical pattern throughout *Gods Go Begging* that is also represented in various characters, including the childless Persephone Flyer. The family history of this African American female character is narrated in chapter 11, titled "The Women's Chorus." Persephone's mother, known as Lizzie, is introduced as the founder of a village that she calls Lysistrata ("named after her favorite Greek play," pp. 235–236); in addition, Persephone's three sisters bear names that are taken from characters in Aristophanes' play: Cleonice Fontenot, Lampi Le Jeune, and Myrinne Thibideau. In *Lysistrata*, the first is named Calonice and the third is called Myrrhine. In *Gods Go Begging*, Lampi Le Jeune's full name is not revealed because, as the narrator argues, the name "was something that she will never disclose" (p. 236). But as the curious reader will discover upon rereading an old copy of *Lysistrata*, Lampi's full name is Lampito; she is the Spartan woman who agrees with Lysistrata and other Athenian women that there should be a ban on sex with their husbands until both Athens and Sparta sign a peace treaty. Allusions to *Lysistrata* appear sometimes as implicit references, as when Persephone wonders if her husband has been killed on a hill in Vietnam; she muses, "I should have withheld sex. . . . You might have stayed home. You might have longed for me" (p. 282).

Congruent with its politics of literacy, *Gods Go Begging* could also be read as a commentary on biblical prophets, such as Elijah (p. 125), and on a literary tradition that includes texts by Ernest J. Gaines (p. 69), Charles Dickens and James Joyce (p. 228), Ralph Ellison, James Baldwin (p. 256), and Jean-Paul Sartre (p. 127); one also reads references to the musical and the

plastic arts: Mozart, Johannes Brahms, Amedeo Modigliani (p. 274). Throughout these references and their implied audience, Véa is consistent with his views on a contemporary market-driven culture; in *The Silver Cloud Café*, Zeferino del Campo tells Stuart, his private investigator, that "clothing labels, professional sports, and pop music do not add up to a culture" (p. 202). Beto learns from his Yaqui grandfather, in *La Maravilla*, to consider the meaning of mainstream culture and majority opinion; the old shaman, about to initiate Beto in Yaqui lore and history, makes a distinction:

> Can you think in all of your *World Books* A through Z of one big leap of humanity that was ever accomplished by the majority, by all those people out there rushing like mad to be the same? Can you think of one great jump of art or thought that was ever accomplished by the mainstream? . . . Stay in the gaps, *mijo*. Love for the land is here. Resistance is here. The company's better in here.
>
> (p. 221)

The critical reception of Alfredo Véa's novels has been, for the most part, at the level of reviews; most of them have been positive but, given the nature of the genre, seldom beyond the level of first impressions. In his review of *Gods Go Begging*, for example, James Lough admits to being rhetorically overwhelmed, as it were, when reading the novel: "All of this high rhetoric gave off a kitschy effect. I thought that maybe I could enjoy it with a sense of irony, of camp, as one enjoys old horror movies or splendidly bad thrift-store table lamps. 'It's so bad it's good.' But I soon realized that the writer was not trying to be kitschy" (*Denver Post*, p. 2). In her review of *Gods Go Begging*, Ann Peterpaul is impressed with the battle and dialogue scenes: "Out of the mouths of the soldiers on that hill come astute commentary and deep philosophizing." (*Weekly Wire*, p. 1) Randall Holdridge, on the other hand, considers Véa's third novel—with its "pervasive influence of 'magical realism'"—to be a "break-out achieve ment," adding that in *Gods Go Begging*, Véa "has conceived a work so ambitious thematically and stylistically, and so timely in its interests, that it surely deserves a broad readership" (*Tucson Weekly*, p. 1).

In his essay on magical realism in the Nuevomexicano narrative, Luis Leal underscores the connection between an immediate reality and the discovery of its richness through the artist's literary act, with examples in the Latin American novel (for example, Alejo Carpentier's), or in Nuevomexicano/Chicano narrative (for instance, those of Fray Angelico Chavez, Rudolfo Anaya, and Sabine Ulibarri). Leal makes a distinction that indirectly allows for a clearer understanding of Véa's novels: "In magical realism the important characteristic is the mystery found in people, nature and objects, a mystery that eludes the understanding of the observer. In *lo real maravilloso* only certain events are considered to be marvelous; in magical realism, all reality is magical." In terms of Chicano literary theory and criticism, Luis Leal proposes that magical realism "offers an alternative theory helpful in analyzing Chicana/o literature. With magical realism, myth and other aspects of imaginative literature can be considered an aspect of the mode, for it combines the two worlds, the real and the imaginary" (*Nuevomexicano Cultural Legacy*, pp. 154, 160–161). As argued earlier, Véa's terms of affiliation are conditioned by a deep sense of belonging to a transhistorical Romantic tradition, ranging from Thoreau and Whitman to Latin American writers whose tradition is no less Romantic, that is to say, visionary, radical, and liberating. Let us recall that as a clear answer to the question "What is the marvelous?" Walt Whitman argues as follows: "Who knows the curious mystery of the eyesight? The other senses corroborate themselves, but this is removed from any proof but its own and foreruns the identities of the spiritual world. A single glance of it mocks all the investigations of man and all the instruments and books of the earth and all reasoning" (*Leaves of Grass*, pp. 9–10).

Véa has completed his fourth novel, with the tentative title *Sleep with Kings*. This novel is about the Mexican-Texas war, the siege of the Alamo, and the fateful figure of the Mexican general Antonio López de Santa Anna. Having paid homage to loved ones in *La Maravilla, The Silver Cloud Café*, and *Gods Go Begging*—that is to say, to grandparents, his bracero friends and caretakers, and to the boys on the hill—Véa has written a novel about one of the founding chapters in Chicano history and a decisive formative phase in the history of U.S. territorial expansion. In his fourth novel, Véa combines the real and the imaginary: a Mexican caudillo and a love affair with an African American female, considered by many to have been a spy for the U.S. government and, to others, the cause of Santa Anna's distraction from military affairs that led to the loss of the Texas-Mexico War in 1836.

Véa's novels are staged in various lands and situations: from Michoacan, Mexico, to Dong Ha in Vietnam, with conflicting characters whose destinies are shaped by fate, hence the timed meetings and well-orchestrated plots, especially noteworthy in novels known to contain several subplots. In addition, the chapters in these novels are framed so as to be reconstructed by the reader, either as integral parts of a novelistic collage or as segments of a mural that is complex in theme and design. Lastly, Véa's characterization reveals a gift for expressionistic detail (for instance, Josephina and Manuel Carvajal, Bambino Reyes, Ted for Short, the Chaplain). With his fourth novel, Véa is now venturing into history, thus away from the autobiographical. Although his novels have yet to produce a contending field of critical perspectives, eventually an informed sense of his literary achievement will warrant the affirmation that, at the level of style and ingenuity of plot construction, Alfredo Véa ranks among the finest novelists currently writing in the Americas.

Selected Bibliography

WORKS OF ALFREDO VÉA JR.

NOVELS
La Maravilla. New York: Dutton, 1993.

The Silver Cloud Café. New York: Dutton, 1996.

Gods Go Begging. New York: Dutton, 1999.

SPECIAL COLLECTIONS
An archive of Alfredo Véa's manuscripts can be found at the John F. Kennedy Memorial Library, Special Collections, at California State University, Los Angeles.

OTHER WORKS
"Caliban and Prospero No More." *(untitled): East Los Angeles Journal of Literature and the Arts* 3, nos. 1–2 (summer–fall 1997).

SECONDARY WORKS

CRITICAL STUDIES AND REVIEWS
Armitt, Lucie. "The Magic Realism of the Contemporary Gothic." In *A Companion to the Gothic.* Edited by David Punter. Oxford; Malden, Mass.: Blackwell Publishers, 2000. Pp. 305–316.

Biggers, Jeff. "Interview with Alfredo Véa, Jr." *Weekly Wire,* September 13, 1999.

Boudreau, John. "In Celebration of All Americans" (review of *La Maravilla*). *Los Angeles Times,* June 28, 1993, sec. E, p. 2.

Cantú, Roberto. "Alfredo Véa, Jr." In *Dictionary of Literary Biography.* Vol. 209, *Chicano Authors, Third Series.* Edited by Francisco A. Lomelí and Carl R. Shirley. Detroit: Gale Research, 1999. Pp. 281–285.

————. "Borders of the Self in Alfredo Véa's *The Silver Cloud Café.*" *Studies in Twentieth Century Literature* 25, no. 1 (winter 2001): 210–245.

Cavell, Stanley. *In Quest of the Ordinary: Lines of Skepticism and Romanticism.* Chicago: University of Chicago Press, 1994.

Harrison, Sam. "Lushly Told Tale from the Desert" (review of *La Maravilla*). *Washington Post,* April 27, 1993, sec. B, p. 2.

Holdridge, Randall. "Crime with Passion: Alfredo Véa's 'Gods Go Begging' Is a Luminous Third Novel." *Tucson Weekly,* September 13, 1999.

Review of *La Maravilla. Publishers Weekly* 240, no. 3 (January 19, 1993): 446.

Leal, Luis. "Magical Realism in Nuevomexicano Narrative." In *Nuevomexicano Cultural Legacy: Forms, Agencies, and Discourse.* Edited by Francisco A. Lomelí, Victor A. Sorell, and Genaro M. Padilla. Albuquerque: University of New Mexico Press, 2002.

Lough, James. "Plot, Point of View Take Back Seat in Ambitious 'Gods'." *Denver Post,* October 31, 1999.

Márquez, María Teresa. "Interview with Alfredo Véa, Jr." (tape-recorded in June 1995, unpublished).

Peterpaul, Ann. "Gods Go Begging." *Weekly Wire,* November 29, 1999.

Porter, Kathleen Sullivan. "The Amazement of Reality: An Interview with Alfredo Véa, Jr." *Hayden's Ferry Review* 22 (spring–summer 1998): 81–92.

Quintero, Ruben. "Chance Images." *Vietnam War Generation Journal* 1, no. 1 (April 2001): 3–23.

Rodríguez, Joe. *The Oddsplayer.* Houston: Arte Público Press, 1989.

See, Carolyn. "Cardboard Community's Cosmic Truths" (review of *La Maravilla*). *Los Angeles Times,* May 10, 1993, sec. E, p. 2.

Sommerstein, Alan H. Introduction to *Lysistrata, The Acharnians, The Clouds,* by Aristophanes. New York: Penguin Books, 1973.

Whitman, Walt. *Leaves of Grass: The First Edition, 1855.* Edited by Malcolm Cowley. New York: Barnes and Noble, 1997.

Zarazua, Daniel D. "Interview with Alfredo Véa." *Mi Gente,* April 2000.

Tino Villanueva

(1941–)

ALBERTO JULIÁN PÉREZ

THE POET Tino Villanueva uses two languages to speak from two worlds, Mexican and American, distinguishing himself in both English- and Spanish-language poetry. Born 11 December 1941 to a family of Mexican American migrant farmworkers, he faced as a child and adolescent the poverty, grueling work, and interracial hostility that challenged many Mexican Americans during those turbulent times. Drawing on his own youthful struggles, Villanueva's poetry personalizes and illuminates his racially and linguistically divided society's struggle for wholeness.

Villanueva did not enjoy the leisure of the kind of middle-class upbringing so many American writers remember as the cradle of their literary taste, as they read books guided by educated parents or wise teachers from good schools. Those were privileges the child of migrant farmworkers did not have. These circumstances mark an important distinction in the education, the sensibility, and the morals of Villanueva. As a member of a rural working-class family, he had a particularly hard upbringing. Migrant workers moved from field to field across Texas following the picking of cotton—long days of backbreaking labor for the whole extended family. He remembered those days in

his poem "Haciendo apenas la recolección" from *Shaking Off the Dark* (1984):

> Let me see: I would start from San Marcos,
> moving northward. . .
> I am hauled among family
> extended across the back seat,
> as the towns bury themselves forever
> in my eyes: Austin, Lampasas, Brownwood,
> past Abilene, Sweetwater,
> along
> the Panhandle's alien tallness.
>
> (p. 49)

Tino Villanueva attended schools in those little towns he names in many of his poems—El Campo, Wharton, Littlefield. His family stayed in housing with outhouses, in squalid living conditions. They were Presbyterians with firm beliefs and strong religious sentiments, but family life was not easy for them. Villanueva kept in his memory vivid scenes of the family quarrels and hostilities that broke out occasionally among them. Poverty, an inferior education, and racial discrimination also burdened him. After following the migrant stream around Texas, the family would return to the segregated life of the Mexican barrio in San Marcos to go back to the fields with the next cotton season. This cycle shaped Villanueva's life until he finished high school in 1960. Limited by his background and preparation, he became a worker in a furniture factory for four years.

Then he was drafted by the Army and served in the Panama Canal Zone for two years, 1964–1966. In Panama he befriended locals who introduced him to Spanish-language poetry. After his military service Villanueva returned to his small hometown in Texas. At a relatively late age, twenty-four, he decided to start his college education and enrolled at Southwest Texas State University in San Marcos. In the university's classrooms he soon found his true vocation, poetry. He took courses in both English and Spanish poetry (Spanish was his undergraduate major and English his minor). After discovering the works of Dylan Thomas, he adopted the Welsh poet as a distant but effective literary mentor—Thomas's way of writing, his respect for the poetic word, his love both for form and for anecdote, became precious lessons for Villanueva as an aspiring writer.

During the 1960s, life was changing fast in America. Numerous social conflicts erupted, including the black civil rights movement against racism and segregation, the heavily Hispanic farmworkers union strikes, and widespread protests against the Vietnam War. These movements of civil resistance found on their side youths ready to agitate for social and economic justice and confront the American government on issues they considered essential to the values and freedoms of their society. The Mexican American community was prepared to assert itself through militancy and protest. The Chicano political movement and cultural renaissance began. Unlike the rebellious and individualistic but marginal Pachuco countercultural Hispanic group of the 1950s, the Chicano movement became engaged in social militancy. Chicanos participated in the student protests on the university campuses of America during the 1960s. They felt the urgency of understanding and explaining the situation of Mexican Americans and extending their social gains. The Chicano movement had a lasting cultural impact on the life of Mexican Americans and Hispanics in the whole country. While the political force of the movement diminished with time after some social gains were achieved, the cultural transformations it produced outlasted its specific social circumstances and remained a vital part of the Hispanic experience in America. The Chicano movement also helped shape the way minorities are seen in the United States by the political elites. Some of its early student militants became university professors and writers whose books became part of the university curriculum.

Many Hispanics who had not been socially committed before the movement became active when they saw its positive results. Villanueva started writing and publishing a few poems in his late twenties in Texas and got more involved in Chicano culture after he began his graduate studies in Spanish at the State University of New York at Buffalo in 1969. After obtaining his master's, he began his doctoral studies at Boston University in 1971. By then, at age twenty-nine, Villanueva was getting ready to publish his first book, *Hay otra voz* [There is another voice]: *Poems (1968–1971)*. This book of poetry was his apprenticeship into literary writing, not just because it was his first but also because of the particular way he approached the act of writing poetry, bringing to it a love of study and apprenticeship. He realized that poetry depends not only on inspiration but on trial and error and hard work as well. He understood the writing of poetry as a craft and believed the poet should be a great craftsman, as his inspiration Dylan Thomas was.

We witness in Villanueva's poetry a constant process of development and growth of his literary skills. At the beginning he published very little but studied hard. Essential to his education were the many courses in British, American, and Spanish poetry he took at college and the courses in Spanish poetry he completed during his graduate career. In 1981 he defended his doctoral dissertation on post–Spanish Civil War poetry, later published in 1988 as *Tres poetas de pos-*

guerra: Celaya, González, y Caballero Bonald (Estudio y Entrevistas) (Three Post-War Poets: Celaya, González, and Caballero Bonald—Study and Interviews). Villanueva explained in an unpublished interview with James Hoggard that he learned a lot from all these poets he read: "each and every one of these poets—English-speaking or Spanish-speaking—have been pertinent to me, for they've taught me something about subject matter, figurative language, line and stanza breaks, typographical layout, tone, punctuation, etc. . . . And to this I've added my own particularities." Attracted by the Chicano movement, he studied it and in 1980 edited an excellent anthology of Chicano literature in Spanish, also contributing a long introduction: *Chicanos Antología histórica y literaria* (Chicanos Historical and Literary Anthology). He also founded *Imagine: International Chicano Poetry Journal,* which lasted from 1982 to 1986. Far from limiting himself, inspired in his search for creative freedom, Villanueva became a painter as well.

This personal growth and exploration is apparent in his work and became a trademark of his art and poetry. His decided to be a poet of two languages and two cultures—the English-speaking mainstream American culture and the Spanish-speaking Chicano culture. He began the difficult process of mastering two literary cultures (the American and the Hispanic) and two poetic traditions in two different languages. Many years of Villanueva's literary career were spent at this effort, with excellent results. The more difficult of these two tasks was to master poetry in Spanish, a language he had learned and used only colloquially, at home and in the culturally isolated barrio, before studying it formally in college. Literary Spanish was in a sense a foreign language for him. He did not live in a Spanish-speaking country until he went to Panama with the Army and later to Spain, where he attended a Spanish literature program during his graduate education. Otherwise he depended entirely on his university studies in America to gain mastery of Spanish literary language and

poetic technique. The struggle to master these and their English counterparts at the same time, present throughout his poetry, constitutes by itself a statement on the vitality of the Spanish culture in the heart of English-speaking America.

His first book, *Hay otra voz,* published in 1972, is divided into three parts: "Por ejemplo, las intimidades"("For Example, Intimacies"), "Pausas de ayer y hoy" ("Pauses of Yesterday and Today") and "Mi raza" ("My Race"). Most of the poems are written in English, with a few in Spanish, and poems in the last section combine Spanish with English. This book and his second, *Shaking Off the Dark,* differ in their approaches to poetry. We find in *Hay otra voz* poems with very sophisticated and complex imagery, such as "My Certain Burn toward Pale Ashes," "Live, Die, and Live," and "This Place," inspired by Dylan Thomas's poetry, and poems written in Spanish where the poet tried to transpose the imagery of English poetry into Spanish, with limited success.

His struggle to master Spanish poetry's rich tradition was a difficult one. *Hay otra voz* shows a poet with an ambiguous style in search of an independent voice. Villanueva did not feel comfortable with either the English or the Spanish poetic traditions yet. In his poetry, America becomes a dual-voiced culture; the national myth of the monoglot society is shattered. In that collection his most successful bilingual poem is "Que hay otra voz" ("That There Is Another Voice"), included in the third part, My Race. In this poem Villanueva writes about the social problems of Chicanos without burdening the reader with heavy moral rhetoric. His imagery is always elegant, with well-chosen adjectives. His approach is restrained and formalistic. The poem revolves around an anecdote drawn from Chicano life, and it has both moral and poetic objectives. He says about the South Plains of Texas:

El aplastante verano se ha quedado en
los ayeres: el perenne azadón se recuesta,

sediento, en la topografía de tu memoria;
las ampollas hoy son callos.
Es el golpe helado del Panhandle que
penetra ahora
tu chaqueta desteñida
tu injuriada sangre
tu rodillera desgastada.

(p. 36)

The suffocating summer lives in
yesterday—the omnipresent hoe rests
thirsty in the topography of your memory;
your blisters today are calluses.
It is the icy blow of the Panhandle that
enters now
your faded jacket
your insulted blood
your worn-out knee patches.

The poet never forgets that the poem is an
aesthetic act, justified by its imagery and its
language, and cannot rely merely on its ideas.
Thus his poems always have a unique linguistic
density.

"Que hay otra voz" is relatively long, and
Villanueva would continue developing his
poetry in this direction—long, autobiographical
poems of self-inquiry. His next book, *Shaking
Off the Dark,* bears much resemblance to the
first: it contains short poems of personal reflection, in English or in Spanish, and other poems
where the poet meditates about his life as a
member of the Mexican American community,
such as "Jugábamos / We Played," in which he
uses expressions of both languages. The imagery
is simpler than in his first book, and more direct,
especially in the intimate poems. In his first
book, for example, he resorts to ornate images
and an oblique use of language in "My Certain
Burn toward Pale Ashes":

My certain burn
       toward pale ashes, is told by the
       hand that whirls the sun; each

driving breath beats with the quick
pulsing face.

(p. 8)

In the second book, in "Resolution, II," he
writes,

Nowhere shall it be written
I cannot write into these lines
pity, lamentation and wild joy,
shift the layers of time
before the morning light,
or against a low sun
in an ochre afternoon.

Already many things have changed.

(p. 13)

This poem is less ornate than the earlier one. His
meditation about time is direct and simple. The
images work around the ideas of time and light.
His poem seems to be looking for symbols to
anchor his poetic intuition.

In the short poem "To Budding Roses," from
Shaking Off the Dark, he re-creates the ancient
poetic motif of transient beauty and the passing
of time as symbolized in the life of a rose:

In this green month
when you are uncaressable
still
budding at every turning second
to burst into our fragile eyes
to spring into our first cupped touch—
you are so ignorant of death.

(p. 25)

It is evident in this poem how carefully Villanueva is looking for precisely the right words,
trying to find the images that can represent his
mood and feelings. It is not surprising to find in
this book a section of haiku, a short Japanese
type of verse—the poet is in search of a direct
poetic form uniting image and idea. The last part
of *Shaking Off the Dark,* "History I Must Wake
to," contains several very moving poems about
his childhood, such as "Haciendo apenas la

recolección" ("A Farm-Worker's Recollection") and "I Too Have Walked My Barrio Streets." He talks about his personal history and the life of his family during the 1940s and 1950s. He employs in these poems either Spanish with some expressions in English, or English with a few Spanish words, but the two languages are never of equal status in the poem—in each case one is prevalent and the other subordinated. This alternation of languages alerts the reader to ethnic difference without destroying the linguistic unity essential to the poem.

These poems contain narrative elements he would continue developing with great success in later books. They are like chapters of a poetic novel of a Chicano adolescent's process of self-awareness and enlightenment. Both *Crónica de mis años peores* (1987), written in Spanish, and *Scene from the Movie* Giant (1993), written in English and winner of a 1994 American Book Award, are variations of an epic of learning, which includes a process of disillusionment, frustration, and search for self. Villanueva centers the action in Texas during the 1950s. *Crónica de mis años peores,* translated into English by James Hoggard in 1994 as *Chronicle of My Worst Years,* begins when the character is a child during the 1940s and finishes in the 1960s when he is a young man. As its title suggests, the book recounts trying episodes in the central character's early life. The character is part of a family of migrant Chicano farm laborers who travel in Texas following the cotton harvest, from the south of the state to the Panhandle and back to the south. The situations presented in the poems resemble many episodes in the life of the young Villanueva, and in that sense the poems are autobiographical. The poet selects and enhances situations he considers significant or symbolic, dressing them in well-crafted poetic images. Villanueva gives form prominence in his verse. The images are taken from daily life, occurrences the memories of which now move the grown man to relate his own history and explain his place in the world.

Memory becomes the real hero of the book. In the process of telling the history of his life, the poet discovers his identity in the theater of memory. Recalling his devastated past as a poor child helps the adult to understand his place in American society, and to understand through poetry what life is all about. Poetry in this sense, and particularly autobiographical poetry, is for Villanueva an instrument of personal salvation. Though introspective and aimed at personal redemption, his verse is also political, and it does not shy from social commentary. Bourgeois poets may find enough satisfaction writing poems to sing of their love or feelings, but a poet such as Villanueva, his experience informed by poverty and deprivation, needs more than that—he considers poetry an instrument of redemption. The child he is talking about is a wounded human being in need of healing, which the poet seeks in his memory. The adult Villanueva also discovered in poetry something else—beauty, and that truth and beauty in poetry can become one. He is not merely confessing his limitations and suffering—he is rescuing from his past what is meaningful in a beautiful way. Form also has a redemptive function; the poetic word is the instrument of the poet's search for freedom.

We witness a process of transvaluation. The character discovers who he was—an underprivileged youth—and the reader perceives the injustices the character suffered growing up. Villanueva is careful not to blame his misery all on the American government but recognizes the complexity of the web of injustice and discrimination that trapped his family. Poverty, menial jobs, inadequate schools, the prejudices of teachers and other authorities, frustration and violence within his own family, and long hours of labor under the sun all contributed to a tortured adolescence, the inferno of poverty aggravated by ethnic prejudice.

The character is able to be rescued from this nightmare through poetry, which also becomes his existential project. In "Tú, por si no otro" ("You, If No One Else") he gives advice to those readers who may be in the same underprivileged situation he once was in:

Pon la voz
donde tengas la memoria,
hombre, que transformaste
la congoja en conciencia
saludable.
Defiende con palabras
cuanto entiendas,
tú, que tragaste el polvo
de las tardes.
Tú, por si no otro,
condenarás desde tu lengua
la erosión de cada contratiempo.

Listen, you
who transformed your anguish
into healthy awareness,
put your voice
where your memory is.
You who swallowed
the afternoon dust
defend everything you understand
with words.
You, if no one else,
will condemn with your tongue
the erosion each disappointment brings.

(pp. 34–35)

The poet sings his disillusionment and pain, and this cathartic process restores his faith in the world, at least in the world of poetry. The poems describe painful adolescent experiences—the boy's resentment when sent on an errand, discrimination in history class by a teacher who despised Chicanos, daily hard labor in the fields with his relatives, anger and fighting within his extended family. The person recalling those events wants to forgive his society and find peace. His understanding of his situation is full of subtleties, not a black and white picture. Villanueva observes the human condition carefully and renders it vividly, and readers identify with the youth's feelings of humiliation—he is powerless in a world of adults and in white society, powerless because of his family's poverty and the backbreaking labor they have to do, and powerless also because of his youthful lack of self-awareness. The adult returning to those memories, however, is in charge of his destiny. He ponders his memories from a situation of privilege, having escaped the social circumstances that frustrated and hurt him. Made materially comfortable with the help of his poetry, and with his pain transformed through self-awareness and cathartic memory, he is a witness of the saving power of the poetic word.

In his next book of poetry, *Scene from the Movie* Giant (1993), Villanueva started with a well-defined narrative situation, as before. *Crónica* was written in Spanish with a Hispanic audience in mind; *Scene* is in English and addressed to the English-speaking reader. This is a major change of task—Hispanic readers, particularly Mexican Americans, know the problems Chicanos face in America, while the non-Chicano outsider is not so familiar with the discrimination faced by Chicanos, historically and currently. With a great sense for communicating across cultural boundaries, Villanueva chose to reflect on *Giant,* George Stevens's 1956 Texas epic of interclass rivalry, sudden oil wealth, shifting social landscapes, and interethnic love and hate. The narrative voice is that of the adult remembering the film's impact on him when as a teenager he went to see it in his hometown Holiday Theater in 1956.

The movie tells the story of a Texas rancher whose son, a Harvard-trained doctor, marries a Chicana. Villanueva's focus is the scene of a fight between the rancher and the racist owner of a hamburger joint. He crafts verses analyzing this scene from different angles and tracing its effects on his understanding of his place in American society. The rancher Bick Benedict, played by Rock Hudson, argues with the racist Sarge, who refuses to serve some Mexican customers and insults his grandson. The adolescent watching the movie finds that scene powerful and emblematic of his situation. The poem transforms the scene into a modern allegory from which the boy, and the reader, can learn about racial discrimination in America and liberate themselves in a catharsis of the negative feelings of impotence (or shame, depending upon which parties to the conflict—privileged or marginalized, Chicano or Anglo—the reader identifies with). The teenage moviegoer can view the ugly incident as a passive outsider witnessing it or from the conflicted perspective of the rancher: in spite of his prejudices, the rancher has a mixed-race grandson, compelling him to admit the need for a racially integrated country. In the final scene, Rock Hudson is willing to defend the Chicanos against racial aggression, by implication taking the side of the young Chicano in the cinema.

Because of the passive position of the observer and narrator in this book, the poetry is more richly and rigorously descriptive than in *Crónica.* The sensibility and consciousness of the observer bring moral and psychological awareness to the situation he depicts. After recounting the film to the readers, the poet turns inward and describes the effect it had on the observer:

> you turn back to when your offended
> little world was unresolved. Each
>
> thought is longing to become another,
> longing to sing, once again and always,
> deep into a song of what memory still
>
> might know. . . .

(p. 51)

The past has a lesson to teach and a hunger for learning pervades Villanueva's poetry and life. He shares the appetite of the working masses to transform the world around them, to redeem themselves, and to embrace a new hope. Villanueva, like many of the participants in the Chicano movement, found a place for himself in the education system as universities opened their doors to the children of the underprivileged. The artists, writers, and intellectuals of the Chicano Renaissance discovered in the American universities institutional support for intellectual freedom, and many of them went on to employment as professors (Villanueva, for example, at Boston University).

Scene from the Movie Giant secured for Villanueva an important place in American poetry outside of Chicano poetry. Villanueva wants to be considered an all-American poet, not just a literary ethnic token. After *Scene* he developed new themes beyond the worn Chicano topics of social protest, publishing in 1997 a long poem, "At the Holocaust Museum: Washington, D.C." Just as in *Scene,* he uses the cinematic experience of the single scene to comment about his own situation. In this poem the poet's experiences as a spectator in the museum of specific exhibits (a freight car, a group of photographs of victims) frame his meditations about the horror of the Holocaust.

As his earlier poems illuminated the marginalization of Chicanos, he now considers the victimization and scapegoating of Jews, and why it is vital for history and society to understand and remember their tragedy. This time he is not part of the victimized group, but a sympathetic outsider. He again shares with his readers feelings of powerlessness and guilt. As a poet his only way to help is to tell the story so others will remember, in hope that history will not repeat itself. He finishes the poem thus:

> Five decades, and in another country,
> I am too late as in a blazing nightmare
> where I reach out,
> but cannot save you, cannot save you.
> Sarah, Rachel, Benjamin, in this light you have
>   risen
> where the past is construed as present.
> For all that is in me: Let the dead go on living,
> let these words become human.
> I am your memory now.

In 1999 he published a small book of ten poems in Spanish, *Primera causa (First Cause).* If "At the Holocaust Museum: Washington,

D.C." was Villanueva's attempt at a narrative poem with a non-Chicano topic of broad interest, *Primera causa* marks a venture into a new poetic territory. This book's short poems are both lyrical and conceptual, elegiac and intellectual. It is a type of poetry dear to the Spanish literary tradition, forged during the Renaissance and Baroque periods in Spain and Spanish America, by poets such as Garcilaso de la Vega (1501–1536), Francisco de Quevedo Villegas (1580–1645), and Sor Juana Inés de la Cruz (1648–1695). One of the poems, "Así dijo el Señor" ("And Thus He Spoke"), makes specific reference to his upbringing as a Mexican American in Texas, but the other poems deal with the act of writing poetry and of memory in a more general way, ignoring specific ethnic situations, as in "Más la voz que el tiempo" ("Voice over Time"), where he writes,

> Memoria mía, memoria mía,
> dame lo que es mío y enséñame
> la pura manera de contar lo que se ha ido
> —que pueda más la voz que el tiempo

> Oh memory, my memory,
> give me back what is mine and guide me
> in the very telling of everything that stayed
>   behind
> —may my voice win out over time.

All the poems of *Primera causa* develop around the core idea of writing and memory. He organized his poems with a thematic center and enriched them with new motives. His next project at this writing was to be an ambitious new book recounting the memories of Penelope, the wife of Ulysses.

There are major themes in Villanueva's poetry—social conflicts, memory, self-awareness, understanding, and resistance to oppression—that continue evolving in his work. He develops his poetic projects and ideas during long periods of incubation; the results are of consistently high quality, careful yet innovative in the use of language and image. Although

many examples of lyric love poems appear in his first two books, his major poetry is descriptive and narrative, with an elegiac tone. This poetry evolved from fairly consistent thematic interests associated with his original poetic treatment of personal autobiographical situations. Happily, he avoided becoming a purely dramatic or narrative poet—his careful and conscientious crafting of form and image give his poetry a richness uncommon in today's verse. Villanueva is a perfectionist, patiently reworking his language for a long time before presenting a poem to the public. He is a voracious reader, able to enrich his own writing with his intellectual discoveries without being overbearing in his erudition. He remains an emotional poet, aiming to touch the heart of the reader.

Although Villanueva's poetry continued to evolve, with some of his best compositions written during his mature years, his place in American poetry was already secured with *Scene from the Movie* Giant. His impact in Spanish poetry has grown despite difficulties that limit his reception. He is an American poet writing in Spanish, and Spanish-language readers outside the United States find this situation extraordinary and difficult to understand. He does not belong to a nation whose main language is Spanish. Readers in Spanish-speaking countries far away from the United States such as Uruguay or Argentina are not familiar with the historical odyssey of the Chicano people. They may resist the idea that a Chicano writer in the United States reflects a new social phenomenon affecting many countries, namely the coexistence of several languages within a national territory, all of which are vital for the future of that society. Instead, they may see a Chicano as a misplaced immigrant who has lost his place of origin.

In spite of this difficulty in its reception, appreciation of Villanueva's Spanish-language poetry will continue growing in the Spanish-speaking countries because it brings to the Spanish language a distinctive new voice and a new history—Spanish used as a minor language, as a language of resistance against social oppression by an Anglophone majority. This language of resistance cannot be ignored because it represents a social difference omnipresent in that society, and it is associated with a set of distinctive customs and diverse personalities. In advanced industrial societies, language does not always represent the nation, and it will become more and more difficult for the modern nation to rely on the use of a single language. Villanueva is a product of this postmodern crisis—a poet who struggles between languages and cultures that tolerate each other without absorbing each other entirely.

Selected Bibliography

WORKS OF TINO VILLANUEVA

POETRY
Hay otra voz: Poems (1968–1971). Staten Island and Madrid: Editorial Mensaje, 1972.

Shaking Off the Dark. Houston: Arte Público Press, 1984.

Crónica de mis años peores. La Jolla, Calif.: Lalo Press, 1987.

Scene from the Movie Giant. Willimantic, Conn.: Curbstone Press, 1993.

Crónica de mis años peores / Chronicle of My Worst Years. Translated by James Hoggard. Evanston, Ill.: Northwestern University Press, 1994.

"At the Holocaust Museum: Washington D.C." *Partisan Review* 4 (1997): 582–585.

Primera causa / First Cause. Translated by Lisa Horowitz. Merrick, N.Y.: Cross-Cultural Communications, 1999.

EDITIONS AND CRITICISM
Chicanos: Antología histórica y literaria. Mexico City: Fondo de Cultura Económica, 1980.

Tres poetas de posguerra: Celaya, González, y Caballero Bonald (Estudio y Entrevistas). London: Tamesis Books, 1988.

CRITICAL AND BIOGRAPHICAL STUDIES

Bruce-Novoa, Juan. "The Other Voice of Silence: Tino Villanueva." In *Modern Chicano Writers: A Collection of Critical Essays*. Edited by Joseph Sommers and Tomás Ybarra-Frausto. Englewood Cliffs, N.J.: Prentice Hall, 1979. Pp. 133–140.

———. "Tino Villanueva." In *Chicano Authors: Inquiry by Interview*. Edited by Juan Bruce-Novoa. Austin: University of Texas Press, 1980. Pp. 253–264.

Costa Picazo, Rolando. "Villanueva: El número dos; o, La palabra y el silencio." In his *Estados Unidos y América Latina: Relaciones interculturales*. Buenos Aires: Asociación Argentina de Estudios Americanos, 1994. Pp. 245–251.

García, Concha. "Entrevista con Tino Villanueva." *Revista de diálogo cultural entre las fronteras de México* 3 (1996): 2–9.

Hoggard, James. "The Expansive Self: The Poetry of Tino Villanueva." *The Texas Observer*, May 12, 2000, pp. 23–25.

Mildonian, Paola. "Introduzione." In *Il Canto del Cronista: Antologia poetica.* Florence: Casa Editrice Le Lettere, 2002. Pp. 5–42.

Olivares, Julián. "Self and Society in Tino Villanueva's *Shaking Off the Dark.*" *Confluencia* 1–2 (spring 1986): 98–110.

———. "Tino Villanueva." *Chicano Writers: First Series.* Edited by Francisco Lomelí and Carl Shirley. Detroit: Gale Research, 1989. Pp. 275–281.

Pérez, Alberto Julián. "Tino Villanueva escribe en español." *Alba de América* 39–40 (July 2002): 369–385.

Rodríguez, Alfonso. "Crónica de mis años peores de Tino Villanueva: La memoria como voluntad creadora." *Foro Hispánico: Revista Hispánica de los Países Bajos,* 9 (July 1995): 91–98.

West, Alan. "Latin American Writing: Language and Spices, Resistance and Redemption." *Agni* 28 (1989): 248–263.

Victor Villaseñor

(1940–)

ELISABETH GUERRERO

THE LIFE AND work of Victor Villaseñor comprise a tale of triumph over adversity. Challenged with having to renounce his native Spanish language when entering school and struggling to succeed academically despite severe dyslexia, Victor Villaseñor has nevertheless come to be a recognized writer of narrative and screenplays. A gifted storyteller whose nonfiction reads like novels, Villaseñor devotes his writing to recounting the experiences of Chicanos in the southwestern borderlands, recovering a sense of historical pride for many of his readers.

Born in 1940 in Carlsbad, California, the son of businessman Juan Salvador Villaseñor and bookkeeper Guadalupe Gómez Villaseñor, the writer grew up on the ranch where he continues to live today. As children, his parents came north with the wave of immigrants who fled the hunger and violence of the Mexican revolution (1910–1920), only to encounter poverty and ethnic prejudice on the other side of the border. Coming from a Spanish-speaking home, Villaseñor struggled in school, and while he mastered English, he continued to face difficulties with reading. In addition, he confronted an ideology of exclusion that dishonored his Mexican heritage; Villaseñor recalls that on his first day of school, "The teachers smacked me on the head when I spoke Spanish and said, 'None of that Mexican stuff'" (Hubbard, *People Magazine,* p. 9).

Before finishing high school, Villaseñor abandoned his studies and became a manual laborer. However, at the age of nineteen the young Californian visited relatives in Mexico; his stay there was pivotal. "For the first time, I saw Mexicans who were doctors, lawyers—heroes" (Hubbard, *People Magazine,* p. 9). There Villaseñor not only met Mexican professionals and intellectuals but also experienced a second epiphany when he was introduced to the works of writers such as Homer and James Joyce. He returned to California with a renewed determination to complete his studies and to communicate his thoughts and feelings to the reading public. Villaseñor continued to struggle with dyslexia, but he finished his high school degree, enrolled in the University of San Diego, and began to write, primarily in English.

After many rejections, the novel *Macho!* appeared in print in 1973. *Macho!* is thus far Villaseñor's only work of fiction. Following the novel, Villaseñor published the nonfiction study *Jury: The People vs. Juan Corona* (1977), the screenplay *The Ballad of Gregorio Cortez* (1983), and then his best-known work, the nonfiction family saga that began with the epic best-seller *Rain of Gold* (1991). *Rain of Gold* was followed by the shorter family tales in *Walking Stars* (1994), and the series concluded with the prequel, *Wild Steps of Heaven* (1996), and the final volume, *Thirteen Senses* (2001). Taken as a whole, Villaseñor's narratives are accessible, with vividly drawn characters. While both academic critics and book reviewers have at times found his writing style to be uneven, occasionally heavy-handed, and laden with clichés and sentimentality, the majority nevertheless celebrate his writing as inspiring and warm-hearted and commend his narratives for their fast-paced and believable social history. Villaseñor has developed a unique style that blurs the divisions between memoir and fiction and is consistently life-affirming.

Despite earning positive book reviews, Villaseñor's work has merited little critical attention in the academic world; he has received no literary prizes, rarely appears on university course reading lists, and is the focus of few critical studies in academic journals. Prominent critics of Chicano literature such as Juan Bruce-Novoa and Carl Shirley have written of their disappointment in Villaseñor's work, labeling it as trite and accusing it of perpetuating stereotypes. To give one example of such stereotypes pointed out by critics, Roberto, a Mexican *campesino* in *Macho!* confuses soap with toothpaste, and the primary activities of the men in his village appear to be confined to cockfights and gunfights.

The lack of accolades for Villaseñor's writing in academia may also be due in part to the approachability of his work, which has won over a wide popular audience but fewer academic readers. The omniscient narrators in Villaseñor's work tend to guide the reader along on a clear path; the narratives follow a straightforward linear chronology; and they are highly engaging "page-turners" written for a broad public rather than for an intellectual élite. Some academic critics have also found fault with overly schmaltzy moments in the texts. Here is one example of a chapter epigraph that demonstrates what some

critics have described as sentimentality in Villaseñor's writing: "And so she dreamed of her truelove coming to get her on his orange-red stallion to take her to his home on the top of a small white cloud" (*Rain of Gold*, p. 79).

The approachable style of Villaseñor's *oeuvre* comprises what French literary theorist Roland Barthes would term "readerly." Barthes describes "readerly" texts as static and predictable, while "writerly" texts are open and complex, inviting the reader to participate in the act of interpretation and in the construction of meaning. Barthes declares: "The goal of literary work (of literature as work) is to make the reader no longer a consumer, but a producer of the text" (*S/Z*, p. 4). In what Barthes would deem a "writerly" text, the reader is challenged by the book as an intellectual puzzle; the answers are not handed to her, and she must participate in the interpretation of the work. One example of a more "writerly" text would be the novel . . . *Y no se lo tragó la tierra* by Tomás Rivera, winner of the prestigious Quinto Sol prize for Chicano literature in 1970; this work merited praise for its concise, tightly wrought language and the multitude of narrative voices and fragments which the reader must piece together and interpret.

Villaseñor's first novel appeared during the same period as Rivera's . . . *Y no se lo tragó la tierra*, during the late 1960s and early 1970s, when the civil rights movement prevailed and interest began to bloom in literature depicting Chicano experiences. Villaseñor's publisher hoped to take advantage of this interest by issuing the book under the rather unfortunate title *Macho!* Despite being stylistically a "readerly" text and despite typecasting Mexicans at times, overall the novel makes a valuable contribution through the sociohistorical content that it offers. In the novel, a young man from Michoacán named Roberto leaves his village under the wing of a *norteño*, a man with experience crossing the northern border of Mexico. Young Roberto hopes to enter the United States under the bracero program (1942–1964), in which the

United States government encouraged and permitted the immigration from Mexico of experienced agricultural workers needed in the fields. The main character trusts that such work will enable him to earn enough money to feed his parents and the siblings that he leaves behind.

After a long and brutal wait for legalization in a town of desperate men waiting to enter the United States, Roberto instead crosses the desert illegally, *a la brava.* During this treacherous crossing, his companions collapse from dehydration in the desert; of those who survive, many more die from suffocation in the stifling cargo of a truck. Villaseñor's novel offers a beneficial contribution in this aspect, as it conveys experiences that are still relevant today; more than three decades after the publication of *Macho!*, many Mexican families continue to cross the border illegally in much the same way, looking for work. Indeed, given the recent crackdown on immigration, border crossing has become a more dangerous ordeal than ever. Those who attempt it in hopes of feeding their families continue to risk betrayal or abandonment by their guides (also known as *coyotes*), robbery or violent attacks while they are unprotected in a harsh environment, and death in the treacherous desert or while sealed in the suffocating trailer of a semi-truck.

Macho! also attempts to provide useful context by including brief informative passages between each chapter. These passages provide historical and cultural explanations of aspects of the life of migrant workers and of Cesar Chavez's labor movement in the 1960s, in which protesters used forms of civil disobedience to obtain better working conditions in the fields and vineyards of California. However, the protagonist of *Macho!* responds to Chavez's struggle with mixed emotions. As the novel indicates, the United Farm Workers discouraged the importation of braceros from Mexico, favoring instead the hiring of Mexican American workers who were U.S. citizens or legal residents.

Roberto must face dual conflicts, both with the transformations that the civil rights movement brings, and with the resistance to change that his village traditions represent. The novel ends on a positive note when Roberto returns to rural Mexico and begins to question the violent custom of the honor code; he decides not to take blood vengeance on the man who killed his father. He chooses not only to abandon the "macho" tradition but also to stay in the village to work the land, feed his family, and improve conditions at home. As one critic observes, this ending neatly erases the conflict between Mexican migrant farmworkers and the Mexican American farm labor movement as depicted in the novel, as now the Mexican citizen stays home for the benefit of the people in his own village and thereby also conveniently ceases to compete with Mexican American farmworkers for jobs and labor rights.

It is interesting to note that in the 1991 reissue of *Macho!* with Arte Público Press, Villaseñor writes: "I'm not the same person who wrote that book twenty years ago. I thought of rewriting parts of it—feeling almost ashamed of some sections" (p. 5). Despite this reevaluation of his previous work, Villaseñor concludes that "the 60s were the 60s" and compares the work to that of Bob Dylan, who while he sings off-key, still conveys an important message. There are some unfortunate passages in the novel, such as when Villaseñor depicts Mexico as a backward and violent nation, writing that "Mexico is the leading nation of violent deaths" (p. 49) and attributing this questionable statistic to ignorance and to the obstinate adherence to a brutal code of honor. Francisco Lomelí and Donaldo Urioste wrote in 1976 of such cultural faux pas in the novel: "The author's many biases of cultural determinism overwhelm his creative talents, exhibiting damaging attitudes towards his Mexican culture in considering it traditional, static and outdated" (*Chicano Perspectives in Literature,* p. 50).

In his study "Macho! de Victor Villaseñor, en el canon chicano," Juan Antonio Perles Rochel attempts to explain why this novel failed to capture academic critics' attention and to become a major part of the Chicano literary canon. *Macho!* fulfilled several characteristics of the genre, including a rural focus, a heroic depiction of Cesar Chavez's labor movement, and a structure of the bildüngsroman, or coming-of-age tale. Also in this list is the incorporation of the bilingual or code-switching linguistic style common in Chicano writing, as *Macho!* includes occasional words in Spanish when appropriate. Bruce-Novoa has termed this technique "interlingualism"; this term points to how the practice celebrates the richness of sound and meaning that arises from the blending of two languages.

According to Perles Rochel, despite sharing the characteristics listed above that won the Quinto Sol Prize for other Chicano novels of the period, such as Tomás Rivera's *. . . Y no se lo tragó la tierra* and Rudolfo Anaya's *Bless Me, Ultima,* two factors prevented *Macho!* from earning similar accolades. First, the main character, Roberto, was Mexican rather than Mexican American; and the novel thereby depicted a Mexican experience rather than a Chicano experience. Secondly, the protagonist's interests as an illegal migrant laborer were at odds with those of Chavez's movement. Therefore, Perles Rochel argues, the novel does not fall easily into the category of Chicano literature and was thus less recognized in the body of Chicano literary criticism that was developing during the period. The novel may have merited less attention from critics not only due to its social context but also due to the stylistic flaws mentioned earlier.

Villaseñor's next book, *Jury: The People vs. Juan Corona,* also does not fall easily into the category of Chicano literature as described by Perles Rochel and defined by Martínez and Lomelí: "Chicano literature . . . is the literature written since 1848 by Americans of Mexican descent or by Mexicans in the United States who write about the Mexican-American experience" (*Chicano Literature,* p. xi). Under this definition, while *Jury* fulfills the first requisite of being written by a Chicano writer, it does not fulfill the second requisite of depicting Chicano experiences or building a Chicano community in the narrative.

Jury focuses primarily on the experiences and perspectives of the jury members rather than on the Mexican American accused man or the family members and protesters who supported him. A nonfiction work of psychological drama, *Jury* provides a play-by-play of the grueling jury deliberations in the case of *The People vs. Juan Corona,* in which a Mexican American labor contractor in California was accused of murdering and burying twenty-five drifters over the course of three months. The account devotes little attention to the background of Corona himself, instead focusing on the jury deliberations that Villaseñor reconstructed from extensive interviews of each of the jurors, ten of whom were Anglo, one of whom was African American, and one of whom was Mexican American. Perhaps due to the legalistic nature of the study, *Jury* is a tightly wrought text that avoids the sentimentality and clichés that sometimes appear in Villaseñor's other works.

A carefully constructed report that permits each of the jury members to have a voice in the account, the narrative depicts the psychological and moral conflicts of the group and ultimately redeems the jury system. The lone unsympathetic figure in the text is Naomi, a juror who held out for a verdict of innocent. Indeed, despite accusations of racism in this case, Villaseñor's study affirms his faith in the best efforts and forthright intentions of the jury members, who ultimately found Corona guilty. *Jury: The People vs. Juan Corona* demonstrates that although the jurors were unable to think of a convincing motive for the murders, there was much evidence to demonstrate Corona's responsibility, including a signed receipt buried with one of the bodies and a ledger with a list of victims. Although *Jury* differs from Villaseñor's other published works, its thoroughness earned him the respect of book critics and opened new doors to him as a writer.

Villaseñor's next major project, the screenplay for the feature film *The Ballad of Gregorio Cortez,* expanded his literary horizons into a new genre for him as a screenwriter. Although the movie, starring Edward James Olmos, was not a blockbuster, it was met with critical acclaim for its "accuracy and authenticity" (Hoffman, *MELUS,* p. 47), was featured on public television, and was reissued on video/DVD in 2000. Based upon Mexican American writer Américo Paredes's *With His Pistol in His Hand* (1958), a seminal study of the historical ballad, or *corrido,* of Gregorio Cortez, the film tells the tale of a Mexican American cowhand who killed an Anglo-Texan sheriff in self-defense in 1901, when the Texas Rangers had free reign over the southwest. Cortez eludes chase for days but is eventually captured, tried, and imprisoned.

As Paredes explains in his study and as eventually comes clear in the film, Cortez's adventure all begins with a linguistic and cultural misunderstanding. When the sheriff's translator, whose Spanish is poor, asks Cortez if he had recently traded a horse, *un caballo,* Cortez answers no. The sheriff and his assistant take this as evidence that Cortez is lying, as they know that he recently acquired a new horse. Nevertheless, court proceedings later reveal in the film that Cortez truthfully answered no because he had not traded *un caballo,* a male horse; instead he had traded *una yegua,* a mare, and for him there is a clear difference.

In addition to this linguistic misunderstanding, the film deftly shows in other ways as well the contested narratives of Anglos and Mexicans. For instance, while an Anglo newspaper reporter records the (Anglo) marshal's testimony of a Mexican thief murdering an officer as unimpeachable fact, the visual cues and the *corrido* itself, in contrast, portray Cortez as the hero. The film brings forth the version of the story that did not appear in the press but that was sustained in the Mexican community's oral tradition; in the *corrido,* as in the film, the Rang-ers are villains who abuse their power and mistreat Texans of Mexican origin.

Cultural studies critic Donald Hoffman commends *The Ballad of Gregorio Cortez* for transforming the Western film genre and neither excluding nor dehumanizing Mexican Americans as prostitutes and ruthless *bandidos.* This transformation of the Western is important, because, as Hoffman notes, "Hollywood . . . seems to treat Mexicans and Mexican-Americans to an unusually vindictive program of degradation and defamation" (*MELUS,* p. 47). This history of the sordid depiction of Mexicans as cowardly villains, Native Americans as wild scalpers, and African Americans as invisible in Westerns may go far in explaining why Villaseñor was averse to his original publisher's plans to change the title of his next work, *Rain of Gold,* to *Rio Grande,* the name of a 1950 John Wayne cowboy movie. That movie and *Rio Bravo* (1959), *The Alamo* (1960), and *The Comancheros* (1961) form a series of films in which, not surprisingly, Anglo soldiers and Texas Rangers are the good guys, protecting their newly acquired territory from the barbarous Native American raiders and from the perfidious Mexicans.

Hoffman explains that *The Ballad of Gregorio Cortez* is an exemplary model of the revisionist Western film due to its balance between depicting discrimination and injustice, while also presenting a guarded optimism that opens the possibility of absolution and the cessation of hostilities: "Only *Ballad* opens a site of negotiation, however fragile, that recognizes that while not all languages are symmetrical, and not all cultures identical, an imperfect understanding, free of the need to dominate, may, in fact, be possible" (*MELUS,* p. 51). Many hands took part in creating the film, particularly those of the director Robert Young (who also directed the film version of Miguel Piñero's *Short Eyes*) and the folklorist Américo Paredes. Nonetheless, the contribution of Villaseñor is also visible precisely here, in the negotiation of the borderlands as a contested space where violence and injustice take place and yet where there remains a resilience and an unshakable zeal for life.

Villaseñor's bestseller *Rain of Gold* continued his literary trajectory of maintaining indomitable spirits in the face of adversity. *Rain of Gold* received considerable advance publicity due to the controversy of its publication. The work appeared in the wake of Cuban American writer Oscar Hijuelos's 1990 Pulitzer Prize for the novel *The Mambo Kings Play Songs of Love.* Many hoped that Hijuelos's success would open the gates for other Latino writers to be more aggressively marketed by mainstream publishers. However, although originally under a generous contract with the major New York publishing house Putnam, Villaseñor pulled out of the deal. He refused to change the title to *Río Grande,* declaring that the work was not a John Wayne movie, and he also refused to cut 150 pages from the 550-page narrative and to market the book as a novel, asserting that he wanted to remain faithful to his extensive research based upon the oral testimony of his relatives. He preferred to market *Rain of Gold* as a "Latino *Roots,*" a nonfiction family epic aiming to celebrate an ethnic group's history and dignity. He was able to buy back the rights to the book and to find a publisher with Nicolás Kanellos in the small editorial house Arte Público Press in Houston. Despite Arte Público's limitations regarding publicity, the book met with great success and was later published in paperback with Dell.

Villaseñor's emphasis on the importance of marketing the work as a family history rather than as fiction continues in the text itself. Despite the novelistic style of his writing, Villaseñor includes black-and-white family photos in the book as evidence of the characters' existence and contends in the prologue: "This . . . isn't fiction. This is a history of a people—a tribal heritage, if you will—of my Indian-European culture as handed down to me by my parents, aunts, uncles and godparents. The people in this story are real. The places are true. And the incidents did really happen" (pp. 10–

11). While the integration of fiction and historiography is not new, and indeed is a current trend in the historical novel, Villaseñor's work is unusual in applying this approach to memoir. His work is a conscious blending of genres, drawing upon novelistic techniques while emphasizing the historical reality of the autobiography. Critic Yves-Charles Grandjeat notes the lengths to which Villaseñor went in order to market *Rain of Gold* as an "'authentique' roman chicano," an authentic Chicano novel, foregoing a generous contract with a major publisher to avoid compromising *Rain of Gold*'s "authenticity" and in order to emphasize its exactitude and veracity (*Caliban,* p. 65). Nevertheless, Grandjeat also observes that, paradoxically, in many ways Villaseñor's "ethnic autobiography" resembles a western movie, replete with Hollywood clichés, "comme si Villaseñor écrivait en ayant a' l'esprit l'adaptation cinématographique du récit" (as if Villaseñor had written the text with the cinematographic adaptation in mind; *Caliban,* p. 70).

Although *Rain of Gold* reads like a "cinematic" novel and has been analyzed as such, as noted above, Villaseñor emphasizes that his narrative is nonfiction, and it falls easily into the genre of family memoir. This emphasis on the family distinguishes Villaseñor's memoirs from those of fellow Chicano writers such as Richard Rodríguez, Gary Soto, and Luis Alberto Urrea, whose autobiographical accounts chronicle the development of a personal (and ethnic) identity and of a writer's vocation. Rather than exploring individual subjectivity, the *Rain of Gold* series instead delves into the experiences of the Villaseñor family as a whole. The title comes from Lluvia de Oro, the name of the goldmining town where Villaseñor's mother's family had lived before crossing the border. *Rain of Gold* is an account of the trials, travails, and joys of his mother's and father's childhoods in Mexico and in the United States. This text alternates between the stories of the two sides of the family until the bookish, romantic Lupe and the charming, quick-tempered Salvador, each determined survivors in their own way, fall in love and marry.

Rain of Gold is particularly gripping in passages that recount the horrors of the Mexican Revolution: as a little girl Villaseñor's mother hides from raping and marauding soldiers under a pile of manure; as a little boy his father risks capture and hanging to steal corn for his starving family. As a *New York Times Book Review* critic states: "What *Rain of Gold* shows best . . . is how the Porfirio Díaz regime, and the revolution it provoked in 1910, affected day-to-day family life" (p. 20). For Villaseñor, the *rurales* of the Porifirio Díaz regime (1876–1910), as well as the revolutionary factions that deposed him, caused chaos and suffering; both were destructive forces that the family had to endure. Like many during the 1910s and 1920s, both sides of the author's family fled their homes in Mexico and continued to fight for survival when they crossed the border and faced unemployment, prejudice, and brutality.

The saga continues when the two families arrive in California. There, amidst much struggle, Lupe and her family make a simple living as migrant farmworkers. Meanwhile, after Salvador, his mother, and his sister Luisa have nearly died of starvation on the border, he relies upon his street smarts and quick wits to keep alive. Salvador frequents brothels and pool halls, undergoes a stint in prison, and makes his living as a miner, gambler, and bootlegger before finally settling down with Lupe.

Rain of Gold was very well received by reviewers and was celebrated for its epic proportions and its incorporation of oral traditions. Villaseñor's writing style was particularly effective in holding readers' attention when alternating suspenseful passages of war and danger with peaceful, evocative descriptions such as this:

> Up ahead, by a scattering of yellow and pink wildflowers, Lupe found a small formation of rock piled up like a stack of tortillas with a twisted little pine tree on top of it. The little high country pine tree was no more than eight feet tall, fully grown, and Lupe could see where its roots had split the rock, looking for soil.
>
> (p. 59)

As a result of these strengths the book sold well, was published in paperback by Dell in 1992, and has appeared in a Spanish translation as well. Nevertheless, *Rain of Gold* has not won a place of honor for Villaseñor in the Chicano literary canon. In *World Literature Today,* the influential critic Juan Bruce-Novoa reviewed the narrative as an ineffective work of fiction, stating, "*Rain of Gold* is not the great Chicano novel" (p. 346). Bruce-Novoa finds fault with the work for resorting to the "clichés of U.S. immigration writing" and what he calls the "ethnic shtick" of basing truth-claims on the oral tradition that supplies the story. Despite Bruce-Novoa's and other prominent critics' negative response to the occasional banality of *Rain of Gold,* most readers and reviewers in popular periodicals received the work favorably overall. A particularly enthusiastic book reviewer wrote: "My grandparents came from the back streets of Copenhagen and Dublin. But Villaseñor has written my family history, too. And yours. *Rain of Gold* is one of the best—and most American—books of this or any other year" (Ryan, *USA Today,* p. 4D). As the book critic notes, the humanization of the immigrant experience is decidedly one of *Rain of Gold*'s strengths.

Villaseñor's next work, *Walking Stars,* was also extremely well received in book reviews. *Walking Stars* is a modest volume compared to the epic proportions of *Rain of Gold.* A series of short narratives designed primarily for young-adult readers, the stories in *Walking Stars* aim to inspire the young reader to have faith in the mysteries of love and survival in the face of hardships. As in *Rain of Gold,* several of the tales are taken from the childhood experiences of the writer's parents; for example, his mother faces her fears on her first day of school, and his father's endurance and love for his mother enable him to win a hundred-mile race with a train. A few of the stories also offer new material from Villaseñor's own childhood on his parents' ranch in California. In one story, a dog behaves erratically when he senses that his beloved companion, Villaseñor's older brother Joseph, has died. In another short narrative, a gelded horse, unable to have his own offspring, valiantly protects each of the mares and her colts on the ranch.

The overall emphasis in these stories is clear in the subtitle of the volume, "Stories of Magic and Power." As Villaseñor states in the preface:

> These are true stories about real life and real people, not made-up, phony, movie heroes with big muscles who always know all the answers, but stories of people like you and me: ordinary people who don't quite know where they're going or how to get there, but always seem to find the way to survive and flourish.
>
> (p. 11)

Villaseñor further guides the young reader by interpolating brief explanations between each story, explaining how each tale inspired his own faith and strength.

Villaseñor's tales of his father's childhood bravery in *Walking Stars* gave impetus to his next volume, *Wild Steps of Heaven*. A "prequel" to *Rain of Gold*, *Wild Steps of Heaven* tells the story of the author's father's family in the mountains of Jalisco during Porfirio Díaz's reign at the turn of the twentieth century. Villaseñor's father, Juan Salvador, is the cheerful, loquacious youngest child, nurtured by his indigenous mother doña Margarita and encouraged to revere the earth and respect women rather than follow the destructive footsteps of the other men in the family. Juan's father is a big-boned, redheaded, blue-eyed man, exceedingly proud of his Spanish origins and cursed with a vile temper. The family is painfully divided when the father turns his anger and hatred toward those of his children who are small and dark like their mother. Calling Juan and his older brother José "backward

Indians," he banishes the gentle horse trainer José to live in the barn, where the young man turns to contemplation and becomes a master horseman and marksman.

Meanwhile, there is a ruthless *coronel* leading a troop of Porfirio Díaz's notorious *rurales* in the area, and José's talents, coupled with his relationship with the desirable Mariposa, turn the Coronel's wrath upon him. Few members of the family survive the brutalities of the *rurales* on the cusp of the revolution, as the *coronel* and his soldiers rape, mutilate, and burn in an attempt to quash the spirits of the indigenous villagers. The remaining fair-skinned brothers are killed or disappear across the border, and Juan's father, screaming "I have no sons," disappears into the mountains. Nevertheless, Juan's wizened but faithful mother, doña Margarita, struggles to respond to hatred and fear with love and magic. The narrative ends just before Juan and his ravaged family, of whom remain only he, his feisty sister Luisa, his brutalized sister Emilia, and his elderly mother, leave for the border.

Thirteen Senses continues where *Rain of Gold* left off, when Villaseñor's father, the passionate Juan Salvador, is grown and living in California. There he marries the graceful Lupe (Guadalupe), who will be Villaseñor's mother. Like *Rain of Gold*, *Thirteen Senses* is in many ways an ode to the mother, in homage both to Salvador's young wife Lupe and to his elderly mother doña Margarita. Salvador uses his wits to support the family by bootlegging whiskey during Prohibition (1920–1933), when alcohol production and consumption were illegal in the United States. A series of violent and dangerous episodes keep the reader in suspense, as Salvador narrowly escapes a police chase on more than one occasion, Lupe drags her husband from a burning house after his still explodes, and the two nearly die of dehydration when crossing the desert with their newborn baby while fleeing to Mexico.

Thirteen Senses is classified as a nonfiction memoir, but it also has elements of magical realism, a genre of fiction that predominated in the "boom" of Latin American novels in the 1960s. Magical realism is the incorporation of magical, dreamlike elements in otherwise realistic narratives; the best-known example is the novel *Cien años de soledad* (*One Hundred Years of Solitude;* 1967) by Colombian writer Gabriel García Márquez. Just as Villaseñor has explained that seemingly incredible scenes, such as his father roping a man-eating snake, are true stories passed down by his elders, García Márquez has argued that seemingly fantastic elements in his novel, such as levitation, are part of the reality that he lived and that his grandparents told him about in Colombia.

In addition to the debt *Thirteen Senses* owes to magical realism, the passages in the narrative in which the grandmother provides spiritual guidance and engages in shape-shifting resemble another genre that, like magical realism, took readers by storm in the 1960s: Carlos Castañeda's best-selling series that began with *The Teachings of Don Juan: A Yaqui Way of Knowledge* (1968). Classified as cultural anthropology but resembling mystical fiction, Castañeda's books provide an ethnographic account of his apprenticeship under Don Juan, a Yaqui Indian healer of northern Mexico.

The title of *Thirteen Senses* comes from Villaseñor's paternal grandmother's teachings of thirteen ways of feeling or perceiving. While they are not clearly spelled out in the narrative, it becomes apparent that in addition to the five familiar senses, the thirteen senses include balance, intuition, harmony, and the union of two loving individuals. In *Rain of Gold,* Lupe and Salvador's Yaqui Indian mothers, doña Guadalupe and doña Margarita, appear as remarkable figures who manage to keep their families alive in the direst of circumstances. Villaseñor further explores this concept of the matriarch who draws upon powerful Native American traditions in *Thirteen Senses.* Like Don Juan in Castañeda's series, in *Thirteen Senses* the paternal grandmother, Juan Salvador's mother doña Margarita, is a wise and powerful spiritual guide, dispensing advice to her family, trusting in visions, and transforming herself into an owl or a fox to protect her loved ones.

Doña Margarita is an unforgettable figure in the narrative, a comical and yet inspiring spiritual guide whose intimate connections with the divine permit her an amusing informality, if not irreverence, toward her celestial associates. Her activities in *Thirteen Senses* include communing with the Virgin Mary daily as she defecates in the outhouse, massaging a wicked rich man's feet to arouse him into repentance, and chugging bootleg whiskey with the local priest. Most spectacularly, doña Margarita negotiates with God and the devil and convinces God to take his fallen angel back into heaven. It is in moments such as these that the narrative interjects hyperbolic expressions in capital letters such as "The drums were beat, Beat, BEATING! The One Collective HEART-*CORAZÓN* of HUMANITY was BEAT BEATING, POUNDING *CON AMOR!*" (p. 161). Also, as in *Rain of Gold, The Thirteen Senses* incorporates epigraphs before each chapter that may seem new-agey or overly sentimental to some readers: "All was back in Balance, All was back in Harmony and at Peace, generating Wisdom through our Thirteen Senses from HEAVEN to EARTH—ALL ONE SONG!" (p. 497).

Victor Villaseñor's writing style is one that many readers may love and a few academic critics may disdain, but regardless of one's response, it cannot be denied that Victor Villaseñor has come into his own as writer. It is clearly apparent that Villaseñor's body of work never fails to convey a passion for life and a belief in the human ability to overcome difficult odds and reach for the stars, even in one's darkest hours. Additionally, his writing provides readers with the opportunity for a greater understanding of the sociohistorical context of the Mexican Revolution and the consequent northern exodus. Villaseñor's exploration of his own family's remarkable history has come to be a source of identity and pride for many readers in the United States, all of whom, in one way or another, share a history of immigration and of border-crossing each day in this contested space.

Selected Bibliography

WORKS OF VICTOR VILLASEÑOR

MEMOIRS

Rain of Gold. Houston: Arte Público Press, 1991. Spanish edition published as *Lluvia de oro.* Mexico: Planeta, 1993.

Wild Steps of Heaven. New York: Delacorte Press, 1996.

Thirteen Senses: A Memoir. New York: Rayo, 2001. Spanish edition published as *Trece sentidos: Una memoria.* New York: Rayo, 2001.

NOVELS AND SHORT STORIES

Macho! Toronto, New York: Bantam Books, 1973. New edition with introduction by the author. Houston: Arte Público Press, 1991.

Walking Stars: Stories of Magic and Power. Houston: Piñata Books, 1994.

OTHER WORKS

Jury: The People vs. Juan Corona. Boston: Little, Brown, 1977 (nonfiction).

The Ballad of Gregorio Cortez. Embassy Pictures, 1983 (screenplay; based on Américo Paredes's 1958 study *With His Pistol in His Hand*).

Snow Goose Global Thanksgiving. Oceanside, Calif.: Snow Goose Publications, 1993.

CRITICAL STUDIES

ARTICLES AND BOOK REVIEWS

Barbato, Joseph. "The Big Latino Book That Wasn't." *Publishers Weekly* 238, no. 6: 21 (February 1, 1991).

Barthes, Roland. *S/Z.* Translated by Richard Miller. New York: Hill & Wang, 1974.

Bruce-Novoa, John. "*Rain of Gold.*" *World Literature Today* 66, no. 2 (spring 1992): 346.

Day, Frances Ann. *Latina and Latino Voices in Literature for Children and Teenagers.* Portsmouth, N.H.: Heinemann, 1997.

Epstein, Robert. "Igniting an Explosion of Culture." *Los Angeles Times,* August 5, 1991, p. 1.

Grandjeat, Yves Charles. "Montage et décodage dans *Rain of Gold:* 'Authentique' roman chicano." *Caliban* 31 (1994): 65–73.

Hoffman, Donald. "Whose Home on the Range? Finding Room for Native Americans, African Americans, and Latino Americans in the Revisionist Western." *MELUS* 22, no. 2 (summer 1997): 45–60.

Hubbard, Kim. "Rain Maker." *People Weekly* 38, no. 13 (September 28, 1992): 95–96.

Kanellos, Nicolás, ed. *Short Fiction by Hispanic Writers of the United States.* Houston: Arte Público Press, 1993.

Kelsey, Verlene. "Mining for a Usable Past: Acts of Recovery, Resistance, and Continuity in Victor Villaseñor's *Rain of Gold.*" *Bilingual Review/La Revista Bilingüe* 18, no. 1 (January–April 1993): 79–85.

Lomelí, Franciso, and Carl Shirley, editors. *Dictionary of Literary Biography,* Vol. 209: *Chicano Writers, Third Series.* Detroit: Gale Group, 1999. Pp. 291–294.

Lomelí, Francisco A., and Donaldo W. Urioste. *Chicano Perspectives in Literature: A Critical and Annotated Bibliography.* Albuquerque: Pajarito Publications, 1976.

Martínez, Julio, and Francisco Lomelí, eds. *Chicano Literature: A Reference Guide.* Westport, Conn.: Greenwood Press, 1985.

Miller, Susan. "Caught between Two Cultures." *Newsweek* 119, no. 16 (April 20, 1992): 78–79.

Miller, Tom. "Children of Another Revolution." *New York Times Book Review,* September 8, 1991, p. 20.

Perles Rochel, Juan Antonio. "*Macho!* de Victor Villaseñor, en el canon chicano." *La Coruña, Interpretations of English: Essays on Literature, Culture and Film.* 1998: 113–119.

Ryan, Alan. "*Rain of Gold:* A Family's History Is America's." *USA Today,* January 9, 1992, p. 4D.

Urrea, Luis Albert. "Of Mexico, of Ourselves: A Review of *Wild Steps of Heaven.*" *San Diego Union,* March 1996.

VIDEO RECORDINGS AND SOUND RECORDINGS

Interview with Carl Mueller and Juan Gomez. *The Chicano Novel: Victor Villaseñor discusses Macho, His Novel about Farm Workers.* Audiocassette/Videocassette Center for Cassette Studies, 1974.

Interview with Betsy Aaron. Videocassette. Ambrose Video, 1992.

Interview with Shauna Hawkins. Videocassette. Evanston Community Television Corp., 1992.

Helena María Viramontes
(1954–)

DEBRA A. CASTILLO

ONE OF THE most important contributions of the contemporary Chicana writer, Tey Diana Rebolledo wrote a few years ago, is "dealing with the significance of language use and silence within our literature" (p. 351). It is here that Helena María Viramontes makes her most distinct and important contribution to this growing body of work. She is the author of a still-slim published corpus of creative texts (to date, one collection of short stories, a short film, and a single novel) along with a group of scattered essays, but each of her anxiously awaited published works is a polished jewel, meticulously written and rewritten until every word is exact. An extremely disciplined writer, she famously rises each day before dawn to work on her creations, and will not succumb to pressure from her fans to release any new work until she feels entirely comfortable that it is ready. She is particularly known for the beauty of her language and the lyricism of her descriptive set pieces. The result is that her limpid prose reveals metaphorical structures of great depth and complexity while remaining clear and accessible to the average reader.

In the same study quoted above, Rebolledo reminds us of another important context for thinking about Viramontes's work. Rebolledo says: "I think we would all agree that Chicana criticism and theory are still in a state of flux, looking for a theoretical, critical framework that is our own" (p. 350). In reminding us of this point, she also reminds us that the evolving Chicano canon, up until the 1980s, was associated nearly exclusively with important male writers like Rudolfo Anaya, Rolando Hinojosa, and Tomás Rivera. Likewise, Angie Chabram-Dernersesian evokes Margarita Cota-Cárdenas and Viola Correa as well as the work of politically committed poets, artists, and community activists to explore the question of what happens when writing women enter the Chicano script. They all agree: writing women cannot merely be written into an existing story about Chicano literature; by existing, and in the acknowledgment of their existence, they rewrite the script itself.

Helena María Viramontes is the product of this formative period in Chicana literature, and her works—like those of cohort members Denise Chávez and Sandra Cisneros—all provide a nuanced view of some facet of a woman's struggle against the restrictions imposed by gender roles in a racialized society. At the same time, subtly, her critique is sharpened by an undercurrent of unmistakable political commitment. Like other Chicana writers from the same generation, Viramontes's strategic reflection on these concerns in her narratives involves a conscious shift from a male to a female narrative point of view and a focus on circumstances and metaphors drawn from a woman's life, often focusing on the very narrow range of options that are allowed Chicanas in an impoverished, still *machista* society. She also frequently employs metaphors drawn from, and based on the rewriting of, feminocentric legends like those of La Malinche and La Llorona.

Viramontes's works tend to be austere, pared-down productions. Many of her narratives are set in the 1960s, the time period of her own youth, and feature culturally and spiritually torn adolescent girls coming into a sharp awareness of the restrictions in their worlds. The adult characters that surround them and complete this worldview speak little, keep secrets, reveal as little of themselves as possible, and are often haunted by tragedy. The combination of this harshness in her characters' daily lives and the stark beauty of Viramontes's prose is the hallmark of her style. Viramontes herself describes her work as a painful tiptoe act on very difficult ground. She says in "Why I Write," "Through writing, I have learned to protect the soles of my feet from the broken glass I shatter within myself. I have no intention of succumbing to the pull of despair. I must be fit, ready for the symbols to ebb and flow throughout the moment, hour, day, ready to read them, learn from them with urgency, point them out to you. . . . I must have faith. Writing is the only way I know how to pray."

In her poetically conceived short story "The Jumping Bean," she uses similar imagery for one of her characters and gives language an unexpectedly literal shape: "The young girl cried. If only she had the capacity to walk barefoot on broken and jagged words like María, then she wouldn't have to release the words, and she could smash them into a thousand pieces of glass, just like she wanted to smash the window" (p. 9). In both quotes the words that cut like glass have a precise and diamond-like beauty, but at the same time they are inherently painful.

While leaving no physical injury, the cut-glass-words in these the quotes metaphorically evoke the deep spiritual wounding that defines and determines the coming-to-consciousness of the Chicana woman in Viramontes's world.

Viramontes was born on 26 February 1954 in East Los Angeles, where she spent her youth. The granddaughter of immigrants, she has nine siblings. Her family was often extended even more, as it offered a home to relatives and friends crossing the border from Mexico. Her father worked in construction, her mother was a housewife, and the whole family would occasionally increase its meager resources by working summers in the agricultural fields, an experience that she recalls in her novel *Under the Feet of Jesus* (1996). Other works, especially those in the still-uncollected stories of *Paris Rats in East L.A.* (forthcoming) and the novel *Their Dogs Came with Them,* speak to the urban experience of a young woman growing up at the edges of the sprawling California metropolis. In one of her personal essays, she says of her barrio: "It was an impoverished area, and in many ways our homes resembled ornate Easter eggs of brilliant colors and chaotic designs improvised with building material found, worked for, or bartered. . . . I still recall the absence of sidewalks when I walked to Elementary School or being held in utter fascination by the old man and his mule who would arrive once a week to pick up metal scraps" ("Four Guiding Principles"). After graduating from Marianna Elementary School, Belvedere Middle School, and Garfield High School, she attended Immaculate Heart College—much to the chagrin of her family, which was puzzled by her insistence on wanting to continue her education. The transition to college became the first big culture shock of her life, since her basic education had taken place in schools that were "99.9 [percent] Mexican-American, and all sites readied for educational discontent" ("Four Guiding Principles"). In Immaculate Heart, she was one of only five Chicanas in her class. In 1975 she earned her bachelor's degree in English literature while working twenty hours a week.

During her college years, she began writing poetry and short stories more seriously. She became one of the coordinators of the Los Angeles Latino Writers Association. With great dedication she and her colleagues hosted Thursday workshops in a downtown Los Angeles studio, and together they produced *XhismeArte,* one of the most important little magazines of that time. Four years later, in September 1979, Viramontes was forced to cut back on this commitment when she joined the creative writing program at the University of California in Irvine. As the first Chicana admitted to this prestigious program, Viramontes found herself once again confronting ignorance and racial stereotyping. In "Four Guiding Principles," her passionate address to young Latino and Latina writers, she describes an encounter with her adviser that drove her to sever her ties with the Irvine program: At this particular meeting, he "began to explain why he thought I was a cheap imitation of Gabriel García Márquez. . . . [He said,] the trouble is that you write about Chicanos. You should be writing about people." Viramontes comments that she left her adviser's office and "never returned to the program and for another ten years never ever entered the Humanities building again." She eventually completed the requirements for the MFA after publishing her short story collection, *The Moths and Other Stories* (1985).

Since that time, she has received a fellowship from the National Endowment for the Arts, a John Dos Passos Prize, and numerous other forms of recognition for her work, and she has participated in the Sundance Institute under the mentorship of Colombian Nobel Prize–winner Gabriel García Márquez, always someone who had greatly influenced her. As she said in "Four Guiding Principles," in reaction to her adviser's slur about that famous author, "I was only offended by the word cheap." She still continues to advise her students to "be angry at institu-

tions, not at the people. The ignorance of others teaches you many things. . . . Make sure your pencil is sharpened enough to cut flesh." Now an associate professor of creative writing at Cornell University, Viramontes continues to organize conferences and support programs for young writers. Her activism has focused especially on work to improve educational access for students of color and to ensure the maintenance of inner-city libraries, which she sees as a crucial resource.

During her years in Irvine, Viramontes was extremely active in promoting Latino and Latina cultural events, and she helped organize two national conferences in that university devoted to the study of Chicana writers. The volumes *Beyond Stereotypes: The Critical Analysis of Chicana Literature* (1985) and *Chicana Creativity and Criticism: New Frontiers in American Literature* (1988) were the direct results of these important early conferences (Viramontes coedited the second of these volumes with longtime collaborator María Herrera Sobek). These conferences, and the volumes they produced, respond as well to Viramontes's understanding that the serious study of Chicana literature requires the kind of critical insights hinted at in the comments by Rebolledo that open this chapter, and a rapid survey of these books' tables of contents offers a useful hint as to how Viramontes defines her theoretical tools. The two volumes she coedited with Herrera Sobek include a combination of poetry, stories, personal essays, critical essays, and visual arts documents, and the artists and writers involved in these projects explore questions of economic, social, and gender-based injustice in innovative and passionate ways.

There are eight stories in her 1985 collection, *The Moths and Other Stories,* her first published book. As a group, these stories could be said to document the struggles of Chicana and Mexicana women to survive, if not always to overcome, the repression wrought by local and dominant cultures, by the church, and by traditional family structures. Domineering husbands and fathers in these tales demand respect and instant, unquestioning compliance from wives and daughters. Any breaking of the unspoken code of obedience and silence tends to take extreme forms: murder, for example. Yet there is no heavy-handed proselytizing about women's oppression in these stories. Clearly, repressive social and cultural values circumscribe women's lives, but Viramontes focuses on the haunting shape of the woman's response in shaping her life meaningfully in the face of such limitations, often in a style that demands careful attention from her reader.

The story "Growing" captures perfectly the difficult transition of an adolescent girl caught between childhood freedom and adult responsibilities. The story's narrator says of Naomi, "She could no longer be herself and her father could no longer trust her, because she was a woman" (p. 38). Early in the story, she asks herself plaintively, with a question that echoes through the entire volume, "What's wrong with being a mujer?" (p. 32). A slightly older woman, Alice Johnson, the protagonist of "Birthday," has an answer to this question. She has learned to her sorrow the costs of expressing her youthful sexuality. Unmarried, pregnant, she sees no recourse other than an abortion. Her boyfriend, Mike, knows nothing of her dilemma; when she confides in her girlfriend Terry, the friend is brutally honest, telling her to cut out the dreamy silliness and accept the inevitable. The unlovely realism of the conversation between the two women contrasts profoundly with the experience of the abortion itself. Here Viramontes's prose is both chillingly premonitory of potential tragedy and at the same time gorgeously lyrical. The story ends on the operating table: "Now the doctor will insert . . . *brimming baptism waters roll. swell. thunder.* Relax, Alice, and try not to move again. *reaching up to the vastness. calm. i relax under the fluids that thicken like jelly.* i am still; my body is transparent and light, ounceless" (p. 46). The use of the word "ounceless" where the reader expects to see "weightless" adds a distinctive poetic quality, while evoking

the almost infinitesimal weight of the aborted fetus. In a larger sense, in these coming-of-age stories, Viramontes points to the necessity for a more nuanced reading of femininity that requires a reexamination of social intersections, a reexploration of Chicana sexuality, and a revised theory of representation of the Chicana subject.

In "The Moths," one of the most frequently anthologized stories from this volume, the teenage girl shares her grandmother's dying as an act of love and the repayment of a debt. The fourteen-year-old girl defines herself as congenitally rebellious, yet respectful silences condition the narrator's loving relationship with her "Abuelita": "We hardly spoke, hardly looked at each other" (p. 24). Breaking the tacit code of silence is reprimanded, equally silently: "Regretful that I had let secret questions drop out of my mouth, I couldn't look into her eyes" (p. 23). The relationship between the women in this family is strained and formal; the young girl is reluctant to touch or kiss either her mother or her grandmother and never allows them to see her tears. Yet, by the end of the story, the awkward fourteen-year-old comes into a recognition, though still a vexed one, of crossing a threshold into full womanhood in the act of washing her grandmother's body for burial. Part of this change also involves taking on the burden and responsibility of her grief. As the room fills with moths, the narrator rocks her grandmother in her arms: "crying for her, for me . . . the misery of feeling half born, sobbing until finally the sobs rippled into circles and circles of sadness and relief" (p. 28).

On the other end of a woman's life, "Neighbors," "Snapshots," and "A Broken Web" all to some extent deal with elders who have borne the heavy costs of marriage and carry deep scars on their souls. "Snapshots" offers the most straightforward critique. Focusing on the story of Olga Ruiz, a woman whose life is defined by devotion to her family, Viramontes provides a strong indictment of the expectations for self-sacrifice inculcated into Chicanas of her generation. Olga tries to convince herself that "it was the small things in life . . . that made me happy" (p. 92), while at the same time her fascination with the constructed small happinesses revealed in photo albums reminds the reader (and her) of the conflict and unhappiness occurring just outside the picture frame. The metaphor of the framed life is important to Aura Rodríguez, the uncurious homemaker of "Neighbors," as well. She has a clearly established set of limits to her life: she "always stayed within her perimeters, both personal and otherwise, and expected the same of her neighbors" (p. 102).

Olivia, of "The Broken Web," keeps an unspoken agreement with her children, "a silent contract that they had with one another; she never played mother and they, in turn, never asked her to" (p. 54). Olivia's lover's wife, referred to throughout the story only as "Tomás's wife" and as the mother of his five legitimate children, floats in a "zombie-like" existence, speaking mostly when no one, not even the reader of the story, can hear her. Her "puzzle-piece heart" (p. 56) remains a silent, unresolved mystery. Inevitably, violence lurks just out of sight in all these domestic arrangements. Olga's pleasure in photographs is tempered by her guilty suspicion, inherited from her grandmother, that snapshots steal people's souls: "It scares me to think that my grandmother may have been right. It scares me even more to think that I don't have a snapshot of her. If I find one, I'll tear it up for sure" (p. 99). Olga's ambivalence about her genealogical heritage is fraught with contradiction and small violent gestures, fitting for this woman of small pleasures. In "Neighbors," the terrified and solitary protagonist ends up sitting inside her front door, ready to shoot the unwelcome visitor whose footsteps she has just heard on the porch. Finally, Tomás's unnamed wife in "The Broken Web" unexpectedly explodes, killing her husband in the midst of a violent argument.

"The Long Reconciliation" is one of the most stunning and beautiful stories in the volume. In it, Viramontes documents Chato and Amanda's brief marriage and fifty-eight-year separation, a marriage conditioned by mutual incomprehension and lack of communication despite their profound and enduring love for each other. Fittingly, this story is one of the more difficult for the reader to piece together because of its shifting narrative and temporal frames. Set in the time of the Mexican Revolution, the story revolves around a couple that is deeply in love and marries too young, too poor to afford children. When Amanda becomes pregnant, she decides to abort their child. Chato is horrified and abandons her emotionally and sexually; for reasons that combine hate and sexual desire, she eventually accepts the importunities of the local landowner. After stabbing the man who cuckolded him, Chato abandons Amanda without a word, forced to leave the country: "We both knew I was never returning; you stood there without a word, immovable as the mountain watching me ride off on a borrowed cloud" (p. 90). In penance and grief, Amanda hastens the death of her erstwhile lover by ripping open his wound and filling it with maggots. During their fifty-eight-year separation the only point of contact between the spouses is a toy carousel that each endows with a quite different symbolic burden related to their distinct obsessions, a metaphorical legacy revealed in parallel monologues, overheard by no one but the reader. Likewise, their long reconciliation is a silent one, occurring—from Chato's point of view at least—on the Day of the Dead, on his deathbed in the alien north, where he lived during the long years of their separation. "I killed for honor," he imagines telling her, at last, unburdening himself; "Then I killed for life," is Amanda's imagined answer, recalling the abortion that she underwent long ago as a desperate response to grinding poverty. But they never meet again in life.

In "Cariboo Cafe," which along with "The Moths" is the most frequently discussed story in this collection, this technique of using unheard parallel monologues is given its most striking expression. The story offers an overtly sociopolitical commentary on the horrors of Central America's undeclared wars in the mid-1980s and carries this story into those other undeclared war zones of U.S. ghettos. Central American refugees, displaced from their native lands, transfer the daily fear of repressive regimes into fear of the police, the Migra, and the drunks, pushers, and prostitutes that make up their current neighborhood. Like other illegal immigrants who have come to this blasted ghetto region: "They arrived in the secrecy of night, as displaced people often do, stopping over for a week, a month, eventually staying a lifetime. The plan was simple. Mother would work too until they saved enough to move into a finer future" (p. 61). In a larger sense, they struggle to survive, to raise their children, and to follow the sometimes labyrinthine code of the new laws of the land: "Rule one: never talk to strangers, not even the neighbor who paced up and down the hallways talking to himself. Rule two: the police, or 'polie' . . . was la Migra in disguise and thus should always be avoided. Rule three: keep your key with you at all times" (p. 61).

The common meeting place for all the varied inhabitants of the barrio is the Cariboo Café, though it would be safe to say that the café's "customers" are not customers in a traditional sense. They go to the café primarily neither to eat nor drink, but to seek sanctuary from the streets, to conceal themselves from the immigration authorities, to escape from the police. And they try to shrink into themselves, to pass as invisible to the bureaucracy. In Viramontes's text, indicators of smallness serve as stand-ins for what in Spanish would be marked by the ubiquitous use of the diminutive form, and their representations in the story include the drunk on the bus bench, discarded like the crumpled ball of paper he resembles, the newspaperman who sits in lonely isolation "in a little house with a little T.V. on and selling magazines with naked girls holding beach balls" (p. 63), and the illegal workers from the garment factory who

order small cokes in the café and eat their home-packed lunches in silence.

The story is multiply voiced and ambiguously located; narrative consciousness slips from a near-omniscient third person to the direct reflections of various characters: a lost child named Sonya, an Anglo cook in the ghetto greasy spoon restaurant of the title, a Central American woman traumatized by grief who precipitates the tragedy by kidnapping Sonya's little brother. The two main parallel monologues, of the cook and the Central American washerwoman, are closely interwoven in the story as a kind of unrecognized and unresolvable dialogue. Their distinct styles, and the overall style of the story, are realistic, to the degree that they present themselves as true-to-life: actual people using their own words, artistically organized to create a political, committed prose.

The story takes place over two days. From the perspective of the cook, the first day is relatively calm. Highlights include the arrival of Paulie, a drug addict and regular customer, who has to be pacified with coffee and yesterday's donut holes; soon after Paulie leaves, more trouble walks in the door in the form of a Latina woman—"She looks street to me. . . . Right off I know she's illegal, which explains why she looks like a weirdo" (pp. 65–66)—who surprisingly has enough money to pay for hamburgers for herself and the two children who accompany her. The next day is more eventful. Paulie OD's in the bathroom and dies. As a result, complains the cook, "I had the cops looking up my ass for the stash," and in addition to suffering this humiliation he still had to clean the vomit and excrement off the walls (p. 67). Then, several illegals hired by the garment factory across the street run into the same bathroom to hide from a Migra raid. When the Migra agents arrive, the cook's reaction is to betray the workers: "I was all confused, you know. That's how it was, and well, I haven't seen Nell for years, and I guess that's why I pointed to the bathroom" (p. 68). Shortly after that, the illegal Central American refugee woman returns to the café with the two children, whom the cook now identifies as kidnap victims, and the owner, once again acting against the dictates of his conscience and his inbred ghetto fear of authorities, calls the police, because he "doesn't know where [Nell] is at or what part of Vietnam JoJo is all crumbled up in" (p. 73). The Central American woman, confusing the police with the thugs from her homeland who disappeared her son, dies in the subsequent shoot-out.

While the Central American woman is eventually goaded into action, her role throughout most of the tale is essentially a passive one. The cook's story is one of apparent reluctance to get involved in the events unfolding around him, followed by a sequence of weakly rationalized actions that always involve violent responses from the authorities; in contrast, she is acted upon by others. Her narrative is scattered and fragmentary, and piecing it together we learn that she blames herself for the death of her small son in the seemingly endless and purposeless war. Through the tortured structure of the woman's thoughts, Viramontes is able to show the psychological effects of war without the literal battlefield descriptions. What the washerwoman describes in this broken, hesitant narrative is the reality of her son's death and the miracle of his supposed return, as well as her own yearning to protect him:

> She wants to conceal him in her body again, return him to her belly so that they will not castrate him and hang his small, blue penis on her door, not crush his face so that he is unrecognizable, not bury him among the heaps of bones, and ears, and teeth, and jaws, because no one, but she, cared to know that he cried. For years he cried and she could hear him day and night. Screaming, howling, sobbing, shriveling and crying because he is only five years old, and all she wanted was a mango.
>
> (p. 74)

Maternal love, maternal need, is her death sentence. At the end of the story, she gives up her life rather than sacrifice her fantasy.

The woman's narrative also has a mythic dimension. As the washerwoman herself recognizes, her life parallels the story of "La Llorona," the folkloric figure of the unnatural mother who, having selfishly abandoned her children, realizes her love for them only after their death and is condemned to search for them endlessly: "It is the night of La Llorona. The women come up from the depths of sorrow to search for their children. I join them, frantic, desperate, and our eyes become scrutinizers, our bodies opiated with the scent of their smiles" (pp. 68–69). Thus, at all times in this story, behind the life-giving mother stands the shadowy nighttime figure of that other woman, the hovering figure of death, the bad mother responsible for murder.

Helena María Viramontes's second collection of short stories, *Paris Rats in East L.A.* (still unavailable in a single volume as of this writing), returns to the barrio and to the mid-sixties time period familiar to us from several of the stories in the earlier collection, *The Moths,* and picks up on both the urban environment and the adolescent experience we have seen in such stories as "The Moths" and "Growing." This volume offers a series of linked stories focusing on a pair of East Los Angeles siblings. If the rich cultural substratum to the stories suggests a prehistory of cultural dislocation and an immigrant's nightmares, that experience is no longer the daily reality lived by Champ and her brother, or even by their larger-than-life and all-too-real *amá,* Arlene. Throughout this sequence of stories, the point-of-view character is Champ, a child notable for her testing of boundaries of self and world. She is an altogether more self-confident and brash protagonist than the characters in the earlier collection, at home with herself and with her East L.A. streets, able to juggle poodle skirts, rock songs, and Miss Clairol hair colors, along with La Llorona and other cultural markers of her Mexican heritage.

The given names of the two central characters in this series of stories are "Ofelia" and "Gregorio," both of which are names that carry the typical Spanish gender marker of "-a" for the feminine and "-o" for the masculine. This gender marker is hidden, but not forgotten, under the nicknames "Champ" and "Spider." Indeed, throughout the stories, readers are aware of the double world these characters inhabit: the performances that they present to the public and that are tied to their street names versus the more tender, disguised selves that they reveal only in moments of intimacy. Viramontes moves back and forth between these spaces, and the linked nature of the stories allows her to develop the characters with a depth more typical of the extended treatment in a novel.

These stories speak lovingly about ordinary people and situations and deal with everyday life in the barrio without romanticizing or pathologizing it. There are no easy answers here; instead, we are allowed into lives that in turn are tragic and funny, seen from the inside through an unblinking eye and entirely free of self-pity. The streets and houses of East L.A. define the boundaries of this reality, and the characters deal comfortably with their stridencies, since those streets and those unlovely interiors comprise their intimate domestic spaces, and in them a moment is always found for beauty, for the expansion of the soul. Each story offers another facet of this life, and in delving into the roots of Champ's story, Viramontes reconstructs the historical and cultural conjuncture that implicitly led to today's Chicana's sense of cultural and political agency.

Each of the stories in this collection focuses on a moment, often shocking for the readers, in which two readings of cultures that the reader is bound to see as conflicting clash and absorb each other. The clash may present itself between inner and outer visions of a character, between Anglo dominant culture and ghetto Chicano understandings, or between highly stylized performances of expectations about masculine and feminine identity. In these clashes, a loving acceptance is the outcome more often than an explosion of violence. "Miss Clairol," for example, starts this way:

Arlene and Champ walk to K-Mart. The store is full of bins mounted with bargain buys from T-shirts to rubber sandals. They go to aisle 23, Cosmetics. Arlene, wearing bell bottom jeans two sizes too small, can't bend down to the Miss Clairol boxes, asks Champ.

—Which one amá?—asks Champ, chewing her thumb nail.

—Shit, mija, I dunno.—Arlene smacks her gum, contemplating the decision.—Maybe I need a change, tú sabes. What do you think?—

. . .

—I dunno— responds Champ. . . . She is too busy thinking of things people otherwise dismiss like parentheses, but sticks to her like gum, . . . and sometimes she wishes she weren't born with such adhesiveness.

(pp. 101–102)

Neither Champ nor Arlene makes any judgment about the cultural realities represented by K-Mart, too-tight bell-bottom jeans, cheap cosmetics, and chewing gum—stereotypical markers of a young working-class woman from the U.S. dominant culture. Nor do they comment on the very different cultural realities hinted at by the interjection of working-class Mexican Spanish—"amá," "mija," "tú sabes." Champ and Arlene control this working-class space as fully empowered citizens of their small world and negotiate its contradictions without a second thought.

At the same time, with her perfect command of tone and figurative language, Viramontes offers a subtle reflection on this cultural intersection, by slipping her reader between this unlovely reality and an unexpected metaphor of striking appropriateness. Champ's function is to serve as the adhesive that holds these various tales together and that mediates among disparate cultural expectations: to share with us her understanding of the gum-chewing *amá,* for instance, instead of the long-suffering mother who more familiarly populates the tales in *The Moths.* Champ is well positioned for her role as protagonist in this sequence of stories. Her fictive character is perfectly delineated in that lovely word "adhesiveness," and if she sometimes feels herself to be the victim of circumstance (things stick to her), she is likewise compelled by her inborn nature to stick to things (and people) until she can puzzle them out. In a constantly shifting world, Champ fights to keep the homely qualities of her existence from slipping away into the evasive margins of ghetto life. She cannily weighs, and Viramontes plays back for us, the potentialities and resistances of people and things in this setting. In a larger sense, Viramontes hints that the contemporary Chicana might well be seen as a product of the strategies developed, unconsciously or consciously, to deal with these constant shocks, these continual conflations of strange and disparate social and cultural borders. Unlike, say, the protagonist of "Jumping Bean," who imagines language as spiky shards of glass that pierce her skin, Champ's chewing-gum stick-to-itiveness helps her to negotiate her difficult terrain with panache.

Furthermore, with Arlene, Viramontes deftly outlines a specific version of 1960s Chicana motherhood that implicitly decries the established literary tradition limiting Mexican women over the age of eighteen to saintly motherhood in all its stereotypical glory of tortilla-rolling, homebody self-abnegation. Despite Arlene's propensity for too-tight clothes and too many men, her brash and vital character points toward a reclaiming of female subjectivity too often denied the well-bred (or even the politically committed) woman of Mexican heritage. Arlene's aggressive, bell-bottom, platinum-tipped presence leaves the reader slightly off balance. She is the very figure of the acculturated Chicana, an unashamed social and spiritual mestiza. At the same time, she can only imagine herself as a woman in relation to a heterosexual system of thought that, in her own mestiza culture as well as in the white dominant culture she mimics, exploits women's bodies through their dreams. Viramontes says it explicitly when she has Arlene meditate on two contrasting stories of her sexual initiation:

Arlene is a romantic. When Champ begins her period, she will tell her things that only women can know. She will tell about the first time she made love with a boy, her awkwardness and shyness forcing them to go under the house, where the cool, refined soil made a soft mattress. . . . She was eleven and his name was Harry.

She will not tell Champ that her first fuck was a guy named Puppet who ejaculated prematurely, at the sight of her apricot vagina, so plump and fuzzy. —Pendejo—she said—you got it all over me.

(p. 104)

It is very much to the point that Arlene retains her romantic perspective despite a lifetime of experiences that to this point more closely approximate the unbeautiful story of sex with Puppet rather than love with Harry. Each time she colors her hair, she washes away the unpleasantness of her past and can rewrite her life. Once a week she can "dance spinning herself into Miss Clairol, and stopping only when it is time to return to the sewing factory, time to wait out the next date, time to change hair color. Time to remember or to forget" (p. 105). If Arlene the woman is not a particularly attractive role model, she nevertheless makes us think about the conventions of the beauty system, about the stifling constructions of femininity, and about the way that female empowerment operates, albeit ambiguously, outside the structures and strictures of middle-class feminist thought.

Sometimes, Viramontes suggests, strength and worth can be defined in these transient moments, when the characters overcome the frustration of having to make a meaning out of a broken dream, a hole in a shirt, a tattoo, a missing dress, or even nothing at all. Champ is a master of such bricolage:

Champ is in the closet. There are piles of clothes on the floor, hangers thrown askew and tangled, shoes all piled up or thrown on the top shelf. Champ is looking for her mother's special dress. Pancha says every girl has one at the end of her closet.

—Goddamn it Champ.—

Amidst the dirty laundry, the black hole of the closet, she finds nothing.

("Miss Clairol," pp. 102–103)

Faced with "nothing," Champ pulls together her resources: imagination, the power of language, adaptability, and resilience.

"Tears on My Pillow" melds Viramontes's revisiting of the tale of La Llorona with the maudlin lyrics of the rock song that give the story its title. In Champ's version of the La Llorona story, the hapless ghost-mother wanders around with no feet, seeking victims whom she pulls out of their rooms if they are so careless as to sleep with their feet towards a window. The story, appropriately for its weepy title, offers, first of all, an accounting for loss through death—of La Llorona's children, Grandpa Ham, Lil Mary G.—or, more generally, through unpredictable and unexplained disappearances:

> Just they never say hello and they never say goodbye. Mama María never said goodbye, she just left and that's that and nobody to tell me why tío Benny don't live with tía Olivia any more or when is Gregorio gonna come home or if Arlene is fixed up to go dancing at the Palladium tonight. No one to say nuthin'. . . .
>
> See what I mean? They just never say hello and never say goodbye. They just disappear, leaving you all alone all ascared with your burns and La Llorona hungry for you.
>
> (p. 115)

All sorts of people in Champ's world disappear—or are disappeared—but the story focuses particularly on the women. In the central incident of the story, Lil Mary G., a classmate's mother, is raped and murdered. Champ arrives late to the scene of the crime and catches only a glimpse of bloodstained sheets as the ambulance pulls away. This incident triggers another memory. Since for the classmate the mother's death is experienced as abandonment, that to Champ's mind recalls other, more mythic tales of mothers who abandon their children. These disappearances somehow, in Champ's mind, are tied to excess, and especially to the fleshy excess involved in those strange and awkward protuberances from a woman's body: her breasts.

The presence or absence of *chichis* defines a womanly existence even as they deform the female. Arlene takes Champ shopping again in this story—this time she needs a new bra: "cause the thing that makes the straps go up and down broke and so her chichis hang down like a cow's" (p. 112). Earlier, Champ crawls into bed with her mother when they hear La Llorona screaming, and seeks safety by pressing her head to those generously comforting breasts (p. 111). Moreover, after Lil Mary G.'s murder, her daughter Veronica "just wants to be left alone til everybody forgets she's around. . . . Then she can disappear like Lil Mary G. without no one paying no attention. You don't need bras or nuthin' when you just air" (p. 113). Champ's fear of disappearing at the hands of La Llorona is the other side of the coin of Veronica's desire to disappear with her mother; both derive from the same nightmares and the same yearning for protection. The woman's body, especially her breasts, define her role as caretaker and protector of children; at the same time, they are the physical marker of her difference, what makes her into a potential murderess or child abandoner.

While the woman's body receives ample attention, the men in these stories (Grandpa Ham, tío Benny, Willy the schoolkid) are in general referenced only sketchily. The exception is the most important male character, Champ's brother, Gregorio / Spider. In contrast with Arlene's blowsy presence, "to me," Champ tells us in the opening of "Paris Rats," Gregorio looks "like a balloon not blowed up all the way, like his bones need more air" (p. 1). More extended descriptions of him focus on his scarred face, "what makes him look always real mad, jest real mean, like he ain't ascared of no knife no gun no nobody" (p. 1), and on the tattoo of a spider-woman covering his back. The spider-woman is, if anything, still more ominous than the scar: "The woman's purple hair extend[s] like tentacles into a web," and when he "takes off his white tank top . . . the young girl sees the spider-woman transform from insect to woman, light to dark, woman to insect, dark to light, taunting her with his every move" ("Spider's Face," p. 33).

The visual aggressivity of the scar and the tattoo tend to obscure Gregorio, the thin, frightened boy, and turn Spider into an instantly readable figure of criminality. In accordance with this image, Spider emphasizes his homeboy side with the impeccable T-shirts he bleaches and irons by himself to a pristine sharp whiteness, and with his trademark "pendleton . . . ironed real smooth, looking bitchen. Gregorio likes it buttoned up to the neck and even up to his hands, even when the hot so hot you could fry your toes on the tar street" ("Paris Rats," p. 1). The clothes articulate a powerful masculine identity and put that identity into play on the streets, creating a structure of meaning out of his youthful body, turning him into the strong, streetwise figure that people expect when they see the scar. In this way, Viramontes reminds us that Spider's body is a text, already written and rewritten in the facial scars and spider-woman tattoo, in the pain and violence that reaffirms his masculinity and his worth in the HM gang. The streets belong to him, at least in that part of the barrio upon which he has staked territorial claim, and that space remains intimately his, even if the boundaries are defined and policed by others.

Poignantly, Spider too reads himself against others. In his case, he defines his public self through the discomfort of passersby, in their recognition of him and in their silence when he lights up an illegal Camel cigarette on the bus, in their refusal to look at him for fear of drawing attention from that scarred face. He reads himself as that empty space opened in front of him for his passage: "He was dragged into the dark ages years ago, catacombs of the nightmare, since. Of course, he must have been afraid. Because he's not really a spider, although at times

he wishes he were. . . . But that's enough for the street warrior. It confirms his existence, like the placas on the walls. He is tired of being invisible" ("Face," p. 34). "Spider" defines at once a gang member's visibility and his invisibility; it allows him to take charge of his home, to own his streets through his symbolic presence. But in order for Spider to survive, he must repress Gregorio, the frightened and tortured boy. And it is Gregorio that both Champ and Viramontes insist upon in these stories. While Spider writes his *placa* (tag) on the walls, taking measure of his world and bringing it within his control, Viramontes's storytelling bends her talents to unwriting Spider, the aggressive gang-banging street fighter, and to writing Gregorio, the loving brother, the boy-child who may never survive to become a man.

Spider has two faces that he shows the world: the mean, scarred face of the frightening gang member and the cruel, purple-lipped face of the fiendish spider-woman tattoo on his back. And while Champ fears the tattoo and knows what the scar portends, she loves the boy who comes into the house for the night, when he is Gregorio and not Spider. The homeboy image, then, is reread in the peace of the evening and in Champ's gaze when she sees past the cruel spider to her beloved brother. Here again, as with her portrayal of Arlene, as with Champ, Viramontes describes a *mestizaje* that goes much further than an identity constructed against U.S. dominant and traditional Mexican customs. Spider is not adequately captured in the stylized figure of an ambiguously expressed phallic potency; he is not an Aztec warrior, nor a Chicano militant, nor a *pachuco* rebel. Like his mother and sister, he is a romantic; susceptible to sentimental songs and the stirring sexuality of the dance.

Especially interesting in this regard is a scene in "Dance Me Forever." In this story, it is Champ and Gregorio's tía Olivia who allows herself to be seduced away from her bitterness and sense of failure by the stories and the dreams

Gregorio outlines. Olivia recalls a poignant moment from her wedding:

> "When Benny and me married, we had a big wedding. . . . Anyways, Gregorio, come the dollar dance, Arlene gives you a dollar to dance with me. You looked so sharp, mijo. I get your dollar and we dance. Kinda dance. And then someone else comes with another dollar to dance with me. But you got so jealous, mijo, you wanted to dance with me forever, and Arlene ended up dragging you off the dance floor. . . .
>
> Sabes que? Afterwards I tell Benny. Dance me like that, like it's forever."
>
> "Some things change, Tía," Gregorio offers, leans forward and removes the butt from her hand. . . . "And some things don't," Gregorio finishes.
>
> And Champ notices that Gregorio's scar is gone. It is hidden under Olivia's cheek and for once his face is whole.
>
> (p. G20)

As in "Spider's Face," the narrative of "Dance Me Forever" offers a temporary and healing wholeness, where the contradictions of a harsh life can be briefly reconciled. Gregorio makes his aunt a present of the attractive self he imagines for her; she, likewise, gifts him with the young man he could be, freed from Spider's disfigurement.

Estrella, the protagonist of Viramontes's first novel, *Under the Feet of Jesus,* is a young woman very much in the same mold as Champ. She is a member of a constantly moving Mexican American family that follows the crops in mid-twentieth-century California, and the novel focuses on the summer of her thirteenth year. Scrappy and assertive, she is also deeply sensitive to the heartbreaking loveliness of the natural world that surrounds her. Often, however, the day-to-day lives of the workers in this apparently ideal setting come accompanied by both danger and suffering, so that beauty and poison overlap and shadow each other. The change of pace between these two extremes is disconcertingly apt. Thus, for example, at one of the most emotionally difficult moments in the novel, during the family's desperate trip to the hospital to try to get medical care for Estrella's dangerously ill friend Alejo, Estrella pauses mentally to recall and to appreciate the swooningly beautiful sensuousness of a red bell pepper, which Viramontes lovingly dissects almost as if it were a cubist painting (p. 153).

The title of the novel astutely brings together the literal and symbolic suggestions raised by the reference to the migrant workers' spiritual lives. Though all of the members of Estrella's family are U.S.-born, they constantly have to worry about being taken up by the INS as illegal immigrants. Petra lectures her children: "Don't run scared. You stay there and look them in the eye. . . . If they stop you, if they try to pull you into the green vans, you tell them the birth certificates are under the feet of Jesus, just tell them" (p. 63). And, of course, the plaster statue of Jesus does hold down the precious envelope of family documents, carefully replaced from glove compartment of the car to the makeshift altar with each of the family's moves.

The novel—dedicated to the memory of Cesar Chavez and to Viramontes's parents, who met while they labored in the fields of California—focuses on the story of Estrella and her family, as well as her taste of what her incipient womanhood might mean in the tender story of first love with Alejo. Estrella, her siblings, "the mother," and "the man who was not her father . . . the man whom they called Perfecto" (pp. 3–4) follow the crop cycles up and down the vast California farmlands, barely earning enough at each stop to eke out a bare existence on the margins of society. At each stop in the circuit, they earn just enough money to pay for their basic sustenance (beans and potato-filled tortillas are a staple) and the minimum necessary gas money to nurse their failing automobile along to the next stop along the migrant trail. Viramontes's descriptions bring home the physical effects of fieldwork—heat and sunstroke and utter exhaustion dragging down every bone in the body. Added to this are the dangers of pesticide exposure, always a worry in the back of people's minds, the cause of the dreaded "*daño* of the fields." Despite these shared difficulties, solidarity and support are scarce commodities, parsimoniously doled out. The narrative hints at the impossibility of community within a people defined by their hardscrabble life so close to the margin, with competition for the best fruit-picking sites and the constant movement between farms disrupting budding friendships. And yet, when necessity drags deep, the members of the migrant community pool their meager resources to help out the person in need.

In this bleak world, family is the only constant. Despite this family-centered structure, however, Viramontes hints at the fault lines and fractures among the siblings and especially between Estrella and the adults in her recombined family. Thus, the narrative is very spare in the use of possessives for family members, who are tightly bound together as the only unit that can confront the difficulties the world puts in their path, but nevertheless seems plagued by unspoken resentments. Petra, for example, is invariably referred to as "the mother" rather than by any affectionate diminutive; similarly, Estrella has a strained and often distant relationship with Perfecto, the mother's much older lover. Meanwhile, we learn that "her real father" had left for Mexico to bury an uncle and never returned to his struggling family in California, or if he did return (neither Estrella nor Petra know for sure, nor can they afford the mental energy to worry about it), he could not find his family, who was constantly on the move and had no concept of forwarding addresses.

The novel's central plot involves a tale of doomed first love. Poised on the threshold of adulthood, Estrella feels the first stirrings of adult attraction for a young fellow field worker, Alejo, who works the fields by day with his cousin Gumersindo and adds to his meager nest egg for high school back home in Texas with surreptitious peach-burgling in the off hours. Estrella's affection is fully corresponded, as

Alejo also falls deeply in love with her: "What he saw was the woman who swam in the magnetic presence of the full moon, a woman named Star" (p. 46). The tale quickly moves into tragedy when Alejo is sprayed by a passing crop duster and becomes progressively sicker as the novel advances, eventually falling so ill that Estrella's family sees no recourse but to take him to a clinic. This foreign space is both frightening and alienating to the anxious family members. Not only do they have to deal with a white woman nurse, but everything in the clinic is too white, including the cotton balls. The whiteness is only superficial, though, as Estrella almost immediately intuits. Apparent cleanliness covers a deep rot. While she is self-conscious about her own odor of sweat, as she enters the clinic she realizes that the clinic's smell of disinfectant is undercut by bad plumbing and the odor of a backed-up toilet. Unsurprisingly, the nurse in the clinic takes Alejo's temperature but is unable to be of any real assistance, so the family finally has to take him to the hospital in Corazon and leave him there, perhaps—probably, they suspect—to die.

Wound around this story are a series of set pieces describing crucial visual images. In counterpoint to the paperweight Jesus who guards family papers are other affectionately described, yet homely, spiritual figures. Thus, for example, the scruffy grocery store is decorated with a

> lopsided poster of the holy Virgen, Our Lady of Guadalupe [that] was tacked between the posters of Elvis Presley and Marilyn Monroe holding her white billowing dress down. La Virgen was adorned by red and green and white twinkling Christmas lights which surrounded the poster like a sequin necklace. . . . La Virgen was raised, it seemed to Petra, above a heavenly mound of bulbous garlic.
>
> (p. 110)

The garlic at the feet of la Virgen—an essential remedy that Petra uses to keep her varicose veins under control—seems a perfect companion to the plaster Jesus, who in the course of this novel accidentally loses his head.

Another crucial visual image is Perfecto's red tool chest. Perfecto Flores is a talented handyman, and while Estrella struggles against accepting him as a father figure, she shares with him his love of tools. Learning about tools also serves as a metaphor for learning per se. Thus the toolbox becomes for Estrella a metaphor to describe her own yearning for information and her dissatisfaction with a school system that does not come close to meeting her needs. Estrella expresses her anger when she is not given access to knowledge about things, and is particularly frustrated with the schools that intermittently serve the migrant population, since none of the teachers find it worth their while to quench her thirst for information. As she struggles to make out the foreign shapes of the letters of the alphabet, the toolbox serves as an essential referent: "The script A's had the curlicue of a pry bar, a hammerhead split like a V. The small i's resembled nails" (p. 24). Estrella puzzles over these shapes on her own; she notes that the teachers would scrub her fingernails but not teach her anything: "They said good luck to her when the pisca was over, reserving the desks in the back of the classroom for the next batch of migrant children. Estrella often wondered what happened to all the things they boxed away in tool chests and kept to themselves" (p. 25). It is Perfecto Flores who finally gives her some useful knowledge, in teaching her the names and uses of tools, and it is in understanding the function of hammers and pliers and crowbars that Estrella makes the leap: "That was when she began to read" (p. 26).

Finally, one of the most mysterious and most discussed images in the novel is the barn that opens and closes *Under the Feet of Jesus.* Early in the novel, the narrator says, "The silence and the barn and the clouds meant many things" (p. 4). At the end of the novel the barn appears again, to close the narrative, when Estrella overcomes her fear and climbs to the top of that dilapidated structure, achieving a bird's-eye view of the surrounding landscape: "Estrella remained as immobile as an angel standing on the verge of faith. Like the chiming bells of the great cathedrals, she believed her heart powerful enough to summon home all those who strayed" (p. 176). In its parallel to the cathedral, the barn suggests a spiritually laden structure of great power and resonance; yet in the novel proper it is both a forbidden and forbidding place, as well as nothing more extraordinary than a dilapidated building. The children avoid it because it seems haunted, and they are also, almost redundantly, told they must stay away from it because it is potentially dangerous. The barn looms large in the novel as a project for Perfecto Flores and Estrella; they have been contracted to tear it down and desperately need the money that this work will bring them. In finally conceding to Perfecto's importunities and agreeing to help tear down the barn, Estrella implicitly also moves forward another step in her path to adulthood and in her ability to handle both real and metaphorical tools.

Viramontes's eagerly awaited next novel, *Their Dogs Came with Them,* is dedicated to the "rememory of East L.A." and begins with an epigraph from Miguel León Portilla's *The Broken Spears,* which tells the indigenous version of the story of the Spanish conquest of Mexico:

> They came in battle array, as conquerors, and the dust rose in whirlwinds on the roads. Their spears glinted in the sun, and their pennons fluttered like bats. They made a clamor as they marched, for their coats of mail and their weapons clashed and rattled. Some of them were dressed in glistening iron from head to foot; they terrified everyone who saw them. Their dogs came with them running ahead of the column. They raised their muzzles high; they lifted their muzzles to the wind. They raced on before with saliva dripping from their jaws.

The epigraph helps the reader understand the menace underlying the novel's title, and, indeed, throughout the entire text Viramontes uses the image of dogs as a leitmotiv to underscore the persistent threat of violence that lurks just out of sight through most of the narration. Because there is supposedly a rabies threat in the area, the city has set up roadblocks and instituted helicopter surveillance to control all passage into and out of the affected zone. People, in this way, are treated as potentially rabid, dangerous animals. Additionally, all of the main characters have symbolically important encounters with dogs—they are bitten by dogs, their attention is caught by the Coppertone billboard of a dog pulling down a child's underwear—or they become dogs themselves (the gang members are likened to a pack of "asphalt jungle dogs" emerging in the night to threaten the have-nots; the children in the soup kitchen are described as displaying "rabid hunger").

The novel is set in the east side of Los Angeles during the period of the Vietnam war, in the 1960s–1970s, and that war, with the all-consuming worry about young fighting men and the inconsolable grief for young men lost, is one of the major referents for the novel as a whole. More immediately, however, looms the ongoing destruction of the east-side neighborhood, as bulldozers and earth-moving machinery grind up houses and stores to make way for the expanding freeway system, as the mysterious Quarantine Authority creates a police-state atmosphere in its supposed concern about the spread of rabies, as young men and women destroy themselves and each other in futile gang rivalries over a shrinking territory. The roar of the earthmovers during the day and the sounds of helicopters and gunfire at night punctuate this novel, inevitably creating an overlay of Vietnam and Los Angeles as similarly tortured jungle war zones.

Three main stories interweave in this text. Fifteen-year-old Ermila Zumaya is perhaps the closest to a central point-of-view character. She had been bounced around in a series of foster families, most recently with Mrs. M., but now lives with her grandparents and a visiting relative from Mexico, cousin Nacho, whose English is too scattershot to be able to convey his grow-

ing uncousinly interest in her. Ermila for her part is an indifferent student at Garfield High School, which serves mostly as a social gathering point for her and her group of friends: Mousie, Lollie, and Rini. "Lest they forget that silence is destructive, they pitted each other against the sorrowful and infinite solitude, each and every hour because that's what friends *por vida* are for." All four girls are attracted to one or another of the members of the two main rival gangs: the McBride Boys or the Lote M (for Maravilla) *vatos.* She has problems with her family because of her drinking and staying out late and is completely incapable of imagining a way to escape from her ongoing but unsatisfactory sexual relationship with her boyfriend, "Alfonso AKA Big Al." Meanwhile, "she listened to the litany of Alfonso's lies . . . and then said she loved him too, which was also a lie." Pushed too fast into a pseudomaturity, Ermila and her friends depend on the cryptic and unreliable advice of Lollie's aunt, a failed restaurateur and illegal beautician: "The best that could be said about Concha was her glorious indifference about the shape of things now. . . . Ermila felt that Concha's advice clearly derived from a manual different than the appliance."

Ermila's point of view opens the novel, as she briefly visits Chavela, an elderly neighbor woman suffering from apparent Alzheimer's who is about to be evicted from her home. Chavela leaves notes for herself in her "scratchy" writing, creating an elementary narrative of her life: "Leve massage for Josie. Basura on Wetsday. J work # AN 54389. Water flours. Chek gas off." The child contrasts "her own house and all the other houses on Grandfather's side of First Street; the houses on the saved side were bright and ornamental like big Easter eggs on display at the Segunda store counter. . . . In a few weeks, Chavela's side of the neighborhood, the dead side of the street would disappear forever." The novel is located precisely on this site of imminent destruction, the disruption not only of a community but also a narrative: the Top Hat, Concha's (illegal) Beauty Shop (dispenser of haircuts and folk therapy), El Zocalo Fine Meats (at the crossroads of much of the novel's action), El Gallo Bakers, Val U Mini Mart, Salas Used Cars (where Ermila sometimes works), the now-boarded-up Los Jalisco Mariscos (once a favorite eating spot for wrestlers, such that the local challenge was trying to recognize them without their masks). From her porch, Ermila watches the houses "disappearing inch by inch" in order to make room for the machinery that is "methodically unspooling the freeways."

Turtle (Antonia/o) Gamboa is a rough, head-shaved youth whose only support group is the other members of the McBride Boys. Technically a girl, Turtle is taller and stronger than most of her companions, and has always preferred the strength and independence of a boy's life to the humiliation of being a "pussy." She is generally treated as a man and referred to with a masculine pronoun in the text. Scarred and gang-tattooed, Turtle and his/her brother Luis Lil Lizard were a feared combination in the barrio, but by the time the novel opens Luis has been drafted to serve in Vietnam and Turtle wanders the streets alone, becoming increasingly desperate, starving, and violent. Throughout the third part of the novel, Turtle reviews the lessons learned from Luis Lil Lizard's Army "Field Manual 21-71, SURVIVAL," applying the tenets of combat to her current situation. Turtle's life, almost inevitably, ends tragically; yet Viramontes is able to develop sympathy in her reader for the plight of this lost child, this "pinche malflora," this cold-blooded killer.

The third major story centers on Tranquilina, the daughter of evangelical ministers who operate a shoestring soup kitchen and church out of their home. Barefoot and raggedly dressed, she chops cabbage for soup and moves back and forth among her charges with a high stack of used bowls, "a porcelain spine of vertebrae between her two hands." Her mother and her foster father, Papá Tomás, were indentured servants in Mexico who escaped north, first to Texas, where Tranquilina is raped by a rancher's

son-in-law, and eventually to California. Her orbit includes a severely psychotic and intermittently violent young man named Ben Brady and his sister Ana. "He's not safe, is he?" asks Tranquilina at one point, and "Ana didn't know how to respond. Ben's not safe, as he is not *in* a safe place, or he's not safe, as he *is* dangerous." Both meanings of the phrase turn out to be true: "Ben's condition was beyond love and prayer and beyond a cocktail of experimental medication, even beyond the saving grace of poetry." Later, Viramontes adds, now from Ben's perspective, "it seemed indescribable except to say that on bad days, the days were indescribably bad."

In the course of the novel, Ben, for reasons confused even to himself, kidnaps a small boy, who is killed while the pair of them are running across a street. In the aftermath, Ben is declared a hero since witnesses assume that he was seriously injured trying to save the child. If Tranquilina, as her name suggests, is the still center of this narrative, the figure that all the other lives brush up against, at least at a tangent, Ben is the only individual able to document those lives. Unlike Chavela, whose writings are scratchy, futile stitchings-together of a life almost forgotten, Ben is a damaged warrior whose weapons are pencils and whose words, when reproduced in the text, invariably match those of the anonymous narrator. Implicitly the major storyteller of the novel, he knows that "stories, like life, had no logical conclusion." And so it is with this novel.

The individuals who people this work have elaborately mended and stitched together lives, yet they remain almost mute or serve only to reiterate over and over the same unhappy tale. The novel is filled with appearances by mysterious characters, like the silent homeless woman, discarded herself, who wanders through the novel and into Tranquilina's mission collecting bottles and other trash. Ben, for example, is not used to speaking, so that when he does try to talk, "vocal irregularities occurred, audible or inaudible malfunctions like a radio needle in pursuit of a clear station." For Ermila and her friends, "the only real estate they cherished, their only private property, were the stories they continued to create and re-create in a world which only gave them one to tell." Turtle, who almost never speaks in the novel, "tried to remember her Spanish, words that were boxed in storage."

And yet, stories are the only means to create a "rememory" of lost people and places. Ermila's friend Mousie grasps this fact firmly. Mousie's brother YoYo was sent back from Vietnam in so many pieces that her mother, against the advice of the Church, decides on cremation. Worried about the Last Judgment, it is left to Mousie "to cross-stitch him back together to recapture his soul." Viramontes too, in this novel, has a similar purpose. Out of the apocalyptic violence and destruction, her own "stitched" language (a favorite term of hers) pulls together the fragments and hands the reader an unflinching portrait of the East Los Angeles soul.

At four hundred manuscript pages, this is Viramontes's most ambitious work to date; it is also her darkest, and while the reader will note threads of continuity with the bleaker stories in *The Moths*, and with the urban landscapes of *Paris Rats*, the novel works on a broader and more complex canvas. In contrast with the much shorter, more tentatively optimistic worlds of *Jesus*'s Estrella and *Rats*'s Champ, this is the work that represents the direction of Viramontes's mature vision, and if that vision is apocalyptic, then her gaze is unflinching and free of false pieties.

Selected Bibliography

WORKS OF HELENA MARÍA VIRAMONTES

PROSE VOLUMES
The Moths and Other Stories. Houston: Arte Público Press, 1985.

Under the Feet of Jesus. New York: Dutton, 1995.

Their Dogs Came with Them. (Forthcoming.)

UNCOLLECTED SHORT STORIES
"The Jumping Bean." In *Pieces of the Heart: New Chicano Fiction.* Edited by Gary Soto. San Francisco: Chronicle Books, 1993. Pp. 122–132.

Paris Rats in East L.A. and Other Stories (unpublished as of this writing) will include the following published stories along with others still in manuscript draft:

"Miss Clairol." *Americas Review* 15, no. 3–4 (1987): 101–105.

"Spider's Face." *Americas 2001* 1, no. 5 (March / April 1988): 33–34. "Dance Me Forever." *L.A. Weekly,* June 24–30, 1988.

"Tears On My Pillow." In *New Chicana / Chicano Writing.* Edited by Charles M. Tatum. Tucson: University of Arizona Press, 1992–1993. Pp. 110–115.

VOLUMES COEDITED WITH MARÍA HERRERA-SOBEK
Chicana Creativity and Criticism: New Frontiers in American Literature. Albuquerque: University of New Mexico Press, 1988.

Chicana (W)rites: On Word and Film. Berkeley: Third Woman Press, 1995.

FILMSCRIPTS

"Paris Rats in East L.A." Directed by Ana Maria Garcia. Produced by the American Film Institute.

INTERVIEWS, PERSONAL ESSAYS

Heredia, Juanita, and Silvia Pellarolo. "East of Downtown and Beyond: Interview with Helena María Viramontes." *Mester* 22–23, nos. 2–1 (1993 fall–1994 spring): 165–180.

Short, Kayann. "Bitter Harvest: A Talk with Helena María Viramontes." *Bloomsbury Review* 16, no. 1 (January–February 1996): 5.

Sitesh, Aruna. *Her Testimony: American Women Writers of the 90s in Conversation.* New Delhi: Affiliated East-West, 1994.

Viramontes, Helena María. "Four Guiding Principles." http://www.chicanovista.com/text/grey/helena1.html (accessed June 3, 2003).

———. "'Nopalitos': The Making of Fiction: Testimonio." In *Breaking Boundaries: Latina Writing and Critical Readings.* Edited by Asunción Horno-Delgado et al. Amherst: University of Massachusetts Press, 1989.

———. "The Writes Ofrenda." In *Máscaras.* Edited by Lucha Corpi. Berkeley: Third Woman Press, 1997.

CRITICAL STUDIES

Alarcon, Norma. "Making 'Familia' from Scratch: Split Subjectivities in the Work of Helena Maria Viramontes and Cherríe Moraga." In *Chicana Creativity and Criticism: Charting New Frontiers in American Literature.* Edited by María Herrerra-Sobek and Helena María Viramontes. Houston: Arte Público Press, 1988. Pp. 147–159.

Avendaño, Nadia. "El discurso femenino en 'The Long Reconciliation' de Helena María Viramontes." *Explicación de Textos Literarios* 29, no. 1 (2000-2001): 53–59.

Calderón, Héctor, and José David Saldívar, eds. *Criticism in the Borderlands.* Durham: Duke University Press, 1991.

Carbonell, Ana Maria. "From Llorona to Gritona: (1) Coatlicue In Feminist Tales by Viramontes and Cisneros." *MELUS* 24, no. 2 (summer 1999): 53–74. http://www.findarticles.com/cf_0/m2278/2_24/59211507/p1/article.jhtml (accessed June 3, 2003).

Castillo, Debra A., and María Socorro Tabuenca Córdoba. *Border Women: Writing from La Frontera.* Minneapolis: University of Minnesota Press, 2002.

Castillo, Debra A. *Talking Back: Toward a Latin American Feminist Literary Criticism.* Ithaca, N.Y.: Cornell University Press, 1992.

Chabram-Dernersesian, Angie. "I Throw Punches for My Race, but I Don't Want to Be a Man: Writing Us—Chica-nos (Girl, Us)/Chica*nas*—into the Movement Script." In *Cultural Studies.* Edited by Lawrence Grossberg, Cary Nelson, and Paula Treichler. New York: Routledge, 1992. Pp. 81–95.

Davidson, Cathy N., and Linda Wagner-Martin, eds. *The Oxford Companion to Women's Writing in the United States.* New York: Oxford University Press, 1995.

Dulfano, Isabel. "Some Thoughts Shared with Helena Maria Viramontes." *Women's Studies: An Interdisciplinary Journal* 30, no. 5 (2001): 647–662.

Fernandez, Roberta. "The Cariboo Cafe: Helena Maria Viramontes Discourses with Her Social and Cultural Contexts." *Women's Studies* 17, no. 2 (1989): 71–85.

Fox, L.C. "Chicana Creativity and Criticism: Charting New Frontiers in America." *College Literature* 18, no. 1 (1991): 103–106.

Franklet, Duane. "Social Language: Bakhtin and Viramontes." *The Americas Review: A Review of Hispanic Literature and Art of the USA.* 17, no. 2 (summer 1989): 110–114.

Gutierrez-Jones, Carl. *Rethinking the Borderlands: Between Chicano Culture and Legal Discourse.* Berkeley: University of California Press, 1995.

Hassett, J. J. "Under the Feet of Jesus—Viramontes, HM." *Chasqui-Revista de Literatura Latinoamericana* 25, no. 2 (1996): 147–148.

Herrera-Sobek, María, ed. *Beyond Stereotypes: The Critical Analysis of Chicana Literature.* Binghamton, N.Y.: Bilingual Press, 1985.

———. "The Nature of Chicana Literature: Feminist Ecological Literary Criticism and Chicana Writers." *Revista Canaria de Estudios Ingleses* 37 (November 1998): 89–100.

Johannessen, Lene. "The Meaning of Place in Viramontes' *Under the Feet of Jesus.*" In *Holding Their Own: Perspectives on the Multi-Ethnic Literatures of the United States.* Edited by Dorothea Fischer-Hornung and Heike Raphael-Hernandez. Tübingen, Germany: Stauffenburg, 2000.

Lawless, Cecelia. "Helena María Viramontes' Homing Devices in Under the Feet of Jesus." In *Homemaking: Women Writers and the Politics and Poetics of Home.* Edited by Catherine Wiley and Fiona R. Barnes. New York: Garland, 1996.

León Portilla, Miguel. *The Broken Spears: The Aztec Account of the Conquest of Mexico.* Translated by Lysander Kemp. Boston: Beacon Press, 1962.

Magill, Frank N., ed. *Masterpieces of Latino Literature.* New York: Salem Press, 1994.

Moore, Deborah Owen. "La Llorona Dines at the Cariboo Cafe: Structure and Legend in the Work of Helena María Viramontes." *Studies in Short Fiction* 35, no. 3 (summer 1998): 277–286.

Pavletich, J. A., and M. G. Backus. "With His Pistol in Her Hand: Rearticulating the Corrido Narrative." *Cultural Critique* 27 (1994): 127–152.

Peck, David. "Teaching Notes." *Radical Teacher: A Newsjournal of Socialist Theory and Practice* 59 (fall 2000): 41.

Peck, David and Eric Howards, eds. *Identities and Issues in Literature.* Pasadena, Calif.: Salem Press, 1997.

Rebolledo, Tey Diana. "The Politics of Poetics: Or, What am I, a Critic, Doing in This Text Anyhow." In *Making Face, Making Soul/Haciendo caras: Creative and Critical Perspectives by Feminists of Color.* Edited by Gloria Anzaldúa. San Francisco: Aunt Lute, 1990. Pp. 346–355.

Rodríguez, Ana Patricia. "Refugees of the South: Central Americans in the U. S. Latino Imaginary." *American Literature: A Journal of Literary History, Criticism, and Bibliography* 73, no. 2 (June 2001): 387–412.

Saldívar, José David. *Border Matters: Remapping American Cultural Studies.* Berkeley: University of California Press, 1997.

———. *The Dialectics of Our America.* Durham: Duke University Press, 1991.

———. "Frontera Crossings: Sites of Cultural Contestation." *Mester* 22–23, nos. 2, 1 (fall 1993–spring 1994): 81–91.

Saldívar-Hull, Sonia. *Feminism on the Border: Chicana Gender Politics and Literature.* Berkeley: University of California Press, 2000.

———. "Political Identities in Contemporary Chicana Literature: Helena María Viramontes's Visions of the U.S. Third World." In *'Writing' Nation and 'Writing' Region in America*. Edited by Theo D'haen and Hans Bertens. Amsterdam: VU University Press, 1996.

Simal, Begoña. "'The Cariboo Cafe' as a Border Text: The Holographic Model." In *Literature and Ethnicity in the Cultural Borderlands*. Edited by Jesús Benito and Anna Manzanas. Amsterdam: Rodopi, 2002.

Stockton, Sharon. "Rereading the Maternal Body: Viramontes' The Moths and the Construction of the New Chicana." *The Americas Review: A Review of Hispanic Literature and Art of the USA* 22, nos. 1–2 (spring–summer 1994): 212–229.

Wilson, Ian Randall. "The Outsiders: Helena María Viramontes' 'The Cariboo Cafe.'" *Americas Review: A Review of Hispanic Literature and Art of the USA* 25 (1999): 179–201.